BRICE CARNAHAN

*Departments of Chemical Engineering
and Biostatistics
The University of Michigan*

H. A. LUTHER

*Department of Mathematics
Texas A & M University*

JAMES O. WILKES

*Department of Chemical Engineering
The University of Michigan*

Applied

Applied Numerical Methods

JOHN WILEY & SONS, INC.

NEW YORK · LONDON · SYDNEY · TORONTO

Preface

This book is intended to be an intermediate treatment of the theory and applications of numerical methods. Much of the material has been presented at the University of Michigan in a course for senior and graduate engineering students. The main feature of this volume is that the various numerical methods are not only discussed in the text but are also illustrated by completely documented computer programs. Many of these programs relate to problems in engineering and applied mathematics. The reader should gain an appreciation of what to expect during the implementation of particular numerical techniques on a digital computer.

Although the emphasis here is on numerical *methods* (in contrast to numerical *analysis*), short proofs or their outlines are given throughout the text. The more important numerical methods are illustrated by worked computer examples. The appendix explains the general manner in which the computer examples are presented, and also describes the flow-diagram convention that is adopted. In addition to the computer examples, which are numbered, there are several much shorter examples appearing throughout the text. These shorter examples are not numbered, and usually illustrate a particular point by means of a short hand-calculation. The computer programs are written in the FORTRAN-IV language and have been run on an IBM 360/67 computer. We assume that the reader is already moderately familiar with the FORTRAN-IV language.

There is a substantial set of unworked problems at the end of each chapter. Some of these involve the derivation of formulas or proofs; others involve hand calculations; and the rest are concerned with the computer solution of a variety of problems, many of which are drawn from various branches of engineering and applied mathematics.

Brice Carnahan
H. A. Luther
James O. Wilkes

Contents

CHAPTER 3

CHAPTER 4

Computer Examples

CHAPTER 5

CHAPTER 6

CHAPTER 7

CHAPTER 8

Applied Numerical Methods

CHAPTER 1

Interpolation and Approximation

1.1 Introduction

This text is concerned with the practical solution of problems in engineering, science, and applied mathematics. Special emphasis is given to those aspects of problem formulation and mathematical analysis which lead to the construction of a solution *algorithm* or procedure suitable for execution on a digital computer. The identification and analysis of computational errors resulting from mathematical approximations present in the algorithms will be emphasized throughout.

To the question, "Why approximate?", we can only answer, "Because we must!" Mathematical models of physical or natural processes inevitably contain some *inherent* errors. These errors result from incomplete understanding of natural phenomena, the stochastic or random nature of many processes, and uncertainties in experimental measurements. Often, a model includes only the most pertinent features of the physical process and is deliberately stripped of superfluous detail related to second-level effects.

Even if an error-free mathematical model could be developed, it could not, in general, be solved *exactly* on a digital computer. A digital computer can perform only a limited number of simple *arithmetic* operations (principally addition, subtraction, multiplication, and division) on finite, rational numbers. Fundamentally important *mathematical* operations such as differentiation, integration, and evaluation of infinite series cannot be implemented directly on a digital computer. All such computers have finite memories and computational registers; only a discrete subset of the real, rational numbers may be generated, manipulated, and stored. Thus, it is impossible to represent infinitesimally small or infinitely large quantities, or even a continuum of the real numbers on a finite interval.

Algorithms that use only arithmetic operations and certain logical operations such as algebraic comparison are called *numerical methods*. The error introduced in approximating the solution of a mathematical problem by a numerical method is usually termed the *truncation error* of the method. We shall devote considerable attention to the truncation errors associated with the numerical approximations developed in this text.

When a numerical method is actually run on a digital computer after transcription to computer program form,

another kind of error, termed *round-off error*, is introduced. Round-off errors are caused by the rounding of results from individual arithmetic operations because only a finite number of digits can be retained after each operation, and will differ from computer to computer, even when the same numerical method is being used.

We begin with the important problem of approximating one function $f(x)$ by another "suitable" function $g(x)$. This may be written

$$f(x) \doteq g(x).$$

There are two principal reasons for developing such approximations. The first is to replace a function $f(x)$ which is difficult to evaluate or manipulate (for example, differentiate or integrate) by a simpler, more amenable function $g(x)$. Transcendental functions given in closed form, such as $\ln x$, $\sin x$, and $\operatorname{erf} x$, are examples of functions which cannot be evaluated by strictly arithmetic operations without first finding approximating functions such as finite power series. The second reason is for interpolating in tables of functional values. The function $f(x)$ is known quantitatively for a finite (usually small) number of arguments called *base points*; the sampled functional values may then be tabulated at the $n + 1$ base points $x_0, x_1, \ldots, x_n$ as follows:

$$
\begin{array}{cc}
x_0 & f(x_0) \\
x_1 & f(x_1) \\
x_2 & f(x_2) \\
\vdots & \vdots \\
x_i & f(x_i) \\
\vdots & \vdots \\
x_n & f(x_n).
\end{array}
$$

We wish to generate an approximating function that will allow an estimation of the value of $f(x)$ for $x \neq x_i$, $i = 0, 1, \ldots, n$. In some cases, $f(x)$ is known analytically but is difficult to evaluate. We have tables of functional values for the trigonometric functions, Bessel functions, etc. In others, we may know the general class of functions to which $f(x)$ belongs, without knowing the values of specific functional parameters.

In the general case, however, only the base-point functional information is given and little is known about $f(x)$ for other arguments, except perhaps that it is continuous in some interval of interest, $a \leqslant x \leqslant b$. The tabulated functional values $f(x_0)$, ..., $f(x_n)$, or even the base-point values x_0, ..., x_n may themselves be approximations to true values, particularly when the table entries are the results of experimental measurements.

The synthesis of a new analytical function $g(x)$ that approximates the original function $f(x)$ depends upon many factors such as knowledge of the function, the source and accuracy of the tabulated functional values, the intended use of the approximating function $g(x)$, and accuracy requirements for the approximation. It is intuitively obvious that the more we know about $f(x)$, the greater is the likelihood of finding a suitable function $g(x)$. For example, if a theoretical model suggests that $f(x)$ should behave as a cubic in x, then we would probably begin by attempting to fit the tabulated information with a third-degree polynomial. If $f(x)$ is a measure of activity in a process involving radioactive decay, then it is quite probable that $g(x)$ will be exponential in character.

Information about the reliability of the $f(x_i)$ values ($i = 0, 1, ..., n$) is essential. It would be unrealistic to expect an approximation $g(x)$ to produce estimates of $f(x)$ accurate to four significant figures, if the values $f(x_0)$, $f(x_1)$, ..., $f(x_n)$ used to generate $g(x)$ were accurate to no more than two figures. Even tabulated values of "known" functions are normally only approximate values because of rounding, that is, the representation of any real number by a finite number of digits. Numerical mathematics is not immune to the laws of thermodynamics. We never get something for nothing (although it is often possible to get more than is apparent at first glance).

In some cases, the synthesized function will not be used directly for functional estimation, but instead will be manipulated further. For example, suppose that the integral

$$\int_a^b f(x)\, dx \doteq \int_a^b g(x)\, dx$$

is required. Assuming that alternative formulations for $g(x)$ are possible, the natural choice would be one that is easy to integrate.

If the function $f(x)$ is not known precisely, then there is certainly *no* way of evaluating the error committed in replacing $f(x)$ by $g(x)$. Fortunately, it is often possible to find some order-of-magnitude estimate for the error by making reasonable assumptions about $f(x)$ (for example, that $f(x)$ is smooth, that it is monotonic, that its high-order derivatives are small, etc.). If the function $f(x)$ is known precisely or analytically, then it is often possible to establish an upper bound for the error.

1.2 Approximating Functions

The most common approximating functions $g(x)$ are those involving linear combinations of simple functions drawn from a class of functions $\{g_i(x)\}$ of the form

$$g(x) = a_0 g_0(x) + a_1 g_1(x) + \cdots + a_n g_n(x).$$

The classes of functions most often encountered are the monomials $\{x^i\}$, $i = 0, 1, ..., n$, the Fourier functions $\{\sin kx, \cos kx\}$, $k = 0, 1, ..., n$, and the exponentials $\{e^{b_i x}\}$, $i = 0, 1, ..., n$. Linear combinations of the monomials lead to polynomials of degree n, $p_n(x)$:

$$f(x) \doteq g(x) = a_0 + a_1 x + a_2 x^2 + \cdots + a_n x^n$$

or

$$g(x) = p_n(x) = a_0 + \sum_{i=1}^n a_i x^i = \sum_{i=0}^n a_i x^i.*$$

Linear combination of the Fourier functions leads to approximations of the form

$$f(x) \doteq g(x) = a_0 + a_1 \cos x + a_2 \cos 2x + $$
$$\cdots + a_n \cos nx$$
$$+ b_1 \sin x + b_2 \sin 2x + $$
$$\cdots + b_n \sin nx,$$

or

$$g(x) = a_0 + \sum_{k=1}^n a_k \cos kx + \sum_{k=1}^n b_k \sin kx.$$

Approximations employing exponentials are usually of the form

$$f(x) \doteq g(x) = a_0 e^{b_0 x} + a_1 e^{b_1 x} + \cdots + a_n e^{b_n x} = \sum_{i=0}^n a_i e^{b_i x}.$$

Rational approximations,

$$f(x) \doteq g(x) = \frac{a_0 + a_1 x + a_2 x^2 + \cdots + a_n x^n}{b_0 + b_1 x + b_2 x^2 + \cdots + b_m x^m} = \frac{p_n(x)}{p_m(x)},$$

are also used, although less frequently than are the polynomials and Fourier functions.

The algebraic polynomials $p_n(x)$ are by far the most important and popular approximating functions. The case for their use is strong, although not overwhelming. The theory of polynomial approximation is well developed and fairly simple. Polynomials are easy to evaluate and their sums, products, and differences are also polynomials. Polynomials can be differentiated and integrated with little difficulty, yielding other polynomials in both cases. In addition, if the origin of the coordinate system is shifted or if the scale of the independent variable is changed, the transformed polynomials remain polynomials, that is, if $p_n(x)$ is a polynomial, so are $p_n(x + a)$ and $p_n(ax)$. Some, but not all, of these favorable properties

---

* The conventional compact polynomial notation will be used throughout, it being understood that $p_n(0) = a_0$.

are possessed by the Fourier approximations as well. As we shall see later, most of the other functions considered as potential candidates for approximating functions (sines, cosines, exponentials, etc.) must themselves be evaluated by using approximations; almost invariably, these approximations are given in terms of polynomials or ratios of polynomials.

All these obvious advantages of the polynomials would be of little value if there were no analytical justification for believing that polynomials can, in fact, yield good approximations for a given function $f(x)$. Here, "good" implies that the discrepancy between an approximating polynomial $p_n(x)$ and $f(x)$, that is, the error in the approximation, can be made arbitrarily small. Fortunately, this theoretical justification does exist. *Any* continuous function $f(x)$ can be approximated to *any* desired degree of accuracy on a specified closed interval by *some* polynomial $p_n(x)$. This follows from the *Weierstrass approximation theorem* stated here without proof [6]:

If $f(x)$ is continuous in the closed interval $[a,b]$, (that is, $a \leqslant x \leqslant b$) then, given any $\epsilon > 0$, there is some polynomial $p_n(x)$ of degree $n \equiv n(\epsilon)$ such that

$$|f(x) - p_n(x)| < \epsilon, \qquad a \leqslant x \leqslant b.$$

Unfortunately, although it is reassuring to know that *some* polynomial will approximate $f(x)$ to a specified accuracy, the usual criteria for generating approximating polynomials in no way guarantee that the polynomial found is the one which the Weierstrass theorem shows must exist. If $f(x)$ is in fact unknown except for a few sampled values, then the theorem is of little relevance. (It is comforting nonetheless!)

The case for polynomials as approximating functions is not so strong that other possibilities should be ruled out completely. Periodic functions can often be approximated very efficiently with Fourier functions; functions with an obvious exponential character will be described more compactly with a sum of exponentials, etc. Nevertheless, for the general approximation problem, polynomial approximations are usually adequate and reasonably easy to generate.

The remainder of this chapter will be devoted to polynomial approximations of the form

$$f(x) \doteq p_n(x) = \sum_{i=0}^{n} a_i x^i. \qquad (1.1)$$

For a thorough discussion of several other approximating functions, see Hamming [2].

1.3   Polynomial Approximation—A Survey

After selection of an nth-degree polynomial (1.1) as the approximating function, we must choose the criterion for "fitting the data." This is equivalent to establishing the procedure for computing the values of the coefficients $a_0, a_1, \ldots, a_n$.

The Interpolating Polynomial. Given the paired values $(x_i, f(x_i))$, $i = 0, 1, \ldots, n$, perhaps the most obvious criterion for determining the coefficients of $p_n(x)$ is to require that

$$p_n(x_i) = f(x_i), \qquad i = 0, 1, \ldots, n. \qquad (1.2)$$

Thus the nth degree polynomial $p_n(x)$ must reproduce $f(x)$ *exactly* for the $n + 1$ arguments $x = x_i$. This criterion seems especially pertinent since (from a fundamental theorem of algebra) there is one and only one polynomial of degree n or less which assumes specified values for $n + 1$ distinct arguments. This polynomial, called the *nth degree interpolating polynomial*, is illustrated schematically for $n = 3$ in Fig. 1.1. Note that requirement (1.2)

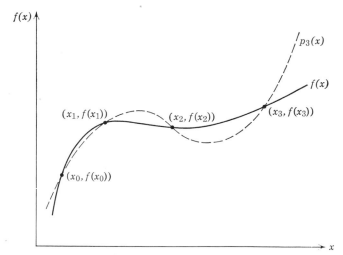

Figure 1.1   *The interpolating polynomial.*

establishes the value of $p_n(x)$ for *all* x, but in no way guarantees accurate approximation of $f(x)$ for $x \neq x_i$, that is, for arguments other than the given base points. If $f(x)$ should be a polynomial of degree n or less, agreement is of course *exact* for all x.

The interpolating polynomial will be developed in considerable detail in Sections 1.5 to 1.9.

The Least-Squares Polynomial. If there is some question as to the accuracy of the individual values $f(x_i)$, $i = 0, 1, \ldots, n$ (often the case with experimental data), then it may be unreasonable to require that a polynomial fit the $f(x_i)$ exactly. In addition, it often happens that the desired polynomial is of low degree, say m, but that there are many data values available, so that $n > m$. Since the exact matching criterion of (1.2) for $n + 1$ functional values can be satisfied only by one polynomial of degree n or less, it is generally impossible to find an interpolating polynomial of degree m using all $n + 1$ of the sampled functional values.

Some other measure of goodness-of-fit is needed. Instead of requiring that the approximating polynomial reproduce the given functional values exactly, we ask only that it fit the data as closely as possible. Of the many meanings which might be ascribed to "as closely as possible," the most popular involves application of the *least-squares* principle. We fit the given $n + 1$ functional values with $p_m(x)$, a polynomial of degree m, requiring that the sum of the squares of the discrepancies between the $f(x_i)$ and $p_m(x_i)$ be a minimum. If the discrepancy at the ith base point x_i is given by $\delta_i = p_m(x_i) - f(x_i)$, the least-squares criterion requires that the $a_j, j = 0, 1, \ldots, m$, be chosen so that the aggregate squared error

$$E = \sum_{i=0}^{n} \delta_i^2 = \sum_{i=0}^{n} [p_m(x_i) - f(x_i)]^2$$

$$= \sum_{i=0}^{n} \left[\sum_{j=0}^{m} a_j x_i^j - f(x_i) \right]^2 \qquad (1.3)$$

be as small as possible. If m should equal n, the minimum error E is exactly zero, and the least-squares polynomial is identical with the interpolating polynomial. Figure 1.2

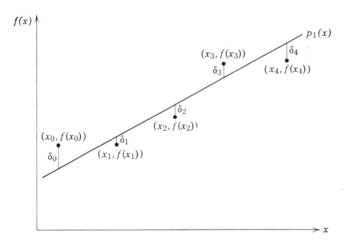

Figure 1.2   *The least-squares polynomial.*

illustrates the fitting of five functional values ($n = 4$) with a *least-squares polynomial* of degree one ($m = 1$), that is, a straight line.

When the values $f(x_i)$ are thought to be of unequal reliability or precision, the least-squares criterion is sometimes modified to require that the squared error at x_i be multiplied by a nonnegative *weight factor* $w(x_i)$ before the aggregate squared error is calculated, that is, (1.3) assumes the form

$$E = \sum_{i=0}^{n} w(x_i) \delta_i^2.$$

The weight $w(x_i)$ is thus a measure of the degree of precision or relative importance of the value $f(x_i)$ in determining the coefficients of the *weighted least-squares polynomial* $p_m(x)$.

The least-squares principle may also be used to find an approximating polynomial $p_m(x)$ for a known continuous function $f(x)$ on the interval $[a,b]$. In this case the object is to choose the coefficients of $p_m(x)$ which minimize E where

$$E = \int_a^b w(x)[p_m(x) - f(x)]^2 \, dx.$$

Here, $w(x)$ is a nonnegative weighting function; in many cases, $w(x) = 1$.

Since the motivation for the least-squares criterion is essentially statistical in nature, further description of the least-squares polynomial will be delayed until Chapter 8.

The Minimax Polynomial. Another popular criterion, termed the *minimax principle*, requires that the coefficients of the approximating polynomial $p_m(x)$ be chosen so that the maximum magnitude of the differences $f(x_i) - p_m(x_i)$, $i = 0, 1, \ldots, n$, $(m < n)$ be as small as possible. Then the *minimax polynomial* of degree m must satisfy the condition

$$\max_i |f(x_i) - p_m(x_i)| = \text{minimum}, \qquad (1.4)$$

that is, $p_m(x)$ must *minimize* the *maximum* error. In more general form, this condition may be written

$$\max_{a \leqslant x \leqslant b} |f(x) - p_m(x)| = \text{minimum}.$$

The minimax polynomial is often called the *optimal* polynomial approximation.

The minimax principle is attributed to Chebyshev, and the minimax polynomials are closely related to the Chebyshev polynomials described in Section 1.10.

Power Series. If a function $f(x)$ is continuous and suitably differentiable, it can be written in terms of a Taylor's series. We assume that the reader is familiar with the Taylor's (power) series expansion of a function; the development may be found in any elementary calculus text. One of the most useful and easily generated polynomial approximations $p_n(x)$ of a function (provided that the required derivative terms can be evaluated) results from truncation of its power series expansion after the nth-degree term. In order to establish a bound for the error introduced by the truncation process, we make use of *Taylor's formula with remainder* [8]:

If a continuous function $f(x)$ possesses a continuous $(n + 1)$th derivative everywhere on the interval $[x_0, x]$, it can be represented by a finite power series

$$f(x) = f(x_0) + (x - x_0)f'(x) + (x - x_0)^2$$

$$\times \frac{f''(x_0)}{2!} + (x - x_0)^3 \frac{f^{(3)}(x_0)}{3!}$$

$$+ \cdots + (x - x_0)^i \frac{f^{(i)}(x_0)}{i!} + \cdots$$

$$+ (x - x_0)^n \frac{f^{(n)}(x_0)}{n!} + R(x)$$

$$= p_n(x) + R(x), \qquad (1.5)$$

where $R(x)$, the *remainder*, is given by

$$R(x) = (x - x_0)^{n+1} \frac{f^{(n+1)}(\xi)}{(n + 1)!}. \qquad (1.6)$$

Here $x_0 < \xi < x$, or, if $x < x_0$, $x < \xi < x_0$. Henceforth* this will be written more succinctly as ξ in (x,x_0).

The parameter ξ in (1.6) is an unknown function of x. Hence, except in very special cases (for example, when $f^{(n+1)}(\xi)$ is a constant), it is impossible to evaluate the error or remainder term $R(x)$ exactly. Nevertheless, we shall see that (1.6) can prove useful in establishing an *upper bound* for the error incurred when $p_n(x)$ is used to approximate $f(x)$. Provided that $f(x)$ meets the continuity and differentiability requirements of the formula, the polynomial $p_n(x)$ given by (1.5) may be viewed as fitting exactly the $n + 1$ paired values $(x_0,f(x_0)),(x_0,f'(x_0))$, $(x_0,f''(x_0)), \ldots, (x_0,f^{(n)}(x_0))$, since $p_n^{(i)}(x_0) = f^{(i)}(x_0)$.

For the most commonly encountered polynomial approximation problem, in which only the functional values $f(x_i)$ are known at $n + 1$ distinct base points $x_i, i = 0, 1, \ldots, n$, the Taylor's expansion of (1.5) is of little use, since it is usually not possible to evaluate the required derivatives. However, if the function $f(x)$ is known analytically and is simply differentiable, then useful approximations $p_n(x)$ can be found easily. By establishing an upper bound for the magnitude of the remainder $R(x)$, and hence of the error in $p_n(x)$, we can use the approximating polynomial with complete confidence in the region of interest.

Example. Expand the function $f(x) = \cos x$ in a Taylor's series. Use Taylor's formula with remainder to find a third-degree polynomial approximation $p_3(x) \doteq \cos x$. For $x_0 = 0$ and $x_0 = \pi/4$, estimate $\cos(\pi/2)$ from $p_3(x)$; establish bounds on the errors in the estimated values, using (1.6).

Cos x and its first four derivatives are:

$$f(x) = \cos x \qquad f'''(x) = \sin x$$
$$f'(x) = -\sin x \qquad f^{(4)}(x) = \cos x$$
$$f''(x) = -\cos x.$$

Substitution into (1.5) and (1.6) with $n = 3$ yields:

$$\cos(x) \doteq p_3(x) = \cos x_0 - (x - x_0) \sin x_0$$
$$-\frac{(x - x_0)^2}{2!} \cos x_0 + \frac{(x - x_0)^3}{3!} \sin x_0, \quad (1.7)$$

$$R(x) = \frac{(x - x_0)^4}{4!} \cos \xi, \qquad \xi \text{ in } (x,x_0).$$

For $x_0 = 0$:

$$\sin(0) = 0, \cos(0) = 1$$

$$\cos x \doteq 1 - \frac{x^2}{2!}, \qquad\qquad (1.8)$$

$$R(x) = \frac{x^4}{4!} \cos \xi, \qquad \xi \text{ in } (x,0).$$

* In general, the notation ξ in $(x,x_0,x_1, \ldots, x_n)$ will indicate that ξ is in the *open* interval determined by the smallest and largest of the enclosed arguments.

For $x_0 = \pi/4$:

$$\sin(\pi/4) \doteq 0.7071, \cos(\pi/4) \doteq 0.7071,$$

$$\cos x \doteq 0.7071 \left[1 - (x - \pi/4) - \frac{(x - \pi/4)^2}{2!} + \frac{(x - \pi/4)^3}{3!} \right],$$

$$R(x) = \frac{(x - \pi/4)^4}{4!} \cos \xi, \qquad \xi \text{ in } (x,\pi/4). \quad (1.9)$$

We now use (1.8) and (1.9) to estimate $\cos(\pi/2)$. From (1.8), $\cos(\pi/2) \doteq 1 - \pi^2/8 \doteq -0.2337$. Since ξ is unknown, but $0 < \xi < \pi/2$, an estimate of the error bound is given by

$$R(x)_{max} = \frac{x^4}{4!} (\cos \xi)_{max} = \frac{(\pi/2)^4}{4!} (1) \doteq 0.2537.$$

In this case, since the sign of the error is known (because $\cos \xi$ is positive for all x, $0 < x < \pi/2$), we could also write:

$$-0.2337 \leqslant \cos(\pi/2) \leqslant 0.0200.$$

Note that although the error is sizeable [$\cos(\pi/2) = 0.0$], it is smaller than the predicted upper bound.

From (1.9),

$$\cos(\pi/2) \doteq 0.7071 \left[1 - \frac{\pi}{4} - \frac{\pi^2}{16 \times 2!} + \frac{\pi^3}{64 \times 3!} \right] \doteq -0.00953.$$

Since $\cos \xi$ has a maximum value 0.7071 on the interval $\pi/4 < \xi < \pi/2$,

$$R(x)_{max} = \frac{(x - \pi/4)^4}{4!} (\cos \xi)_{max} \doteq \frac{(\pi/4)^4}{4!} (0.7071) \doteq 0.01121.$$

As before, the sign of R is known to be positive, and the approximation could be written:

$$-0.00953 \leqslant \cos(\pi/2) \leqslant 0.00168.$$

The error is again smaller than the upper bound. The approximation is much better than in the previous case.

The preceding example illustrates the influence of the polynomial $(x - x_0)^{n+1}$ on the remainder term of (1.6), $R(x)$. Normally, to approximate best a function $f(x)$ on the interval $[a,b]$, x_0 should be chosen near the middle of the interval; we can show that the choice $x_0 = (a + b)/2$ minimizes the maximum contribution of the term $(x - x_0)^{n+1}$ to the remainder for $a \leqslant x \leqslant b$. For a fixed value of n (that is, for a fixed number of terms retained in the series), this is about the only practical way of reducing the magnitude of the error in the approximating polynomial $p_n(x)$. The value of $f^{(n+1)}(\xi)$ for a given x in $[a,b]$ cannot be computed, in general, since ξ is an unknown function of x. Consequently, in estimating the error $R(x)$, we can only be certain that $|f^{(n+1)}(\xi)|$ can be no greater than the maximum value of $|f^{(n+1)}(x)|$ for x in $[a,b]$. Of course, if each successive term in the Taylor's expansion is smaller in magnitude than the previous ones (often but not always the case), another way to lower the upper bound on the magnitude of $R(x)$ is to include additional terms in the approximation, that is, to increase the degree of the approximating polynomial.

1.4 Evaluation of Polynomials and Their Derivatives

Efficient evaluation of a polynomial

$$p_n(x) = \sum_{i=0}^{n} a_i x^i = a_0 + a_1 x + a_2 x^2 + \cdots + a_n x^n$$

may be important if $p_n(x)$ is to be computed many times for different values of x. Straightforward term-by-term evaluation is inefficient, particularly for large values of n. If each factor x^k is computed by $k - 1$ repeated multiplications of x, then $n(n + 1)/2$ multiplications and n additions are required to evaluate $p_n(x)$. If each factor x^k is calculated by successive multiplications, $x \cdot x^{k-1}$, then $2n - 1$ multiplications and n additions are required. However, if the *nested* form of $p_n(x)$,

$$p_n(x) = a_0 + x(a_1 + x(a_2 + \cdots + x(a_{n-1} + xa_n)\cdots)),$$

$$(1.10)$$

is used, then only n multiplications and n additions are required per evaluation. The procedure described by (1.10) is called *Horner's rule*. It has been shown [5] that for $n \leqslant 4$, the nested evaluation requires the minimum possible number of arithmetic operations. For polynomials of higher degree, other schemes which require fewer than $2n$ operations (on the average) are known, particularly when $p_n(x)$ is to be evaluated many times. The procedure is generally different for each n [4,19]. For most applications, the nested computing scheme of (1.10) is adequate.

Since the calculations in the innermost parentheses must be performed first, the computing procedure for

---

```
                .
        P = A(N + 1)
        IF (N.LT.1)     GO TO 2
        DO 1    J = 1, N
        I = N − J
      1 P = P*X + A(I + 1)
      2 .
                .
                .
```

Algorithm 1

---

evaluating $p_n(x)$ can be seen more easily if the terms on the right-hand side of (1.10) are written in reversed order as follows:

$$p_n(x) = ((\cdots(a_n x + a_{n-1})x + a_{n-2})x + \cdots + a_1)x + a_0.$$

For example, for $n = 4$,

$$p_4(x) = (((a_4 x + a_3)x + a_2)x + a_1)x + a_0.$$

Using the flow diagram conventions outlined in the appendix, two algorithms for implementing the computation of (1.10) are shown in Fig. 1.3. In each case, the value of $p_n(x)$ is assigned to the symbol p.

Transcription of these two flow diagrams into two FORTRAN IV statement sequences is complicated somewhat by the following restrictions in the FORTRAN IV language as implemented on most of the digital computers now in use [10,11]:

1. Zero is not a permitted subscript for subscripted variables.

2. Subscripts are limited to simple arithmetic expressions of the form $c_1 v \pm c_2$ where c_1 and c_2 are non-negative integer constants and v is a nonsubscripted integer variable.

3. The initial value, increment, and terminal value of the iteration variable in the iteration (DO) statement must be positive integer constants or variables.

4. The iteration (DO) loop is executed at least once, even when the upper limit of the iteration variable is smaller than the initial value of the iteration variable.

Some of these difficulties can be avoided if a different subscription convention is used in (1.10). However, given the subscription convention of (1.10), assume that FORTRAN variables N and X have been assigned the values of n and x, respectively; let the values of the coefficients $a_0, \ldots, a_n$ be assigned in sequence to the elements of the FORTRAN subscripted variable A from A(1) to A(N + 1). Thus coefficient a_i is assigned to array element A(I + 1), where problem variable i is equivalent to program variable I. If J is a counting variable and NP1 is a variable assigned the value $n + 1$, FORTRAN IV statement sequences which describe algorithms 1 and 2 and assign the computed value of $p_n(x)$ to the FORTRAN variable P are:

```
                .
        P = 0.0
        NP1 = N + 1
        DO 1    J = 1, NP1
        I = N − J + 1
      1 P = P*X + A(I + 1)
      2 .
                .
                .
```

Algorithm 2

In both FORTRAN sequences a few integer operations could be eliminated, but not without destroying the equivalence of program variable I and problem variable i.

McCracken and Dorn [9] show that in addition to saving computing time, the nested scheme leads to a lower bound for the total round-off error than straightforward term-by-term evaluation when the coefficients a_i become smaller with increasing i. The term *round-off error* refers to those errors resulting from the rounding and/or truncation of the results of individual arithmetic operations on a computing machine. They are generated because the memories of all real machines are finite and

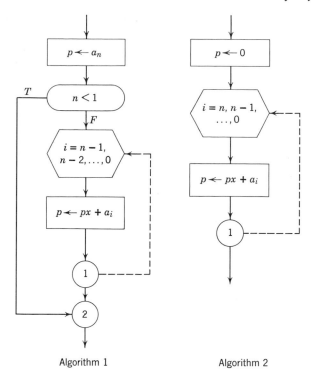

Algorithm 1   Algorithm 2

Figure 1.3 *Evaluation of a polynomial $p_n(x)$ using Horner's rule.*

only a fixed, usually small, number of digits can be retained after each arithmetic operation. The extent of round-off error associated with any algorithm depends upon the computing machine used (the number of digits retained, whether numbers are rounded or truncated, etc.), the particular sequence of machine operations used, and the values of the various numbers involved in these machine operations.

Analysis of the round-off error present in the final result of a numerical computation, usually termed the *accumulated* round-off error, is difficult, particularly when the algorithm used is of some complexity. Except in very simple cases, the accumulated error is not simply the sum of the *local* round-off errors, that is, errors resulting from individual rounding or truncation operations. The local error at any stage of the calculation is propagated (either magnified or diminished) throughout the remaining part of the computation. In order to establish a round-off error *bound*, one must assume the worst possible outcome for the result of each arithmetic operation and follow the propagation of all such errors throughout the remaining calculations. In cases where it is possible to do this, the resulting bounds are almost invariably very conservative; the observed errors are usually much smaller than the calculated bounds, although they can be very considerable in some problems (we shall attempt to point out those algorithms in which round-off error may be a serious problem). In recent years, numerical analysts have attempted to create statistical models of the propagation of rounding errors [12],

wherein local round-off errors are treated as if they were random variables. Such models produce much smaller and usually more realistic estimates of round-off error actually observed than do the round-off error bounds.

The sequence of factors computed during evaluation of $p_n(x)$ for a particular argument $x = t$ is closely related to that involved in removing the factor $(x - t)$ from $p_n(x)$ by *synthetic division*. Using the notation of (1.10), let

$$b_n = a_n,$$
$$b_i = b_{i+1}t + a_i, \qquad i = n - 1, \ldots, 0. \qquad (1.11)$$

The sequence of values of the b_i in (1.11) is exactly the sequence of values assumed by the FORTRAN variable P in the two FORTRAN program segments of page 6, and b_0 is equivalent to the right-hand side of (1.10) with $x = t$, that is, $b_0 = p_n(t)$. For example, for $n = 4$,

$$b_4 = a_4$$
$$b_3 = b_4t + a_3 = a_4t + a_3$$
$$b_2 = b_3t + a_2 = (a_4t + a_3)t + a_2$$
$$b_1 = b_2t + a_1 = ((a_4t + a_3)t + a_2)t + a_1$$
$$b_0 = b_1t + a_0 = (((a_4t + a_3)t + a_2)t + a_1)t + a_0.$$

Now let us divide $p_n(x)$ by the factor $(x - t)$ to yield

$$\frac{p_n(x)}{(x - t)} = q_{n-1}(x) + \frac{R_0}{(x - t)},$$

or

$$p_n(x) = (x - t)q_{n-1}(x) + R_0.$$

Here $q_{n-1}(x)$ is a polynomial of degree $n - 1$ and R_0 is the constant remainder. The coefficients of $q_{n-1}(x)$ and R_0 depend on t. By carrying out the indicated division in longhand or, more simply, by equating coefficients of like powers of x on both sides of the last equation, it can be seen that

$$q_{n-1}(x) = b_nx^{n-1} + b_{n-1}x^{n-2} + \cdots + b_2x + b_1,$$
$$R_0 = b_0 = p_n(t),$$

where the b_i are given by (1.11).

If we divide $q_{n-1}(x)$ by the factor $(x - t)$ in similar fashion we get a polynomial $q_{n-2}(x)$ of degree $n - 2$ with constant remainder R_1 such that

$$q_{n-1}(x) = (x - t)q_{n-2}(x) + R_1.$$

Let $q_{n-2}(x)$ be written as

$$q_{n-2}(x) = c_nx^{n-2} + c_{n-1}x^{n-3} + \cdots + c_3x + c_2.$$

By analogy with (1.11), we may write

$$c_n = b_n,$$
$$c_i = c_{i+1}t + b_i, \qquad i = n - 1, \ldots, 1,$$

where $c_1 = R_1 = q_{n-1}(t)$. The original polynomial becomes

$$p_n(x) = (x - t)^2q_{n-2}(x) + (x - t)R_1 + R_0$$

and its first derivative becomes

$$p_n'(x) = 2(x - t)q_{n-2}(x) + (x - t)^2 q_{n-2}'(x) + R_1,$$

so that $p_n'(t) = R_1 = c_1$. The process of using the nested form of (1.10) for $q_{n-2}(x)$, followed by division by a factor $(x - t)$ to generate a new polynomial $q_{n-3}(x)$ with remainder R_2, is continued until the original polynomial is written in the form

$$p_n(x) = (x - t)^n R_n + (x - t)^{n-1} R_{n-1}$$
$$+ \cdots + (x - t)R_1 + R_0.$$

Then $p_n(t) = R_0$, $p_n'(t) = R_1$, $p_n''(t) = 2R_2$, etc. In general, $p_n^{(i)}(t) = i! R_i$. This procedure is best illustrated by preparing a table of the a_i, b_i, c_i, and coefficients of the other intermediate polynomials $q_{n-3}(x)$, $q_{n-4}(x)$, etc., as follows:

$$
\begin{array}{llllll}
a_0 & b_0 = R_0 \\
a_1 & b_1 & c_1 = R_1 \\
a_2 & b_2 & c_2 & R_2 \\
a_3 & b_3 & c_3 & . & R_3 \\
. & . & . & . & . & R_4 \\
. & . & . & . & . \\
. & . & . & . & . \\
a_{n-1} & b_{n-1} & c_{n-1} & . & . & . & R_{n-1} \\
a_n & b_n & c_n & . & . & . & . & R_n
\end{array}
$$

If we let $T_{i,j}$ be the entry in the ith row and jth column of the table, then the procedure for calculating the non-zero table elements is:

1. $T_{i,0} = a_i$, $i = 0, 1, \ldots, n$.
2. $T_{n,j} = a_n$, $j = 1, 2, \ldots, n + 1$.
3. $T_{i,j} = T_{i+1,j} t + T_{i,j-1}$, $j = 1, 2, \ldots, n$; $i = n - 1, n - 2, \ldots, j - 1$.
4. $p_n^{(i)}(t) = i! T_{i,i+1}$, $i = 0, 1, \ldots, n$.   (1.12)

Example. Use the algorithm of (1.12) to evaluate the polynomial

$$p_4(x) = 3x^4 + 2x^3 - x^2 + 2x - 5$$

and its derivatives of order 1 through 4 for $x = 2$.

The elements of the T table computed using the first three steps of (1.12) are shown below:

i	$j = 0$	1	2	3	4	$5 = n+1$
0	-5	59				
1	2	32	118			
2	-1	15	43	83		
3	2	8	14	20	26	
$4 = n$	3	3	3	3	3	3

Using step 4 of (1.12), the values of the polynomial and its first four derivatives for $x = 2$ are:

$$p_4(2) = R_0 = 59$$
$$p_4'(2) = R_1 = 118$$
$$p_4''(2) = 2R_2 = 166$$
$$p_4^{(3)}(2) = 6R_3 = 156$$
$$p_4^{(4)}(2) = 24R_4 = 72.$$

1.5 The Interpolating Polynomial

It is important to reiterate that there is *one and only one* polynomial of degree n or less which assumes the exact values $f(x_0), f(x_1), \ldots, f(x_n)$ at $n + 1$ distinct base points $x_0, x_1, \ldots, x_n$, that is, satisfies (1.2). Therefore, although the many polynomial interpolation formulas to be found in the literature *appear* to be different, those which use the same base-point information and the same criterion (1.2) for computing the coefficients $a_0, a_1, \ldots, a_n$ *must* be fundamentally the same. The interpolating polynomial has coefficients a_i which are the solutions of the set of $n + 1$ simultaneous linear equations:

$$a_0 + a_1 x_0 + a_2 x_0^2 + \cdots + a_n x_0^n = f(x_0)$$
$$a_0 + a_1 x_1 + a_2 x_1^2 + \cdots + a_n x_1^n = f(x_1)$$
$$a_0 + a_1 x_2 + a_2 x_2^2 + \cdots + a_n x_2^n = f(x_2)$$
$$\vdots \qquad\qquad\qquad\qquad \vdots$$
$$a_0 + a_1 x_n + a_2 x_n^2 + \cdots + a_n x_n^n = f(x_n).$$

The determinant of the matrix of coefficients for these equations

$$
\begin{vmatrix}
1 & x_0 & x_0^2 & \cdots & x_0^n \\
1 & x_1 & x_1^2 & \cdots & x_1^n \\
1 & x_2 & x_2^2 & \cdots & x_2^n \\
\vdots & & & & \vdots \\
1 & x_n & x_n^2 & \cdots & x_n^n
\end{vmatrix}
$$

is known as the Vandermonde determinant and is nonzero if $x_i \neq x_j$, $i \neq j$. Thus (see Chapter 4) there is a unique solution for the a_i, that is, there is a unique polynomial $p_n(x)$ which exactly reproduces $f(x)$ at the sample points.

Since the coefficients of the desired polynomial may be computed by solving this set of simultaneous linear equations, there is some question as to the need for interpolating formulas. One reason for not using the simultaneous equations approach is that solving a linear system of any size is not an easy task (see Chapter 5), particularly if hand methods are being used. More important, perhaps, the development of an interpolating formula often produces an error term as a by-product. While it is not possible to evaluate this error term exactly, one can frequently find an upper bound for the error, or barring that, some order-of-magnitude estimate of the error. The importance of such information can hardly be overstated.

Obviously, the smaller the error bound, the greater confidence one has in using the derived polynomial.

Most numerical analysis textbooks cover in great detail the subject of interpolation by formulas derived from the criterion of (1.2). All can be classified into one of two groups: those applicable for arbitrarily spaced base points and those for evenly spaced base points, that is, for base points,

$$
\begin{aligned}
x_0 & \\
x_1 &= x_0 + h \\
x_2 &= x_0 + 2h \\
&\vdots \\
x_i &= x_0 + ih \\
&\vdots \\
x_n &= x_0 + nh,
\end{aligned}
$$

where h is the constant spacing or stepsize between adjacent ordered x_i values.

In what follows, the two most common forms of the interpolating polynomial for arbitrarily spaced base points, *Newton's divided-difference interpolating polynomial* and *Lagrange's interpolating polynomial* will be developed in some detail. Both permit arbitrary ordering of the base points $x_0, x_1, x_2, \ldots, x_n$ as well. Duplicate base-point values are not permitted, since the Vandermonde determinant would vanish and the system of equations in the unknown coefficients would have no unique solution.

The equal-interval formulas have been developed to simplify interpolation in tables of functions with evenly spaced arguments. Some have been developed specifically for interpolation near the beginning, middle, or end of a table. All can be derived from either Lagrange's or Newton's divided-difference interpolating polynomial. With the widespread use of high-speed computers, tabular interpolation of this sort has lost much of its importance. Almost without exception, functional values needed for digital computation are generated directly by subroutines from the computer's program library. As a consequence, only a few of the most important equal-interval formulas will be shown, primarily because of their use in the development of numerical integration formulas (see Chapter 2).

1.6 Newton's Divided-Difference Interpolating Polynomial

Consider the definition of the derivative:

$$
\left[\frac{df(x)}{dx}\right]_{x_0} = f'(x_0) = \lim_{x \to x_0} \frac{f(x) - f(x_0)}{x - x_0}.
$$

For the finite or discrete mathematics, it is useful to define an approximation to the derivative,

$$
f[x, x_0] = \frac{f(x) - f(x_0)}{x - x_0}, \qquad x \neq x_0, \qquad (1.13)
$$

where $f[x, x_0]$ is termed the *first finite divided difference* or the *finite divided difference of order one* relative to arguments x, x_0.

The relationship of the first finite divided difference and the first derivative is clearly indicated by the *differential mean-value theorem* from the elementary calculus:

Let $f(x)$ be continuous for $a \leqslant x \leqslant b$ and differentiable for $a < x < b$; then there exists at least one ξ, $a < \xi < b$, for which

$$
f'(\xi) = \frac{f(b) - f(a)}{b - a}.
$$

Graphically (see Fig. 1.4), this simply means that if $f(x)$ is continuous and suitably differentiable on some interval in x, then there is at least one point $x = \xi$ on the interval for which the slope of the line tangent to $f(x)$ [that is, the derivative, $f'(\xi)$] is the same as the slope of the line joining the functional values at the ends of the interval.

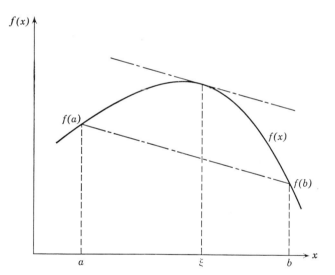

Figure 1.4 Illustration of the differential mean-value theorem.

Thus the first finite divided difference of (1.13) is related to the first derivative (provided that the continuity and differentiability restrictions of the theorem are met) as follows:

$$
f[x, x_0] = \frac{f(x) - f(x_0)}{x - x_0} = f'(\xi), \qquad \xi \text{ in } (x, x_0).
$$

$$(1.14)$$

In order to permit similar approximations for higher-order derivatives as well, the concept of the finite divided difference is extended as shown in Table 1.1, where it is

Table 1.1   The Finite Divided Differences

Order	Difference Notation	Definition
0	$f[x_0]$	$f(x_0)$
1	$f[x_1,x_0]$	$\dfrac{f[x_1] - f[x_0]}{x_1 - x_0}$
2	$f[x_2,x_1,x_0]$	$\dfrac{f[x_2,x_1] - f[x_1,x_0]}{x_2 - x_0}$
3	$f[x_3,x_2,x_1,x_0]$	$\dfrac{f[x_3,x_2,x_1] - f[x_2,x_1,x_0]}{x_3 - x_0}$
$\vdots$		
n	$f[x_n,x_{n-1},x_{n-2}, \ldots, x_1,x_0]$	$\dfrac{f[x_n,x_{n-1}, \ldots, x_1] - f[x_{n-1},x_{n-2}, \ldots, x_0]}{x_n - x_0}.$

assumed that tabulated sample values at $n + 1$ discrete base points are available as follows:

$$\begin{aligned} x_0 \quad & f(x_0) \\ x_1 \quad & f(x_1) \\ & \vdots \\ x_i \quad & f(x_i) \\ & \vdots \\ x_n \quad & f(x_n). \end{aligned}$$

The general relationship between higher-order finite divided differences and the derivatives of corresponding orders is shown later in (1.41). Note that the divisor in each divided difference involves the difference of the two arguments which are not common to the two divided differences in the numerator.

It is apparent from the definition of the divided difference of order one that

$$f[x_1,x_0] = f[x_0,x_1], \qquad (1.15)$$

that is, the order of the two arguments is immaterial. With a little algebraic manipulation it can be shown that

$$f[x_2,x_1,x_0] = f[x_{\alpha_0},x_{\alpha_1},x_{\alpha_2}],$$

where α_0, α_1, α_2 is any permutation of the integers 2, 1, 0. In general it follows by induction that

$$f[x_n,x_{n-1}, \ldots, x_0] = f[x_{\alpha_0},x_{\alpha_1}, \ldots, x_{\alpha_n}] \qquad (1.16)$$

where the sequence of integers α_0, α_1, α_2, ..., α_n is any permutation of n, $n - 1$, $n - 2$, ..., 0.

It is also apparent from the definition that

$$f[x_0,x_1] = f[x_1,x_0] = \frac{f(x_1)}{(x_1 - x_0)} + \frac{f(x_0)}{(x_0 - x_1)}.$$

Algebraic manipulation of differences of increasing order leads by induction to a similar *symmetric* form for the nth divided difference in terms of the tabulated arguments and functional values:

$$\begin{aligned} f[x_n,x_{n-1}, \ldots, x_0] = & \frac{f(x_n)}{(x_n - x_{n-1})(x_n - x_{n-2}) \cdots (x_n - x_0)} \\ & + \frac{f(x_{n-1})}{(x_{n-1} - x_n)(x_{n-1} - x_{n-2}) \cdots (x_{n-1} - x_0)} \\ & + \cdots \\ & + \frac{f(x_0)}{(x_0 - x_n)(x_0 - x_{n-1}) \cdots (x_0 - x_1)}. \end{aligned}$$

This symmetric form can be written more compactly as

$$f[x_n,x_{n-1}, \ldots, x_0] = \sum_{i=0}^{n} \frac{f(x_i)}{\prod\limits_{\substack{j=0 \\ j \neq i}}^{n} (x_i - x_j)}. \qquad (1.17)$$

Consider the problem of *linear* interpolation to evaluate the *linear* function $f(x)$ at argument x, $x_0 < x < x_1$, given only the base-point information:

$$\begin{aligned} x_0 \quad & f(x_0) \\ x_1 \quad & f(x_1). \end{aligned}$$

This situation is shown schematically in Fig. 1.5. From geometric considerations alone, it is apparent that, for this case,

$$f[x,x_0] = f[x_1,x_0]. \qquad (1.18)$$

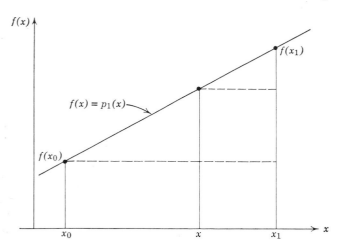

Figure 1.5 *Linear interpolation—f(x) linear.*

Replacing $f[x,x_0]$ by its definition from Table 1.1 yields

$$\frac{f(x) - f(x_0)}{x - x_0} = f[x_1,x_0]$$

or

$$\begin{aligned}
f(x) &= f(x_0) + (x - x_0)f[x_1,x_0] \\
&= f[x_0] + (x - x_0)f[x_1,x_0] \\
&= p_1(x).
\end{aligned} \tag{1.19}$$

Since all the elements on the right-hand side of (1.19), which defines a straight line or first-degree interpolating polynomial $p_1(x)$, can be evaluated from known quantities, the linear interpolant $f(x)$ can be computed directly. The procedure or algorithm of (1.19) is, of course, the one commonly used for linear interpolation, disguised somewhat by the presence of the divided-difference notation.

Consider linear interpolation between the tabulated points (1,1) and (3,5), shown schematically (Fig. 1.6a) and in tabular form (Fig. 1.6b).

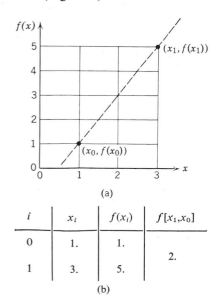

(a)

i	x_i	$f(x_i)$	$f[x_1,x_0]$
0	1.	1.	
			2.
1	3.	5.	

(b)

Figure 1.6 *Numerical example for linear interpolation.*

Substituting the tabular values into (1.19) yields

$$p_1(x) = f(x) = 1 + (x - 1)(2) = 2x - 1,$$

which is the straight line (first-degree polynomial) passing through the points (1,1) and (3,5).

Now let us reexamine the case of linear interpolation shown above. Suppose that $f(x)$ is *not* linear, that is, that equation (1.18) is only an *approximation*,

$$f[x,x_0] \doteq f[x_1,x_0]. \tag{1.20}$$

Equation (1.19) is then, of course, also only an approximation. This situation is shown schematically in Fig. 1.7.

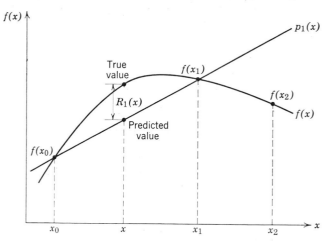

Figure 1.7 *Linear interpolation—f(x) not linear.*

To account for any discrepancy and to restore the desired equality, an error or remainder term $R_1(x)$ can be appended to (1.19). Then

$$f(x) = f[x_0] + (x - x_0)f[x_1,x_0] + R_1(x). \tag{1.21}$$

Solving (1.21) for $R_1(x)$ and collecting factors in terms of the finite divided differences yields

$$\begin{aligned}
R_1(x) &= (x - x_0)(f[x,x_0] - f[x_1,x_0]) \\
&= (x - x_0)(x - x_1)f[x,x_1,x_0].
\end{aligned} \tag{1.22}$$

Then (1.21) has the form

$$\begin{aligned}
f(x) &= f[x_0] + (x - x_0)f[x_1,x_0] \\
&\quad + (x - x_0)(x - x_1)f[x,x_1,x_0] \\
&= p_1(x) + R_1(x),
\end{aligned} \tag{1.23}$$

where $p_1(x)$ [see (1.19)] is, as before, the first-degree interpolating polynomial passing through the sample points $(x_0,f(x_0))$ and $(x_1,f(x_1))$. $R_1(x)$ is the discrepancy between $f(x)$ and $p_1(x)$ and will be termed the *remainder* or *error* term for the first-degree polynomial approximation of $f(x)$.

It is, of course, impossible to compute $f[x,x_1,x_0]$ exactly since $f(x)$, required for its evaluation, is unknown (otherwise there would be no need for interpolation in the first place). However, if an additional value of $f(x)$ is

where

$$R_n(x) = \left[\prod_{i=0}^{n}(x - x_i)\right]f[x,x_n,x_{n-1},\ldots,x_0] \quad (1.39a)$$

or

$$R_n(x) = \left[\prod_{i=0}^{n}(x - x_i)\right]\frac{f^{(n+1)}(\xi)}{(n+1)!},$$

$$\xi \text{ in } (x,x_n,x_{n-1},\ldots,x_0). \quad (1.39b)$$

The value of ξ is unknown, except that it is somewhere on the interval containing x and the base-point values $x_0, x_1, \ldots, x_n$. If the function $f(x)$ is given only in tabular form, then the second form (1.39b) of $R_n(x)$ is of little value since $f^{(n+1)}(\xi)$ cannot be determined. However, if $f(x)$ should be known analytically, then (1.39b) is useful in establishing an upper bound for the error.

Example. Several values of the cosine function and the corresponding divided differences of orders one through five are shown in Table 1.3. The differences have been computed by retaining only significant digits (equal to the number of digits in the numerator for each divided difference) at each stage of the calculation. Notice that each differencing operation tends to reduce the number of meaningful figures in a divided-difference table (see Example 1.1). Evaluate the second-degree interpolating polynomial passing through the functional values at θ_1, θ_2, and θ_3, for interpolation argument $\theta = 0.25$, that is, estimate the value cos (0.25).

The error given by (1.39a) is

$$R_2(\theta) = (\theta - \theta_3)(\theta - \theta_2)(\theta - \theta_1)\cos[\theta,\theta_3,\theta_2,\theta_1].$$

If we estimate $\cos[\theta,\theta_3,\theta_2,\theta_1]$ as the average of the three calculated third-order differences, an estimate of the error in the calculated cos(0.25) is

$$(0.05)(-0.05)(-0.15)(0.0371062 + 0.0609082$$
$$+ 0.0797050)/3 \doteq 2.22 \times 10^{-5}.$$

In this case we know that the functional values are for the function $\cos\theta$. Since we know that the third derivative is the function $\sin\theta$ and can establish its upper bound on the interval $[\theta_1,\theta_3] = [0.2,0.4]$, an upper bound for the interpolation error is given by (1.39b) as

$$\left|(\theta - \theta_3)(\theta - \theta_2)(\theta - \theta_1)\frac{\sin\xi}{3!}\right|$$

$$< \left|(0.05)(-0.05)(-0.15)\frac{\sin(0.4)}{3!}\right| \doteq 2.44 \times 10^{-5}.$$

Since the true value of cos(0.25) to seven significant figures is 0.9689124, the actual error is 1.77×10^{-5}.

Note that (1.39b) shows that if $f(x)$ is a polynomial of degree n or less, then $R_n(x)$ vanishes for all x. This is evidenced by the appearance of zeros in a table of divided differences. For example, consider the divided-difference table (Table 1.4).

Table 1.3   Divided-Difference Table for cos θ

i	θ_i Radians	$\cos\theta_i$	$f_1[\ ]$	$f_2[\ ]$	$f_3[\ ]$	$f_4[\ ]$	$f_5[\ ]$
0	0.0	1.00000000					
			−0.09966715				
1	0.2	0.98006657		−0.4921125			
			−0.2473009		0.0371062		
2	0.3	0.95533648		−0.4772700		0.0396700	
			−0.3427549		0.0609082		−0.0029662
3	0.4	0.92106099		−0.4529067		0.0375936	
			−0.4786269		0.0797050		
4	0.6	0.82533561		−0.4210247			
			−0.6049343				
5	0.7	0.76484218					

In terms of θ and the three base points θ_1, θ_2, and θ_3, (1.31) becomes

$$\cos\theta \doteq p_2(\theta) = \cos\theta_1 + (\theta - \theta_1)\cos[\theta_2,\theta_1]$$
$$+ (\theta - \theta_1)(\theta - \theta_2)\cos[\theta_3,\theta_2,\theta_1].$$

Then

$$\cos(0.25) \doteq 0.98006657 + (0.05)(-0.2473009)$$
$$+ (0.05)(-0.05)(-0.4772700)$$

or

$$\cos(0.25) \doteq 0.9688947.$$

The constant third differences and zero higher-order differences indicate that all six points can be fitted exactly with a third-degree polynomial. Without other information, however, it is not certain that $f(x)$ itself is a third-degree polynomial. In this case (1.33) would yield an estimated error of zero, which is the true error *only* if $f(x)$ is in fact a polynomial of degree three.

Some comments concerning the relationship of derivatives and the finite divided differences are in order.

Table 1.4   Divided-Difference Table

i	x_i	$f(x_i)$	$f_1[\ ]$	$f_2[\ ]$	$f_3[\ ]$	$f_4[\ ]$	$f_5[\ ]$
0	0.	−5.					
			6.				
1	1.	1.		2.			
			12.		1.		
2	3.	25.		6.		0.	
			30.		1.		0.
3	4.	55.		11.		0.	
			63.		1.		
4	6.	181.		15.			
			108.				
5	7.	289.					

Consider equation (1.30),

$$f(x) = p_n(x) + R_n(x).$$

Since $f(x)$ agrees exactly with $p_n(x)$ at the $n+1$ base points $x_0, x_1, \ldots, x_n$, $R_n(x)$ must vanish at least $n+1$ times on the interval determined by the base points. Rolle's theorem, applied repeatedly, shows that $R_n'(x)$ must vanish at least n times, $R_n''(x)$ at least $n-1$ times, etc., and that $R_n^{(n)}(x)$ must vanish at least once, say at $x = \xi$. Then differentiation of (1.30) n times and evaluation at $x = \xi$ yields

$$f^{(n)}(\xi) = p_n^{(n)}(\xi) + R_n^{(n)}(\xi) = p_n^{(n)}(\xi). \qquad (1.40)$$

But

$$p_n^{(n)}(\xi) = n!\, f[x_n, x_{n-1}, \ldots, x_0],$$

so that

$$f[x_n, x_{n-1}, \ldots, x_0] = \frac{f^{(n)}(\xi)}{n!},$$

$$\xi \text{ in } (x_n, x_{n-1}, \ldots, x_0). \qquad (1.41)$$

In general, a finite divided difference of any order is similarly related to the derivative of corresponding order evaluated at some point ξ on the interval containing all its arguments.

The order of the base-point indices is immaterial. For example, consider the divided-difference table of Table 1.2 with the base-point indices interchanged (Table 1.5).

As before, the third-degree polynomial generated by the information in the table is given by

$$\begin{aligned} p_3(x) = {} & f[x_0] + (x - x_0)f[x_1, x_0] \\ & + (x - x_0)(x - x_1)f[x_2, x_1, x_0] \\ & + (x - x_0)(x - x_1)(x - x_2)f[x_3, x_2, x_1, x_0] \end{aligned}$$

or (following the indicated path through the table),

$$\begin{aligned} p_3(x) = {} & 25 + (x - 3)12 + (x - 3)(x - 1)6 \\ & + (x - 3)(x - 1)(x - 4)1 = x^3 - 2x^2 + 7x - 5. \end{aligned}$$

With additional interchanges of the base-point indices, it becomes apparent that *any* path through the divided-difference table which terminates with the same higher-order difference yields the same polynomial. Figure 1.8 shows the eight different paths which could be taken across this table; all terminate with the third-order difference $f[x_3, x_2, x_1, x_0] = 1$.

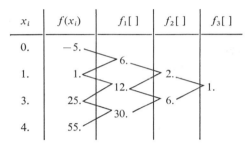

Figure 1.8   Equivalent paths across the divided-difference table.

That the same polynomial is produced for all possible paths across the table is a natural consequence of the fact that any particular high-order difference is a function of all sample values in the triangular segment subtended to its left in the table (all four sample values are used to compute $f[x_3, x_2, x_1, x_0] = 1$). Therefore, all $p_3(x)$ which terminate with the difference $f[x_3, x_2, x_1, x_0]$ must pass through the points x_0, x_1, x_2, and x_3. Since there is only one such polynomial, all third-degree polynomials generated must be the same, regardless of the path taken.

Table 1.2 can be modified as well by arbitrarily ordering the base points. Consider the same sample values in different order (Table 1.6).

Table 1.5   Divided-Difference Table—Base-point Indices Interchanged

i	x_i	$f(x_i)$	$f_1[\ ]$	$f_2[\ ]$	$f_3[\ ]$
3	0.	−5.			
			6.		
1	1.	1.		2.	
			12.		1.
0	3.	25.		6.	
			30.		
2	4.	55.			

Table 1.6   Divided-Difference Table—Functional Values in Arbitrary Order

i	x_i	$f(x_i)$	$f_1[\ ]$	$f_2[\ ]$	$f_3[\ ]$
0	3.	25.			
			10.		
1	0.	−5.		5.	
			15.		1.
2	4.	55.		3.	
			18.		
3	1.	1.			

The third-degree interpolating polynomial is given (taking the upper diagonal path) by (1.29) as

$$p_3(x) = 25 + (x - 3)10 + (x - 3)(x - 0)5$$
$$+ (x - 3)(x - 0)(x - 4)1 = x^3 - 2x^2 + 7x - 5.$$

When a divided-difference table for $n + 1$ base points has been prepared for all differences of order n or less, interpolating polynomials of any degree m where $m \leqslant n$ may be found. If the full difference table is not used ($m < n$), there is a choice of base points. It is intuitively obvious that one should use base-point information near the desired interpolation argument. That this is the case may be seen by examining the form of the error term (1.39b). In general, since $f^{(n+1)}(\xi)$ is unknown, the best that can be done to reduce the error is to make that part of the error term given by the polynomial

$$\prod_{i=0}^{n} (x - x_i) \tag{1.42}$$

as small as possible in magnitude. Clearly the interpolation argument should be centered as nearly as possible on the interval containing the base points used in the interpolation, that is, the base points should be distributed about the interpolation argument as "evenly" as possible. In general, (1.42) shows that when the interpolation argu-ment is near the endpoints x_0 or x_n, the error is likely to be larger than when it is near $x_{n/2}$, assuming that the base points are in algebraic order. It also indicates that when x is outside the interval $[x_0, \ldots, x_n]$, that is, when the inter-polating polynomial is used for *extrapolation*, the error may be very large.

The divided-difference form of the interpolating poly-nomial is especially well suited for computing interpolant values for polynomials of different degree. Altering the degree of the polynomial from j to $j + 1$ requires the evaluation of just one additional term, and no previous calculations need be repeated or modified. This feature is important when the degree of the desired polynomial is not known at the beginning of the calculation. New terms can be added one at a time (equivalent to increasing the degree by one) until the bound on the remainder term or the error estimate given by the first term dropped is small enough, without invalidating the calculations already done.

In addition, when many interpolations with the same data set but different interpolation arguments must be carried out, considerable computing time is saved (over the Lagrange formulation of the next section), since a large part of the computation, involved in setting up the divided-difference table, need be done just once.

EXAMPLE 1.1

INTERPOLATION WITH FINITE DIVIDED DIFFERENCES

Problem Statement

Write a subroutine named DTABLE that will calculate all divided differences of order m or less for the paired values (x_i, y_i), $i = 1, 2, \ldots, n$, where $m < n$. Elements of the divided-difference table should be assigned to the first m columns of the first $n - 1$ rows of the lower triangular matrix† T, so that

$$T_{i,j} = f[x_{i+1}, x_i, \ldots, x_{i+1-j}], \quad \begin{cases} i = 1, 2, \ldots, n-1, \\ j = 1, 2, \ldots, m, \end{cases}$$

$$(1.1.1)$$

where $f(x_i) = y_i$.

$$
\begin{array}{llll}
x_1 & y_1 & T_{1,1} = f[x_2, x_1] \\
x_2 & y_2 & T_{2,1} = f[x_3, x_2] & T_{2,2} = f[x_3, x_2, x_1] \\
x_3 & y_3 & T_{3,1} = f[x_4, x_3] & T_{3,2} = f[x_4, x_3, x_2] \\
\vdots & \vdots & \vdots & \vdots \\
x_m & y_m & T_{m,1} = f[x_{m+1}, x_m] & T_{m,2} = f[x_{m+1}, x_m, x_{m-1}] & \quad T_{m,m} = f[x_{m+1}, \ldots, x_1] \\
\vdots & \vdots & \vdots & \vdots & \qquad \vdots \\
x_{n-1} & y_{n-1} & T_{n-1,1} = f[x_n, x_{n-1}] & T_{n-1,2} = f[x_n, x_{n-1}, x_{n-2}] & \quad T_{n-1,m} = f[x_n, \ldots, x_{n+1-m}] \\
x_n & y_n
\end{array}
$$

Assume that the values x_i are in ascending algebraic order but of arbitrary spacing. Write a function named FNEWT that evaluates a divided-difference interpolating polynomial of degree d for interpolation argument $\bar{x}$, using the appropriate divided differences from the matrix† T of (1.1.1). The function should search the x vector to establish which $d + 1$ of the n possible base points x_i should be used to determine the interpolating polynomial, so that $\bar{x}$ is as nearly central to the selected points as possible. This will make (1.42) as small as possible and, hopefully, make the error term (1.32) for the interpolation acceptably small. Should $\bar{x}$ be smaller than x_1 or larger than x_n, the base points should be the first or last $d + 1$ of the x_i, respectively; for these cases, the interpolating polynomial will be used to extrapolate, since $\bar{x}$ lies outside the range of available base points.

To test the two programs, write a main program that reads values for m, n, and x_i, $i = 1, 2, \ldots, n$, computes the elements of the y vector as $y_i = \cos x_i$, and calls on DTABLE to calculate entries in the divided-difference table

T as given by (1.1.1). The program should then read values for $\bar{x}$ and d, should call on FNEWT to evaluate the appropriate divided-difference interpolating polynomial, and then should compare the interpolant value, $\bar{y}(\bar{x})$, with the value of $\cos \bar{x}$ computed by the library function COS.

Method of Solution

Using (1.1.1), the complete divided-difference table will have the following appearance:

Note that, unlike the divided-difference tables such as Table 1.2, there is no base point $(x_0, y_0 = f(x_0))$. In order to facilitate the simple subscription scheme of (1.1.1), the divided-difference portion of the table is no longer symmetric about the base points near the middle of the table. All elements of the T matrix, $T_{i,j}$ for $j > i$, $j > m$, and $i \geq n$, are unused. The subroutine DTABLE assumes that T is a k by k matrix, and checks for argument consistency to insure that $m < n$.

The function FNEWT searches the vector of base points to find that value of i for which $\bar{x} \leq x_i$; if $\bar{x} > x_n$, i is assigned the value n. The base points used to determine the interpolating polynomial are normally $x_{max-d}, \ldots, x_{max}$, where $max = i + d/2$ for d even and $max = i + (d-1)/2$ for d odd. Should max be smaller than $d + 1$ or larger than n, then max is reassigned the value $d + 1$ or n, respectively. This insures that only given base points are used to fit the polynomial.

In terms of the divided differences, the interpolant value, $\bar{y}(\bar{x})$, is described by the polynomial of degree d:

$$\bar{y}(\bar{x}) = y_{max-d} + (\bar{x} - x_{max-d}) f[x_{max-d+1}, x_{max-d}]$$

$$+ (\bar{x} - x_{max-d+1})(\bar{x} - x_{max-d})$$

$$\times f[x_{max-d+2}, x_{max-d+1}, x_{max-d}]$$

$$+ \cdots + (\bar{x} - x_{max-1}) \cdots (\bar{x} - x_{max-d})$$

$$\times f[x_{max}, \ldots, x_{max-d}]. \qquad (1.1.2)$$

---

† The term *vector* will be used throughout to describe a *linear* array (a column) of numbers identified by a common *name*. Individual elements of the vector are identified by a *single subscript* attached to the name. In this case, the x and y vectors consist of the elements $x_1, x_2, \ldots, x_n$ and $y_1, y_2, \ldots, y_n$, respectively.

The term *matrix* will describe a *rectangular* array (rows and columns) of numbers identified by a common name. Individual elements of the matrix are identified by *two* subscripts, the first to indicate the *row* index and the second to indicate the *column* index. Thus $T_{i,j}$ is the element appearing in the ith row and jth column of the matrix T (see Chapter 4).

The corresponding error term, from (1.32) and (1.39), is

$$R_d(\bar{x}) = f(\bar{x}) - \bar{y}(\bar{x}) = (\bar{x} - x_{max}) \cdots (\bar{x} - x_{max-d})$$
$$\times f[\bar{x}, x_{max}, \ldots, x_{max-d}], \quad (1.1.3)$$

or

$$R_d(\bar{x}) = (\bar{x} - x_{max}) \cdots (\bar{x} - x_{max-d}) \frac{f^{(d+1)}(\xi)}{(d+1)!},$$
$$\xi \text{ in } (\bar{x}, x_{max-d}, \ldots, x_{max}). \quad (1.1.4)$$

Rewritten in the nested form of (1.10), (1.1.2) becomes

$$\bar{y}(\bar{x}) = \{\{ \cdots \{f[x_{max}, \ldots, x_{max-d}](\bar{x} - x_{max-1})$$
$$+ f[x_{max-1}, \ldots, x_{max-d}]\}(\bar{x} - x_{max-2})$$
$$+ f[x_{max-2}, \ldots, x_{max-d}]\}(\bar{x} - x_{max-3})$$
$$+ \cdots + f[x_{max-d+1}, x_{max-d}]\}$$
$$\times (\bar{x} - x_{max-d}) + y_{max-d}, \quad (1.1.5)$$

or, from (1.1.1),

$$\bar{y}(\bar{x}) = \{\{ \cdots \{T_{max-1,d}(\bar{x} - x_{max-1}) + T_{max-2,d-1}\}$$
$$\times (\bar{x} - x_{max-2})$$
$$+ T_{max-3,d-2}\}(\bar{x} - x_{max-3}) + \cdots + T_{max-d,1}\}$$
$$\times (\bar{x} - x_{max-d})$$
$$+ y_{max-d}. \quad (1.1.6)$$

FNEWT uses this nested form to evaluate $\bar{y}(\bar{x})$. Should there be an inconsistency in the function arguments, that is, if $d > m$, the value assigned to FNEWT is zero; otherwise, the value is $\bar{y}(\bar{x})$.

In both DTABLE and FNEWT, a computational switch, *trubl*, is set to 1 when argument inconsistency is found; otherwise, *trubl* is set to 0. FNEWT does not check to insure that the elements x_i, $i = 1, 2, \ldots, n$, are in ascending order, although such a test could be incorporated easily.

Flow Diagram

Main Program

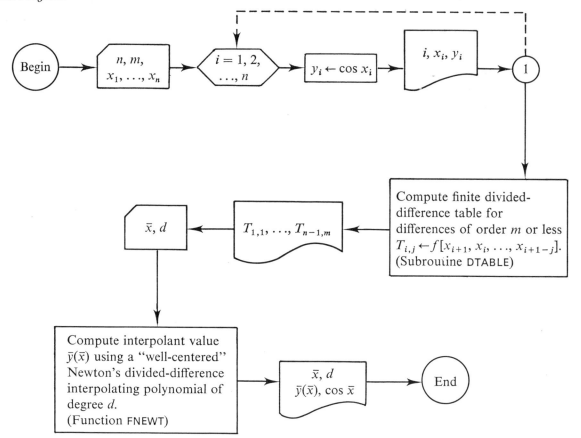

Subroutine DTABLE (Arguments: x, y, T, n, m, $trubl$, k)

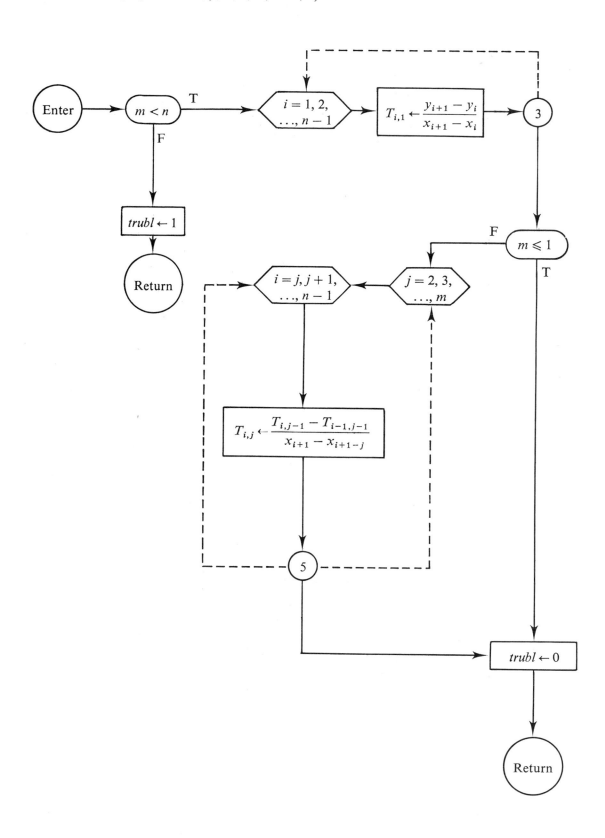

Function FNEWT (Arguments: x, y, T, n, m, d, $\bar{x}$, *trubl*, k)

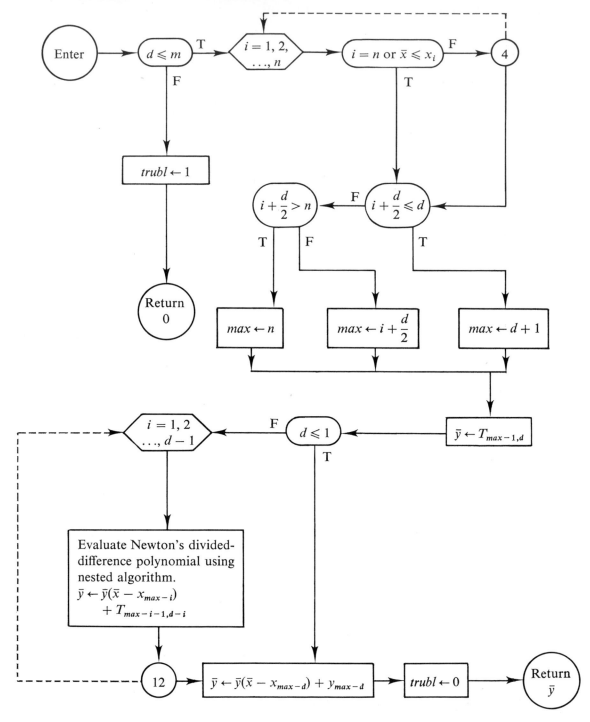

Example 1.1   Interpolation with Finite Divided Differences   **21**

FORTRAN *Implementation*

List of Principal Variables

Program Symbol	Definition

(Main)

I, J, L	Subscripts i, j, l.
IDEG	Degree, d, of the interpolating polynomial.
M	m, highest-order divided difference to be computed by DTABLE.
N	n, the number of paired values $(x_i, y_i = f(x_i))$.
NM1	$n - 1$.
TABLE	Matrix of divided differences, $T_{i,j}$.
TRUBL	Computational switch: set to 1 if argument inconsistency is encountered, otherwise set to 0.
TRUVAL	Value of $\cos \bar{x}$ computed by the library function COS.
X	Vector of base points, x_i.
XARG	Interpolation argument, $\bar{x}$.
Y	Vector of functional values, $y_i = f(x_i)$.
YINTER	Interpolant value, $\bar{y}(\bar{x})$.

(Subroutine
  DTABLE)

ISUB	Subscript, $i + 1 - j$.
K	Row and column dimensions, k, of matrix T.

(Function
  FNEWT)

IDEGM1	$d - 1$.
ISUB1, ISUB2	Subscripts, $max - i$, $d - i$.
MAX	Subscript of largest base point used to determine the interpolating polynomial, max.
YEST	Variable used in nested evaluation of interpolating polynomial, (1.1.6).

Program Listing

Main Program

```
C        APPLIED NUMERICAL METHODS, EXAMPLE 1.1
C        NEWTON'S DIVIDED-DIFFERENCE INTERPOLATING POLYNOMIAL
C
C        TEST PROGRAM FOR THE SUBROUTINE DTABLE AND THE FUNCTION
C        FNEWT.  THIS PROGRAM READS A SET OF N VALUES X(1)...X(N),
C        COMPUTES A CORRESPONDING SET OF VALUES Y(1)...Y(N) WHERE
C        Y(I) = COS(X(I)), AND THEN CALLS ON SUBROUTINE DTABLE
C        TO CALCULATE ALL FINITE DIVIDED DIFFERENCES OF ORDER M OR
C        LESS.   WITH THE DIVIDED DIFFERENCES STORED IN MATRIX TABLE,
C        THE PROGRAM READS VALUES FOR XARG, THE INTERPOLATION
C        ARGUMENT, AND IDEG, THE DEGREE OF THE INTERPOLATING
C        POLYNOMIAL TO BE EVALUATED BY THE FUNCTION FNEWT.
C        FNEWT COMPUTES THE INTERPOLANT VALUE, YINTER, WHICH IS
C        COMPARED WITH THE TRUE VALUE, TRUVAL = COS(XARG).
C
         DIMENSION X(20), Y(20), TABLE(20,20)
C
C        ..... READ DATA, COMPUTE Y VALUES, AND PRINT .....
         READ (5,100)  N, M, (X(I), I=1,N)
         WRITE (6,200)
         DO 1  I=1,N
         Y(I) = COS(X(I))
    1    WRITE (6,201)  I, X(I), Y(I)
C
C        ..... COMPUTE AND PRINT DIVIDED DIFFERENCES .....
         CALL DTABLE( X,Y,TABLE,N,M,TRUBL,20 )
         IF (TRUBL.NE.0.0)  CALL EXIT
         WRITE (6,202)  M
         NM1 = N - 1
         DO 6  I=1,NM1
         L = I
         IF (I.GT.M)  L = M
    6    WRITE (6,203)  (TABLE(I,J), J=1,L)
C
C        ..... READ XARG AND IDEG, CALL ON FNEWT TO INTERPOLATE .....
         WRITE (6,204)
    7    READ (5,101)  XARG, IDEG
         YINTER = FNEWT( X,Y,TABLE,N,M,IDEG,XARG,TRUBL,20 )
C
C        ..... COMPUTE TRUE VALUE OF COS(XARG) AND PRINT RESULTS .....
         TRUVAL = COS(XARG)
         WRITE (6,205)  XARG, IDEG, YINTER, TRUVAL, TRUBL
         GO TO 7
C
C        ..... FORMATS FOR INPUT AND OUTPUT STATEMENTS .....
  100    FORMAT ( 4X, I3, 10X, I3 / (15X, 5F10.4) )
  101    FORMAT ( 7X, F8.4, 13X, I3 )
  200    FORMAT ( 33H1THE SAMPLE FUNCTIONAL VALUES ARE / 5H0   I, 8X,
        1  4HX(I), 9X, 4HY(I) / 1H  )
  201    FORMAT ( 1H , I4, 2F13.6 )
  202    FORMAT ( 9H1FOR M = , I2, 29H, THE DIVIDED DIFFERENCES ARE )
  203    FORMAT ( 1H / (1H , 8E16.7) )
  204    FORMAT ( 25H1THE DATA AND RESULTS ARE / 1H0, 5X, 4HXARG, 5X,
        1  4HIDEG, 5X, 6HYINTER, 6X, 6HTRUVAL, 3X, 5HTRUBL / 1H  )
  205    FORMAT ( 1H , F9.4, I8, 2F12.6, F7.1 )
C
         END
```

Subroutine DTABLE

```
         SUBROUTINE DTABLE ( X,Y,TABLE,N,M,TRUBL,K )
C
C        DTABLE COMPUTES THE FINITE DIVIDED DIFFERENCES OF
C        Y(1)...Y(N) FOR ALL ORDERS M OR LESS AND STORES THEM IN
C        THE LOWER TRIANGULAR PORTION OF THE FIRST M COLUMNS OF THE FIRST
C        N-1 ROWS OF THE MATRIX TABLE.  FOR INCONSISTENT ARGUMENTS,
C        TRUBL = 1.0 ON EXIT.  OTHERWISE, TRUBL = 0.0 ON EXIT.
C
         DIMENSION X(N), Y(N), TABLE(K,K)
```

Example 1.1 *Interpolation with Finite Divided Differences*   **23**

Program Listing (*Continued*)

```
C
C           ..... CHECK FOR ARGUMENT CONSISTENCY .....
            IF (M.LT.N)  GO TO 2
            TRUBL = 1.0
            RETURN
C
C           ..... CALCULATE FIRST-ORDER DIFFERENCES .....
      2     NM1 = N - 1
            DO 3    I=1,NM1
      3     TABLE(I,1) = (Y(I+1) - Y(I))/(X(I+1) - X(I))
            IF (M.LE.1)  GO TO 6
C
C           ..... CALCULATE HIGHER-ORDER DIFFERENCES .....
            DO 5    J=2,M
            DO 5    I=J,NM1
            ISUB = I+1-J
      5     TABLE(I,J) = (TABLE(I,J-1) - TABLE(I-1,J-1))/(X(I+1) - X(ISUB))
C
      6     TRUBL = 0.0
            RETURN
C
            END
```

Function FNEWT

```
            FUNCTION FNEWT ( X,Y,TABLE,N,M,IDEG,XARG,TRUBL,K )
C
C           FNEWT ASSUMES THAT X(1)...X(N) ARE IN ASCENDING ORDER AND
C           FIRST SCANS THE X VECTOR TO DETERMINE WHICH ELEMENT IS
C           NEAREST (.GE.) THE INTERPOLATION ARGUMENT, XARG.
C           THE IDEG+1 BASE POINTS NEEDED FOR THE EVALUATION OF THE
C           DIVIDED-DIFFERENCE POLYNOMIAL OF DEGREE IDEG+1 ARE THEN
C           CENTERED ABOUT THE CHOSEN ELEMENT WITH THE LARGEST HAVING
C           THE SUBSCRIPT MAX.  IT IS ASSUMED THAT THE FIRST M DIVIDED
C           DIFFERENCES HAVE BEEN COMPUTED BY THE SUBROUTINE
C           DTABLE AND ARE ALREADY PRESENT IN THE MATRIX TABLE.
C           MAX IS CHECKED TO INSURE THAT ALL REQUIRED BASE POINTS ARE
C           AVAILABLE, AND THE INTERPOLANT VALUE IS COMPUTED USING NESTED
C           POLYNOMIAL EVALUATION.  THE INTERPOLANT IS RETURNED AS
C           THE VALUE OF THE FUNCTION.  FOR INCONSISTENT ARGUMENTS,
C           TRUBL = 1.0 ON EXIT.  OTHERWISE, TRUBL = 0.0 ON EXIT.
C
            DIMENSION X(N), Y(N), TABLE(K,K)
C
C           ..... CHECK FOR ARGUMENT INCONSISTENCY .....
            IF (IDEG.LE.M)  GO TO 2
            TRUBL = 1.0
            FNEWT = 0.0
            RETURN
C
C           ..... SEARCH X VECTOR FOR ELEMENT .GE. XARG .....
      2     DO 4    I=1,N
      4     IF (I.EQ.N .OR. XARG.LE.X(I))  GO TO 5
      5     MAX = I + IDEG/2
C
C           ..... INSURE THAT ALL REQUIRED DIFFERENCES ARE IN TABLE .....
            IF (MAX.LE.IDEG)  MAX = IDEG + 1
            IF (MAX.GT.N)  MAX = N
```

Program Listing (*Continued*)

```
C
C        ..... COMPUTE INTERPOLANT VALUE .....
         YEST = TABLE(MAX-1,IDEG)
         IF (IDEG.LE.1)  GO TO 13
         IDEGM1 = IDEG - 1
         DO 12   I=1,IDEGM1
         ISUB1 = MAX - I
         ISUB2 = IDEG - I
   12    YEST = YEST*(XARG - X(ISUB1)) + TABLE(ISUB1-1,ISUB2)
   13    ISUB1 = MAX - IDEG
         TRUBL = 0.0
         FNEWT = YEST*(XARG - X(ISUB1)) + Y(ISUB1)
         RETURN
C
         END
```

Data

```
N =   8      M =   6
X(1)...X(5) =        0.0000     0.2000     0.3000     0.4000     0.6000
X(6)...X(8) =        0.7000     0.9000     1.0000
XARG =    0.2500     IDEG =   1
XARG =    0.2500     IDEG =   2
XARG =    0.2500     IDEG =   3
XARG =    0.2500     IDEG =   4
XARG =    0.2500     IDEG =   5
XARG =    0.2500     IDEG =   6
XARG =    0.4500     IDEG =   1
XARG =    0.4500     IDEG =   2
XARG =    0.4500     IDEG =   3
XARG =    0.0500     IDEG =   1
XARG =    0.0500     IDEG =   2
XARG =    0.0500     IDEG =   3
XARG =    0.9500     IDEG =   1
XARG =    0.9500     IDEG =   2
XARG =    0.9500     IDEG =   3
XARG =    0.1000     IDEG =   4
XARG =   -0.1000     IDEG =   4
XARG =    0.5500     IDEG =   7
XARG =    1.1000     IDEG =   1
XARG =    2.0000     IDEG =   1
XARG =    2.0000     IDEG =   2
XARG =    2.0000     IDEG =   3
XARG =    2.0000     IDEG =   4
XARG =    2.0000     IDEG =   5
XARG =    2.0000     IDEG =   6
```

Example 1.1 Interpolation with Finite Divided Differences　　　　**25**

Computer Output

```
THE SAMPLE FUNCTIONAL VALUES ARE

   I        X(I)         Y(I)

   1       0.0         1.000000
   2       0.200000    0.980067
   3       0.300000    0.955337
   4       0.400000    0.921061
   5       0.600000    0.825336
   6       0.700000    0.764842
   7       0.900000    0.621610
   8       1.000000    0.540302


FOR M =  6, THE DIVIDED DIFFERENCES ARE

 -0.9966671E-01

 -0.2473003E 00   -0.4921121E 00

 -0.3427552E 00   -0.4772744E 00     0.3709435E-01

 -0.4786271E 00   -0.4529063E 00     0.6092027E-01    0.3970985E-01

 -0.6049339E 00   -0.4210227E 00     0.7970881E-01    0.3757709E-01   -0.3046803E-02

 -0.7161614E 00   -0.3707584E 00     0.1005287E 00    0.3469983E-01   -0.4110366E-02   -0.1181737E-02

 -0.8130769E 00   -0.3230514E 00     0.1192673E 00    0.3123104E-01   -0.4955415E-02   -0.1056310E-02


THE DATA AND RESULTS ARE

      XARG      IDEG      YINTER      TRUVAL     TRUBL

     0.2500      1       0.967702    0.968913    0.0
     0.2500      2       0.968895    0.968913    0.0
     0.2500      3       0.968909    0.968913    0.0
     0.2500      4       0.968912    0.968913    0.0
     0.2500      5       0.968913    0.968913    0.0
     0.2500      6       0.968913    0.968913    0.0
     0.4500      1       0.897130    0.900447    0.0
     0.4500      2       0.900287    0.900447    0.0
     0.4500      3       0.900437    0.900447    0.0
     0.0500      1       0.995017    0.998750    0.0
     0.0500      2       0.998708    0.998750    0.0
     0.0500      3       0.998777    0.998750    0.0
     0.9500      1       0.580956    0.581683    0.0
     0.9500      2       0.581764    0.581683    0.0
     0.9500      3       0.581689    0.581683    0.0
     0.1000      4       0.995005    0.995004    0.0
    -0.1000      4       0.994996    0.995004    0.0
     0.5500      7       0.0         0.852525    1.0
     1.1000      1       0.458995    0.453597    0.0
     2.0000      1      -0.272774   -0.416147    0.0
     2.0000      2      -0.628129   -0.416147    0.0
     2.0000      3      -0.457578   -0.416147    0.0
     2.0000      4      -0.395053   -0.416147    0.0
     2.0000      5      -0.410927   -0.416147    0.0
     2.0000      6      -0.416679   -0.416147    0.0
```

Discussion of Results

The programs have been written to allow calculation of the desired table of divided differences just once (by calling DTABLE once). Subsequently, an interpolating polynomial of any degree $d \le m$ can be evaluated for any argument, without recomputing the divided-difference table, by calling only on FNEWT.

The programs were compiled and executed on an IBM 360/67 computer using single-precision arithmetic, equivalent to a computer word-size of approximately seven decimal digits. Note that the calculated higher-order divided differences differ considerably from those of Table 1.3 which were computed using significant-digit arithmetic. Yet different values are found using double-precision arithmetic, equivalent to a word-size of approximately 16 decimal digits for computers of the IBM 360 type. The results for calculation of the divided differences using double-precision arithmetic are:

Comparison of the *interpolated* estimates of the cosine function with those computed by the library function COS (accurate to the number of figures shown) shows that interpolation of degree three or more in general yields results accurate to five or more figures. Interpolant values resulting from double-precision calculations (not shown) do not differ from the single-precision results in the first six digits, indicating that the higher-order divided differences contribute little to the significant part of the computed interpolant values. On the other hand, the *extrapolated* estimates of the cosine function for the 17th and 19th–25th data sets are in considerable error, with at best two digits of accuracy, even for evaluation of the interpolating polynomial of degree six.

Although the function FNEWT assumes that the base-point values are ordered in ascending sequence, this is not an essential feature of Newton's divided-difference interpolating polynomial. Modification of FNEWT to

```
FOR M =   6, THE DIVIDED DIFFERENCES ARE

  -0.9966711D-01

  -0.2473009D 00   -0.4921126D 00

  -0.3427550D 00   -0.4772703D 00    0.3710567D-01

  -0.4786269D 00   -0.4529065D 00    0.6090960D-01    0.3967322D-01

  -0.6049343D 00   -0.4210246D 00    0.7970470D-01    0.3759019D-01   -0.2975748D-02

  -0.7161611D 00   -0.3707561D 00    0.1005371D 00    0.3472064D-01   -0.4099361D-02   -0.1248458D-02

  -0.8130766D 00   -0.3230518D 00    0.1192607D 00    0.3120612D-01   -0.5020751D-02   -0.1151737D-02
```

In the computer output the letters E and D should be interpreted as "times ten to the power." These examples illustrate the important point that computer characteristics may affect calculated results significantly, even for the same algorithm.

permit arbitrary ordering of the elements of the x vector would involve only minor changes. In particular, it would be necessary to specify which base points are to be used to determine the interpolating polynomial, probably by addition of another dummy argument.

1.7   Lagrange's Interpolating Polynomial

Lagrange's form of the interpolating polynomial [3] is given by

$$p_n(x) = \sum_{i=0}^{n} L_i(x)f(x_i), \qquad (1.43)$$

where

$$L_i(x) = \prod_{\substack{j=0 \\ j \neq i}}^{n} \frac{(x - x_j)}{(x_i - x_j)}, \qquad i = 0, 1, \ldots, n. \quad (1.44)$$

Each functional value $f(x_i)$ included in the polynomial fit is multiplied by L_i, an nth-degree polynomial in x [since there are n factors $(x - x_j)$].

As before [see (1.30) and (1.39)],

$$f(x) = p_n(x) + R_n(x),$$

where

$$R_n(x) = \left[\prod_{i=0}^{n} (x - x_i) \right] \frac{f^{(n+1)}(\xi)}{(n+1)!}, \qquad \xi \text{ in } (x, x_0, x_1, \ldots, x_n),$$

or

$$R_n(x) = \left[\prod_{i=0}^{n} (x - x_i) \right] f[x, x_n, x_{n-1}, \ldots, x_0].$$

The Lagrange form for $p_n(x)$ can be derived directly from Newton's divided-difference polynomial of equivalent degree by first writing the divided differences in the symmetric form of (1.17). For example, consider the second-degree divided-difference polynomial,

$$p_2(x) = f[x_0] + (x - x_0)f[x_1, x_0]$$
$$+ (x - x_0)(x - x_1)f[x_2, x_1, x_0].$$

Substituting the equivalent symmetric forms for the divided differences yields

$$p_2(x) = f(x_0) + (x - x_0)\frac{f(x_0)}{(x_0 - x_1)} + (x - x_0)\frac{f(x_1)}{(x_1 - x_0)} + \frac{(x - x_0)(x - x_1)}{(x_0 - x_1)(x_0 - x_2)}f(x_0)$$

$$+ \frac{(x - x_0)(x - x_1)}{(x_1 - x_0)(x_1 - x_2)}f(x_1) + \frac{(x - x_0)(x - x_1)}{(x_2 - x_0)(x_2 - x_1)}f(x_2) \qquad (1.45)$$

$$= \frac{(x - x_1)(x - x_2)}{(x_0 - x_1)(x_0 - x_2)}f(x_0) + \frac{(x - x_0)(x - x_2)}{(x_1 - x_0)(x_1 - x_2)}f(x_1) + \frac{(x - x_0)(x - x_1)}{(x_2 - x_0)(x_2 - x_1)}f(x_2)$$

or

$$p_2(x) = \left[\prod_{\substack{j=0 \\ j \neq 0}}^{2} \frac{(x - x_j)}{(x_0 - x_j)} \right]f(x_0) + \left[\prod_{\substack{j=0 \\ j \neq 1}}^{2} \frac{(x - x_j)}{(x_1 - x_j)} \right]f(x_1) + \left[\prod_{\substack{j=0 \\ j \neq 2}}^{2} \frac{(x - x_j)}{(x_2 - x_j)} \right]f(x_2)$$

$$= \sum_{i=0}^{2} \left[\prod_{\substack{j=0 \\ j \neq i}}^{2} \frac{(x - x_j)}{(x_i - x_j)} \right]f(x_i) = \sum_{i=0}^{2} L_i(x)f(x_i). \qquad (1.46)$$

The higher-degree Lagrange formulations can be derived in an analogous way from the corresponding divided-difference polynomial, although the algebra is quite tedious. A somewhat simpler alternative development is as follows: Assume that the interpolation polynomial has the form

$$p_n(x) = a_0(x - x_1)(x - x_2)(x - x_3) \cdots (x - x_n)$$
$$+ a_1(x - x_0)(x - x_2)(x - x_3) \cdots (x - x_n)$$
$$+ a_2(x - x_0)(x - x_1)(x - x_3) \cdots (x - x_n)$$
$$\vdots$$
$$+ a_i(x - x_0)(x - x_1) \qquad (1.47)$$
$$\cdots (x - x_{i-1})(x - x_{i+1}) \cdots (x - x_n)$$
$$\vdots$$
$$+ a_{n-1}(x - x_0)(x - x_1) \cdots (x - x_{n-2})(x - x_n)$$
$$+ a_n(x - x_0)(x - x_1) \cdots (x - x_{n-2})(x - x_{n-1}),$$

where the coefficients $a_0, a_1, \ldots, a_n$ are determined by requiring, as before, that $p_n(x_i) = f(x_i)$, $i = 0, 1, \ldots, n$. Examination of (1.47) shows that this can be the case only if

$$a_0 = \frac{f(x_0)}{(x_0 - x_1)(x_0 - x_2) \cdots (x_0 - x_n)}$$

$$a_1 = \frac{f(x_1)}{(x_1 - x_0)(x_1 - x_2) \cdots (x_1 - x_n)},$$

or, in general,

$$a_i = \frac{f(x_i)}{(x_i - x_0)(x_i - x_1) \cdots (x_i - x_{i-1})(x_i - x_{i+1}) \cdots (x_i - x_n)}. \qquad (1.48)$$

In condensed form, (1.47), with the coefficients of (1.48) substituted, yields the Lagrange form of (1.43).

Note that the Lagrange form involves only the base points x_i and the corresponding functional values $f(x_i)$. The divided differences of Newton's fundamental formula need not be computed at all. When only one interpolation is to be carried out, the amount of computation required by the divided-difference and Lagrange formulas is roughly equivalent. Less computer storage is required for the Lagrange formula, of course, since there is no need to save the divided-difference table.

The Lagrange form has two significant disadvantages aside from the excessive amount of calculation required when many interpolations are to be done using the same data set. Since the divided differences are not computed, the error estimate of (1.33) has little relevance. Normally, no estimate of the error can be made, since the error bound of (1.39b) is not applicable unless high-order derivatives can be evaluated (not the usual case). Also, the addition of a new term (that is, increasing the degree of the polynomial by one), which is a simple matter when using Newton's form, requires complete recomputation of all the $L_i(x)$ values for Lagrange's form. Thus the Lagrange form is not well-suited for cases in which the desired polynomial degree is not known *a priori*.

Example. Use the Lagrange form of (1.43) and (1.44) to find the second-degree interpolating polynomial passing through the three points in Table 1.7 (see Table 1.2).

Table 1.7   Functional Values

i	x_i	$f(x_i)$
0	0.	-5.
1	1.	1.
2	3.	25.

For this case,

$$L_0 = \frac{(x-1)(x-3)}{(0-1)(0-3)} = \frac{x^2 - 4x + 3}{3}$$

$$L_1 = \frac{(x-0)(x-3)}{(1-0)(1-3)} = \frac{-x^2 + 3x}{2}$$

$$L_2 = \frac{(x-0)(x-1)}{(3-0)(3-1)} = \frac{x^2 - x}{6},$$

and

$$p_2(x) = L_0(-5) + L_1(1) + L_2(25) = 2x^2 + 4x - 5,$$

which is identical with the polynomial found previously for the same data using the divided-difference form of the interpolating polynomial.

EXAMPLE 1.2

LAGRANGIAN INTERPOLATION

Problem Statement

Write a function named FLAGR that evaluates for interpolation argument $\bar{x}$ the Lagrangian interpolating polynomial of degree d passing through the points (x_{min}, y_{min}), (x_{min+1}, y_{min+1}), ..., (x_{min+d}, y_{min+d}).

In addition, write a main program that reads data values n, x_1, x_2, ..., x_n, y_1, y_2, ..., y_n, $\bar{x}$, d, and min, and then calls upon FLAGR to evaluate the appropriate interpolating polynomial and return the interpolant value, $\bar{y}(\bar{x})$. As test data, use information from Table 1.2.1 relating observed voltage and temperature for the Platinum to Platinum-10 percent Rhodium thermocouple with cold junctions at 32°F.

Table 1.2.1   Reference Table for the Pt-10% Rh Thermocouple [21]

emf (microvolts)	Temperature (°F)
0	32.0
300	122.4
500	176.0
1000	296.4
1500	405.7
1700	447.6
2000	509.0
2500	608.4
3000	704.7
3300	761.4
3500	799.0
4000	891.9
4500	983.0
5000	1072.6
5300	1125.7
5500	1160.8
5900	1230.3
6000	1247.5

Read tabulated values for the 13 selected base points $x_1 = 0$, $x_2 = 500$, $x_3 = 1000$, ..., $x_{13} = 6000$, and the

corresponding functional values y_1, y_2, ..., y_{13}, where $y_i = f(x_i)$. Then call on FLAGR to evaluate $\bar{y}(\bar{x})$ for arguments $\bar{x} = 300$, 1700, 2500, 3300, 5300, and 5900, with various values for d and min. Compare the results with the experimentally observed values from Table 1.2.1.

Method of Solution

In terms of the problem parameters, Lagrange's form of the interpolating polynomial (1.43) becomes:

$$\bar{y}(\bar{x}) = \sum_{i=min}^{min+d} L_i(\bar{x}) y_i, \qquad (1.2.1)$$

where

$$L_i(\bar{x}) = \prod_{\substack{j=min \\ j \neq i}}^{min+d} \frac{(\bar{x} - x_j)}{(x_i - x_j)}, \qquad (1.2.2)$$

$$i = min, min + 1, \ldots, min + d.$$

The program that follows is a straightforward implementation of (1.2.1) and (1.2.2), except that some calculations (about d^2 multiplications and d^2 subtractions, at the expense of $d + 1$ divisions) are saved by writing (1.2.2) in the form

$$L_i(\bar{x}) = \frac{c/(\bar{x} - x_i)}{\prod_{\substack{j=min \\ j \neq i}}^{min+d} (x_i - x_j)}, \qquad (1.2.3)$$

$$i = min, min + 1, \ldots, min + d, \bar{x} \neq x_i,$$

where

$$c = \prod_{j=min}^{min+d} (\bar{x} - x_j). \qquad (1.2.4)$$

The restriction in (1.2.3), $\bar{x} \neq x_i$, causes no difficulty, since, if $\bar{x} = x_i$, the interpolant $\bar{y}(\bar{x})$ is known to be y_i; no additional computation is required.

Flow Diagram

Main Program

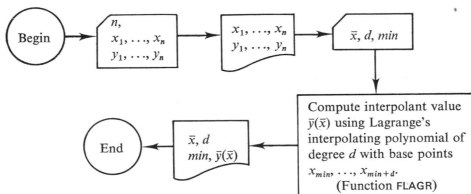

29

Function FLAGR (Arguments: x, y, $\bar{x}$, d, min, n)

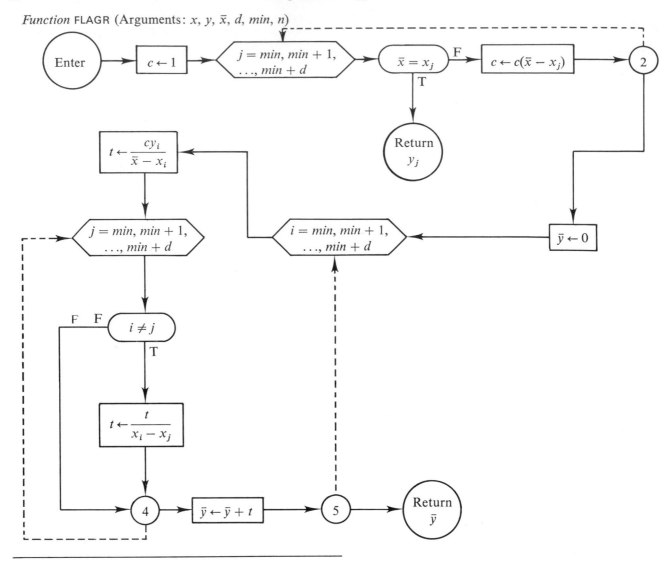

FORTRAN *Implementation*

List of Principal Variables

Program Symbol	Definition
(Main)	
I	Subscript, i.
IDEG	Degree, d, of the interpolating polynomial.
MIN	Smallest subscript for base points used to determine the interpolating polynomial, *min.*
N	n, the number of paired values $(x_i, y_i = f(x_i))$.
X	Vector of base points, x_i.
XARG	Interpolation argument, $\bar{x}$.
Y	Vector of functional values, $y_i = f(x_i)$.
YINTER	Interpolant value, $\bar{y}(\bar{x})$.
(Function FLAGR)	
FACTOR	The factor c (see (1.2.4)).
J	Subscript, j.
MAX	Largest subscript for base points used to determine the interpolating polynomial, $min + d$.
TERM	t, a variable that assumes successively the values $L_i(\bar{x})y_i$ in (1.2.1).
YEST	Interpolant value, $\bar{y}(\bar{x})$.

Example 1.2 *Lagrangian Interpolation* **31**

Program Listing

Main Program

```
C         APPLIED NUMERICAL METHODS, EXAMPLE 1.2
C         LAGRANGE'S INTERPOLATING POLYNOMIAL
C
C         TEST PROGRAM FOR THE FUNCTION FLAGR.  THIS PROGRAM READS A
C         SET OF N VALUES X(1)...X(N) AND A CORRESPONDING SET OF
C         FUNCTIONAL VALUES Y(1)...Y(N) WHERE Y(I) = F(X(I)). THE
C         PROGRAM THEN READS VALUES FOR XARG, IDEG, AND MIN (SEE FLAGR
C         FOR MEANINGS) AND CALLS ON FLAGR TO PRODUCE THE INTERPOLANT
C         VALUE, YINTER.
C
          IMPLICIT  REAL*8(A-H, O-Z)
          DIMENSION X(100), Y(100)
C
C         ..... READ N, X AND Y VALUES, AND PRINT .....
          READ (5,100)  N, (X(I), I=1,N)
          READ (5,101)  (Y(I), I=1,N)
          WRITE (6,200)
          DO 1  I=1,N
        1 WRITE (6,201)  I, X(I), Y(I)
C
C         ..... READ INTERPOLATION ARGUMENTS, CALL ON FLAGR, AND PRINT .....
          WRITE (6,202)
        2 READ (5,102)  XARG, IDEG, MIN
          YINTER = FLAGR ( X,Y,XARG,IDEG,MIN,N )
          WRITE (6,203)  XARG, IDEG, MIN, YINTER
          GO TO 2
C
C         ..... FORMATS FOR INPUT AND OUTPUT STATEMENTS .....
      100 FORMAT ( 4X, I3 / (15X, 5F10.4) )
      101 FORMAT ( 15X, 5F10.4 )
      102 FORMAT ( 7X, F10.4, 13X, I2, 12X, I2 )
      200 FORMAT ( 33H1THE SAMPLE FUNCTIONAL VALUES ARE / 5H0   I, 8X,
        1 4HX(I), 9X, 4HY(I) / 1H  )
      201 FORMAT ( 1H , I4, 2F13.4 )
      202 FORMAT ( 25H1THE DATA AND RESULTS ARE / 1H0, 5X, 4HXARG, 5X,
        1 4HIDEG, 5X, 3HMIN, 5X, 6HYINTER / 1H )
      203 FORMAT ( 1H , F9.4, I8, I8, F12.4 )
C
          END
```

Function FLAGR

```
          FUNCTION FLAGR ( X,Y,XARG,IDEG,MIN,N )
C
C         FLAGR USES THE LAGRANGE FORMULA TO EVALUATE THE INTERPOLATING
C         POLYNOMIAL OF DEGREE IDEG FOR ARGUMENT XARG USING THE DATA
C         VALUES X(MIN)...X(MAX) AND Y(MIN)...Y(MAX) WHERE
C         MAX = MIN + IDEG.   NO ASSUMPTION IS MADE REGARDING ORDER OF
C         THE X(I), AND NO ARGUMENT CHECKING IS DONE.   TERM IS
C         A VARIABLE WHICH CONTAINS SUCCESSIVELY EACH TERM OF THE
C         LAGRANGE FORMULA.  THE FINAL VALUE OF YEST IS THE INTERPOLATED
C         VALUE.  SEE TEXT FOR A DESCRIPTION OF FACTOR.
C
          IMPLICIT  REAL*8(A-H, O-Z)
          REAL*8  X, Y, XARG, FLAGR
          DIMENSION X(N), Y(N)
C
C         ..... COMPUTE VALUE OF FACTOR .....
          FACTOR = 1.0
          MAX = MIN + IDEG
          DO 2  J=MIN,MAX
          IF (XARG.NE.X(J))  GO TO 2
          FLAGR = Y(J)
          RETURN
        2 FACTOR = FACTOR*(XARG - X(J))
```

Program Listing (*Continued*)

```
C
C        ..... EVALUATE INTERPOLATING POLYNOMIAL .....
         YEST = 0.
         DO 5    I=MIN,MAX
         TERM = Y(I)*FACTOR/(XARG - X(I))
         DO 4    J=MIN,MAX
   4     IF (I.NE.J)   TERM = TERM/(X(I)-X(J))
   5     YEST = YEST + TERM
         FLAGR = YEST
         RETURN
C
         END
```

Data

```
N =  13
X(1)...X(5) =        0.       500.      1000.      1500.      2000.
X(6)...X(10) =    2500.      3000.      3500.      4000.      4500.
X(11)...X(13) =   5000.      5500.      6000.
Y(1)...Y(5) =       32.0      176.0      296.4      405.7      509.0
Y(6)...Y(10) =     608.4      704.7      799.0      891.9      983.0
Y(11)...Y(13) =   1072.6     1160.8     1247.5
XARG =    300.        IDEG =   1      MIN =   1
XARG =    300.        IDEG =   2      MIN =   1
XARG =    300.        IDEG =   3      MIN =   1
XARG =    300.        IDEG =   4      MIN =   1
XARG =   1700.        IDEG =   1      MIN =   4
XARG =   1700.        IDEG =   2      MIN =   3
XARG =   1700.        IDEG =   2      MIN =   4
XARG =   1700.        IDEG =   3      MIN =   3
XARG =   1700.        IDEG =   4      MIN =   2
XARG =   1700.        IDEG =   4      MIN =   3
XARG =   2500.        IDEG =   1      MIN =   5
XARG =   2500.        IDEG =   1      MIN =   6
XARG =   2500.        IDEG =   2      MIN =   5
XARG =   2500.        IDEG =   3      MIN =   4
XARG =   2500.        IDEG =   3      MIN =   5
XARG =   2500.        IDEG =   4      MIN =   4
XARG =   3300.        IDEG =   1      MIN =   7
XARG =   3300.        IDEG =   2      MIN =   6
XARG =   3300.        IDEG =   2      MIN =   7
XARG =   3300.        IDEG =   3      MIN =   6
XARG =   3300.        IDEG =   4      MIN =   5
XARG =   3300.        IDEG =   4      MIN =   6
XARG =   3300.        IDEG =   5      MIN =   5
XARG =   3300.        IDEG =   6      MIN =   4
XARG =   3300.        IDEG =   6      MIN =   5
XARG =   3300.        IDEG =   7      MIN =   4
XARG =   3300.        IDEG =   8      MIN =   3
XARG =   3300.        IDEG =   8      MIN =   4
XARG =   3300.        IDEG =   9      MIN =   3
XARG =   5300.        IDEG =   1      MIN =  11
XARG =   5300.        IDEG =   2      MIN =  10
XARG =   5300.        IDEG =   2      MIN =  11
XARG =   5300.        IDEG =   3      MIN =  10
XARG =   5300.        IDEG =   4      MIN =   9
XARG =   5900.        IDEG =   1      MIN =  12
XARG =   5900.        IDEG =   2      MIN =  11
XARG =   5900.        IDEG =   3      MIN =  10
XARG =   5900.        IDEG =   4      MIN =   9
```

Example 1.2 *Lagrangian Interpolation*   **33**

Computer Output

```
THE SAMPLE FUNCTIONAL VALUES ARE
```

I	X(I)	Y(I)
1	0.0	32.0000
2	500.0000	176.0000
3	1000.0000	296.4000
4	1500.0000	405.7000
5	2000.0000	509.0000
6	2500.0000	608.4000
7	3000.0000	704.7000
8	3500.0000	799.0000
9	4000.0000	891.9000
10	4500.0000	983.0000
11	5000.0000	1072.6000
12	5500.0000	1160.8000
13	6000.0000	1247.5000

```
THE DATA AND RESULTS ARE
```

XARG	IDEG	MIN	YINTER
300.0000	1	1	118.4000
300.0000	2	1	121.2320
300.0000	3	1	121.9320
300.0000	4	1	122.1806
1700.0000	1	4	447.0200
1700.0000	2	3	447.7400
1700.0000	2	4	447.4880
1700.0000	3	3	447.6224
1700.0000	4	2	447.5552
1700.0000	4	3	447.5933
2500.0000	1	5	608.4000
2500.0000	1	6	608.4000
2500.0000	2	5	608.4000
2500.0000	3	4	608.4000
2500.0000	3	5	608.4000
2500.0000	4	4	608.4000
3300.0000	1	7	761.2800
3300.0000	2	6	761.5200
3300.0000	2	7	761.4480
3300.0000	3	6	761.4816
3300.0000	4	5	761.4704
3300.0000	4	6	761.4592
3300.0000	5	5	761.4646
3300.0000	6	4	761.4632
3300.0000	6	5	761.4543
3300.0000	7	4	761.4586
3300.0000	8	3	761.4578
3300.0000	8	4	761.4518
3300.0000	9	3	761.4547
5300.0000	1	11	1125.5200
5300.0000	2	10	1125.6880
5300.0000	2	11	1125.7000
5300.0000	3	10	1125.6944
5300.0000	4	9	1125.6899
5900.0000	1	12	1230.1600
5900.0000	2	11	1230.2800
5900.0000	3	10	1230.2848
5900.0000	4	9	1230.2915

Discussion of Results

All computations have been carried out using double-precision arithmetic (8 byte REAL operands); for the test data used, however, single-precision arithmetic would have yielded results of comparable accuracy. Since the true function $f(x)$, for which $y_i = f(x_i)$, is unknown, it is not possible to determine an upper bound for the interpolation error from (1.39b). However, comparison of the interpolant values with known functional values from Table 1.2.1 for the arguments used as test data, shows that interpolation of degree 2 or more when the argument is well-centered with respect to the base points, generally yields results comparable in accuracy to the experimentally measured values. The results for $\bar{x} = 300$ are less satisfactory than for the other arguments, possibly because the argument is near the beginning of the table where the function appears to have considerable curvature, and because centering of the argument among the base points is not practicable for large d.

While the base points used as test data were ordered in ascending sequence and equally spaced, the program is not limited with respect to either ordering or spacing of the base points. For greater accuracy, however, one would normally order the base points in either ascending or descending sequence, and attempt to center the interpolation argument among those base points used to determine the interpolating polynomial. This tends to keep the polynomial factor

$$\prod_{i=min}^{min+d} (\bar{x} - x_i), \qquad (1.2.5)$$

and hence the error term comparable to (1.39b), as small as possible. This practice will usually lead to more satisfactory low-order interpolant values as well. The program does not test to insure that the required base points are in fact available, although a check to insure that $min > 0$ and $max \leqslant n$ could be inserted easily.

1.8 Polynomial Interpolation with Equally Spaced Base Points

When the base-point values are equally spaced so that $x_1 - x_0 = x_2 - x_1 = x_3 - x_2 = \cdots = x_n - x_{n-1} = h$, then, as we would expect, some simplification of the divided-difference or Lagrange formulation is possible. The interpolating polynomial will be developed in terms of the forward (Δ), backward (∇), and central (δ) difference operators. These are linear operators, that is,

$$\Delta(\alpha f(x) + \beta g(x)) = \alpha \Delta f(x) + \beta \Delta g(x)$$
$$\nabla(\alpha f(x) + \beta g(x)) = \alpha \nabla f(x) + \beta \nabla g(x)$$
$$\delta(\alpha f(x) + \beta g(x)) = \alpha \delta f(x) + \beta \delta g(x), \quad (1.49)$$

and will be defined individually in subsequent sections. The principal reason for using *finite differences* is notational compactness. In addition, use of these operators permits a considerable reduction in computation compared with the Newton or Lagrange forms.

Forward Differences. The *forward-difference operator* (Δ) is defined as follows:

$$\Delta f(x) = f(x + h) - f(x)$$
$$\Delta^2 f(x) = \Delta(\Delta f(x)) = \Delta(f(x + h) - f(x))$$
$$= \Delta f(x + h) - \Delta f(x)$$
$$\Delta^3 f(x) = \Delta^2 f(x + h) - \Delta^2 f(x) \quad (1.50)$$
$$\vdots$$
$$\Delta^n f(x) = \Delta^{n-1} f(x + h) - \Delta^{n-1} f(x).$$

$\Delta f(x)$ is termed the *first forward difference*, $\Delta^2 f(x)$ the *second forward difference*, etc.

The forward finite differences can be computed and saved in a *forward-difference table* in much the same manner as shown earlier for the divided differences. As an example, consider the polynomial $(x^3 - 2x^2 + 7x - 5)$, used earlier, tabulated at five base points with $h = 1.0$ (Table 1.8).

Table 1.8   *Forward-Difference Table*

i	x_i	$f(x_i)$	Δf	$\Delta^2 f$	$\Delta^3 f$	$\Delta^4 f$
0	0.	−5.				
			6.			
1	1.	1.		2.		
			8.		6.	
2	2.	9.		8.		0.
			16.		6.	
3	3.	25.		14.		
			30.			
4	4.	55.				

Notice that for this third-degree polynomial, the third forward differences are constant and the fourth forward difference is zero.

The relationship between a given forward finite difference and the corresponding finite divided difference of Table 1.1 is a simple one:

$$f[x_1,x_0] = \frac{f(x_1) - f(x_0)}{x_1 - x_0} = \frac{f(x_0 + h) - f(x_0)}{h} = \frac{\Delta f(x_0)}{h}.$$

Similarly,

$$f[x_2,x_1,x_0] = \frac{\dfrac{f(x_2) - f(x_1)}{x_2 - x_1} - \dfrac{f(x_1) - f(x_0)}{x_1 - x_0}}{x_2 - x_0} = \frac{\Delta^2 f(x_0)}{2h^2}.$$

In general,

$$f[x_n,x_{n-1}, \ldots, x_0] = \frac{\Delta^n f(x_0)}{n!\, h^n}. \quad (1.51)$$

In order to rewrite the divided-difference polynomial in terms of the forward finite differences in compact form, we introduce a parameter α, so that

$$x = x_0 + \alpha h, \quad (1.52)$$

where $0 \leqslant \alpha \leqslant n$ for values of x in the interval $x_0 \leqslant x \leqslant x_n$. Since the base-point values x_0, x_1, x_2, ..., x_n are evenly spaced at intervals h,

$$\begin{aligned} x - x_0 &= \alpha h \\ x - x_1 &= \alpha h - h = h(\alpha - 1) \\ x - x_2 &= h(\alpha - 2) \\ &\vdots \\ x - x_i &= h(\alpha - i) \\ &\vdots \\ x - x_n &= h(\alpha - n). \end{aligned} \quad (1.53)$$

The finite divided-difference formulation (Newton's fundamental formula) is rewritten here for convenience see (1.30), (1.31), and (1.39)]:

$$f(x) = p_n(x) + R_n(x),$$

where

$$\begin{aligned} p_n(x) = &f[x_0] + (x - x_0)f[x_1,x_0] \\ &+ (x - x_0)(x - x_1)f[x_2,x_1,x_0] \\ &+ (x - x_0)(x - x_1)(x - x_2)f[x_3,x_2,x_1,x_0] \\ &+ \cdots \\ &+ (x - x_0)(x - x_1) \\ &\qquad \cdots (x - x_{n-1})f[x_n,x_{n-1}, \ldots, x_0], \end{aligned}$$

and

$$R_n(x) = (x - x_0)(x - x_1) \cdots (x - x_{n-1})(x - x_n) \\ \times f[x,x_n,x_{n-1}, \ldots, x_0],$$

or

$$R_n(x) = (x - x_0)(x - x_1) \cdots (x - x_{n-1})(x - x_n) \\ \times \frac{f^{(n+1)}(\xi)}{(n+1)!}, \quad \xi \text{ in } (x,x_n,x_{n-1}, \ldots, x_0).$$

In terms of α and the forward-difference operator, Newton's fundamental formula assumes the form

$$f(x_0 + \alpha h) = f(x_0) + \alpha \Delta f(x_0) + \frac{\alpha(\alpha - 1)}{2!} \Delta^2 f(x_0)$$

$$+ \frac{\alpha(\alpha - 1)(\alpha - 2)}{3!} \Delta^3 f(x_0) + \cdots$$

$$+ \frac{\alpha(\alpha - 1)(\alpha - 2)\cdots(\alpha - n + 1)}{n!}$$

$$\times \Delta^n f(x_0) + R_n(x_0 + \alpha h) \qquad (1.54)$$

$$= p_n(x_0 + \alpha h) + R_n(x_0 + \alpha h)$$

where

$$R_n(x_0 + \alpha h) = h^{n+1} \alpha(\alpha - 1)(\alpha - 2)\cdots(\alpha - n)$$

$$\times \frac{f^{(n+1)}(\xi)}{(n+1)!}, \qquad \xi \text{ in } (x, x_0, x_1, \ldots, x_n), \quad (1.55a)$$

or

$$R_n(x_0 + \alpha h) = h^{n+1} \alpha(\alpha - 1)(\alpha - 2)\cdots(\alpha - n)$$

$$\times f[x, x_n, x_{n-1}, \ldots, x_0]. \quad (1.55b)$$

As before, an estimate of the error can be made if an additional base point x_{n+1} is given, by assuming that

$$f[x, x_n, x_{n-1}, \ldots, x_0] \doteq f[x_{n+1}, x_n, x_{n-1}, \ldots, x_0].$$

Since

$$f[x_{n+1}, x_n, x_{n-1}, \ldots, x_0] h^{n+1} = \frac{\Delta^{n+1} f(x_0)}{(n+1)!},$$

an estimate of $R_n(x_0 + \alpha h)$ is given by

$$R_n(x_0 + \alpha h) \doteq \alpha(\alpha - 1)(\alpha - 2)\cdots(\alpha - n) \frac{\Delta^{n+1} f(x_0)}{(n+1)!}.$$

$$(1.56)$$

Equation (1.54) is known as *Newton's forward formula* (NFF). Notice that NFF uses only the differences along the upper diagonal of the difference table (marked with solid lines in Table 1.8). Consequently, NFF is most useful for interpolation near the *beginning* of an equal-interval table. Of course, the same formula can be applied in other parts of a table by a suitable translation of the zero subscript. The necessary forward differences, starting with the shifted origin $x_0 = 1.0$, $y_0 = 1.0$, would be those along the dotted diagonal of Table 1.8.

Example. Apply Newton's fundamental formula to the data of Table 1.8 and evaluate the second-degree polynomial for interpolation argument $x = 1.5$.

For this case, $h = 1$ and

$$\alpha = \frac{x - x_0}{h} = \frac{1.5 - 0}{1} = 1.5.$$

Substitution into (1.54) yields

$$p_2(1.5) = -5 + (1.5)6 + (1.5)(0.5)\frac{2}{2!} = 4.75.$$

As a check, use the second-degree Lagrange formula (1.46):

$$p_2(1.5) = \frac{(1.5-1)(1.5-2)}{(0-1)(0-2)}(-5) + \frac{(1.5-0)(1.5-2)}{(1-0)(1-2)}(1)$$

$$+ \frac{(1.5-0)(1.5-1)}{(2-0)(2-1)}(9) = 4.75.$$

The error estimate from the first difference dropped would be given by (1.56):

$$R_2(x_0 + \alpha h) \doteq \alpha(\alpha - 1)(\alpha - 2)\frac{\Delta^3 f(x_0)}{3!}$$

$$= \left(\frac{3}{2}\right)\left(\frac{1}{2}\right)\left(\frac{-1}{2}\right)\frac{6}{3!} = -\frac{3}{8}.$$

In this case, $-\frac{3}{8}$ happens to be exactly the error, since $f(x)$ is a third-degree polynomial and the higher-order differences vanish.

Backward Differences. The *backward-difference operator* (∇) is defined as follows:

$$\nabla f(x) = f(x) - f(x - h)$$
$$\nabla^2 f(x) = \nabla f(x) - \nabla f(x - h)$$
$$\nabla^3 f(x) = \nabla^2 f(x) - \nabla^2 f(x - h) \qquad (1.57)$$
$$\vdots$$
$$\nabla^n f(x) = \nabla^{n-1} f(x) - \nabla^{n-1} f(x - h).$$

$\nabla f(x)$ is termed the *first backward difference*, $\nabla^2 f(x)$, the *second backward difference*, etc. Define a parameter α, this time by using as the origin the base point x_n, so that

$$x = x_n + \alpha h. \qquad (1.58)$$

α is zero or negative ($-n \leqslant \alpha \leqslant 0$) for values of x in the table, $x_0 \leqslant x \leqslant x_n$. Table 1.9 indicates the backward differences for the data of Table 1.8 with the base-point indices renumbered.

Table 1.9   Backward-Difference Table

i	x_i	$f(x_i)$	∇f	$\nabla^2 f$	$\nabla^3 f$	$\nabla^4 f$
$n-4$	0.	-5.				
			6.			
$n-3$	1.	1.		2.		
			8.		6.	
$n-2$	2.	9.		8.		0.
			16.		6.	
$n-1$	3.	25.		14.		
			30.			
n	4.	55.				

Notice that the backward differences of Table 1.9 are identical with the forward differences of Table 1.8; only the indices of the base points differ.

If Newton's fundamental formula is written in terms of the divided differences along the lower diagonal path of a divided-difference table, (1.30) has the form

$$f(x) = p_n(x) + R_n(x)$$

where

$$
\begin{aligned}
p_n(x) =\ & f[x_n] + (x - x_n)f[x_n, x_{n-1}] \\
& + (x - x_n)(x - x_{n-1})f[x_n, x_{n-1}, x_{n-2}] \\
& + \cdots + (x - x_n)(x - x_{n-1})(x - x_{n-2}) \\
& \cdots (x - x_1)f[x_n, x_{n-1}, \ldots, x_0]
\end{aligned}
\tag{1.59}
$$

and

$$
\begin{aligned}
R_n(x) =\ & (x - x_n)(x - x_{n-1}) \cdots (x - x_0) \\
& \times f[x, x_n, x_{n-1}, \ldots, x_0],
\end{aligned}
$$

or

$$
\begin{aligned}
R_n(x) =\ & (x - x_n)(x - x_{n-1}) \cdots (x - x_0) \\
& \times \frac{f^{(n+1)}(\xi)}{(n+1)!}, \qquad x_0 < \xi < x_n.
\end{aligned}
\tag{1.60}
$$

In terms of α and the backward differences, (1.60) becomes

$$
\begin{aligned}
f(x_n + \alpha h) =\ & f(x_n) + \alpha \nabla f(x_n) + \frac{\alpha(\alpha + 1)}{2!} \nabla^2 f(x_n) \\
& + \frac{\alpha(\alpha + 1)(\alpha + 2)}{3!} \nabla^3 f(x_n) \\
& + \cdots + \frac{\alpha(\alpha + 1)(\alpha + 2) \cdots (\alpha + n - 1)}{n!} \\
& \times \nabla^n f(x_n) + R_n(x_n + \alpha h)
\end{aligned}
\tag{1.61}
$$

where

$$
\begin{aligned}
R_n(x_n + \alpha h) =\ & h^{n+1} \alpha(\alpha + 1)(\alpha + 2) \cdots (\alpha + n) \\
& \times f[x, x_n, x_{n-1}, \ldots, x_0],
\end{aligned}
\tag{1.62}
$$

or

$$
\begin{aligned}
R_n(x_n + \alpha h) =\ & h^{n+1} \alpha(\alpha + 1)(\alpha + 2) \cdots (\alpha + n) \\
& \times \frac{f^{(n+1)}(\xi)}{(n+1)!}, \qquad x_0 < \xi < x_n.
\end{aligned}
$$

If an additional base point $x_{-1} = x_0 - h$ should be available, then the $(n + 1)$th divided difference may be approximated by

$$f[x, x_n, x_{n-1}, \ldots, x_0] \doteq f[x_n, x_{n-1}, \ldots, x_0, x_{-1}],$$

leading to an estimate for $R_n(x_n + \alpha h)$ of

$$R_n(x_n + \alpha h) \doteq \frac{\alpha(\alpha + 1)(\alpha + 2) \cdots (\alpha + n)\nabla^{n+1}f(x_n)}{(n+1)!}.$$

$$\tag{1.63}$$

Equation (1.61) is known as *Newton's backward formula* (NBF). Since NBF uses differences along the lower diagonal of the difference table, it is most useful for interpolation near the end of a set of tabulated values. As before, a shifting of subscripts, say the labeling of the point (3,25) in Table 1.9 as $(x_n, f(x_n))$, allows the formula to be used elsewhere in the table. In Chapter 6, we shall show that this form of the interpolating polynomial is quite useful in creating algorithms for stepwise solution of ordinary differential equations.

Example. By using the differences of Table 1.9, find the interpolant value predicted by the third-degree NBF formula (1.61) for the argument $x = 3.5$.

For this case, $\alpha = (x - x_n)/h = (3.5 - 4)/1 = -0.5$. Then NBF yields

$$p_3(3.5) = 55 + (-0.5)(30) + \frac{(-0.5)(0.5)}{2!}(14)$$

$$+ \frac{(-0.5)(0.5)(1.5)}{3!}(6) = 37\tfrac{7}{8}.$$

Since $f(x) = x^3 - 2x^2 + 7x - 5$ is a third-degree polynomial, this predicted value is the exact value, that is, the higher-order differences vanish as before.

Central Differences. In Section 1.6 it was shown that the interpolation error tends to be smallest when we fit the interpolating polynomial with base points on both sides of the interpolation argument. This can be effected by choosing a path through the divided-difference table which zizgags about some base point near the interpolation argument. Stated another way, this means that if a central path is taken across the difference table, more of the functional value is represented by leading terms in the difference formulation (the sequence converges faster). Consequently, a low-order central interpolation may produce answers with remainder terms no larger than a higher-order fit using the forward or backward paths. Of course, if the same base points are used to produce polynomials of equivalent degree, then all paths are equivalent.

A simple notation which describes differences along a zigzag path near the center of the difference table is needed. The *central-difference operator* (δ) is defined as follows:

$$\delta f(x) = f\left(x + \frac{h}{2}\right) - f\left(x - \frac{h}{2}\right)$$

$$\delta^2 f(x) = \delta f\left(x + \frac{h}{2}\right) - \delta f\left(x - \frac{h}{2}\right)$$

$$\vdots$$

$$\delta^n f(x) = \delta^{n-1} f\left(x + \frac{h}{2}\right) - \delta^{n-1} f\left(x - \frac{h}{2}\right).$$

$$\tag{1.64}$$

There is a notational difficulty for the odd differences, since there are no tabulated values at the half-interval values $x_i + h/2$, $x_i - h/2$, etc. However, these "fictional" values are simply ignored and instead the odd differences are evaluated at mid-interval. Thus the even and odd differences are evaluated separately as follows:

For $2r = n$ (even):

$$\frac{\delta^n f(x_i)}{n! h^n} = f[x_i, x_{i+1}, x_{i-1}, \ldots, x_{i+r}, x_{i-r}].$$

For $2r + 1 = n$ (odd):

$$\frac{\delta^n f\left(x_i + \dfrac{h}{2}\right)}{n! h^n} = f[x_{i+1}, x_i, x_{i+2}, x_{i-1}, \ldots, x_{i+r+1}, x_{i-r}].$$

The central-difference table (entries are identical with the forward- and backward-difference tables, except for the subscripts of the base points) then takes the form of Table 1.10.

Table 1.10   Central-Difference Table

If the zigzag path along the solid lines is taken, the formulation is termed the *Gauss forward formula* and is given by

$$f(x_0 + \alpha h) = f(x_0) + \alpha \delta f(x_0 + h/2)$$
$$+ \alpha(\alpha - 1)\delta^2 f(x_0)/2!$$
$$+ \alpha(\alpha - 1)(\alpha + 1)\delta^3 f(x_0 + h/2)/3!$$
$$+ \cdots + R_n(x_0 + \alpha h), \tag{1.65}$$

where $\alpha = (x - x_0)/h$. When the dotted path is used, the *Gauss backward formula* is generated instead:

$$f(x_0 + \alpha h) = f(x_0) + \alpha \delta f(x_0 - h/2)$$
$$+ \alpha(\alpha + 1)\delta^2 f(x_0)/2!$$
$$+ \alpha(\alpha - 1)(\alpha + 1)\delta^3 f(x_0 - h/2)/3!$$
$$+ \cdots + R_n(x_0 + \alpha h). \tag{1.66}$$

An estimate of $R_n(x_0 + \alpha h)$ can be made, as before, by evaluating the first term dropped. If the last retained term is of even order $n = 2r$, then the two formulas are equivalent (since the same base points are involved in the fit) and yield identical results for all α. The polynomial agrees with the data at $x_{-r}, x_{-r+1}, \ldots, x_0, \ldots, x_{r-1}, x_r$. If

$n = 2r + 1$ is odd, then the forward formula agrees exactly with the data at $x_{-r}, x_{-r+1}, \ldots, x_0, \ldots, x_{r-1}, x_r, x_{r+1}$, and the backward formula agrees at $x_{-r-1}, x_{-r}, x_{-r+1}, \ldots, x_0, \ldots, x_{r-1}, x_r$. *Stirling's formula*, occasionally mentioned in the literature, is simply the average of these two Gauss central-difference formulas:

$$f(x_0 + \alpha h) = f(x_0) + \frac{\alpha}{2}\left[\delta f(x_0 + h/2)\right.$$
$$\left. + \delta f(x_0 - h/2)\right] + \alpha^2 \frac{\delta^2 f(x_0)}{2!}$$
$$+ \frac{\alpha(\alpha - 1)(\alpha + 1)}{2}$$
$$\times \frac{\delta^3 f(x_0 + h/2) + \delta^3 f(x_0 - h/2)}{3!} + \cdots$$
$$\tag{1.67}$$

The differences of Table 1.8 with subscripts adjusted as shown in Table 1.10 are illustrated in Table 1.11.

Table 1.11   Central-Difference Table

i	x_i	$f(x_i)$	δ	δ^2	δ^3	δ^4
-2	0.	$-5.$				
			6			
-1	1.	1.		2.		
			8.		6.	
0	2.	9.		8.		0.
			16.		6.	
1	3.	25.		14.		
			30.			
2	4.	55.				

Example. Use the Gauss forward formula of (1.65) and central-differences of Table 1.11 to compute the interpolant value for interpolation argument $x = 2.5$ with $n = 3$.

Following the zigzag path across the table,

$$\alpha = (x - x_0)/h = (2.5 - 2)/1 = 0.5,$$
$$p_3(2.5) = 9 + (0.5)(16) + (0.5)(-0.5)(8)/2!$$
$$+ (0.5)(-0.5)(1.5)(6)/3! = 15\tfrac{5}{8}.$$

Evaluation of the generating function

$$f(x) = p_3(x) = x^3 - 2x^2 + 7x - 5$$

for $x = 2.5$ yields the same value, as expected.

1.9 Concluding Remarks on Polynomial Interpolation

Approximating polynomials, which use information about derivatives as well as functional values, may also be constructed. For example, a third-degree polynomial could be found which reproduces functional values $f(x_0)$ and $f(x_1)$ and derivative values $f'(x_0)$ and $f'(x_1)$ at x_0 and x_1 respectively. The simultaneous equations to be solved in this case would be (for $p_3(x) = \sum_{i=0}^{3} a_i x^i$):

$$a_0 + a_1 x_0 + a_2 x_0^2 + a_3 x_0^3 = f(x_0)$$
$$a_0 + a_1 x_1 + a_2 x_1^2 + a_3 x_1^3 = f(x_1)$$
$$a_1 + 2a_2 x_0 + 3a_3 x_0^2 = f'(x_0)$$
$$a_1 + 2a_2 x_1 + 3a_3 x_1^2 = f'(x_1).$$

This system has the determinant

$$\begin{vmatrix} 1 & x_0 & x_0^2 & x_0^3 \\ 1 & x_1 & x_1^2 & x_1^3 \\ 0 & 1 & 2x_0 & 3x_0^2 \\ 0 & 1 & 2x_1 & 3x_1^2 \end{vmatrix}.$$

Higher-order derivatives may be used as well, subject to the restriction that the determinant of the system of equations may not vanish. The logical limit to this process, when $f(x_0), f'(x_0), f''(x_0), \ldots, f^{(n)}(x_0)$ are employed, yields the nth-degree polynomial produced by Taylor's expansion, truncated after the term in x^n. The generation of appropriate interpolation formulas for these special cases is somewhat more tedious, but fundamentally no more difficult than cases for which only the $f(x_i)$ are specified.

Unfortunately, there are no simple ground rules for deciding what degree interpolation will yield best results. When it is possible to evaluate higher-order derivatives, then, of course, an error bound can be computed using (1.39b). In most situations, however, it is not possible to compute such a bound and the error estimate of (1.33) is the only information available. As the degree n of the interpolating polynomial increases, the interval containing the points $x_0, x_1, \ldots, x_n$ also increases in size, tending, for a given x, to increase the magnitude of the polynomial term $\prod_{i=0}^{n} (x - x_i)$ in the error (1.39) or error estimate (1.33). And, of course, the derivatives and divided differences do not necessarily become smaller as n increases; in fact, for many functions [13] the derivatives at first tend to decrease in magnitude with increasing n and then eventually increase without bound as n becomes larger and larger. Therefore the error may well increase rather than decrease as additional terms are retained in the approximation, that is, as the degree of the interpolating polynomial is increased.

One final word of caution. The functional values $f(x_i)$ are usually known to a few significant figures at best. Successive differencing operations on these data, which are normally of comparable magnitude, inevitably lead to loss of significance in the computed results; in some cases, calculated high-order differences may be completely meaningless.

On the reassuring side, low-degree interpolating polynomials usually have very good convergence properties, that is, most of the functional value can be represented by low-order terms. In practice, we can almost always achieve the desired degree of accuracy with low-degree polynomial approximations, provided that base-point functional values are available on the interval of interest.

1.10 Chebyshev Polynomials

The only approximating functions employed thus far have been the polynomials, that is, linear combinations of the monomials $1, x, x^2, \ldots, x^n$. An examination of the monomials on the interval $[-1,1]$ shows that each achieves its maximum magnitude (1) at $x = \pm 1$ and its minimum magnitude (0) at $x = 0$. If a function $f(x)$ is approximated by a polynomial

$$p_n(x) = a_0 + a_1 x + a_2 x^2 + \cdots + a_n x^n,$$

where $p_n(x)$ is presumably a good approximation, the dropping of high-order terms or modification of the coefficients $a_1, \ldots, a_n$ will produce little error for small x (near zero), but probably substantial error near the ends of the interval (x near ± 1).

Unfortunately it is in general true that polynomial approximations (for example those following from Taylor's series expansions) for arbitrary functions $f(z)$ exhibit this same uneven error distribution over arbitrary intervals $a \leqslant z \leqslant b$. Since any such arbitrary finite interval can be transformed to the interval $-1 \leqslant x \leqslant 1$ by the change of variable

$$x = \frac{2z - b - a}{b - a}, \qquad z \text{ in } [a,b],$$
$$x \text{ in } [-1,1], \qquad (1.68)$$

it is sufficient to examine the behavior of functions potentially better than $1, x, x^2, \ldots, x^n$ on the interval $[-1,1]$. In particular, it seems reasonable to look for other sets of simple, related functions that have their extreme values well distributed on the interval $[-1,1]$. We hope that if we approximate an arbitrary function using a linear combination of such functions, the error in the approximation will be distributed more evenly over the interval. In particular, we want to find approximations which are fairly easy to generate and which reduce the *maximum* error to the *minimum* (or near minimum) value.

The cosine functions, $\cos \theta$, $\cos 2\theta$, ..., $\cos n\theta$, appear to be good candidates. Each of the functions has identical maximum and minimum values distributed regularly over an arbitrary interval, say $0 \leqslant \theta \leqslant \pi$; in addition, the extreme values for two functions $\cos j\theta$, $\cos k\theta$, $j \neq k$, do not, in general, occur at the same values of x (see Fig. 1.9).

As shown earlier (1.7), the cosine function requires an approximation for its numerical evaluation. A simpler and more useful form results from the transformation of $\cos n\theta$ on the interval $0 \leqslant \theta \leqslant \pi$ into an nth-degree polynomial in x on the interval $-1 \leqslant x \leqslant 1$. The set of poly-

Table 1.12   The Chebyshev Polynomials

$T_0 = 1$,
$T_1 = x$,
$T_2 = 2x^2 - 1$,
$T_3 = 4x^3 - 3x$,
$T_4 = 8x^4 - 8x^2 + 1$,
$T_5 = 16x^5 - 20x^3 + 5x$,
$T_6 = 32x^6 - 48x^4 + 18x^2 - 1$,
$T_7 = 64x^7 - 112x^5 + 56x^3 - 7x$,
$T_8 = 128x^8 - 256x^6 + 160x^4 - 32x^2 + 1$,
$T_9 = 256x^9 - 576x^7 + 432x^5 - 120x^3 + 9x$.

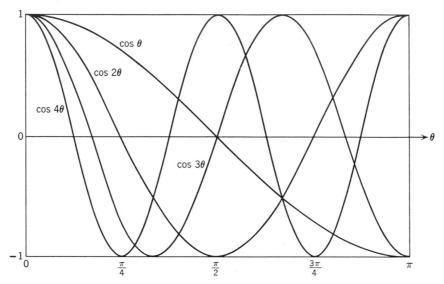

Figure 1.9 $\cos n\theta$, $n = 1, 2, 3, 4$, *on the interval* $0 \leqslant \theta \leqslant \pi$.

nomials $T_n(x) = \cos n\theta$, $n = 0, 1, \ldots$, generated from the sequence of cosine functions using the transformation

$$\theta = \cos^{-1} x, \qquad (1.69)$$

is known as the Chebyshev polynomials. Clearly $T_0(x) = \cos(0) = 1$. On introducing (1.69), the first cosine function is transformed into the Chebyshev polynomial of degree one,

$$T_1(x) = \cos \theta = \cos(\cos^{-1} x) = x. \qquad (1.70)$$

To find $T_2(x)$, the Chebyshev polynomial of degree two, apply the trigonometric identity, $\cos 2\theta = 2 \cos^2 \theta - 1$ to yield

$$\cos 2\theta = \cos(2 \cos^{-1} x) = 2 \cos^2(\cos^{-1} x) - 1$$

or

$$T_2(x) = 2x^2 - 1. \qquad (1.71)$$

In general, repeated application of the trigonometric identity,

$$\cos n\theta = 2 \cos \theta \cos(n - 1)\theta - \cos(n - 2)\theta,$$

can be used to compute higher-order Chebyshev polynomials, yielding the recursion relation,

$$T_n(x) = 2xT_{n-1}(x) - T_{n-2}(x). \qquad (1.72)$$

The algebraic functions $1, x, x^2, x^3, \ldots, x^9$ can be expressed as functions of the Chebyshev polynomials by simple algebraic manipulation and are shown in Table 1.13. Notice that the Chebyshev polynomials (because of their $\cos n\theta$ origin) have a maximum magnitude of 1 on the interval $[-1,1]$. The $T_i(x)$ of degrees 0 to 3 are shown in Fig. 1.10. The n roots of $T_n(x)$ are real, occur on the interval $[-1,1]$, and are given by

$$\lambda_i = \cos\left[\frac{(2i - 1)\pi}{2n}\right], \qquad i = 1, \ldots, n. \qquad (1.73)$$

A very useful property of these polynomials is that of all the possible monic polynomials $p_n(x)$, that is, of all polynomials of degree n with the coefficient of the nth-power term equal to 1, the polynomial

$$\phi_n(x) = \frac{T_n(x)}{2^{n-1}} \qquad (1.74)$$

has the *smallest* upper bound for its absolute value on the interval $[-1,1]$.

Examination of the recursion relation or of Table 1.12 shows that the leading coefficient of the nth Chebyshev polynomial is 2^{n-1}, so that $\phi_n(x)$ is simply the normalized nth Chebyshev polynomial, that is, $T_n(x)$ divided by its

Table 1.13   Powers of x in Terms of the Chebyshev Polynomials

$1 = T_0,$

$x = T_1,$

$x^2 = \dfrac{1}{2}(T_0 + T_2),$

$x^3 = \dfrac{1}{4}(3T_1 + T_3),$

$x^4 = \dfrac{1}{8}(3T_0 + 4T_2 + T_4),$

$x^5 = \dfrac{1}{16}(10T_1 + 5T_3 + T_5),$

$x^6 = \dfrac{1}{32}(10T_0 + 15T_2 + 6T_4 + T_6),$

$x^7 = \dfrac{1}{64}(35T_1 + 21T_3 + 7T_5 + T_7),$

$x^8 = \dfrac{1}{128}(35T_0 + 56T_2 + 28T_4 + 8T_6 + T_8),$

$x^9 = \dfrac{1}{256}(126T_1 + 84T_3 + 36T_5 + 9T_7 + T_9).$

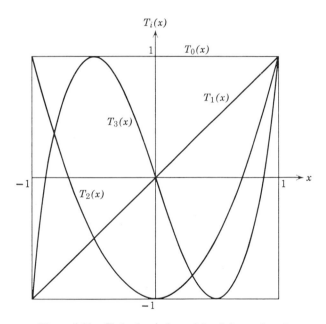

Figure 1.10   Chebyshev polynomials of degree 0 to 3.

high-order coefficient. Since the maximum magnitude of $T_n(x)$ is 1 for $-1 \leqslant x \leqslant 1$, the maximum magnitude of $\phi_n(x)$ is $1/2^{n-1}$ for $-1 \leqslant x \leqslant 1$. A study of $\phi_n(x)$ on this interval shows that all the extreme values have the same magnitude, namely $1/2^{n-1}$, and that there are exactly $n + 1$ of them, alternately relative maxima and minima. The proof that $\phi_n(x)$ has the property of minimum upper bound follows.

Assume that there is some other monic polynomial

$S_n(x)$, which has a smaller maximum magnitude on the indicated interval, and determine the difference

$$D(x) = \phi_n(x) - S_n(x) \tag{1.75}$$

at the local extrema of $\phi_n(x)$. $\phi_n(x)$ has exactly $n + 1$ extreme values and crosses the x axis exactly n times (has n roots) in the interval $-1 \leqslant x \leqslant 1$. At each of these extreme values (let the abscissas be $x_0, x_1, \ldots, x_n$), $S_n(x)$ must be smaller in magnitude than $\phi_n(x)$ because of the initial assumption. This requires that the differences evaluated at the x_i,

$$D(x_i) = \phi_n(x_i) - S_n(x_i), \tag{1.76}$$

change sign for each successive value of i, that is, if $D(x_0) < 0$, then $D(x_1) > 0$, $D(x_2) < 0$, etc., and if $D(x_0) > 0$, then $D(x_1) < 0$, $D(x_2) > 0$, etc. Thus $D(x)$ must change sign n times, or equivalently, have n roots in the interval $[-1,1]$. But $D(x)$ is a polynomial of degree $n - 1$, because both $\phi_n(x)$ and $S_n(x)$ have leading coefficient unity. Since an $(n - 1)$th-degree polynomial has only $n - 1$ roots, there is no polynomial $S_n(x)$. The proposition that $\phi_n(x)$ is the monic polynomial that deviates least from zero on $[-1,1]$ is thus proved by contradiction.

Consider the illustration of the proof for $\phi_2(x) = T_2(x)/2$ shown in Fig. 1.11. The solid curve is $\phi_2(x)$, that is, $T_2(x)/2 = x^2 - \frac{1}{2}$, which has three extreme values at $x_0 = -1$, $x_1 = 0$, and $x_2 = 1$. The dotted curve shows a proposed $S_n(x)$ which has a maximum magnitude on the interval smaller than $\phi_2(x)$. The difference in the ordinates $\phi_2(x)$ and $S_2(x)$ at x_0, x_1, and x_2 are shown as $D(x_0)$, $D(x_1)$, and $D(x_2)$. As indicated by the direction of the arrows, $D(x)$ must change sign twice on the interval, an impossibility since $\phi_2(x) - S_2(x)$ is only a first-degree polynomial.

1.11   Minimizing the Maximum Error

Since the nth-degree polynomial $\phi_n(x) = T_n(x)/2^{n-1}$ has the smallest maximum magnitude of all possible nth-degree monic polynomials on the interval $[-1,1]$, any error that can be expressed as an nth-degree polynomial can be minimized for the interval $[-1,1]$ by equating it with $\phi_n(x)$. For example, the error term for the interpolating polynomial has been shown to be of the form (see 1.39b)

$$R(x) = \left[\prod_{i=0}^{n} (x - x_i) \right] \frac{f^{(n+1)}(\xi)}{(n+1)!}.$$

We can do very little about $f^{(n+1)}(\xi)$. The only effective way of minimizing $R(x)$ is to minimize the maximum magnitude of the $(n + 1)$th-degree polynomial $\prod_{i=0}^{n}(x - x_i)$. Treat $f^{(n+1)}(\xi)$ as though it were constant. Now equate $\prod_{i=0}^{n}(x - x_i)$ with $\phi_{n+1}(x)$, and notice that the $(x - x_i)$ terms are simply the $n + 1$ factors of $\phi_{n+1}(x)$; the x_i are therefore roots of $\phi_{n+1}(x)$, or equivalently, the

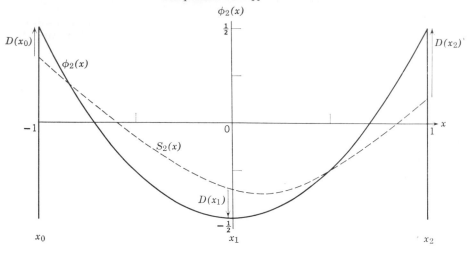

Figure 1.11   *$\phi_2(x)$, the second-degree monic polynomial that deviates least from zero on* $[-1,1]$.

roots of the corresponding Chebyshev polynomial $T_{n+1}(x)$, given by

$$x_i = \cos\left[\frac{(2i+1)\pi}{2n+2}\right], \qquad i = 0, 1, \ldots, n. \quad (1.77)$$

For an arbitrary interval, $a \leqslant z \leqslant b$, the appropriate z_i values may be computed by transforming these root values from $[-1,1]$ to $[a,b]$, using the inverse of (1.68),

$$z_i = \frac{x_i(b-a)+(b+a)}{2}. \quad (1.78)$$

This minimization of maximum error is sometimes termed the *minimax principle*.

However, the application of the minimax principle is possible only when there is a freedom of choice in selecting the base points x_i. Fortunately, this is often the case in experimental work where one has control over the independent variable values which may be used subsequently as base points for polynomial interpolation. For example, the sampling time for an experiment may be the independent variable of interest. Then for a fixed total time interval, during which a fixed number of samples are to be taken, the best times for taking sample measurements are given by the transformed roots of the appropriate Chebyshev polynomial.

A more general but related problem is to find that approximating polynomial $p_n^*(x)$ of degree n which satisfies

$$D = \max_{-1 \leqslant x \leqslant 1} |f(x) - p_n^*(x)| \leqslant \max_{-1 \leqslant x \leqslant 1} |f(x) - p_n(x)|, \quad (1.79)$$

that is, *minimizes* the *maximum* deviation from $f(x)$ on $[-1,1]$ (or, in general, on $[a,b]$). One can show [14] that $p_n^*(x)$ is unique and that the deviation, $d^*(x) = f(x) - p_n^*(x)$, must attain its maximum magnitude at not less than $n + 2$ distinct points in $[-1,1]$ (or $[a,b]$) and be alternately positive and negative at these points. The

argument is straightforward. Suppose that $p_n(x) = f(x) - d(x)$ is a better approximation to $f(x)$ than is a given polynomial $p_n^*(x)$ that exhibits the equal-magnitude oscillatory behavior for its error (such an error function is said to possess the *equal ripple* property). Then $d^*(x) - d(x) = p_n(x) - p_n^*(x)$ is evidently a polynomial of degree n, alternately positive and negative at the $n + 2$ or more points where $d^*(x)$ passes through its extreme values, since at these points, by hypothesis, $|d(x)| < |d^*(x)|$. Since no polynomial of degree n possesses $n + 1$ roots (changes in sign), the contention that $p_n^*(x)$ is the polynomial of degree n that minimizes the maximum deviation from $f(x)$ on the interval of interest is proved by contradiction. The polynomial $p_n^*(x)$ is called the *minimax polynomial* of degree n.

We assume that $f(x)$ is a single-valued continuous function on the closed interval $[a,b]$. Then $d^*(x)$ is continuous and $p_n^*(x)$ must be equal to $f(x)$ at $n + 1$ distinct points $x_0, x_1, \ldots, x_n$, where each x_i lies between two points at which the error achieves its extreme value. Thus the minimax polynomial $p_n^*(x)$ is an nth-degree interpolating polynomial. When $f(x)$ possesses an $(n + 1)$th-order derivative, the error term (1.39b) applies, and the problem reverts to that of the early paragraphs of this section. If $f^{(n+1)}(x)$ is a constant, then the interpolating polynomial using the base points given by (1.77) is precisely $p_n^*(x)$; if not, then the interpolating polynomial so generated is only an approximation to $p_n^*(x)$.

The problem of finding $p_n^*(x)$ when $f^{(n+1)}(\xi)$ in (1.39b) is unknown or variable in $[-1,1]$, becomes an iterative one. The procedures commonly used (see for example [16]) follow from the work of Remes [15] and are rather complex; they will not be described here.

Clenshaw [17] shows that if the function $f(x)$ can be expanded in terms of the Chebyshev polynomials as

$$f(x) = \sum_{i=0}^{\infty} a_i T_i(x), \quad (1.80)$$

then the partial sum

$$p_n(x) = \sum_{i=0}^{n} a_i T_i(x) \qquad (1.81)$$

will usually be a very good approximation to $p_n^*(x)$, that is, $p_n(x)$ given by (1.81) will be *near-minimax*. Note that (1.80) is just the Fourier cosine series expansion of the function $f(\cos \theta)$. Clenshaw suggests that the improvement one can get in the approximation using $p_n^*(x)$ is seldom worth the required effort to find it and that the addition of one more term in (1.81), that is, increasing the degree of the polynomial by one, will usually produce a greater improvement in accuracy. Unfortunately, the procedure for generating the coefficients in (1.80), described in detail in [17], is rather tedious for arbitrary functions. Clenshaw lists extensive tabulations of the a_i for the common trigonometric functions, inverse trigonometric functions, exponential and hyperbolic functions, logarithmic and inverse hyperbolic functions, the gamma function, the error function, and several of the Bessel functions.

Snyder [18] describes procedures for generating minimax or near-minimax rational approximations (see Section 1.2) to arbitrary functions. His book contains a substantial bibliography of recent work in the general area of minimax approximations and Chebyshev polynomials.

1.12 Chebyshev Economization—Telescoping a Power Series

Coefficients of the Chebyshev polynomials in (1.81) for arbitrary functions $f(x)$ can be computed with some effort using methods similar to those outlined in Example 2.2 in Chapter 2. If $f(x)$ is a polynomial of degree n, then it is a simple matter to determine the coefficients in (1.81) using Table 1.13; we simply replace each term x^j by its expansion in terms of the Chebyshev polynomials and collect coefficients of like polynomials $T_i(x)$. It often happens that when polynomials, particularly those resulting from truncated Taylor's series expansions, are expressed using Chebyshev polynomials, some of the high-order Chebyshev polynomials can be dropped with the knowledge that the error involved is small (since the upper bound for $|T_n(x)|$ in $[-1,1]$ is known to be 1). The truncated series can then be retransformed to a polynomial in x with fewer terms than the original, and, of course, modified coefficients. This procedure, termed *Chebyshev economization* or *telescoping a power series*, is probably best illustrated with some examples.

Suppose we want to find a three-term approximation for the cosine on the interval $[-1,1]$ of the form

$$\cos x \doteq a + bx^2 + cx^4 \qquad (1.82)$$

which is in error by no more than 5×10^{-5} (see the results of Example 1.3). The logical starting place is with the power series expansion

$$\cos x = 1 - \frac{x^2}{2!} + \frac{x^4}{4!} - \frac{x^6}{6!} + \frac{x^8}{8!} - \frac{x^{10}}{10!} +$$

$$\cdots \pm \frac{x^n}{n!} \mp \cdots, \qquad (1.83)$$

with n even. Examination of the remainder term for truncation after the nth-degree term, $x^{n+2}/(n+2)! \cos \xi$, $|\xi| < 1$, shows that truncation of the series results in a total error smaller than the first term dropped. Truncation after the term in x^8 will produce an error of magnitude less than $1/10! \doteq 2.76 \times 10^{-7}$ for x in $[-1,1]$.

Rewriting the remaining five-term series in terms of the Chebyshev polynomials by using Table 1.13 yields:

$$\cos x \doteq T_0$$

$$-\frac{1}{2} \times \frac{1}{2!} (T_0 + T_2)$$

$$+\frac{1}{8} \times \frac{1}{4!} (3T_0 + 4T_2 + T_4) \qquad (1.84)$$

$$-\frac{1}{32} \times \frac{1}{6!} (10T_0 + 15T_2 + 6T_4 + T_6)$$

$$+\frac{1}{128} \times \frac{1}{8!} (35T_0 + 56T_2 + 28T_4 + 8T_6 + T_8).$$

Collecting coefficients of the T_i,

$$\cos x \doteq 0.76519775 T_0 - 0.22980686 T_2$$
$$+ 0.0049533419 T_4 - 4.185265 \times 10^{-5} T_6$$
$$+ 1.937624 \times 10^{-7} T_8. \qquad (1.85)$$

Since the maximum magnitude of the Chebyshev polynomials in $[-1,1]$ is 1.0, the terms in T_6 and T_8 can be dropped without incurring an additional error larger than $4.186 \times 10^{-5} + 1.938 \times 10^{-7} \doteq 4.206 \times 10^{-5}$. When added to the maximum Taylor's series error, 2.76×10^{-7}, the maximum total error must be smaller than 4.234×10^{-5}. Since this is less than the prescribed error, a suitable approximation for the cosine is given by

$$\cos x \doteq 0.76519775 T_0$$
$$- 0.22980686 T_2 + 0.0049533419 T_4. \qquad (1.86)$$

Table 1.12 can be used to retransform the series into a polynomial in x, yielding

$$\cos x \doteq 0.99995795 - 0.49924045\, x^2 + 0.03962674 x^4. \qquad (1.87)$$

If the original power series had been truncated after the term in x^4, the error bound would have been

$$\frac{1}{6!} = \frac{1}{720} \doteq 1.39 \times 10^{-3},$$

some 28 times the specified value. While it would appear at first glance that the original series could be truncated after the term in x^6 (since $1/8! \doteq 2.5 \times 10^{-5} < 5 \times 10^{-5}$)

EXAMPLE 1.3

CHEBYSHEV ECONOMIZATION

Problem Statement

Write a program that reads as data the following:

$$n, \varepsilon, L, R, a_0, a_1, \ldots, a_n.$$

Here, the a_i are the coefficients of the nth-degree polynomial

$$p_n(z) = \sum_{i=0}^{n} a_i z^i, \qquad (1.3.1)$$

where $L \leqslant z \leqslant R$. The program should transform (1.3.1) to the nth-degree polynomial in a new variable x having coefficients a_i^*,

$$p_n(x) = \sum_{i=0}^{n} a_i^* x^i, \qquad (1.3.2)$$

where $-1 \leqslant x \leqslant 1$, and x and z are related (see (1.68)) by

$$x = \frac{2z - R - L}{R - L}. \qquad (1.3.3)$$

Next, the program should expand (1.3.2) in terms of the Chebyshev polynomials of Tables 1.12 and 1.13 as

$$p_n(x) = \sum_{i=0}^{n} b_i T_i(x), \qquad (1.3.4)$$

and then carry out the Chebyshev economization procedure, dropping all those high-order polynomials $T_i(x)$ which can, in sum, contribute no more than an amount ε to the value of $p_n(x)$ on $[-1,1]$. Let m be the degree of the truncated polynomial, so that

$$p_n(x) = p_m(x) + E = \sum_{i=0}^{m} b_i T_i(x) + E, \qquad (1.3.5)$$

where

$$E = \sum_{i=m+1}^{n} b_i T_i(x), \qquad (1.3.6)$$

and

$$E_{max} = \sum_{i=m+1}^{n} |b_i| \leqslant \varepsilon. \qquad (1.3.7)$$

The economized polynomial $p_m(x)$ should be rewritten as

$$p_m(x) = \sum_{i=0}^{m} c_i^* x^i, \qquad (1.3.8)$$

using Table 1.12. Finally, (1.3.8) should be transformed to the original variable z on the interval $[L,R]$, using (1.3.3), to yield

$$p_m(z) = \sum_{i=0}^{m} c_i z^i. \qquad (1.3.9)$$

The program should print the input data, the coefficients of the various polynomials as they are computed, and the value of E_{max}.

To simplify the transformation from (1.3.1) to (1.3.2) and from (1.3.8) to (1.3.9), write a general purpose subroutine named TRANS that converts an nth-degree polynomial in any variable (z for example) on an arbitrary interval $[L_1, R_1]$,

$$p_n(z) = \sum_{i=0}^{n} d_i z^i, \qquad (1.3.10)$$

to an nth-degree polynomial in any other variable (x, for example) on another arbitrary interval $[L_2, R_2]$,

$$p_n(x) = \sum_{i=0}^{n} d_i^* x^i, \qquad (1.3.11)$$

using the transformation

$$z = \frac{(R_1 - L_1)x + (L_1 R_2 - R_1 L_2)}{R_2 - L_2}. \qquad (1.3.12)$$

Note that (1.3.3) is a special case of (1.3.12), for which $L_1 = L$, $R_1 = R$, $L_2 = -1$, and $R_2 = 1$.

Method of Solution

Substituting (1.3.12) into (1.3.10), collecting terms in like powers of x, and equating them with the coefficients of (1.3.11) leads, after some tedious algebra, to the following relationship between d_i and d_i^*:

$$d_i^* = \left[\frac{R_1 - L_1}{R_2 - L_2}\right]^i \sum_{j=i}^{n} \binom{j}{i} \left[\frac{L_1 R_2 - R_1 L_2}{R_2 - L_2}\right]^{j-i} d_j,$$

$$L_1 R_2 \neq R_1 L_2,$$

$$d_i^* = \left[\frac{R_1 - L_1}{R_2 - L_2}\right]^i d_i, \qquad L_1 R_2 = R_1 L_2. \qquad (1.3.13)$$

Here,

$$\binom{j}{i} = \frac{j!}{i!(j-i)!}$$

is the binomial coefficient.

The subroutine TRANS computes values for the d_i^*, given the d_i, n, L_1, R_1, L_2, and R_2. A function called NOMIAL evaluates the binomial coefficient of (1.3.13), when needed by TRANS.

To implement the transformations from (1.3.2) to (1.3.4) and from the economized polynomial $p_m(x)$ in terms of the Chebyshev polynomials to (1.3.8), it is convenient to set up two 10×10 matrices $\bar{X}$ and $\bar{T}$, containing the coefficients from Tables 1.12 and 1.13. The matrix $\bar{X}$ contains the coefficients from Table 1.13 arranged so that element $\bar{X}_{i,j}$ contains the coefficient of T_j for the expansion of x^i in terms of the Chebyshev polynomials, as illustrated in Table 1.3.1.

The matrix $\bar{T}$ contains the coefficients from Table 1.12, arranged so that $\bar{T}_{i,j}$ is equal to the coefficient of the jth power of x for the ith Chebyshev polynomial, T_i, and is illustrated by Table 1.3.2. This organization of the matrices $\bar{X}$ and $\bar{T}$ leads to rather simple subscription schemes for carrying out the economization process, but is not essential. To economize on computer memory

Example 1.3 Chebyshev Economization **47**

Table 1.3.1 The Matrix $\overline{X}$

i Row Subscript	j - Column Subscript									
	0	1	2	3	4	5	6	7	8	9
0	1									
1	0	1								
2	1/2	0	1/2							
3	0	3/4	0	1/4						
4	3/8	0	4/8	0	1/8					
5	0	10/16	0	5/16	0	1/16				
6	10/32	0	15/32	0	6/32	0	1/32			
7	0	35/64	0	21/64	0	7/64	0	1/64		
8	35/128	0	56/128	0	28/128	0	8/128	0	1/128	
9	0	126/256	0	84/256	0	36/256	0	9/256	0	1/256

Table 1.3.2 The Matrix $\overline{T}$

i Row Subscript	j - Column Subscript									
	0	1	2	3	4	5	6	7	8	9
0	1									
1	0	1								
2	−1	0	2							
3	0	−3	0	4						
4	1	0	−8	0	8					
5	0	5	0	−20	0	16				
6	−1	0	18	0	−48	0	32			
7	0	−7	0	56	0	−112	0	64		
8	1	0	−32	0	160	0	−256	0	128	
9	0	9	0	−120	0	432	0	−576	0	256

requirements, the tables could be packed tightly to eliminate all nonzero entries; this would, of course, lead to a different subscription scheme.

Having found the a_i^* in (1.3.2), the coefficients of (1.3.4) can be computed from

$$b_j = \sum_{\substack{i=j \\ \Delta i = 2}}^{n} a_i^* \overline{X}_{i,j}, \quad j = 0, 1, \ldots, n, \quad (1.3.14)$$

where $\Delta i = 2$ indicates that i is to be incremented by 2; this allows the zero entries in $\overline{X}$ to be ignored.

Once the economized polynomial $p_m(x)$ has been found, using criterion (1.3.7), the coefficients of (1.3.8) can be computed from

$$c_j^* = \sum_{\substack{i=j \\ \Delta i = 2}}^{m} b_i \overline{T}_{i,j}, \quad j = 0, 1, \ldots, m. \quad (1.3.15)$$

Flow Diagram

Main Program

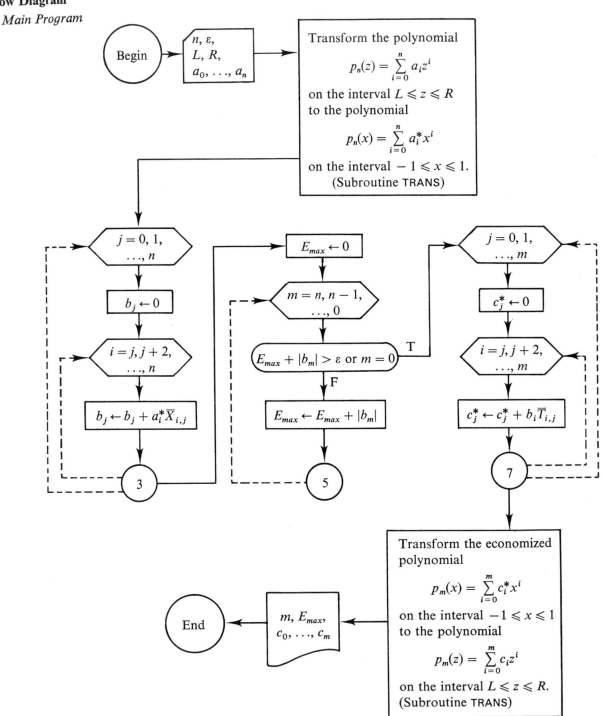

Example 1.3 *Chebyshev Economization* **49**

Subroutine TRANS (Dummy arguments: n, d, d^*, L_1, R_1, L_2, R_2;

calling arguments: $\begin{Bmatrix} n, a, a^*, L, R, -1, 1 \\ m, c^*, c, -1, 1, L, R \end{Bmatrix}$)

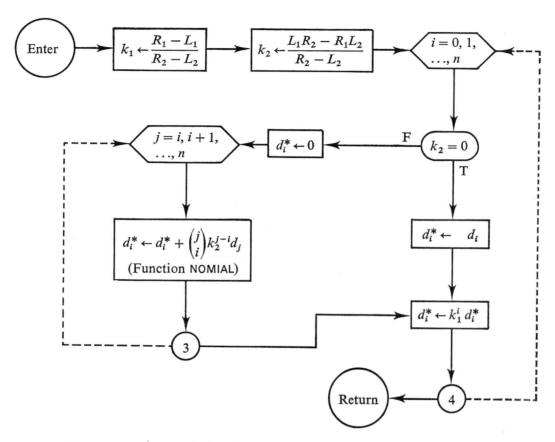

Function NOMIAL (Dummy arguments: k, l; calling arguments: j, i)

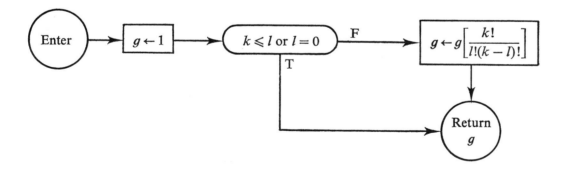

FORTRAN *Implementation*

List of Principal Variables

Program Symbol	Definition

(Main)

A, ASTAR, B, C, CSTAR†   Vectors of polynomial coefficients a_i, a_i^*, b_i, c_i, and c_i^*.

AL, AR   Lower bound, L, and upper bound, R, for the interval of interest in the variable z.

EMAX E_{max}, maximum possible error introduced by the economization procedure.

EPS ε, maximum allowable error to be introduced by the economization process.

I, ISUB, J, NP1, MP1†   Subscripts, i, $n + 2 - i$, j, $n + 1$, and $m + 1$.

M m, degree of the economized polynomial.

N n, degree of the starting polynomial.

ONE, ONEM   1.0, -1.0 (double-precision).

TTOX†   Matrix of coefficients for converting from a polynomial in terms of $T_i(x)$ to a polynomial in terms of x^j, $\overline{T}_{i,j}$ (see Table 1.3.2).

XTOT†   Matrix of coefficients for converting from a polynomial in terms of x^i to a polynomial in terms of $T_j(x)$, $\overline{X}_{i,j}$ (see Table 1.3.1).

(Subroutine TRANS)

BINOM   Binomial coefficient calculated by function NOMIAL.

COEFFI, COEFFT†   Vectors of coefficients for the initial and transformed polynomials, d_i and d_i^*, respectively.

CON1, CON2   Constants $k_1 = (R_1 - L_1)/(R_2 - L_2)$ and $k_2 = (L_1 R_2 - R_1 L_2)/(R_2 - L_2)$.

ENDLI, ENDLT   Lower bounds for the initial and terminal intervals, respectively.

ENDRI, ENDRT   Upper bounds for the initial and terminal intervals, respectively.

(Function NOMIAL)

ICOUNT   Counting variable.

K, L   Arguments for the binomial coefficient, k, l.

NOM   Binomial coefficient $g = \binom{k}{l}$.

---

† Because of FORTRAN limitations (subscripts smaller than one are not allowed), all subscripts in the text and flow diagrams are advanced by one when they appear in the programs: for example, a_0, a_n, $\overline{T}_{0,0}$, and $\overline{T}_{n,n}$ become A(1), A(N + 1), TTOX(1, 1) and TTOX(N + 1, N + 1) respectively.

Example 1.3   Chebyshev Economization

51

Program Listing

Main Program

```
C           APPLIED NUMERICAL METHODS, EXAMPLE 1.3
C           CHEBYSHEV ECONOMIZATION
C
C           THIS PROGRAM READS THE N+1 COEFFICIENTS A(1)...A(N+1) OF AN
C           N-TH DEGREE POLYNOMIAL IN Z ON THE INTERVAL (AL,AR) AND
C           EPS, THE MAXIMUM TOLERABLE ERROR PERMITTED IN THE
C           ECONOMIZED POLYNOMIAL.   THE COEFFICIENTS ARE ASSUMED TO
C           BE IN ORDER OF ASCENDING POWERS OF Z.  THE PROGRAM
C           CALLS ON THE SUBROUTINE TRANS TO COMPUTE THE COEFFICIENTS
C           ASTAR(1)...ASTAR(N+1) OF THE TRANSFORMED POLYNOMIAL IN X
C           ON THE INTERVAL (-1,1).   THE TRANSFORMED POLYNOMIAL IS
C           EXPANDED IN TERMS OF THE CHEBYSHEV POLYNOMIALS OF DEGREE N
C           OR LESS, WHERE B(J+1) IS THE COEFFICIENT OF THE J-TH CHEBYSHEV
C           POLYNOMIAL.   THIS POLYNOMIAL IS THEN TRUNCATED TO ONE
C           OF DEGREE M BY DROPPING HIGH ORDER TERMS OF THE POLYNOMIAL.
C           TERMS ARE DROPPED IN REVERSE ORDER SO LONG AS THE MAGNITUDE OF
C           THE POSSIBLE ERROR, EMAX, IS NOT GREATER THAN EPS. AFTER THE
C           ECONOMIZATION PROCESS IS COMPLETED, THE TRUNCATED POLYNOMIAL
C           IS CONVERTED TO A POLYNOMIAL IN THE VARIABLE X WITH THE
C           M+1 COEFFICIENTS IN CSTAR(1)...CSTAR(M+1).   THE SUBROUTINE
C           TRANS IS CALLED TO TRANSFORM THE ECONOMIZED POLYNOMIAL
C           IN X ON THE INTERVAL (-1,1) TO A POLYNOMIAL IN THE ORIGINAL
C           VARIABLE Z ON THE INTERVAL (AL,AR).   THE COEFFICIENTS OF THE
C           ECONOMIZED POLYNOMIAL ARE IN C(1)...C(M+1).  ELEMENTS OF THE
C           CONVERSION MATRICES XTOT AND TTOX ARE PRESET WITH VALUES
C           FROM TABLES 1.2 AND 1.3 IN THE TEXT.  AS WRITTEN, THE PROGRAM
C           CAN HANDLE STARTING POLYNOMIALS OF DEGREE NINE AT MOST.
C
      IMPLICIT  REAL*8(A-H, O-Z)
      DIMENSION A(10), ASTAR(10), B(10), CSTAR(10), C(10), XTOT(10,10),
     1 TTOX(10,10)
C
C     ..... PRESET CONVERSION MATRICES XTOT AND TTOX .....
      DATA  XTOT  / 1.0,  0.0,  0.5,  0.0,  0.375,  0.0,  0.3125,  0.0,
     1 0.2734375, 2*0.0,  1.0,  0.0,  0.75,  0.0,  0.625,  0.0,  0.546875,  0.0,
     2 0.4921875, 2*0.0,  0.5,  0.0,  0.5,  0.0,  0.46875,  0.0,  0.4375,
     3 4*0.0,  0.25,  0.0,  0.3125,  0.0,  0.328125,  0.0,  0.328125,  4*0.0,
     4 0.125,  0.0,  0.1875,  0.0,  0.21875,  6*0.0,  0.0625,  0.0,  0.109375,
     5 0.0,  0.140625,  6*0.0,  0.03125,  0.0,  0.0625,  8*0.0,  0.015625,  0.0,
     6 0.03515625,  8*0.0,  0.0078125,  10*0.0,  0.00390625 /
C
      DATA  TTOX  / 1.0,  0.0,  -1.0,  0.0,  1.0,  0.0,  -1.0,  0.0,  1.0,
     1 2*0.0,  1.0,  0.0,  -3.0,  0.0,  5.0,  0.0,  -7.0,  0.0,  9.0,  2*0.0,
     2 2.0,  0.0,  -8.0,  0.0,  18.0,  0.0,  -32.0,  4*0.0,  4.0,  0.0,  -20.0,
     3 0.0,  56.0,  0.0,  -120.0,  4*0.0,  8.0,  0.0,  -48.0,  0.0,  160.0,
     4 6*0.0,  16.0,  0.0,  -112.0,  0.0,  432.0,  6*0.0,  32.0,  0.0,  -256.0,
     5 8*0.0,  64.0,  0.0,  -576.0,  8*0.0,  128.0,  10*0.0,  256.0 /
C
      DATA  ONE, ONEM  /  1.0,  -1.0  /
C
C     ..... READ AND PRINT DATA .....
    1 READ (5,100)  N, EPS, AL, AR
      IF ( N.GT.9 )  CALL EXIT
      NP1 = N + 1
      READ (5,101)  (A(I), I=1,NP1)
      WRITE (6,200)  N, EPS, AL, AR, NP1, (A(I), I=1,NP1)
C
C     ..... TRANSFORM POLYNOMIAL IN Z ON INTERVAL (AL,AR)
C           TO A POLYNOMIAL IN X ON THE INTERVAL (-1,1) .....
      CALL TRANS( N,A,ASTAR,AL,AR,ONEM,ONE )
      WRITE (6,201)  NP1, (ASTAR(I), I=1,NP1)
C
C     ..... EXPAND TRANSFORMED POLY. IN TERMS OF CHEBY. POLYS. .....
      DO 3  J=1,NP1
      B(J) = 0.0
      DO 3  I=J,NP1,2
    3 B(J) = B(J) + ASTAR(I)*XTOT(I,J)
      WRITE (6,202)  NP1, (B(I), I=1,NP1)
```

Program Listing (*Continued*)

```
C
C        ..... CARRY OUT THE ECONOMIZATION PROCEDURE .....
         EMAX = 0.0
         MP1 = NP1
         DO 5  I=1,N
         ISUB = NP1 + 1 - I
         IF ( EMAX + DABS(B(ISUB)).GT.EPS )    GO TO 6
         MP1 = NP1 - I
    5    EMAX = EMAX + DABS(B(ISUB))
C
C        ..... CONVERT ECONOMIZED POLYNOMIAL TO POWERS OF X .....
    6    M = MP1 - 1
         DO 7   J=1,MP1
         CSTAR(J) = 0.0
         DO 7  I=J,MP1,2
    7    CSTAR(J) = CSTAR(J) + B(I)*TTOX(I,J)
         WRITE (6,203)  MP1, (CSTAR(I), I=1,MP1)
C
C        ..... TRANSFORM ECONOMIZED POLYNOMIAL IN X ON INTERVAL
C              (-1,1) TO A POLYNOMIAL IN Z ON INTERVAL (AL,AR) .....
         CALL TRANS( M,CSTAR,C,ONEM,ONE,AL,AR )
         WRITE (6,204)  AL, AR, M, EMAX, MP1, (C(I), I=1,MP1)
         GO TO 1
C
C        ..... FORMATS FOR THE INPUT AND OUTPUT STATEMENTS .....
  100    FORMAT ( 4X, I2, 12X, E12.5, 2(10X, F10.5) )
  101    FORMAT ( 16X, 4E14.6 )
  200    FORMAT (6H1N   =,I5/6H EPS =, E15.5/6H AL  =,F10.4/6H AR  =,F10.4/
        11H0/27H THE COEFFICIENTS A(1)...A(, I1, 5H) ARE// (1H ,1P5E16.6))
  201    FORMAT ( 1H0/ 1H0/ 35H THE COEFFICIENTS ASTAR(1)...ASTAR(,I1,
        1 5H) ARE/ 1H / (1H , 1P5E16.6))
  202    FORMAT ( 1H0/ 1H0/ 27H THE COEFFICIENTS B(1)...B(, I1, 5H) ARE/
        1  1H / (1H , 1P5E16.6))
  203    FORMAT ( 1H0/ 1H0/ 35H THE COEFFICIENTS CSTAR(1)...CSTAR(, I1,
        1 5H) ARE/ 1H / (1H , 1P5E16.6))
  204    FORMAT ( 1H0/ 1H0/ 49H THE ECONOMIZED POLYNOMIAL ON THE INTERVAL (
        1 AL = ,F10.4,2H, ,5H AR = ,F10.4,8H ) IS OF/11H DEGREE M =,I2,2H.
        2 53H THE MAXIMUM ERROR ON THIS INTERVAL IS NO LARGER THAN,1PE15.7,
        3 1H./27H0THE COEFFICIENTS C(1)...C(, I1, 5H) ARE/ 1H /
        4 (1H , 1P5E16.6))
C
         END
```

Subroutine TRANS

```
         SUBROUTINE TRANS( N,COEFFI,COEFFT,ENDLI,ENDRI,ENDLT,ENDRT )
C
C        TRANS CONVERTS AN N-TH DEGREE POLYNOMIAL IN ONE VARIABLE
C        (SAY Z) ON THE INTERVAL (ENDLI,ENDRI) HAVING COEFFICIENTS
C        COEFFI(1)...COEFFI(N+1) INTO AN N TH DEGREE POLYNOMIAL
C        IN A SECOND VARIABLE (SAY X) ON THE INTERVAL (ENDLT,ENDRT)
C        WITH COEFFICIENTS COEFFT(1)...COEFFT(N+1) WHERE THE TWO
C        VARIABLES X AND Z ARE RELATED BY THE TRANSFORMATION
C
C        Z = ((ENDRI-ENDLI)*X + (ENDLI*ENDRT-ENDRI*ENDLT))/(ENDRT-ENDLT)
C        X = ((ENDRT-ENDLT)*Z + (ENDRI*ENDLT-ENDLI*ENDRT))/(ENDRI-ENDLI)
C
         IMPLICIT  REAL*8(A-H, O-Z)
         REAL*8  COEFFI, COEFFT, ENDLI, ENDRI, ENDLT, ENDRT
         DIMENSION COEFFI(10), COEFFT(10)
C
C        ..... COMPUTE CONSTANT PARAMETERS .....
         CON1 = (ENDRI-ENDLI)/(ENDRT-ENDLT)
         CON2 = (ENDLI*ENDRT-ENDRI*ENDLT)/(ENDRT-ENDLT)
         NP1 = N + 1
```

Example 1.3   Chebyshev Economization   **53**

Program Listing (*Continued*)

```
C
      DO 4  I=1,NP1
C     ..... CHECK FOR CON2=0 TO AVOID COMPUTING 0.**0 .....
      IF ( CON2.NE.0.0 )  GO TO 2
      COEFFT(I) = COEFFI(I)
      GO TO 4
    2 COEFFT(I) = 0.0
      DO 3  J=I,NP1
      BINOM = NOMIAL(J-1,I-1)
    3 COEFFT(I) = COEFFT(I) + COEFFI(J)*CON2**(J-I)*BINOM
    4 COEFFT(I) = COEFFT(I)*CON1**(I-1)
      RETURN
C
      END
```

Function NOMIAL

```
      FUNCTION NOMIAL (K,L)
C
C        NOMIAL COMPUTES THE BINOMIAL COEFFICIENT (K,L).
C
      NOM = 1
      IF ( K.LE.L .OR. L.EQ.0 )  GO TO 4
      DO 3  ICOUNT=1,L
    3 NOM = NOM*(K-ICOUNT+1)/ICOUNT
    4 NOMIAL = NOM
      RETURN
C
      END
```

Data

```
N =  3      EPS =    0.000000E00      AL =     1.00000    AR =     3.00000
A(1)...A(4) =        0.000000E00   0.000000E00   0.000000E00   1.000000E00
N =  3      EPS =    3.260000E00      AL =     1.00000    AR =     3.00000
A(1)...A(4) =        0.000000E00   0.000000E00   0.000000E00   1.000000E00
N =  3      EPS =    0.000000E00      AL =    -1.00000    AR =     1.00000
A(1)...A(4) =        2.000000E00   3.000000E00   1.000000E00   0.500000E00
N =  3      EPS =    0.400000E00      AL =    -1.00000    AR =     1.00000
A(1)...A(4) =        2.000000E00   3.000000E00   1.000000E00   0.500000E00
N =  3      EPS =    0.700000E00      AL =    -1.00000    AR =     1.00000
A(1)...A(4) =        2.000000E00   3.000000E00   1.000000E00   0.500000E00
N =  8      EPS =    0.000000E00      AL =     0.00000    AR =     1.57080
A(1)...A(4) =        1.000000E00   0.000000E00  -0.500000E00   0.000000E00
A(5)...A(8) =        4.166667E-2   0.000000E00  -1.388888E-3   0.000000E00
A(9) =               2.480159E-5
N =  8      EPS =    5.000000E-5      AL =     0.00000    AR =     1.57080
A(1)...A(4) =        1.000000E00   0.000000E00  -0.500000E00   0.000000E00
A(5)...A(8) =        4.166667E-2   0.000000E00  -1.388888E-3   0.000000E00
A(9) =               2.480159E-5
N =  8      EPS =    0.000000E00      AL =    -1.00000    AR =     1.00000
A(1)...A(4) =        1.000000E00   0.000000E00  -0.500000E00   0.000000E00
A(5)...A(8) =        4.166667E-2   0.000000E00  -1.388888E-3   0.000000E00
A(9) =               2.480159E-5
N =  8      EPS =    5.000000E-5      AL =    -1.00000    AR =     1.00000
A(1)...A(4) =        1.000000E00   0.000000E00  -0.500000E00   0.000000E00
A(5)...A(8) =        4.166667E-2   0.000000E00  -1.388888E-3   0.000000E00
A(9) =               2.480159E-5
N =  2      EPS =    0.100000E00      AL =    -1.00000    AR =     1.00000
A(1)...A(3) =        8.250000E00   0.390000E00  -0.086300E00
N =  2      EPS =    0.000000E00      AL = 1000.00000    AR = 2000.00000
A(1)...A(3) =        6.300000E00   1.820000E-3  -0.345000E-6
N =  2      EPS =    0.050000E00      AL = 1000.00000    AR = 2000.00000
A(1)...A(3) =        6.300000E00   1.820000E-3  -0.345000E-6
```

Computer Output

Results for the 2nd Data Set

```
N   =     3
EPS =     0.32600D 01
AL  =     1.0000
AR  =     3.0000


THE COEFFICIENTS A(1)...A(4) ARE
     0.0                0.0                0.0            1.000000D 00



THE COEFFICIENTS ASTAR(1)...ASTAR(4) ARE

     8.000000D 00     1.200000D 01     6.000000D 00     1.000000D 00



THE COEFFICIENTS B(1)...B(4) ARE

     1.100000D 01     1.275000D 01     3.000000D 00     2.500000D-01



THE COEFFICIENTS CSTAR(1)...CSTAR(2) ARE

     1.100000D 01     1.275000D 01



THE ECONOMIZED POLYNOMIAL ON THE INTERVAL ( AL =    1.0000,  AR =    3.0000 ) IS OF
DEGREE M = 1.   THE MAXIMUM ERROR ON THIS INTERVAL IS NO LARGER THAN  3.2500000D 00.

THE COEFFICIENTS C(1)...C(2) ARE

    -1.450000D 01     1.275000D 01
```

Results for the 7th Data Set

```
N   =     8
EPS =     0.50000D-04
AL  =     0.0
AR  =     1.5708


THE COEFFICIENTS A(1)...A(9) ARE
     1.000000D 00     0.0            -5.000000D-01     0.0            4.166667D-02
     0.0            -1.388888D-03     0.0             2.480159D-05



THE COEFFICIENTS ASTAR(1)...ASTAR(9) ARE

     7.071055D-01    -5.553624D-01    -2.180890D-01     5.709914D-02     1.121591D-02
    -1.754886D-03    -2.254503D-04     2.872742D-05     3.590928D-06



THE COEFFICIENTS B(1)...B(9) ARE

     6.021975D-01    -5.136192D-01    -1.035407D-01     1.373581D-02     1.360503D-03
    -1.065383D-04    -6.820888D-06     4.488660D-07     2.805413D-08
```

Example 1.3   *Chebyshev Economization*   **55**

Computer Output (*Continued*)

```
    THE COEFFICIENTS CSTAR(1)...CSTAR(6) ARE

      7.070987D-01    -5.553593D-01    -2.179653D-01     5.707401D-02    1.088402D-02
     -1.704613D-03
```

```
    THE ECONOMIZED POLYNOMIAL ON THE INTERVAL ( AL =      0.0    , AR =    1.5708 ) IS OF
    DEGREE M = 5.   THE MAXIMUM ERROR ON THIS INTERVAL IS NO LARGER THAN  7.2978080D-06.

    THE COEFFICIENTS C(1)...C(6) ARE

      1.000007D 00    -3.383638D-04    -4.974232D-01    -7.241249D-03     5.100312D-02
     -5.703891D-03
```

Results for the 8th Data Set

```
    N   =    8
    EPS =    0.0
    AL  =   -1.0000
    AR  =    1.0000


    THE COEFFICIENTS A(1)...A(9) ARE
      1.000000D 00    0.0            -5.000000D-01     0.0            4.166667D-02
      0.0            -1.388888D-03    0.0             2.480159D-05
```

```
    THE COEFFICIENTS ASTAR(1)...ASTAR(9) ARE

      1.000000D 00    0.0            -5.000000D-01     0.0            4.166667D-02
      0.0            -1.388888D-03    0.0             2.480159D-05
```

```
    THE COEFFICIENTS B(1)...B(9) ARE

      7.651978D-01    0.0            -2.298069D-01     0.0            4.953343D-03
      0.0            -4.185265D-05    0.0             1.937624D-07
```

```
    THE COEFFICIENTS CSTAR(1)...CSTAR(9) ARE

      1.000000D 00    0.0            -5.000000D-01     0.0            4.166667D-02
      0.0            -1.388888D-03    0.0             2.480159D-05
```

```
    THE ECONOMIZED POLYNOMIAL ON THE INTERVAL ( AL =   -1.0000,  AR =    1.0000 ) IS OF
    DEGREE M = 8.   THE MAXIMUM ERROR ON THIS INTERVAL IS NO LARGER THAN  0.0

    THE COEFFICIENTS C(1)...C(9) ARE

      1.000000D 00    0.0            -5.000000D-01     0.0            4.166667D-02
      0.0            -1.388888D-03    0.0             2.480159D-05
```

Computer Output (*Continued*)

Results for the 9th Data Set

```
N   =    8
EPS =    0.50000D-04
AL  =   -1.0000
AR  =    1.0000


THE COEFFICIENTS A(1)...A(9) ARE
    1.000000D 00     0.0           -5.000000D-01     0.0           4.166667D-02
    0.0             -1.388888D-03   0.0              2.480159D-05


THE COEFFICIENTS ASTAR(1)...ASTAR(9) ARE

    1.000000D 00     0.0           -5.000000D-01     0.0           4.166667D-02
    0.0             -1.388888D-03   0.0              2.480159D-05


THE COEFFICIENTS B(1)...B(9) ARE

    7.651978D-01     0.0           -2.298069D-01     0.0           4.953343D-03
    0.0             -4.185265D-05   0.0              1.937624D-07


THE COEFFICIENTS CSTAR(1)...CSTAR(5) ARE

    9.999580D-01     0.0           -4.992405D-01     0.0           3.962674D-02
```

```
THE ECONOMIZED POLYNOMIAL ON THE INTERVAL ( AL =   -1.0000,  AR =    1.0000 ) IS OF
DEGREE M = 4.   THE MAXIMUM ERROR ON THIS INTERVAL IS NO LARGER THAN   4.2046413D-05.

THE COEFFICIENTS C(1)...C(5) ARE

    9.999580D-01     0.0           -4.992405D-01     0.0           3.962674D-02
```

Results for the 12th Data Set

```
N   =    2
EPS =    0.50000D-01
AL  = 1000.0000
AR  = 2000.0000


THE COEFFICIENTS A(1)...A(3) ARE
    6.300000D 00    1.820000D-03   -3.450000D-07


THE COEFFICIENTS ASTAR(1)...ASTAR(3) ARE

    8.253750D 00    3.925000D-01   -8.625000D-02


THE COEFFICIENTS B(1)...B(3) ARE

    8.210625D 00    3.925000D-01   -4.312500D-02
```

Example 1.3   *Chebyshev Economization*   **57**

Computer Output (*Continued*)

```
THE COEFFICIENTS CSTAR(1)...CSTAR(2) ARE

   8.210625D 00    3.925000D-01
```

```
THE ECONOMIZED POLYNOMIAL ON THE INTERVAL ( AL = 1000.0000,  AR = 2000.0000 ) IS OF
DEGREE M = 1.   THE MAXIMUM ERROR ON THIS INTERVAL IS NO LARGER THAN  4.3125000D-02.

THE COEFFICIENTS C(1)...C(2) ARE

   7.033125D 00    7.850000D-04
```

Discussion of Results

Five different polynomials were used in the twelve test data sets as follows:

Data Set	Interval [L, R]	Maximum Allowable Error, ε	Polynomial
1	[1, 3]	0	$p_3(z) = z^3$
2	[1, 3]	3.26	
3	[−1, 1]	0	$p_3(z) = 2 + 3z + z^2 + \frac{1}{2}z^3$
4	[−1, 1]	0.4	
5	[−1, 1]	0.7	
6	[0, π/2]	0	$p_8(z) = 1 - \dfrac{z^2}{2!} + \dfrac{z^4}{4!} - \dfrac{z^6}{6!} + \dfrac{z^8}{8!}$
7	[0, π/2]	0.00005	
8	[−1, 1]	0	
9	[−1, 1]	0.00005	
10	[−1, 1]	0.1	$p_2(z) = 8.25 + 0.39z - 0.0863z^2$
11	[1000, 2000]	0	$p_2(z) = 6.3 + 0.00182z - 3.45 \times 10^{-7}z^2$
12	[1000, 2000]	0.05	

Data sets 1, 3, 6, 8, and 11 allow no error to be introduced by the economization process. Hence, the economized polynomial for these cases must be equivalent to the original polynomials; significant discrepancies could be accounted for only as errors in one or more elements of the $\overline{X}$ or $\overline{T}$ matrices, assuming that the executable portion of the program is free of error. Results for the 8th data set, included in the computer output, illustrate these cases. Results for data set 2, shown in the computer output, are those outlined in (1.88) to (1.92). Results for data sets 4 and 5, not shown, are, respectively:

$$m = 2, E_{max} = 0.125, \qquad p_2(z) = 2 + 3.375z + z^2,$$

and

$$m = 1, E_{max} = 0.625, \qquad p_1(z) = 2.5 + 3.375z.$$

The starting polynomial for data sets 6–9 is the power series for cos z, expanded about $z_0 = 0$, and truncated after the term in z^8; it has been used as an example in Section 1.12. The results for data set 9, shown in the computer output, correspond to those of (1.82) to (1.87).

The results for data set 7, shown in the computer output, are similar to those for data set 9, except that the interval is $0 \leqslant z \leqslant \pi/2$. The economized polynomial is

$$\cos z \doteq 1.000007 - 3.383638 \times 10^{-4}z - 0.4974232z^2$$
$$- 7.241249 \times 10^{-3}z^3 + 5.100312 \times 10^{-2}z^4$$
$$- 5.703891 \times 10^{-3}z^5. \qquad (1.3.16)$$

In this case, $E_{max} = 7.298 \times 10^{-6}$. The total possible error in the approximation is given by E_{max} plus the maximum possible error introduced in truncating the power series expansion after the term in z^8, that is, by

$$E_{max} + \left[\frac{z^{10}}{10!} \cos \xi\right]_{max}, \qquad z, \xi \text{ in } [0, \pi/2]. \qquad (1.3.17)$$

Thus, the maximum possible magnitude of the error in (1.3.16) for the interval $[0,\pi/2]$ is

$$7.298 \times 10^{-6} + (\pi/2)^{10}/10! \doteq 3.25 \times 10^{-5}. \qquad (1.3.18)$$

By taking advantage of the fact that cos z is periodic with period 2π, that $\cos(\pi/2 + \alpha) = -\cos(\pi/2 - \alpha)$, and that $\cos(\pi + \beta) = \cos(\pi - \beta)$, (1.3.16) may, after suitable adjustment of the argument, be used to find the cosine of *any* angle within the accuracy of (1.3.18). In fact, since cos $z = \sin(z + \pi/2)$, (1.3.16), with an appropriate transformation of variable, could be used to calculate the *sine* of any angle as well, with the same bound for the error.

Results of the economization process for the 10th data set, not shown, are:

$$m = 1, E_{max} = 0.04315, p_1(z) = 8.206850 + 0.39z.$$

Results for the 12th data set (see the computer output) show the first-order minimax polynomial approximation to a second-degree polynomial representation of the molar heat capacity for gaseous nitrogen at low pressures in the temperature range 1000–2000°K. See Problem 1.46 at the end of the chapter for more details.

Double-precision arithmetic has been used for all calculations. In order to generate accurate coefficients for the economized polynomial, particularly when only small errors, ε, are allowed, it is important to carry as many digits as possible throughout the calculations; double-precision arithmetic should be used, if available.

As written, the program can handle only starting

Example 1.3 *Chebyshev Economization* **59**

polynomials of degree nine or less. The matrices $\overline{T}$ and $\overline{X}$ could be expanded to allow higher-degree starting polynomials, although the storage requirements for $\overline{T}$ and $\overline{X}$ could become prohibitive for large n, if the subscription scheme outlined earlier were used. An alternative approach would be to pack the coefficients from Tables 1.12 and 1.13 using a more efficient assignment of memory.

Yet another, more elegant, approach to the economization process is to use the recursion relation of (1.72) to generate the needed coefficients. This avoids the need for saving tabulated information. In addition, since truncation always starts with the highest-order term of (1.3.4), $a_n^* x^n$ can be expanded to yield b_n directly. If the term $b_n T_n$ can be dropped without exceeding the maximum allowable error, the a_i^*, $i = 0, 1, \ldots, n - 1$, can be modified appropriately, to $\bar{a}_i^*$ for example, using the recursion relation. Next, $\bar{a}_{n-1}^* x^{n-1}$ can be expanded to yield b_{n-1} directly. If $b_{n-1} T_{n-1}$ can be dropped, the $\bar{a}_i^*$, $i = 0, 1, \ldots, n - 2$, can be modified appropriately, again using the recursion relation. This process of expanding only the highest-order untruncated power of x in terms of the Chebyshev polynomials, followed by proper adjustment of the coefficients of lower powers of x, leads directly to the economized polynomial (1.3.8), without ever evaluating $b_0, \ldots, b_{m-1}$. Arden [1] and Hamming [2] suggest some other approaches to the economization process which use only the recursion relation of (1.72).

Problems

1.1 In the expansion

$$e^x \doteq 1 + x + \frac{x^2}{2!} + \frac{x^3}{3!} + \cdots + \frac{x^n}{n!},$$

how large must n be to yield an approximation for $e^{3.1}$ that is accurate within 10^{-6}?

1.2 For small values of x, the approximations

$$e^x \doteq 1 + x, \qquad \sin x \doteq x$$

are sometimes employed. In each case, use the error term from Taylor's expansion to estimate how large a value of x (to the nearest 0.001) may be employed with the assurance that the error in the approximation is smaller than 0.01. Check your conclusions against tables of exponentials and sines.

1.3 Let M be the maximum magnitude of $f''(x)$ on the interval (x_0, x_1). Show that the error for linear interpolation for $f(x)$, using the functional values at x_0 and x_1, is bounded by

$$\tfrac{1}{8}M(x_1 - x_0)^2$$

for $x_0 \leqslant x \leqslant x_1$. Does this same error bound apply for linear extrapolation, that is, for $x < x_0$ or $x > x_1$?

1.4 Use the algorithm of (1.12) to evaluate

$$p_5(x) = 3x^5 + 4x^4 - 2x^3 + 5x - 7$$

and each of its derivatives at $x = 2.5$.

1.5 Write a function, named POLY, that implements the algorithm of (1.12) to evaluate an nth-degree polynomial $p_n(x) = \sum_{i=0}^{n} a_i x^i$, and each of its derivatives of order 1 through n at $x = \bar{x}$. The function should have the dummy argument list

(N, A, XBAR, DVAL)

where N is the degree of the polynomial, n, A is a vector (one-dimensional array) containing the coefficients $a_0, a_1, \ldots, a_n$ in elements A(1), A(2), ..., A(N + 1), XBAR is the independent variable value, $\bar{x}$, and DVAL is a vector containing $p_n'(\bar{x})$, $p_n''(\bar{x}), \ldots, p_n^{(n)}(\bar{x})$ in elements DVAL (1), DVAL(2), ..., DVAL(N) upon return from the function. The *value* of POLY should be $p_n(\bar{x})$.

Write a short main program that reads values for n, a_0, $a_1, \ldots, a_n$, and $\bar{x}$, calls on POLY, prints the values returned for $p_n(\bar{x})$, $p_n'(\bar{x}), \ldots, p_n^{(n)}(\bar{x})$, and then reads another data set. Test POLY with several different polynomials, including that of Problem 1.4.

1.6 (a) Show that the nth divided difference of $y = x^n$ is unity, no matter which base points $x_0, x_1, \ldots, x_n$ are chosen.

(b) Show that the nth divided difference of any polynomial $p_n(x) = \sum_{i=0}^{n} a_i x^i$ is given by a_n, regardless of the choice of base points.

1.7 Investigate the relation, if any, between the number of significant figures to which tabulated values of $f(x)$ vs x are given, and the highest order for which finite divided differences are likely to be meaningful.

1.8 Consider the divided differences in Table P1.8.

(a) What is the significance of the zero at the top of the seventh column?

Table P1.8

i	x_i	$f(x_i)$	$f_1[\ ]$	$f_2[\ ]$	$f_3[\ ]$	$f_4[\ ]$	$f_5[\ ]$
0	−1	13					
			−11				
1	0	2		1			
			−8		1*		
2	2	−14*		6*		0*	
			16*		1		−$\frac{5}{336}$
3	4	18		11		−$\frac{5}{48}$	
			49		$\frac{3}{8}$		
4	5	67		12½			
			24				
5	6	91					

(b) Without renumbering the abscissas, write down the divided-difference polynomial that uses the elements denoted by asterisks.

(c) What is the likely error bound for a fourth-degree interpolation with $x_0 \leqslant x \leqslant x_5$?

(d) Find the value of $f(x)$ predicted by the polynomial of (b) for $x = 1.0$.

(e) Find the value of $f(x)$ predicted by Lagrange's second-degree interpolating polynomial at $x = 1.0$, using the three base points x_1, x_2, and x_3.

1.9 Form the divided-difference table for the data in Table P1.9.

Table P1.9

x	$f(x)$
1.70	4.5624893
1.75	4.5974591
1.80	4.6321700
1.85	4.6666663
1.90	4.7009872
1.95	4.7351677
2.00	4.7692389

(a) Estimate the magnitude of the error terms for linear interpolation using successive ordinates.

(b) Given the additional information that the tabulated function is $f(x) = \cos(\ln x) + x + 2$, show that the maximum error for any interpolant value approximating $f(x)$ using linear interpolation with successive base points is smaller than 0.00004.

1.10 Form the finite-difference table for the data of Table P1.10.

(a) Write Newton's forward formula (1.54) for the interpolating polynomial that reproduces exactly the first four functional values in Table P1.10.

(b) Write Newton's backward formula (1.61) that uses the last three entries in the table.

(c) Write the Gauss forward formula (1.65) with base points $x_{-1} = 2.5$, $x_0 = 3.0$, $x_1 = 3.5$, $x_2 = 4.0$.

(d) Estimate the error when the polynomial of part (a) is used for interpolation (or extrapolation) with arguments $x = 1.75$, 2.3, and 4.0.

Table P1.10

x	$f(x)$
1.0	1.841471
1.5	6.180399
2.0	10.708933
2.5	20.173274
3.0	32.905180
3.5	48.827695
4.0	70.643568
4.5	99.630912
5.0	132.914840

(e) Given the information that the tabulated function of Table P1.10 is $f(x) = 6x + 2\cos x^2 - 4x^2 \sin x^2 - 5x^{-2}$, find the error bound for quadratic interpolation (interpolating polynomials of degree 2) using three successive base points x_i, x_{i+1}, x_{i+2}, with $x_i < x < x_{i+2}$. Does the bound change appreciably over the range of the table?

1.11 Let $y_i = f(x_i)$, $i = 0, 1, \ldots, n$. Show that Newton's fundamental formula (1.30) for the polynomial of degree one passing through the points (x_j, y_j) and (x_k, y_k) may be written in the form

$$y_{j,k}(x) = \frac{1}{x_k - x_j} \begin{vmatrix} y_j & x_j - x \\ y_k & x_k - x \end{vmatrix}$$

where the vertical bars indicate the determinant (see Chapter 4). Let $y_{p_0, p_1, \ldots, p_m}(x)$ be the interpolating polynomial of degree m passing through the points $p_0, p_1, \ldots, p_m$. Show that

$$y_{0,1,2}(x) = \frac{1}{x_2 - x_0} \begin{vmatrix} y_{0,1} & x_0 - x \\ y_{1,2} & x_2 - x \end{vmatrix} = \frac{1}{x_2 - x_1} \begin{vmatrix} y_{0,1} & x_1 - x \\ y_{0,2} & x_2 - x \end{vmatrix},$$

$$y_{0,1,3}(x) = \frac{1}{x_3 - x_0} \begin{vmatrix} y_{0,1} & x_0 - x \\ y_{1,3} & x_3 - x \end{vmatrix} = \frac{1}{x_3 - x_1} \begin{vmatrix} y_{0,1} & x_1 - x \\ y_{0,3} & x_3 - x \end{vmatrix},$$

$$y_{0,1,2,3}(x) = \frac{1}{x_3 - x_2} \begin{vmatrix} y_{0,1,2} & x_2 - x \\ y_{0,1,3} & x_3 - x \end{vmatrix}.$$

Note that each of the second-degree interpolating polynomials can be described in terms of linear interpolation on two linear interpolating polynomials, and that the third-degree interpolating polynomial can be described in terms of linear interpolation on two second-degree interpolating polynomials.

1.12 (a) Using the definitions of Problem 1.11, consider Table P1.12:

Table P1.12

x_0	y_0					
x_1	y_1	$y_{0,1}$				
x_2	y_2	$y_{0,2}$	$y_{0,1,2}$			
x_3	y_3	$y_{0,3}$	$y_{0,1,3}$	$y_{0,1,2,3}$		
x_4	y_4	$y_{0,4}$	$y_{0,1,4}$	$y_{0,1,2,4}$	$y_{0,1,2,3,4}$	
x_5	y_5	$y_{0,5}$	$y_{0,1,5}$	$y_{0,1,2,5}$	$y_{0,1,2,3,5}$	$y_{0,1,2,3,4,5}$
$\vdots$	$\vdots$					$\vdots$
x_n	y_n	$y_{0,n}$	$y_{0,1,n}$	$y_{0,1,2,n}$	$y_{0,1,2,3,n}$	$y_{0,1,2,3,4,n}\cdots$

Show that if each of the quantities $(x_i - x)$, $i = 0, 1, \ldots, n$, is computed first, and that if entries in the table following the first two columns are calculated one column at a time, then each entry may be evaluated using just two multiplications, two subtractions, and two divisions.

(b) Generate a table comparable to that of part (a) for the functional values of Tables 1.2 and 1.4 with interpolant value $x = 0.5$, and compare with the results for various degrees of interpolation shown in Section 1.6.

1.13 The interpolation method suggested in Problems 1.11 and 1.12 is known as *iterated linear interpolation* or *Aitken's method*. Implement the method by writing a subroutine, named AITKEN, that could be called from another program with the statement

CALL AITKEN (X, Y, NMAX, N, ATABLE, XARG)

where the data points (x_i, y_i) are available in the arrays X and Y with subscripts 1, 2, ..., NMAX, and the X array is arranged in ascending sequence. The subroutine should scan the X array to find the element nearest the argument, $x = $ XARG, and designate it as x_0 for Aitken's interpolation. AITKEN should then develop the appropriate entries for columns 3 through $n + 2$ of Aitken's table in columns 1 through N of the matrix ATABLE, and return to the calling program.

Write a short main program that reads values for NMAX, X(1), ..., X(NMAX), and Y(1), ..., Y(NMAX) just once, and then repeatedly reads values for N and XARG, calls upon AITKEN to compute the elements of ATABLE, and prints the matrix ATABLE.

1.14 When $f(x)$ is a single-valued function of x, and a value of x is required for which the dependent variable $f(x)$ assumes a specified value, the role of independent and dependent variable may be interchanged, and any of the appropriate interpolation formulas may be used. The process is usually termed *inverse interpolation*.

Chose the thermocouple emf and temperature data from Table 1.2.1 corresponding to $x_0 = 0$, $x_1 = 500$, $x_2 = 1000$, etc., and use inverse interpolation to find approximations of the emf corresponding to temperatures of 122.4, 118.4, 121.932, 447.6, and 447.02°F for interpolation of degrees 1, 2, and 3. Compare your results with Table 1.2.1 and the computer output for Example 1.2.

1.15 Suppose that $\bar{y}(\bar{x})$ is the value of the nth-degree interpolating polynomial passing through the points (x_k, y_k), $(x_{k+1}, y_{k+1}), \ldots, (x_{k+n}, y_{k+n})$, where $y_i = f(x_i)$ and $f(x)$ is a single-valued function of x. Carry out an inverse interpolation using the same points with $\bar{y}$ as the argument and let the interpolated result be denoted by $\bar{x}^*$. Comment on the following statements:

(a) $\bar{x}^*$ will be identical to $\bar{x}$.

(b) the smaller the value of $|\bar{x}^* - \bar{x}|$, the better the value of $\bar{y}$ will approximate $f(x)$.

1.16 Show that Lagrange's interpolating polynomial (1.43) can be written in the form

$$p_n(x) = \prod(x) \sum_{i=0}^{n} \frac{f(x_i)}{(x - x_i) \prod'(x_i)},$$

where

$$\prod(x) = \prod_{j=0}^{n}(x - x_j) \quad \text{and} \quad \prod'(x) = \frac{d\prod(x)}{dx}.$$

1.17 In Example 1.1, how would you modify the main program, the subroutine DTABLE, and the function FNEWT, so that the matrix TABLE could be eliminated and replaced by a vector (one-dimensional array) TABLE?

Hint: Only the elements on the appropriate diagonal of TABLE are actually used in the evaluation of Newton's fundamental formula (1.1.6).

1.18 How could you modify the function FLAGR of Example 1.2 so that the function would choose the appropriate base points, and the argument MIN would be unnecessary?

1.19 The values shown in Table P1.19 are available [24] for the thermal conductivity, k (BTU/hr ft °F), of carbon dioxide gas and for the viscosity, μ (lb/ft hr), of liquid ethylene glycol, at various temperatures T (°F).

Table P1.19

T	k	T	μ
32	0.0085	0	242
212	0.0133	50	82.1
392	0.0181	100	30.5
572	0.0228	150	12.6
		200	5.57

In each case, determine the simplest interpolating polynomial that is likely to predict k and μ within 1% over the specified ranges of temperature. These polynomials will be needed in Problem 2.15.

Hint: ln μ is more nearly a simple function of T than μ is itself.

1.20 Suppose we wish to prepare a table of functional values of $e^x \sin x$ for subsequent quadratic interpolation using Newton's forward formula (1.54) on the interval $0 \leqslant x \leqslant 2$. What base-point spacing should be used to insure that interpolation will be accurate to four decimal places for any argument in the indicated range?

1.21 In a table of values of $f(x)$ vs x, a few entries may be in error. By forming a divided-difference table, investigate the feasibility of locating the errors and, if possible, correcting them. Assume that $f(x)$ is a smooth function of x. Before checking against published values, attempt to locate the errors in Table P1.21, allegedly of sin x vs x.

Table P1.21

x	sin x?
0.2	0.19867
0.25	0.24740
0.3	0.29552
0.35	0.34920
0.4	0.38492
0.45	0.43497
0.5	0.47943
0.55	0.52269
0.6	0.56464
0.65	0.60529
0.7	0.64422
0.75	0.68164
0.8	0.72736

1.22 If the method of Problem 1.21 appears feasible and can be applied generally, write a subroutine, named CHECK, that will implement it. Also write a short main program to handle input and output and call on the subroutine as follows:

CALL CHECK (X, F, N, ANSWER, TRUEF)

Here, X and F are the vectors that contain the tabulated values of x and $f(x)$, and N is the subscript corresponding to the last entry in the table. ANSWER is a logical vector; according to whether an entry F(I) is found to be in error or not, the subroutine should store the logical value .FALSE. or .TRUE. in the corresponding element ANSWER(I). The vector TRUEF should ultimately contain the corrected table of values for $f(x)$. Since it is generally impossible to distinguish between an error in x and one in $f(x)$, attempt only to correct the latter if a discrepancy is found.

1.23 Write a function, named STIRL, that uses Stirling's formula, equation (1.67), to implement an mth-degree central-difference interpolation on the data values $(x_i, f(x_i))$, $i = 1, 2, \ldots, n$. Assume that the x_i are evenly spaced and are arranged in ascending order. The calling sequence should be of the form

FVAL = STIRL (X, F, M, N, TEMP, XVAL, NOGOOD)

where X and F are vectors containing the data values, M and N have obvious meanings, and XVAL is the interpolation argument. TEMP is a vector, dimensioned in the calling program to have maximum subscript $2 \times N$, that will be used for working storage. NOGOOD is an integer, returned as 0 in case of computational difficulties (see below), and as 1 otherwise.

The routine should center the central-difference paths across the table as closely as possible about the interpolation argument. Only those differences that are actually needed for the evaluation should be computed, and no working vectors other than TEMP should be used in the function. The interpolated value should be returned as the value of the function. The function should check for any argument inconsistencies and should forbid extrapolation beyond the limits of the table.

To test the function STIRL, also write a main program that reads data sets of the form: N, X(1) ...X(N), F(1) .... F(N), M, XVAL.

Suggested Test Data

(a) The values shown in Table P1.23a are available [24] for the density of water, ρ (g/ml), at various temperatures T (°C).

Table P1.23a

T	ρ	T	ρ
0	0.9998679	30	0.9956756
5	0.9999919	35	0.9940594
10	0.9997277	40	0.9922455
15	0.9991265	45	0.99024
20	0.9982323	50	0.98807
25	0.9970739	55	0.98573
		60	0.98324

Interpolate using several different values for T and m (degree of the polynomial).

(b) The values shown in Table P1.23b are available [20] for the refractive index, n, of aqueous sucrose solutions at 20°C, containing various percentages, P, of water.

Table P1.23b

P	n	P	n
15	1.5033	60	1.3997
20	1.4901	65	1.3902
25	1.4774	70	1.3811
30	1.4651	75	1.3723
35	1.4532	80	1.3639
40	1.4418	85	1.3557
45	1.4307	90	1.3479
50	1.4200	95	1.3403
55	1.4096	100	1.3330

Interpolate using several different values for P and m.

1.24 Suppose we wish to approximate a continuous and differentiable function $f(x)$ on the interval $[a,b]$ in a piecewise fashion, using low-degree interpolating polynomials over non-overlapping subintervals of $[a,b]$. Let the base points be $a = x_0 < x_1 < \cdots < x_{n-1} < x_n = b$, the corresponding functional values be $y_i = f(x_i)$, $i = 0, 1, \ldots, n$, and the approximating function for $[a,b]$ be $S_{\bar{x}}(\bar{y},x)$, where $\bar{x} = [x_0, x_1, \ldots, x_n]^t$ and $\bar{y} = [y_0, y_1, \ldots, y_n]^t$. We shall require that $S_{\bar{x}}(\bar{y},x)$ be continuous on $[a,b]$, possess continuous first and second derivatives for all x in $[a,b]$, and satisfy the $n+1$ conditions

$$S_{\bar{x}}(\bar{y},x) = f(x_i) = y_i, \qquad i = 0, 1, \ldots, n.$$

Let $S_{\bar{x}}(\bar{y},x)$ coincide with a third-degree polynomial $p_{3,i}(x)$ on each subinterval $[x_i, x_{i+1}]$, $i = 0, 1, \ldots, n-1$. Then each of the n functions $p''_{3,i}(x)$, $i = 0, 1, \ldots, n-1$, can be written as a linear combination of $p''_{3,i}(x_i)$ and $p''_{3,i}(x_{i+1})$, since the $p''_{3,i}(x)$ are linear functions:

$$p''_{3,i}(x) = \frac{(x_{i+1} - x)}{h_i} p''_{3,i}(x_i)$$

$$+ \frac{(x - x_i)}{h_i} p''_{3,i}(x_{i+1}), \qquad i = 0, 1, \ldots, n-1.$$

Here, $h_i = x_{i+1} - x_i$.

Show that integrating the functions $p''_{3,i}(x)$ twice and imposing the conditions

$$\left. \begin{array}{l} p_{3,i}(x_i) = y_i, \\ p_{3,i}(x_{i+1}) = y_{i+1}, \end{array} \right\} \qquad i = 0, 1, \ldots, n-1,$$

leads to the following interpolating functions:

$$p_{3,i}(x) = \frac{p''_{3,i}(x_i)}{6h_i} (x_{i+1} - x)^3 + \frac{p''_{3,i}(x_{i+1})}{6h_i} (x - x_i)^3$$

$$+ \left[\frac{y_{i+1}}{h_i} - \frac{h_i p''_{3,i}(x_{i+1})}{6} \right] (x - x_i)$$

$$+ \left[\frac{y_i}{h_i} - \frac{h_i p''_{3,i}(x_i)}{6} \right] (x_{i+1} - x), \qquad i = 0, 1, \ldots, n-1.$$

Next, show that the continuity conditions for the derivative of $S_{\bar{x}}(\bar{y},x)$, that is,

$$p'_{3,i}(x_i) = p'_{3,i-1}(x_i), \qquad i = 1, 2, \ldots, n-1,$$

lead to a system of $n-1$ linear difference equations,

$$\frac{h_{i-1}}{h_i} p''_{3,i-1}(x_{i-1}) + \frac{2(h_i + h_{i-1})}{h_i} p''_{3,i}(x_i) + p''_{3,i}(x_{i+1})$$

$$= \frac{6}{h_i} \left[\frac{(y_{i+1} - y_i)}{h_i} - \frac{(y_i - y_{i-1})}{h_{i-1}} \right], \qquad i = 1, 2, \ldots, n-1,$$

in the $n+1$ unknown derivatives $S''_{\bar{x}}(\bar{y},x_i)$, $i = 0, 1, \ldots, n$. If two additional conditions are specified, for example, $S''_{\bar{x}}(\bar{y},x_0)$ and $S''_{\bar{x}}(\bar{y},x_n)$, then the simultaneous linear equations can be solved for the $p''_{3,i}(x_i)$, $i = 1, 2, \ldots, n-1$, using methods described in Chapter 5, and the necessary interpolating functions $p_{3,i}(x)$, $i = 0, 1, \ldots, n-1$, are then known.

1.25 The approximating function $S_{\bar{x}}(\bar{y},x)$ of Problem 1.24 is known as the *cubic spline function* [22]. Show that if $p''_{3,0}(x_0) = 0$ and if $p''_{3,n-1}(x_n) = 0$, then the generated spline function possesses the property of *least mean-squared curvature*, that is, that for all other twice-differentiable interpolating functions, $g(x)$, the property

$$\int_a^b [S''_{\bar{x}}(\bar{y},x) - f''(x)]^2 \, dx \leqslant \int_a^b [g''(x) - f''(x)]^2 \, dx$$

holds. Thus, in the sense of the integral, the cubic spline may be viewed as the "smoothest" of all possible interpolating functions.

1.26 Show that the linear difference equations of Problem 1.24 may be written in the form

$$p''_{3,i-1}(x_{i-1}) + 4p''_{3,i}(x_i) + p''_{3,i}(x_{i+1})$$

$$= \frac{6}{h^2} \Delta^2 f(x_{i-1}), \qquad i = 1, 2, \ldots, n-1,$$

when the base points x_i, $i = 0, 1, \ldots, n$, are equally spaced with spacing h.

1.27 Write a function, named SPLINE, that evaluates the cubic spline function of Problem 1.24. The dummy argument list should be

(N, X, Y, XARG)

where the $N + 1$ base points for the spline fit are available in X(1), ..., X(N + 1), the corresponding functional values are available in Y(1), ..., Y(N + 1), and XARG is the interpolation argument. The value of $S_{\bar{x}}(\bar{Y}, \text{XARG})$ should be returned as the value of SPLINE. Test the function with data from Table P1.19.

1.28 This problem deals with two-dimensional interpolation, in which we consider the approximation of a function $f = f(x,y)$. Suppose that a total of mn functional values $f(x_i, y_j)$ are available, for all possible combinations of m levels of x_i ($i = 1, 2, \ldots, m$), and n levels of y_j ($j = 1, 2, \ldots, n$). For convenience, arrange these values $f_{ij} \equiv f(x_i, y_j)$ in a two-dimensional table, so that row i corresponds to $x = x_i$, and column j corresponds to $y = y_j$. Then, given arbitrary x and y, the problem is to interpolate in the table to find an approximation to $f(x,y)$.

Here, we consider linear interpolation. Let $x_i \leqslant x \leqslant x_{i+1}$, and $y_j \leqslant y \leqslant y_{j+1}$, as shown in Fig. P1.28. The symbol □ indicates points at which functional values are available.

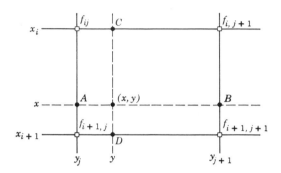

Figure P1.28

First, interpolate linearly through f_{ij} and $f_{i+1,j}$, and through $f_{i,j+1}$ and $f_{i+1,j+1}$, to obtain approximations f_A and f_B to $f(x,y)$ at the points A and B. Then interpolate linearly through f_A and f_B to obtain the final approximation to $f(x,y)$. If $\alpha = (x - x_i)/(x_{i+1} - x_i)$, and $\beta = (y - y_j)/(y_{j+1} - y_j)$, show that the result is

$$f(x,y) \doteq (1 - \alpha)(1 - \beta)f_{ij} + \beta(1 - \alpha)f_{i,j+1}$$
$$+ \alpha(1 - \beta)f_{i+1,j} + \alpha\beta f_{i+1,j+1}.$$

What would be the corresponding formula if the first interpolation were in the y direction, to give f_C and f_D, followed by interpolation in the x direction?

Give a simple graphical interpretation, based on relative areas, to the weight factors assigned in the above formula to $f_{ij}, f_{i,j+1}, f_{i+1,j}$, and $f_{i+1,j+1}$.

1.29   Write a function, named LIN2D, that will perform the two-dimensional linear interpolation discussed in Problem 1.28. A typical call will be

    FXY = LIN2D (F, X, Y, M, N, XVAL, YVAL)

Here, F, X, and Y are the arrays that have been preset with the tabulated values f_{ij}, x_i, and y_j, M and N have obvious meanings, and XVAL and YVAL correspond to the values x and y for which $f(x,y)$ is to be estimated. If x and/or y lie outside the range of the table, the function should print a message to this effect and return the value zero.

Also, write a main program that will read values for M, N, the matrix F, the vectors X and Y, and XVAL and YVAL. The main program should call on LIN2D as indicated above, then

Table P1.29a

| Temp. | Pressure, psia | | | | | | |
°F	10	20	30	40	60	80	100
−200	17.15	8.47	5.57	4.12	2.678	1.954	1.518
−100	23.97	11.94	7.91	5.91	3.91	2.903	2.301
0	30.72	15.32	10.19	7.63	5.06	3.78	3.014
100	37.44	18.70	12.44	9.33	6.21	4.65	3.71
200	44.13	22.07	14.70	11.03	7.34	5.50	4.40
300	50.83	25.42	16.94	12.71	8.46	6.35	5.07
400	57.51	28.76	19.17	14.38	9.58	7.19	5.75
500	64.20	32.10	21.40	16.05	10.70	8.03	6.42

print the interpolated value FXY, and finally return to read additional pairs of values for XVAL and YVAL.

Suggested Test Data

(a) The values shown in Table P1.29a are given by Perry [24] for the specific volume, v (cu ft/lb), of superheated methane, at various temperatures and pressures. Estimate the specific volume of methane at (56.4°F, 12.7 psia), (56.4, 22.7), (56.4,100), (411.2, 12.7), (411.2, 30.1), (−200, 10), and (0, 84.3). To test LIN2D completely, also try a few temperatures and pressures beyond the scope of the table.

(b) The values shown in Table P1.29b are given by Perry [24] for the total vapor pressures, p (psia), of aqueous solutions of ammonia, at various temperatures and molal concentrations of ammonia.

Table P1.29b

| Temp. | Percentage Molal Concentration of Ammonia | | | | | |
°F	0	10	20	25	30	35
60	0.26	1.42	3.51	5.55	8.65	13.22
80	0.51	2.43	5.85	9.06	13.86	20.61
100	0.95	4.05	9.34	14.22	21.32	31.16
140	2.89	9.98	21.49	31.54	45.73	64.78
180	7.51	21.65	44.02	62.68	88.17	121.68
220	17.19	42.47	81.91	113.81	156.41	211.24
250	29.83	66.67	124.08	169.48	229.62	305.60

Estimate the total vapor pressure at (126.5°F, 28.8 mole %), (126.5, 6.7), (126.5, 25.0), (60, 0), (237.5, 17.6), and (237.5, 35.0).

1.30   Extend the scheme outlined in Problem 1.28 to two-dimensional *cubic* interpolation. The known functional values that will be involved are denoted by the symbol □ in Fig. P1.30. The successive values x_i and y_j need not be equally spaced.

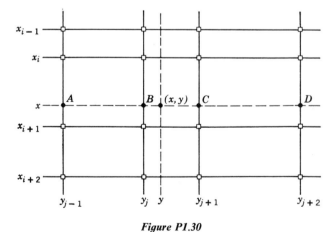

Figure P1.30

First, interpolate four times in the x direction to give four third-degree polynomials that will yield estimates for f_A, f_B, f_C, and f_D. Then interpolate these four values in the y direction for the final approximation to $f(x,y)$.

Establish a computational algorithm for the above procedure. Would the final result be different if the interpolation proceeded in the y direction first?

1.31 Write a function, named CUB2D, that will perform the two-dimensional cubic interpolation discussed in Problem 1.30. A typical call will be

FXY = CUB2D (F, X, Y, M, N, XVAL, YVAL)

in which the arguments have the same meanings as in Problem 1.29. Test the function with a main program and data similar to those used in Problem 1.29.

1.32 Following in the same vein as Problems 1.28 and 1.30, investigate the following alternative procedure for two-dimensional approximation. Referring to Fig. P1.32, consider the nine points within which the point of approximation (x,y), is most nearly centered.

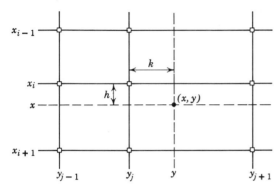

Figure P1.32

Taylor's expansion in two dimensions (see, for example, equation (7.1)) gives

$$f(x,y) \doteq f_{ij} + hf_x + kf_y + \frac{h^2}{2}f_{xx} + hkf_{xy} + \frac{k^2}{2}f_{yy},$$

in which the derivatives $f_x \ (\equiv \partial f/\partial x)$, f_y, etc., are to be evaluated at the point (x_i,y_j). These five partial derivatives may be estimated from the nine functional values by using equations (7.6), (7.7), and (7.8), if the x_i and y_j are spaced uniformly, or by somewhat different forms if they are spaced unevenly.

Develop a computational algorithm for this type of approximation. Does the final approximation value differ from that predicted by a quadratic-type interpolation similar to the linear and cubic interpolation procedures discussed in Problems 1.28 and 1.30?

1.33 Write a function, named TAYLOR, that implements the two-dimensional approximation procedure developed in Problem 1.32. A typical call will be

FXY = TAYLOR (F, X, Y, M, N, XVAL, YVAL)

in which the arguments have the same meanings as in Problem 1.29. Test the function with a main program and data similar to those used in Problem 1.29.

1.34 Following lines similar to those of Problems 1.28 through 1.31, develop an algorithm for interpolating in three dimensions at the point (x,y,z). Write a function, such as LIN3D (if linear interpolation is used), that implements the procedure, for which a typical call will be

ANS = LIN3D (F, X, Y, Z, M, N, P, XVAL, YVAL, ZVAL)

The arguments are the same as before, with the addition of Z, the vector containing the several levels z_k, P, the number of such levels, and ZVAL, the particular value of z.

1.35 Suppose that $(m+1)(n+1)$ functional values $f(x_i,y_j)$ are available for all combinations of $m+1$ levels of $x_i, i = 0, 1, \ldots, m$, and $n+1$ levels of $y_j, j = 0, 1, \ldots, n$. Define Lagrangian interpolation coefficients comparable to (1.44) as follows:

$$X_{m,i}(x) = \prod_{\substack{k=0 \\ k \neq i}}^{m} \frac{x - x_k}{x_i - x_k}, \qquad i = 0, 1, \ldots, m,$$

$$Y_{n,j}(y) = \prod_{\substack{k=0 \\ k \neq j}}^{n} \frac{y - y_k}{y_j - y_k}, \qquad j = 0, 1, \ldots, n.$$

Show that

$$p_{m,n}(x,y) = \sum_{i=0}^{m} \sum_{j=0}^{n} X_{m,i}(x) \, Y_{n,j}(y) \, f(x_i,y_j)$$

is a two-dimensional polynomial of degree m in x and degree n in y of the form

$$p_{m,n}(x,y) = \sum_{i=0}^{m} \sum_{j=0}^{n} a_{i,j} x^i y^j,$$

and satisfies the $(m+1)(n+1)$ conditions

$$p_{m,n}(x_i,y_j) = f(x_i,y_j), \qquad \begin{aligned} i &= 0, 1, \ldots, m, \\ j &= 0, 1, \ldots, n, \end{aligned}$$

and therefore that $p_{m,n}(x,y)$ may be viewed as a two-dimensional interpolating polynomial passing through the $(m+1)(n+1)$ points $(x_i,y_j,f(x_i,y_j))$, $i = 0, 1, \ldots, m, j = 0, 1, \ldots, n$.

1.36 Use the two-dimensional interpolating polynomial of Problem 1.35 with $n = m = 1$ and $n = m = 2$ to find estimates of the specific volume of methane at (100°F, 40 psia) using the information from Table P1.29a at temperatures of —100, 0, 200, and 300°F and pressures of 20, 30, 60, and 80 psia. Compare the results with the reported value of 9.33 cu ft/lb.

1.37 Find a three-dimensional interpolating polynomial of degree m in x, n in y, and q in z of the form

$$p_{m,n,q}(x,y,z) = \sum_{i=0}^{m} \sum_{j=0}^{n} \sum_{k=0}^{q} a_{i,j,k} x^i y^j z^k,$$

that satisfies the $(m+1)(n+1)(q+1)$ conditions

$$p_{m,n,q}(x_i,y_j,z_k) = f(x_i,y_j,z_k), \qquad \begin{aligned} i &= 0, 1, \ldots, m, \\ j &= 0, 1, \ldots, n, \\ k &= 0, 1, \ldots, q. \end{aligned}$$

Develop a comparable interpolating polynomial for any number of independent variables.

1.38 Show that the remainder term for the two-dimensional interpolating polynomial of Problem 1.35, analogous to (1.39b) for the one-dimensional case, is given by

$$R_{m,n}(x,y) = \frac{\left[\prod_{i=0}^{m}(x - x_i)\right]}{(m+1)!} \frac{\partial^{m+1} f(\xi,y)}{\partial x^{m+1}}$$
$$+ \frac{\left[\prod_{j=0}^{n}(y - y_j)\right]}{(n+1)!} \frac{\partial^{n+1} f(x,\eta)}{\partial y^{n+1}}$$
$$- \frac{\left[\prod_{i=0}^{m}(x - x_i)\right]\left[\prod_{j=0}^{n}(y - y_j)\right]}{(m+1)!(n+1)!} \frac{\partial^{m+n+2} f(\xi',\eta')}{\partial x^{m+1} \partial y^{n+1}}$$

where ξ and ξ' are in $(x,x_0,x_1,\ldots,x_m)$ and η and η' are in $(y,y_0,y_1,\ldots,y_n)$.

1.39 Write a function, named POLY2D, that evaluates the two-dimensional interpolating polynomial $p_{m,n}(x,y)$ of Problem 1.35 for arguments $x = \bar{x}$ and $y = \bar{y}$. The function should have the dummy argument list

(IMAX, JMAX, X, Y, F, M, N, XBAR, YBAR)

Here, F is a matrix having IMAX rows and JMAX columns of functional values $f(x_i,y_j)$, X is a vector containing the corresponding values of x_i in ascending sequence in X(1), ..., X(IMAX), and Y is a vector containing the y_j in ascending sequence in Y(1), ..., Y(JMAX); F is arranged so that F(I,J) is the functional value corresponding to X(I) and Y(J). The function should scan the vectors X and Y to determine which $(M+1)(N+1)$ of the functional values F(I,J) should be selected to make the point (XBAR, YBAR) (that is, the point $(\bar{x},\bar{y})$) as nearly central as possible to the base points for evaluating the interpolating polynomial $p_{m,n}(\bar{x},\bar{y})$ of degree M in x and of degree N in y. The value $p_{m,n}(\bar{x},\bar{y})$ should be returned as the value of POLY2D. Should XARG or YARG fall outside the range of base points, the interpolating polynomial should be used for extrapolation.

Write a short main program that reads values for IMAX, JMAX, X(1), ..., X(IMAX), Y(1), ..., Y(JMAX), F(1,1), ..., F(IMAX, JMAX) once, then reads values for M, N, XBAR, and YBAR, calls on POLY2D to evaluate the appropriate interpolating polynomial, prints the result, and returns to read another set of values for M, N, XBAR, and YBAR. Test the function with the data of Problem 1.29 using different combinations of M and N. Compare the interpolated results with those found using the functions LIN2D and CUB2D of Problems 1.29 and 1.31, respectively.

1.40 Using the properties of the cubic spline function discussed in Problem 1.24, develop a two dimensional *doubly-cubic spline* function (see [22]) for interpolation in rectangular regions with base points and functional values arranged as described in Problem 1.35.

Table P1.42

$-v_g$	v_a	i_a	$-v_g$	v_a	i_a
0	0	0	12	200	0.2
0	25	2.1	12	225	0.7
0	50	4.7	12	250	1.7
0	75	7.9	12	275	3.3
0	100	11.6	12	300	5.3
			12	325	7.9
4	75	0.3	16	275	0.2
4	100	1.7	16	300	0.8
4	125	3.9	16	325	1.7
4	150	6.8	16	350	3.1
4	175	10.1	16	375	5.0
4	200	13.8	16	400	7.5
8	125	0.1	20	325	0.1
8	150	0.6	20	350	0.4
8	175	1.7	.20	375	1.1
8	200	3.6	20	400	2.0
8	225	6.0	20	425	3.4
8	275	12.3			

1.41 Write a function, named SPLIN2, with dummy argument list (IMAX, JMAX, X, Y, F, XBAR, YBAR) that evaluates the doubly-cubic spline function developed in Problem 1.40. The arguments have the meanings of like arguments for the function POLY2D described in Problem 1.39. Write a short main program similar to that outlined in Problem 1.39, and test the function SPLIN2 with the data of Problem 1.29.

1.42 The characteristics in Table P1.42 are available for the 6J5 triode electronic vacuum tube [23[(v_a = anode voltage, v_g = grid voltage, i_a = anode current, mA).

Write a function with three different entries, such that given any two of v_g, v_a, and i_a, the function will compute the third, using an appropriate two-dimensional interpolation procedure. Let the three function names be VGRID, VANODE, IANODE (real). If VG, VA, and IA (real) are program variables equivalent to v_g, v_a, and i_a, respectively, then typical statements referencing the function might be

VG = VGRID (VA, IA)

VA = VANODE (VG, IA)

IA = IANODE (VA, VG)

Test the function thoroughly with a short calling program. The functions can be used in Problem 2.48 and Problem 3.20.

1.43 Suppose that you wish to minimize the maximum magnitude of the error-term factor

$$\prod_{i=0}^{n} (x - x_i)$$

in the Lagrange or divided-difference interpolation formulas, to be used over the interval $[a,b]$. You are free to choose the base points $x_0, x_1, \ldots, x_n$.

If $a = 2$, $b = 6$, and $n = 3$, what values would you select for x_0, x_1, x_2, and x_3?

1.44 Find the near-minimax quadratic, and minimax cubic, polynomial approximations to x^4 on the interval [2,8].

1.45 Use the Chebyshev economization procedure to yield an approximation of the form

$$e^x \doteq a_0 + a_1 x + a_2 x^2 + a_3 x^3,$$

which is in error by 0.0095, at most, on the interval $-1 \leqslant x \leqslant 1$.

1.46 Hougen and Watson [7] suggest that the following empirical equation describes the molal heat capacity of nitrogen accurately (within 1.2%) between 300 and 2100°K:

$$c_p = 6.3 + 1.82 \times 10^{-3}T - 0.345 \times 10^{-6}T^2.$$

Here, c_p has units of cal/gm mole °K and T is in °K ($= °C + 273.15°$).

(a) Find the linear approximation to c_p that minimizes the maximum additional error in c_p between 1000 and 2000 °K.

(b) What is the upper limit on the total percentage error for the approximation of part (a)?

1.47 The coefficient of expansion, k, for aluminum between 0 and 100°C is given by

$$k(T) = 0.22 \times 10^{-4}T + 0.009 \times 10^{-6}T^2,$$

where T is in °C and the reference temperature is 0 °C (that is, k is zero at 0 °C).

(a) Rewrite the expression for k in terms of the Chebyshev polynomials of Table 1.12, and truncate to the constant term.

(b) Calculate the integrated average value of k between 0 and 100 °C, and the arithmetic average of the values of $k(0)$ and $k(100)$, and compare with the results of part (a).

1.48 Write a function, named CHEB, that implements the Chebyshev economization procedure outlined in Section 1.12, by making direct use of the recursion relation (1.72). The routine should *not* require tabular information such as that of Tables 1.3.1 and 1.3.2. The function should have the arguments

(N, A, AL, AR, EPS, M, C)

where all variables have the meanings ascribed to the program variables of Example 1.3. The *value* of CHEB should be the maximum possible error introduced by the economization process (comparable to program variable E of Example 1.3).

1.49 Show that equation (1.3.13) follows from (1.3.10), (1.3.11), and (1.3.12).

1.50 Show that the coefficients a_i in (1.80) and (1.81) are given by

$$a_0 = \frac{1}{\pi} \int_{-1}^{1} \frac{f(x)}{\sqrt{1-x^2}}\, dx = \frac{1}{\pi} \int_0^{\pi} f(\cos\theta)\, d\theta,$$

$$a_i = \frac{2}{\pi} \int_{-1}^{1} \frac{f(x)\, T_i(x)}{\sqrt{1-x^2}}\, dx = \frac{2}{\pi} \int_0^{\pi} f(\cos\theta) \cos i\,\theta\, d\theta,$$

$$i = 1, 2, \ldots.$$

Using these definitions, find an approximation of the form of (1.81) for $n = 4$ and $f(x) = \cos x$, $-1 \leqslant x \leqslant 1$. Compare the result with the economized power-series approximation of (1.87).

1.51 Snyder [18] shows that when the integrals of Problem 1.50 are difficult to evaluate, they may be approximated by

$$a_0 \doteq \frac{1}{n+1} \sum_{j=0}^{n} f(x_j), \quad a_i \doteq \frac{2}{n+1} \sum_{j=0}^{n} f(x_j) T_i(x_j), \quad i = 1, 2, \ldots, n,$$

where the $x_j, j = 0, 1, \ldots, n$, are the $n+1$ roots of $T_{n+1}(x)$ (see (1.77)). Use these relationships to estimate the coefficients $a_i, i = 0, 1, \ldots, 4$, for the function $f(x) = \cos x$, $-1 \leqslant x \leqslant 1$, and compare with the results of Problem 1.50 and with the economized power-series approximation of (1.87).

Bibliography

1. B. W. Arden, *An Introduction to Digital Computing*, Addison-Wesley, Reading, Massachusetts, 1963.
2. R. W. Hamming, *Numerical Methods for Scientists and Engineers*, McGraw-Hill, New York, 1962.
3. F. B. Hildebrand, *Introduction to Numerical Analysis*, McGraw-Hill, New York, 1956.
4. D. E. Knuth, "Evaluation of Polynomials by Computer," *Communications of the A.C.M.*, **5**, 595–599 (1962).
5. A. M. Ostrowski, *Studies in Mathematics and Mechanics Presented to R. Von Mises*, pp. 40–48, Academic Press, New York, 1954.
6. J. Todd, *A Survey of Numerical Analysis*, McGraw-Hill, New York, 1962.
7. O. A. Hougen and K. M. Watson, *Chemical Process Principles, Part One, Material and Energy Balances*, Wiley, New York, 1953.
8. W. Kaplan, *Advanced Calculus*, Addison-Wesley, Cambridge, Massachusetts, 1953.
9. D. D. McCracken and W. S. Dorn, *Numerical Methods and FORTRAN Programming*, Wiley, New York, 1964.
10. E. I. Organick, *A FORTRAN IV Primer*, Addison-Wesley, Reading, Massachusetts, 1966.
11. D. D. McCracken, *A Guide to FORTRAN IV Programming*, Wiley, New York, 1965.
12. P. H. Henrici, *Elements of Numerical Analysis*, Wiley, New York, 1964.
13. A. Ralston, *A First Course in Numerical Analysis*, McGraw-Hill, New York, 1965.
14. E. Isaacson and H. B. Keller, *Analysis of Numerical Methods*, Wiley, New York, 1966.
15. E. Remes, "Sur le calcul effectif des polynomes d'approximation de Tchebichef," *C.R. Acad. Sci. Paris*, **199**, 337–340 (1934).
16. F. D. Murnaghan and J. W. Wrench, Jr., "The Determination of the Chebyshev Approximating Polynomial for a Differentiable Function," *Math. Tables Aids Comput.*, **13**, 185–193 (1959).
17. C. W. Clenshaw, "Chebyshev Series for Mathematical Functions," *Math. Tables*, Vol. 5, Nat. Phys. Lab., G. Britain, 1962.
18. M. A. Snyder, *Chebyshev Methods in Numerical Approximation*, Prentice-Hall, Englewood Cliffs, New Jersey, 1966.
19. C. T. Fike, "Methods of Evaluating Polynomial Approximations in Function Evaluation Routines," *Communications of the A.C.M.*, **10**, 175–178, (1967).
20. *International Critical Tables*, Vol. II, p. 337, McGraw-Hill, New York, 1927.
21. C. D. Hodgman, ed., *Handbook of Chemistry and Physics*, 33rd ed., Chemical Rubber, Cleveland, Ohio, 1951.
22. J. H. Ahlberg, E. N. Nilson, and J. L. Walsh, *The Theory of Splines and their Applications*, Academic Press, New York, 1967.
23. R. J. Smith, *Circuit, Devices, and Systems*, Wiley, New York, 1966.
24. J. H. Perry, ed., *Chemical Engineers' Handbook*, 3rd ed., McGraw-Hill, New York, 1950.

CHAPTER 2

Numerical Integration

2.1 Introduction

The evaluation of a definite integral

$$\int_a^b f(x)\,dx \qquad (2.1)$$

by formal methods is often difficult or impossible, even when $f(x)$ is of a relatively simple analytical form. For these intractable cases, and for the more general integration problem in which only a few sample values of $f(x)$ are available at distinct base-point arguments x_i, $i = 0$, $1, \ldots, n$, some other approach is necessary. An obvious alternative is to find a function $g(x)$ that is both a suitable approximation of $f(x)$ and simple to integrate formally. Then (2.1) can be estimated as

$$\int_a^b g(x)\,dx. \qquad (2.2)$$

Fortunately the interpolating polynomials $p_n(x)$, already developed in Chapter 1, often produce adequate approximations and possess the desired property of simple integrability. In fact, this combination of characteristics is a principal reason for the great emphasis given to polynomials throughout much of numerical mathematics.

Figure 2.1 illustrates the approximation of the function $f(x)$ by the polynomial $p_4(x)$ that exactly reproduces the value of $f(x)$ at the indicated base points $x_0, x_1, \ldots, x_4$.

The true value of

$$\int_{x_0}^{x_4} f(x)\,dx$$

is given by the area under the solid curve $f(x)$, whereas the approximation

$$\int_{x_0}^{x_4} p_4(x)\,dx$$

is given by the area under the dotted curve $p_4(x)$. Note that if the difference between $f(x)$ and $p_4(x)$,

$$\delta(x) = f(x) - p_4(x),$$

differs in sign on various segments of the integration interval (the usual case), then the overall integration error

$$\int_{x_0}^{x_4} \delta(x)\,dx = \int_{x_0}^{x_4} f(x)\,dx - \int_{x_0}^{x_4} p_4(x)\,dx$$

may be small, even when $p_4(x)$ is not a particularly good approximation of $f(x)$. Positive errors in one segment tend to cancel negative errors in others. For this reason, integration is often termed a *smoothing* process.

Texts on numerical mathematics abound with formulas for numerical integration (sometimes called *quadrature* or *mechanical quadrature*). This is not surprising, since there are so many possibilities for selecting the base-point spacing, the degree of the interpolating polynomial, and

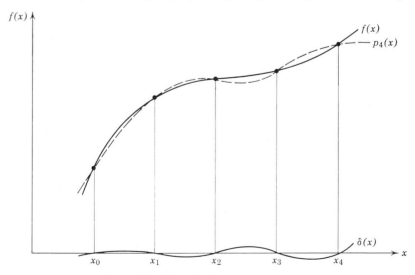

Figure 2.1 Numerical integration.

69

the location of base points with respect to the interval of integration. The commonly used integration methods can be classified into two groups: the Newton-Cotes formulas that employ functional values at equally spaced base points, and the Gaussian quadrature formulas that employ unequally spaced base points, determined by certain properties of orthogonal polynomials.

2.2 Numerical Integration with Equally Spaced Base Points

Consider the four parts of Fig. 2.2, in which $f(x)$ is known only at the indicated set of equally spaced base points.

In each case, the same integral,

$$\int_a^b f(x)\, dx,$$

is to be evaluated by the approximation

$$\int_a^b p_n(x)\, dx. \tag{2.3}$$

Since a different interpolating polynomial $p_n(x)$ is used in each of the four cases, (2.3) yields four different approximations (the shaded areas) of the true integral. In Fig. 2.2a, the polynomial is fitted by using only functional values on the interval $[a,b]$, with base points at both a and b. Figure 2.2b illustrates a similar situation, except that functional values at base points outside the integration interval are also used to determine the approximating polynomial. In Fig. 2.2c, the polynomial is determined by functional values between the integration limits, with no base points at the ends of the interval; Fig. 2.2d is similar, except that there is a base point at one end of the interval, $x = a$. Obviously, many other combinations are also possible. For example, a and b could be arbitrarily located with respect to the base points, that is, a and/or b need not coincide with base point values.

The two most frequently used classes of equal-interval integration formulas are called *closed* and *open*. In both classes, the integration limits a and b are either coincident

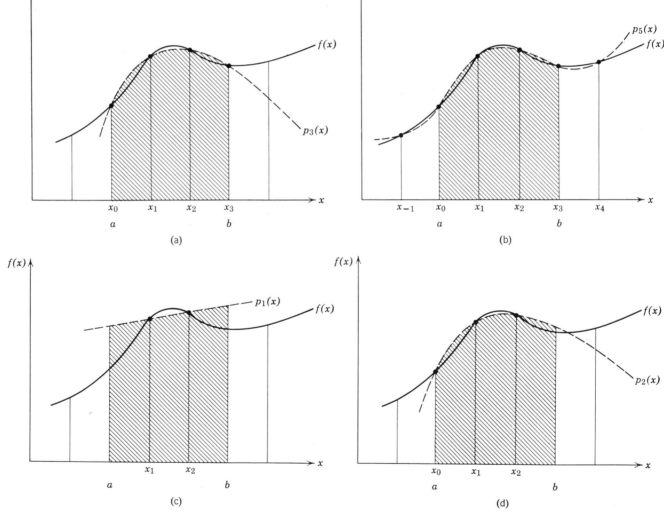

Figure 2.2 Numerical integration—four different polynomial approximations of $f(x)$.

with base points or are displaced from base points by integral multiples of the base-point spacing h. The *closed* integration formulas use information about $f(x)$, that is, they have base points, at both limits of integration, and are illustrated in Fig. 2.2a. The *open* integration formulas do not require information about $f(x)$ at the limits of integration (see Fig. 2.2c).

All of the closed and open formulas can be generated by integrating one of the general interpolating polynomials $p_n(x)$ from Chapter 1 with appropriate base points and integration limits. Since it is assumed here that $f(x)$ can be computed or is known only at the base points $x_0, x_1, x_2, \ldots, x_n$, equally spaced by stepsize h, the logical choice for the polynomial representation is one of the finite-difference (forward, backward, or central) forms. Let the polynomial be given in terms of the forward finite differences by Newton's forward formula of (1.54),

$$f(x_0 + \alpha h) = f(x_0) + \alpha\, \Delta f(x_0) + \frac{\alpha(\alpha - 1)}{2!}\, \Delta^2 f(x_0)$$

$$+ \frac{\alpha(\alpha - 1)(\alpha - 2)}{3!}\, \Delta^3 f(x_0) + \cdots$$

$$+ \frac{\alpha(\alpha - 1)(\alpha - 2)\ldots(\alpha - n + 1)}{n!}$$

$$\times \Delta^n f(x_0) + R_n(x_0 + \alpha h)$$

$$= p_n(x_0 + \alpha h) + R_n(x_0 + \alpha h).$$

Here, as before, $\alpha = (x - x_0)/h$, $p_n(x_0 + \alpha h)$ is the nth-degree interpolating polynomial, and $R_n(x_0 + \alpha h)$ is the remainder or error term (1.55),

$$R_n(x_0 + \alpha h) = h^{n+1}\alpha(\alpha - 1)(\alpha - 2)\cdots(\alpha - n)$$

$$\times \frac{f^{(n+1)}(\xi)}{(n + 1)!}, \qquad \xi \text{ in } (x, x_0, \ldots, x_n),$$

or

$$R_n(x_0 + \alpha h) = h^{n+1}\alpha(\alpha - 1)(\alpha - 2)$$

$$\cdots (\alpha - n)f[x, x_n, x_{n-1}, \ldots, x_0].$$

2.3 Newton-Cotes Closed Integration Formulas

The simplest case of closed integration is shown schematically in Fig. 2.3. Here, the two base points $x_0 = a$ and $x_1 = b$ are used to determine a first-degree polynomial, $p_1(x) = p_1(x_0 + \alpha h)$ or straight-line approximation of $f(x)$. The appropriate form of (1.54) is given by

$$f(x) = f(x_0 + \alpha h) = f(x_0) + \alpha\, \Delta f(x_0) + R_1(x_0 + \alpha h)$$

$$= p_1(x_0 + \alpha h) + R_1(x_0 + \alpha h) \qquad (2.4)$$

where

$$R_1(x_0 + \alpha h) = h^2\alpha(\alpha - 1)\frac{f''(\xi)}{2!},$$

$$\xi \text{ in } (x_0, x_1), \quad (2.5)$$

or

$$R_1(x_0 + \alpha h) = h^2\alpha(\alpha - 1)f[x, x_0, x_1].$$

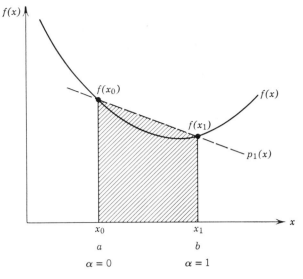

Figure 2.3   The trapezoidal rule.

Using this polynomial approximation for $f(x)$ and transforming the integration variable from x to α, $(\alpha = (x - x_0)/h)$, we have

$$\int_a^b f(x)\, dx = \int_{x_0}^{x_1} f(x)\, dx \doteq \int_{x_0}^{x_1} p_1(x)\, dx$$

$$\doteq h \int_0^1 p_1(x_0 + \alpha h)\, d\alpha, \qquad (2.6)$$

where the integral on the right, is given, from (2.4), by

$$h \int_0^1 [f(x_0) + \alpha\, \Delta f(x_0)]\, d\alpha =$$

$$h\left[\alpha f(x_0) + \frac{\alpha^2}{2}\, \Delta f(x_0)\right]_0^1$$

$$= h\left[f(x_0) + \frac{\Delta f(x_0)}{2}\right]. \quad (2.7)$$

From the definition of the first forward difference, $\Delta f(x_0) = f(x_0 + h) - f(x_0)$, (2.7) assumes the final form,

$$\int_{a=x_0}^{b=x_1} f(x)\, dx \doteq h\left[f(x_0) + \frac{f(x_0 + h) - f(x_0)}{2}\right]$$

$$\doteq \frac{h}{2}[f(x_0) + f(x_1)], \qquad (2.8)$$

the familiar *trapezoidal rule*. The required area under the solid curve of Fig. 2.3 is approximated by the area under the dotted straight line (the shaded trapezoid).

The error involved in using the trapezoidal approximation is given by the integral of the remainder term (2.5),

$$\int_{x_0}^{x_1} R_1(x)\, dx$$

$$= h \int_0^1 R_1(x_0 + \alpha h)\, d\alpha$$

$$= h^3 \int_0^1 \alpha(\alpha - 1)\frac{f''(\xi)}{2!}\, d\alpha, \qquad \xi \text{ in } (x_0, x_1). \quad (2.9)$$

If $f(x)$ is a continuous function of x, then $f''(\xi)$ or its equivalent, $2! f[x,x_0,x_1]$ [see (2.5)], is a continuous, but unknown, function of x, so direct evaluation of (2.9) is impossible. Since α is simply a transformed value of x, $f''(\xi)$ is a continuous function of the integration variable α; this property simplifies the estimation of (2.9). The factor $f''(\xi)$ can be taken outside the integral sign by applying the *integral mean-value theorem* from the calculus:

If two functions, $q(x)$ and $g(x)$, are continuous for $a \leqslant x \leqslant b$ and $g(x)$ is of constant sign for $a < x < b$, then

$$\int_a^b q(x)g(x)\,dx = q(\bar{\xi}) \int_a^b g(x)\,dx,$$

where $a < \bar{\xi} < b$.

Since the factor $\alpha(\alpha - 1)$ is negative for all α in the

The trapezoidal rule with error term is then given by

$$\int_{x_0}^{x_1} f(x)\,dx = \frac{h}{2}[f(x_0) + f(x_1)]$$
$$- \frac{h^3}{12}f''(\xi), \qquad \xi \text{ in } (x_0,x_1). \quad (2.11)$$

Thus the error term from the trapezoidal rule is zero only if $f''(\bar{\xi})$ vanishes. If $f(x)$ is linear, that is, a first-degree polynomial, the trapezoidal rule yields exactly $\int_a^b f(x)dx$, as expected (see Fig. 2.3).

A more general problem is illustrated in Fig. 2.4. Here, the interpolating polynomial is of degree n; the $n + 1$ evenly spaced base points are $x_0, x_1, \ldots, x_n$. Let a, the lower limit of integration, coincide with the base point x_0. Let b, the upper limit of integration, be arbitrary for the moment. Then the approximation is given by the integral

$$\int_a^b f(x)\,dx \doteq \int_{x_0}^b p_n(x)\,dx = h\int_0^{\bar{\alpha}} p_n(x_0 + \alpha h)\,d\alpha \qquad (2.12)$$

$$\doteq h\int_0^{\bar{\alpha}} \left[f(x_0) + \alpha\,\Delta f(x_0) + \frac{\alpha(\alpha-1)}{2!}\Delta^2 f(x_0) + \frac{\alpha(\alpha-1)(\alpha-2)}{3!}\Delta^3 f(x_0) \right.$$
$$\left. + \cdots + \frac{\alpha(\alpha-1)(\alpha-2)\cdots(\alpha-n+1)}{n!}\Delta^n f(x_0) \right]d\alpha,$$

where $\bar{\alpha} = (b - x_0)/h$. Carrying out the indicated integration for the first few terms yields

$$h\int_0^{\bar{\alpha}} p_n(x_0 + \alpha h)\,d\alpha = h\left[\alpha f(x_0) + \frac{\alpha^2}{2}\Delta f(x_0) + \left(\frac{\alpha^3}{6} - \frac{\alpha^2}{4}\right)\Delta^2 f(x_0) \right.$$
$$\left. + \left(\frac{\alpha^4}{24} - \frac{\alpha^3}{6} + \frac{\alpha^2}{6}\right)\Delta^3 f(x_0) + \left(\frac{\alpha^5}{120} - \frac{\alpha^4}{16} + \frac{11\alpha^3}{72} - \frac{\alpha^2}{8}\right)\Delta^4 f(x_0) + \cdots \right]_0^{\bar{\alpha}}. \quad (2.13)$$

All terms vanish when evaluated at the lower integration limit, so that

$$\int_a^b f(x)\,dx \doteq h\left[\bar{\alpha} f(x_0) + \frac{\bar{\alpha}^2}{2}\Delta f(x_0) + \left(\frac{\bar{\alpha}^3}{6} - \frac{\bar{\alpha}^2}{4}\right)\Delta^2 f(x_0) \right.$$
$$\left. + \left(\frac{\bar{\alpha}^4}{24} - \frac{\bar{\alpha}^3}{6} + \frac{\bar{\alpha}^2}{6}\right)\Delta^3 f(x_0) + \left(\frac{\bar{\alpha}^5}{120} - \frac{\bar{\alpha}^4}{16} + \frac{11\bar{\alpha}^3}{72} - \frac{\bar{\alpha}^2}{8}\right)\Delta^4 f(x_0) + \cdots \right]. \quad (2.14)$$

The corresponding error term [see (1.55a)] is given by

$$h\int_0^{\bar{\alpha}} R_n(x_0 + \alpha h)\,d\alpha = h^{n+2}\int_0^{\bar{\alpha}} \left[\alpha(\alpha-1)(\alpha-2)\cdots(\alpha-n)\frac{f^{(n+1)}(\xi)}{(n+1)!} \right]d\alpha, \quad (2.15)$$

with ξ in $(x_0,x_1,\ldots,b)$.

interval $0 < \alpha < 1$, the integral mean-value theorem allows (2.9) to be rewritten as

$$h^3 \int_0^1 \alpha(\alpha - 1)\frac{f''(\xi)}{2!}\,d\alpha$$
$$= h^3 \frac{f''(\bar{\xi})}{2!}\int_0^1 (\alpha^2 - \alpha)\,d\alpha$$
$$= -\frac{h^3}{12}f''(\bar{\xi}), \qquad \xi, \bar{\xi} \text{ in } (x_0,x_1). \quad (2.10)$$

Equations (2.14) and (2.15) describe a family of related integration formulas. If the upper limit b is chosen to coincide with one of the base points so that the integration is across m intervals, each of width h (that is, the integration is between $a = x_0$ and $b = x_m$), then $\bar{\alpha}$ in (2.14) and (2.15) assumes the integral value m.

Note that the trapezoidal rule already developed follows from (2.14) and (2.15) when $\bar{\alpha} = m = n = 1$. To find similar formulas for integration across $m = 2, 3, 4$ or more intervals, let $\bar{\alpha} = 2, 3, 4$, etc. in (2.14). The choice of

n is still open, and, although $n = \bar{\alpha}$ seems the most natural, there is no reason why points outside the integration interval could not also be used to determine the interpolating polynomial.

When $\bar{\alpha}$ is an even integer, that is, when the overall integration interval contains an even number of steps of

$$h^5 \int_0^2 \alpha(\alpha - 1)(\alpha - 2)(\alpha - 3)\frac{f^{(4)}(\xi)}{4!}\,d\alpha = h^5 \frac{f^{(4)}(\bar{\xi})}{4!} \int_0^2 \alpha(\alpha - 1)(\alpha - 2)(\alpha - 3)\,d\alpha,$$
$$= \frac{-h^5 f^{(4)}(\bar{\xi})}{90}, \qquad \xi, \bar{\xi} \text{ in } (x_0, x_2).$$
$$(2.19)$$

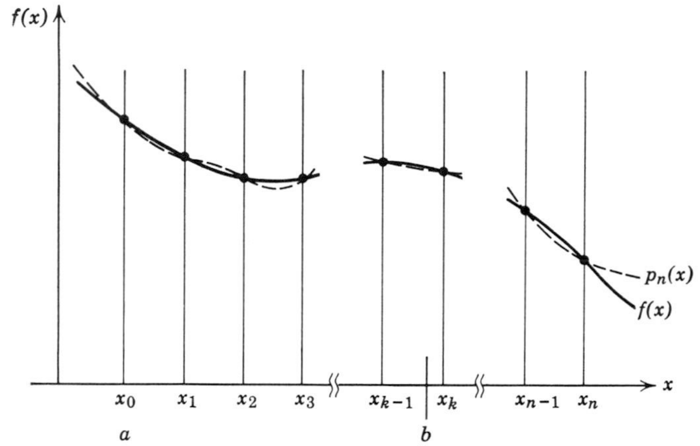

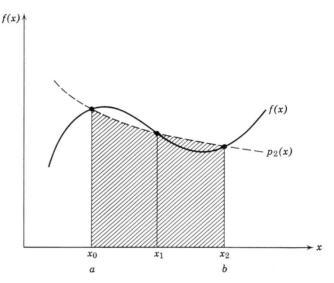

Figure 2.4   General case for closed integration.

width h, (2.14) yields an unexpected dividend which is illustrated by the choice $\bar{\alpha} = 2$:

$$\int_{x_0}^{x_2} f(x)\,dx = h \int_0^2 f(x_0 + \alpha h)\,d\alpha \doteq h\left[2f(x_0) + 2\Delta f(x_0) \right.$$
$$\left. + \frac{1}{3}\Delta^2 f(x_0) + 0\,\Delta^3 f(x_0) - \frac{1}{90}\Delta^4 f(x_0) + \cdots \right]. \quad (2.16)$$

Note that the coefficient of $\Delta^3 f(x_0) = \Delta^{\bar{\alpha}+1} f(x_0)$ is zero. On substitution of the appropriate ordinate values from the forward-difference definitions of (1.50) and retention of the first three terms, that is, for the choice $n = 2$, (2.16) becomes

$$\int_{x_0}^{x_2} f(x)\,dx \doteq \frac{h}{3}\left[f(x_0) + 4f(x_1) + f(x_2) \right]. \quad (2.17)$$

Equation (2.17) is the well-known *Simpson's rule*, probably the most frequently used of all the numerical integration formulas. Because of the appearance of the zero coefficient in (2.16), the error term for Simpson's rule is not given by (2.15) with $n = 2$ as might be expected, but rather with $n = 3$, that is,

$$h \int_0^2 R_3(x_0 + \alpha h)\,d\alpha \doteq h^5 \int_0^2 \alpha(\alpha - 1)(\alpha - 2)(\alpha - 3)$$
$$\times \frac{f^{(4)}(\xi)}{4!}\,d\alpha, \qquad \xi \text{ in } (x_0, x_2). \quad (2.18)$$

Note that the error of (2.18) cannot be evaluated directly by simple application of the integral mean-value theorem as was done with the trapezoidal rule error (2.10), since the factor $\alpha(\alpha - 1)(\alpha - 2)(\alpha - 3)$ does not have a constant sign over the interval of integration. However, Steffensen [5] has shown that the error can be written in analogous fashion, that is, as

Henceforth the bar on $\bar{\xi}$ in (2.11) and (2.19) will be dropped, since both ξ and $\bar{\xi}$ are simply unknown values of the independent variable on the integration interval.

Simpson's rule with error term is then given by

$$\int_{x_0}^{x_2} f(x)\,dx = \frac{h}{3}\left[f(x_0) + 4f(x_1) + f(x_2) \right]$$
$$- \frac{h^5}{90} f^{(4)}(\xi), \qquad \xi \text{ in } (x_0, x_2). \quad (2.20)$$

Figure 2.5   Simpson's rule.

Only three points are used to determine the polynomial (see Fig. 2.5). Hence one would expect the integration to be exact for $f(x)$ a polynomial of degree two or less. In fact, (2.20) shows that Simpson's rule is exact when $f(x)$ is a polynomial of degree three or less. The set of closed formulas generated by (2.14) and (2.15) are known as the *Newton-Cotes closed integration formulas*. A list for the cases $\bar{\alpha} = 1, 2, \ldots, 6$ follows.

$\bar{\alpha} = 1$ (trapezoidal rule):

$$\int_{x_0}^{x_1} f(x)\,dx = \frac{h}{2}\left[f(x_0) + f(x_1) \right] - \frac{h^3}{12} f''(\xi). \quad (2.21a)$$

$\bar{\alpha} = 2$ (Simpson's rule):

$$\int_{x_0}^{x_2} f(x)\, dx = \frac{h}{3}\left[f(x_0) + 4f(x_1) + f(x_2) \right] - \frac{h^5}{90} f^{(4)}(\xi).$$

$$(2.21b)$$

$\bar{\alpha} = 3$ (Simpson's second rule):

$$\int_{x_0}^{x_3} f(x)\, dx = \frac{3h}{8}\left[f(x_0) + 3f(x_1) \right.$$

$$\left. + 3f(x_2) + f(x_3) \right] - \frac{3h^5}{80} f^{(4)}(\xi). \quad (2.21c)$$

$\bar{\alpha} = 4$:

$$\int_{x_0}^{x_4} f(x)\, dx = \frac{2h}{45}\left[7f(x_0) + 32f(x_1) + 12f(x_2) \right.$$

$$\left. + 32f(x_3) + 7f(x_4) \right] - \frac{8h^7}{945} f^{(6)}(\xi). \quad (2.21d)$$

$\bar{\alpha} = 5$:

$$\int_{x_0}^{x_5} f(x)\, dx = \frac{5h}{288}\left[19f(x_0) + 75f(x_1) + 50f(x_2) \right.$$

$$+ 50f(x_3) + 75f(x_4) + 19f(x_5) \left. \right] - \frac{275h^7}{12096} f^{(6)}(\xi).$$

$$(2.21e)$$

$\bar{\alpha} = 6$:

$$\int_{x_0}^{x_6} f(x)\, dx = \frac{h}{140}\left[41f(x_0) + 216f(x_1) + 27f(x_2) \right.$$

$$+ 272f(x_3) + 27f(x_4) + 216f(x_5)$$

$$+ 41f(x_6) \left. \right] - \frac{9h^9}{1400} f^{(8)}(\xi). \quad (2.21f)$$

Note that when $\bar{\alpha}$ is *even* (that is, when there is an even number of intervals or an odd number of base points) the formulas are exact for $f(x)$ a polynomial of degree $\bar{\alpha} + 1$ or less; when $\bar{\alpha}$ is *odd*, the formulas are exact for $f(x)$ a polynomial of degree $\bar{\alpha}$ or less. For all even values of $\bar{\alpha}$, the coefficient of $\Delta^{\bar{\alpha}+1} f(x_0)$ in (2.14) assumes a zero value. Hence in each such case, the error term involves a derivative of order $\bar{\alpha} + 2$ rather than of order $\bar{\alpha} + 1$ as might be expected. For this reason the odd-point formulas are more frequently used than the even-point formulas. For example, consider the error terms in the formulas for $\bar{\alpha} = 2$ and $\bar{\alpha} = 3$:

$\bar{\alpha} = 2$ (Simpson's rule):

$$-\frac{h^5}{90} f^{(4)}(\xi),$$

$\bar{\alpha} = 3$ (Simpson's second rule):

$$-\frac{3h^5}{80} f^{(4)}(\xi).$$

On first glance, it would appear that the error for $\bar{\alpha} = 2$ is actually smaller than for $\bar{\alpha} = 3$. However, allowance must be made for the fact that for integration over the same interval $[a,b]$, the stepsize $(b - a)/\bar{\alpha}$ for the second case is only two-thirds the stepsize for the first. In terms of a and b, remembering that the values of ξ in the two will not normally be the same, the error terms become:

$\bar{\alpha} = 2$:

$$-\frac{(b - a)^5}{2880} f^{(4)}(\xi_1),$$

$\bar{\alpha} = 3$:

$$-\frac{(b - a)^5}{6480} f^{(4)}(\xi_2).$$

The error bound for the second case is smaller (assuming that $f^{(4)}(\xi_1)$ is not appreciably different from $f^{(4)}(\xi_2)$), but only moderately so.

None of the formulas of (2.21) requires the computation of differences, or the coefficients of the interpolating polynomial. Each involves only the calculation of a weighted sum of the base-point functional values, that is,

$$\int_a^b f(x)\, dx \doteq \sum_{i=0}^{n} w_i f(x_i), \quad (2.22)$$

where the w_i are the weights assigned to the functional values, $f(x_i)$, $i = 0, 1, \ldots, n$.

Example. Use the trapezoidal and Simpson's rules to estimate the integral

$$\int_1^3 f(x)\, dx = \int_1^3 (x^3 - 2x^2 + 7x - 5)\, dx$$

$$= \left[\frac{x^4}{4} - \frac{2x^3}{3} + \frac{7x^2}{2} - 5x \right]_1^3 = 20\tfrac{2}{3}. \quad (2.23)$$

Functional values from (2.23) for several values of x on the integration interval are:

x	$f(x)$
1.0	1
1.5	$4\tfrac{3}{8}$
2.0	9
2.5	$15\tfrac{5}{8}$
3.0	25

For the trapezoidal rule (see Fig. 2.6a), $h = 2$, $x_0 = 1$, $x_1 = 3$, $f(x_0) = 1$, and $f(x_1) = 25$. From (2.21a),

$$\int_{x_0=1}^{x_1=3} f(x)\, dx = \frac{h}{2}\left[f(x_0) + f(x_1) \right] - \frac{h^3}{12} f''(\xi)$$

$$= \frac{2}{2}[1 + 25] - \frac{8}{12} f''(\xi)$$

$$= 26 - \frac{2}{3} f''(\xi).$$

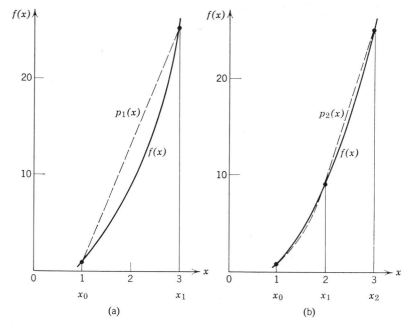

Figure 2.6 *Numerical approximation of* $\int_1^3 (x^3 - 2x^2 + 7x - 5)\, dx$. **(a)** *Trapezoidal rule.* **(b)** *Simpson's rule.*

Since $f''(x) = 6x - 4$, the error is given by

$$-\frac{2}{3} f''(\xi) = -\frac{2}{3}(6\xi - 4), \qquad 1 < \xi < 3,$$

which has an extreme value $-9\frac{1}{3}$. The true error is $20\frac{2}{3} - 26 = -5\frac{1}{3}$, smaller than the bound as expected, but still quite large.

For Simpson's rule (see Fig. 2.6*b*), $h = 1$, $x_0 = 1$, $x_1 = 2$, $x_2 = 3$, $f(x_0) = 1$, $f(x_1) = 9$, and $f(x_2) = 25$. From (2.20),

$$\int_{x_0=1}^{x_2=3} f(x)\, dx = \frac{h}{3}[f(x_0) + 4f(x_1) + f(x_2)] - \frac{h^5}{90} f^{(4)}(\xi)$$

$$= \frac{1}{3}(1 + 36 + 25) - \frac{h^5}{90} f^{(4)}(\xi) = 20\frac{2}{3} - \frac{1}{90} f^{(4)}(\xi).$$

Since the fourth derivative of $f(x)$ vanishes for all x, the error term vanishes and the result is exact.

2.4 Newton-Cotes Open Integration Formulas

We can derive integration formulas which employ equally spaced base points but which do not require base-point functional values at one or both of the integration limits (see Figs. 2.2*c* and 2.2*d*). The general open integration problem is illustrated in Fig. 2.7. Here the interpolating polynomial is of degree $n - 2$; the $n - 1$ evenly spaced base points are $x_1, \ldots, x_{n-1}$. Let a, the lower integration limit, coincide with $x_0 = x_1 - h$, where h, as before, is the base-point spacing. Let b, the upper-integration limit, be arbitrary for the moment. Then the approximation is given by

$$\int_a^b f(x)\, dx \doteq \int_a^b p_{n-2}(x)\, dx. \qquad (2.24)$$

A simple representation of $p_{n-2}(x)$ is given by the forward finite-difference polynomial, Newton's forward formula (1.54), where the forward differences of $f(x_1)$ rather than of $f(x_0)$ are used, giving

$$\int_a^b f(x)\, dx \doteq \int_{x_0}^b p_{n-2}(x)\, dx$$

$$\doteq h \int_0^{\bar{\alpha}} p_{n-2}(x_0 + \alpha h)\, d\alpha. \qquad (2.25)$$

Here, $\alpha = (x - x_0)/h$ and $\bar{\alpha} = (b - x_0)/h$. In terms of the forward differences of $f(x_1)$, $p_{n-2}(x_0 + \alpha h)$ is given by

$$p_{n-2}(x_0 + \alpha h) = f(x_1) + (\alpha - 1)\Delta f(x_1)$$

$$+ \frac{(\alpha - 1)(\alpha - 2)}{2!} \Delta^2 f(x_1)$$

$$+ \frac{(\alpha - 1)(\alpha - 2)(\alpha - 3)}{3!} \Delta^3 f(x_1)$$

$$+ \cdots + \frac{(\alpha - 1)(\alpha - 2)\cdots(\alpha - n + 2)}{(n - 2)!}$$

$$\times \Delta^{n-2} f(x_1). \qquad (2.26)$$

Then the integral of (2.25) becomes

$$\int_a^b f(x)\, dx \doteq h \int_0^{\bar{\alpha}} [f(x_1) + (\alpha - 1)\Delta f(x_1) + \cdots]\, d\alpha$$

$$\doteq h \left[\alpha f(x_1) + \left(\frac{\alpha^2}{2} - \alpha \right) \Delta f(x_1) \right.$$

$$\left. + \left(\frac{\alpha^3}{6} - \frac{3\alpha^2}{4} + \alpha \right) \Delta^2 f(x_1) + \cdots \right]_0^{\bar{\alpha}}. \quad (2.27)$$

All terms vanish at the lower limit. Hence

$$\int_a^b f(x)\,dx \doteq h\left[\bar{\alpha}f(x_1) + \left(\frac{\bar{\alpha}^2}{2} - \bar{\alpha}\right)\Delta f(x_1)\right.$$

$$\left. + \left(\frac{\bar{\alpha}^3}{6} - \frac{3\bar{\alpha}^2}{4} + \bar{\alpha}\right)\Delta^2 f(x_1) + \cdots\right].$$

$$(2.28)$$

The corresponding error term is given by

$$h\int_0^{\bar{\alpha}} R_{n-2}(x_0 + \alpha h)\,d\alpha$$

$$= h^n\int_0^{\bar{\alpha}} \frac{(\alpha-1)(\alpha-2)\cdots(\alpha-n+1)}{(n-1)!}f^{(n-1)}(\xi)\,d\alpha,$$

$$(2.29)$$

where $x_0 < \xi < b$.

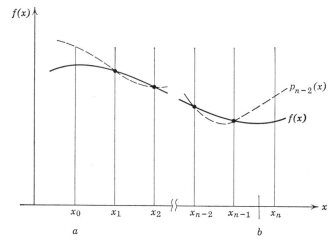

Figure 2.7   General case for open integration.

Equations (2.28) and (2.29) describe a family of related integration formulas. If the upper limit b is chosen to coincide with one of the base points so that integration is across m intervals, each of width h (that is, the integral is evaluated between $a = x_0$ and $b = x_m$), then $\bar{\alpha}$ in (2.28) and (2.29) assumes the integral value m. The choice of n is still open. The usual choice is $n = \bar{\alpha}$, that is, the integral corresponds to that shown in Fig. 2.2c.

Evaluation of (2.28) and (2.29) for integral values of $\bar{\alpha}$ and $n = \bar{\alpha}$ leads to the family of *Newton-Cotes open integration formulas*:

$\bar{\alpha} = 2$:

$$\int_{x_0}^{x_2} f(x)\,dx = 2hf(x_1) + \frac{h^3}{3}f''(\xi). \quad (2.30a)$$

$\bar{\alpha} = 3$:

$$\int_{x_0}^{x_3} f(x)\,dx = \frac{3h}{2}\left[f(x_1) + f(x_2)\right] + \frac{3h^3}{4}f''(\xi). \quad (2.30b)$$

$\bar{\alpha} = 4$:

$$\int_{x_0}^{x_4} f(x)\,dx = \frac{4h}{3}\left[2f(x_1) - f(x_2) + 2f(x_3)\right]$$

$$+ \frac{14h^5}{45}f^{(4)}(\xi). \quad (2.30c)$$

$\bar{\alpha} = 5$:

$$\int_{x_0}^{x_5} f(x)\,dx = \frac{5h}{24}\left[11f(x_1) + f(x_2)\right.$$

$$\left. + f(x_3) + 11f(x_4)\right] + \frac{95h^5}{144}f^{(4)}(\xi). \quad (2.30d)$$

$\bar{\alpha} = 6$:

$$\int_{x_0}^{x_6} f(x)\,dx = \frac{3h}{10}\left[11f(x_1) - 14f(x_2) + 26f(x_3)\right.$$

$$\left. - 14f(x_4) + 11f(x_5)\right] + \frac{41h^7}{140}f^{(6)}(\xi). \quad (2.30e)$$

When $\bar{\alpha}$ is *even*, that is, when the formulas involve an even number of intervals or an odd number of base points, they are exact for $f(x)$ a polynomial of degree $\bar{\alpha} - 1$ or less. When $\bar{\alpha}$ is *odd*, the formulas are exact for $f(x)$ a polynomial of degree $\bar{\alpha} - 2$ or less. For even values of $\bar{\alpha}$, the coefficient of $\Delta^{\bar{\alpha}-1}f(x_1)$ in (2.28) becomes zero. Then the error term of (2.29) involves a derivative of order $\bar{\alpha}$ rather than of $\bar{\alpha} - 1$, as would be expected. For this reason the odd-point formulas are more frequently used than the even-point formulas.

2.5   Integration Error Using the Newton-Cotes Formulas

Provided that $f(x)$ is continuous and has derivatives of suitably high order, the error terms for the closed and open formulas of (2.21) and (2.30) apply. Error terms for the Newton-Cotes formulas are of the form $ch^k f^{(k-1)}(\xi)$, ξ in (a,b), where c is some constant, different for each formula. Comparison of closed and open formulas, requiring the same number of functional values, shows the open formulas to be slightly better when two or three points are used; for more than three points the closed formulas are considerably more accurate than the open ones. This conclusion requires the assumption that the derivative terms $f^{(k-1)}(\xi)$ are roughly the same for the two formulas. Therefore, where applicable, closed rather than open formulas should be used.

The m-point formulas for odd m are of the same order of accuracy as the $m + 1$-point formulas; both are said to have *degree of precision* m. A formula with degree of precision m will integrate all polynomials of degree m or less exactly. Polynomials of higher degree will not be integrated exactly. Thus Simpson's rule possesses degree of precision three since it will produce exactly the integral of all polynomials of degree three or less. Except for the trapezoidal rule, which is often used because of its simplicity, formulas with an odd number of base-point functional values are usually preferred over those with an even number of points.

Because the degree of precision of the Newton-Cotes formulas increases with the number of points, we might suspect that a very high-order formula would be more accurate than a low-order formula. Unfortunately, the *m*-point formulas for large *m* have some very undesirable properties from the computational standpoint. The weight factors tend to be large with alternating signs, which can lead to serious rounding errors, that is, errors introduced because only a fixed, usually small, number of digits can be retained after each computer operation. In addition there exist many functions for which the magnitude of the derivative increases without bound as the order of differentiation increases. Therefore, a high-order formula may produce a larger error than a low-order one. Formulas employing more than eight points are almost never used.

If $f(x)$ is known analytically, then it may be possible to determine the appropriate high-order derivative and examine its behavior on the interval $[a,b]$ to establish an error bound for the particular formula chosen. In many practical situations, however, the error formula is of little direct value since an expression for the derivative may not be available. In some cases, it might be possible to estimate the required derivative value from high-order, finite divided differences of the functional values.

Even when one has no information about higher-order derivatives, it may be possible to estimate the error if the integral is computed using two different integration formulas with comparable degrees of precision. For example, consider the evaluation of

$$I^* = \int_a^b f(x)\, dx$$

by using the three- and four-point closed formulas of (2.21b) and (2.21c), that is, Simpson's first and second rules, each of degree of precision three. Let I_1 and E_1 be the estimate of I^* and the error, respectively, resulting from the use of Simpson's first rule, and let I_2 and E_2 be like quantities, resulting from the use of Simpson's second rule. Then

$$I^* = I_1 + E_1 = I_2 + E_2. \qquad (2.31)$$

In terms of the integration limits a and b, we can write

$$\frac{E_1}{E_2} = \frac{-\dfrac{(b-a)^5}{2880} f^{(4)}(\xi_1)}{-\dfrac{(b-a)^5}{6480} f^{(4)}(\xi_2)} \qquad (2.32)$$

where ξ_1 and ξ_2 are different values of ξ in (a,b). If we

assume that $f^{(4)}(\xi_1)$ approximately equals $f^{(4)}(\xi_2)$, then (2.32) reduces to

$$E_1 = \tfrac{9}{4} E_2 \qquad (2.33)$$

and (2.31) becomes

$$I^* = \tfrac{9}{5} I_2 - \tfrac{4}{5} I_1. \qquad (2.34)$$

The validity of (2.34) hinges completely upon the assumption that $f^{(4)}(\xi_1)$ and $f^{(4)}(\xi_2)$ are equal.

Example. Evaluate

$$\int_a^b \mathrm{f}(x)\, dx = \int_1^3 (x^3 - 2x^2 + 7x + 5)\, dx = 20\tfrac{2}{3} \qquad (2.35)$$

by using the trapezoidal rule (2.21a) and the one-point open formula of (2.30a), each with degree of precision one. Then estimate I^* by using the technique outlined above. For this polynomial function [see (2.23)], the estimates of I^* computed from (2.21a) and (2.30a) are, respectively, $I_1 = 26$ and $I_2 = 18$. The ratio of error terms is

$$\frac{E_1}{E_2} = \frac{-\dfrac{(b-a)^3}{12} f''(\xi_1)}{\dfrac{(b-a)^3}{24} f''(\xi_2)}, \qquad \xi_1, \xi_2 \text{ in } (a,b). \qquad (2.36)$$

Assuming that $f''(\xi_1)$ is equal to $f''(\xi_2)$ leads to

$$E_1 = -2E_2. \qquad (2.37)$$

Note that for this case, the open formula is apparently more accurate than the closed formula of identical degree of precision (not the usual case). Substitution of (2.37) into (2.31) leads to

$$I^* = \frac{1}{3} I_1 + \frac{2}{3} I_2 = \frac{26}{3} + \frac{2 \times 18}{3} = 20\tfrac{2}{3}, \qquad (2.38)$$

which is the true value of the integral in this case. Upon closer examination, (2.38) is seen to reduce to

$$I^* = \tfrac{1}{3}[f(1) + 4f(2) + f(3)], \qquad (2.39)$$

[Simpson's rule (2.21b)]. Thus the expression of the error in terms of two formulas with degree of precision one has resulted in a compound formula with degree of precision three.

2.6 Composite Integration Formulas

One way to reduce the error associated with a low-order integration formula is to subdivide the interval of integration $[a,b]$ into smaller intervals and then to use the formula separately on each subinterval. Repeated application of a low-order formula is usually preferred to the single application of a high-order formula, partly because of the simplicity of the low-order formulas and partly because of computational difficulties, already mentioned in the previous section, associated with the high-order formulas. Integration formulas resulting from interval subdivision and repeated application of a low-order formula are called *composite* integration formulas.

Although any of the Newton-Cotes or other simple (one-application) formulas can be written in composite form, the closed formulas are especially attractive since, except for the base points $x = a$ and $x = b$, base points at the ends of each subinterval are also base points for adjacent subintervals. Thus, although one might suspect that n repeated applications of an m-point formula would require nm functional evaluations, in fact only $n(m-1)+1$ such evaluations are needed, a considerable saving, especially when m is small.

The simplest composite formula is generated by repeated application of the trapezoidal rule of (2.21a). For n applications of the rule, each subinterval is of length $h = (b - a)/n$. Let $x_i = x_0 + ih$, $i = 0, 1, \ldots, n$. Then

$$\int_a^b f(x)\,dx = \int_{x_0}^{x_n} f(x)\,dx = \int_{x_0}^{x_1} f(x)\,dx$$

$$+ \int_{x_1}^{x_2} f(x)\,dx + \cdots + \int_{x_{n-1}}^{x_n} f(x)\,dx$$

$$= \frac{h}{2} [f(x_0) + f(x_1)]$$

$$+ \frac{h}{2} [f(x_1) + f(x_2)] + \cdots$$

$$+ \frac{h}{2} [f(x_{n-1}) + f(x_n)]$$

$$- \frac{h^3}{12} \sum_{i=1}^n f''(\xi_i), \qquad x_{i-1} < \xi_i < x_i.$$

$$(2.40)$$

Collecting common terms in (2.40) leads to

$$\int_{x_0}^{x_n} f(x)\,dx = \frac{h}{2} [f(x_0) + 2f(x_1) + 2f(x_2) + \cdots$$

$$+ 2f(x_{n-1}) + f(x_n)]$$

$$- \frac{h^3}{12} \sum_{i=1}^n f''(\xi_i)$$

$$= \frac{h}{2} [f(x_0) + f(x_n)] + h \sum_{i=1}^{n-1} f(x_i)$$

$$- \frac{h^3}{12} \sum_{i=1}^n f''(\xi_i), \qquad x_{i-1} < \xi_i < x_i.$$

$$(2.41)$$

In terms of n, the number of applications of the rule, and a and b, the integration limits, the composite formula is

$$\int_a^b f(x)\,dx = \frac{(b - a)}{n} \left[\frac{1}{2}f(a) + \frac{1}{2}f(b) \right.$$

$$\left. + \sum_{i=1}^{n-1} f\left(a + \frac{(b - a)}{n} i \right) \right]$$

$$- \frac{(b - a)^3}{12n^2} f''(\xi), \qquad a < \xi < b.$$

$$(2.42)$$

The error term of (2.41) simplifies to that of (2.42) because the continuous function $f''(x)$ assumes all values between its extreme values. Therefore, there must be some ξ in (a,b) for which

$$n f''(\xi) = \sum_{i=1}^n f''(\xi_i), \qquad x_{i-1} < \xi_i < x_i.$$

The error for the composite trapezoidal formula is proportional to $1/n^2$. Therefore, if we double the number of applications, the error will decrease *roughly* by a factor of four [$f''(\xi)$ will usually be different for two different values of n]. This form of the error term suggests a technique, similar to that outlined in (2.31) to (2.34), for estimating the error. In this case, the same composite formula is used with two different values of n; in (2.31) to (2.34) two different simple (one-application) formulas are used.

Let I_n and E_n be, respectively, the estimate of the integral and the associated error for n applications of the composite trapezoidal formula. Then the true value of the integral is

$$I^* = I_{n_1} + E_{n_1} = I_{n_2} + E_{n_2} \qquad (2.43)$$

where n_1 and n_2 are two different values of n. From (2.42),

$$\frac{E_{n_2}}{E_{n_1}} = \frac{- \dfrac{(b - a)^3}{12n_2^2} f''(\xi_2)}{- \dfrac{(b - a)^3}{12n_1^2} f''(\xi_1)}, \qquad \xi_1, \xi_2 \text{ in } (a,b).$$

$$(2.44)$$

Assuming that $f''(\xi_1)$ and $f''(\xi_2)$ are equal, (2.44) reduces to

$$E_{n_2} = \left[\frac{n_1}{n_2} \right]^2 E_{n_1}. \qquad (2.45)$$

Substitution of (2.45) into (2.43) leads to

$$I^* = I_{n_1} + \frac{I_{n_2} - I_{n_1}}{1 - \left[\dfrac{n_1}{n_2} \right]^2}. \qquad (2.46)$$

For $n_2 = 2n_1$, (2.46) becomes

$$I^* = \tfrac{4}{3} I_{n_2} - \tfrac{1}{3} I_{n_1}. \qquad (2.47)$$

This kind of approach in which two approximations to an integral are used to get a third (hopefully better) approximation is called *Richardson's deferred approach to the limit* or *Richardson's extrapolation*.

For n applications of Simpson's rule, functional values are required at $2n + 1$ base points $x_0, x_1, \ldots, x_{2n}$. The composite Simpson's rule formula is

$$\int_a^b f(x)\,dx = \int_{x_0}^{x_{2n}} f(x)\,dx = \frac{h}{3}\left[f(x_0) + 4f(x_1) + 2f(x_2) + 4f(x_3) + 2f(x_4)\right.$$

$$\left. + \cdots + 2f(x_{2n-2}) + 4f(x_{2n-1}) + f(x_{2n})\right] - \frac{h^5}{90}\sum_{i=1}^{n} f^{(4)}(\xi_i) \tag{2.48}$$

where

$$x_{2i-2} < \xi_i < x_{2i}, \qquad h = \frac{b-a}{2n}, \qquad \text{and} \quad x_i = x_0 + ih,\ i = 0, 1, \ldots, 2n.$$

In terms of a, b, and n, (2.48) is given by

$$\int_a^b f(x)\,dx = \frac{(b-a)}{6n}\left[f(a) + f(b) + 2\sum_{i=1}^{n-1} f\left(a + \frac{(b-a)}{n}i\right)\right.$$

$$\left. + 4\sum_{\substack{i=1 \\ \Delta i = 2}}^{2n-1} f\left(a + \frac{(b-a)}{2n}i\right)\right] - \frac{(b-a)^5}{2880n^4} f^{(4)}(\xi) \tag{2.49}$$

where $a < \xi < b$. In the second sum, $\Delta i = 2$ indicates that the index i should assume only odd values.

If Richardson's extrapolation technique is applied to (2.49), the relationship corresponding to equation (2.46) for the composite trapezoidal rule is

$$I^* = I_{n_1} + \frac{I_{n_2} - I_{n_1}}{1 - \left[\dfrac{n_1}{n_2}\right]^4}. \tag{2.50}$$

For $n_2 = 2n_1$, (2.50) becomes

$$I^* = \frac{16}{15} I_{n_2} - \frac{1}{15} I_{n_1}. \tag{2.51}$$

Composite formulas similar to those of (2.42) and (2.49) can be generated for any of the low-order integration formulas.

Example. Evaluate the integral of (2.35) by using first two and then four applications of the composite trapezoidal rule. Then perform Richardson's extrapolation, given by (2.47), to find a third estimate of the integral.

Let $n_1 = 2$ and $n_2 = 4$. Then (2.42) yields (see Fig. 2.8),

$$I_{n_1} = \frac{(3-1)}{2}\left[\frac{1}{2} + \frac{25}{2} + 9\right] = 22$$

$$I_{n_2} = \frac{(3-1)}{4}\left[\frac{1}{2} + \frac{25}{2} + 4\tfrac{3}{8} + 9 + 15\tfrac{5}{8}\right] = 21$$

and substitution into (2.47) gives a third estimate,

$$I^* = \tfrac{4}{3}(21) - \tfrac{1}{3}(22) = 20\tfrac{2}{3}.$$

The true value of the integral is $20\tfrac{2}{3}$ and the actual errors for these three estimates of the integral are $4/3$, $1/3$, and 0. On closer examination (2.47) is seen to be equivalent to Simpson's rule; hence I^* should be free of error in this case, since $f(x)$ is a polynomial of degree three.

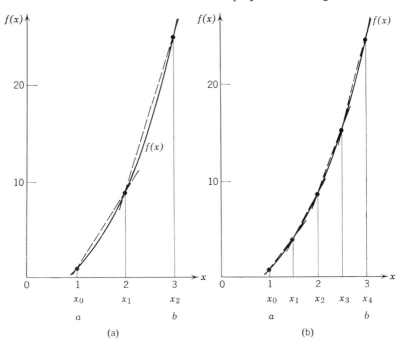

Figure 2.8   *Repeated application of the trapezoidal rule.*   **(*a*) *Two applications.***   **(*b*) *Four applications.***

EXAMPLE 2.1

RADIANT INTERCHANGE BETWEEN PARALLEL PLATES
COMPOSITE SIMPSON'S RULE

Introduction

Two infinitely long parallel plates of width w are separated by a distance d, as shown in Fig. 2.1.1. Their surfaces are gray, isothermal, diffusely radiating and reflecting, and have temperatures T_1 and T_2 and emissivities ε_1 and ε_2.

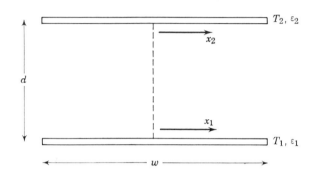

Figure 2.1.1   Geometry of parallel plates.

It can be shown that the local *radiosities* B_1 and B_2 (defined as the rates at which emitted plus reflected radiation leave unit area of each surface) are the solution of the simultaneous integral equations:

$$B_1(x_1) = \varepsilon_1\sigma T_1^4 + (1 - \varepsilon_1)\int_{-w/2}^{w/2} B_2(x_2)f(x_1, x_2, d)\,dx_2,$$

$$(2.1.1)$$

$$B_2(x_2) = \varepsilon_2\sigma T_2^4 + (1 - \varepsilon_2)\int_{-w/2}^{w/2} B_1(x_1)f(x_1, x_2, d)\,dx_1,$$

$$(2.1.2)$$

in which σ is the Stefan-Boltzmann constant, and

$$f(x_1, x_2, d) = \frac{1}{2}\frac{d^2}{[d^2 + (x_1 - x_2)^2]^{3/2}}. \quad (2.1.3)$$

The integral in equation (2.1.1) is the *irradiosity*, $I_1 = I_1(x_1)$, being the rate per unit area of incident radiation at a point x_1 on the lower plate. The integral arises because radiation emitted from all points along the upper plate has been taken into account. Similarly, the integral in (2.1.2) is I_2, the irradiosity at the upper plate.

The net rates at which heat must be supplied to unit length of the lower and upper surfaces, to keep them at steady temperatures, are

$$Q_1 = \int_{-w/2}^{w/2} (B_1 - I_1)\,dx_1, \quad (2.1.4)$$

$$Q_2 = \int_{-w/2}^{w/2} (B_2 - I_2)\,dx_2. \quad (2.1.5)$$

Problem Statement

Write a computer program that will accept values for T_1, T_2, ε_1, ε_2, d, w, σ, and n (see below), and that will proceed to compute:

(a) The emissive powers, $E_1 = \varepsilon_1\sigma T_1^4$ and $E_2 = \varepsilon_2\sigma T_2^4$, for the two plates.
(b) The local radiosities B_1 and B_2 at the discrete points having x_1 and x_2 equal to 0, Δx, $2\Delta x$, ..., $n\Delta x$, where $\Delta x = w/2n$.
(c) The local irradiosities I_1 and I_2 at the same points as in (b).
(d) The net heat inputs Q_1 and Q_2 at the two plates.

Use Simpson's rule for approximating the integrals in the above equations. Assume symmetry of B_1 and I_1 about the centerline $x_1 = 0$, and of B_2 and I_2 about $x_2 = 0$.

Method of Solution

We first write a function, named SIMPS, that will evaluate the general integral $\int_a^b f(x)dx$ by n repeated applications of Simpson's rule, as discussed in Section 2.6. The appropriate composite integration formula is readily derived from equation (2.49):

$$\int_a^b f(x)\,dx \doteq \frac{h}{3}\left[2\sum_{\substack{i=0\\ \Delta i=2}}^{2n-2} f(x_i) + 4\sum_{\substack{i=1\\ \Delta i=2}}^{2n-1} f(x_i) - f(a) + f(b)\right],$$

$$(2.1.6)$$

where $h = (b - a)/2n$ and $x_i = a + ih$. An appropriate call for the function could be

$$\text{AREA} = \text{SIMPS}\,(A, B, N, F)$$

in which A, B, and N have obvious interpretations, and F is the name of the function to be integrated.

Figure 2.1.2, corresponding to $n = 2$, emphasizes that we compute B_1, for example, at only $n + 1$ points, to which we can assign subscripts $i = 0, 1, ..., n$. From symmetry, $B_{1(-i)} = B_{1i}$.

The basic approach is straightforward. As a starting guess, assume $B_1 = E_1$ and $B_2 = E_2$ everywhere. The

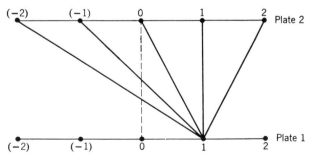

Figure 2.1.2 B_1 and B_2 are computed at discrete points only.

right-hand sides of (2.1.1) and (2.1.2) can then be evaluated, enabling new estimates to be made of the distributions of B_1 and B_2. These values are cycled back into the two integrals, giving revised estimates, and so on. Iterations are discontinued either when *itmax* iterations have been made or when B_1 and B_2 at all points do not change by more than a fractional amount δ. This approach to the solution is an example of a successive substitution method for solution of simultaneous nonlinear equations. Successive substitution methods are discussed in Chapter 5.

Note that the number of applications of Simpson's rule is n, which is also the number of increments Δx along each half of the plate. For example, if $n = 2$, an estimation of B_{11} from (2.1.1) will involve five values of B_2: $B_{2(-2)}$, $B_{2(-1)}$, B_{20}, B_{21}, and B_{22}, which are just enough for two applications of Simpson's rule.

Since the function SIMPS evaluates the integrand at definite values of the continuous variables x_1 and x_2, a translation must be made (achieved in the program by the function ISUB) between these continuous variables and the appropriate subscripts for the point values such as B_{1i}. For this purpose we use, for example, $i = |x_1/\Delta x| + 0.001$, rounded down to the next lower integer. Here, the absolute value sign accounts for symmetry, and the small increment of 0.001 avoids any complications of round-off error when $x_1/\Delta x$ is evaluated. There are also other complications in the programming, mainly arising from the fact that SIMPS needs a single function name for the integrand, whereas the integrands of (2.1.1), (2.1.2), (2.1.4), and (2.1.5) involve either the product or difference of *two* functions. This difficulty is overcome by defining additional functions, such as FB1, which stands for the product of $B_1(x_1)$ and $f(x_1, x_2, d)$.

Flow Diagram
Main Program

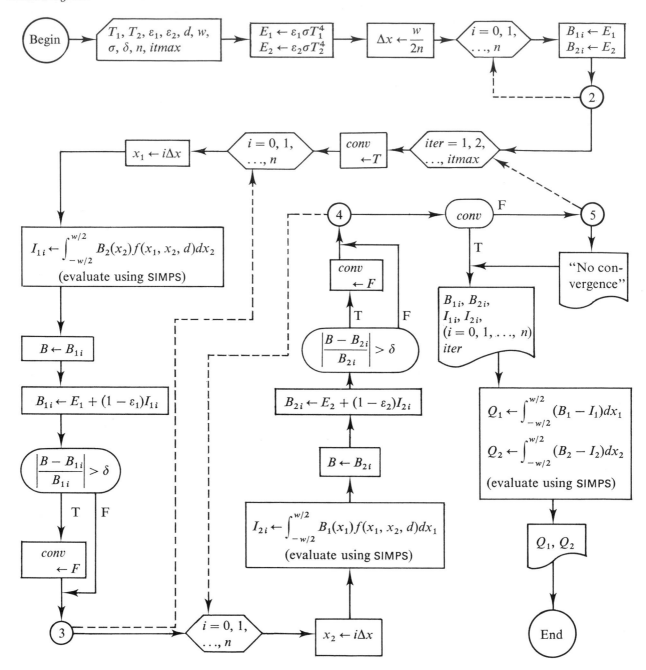

Function SIMPS (Arguments: a, b, n, f)

FORTRAN *Implementation*

List of Principal Variables

Program Symbol	Definition
(Main)	
B1, B2†	Vectors, containing the radiosities B_{1i} and B_{2i} at each point i (BTU/hr sq ft).
CONV	Logical variable used in testing for convergence.
D	Separation between the plates, d (ft).
DIF1, DIF2	Functions, giving the differences $(B_1(x_1) - I_1(x_1))$ and $(B_2(x_2) - I_2(x_2))$, respectively.
DX	Spacing, Δx, between points at which radiosities are computed (ft).
E1, E2	Emissive powers, $E_1 = \varepsilon_1 \sigma T_1^4$ and $E_2 = \varepsilon_2 \sigma T_2^4$ (BTU/hr sq ft).
EPS1, EPS2	Emissivities, ε_1 and ε_2, of the lower and upper plates, respectively.
FB1, FB2	Functions, giving the products $B_1(x_1)f(x_1, x_2, d)$ and $B_2(x_2)f(x_1, x_2, d)$, respectively.
I†	Subscript, indicating point at which radiosity is being computed.
INT1, INT2†	Vectors, containing the irradiosities I_{1i} and I_{2i} at each point i (BTU/hr sq ft).
ITER	Counter on the number of iterations, *iter*.
ITMAX	Maximum number of iterations allowed, *itmax*.
N	Number of increments, n, into which one half of each plate is subdivided.
Q1, Q2	Heat supplied to the lower and upper plates, Q_1 and Q_2, respectively (BTU/hr ft).
SAVE	Temporary storage for radiosities, B.
SIGMA	Stefan-Boltzmann constant, σ (1.712×10^{-9} BTU/hr sq ft $°R^4$).
SIMPS	Function for implementing Simpson's rule.
T1, T2	Temperatures, T_1 and T_2 ($°R$), of the lower and upper plates, respectively.
TOL	Tolerance, δ, used in convergence testing.
W	Plate width, w (ft).
X	Distance from centerline (ft), either x_1 or x_2.
XHIGH, XLOW	Upper and lower limits on X.
(Function FB1)	
ISUB	Function for converting distance to corresponding subscript.
F	Function for evaluating equation (2.1.3).
(Function SIMPS)	
H	Stepsize, h.
SUMEND, SUMMID	The first and second summations of (2.1.6), S_e and S_m, respectively.

† Because of FORTRAN limitations, we have $1 \leqslant I \leqslant N + 1$, corresponding to $0 \leqslant i \leqslant n$; thus, B_{10} through B_{1n} in the text correspond to B1(1) through B1(N + 1) in the program.

Program Listing

Main Program

```
C           APPLIED NUMERICAL METHODS, EXAMPLE 2.1
C           SIMULTANEOUS INTEGRAL EQUATIONS - COMPOSITE SIMPSON'S RULE
C
C           THIS PROGRAM COMPUTES THE RADIANT HEAT TRANSFER BETWEEN TWO
C           INFINITE, ISOTHERMAL, OPPOSED PARALLEL PLATES OF WIDTH W,
C           SEPARATED BY A DISTANCE D.   THE PLATES HAVE TEMPERATURES
C           T1 AND T2, AND EMISSIVITIES EPS1 AND EPS2.  SIGMA IS THE
C           STEFAN-BOLTZMANN CONSTANT.  THE ITERATIVE SOLUTION OF TWO
C           SIMULTANEOUS INTEGRAL EQUATIONS GIVES VALUES FOR THE RADIO-
C           SITIES, B1 AND B2, AND THE IRRADIOSITIES, I1 AND I2, AS FUNC-
C           TIONS OF POSITION.  THESE VALUES ARE OBTAINED AT A SERIES OF
C           N+1 POINTS EQUALLY SPACED BETWEEN THE CENTER (B1(1), FOR
C           EXAMPLE) AND THE EDGE (B1(N+1)) OF EACH PLATE.  THE FUNCTION
C           SIMPS IS USED TO EVALUATE INTEGRALS BY N REPEATED APPLICATIONS
C           OF SIMPSON'S RULE.  Q1 AND Q2 ARE THE NET RATES OF HEAT TRANS-
C           FER TO THE PLATES TO MAINTAIN THEM AT CONSTANT TEMPERATURES.
C           THE ITERATIONS STOP EITHER WHEN ITMAX ITERATIONS HAVE BEEN
C           PERFORMED OR WHEN NO COMPUTED RADIOSITY CHANGES BY MORE THAN
C           A FRACTIONAL AMOUNT TOL FROM ONE ITERATION TO THE NEXT.
C
      REAL INT1, INT2
      LOGICAL CONV
      COMMON B1, B2, W, N, X, DSQ, INT1, INT2
      DIMENSION B1(1025), B2(1025), INT1(1025), INT2(1025)
      EXTERNAL FB1, FB2, DIF1, DIF2
C
C      ..... READ INPUT DATA AND COMPUTE EMISSIVE POWERS .....
    1 READ (5,100)  T1, T2, EPS1, EPS2, D, W, SIGMA, TOL, N, ITMAX
      E1 = EPS1*SIGMA*T1**4
      E2 = EPS2*SIGMA*T2**4
      XHIGH = W/2.
      XLOW = - XHIGH
      WRITE (6,200)   T1, T2, EPS1, EPS2, D, W, SIGMA, TOL, N, ITMAX,
    1    E1, E2, XLOW, XHIGH
C
C      ..... COMPUTE CONSTANTS, GUESS INITIAL RADIOSITIES .....
      DSQ = D*D
      DX = W/FLOAT(2*N)
      NP1 = N + 1
      DO 2   I=1,NP1
      B1(I) = E1
    2 B2(I) = E2
C
C      ..... PERFORM SUCCESSIVE ITERATIONS .....
      DO 5   ITER=1,ITMAX
      CONV = .TRUE.
C
C      ..... COMPUTE RADIOSITIES ACROSS STRIP ONE .....
      DO 3   I=1,NP1
      X = FLOAT(I-1)*DX
      INT1(I) = SIMPS(XLOW,XHIGH,N,FB2)
      SAVE = B1(I)
      B1(I) = E1 + (1.0-EPS1)*INT1(I)
    3 IF ( ABS((SAVE-B1(I))/B1(I)) .GT. TOL )   CONV = .FALSE.
C
C      ..... COMPUTE RADIOSITIES ACROSS STRIP TWO .....
      DO 4   I=1,NP1
      X = FLOAT(I-1)*DX
      INT2(I) = SIMPS(XLOW,XHIGH,N,FB1)
      SAVE = B2(I)
      B2(I) = E2 + (1.0-EPS2)*INT2(I)
    4 IF ( ABS((SAVE-B2(I))/B2(I)) .GT. TOL )   CONV = .FALSE.
C
C      ..... TEST FOR CONVERGENCE OF ITERATION SCHEME .....
    5 IF ( CONV )   GO TO 6
C
C      ..... PRINT OUTPUT .....
      WRITE (6,201)
    6 WRITE (6,202)  ITER, (I,B1(I),B2(I),INT1(I),INT2(I), I=1,NP1)
```

Program Listing *(Continued)*

```
C
C        ..... COMPUTE HEAT TRANSFER RATE PER UNIT PLATE LENGTH .....
         Q1 = SIMPS(XLOW,XHIGH,N,DIF1)
         Q2 = SIMPS(XLOW,XHIGH,N,DIF2)
         WRITE (6,203)   Q1, Q2
C
         GO TO 1
C
C        ..... FORMATS FOR INPUT AND OUTPUT STATEMENTS .....
  100    FORMAT( 4X, F8.2, 12X, F8.2, 2(14X, F6.2)/4X, F8.2, 12X, F8.2,
     1      14X,E10.3,10X, E6.1/ 5X, I5, 20X, I5 )
  200    FORMAT(55H1RADIANT HEAT TRANSFER BETWEEN INFINITE PARALLEL PLATES/
     1      10H0T1      = ,F12.2/ 10H T2      = ,F12.2/ 10H EPS1   = ,F12.2/
     2      10H EPS2    = ,F12.2/ 10H D       = ,F12.2/ 10H W      = ,F12.2/
     3      10H SIGMA   = ,E18.4/ 10H TOL     = ,E18.4/ 10H N      = ,I9/
     4      10H ITMAX   = ,I9  / 10H E1       = ,E18.4/ 10H E2     = ,E18.4/
     5      10H XLOW    = ,F12.2/ 10H XHIGH   = ,F12.2 )
  201    FORMAT( 36H0CONVERGENCE CRITERION NOT SATISFIED )
  202    FORMAT( 1H0/ 10H ITER     = , I9/ 6H0    I,5X, 5HB1(I), 10X,5HB2(I),
     1      10X,7HINT1(I), 8X, 7HINT2(I)/ (1H , I5, 4E15.6) )
  203    FORMAT( 1H0/10H0Q1       = , E15.6/ 10H Q2       = , E15.6 )
C
         END
```

Functions FB1, FB2, DIF1, DIF2,

```
         FUNCTION FB1(Y)
C
         REAL INT1, INT2
         COMMON B1, B2, W, N, X, DSQ, INT1, INT2
         DIMENSION B1(1025), B2(1025), INT1(1025), INT2(1025)
C
C        ..... STATEMENT FUNCTION DEFINITIONS .....
         ISUB(P) = INT(ABS(2.0*P/W)*FLOAT(N) + 0.001) + 1
         F(P) = 0.5*DSQ/(DSQ + (X-P)**2)**1.5
C
         I = ISUB(Y)
         FB1 = B1(I)*F(Y)
         RETURN
C
         ENTRY FB2(Y)
         I = ISUB(Y)
         FB2 = B2(I)*F(Y)
         RETURN
C
         ENTRY DIF1(Y)
         I = ISUB(Y)
         DIF1 = B1(I) - INT1(I)
         RETURN
C
         ENTRY DIF2(Y)
         I = ISUB(Y)
         DIF2 = B2(I) - INT2(I)
         RETURN
C
         END
```

Function SIMPS

```
         FUNCTION SIMPS( A, B, N, F )
C
C        THE FUNCTION SIMPS USES N APPLICATIONS OF SIMPSON'S RULE
C        TO CALCULATE NUMERICALLY THE INTEGRAL OF F(X)*DX BETWEEN
C        INTEGRATION LIMITS A AND B.   SUMEND IS THE SUM OF ALL F(X(I))
C        FOR EVEN I (EXCEPT FOR F(X(2*N)) WHILE SUMMID IS THE SUM OF
C        ALL F(X(I)) FOR I ODD.    H IS THE STEPSIZE BETWEEN ADJACENT
C        X(I) AND TWOH IS THE LENGTH OF THE INTERVAL OF INTEGRATION
```

Program Listing (*Continued*)

```
C            FOR EACH INDIVIDUAL APPLICATION OF SIMPSON'S RULE.  K IS THE
C            ITERATION COUNTER.
C
C        ..... INITIALIZE PARAMETERS .....
         TWOH = (B-A)/N
         H = TWOH/2.
         SUMEND = 0.
         SUMMID = 0.
C
C        ..... EVALUATE SUMEND AND SUMMID .....
         DO 1   K=1,N
         X = A + FLOAT(K-1)*TWOH
         SUMEND = SUMEND + F(X)
       1 SUMMID = SUMMID + F(X+H)
C
C        ..... RETURN ESTIMATED VALUE OF THE INTEGRAL .....
         SIMPS = (2.0*SUMEND + 4.0*SUMMID - F(A) + F(B))*H/3.
         RETURN
C
         END
```

Data

```
T1 = 1000.00        T2 =  500.00        EPS1 =  0.80        EPS2 =  0.60
D  =    1.00        W  =    1.00        SIGMA= 1.712E-9     TOL  =1.0E-6
N  =    2           ITMAX =     25
T1 = 1000.00        T2 =  500.00        EPS1 =  0.80        EPS2 =  0.60
D  =    1.00        W  =    1.00        SIGMA= 1.712E-9     TOL  =1.0E-6
N  =    8           ITMAX =     25
T1 = 1000.00        T2 =  800.00        EPS1 =  0.20        EPS2 =  0.60
D  =    1.00        W  =    1.00        SIGMA= 1.712E-9     TOL  =1.0E-6
N  =    2           ITMAX =     25
```

Computer Output

Results for the 1st Data Set

```
RADIANT HEAT TRANSFER BETWEEN INFINITE PARALLEL PLATES

T1      =        1000.00
T2      =         500.00
EPS1    =           0.80
EPS2    =           0.60
D       =           1.00
W       =           1.00
SIGMA   =        0.1712E-08
TOL     =        0.1000E-05
N       =        2
ITMAX   =       25
E1      =        0.1370E 04
E2      =        0.6420E 02
XLOW    =         -0.50
XHIGH   =          0.50


ITER    =        1

    I      B1(I)           B2(I)           INT1(I)          INT2(I)
    1   0.137534E 04    0.310218E 03    0.287179E 02    0.615045E 03
    2   0.137501E 04    0.295956E 03    0.270533E 02    0.579390E 03
    3   0.137414E 04    0.258636E 03    0.226972E 02    0.486090E 03


ITER    =        2

    I      B1(I)           B2(I)           INT1(I)          INT2(I)
    1   0.139587E 04    0.313637E 03    0.131350E 03    0.623594E 03
    2   0.139432E 04    0.299172E 03    0.123582E 03    0.587430E 03
    3   0.139027E 04    0.261324E 03    0.103378E 03    0.492810E 03
```

Computer Output (*Continued*)

```
ITER    =       3

     I      B1(I)          B2(I)          INT1(I)        INT2(I)
     1   0.139615E 04   0.313685E 03   0.132774E 03   0.623712E 03
     2   0.139458E 04   0.299217E 03   0.124922E 03   0.587542E 03
     3   0.139050E 04   0.261361E 03   0.104497E 03   0.492903E 03


ITER    =       4

     I      B1(I)          B2(I)          INT1(I)        INT2(I)
     1   0.139616E 04   0.313685E 03   0.132794E 03   0.623714E 03
     2   0.139459E 04   0.299218E 03   0.124940E 03   0.587544E 03
     3   0.139050E 04   0.261362E 03   0.104512E 03   0.492904E 03


ITER    =       5

     I      B1(I)          B2(I)          INT1(I)        INT2(I)
     1   0.139616E 04   0.313685E 03   0.132794E 03   0.623714E 03
     2   0.139459E 04   0.299218E 03   0.124941E 03   0.587544E 03
     3   0.139050E 04   0.261362E 03   0.104513E 03   0.492904E 03



Q1      =    0.127132E 04
Q2      =   -0.282479E 03
```

Partial Results for the 2nd Data Set (Same as 1st Set, with N=8)

```
ITER    =       5

     I      B1(I)          B2(I)          INT1(I)        INT2(I)
     1   0.139614E 04   0.313623E 03   0.132720E 03   0.623557E 03
     2   0.139604E 04   0.312689E 03   0.132211E 03   0.621222E 03
     3   0.139574E 04   0.309910E 03   0.130698E 03   0.614276E 03
     4   0.139524E 04   0.305357E 03   0.128221E 03   0.602894E 03
     5   0.139457E 04   0.299145E 03   0.124847E 03   0.587362E 03
     6   0.139373E 04   0.291429E 03   0.120666E 03   0.568073E 03
     7   0.139276E 04   0.282407E 03   0.115787E 03   0.545517E 03
     8   0.139167E 04   0.272303E 03   0.110338E 03   0.520258E 03
     9   0.139049E 04   0.261365E 03   0.104454E 03   0.492914E 03



Q1      =    0.127141E 04
Q2      =   -0.282314E 03
```

Partial Results for the 3rd Data Set

```
RADIANT HEAT TRANSFER BETWEEN INFINITE PARALLEL PLATES

T1      =        1000.00
T2      =         800.00
EPS1    =           0.20
EPS2    =           0.60
D       =           1.00
W       =           1.00
SIGMA   =        0.1712E-08
TOL     =        0.1000E-05
N       =        2
ITMAX   =       25
E1      =        0.3424E 03
E2      =        0.4207E 03
XLOW    =          -0.50
XHIGH   =           0.50
```

Computer Output (*Continued*)

```
ITER    =          6

  I      B1(I)           B2(I)            INT1(I)          INT2(I)
  1    0.523475E 03    0.512213E 03    0.226344E 03    0.228681E 03
  2    0.512933E 03    0.506865E 03    0.213167E 03    0.215312E 03
  3    0.485382E 03    0.492907E 03    0.178728E 03    0.180417E 03


Q1     =     0.300475E 03
Q2     =     0.293706E 03
```

Discussion of Results

The first two sets of results are for $T_1 = 1000°R$, $T_2 = 500°R$, $\varepsilon_1 = 0.8$, and $\varepsilon_2 = 0.6$. Convergence within the specified tolerance is rapid, occurring after five iterations. The results for $n = 2$ are almost identical with those for $n = 8$, indicating that good accuracy can be obtained with just a few subdivisions. The radiant fluxes are most intense at the center of the plate ($\iota = 1$), since

end leakage is least important at this point. Q_2 is negative, since the upper plate receives more energy from the lower plate than it can radiate and reflect to its surroundings, and so must be cooled to maintain its temperature constant.

The third set of results is for $T_1 = 1000$, $T_2 = 800$, $\varepsilon_1 = 0.2$, and $\varepsilon_2 = 0.6$. These conditions are such that heat must be supplied to *both* plates at approximately equal rates.

2.7 Repeated Interval-Halving and Romberg Integration

Let $T_{N,1}$ be the computed estimate of an integral

$$\int_a^b f(x)\,dx$$

by using the composite trapezoidal rule of (2.42) with $n = 2^N$. Then $T_{0,1}$ is the estimate of the integral using the simple trapezoidal rule, $T_{1,1}$ the estimate for two applications, $T_{2,1}$ the estimate for four applications, etc. $T_{N,1}$ involves twice as many subintervals as $T_{N-1,1}$. Hence N can be viewed as the number of times the initial integration interval $[a,b]$ has been halved to produce subintervals of length $h = (b - a)/2^N$. From (2.42):

$$T_{0,1} = \frac{(b-a)}{1}\left\{\frac{1}{2}\left[f(a)+f(b)\right]\right\} \tag{2.52a}$$

$$T_{1,1} = \frac{(b-a)}{2}\left\{\frac{1}{2}[f(a)+f(b)]+f\left(a+\frac{(b-a)}{2}\right)\right\}$$

$$= \frac{1}{2}\left\{T_{0,1}+(b-a)f\left(a+\frac{(b-a)}{2}\right)\right\} \tag{2.52b}$$

$$T_{2,1} = \frac{(b-a)}{4}\left\{\frac{1}{2}[f(a)+f(b)]+\sum_{i=1}^{3}f\left(a+\frac{(b-a)}{4}i\right)\right\}$$

$$= \frac{1}{2}\left\{T_{1,1}+\frac{(b-a)}{2}\sum_{\substack{i=1\\ \Delta i=2}}^{3}f\left(a+\frac{(b-a)}{4}i\right)\right\} \tag{2.52c}$$

$$T_{3,1} = \frac{(b-a)}{8}\left\{\frac{1}{2}[f(a)+f(b)]+\sum_{i=1}^{7}f\left(a+\frac{(b-a)}{8}i\right)\right\}$$

$$= \frac{1}{2}\left\{T_{2,1}+\frac{(b-a)}{4}\sum_{\substack{i=1\\ \Delta i=2}}^{7}f\left(a+\frac{(b-a)}{8}i\right)\right\} \tag{2.52d}$$

$$T_{4,1} = \frac{(b-a)}{16}\left\{\frac{1}{2}[f(a)+f(b)]+\sum_{i=1}^{15}f\left(a+\frac{(b-a)}{16}i\right)\right\}$$

$$= \frac{1}{2}\left\{T_{3,1}+\frac{(b-a)}{8}\sum_{\substack{i=1\\ \Delta i=2}}^{15}f\left(a+\frac{(b-a)}{16}i\right)\right\}. \tag{2.52e}$$

By induction, the general recursion relation for $T_{N,1}$ in terms of $T_{N-1,1}$ is

$$T_{N,1} = \frac{1}{2}\left\{T_{N-1,1}+\frac{(b-a)}{2^{N-1}}\sum_{\substack{i=1\\ \Delta i=2}}^{2^N-1}f\left(a+\frac{(b-a)}{2^N}i\right)\right\}. \tag{2.53}$$

The recursion relation of (2.53) can be used to compute the sequence $T_{1,1}, T_{2,1}, \ldots, T_{N,1}$ once $T_{0,1}$ has been calculated. The function $f(x)$ need be evaluated just $2^N + 1$ times to compute the entire sequence.

Corresponding to $T_{N,1}$, the error term given by (2.42) is

$$-\frac{(b-a)^3}{12(2)^{2N}}f''(\xi), \qquad \xi \text{ in } (a,b). \tag{2.54}$$

Provided that $f(x)$ has a continuous and bounded second derivative on the interval (a,b), (2.54) assures that the sequence $T_{0,1}\ldots T_{N,1}$ converges to the true integral, assuming that no round-off error enters into the calculations.

The Richardson extrapolation technique of (2.47) can now be applied to each pair of adjacent elements in the sequence $T_{0,1}, T_{1,1}, \ldots$ to produce a third (hopefully improved) estimate of the integral. Let I^* in (2.47), corresponding to the pair of estimates $T_{N,1}, T_{N+1,1}$, be denoted $T_{N,2}$ so that

$$T_{N,2} = \frac{4T_{N+1,1}-T_{N,1}}{3}. \tag{2.55}$$

For example, from (2.52a) and (2.52b),

$$T_{0,2} = \frac{4T_{1,1}-T_{0,1}}{3}$$

$$= \frac{(b-a)}{6}\left\{f(a)+4f\left(a+\frac{(b-a)}{2}\right)+f(b)\right\}, \tag{2.56}$$

which is just the integral predicted by one application of Simpson's rule. Investigation of the sequence $T_{0,2}, T_{1,2}, \ldots, T_{N,2}$ leads, by induction, to the conclusion that $T_{N,2}$ is the estimate of the integral which would be computed by using the composite Simpson's rule of (2.49) with $n = 2^N$. Thus $T_{N,2}$ is the value computed for the integral by Simpson's rule after halving the initial interval, $[a,b]$, N times.

From (2.49), the error in $T_{N,2}$ is given by

$$-\frac{(b-a)^5}{2880(2)^{4N}}f^{(4)}(\xi), \qquad \xi \text{ in } (a,b). \tag{2.57}$$

Provided that $f(x)$ has a continuous and bounded fourth derivative on the interval $[a,b]$, (2.57) assures that the sequence $T_{02}\ldots T_{N,2}$ converges to the true integral, assuming no round-off error.

The Richardson extrapolation technique of (2.51) can now be applied to each pair of adjacent elements in the sequence $T_{0,2}, T_{1,2}, \ldots$ to produce yet another sequence of estimates,

$$T_{N,3} = \frac{16T_{N+1,2}-T_{N,2}}{15}. \tag{2.58}$$

Investigation of the sequence $T_{0,3}, T_{1,3}\ldots$ shows that $T_{N,3}$ is the estimate of the integral that would be computed by using the composite version of the five-point Newton-Cotes closed formula of (2.21d) with 2^N repeated applications or, alternatively, after halving the original integration interval, $[a,b]$, N times. The error term for $T_{N,3}$ has the form

$$-\frac{(b-a)^7}{1935360(2)^{6N}}f^{(6)}(\xi), \qquad \xi \text{ in } (a,b). \tag{2.59}$$

Provided that $f(x)$ has a continuous and bounded sixth derivative on the interval (a,b), (2.59) assures that the sequence $T_{0,3}\ldots T_{N,3}$ converges to the true integral, assuming no round-off error.

The Richardson extrapolation technique can be applied to each pair of adjacent elements in the sequence $T_{0,3}, T_{1,3} \ldots$ to produce another sequence of estimates,

$$T_{N,4} = \frac{64 T_{N+1,3} - T_{N,3}}{63}, \qquad (2.60)$$

which can be shown (see Bauer *et al.* [6]) to converge to the true integral.

The relationships of (2.55), (2.58), and (2.60) are special cases of the general extrapolation formula,

$$T_{N,j} = \frac{4^{j-1} T_{N+1,j-1} - T_{N,j-1}}{4^{j-1} - 1}, \qquad (2.61)$$

credited to Romberg and described in detail by Bauer *et al.* [6], who show that each of the sequences $T_{N,j}$, for $j = 1, 2, \ldots$, converges to the true integral with increasing N. In addition, the sequence $T_{0,1} T_{0,2}, \ldots, T_{0,j}$ also converges to the true integral for increasing j. The sequences $T_{N,j}$ for $j > 3$ do not correspond to composite rules for Newton-Cotes closed integration as do those for $j \leqslant 3$.

These Romberg sequences can be arranged in simple tabular form as follows:

$$
\begin{array}{cccccc}
T_{0,1} & T_{0,2} & T_{0,3} & T_{0,4} & T_{0,5} & \cdots & T_{0,j} \\
T_{1,1} & T_{1,2} & T_{1,3} & T_{1,4} & T_{1,5} & & \\
T_{2,1} & T_{2,2} & T_{2,3} & & & & \\
\vdots & \vdots & \vdots & & & & \\
T_{N-2,1} & T_{N-2,2} & T_{N-2,3} & & & & \\
T_{N-1,1} & T_{N-1,2} & & & & & \\
T_{N,1} & & & & & & (2.62)
\end{array}
$$

To use this technique, we simply compute the elements of the first column using (2.52a) and (2.53), fill out the remaining elements of the triangular array using (2.61), and then examine the number sequences down each column and across each row. Each of the sequences should converge to the true integral.

The error corresponding to $T_{N,j}$, as defined in (2.61), can be shown [6] to be equal to

$$\frac{k(j)}{2^{2jN}} f^{(2j)}(\xi), \qquad \xi \text{ in } (a,b),$$

where $k(j)$ is a constant that depends on a, b and j, but is independent of N.

Example. Use the Romberg integration scheme to estimate the value of ln 137.2 from the integral

$$\ln 137.2 = \int_1^{137.2} \frac{1}{x}\, dx.$$

Table 2.1 shows the results in the tabular form of (2.62). The first column contains the results for evaluation of the integral using the composite trapezoidal rule of (2.53), after computing the first entry with the simple trapezoidal rule of (2.52a). The remaining entries in the Romberg tableau are the results of repeated extrapolation using (2.61).

The true integral to six figures is 4.92144. Clearly, each column sequence is converging to this value. The sequence across the top row is also converging to this value. The apparent divergence of the last entry or two in each column results from round-off errors in the calculations (recall that the last entry in the first column involves $2^{13} = 8192$ repeated applications of the trapezoidal rule).

Table 2.1   Romberg Tableau for Evaluation of ln 137.2

N	j= 1	2	3	4	5	6	7	8	9	10
0	68.5964	24.1795	12.7845	8.05264	6.02881	5.24048	4.98842	4.93035	4.92208	4.92146
1	35.2837	13.4967	8.12658	6.03672	5.24125	4.98848	4.93035	4.92208	4.92146	4.92144
2	18.9434	8.46221	6.06937	5.24436	4.98873	4.93037	4.92208	4.92146	4.92144	4.92144
3	11.0825	6.21893	5.25725	4.98973	4.93042	4.92209	4.92146	4.92144	4.92144	4.92143
4	7.43482	5.31736	4.99391	4.93065	4.92209	4.92146	4.92144	4.92144	4.92143	4.92143
5	5.84672	5.01412	4.93164	4.92213	4.92146	4.92144	4.92144	4.92143	4.92143	
6	5.22227	4.93680	4.92228	4.92146	4.92144	4.92144	4.92143	4.92143		
7	5.00817	4.92318	4.92148	4.92144	4.92144	4.92143	4.92143			
8	4.94443	4.92158	4.92144	4.92144	4.92143	4.92143				
9	4.92730	4.92145	4.92144	4.92143	4.92143					
10	4.92291	4.92144	4.92143	4.92143						
11	4.92181	4.92144	4.92143							
12	4.92153	4.92143								
13	4.92145									

EXAMPLE 2.2

FOURIER COEFFICIENTS USING ROMBERG INTEGRATION

Problem Statement

Write a general-purpose subroutine named TROMB that uses the Romberg integration algorithm outlined in Section 2.7 to evaluate numerically the integral

$$\int_a^b f(x)\,dx \qquad (2.2.1)$$

where $f(x)$ is any single-valued function and a and b are finite. The program should first use the trapezoidal rule with repeated interval halving to determine $T_{0,1}, T_{1,1}, \ldots, T_{N_{max},1}$ from (2.52a) and the recursion relation (2.53). Then the Romberg sequences $\{T_{N,j}\}$ should be computed from the general extrapolation formula (2.61) for all $j \leq j_{max}$. The Romberg Tableau should be organized as illustrated in Table 2.1.

To test the subroutine, write a general purpose program that calls on TROMB to evaluate the coefficients of the Fourier expansion for any arbitrary function $g(x)$, periodic with period 2π, such that $g(x) = g(x + 2k\pi)$ for integral k. The Fourier expansion may be written [14]

$$g(x) = \sum_{m=0}^{\infty} c_m \cos mx + \sum_{m=0}^{\infty} d_m \sin mx, \qquad (2.2.2)$$

where

$$c_m = \frac{1}{\pi} \int_{-\pi}^{\pi} g(x) \cos mx\,dx \qquad (2.2.3)$$

$$d_m = \frac{1}{\pi} \int_{-\pi}^{\pi} g(x) \sin mx\,dx. \qquad (2.2.4)$$

Write the program so that the coefficients (c_m, d_m) are calculated in pairs, for $m = 0, 1, \ldots, m_{max}$.

As a test periodic function, $g(x)$, use the sawtooth function of Fig. 2.2.1.

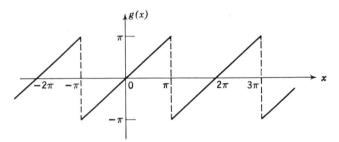

Figure 2.2.1 A periodic sawtooth function.

Method of Solution

The subroutine TROMB is a straightforward implementation of the trapezoidal rule of (2.52a),

$$T_{0,1} = (b - a)[f(a) + f(b)]/2,$$

followed by repeated interval halving using the recursion relation of (2.53),

$$T_{N,1} = \frac{1}{2}\left\{ T_{N-1,1} + \frac{(b-a)}{2^{N-1}} \sum_{\substack{i=1 \\ \Delta i=2}}^{2^N - 1} f\left(a + \frac{(b-a)}{2^N}\,i\right) \right\},$$

for $N = 1, 2, \ldots, N_{max}$. The Romberg extrapolation formula of (2.61),

$$T_{N,j} = \frac{4^{j-1} T_{N+1,j-1} - T_{N,j-1}}{4^{j-1} - 1},$$

is then employed for $j = 2, 3, \ldots, j_{max}$, with $N = 0, 1, \ldots, N_{max} - j + 1$, to fill out the remaining elements in the first j_{max} columns of the matrix T.

The integrands for the integrals of (2.2.3) and (2.2.4),

$$f_c(x) = [g(x) \cos mx]/\pi, \qquad (2.2.5)$$

$$f_d(x) = [g(x) \sin mx]/\pi, \qquad (2.2.6)$$

are evaluated by the functions FUNCTC and FUNCTD, respectively, defined in one multiple-entry function. The periodic function $g(x)$, which for the suggested function of Fig. 2.2.1 is given by

$$g(x) = x, \qquad (2.2.7)$$

is also defined in the multiple-entry function.

From (2.2.4), it is clear that for all $g(x)$, $d_0 = 0$. For the periodic function of (2.2.7), the coefficients c_m and d_m of (2.2.3) and (2.2.4) may be found analytically, and are given by

$$c_m = \frac{1}{\pi} \int_{-\pi}^{\pi} x \cos mx\,dx = 0, \qquad m = 0, 1, \ldots \qquad (2.2.8)$$

$$d_m = \frac{1}{\pi} \int_{-\pi}^{\pi} x \sin mx\,dx = -\frac{2}{m}\cos m\pi = -\frac{2}{m}(-1)^m,$$

$$m = 1, 2, \ldots \qquad (2.2.9)$$

Then the Fourier expansion of (2.2.7) is

$$g(x) = x = 2\left(\sin x - \frac{\sin 2x}{2} + \frac{\sin 3x}{3} - \ldots\right). \qquad (2.2.10)$$

In the programs that follow, all c_m and d_m are evaluated for $m = 0, 1, \ldots, m_{max}$. The Romberg tableaus for c_m and d_m are stored in the matrices C and D respectively.

Example 2.2   Fourier Coefficients using Romberg Integration   **93**

Flow Diagram
Main Program

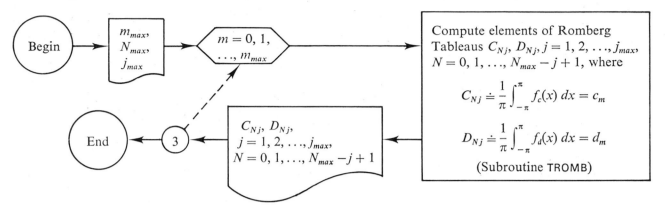

Functions FUNCTC, FUNCTD, G (Argument: x)

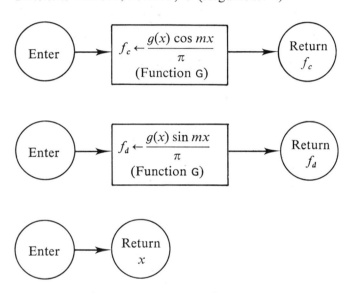

Subroutine TROMB (Dummy arguments: $N_{max}, a, b, f, T, j_{max}, n$;
       calling arguments: $N_{max}, -\pi, \pi$, FUNCTC or FUNCTD, C or D, j_{max}, n)

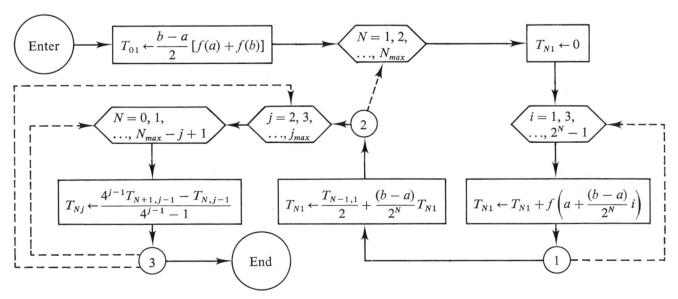

FORTRAN *Implementation*

List of Principal Variables

Program Symbol   Definition

(Main)

C, D†	Matrices C and D, containing the Romberg tableaus for c_m and d_m, respectively.
J	Column subscript for tableaus, j.
JM	Maximum column subscript in Nth row of tableau.
JMAX	j_{max}, number of columns in tableau.
M	m, index on Fourier coefficients c_m and d_m.
MMAX	m_{max}, maximum value of m.
N†	Row subscript for tableaus, N.
NMAX	N_{max}, maximum value of N.
NMAXP1	$N_{max} + 1$.
PI	π.
MMAXP1	$m_{max} + 1$.
MPLUS1	$m + 1$.

**(Functions
   FUNCTC,
   FUNCTD,
   G)**

X	The variable of integration, x.

**(Subroutine
   TROMB)**

A, B	Lower and upper limits of integration, a and b.
F	The integrand function, f.
FR	$(b - a)/2^N$.
FORJM1	4^{j-1}.
H	$b - a$.
I	i, index on repeated sum of (2.53).
IMAX	$2^N - 1$.
NRC	n, number of rows and columns in tableau T.
NXMJP2	$N_{max} - j + 2$.
T†	Matrix containing the Romberg tableau, T.

† Because of FORTRAN limitations, the row subscripts of the text and flow diagrams are advanced by one when they appear in the program. For example, N assumes values 1, 2, …, $N_{max} + 1$, so that $T_{0,1} = $ T(1, 1), $T_{Nmax,1} = $ T($N_{max} + 1$, 1), etc.

Example 2.2   Fourier Coefficients using Romberg Integration   **95**

Program Listing

Main Program

```
C           APPLIED NUMERICAL METHODS, EXAMPLE 2.2
C           FOURIER COEFFICIENTS USING ROMBERG INTEGRATION
C
C           THIS TEST PROGRAM CALLS ON THE SUBROUTINE TROMB TO COMPUTE
C           THE INTEGRALS NECESSARY TO DETERMINE THE COEFFICIENTS
C           OF THE FOURIER EXPANSION FOR A FUNCTION G(X) ON THE
C           INTERVAL (-PI,PI) WHERE THE FUNCTION IS PERIODIC FOR ALL
C           X SUCH THAT G(X) = G(X + 2*K*PI), K BEING AN
C           INTEGER.  THE FIRST MMAX COEFFICIENTS OF THE COSINE AND
C           SINE TERMS (THE C(M) AND D(M) OF THE TEXT) ARE COMPUTED
C           USING THE TRAPEZOIDAL RULE WITH REPEATED INTERVAL HALVING
C           FOLLOWED BY THE ROMBERG EXTRAPOLATION PROCEDURE.  THE ROMBERG
C           TABLEAUS FOR C(M) AND D(M) ARE STORED IN THE UPPER TRIANGULAR
C           PORTIONS OF THE FIRST NMAX+1 ROWS OF THE FIRST JMAX COLUMNS OF
C           THE C AND D MATRICES RESPECTIVELY.  FOURIER COEFFICIENTS
C           FOR ANY ARBITRARY PERIODIC FUNCTION CAN BE FOUND BY DEFINING
C           G(X) APPROPRIATELY (SEE THE FUNCTIONS FUNCTC AND FUNCTD).
C
      IMPLICIT  REAL*8(A-H, O-Z)
      DIMENSION C(20,20), D(20,20)
      EXTERNAL  FUNCTC, FUNCTD
      COMMON M
      DATA  PI / 3.1415926535898 /
C
C     ..... READ DATA, CALL TROMB TO COMPUTE INTEGRALS .....
    1 READ (5,100)  MMAX, NMAX, JMAX
      WRITE (6,200)  MMAX, NMAX, JMAX
      MMAXP1 = MMAX + 1
      DO 3  MPLUS1=1,MMAXP1
      M = MPLUS1 - 1

      CALL TROMB( NMAX, -PI, PI, FUNCTC, C, JMAX, 20 )
      CALL TROMB( NMAX, -PI, PI, FUNCTD, D, JMAX, 20 )
C
C     ..... PRINT OUT ROMBERG TABLEAUS .....
      WRITE (6,201)  M
      NMAXP1 = NMAX + 1
      DO 2  N=1,NMAXP1
      JM = JMAX
      IF ( N.GT.NMAXP1+1-JMAX )   JM = NMAXP1 + 1 - N
    2 WRITE (6,202)   (C(N,J), J=1,JM)
      WRITE (6,203)  M
      DO 3  N=1,NMAXP1
      JM = JMAX
      IF ( N.GT.NMAXP1+1-JMAX )   JM = NMAXP1 + 1 - N
    3 WRITE (6,202)   (D(N,J), J=1,JM)
      GO TO 1
C
C     ..... FORMATS FOR INPUT AND OUTPUT STATEMENTS .....
  100 FORMAT( 7X, I3, 2(12X, I3) )
  200 FORMAT( 8H1MMAX = , I2/ 8H NMAX = , I2/ 8H JMAX = , I2 )
  201 FORMAT( 1H0/ 1H0,9X,2HC(,I2,1H)/ 1H  )
  202 FORMAT( 1H , 1P7E17.8 )
  203 FORMAT( 1H0/ 1H0,9X,2HD(,I2,1H)/ 1H  )
C
      END
```

Functions FUNCTC, FUNCTD, G

```
      FUNCTION FUNCTC( X )
C
C           THE FUNCTIONS FUNCTC AND FUNCTD COMPUTE RESPECTIVELY THE
C           INTEGRAND FOR THE M(TH) COEFFICIENT OF THE COSINE AND SINE
C           TERMS OF THE FOURIER EXPANSION OF THE PERIODIC FUNCTION
C           G(X) = X.
```

Program Listing (*Continued*)

```
C
      IMPLICIT  REAL*8(A-H, O-Z)
      REAL*8   X, FUNCTC, FUNCTD
      COMMON M
      DATA  PI / 3.1415926535898 /
C
C     ..... DEFINE PERIODIC FUNCTION .....
      G(X) = X
C
      FUNCTC = G(X)*DCOS(FLOAT(M)*X)/PI
      RETURN
C
      ENTRY FUNCTD( X )
      FUNCTD = G(X)*DSIN(FLOAT(M)*X)/PI
      RETURN
C
      END
```

Subroutine TROMB

```
      SUBROUTINE TROMB( NMAX, A, B, F, T, JMAX, NRC )
C
C         THE SUBROUTINE TROMB FIRST APPROXIMATES THE INTEGRAL OF
C         F(X)*DX ON THE INTERVAL (A,B) USING THE TRAPEZOIDAL
C         RULE WITH REPEATED INTERVAL HALVING.  T(N+1,1) IS THE VALUE
C         OF THE INTEGRAL COMPUTED AFTER THE N(TH) INTERVAL-HALVING
C         OPERATION.   ALL T(N+1,1) VALUES ARE COMPUTED FOR N = 0 TO
C         N = NMAX.  H IS THE LENGTH OF THE STARTING INTERVAL (A,B).
C         REMAINING ELEMENTS OF THE ROMBERG TABLEAU ARE THEN ENTERED
C         INTO THE FIRST JMAX COLUMNS OF THE FIRST NMAX+1 ROWS OF THE
C         MATRIX T.
C
      IMPLICIT  REAL*8(A-H, O-Z)
      REAL*8   A, B, F, T
      DIMENSION T(NRC,NRC)
C
C     ..... COMPUTE H AND FIRST INTEGRAL APPROXIMATION .....
      H = B - A
      T(1,1) = (F(A) + F(B))*H/2.0
C
C     ..... HALVE INTERVAL REPEATEDLY, COMPUTE T(N+1,1) .....
      DO 2   N=1,NMAX
      T(N+1,1) = 0.0
      FR = H/2.0**N
      IMAX = 2**N - 1
      DO 1   I = 1,IMAX,2
    1 T(N+1,1) = T(N+1,1) + F(FLOAT(I)*FR + A)
    2 T(N+1,1) = T(N,1)/2.0 + H*T(N+1,1)/2.0**N
C
C     ..... COMPUTE ROMBERG TABLEAU .....
      DO 3   J=2,JMAX
      NXMJP2 = NMAX - J + 2
      FORJM1 = 4.0**(J-1)
      DO 3   N=1,NXMJP2
    3 T(N,J) = (FORJM1*T(N+1,J-1) - T(N,J-1))/(FORJM1 - 1.0)
C
      RETURN
C
      END
```

Data

MMAX = 10   NMAX = 13   JMAX =   7

Computer Output (*abbreviated*)

```
MMAX = 10
NMAX = 13
JMAX =  7
```

C(0)

```
 0.0               -4.44089210D-15   -8.88178420D-16   -5.90968360D-16   -3.54160573D-16   -1.11505611D-15   -1.56736905D-15
-3.33066907D-15    -1.11022302D-15   -5.95612267D-16   -3.55085603D-16   -1.14313304D-15   -1.56725862D-15   -6.13269043D-16
-1.66533454D-15    -6.27754339D-16   -3.58843832D-16   -1.11134731D-15   -1.56681629D-15   -6.13501951D-16   -3.10371843D-15
-8.87165214D-16    -3.75652058D-16   -1.09958945D-15   -6.14432922D-16   -1.03110047D-15   -3.62401184D-15
-5.03530347D-16    -1.05434336D-15   -1.55776450D-15   -1.56503712D-15   -3.10068012D-16   -3.62388466D-15   -3.91411263D-15
-9.16640106D-16    -1.52630068D-15   -6.32827755D-16   -3.09098272D-16   -3.62337372D-15   -3.91404177D-15   -3.93647376D-15
-1.37388553D-15    -6.88669813D-16   -3.05257405D-15   -3.62129407D-15   -3.91375792D-15   -3.93646828D-15   -4.57441915D-14
-6.88669813D-16    -2.90483004D-15   -3.61240782D-15   -3.91261548D-15   -3.93644610D-15   -4.57338450D-15   -5.37800861D-14
-2.90483004D-15    -3.56818421D-15   -3.90792474D-15   -3.93635302D-15   -4.56931666D-14   -5.37781217D-14
-2.59361596D-15    -3.88669095D-15   -3.93590882D-15   -3.93590882D-15   -5.37702262D-14
-3.27454215D-15    -3.93283271D-15   -3.93590882D-15   -4.45530054D-15
-3.73365375D-15    -3.93283271D-15   -4.48801456D-14   -5.37380380D-14
-3.88303797D-15    -4.23209385D-14   -5.35996335D-14
-3.27114634D-14    -5.28947150D-14
-4.78489021D-14
```

D(0)

```
0.0   0.0   0.0   0.0   0.0   0.0   0.0
0.0   0.0   0.0   0.0   0.0   0.0   0.0
0.0   0.0   0.0   0.0   0.0   0.0   0.0
0.0   0.0   0.0   0.0   0.0   0.0   0.0
0.0   0.0   0.0   0.0   0.0   0.0   0.0
0.0   0.0   0.0   0.0   0.0   0.0   0.0
0.0   0.0   0.0   0.0   0.0   0.0   0.0
0.0   0.0   0.0   0.0   0.0   0.0
0.0   0.0   0.0   0.0   0.0
0.0   0.0   0.0   0.0
0.0   0.0   0.0
0.0   0.0
0.0
0.0
```

D(1)

```
-2.08191779D-14   -6.93972597D-15    2.23402144D 00    1.99483342D 00    2.00002583D 00    1.99999997D 00    2.00000000D 00
-1.04095889D-14    2.09439510D 00    1.99857073D 00    2.00000555D 00    1.99999999D 00    2.00000000D 00    2.00000000D 00
 1.57079633D 00    2.00455975D 00    1.99998313D 00    2.00000002D 00    2.00000000D 00    2.00000000D 00    2.00000000D 00
 1.89611890D 00    2.00026917D 00    1.99999975D 00    2.00000000D 00    2.00000000D 00    2.00000000D 00    2.00000000D 00
 1.97423160D 00    2.00001659D 00    2.00000000D 00    2.00000000D 00    2.00000000D 00    2.00000000D 00    2.00000000D 00
 1.99357034D 00    2.00000103D 00    2.00000000D 00    2.00000000D 00    2.00000000D 00    2.00000000D 00    2.00000000D 00
 1.99839336D 00    2.00000006D 00    2.00000000D 00    2.00000000D 00    2.00000000D 00    2.00000000D 00
 1.99959839D 00    2.00000000D 00    2.00000000D 00    2.00000000D 00
 1.99989960D 00    2.00000000D 00
 1.99997490D 00    2.00000000D 00
 1.99999373D 00    2.00000000D 00
 1.99999843D 00    2.00000000D 00
 1.99999961D 00
 1.99999990D 00
```

D(5)

```
-1.92851332D-13  -6.42837774D-14   2.23402144D 00  -1.21469895D 00   5.86911516D-01   3.95243093D-01   4.00029338D-01
-9.64256660D-14   2.09439510D 00  -1.16081269D 00   5.79873975D-01   3.95430270D-01   4.00028169D-01   3.99999957D-01
 1.57079633D 00  -9.57362204D-01   5.52675746D-01   3.96150753D-01   4.00023679D-01   3.99999964D-01   4.00000000D-01
-3.25322571D-01   4.58298374D-01   3.98596456D-01   4.00008550D-01   3.99999987D-01   4.00000000D-01   4.00000000D-01
 2.62393138D-01   4.02327826D-01   3.99986486D-01   4.00000020D-01   4.00000000D-01   4.00000000D-01   4.00000000D-01
 3.67344154D-01   4.00132820D-01   3.99999809D-01   4.00000000D-01   4.00000000D-01   4.00000000D-01   4.00000000D-01
 3.91935653D-01   4.00008122D-01   3.99999997D-01   4.00000000D-01   4.00000000D-01   4.00000000D-01
 3.97990005D-01   4.00000505D-01   4.00000000D-01   4.00000000D-01   4.00000000D-01
 3.99497880D-01   4.00000032D-01   4.00000000D-01   4.00000000D-01   4.00000000D-01
 3.99874494D-01   4.00000002D-01   4.00000000D-01   4.00000000D-01
 3.99968625D-01   4.00000000D-01   4.00000000D-01   4.00000000D-01
 3.99992156D-01   4.00000000D-01   4.00000000D-01
 3.99998039D-01   4.00000000D-01   4.00000000D-01
 3.99999510D-01
```

D(7)

```
-2.80511028D-13  -9.35036762D-14  -2.23402144D 00  -1.99483342D 00   9.76823748D-01   2.49509838D-01   2.86156743D-01
-1.40255514D-13  -2.09439510D 00  -1.99857073D 00   9.65215712D-01   2.50220105D-01   2.86147796D-01   2.85712983D-01
 1.57079633D 00  -2.00455975D 00   9.18906549D-01   2.53013057D-01   2.86112710D-01   2.85713089D-01   2.85714287D-01
-1.89611890D 00   7.36189905D-01   2.63417643D-01   2.85983415D-01   2.85714533D-01   2.85714286D-01   2.85714286D-01
 7.81127040D-02   2.92965909D-01   2.85983415D-01   2.85713479D-01   2.85714286D-01   2.85714286D-01   2.85714286D-01
 2.39252608D-01   2.86089267D-01   2.85713225D-01   2.85714286D-01   2.85714286D-01   2.85714286D-01   2.85714286D-01
 2.74380102D-01   2.85736728D-01   2.85714270D-01   2.85714286D-01   2.85714286D-01   2.85714286D-01
 2.82897572D-01   2.85715674D-01   2.85714285D-01   2.85714286D-01   2.85714286D-01
 2.85011148D-01   2.85714372D-01   2.85714286D-01   2.85714286D-01   2.85714286D-01
 2.85538566D-01   2.85714291D-01   2.85714286D-01   2.85714286D-01
 2.85670360D-01   2.85714286D-01   2.85714286D-01   2.85714286D-01
 2.85703305D-01   2.85714286D-01   2.85714286D-01
 2.85711540D-01   2.85714286D-01   2.85714286D-01
 2.85713599D-01
```

D(10)

```
 4.03234603D-13   1.34411534D-13  -8.96076897D-15  -1.13474105D 00   6.14181201D-01  -2.94342988D-01  -1.97597927D-01
 2.01617302D-13   1.68290326D-13  -1.11701072D-13   6.07349473D-01  -2.93455758D-01  -1.97621547D-01  -2.00014669D-01
 5.04043254D-14  -1.04719755D 00   5.80406345D-01  -2.89936987D-01  -1.97715135D-01  -2.00014085D-01  -1.99999978D-01
-7.85398163D-01   4.78681102D-01  -2.76337873D-01  -1.98075376D-01  -2.00011839D-01  -1.99999982D-01  -2.00000000D-01
 1.62661286D-01  -2.29149187D-01  -1.99298243D-01  -2.00004275D-01  -1.99999993D-01  -2.00000000D-01  -2.00000000D-01
-1.31196569D-01  -2.01163913D-01  -1.99999904D-01  -2.00000010D-01  -2.00000000D-01  -2.00000000D-01  -2.00000000D-01
-1.83672077D-01  -2.00664410D-01  -1.99999999D-01  -2.00000000D-01  -2.00000000D-01  -2.00000000D-01
-1.95967827D-01  -2.00040610D-01  -2.00000000D-01  -2.00000000D-01  -2.00000000D-01
-1.98995002D-01  -2.00002520D-01  -2.00000000D-01  -2.00000000D-01  -2.00000000D-01
-1.99748940D-01  -2.00000160D-01  -2.00000000D-01  -2.00000000D-01
-1.99937247D-01  -2.00000000D-01  -2.00000000D-01  -2.00000000D-01
-1.99984312D-01  -2.00000000D-01  -2.00000000D-01
-1.99996078D-01  -2.00000000D-01  -2.00000000D-01
-1.99999020D-01
```

Example 2.2   Fourier Coefficients using Romberg Integration   **99**

Discussion of Results

Romberg tableaus are shown only for the coefficients c_0, d_0, d_1, d_5, d_7, and d_{10} to conserve space. All calculations were performed in double-precision arithmetic. The results shown for c_0 are typical of those found for all the c_m, $m = 0, 1, \ldots, 10$. All entries in the C matrices are in the range 10^{-16} to 5×10^{-14}, giving exceptionally good agreement with the true values, $c_m = 0$. Assuming that D(8,7), corresponding to $T_{7,7}$, is the most accurate approximation to d_m, the best estimates found by the program are shown in Table 2.2.1. In every case, there is at least nine-figure agreement (the number of figures printed) between the results of the Romberg integration and the exact value of the integral.

Table 2.2.1
Calculated Estimates of d_m

m	d_m (Calculated)	d_m (Exact)
0	0.00000000	0
1	2.00000000	2
2	−1.00000000	−1
3	0.666666667	2/3
4	−0.500000000	−1/2
5	0.400000000	2/5
6	−0.333333333	−1/3
7	0.285714286	2/7
8	−0.250000000	−1/4
9	0.222222222	2/9
10	−0.200000000	−1/5

2.8 Numerical Integration with Unequally Spaced Base Points

All the integration formulas developed in the preceding sections are of the form given by (2.22)

$$\int_a^b f(x)\, dx \doteq \sum_{i=0}^n w_i f(x_i),$$

where the $n + 1$ values w_i are the weights to be given to the $n + 1$ functional values $f(x_i)$. The x_i have been specified to be equally spaced so there is no choice in the selection of the base points. If the x_i are not so fixed and if we place no other restrictions on them, it follows that there are $2n + 2$ undetermined parameters (the w_i and x_i), which apparently might suffice to define a polynomial of degree $2n + 1$. The Gaussian quadrature formulas to be developed in Section 2.10 have a form identical with (2.22), that is, they involve the weighted sum of $n + 1$ functional values. The x_i values to be used are not evenly spaced, however, but are chosen so that the sum of the $n + 1$ appropriately weighted functional values in (2.22) yields the integral exactly when $f(x)$ is a polynomial of degree $2n + 1$ or less. Before proceeding with the development, some background material on orthogonal polynomials is required.

2.9 Orthogonal Polynomials

Two functions $g_n(x)$ and $g_m(x)$ selected from a family of related functions $g_k(x)$ are said to be orthogonal with respect to a weighting function $w(x)$ on the interval $[a,b]$ if

$$\int_a^b w(x)g_n(x)g_m(x)\, dx = 0, \qquad n \neq m,$$
$$\int_a^b w(x)[g_n(x)]^2\, dx = c(n) \neq 0. \tag{2.63}$$

In general, c depends on n. If these relationships hold for all n, the family of functions $\{g_k(x)\}$ constitutes a set of orthogonal functions. Some common families of orthogonal functions are the sets $\{\sin kx\}$ and $\{\cos kx\}$. Orthogonality can be viewed as a generalization of the perpendicularity property for two vectors in n dimensional space where n becomes very large and the elements (coordinates) of the vectors can be represented as continuous functions of some independent variable (see [1] for an interesting discussion and geometric interpretation). For our purposes, the definition (2.63) is adequate. The functions $1, x, x^2, x^3, \ldots, x^n$ are not orthogonal. However, several families of well-known polynomials do possess a property of orthogonality. Four such sets are the Legendre, Laguerre, Chebyshev, and Hermite polynomials.

Legendre Polynomials: $P_n(x)$. The Legendre polynomials are orthogonal on the interval $[-1,1]$ with respect to the weighting function $w(x) = 1$, that is,

$$\int_{-1}^{+1} P_n(x)P_m(x)\, dx = 0, \qquad n \neq m,$$
$$\int_{-1}^{+1} [P_n(x)]^2\, dx = c(n) \neq 0. \tag{2.64}$$

The first few Legendre polynomials are:

$$\begin{aligned}
P_0(x) &= 1, \\
P_1(x) &= x, \\
P_2(x) &= \tfrac{1}{2}(3x^2 - 1), \\
P_3(x) &= \tfrac{1}{2}(5x^3 - 3x), \\
P_4(x) &= \tfrac{1}{8}(35x^4 - 30x^2 + 3).
\end{aligned} \tag{2.65}$$

The general recursion relation is

$$P_n(x) = \frac{2n - 1}{n} xP_{n-1}(x) - \frac{n - 1}{n} P_{n-2}(x). \tag{2.66}$$

Laguerre Polynomials: $\mathscr{L}_n(x)$. The Laguerre polynomials are orthogonal on the interval $[0,\infty]$ with respect to the weighting function $w(x) = e^{-x}$, that is,

$$\int_0^\infty e^{-x}\mathscr{L}_n(x)\mathscr{L}_m(x)\, dx = 0, \qquad n \neq m,$$
$$\int_0^\infty e^{-x}[\mathscr{L}_n(x)]^2\, dx = c(n) \neq 0. \tag{2.67}$$

The first few Laguerre polynomials are:

$$\begin{aligned}
\mathscr{L}_0(x) &= 1, \\
\mathscr{L}_1(x) &= -x + 1, \\
\mathscr{L}_2(x) &= x^2 - 4x + 2, \\
\mathscr{L}_3(x) &= -x^3 + 9x^2 - 18x + 6.
\end{aligned} \tag{2.68}$$

The general recursion relation is

$$\mathscr{L}_n(x) = (2n - x - 1)\mathscr{L}_{n-1}(x) - (n - 1)^2\mathscr{L}_{n-2}(x). \tag{2.69}$$

Chebyshev Polynomials: $T_n(x)$. The Chebyshev polynomials, already described in some detail in Chapter 1, are orthogonal on the interval $[-1,1]$ with respect to the weighting function $w(x) = 1/\sqrt{1 - x^2}$, that is,

$$\int_{-1}^{+1} \frac{1}{\sqrt{1 - x^2}} T_n(x)T_m(x)\, dx = 0, \qquad n \neq m,$$
$$\int_{-1}^{+1} \frac{1}{\sqrt{1 - x^2}} [T_n(x)]^2\, dx = c(n) \neq 0. \tag{2.70}$$

The first few polynomials (see Table 1.12 for a more complete list) are:

$$\begin{aligned}
T_0(x) &= 1, \\
T_1(x) &= x, \\
T_2(x) &= 2x^2 - 1, \\
T_3(x) &= 4x^3 - 3x.
\end{aligned} \tag{2.71}$$

The general recursion relation is

$$T_n(x) = 2xT_{n-1}(x) - T_{n-2}(x). \qquad (2.72)$$

Hermite Polynomials: $H_n(x)$. The Hermite polynomials are orthogonal on the interval $[-\infty, \infty]$ with respect to the weighting function e^{-x^2}, that is,

$$\int_{-\infty}^{\infty} e^{-x^2} H_n(x) H_m(x)\, dx = 0, \qquad m \neq n,$$

$$\int_{-\infty}^{\infty} e^{-x^2} [H_n(x)]^2\, dx = c(n) \neq 0. \qquad (2.73)$$

The first few Hermite polynomials are:

$$\begin{aligned} H_0(x) &= 1, \\ H_1(x) &= 2x, \\ H_2(x) &= 4x^2 - 2, \\ H_3(x) &= 8x^3 - 12x. \end{aligned} \qquad (2.74)$$

The general recursion relation is

$$H_n(x) = 2xH_{n-1}(x) - 2(n-1)H_{n-2}(x). \qquad (2.75)$$

General Comments on Orthogonal Polynomials. The sequences of polynomials $\{P_n(x)\}$, $\{\mathscr{L}_n(x)\}$, $\{T_n(x)\}$, and $\{H_n(x)\}$, respectively satisfying relationships (2.64), (2.67), (2.70), and (2.73), are unique. Each of the polynomials $P_n(x)$, $\mathscr{L}_n(x)$, $T_n(x)$, and $H_n(x)$ is an nth-degree polynomial in x with real coefficients and n distinct real roots interior to the appropriate interval of integration; for example, all n roots of $P_n(x)$ lie on the open interval $(-1, 1)$. Stroud and Secrest [7] discuss these and other properties of several families of orthogonal polynomials in detail.

An arbitrary nth-degree polynomial $p_n(x) = \sum_{i=0}^{n} \alpha_i x^i$ may be represented by a linear function of any of the above families of orthogonal polynomials. Thus

$$p_n(x) = \beta_0 Z_0(x) + \beta_1 Z_1(x) + \cdots + \beta_n Z_n(x)$$

$$= \sum_{i=0}^{n} \beta_i Z_i(x), \qquad (2.76)$$

where $Z_i(x)$ is the ith-degree polynomial of one of the families of orthogonal polynomials. Expansions for the monomials x^i in terms of the Chebyshev polynomials are given in Table 1.13.

Example. Expand the fourth-degree polynomial $p_4(x)$ in terms of the Legendre polynomials.

Substitution of the polynomials $P_i(x)$ of (2.65) into (2.76) leads to

$$p_4(x) = \beta_0 + \beta_1 x + \beta_2 \left(\frac{3}{2} x^2 - \frac{1}{2} \right) + \beta_3 \left(\frac{5}{2} x^3 - \frac{3}{2} x \right)$$

$$+ \beta_4 \left(\frac{35}{8} x^4 - \frac{30}{8} x^2 + \frac{3}{8} \right).$$

Collecting the coefficients of like powers of x,

$$p_4(x) = \left(\beta_0 - \frac{1}{2} \beta_2 + \frac{3}{8} \beta_4 \right) + \left(\beta_1 - \frac{3}{2} \beta_3 \right) x$$

$$+ \left(\frac{3}{2} \beta_2 - \frac{30}{8} \beta_4 \right) x^2 + \frac{5}{2} \beta_3 x^3 + \frac{35}{8} \beta_4 x^4.$$

Thus

$$\beta_4 = \frac{8}{35} \alpha_4,$$

$$\beta_3 = \frac{2}{5} \alpha_3,$$

$$\beta_2 = \frac{2}{3} \left(\alpha_2 + \frac{15}{4} \beta_4 \right) = \frac{2}{3} \left(\alpha_2 + \frac{6}{7} \alpha_4 \right),$$

$$\beta_1 = \alpha_1 + \frac{3}{2} \beta_3 = \alpha_1 + \frac{3}{5} \alpha_3,$$

$$\beta_0 = \alpha_0 + \frac{1}{2} \beta_2 - \frac{3}{8} \beta_4 = \alpha_0 + \frac{1}{3} \alpha_2 + \frac{1}{5} \alpha_4.$$

The reader should verify that the polynomial $p_4(x) = x^4 + 3x^3 - 2x^2 + 2x - 1$ is equivalent to

$$p_4(x) = -\frac{22}{15} P_0(x) + \frac{19}{5} P_1(x)$$

$$- \frac{16}{21} P_2(x) + \frac{6}{5} P_3(x) + \frac{8}{35} P_4(x).$$

2.10 Gaussian Quadrature

Gauss-Legendre Quadrature. As before, we estimate the value of the integral $\int_a^b f(x)\, dx$ by approximating the function $f(x)$ with an nth-degree interpolating polynomial $p_n(x)$, and integrate as follows:

$$\int_a^b f(x)\, dx = \int_a^b p_n(x)\, dx + \int_a^b R_n(x)\, dx. \qquad (2.77)$$

Here, $R_n(x)$ is the error term for the nth-degree interpolating polynomial. Since the x_i are not yet specified, the Lagrangian form of the interpolating polynomial, (1.43), which permits arbitrarily spaced base points, will be used with its error term, (1.39).

$$f(x) = p_n(x) + R_n(x)$$

$$= \sum_{i=0}^{n} L_i(x) f(x_i) + \left[\prod_{i=0}^{n} (x - x_i) \right] \frac{f^{(n+1)}(\xi)}{(n+1)!},$$

$$a < \xi < b, \qquad (2.78)$$

where

$$L_i(x) = \prod_{\substack{j=0 \\ j \neq i}}^{n} \left(\frac{x - x_j}{x_i - x_j} \right).$$

To simplify the development somewhat, but without removing any generality of the result, the interval of integration will be changed from $[a,b]$ to $[-1,1]$ by a suitable transformation of variable. Assume that all the base points are in the interval of integration, that is, $a \leqslant x_0, x_1, \ldots, x_n \leqslant b$. Let the new variable, z, where $-1 \leqslant z \leqslant 1$, be defined by

$$z = \frac{2x - (a+b)}{b-a}. \qquad (2.79)$$

Define also a new function $F(z)$ so that

$$F(z) = f(x) = f\left(\frac{(b-a)z + (a+b)}{2}\right). \qquad (2.80)$$

Then (2.78) becomes

$$F(z) = \sum_{i=0}^{n} L_i(z)F(z_i) + \left[\prod_{i=0}^{n}(z - z_i)\right]\frac{F^{(n+1)}(\xi)}{(n+1)!}, \qquad (2.81)$$

where

$$L_i(z) = \prod_{\substack{j=0 \\ j \neq i}}^{n} \frac{(z - z_j)}{(z_i - z_j)} \quad \text{and} \quad -1 < \xi < 1.$$

Here, z_i is simply the base-point value x_i transformed by (2.79). Now if $f(x)$ is *assumed to be a polynomial of degree* $2n+1$ as suggested earlier, then the term $F^{(n+1)}(\xi)/(n+1)!$ must be a polynomial of degree n, since $\sum_{i=0}^{n} L_i(z)F(z_i)$ is a polynomial of degree n at most, and $\prod_{i=0}^{n}(z - z_i)$ is a polynomial of degree $n+1$. Let

$$\frac{F^{(n+1)}(\xi)}{(n+1)!} = q_n(z),$$

where $q_n(z)$ is a polynomial of degree n. Then

$$F(z) = \sum_{i=0}^{n} L_i(z)F(z_i) + \left[\prod_{i=0}^{n}(z - z_i)\right]q_n(z). \qquad (2.82)$$

Now integration of both sides of (2.82) between the transformed integration limits gives

$$\int_{-1}^{1} F(z)\,dz = \int_{-1}^{1}\sum_{i=0}^{n} L_i(z)F(z_i)\,dz$$
$$+ \int_{-1}^{1}\left[\prod_{i=0}^{n}(z - z_i)\right]q_n(z)\,dz. \qquad (2.83)$$

Since the $F(z_i)$ are fixed values, the summation operator can be taken outside the integral sign. Dropping the right-most integral, (2.83) becomes

$$\int_{-1}^{1} F(z)\,dz \doteq \sum_{i=0}^{n} F(z_i)\int_{-1}^{1} L_i(z)\,dz$$

$$\doteq \sum_{i=0}^{n} w_i F(z_i), \qquad (2.84)$$

where

$$w_i = \int_{-1}^{1} L_i(z)\,dz = \int_{-1}^{1}\prod_{\substack{j=0 \\ j \neq i}}^{n}\left[\frac{z - z_j}{z_i - z_j}\right]dz. \qquad (2.85)$$

Note that (2.84) is of the desired form (2.22) and that the second integral on the right-hand side of (2.83),

$$\int_{-1}^{1}\left[\prod_{i=0}^{n}(z - z_i)\right]q_n(z)\,dz, \qquad (2.86)$$

is then the error term for the integration or quadrature formula of (2.84). The object is to select the z_i in such a way that the error term (2.86) vanishes. The orthogonality property of the Legendre polynomials of (2.64) will be used to establish such values z_i.

First, expand the two polynomials $q_n(z)$ and $\prod_{i=0}^{n}(z - z_i)$ in terms of the Legendre polynomials, as illustrated in Section 2.9:

$$\prod_{i=0}^{n}(z - z_i) = b_0 P_0(z) + b_1 P_1(z) +$$
$$\cdots + b_n P_n(z) + b_{n+1}P_{n+1}(z) = \sum_{i=0}^{n+1} b_i P_i(z), \qquad (2.87)$$

and

$$q_n(z) = c_0 P_0(z) + c_1 P_1(z) + \cdots + c_n P_n(z) = \sum_{i=0}^{n} c_i P_i(z). \qquad (2.88)$$

The product $q_n(z)\prod_{i=0}^{n}(z - z_i)$ is, from (2.87) and (2.88),

$$\sum_{i=0}^{n}\sum_{j=0}^{n} b_i c_j P_i(z)P_j(z) + b_{n+1}\sum_{i=0}^{n} c_i P_i(z)P_{n+1}(z). \qquad (2.89)$$

The integral of (2.86) then assumes the form

$$\int_{-1}^{1}\left[\sum_{i=0}^{n}\sum_{j=0}^{n} b_i c_j P_i(z)P_j(z) + b_{n+1}\sum_{i=0}^{n} c_i P_i(z)P_{n+1}(z)\right]dz. \qquad (2.90)$$

Because of the orthogonality properties of the Legendre polynomials, all terms of this integral that are of the form

$$b_i c_j \int_{-1}^{1} P_i(z)P_j(z)\,dz, \qquad i \neq j, \qquad (2.91)$$

will vanish [see (2.64)]. Thus the error term (2.86) for the quadrature formula of (2.84) may be written

$$\int_{-1}^{1}\left[\prod_{i=0}^{n}(z - z_i)\right]q_n(z)\,dz = \int_{-1}^{1}\sum_{i=0}^{n} b_i c_i [P_i(z)]^2\,dz$$

$$= \sum_{i=0}^{n} b_i c_i \int_{-1}^{1}[P_i(z)]^2\,dz. \qquad (2.92)$$

One way to make this expression vanish is to specify that the first $n+1$ of the b_i, $i = 0, 1, \ldots, n$, are zero. The coefficient b_{n+1} of $P_{n+1}(z)$ is still unspecified, but from (2.87) it must be given by

$$\prod_{i=0}^{n}(z - z_i) = b_{n+1}P_{n+1}(z). \qquad (2.93)$$

For example, for $n = 3$, the coefficient of the high-order (z^4) term of $P_{n+1}(z) = P_4(z)$ is 35/8 [see (2.65)]. Since the high-order coefficient of $\prod_{i=0}^{n}(z - z_i)$ is 1, $b_{n+1} = 8/35$. The important feature of (2.93) is that the polynomial $\prod_{i=0}^{n}(z - z_i)$ is already in factored form, that is, it has the $n + 1$ roots z_i, $i = 0, 1, \ldots, n$. Since $b_{n+1}P_{n+1}(z)$ is the same polynomial, the z_i must be the roots of $b_{n+1}P_{n+1}(z)$ as well, or equivalently, of $P_{n+1}(z)$. Thus the $n + 1$

base points to be used in the integration formula of (2.84) are the $n + 1$ roots of the appropriate [$(n + 1)$th-degree] Legendre polynomial. The relative weight assigned each functional value $F(z_i)$ is given by (2.85). Values of the appropriate base points (roots) and weight factors for $n = 1, 2, 3, 4, 5, 9$, and 14 (corresponding to the 2, 3, 4, 5, 6, 10, and 15-point formulas respectively) are shown in Table 2.2. The integration formulas of (2.84) with base

Table 2.2. Roots of the Legendre Polynomials $P_{n+1}(z)$ and the Weight
Factors for the Gauss-Legendre Quadrature[4]

$$\int_{-1}^{1} F(z)\, dz \doteq \sum_{i=0}^{n} w_i F(z_i)$$

Roots (z_i)	Weight Factors (w_i)
Two-Point Formula $n = 1$	
$\pm$0.57735 02691 89626	1.00000 00000 00000
Three-Point Formula $n = 2$	
0.00000 00000 00000	0.88888 88888 88889
$\pm$0.77459 66692 41483	0.55555 55555 55556
Four-Point Formula $n = 3$	
$\pm$0.33998 10435 84856	0.65214 51548 62546
$\pm$0.86113 63115 94053	0.34785 48451 37454
Five-point Formula $n = 4$	
0.00000 00000 00000	0.56888 88888 88889
$\pm$0.53846 93101 05683	0.47862 86704 99366
$\pm$0.90617 98459 38664	0.23692 68850 56189
Six-Point Formula $n = 5$	
$\pm$0.23861 91860 83197	0.46791 39345 72691
$\pm$0.66120 93864 66265	0.36076 15730 48139
$\pm$0.93246 95142 03152	0.17132 44923 79170
Ten-Point Formula $n = 9$	
$\pm$0.14887 43389 81631	0.29552 42247 14753
$\pm$0.43339 53941 29247	0.26926 67193 09996
$\pm$0.67940 95682 99024	0.21908 63625 15982
$\pm$0.86506 33666 88985	0.14945 13491 50581
$\pm$0.97390 65285 17172	0.06667 13443 08688
Fifteen-Point Formula $n = 14$	
0.00000 00000 00000	0.20257 82419 25561
$\pm$0.20119 40939 97435	0.19843 14853 27111
$\pm$0.39415 13470 77563	0.18616 10001 15562
$\pm$0.57097 21726 08539	0.16626 92058 16994
$\pm$0.72441 77313 60170	0.13957 06779 26154
$\pm$0.84820 65834 10427	0.10715 92204 67172
$\pm$0.93727 33924 00706	0.07036 60474 88108
$\pm$0.98799 25180 20485	0.03075 32419 96117

points given by the roots z_i and weight factors w_i listed in Table 2.2 are called the *Gauss-Legendre quadrature formulas.* Computation of the roots z_i and weight factors w_i for several values of n is illustrated in Example 3.4.

Example. Use the two-point Gauss-Legendre quadrature formula to evaluate

$$\int_{-1}^{1} F(z)\, dz = \int_{-1}^{1} (z^3 + z^2 + z + 1)\, dz = 2\tfrac{2}{3}.$$

From Table 2.2, the two-point formula is

$$\int_{-1}^{1} F(z)\, dz \doteq \sum_{i=0}^{1} w_i F(z_i) = 1 \times F(0.57735\ldots)$$
$$+ 1 \times F(-0.57735\ldots).$$

We have

$$F(-0.57735\ldots) = 0.56353297$$
$$F(+0.57735\ldots) = 2.10313369.$$

Since both weights are 1, $F(z)\, dz \doteq F(z_0) + F(z_1)$, so that

$$\int_{-1}^{1} (z^3 + z^2 + z + 1)\, dz \doteq 2.66666666.$$

To the given number of figures, this result is exact (as would be expected), since the two-point formula ($n = 1$) is exact when $F(z)$ is a polynomial of degree three ($2n + 1$) or less.

Example. Use the five-point Gauss-Legendre quadrature to compute an estimate of ln 2, that is, evaluate

$$\int_{1}^{2} \frac{dx}{x} = \ln x \Big]_{1}^{2} = \ln 2 \doteq 0.69314718.$$

Transforming the variable from $1 \leqslant x \leqslant 3$ to $-1 \leqslant z \leqslant 1$, using (2.79),

$$z = \frac{2x - (b + a)}{b - a} = \frac{2x - 2 - 1}{2 - 1} = 2x - 3.$$

Then

$$f(x) = \frac{1}{x},$$

$$F(z) = \frac{2}{z + 3},$$

and

$$\int_{1}^{2} \frac{dx}{x} = \int_{-1}^{1} \frac{2}{z + 3} \times \frac{dz}{2} = \int_{-1}^{1} \left(\frac{1}{z + 3} \right) dz.$$

The five-point quadrature is given by

$$\int_{-1}^{1} F(z)\, dz \doteq \sum_{i=0}^{4} w_i F(z_i).$$

The evaluation of the five-point formula for the given $F(z)$ is shown in Table 2.3. The computed estimate, $\ln 2 \doteq 0.69314712$, is accurate to six figures.

Normally the limits of integration will not be -1 and 1, as required by the Gauss-Legendre quadrature formulas. One approach to the evaluation of

$$\int_{a}^{b} f(x)\, dx, \qquad (2.94)$$

where a and b are arbitrary but finite, is to transform the function $f(x)$, $a \leqslant x \leqslant b$, to the interval $-1 \leqslant z \leqslant 1$, using the transformation of (2.79) as illustrated in the last example. An alternative and usually much simpler approach is to transform the Gauss-Legendre quadrature formula from the standard interval $-1 \leqslant z \leqslant 1$ to the desired interval $a \leqslant x \leqslant b$, using the inverse of (2.79),

$$x = \frac{z(b - a) + b + a}{2}. \qquad (2.95)$$

Then (2.94) becomes

$$\int_{a}^{b} f(x)\, dx = \frac{(b - a)}{2} \int_{-1}^{1} f\left(\frac{z(b - a) + b + a}{2} \right) dz. \qquad (2.96)$$

Since the standard Gauss-Legendre quadrature is given by

$$\int_{-1}^{1} F(z)\, dz \doteq \sum_{i=0}^{n} w_i F(z_i), \qquad (2.97)$$

the integral of (2.96) can be approximated by

$$\int_{a}^{b} f(x)\, dx \doteq \frac{(b - a)}{2} \sum_{i=0}^{n} w_i f\left(\frac{z_i(b - a) + b + a}{2} \right). \qquad (2.98)$$

Table 2.3   Five-Point Gauss-Legendre Quadrature

i	z_i	w_i	$F(z_i) = \dfrac{1}{z_i + 3}$	$w_i F(z_i)$
0	0.00000000	0.56888889	0.33333333	0.18962962
1	+0.53846931	0.47862867	0.28260808	0.13526433
2	−0.53846931	0.47862867	0.40625128	0.19444351
3	+0.90617985	0.23692689	0.25600460	0.06065437
4	−0.90617985	0.23692689	0.47759593	0.11315529
			$\sum_{i=0}^{4} w_i F(z_i) \quad =$	0.69314712

The general formulation of the Gauss-Legendre quadrature given by (2.98) is particularly suitable for machine computation because it does not require *symbolic* transformation of $f(x)$; instead, the base points z_i are transformed and the weight factors w_i are modified by the constant $(b - a)/2$.

Example. Use the two-point Gauss-Legendre quadrature formula to evaluate

$$\int_1^3 (x^3 + x^2 + x + 1)\, dx = 34\tfrac{2}{3}.$$

Using (2.98) with $a = 1$, $b = 3$, and the w_i and z_i from Table 2.2 for $n = 1$,

$$\int_1^3 f(x)\, dx \doteq \frac{(3 - 1)}{2}$$

$$\times \left[1.0 f\left(\frac{-0.577350269189626(3 - 1) + 3 + 1}{2} \right) \right.$$

$$\left. + 1.0 f\left(\frac{0.577350269189626(3 - 1) + 3 + 1}{2} \right) \right]$$

$$= f(1.4226497309) + f(2.5773502691)$$

$$= 7.32592866 + 27.34073801 = 34.66666667.$$

To the number of figures retained in the calculation, the results are exact, as expected, since $f(x)$ is a polynomial of degree $2n + 1$.

The preceding example illustrates why the Gauss-Legendre quadrature formulas have been little used in the past. The weight factors and base points for the computation are inconvenient numbers for hand calculation. On a digital computer, however, the presence of such numbers makes no difference in calculations, provided that the function can be evaluated at the necessary arguments (if the function is available only in tabulated form, then it will probably be necessary to interpolate on the table).

In the derivation of the quadrature formulas, great emphasis has been placed on accurate integration of polynomial functions, so that (2.84) yields exactly the integral when $F(z)$ is a polynomial of degree $2n + 1$ or less. In most real situations, of course, $F(z)$ is not a polynomial at all; the question of formula accuracy is, as always, of prime importance. Unfortunately the derivation of the error term corresponding to (2.84) is quite tedious. The development is not included here, but a complete description may be found on pages 314–325 of [2]. The error term for the Gauss-Legendre quadrature formula of (2.84) is

$$E_n(z) = \frac{2^{2n+3}[(n + 1)!]^4}{(2n + 3)[(2n + 2)!]^3} F^{(2n+2)}(\xi), \qquad \xi \text{ in } (-1,1).$$

$$(2.99)$$

Provided that the magnitudes of high-order derivatives decrease or do not increase substantially with increasing n, the Gauss-Legendre formulas are significantly more accurate than the equal-interval formulas of the preceding sections for comparable values of n.

EXAMPLE 2.3

GAUSS-LEGENDRE QUADRATURE

Problem Statement

Write a general-purpose function named GAUSS that uses the m-point Gauss-Legendre quadrature formula to evaluate numerically the integral

$$\int_a^b f(x)\, dx, \qquad (2.3.1)$$

where $f(x)$ is any single-valued function and a and b are finite. The function should incorporate the necessary Legendre polynomial roots, z_i, and the corresponding weight factors, w_i, from Table 2.2 for the 2, 3, 4, 5, 6, 10, and 15-point quadrature formulas.

Method of Solution

The integral of (2.3.1) can be evaluated numerically by implementing the algorithm of (2.98), provided the appropriate w_i and z_i values are available. An examination of Table 2.2 shows that the roots z_i for the m-point formula are placed symmetrically about the origin. For m odd, there is one root $z_0 = 0$ and $(m - 1)/2$ root pairs $z_i = -z_{i+1}$, $i = 1, 3, \ldots, m - 2$. The weights w_i and w_{i+1} associated with the root pairs are identical. For m even, there are $m/2$ root pairs, and no zero root.

Because nearly half of the z_i in Table 2.2 appear in root pairs, only the magnitudes of the z_i and the corresponding weight factors need be available to the function GAUSS.

Table 2.3.1 *Assignment of the Roots and Weight Factors to the z and w vectors*

j	z_j	w_j	m
1	0.57735..	1.0	2
2	0.0	0.88888..	3
3	0.77459..	0.55555..	3
4	0.33998..	0.65214..	4
5	0.86113..	0.34785..	4
6	0.0	0.56888..	5
7	0.53846..	0.47862..	5
8	0.90617..	0.23692	5
9	0.23861..	0.46791..	6
10	0.66120..	0.36076..	6
11	0.93246..	0.17132..	6
12	0.14887..	0.29552..	10
13	0.43339..	0.26926..	10
14	.	.	
15	.	.	
16	0.97390..	0.06667..	10
17	0.0	0.20257..	15
18	0.20119..	0.19843..	15
.	.	.	
.	.	.	
24	0.98799..	0.03075..	15

Let the magnitudes of the roots and the corresponding weight factors from Table 2.2 be assigned to elements of two vectors, z and w, as shown in Table 2.3.1.

In order to locate the roots and weight factors for the m-point formula, it is convenient to assign the following values to two vectors, p and k:

i	p_i	k_i
1	2	1
2	3	2
3	4	4
4	5	6
5	6	9
6	10	12
7	15	17
8	—	25

To find the elements of the z and w vectors for the m-point formula, the p array is searched for an element equal to m, i.e. for $p_i = m$. The desired roots and weight factors are $z_{k_i}, \ldots, z_{k_{i+1}-1}$, and $w_{k_i}, \ldots, w_{k_{i+1}-1}$, respectively. For example, the proper constants for the 5-point formula can be found by scanning the p vector and noting that $p_4 = 5$. Then $k_4 = 6$ and $k_5 = 9$. The desired elements of the z and w vectors are z_6, z_7, z_8 and w_6, w_7, w_8 respectively.

Let $c = (b - a)/2$ and $d = (b + a)/2$. Then (2.98) may be rewritten as

$$\int_a^b f(x)\, dx = c \sum_{j=k_i}^{k_{i+1}-1} w_j[f(cz_j + d) + f(-cz_j + d)], \qquad (2.3.2)$$

for even values of m. For odd values of m, (2.3.2) also applies except when $j = k_i$. In this case z_j has a zero value and does not occur in a root pair; the factor $w_j f(d)$ should be added just once to the accumulated sum.

In the program that follows, the function GAUSS checks to insure that m has been assigned one of the legitimate values 2, 3, 4, 5, 6, 10, or 15. If not, GAUSS returns a true zero as its value.

A short calling program is included to test GAUSS. It reads values for a, b, and m, calls on GAUSS to compute the required integral, and prints the results. The function $f(x)$ is defined as a function named FUNCTN. In this example, $f(x) = 1/x$, i.e., the integral to be evaluated is

$$\int_a^b \frac{dx}{x} = \ln b - \ln a. \qquad (2.3.3)$$

When $a = 1$, the results can be compared directly with tabulated values of $\ln b$.

Example 2.3   Gauss-Legendre Quadrature   **107**

Flow Diagram

Main Program

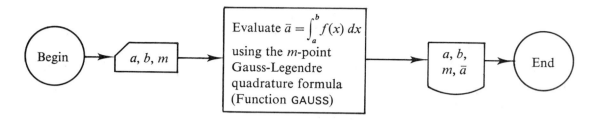

Function FUNCTN (Dummy argument: x)

Entry → Return $1/x$

Function GAUSS* (Dummy arguments: a, b, m, f; calling arguments: $a, b, m,$ FUNCTN)

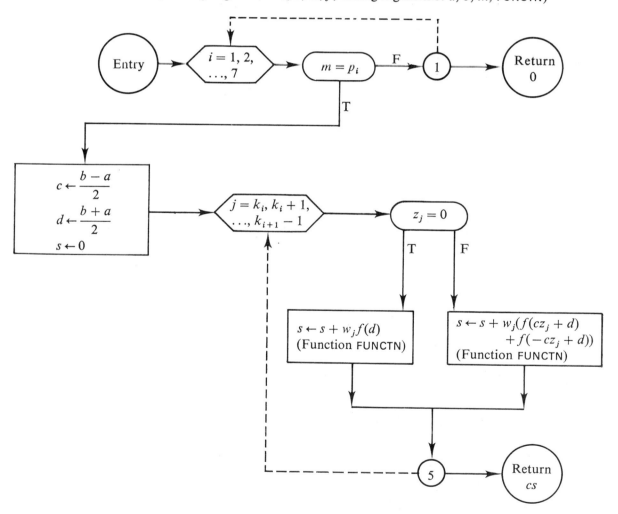

* The vectors p, k, w, and z are assumed to have appropriate values upon entry (see text).

FORTRAN *Implementation*

List of Principal Variables

Program Symbol	Definition
(Main)	
A, B	Integration limits, a and b.
AREA	Computed value of integral (2.3.1), $\bar{a}$.
M	Number of points in the Gauss-Legendre quadrature formula, m.
(Function GAUSS)	
C	$c = (b - a)/2$.
D	$d = (b + a)/2$.
I	Subscript for vectors p and k, i.
J	Index on the repeated sum of (2.3.2).
JFIRST	Initial value of j, k_i.
JLAST	Final value of j, $k_{i+1} - 1$.
KEY	Vector k.
NPOINT	Vector p.
SUM	Repeated sum of (2.3.2).
WEIGHT	Vector of weight factors, w_i.
Z	Vector of Legendre polynomial roots, z_i.
(Function FUNCTN)	
X	Integration variable, x.

Example 2.3   Gauss-Legendre Quadrature   **109**

Program Listing

Main Program

```
C           APPLIED NUMERICAL METHODS, EXAMPLE 2.3
C           GAUSS-LEGENDRE QUADRATURE
C
C           THIS CALLING PROGRAM READS VALUES FOR A, B, AND M, CALLS
C           ON THE FUNCTION GAUSS TO COMPUTE THE NUMERICAL APPROXIMATION
C           OF THE INTEGRAL OF FUNCTN(X)*DX BETWEEN INTEGRATION LIMITS
C           A AND B USING THE M POINT GAUSS-LEGENDRE QUADRATURE FORMULA,
C           PRINTS THE RESULTS, AND RETURNS TO READ A NEW SET OF
C           DATA VALUES.
C
            IMPLICIT  REAL*8(A-H, O-Z)
            EXTERNAL FUNCTN
C
            WRITE (6,200)
      1     READ (5,100)  A, B, M
            AREA = GAUSS ( A, B, M, FUNCTN )
            WRITE (6,201)  A, B, M, AREA
            GO TO 1
C
C     ..... FORMATS FOR INPUT AND OUTPUT STATEMENTS .....
    100     FORMAT ( 4X, F8.4, 10X, F8.4, 10X, I3 )
    200     FORMAT ( 1H1,10X, 1HA, 14X, 1HB, 10X, 1HM, 9X, 4HAREA / 1H  )
    201     FORMAT ( 1H , 2F15.6, I7, F15.6 )
C
            END
```

Function FUNCTN

```
            FUNCTION FUNCTN( X )
C
C     ..... THIS FUNCTION RETURNS 1/X AS ITS VALUE .....
            REAL*8  X, FUNCTN
            FUNCTN = 1.0/X
            RETURN
C
            END
```

Function GAUSS

```
            FUNCTION GAUSS( A, B, M, FUNCTN )
C
C           THE FUNCTION GAUSS USES THE M-POINT GAUSS-LEGENDRE QUADRATURE
C           FORMULA TO COMPUTE THE INTEGRAL OF FUNCTN(X)*DX BETWEEN
C           INTEGRATION LIMITS A AND B.  THE ROOTS OF SEVEN LEGENDRE
C           POLYNOMIALS AND THE WEIGHT FACTORS FOR THE CORRESPONDING
C           QUADRATURES ARE STORED IN THE Z AND WEIGHT ARRAYS
C           RESPECTIVELY.  M MAY ASSUME VALUES 2,3,4,5,6,10, AND 15
C           ONLY.  THE APPROPRIATE VALUES FOR THE M-POINT FORMULA ARE
C           LOCATED IN ELEMENTS Z(KEY(I))...Z(KEY(I+1)-1) AND
C           WEIGHT(KEY(I))...WEIGHT(KEY(I+1)-1) WHERE THE PROPER
C           VALUE OF I IS DETERMINED BY FINDING THE SUBSCRIPT OF THE
C           ELEMENT OF THE ARRAY NPOINT WHICH HAS THE VALUE M.  IF AN
C           INVALID VALUE OF M IS USED, A TRUE ZERO IS RETURNED AS THE
C           VALUE OF GAUSS.
C
            IMPLICIT  REAL*8(A-H, O-Z)
            REAL*8  GAUSS, A, B, FUNCTN
            DIMENSION NPOINT(7), KEY(8), Z(24), WEIGHT(24)
```

Program Listing (*Continued*)

```
C
C       ..... PRESET NPOINT, KEY, Z, AND WEIGHT ARRAYS .....
        DATA  NPOINT / 2, 3,  4,  5,  6,  10,  15 /
C
        DATA  KEY  / 1, 2,  4,  6,  9,  12,  17,  25 /
C
        DATA  Z          / 0.577350269,0.0           ,0.774596669,
       1          0.339981044,0.861136312,0.0          ,0.538469310,
       2          0.906179846,0.238619186,0.661209387,0.932469514,
       3          0.148874339,0.433395394,0.679409568,0.865063367,
       4          0.973906529,0.0           ,0.201194094,0.394151347,
       5          0.570972173,0.724417731,0.848206583,0.937273392,
       6          0.987992518 /
C
        DATA  WEIGHT     / 1.0          ,0.888888889,0.555555556,
       1          0.652145155,0.347854845,0.568888889,0.478628671,
       2          0.236926885,0.467913935,0.360761573,0.171324493,
       3          0.295524225,0.269266719,0.219086363,0.149451349,
       4          0.066671344,0.202578242,0.198431485,0.186161000,
       5          0.166269206,0.139570678,0.107159221,0.070366047,
       6          0.030753242 /
C
C       ..... FIND SUBSCRIPT OF FIRST Z AND WEIGHT VALUE .....
        DO 1   I=1,7
      1 IF (M.EQ.NPOINT(I))  GO TO 2
C
C       ..... INVALID M USED .....
        GAUSS = 0.0
        RETURN
C
C       ..... SET UP INITIAL PARAMETERS .....
      2 JFIRST = KEY(I)
        JLAST = KEY(I+1) - 1
        C = (B-A)/2.0
        D = (B+A)/2.0
C
C       ..... ACCUMULATE THE SUM IN THE M-POINT FORMULA .....
        SUM = 0.0
        DO 5   J=JFIRST,JLAST
        IF ( Z(J).EQ.0.0 )  SUM = SUM + WEIGHT(J)*FUNCTN(D)
      5 IF ( Z(J).NE.0.0 )  SUM = SUM + WEIGHT(J)*(FUNCTN(Z(J)*C + D)
       1    + FUNCTN(-Z(J)*C + D))
C
C       ..... MAKE INTERVAL CORRECTION AND RETURN .....
        GAUSS = C*SUM
        RETURN
C
        END
```

Data

A =		B =		M =	
A =	1.0000	B =	2.0000	M =	2
A =	1.0000	B =	2.0000	M =	3
A =	1.0000	B =	2.0000	M =	4
A =	1.0000	B =	2.0000	M =	5
A =	1.0000	B =	2.0000	M =	6
A =	1.0000	B =	2.0000	M =	10
A =	1.0000	B =	2.0000	M =	15
A =	1.0000	B =	5.0000	M =	2
A =	1.0000	B =	5.0000	M =	3
A =	1.0000	B =	5.0000	M =	4
A =	1.0000	B =	5.0000	M =	5
A =	1.0000	B =	5.0000	M =	6
A =	1.0000	B =	5.0000	M =	10
A =	1.0000	B =	5.0000	M =	15
A =	1.0000	B =	10.0000	M =	2
A =	1.0000	B =	10.0000	M =	3
A =	1.0000	B =	10.0000	M =	4

Example 2.3 Gauss-Legendre Quadrature **111**

Program Listing (*Continued*)

```
A =    1.0000    B =   10.0000    M =    5
A =    1.0000    B =   10.0000    M =    6
A =    1.0000    B =   10.0000    M =   10
A =    1.0000    B =   10.0000    M =   15
A =    1.0000    B =   20.0000    M =    2
A =    1.0000    B =   20.0000    M =    3
A =    1.0000    B =   20.0000    M =    4
A =    1.0000    B =   20.0000    M =    5
A =    1.0000    B =   20.0000    M =    6
A =    1.0000    B =   20.0000    M =   10
A =    1.0000    B =   20.0000    M =   15
A =    1.0000    B =   20.0000    M =    1
A =    1.0000    B =   20.0000    M =    8
A =    1.0000    B =   20.0000    M =   17
```

Computer Output

A	B	M	AREA
1.000000	2.000000	2	0.692308
1.000000	2.000000	3	0.693122
1.000000	2.000000	4	0.693146
1.000000	2.000000	5	0.693147
1.000000	2.000000	6	0.693147
1.000000	2.000000	10	0.693147
1.000000	2.000000	15	0.693147
1.000000	5.000000	2	1.565217
1.000000	5.000000	3	1.602694
1.000000	5.000000	4	1.608430
1.000000	5.000000	5	1.609289
1.000000	5.000000	6	1.609416
1.000000	5.000000	10	1.609438
1.000000	5.000000	15	1.609438
1.000000	10.000000	2	2.106383
1.000000	10.000000	3	2.246610
1.000000	10.000000	4	2.286970
1.000000	10.000000	5	2.298283
1.000000	10.000000	6	2.301408
1.000000	10.000000	10	2.302579
1.000000	10.000000	15	2.302585
1.000000	20.000000	2	2.488565
1.000000	20.000000	3	2.779872
1.000000	20.000000	4	2.905192
1.000000	20.000000	5	2.958221
1.000000	20.000000	6	2.980324
1.000000	20.000000	10	2.995311
1.000000	20.000000	15	2.995728
1.000000	20.000000	1	0.0
1.000000	20.000000	8	0.0
1.000000	20.000000	17	0.0

Discussion of Results

The program has been tested for the integrand function $f(x) = 1/x$ with integration limits $a = 1$ and $b = 2$, 5, 10, 20 leading to the true integrals ln 2, ln 5, ln 10, and ln 20 respectively (see Table 2.3.2). Each integral has been evaluated numerically using the 2, 3, 4, 5, 6, 10, and 15-point Gauss-Legendre quadrature formulas.

In terms of the transformed variable z, $-1 \leqslant z \leqslant 1$ (see (2.95)), the integrand function is given by

$$F(z) = \frac{2}{z(b-1) + b + 1}. \tag{2.3.4}$$

Then, from (2.99), the error for the m-point quadrature is

$$|E(z)| = \frac{2^{2m+2}(m!)^4(b-1)^{2m}}{(2m+1)[(2m)!]^2[\xi(b-1) + b + 1]^{2m+1}},$$
$$-1 < \xi < 1. \tag{2.3.5}$$

Since $\xi(b-1) + b + 1$ has a minimum value of 2 for $b \geqslant 1$, the maximum truncation errors for the computed logarithms are given by

$$|E_{max}(b,m)| = \frac{2(m!)^4(b-1)^{2m}}{(2m+1)[(2m)!]^2}, \qquad b \geqslant 1. \tag{2.3.6}$$

The error bound increases with increasing b, i.e., as the length of the integration interval increases, and decreases with increasing m, the number of points in the quadrature formula. The computed approximations for ln 2, ln 5, ln 10, and ln 20 show similar trends for the actual error.

Table 2.3.2   *True Integral Values*

Data Sets	True Integral
1–7	0.693147
8–14	1.609438
15–21	2.302585
22–28	2.995732
29–31	Illegal data values

An alternative, though computationally less efficient, approach to integration by Gauss-Legendre quadrature is illustrated in example 3.4. Recursion relation (2.66) is used to generate the coefficients of the appropriate Legendre polynomial, and the base points z_i are found by using the half-interval root-finding method of Section 3.8. The corresponding weight factors w_i are generated by evaluating the integral of (2.85), which can be determined analytically.

With only minor modifications, GAUSS could be changed to allow evaluation of Gauss-Legendre quadrature formulas of the composite type.

Gauss-Laguerre Quadrature. The Laguerre polynomials of (2.68) can be used to generate a Gaussian quadrature formula to evaluate integrals of the form

$$\int_0^\infty e^{-z}F(z)\,dz \doteq \sum_{i=0}^n w_iF(z_i). \qquad (2.100)$$

The derivation of the integration formula of (2.100), which is known as the *Gauss-Laguerre quadrature*, is very similar to that for the Gauss-Legendre quadrature of the preceding section. As before, the Lagrange form of the interpolating polynomial (1.43) with its error term (1.39) is used to approximate the function $F(z)$, since the z_i are as yet unspecified. Thus

$$F(z) = \sum_{i=0}^n L_i(z)F(z_i) + \left[\prod_{i=0}^n (z - z_i)\right]\frac{F^{(n+1)}(\xi)}{(n+1)!},$$
$$0 < \xi < \infty, \qquad (2.101)$$

where

$$L_i(z) = \prod_{\substack{j=0 \\ j \ne i}}^n \left[\frac{z - z_j}{z_i - z_j}\right]. \qquad (2.102)$$

Assume that $F(z)$ is a polynomial of degree $2n + 1$; then $F^{(n+1)}(\xi)/(n+1)!$ must be a polynomial of degree n. Let this polynomial be $q_n(z)$, so that

$$F(z) = \sum_{i=0}^n L_i(z)F(z_i) + \left[\prod_{i=0}^n (z - z_i)\right]q_n(z). \qquad (2.103)$$

To compute $\int_0^\infty e^{-z}F(z)\,dz$, multiply each term of (2.103) by e^{-z} and integrate both sides:

$$\int_0^\infty e^{-z}F(z)\,dz = \sum_{i=0}^n F(z_i)\int_0^\infty e^{-z}L_i(z)\,dz$$
$$+ \int_0^\infty e^{-z}\left[\prod_{i=0}^n (z - z_i)\right]q_n(z)\,dz. \qquad (2.104)$$

By the orthogonality property of the Laguerre polynomials, the remainder term on the right can be made to vanish if $\prod_{i=0}^n(z - z_i)$ is a constant multiple of the Laguerre polynomial, $\mathcal{L}_{n+1}(z)$. The argument used here is identical with that used previously [see (2.86)–(2.92)] for the Gauss-Legendre quadrature. Expand $q_n(z)$ in terms of the Laguerre polynomials of degree n or less. Then if $\prod_{i=0}^n(z - z_i)$ is $(-1)^{n+1}\mathcal{L}_{n+1}(z)$, the integral on the right of (2.104) vanishes. Thus the base points z_i to be used for the $n + 1 = m$-point Gauss-Laguerre quadrature are simply the roots of the $(n + 1)$th-degree Laguerre polynomial $\mathcal{L}_{n+1}(z)$. The corresponding weight factors are given by the coefficients of the $F(z_i)$ in (2.104), that is,

$$w_i = \int_0^\infty e^{-z}L_i(z)\,dz = \int_0^\infty e^{-z}\prod_{\substack{j=0 \\ j \ne i}}^n \left[\frac{z - z_j}{z_i - z_j}\right]dz. \qquad (2.105)$$

The appropriate base points z_i and weight factors w_i for $n = 1, 2, 3, 4, 5, 9$, and 14 (for the $m = 2, 3, 4, 5, 6, 10$, and 15-point formulas respectively) are shown in Table 2.4.

Table 2.4   Roots of the Laguerre Polynomials $\mathcal{L}_{n+1}(z)$ and the Weight Factors[a] for the Gauss-Laguerre Quadrature[4]

$$\int_0^\infty e^{-z}F(z)\,dz \doteq \sum_{i=0}^n w_iF(z_i)$$

Roots (z_i)	Weight Factors (w_i)
Two-Point Formula	
$n = 1$	
.58578 64376 27	.85355 33905 93
3.41421 35623 73	.14644 66094 07
Three-Point Formula	
$n = 2$	
.41577 45567 83	.71109 30099 29
2.29428 03602 79	.27851 77335 69
6.28994 50829 37	.(1) 10389 25650 16
Four-Point Formula	
$n = 3$	
.32254 76896 19	.60315 41043 42
1.74576 11011 58	.35741 86924 38
4.53662 02969 21	.(1) 38887 90851 50
9.39507 09123 01	.(3) 53929 47055 61

Numerical Integration

Table 2.4 (continued)

Roots (z_i)	Weight Factors (w_i)
Five-Point Formula $n = 4$	
.26356 03197 18	.52175 56105 83
1.41340 30591 07	.39866 68110 83
3.59642 57710 41	.(1) 75942 44968 17
7.08581 00058 59	.(2) 36117 58679 92
12.64080 08442 76	.(4) 23369 97238 58
Six-Point Formula $n = 5$	
.22284 66041 79	.45896 46739 50
1.18893 21016 73	.41700 08307 72
2.99273 63260 59	.11337 33820 74
5.77514 35691 05	.(1) 10399 19745 31
9.83746 74183 83	.(3) 26101 72028 15
15.98287 39806 02	.(6) 89854 79064 30
Ten-Point Formula $n = 9$	
.13779 34705 40	.30844 11157 65
.72945 45495 03	.40111 99291 55
1.80834 29017 40	.21806 82876 12
3.40143 36978 55	.(1) 62087 45609 87
5.55249 61400 64	.(2) 95015 16975 18
8.33015 27467 64	.(3) 75300 83885 88
11.84378 58379 00	.(4) 28259 23349 60
16.27925 78313 78	.(6) 42493 13984 96
21.99658 58119 81	.(8) 18395 64823 98
29.92069 70122 74	.(12) 99118 27219 61
Fifteen-Point Formula $n = 14$	
.09330 78120 17	.21823 48859 40
.49269 17403 02	.34221 01779 23
1.21559 54120 71	.26302 75779 42
2.26994 95262 04	.12642 58181 06
3.66762 27217 51	.(1) 40206 86492 10
5.42533 66274 14	.(2) 85638 77803 61
7.56591 62266 13	.(2) 12124 36147 21
10.12022 85680 19	.(3) 11167 43923 44
13.13028 24821 76	.(5) 64599 26762 02
16.65440 77083 30	.(6) 22263 16907 10
20.77647 88994 49	.(8) 42274 30384 98
25.62389 42267 29	.(10) 39218 97267 04
31.40751 91697 54	.(12) 14565 15264 07
38.53068 33064 86	.(15) 14830 27051 11
48.02608 55726 86	.(19) 16005 94906 21

[a] The numbers in parentheses indicate the number of zeros between the decimal point and the first significant digit.

The error for the Gauss-Laguerre quadrature is given [8] by

$$E_n = \frac{[(n+1)!]^2}{(2n+2)!} F^{(2n+2)}(\xi), \qquad \xi \text{ in } (0,\infty). \tag{2.106}$$

Example. Use the Gauss-Laguerre quadrature formula to estimate $\Gamma(2.0)$ and $\Gamma(1.8)$, where

$$\Gamma(\alpha) = \int_0^\infty e^{-z} z^{\alpha-1} \, dz.$$

For integral arguments, α,

$$\Gamma(\alpha) = (\alpha - 1)!$$

From (2.100),

$$\Gamma(\alpha) \doteq \sum_{i=0}^n w_i z_i^{\alpha-1}.$$

For $\alpha = 2$,

$$\Gamma(2) \doteq \sum_{i=0}^n w_i z_i.$$

Examination of Table 2.4 shows that $\sum_{i=0}^n w_i z_i = 1$ for all n. Therefore, $\Gamma(2) = 1! = 1$. In this case, the solution is exact since $F(z) = z$ is a polynomial of degree less than $2n + 1$ for all n.

For $\alpha = 1.8$,

$$\Gamma(1.8) \doteq \sum_{i=0}^n w_i x_i^{0.8}.$$

Since $F(z) = z^{0.8}$ is not a polynomial, the quadrature will be inexact. The true value is $\Gamma(1.8) \doteq 0.931384$. Results for the quadrature with $n = 1, 2, 3, 4, 5, 9$, and 14 are listed in Table 2.5.

Table 2.5 $\Gamma(1.8)$ *by Gauss-Laguerre Quadrature*

n	$\sum_{i=0}^n w_i z_i^{0.8}$
1	0.947566
2	0.938834
3	0.935734
4	0.934261
5	0.933441
9	0.932192
14	0.931771

The Gauss-Laguerre quadrature of (2.100) can be used to evaluate integrals of the form

$$\int_a^\infty e^{-x} f(x) \, dx, \tag{2.107}$$

where a is arbitrary and finite, by means of the linear transformation $x = z + a$. Then (2.107) becomes

$$\int_a^\infty e^{-x} f(x) \, dx = \int_0^\infty e^{-(z+a)} f(z + a) \, dz$$

$$= e^{-a} \int_0^\infty e^{-z} f(z + a) \, dz, \tag{2.108}.$$

and the general formulation of the Gauss-Laguerre quadrature for arbitrary lower limit of integration a is

$$\int_a^\infty e^{-x} f(x) \, dx \doteq e^{-a} \sum_{i=0}^n w_i f(z_i + a), \tag{2.109}$$

where the w_i and z_i are those tabulated in Table 2.4.

Example. Use (2.109) to evaluate

$$\int_1^\infty e^{-x} x^2 \, dx,$$

for which the analytical value is $5/e$.

From (2.109), the integral is approximated by

$$e^{-1} \sum_{i=0}^n w_i (z_i + 1)^2$$

$$= e^{-1} \left[\sum_{i=0}^n w_i z_i^2 + 2 \sum_{i=0}^n w_i z_i + \sum_{i=0}^n w_i \right]. \tag{2.110}$$

Examination of Table 2.4 shows that

$$\sum_{i=0}^n w_i z_i^2 = 2, \qquad \sum_{i=0}^n w_i z_i = 1, \qquad \text{and} \qquad \sum_{i=1}^n w_i = 1,$$

for all n. The solution is exact, as expected, since $f(x)$ is a polynomial of degree less than $2n + 1$ for all n.

Gauss-Chebyshev Quadrature. Yet another Gaussian quadrature formula can be developed by using the orthogonality property of the Chebyshev polynomials. The development is completely analogous to that followed in producing the Gauss-Legendre and Gauss-Laguerre quadratures. In this case, the pertinent integral and corresponding *Gauss-Chebyshev quadrature* formula are given by

$$\int_{-1}^1 \frac{1}{\sqrt{1 - z^2}} F(z) \, dz \doteq \sum_{i=0}^n w_i F(z_i). \tag{2.111}$$

The integration is exact if $F(z)$ is a polynomial of degree $2n + 1$ or less. Here, the $n + 1$ values z_i are the roots of the $(n+1)$th-degree Chebyshev polynomial $T_{n+1}(z)$, [see (1.77)], so that

$$z_i = \cos \frac{(2i + 1)\pi}{(2n + 2)}, \qquad i = 0, 1, \dots, n. \tag{2.112}$$

The w_i in this case are equal and have the value $\dfrac{\pi}{n + 1}$. Then (2.111) simplifies to

$$\int_{-1}^1 \frac{1}{\sqrt{1 - z^2}} F(z) \, dz \doteq \left(\frac{\pi}{n + 1} \right) \sum_{i=0}^n F(z_i). \tag{2.113}$$

The corresponding error term [8] is

$$E_n = \frac{2\pi}{2^{2n+2}(2n+2)!} F^{(2n+2)}(\xi), \qquad \xi \text{ in } (-1,1).$$

$$(2.114)$$

Any integral of the form

$$\int_a^b \frac{1}{\sqrt{1-x^2}} f(x)\, dx \qquad \text{or} \qquad \int_a^b f(x)\, dx,$$

where a and b are finite, can be expressed in the form of (2.111) by a suitable transformation.

Gauss-Hermite Quadrature. Based upon the orthogonality property of the Hermite polynomials of (2.74), one can develop a useful Gaussian formula,

$$\int_{-\infty}^{\infty} e^{-x^2} f(x)\, dx \doteq \sum_{i=0}^{n} w_i f(x_i), \qquad (2.115)$$

which is known as the *Gauss-Hermite quadrature*. Here, the x_i are the roots of the Hermite polynomial of degree $n+1$. The weight factors and appropriate roots for the first few quadrature formulas are listed in Table 2.6. The corresponding error term [8] is

$$E_n = \frac{(n+1)!\sqrt{\pi}}{2^{n+1}(2n+2)!} f^{(2n+2)}(\xi). \qquad (2.116)$$

Table 2.6   *Roots of the Hermite Polynomials $H_{n+1}(x)$ and Weight Factors for the Gauss-Hermite Quadrature* [3]

$$\int_{-\infty}^{\infty} e^{-x^2} f(x)\, dx \doteq \sum_{i=0}^{n} w_i f(x_i)$$

Roots (x_i)	Weight Factors (w_i)
Two-Point Formula $n = 1$	
$\pm 0.70710\ 67811$	$0.88622\ 69255$
Three-Point Formula $n = 2$	
$\pm 1.22474\ 48714$	$0.29540\ 89752$
$0.00000\ 00000$	$1.18163\ 59006$
Four-Point Formula $n = 3$	
$\pm 1.65068\ 01239$	$0.08131\ 28354$
$\pm 0.52464\ 76233$	$0.80491\ 40900$
Five-Point Formula $n = 4$	
$\pm 2.02018\ 28705$	$0.01995\ 32421$
$\pm 0.95857\ 24646$	$0.39361\ 93232$
$0.00000\ 00000$	$0.94530\ 87205$

Other Gaussian Quadrature Formulas. By a suitable transformation of the variable of integration or of the function to be integrated, the four Gaussian quadrature formulas developed in this section allow the numerical evaluation of many well-behaved integrals over finite, semi-infinite, or infinite intervals of integration. For example, we might write

$$\int_a^b f(x)\, dx = \int_a^b w(x) \frac{f(x)}{w(x)}\, dx$$

$$= \int_a^b w(x) g(x)\, dx \qquad (2.117)$$

and then use the quadrature appropriate for integrals of the form on the right of (2.117). In some cases, it may be possible to evaluate integrals in which the integrand has a singularity on the integration interval by relegating the singular term to the weighting function. For example, integrands containing the factor $1/\sqrt{1-x^2}$ over the integration interval $[-1,1]$ can be handled by using the Gauss-Chebyshev quadrature.

A variety of other quadrature formulas of the Gaussian type can be generated for particular weighting functions, limits of integration, and sets of orthogonal polynomials. Two well-known quadrature formulas of the Gaussian type have been developed that include one or both end points of the integration interval as base points. When $x_0 = a$ and $x_n = b$, the remaining base points $x_1, \ldots, x_{n-1}$ are found to be the roots of $P_n'(x)$, the derivative of the Legendre polynomial of degree n. The formula is called the *Lobatto quadrature* and produces exactly the integral if $f(x)$ is a polynomial of degree $2n-1$ or less. When only one integration limit is specified to be a base point, the analogous formula is called the *Radau quadrature* and is exact when $f(x)$ is a polynomial of degree $2n$ or less.

The reader interested in the development of many other Gaussian formulas is referred to [7], which also contains extensive tabulations of base points and weight factors for a variety of quadratures. The tabulated values are accurate to 30 significant figures in all cases. Tables for the Legendre, Laguerre, and Hermite formulas are particularly complete (for example, base points and weight factors for the Gauss-Legendre quadrature for over 80 values of n from 1 to 511).

The Gaussian quadrature formulas can also be used repeatedly over subintervals of the integration interval to create composite formulas similar to those of Section 2.6. Since most of the Gaussian formulas do not have base points at the ends of the integration interval, there is usually no saving in the number of function evaluations per subinterval, as occurs when composite formulas are constructed from the low-order Newton-Cotes closed formulas. On the other hand, the inconvenient form of values of the weight factors and base points makes use of the high-order formulas virtually impossible for hand calculation; even the preparation of computer programs to implement a quadrature for several values of n can be tedious, because of the large amount of tabular information required (alternatively, we might compute the essential polynomial roots by using methods described in Chapter 3, and then evaluate the necessary weight factors, probably too wasteful of computing time for a frequently used integration program).

EXAMPLE 2.4

VELOCITY DISTRIBUTION USING GAUSSIAN QUADRATURE

Introduction

Gill and Scher [11] have derived an expression for the velocity distribution for a fluid flowing in a smooth circular pipe by modifying Prandtl's mixing-length expression. The dimensionless velocity in the axial direction, u^+, is given as a function of the dimensionless distance from the inside wall of the tube, y^+, by the following integral:

$$u^+ = \int_0^{y^+} \frac{-1 + \sqrt{1 + 4cd}}{2c} \, dy^+, \qquad (2.4.1)$$

where

$$c = (0.36)^2 (y^+)^2 (1 - e^{-\phi(y^+/\bar{y}^+)})^2 \qquad (2.4.2)$$

and

$$d = 1 - \frac{y^+}{\bar{y}^+}. \qquad (2.4.3)$$

Here, $\bar{y}^+$ is the dimensionless distance corresponding to the centerline of the tube, and is given by

$$\bar{y}^+ = \frac{N_{Re}}{2} \sqrt{\bar{f}/2}, \qquad (2.4.4)$$

and ϕ, a function of $\bar{y}^+$ and some empirically determined constants, is given by

$$\phi = \frac{\bar{y}^+ - 60}{22}. \qquad (2.4.5)$$

N_{Re}, the *Reynolds number*, and $\bar{f}$, the *Fanning friction factor*, are dimensionless parameters that are functions of the physical properties and the bulk velocity of the fluid and also of the physical dimensions and surface roughness of the tube. The Reynolds number is given by

$$N_{Re} = \frac{vD\rho}{\mu}, \qquad (2.4.6)$$

where v is the mean fluid velocity, D is the inside diameter of the tube, and ρ and μ are the density and viscosity of the fluid, respectively, all in compatible units. For smooth circular tubes in the range of Reynolds number from 2000 to 50000, $\bar{f}$ is adequately represented [12] by the *Blasius equation*,

$$\bar{f} = 0.079 \, N_{Re}^{-0.25}. \qquad (2.4.7)$$

Problem Statement

Using an approach suggested by (2.117), derive a variant of the Gauss-Chebyshev quadrature (2.111) for estimating the value of the integral

$$\int_a^b f(x) \, dx, \qquad (2.4.8)$$

where $f(x)$ is any single-valued function and a and b are finite. Write a general-purpose function named CHEBY that evaluates (2.4.8) using the m-point version of the derived quadrature formula.

Write a main program that reads the appropriate data and then calls on both CHEBY and GAUSS (the function developed in Example 2.3) to implement the Gauss-Chebyshev and Gauss-Legendre quadratures, respectively, for evaluating the integral of (2.4.1). Compare the two resulting estimates of (2.4.1) for $N_{Re} = 5000$, 10000, 25000, and 50000, with $y^+ = 1$, 2, 5, 10, 20, 50, 100, 200, 500, and 1000, using the 2, 4, 6, 10, and 15-point quadratures.

Method of Solution

The integral of (2.4.8), where $a \leqslant x \leqslant b$, can be transformed to the standard interval for the Gauss-Chebyshev quadrature, $-1 \leqslant z \leqslant 1$, by the transformation (2.95)

$$x = \frac{z(b-a) + b + a}{2},$$

to yield

$$\int_a^b f(x) \, dx = \frac{(b-a)}{2} \int_{-1}^1 f\left(\frac{z(b-a) + b + a}{2}\right) dz. \qquad (2.4.9)$$

Rewriting (2.4.9) in the form of (2.117), with the weighting factor for the Gauss-Chebyshev quadrature,

$$w(z) = \frac{1}{\sqrt{1 - z^2}}, \qquad (2.4.10)$$

yields

$$\int_a^b f(x) \, dx = \frac{(b-a)}{2} \int_{-1}^1 \frac{1}{\sqrt{1 - z^2}} F(z) \, dz, \qquad (2.4.11)$$

where

$$F(z) = \sqrt{1 - z^2} f\left(\frac{z(b-a) + b + a}{2}\right). \qquad (2.4.12)$$

The Gauss-Chebyshev quadrature formula of (2.113) then becomes

$$\int_a^b f(x) \, dx \doteq \frac{\pi(b-a)}{2m} \sum_{i=1}^m \sqrt{1 - z_i^2} f(x_i), \qquad (2.4.13)$$

where

$$z_i = \cos\left(\frac{[2(i-1) + 1]\pi}{2m}\right), \qquad i = 1, 2, \ldots, m,$$

$$x_i = \frac{z_i(b-a) + b + a}{2}, \qquad i = 1, 2, \ldots, m,$$

$$(2.4.14)$$

and m is the number of points in the quadrature formula. Here, x_i is simply a root, z_i, of the mth-degree Chebyshev polynomial transformed to the interval $[a,b]$ using (2.95).

The integrand of (2.4.1), as written, is indeterminate at the lower limit of integration. An equivalent form which avoids this difficulty is

$$u^+ = \int_0^{y^+} \frac{2d}{1 + \sqrt{1 + 4cd}}\, dy^+ \qquad (2.4.15)$$

The integrand of (2.4.15) is evaluated by a function named FUNCTN, which is called upon by both CHEBY and GAUSS in the programs that follow. To improve the accuracy of the numerical integrations of (2.4.15), the integral is rewritten as

$$u_i^+ = u_{i-1}^+ + \Delta u_i^+$$

$$= u_{i-1}^+ + \int_{y_{i-1}^+}^{y_i^+} \frac{2d}{1 + \sqrt{1 + 4cd}}\, dy^+, \quad i = 2, 3, \ldots, N,$$

$$(2.4.16)$$

where $u_1^+ = y_1^+ = 0$. The program that follows reads, as data, values for N, and $y_2^+, y_3^+, \ldots, y_N^+$ just once. Thereafter, a series of values are read for N_{Re} and m; for each data set, CHEBY and GAUSS are called to evaluate the $N - 1$ integrals of (2.4.16). Since a value y_i^+ that is larger than $\bar{y}^+$ is physically meaningless, fewer than $N - 1$ integrals in (2.4.16) may be evaluated for some data sets.

Flow Diagram

Main Program

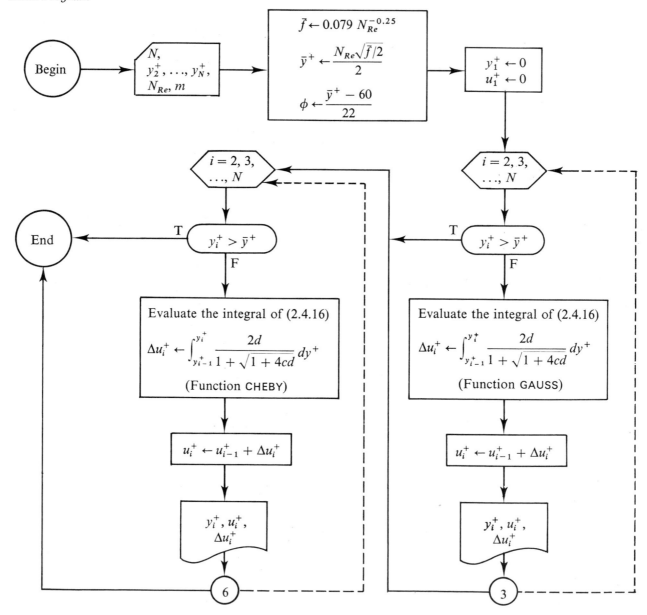

Example 2.4   Velocity Distribution using Gaussian Quadrature   **119**

Function FUNCTN (Dummy argument: y^+; calling argument: x_i)

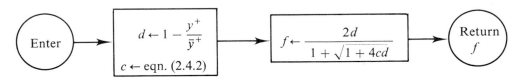

Function CHEBY (Dummy arguments: a, b, m, f;
calling arguments: y_{i-1}^+, y_i^+, m, FUNCTN)

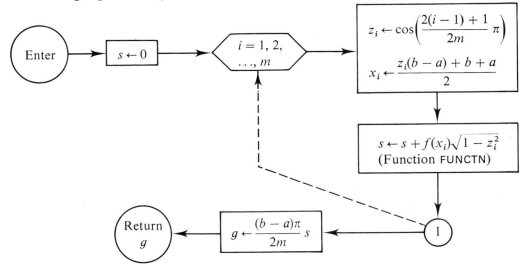

FORTRAN *Implementation*

List of Principal Variables

Program Symbol	Definition

(Main)

DUPLUS	Δu_i^+, the integral of (2.4.16).
FF	Fanning friction factor, $\bar{f}$.
I	Subscript, i.
M	Number of points to be used in the quadrature formulas, m.
NYPL	N, the number of values of y_i^+.
PHI	ϕ, the function of equation (2.4.5).
RE	The Reynolds number, N_{Re}.
UPLUS	The dimensionless axial velocity $u_{i,}^+$ corresponding to dimensionless distance y_i^+.
YPLUS	The dimensionless distance from the tube wall, y_i^+.
YPLUSM	The dimensionless distance corresponding to the centerline of the tube, $\bar{y}^+$.

(Function FUNCTN)

C, D	Parameters c and d given by (2.4.2) and (2.4.3).
YPL	y^+, dimensionless distance from the tube wall.

(Function CHEBY)

A, B	Lower and upper limits of integration, a and b, respectively (see (2.4.13)).
F	Integrand, f (see (2.4.13)).
SUM	s, the repeated sum of (2.4.13).
XI	x_i, the root z_i transformed to the interval $[a, b]$.
ZI	z_i, a root of the mth-degree Chebyshev polynomial.

Numerical Integration

Program Listing

Main Program

```
C          APPLIED NUMERICAL METHODS, EXAMPLE 2.4
C          VELOCITY DISTRIBUTION USING GAUSSIAN QUADRATURE
C
C          THIS PROGRAM COMPUTES DIMENSIONLESS VELOCITY DISTRIBUTIONS
C          FOR A FLUID FLOWING INSIDE A SMOOTH CIRCULAR TUBE BY
C          INTEGRATION OF A RELATIONSHIP DEVELOPED BY GILL AND SCHER (SEE
C          AICHE JOURNAL, VOL 7, NO 1, P 61 (1961)).  RE IS THE REYNOLDS
C          NUMBER, YPLUS THE DIMENSIONLESS DISTANCE FROM THE TUBE WALL,
C          AND UPLUS THE DIMENSIONLESS VELOCITY IN THE AXIAL DIRECTION AT
C          DISTANCE YPLUS.  YPLUSM IS THE VALUE OF YPLUS WHICH CORRESPONDS
C          TO THE CENTERLINE DISTANCE.  FF, THE FANNING FRICTION FACTOR,
C          IS COMPUTED AS A FUNCTION OF RE USING THE BLASIUS EQUATION.
C          PHI IS DESCRIBED IN THE PROBLEM STATEMENT.  THE INTEGRAL
C          IS EVALUATED USING BOTH THE GAUSS-LEGENDRE AND GAUSS-
C          CHEBYSHEV QUADRATURES, PERFORMED BY THE FUNCTIONS GAUSS (SEE
C          EXAMPLE 2.3) AND CHEBY RESPECTIVELY.  THE FUNCTIONAL VALUES FOR
C          THE QUADRATURES ARE COMPUTED BY THE FUNCTION FUNCTN.  FOR A
C          GIVEN RE AND A SET OF NYPL VALUES OF YPLUS, THE INTEGRATIONS
C          ARE CARRIED OUT USING SUCCESSIVE YPLUS VALUES AS THE LIMITS
C          OF INTEGRATION WITH THE M POINT QUADRATURE FORMULA.  PHI AND
C          YPLUSM ARE ASSIGNED TO COMMON STORAGE TO SIMPLIFY COMMUNICATION
C          AMONG THE PROGRAMS.
C
       IMPLICIT  REAL*8(A-H, O-Z)
       DIMENSION YPLUS(100)
       COMMON PHI, YPLUSM
       EXTERNAL FUNCTN
C
C          ..... READ DATA, COMPUTE CONSTANT PARAMETERS .....
       READ (5,100)    NYPL, (YPLUS(I), I=2,NYPL)
     1 READ (5,101)    RE, M
       FF = 0.079/RE**0.25
       YPLUSM = RE*DSQRT(FF/2.)/2.
       PHI = (YPLUSM-60.)/22.
C
C          ..... EVALUATE INTEGRAL USING GAUSS-LEGENDRE QUADRATURE .....
       YPLUS(1) = 0.
       UPLUS = 0.
       WRITE (6,200)    RE, YPLUSM, M, YPLUS(1), UPLUS
       DO 3  I = 2, NYPL
       IF (YPLUS(I).GT.YPLUSM)  GO TO 4
       DUPLUS = GAUSS( YPLUS(I-1), YPLUS(I), M, FUNCTN )
       UPLUS = UPLUS + DUPLUS
     3 WRITE (6,201)    YPLUS(I), UPLUS, DUPLUS
C
C          ..... EVALUATE INTEGRAL USING GAUSS-CHEBYSHEV QUADRATURE .....
     4 UPLUS = 0.
       WRITE (6,202)    YPLUS(1), UPLUS
       DO 6  I = 2, NYPL
       IF (YPLUS(I).GT.YPLUSM)  GO TO 1
       DUPLUS = CHEBY( YPLUS(I-1), YPLUS(I), M, FUNCTN )
       UPLUS = UPLUS + DUPLUS
     6 WRITE (6,201)    YPLUS(I), UPLUS, DUPLUS
       GO TO 1
C
C          ..... FORMATS FOR INPUT AND OUTPUT STATEMENTS .....
   100 FORMAT ( 10X, I2/ (20X, 5F10.3) )
   101 FORMAT ( 10X, F10.3, 20X, I2 )
   200 FORMAT ( 10H1RE      = ,F10.1/ 10H YPLUSM = ,F11.2/ 10H M        = ,
     1    I8/ 54H0VELOCITY DISTRIBUTION USING GAUSS-LEGENDRE QUADRATURE
     2    / 1H0,5X,5HYPLUS,8X,5HUPLUS,10X,6HDUPLUS/ 1H0,F10.2,F15.7 )
   201 FORMAT ( 1H , F10.2, 2F15.7 )
   202 FORMAT ( 55H0VELOCITY DISTRIBUTION USING GAUSS-CHEBYSHEV QUADRATUR
     1E  / 1H0,5X,5HYPLUS,8X,5HUPLUS,10X,6HDUPLUS/ 1H0,F10.2,F15.7 )
C
       END
```

Example 2.4   Velocity Distribution using Gaussian Quadrature   **121**

Program Listing (*Continued*)

Function FUNCTN

```
          FUNCTION FUNCTN( YPL )
C
C             THE FUNCTION FUNCTN COMPUTES THE INTEGRAND FOR THE QUADRATURE
C             FUNCTIONS GAUSS AND CHEBY.  C, D, YPLUSM AND PHI ARE DESCRIBED
C             IN THE PROBLEM STATEMENT.  YPL IS THE DIMENSIONLESS DISTANCE
C             FROM THE TUBE WALL.
C
          IMPLICIT  REAL*8(A-H, O-Z)
          REAL*8  FUNCTN, YPL
          COMMON PHI, YPLUSM
C
          D = 1. - YPL/YPLUSM
          C = 0.36*0.36*YPL*YPL*(1.-DEXP(-PHI*YPL/YPLUSM))**2
          FUNCTN = 2.*D/(1. +DSQRT(1. + 4.*C*D))
          RETURN
C
          END
```

Function CHEBY

```
          FUNCTION CHEBY( A, B, M, F )
C
C             THE FUNCTION CHEBY COMPUTES THE VALUE OF THE INTEGRAL OF
C             F(X)*DX BETWEEN THE INTEGRATION LIMITS A AND B USING THE
C             M-POINT GAUSS-CHEBYSHEV QUADRATURE FORMULA.  ZI IS THE I-TH ROOT
C             OF THE CHEBYSHEV POLYNOMIAL OF DEGREE M ON THE INTERVAL
C             (-1,1) AND XI IS THE VALUE OF ZI TRANSFORMED TO THE INTERVAL
C             (A,B).  SUM IS THE SUM OF THE FUNCTIONAL VALUES AT THE M
C             VALUES OF XI CORRECTED FOR THE WEIGHTING FUNCTION.  THE
C             UNIFORM WEIGHT FACTOR IS THEN APPLIED AND THE APPROXIMATED
C             VALUE OF THE INTEGRAL IS RETURNED AS THE VALUE OF THE FUNCTION.
C
          IMPLICIT  REAL*8(A-H, O-Z)
          REAL*8  CHEBY, A, B, F
C
          SUM = 0.
          DO 1  I = 1, M
          ZI = DCOS(FLOAT(2*(I-1) + 1)*3.1415927/FLOAT (2*M))
          XI = (ZI*(B-A) + B + A)/2.
    1     SUM = SUM + F(XI)*DSQRT(1.-ZI*ZI)
          CHEBY = (B-A)*3.1415927*SUM/FLOAT(2*M)
          RETURN
C
          END
```

Data

```
          NYPL    =   11
          YPLUS(2)...YPLUS(6)      1.000      2.000      5.000     10.000     20.000
          YPLUS(7)...YPLUS(11)    50.000    100.000    200.000    500.000   1000.000
          RE      =    5000.000          M     =     2
          RE      =    5000.000          M     =     4
          RE      =    5000.000          M     =     6
          RE      =    5000.000          M     =    10
          RE      =    5000.000          M     =    15
          RE      =   10000.000          M     =     2
          RE      =   10000.000          M     =     4
          RE      =   10000.000          M     =     6
          RE      =   10000.000          M     =    10
          RE      =   10000.000          M     =    15
          RE      =   25000.000          M     =     2
          RE      =   25000.000          M     =     4
          RE      =   25000.000          M     =     6
          RE      =   25000.000          M     =    10
          RE      =   25000.000          M     =    15
```

Program Listing (*Continued*)

RE	=	50000.000	M	=	2
RE	=	50000.000	M	=	4
RE	=	50000.000	M	=	6
RE	=	50000.000	M	=	10
RE	=	50000.000	M	=	15

Computer Output

Results for the 11th Data Set

```
RE     =     25000.0
YPLUSM =       700.59
M      =          2
```

VELOCITY DISTRIBUTION USING GAUSS-LEGENDRE QUADRATURE

YPLUS	UPLUS	DUPLUS
0.0	0.0	
1.00	0.9992443	0.9992443
2.00	1.9958208	0.9965765
5.00	4.8776166	2.8817958
10.00	8.4823031	3.6046865
20.00	11.8944744	3.4121713
50.00	15.1074984	3.2130241
100.00	16.9996247	1.8921263
200.00	18.7004495	1.7008247
500.00	20.5245821	1.8241326

VELOCITY DISTRIBUTION USING GAUSS-CHEBYSHEV QUADRATURE

YPLUS	UPLUS	DUPLUS
0.0	0.0	
1.00	1.1098645	1.1098645
2.00	2.2166574	1.1067930
5.00	5.4059707	3.1893133
10.00	9.4129422	4.0069715
20.00	13.3053378	3.8923955
50.00	17.0892826	3.7839448
100.00	19.2499871	2.1607046
200.00	21.1825355	1.9325484
500.00	23.2999976	2.1174622

Results for the 12th Data Set

```
RE     =     25000.0
YPLUSM =       700.59
M      =          4
```

VELOCITY DISTRIBUTION USING GAUSS-LEGENDRE QUADRATURE

YPLUS	UPLUS	DUPLUS
0.0	0.0	
1.00	0.9992432	0.9992432
2.00	1.9958190	0.9965758
5.00	4.8779561	2.8821371
10.00	8.4806276	3.6026716
20.00	11.8947849	3.4141572
50.00	15.1339481	3.2391632
100.00	17.0306282	1.8966801
200.00	18.7343299	1.7037017
500.00	20.5672100	1.8328801

Example 2.4   Velocity Distribution using Gaussian Quadrature   **123**

Computer Output (*Continued*)

VELOCITY DISTRIBUTION USING GAUSS-CHEBYSHEV QUADRATURE

YPLUS	UPLUS	DUPLUS
0.0	0.0	
1.00	1.0253935	1.0253935
2.00	2.0480377	1.0226442
5.00	5.0043534	2.9563157
10.00	8.7014534	3.6971001
20.00	12.2166106	3.5151572
50.00	15.5693084	3.3526979
100.00	17.5230004	1.9536919
200.00	19.2766312	1.7536309
500.00	21.1692723	1.8926411

Results for the 13th Data Set

RE   =   25000.0
YPLUSM =   700.59
M   =   6

VELOCITY DISTRIBUTION USING GAUSS-LEGENDRE QUADRATURE

YPLUS	UPLUS	DUPLUS
0.0	0.0	
1.00	0.9992432	0.9992432
2.00	1.9958190	0.9965758
5.00	4.8779561	2.8821372
10.00	8.4806278	3.6026716
20.00	11.8947777	3.4141500
50.00	15.1340019	3.2392242
100.00	17.0306880	1.8966861
200.00	18.7343936	1.7037056
500.00	20.5672992	1.8329056

VELOCITY DISTRIBUTION USING GAUSS-CHEBYSHEV QUADRATURE

YPLUS	UPLUS	DUPLUS
0.0	0.0	
1.00	1.0107488	1.0107488
2.00	2.0187947	1.0080459
5.00	4.9336171	2.9148224
10.00	8.5778446	3.6442275
20.00	12.0359425	3.4580979
50.00	15.3233605	3.2874179
100.00	17.2447373	1.9213768
200.00	18.9701337	1.7253964
500.00	20.8286561	1.8585224

Results for the 14th Data Set

RE   =   25000.0
YPLUSM =   700.59
M   =   10

Computer Output (*Continued*)

VELOCITY DISTRIBUTION USING GAUSS-LEGENDRE QUADRATURE

YPLUS	UPLUS	DUPLUS
0.0	0.0	
1.00	0.9992432	0.9992432
2.00	1.9958190	0.9965758
5.00	4.8779561	2.8821372
10.00	8.4806278	3.6026716
20.00	11.8947777	3.4141500
50.00	15.1340019	3.2392242
100.00	17.0306880	1.8966861
200.00	18.7343936	1.7037056
500.00	20.5672993	1.8329057

VELOCITY DISTRIBUTION USING GAUSS-CHEBYSHEV QUADRATURE

YPLUS	UPLUS	DUPLUS
0.0	0.0	
1.00	1.0033640	1.0033640
2.00	2.0040479	1.0006839
5.00	4.8978994	2.8938515
10.00	8.5154558	3.6175564
20.00	11.9452665	3.4298107
50.00	15.2015168	3.2562503
100.00	17.1069899	1.9054731
200.00	18.8184241	1.7114342
500.00	20.6604113	1.8419872

Results for the 5th Data Set

RE	=	5000.0
YPLUSM	=	171.34
M	=	15

VELOCITY DISTRIBUTION USING GAUSS-LEGENDRE QUADRATURE

YPLUS	UPLUS	DUPLUS
0.0	0.0	
1.00	0.9970600	0.9970600
2.00	1.9876531	0.9905930
5.00	4.8710430	2.8833900
10.00	8.7551440	3.8841010
20.00	12.7210159	3.9658719
50.00	16.2539475	3.5329316
100.00	17.8935831	1.6396356

VELOCITY DISTRIBUTION USING GAUSS-CHEBYSHEV QUADRATURE

YPLUS	UPLUS	DUPLUS
0.0	0.0	
1.00	0.9988846	0.9988846
2.00	1.9912901	0.9924054
5.00	4.8799113	2.8886212
10.00	8.7710440	3.8911327
20.00	12.7448483	3.9738043
50.00	16.2862123	3.5413640
100.00	17.9293563	1.6431440

Example 2.4   Velocity Distribution using Gaussian Quadrature   **125**

Computer Output (*Continued*)

Results for the 10th Data Set

```
RE     =     10000.0
YPLUSM =       314.25
M      =          15
```

VELOCITY DISTRIBUTION USING GAUSS-LEGENDRE QUADRATURE

YPLUS	UPLUS	DUPLUS
0.0	0.0	
1.00	0.9983751	0.9983751
2.00	1.9925942	0.9942191
5.00	4.8764971	2.8839029
10.00	8.5858104	3.7093133
20.00	12.1847202	3.5989098
50.00	15.5076555	3.3229353
100.00	17.3040266	1.7963711
200.00	18.7074839	1.4034573

VELOCITY DISTRIBUTION USING GAUSS-CHEBYSHEV QUADRATURE

YPLUS	UPLUS	DUPLUS
0.0	0.0	
1.00	1.0002020	1.0002020
2.00	1.9962400	0.9960379
5.00	4.8853570	2.8891170
10.00	8.6014337	3.7160767
20.00	12.2076236	3.6061899
50.00	15.5383625	3.3307388
100.00	17.3384711	1.8001086
200.00	18.7448067	1.4063356

Results for the 15th Data Set

```
RE     =     25000.0
YPLUSM =       700.59
M      =          15
```

VELOCITY DISTRIBUTION USING GAUSS-LEGENDRE QUADRATURE

YPLUS	UPLUS	DUPLUS
0.0	0.0	
1.00	0.9992432	0.9992432
2.00	1.9958190	0.9965758
5.00	4.8779561	2.8821372
10.00	8.4806278	3.6026716
20.00	11.8947777	3.4141500
50.00	15.1340019	3.2392242
100.00	17.0306880	1.8966861
200.00	18.7343936	1.7037056
500.00	20.5672993	1.8329057

VELOCITY DISTRIBUTION USING GAUSS-CHEBYSHEV QUADRATURE

YPLUS	UPLUS	DUPLUS
0.0	0.0	
1.00	1.0010717	1.0010717
2.00	1.9994704	0.9983987
5.00	4.8868067	2.8873362
10.00	8.4960833	3.6092766
20.00	11.9171720	3.4210887
50.00	15.1639220	3.2467499
100.00	17.0645000	1.9005780
200.00	18.7716300	1.7071299
500.00	20.6085537	1.8369237

Computer Output (*Continued*)

Results for the 20th Data Set

```
RE     =      50000.0
YPLUSM =      1284.89
M      =      15
```

VELOCITY DISTRIBUTION USING GAUSS-LEGENDRE QUADRATURE

YPLUS	UPLUS	DUPLUS
0.0	0.0	
1.00	0.9995640	0.9995640
2.00	1.9970033	0.9974393
5.00	4.8781194	2.8811161
10.00	8.4432825	3.5651631
20.00	11.7980046	3.3547220
50.00	15.0140866	3.2160820
100.00	16.9474237	1.9333371
200.00	18.7487224	1.8012987
500.00	20.9321366	2.1834143
1000.00	22.1922505	1.2601138

VELOCITY DISTRIBUTION USING GAUSS-CHEBYSHEV QUADRATURE

YPLUS	UPLUS	DUPLUS
0.0	0.0	
1.00	1.0013931	1.0013931
2.00	2.0006568	0.9992637
5.00	4.8869659	2.8863091
10.00	8.4586789	3.5717129
20.00	11.8202279	3.3615491
50.00	15.0437528	3.2235249
100.00	16.9810396	1.9372868
200.00	18.7859387	1.8048991
500.00	20.9740274	2.1880887
1000.00	22.2367209	1.2626935

Example 2.4   Velocity Distribution using Gaussian Quadrature   **127**

Discussion of Results

Complete computer output is shown for data sets 11, 12, 13, 14, and 15 to illustrate the influence of the number of points in the quadrature formula on the results for $N_{Re} = 25000$, and for data sets 10, 15, 20, and 25 to show results for the 15-point quadrature formulas (probably the most accurate of those used) for $N_{Re} = 5000, 10000, 25000,$ and 50000. All computations were done using double-precision arithmetic.

The values of u^+ predicted by the various quadratures for $y^+ = 500$ and $N_{Re} = 25000$ are shown in Table 2.4.1.

Table 2.4.1   Predicted u^+ for $y^+ = 500$ and $N_{Re} = 25000$

m	u^+ (Gauss-Legendre Quadrature)	u^+ (Gauss-Chebyshev Quadrature)
2	20.5245821	23.2999976
4	20.5672100	21.1692723
6	20.5672992	20.8286561
10	20.5672993	20.6604113
15	20.5672993	20.6085537

The results for the Gauss-Legendre quadratures are nearly constant, indicating that the integrand function of (2.4.1) can probably be represented adequately by polynomials of low degree, at least for the short intervals of integration used. Since

$$\lim_{y^+ \to 0} f(y^+) = \lim_{y^+ \to 0} \frac{2d}{1 + \sqrt{1 + 4cd}} = 1,$$

and since $f(y^+) < 1$ for $y^+ > 0$, any result that gives

$u^+ > y^+$ is clearly in error (see, for example, the results for small y^+ values for the 2-point Gauss-Chebyshev quadrature). It appears that the Gauss-Legendre quadratures yield better values for the integrals, although the results for all N_{Re} using the 15-point quadrature formulas are quite consistent (in no case differing by more than 0.25 percent).

The results for the 15-point quadratures with $N_{Re} = 50000$ are shown in Fig. 2.4.1. They agree in every case with the plotted values reported by Gill and Scher. Unfortunately, the authors failed to indicate how they evaluated the integral, and did not report the results in tabular form. Thus it was possible to check only the most significant digits of the results.

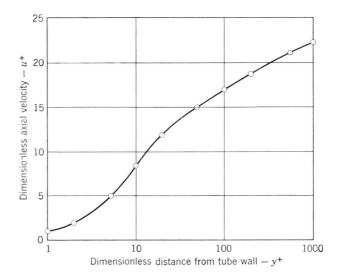

Figure 2.4.1   **Dimensionless velocity distribution in smooth circular tubes—$N_{Re} = 50000$.**

2.11 Numerical Differentiation

Having described numerical integration in some detail, a few words about numerical differentiation are in order. The differentiation problem involves the evaluation of

$$\frac{df(x)}{dx}$$

at some arbitrary x, given only a few sample values of $f(x)$ at the base points $x_0, x_1, \ldots, x_n$. The problem seems intuitively no more difficult than the integration problem of (2.1). The obvious solution is to find a suitable approximation of $f(x)$, say $g(x)$, which is simple to differentiate and evaluate, that is,

$$\frac{df(x)}{dx} \doteq \frac{dg(x)}{dx}. \qquad (2.118)$$

The usual choice for the approximating function is $p_n(x)$, the nth-degree interpolating polynomial which passes through the points $(x_0, f(x_0)), (x_1, f(x_1)), \ldots, (x_n, f(x_n))$. Then (2.118) is given by

$$\frac{df(x)}{dx} \doteq \frac{dp_n(x)}{dx}. \qquad (2.119)$$

Provided that $f(x)$ is m times differentiable, higher-order derivatives may be approximated by evaluating the higher-order derivatives of $p_n(x)$, $n \leqslant m$,

$$\frac{d^m f(x)}{dx^m} \doteq \frac{d^m p_n(x)}{dx^m}. \qquad (2.120)$$

Unfortunately, considerable care is required if serious errors are to be avoided. The inherent difficulty with this approach is that differentiation tends to magnify small discrepancies or errors in the approximating function (just as the integration process tends to damp or smooth them out). Figure 2.9 shows the situation.

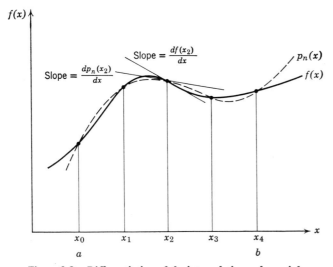

Figure 2.9 Differentiation of the interpolating polynomial.

Note that if the polynomial approximation $p_n(x)$ is reasonably good, the integral $\int_a^b p_n(x)\,dx$ may be an excellent approximation to $\int_a^b f(x)\,dx$. On the other hand, $dp_n(x)/dx$, which is simply the slope of the line tangent to $p_n(x)$, may vary significantly in magnitude from $df(x)/dx$, even at the base points, where $p_n(x)$ and $f(x)$ agree exactly; the *sign* of the derivative might even be in error. Higher-order differentiation tends to magnify these discrepancies still further. Admittedly, the deviations may be exaggerated in the figure, but the point is clear. Numerical differentiation is an inherently less accurate process than numerical integration.

Because of this tendency toward error, numerical differentiation should be avoided wherever possible. This is particularly true when the $f(x_i)$ values are themselves subject to some error, as they would probably be if determined experimentally (engineers and scientists, in fact, often use differentiation tests on laboratory data as an indication of experimental precision). If derivative values must be computed in such cases, particularly when the results are to be used in subsequent calculations, it is usually better to use one of the least-squares polynomials (see Chapter 8) to smooth the data before differentiating them.

In spite of the problems associated with the differentiation process, the approximation of (2.120) is often used. Then

$$f(x) = p_n(x) + R_n(x), \qquad (2.121)$$

where $R_n(x)$ is the error associated with the nth-degree interpolating polynomial for which $p_n(x_i) = f(x_i)$. We can then write

$$\frac{df(x)}{dx} = \frac{dp_n(x)}{dx} + \frac{dR_n(x)}{dx}. \qquad (2.122)$$

Any of the several formulations of the interpolating polynomial from Chapter 1 may be used for $p_n(x)$. To illustrate, assume that the base points $x_0, x_1, \ldots, x_n$ are evenly spaced by intervals of length h, so that $p_n(x)$ may be written as

$$p_n(x) = f(x_0) + (x - x_0)\frac{\Delta f(x_0)}{h} + \cdots$$
$$+ (x - x_0)(x - x_1)\cdots(x - x_{n-1})\frac{\Delta^n f(x_0)}{h^n n!}.$$

Then

$$\frac{df(x)}{dx} \doteq \frac{\Delta f(x_0)}{h} + (2x - x_0 - x_1)\frac{\Delta^2 f(x_0)}{2!\,h^2}$$
$$+ [3x^2 - 2(x_0 + x_1 + x_2)x$$
$$+ (x_0 x_1 + x_0 x_2 + x_1 x_2)]\frac{\Delta^3 f(x_0)}{3!\,h^3} + \cdots.$$
$$(2.123)$$

Now we must choose an appropriate value for n. For example, for $n = 1$ and $n = 2$, (2.123) becomes, respectively,

$$\frac{df(x)}{dx} \doteq \frac{\Delta f(x_0)}{h} = f[x_0, x_1]$$

$$= \frac{1}{h} f(x_1) - \frac{1}{h} f(x_0), \qquad (2.124a)$$

$$\frac{df(x)}{dx} \doteq \frac{\Delta f(x_0)}{h} + (2x - x_0 - x_1) \frac{\Delta^2 f(x_0)}{2! \, h^2}$$

$$\doteq \left[\frac{2x - x_0 - x_1 - 2h}{2h^2} \right] f(x_0)$$

$$+ \left[\frac{2x_0 - 4x + 2x_1 + 2h}{2h^2} \right] f(x_1)$$

$$+ \left[\frac{2x - x_0 - x_1}{2h^2} \right] f(x_2). \qquad (2.124b)$$

Second derivatives can be computed similarly; for example, for $n = 2$,

$$\frac{d^2 f(x)}{dx} \doteq \frac{\Delta^2 f(x_0)}{h^2} = 2 f[x_2, x_1, x_0]$$

$$\doteq \frac{1}{h^2} f(x_0) - \frac{2}{h^2} f(x_1) + \frac{1}{h^2} f(x_2). \qquad (2.125)$$

Other derivatives follow in obvious fashion, although the formulas quickly become rather cumbersome when written in general form.

Error terms for the differentiation formulas are given by the appropriate derivative of the remainder term for the nth-degree interpolating polynomial $R_n(x)$, given by (1.39b) as

$$R_n(x) = \left[\prod_{i=0}^{n} (x - x_i) \right] \frac{f^{(n+1)}(\xi)}{(n+1)!}, \qquad (2.126)$$

where $\xi = \xi(x)$ is an unknown point on the interval $(x, x_0, \ldots, x_n)$. Unfortunately, $\xi(x)$ may not be single-valued or differentiable, although $f^{(n+1)}(\xi)$ is, provided $f(x)$ itself possesses derivatives of higher order. If we let $\pi(x) = \prod_{i=0}^{n}(x - x_i)$ and use the finite divided-difference equivalent of $f^{(n+1)}(\xi)$, [see (1.39a)], then $R_n(x)$ is given by

$$R_n(x) = \pi(x) f[x, x_n, x_{n-1}, \ldots, x_0], \qquad (2.127)$$

and its first derivative is

$$\frac{dR_n}{dx} = \frac{d\pi(x)}{dx} f[x, x_n, x_{n-1}, \ldots, x_0]$$

$$+ \pi(x) \frac{df}{dx} [x, x_n, x_{n-1}, \ldots, x_0]. \qquad (2.128)$$

We can show (see [2]) that

$$\frac{df}{dx} [x, x_n, x_{n-1}, \ldots, x_0] = \frac{f^{(n+2)}(\xi)}{(n+2)!}, \qquad (2.129)$$

with ξ in $(x, x_0, \ldots, x_n)$. Then (2.128) can be written as

$$\frac{dR_n}{dx} = \frac{d\pi(x)}{dx} \frac{f^{(n+1)}(\xi_1)}{(n+1)!} + \pi(x) \frac{f^{(n+2)}(\xi_2)}{(n+2)!},$$

$$\xi_1, \xi_2 \text{ in } (x, x_0, \ldots, x_n). \qquad (2.130)$$

For $x = x_j$, that is, when x is one of the base points,

$$\frac{dR_n}{dx}(x_j) = \frac{d\pi(x_j)}{dx} \frac{f^{(n+1)}(\xi_1)}{(n+1)!}$$

$$= \left[\prod_{\substack{i=0 \\ i \neq j}}^{n} (x_j - x_i) \right] \frac{f^{(n+1)}(\xi_1)}{(n+1)!}. \qquad (2.131)$$

For example, (2.124b) can be written with its error term as:

$$\frac{df(x_0)}{dx} = \frac{1}{2h} [-3f(x_0) + 4f(x_1) - f(x_2)] + \frac{h^2}{3} f^{(3)}(\xi)$$

$$(2.132a)$$

$$\frac{df(x_1)}{dx} = \frac{1}{2h} [f(x_2) - f(x_0)] - \frac{h^2}{6} f^{(3)}(\xi) \qquad (2,132b)$$

$$\frac{df(x_2)}{dx} = \frac{1}{2h} [f(x_0) - 4f(x_1) + 3f(x_2)] + \frac{h^2}{3} f^{(3)}(\xi).$$

$$(2.132c)$$

Notice that the leading factor in the error term for the derivative at x_1 is just half that for the error term at x_0 and at x_2. We would expect that the computed derivative estimate at the midpoint would be more accurate than those computed at the end points, since functional values on *both* sides of the midpoint are used in the midpoint formula (2.132b) but not in the end-point formulas. Comparison of the first derivative approximations, using higher-degree interpolating polynomials (see, for example, the extensive tables in [9]), shows that the magnitudes of the coefficients of $f^{(n+1)}(\xi)$ at the base points decrease monotonically as x approaches the midpoint of the interval. In addition, the midpoint formula with n even is invariably simpler [for example, (2.132b)] than formulas for other base points. For these reasons, the odd-point formulas (n even) are usually favored over the even-point ones, and the base-point values should, if possible, lie on both sides of the argument at which $df(x)/dx$ is to be approximated.

To determine $d^m f(x)/dx^m$ for $m \leq n$, we use (2.120). The corresponding error term, assuming that $f(x)$ possesses derivatives of order $n + m + 1$, is given [9] by the rather complicated expression

$$\frac{d^m R_n(x)}{dx^m} = \sum_{k=0}^{m} \frac{m!}{(m-k)!(n+k+1)!}$$

$$\times f^{(n+k+1)}(\xi_k) \frac{d^{(m-k)}}{dx^{(m-k)}} \left[\prod_{i=0}^{n} (x - x_i) \right],$$

$$(2.133)$$

where the ξ_k are all in the interval $(x, x_0, \ldots, x_n)$. At the base points $x = x_j, j = 0, 1, \ldots, n$, (2.133) simplifies somewhat since the term in $f^{(n+m+1)}(\xi_m)$ vanishes. This formulation is not particularly useful unless one can establish upper bounds for the derivatives

$$f^{(n+1)}(x), f^{(n+2)}(x), \ldots, f^{(n+m+1)}(x)$$

on the interval containing the base points.

In general, we can show that $p_n(x)$, the nth-degree interpolating polynomial, has error of order h^{n+1}, written as $O(h^{n+1})$ [see (1.62)], and that each successive differentiation reduces by one the order of the associated error. Thus

$$R_n(x) = O(h^{n+1}),$$

$$\frac{dR(x)}{dx} = O(h^n),$$

$$\frac{d^2 R(x)}{dx^2} = O(h^{n-1}), \qquad (2.134)$$

$$\ldots$$

$$\frac{d^m R(x)}{dx^m} = O(h^{n-m+1}),$$

$$\ldots$$

$$\frac{d^n R(x)}{dx^n} = O(h),$$

clearly showing the deterioration in accuracy resulting from successive differentiation operations. To decrease the error, we can reduce the stepsize h, that is, choose the base points on a smaller total interval. In practical situations where we have a given set of tabular values for $f(x)$, this may be impossible. Unfortunately, small values of h tend to magnify the round-off error in the evaluation of a differentiation formula, since h appears in the denominator with positive powers. This suggests that for a given function, a given differentiation formula, and a given argument x, there is an optimal choice for the value of h [8]. Unfortunately, one would rarely have

available the information required to determine the optimal h.

Example. As an example of numerical differentiation, consider a study involving simultaneous fluid flow and heat transfer. Values of temperature $T_0, T_1, T_2, T_3 \ldots$ are determined at a series of fixed points $x_0, x_1, x_2, x_3 \ldots$ extending normally from a solid wall into the fluid. The point x_0 coincides with the wall, and the points are equally spaced by a distance h. The problem is to estimate the temperature gradient dT/dx at the wall, since a knowledge of the fluid thermal conductivity then enables the rate of heat transfer between the wall and fluid to be determined.

The method attempted here is that suggested by equation (2.122), namely, to differentiate the interpolating polynomial passing through two or more of the points (T_i, x_i), $i = 0, 1, 2, \ldots$. Without going into the details of constructing the interpolating polynomial, the resulting approximations for dT/dx at $x = x_0$ are given in Table 2.7, for polynomial orders $n = 1, 2, 3,$ and 4.

As an illustration, the temperature gradient at the wall is evaluated for a set of temperatures computed during a recent finite-difference investigation [10] into a problem involving natural convection; the appropriate values (here limited to five points) are $T_0 = -1.000$, $T_1 = -0.588$, $T_2 = -0.295$, $T_3 = -0.259$ and $T_4 = -0.305$, with $h = 0.1$.

Clearly, the value of dT/dx at $x = x_0$ is in considerable doubt. The trouble stems mainly from the inherent inaccuracy of numerically differentiating any function that is not closely approximated by a polynomial of low order; it is further aggravated by the fact that information is being sought at the extreme end of an interval. Barring some special knowledge about the form of $T(x)$, the only satisfactory way in which the temperature gradient at the wall can be estimated more precisely is to have temperatures available at points spaced more closely together, that is, for a smaller value of h. The use of the higher-order formulas in conjunction with a relatively large point spacing can easily introduce undesirable oscillations into the approximation for a function which is essentially smooth. The full advantage of the higher-order formulas, as evidenced by their error terms, may only be realized as h becomes progressively smaller.

Table 2.7   Estimation of Temperature Gradient

Order of Polynomial	Approximation to dT/dx at $x = x_0$	Error Term	Numerical Value
1	$\dfrac{T_1 - T_0}{h}$	$O(h)$	4.12
2	$\dfrac{-T_2 + 4T_1 - 3T_0}{2h}$	$O(h^2)$	4.71
3	$\dfrac{2T_3 - 9T_2 + 18T_1 - 11T_0}{6h}$	$O(h^3)$	4.25
4	$\dfrac{-3T_4 + 16T_3 - 36T_2 + 48T_1 - 25T_0}{12h}$	$O(h^4)$	3.47

Problems

2.1 Show that if the curve $f(x)$ has no inflection point on (x_0, x_1), that is, $f''(x) \neq 0$ on (x_0, x_1), then the error in the trapezoidal rule (2.11) is bounded as follows:

$$\left| \frac{h^3}{12} f''(\xi) \right| = \left| \int_{x_0}^{x_1} f(x)\, dx - \frac{h}{2} [f(x_0) + f(x_1)] \right|$$
$$\leqslant \frac{h^2}{8} \left| [f'(x_0) + f'(x_1)] \right|,$$

where $x_0 < \xi < x_1$.

2.2 Show that if $f'(x_0)$ and $f'(x_1)$ are available, then the *improved trapezoidal rule* (see (2.8)), given by

$$\int_{x_0}^{x_1} f(x)\, dx \doteq \frac{h}{2} [f(x_0) + f(x_1)] - \frac{h^2}{12} [f'(x_0) + f'(x_1)],$$

has degree of precision three; that is, it is exact if $f(x)$ is a polynomial of degree three or less.

2.3 Find the error term for the improved trapezoidal rule of Problem 2.2.

2.4 The integral $I = \int_a^b f(x)\, dx$ is to be estimated by a trapezoidal-type rule, using two base points, x_1 and x_2, that do not necessarily coincide with the integration limits a and b. Show that the required approximation is

$$I \doteq \frac{b-a}{x_2 - x_1} \left[x_2 f(x_1) - x_1 f(x_2) + \frac{b+a}{2} [f(x_2) - f(x_1)] \right].$$

What is the corresponding error term?

2.5 The integral $I = \int_a^b f(x)\, dx$ is to be estimated by a quadratic-type rule, using three base points, x_1, x_2, and x_3, that are not necessarily equally spaced, and none of which necessarily coincides with a or b. Derive the appropriate integration formula and its associated error term. Check that the formula reduces to Simpson's rule when $x_1 = a$, $x_3 = b$, and $(x_2 - x_1) = (x_3 - x_2) = h$.

2.6 Functional values $f(x_1), f(x_2), \ldots, f(x_n)$ are available at the base points $x_1, x_2, \ldots, x_n$ (arranged in ascending order, but not necessarily equally spaced). The integral

$$I = \int_a^b f(x)\, dx$$

is to be estimated by repeated application of the trapezoidal-type rule discussed in Problem 2.4. Write a function, named AREA1, to perform the required integration. A typical call will be

ANS = AREA1 (F, X, N, A, B)

in which F and X are the vectors used to store the functional values and base points, N is the number of points, and A and B are the integration limits. If possible, always arrange for the subintervals of integration to coincide with the known base points. In general this will not be the case for the extreme subintervals involving the integration limits a and b. Avoid extrapolation if possible; that is, use a base less than a and another greater than b, if available. The function AREA1 may be used in Problem 2.16.

2.7 Write a function, named AREA2, similar to AREA1 of Problem 2.6, but now using repeated application of the quadratic-type integration formula developed in Problem 2.5. A typical call will be

ANS = AREA2 (F, X, N, A, B)

If possible, again completely embrace the limits of integration by known base points. The function AREA2 may be used in Problem 2.16.

2.8 The Newton-Cotes closed integration formula for $\alpha = 6$, given by equation (2.21f), is inconvenient for hand calculations because of the rather unusual coefficients. An alternative approximation that is sometimes used is

$$\int_{x_0}^{x_6} f(x)\, dx \doteq \frac{3h}{10} [f(x_0) + 5f(x_1) + f(x_2) + 6f(x_3) + f(x_4) + 5f(x_5) + f(x_6)].$$

What is the error term for this approximation, and for what degrees of polynomial will the formula be exact?

2.9 What is the formulation of the quadrature given in Problem 2.8 when using n applications of the rule in the evaluation of

$$\int_a^b f(x)\, dx?$$

2.10 Consider the computation of the integral

$$\int_a^b f(x)\, dx$$

using Simpson's rule (2.21b) repeatedly, each time halving the interval h. This is equivalent to the composite Simpson's rule of (2.49) for $n = 1, 2, 4, 8, 16, \ldots$. Let j be the number of interval-halving operations. Then n and j are related by $n = 2^j$. Let I_j be the estimate of the integral for j repeated interval halvings, and I_j^* be the improved estimate

$$I_j^* = \frac{16}{15} I_j - \frac{1}{15} I_{j-1},$$

using Richardson's extrapolation technique (see (2.51)).

Write a function, named SIMPRH, with argument list

(A, B, F, EPS, JMAX, J)

to implement the method outlined in the preceding paragraph, where A and B are the lower and upper integration limits, respectively, and F is the name of another function that evaluates the integrand, $f(x)$. SIMPRH should calculate, in order, the I_j^*, $j = 0, 1, 2, \ldots$, until

$$j > \text{JMAX}$$

or

$$|I_j^* - I_j| < \text{EPS}.$$

Thus EPS may be considered to be a tolerance on the estimated error. The number of interval-halving steps carried out should be stored in J upon exit. The final I_j^* should be returned as the value of the function.

2.11 The truncated Chebyshev expansion of $f(x)$ on $[-1, 1]$ is given by (1.81),

$$f(x) \doteq p_n(x) = \sum_{i=0}^{n} b_i x^i = \sum_{i=0}^{n} a_i T_i(x),$$

where the coefficients a_i (see Problem 1.50) are

$$a_0 = \frac{1}{\pi} \int_0^\pi f(\cos\theta)\, d\theta,$$

$$a_i = \frac{2}{\pi} \int_0^\pi f(\cos\theta)\cos i\theta\, d\theta, \qquad i = 1, 2, \ldots, n.$$

Write a subroutine, named CHEBCO, with argument list

(F, N, A, B, EPS)

that finds the coefficients a_i and b_i, $i = 0, 1, \ldots, n$. Essential values of $f(x)$ should be supplied by another function, with dummy argument name F. The integrals should be evaluated by the function SIMPRH of Problem 2.10 with the error estimate tolerance EPS (see Problem 2.10). The coefficients $a_0, \ldots, a_n$, and $b_0, \ldots, b_n$ should be stored in A(1), ..., A(N + 1) and B(1), ..., B(N + 1), respectively, upon return.

Test CHEBCO with an appropriate calling program to evaluate the coefficients a_i and b_i, $i = 0, 1, \ldots, 6$, for $f(x) = \tan^{-1} x$. Compare your results with values reported by Snyder [20]:

$$\tan^{-1} x \doteq 0.994949366x - 0.287060636x^3 + 0.078937176x^5.$$

Note that the value selected for EPS and the number of digits retained in the computations will be limited by the word size for the particular computer being used. Double-precision arithmetic should be used, if available.

2.12 Let A, B, and C be points on the x axis such that $AB = BC$. Raise ordinates from these points to intersect the curve $y = y(x)$ at D, E, and F, respectively. Let P be the intersection of DF and BE, and let Q be the point between E and P such that $2EQ = PQ$.

Show that Simpson's rule amounts to saying that the area under the curve approximately equals $AC \times BQ$.

2.13 The distribution with wavelength λ of the intensity q of radiation leaving unit area of the surface of a black body is given in Problem 3.43. Write a program that will compute the total rate Q at which radiation is being emitted between wavelengths λ_1 and λ_2, that is,

$$Q = \int_{\lambda_1}^{\lambda_2} q\, d\lambda.$$

The integration routine used can be checked by noting that the total rate over all wavelengths, $\int_0^\infty q\, d\lambda$, has the exact value σT^4, where σ is the Stefan-Boltzmann constant,

$$\sigma \doteq \frac{2\pi^5 k^4}{15c^2 h^3},$$

and T, k, c, and h are defined in Problem 3.43. The program should also compute the fractional emission, $Q/\sigma T^4$.

Suggested Test Data

$T = 2000°K$, $6000°K$; $\lambda_1 = 3933.666$ Å (Ca^+ K line); $\lambda_2 = 5895.923$ Å (Na D_1 line). Note that 1 Å (angstrom unit) = 10^{-8} cm.

2.14 Consider the condensation of a pure vapor on the outside of a single cooled horizontal tube. According to the simple Nusselt theory of film condensation, the mean heat transfer coefficient h is given by

$$h = \left(\frac{k^3\rho y\lambda}{vr\Delta T}\right)^{1/4} \left(\frac{2^{3/2}}{3\pi}\right) I^{3/4},$$

where

$$I = \int_0^\pi (\sin\beta)^{1/3}\, d\beta.$$

Here, k, ρ, and v are the thermal conductivity, density, and kinematic viscosity of the condensed liquid film, r is the tube radius, λ is the latent heat of condensing vapor, g is the gravitational acceleration, ΔT is the difference between the vapor saturation temperature (T_v) and the tube wall temperature (T_w), and all these quantities are in consistent units.

For water, the group $\phi = (k^3\rho g\lambda/v)$, in BTU⁴/hr⁴ °F³ ft⁷, varies with temperature T (°F) as follows:

T:	100	110	120	130	140	150	160	170
$\phi \times 10^{-14}$:	0.481	0.536	0.606	0.670	0.748	0.820	0.892	0.976

T:	180	190	200	210	220	230	240	250
$\phi \times 10^{-14}$:	1.051	1.130	1.218	1.280	1.327	1.376	1.430	1.503

When used in the above formula for h, ϕ should be evaluated at the mean film temperature $\bar{T} = (T_v + T_w)/2$.

Write a program that uses the above equations to compute h. The input data should include values for T_v, T_w (both in °F), and d (tube diameter in inches); these values should also appear in the printed output. The program should then compute and print values of the integral I, the mean film temperature $\bar{T}$, the corresponding value of ϕ, and the resulting heat transfer coefficient h. The four sets of test data in Table P2.14 are suggested.

Table P2.14

T_v	T_w	d
212	208	0.75
212	208	2.00
212	210	0.75
120	116	0.75

2.15 The shell-and-tube heat exchanger shown in Fig. P2.15 is employed for heating a steady stream of m lb/hr of a fluid from an inlet temperature T_1 to an exit temperature T_2. This is achieved by continuously condensing a saturated vapor in the shell, maintaining its temperature at T_s.

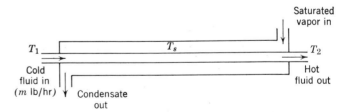

Figure P2.15

By integrating a heat balance on a differential element of length, the required exchanger length is found to be

$$L = \frac{m}{\pi D} \int_{T_1}^{T_2} \frac{c_p\, dT}{h(T_s - T)},$$

where D is the tube diameter. The local heat-transfer co-efficient h is given by the correlation

$$h = \frac{0.023k}{D}\left(\frac{4m}{\pi D\mu}\right)^{0.8}\left(\frac{\mu c_p}{k}\right)^{0.4},$$

where c_p, μ, and k (the specific heat, viscosity, and thermal conductivity of the fluid, respectively) are functions of temperature T. All quantities in the above formulas must be in consistent units.

Write a program that will read values for m, T_1, T_2, T_s, D, and information concerning the temperature dependency of c_p, μ, and k, as data. The program should then compute the required exchanger length, L.

In making approximate heat-exchanger calculations, one often assumes mean values for c_p, μ, and k, evaluating them just once, at the mean fluid temperature $(T_1 + T_2)/2$. Let the program estimate the error involved in making this assumption.

Suggested Test Data

Fluid	Case A	Case B
Fluid	Carbon dioxide gas	Ethylene glycol liquid
m, lb/hr	22.5	45,000
T_1, °F	60	0
T_2, °F	280 and 500	90 and 180
T_s, °F	550	250
D, in.	0.495	1.032

c_p, BTU/lb °F: $\quad 0.251 + 3.46 \times 10^{-5}T - \dfrac{14,400}{(T+460)^2}$

$\qquad\qquad\qquad 0.53 + 0.00065\,T$

k, BTU/hr ft °F: $\quad\begin{cases} 0.0085 & (32°\text{F}) \\ 0.0133 & (212) \\ 0.0181 & (392) \\ 0.0228 & (572) \end{cases}$ $\quad 0.153$ (constant)

μ, lb/ft hr: $\quad 0.0332\left(\dfrac{T+460}{460}\right)^{0.935}$ $\quad\begin{cases} 242 & (0°\text{F}) \\ 82.1 & (50) \\ 30.5 & (100) \\ 12.6 & (150) \\ 5.57 & (200) \end{cases}$

The above physical properties have been derived from Perry [15]. See Problem 1.19, concerning the interpolating polynomials resulting from the tabulated values of k for carbon dioxide and μ for ethylene glycol.

2.16 The *fugacity f* (atm) of a gas at a pressure P (atm) and a specified temperature T is given by Denbigh [16] as

$$\ln\frac{f}{P} = \int_0^P \frac{C-1}{p}\,dp,$$

where $C = Pv/RT$ is the experimentally determined *compressibility factor* at the same temperature T, R is the gas constant, and v is the molal volume. For a perfect gas, $C = 1$, and the fugacity is identical with the pressure.

Suppose that n values are available for C, namely, C_1, C_2,

..., C_n, for which the corresponding pressures are p_1, p_2, ..., p_n (not necessarily equally spaced, but arranged in ascending order of magnitude). Assume that the value of p_1 (typically, 1 atm) is sufficiently low for the gas to be perfect in the range $0 \leq p \leq p_1$, so that

$$\ln\frac{f}{P} = \int_{p_1}^P \frac{C-1}{p}\,dp.$$

Write a program that will read data values for n, C_i and p_i ($i = 1, 2, \ldots, n$), and P, and that will proceed to use one of the unequal-interval integration functions developed in Problems 2.6 and 2.7 to evaluate f.

Suggested Test Data

$P = 50$, 100, 150, 200, 250, 500, 750, 1000, 1500, and 2000 atm, with compressibility factors, derived from Perry [15], given in Table P2.16.

Table P2.16

	Compressibilty Factor, C	
p (atm)	Methane $(-70°\text{C})$	Ammonia $(200°\text{C})$
1	0.9940	0.9975
10	0.9370	0.9805
20	0.8683	0.9611
30	0.7928	0.9418
40	0.7034	0.9219
50	0.5936	0.9020
60	0.4515	0.8821
80	0.3429	0.8411
100	0.3767	0.8008
120	0.4259	—
140	0.4753	—
160	0.5252	—
180	0.5752	—
200	0.6246	0.5505
250	0.7468	—
300	0.8663	0.4615
400	1.0980	0.4948
500	1.3236	0.5567
600	1.5409	0.6212
800	1.9626	0.7545
1000	2.3684	0.8914

2.17. If $T_n(x)$ is the nth-degree Chebyshev polynomial, use the orthogonality property of equation (2.70) to show that

$$\int_{-1}^1 \frac{T_n(x)x^m}{\sqrt{1-x^2}}\,dx = 0, \qquad m < n.$$

2.18 As an engineer with a background in numerical methods, you have been asked to obtain the best average value for the percentage of impurity in a product stream over a certain time period during which this percentage is likely to fluctuate, although not very erratically. You may take a maximum of four samples and conduct, at most, two precise chemical analyses. If desired, samples may be mixed before analysis. What strategy do you recommend, and why?

2.19   The error function, erf x, is defined by

$$\operatorname{erf} x = \frac{2}{\sqrt{\pi}} \int_0^x e^{-t^2}\, dt$$

$$= 1 - \frac{2}{\sqrt{\pi}} \int_x^\infty e^{-t^2}\, dt.$$

By using appropriate four-point Gaussian quadrature formulas, evaluate both of these integrals for $x = 0.5$, and compare with the tabulated value, erf $(0.5) \doteq 0.520500$.

2.20   Since $\Gamma(n + 1) = n!$, the Gauss-Laguerre three-point formula could be used to approximate $n!$:

$$n! = \int_0^\infty e^{-x} x^n\, dx \doteq \sum_{i=0}^2 a_i x_i^n.$$

What is the largest integer n for which this formula would be exact?

2.21   Modify the function GAUSS of Example 2.3 so that integrals of the form

$$\int_a^b f(x)\, dx$$

are evaluated using a composite formula, equivalent to repeated application of the m-point Gauss-Legendre quadrature over nonoverlapping subintervals of $[a,b]$ of length $(b - a)/n$.

2.22   Write a function, named LAGUER, that employs the m-point Gauss-Laguerre quadrature formula (2.109) to evaluate numerically an integral of the form

$$\int_a^\infty e^{-x} f(x)\, dx,$$

where $f(x)$ is an arbitrary function and a is finite. The function should incorporate the necessary Laguerre polynomial roots and the corresponding weight factors (see Table 2.4) for the m-point quadrature where m may be any of 2, 3, 4, 5, 6, 10, or 15. Let the argument list be (A, M, F), where A and M have obvious interpretations, and F is a function that evaluates $f(x)$ for any x.

To test the routine, write a short main program and appropriate functions to compute:
(a) the gamma function

$$\Gamma(\alpha) = \int_0^\infty e^{-x} x^{\alpha - 1}\, dx,$$

for $\alpha = 1.0, 1.2, 1.4, 1.6, 1.8, 2.0$.
(b) the exponential integral,

$$E_1(\alpha) = \int_\alpha^\infty \frac{e^{-x}}{x}\, dx,$$

for $\alpha = 0.5, 1.0, 1.5, 2.0$. In each case the integral should be evaluated using the 2, 3, 4, 5, 6, 10, and 15-point quadratures. Compare the results with tabulated values.

2.23   Write and test a function, named HERMIT, that implements the Gauss-Hermite quadrature of (2.115) for $n = 1, 2, 3, 4, 9$, and 19 (see Table 2.6 and reference [3]). Let the argument list be (N, F), where N and F correspond to n and f in (2.115). Use HERMIT to evaluate the integral

$$\int_{-\infty}^\infty \frac{x^2}{1 + x^4}\, dx,$$

and compare with the true value, $\pi / [2 \sin(\pi/4)]$.

2.24   In a study by Carnahan [17], the fraction f_{Th} of certain fission neutrons having energies above a threshold energy E_{Th} (Mev) was found to be

$$f_{Th} = 1 - 0.484 \int_0^{E_{Th}} \sinh(\sqrt{2E}) e^{-E}\, dE.$$

Evaluate f_{Th} within ± 0.001 for $E_{Th} = 0.5, 2.9, 5.3$, and 8.6 Mev.

2.25   The following relation is available [3] for $P_n'(x)$, the derivative of the nth-degree Legendre polynomial:

$$(x^2 - 1) P_n'(x) = nx P_n(x) - n P_{n-1}(x).$$

Show that the family of polynomials $P_n'(x)$ is orthogonal on the interval $[-1, 1]$ with respect to the weighting function $(x^2 - 1)$.

Show also that a Gaussian quadrature of the form

$$\int_{-1}^1 f(x)\, dx \doteq \sum_{i=0}^n w_i f(x_i)$$

can be developed for the case in which two base points are preassigned $(x_0 = -1, x_n = 1)$, that the quadrature is exact when $f(x)$ is a polynomial of degree $2n - 1$ or less, that $x_1, x_2, \ldots, x_{n-1}$ are the zeros of $P_n'(x)$, and that the weight factors are

$$w_0 = \frac{1}{2 P_n'(-1)} \int_{-1}^1 (1 - x) P_n'(x)\, dx,$$

$$w_n = \frac{1}{2 P_n'(+1)} \int_{-1}^1 (1 + x) P_n'(x)\, dx,$$

$$w_i = \frac{1}{(x_i^2 - 1) P_n''(x_i)} \int_{-1}^1 \frac{(x^2 - 1) P_n'(x)}{x - x_i}\, dx, \quad i = 1, 2, \ldots, n-1.$$

Note.   It can be shown by further manipulation that

$$w_0 \doteq w_n = \frac{2}{n(n+1)}, \qquad w_i = \frac{2}{n(n+1)[P_n(x_i)]^2}.$$

The above is known as *Lobatto quadrature*.

2.26   Show that a Gaussian quadrature,

$$\int_{-1}^1 f(x)\, dx = \sum_{i=0}^n w_i f(x_i),$$

for which $x_0 = -1$ and the remaining base points are the n roots of

$$\phi_n(x) = \frac{P_n(x) + P_{n+1}(x)}{1 + x},$$

is exact when $f(x)$ is a polynomial of degree $2n$ or less. Find the weight factors w_i, $i = 0, 1, \ldots, n$, for $n = 1, 2, 3$.

2.27   A useful quadrature formula, attributed to Chebyshev, is given by

$$\int_{-1}^1 f(x)\, dx \doteq \frac{2}{n+1} \sum_{i=0}^n f(x_i),$$

where the x_i are the $n+1$ roots of an $(n+1)$th-degree polynomial $C_{n+1}(x)$. The first few of these polynomials are:

$$C_0(x) = 1,$$
$$C_1(x) = x,$$
$$C_2(x) = x^2 - \tfrac{1}{3},$$
$$C_3(x) = x^3 - \tfrac{1}{2}x,$$
$$C_4(x) = x^4 - \tfrac{2}{3}x^2 + \tfrac{1}{45},$$
$$C_5(x) = x^5 - \tfrac{5}{6}x^3 + \tfrac{7}{72}x,$$
$$C_6(x) = x^6 - x^4 + \tfrac{1}{5}x^2 - \tfrac{1}{105},$$
$$C_7(x) = x^7 - \tfrac{7}{6}x^5 + \tfrac{119}{360}x^3 - \tfrac{149}{6480}x,$$
$$C_9(x) = x^9 - \tfrac{3}{2}x^7 + \tfrac{27}{40}x^5 - \tfrac{57}{560}x^3 + \tfrac{53}{22400}x.$$

It can be shown [26] that the roots of these polynomials all lie in $(-1,1)$ and are real, whereas some of the roots of $C_n(x)$, for $n=8$ and $n>10$ are complex. Note that this quadrature has the attractive feature that all the weight factors are equal, and the weighting function for the integral is $w(x)=1$.

(a) Show that the polynomials $C_n(x)$ are *not* orthogonal with respect to the weighting function $w(x)=1$ on the interval $[-1,1]$.

(b) Find the error term for the quadrature.

(c) What is the degree of precision of the formula for n even and n odd?

(d) Show that the two-point formula is identical to the two-point Gauss-Legendre quadrature of (2.84).

(e) Modify the quadrature to allow estimation of integrals of the form

$$\int_a^b f(x)\,dx,$$

where a and b are finite.

2.28 Using the roots of the polynomials $C_n(x)$ of Problem 2.27 and found by the program developed in Problem 3.32, write a function, named CHEB2, with argument list (A, B, F, M, R) that implements the composite version of the quadrature developed in part (e) of Problem 2.27. Here, A and B are the lower and upper integration limits, M is the number of points in the quadrature formula, and R (integer) is the number of repeated applications of the quadrature. Thus the M-point quadrature is to be applied to R nonoverlapping subintervals of [A, B], each of length (B − A)/R. F is another function that evaluates $f(x)$ for any x.

Write a main program and accompanying function F to allow computation of the complete elliptic integral of the second kind,

$$E(\alpha) = \int_0^{\pi/2} (1 - \alpha \sin^2 x)^{1/2}\,dx.$$

The main program should read values for ALPHA (α), M, and R, call upon CHEB2 to return the estimated value of the integral, print the results, and return to read another data set. Since CHEB2 should be a general routine, F should have only one argument (say X). ALPHA should be available to the function F through a COMMON (or equivalent) declaration.

For a variety of values for M and R, calculate values of $E(\alpha)$, for $\alpha = 0., 0.1, 0.25,$ and 0.5. Compare your results with the tabulated values [3]:

$$E(0.00) = 1.570796327$$
$$E(0.10) = 1.530757637$$
$$E(0.25) = 1.467462209$$
$$E(0.50) = 1.350643881$$

2.29 A very light spring of length L has Young's modulus E and cross-sectional moment of inertia I; it is rigidly clamped at its lower end B and is initially vertical (Fig. P2.29). A downward force P at the free end A causes the spring to bend over. If θ is the angle of slope at any point and s is the distance *along the spring* measured from A, then integration of the exact governing equation $EI(d\theta/ds) = -Py$, noting that $dy/ds = \sin\theta$, leads to [21]:

$$ds = -\frac{d\theta}{[(2P/EI)(\cos\theta - \cos\alpha)]^{1/2}},$$

and

$$L = \sqrt{\frac{EI}{P}} \int_0^{\pi/2} [1 - \sin^2(\alpha/2)\sin^2\phi]^{-1/2}\,d\phi,$$

where α is the value of θ at A.

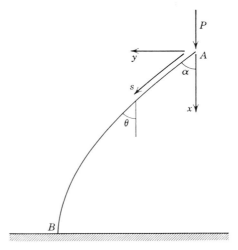

Figure P2.29

Show from the above that the Euler load P_e for which the spring just begins to bend is given by

$$P_e = \frac{\pi^2 EI}{4L^2}.$$

Let x_g and y_b denote the vertical distance of A above the datum plane and the horizontal distance of B from A, respectively. Compute the values of P/P_e for which $x_g/L = 0.99, 0.95, 0.9, 0.5,$ and 0. What are the corresponding values of y_b/L and α?

(Note that the above expression for L and a related expression for x_g/L involve elliptic integrals.)

2.30 A semiinfinite medium $(x \geqslant 0)$ has a thermal diffusivity α and a zero initial temperature at time $t = 0$. For $t > 0$, the surface at $x = 0$ is maintained at a temperature $T_s = T_s(t)$. By using Duhamel's theorem (see p. 62 of Carslaw and Jaeger

[22], for example), the subsequent temperature $T(x,t)$ inside the medium can be shown to be given by

$$T(x,t) = \frac{x}{2\sqrt{\pi\alpha}} \int_0^t T_s(\lambda) \frac{e^{-[x^2/4\alpha(t-\lambda)]}}{(t-\lambda)^{3/2}} \, d\lambda.$$

(An alternative form of the integral can be obtained by introducing a new variable: $\mu = x/[2\sqrt{\alpha(t-\lambda)}]$.)

Let T_s represent the periodic temperature in °F at a point on the earth's surface. For example, the mean monthly air temperatures in Table P2.30 have been reported [23] at the locations indicated.

Table P2.30

	Nagpur	Cape Royds	Yakutsk
January	66.9	26.1	−45.0
February	73.9	20.4	−35.4
March	82.5	4.9	−11.4
April	89.9	−10.9	14.0
May	92.4	−5.5	40.0
June	86.4	−7.1	58.0
July	80.4	−17.0	65.7
August	80.3	−15.7	59.0
September	80.2	−5.7	42.0
October	78.3	4.5	16.5
November	72.3	17.0	−22.1
December	67.7	30.0	−41.2

Compute the likely mean monthly ground temperatures at 5, 10, 20, and 50 feet below the earth's surface at each of the above locations. Plot these computed temperatures to show their relation to the corresponding surface temperatures. In each case, assume: (a) dry ground with $\alpha = 0.0926$ sq ft/hr, (b) the mean monthly ground and air temperatures at the surface are approximately equal, and (c) the pattern of air temperatures repeats itself indefinitely from one year to the next.

2.31 Suppose that $(m+1)(n+1)$ functional values $f(x_i,y_j)$ are available for all combinations of $m+1$ levels of x_i, $i = 0, 1, \ldots, m$, and $n+1$ levels of y_j, $j = 0, 1, \ldots, n$. Define Lagrangian interpolation coefficients $X_{m,i}(x)$, $i = 0, 1, \ldots, m$, and $Y_{n,j}(y)$, $j = 0, 1, \ldots, m$, as in Problem 1.35. Let the integral in the rectangular domain $a \leqslant x \leqslant b$, $c \leqslant y \leqslant d$,

$$I = \int_a^b \int_c^d f(x,y) \, dy \, dx$$

be approximated by the integral of the two-dimensional interpolating polynomial of degree m in x and of degree n in y,

$$p_{m,n}(x,y) = \sum_{i=0}^m \sum_{j=0}^n a_{i,j} x^i y^j = \sum_{i=0}^m \sum_{j=0}^n X_{m,i}(x) Y_{n,j}(y) f(x_i,y_j),$$

that is, let

$$I \doteq \int_a^b \int_c^d p_{m,n}(x,y) \, dy \, dx.$$

Show that the latter integral may be rewritten as

$$I \doteq \sum_{i=0}^m \sum_{j=0}^n A_{i,j} f(x_i,y_j),$$

where

$$A_{i,j} - \alpha_i \beta_j,$$

$$\alpha_i = \int_a^b X_{m,i}(x) \, dx,$$

$$\beta_j = \int_c^d Y_{n,j}(y) \, dy.$$

2.32 Show that if the x_i are equally spaced on the interval $[a,b]$, and the y_j are equally spaced on the interval $[c,d]$, then the coefficients α_i and β_j of Problem 2.31 are the coefficients of the $(m+1)$- and $(n+1)$-point Newton-Cotes closed integration formulas of (2.21).

2.33 Find the error term for the quadrature formula developed in Problem 2.32.

2.34 Write a function, named SIMPS2, that evaluates the double integral

$$\int_a^b \int_c^d f(x,y) \, dy \, dx,$$

using the two-dimensional quadrature formula developed in Problem 2.31 with $m = n = 2$, $x_0 = a$, $x_1 = (a+b)/2$, $x_2 = b$, $y_0 = c$, $y_1 = (c+d)/2$, and $y_2 = d$. The function should have arguments

(A, B, C, D, F)

where A, B, C, and D have obvious interpretations, and F is the name of another function with arguments (X, Y) that calculates $f(x,y)$ when necessary. What is the error term for this two-dimensional implementation of Simpson's rule?

2.35 Develop a composite quadrature formula for the two-dimensional Simpson's rule described in Problem 2.34. In this case, the integral over the rectangular domain $a \leqslant x \leqslant b$, $c \leqslant y \leqslant d$, is computed as the sum of integrals evaluated for nonoverlapping rectangular domains. Let the individual rectangles have dimensions $(b-a)/N_x$ and $(d-c)/N_y$, so that the simple rule is repeated $N_x N_y$ times.

2.36 Write a function, named SIMPC2, that implements the composite two-dimensional Simpson's rule developed in Problem 2.35. The argument list should be

(A, B, C, D, F, NX, NY)

where NX and NY are N_x and N_y, respectively, and the other arguments are those described in Problem 2.34. Although each application of the two-dimensional Simpson's rule requires the evaluation of nine functional values, eight of these functional values are, in general, on the "boundaries" of other rectangular domains as well. Show that, while straightforward repeated applications of the rule might require as many as $9N_x N_y$ evaluations of the function, the minimum number of functional evaluations required is only $(2N_x + 1)(2N_y + 1)$. Your function should require as few functional evaluations as possible. The estimate of the integral should be returned as the value of the function.

2.37 Develop an algorithm, based on the one-dimensional Gauss-Legendre quadrature formula (2.96), for numerical evaluation of integrals of the form

$$\int_a^b \int_{y_1(x)}^{y_2(x)} f(x,y) \, dy \, dx.$$

2.38 Implement the algorithm developed in Problem 2.37 as a function named INT2D. Use the function to evaluate the integral

$$\int_{-1}^{1}\int_{-1+x^2}^{1-x^2}\sqrt{x^2+y^2}\,dy\,dx,$$

and compare with the exact value, $2\pi/3$.

2.39 As shown in Fig. P2.39, a differential element of area dA_1 (a plane source) is situated at a distance L from the center O of a circular disc (surface "2") of radius a. The line joining O to dA_1 is normal to dA_1 and also makes an angle α with the plane of the disc. From Problem 2.41, the fraction of radiation leaving dA_1 that impinges on the disc is given by

$$F_{dA_1\to A_2}=\frac{1}{\pi}\int_{A_2}\frac{\cos\phi_1\cos\phi_2}{r^2}\,dA_2,$$

where the integral is taken over the area A_2 of the disc. Polar coordinates should be used to span A_2, that is, let $dA_2 = R\,dR\,d\theta$, where R is the radial measure ($0 \le R \le a$) and θ is the angular measure ($0 \le \theta \le 2\pi$) in A_2.

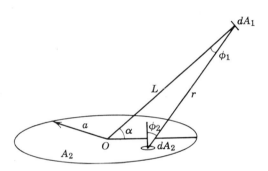

Compute $F_{dA_1\to A_2}$ for all combinations of $L/a = 1, 2, 3$, and 5, $\alpha = 30°, 60°$, and $90°$, using the function SIMPC2 from Problem 2.36. For $\alpha = 90°$, check the results against the known analytical value:

$$F_{dA_1\to A_2}=1-\frac{L^2}{a^2+L^2}.$$

2.40 Express the integral of Problem 2.39 in terms of Cartesian coordinates and use the function INT2D developed in Problem 2.38 to evaluate the integral for the data of Problem 2.39. Compare the results with the analytical solution.

2.41 Consider radiant heat transfer between surface 1 and surface 2, of total areas A_1 and A_2, respectively. The *view factor* F_{12} is defined as the fraction of the total radiation leaving surface 1 that impinges on surface 2 directly. If surface 1 is diffuse, radiating uniformly in all directions, it can be shown that

$$F_{12}=\frac{1}{\pi A_1}\int_{A_1}\int_{A_2}\frac{\cos\phi_1\cos\phi_2}{r^2}\,dA_1\,dA_2,$$

where r is the distance between two elements dA_1 and dA_2 on the respective surfaces, and ϕ_1 and ϕ_2 are the angles between the line joining dA_1 and dA_2 and their respective normals.

Next consider two adjacent rectangles, mutually inclined at 90°, illustrated in Fig. P2.41. For the elements shown, $r^2 = (w-y)^2 + x^2 + z^2$, $\cos\phi_1 = x/r$, and $\cos\phi_2 = z/r$, and

the view factor becomes

$$F_{12}=\frac{1}{\pi W_1 L}\int_{y=0}^{L}\int_{z=0}^{W_1}\int_{w=0}^{L}\int_{x=0}^{W_2}\frac{xz}{r^4}\,dw\,dx\,dy\,dz.$$

Write a program that will read values for L, W_1, and W_2, and that will use numerical integration to estimate F_{12}.

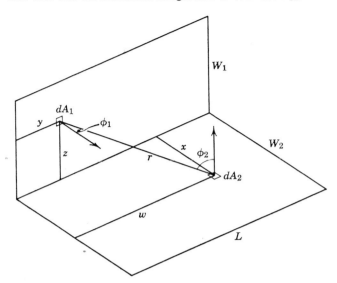

Suggested Test Data

$L = 1$, with $W_1 = W_2$ having the values 0.5, 1, and 2 in sequence.

2.42 Repeat Problem 2.41, now with an absorbing (but not reradiating or scattering) gas intervening between the two surfaces. In this case, the integrand will have to be multiplied by an additional factor $e^{-\beta r}$, where β is an attenuation coefficient. Suggested values are $\beta L = 0.5, 1$, and 2.

2.43 Two parallel squares of side L are opposite each other, a distance d apart. Starting from the definition given in Problem 2.41, evaluate F_{12} for radiant interchange between the two squares for $d/L = 0.5, 1$, and 2.

2.44 A beam of radiation of intensity πF is incident at an angle θ_0 to the normal of the surface of a semiinfinite medium that scatters isotropically with an albedo ω_0 (fraction of a pencil of radiation that is scattered at any point). Because of scattering within the medium, some of the radiation will reemerge from the surface. It can be shown (see, for example, Chandrasekhar [25]) that the intensity of radiation emerging at an angle θ to the normal is given by

$$I(\theta,\theta_0)=\frac{1}{4}\omega_0 F\frac{\mu_0}{\mu+\mu_0}H(\mu)H(\mu_0),$$

where $\mu = \cos\theta$ and $\mu_0 = \cos\theta_0$. The function H satisfies the following integral equation, which is of general importance in theories of radiation scattering:

$$H(\mu)=1+\mu H(\mu)\int_0^1\frac{\Psi(\mu')}{\mu+\mu'}H(\mu')\,d\mu'.$$

In the present application, the characteristic function is simply $\Psi(\mu) = \frac{1}{2}\omega_0$ (constant).

Write a program that will compute and tabulate the function H for all combinations of μ and ω_0, both ranging from 0 to 1 in increments of 0.1. Then, evaluate I/F for several test values of θ, θ_0, and ω_0.

2.45 As shown in Fig. P2.45, two infinite black parallel plates at absolute temperatures T_h and T_c are separated by an optical thickness $\tau = L$ of a gray gas that absorbs and emits (but does not scatter) radiant energy. (Optical thickness measures the ability of a gas path of length z to attenuate radiation, and is defined as $\tau = \int_0^z \kappa\rho\,dz$, where $\rho = $ density and $\kappa = $ mass absorption coefficient.)

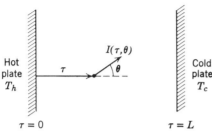

Figure P2.45

The intensities of radiation in the outward (τ increasing) and inward (τ decreasing) directions depend both on τ and on the angular direction θ; from the basic transfer equation (see, for example, Chandrasekhar [25]), it may be shown that these intensities I are given by the solution of the simultaneous integral equations

$$I(\tau,\mu) = \frac{E_h}{\pi} e^{-\tau/\mu} + \int_0^\tau \frac{E(t)}{\pi}\left[e^{-(\tau-t)/\mu}\right]\frac{dt}{\mu} \quad \text{(outward, } 0 < \mu \leqslant 1),$$

$$I(\tau,\mu) = \frac{E_c}{\pi} e^{(L-\tau)/\mu} + \int_L^\tau \frac{E(t)}{\pi} e^{(t-\tau)/\mu}\frac{dt}{\mu} \quad \text{(inward, } -1 \leq \mu < 0).$$

In both cases, $\mu = \cos\theta$. Also, $E_h = \sigma T_h^4$ and $E_c = \sigma T_c^4$ are the emissive powers of the hot and cold plates, where $\sigma = 1.355 \times 10^{-12}$ cal/sec sq cm °K⁴ is the Stefan-Boltzmann constant. E is the emissive power of the gas and is given as a function of τ by

$$\frac{E}{\pi} = \frac{1}{2}\int_{-1}^1 I(\tau,\mu)\,d\mu,$$

in which the right-hand side is actually the average intensity of radiation at any point.

Write a program that will solve the above equations to give the outward and inward intensities as functions of τ and μ, and E as a function of τ. The accuracy of the computations should be checked by computing the net radiant flux density in the $+\tau$ direction,

$$q = 2\pi\int_{-1}^1 I(\tau,\mu)\mu\,d\mu,$$

which should be constant for all τ. Solutions should be obtained at points that subdivide L into n equal increments $\Delta\tau = L/n$, and for angular directions whose cosines are equally spaced by an amount $\Delta\mu$ in the range $-1 \leqslant \mu \leqslant 1$.

Suggested Test Data

$T_h = 1500°$K, $T_c = 1000°$K, $n = 10$, $\Delta\mu = 0.1$, with $L = 0.1$, 0.5, and 2.0 in turn.

(The above equations can be written in dimensionless form, if required, by introducing $X = \tau/L$, $\xi = \xi(X,L) = (E - E_c)/$ $(E_h - E_c)$, $\alpha = \alpha(X,L,\mu) = (\pi I - E_c)/(E_h - E_c)$, and $\psi = \psi(L) = q/(E_h - E_c)$.)

2.46 Referring to Table 2.7, verify the algebraic approximations to the derivative and their associated error terms.

2.47 Jenkins and White [24] give values, reproduced here in Table P2.47, for the refractive index, n, and the dispersion, $dn/d\lambda$, of barium flint glass. The wavelength, λ, is in angstrom units.

Table P2.47

λ	n	$dn/d\lambda$
6563	1.58848	0.38×10^{-5}
6439	1.58896	0.39×10^{-5}
5890	1.59144	0.50×10^{-5}
5338	1.59463	0.68×10^{-5}
5086	1.59644	0.78×10^{-5}
4861	1.59825	0.89×10^{-5}
4340	1.60367	1.23×10^{-5}
3988	1.60870	1.72×10^{-5}

Make a critical evaluation of these tabulated values of dispersion, under each of the following circumstances:

(a) If the only additional information is that n is a monotonic function of λ.

(b) If n is known to vary approximately with λ according to the simplified Cauchy equation, $n = A + B/\lambda^2$, where A and B are constants.

2.48 The following quantities find application in the study of certain electronic vacuum tubes: (a) *dynamic plate resistance*, $r_p = (\partial v_a/\partial i_a)_{v_g}$, (b) *amplification factor*, $\mu = -(\partial v_a/\partial v_g)_{i_a}$, and (c) *transconductance*, $g_m = (\partial i_a/\partial v_g)_{v_a}$. Here, $v_a = $ anode voltage, $v_g = $ grid voltage, and $i_a = $ anode current; representative values for the triode 6J5 can be found in Problem 1.42.

Write a function with three entries, RP6J5, MU6J5, and GM6J5, that will compute r_p, μ, and g_m, respectively, when supplied with any two of the following variables: (1) v_g, (2) v_a, and (3) i_a. The first calling argument should be an integer, having the value 1, 2, or 3, indicating which of these three variables is *omitted*. For example, we might have:

RP = RP6J5 (1, VA, IA)

RP = RP6J5 (2, VG, IA)

GM = GM6J5 (3, VG, VA)

The a-c signal voltage amplification A for a triode with a load resistance R in the anode circuit is readily shown (see Smith [19], for example) to be

$$A = -\frac{g_m r_p R}{r_p + R}.$$

To test the above functions, write a short calling program that will accept values for v_g, v_a, and R, and then compute and print the corresponding values of r_p, μ, g_m, A, and the product $r_p g_m$ (which theoretically should equal μ, thus affording a check on the accuracy of the calculations). Suggested test data, $R = 1.5$, 8.2, and 22.0 $k\Omega$ for each of the following combinations: $v_g = -2.7$, $v_a = 130$ volts; $v_g = -10.0$, $v_a = 287$; $v_g = -20.9$, $v_a = 405$.

The case of specified high-tension supply voltage (instead of the actual anode voltage) is discussed in Problem 3.20.

2.49 Show that for $m = 1$, $n = 4$, and $x_i = x_0 + ih$, (2.120) leads to the following formulations for $f'(x_i)$:

$$f'(x_0) = \frac{1}{12h}[-25f(x_0) + 48f(x_1) - 36f(x_2)$$
$$+ 16f(x_3) - 3f(x_4)] + \frac{h^4}{5} f^{(5)}(\xi),$$

$$f'(x_1) = \frac{1}{12h}[-3f(x_0) - 10f(x_1) + 18f(x_2)$$
$$- 6f(x_3) + f(x_4)] - \frac{h^4}{20} f^{(5)}(\xi),$$

$$f'(x_2) = \frac{1}{12h}[f(x_0) - 8f(x_1) + 8f(x_2) - f(x_3)] + \frac{h^4}{30} f^{(5)}(\xi),$$

$$f'(x_3) = \frac{1}{12h}[-f(x_0) + 6f(x_1) - 18f(x_2) + 10f(x_3)$$
$$+ 3f(x_4)] + \frac{h^4}{20} f^{(5)}(\xi),$$

$$f'(x_4) = \frac{1}{12h}[3f(x_0) - 16f(x_1) + 36f(x_2) - 48f(x_3)$$
$$+ 25f(x_4)] + \frac{h^4}{5} f^{(5)}(\xi).$$

2.50 Show that for $m = 2$, $n = 4$, and $x_i = x_0 + ih$, (2.120) leads to the following formulations for $f''(x_i)$:

$$f''(x_0) = \frac{1}{24h^2}[70f(x_0) - 208f(x_1) + 228f(x_2) - 112f(x_3)$$
$$+ 22f(x_4)] - \frac{5}{6} h^3 f^{(5)}(\xi_1) + \frac{h^4}{15} f^{(6)}(\xi_2),$$

$$f''(x_1) = \frac{1}{24h^2}[22f(x_0) - 40f(x_1) + 12f(x_2) + 8f(x_3)$$
$$- 2f(x_4)] + \frac{1}{12} h^3 f^{(5)}(\xi_1) - \frac{h^4}{60} f^{(6)}(\xi_2),$$

$$f''(x_2) = \frac{1}{24h^2}[-2f(x_0) + 32f(x_1) - 60f(x_2) + 32f(x_3)$$
$$- 2f(x_4)] + \frac{1}{90} h^4 f^{(6)}(\xi),$$

$$f''(x_3) = \frac{1}{24h^2}[-2f(x_0) + 8f(x_1) + 12f(x_2) - 40f(x_3)$$
$$+ 22f(x_4)] - \frac{1}{12} h^3 f^{(5)}(\xi_1) + \frac{h^4}{60} f^{(6)}(\xi_2),$$

$$f''(x_4) = \frac{1}{24h^2}[22f(x_0) - 112f(x_1) + 228f(x_2) - 208f(x_3)$$
$$+ 70f(x_4)] + \frac{5}{6} h^3 f^{(5)}(\xi_1) - \frac{h^4}{15} f^{(6)}(\xi_2).$$

2.51 Show that for $x = x_i$, (2.120) may be written in the form

$$\left.\frac{d^m f(x)}{dx^m}\right|_{x_i} \doteq \left.\frac{d^m p_n(x)}{dx^m}\right|_{x_i} = \sum_{j=0}^{n} a_j f(x_j),$$

where the a_j are solutions of the simultaneous linear equations

$$a_0 + a_1 + a_2 + \cdots + a_n = 0$$
$$x_0 a_0 + x_1 a_1 + x_2 a_2 + \cdots + x_n a_n = 0$$
$$\cdots\cdots\cdots\cdots\cdots\cdots\cdots\cdots\cdots\cdots$$
$$x_0^{m-1} a_0 + x_1^{m-1} a_1 + x_2^{m-1} a_2 + \cdots + x_n^{m-1} a_n = 1$$
$$x_0^m a_0 + x_1^m a_1 + x_2^m a_2 + \cdots + x_n^m a_n = m!$$
$$x_0^{m+1} a_0 + x_1^{m+1} a_1 + x_2^{m+1} a_2 + \cdots + x_n^{m+1} a_n = (m+1)! x_i$$
$$\cdots\cdots\cdots\cdots\cdots\cdots\cdots\cdots\cdots\cdots$$
$$x_0^n a_0 + x_1^n a_1 + x_2^n a_2 + \cdots + x_n^n a_n = \frac{n!}{(n-m)!} x_i^{n-m}.$$

Hint: Equation (2.120) must be satisfied exactly if $f(x)$ is a polynomial of degree n or less, in particular, if $f(x) = 1, x, x^2, \ldots, x^n$. This approach is known as the *method of undetermined coefficients*. Note that the formulation does not assume equal spacing for the base points, $x_i, i = 0, 1, \ldots, n$. (See also Problem 5.9.).

2.52 Write a function, named DSPLIN, with argument list

$$(\text{N, X, Y, XARG})$$

that will evaluate the derivative of the cubic spline function (see Problems 1.24, 1.25, and 1.26) at $x = $ XARG where the $N + 1$ base points for the spline fit are available in X(1), ..., X(N + 1), and the corresponding functional values are available in Y(1), ..., Y(N + 1). The value of $S'_{\bar{x}}(\bar{Y}, \text{XARG})$ should be returned as the value of DSPLIN.

Bibliography

1. B. W. Arden, *An Introduction to Digital Computing*, Addison-Wesley, Reading, Massachusetts, 1963.
2. F. B. Hildebrand, *Introduction to Numerical Analysis*, McGraw-Hill, New York, 1956.
3. "Handbook of Mathematical Functions," *Natl. Bur. Standards Appl. Math. Series*, **55**, Washington, D.C., 1964.
4. "Tables of Functions and Zeros of Functions," *Natl. Bur. Standards Appl. Math. Series*, **37**, Washington, D.C., 1954.
5. J. F. Steffensen, *Interpolation*, Williams and Wilkins, Baltimore, 1927; 2nd ed., Chelsea, New York, 1950.
6. F. L. Bauer, H. Rutishauser, and E. Stiefel, "New Aspects in Numerical Quadrature," *Proceedings of Symposia in Applied Mathematics*, XV, pp. 199–218, American Mathematical Society, Providence, R. I., 1963.
7. A. H. Stroud and D. Secrest, *Gaussian Quadrature Formulas*, Prentice-Hall, Englewood Cliffs, New Jersey, 1966.
8. A. Ralston, *A First Course in Numerical Analysis*, McGraw-Hill, New York, 1965.
9. I. S. Berezin and N. P. Zhidkov, *Computing Methods*, Vol. I, (English translation), Pergamon Press, London, 1965.
10. J. O. Wilkes, *The Finite-Difference Computation of Natural Convection in an Enclosed Rectangular Cavity*, Ph.D. Thesis, University of Michigan, 1963.
11. W. N. Gill and M. Scher, "A Modification of the Momentum Transport Hypothesis," *A.I.Ch.E. Journal*, **7**, 61–65 (1961).
12. J. G. Knudsen and D. L. Katz, *Fluid Dynamics and Heat Transfer*, McGraw-Hill, New York, 1954.
13. P. S. Davis and P. Rabinowitz, *Numerical Integration*, Blaisdell, Waltham, Massachusetts, 1967.
14. C. W. Clenshaw, "Chebyshev Series for Mathematical Functions," *Math. Tables*, Vol. 5, Nat. Phys. Lab., G. Britain, 1962.
15. J. H. Perry, ed., *Chemical Engineers' Handbook*, 3rd ed., McGraw-Hill, New York, 1950.
16. K. G. Denbigh, *The Principles of Chemical Equilibrium*, Cambridge University Press, London, 1957.
17. B. Carnahan, *Radiation Induced Cracking of Pentanes and Dimethylbutanes*, Ph.D. Thesis, University of Michigan, 1964.
18. I. S. and E. S. Sokolnikoff, *Higher Mathematics for Engineers and Physicists*, 2nd ed., McGraw-Hill, New York, 1941.
19. R. J. Smith, *Circuits, Devices, and Systems*, Wiley, New York, 1966.
20. M. A. Snyder, *Chebyshev Methods in Numerical Approximation*, Prentice-Hall, Englewood Cliffs, New Jersey, 1966.
21. S. Timoshenko, *Theory of Elastic Stability*, McGraw-Hill, New York, 1936.
22. H. S. Carslaw and J. C. Jaeger, *Conduction of Heat in Solids*, 2nd ed., Oxford University Press, London, 1959.
23. "Polar Regions" and "Climate and Climatology," *Encyclopaedia Britannica*, 11th ed., Cambridge University Press, London, 1910.
24. F. A. Jenkins and H. E. White, *Fundamentals of Optics*, McGraw-Hill, New York, 1951.
25. S. Chandrasekhar, *Radiative Transfer*, Dover, New York, 1960.
26. V. I. Krylov, *Approximate Calculation of Integrals*, Macmillan, New York, 1962.

CHAPTER 3

Solution of Equations

3.1 Introduction

This chapter discusses methods for finding the roots of equations such as $x^3 - 3x + 1 = 0$, or $\cos x - x = 0$. While the emphasis will be on polynomial equations, several of the techniques to be discussed will also be applicable to transcendental equations, such as the second example above.

The problems to be discussed will range from the finding of all roots of the equation, with no prior information about their locations, to the more precise evaluation of a single real root already known to be the only one lying within some fairly short interval. Sometimes, real roots are the only ones of interest; in other cases, complex roots are also sought. The coefficients of the equations will usually be regarded as real in the present discussion, although parts of it will be valid without this restriction.

For the remainder of the chapter, the equation to be solved, if not specifically designated, will be written

$$f(x) = 0, \qquad (3.1)$$

and f will consistently denote the function appearing on the left-hand side of (3.1). Since some of the methods of solution to be discussed are applicable only to algebraic equations, we shall regard $f(x)$ as a polynomial throughout the discussion. The extent to which this restriction may be lifted at various points will be apparent from the context. With this understanding, $f(x)$ may be expressed in any of the forms

$$f(x) = x^n + a_1 x^{n-1} + \cdots + a_{n-1} x + a_n,$$
$$f(x) = \sum_{i=0}^{n} a_i x^{n-i}, \ a_0 = 1,$$
$$f(x) = (x - \alpha_1)(x - \alpha_2) \ldots (x - \alpha_n), \qquad (3.2)$$
$$f(x) = \prod_{i=1}^{n} (x - \alpha_i).$$

Here n is the *degree* of the equation, $a_0, a_1, \ldots, a_n$ are the *coefficients*, and $\alpha_1, \alpha_2, \ldots, \alpha_n$ are the *roots*. It is understood throughout that $|\alpha_1| \geqslant |\alpha_2| \geqslant \cdots \geqslant |\alpha_n|$ and $a_n \neq 0$.

3.2 Graeffe's Method

Of the numerous methods of solution that have been suggested, the most completely "global" ones, in the sense of yielding simultaneous approximations to all roots, are probably Graeffe's root-squaring technique [11] and the QD method of Section 3.9.

Consider the function ϕ defined by

$$\phi(x) = (-1)^n f(x) f(-x)$$
$$= (x^2 - \alpha_1^2)(x^2 - \alpha_2^2) \cdots (x^2 - \alpha_n^2). \qquad (3.3)$$

Since $\phi(x)$ is a polynomial containing only even powers, we may define the polynomial

$$f_2(x) = \phi(\sqrt{x}) = (x - \alpha_1^2)(x - \alpha_2^2) \cdots (x - \alpha_n^2),$$

which has the property that the roots of $f_2(x) = 0$ are the squares of the roots of (3.2). Repeating this operation, we obtain a sequence of polynomials $f_2, f_4, f_8, f_{16}, \ldots$ such that the equation

$$f_m(x) \equiv (x - \alpha_1^m)(x - \alpha_2^m) \cdots (x - \alpha_n^m) = 0, \qquad (3.4)$$

where m is a positive integral power of 2, has the roots $\alpha_1^m, \alpha_2^m, \ldots, \alpha_n^m$. The coefficients of f_m are determined from the coefficients of the preceding polynomial by an algorithm that is described later.

The object of this procedure is to produce an equation having roots differing greatly in magnitude, since the roots of such an equation can be approximated by simple functions of its coefficients. If the roots of (3.2) are real and $|\alpha_1| > |\alpha_2| > \cdots > |\alpha_n|$, then the ratios

$$|\alpha_2^m/\alpha_1^m|, \ |\alpha_3^m/\alpha_2^m|, \ \ldots, \ |\alpha_n^m/\alpha_{n-1}^m|$$

can all be made as small as desired by making m large enough. Expanding (3.4) leads to

$$f_m(x) = x^n - (\alpha_1^m + \cdots)x^{n-1} + (\alpha_1^m \alpha_2^m + \cdots)x^{n-2}$$
$$- (\alpha_1^m \alpha_2^m \alpha_3^m + \cdots)x^{n-3} + \cdots + (-1)^n \alpha_1^m \alpha_2^m \cdots \alpha_n^m. \qquad (3.5)$$

Writing the right-hand side of (3.5) in the form

$$x^n - A_1 x^{n-1} + A_2 x^{n-2} + \cdots + (-1)^n A_n, \qquad (3.6)$$

we derive the approximations

$$\alpha_1^m \doteq A_1, \ \alpha_2^m \doteq \frac{A_2}{A_1}, \ \ldots, \ \alpha_n^m \doteq \frac{A_n}{A_{n-1}}. \qquad (3.7)$$

From these, by taking mth roots, we may approximate the values of the roots $\alpha_1, \alpha_2, \ldots, \alpha_n$ of (3.2).

Since the signs of the roots are not determined, they must be checked by substitution or otherwise. If the roots do not all have different absolute values, as will be true if multiple or complex roots are present, the situation is more complicated. If $|\alpha_1| = |\alpha_2|$, while the other roots are of lesser magnitude, the first terms on the right of (3.5) are approximated by $x^n - (\alpha_1^m + \alpha_2^m)x^{n-1} + (\alpha_1^m\alpha_2^m)x^{n-2}$. It is seen from the above that in this case α_1^m and α_2^m are approximated by the roots of the quadratic equation $x^2 - A_1 x + A_2 = 0$, while if α_r and α_{r+1} are the roots of equal magnitude, the equation

$$A_{r-1}x^2 - A_r x + A_{r+1} = 0 \tag{3.8}$$

yields approximations to α_r^m and α_{r+1}^m. Of course, this leaves m possible values from which α_r must be calculated by reference to the original equation. Should α_r be real, this offers no computational difficulty.

After a sufficient number of steps have been taken, it is clear from (3.5) that if the roots are real and distinct, the coefficients $A_1, A_2, \ldots, A_n$ will be approximately squared at each iteration. However, if $|\alpha_r| = |\alpha_{r+1}|$, this will not be true of the coefficient A_r.

In spite of its advantage of furnishing approximations to all roots simultaneously, Graeffe's method does not seem to have aroused great enthusiasm among users of automatic equipment. One drawback is the need for making decisions not readily mechanized. The difficulties in locating complex roots have already been mentioned. Moreover, errors introduced at any stage have the effect of replacing the original problem with a new one, thus affecting the correctness of the roots arrived at rather than merely the rate of convergence. A technique for obviating this last difficulty will be explained in Section 3.4. Another feature of concern is that coefficients developed can quickly leave the usual floating-point range.

The coefficients in (3.6) can be found by performing the polynomial multiplication $(-1)^n f(x) f(-x)$ and then compressing the result by ignoring the zero contents of alternate locations, starting with that corresponding to x^{2n-1}, and storing the contents of the remaining locations in some suitable sequence of locations.

If desired, the coefficients may be found iteratively by the relations

$$_{j+1}A_i = (-1)^i\left[_jA_i^2 + 2\sum_{l=1}^{i}(-1)^l\,_jA_{i+l}\,_jA_{i-l}\right],$$
$$0 \leq i \leq n,$$

where $_0A_i = a_i$ and

$$f_{(2^j)}(x) = \sum_{i=0}^{n}\,_jA_i x^{n-i}.$$

In the above formula, the presubscripts on A refer to the iteration counter, that is, $_jA_i$ is the value of A_i found on the jth pass of the iterative scheme; $_0A_i$ is the initial value of A_i, etc. Indices greater than n mean that the number to be used is zero.

One application of value lies in the use of the root-squaring technique over a few iterations. When roots are distinct but nearly equal, the result may be a useful equation in which the roots have better separation. Then the method of Section 3.3 can be applied.

Example. Consider $f(x) = x^4 - 2x^3 + 1.25x^2 - 0.25x - 0.75$, which has the factors $(x-1.5)$, $(x+0.5)$, and $(x^2 - x + 1)$. Using the algorithm above, it is found that

$$f_2(x) = x^4 - 1.5x^3 - 0.9375x^2 - 1.9375x + 0.5625,$$
$$f_4(x) = x^4 - 4.125x^3 - 3.80859375x^2 - 4.80859375x$$
$$+ 0.31640625,$$
$$f_8(x) = x^4 - 24.6328125x^3 - 24.53269958x^2 - 25.5327025x$$
$$+ 0.10011292.$$

Thus the predicted values of $\alpha_1^8, \alpha_2^8, \alpha_3^8$, and α_4^8 are, respectively, 24.6, $-0.498 + 0.888i$, $-0.498 - 0.888i$, and 0.00392. These compare fairly well with the truncated true values 25.63, $-0.5 + 0.866i$, $-0.5 - 0.866i$, and 0.00391.

3.3 Bernoulli's Method

Let u_k, $0 \leq k \leq n-1$, be real numbers that we can choose somewhat arbitrarily (freedom of choice is discussed below). For $k \geq n$, define

$$u_k = -\sum_{j=1}^{n} a_j u_{k-j}. \tag{3.9}$$

Bernoulli's method for finding a zero of

$$f(x) = \sum_{i=0}^{n} a_i x^{n-i}$$

is to observe relations involving the sequence $\{u_k\}$ and certain related sequences of which we use only those given by

$$v_k = u_k^2 - u_{k+1}u_{k-1},$$
$$t_k = u_k u_{k-1} - u_{k+1}u_{k-2}. \tag{3.10}$$

The simplest theorem states that if $|\alpha_1| > |\alpha_2|$, then

$$\alpha_1 = \lim_{k\to\infty} \frac{u_k}{u_{k-1}}. \tag{3.11}$$

An important advantage of Bernoulli's method over Graeffe's method is that (3.11) remains true, if suitable initial values are used, for the case $\alpha_1 = \alpha_2 = \cdots = \alpha_i$, provided $|\alpha_i| > |\alpha_{i+1}|$. In addition, if two or more roots are of equal modulus and one is of greater multiplicity than the others, the limit in (3.11) exists and is that root of greater multiplicity. Moreover, the technique for finding a conjugate pair of complex roots can be considerably simpler than when using the root-squaring method. The price paid is lack of knowledge of other roots.

If there are no multiple roots, it can be shown [1] that the unique solution of (3.9) for $k \geq 0$ is of the form

$$u_k = c_1\alpha_1^k + c_2\alpha_2^k + \cdots + c_n\alpha_n^k, \tag{3.12}$$

where the character of the c_i is controlled by the initial choice of the u_k, $0 \leq k \leq n-1$. This being so, it is clear that the conclusion of (3.11) is warranted provided that c_1 is not zero. Should $\alpha_1 = \alpha_2$ and $|\alpha_2| > |\alpha_3|$, then the character of the solution is

$$u_k = c_1\alpha_1^k + c_2 k\alpha_1^k + c_3\alpha_3^k + \cdots + c_n\alpha_n^k.$$

Similar relations hold for the general case, and the truth of (3.11) for the conditions described is then clear, provided that a properly chosen coefficient does not vanish.

Suppose next that $|\alpha_1| = |\alpha_2| > |\alpha_3|$. It follows that

$$\lim_{k \to \infty} \frac{v_k}{v_{k-1}} = \alpha_1 \alpha_2,$$

$$\lim_{k \to \infty} \frac{t_{k+1}}{v_k} = \alpha_1 + \alpha_2. \qquad (3.13)$$

The discussion is given only for $\alpha_1 \neq \alpha_2$, although the proposition is valid as stated. (Indeed, it is true for $\alpha_1 = \alpha_2 = \cdots = \alpha_i$; $\alpha_{i+1} = \alpha_{i+2} = \cdots = \alpha_{2i}$; $|\alpha_1| = |\alpha_{2i}| > |\alpha_{2i+1}|$, as well as when $\alpha_1 = \alpha_2 = \cdots = \alpha_i$; $\alpha_{i+1} = \alpha_{i+2} = \cdots = \alpha_{2i}$; $|\alpha_1| = |\alpha_{2i}| = |\alpha_{2i+1}|$, provided that α_{2i+1} and following roots of equal modulus have multiplicity less than i.) Note that the limit of v_k/v_{k-1} is v_k'/v_{k-1}' where

$$v_k' = (c_1\alpha_1^k + c_2\alpha_2^k)^2$$
$$- (c_1\alpha_1^{k+1} + c_2\alpha_2^{k+1})(c_1\alpha_1^{k-1} + c_2\alpha_2^{k-1})$$
$$= c_1 c_2 \alpha_1^{k-1} \alpha_2^{k-1}(2\alpha_1\alpha_2 - \alpha_1^2 - \alpha_2^2).$$

Also, the limit of t_{k+1}/v_k is t_{k+1}'/v_k', where

$$t_k' = (c_1\alpha_1^k + c_2\alpha_2^k)(c_1\alpha_1^{k-1} + c_2\alpha_2^{k-1})$$
$$- (c_1\alpha_1^{k+1} + c_2\alpha_2^{k+1})(c_1\alpha_1^{k-2} + c_2\alpha_2^{k-2})$$
$$= c_1 c_2 \alpha_1^{k-2} \alpha_2^{k-2}(\alpha_1 + \alpha_2)(2\alpha_1\alpha_2 - \alpha_1^2 - \alpha_2^2).$$

Consider next the problem of choosing $u_0, u_1, \ldots, u_{n-1}$ so that none of the coefficients of dominant powers vanish. Since the relations of (3.12) (or similar ones in the case of multiple roots) hold for $0 \leqslant k \leqslant n-1$, and since the determinants involved are non-vanishing Vandermonde determinants, it suffices to choose u_{n-1} to be non-zero and $u_k = 0$ for $k < n-1$. In that event, for each root, the coefficient indicative of the multiplicity of the root cannot vanish.

It should be borne in mind that a limit of the form (3.11) can correspond to a multiple root. When limits of the form (3.13) occur, α_1 and α_2 are found by solving $x^2 - (\alpha_1 + \alpha_2)x + \alpha_1\alpha_2 = 0$. Here, too, the roots may be multiple.

Note that the numbers formed often exceed the usual floating-point range. The difficulty can be remedied by dividing the last n values of the u_k by some constant and then proceeding.

As previously indicated, Graeffe's method may be used prior to applying Bernoulli's method in order to increase the root-separation. Since convergence may be slow, and since multiple roots must be considered, we suggest that as soon as convergence seems to be established, the procedures of Section 3.4 on the iterative factorization of polynomials be employed.

A few further remarks concerning both Bernoulli's and Graeffe's methods will be found in the next chapter when companion matrices are discussed. Additional references to Bernoulli's method are given on page 161 of Henrici [1].

Example. Now consider the application of Bernoulli's method to the example of the previous section, namely,

$$f(x) = x^4 - 2x^3 + 1.25x^2 - 0.25x - 0.75.$$

The formula for u_k is thus

$$u_k = 2u_{k-1} - 1.25\, u_{k-2} + 0.25\, u_{k-3} + 0.75\, u_{k-4}.$$

Table 3.1 gives u_k and u_k/u_{k-1} for the initial approximation $u_0 = u_1 = u_2 = 0$, $u_3 = 1$. The factors for the polynomial are $(x - 1.5)$, $(x + 0.5)$, and $(x^2 - x + 1)$.

Table 3.1   *Bernoulli's Method—First Example*

k	u_k	$u_k/u_{k-1} \doteq \alpha_1$
4	2.0	2.0
5	2.75	1.375
6	3.25	1.1818
7	4.3125	1.3269
8	6.7500	1.5652
9	10.9844	1.6273
10	17.0469	1.5519
11	25.2852	1.4833
12	37.0703	1.4661
13	55.0342	1.4846
14	82.8369	1.5052
15	125.113	1.5104
16	188.240	1.5046
17	282.075	1.4985
18	422.255	1.4970
19	632.809	1.4986
20	949.497	1.5004

As a second example, take $f(x) = x^4 - x^3 + 0.75x^2 + 0.25x - 0.25 = (x^2 - 0.25)(x^2 - x + 1)$. Again, let $u_0 = u_1 = u_2 = 0$, $u_3 = 1$.

Table 3.2 shows u_k, v_k, t_k, v_k/v_{k-1}, and t_{k+1}/v_k for values of $k = 3, 4, \ldots, 16$.

Table 3.2   *Bernoulli's Method—Second Example*

k	u_k	v_k	t_k	v_k/v_{k-1}	t_k/v_{k-1}
3	1.0	1.0	0		
4	1.0	0.75	1.0	0.75	1.0
5	0.25	0.8125	1.0	1.0833	1.3333
6	−0.75	0.79688	0.7500	0.9808	0.9231
7	−0.9375	0.73828	0.7500	0.9265	0.9412
8	−0.1875	0.75293	0.7500	1.0198	1.0159
9	0.76563	0.76489	0.7500	1.0159	0.9961
10	0.95313	0.76190	0.76563	0.9961	1.0010
11	0.19141	0.76265	0.76563	1.0010	1.0049
12	−0.76172	0.76246	0.76172	0.9998	0.9988
13	−0.95215	0.76153	0.76172	0.9987	0.9990
14	−0.19043	0.76177	0.76172	1.0003	1.0002
15	0.76196	0.76195	0.76172	1.0002	0.99993
16	0.95239				

Thus the dominant roots are found as the solution of $x^2 - 0.99993x + 1.0002$, as compared with the true factor $x^2 - x + 1$.

EXAMPLE 3.1

GRAEFFE'S ROOT-SQUARING METHOD
MECHANICAL VIBRATION FREQUENCIES

Problem Statement

Write a program that implements Graeffe's root-squaring method for finding real and distinct roots of the nth-degree polynomial

$$p_n(x) = \sum_{i=0}^{n} a_i x^{n-i}, \qquad (3.1.1)$$

where the a_i are real and $a_n \neq 0$.

Test the program with several different polynomials, in particular, the polynomial whose roots are related to the frequencies of vibration for the mechanical system illustrated in Figure 3.1.1 (see Problem 4.23 for details). Con-

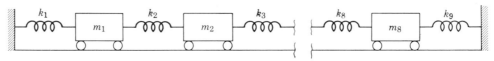

Figure 3.1.1 Mass-spring system.

sider the horizontal motion of eight equal masses, that is, let $m_1 = m_2 = \cdots = m_8 = m$. The spring stiffness coefficient, k_i, $i = 1, 2, \ldots, 9$, is the force required to extend or compress the ith spring by unit length. Find the frequencies of vibration for two cases:

A. $m = 1 \text{ lb}_m$, and $k_1 = k_2 = \cdots = k_9 = 1 \text{ lb}_m/\text{sec}^2$.
B. $m = 4 \text{ lb}_m$, and $k_i = i/4 \text{ lb}_m/\text{sec}^2$, $i = 1, 2, \ldots, 9$.

Method of Solution

Graeffe's method. In the program that follows, Graeffe's method as described by (3.3) and (3.4) is implemented. Data for the program are: n, *itmax*, T, ε, *iprint*, $a_0, \ldots, a_n$. Here, *itmax* is the maximum number of iterative squaring operations permitted. T is the maximum coefficient magnitude allowed, while $1/T$ is the minimum coefficient magnitude allowed (aside from zero); these limits on magnitude insure that all coefficients remain in the floating-point (REAL) number range. ε is a small positive number used in the root test (3.1.9), and *iprint* is a printing control switch.

The program first normalizes the coefficients a_i, $i = 0, 1, \ldots, n$, by dividing each by a_0, that is,

$$a_i \leftarrow a_i/a_0, \qquad i = 1, 2, \ldots, n, \\ a_0 \leftarrow 1, \qquad (3.1.2)$$

where the left arrow is intended to mean assignment or replacement, rather than algebraic equality. Since Graeffe's method yields only the *magnitudes* of possible roots, one way of establishing the proper *sign* for a potential root is to evaluate the original polynomial (or its normalized equivalent) using both the positive and negative arguments. Hence, the values of the a_i should not be destroyed during the root-squaring process.

Let coefficients $_jA_i$ and $_{j+1}A_i$, described in Section 3.2, be rewritten as

$$C_i = {}_jA_i \\ B_i = {}_{j+1}A_i. \qquad (3.1.3)$$

Then, given the initial values for the C_i, where

$$C_i = {}_0A_i = a_i, \qquad (3.1.4)$$

the B_i for one iteration may be evaluated from

$$B_0 = 1 \\ B_i = (-1)^i \left[C_i^2 + 2 \sum_{l=1}^{i} (-1)^l C_{i+l} C_{i-l} \right], \\ i = 1, 2, \ldots, n. \qquad (3.1.5)$$

In (3.1.5), any elements C_k, $k < 0$ or $k > n$, are arbitrarily set to zero. After the computation of the B_i, $i = 1, 2, \ldots, n$, each B_i is tested to insure that its value is well within the floating-point number range. The permitted number range is $[-T, -1/T]$, 0, $[1/T, T]$. The nonzero B_i are subjected to two magnitude tests,

$$\left. \begin{array}{l} |B_i| < T \\ |B_i| > \dfrac{1}{T}, \qquad B_i \neq 0, \end{array} \right\} i = 1, 2, \ldots, n. \qquad (3.1.6)$$

Should all B_i pass both tests, the root-squaring process is continued. The C_i are assigned the newly computed values of the B_i, that is,

$$C_i \leftarrow B_i, \qquad i = 1, 2, \ldots, n. \qquad (3.1.7)$$

Then, the B_i for the next iteration are computed using (3.1.5).

The sequence (3.1.5), (3.1.6), and (3.1.7) is repeated cyclically until at least one B_i fails one of the magnitude tests (3.1.6), at which time the real and distinct roots, α_i, of (3.1.1) should be well separated and such that

$$\bar{\alpha}_i = |\alpha_i| \doteq \left| \frac{B_i}{B_{i-1}} \right|^{1/2^j}, \qquad i = 1, 2, \ldots, n, \qquad (3.1.8)$$

where j is the number of iterations.

The original polynomial (3.1.1) is then evaluated using both $+\bar{\alpha}_i$ and $-\bar{\alpha}_i$ to determine which produces the smallest magnitude, and hence which sign should be assigned to α_i. Of course, the α_i found may not be roots at all ($p_n(x)$ may have multiple or complex roots). A value α_i with proper sign is assumed to be a root if

$$|p_n(\alpha_i)| < \varepsilon, \qquad (3.1.9)$$

that is, if the magnitude of the polynomial evaluated at α_i is smaller than some small number ε.

Mechanical vibration system. Following the method outlined in Problem 4.23, the natural circular frequencies of vibration ω of the above system are given by $\omega^2 = \lambda$, where λ may be any one of the eigenvalues of the following matrix:

$$\frac{1}{m}\begin{bmatrix} k_1 + k_2 & -k_2 & 0 & 0 & \cdot & 0 & 0 \\ -k_2 & k_2 + k_3 & -k_3 & 0 & \cdot & 0 & 0 \\ 0 & -k_3 & k_3 + k_4 & -k_4 & \cdot & 0 & 0 \\ \cdot & \cdot & \cdot & \cdot & \cdot & \cdot & \cdot \\ 0 & 0 & 0 & 0 & \cdot & -k_8 & k_8 + k_9 \end{bmatrix}$$

(3.1.10)

Several methods for obtaining the eigenvalues of matrices are described in Chapter 4. One such method is to solve the *characteristic equation* of the matrix, described on page 220. Using the method of Danilevski, outlined in Section 4.9, the characteristic equations for matrix (3.1.10) for the two situations described in the problem statement are:

Case A. $\lambda^8 - 16\,\lambda^7 + 105\,\lambda^6 - 364\,\lambda^5 + 715\,\lambda^4$
$\qquad\qquad - 792\,\lambda^3 + 462\,\lambda^2 - 120\,\lambda + 9 = 0$ (3.1.11)

Case B. $\lambda^8 - 20\,\lambda^7 + 157.0625\,\lambda^6 - 623.4374\,\lambda^5$
$\qquad\qquad + 1341.4450\,\lambda^4 - 1557.6560\,\lambda^3 + 912.2167\,\lambda^2$
$\qquad\qquad - 227.9003\,\lambda + 15.6643 = 0.$ (3.1.12)

Flow Diagram

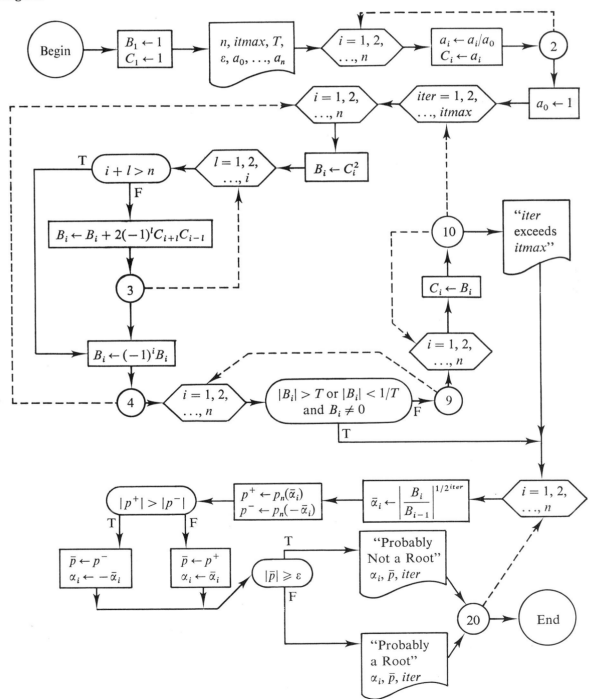

FORTRAN *Implementation*

List of Principal Variables

Program Symbol	Definition
A†	Vector of polynomial coefficients, a_i.
B†	Vector of coefficients, B_i, of the squared polynomial after the current iteration (3.1.3).
C†	Vector of coefficients, C_i, of the squared polynomial prior to the current iteration (3.1.3).
EPS	Small positive number, ε, used in test (3.1.9) to determine if α_i is to be considered a root.
I, IM1, IML, IPL	i, $i-1$, $i-l$, $i+l$, respectively.
IPRINT	Print control variable. If nonzero, coefficients B_i are printed after each iteration.
ITER	Iteration counter, j.
ITMAX	Maximum number of iterations allowed.
J	Subscript (not to be confused with iteration counter).
L	l.
N	n, degree of starting polynomial.
NP1	$n+1$.
PMINUS	p^-, value of $p_n(-\bar{\alpha}_i)$.
PPLUS	p^+, value of $p_n(\bar{\alpha}_i)$.
PVAL	$p_n(\alpha_i)$.
ROOT	α_i, possibly a root of $p_n(x)$.
TOP	T, upper limit on the magnitudes of coefficients B_i, produced by the root-squaring process.

† Because of FORTRAN limitations (subscripts smaller than one are not allowed), all subscripts on the vectors of coefficients a, B, and C that appear in the text and flow diagram are advanced by one when they appear in the program; for example, a_0 becomes A(1), B_n becomes B(N + 1), etc.

Program Listing

```
C           APPLIED NUMERICAL METHODS, EXAMPLE 3.1
C           GRAEFFE'S ROOT-SQUARING METHOD
C
C           THIS PROGRAM USES GRAEFFE'S ROOT SQUARING TECHNIQUE TO FIND
C           THE REAL AND DISTINCT ROOTS OF THE NTH DEGREE POLYNOMIAL WHOSE
C           COEFFICIENTS ARE READ INTO A(1)...A(N+1) IN DECREASING
C           POWERS OF THE VARIABLE WITH THE CONSTANT TERM IN A(N+1).  THE
C           COEFFICIENTS ARE FIRST NORMALIZED BY DIVIDING EACH BY A(1),
C           YIELDING A(1) = 1.  THE ITERATIVE ROOT SQUARING PROCESS USES
C           TWO TEMPORARY VECTORS, C AND B, IN ALTERNATE SUCCESSION AND
C           CONTINUES UNTIL ONE OF THE COEFFICIENTS EXCEEDS TOP IN
C           MAGNITUDE OR UNTIL THE MAXIMUM NUMBER OF ITERATIONS ITMAX
C           IS EXCEEDED.  AT THIS POINT THE MAGNITUDES OF THE POSSIBLE
C           ROOTS ARE COMPUTED (ROOT).  IN ORDER TO DETERMINE THE PROPER
C           SIGN FOR ROOT, THE NORMALIZED POLYNOMIAL IS EVALUATED FOR
C           POSITIVE (PPLUS) AND NEGATIVE (PMINUS) ARGUMENTS.  IF THE
C           MAGNITUDE OF PPLUS OR PMINUS IS SMALLER THAN EPS, IT IS
C           ASSUMED THAT A ROOT HAS BEEN FOUND.  AN APPROPRIATE COMMENT
C           IS PRINTED ALONG WITH THE VALUE OF ROOT (WITH PROPER SIGN)
C           AND THE CORRESPONDING VALUE OF THE POLYNOMIAL, PVAL.
C           IF IPRINT IS NONZERO, COEFFICIENTS OF THE SQUARED POLYNOMIAL
C           ARE PRINTED AFTER EACH ITERATION.
C
      DIMENSION A(100), B(100), C(100)
C
      B(1) = 1.
      C(1) = 1.
    1 READ (5,100) N,ITMAX,TOP,EPS,IPRINT
      NP1 = N + 1
      READ (5,101) (A(I),I=1,NP1)
C
C     ..... NORMALIZE A COEFFICIENTS, INITIALIZE C VECTOR .....
      DO 2   I = 2, NP1
      A(I) = A(I)/A(1)
    2 C(I) = A(I)
      A(1) = 1.
      WRITE (6,200) N,ITMAX,TOP,EPS,IPRINT,NP1,(A(I),I=1,NP1)
C
C     ..... BEGIN GRAEFFE'S ITERATION .....
      DO 10   ITER = 1, ITMAX
C
C     ..... COMPUTE COEFFICIENTS OF F(X)*F(-X) (WITH APPROPRIATE
C           SIGN), IGNORING ALTERNATE ZERO COEFFICIENTS .....
      DO 4   I = 2, NP1
      B(I) = C(I)*C(I)
      IM1 = I - 1
      DO 3   L = 1, IM1
      IPL = I + L
      IML = I - L
      IF ( IPL.GT.NP1 )   GO TO 4
    3 B(I) = B(I) + (-1.)**L*2.*C(IPL)*C(IML)
    4 B(I) = (-1.)**IM1*B(I)
      IF ( IPRINT.EQ.0 ) GO TO 6
      WRITE (6,201) ITER,NP1,(B(I),I=1,NP1)
C
C     ..... HAVE ANY COEFFICIENTS EXCEEDED SIZE LIMITS .....
    6 DO 9   I = 2, NP1
    9 IF ( ABS(B(I)).GT.TOP .OR. ABS(B(I)).LT.1./TOP .AND. B(I).NE.0.0 )
     1    GO TO 11
C
C     ..... SHIFT COEFFICIENTS FROM B TO C FOR NEXT ITERATION .....
      DO 10   I = 2, NP1
   10 C(I) = B(I)
C
      WRITE (6,202)
      ITER = ITMAX
C
C     ..... THE FOLLOWING STATEMENTS COMPUTE THE MAGNITUDES OF THE
C           POSSIBLE ROOTS AND EVALUATE THE ORIGINAL POLYNOMIAL FOR
C           BOTH POSITIVE AND NEGATIVE VALUES OF THESE ROOTS .....
```

Program Listing (*Continued*)

```
C
   11   WRITE (6,203)
        DO 20   I = 2, NP1
C
C       ..... COMPUTE ESTIMATE OF ROOT FROM COEFFICIENTS OF SQUARED
C               POLYNOMIAL .....
        ROOT= ABS(B(I)/B(I-1))**(1./2.**ITER)
C
C       ..... EVALUATE POLYNOMIAL AT ROOT AND -ROOT .....
        PPLUS = 1.
        PMINUS = 1.
        DO 14   J = 2, NP1
        PPLUS = PPLUS*ROOT + A(J)
   14   PMINUS = PMINUS*(-ROOT) + A(J)
C
C       ..... CHOOSE LIKELY ROOT AND MINIMUM POLYNOMIAL VALUE .....
        IF( ABS(PPLUS).GT.ABS(PMINUS) )   GO TO 16
            PVAL = PPLUS
            GO TO 17
   16       PVAL = PMINUS
            ROOT = -ROOT
C
C       ..... IS PVAL SMALLER THAN EPS .....
   17   IF( ABS(PVAL).GE.EPS )   GO TO 19
            WRITE (6,204)   ROOT, PVAL, ITER
            GO TO 20
   19       WRITE (6,205)   ROOT, PVAL, ITER
   20   CONTINUE
        GO TO 1
C
C       ..... FORMATS FOR INPUT AND OUTPUT STATEMENTS .....
  100   FORMAT (10X,I2,18X,I2,18X,E6.1/ 10X,E6.1,14X,I1 )
  101   FORMAT (20X, 5F10.4 )
  200   FORMAT (10H1N       = , I8 / 10H ITMAX  = , I8 / 10H TOP    = ,
     1   1PE14.1/10H EPS      = , 1PE14.1/10H IPRINT = , I8/
     2   20H0          A(1)...A( , I2, 1H), // (1H , 0P5F13.6) )
  201   FORMAT (10H0ITER   = , I8 /20H0             B(1)...B(, I2, 1H)/ 1H /
     1   (1H , 1P5E15.6) )
  202   FORMAT (43H0ITER EXCEEDS ITMAX - CALCULATION CONTINUES )
  203   FORMAT (1H0/ 55H       ROOT      POLYNOMIAL VALUE    ITER             CO
     1MMENT / 1H  )
  204   FORMAT (1H , F10.6, 1PE17.6, I8, 7X, 15HPROBABLY A ROOT )
  205   FORMAT (1H , F10.6, 1PE17.6, I8, 7X, 19HPROBABLY NOT A ROOT )
C
        END
```

Data

```
N       =    2          ITMAX  =   25          TOP    =  1.0E30
EPS     =  1.0E-1        IPRINT =   1
A(1)...A(3) =              1.0000    -3.0000     2.0000
N       =    2          ITMAX  =    3          TOP    =  1.0E30
EPS     =  1.0E-1        IPRINT =   0
A(1)...A(3) =              1.0000    -3.0000     2.0000
N       =    3          ITMAX  =   25          TOP    =  1.0E30
EPS     =  1.0E-1        IPRINT =   0
A(1)...A(4) =              2.0000   -12.0000    22.0000   -12.0000
N       =    4          ITMAX  =   25          TOP    =  1.0E30
EPS     =  1.0E-1        IPRINT =   0
A(1)...A(5) =              1.0000   -10.0000    35.0000   -50.0000    24.0000
N       =    3          ITMAX  =   25          TOP    =  1.0E30
EPS     =  1.0E-1        IPRINT =   0
A(1)...A(4) =              0.5000     4.0000    10.5000     9.0000
N       =    3          ITMAX  =   25          TOP    =  1.0E30
EPS     =  1.0E-1        IPRINT =   0
A(1)...A(4) =              1.0000   -19.0000    55.0000    75.0000
N       =    3          ITMAX  =   25          TOP    =  1.0E30
EPS     =  1.0E-1        IPRINT =   1
A(1)...A(4) =              0.2500    -1.2500     2.0000    -1.0000
```

Program Listing (*Continued*)

```
N       =    4          ITMAX  =   25        TOP    =   1.0E30
EPS     =  1.0E-1       IPRINT =   0
A(1)...A(5) =               1.0000  -35.0000  146.0000 -100.0000    1.0000
N       =    4          ITMAX  =   25        TOP    =   1.0E30
EPS     =  1.0E-1       IPRINT =   0
A(1)...A(5) =               1.0000  -16.0000   78.0000 -412.0000  624.0000
N       =    3          ITMAX  =   25        TOP    =   1.0E30
EPS     =  1.0E-1       IPRINT =   0
A(1)...A(4) =               1.0000    0.0000   -3.0000    1.0000
N       =    4          ITMAX  =   25        TOP    =   1.0E30
EPS     =  1.0E-1       IPRINT =   0
A(1)...A(5) =               1.0000  -24.0000  150.0000 -200.0000 -375.0000
N       =    4          ITMAX  =   25        TOP    =   1.0E30
EPS     =  1.0E-1       IPRINT =   0
A(1)...A(5) =               1.0000   -1.0000    0.7500    0.2500   -0.2500
N       =    4          ITMAX  =   25        TOP    =   1.0E30
EPS     =  1.0E-1       IPRINT =   0
A(1)...A(5) =               1.0000   -2.0000    1.2500   -0.2500   -0.7500
N       =    8          ITMAX  =   25        TOP    =   1.0E30
EPS     =  1.0E-1       IPRINT =   0
A(1)...A(5) =               1.0000  -16.0000  105.0000 -364.0000  715.0000
A(6)...A(9) =            -792.0000  462.0000 -120.0000    9.0000
N       =    8          ITMAX  =   25        TOP    =   1.0E30
EPS     =  1.0E-1       IPRINT =   0
A(1)...A(5) =               1.0000  -20.0000  157.0625 -623.4374 1341.4450
A(6)...A(9) =           -1557.6560  912.2167 -227.9003   15.6643
```

Computer Output

Results for the 1st Data Set

```
N        =          2
ITMAX    =         25
TOP      =       1.0E 30
EPS      =       1.0E-01
IPRINT   =          1


          A(1)...A( 3)
     1.000000    -3.000000     2.000000

ITER   =          1

          B(1)...B( 3)

   1.000000E 00  -5.000000E 00   4.000000E 00

ITER   =          2

          B(1)...B( 3)

   1.000000E 00  -1.700000E 01   1.600000E 01

ITER   =          3

          B(1)...B( 3)

   1.000000E 00  -2.570000E 02   2.560000E 02

ITER   =          4

          B(1)...B( 3)

   1.000000E 00  -6.553700E 04   6.553600E 04
```

Computer Output (*Continued*)

```
ITER    =           5

            B(1)...B( 3)

   1.000000E 00  -4.294967E 09   4.294967E 09
ITER    =           6

            B(1)...B( 3)

   1.000000E 00  -1.844674E 19   1.844674E 19
ITER    =           7

            B(1)...B( 3)

   1.000000E 00  -3.402824E 38   3.402824E 38


     ROOT        POLYNOMIAL VALUE    ITER        COMMENT

   2.000000       0.0                 7         PROBABLY A ROOT
   1.000000       0.0                 7         PROBABLY A ROOT
```

Results for the 2nd Data Set

```
N       =           2
ITMAX   =           3
TOP     =           1.0E 30
EPS     =           1.0E-01
IPRINT  =           0

            A(1)...A( 3)
     1.000000    -3.000000     2.000000

ITER EXCEEDS ITMAX - CALCULATION CONTINUES


     ROOT        POLYNOMIAL VALUE    ITER        COMMENT

   2.000975       9.756088E-04        3         PROBABLY A ROOT
   0.999513       4.882812E-04        3         PROBABLY A ROOT
```

Results for the 7th Data Set

```
N       =           3
ITMAX   =           25
TOP     =           1.0E 30
EPS     =           1.0E-01
IPRINT  =           1

            A(1)...A( 4)
     1.000000    -5.000000     8.000000     -4.000000
ITER    =           1

            B(1)...B( 4)

   1.000000E 00  -9.000000E 00   2.400000E 01  -1.600000E 01
ITER    =           2

            B(1)...B( 4)

   1.000000E 00  -3.300000E 01   2.880000E 02  -2.560000E 02
```

Computer Output (*Continued*)

```
ITER    =         3

            B(1)...B( 4)

   1.000000E 00  -5.130000E 02   6.604800E 04  -6.553600E 04

ITER    =         4

            B(1)...B( 4)

   1.000000E 00  -1.310730E 05   4.295098E 09  -4.294967E 09

ITER    =         5

            B(1)...B( 4)

   1.000000E 00  -8.589935E 09   1.844674E 19  -1.844674E 19

ITER    =         6

            B(1)...B( 4)

   1.000000E 00  -3.689349E 19   3.402824E 38  -3.402824E 38


     ROOT        POLYNOMIAL VALUE     ITER          COMMENT

   2.021778      4.854202E-04          6        PROBABLY A ROOT
   1.978456      4.539490E-04          6        PROBABLY A ROOT
   1.000000      0.0                   6        PROBABLY A ROOT
```

Results for the 9th Data Set

```
N      =         4
ITMAX  =        25
TOP    =         1.0E 30
EPS    =         1.0E-01
IPRINT =         0

            A(1)...A( 5)
    1.000000    -16.000000    78.000000   -412.000000    624.000000


     ROOT        POLYNOMIAL VALUE     ITER          COMMENT

  11.999994     -8.300781E-03          4        PROBABLY A ROOT
   5.324727     -9.699263E 02          4        PROBABLY NOT A ROOT
   4.882880     -8.222861E 02          4        PROBABLY NOT A ROOT
   2.000000      0.0                   4        PROBABLY A ROOT
```

Computer Output (*Continued*)

Results for the 14th Data Set

```
N       =        8
ITMAX   =        25
TOP     =        1.0E 30
EPS     =        1.0E-01
IPRINT  =        0

            A(1)...A( 9)
    1.000000     -16.000000    105.000000   -364.000000    715.000000
 -792.000000     462.000000   -120.000000      9.000000
```

Results for the 15th Data Set

ROOT	POLYNOMIAL VALUE	ITER	COMMENT
3.931828	2.785426E 00	4	PROBABLY NOT A ROOT
3.504101	3.037500E-01	4	PROBABLY NOT A ROOT
2.987610	-5.760479E-02	4	PROBABLY A ROOT
2.344709	1.475048E-02	4	PROBABLY A ROOT
1.652354	-3.833771E-04	4	PROBABLY A ROOT
0.999980	1.506805E-04	4	PROBABLY A ROOT
0.467911	-9.536743E-06	4	PROBABLY A ROOT
0.120615	-4.768372E-06	4	PROBABLY A ROOT

```
N       =        8
ITMAX   =        25
TOP     =        1.0E 30
EPS     =        1.0E-01
IPRINT  =        0

            A(1)...A( 9)
    1.000000     -20.000000    157.062500   -623.437256   1341.444824
 -1557.655762    912.216553   -227.900299     15.664300
```

ROOT	POLYNOMIAL VALUE	ITER	COMMENT
6.595325	5.434601E 01	4	PROBABLY NOT A ROOT
4.708691	-4.292822E-01	4	PROBABLY NOT A ROOT
3.365894	-7.332039E-02	4	PROBABLY A ROOT
2.342498	1.753998E-02	4	PROBABLY A ROOT
1.544105	-1.212120E-03	4	PROBABLY A ROOT
0.912852	1.974106E-04	4	PROBABLY A ROOT
0.425053	-9.536743E-07	4	PROBABLY A ROOT
0.106776	-3.814697E-06	4	PROBABLY A ROOT

Discussion of Results

Single-precision arithmetic was used for all calculations. Results are shown for data sets 1, 2, 7, 9, 14, and 15. In most cases, the printing of intermediate coefficients was not requested. Final results for each data set are listed below, along with the polynomial $p_n(x)$ and the known roots.

Data Set 1 (results shown)	Calculated Roots	True Roots
$p_n(x) = x^2 - 3x + 2$	2.000000	2.000000
Number of iterations,	1.000000	1.000000
ITER = 7		

Data Set 2 (results shown)	Calculated Roots	True Roots
$p_n(x) = x^2 - 3x + 2$	2.000975	2.000000
ITER = 3	0.999513	1.000000

In this case, the maximum number of iterations permitted was 3. Hence the roots of the squared polynomial have not been separated far enough to attain the accuracy shown for the same polynomial in data set 1.

Data Set 3	Calculated Roots	True Roots
$p_n(x) = 2x^3 - 12x^2 + 22x - 12$	2.999999	3.000000
ITER = 6	2.000000	2.000000
	1.000000	1.000000

Data Set 4	Calculated Roots	True Roots
$p_n(x) = x^4 - 10x^3 + 35x^2$	4.000011	4.000000
$- 50x + 24$	2.999990	3.000000
ITER = 5	1.999999	2.000000
	1.000000	1.000000

Data Set 5	Calculated Roots	True Roots
$p_n(x) = 0.5x^3 + 4x^2 + 10.5x$	-3.065690	-3.000000
$+ 9$	-2.935715	-3.000000
ITER = 5	-1.999999	-2.000000

In this case the dominant root has multiplicity 2. The program indicated that -3.065690 and -2.935715 were probably roots, since the polynomial values were -0.00593 and -0.00386, respectively, smaller than the data value read for ε (0.1). Typically, Graeffe's method estimates of multiple real roots will span the true value, that is, $(-3.066 - 2.936)/2 \doteq -3.0$.

Data Set 6	Calculated Roots	True Roots
$p_n(x) = x^3 - 19x^2 + 55x + 75$	14.999993	15.000000
ITER = 4	4.999995	5.000000
	-1.000000	-1.000000

Here the roots are well separated, and good accuracy is attained in just four iterations.

Data Set 7 (results shown)	Calculated Roots	True Roots
$p_n(x) = 0.25x^3 - 1.25x^2$	2.021778	2.000000
$+ 2x - 1$	1.978456	2.000000
ITER = 6	1.000000	1.000000

Again, as in data set 5, there are multiple real roots. If a multiple root were known to exist, then (3.8) could be applied to find better root values from the solution of the quadratic equation

$$x^2 - 3.689349 \times 10^{19}x + 3.402824 \times 10^{38} = 0.$$

The predicted roots are:

$$\alpha_1^{2^6} = \alpha_1^{64} \doteq 1.8446745 \times 10^{19}$$

$$\alpha_2^{64} \doteq 1.8446745 \times 10^{19}$$

which to seven significant figures yields $\alpha_1 \doteq \alpha_2 \doteq$ 2.000000.

Data Set 8	Calculated Roots
$p_n(x) = x^4 - 35x^3 + 146x^2 - 100x + 1$	30.288681
ITER = 4	3.858056
	.843107
	.010150

This polynomial is the characteristic function found by the method of Danilevski (see Chapter 4) for the symmetric matrix

$$\begin{bmatrix} 10 & 9 & 7 & 5 \\ 9 & 10 & 8 & 6 \\ 7 & 8 & 10 & 7 \\ 5 & 6 & 7 & 5 \end{bmatrix}.$$

Calculation of the roots of $p_n(x)$ (the eigenvalues of the matrix) using the Power, Rutishauser, and Jacobi methods (see Examples 4.2, 4.3, and 4.4, respectively) yielded the following results:

Power Method	Rutishauser Method	Jacobi Method
30.288685	30.288685	30.288685
3.858057	3.858057	3.858057
0.843107	0.843107	0.843107
0.010150	0.010150	0.010150

Data Set 9 (results shown)	Calculated Roots	True Roots
$p_n(x) = x^4 - 16x^3 + 78x^2$	11.999994	12.000000
$- 412x + 624$	5.324727 (NR)	1.0 + 5i
ITER = 4	4.882880 (NR)	1.0 - 5i
	2.000000	2.000000

The program indicated correctly that 5.32 and 4.88 were probably not roots (NR). The two real roots were found, but not the pair of complex conjugate roots. The starting polynomial in this case is the characteristic function of the matrix

$$\begin{bmatrix} 4 & -5 & 0 & 3 \\ 0 & 4 & -3 & -5 \\ 5 & -3 & 4 & 0 \\ 3 & 0 & 5 & 4 \end{bmatrix}.$$

Data Set 10	Calculated Roots	True Roots
$p_n(x) = x^3 - 3x + 1$	−1.879385	−1.879385
ITER = 7	1.532089	1.532089
	0.347296	0.347296

The computed roots agree exactly with the roots calculated for $p_n(x)$ by the method of successive substitutions (see Table 3.5).

Data Set 11	Calculated Roots	True Roots
$p_n(x) = x^4 - 24x^3$	14.999993	15.000000
$+ 150x^2 - 200x$	5.221369 (NR)	5.000000
$- 375$	4.788013 (NR)	5.000000
ITER = 4	−1.000000	−1.000000

This is the characteristic function of the matrix

$$\begin{bmatrix} 6 & 4 & 4 & 1 \\ 4 & 6 & 1 & 4 \\ 4 & 1 & 6 & 4 \\ 1 & 4 & 4 & 6 \end{bmatrix}.$$

Data Set 12	Calculated Roots	True Roots
$p_n(x) = x^4 - x^3 + 0.75x^2$	1.000000 (NR)	$0.5 + \dfrac{\sqrt{3}}{2}i$
$+ 0.25x - 0.25$		
ITER = 6	1.000000 (NR)	$0.5 - \dfrac{\sqrt{3}}{2}i$
	0.505445	0.500000
	−0.494614	−0.500000

In this case there are two pairs of roots, one complex conjugate, the other real. As before, the routine fails to find accurately any root from a root pair.

Data Set 13	Calculated Roots	True Roots
$p_n(x) = x^4 - 2x^3 + 1.25x^2$	1.500000	1.500000
$- 0.25x - 0.75$	1.000000 (NR)	
ITER = 8		$0.5 + \dfrac{\sqrt{3}}{2}i$
	1.000000 (NR)	
		$0.5 - \dfrac{\sqrt{3}}{2}i$
	−0.500000	−0.500000

This polynomial is used in the numerical example of Section 3.2. The two real and distinct roots were found. The pair of complex conjugate roots was not found, as before. Equation 3.8 could be used to find them, however.

Data Set 14 (results shown)	Calculated Roots
$p_n(x) = x^8 - 16x^7 + 105x^6 - 364x^5$	3.931828 (NR)
$+ 715x^4 - 792x^3 + 462x^2$	3.504101 (NR)
$- 120x + 9$	2.987610
ITER = 4	2.344709
	1.652354
	0.999980
	0.467911
	0.120615

This polynomial is the characteristic function for the eighth-order striped symmetric matrix (3.1.10) for Case A. It is also used as an example data set for calculation of the roots (eigenvalues) by the Power, Rutishauser, and Jacobi methods (see Examples 4.2, 4.3, 4.4).

Power Method	Rutishauser Method	Jacobi Method
3.879385	3.879385	3.879385
3.532089	3.532089	3.532089
3.000000	3.000000	3.000000
2.347296	2.347296	2.347296
1.652704	1.652704	1.652704
1.000000	1.000000	1.000000
0.467911	0.467911	0.467911
	0.120615	0.120615

The vibrational frequencies predicted by Graeffe's method for the mechanical system of Fig. 3.1.1 with the parameter values for Case A are:

$$1.982884 \text{ sec}^{-1}$$
$$1.871924$$
$$1.728470$$
$$1.531244$$
$$1.285439$$
$$0.999990$$
$$0.684040$$
$$0.347297.$$

The two or three highest frequencies computed using Graeffe's method may not be of adequate accuracy. However, the method has produced good approximations to these roots. These may be used as first estimates in one of the iterative root-finding procedures to be discussed later in this chapter.

Data Set 15 (results shown)	Calculated Roots	True Roots
$p_n(x) = x^8 - 20x^7$	6.595325 (NR)	6.593518
$+ 157.0625x^6$	4.708691 (NR)	4.708399
$- 623.4374x^5$	3.365894	3.366539
$+ 1341.4450x^4$	2.342498	2.342620
$- 1557.6560x^3$	1.544105	1.544235
$+ 912.2167x^2$	0.912852	0.912859
$- 227.9003x$	0.425053	0.425054
$+ 15.6643$	0.106776	0.106776

ITER = 4

This is the characteristic function for matrix (3.1.10) for Case B. Again, the largest root estimates may not be of adequate accuracy, but can serve as very good starting values for some other root-finding method. Based on the Graeffe's method results, the natural frequencies for the mechanical system of Fig. 3.1.1 with the parameter values of Case B are:

$$2.568136 \ \text{sec}^{-1}$$
$$2.169951$$
$$1.834637$$
$$1.530522$$
$$1.242620$$
$$0.955433$$
$$0.651961$$
$$0.326766.$$

3.4 Iterative Factorization of Polynomials

The techniques discussed thus far are usually useful in finding approximate values of one or more roots of $f(x)$. Should a root be located which is not multiple-valued, a procedure such as Newton's method (p.171) can be employed to determine the root more accurately. In such event, a polynomial of reduced degree can be formed for further investigation by ordinary synthetic division (p.7). Proceeding in this manner, if no multiple roots are present, the solution can be completed. However, this procedure can be expected to make approximations to successive roots more and more inaccurate, and the presence of multiple roots causes difficulty. In this section (see also Luther [6]), a method is presented for improving the accuracy for single roots, and for maintaining a balance of accuracy among the various roots as solution progresses.

Bairstow's method [4] is an algorithm for finding quadratic factors iteratively for the polynomial of (3.2). The iterative technique which follows produces factors of arbitrary degree m for this same polynomial. Programming in terms of m as a parameter is simple: when m is unity, the method is Newton's method; for m equal to two, the method is closely related to Bairstow's method, but is somewhat simpler.

Consider first the problem, useful in its own right, of dividing

$$f(x) = \sum_{i=0}^{n} a_i x^{n-i}, \qquad a_0 = 1,$$

by

$$g(x) = \sum_{i=0}^{m} p_i x^{m-i}, \qquad p_0 = 1, \qquad (3.14)$$

it being understood that $m < n$. For $0 \leqslant k \leqslant n$, define numbers b_j by

$$\sum_{i=0}^{m} p_i b_{k-i} = a_k, \qquad b_j = 0 \text{ for } j < 0. \qquad (3.15)$$

Let

$$h(x) = \sum_{i=0}^{n-m} b_i x^{n-m-i};$$

$$\qquad (3.16)$$

$$r_j = \sum_{i=0}^{m-j-1} p_i b_{n-j-i}, \qquad 0 \leqslant j \leqslant m-1.$$

Then it is a straightforward matter to verify that

$$f(x) = g(x)h(x) + \sum_{i=0}^{m-1} r_i x^i. \qquad (3.17)$$

Now apply the Newton-Raphson recursion relations (p. 319) to the quantities $b_{n-m+1}, b_{n-m+2}, \ldots, b_n$ considered as functions of $p_1, p_2, \ldots, p_m$. The results are as follows.

Let $f(x)$ have the factor

$$\sum_{i=0}^{m} \rho_i x^{m-i}, \qquad \rho_0 = 1,$$

and let the Jacobian involved in the Newton-Raphson technique be different from zero at the point $\rho - (\rho_1, \rho_2, \ldots, \rho_m)$. Let $P^{(j)} = (p_1^{(j)}, p_2^{(j)}, \ldots, p_m^{(j)})$ and let the point $P^{(1)}$ be "near enough" to ρ. Then the sequence of points $\{P^{(j)}\}$, defined below, converges to ρ, and

$$f(x) = \sum_{i=0}^{m} \rho_i x^{m-i} \sum_{i=0}^{n-m} \beta_i x^{n-m-i}.$$

$\beta_0 = 1$ and $\beta = (\beta_1, \beta_2, \ldots, \beta_m)$ is given by

$$\beta = \lim_{j \to \infty} (b_1^{(j)}, b_2^{(j)}, \ldots, b_{n-m}^{(j)}).$$

Here the numbers $b_k^{(j)}$ are related to the numbers $p_i^{(j)}$ [see (3.15)] by

$$\sum_{i=0}^{m} p_i^{(j)} b_{k-i}^{(j)} = a_k, \qquad b_s^{(j)} = 0 \text{ for } s < 0. \qquad (3.18)$$

To find the numbers $p_i^{(j+1)}$ from the numbers $p_i^{(j)}$, $(1 \leqslant i \leqslant m)$, first solve, for the numbers $c_s^{(j)}$, the equations $(0 \leqslant k \leqslant n)$:

$$\sum_{i=0}^{m} p_i^{(j)} c_{k-i}^{(j)} = -b_k^{(j)}, \qquad c_s^{(j)} = 0 \text{ for } s < 0. \qquad (3.19)$$

Then, having thus determined the $c_s^{(j)}$ ($0 \leqslant s \leqslant n$), solve, for the $p_i^{(j+1)}$, the simultaneous linear equations:

$$\sum_{i=1}^{m} p_i^{(j+1)} c_{k-i}^{(j)} = -2b_k^{(j)} - c_k^{(j)}, \qquad n-m+1 \leqslant k \leqslant n.$$

$$\qquad (3.20)$$

This method of finding factors, and eventually zeros, can be employed in its own right, and seems especially successful when the degree m of the factor is about half of n. However, in contrast to the Bernoulli method, convergence cannot be guaranteed for any systematic choice of $P^{(1)}$ not based on a knowledge of a zero ρ. Convergence is almost assured when used in conjunction with

Table 3.3 *Iterative Factorization—Starting Factor*
$x^2 - 1.0010x + 0.9961$

	$k=1$	$k=2$	$k=3$
p_1	-1.00100	-0.99997	-1.00000
p_2	0.99610	1.00000	1.00000
b_1	0.00100	-0.00003	0.00000
b_2	-0.24510	-0.25002	-0.25000
b_3	0.00366	0.00001	0.00000
b_4	-0.00219	0.00003	0.00000
c_1	-1.00200	-0.99995	-1.00000
c_2	0.23820	0.25010	0.25000
c_3	1.23287	1.25003	1.25000
c_4	0.99903	0.99986	1.00000
p_1'	-0.99997	-1.00000	-1.00000
p_2'	1.00000	1.00000	1.00000
$b_1' =$			0.00000
$b_2' =$			-0.25000

some method of finding approximately the coefficients of a factor. Thus, let Bernoulli's method be used to approximate the zero α_1 of $f(x)$. Then, with allowance for possible multiple roots, a factor $(x - \alpha_1)^k$ can be removed from $f(x)$. This process also delivers the equation of reduced degree, which can then be studied. Successive factors can be combined so as to maintain a better accuracy balance for successive zeros.

Example. Consider the polynomial of the previous section, namely,

$$f(x) = x^4 - x^3 + 0.75x^2 + 0.25x - 0.25,$$

and use as an approximate factor the result of the tenth step of the Bernoulli process, or $x^2 - 1.0010x + 0.9961$. Using primed letters for the $(k + 1)$th step and unprimed letters for the kth step, the appropriate formulas are:

$$
\begin{aligned}
b_1 &= -1 - p_1, & c_1 &= -b_1 + p_1, \\
b_2 &= 0.75 - b_1 p_1 - p_2, & c_2 &= -b_2 - c_1 p_1 + p_2, \\
b_3 &= 0.25 - b_1 p_2 - b_2 p_1, & c_3 &= -b_3 - c_1 p_2 - c_2 p_1, \\
b_4 &= -0.25 - b_2 p_2 - b_3 p_1, & c_4 &= -b_4 - c_2 p_2 - c_3 p_1, \\
\end{aligned}
$$
$$c_2 p_1' + c_1 p_2' = -2b_3 - c_3,$$
$$c_3 p_1' + c_2 p_2' = -2b_4 - c_4.$$

Table 3.3 illustrates the resulting sequences. Thus, in terms of quadratic factors, the polynomial is

$$f(x) = (x^2 - x + 1)(x^2 - 0.25).$$

For the same polynomial, the sequence using a starting factor $(x^2 + 0x + 0)$ is shown in Table 3.4. Thus, the same quadratic factors,

$$f(x) = (x^2 - 0.25)(x^2 - x + 1),$$

have been found, but this time in reverse order.

Table 3.4   Iterative Factorization—Starting Factor x^2

	$k = 1$	$k = 2$	$k = 3$	$k = 4$	$k = 5$
p_1	0.00000	−0.07692	−0.00613	−0.00321	−0.00000
p_2	0.00000	−0.30769	−0.25434	−0.25002	−0.25000
b_1	−1.00000	−0.92308	−0.99387	−0.99997	−1.00000
b_2	0.75000	0.98669	0.99824	0.99999	1.00000
b_3	0.25000	0.04188	0.00334	0.00002	0.00000
b_4	−0.25000	0.05682	0.00391	0.00002	0.00000
c_1	1.00000	0.84615	0.98774	0.99994	1.00000
c_2	−0.75000	−1.22929	−1.24652	−1.24998	−1.25000
c_3	−0.25000	0.12392	0.24023	0.24995	0.25000
c_4	−0.25000	−0.42553	−0.31947	−0.31254	−0.31250
p_1'	−0.07692	−0.00613	−0.00321	−0.00000	−0.00000
p_2'	−0.30769	−0.25434	−0.25002	−0.25000	−0.25000
					$b_1' = -1.00000$
					$b_2' = 1.00000$

EXAMPLE 3.2

ITERATIVE FACTORIZATION OF POLYNOMIALS

Problem Statement

Write a program that employs the method of iterative factorization outlined in Section 3.4 to find an mth-degree factor,

$$g(x) = \sum_{i=0}^{m} p_i x^{m-i}, \qquad (3.2.1)$$

of the nth-degree polynomial

$$\phi_n(x) = \sum_{i=0}^{n} a_i x^{n-i}. \qquad (3.2.2)$$

Method of Solution

The program that follows reads data values for n, m, $itmax$, ε_1, ε, a_0, ..., a_n, p_1, ..., p_m, where p_1, ..., p_m are the initial estimates of the coefficients of the mth-degree factor $g(x)$; $itmax$ is the maximum number of factorization cycles permitted, ε is the maximum allowable pivot size in the solution of the simultaneous equations (3.20) by Gauss-Jordan reduction (see Example 5.2), and ε_1 is described below.

The program first normalizes the coefficients a_0, ..., a_n by dividing each by the initial a_0, that is,

$$\begin{aligned} a_i &\leftarrow a_i/a_0, \qquad i = 1, 2, \ldots, n, \\ a_0 &\leftarrow 1, \end{aligned} \qquad (3.2.3)$$

---

and assigns the value one to coefficient p_0. Dropping the iteration counter as a superscript, and solving (3.18) and (3.19) for the b_i and c_i, $i = 0, 1, \ldots, n$, leads to:

$$\begin{aligned} X_{i,j} &\leftarrow c_{n-m-j+i}, \qquad n - m - j + i \geq 0, \\ X_{i,j} &\leftarrow 0, \qquad n - m - j + i < 0, \end{aligned} \left.\begin{aligned} \\ \end{aligned}\right\} j = 1, 2, \ldots, m, \left.\begin{aligned} \\ \\ \end{aligned}\right\} i = 1, 2, \ldots, m.$$

$$X_{i,m+1} \leftarrow -(2b_{n-m+i} + c_{n-m+i}), \qquad (3.2.8)$$

$$\left.\begin{aligned} b_0 &= a_0 = 1 \\ b_i &= a_i - \sum_{j=1}^{i} p_j b_{i-j}, \qquad i < m, \\ b_i &= a_i - \sum_{j=1}^{m} p_j b_{i-j}, \qquad i \geq m, \end{aligned}\right\} \qquad (3.2.4)$$

$$\left.\begin{aligned} c_0 &= -b_0 = -1 \\ c_i &= -b_i - \sum_{j=1}^{i} p_j c_{i-j}, \qquad i < m, \\ c_i &= -b_i - \sum_{j=1}^{m} p_j c_{i-j}, \qquad i \geq m. \end{aligned}\right\} \qquad (3.2.5)$$

Note that in (3.2.4) and (3.2.5), j is simply a summation index, and is not the iteration counter of (3.18) and (3.19). One measure of convergence is the magnitude of the coefficients b_{n-m+1}, b_{n-m+2}, ..., b_n, which will vanish when a perfect factor $g(x)$ has been found. After each iteration, the convergence test,

$$\sum_{i=n-m+1}^{n} |b_i| \leq \varepsilon_1, \qquad (3.2.6)$$

is made; if the test is passed, computation is discontinued and the p_i, $i = 0, 1, \ldots, m$ are taken to be the coefficients of $g(x)$.

If convergence test (3.2.6) is failed, then the m simultaneous linear equations of (3.20) are solved for the new p_i, $i = 1, 2, \ldots, m$, here denoted p_i':

$$\begin{aligned} c_{n-m}\, p_1' + c_{n-m-1}p_2' + \cdots + c_{n-2m+1}p_m' &= -(2b_{n-m+1} + c_{n-m+1}) \\ c_{n-m+1}p_1' + c_{n-m}p_2' + \cdots + c_{n-2m+2}p_m' &= -(2b_{n-m+2} + c_{n-m+2}) \\ \cdots \qquad\qquad \cdots \qquad\qquad \cdots \\ \cdots \qquad\qquad \cdots \qquad\qquad \cdots \\ c_{n-1}\, p_1' + \quad c_{n-2}p_2' + \cdots + \quad c_{n-m}p_m' &= -(2b_n - c_n). \end{aligned} \qquad (3.2.7)$$

Any c_k for which $k < 0$ should be assigned the value zero. The coefficients of the linear equations, with the right-hand side vector appended as an additional column, are stored in the $m \times m + 1$ matrix X, such that:

The function SIMUL is called to solve the equations for the p_i', which are then overstored in the p vector,

$$p_i \leftarrow p_i', \qquad i = 1, 2, \ldots, m. \qquad (3.2.9)$$

The iterative factorization process is continued until the convergence test is passed, or until the maximum number of factorization cycles has been completed.

Example 3.2   Iterative Factorization of Polynomials   **159**

Flow Diagram

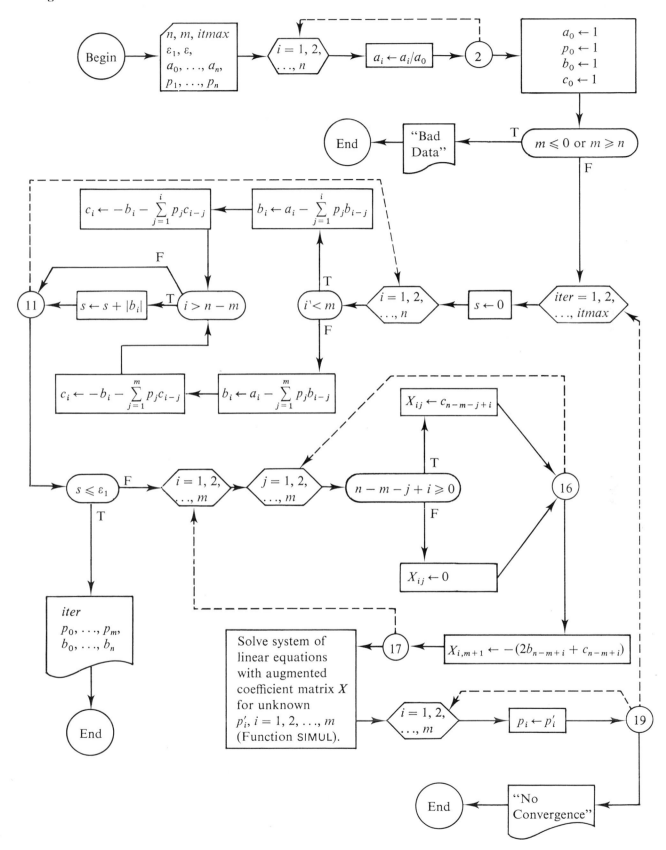

FORTRAN *Implementation*

List of Principal Variables

Program Symbol	Definition
A†	Vector of coefficients, a_i, of the starting polynomial, $\phi_n(x)$.
B, C†	Vector of coefficients, b_i (see (3.2.4)) and c_i (see (3.2.5)), respectively.
CHEK	ε_1, small positive number used in the termination test (3.2.6).
EPS	Minimum pivot magnitude allowed during Gauss-Jordan solution of linear equations (see SIMUL).
I, IMJ, J, K	i, $i - j$, j, and k, respectively.
ITER	Iteration counter for the factorization algorithm, *iter*.
ITMAX	Maximum number of iterative cycles permitted, *itmax*.
M	m, degree of the desired factor, $g(x)$ (see (3.2.1)).
MP1, MP1MI	$m + 1$ and $m + 1 - i$, respectively.
N	n, degree of starting polynomial, $\phi_n(x)$.
NMI1, NMJI, NP1	$n - m + i + 1$, $n - m - j + i$, and $n + 1$, respectively.
P†	Vector of coefficients, p_i, of the polynomial factor, $g(x)$ (see (3.2.1)).
SIMUL	SIMUL implements the Gauss-Jordan reduction scheme with the maximum pivot strategy to solve systems of linear equations (see Example 5.2). For argument list (m, X, p, ε), SIMUL calculates the solutions $p_1, p_2 \ldots, p_m$, for the m simultaneous linear equations whose augmented coefficient matrix is in the $m \times (m + 1)$ matrix X. ε is the minimum pivot magnitude which will be used by function SIMUL.
SUM	The repeated sum in convergence test (3.2.6).
X	X, the $m \times (m + 1)$ augmented coefficient matrix for the linear equations of (3.2.7) (see (3.2.8)).

† Because of FORTRAN limitations (subscripts smaller than one are not allowed), all subscripts on the vectors of coefficients a, b, c, and p that appear in the text and flow diagram are advanced by one when they appear in the program; for example, a_0 becomes A(1), p_m becomes P(M + 1), etc. Limitations on the form of subscript expressions and the absence of a zero subscript in most FORTRAN implementations, result in the introduction of a number of variables that do not appear in the flow diagram.

Example 3.2   Iterative Factorization of Polynomials   **161**

Program Listing

```
C           APPLIED NUMERICAL METHODS, EXAMPLE 3.2
C           ITERATIVE FACTORIZATION OF POLYNOMIALS
C
C           THIS PROGRAM USES AN ITERATIVE PROCEDURE TO FACTOR A POLYNOMIAL
C           OF DEGREE M WITH COEFFICIENTS P(1)...P(M+1) FROM A POLYNOMIAL
C           OF DEGREE N WITH COEFFICIENTS A(1)...A(N+1).  SUBSCRIPTS
C           INCREASE WITH DECREASING POWERS OF THE VARIABLE.  COEFFICIENTS
C           OF THE N TH  DEGREE POLYNOMIAL ARE FIRST NORMALIZED BY
C           DIVIDING EACH BY A(1).    INITIAL ESTIMATES FOR THE COEFFICIENTS
C           P(2)...P(M+1) ARE READ AS DATA.  THE COEFFICIENTS OF THE
C           RESIDUAL POLYNOMIAL ARE SAVED IN B(1)...B(N+1).   THE PROCEDURE
C           INVOLVES ITERATION TO IMPROVE CURRENT VALUES OF THE COEFFI-
C           CIENTS P(2)...P(M+1) IN SUCH A WAY THAT THE COEFFICIENTS OF THE
C           RESIDUAL POLYNOMIAL B(N-M+2)...B(N+1) VANISH.  THE COEFFICIENTS
C           C(1)...C(N+1) (SEE TEXT) ARE SAVED IN THE C VECTOR. CONVERGENCE
C           IS ESTABLISHED WHEN THE ACCUMULATED MAGNITUDE (SUM) OF
C           B(N-M+2)...B(N+1) IS LESS THAN CHEK.  WHEN THE CONVERGENCE TEST
C           FAILS, THE FUNCTION SIMUL (SEE PROBLEM 5.2) IS CALLED TO
C           SOLVE THE SET OF LINEAR EQUATIONS FOR THE UPDATED P VALUES,
C           WITH THE AUGMENTED COEFFICIENT MATRIX IN THE ARRAY X.
C           EPS IS THE MINIMUM PIVOT MAGNITUDE ALLOWED BY SIMUL.
C           ITERATION PROCEEDS UNTIL THE CONVERGENCE TEST IS PASSED OR
C           UNTIL ITER, THE NUMBER OF ITERATIONS, EXCEEDS ITMAX.
C
      IMPLICIT  REAL*8(A-H, O-Z)
      DIMENSION A(20),  B(20),  C(20),  P(20),  X(21,21)
C
C           ..... READ DATA, NORMALIZE A'S, PRINT .....
    1 READ (5,100) N,M,ITMAX,CHEK,EPS,(A(I),I=1,N),A(N+1)
      NP1 = N + 1
      MP1 = M + 1
      READ (5,101) (P(I),I=2,MP1)
      DO 2   I = 2, NP1
    2 A(I) = A(I)/A(1)
      A(1) = 1.
      B(1) = 1.
      C(1) = -1.
      P(1) = 1.
      WRITE (6,200) N,M,ITMAX,CHEK,EPS,NP1,(A(I),I=1,NP1)
      WRITE (6,201) MP1,(P(I),I=1,MP1)
C
C           ..... CHECK FOR ARGUMENT CONSISTENCY .....
      IF ( M.GT.0 .AND. M.LT.N )   GO TO 4
         WRITE (6,202)
         GO TO 1
C
C           ..... BEGIN ITERATIVE FACTORIZATION .....
    4 DO 19   ITER = 1, ITMAX
C
C           ..... COMPUTE COEFFICIENTS IN B AND C ARRAYS AND SUM .....
      SUM = 0.
      K = 1
      DO 11   I = 2, NP1
      B(I) = A(I)
      IF ( K.LT.MP1 )   K = K + 1
    6 DO 7   J = 2, K
      IMJ = I - J
    7 B(I) = B(I) - P(J)*B(IMJ+1)
      IF ( I.GT.NP1-M )   SUM = SUM + DABS(B(I))
      C(I) = -B(I)
      DO 11   J = 2, K
      IMJ = I - J
   11 C(I) = C(I) - P(J)*C(IMJ+1)
C
C           ..... CHECK FOR CONVERGENCE .....
      IF ( SUM.GT.CHEK )   GO TO 13
         WRITE (6,203) ITER,MP1,(P(I),I=1,MP1)
         WRITE (6,204) NP1,(B(I),I=1,NP1)
         GO TO 1
```

Program Listing (*Continued*)

```
C
C       ..... NO CONVERGENCE YET, SET UP COEFFICIENT MATRIX X .....
  13    DO 17    I = 1, M
        DO 16    J = 1, M
        NMJI = N - M - J + I
        X(I,J) = 0.
  16    IF (NMJI.GE.0 )   X(I,J) = C(NMJI+1)
        NMI1 = N - M + I + 1
  17    X(I,MP1) = -(2.0*B(NMI1) + C(NMI1))
C
C       ..... SOLVE LINEAR EQUATIONS FOR NEW P'S - SHIFT SUBSCRIPTS .....
        CALL SIMUL( M, X, P, EPS, 1, 21 )
        DO 18    I = 1, M
        MP1MI = MP1 - I
  18    P(MP1MI+1) = P(MP1MI)
  19    P(1) = 1.
C
        WRITE (6,205)
        GO TO 1
C
C       ..... FORMATS FOR INPUT AND OUTPUT STATEMENTS .....
 100    FORMAT ( 3(10X, I2, 8X)/ 10X, E6.1, 14X, E7.1 / (20X, 5F10.3) )
 101    FORMAT (20X, 5F10.3)
 200    FORMAT ( 10H1N      = ,I8 / 10H M      = , I8 / 10H ITMAX = , I8
       1  /10H CHEK   = , F14.5/ 10H EPS    = ,  E14.1 / 20H0          A(
        21)...A(, I2, 1H)// (1H , 5F15.6) )
 201    FORMAT ( 20H0           P(1)...P(, I2, 1H)/ (1H , 5F15.6) )
 202    FORMAT ( 33H BAD DATA ENCOUNTERED AND IGNORED )
 203    FORMAT ( 35H0CONVERGENCE CRITERION HAS BEEN MET/  10H0ITER   = ,
       1  I8/  20H0           P(1)...P(, I2, 1H)/1H / (1H , 5F15.6) )
 204    FORMAT ( 20H0           B(1)...B(, I2, 1H)/ (1H , 5F15.6) )
 205    FORMAT ( 15H0NO CONVERGENCE )
C
        END
```

Data

```
N      =   4        M       =   2        ITMAX  =  30
CHEK   = 1.0E-2     EPS     =  1.0E-20
A(1)...A(5) =            1.000   -10.000    35.000   -50.000    24.000
P(2)...P(3) =           10.000    10.000
N      =   4        M       =   2        ITMAX  =  30
CHEK   = 1.0E-4     EPS     =  1.0E-20
A(1)...A(5) =            1.000   -10.000    35.000   -50.000    24.000
P(2)...P(3) =           10.000    10.000
N      =   4        M       =   2        ITMAX  =  30
CHEK   = 1.0E-4     EPS     =  1.0E-20
A(1)...A(5) =            1.000   -10.000    35.000   -50.000    24.000
P(2)...P(3) =            0.000     0.000
N      =   4        M       =   3        ITMAX  =  30
CHEK   = 1.0E-4     EPS     =  1.0E-20
A(1)...A(5) =            1.000   -10.000    35.000   -50.000    24.000
P(2)...P(4) =           10.000    10.000    10.000
N      =   4        M       =   3        ITMAX  =  30
CHEK   = 1.0E-4     EPS     =  1.0E-20
A(1)...A(5) =            1.000   -10.000    35.000   -50.000    24.000
P(2)...P(4) =            0.000     0.000     0.000
N      =   4        M       =   1        ITMAX  =  30
CHEK   = 1.0E-4     EPS     =  1.0E-20
A(1)...A(5) =            1.000   -10.000    35.000   -50.000    24.000
P(2)        =           10.000
N      =   4        M       =   1        ITMAX  =  30
CHEK   = 1.0E-4     EPS     =  1.0E-20
A(1)...A(5) =            1.000   -10.000    35.000   -50.000    24.000
P(2)        =            0.000
N      =   4        M       =   4        ITMAX  =  30
CHEK   = 1.0E-4     EPS     =  1.0E-20
A(1)...A(5) =            1.000   -10.000    35.000   -50.000    24.000
P(2)...P(5) =           10.000    10.000    10.000    10.000
```

Example 3.2   Iterative Factorization of Polynomials   **163**

Program Listing (*Continued*)

```
N     =    4        M      =    4         ITMAX  =   30
CHEK  =  1.0E-4      EPS    =  1.0E-20
A(1)...A(5) =                2.000   -20.000     70.000  -100.000     48.000
P(2)...P(5) =               10.000    10.000     10.000    10.000
N     =    4        M      =    0         ITMAX  =   30
CHEK  =  1.0E-4      EPS    =  1.0E-20
A(1)...A(5) =                1.000   -10.000     35.000   -50.000     24.000
NO P'S
N     =    4        M      =    1         ITMAX  =   30
CHEK  =  1.0E-4      EPS    =  1.0E-20
A(1)...A(5) =                1.000   -24.000    150.000  -200.000   -275.000
P(2)        =                0.000
N     =    4        M      =    2         ITMAX  =   30
CHEK  =  1.0E-5      EPS    =  1.0E-20
A(1)...A(5) =                1.000    -1.000      0.750     0.250     -0.250
P(2)...P(3) =               -2.000     2.000
N     =    4        M      =    2         ITMAX  =   30
CHEK  =  1.0E-5      EPS    =  1.0E-20
A(1)...A(5) =                1.000    -1.000      0.750     0.250     -0.250
P(2)...P(3) =                0.000     0.000
```

Computer Output

Results for the 1st Data Set

```
N      =        4
M      =        2
ITMAX  =       30
CHEK   =        0.01000
EPS    =        0.1D-19

          A(1)...A( 5)
   1.000000     -10.000000      35.000000     -50.000000      24.000000

          P(1)...P( 3)
   1.000000      10.000000      10.000000

CONVERGENCE CRITERION HAS BEEN MET

ITER   =       11

          P(1)...P( 3)

   1.000000      -4.999663       3.995807

          B(1)...B( 5)
   1.000000      -5.000337       6.004194      -0.000676       0.005026
```

Computer Output (*Continued*)

Results for the 2nd Data Set

```
N       =        4
M       =        2
ITMAX   =        30
CHEK    =        0.00010
EPS     =        0.1D-19

           A(1)...A( 5)
        1.000000     -10.000000     35.000000     -50.000000     24.000000

           P(1)...P( 3)
        1.000000      10.000000     10.000000

CONVERGENCE CRITERION HAS BEEN MET

ITER    =        12



           P(1)...P( 3)

        1.000000      -4.999999      3.999991

           B(1)...B( 5)
        1.000000      -5.000001      6.000009      -0.000002      0.000006
```

Results for the 9th Data Set

```
N       =        4
M       =        4
ITMAX   =        30
CHEK    =        0.00010
EPS     =        0.1D-19

           A(1)...A( 5)
        1.000000     -10.000000     35.000000     -50.000000     24.000000

           P(1)...P( 5)
        1.000000      10.000000     10.000000     10.000000     10.000000
BAD DATA ENCOUNTERED AND IGNORED
```

Results for the 11th Data Set

```
N       =        4
M       =        1
ITMAX   =        30
CHEK    =        0.00010
EPS     =        0.1D-19

           A(1)...A( 5)
        1.000000     -24.000000     150.000000     -200.000000     -275.000000

           P(1)...P( 2)
        1.000000       0.0

CONVERGENCE CRITERION HAS BEEN MET

ITER    =        6

           P(1)...P( 2)

        1.000000       0.812840

           B(1)...B( 5)
        1.000000     -24.812840     170.168865     -338.320032      0.000000
```

Example 3.2   Iterative Factorization of Polynomials **165**

Computer Output (*Continued*)

Results for the 13th Data Set

```
N      =        4
M      =        2
ITMAX  =       30
CHEK   =        0.00001
EPS    =        0.1D-19

        A(1)...A( 5)
1.000000       -1.000000      0.750000      0.250000      -0.250000

        P(1)...P( 3)
1.000000        0.0           0.0
```

```
CONVERGENCE CRITERION HAS BEEN MET

ITER   =        5

        P(1)...P( 3)

1.000000       -0.000000     -0.250000

        B(1)...B( 5)
1.000000       -1.000000      1.000000      0.000000      0.000000
```

Discussion of Results

All calculations have been made using double-precision arithmetic. Results for the 1st, 2nd, 9th, 11th, and 13th data sets are shown in the computer output. The first ten data sets are for the starting polynomial of fourth degree,

$$\phi_4(x) = x^4 - 10x^3 + 35x^2 - 50x + 24,$$

which in factored form is:

$$
\begin{aligned}
\phi_4(x) &= (x-4)(x-3)(x-2)(x-1) \\
&= (x^3 - 9x^2 + 26x - 24)(x-1) \\
&= (x^3 - 8x^2 + 19x - 12)(x-2) \\
&= (x^3 - 7x^2 + 14x - 8)(x-3) \\
&= (x^3 - 6x^2 + 11x - 6)(x-4) \\
&= (x^2 - 7x + 12)(x^2 - 3x + 2) \\
&= (x^2 - 6x + 8)(x^2 - 4x + 3) \\
&= (x^2 - 5x + 4)(x^2 - 5x + 6).
\end{aligned}
$$

A summary of the results for the first ten data sets follows.

Data Set 1 (results shown)

Starting factor:	$x^2 + 10x + 10$
Iterations required:	11
Factors found:	$x^2 - 4.999663x + 3.995807$
	$x^2 - 5.000337x + 6.004194$

Data Set 2 (results shown)

Starting factor:	$x^2 + 10x + 10$
Iterations required:	12
Factors found:	$x^2 - 4.999999x + 3.999991$
	$x^2 - 5.000001x + 6.000009$

Data Set 3

Starting factor:	x^2
Iterations required:	11
Factors found:	$x^2 - 5.000000x + 4.000000$
	$x^2 - 5.000000x + 6.000000$

Data Set 4

Starting factor:	$x^3 + 10x^2 + 10x + 10$
Iterations required:	12
Factors found:	$x^3 - 9.000000x^2 + 25.999999x$
	$- 23.999998$
	$x \quad - 1.000000$

Data Set 5

Starting factor:	x^3
Iterations required:	9
Factors found:	$x^3 - 7.000000x^2 + 14.000000x$
	$- 8.000000$
	$x \quad - 3.000000$

Data Set 6

Starting factor:	$x + 10$
Iterations required:	13
Factors found:	$x - 1.000000$
	$x^3 - 9.000000x^2 + 26.000000x$
	$- 24.000000$

Data Set 7

Starting factor:	x
Iterations required:	7
Factors found:	$x - 1.000000$
	$x^3 - 9.000000x^2 + 26.000000x$
	$- 24.000000$

Data Set 8: Bad data encountered ($m = n$).

Data Set 9 (results shown): Bad data encountered ($m = n$).

Data Set 10: Bad data encountered ($m = 0$).

Note that although the starting factors for the first and second data sets are identical, an additional iteration is required for the second set because of the more stringent convergence requirement. The results for the fourth and fifth data sets show that different starting factors may lead to different combinations of final factors. The results for data sets 8, 9, and 10 indicate that the program is checking properly for inconsistent values of m and n, while the printed results for the ninth data set show that the coefficients a_i are being normalized as specified in (3.2.3).

The starting polynomial for the eleventh data set is

$$\phi_4(x) = x^4 - 24x^3 + 150x^2 - 200x - 275.$$

The results, shown in the computer output, are:

Starting factor:	x
Iterations required:	6
Factors found:	$x + 0.812840$
	$x^3 - 24.812840x^2$
	$+ 170.168865x - 338.320032$

To six figure accuracy, one root of this polynomial is -0.812840.

The polynomial for the twelfth and thirteenth data sets is

$$
\begin{aligned}
\phi_4(x) &= x^4 - x^3 + 0.75x^2 + 0.25x - 0.25 \\
&= (x^2 - 0.25)(x^2 - x + 1).
\end{aligned}
$$

This is the polynomial used in the examples of Tables 3.3 and 3.4. Results for the two cases are:

Data Set 12

Starting factor:	$x^2 - 2x + 2$
Iterations required:	15
Factors found:	$x^2 - 0.000000x - 0.250000$
	$x^2 - 1.000000x + 1.000000$

Example 3.2   Iterative Factorization of Polynomials   **167**

Data Set 13 (results shown)

Starting factor: x^2
Iterations required: 5
Factors found: $x^2 - 0.000000x - 0.250000$
                         $x^2 - 1.000000x + 1.000000$

The results for these two data sets clearly show the importance of the starting factor on the number of iterations required to converge to the same factors with equivalent accuracy.

3.5 Method of Successive Substitutions

The following discussion is not confined to polynomial equations. We rewrite (3.1) in the form

$$x = F(x), \tag{3.21}$$

such that if $f(\alpha) = 0$, then $\alpha = F(\alpha)$. If an initial approximation x_1 to a root α is provided, a sequence $x_2, x_3, \ldots$ may be defined by the recursion relation

$$x_{j+1} = F(x_j), \tag{3.22}$$

with the hope that the sequence will converge to α. The successive iterations are interpreted graphically in Fig. 3.1a.

previously mentioned. If we set $x_{j+1} = \cos(x_j)$, then $F'(x) = -\sin x$. The reader should establish graphically that $|F'(\alpha)| < 1$ for the unique solution α.

Note that the equation $x = F(x)$ can be formed from the original equation, $f(x) = 0$, in an unlimited number of ways. While the choice of F will depend on the particular situation, one suggestion is offered. If $\alpha = F(\alpha)$, then also $\alpha = (1 - k)\alpha + kF(\alpha)$; therefore, instead of (3.22), we can consider

$$x_{j+1} = (1 - k)x_j + kF(x_j) \tag{3.25}$$

to see whether a suitable choice of k will affect convergence favorably.

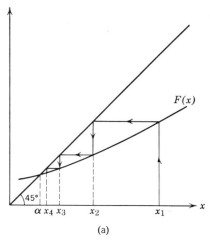

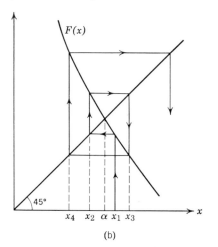

(a)   (b)

Figure 3.1 Graphical interpretation of method of successive substitutions.

Convergence will certainly occur if, for some constant ρ where $0 < \rho < 1$, the inequality

$$|F(x) - F(\alpha)| \leqslant \rho|x - \alpha| \tag{3.23}$$

holds true whenever $|x - \alpha| \leqslant |x_1 - \alpha|$. For, if (3.23) holds, we find that

$$|x_2 - \alpha| = |F(x_1) - \alpha| = |F(x_1) - F(\alpha)| \leqslant \rho|x_1 - \alpha|,$$

since $\alpha = F(\alpha)$. Proceeding,

$$|x_3 - \alpha| = |F(x_2) - F(\alpha)| \leqslant \rho|x_2 - \alpha| \leqslant \rho^2|x_1 - \alpha|.$$

Continuing in this manner, we conclude that $|x_j - \alpha| \leqslant \rho^{j-1}|x_1 - \alpha|$, and thus that $\lim_{j \to \infty} x_j = \alpha$.

Condition (3.23) is clearly satisfied if F possesses a derivative F' such that $|F'(x)| \leqslant \rho < 1$ for $|x - \alpha| < |x_1 - \alpha|$. Figure 3.1b shows how the method of successive substitutions fails to converge for a case in which $|F'(x)| > 1$ in the region of interest. Generally, when x_j is close to α, the approximate relation

$$x_{j+1} - \alpha \doteq F'(\alpha)(x_j - \alpha) \tag{3.24}$$

holds true; $F'(\alpha)$ is called the *asymptotic convergence factor*.

An example is furnished by the equation $\cos x - x = 0$

Further discussion of this and other iterative methods can be found in Traub [14].

Example. Consider the equation

$$f(x) = x^3 - 3x + 1 = 0.$$

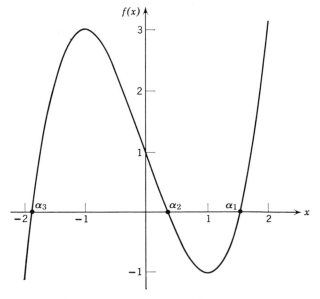

Figure 3.2 Roots of $f(x) = x^3 - 3x + 1 = 0$.

The function $f(x)$ is illustrated in Fig. 3.2; by inspection, $2 > \alpha_1 > 1$, $1 > \alpha_2 > 0$, and $-1 > \alpha_3 > -2$. Consider first the version

$$x_{j+1} = \frac{1}{3}(x_j^3 + 1). \qquad (3.26a)$$

Corresponding to (3.26a), $F'(x) = x^2$, and $|F'(x)| < 1$ if $|x| < 1$. Consequently, (3.26a), if used to define the iterative process, can be expected to yield α_2, but not to yield α_1 or α_3. If, however, in (3.25) we use $k = -\frac{1}{2}$, so that

$$x_{j+1} = \frac{3}{2}x_j - \frac{1}{6}(x_j^3 + 1), \qquad (3.26b)$$

then $F(x)$ becomes $(3/2)x - (x^3 + 1)/6$ and $F'(x) = 3/2 - x^2/2$. In particular, for $1 < |x| < \sqrt{5}$, which includes $1 < |x| < 2$, $|F'(x)| < 1$. Thus, properly started, the approach using (3.26b) yields α_1 and α_3. Complete details of the iterative processes are given in Table 3.5.

neighborhood of a point (x,y) such that $w(x,y) \neq 0$, there exists a point (x',y') such that $w(x',y') < w(x,y)$. The proof assumes that $f(z)$ has certain derivatives, and this is valid for polynomials in particular. At a given step in the process, which is iterative, the current value $w(x,y)$ is compared with the values $w(x+h,y)$, $w(x-h,y)$, $w(x,y+h)$, and $w(x,y-h)$ until a smaller value is found (if possible). The coordinates yielding this smaller value are taken as the values of x and y in the next iterative step. Should these four points yield no decrease in $w = |u| + |v|$, h is replaced by $h/2$ and the process is continued.

There is no guarantee of convergence. For example, the polynomials

$$\sum_{j=0}^{n} c_{4j} z^{4j} + K,$$

Table 3.5   Illustration of Method of Successive Substitutions

Iterative Formula:	(3.26a)	(3.26b)	(3.26b)
Starting Value, x_1:	0.5	1.5	-1.5
j	x_j	x_j	x_j
1	0.5	1.5	-1.5
2	0.375	1.520833	-1.854167
3	0.350911	1.528319	-1.885500
4	0.347737	1.530848	-1.877723
5	0.347350	1.531683	-1.879825
6	0.347303	1.531956	-1.879268
7	0.347297	1.532046	-1.879416
8	0.347296	1.532075	-1.879377
9	0.347296	1.532084	-1.879387
10	—	1.532087	-1.879385
11	—	1.532088	-1.879385
12	—	1.532089	—
13	—	1.532089	—

3.6   Ward's Method

Let the polynomial $f(z)$ be a function of the complex variable $z = x + iy$, so that

$$f(z) = u(x,y) + iv(x,y). \qquad (3.27)$$

Clearly, $f(z)$ has a zero $\alpha = \beta + i\gamma$ if and only if $u(\beta,\gamma) = v(\beta,\gamma) = 0$. This pair of simultaneous equations in $u(x,y)$ and $v(x,y)$ may be used in various ways. One may, for example, seek to minimize $u^2(x,y) + v^2(x,y)$. Ward's method [3] seeks to minimize

$$w(x,y) = |v(x,y)| + |u(x,y)|. \qquad (3.28)$$

Since no derivatives are employed, the method seems well suited for finding multiple roots. The technique is based on the knowledge (subsequently verified) that in every

where K and the c_{4j} are positive, cannot be solved by the process just described if $z = 0$ is the point of departure. One can, of course, introduce variations of the search process described above.

To show that if $w(x,y) \neq 0$, there does exist in every neighborhood of (x,y) a point (x',y') such that $w(x',y') < w(x,y)$, proceed as follows, writing $z = x + iy$ and $z' = x' + iy'$. We have

$$f(z') = f(z) + (z' - z)^m \left[\frac{1}{m!} f^{(m)}(z) + s(z')\right],$$

where $f^{(m)}(z)/m!$ is the second non-zero coefficient in Taylor's expansion of $f(z')$ in powers of $z' - z$. Also, $s(z) = 0$, for $s(z') = (z' - z)[f^{(m+1)}(z) + t(z')]/(m+1)!$ Let $f^{(m)}(z)/m! = ae^{ib}$ and let $z' - z = re^{i\tau}$. Choose r_1 so small that $|s(z')| = k < a/3$ for $r < r_1$. Then if $f(z) = u + iv$,

$$f(z') = u + iv + r^m e^{im\tau}[ae^{ib} + ke^{ic}].$$

Let $\phi = b + m\tau$, $\psi = c + m\tau$. Then

$$w(x',y') = |u + r^m a \cos \phi + r^m k \cos \psi|$$
$$+ |v + r^m a \sin \phi + r^m k \sin \psi|.$$

If $u \neq 0$, choose r_2 so that $r_2 < r_1$ and $r_2^m(a + k) < |u|$. If $u > 0$, choose $\phi = \pi$ and $r < r_2$. Then

$$|u + r^m a \cos \phi + r^m k \cos \psi| = u - r^m a + r^m k \cos \psi$$
$$\leqslant u - r^m a + r^m k$$
$$< u - r^m a + r^m \frac{a}{3}$$
$$< u - \frac{2}{3} a r^m.$$

Also,

$$|v + r^m a \sin \phi + r^m k \sin \psi| < |v| + r^m \frac{a}{3}.$$

Therefore, $w(x',y') < |u| + |v| - \frac{1}{3} a r^m < w(x,y)$.

Suppose next that $u < 0$. Choose $\phi = 0$, Then, for $r < r_2$,

$$|u + r^m a \cos \phi + r^m k \cos \psi| = |u| - r^m(a + k \cos \psi)$$
$$< |u| - r^m a + r^m \frac{a}{3}$$
$$< |u| - \tfrac{2}{3} a r^m.$$

Also,

$$|v + r^m a \sin \phi + r^m k \sin \psi| < |v| + \frac{a}{3} r^m.$$

Then, in this case as well, $w(x'y') < w(x,y)$.

Finally, if $u = 0$, and, of course, $v \neq 0$, choose r_3 so that $r_3 < r_1$ and $r_3^m(a + k) < |v|$. If $v > 0$, choose $\phi = -\pi/2$; if $v < 0$, choose $\phi = \pi/2$. Then for $r < r_3$ we have, as before, $w(x',y') < w(x,y)$.

Example. Starting with $z = 1 + i$, and with an initial step $h = 0.1$, find a zero of the following function:

$$f(z) = z^4 - 2z^3 + 1.25z^2 - 0.25z - 0.75$$
$$= (z - 1.5)(z + 0.5)(z^2 - z + 1)$$
$$= (z - 1.5)(z + 0.5)(z - 0.5\{1 + i\sqrt{3}\})(z - 0.5\{1 - i\sqrt{3}\}).$$

Since $z = x + iy$, $f(z) = u + iv$, where

$$u = x^4 - 6x^2y^2 + y^4 - 2x^3 + 6xy^2 + 1.25x^2 - 1.25y^2$$
$$- 0.25x - 0.75,$$
$$v = 4x^3y - 4xy^3 - 6x^2y + 2y^3 + 2.5xy - 0.25y.$$

Table 3.6 lists the successive values of x, y, $|u|$, $|v|$, and $w(= |u| + |v|)$. Unnecessary calculations are, of course, omitted. The required root is approximately $0.500 + 0.860i$.

Table 3.6   Illustration of Ward's Method

x	y	$|u|$	$|v|$	w
1.0	1.0	1.0	1.75	2.75
1.1	1.0	1.6204	1.836	3.4564
0.9	1.0	0.4744	1.544	2.0184
0.8	1.0	0.0545	1.242	1.2965
0.7	1.0	0.2516	0.868	1.1196
0.6	1.0	0.4376	0.446	0.8836
0.5	1.0	0.5	0.0	0.5
0.4	1.0	0.4376	0.446	0.8836
0.5	1.1	1.0166	—	>1.0166
0.5	0.9	0.1086	0.0	0.1086
0.6	0.9	0.0576	0.333	0.3906
0.4	0.9	0.0576	0.333	0.3906
0.5	0.8	0.1804	—	>0.1804
0.55	0.9	0.0958312	0.16785	0.263681
0.45	0.9	0.0958312	0.16785	0.263681
0.5	0.85	0.0473688	0.0	0.0473688
0.55	0.85	0.058825	—	>0.058825
0.45	0.85	0.058825	—	>0.058825
0.505	0.85	0.0474834	—	>0.0474834
0.495	0.85	0.0474834	—	>0.0474834
0.5	0.855	0.0328462	0.0	0.0328462
0.505	0.855	0.0329621	—	>0.0329621
0.495	0.855	0.0329621	—	>0.0329621
0.5	0.86	0.0180918	0.0	0.0180918

3.7 Newton's Method

Newton's method for finding the zeros of $f(x)$ is the most widely known, and it is not limited to polynomial functions. It will be presented here for the complex case. Consider, then, $z = x + iy$ and $f(z) = u(x,y) + iv(x,y)$. For an iterative process, the complex expression

$$z_{k+1} = z_k - \frac{f(z_k)}{f'(z_k)} \tag{3.29}$$

is equivalent to the two expressions

$$x_{k+1} = x_k + \left(\frac{vu_y - uu_x}{u_x^2 + u_y^2}\right)_{x_k,y_k},$$
$$\tag{3.30}$$
$$y_{k+1} = y_k + \left(\frac{-vu_x - uu_y}{u_x^2 + u_y^2}\right)_{x_k,y_k}.$$

Here, u_x and u_y mean $\partial u/\partial x$ and $\partial u/\partial y$, respectively. The expressions in parentheses are to be evaluated for $x = x_k$, $y = y_k$. The manipulation establishing the equivalence of (3.29) and (3.30) requires only knowledge of the Cauchy-Riemann equations, stating that

$$u_x = v_y, \qquad u_y = -v_x.$$

The expressions (3.30) can alternately be found by considering the simultaneous solution of

$$u(x,y) = 0, \qquad v(x,y) = 0,$$

using the Newton-Raphson technique (p. 319). This may be consulted for an indication of proof of convergence when z_1 is near a zero of $f(z)$.

As previously remarked, Newton's method, when applied to polynomials, can be considered as the case $m = 1$ of the iterative factorization technique.

Yet another approach is to view it in terms of the method of successive substitutions. In (3.21) let

$$F(x) = x - \frac{f(x)}{f'(x)}.$$

Then the asymptotic convergence factor for a zero, α, of $f(x)$ becomes, for x real,

$$F'(\alpha) = \frac{f(\alpha)f''(\alpha)}{[f'(\alpha)]^2} = 0.$$

This means that convergence is guaranteed (for $f'(\alpha) \neq 0$) if the initial value x_1 is near enough to α.

If $f(x)$ is the polynomial (3.2), observe that $f(r)$ may be written in the form

$$(\cdots(((1)r + a_1)r + a_2)r\cdots)r + a_n.$$

This is really synthetic division. It may be phrased iteratively as $f(x) = (x - r)\sum_{i=0}^{n-1} b_i x^{n-1-i} + b_n$, with $b_{i+1} = b_i r + a_{i+1}$ [see equation (3.15), using $m = 1$ and $p_1 = r$]. Observe that $f'(r) = \sum_{i=0}^{n-1} b_i r^{n-1-i}$; therefore, $f(r)$ and $f'(r)$ can be calculated simultaneously.

It can be shown that if α is a simple zero of $f(x)$ and if $\lim_{k\to\infty} x_k = \alpha$, then

$$\lim_{k\to\infty} \frac{x_{k+1} - \alpha}{(x_k - \alpha)^2} = \frac{f''(\alpha)}{2f'(\alpha)}. \tag{3.31}$$

This means that once x_k is near α, the error in the next step is proportional to the *square* of the error in x_k; the resulting *quadratic* convergence is then rapid in comparison with the *linear* convergence of several other methods.

To understand (3.31), recall, by Taylor's theorem, that

$$f(x) - f(\alpha) = (x - \alpha)f'(\alpha) + \tfrac{1}{2}(x - \alpha)^2 f''(\alpha)$$
$$+ \tfrac{1}{6}(x - \alpha)^3 f'''(\xi),$$

where ξ lies between x and α. Then the Newton's method algorithm, modified by subtracting α from both sides and noting that $f(\alpha) = 0$,

$$x_{k+1} - \alpha = x_k - \alpha - \frac{f(x_k) - f(\alpha)}{f'(x_k)},$$

may be written as

$$x_{k+1} - \alpha = x_k - \alpha - \frac{1}{f'(x_k)}\left[(x_k - \alpha)f'(\alpha)\right.$$
$$+ \frac{1}{2}(x_k - \alpha)^2 f''(\alpha) + \frac{1}{6}(x_k - \alpha)^3 f'''(\xi_k)\Big]$$
$$= \frac{(x_k - \alpha)^2}{f'(x_k)}\left[\frac{f'(x_k) - f'(\alpha)}{x_k - \alpha}\right.$$
$$\left. - \frac{1}{2}f''(\alpha) - \frac{1}{6}(x_k - \alpha)f'''(\xi_k)\right].$$

Dividing by $(x_k - \alpha)^2$ and noting that $\lim_{k\to\infty} x_k = \alpha$, (3.31) follows:

$$\lim_{k\to\infty} \frac{x_{k+1} - \alpha}{(x_k - \alpha)^2} = \frac{1}{f'(\alpha)}\left[f''(\alpha) - \frac{1}{2}f''(\alpha)\right] = \frac{f''(\alpha)}{2f'(\alpha)}.$$

Example. Starting at the point $(1,i)$, use Newton's method to find a zero of the following function, in which $z = x + iy$:

$$f(z) = z^4 - 2z^3 + 1.25z^2 - 0.25z - 0.75$$
$$= (z - 1.5)(z + 0.5)(z^2 - z + 1)$$
$$= (z - 1.5)(z + 0.5)(z - 0.5\{1 + i\sqrt{3}\})(z - 0.5\{1 - i\sqrt{3}\}).$$

For this function,

$$u(x,y) = x^4 - 6x^2y^2 + y^4 - 2x^3 + 6xy^2 + 1.25x^2$$
$$- 1.25y^2 - 0.25x - 0.75,$$
$$v(x,y) = 4x^3y - 4xy^3 - 6x^2y + 2y^3 + 2.5xy - 0.25y,$$
$$u_x(x,y) = 4x^3 - 12xy^2 - 6x^2 + 6y^2 + 2.5x - 0.25,$$
$$u_y(x,y) = -12x^2y + 4y^3 + 12xy - 2.5y.$$

Table 3.7 lists x' and y' as the iterative successors of x and y.

Table 3.7   Illustration of Newton's Method

	$k = 1$	$k = 2$	$k = 3$	$k = 4$	$k = 5$	$k = 6$
x	1.0	0.762832	0.459373	0.524586	0.502265	0.500005
y	1.0	0.757522	0.731024	0.897316	0.866673	0.866018
u	-1.0	-0.527593	-0.336523	0.096532	0.001940	-0.000022
v	-1.75	-0.501543	0.078138	-0.082031	-0.006880	-0.000014
u_x	-5.75	-1.86867	0.280573	-0.249786	-0.021549	-0.000044
u_y	1.5	1.48959	1.91366	3.33214	3.03719	3.03102
x'	0.762832	0.459373	0.524586	0.502265	0.500005	0.500000
y'	0.757522	0.731024	0.897316	0.866673	0.866018	0.866025

Therefore, a root is $0.5 + 0.866025i$.

EXAMPLE 3.3

SOLUTION OF AN EQUATION OF STATE USING NEWTON'S METHOD

Introduction

Many equations of state have been developed to describe the P-V-T (pressure, volume, temperature) relationships of gases. One of the better known equations of state is the Beattie-Bridgeman equation,

$$P = \frac{RT}{V} + \frac{\beta}{V^2} + \frac{\gamma}{V^3} + \frac{\delta}{V^4}, \quad (3.3.1)$$

where P is the pressure, V is the molar volume, T is the temperature, $\beta, \gamma,$ and δ are temperature-dependent parameters characteristic of the gas, and R is the universal gas constant in compatible units. The second, third, and fourth terms on the right-hand side of (3.3.1) may be viewed as corrections of the ideal gas law

$$P = \frac{RT}{V}, \quad (3.3.2)$$

ascribable to "non-ideal" behavior.

The parameters $\beta, \gamma,$ and δ are defined by

$$\beta = RT B_0 - A_0 - \frac{Rc}{T^2}, \quad (3.3.3)$$

$$\gamma = -RT B_0 b + A_0 a - \frac{RcB_0}{T^2}, \quad (3.3.4)$$

$$\delta = \frac{RB_0 bc}{T^2}. \quad (3.3.5)$$

$A_0, B_0, a, b,$ and c are widely tabulated constants, determined empirically from experimental data, and are different for each gas.

Equation (3.3.1) is explicit in pressure P but implicit in temperature T and volume V. Hence some iterative root finding procedure is required to find the volume which corresponds to given values of pressure and temperature.

Problem Statement

Write a program that uses Newton's method to solve (3.3.1) for the molar volume of any gas, given the pressure, P, temperature, T, and the constants $R, A_0, B_0, a, b,$ and c. After computing V, calculate the compressibility factor z, where

$$z = \frac{PV}{RT}. \quad (3.3.6)$$

The compressibility factor is a useful index of the departure of real gas behavior from that predicted by the ideal gas law ($z = 1$ for an ideal gas).

As test cases, compute the compressibility factors for gaseous methane (natural gas) at temperatures of 0°C and 200°C for the following pressures (in atmospheres): 1, 2, 5, 10, 20, 40, 60, 80, 100, 120, 140, 160, 180, 200. Compare the calculated results with experimental values.

Method of Solution

Rewriting (3.3.1) in the form

$$f(V) = \frac{RT}{V} + \frac{\beta}{V^2} + \frac{\gamma}{V^3} + \frac{\delta}{V^4} - P = 0, \quad (3.3.7)$$

and differentiating with respect to V at constant T and P yields

$$f'(V) = -\frac{RT}{V^2} - \frac{2\beta}{V^3} - \frac{3\gamma}{V^4} - \frac{4\delta}{V^5}. \quad (3.3.8)$$

The Newton's method algorithm from (3.29) is then

$$V_{k+1} = V_k - \frac{f(V_k)}{f'(V_k)}, \quad (3.3.9)$$

or

$$V_{k+1} = V + \frac{RTV^4 + \beta V^3 + \gamma V^2 + \delta V - PV^5}{RTV^3 + 2\beta V^2 + 3\gamma V + 4\delta}, \quad (3.3.10)$$

where for simplicity the subscripts k have been omitted from the volume terms on the right-hand side. Using units of atmospheres (1 atm $\doteq$ 14.7 lb_f/in^2) for P, liters/g mole (1 g mole of methane (CH_4) is approximately 16 grams) for V, and °K (°K $\doteq$ °C + 273.15) for T, the gas constant R is equal to 0.08205 liter atm/°K g mole. For this set of selected units, the appropriate constants for methane are [15]:

A_0	2.2769
B_0	0.05587
a	0.01855
b	-0.01587
c	12.83 × 10⁴.

The ideal gas law should give a reasonable first estimate for the molar volume V:

$$V_1 = \frac{RT}{P}. \quad (3.3.11)$$

A criterion for terminating the iterative procedure of (3.3.10) is

$$\left| \frac{V_{k+1} - V_k}{V_{k+1}} \right| \leq \varepsilon. \quad (3.3.12)$$

Here ε is a small positive number. For $\varepsilon = 10^{-N}$, the final value of V_{k+1} should be accurate to approximately N significant figures. This does not imply that the calculated volume will agree with experimental measurement to N significant figures, but rather that the equation has been solved this accurately given the set of constants $a, A_0, b, \beta, B_0, c, \delta,$ and γ.

Newton's method may fail to converge to a root, if given a bad starting value. The number of iterations should be limited to a small integer, *itmax*.

173

Flow Diagram

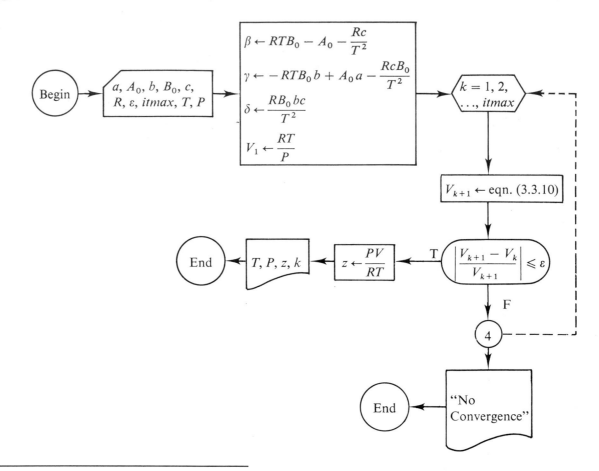

FORTRAN *Implementation*

    List of Principal Variables

Program Symbol	Definition
A, AZERO, B, BZERO, C	Material-dependent constants, a, A_0, b, B_0, c.
BETA, DELTA, GAMMA	Temperature-dependent parameters, β, δ, and γ.
DELTAV	Incremental change in molar volume for the kth iteration, $V_{k+1} - V_k$, liter/g mole.
EPS	Tolerance for convergence criterion, ε.
ITER	Iteration counter, k.
ITMAX	Maximum number of iterations permitted, *itmax*.
P	Pressure, P, atm.
R	Universal gas constant, R, liter atm/°K g mole.
T	Temperature, T, °K.
TC	Temperature, T, °C.
V	Molar volume, V_k, liter/g mole.
Z	Compressibility factor, z.

Example 3.3   Solution of an Equation of State Using Newton's Method   **175**

Program Listing

```
C          APPLIED NUMERICAL METHODS, EXAMPLE 3.3
C          SOLUTION OF AN EQUATION OF STATE USING NEWTON'S METHOD
C
C          GIVEN A TEMPERATURE T AND PRESSURE P, THIS PROGRAM USES
C          NEWTON'S METHOD TO COMPUTE THE MOLAR VOLUME V OF A GAS WHOSE
C          PRESSURE-VOLUME-TEMPERATURE BEHAVIOR IS DESCRIBED BY THE
C          BEATTIE-BRIDGEMAN EQUATION OF STATE.  R IS THE UNIVERSAL GAS
C          CONSTANT.  A, AZERO, B, BZERO AND C ARE EMPIRICAL CONSTANTS,
C          DIFFERENT FOR EACH GAS.  BETA, GAMMA, AND DELTA ARE TEMPERATURE-
C          DEPENDENT PARAMETERS DESCRIBED IN THE PROBLEM STATEMENT.
C          ITER IS THE ITERATION COUNTER AND DELTAV THE CHANGE IN V
C          PRODUCED BY ONE APPLICATION OF NEWTON'S ALGORITHM. FOR
C          CONVERGENCE, THE MAGNITUDE OF DELTAV/V IS REQUIRED TO BE
C          SMALLER THAN SOME SMALL POSITIVE NUMBER EPS. AT MOST ITMAX
C          ITERATIONS ARE ALLOWED.  IF THE CONVERGENCE TEST IS PASSED,
C          THE COMPRESSIBILITY FACTOR Z IS ALSO COMPUTED.  THE IDEAL
C          GAS LAW IS USED TO GET A FIRST ESTIMATE OF V.  IT IS ASSUMED
C          THAT TC, THE TEMPERATURE READ IN AS DATA, HAS UNITS OF
C          DEGREES CENTIGRADE.  T HAS UNITS OF DEGREES KELVIN.  UNITS
C          FOR ALL OTHER PARAMETERS MUST BE DIMENSIONALLY CONSISTENT.
C
   1  READ (5,100) A,AZERO,B,BZERO,C,R,EPS,ITMAX
      WRITE (6,200) A,AZERO,B,BZERO,C,R,EPS,ITMAX
C
   2  READ (5,101) TC,P
C
C          ..... COMPUTE TEMPERATURE-DEPENDENT PARAMETERS FOR GAS .....
      T = TC + 273.15
      BETA = R*T*BZERO - AZERO - R*C/(T*T)
      GAMMA = -R*T*BZERO*B + AZERO*A - R*C*BZERO/(T*T)
      DELTA = R*BZERO*B*C/(T*T)
C
C          .....USE IDEAL GAS LAW FOR FIRST VOLUME ESTIMATE .....
      V = R*T/P
C
C          ..... BEGIN NEWTON METHOD ITERATION .....
      DO 4   ITER = 1, ITMAX
      DELTAV = (((((-P*V+R*T)*V+BETA)*V+GAMMA)*V+DELTA)*V)/
     1  (((R*T*V+2.*BETA)*V+3.*GAMMA)*V+4.*DELTA)
      V = V + DELTAV
C
C          .....CHECK FOR CONVERGENCE .....
      IF( ABS(DELTAV/V).GT.EPS )   GO TO 4
        Z = P*V/(R*T)
        WRITE (6,201) TC,P,Z,ITER
        GO TO 2
   4  CONTINUE
C
      WRITE (6,202)
      GO TO 2
C
C          ..... FORMATS FOR INPUT AND OUTPUT STATEMENTS .....
 100  FORMAT (3(10X,F8.5,2X)/10X,F8.5,12X,F8.0,12X,F8.5/10X,E6.1,14X,I2)
 101  FORMAT (10X,F6.2,14X,F6.2)
 200  FORMAT (10H1A       = , F14.5/ 10H AZERO  = , F14.5/10H B       = ,
     1F14.5/ 10H BZERO  = , F14.5/ 10H C       = , F14.5/ 10H R      = ,
     2F14.5/ 10H EPS     = ,1PE14.1/10H ITMAX  = ,I8/ 51H0       TC
     3       P            Z             ITER  /  )
 201  FORMAT (F10.3, F15.3, F15.6, I10 )
 202  FORMAT (16H0 NO CONVERGENCE)
C
      END
```

Data

```
A     =   0.01855  AZERO  =    2.27690  B     =  -0.01587
BZERO =   0.05587  C      =  128300.    R     =   0.08205
EPS   =   1.0E-6   ITMAX  =  20
TC    =   0.00     P      =    1.00
```

Program Listing (*Continued*)

```
TC    =     0.00    P    =     2.00
TC    =     0.00    P    =     5.00
TC    =     0.00    P    =    10.00
TC    =     0.00    P    =    20.00
TC    =     0.00    P    =    40.00
TC    =     0.00    P    =    60.00
TC    =     0.00    P    =    80.00
TC    =     0.00    P    =   100.00
TC    =     0.00    P    =   120.00
TC    =     0.00    P    =   140.00
TC    =     0.00    P    =   160.00
TC    =     0.00    P    =   180.00
TC    =     0.00    P    =   200.00
TC    =   200.00    P    =     1.00
TC    =   200.00    P    =     2.00
TC    =   200.00    P    =     5.00
TC    =   200.00    P    =    10.00
TC    =   200.00    P    =    20.00
TC    =   200.00    P    =    40.00
TC    =   200.00    P    =    60.00
TC    =   200.00    P    =    80.00
TC    =   200.00    P    =   100.00
TC    =   200.00    P    =   120.00
TC    =   200.00    P    =   140.00
TC    =   200.00    P    =   160.00
TC    =   200.00    P    =   180.00
TC    =   200.00    P    =   200.00
```

Computer Output

```
A      =        0.01855
AZERO  =        2.27690
B      =       -0.01587
BZERO  =        0.05587
C      =   128300.00000
R      =        0.08205
EPS    =        1.0E-06
ITMAX  =       20
```

TC	P	Z	ITER
0.0	1.000	0.997678	3
0.0	2.000	0.995355	3
0.0	5.000	0.988382	3
0.0	10.000	0.976741	3
0.0	20.000	0.953426	4
0.0	40.000	0.906962	4
0.0	60.000	0.861555	4
0.0	80.000	0.818736	5
0.0	100.000	0.780686	5
0.0	120.000	0.749900	5
0.0	140.000	0.728303	5
0.0	160.000	0.716365	6
0.0	180.000	0.713063	6
0.0	200.000	0.716636	7
200.000	1.000	0.999898	2
200.000	2.000	0.999799	2
200.000	5.000	0.999517	2
200.000	10.000	0.999098	2
200.000	20.000	0.998448	3
200.000	40.000	0.997911	3
200.000	60.000	0.998387	3
200.000	80.000	0.999865	2
200.000	100.000	1.002318	3
200.000	120.000	1.005715	3
200.000	140.000	1.010011	3
200.000	160.000	1.015156	3
200.000	180.000	1.021094	3
200.000	200.000	1.027771	4

Example 3.3   Solution of an Equation of State Using Newton's Method   **177**

Discussion of Results

The calculated results shown in the computer output are plotted in Fig. 3.3.1 along with experimental values reported by Brown, Katz, Oberfell, and Alden [16] (the solid lines). In the pressure range 0–200 atm, agreement is quite good at 200°C (maximum deviation is approximately 0.3 percent). Predicted values for 0°C are quite good at pressures below 100 atm, but at higher pressures are in considerable error; the Beattie-Bridgeman equation would have to be used with some caution at higher pressures.

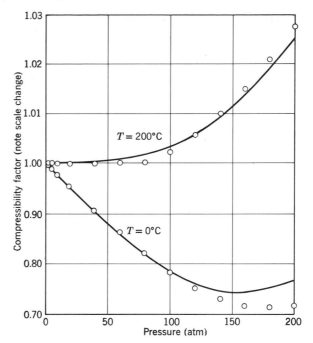

Figure 3.3.1   Compressibility factor for methane (CH_4).
——*Experimental values.*

∘ *Values predicted by Beattie-Bridgeman equation of state with the given set of constants.*

3.8 *Regula Falsi* and Related Methods

For the real case of Newton's method, the expression [see (3.29)]:

$$x_{k+1} = x_k - \frac{f(x_k)}{f'(x_k)}$$

has the interpretation illustrated in Fig. 3.3. We draw a tangent to the curve $y = f(x)$ at the point $(x_k, f(x_k))$. This

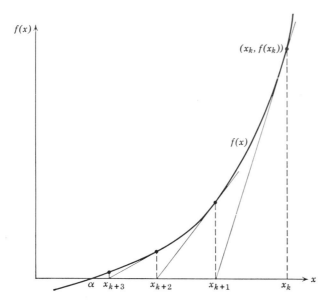

Figure 3.3   Newton's method for the real root $x = \alpha$.

tangent meets the x-axis at the point $(x_{k+1}, 0)$. If, then, the curve crosses the x-axis at a point $(\alpha, 0)$ sufficiently near $(x_k, f(x_k))$, and it is concave up or down in a region including these two points, it may easily be seen that the number x_{k+1} is nearer α than was x_k.

This kind of pictorial approach suggests other methods. One method, sometimes called the rule of *false position*, may be constructed as follows. Referring to Fig. 3.4, let

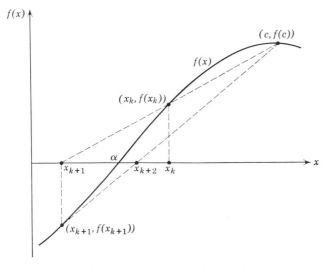

Figure 3.4   Method of false position.

$(c, f(c))$ be a fixed point on $y = f(x)$. Draw a chord through this point and the point $(x_k, f(x_k))$ so that it intersects the x-axis in a point $(x_{k+1}, 0)$. Thus,

$$x_{k+1} = \frac{cf(x_k) - x_k f(c)}{f(x_k) - f(c)}. \tag{3.32}$$

This new point may well yield a better approximation than x_k to α.

The procedure may be justified by the method of successive substitutions. Let

$$F(x) = \frac{cf(x) - xf(c)}{f(x) - f(c)},$$

where $f(c) \neq 0$. It is clear that $f(\alpha) = 0$ implies $F(\alpha) = \alpha$, and that $\alpha = F(\alpha)$ implies $f(\alpha) = 0$. Since

$$F'(x) = f(c) \frac{(x - c)f'(x) + f(c) - f(x)}{[f(x) - f(c)]^2},$$

it follows that in the neighborhood of a zero, α, for $f(x)$, the asymptotic convergence factor is

$$F'(\alpha) = 1 + (\alpha - c)\frac{f'(\alpha)}{f(c)}.$$

Applying the mean-value theorem, together with $f(\alpha) = 0$, we see that $f(c) - f(\alpha) = f(c) = (c - \alpha)f'(\xi)$, in which ξ lies between α and c. Thus,

$$F'(\alpha) = 1 - \frac{f'(\alpha)}{f'(\xi)},$$

so that convergence can be expected for proper values of c.

Since only functional values are involved (no derivative values are required), the resulting iterative formula (3.32) involves little computational effort. Also, in common with the other procedures given in this section, the method of false position is not confined to roots of polynomial equations.

Another technique with a simple graphical explanation is illustrated in Fig. 3.5. It gives a root, if values x_{L1} and x_{R1} are known, such that $f(x_{L1})$ and $f(x_{R1})$ are opposite in sign. For continuous functions, the number $f((x_{L1} + x_{R1})/2)$, being the value of the function at the halfway point, will be either zero or have the sign of $f(x_{L1})$ or the sign of $f(x_{R1})$. If the value is not zero, a second pair x_{L2} and x_{R2} can be chosen from the three numbers x_{L1}, x_{R1}, and $(x_{L1} + x_{R1})/2$ so that $f(x_{L2})$ and $f(x_{R2})$ are opposite in sign, while

$$|x_{L2} - x_{R2}| = \tfrac{1}{2}|x_{L1} - x_{R1}|.$$

Continuing in this manner, there is always a point α in the interval $[x_{Lk}, x_{Rk}]$ for which $f(\alpha) = 0$; α is uniquely determined by the process even though the interval may contain more than one zero for $f(x)$.

Because each new application of the iterative scheme

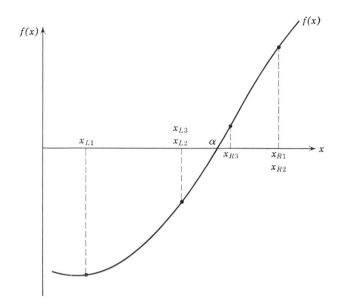

Figure 3.5 Half-interval method.

The process just described is linear inverse interpolation and sometimes bears the name *regula falsi*.

Example. Find the root of $f(x) = x^3 - 3x + 1 = 0$, that is known to lie between $x_{L1} = 1$ and $x_{R1} = 2$.

The results for ten iterations of the *regula falsi* method are given in Table 3.8. Because of the nature of the function and

Table 3.8 Illustration of Regula Falsi *Method*

k	x_{Lk}	x_{Rk}	$f(x_{Lk})$	$f(x_{Rk})$
1	1.000	2.000	−1.000	3.000
2	1.250	2.000	−0.797	3.000
3	1.407	2.000	−0.434	3.000
4	1.482	2.000	−0.190	3.000
5	1.513	2.000	−0.075	3.000
6	1.525	2.000	−0.028	3.000
7	1.529	2.000	−0.011	3.000
8	1.531	2.000	−0.004	3.000
9	1.532	2.000	−0.001	3.000
10	1.532	2.000	−0.001	3.000

reduces by half the length of the interval in x known to contain α, this procedure is called the *half-interval* method. Note that since the interval of uncertainty is always known, we can specify, *a priori*, the number of iterations required to locate the root within a prescribed tolerance. If Δ_1 is the length of the starting interval, then the number n of interval-halving operations required to reduce the interval of uncertainty to Δ_n is given by

$$n = \frac{\ln(\Delta_1/\Delta_n)}{\ln 2}. \qquad (3.33)$$

A technique which in some senses combines the features of the two preceding ones may also be constructed. Referring to Fig. 3.6, let x_{L1} and x_{R1} be numbers such that $f(x_{L1})$ and $f(x_{R1})$ are opposite in sign. Let x_2 be the abscissa of the point of intersection of the x-axis and the chord joining the points $(x_{L1}, f(x_{L1}))$, $(x_{R1}, f(x_{R1}))$; that is,

$$x_2 = \frac{x_{L1}f(x_{R1}) - x_{R1}f(x_{L1})}{f(x_{R1}) - f(x_{L1})}. \qquad (3.34)$$

If $f(x_2) = 0$, the process terminates with a zero of $f(x)$. If $f(x_2)$ has the same sign as $f(x_{R1})$, choose $x_{L2} = x_{L1}$ and $x_{R2} = x_2$. If $f(x_2)$ has the same sign as $f(x_{L1})$, choose $x_{L2} = x_2$, and $x_{R2} = x_{R1}$. The process is then continued to create the sequence of pairs (x_{Lk}, x_{Rk}).

the points chosen, this is also an example of the method of false position; note that x_{Rk} remains unchanged throughout the course of the iteration and this is equivalent to c in equation (3.32). Hence, the required root is approximately 1.532; it is computed more accurately to be 1.532089.

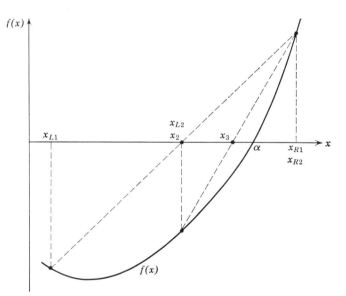

Figure 3.6 Regula falsi method.

EXAMPLE 3.4

GAUSS-LEGENDRE BASE POINTS AND WEIGHT FACTORS BY THE HALF-INTERVAL METHOD

Problem Statement

Write a program that computes the base-point values and weight factors for use in the $(n + 1)$-point $(n \leqslant 9)$ Gauss-Legendre quadrature (see Section 2.10 and Example 2.3):

$$\int_{-1}^{1} F(z)\,dz \doteq \sum_{i=0}^{n} w_i F(z_i). \tag{3.4.1}$$

Use the half-interval method to compute the base-point values, which are the roots z_i of the $(n+1)$th degree Legendre polynomial $P_{n+1}(z)$. Find the corresponding weight factors w_i by evaluating the integral of equation (2.85). As a check on the calculations, use (3.4.1) to evaluate a few simple test integrals.

Method of Solution

The coefficients of all the Legendre polynomials $P_n(z)$, $0 \leqslant n \leqslant 10$, are first generated and stored in successive rows of the lower triangular portion of matrix A. The elements of A, which are such that a_{ij} is the coefficient of z^j in $P_i(z)$, are obtained recursively from (2.66). The actual formulas used are shown in the flow diagram.

For a given n, the roots of $P_{n+1}(z)$ are obtained by first noting that they lie between -1 and 1. Starting from $z = -1$, we proceed in increments of 0.05 (assumed to be smaller than the separation of the roots) until $P_{n+1}(z)$ changes sign, that is, until we reach a point z such that $P_{n+1}(z)P_{n+1}(z + 0.05)$ is negative. By setting a left-hand limit $z_l = z$ and a right-hand limit $z_r = z + 0.05$, the half-interval method of Section 3.8 can then be implemented. By arbitrarily deciding to locate each root within a small interval of 10^{-6}, the required number of iterations is obtained from (3.33) by substituting $\Delta_1 = 0.05$ and $\Delta_2 = 10^{-6}$ and rounding up to the next integer.

When the first root z_0 has been found, we again step to the right in increments of 0.05, until $P_{n+1}(z)$ again changes sign. The procedure is repeated until all $n + 1$ roots $z_0, z_1, \ldots, z_n$ have been located within the required degree of accuracy.

The corresponding weight factors $w_0, w_1, \ldots, w_n$ are given from equation (2.85):

$$w_i = \int_{-1}^{1} \prod_{\substack{j=0 \\ j \neq i}}^{n} \left[\frac{z - z_j}{z_i - z_j} \right] dz. \tag{3.4.2}$$

Since the integrand is an nth-degree polynomial, (3.4.2) can be rewritten as

$$w_i = \int_{-1}^{1} (c_0 + c_1 z + c_2 z^2 + \cdots + c_n z^n)\,dz$$
$$= 2\left(c_0 + \frac{c_2}{3} + \frac{c_4}{5} + \cdots + \frac{c_n}{n+1}\right), \tag{3.4.3}$$

for n even, with a similar form, terminating in c_{n-1}/n, for n odd. The method for obtaining the c's by expanding the repeated product is detailed in the flow diagram.

Finally, the $(n + 1)$-point Gauss-Legendre quadrature of (3.4.1) is used to approximate the following test integrals:

$$I_1 = \int_{-1}^{1} e^z\,dz, \quad I_2 = \int_{-1}^{1} \cos\frac{\pi z}{2}\,dz,$$
$$I_3 = \int_{-1}^{1} z^5\,dz, \quad I_4 = \int_{-1}^{1} z^6\,dz,$$

which have the exact values $e - e^{-1}, 4/\pi, 0$, and $2/7$, respectively.

Flow Diagram

Main Program

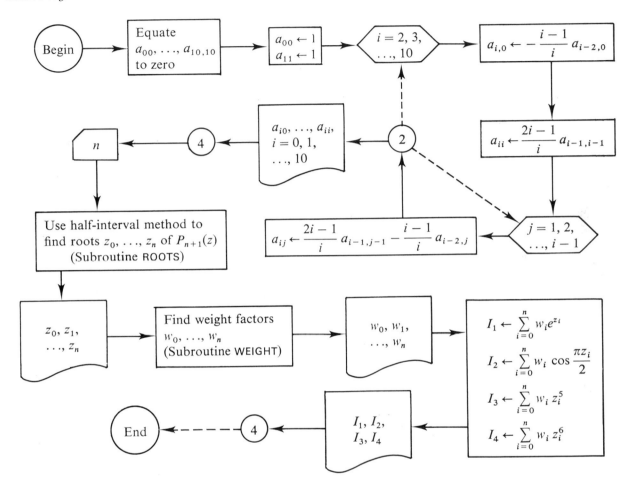

Subroutine ROOTS (Arguments: n, a, z)

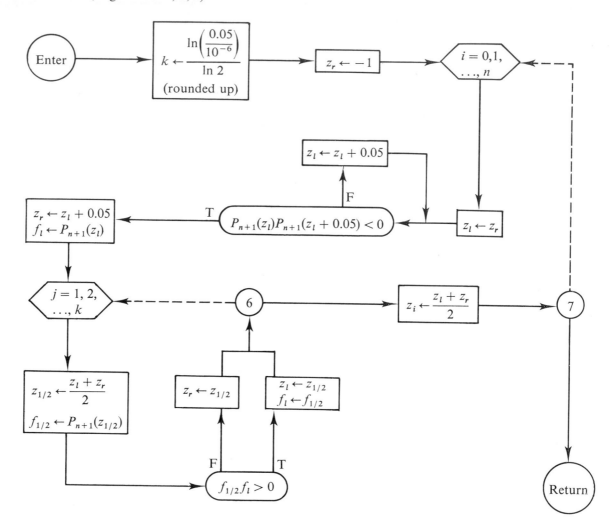

Subroutine WEIGHT (Arguments: n, z, w)

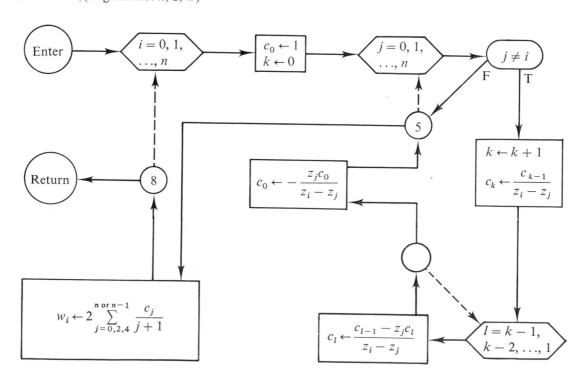

FORTRAN *Implementation*

List of Principal Variables

Program Symbol	*Definition*
(Main)	
A†	Matrix whose rows contain coefficients of the successive Legendre polynomials.
EXACT1, EXACT2, EXACT3, EXACT4	Exact values of the four integrals, I_1, I_2, I_3, and I_4.
FI1, FI2, FI3, FI4	Approximations to the integrals I_1 I_2 I_3 and I_4.
N	n.
ROOTS	Subroutine for determining the roots of $P_{n+1}(z)$.
W†	Vector of weight factors w_i.
WEIGHT	Subroutine for finding the weight factors w_i.
Z†	Vector of roots z_i.
(Subroutine ROOTS)	
FZL, FZHALF	Values of $P_{n+1}(z)$ at the left end and midpoint of the current interval, f_l and $f_{1/2}$, respectively.
ITER	Number of half-interval iterations, k.
POLY	Function for evaluating $P_{n+1}(z)$.
ZL, ZR, ZHALF	Values of z at the left end, right end, and midpoint of the current interval, z_l, z_r, and $z_{1/2}$, respectively.
(Subroutine WEIGHT)	
C†	Vector of coefficients c in (3.4.3).

† Because of FORTRAN limitations, all subscripts in the text are advanced by one when they appear in the program; e.g., the roots z_0 through z_n become Z(1) through Z(N + 1).

Program Listing

Main Program

```
C           APPLIED NUMERICAL METHODS, EXAMPLE 3.4
C           GAUSS-LEGENDRE BASE POINTS AND WEIGHTS BY HALF-INTERVAL METHOD.
C
C           THIS PROGRAM AND ITS ASSOCIATED SUBROUTINES ROOTS AND
C           WEIGHT REPRESENT A COMPLETE PACKAGE FOR GAUSS-LEGENDRE
C           QUADRATURE.   FIRST, THE COEFFICIENTS OF THE LEGENDRE
C           POLYNOMIALS OF ORDERS ZERO THROUGH TEN ARE COMPUTED AND
C           STORED IN THE ARRAY A.   A VALUE FOR N (NOT BIGGER THAN 9)
C           IS THEN READ AND THE ROOTS OF THE (N+1)TH ORDER LEGENDRE
C           POLYNOMIAL ARE COMPUTED AND STORED IN Z(1)...Z(N) BY THE
C           SUBROUTINE ROOTS, WHICH EMPLOYS THE HALF-INTERVAL METHOD.
C           THE CORRESPONDING WEIGHT FACTORS W(1)...W(N) ARE COMPUTED
C           BY THE SUBROUTINE WEIGHT.   FINALLY, THE INTEGRALS OF FOUR
C           COMMON FUNCTIONS ARE ESTIMATED BY AN (N+1)-POINT GAUSS-
C           LEGENDRE QUADRATURE AND ARE COMPARED WITH THEIR ANALYTICAL
C           VALUES.
C
      DIMENSION W(10), Z(10), A(11,11)
      PI = 3.1415926
C
C     ..... ESTABLISH COEFFICIENTS OF LEGENDRE
C           POLYNOMIALS UP TO ORDER N = 10 .....
      DO 1  I = 1, 11
      DO 1  J = 1, 11
    1 A(I,J) = 0.0
      A(1,1) = 1.0
      A(2,2) = 1.0
      DO 2  I = 2, 10
      FI = I
      C1 = (2.0*FI - 1.0)/FI
      C2 = (FI - 1.0)/FI
      A(I+1,1) = - C2*A(I-1,1)
      IP1 = I + 1
      A(IP1,IP1) = A(I,I)*C1
      DO 2  JP1 = 2, I
      J = JP1 - 1
    2 A(IP1,JP1) = A(I,J)*C1 - A(I-1,JP1)*C2
      WRITE (6,200)
      DO 3  I = 1, 11
    3 WRITE (6,201) (A(I,J), J = 1, I)
C
C     ..... READ VALUE OF N AND FIND ROOTS Z(I) .....
    4 READ (5,100) N
      WRITE (6,202) N
      CALL ROOTS (N, A, Z)
      NP1 = N + 1
      WRITE (6,203) (Z(I), I = 1, NP1)
C
C     ..... FIND WEIGHT FACTORS W(I) .....
      CALL WEIGHT (N, Z, W)
      WRITE (6,204) (W(I), I = 1, NP1)
C
C     ..... PERFORM INTEGRATIONS .....
      FI1 = 0.0
      FI2 = 0.0
      FI3 = 0.0
      FI4 = 0.0
      DO 6  I = 1, NP1
      FI1 = FI1 + W(I)*EXP(Z(I))
      FI2 = FI2 + W(I)*COS(PI*Z(I)/2.0)
      IF (ABS(Z(I)) .GT. 1.0E-5) GO TO 5
        Z(I) = 0.0
    5 FI3 = FI3 + W(I)*Z(I)**5
    6 FI4 = FI4 + W(I)*Z(I)**6
```

Program Listing (*Continued*)

```
C
C           ..... PRINT NUMERICAL AND 'EXACT' VALUES OF INTEGRALS .....
            EXACT1 = EXP(1.0) - EXP(-1.0)
            EXACT2 = 4.0/PI
            EXACT3 = 0.0
            EXACT4 = 2.0/7.0
            WRITE (6,205) FI1, FI2, FI3, FI4, EXACT1, EXACT2, EXACT3, EXACT4
            GO TO 4
C
C           ..... FORMATS FOR INPUT AND OUTPUT STATEMENTS .....
  100    FORMAT (6X, I4)
  200    FORMAT (81H1        THE COEFFICIENTS FOR THE LEGENDRE POLYNOMIALS OF
         1ORDER ZERO THROUGH TEN ARE)
  201    FORMAT (1H0, F7.5, 10F10.5)
  202    FORMAT (37H1       GAUSS-LEGENDRE QUADRATURE, WITH/
         1 1H0, 9X, 8HN     = , I6)
  203    FORMAT (51H0       THE ROOTS OF THE (N+1)TH ORDER POLYNOMIAL ARE/
         1(1H0, 5X, 10F10.6))
  204    FORMAT (42H0       THE CORRESPONDING WEIGHT FACTORS ARE/
         1(1H0, 5X, 10F10.6))
  205    FORMAT (39H0       ESTIMATED VALUES OF INTEGRALS ARE/
         1 1H0, 5X, 14H      FI1     = , F10.6, 14H      FI2     = , F10.6,
         2 14H      FI3     = , F10.6, 14H      FI4     = , F10.6/
         3 35H0       EXACT VALUES OF INTEGRALS ARE/
         4 1H0, 5X, 14H      EXACT1 = , F10.6, 14H      EXACT2 = , F10.6,
         5 14H      EXACT3 =   F10.6, 14H      EXACT4 = , F10.6)
C
            END
```

Subroutine ROOTS

```
C               SUBROUTINE TO FIND ROOTS Z(1)...Z(N+1) OF THE (N+1)TH ORDER
C               LEGENDRE POLYNOMIAL, USING THE HALF-INTERVAL METHOD.
C
            SUBROUTINE ROOTS (N, A, Z)
            DIMENSION A(11,11), Z(11)
            NP1 = N + 1
            ITER = ALOG(0.05/1.0E-6)/ALOG(2.0) + 1.0
            WRITE (6,200) ITER
C
C           ..... ESTABLISH INTERVAL WITHIN WHICH ROOT LIES .....
            ZR = - 1.0
            DO 7  I = 1, NP1
            ZL = ZR
   1     IF (POLY(ZL, A, N)*POLY(ZL+0.05, A, N) .LT. 0.0) GO TO 3
            ZL = ZL + 0.05
            GO TO 1
   3     ZR = ZL + 0.05
            FZL = POLY (ZL, A, N)
C
C           ..... BEGIN HALF-INTERVAL ITERATION .....
            DO 6  J = 1, ITER
            ZHALF = (ZL + ZR)/2.0
            FZHALF = POLY (ZHALF, A, N)
C
C           ..... CHOOSE THE SUB-INTERVAL CONTAINING THE ROOT .....
            IF (FZHALF*FZL .LE. 0.0) GO TO 5
            ZL = ZHALF
            FZL = FZHALF
            GO TO 6
   5        ZR = ZHALF
   6     CONTINUE
   7     Z(I) = (ZL + ZR)/2.0
            RETURN
C
C           ..... FORMAT FOR OUTPUT STATEMENT .....
  200    FORMAT (1H0, 9X, 8HITER = , I6)
C
            END
```

Program Listing (*Continued*)

Subroutine WEIGHT

```
C          SUBROUTINE TO ESTABLISH WEIGHT FACTORS W(1)...W(N+1) FOR
C          (N+1)-POINT GAUSS-LEGENDRE QUADRATURE.
C
           SUBROUTINE WEIGHT (N, Z, W)
           DIMENSION C(10), Z(11), W(11)
           NP1 = N + 1
C
C          ..... FIND COEFFICIENTS OF POWERS OF Z IN INTEGRAND .....
           DO 8  I = 1, NP1
           C(1) = 1.0
           K = 1
           DO 5  J = 1, NP1
           IF (J .EQ. I) GO TO 5
             K = K + 1
             DENOM = Z(I) - Z(J)
             C(K) = C(K-1)/DENOM
             L = K - 1
     2     IF (L .LT. 2) GO TO 4
               C(L) = (C(L-1) - Z(J)*C(L))/DENOM
               L = L - 1
               GO TO 2
     4       C(1) = - Z(J)*C(1)/DENOM
     5     CONTINUE
C
C          ..... EVALUATE W(I) AS THE INTEGRAL .....
           W(I) = C(1)
           IF (NP1 .LT. 3) GO TO 8
             DO 7  J = 3, NP1, 2
             FJ = J
     7       W(I) = W(I) + C(J)/FJ
     8     W(I) = 2.0*W(I)
           RETURN
C
           END
```

Function POLY

```
C          FUNCTION FOR EVALUATING (N+1)TH ORDER LEGENDRE POLYNOMIAL.
C
           FUNCTION POLY (X, A, N)
           DIMENSION A(11,11)
           VAL = A(N+2,1)
           NP1 = N + 1
           DO 1  K = 1, NP1
           KP1 = K + 1
     1     VAL = VAL + A(N+2,KP1)*X**K
           POLY = VAL
           RETURN
C
           END
```

Data

```
N  =   1
N  =   2
N  =   3
N  =   4
N  =   5
N  =   6
N  =   7
N  =   8
N  =   9
```

Computer Output

THE COEFFICIENTS FOR THE LEGENDRE POLYNOMIALS OF ORDER ZERO THROUGH TEN ARE

```
 1.00000
 0.0       1.00000
-0.50000  -0.0       1.50000
 0.0      -1.50000  -0.0       2.50000
 0.37500  -0.0      -3.75000  -0.0       4.37500
 0.0       1.87500  -0.0      -8.74999  -0.0       7.87499
-0.31250  -0.0       6.56249  -0.0     -19.68747  -0.0      14.43748
 0.0      -2.18750  -0.0      19.68747  -0.0     -43.31241  -0.0      26.81245
 0.27344  -0.0      -9.84374  -0.0      54.14053  -0.0     -93.84355  -0.0      50.27335
 0.0       2.46093  -0.0     -36.09369  -0.0     140.76532  -0.0    -201.09326  -0.0      94.96072
-0.24609  -0.0      13.53513  -0.0    -117.30446  -0.0     351.91284  -0.0    -427.32275  -0.0     180.42534
```

Results for the 2nd Data Set

GAUSS-LEGENDRE QUADRATURE, WITH

N   =   2

ITER =   16

THE ROOTS OF THE (N+1)TH ORDER POLYNOMIAL ARE

-0.774597 0.000000 0.774596

THE CORRESPONDING WEIGHT FACTORS ARE

0.555555 0.888889 0.555556

ESTIMATED VALUES OF INTEGRALS ARE

FI1 = 2.350336   FI2 = 1.274123   FI3 = -0.000001   FI4 = 0.240000

EXACT VALUES OF INTEGRALS ARE

EXACT1 = 2.350402   EXACT2 = 1.273239   EXACT3 = 0.0   EXACT4 = 0.285714

Computer Output (*Continued*)

Results for the 4th Data Set

```
GAUSS-LEGENDRE QUADRATURE, WITH

    N    =    4

    ITER =    16

THE ROOTS OF THE (N+1)TH ORDER POLYNOMIAL ARE

-0.906180 -0.538469 -0.000000  0.538469  0.906180

THE CORRESPONDING WEIGHT FACTORS ARE

0.236927  0.478628  0.568891  0.478628  0.236927

ESTIMATED VALUES OF INTEGRALS ARE

    FI1  =   2.350401    FI2  =    1.273240    FI3  =   0.000000    FI4  =   0.285714

EXACT VALUES OF INTEGRALS ARE

    EXACT1 =  2.350402    EXACT2 =  1.273239    EXACT3 =  0.0       EXACT4 =  0.285714
```

Results for the 9th Data Set

```
GAUSS-LEGENDRE QUADRATURE, WITH

    N    =    9

    ITER =    16

THE ROOTS OF THE (N+1)TH ORDER POLYNOMIAL ARE

-0.973907 -0.865058 -0.679413 -0.433394 -0.148875  0.148874  0.433394  0.679413  0.865058  0.973909

THE CORRESPONDING WEIGHT FACTORS ARE

0.066670  0.149284  0.219296  0.269215  0.295650  0.295694  0.269552  0.219099  0.149464  0.066672

ESTIMATED VALUES OF INTEGRALS ARE

    FI1  =   2.351203    FI2  =    1.273784    FI3  =   0.000066    FI4  =   0.285669

EXACT VALUES OF INTEGRALS ARE

    EXACT1 =  2.350402    EXACT2 =  1.273239    EXACT3 =  0.0       EXACT4 =  0.285714
```

Discussion of Results

The printout is reproduced above only for the three, five, and ten-point formulas ($n = 2, 4,$ and 9, respectively). Within the specified tolerance, the roots z_i agree with those given in Table 2.2.

The five-point Gauss-Legendre quadrature is highly accurate for all four test integrals. Even the three-point formula fails seriously only for I_4, in which the integrand is z^6; however, as predicted in Section 2.10, it handles I_3 exactly, since the integrand, z^5, is now a polynomial only of degree $2n + 1$. The ten-point formula shows obvious signs of accumulated round-off error; this difficulty could be overcome by working in double-precision arithmetic.

Note that the actual *application* of the Gauss-Legendre quadrature is treated much more thoroughly in Examples 2.3 and 2.4.

EXAMPLE 3.5

DISPLACEMENT OF A CAM FOLLOWER USING THE *REGULA FALSI* METHOD

Problem Statement

Consider the rotating cam with follower shown in Fig. 3.5.1. Let d (inches) be the displacement of the follower tip measured from the center of rotation of the cam. The

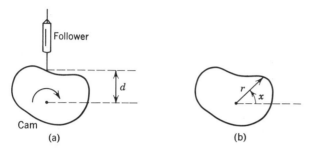

Figure 3.5.1 (a) *Cam and follower*
(b) *Rotation angle, x, and radius, r.*

radius of the cam, r (inches), measured from the center of rotation, is a function of the rotation angle, x (radians):

$$r(x) = 0.5 + 0.5e^{(-x/2\pi)} \sin x, \qquad 0 \leqslant x \leqslant 2\pi. \quad (3.5.1)$$

Figure 3.5.2 shows the displacement of the follower, $d(x)$, corresponding to one complete rotation of the cam.

Write a program that reads values for D, x_L, x_R, ε, and *itmax*, and then uses the *regula falsi* algorithm of (3.34) to find a rotation angle x on the angular interval $[x_L, x_R]$ for which the follower displacement $d(x)$ is equal to D. The convergence criterion for stopping the iterative computation should be

$$|d(x) - D| \leqslant \varepsilon. \quad (3.5.2)$$

If the criterion of (3.5.2) is not satisfied after *itmax* iterations, computation should be discontinued.

Method of Solution

For a given angle of rotation x, the displacement of the follower, $d(x)$, is equal to the radius of the cam, $r(x)$. Then the angle x that produces the desired displacement D is the solution of the equation

$$f(x) = r(x) - D = 0.5 + 0.5e^{(-x/2\pi)} \sin x - D = 0. \quad (3.5.3)$$

The convergence criterion of (3.5.2) is given by

$$|f(x)| \leqslant \varepsilon. \quad (3.5.4)$$

After establishing that $f(x_L)$ and $f(x_R)$ are of opposite sign, to insure that a root of (3.5.3) exists on the interval $[x_L, x_R]$, the *regula falsi* algorithm of (3.34) can be implemented iteratively:

$$x_{k+1} = \frac{x_{L,k}f(x_{R,k}) - x_{R,k}f(x_{L,k})}{f(x_{R,k}) - f(x_{L,k})}. \quad (3.5.5)$$

Here, k is the iteration counter. For the first iteration, $x_{L,1}$ and $x_{R,1}$ are given by x_L and x_R, respectively. Thereafter,

$$\text{if } f(x_{k+1})f(x_{L,k}) < 0, \quad \begin{cases} x_{R,k+1} = x_{k+1}, \\ x_{L,k+1} = x_{L,k}, \end{cases}$$

$$\text{if } f(x_{k+1})f(x_{L,k}) \geqslant 0, \quad \begin{cases} x_{L,k+1} = x_{k+1}. \\ x_{R,k+1} = x_{R,k}. \end{cases}$$

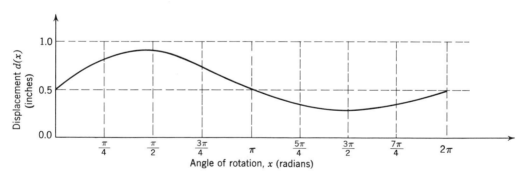

Figure 3.5.2 *Follower displacement, d, as a function of angle of rotation, x.*

Flow Diagram

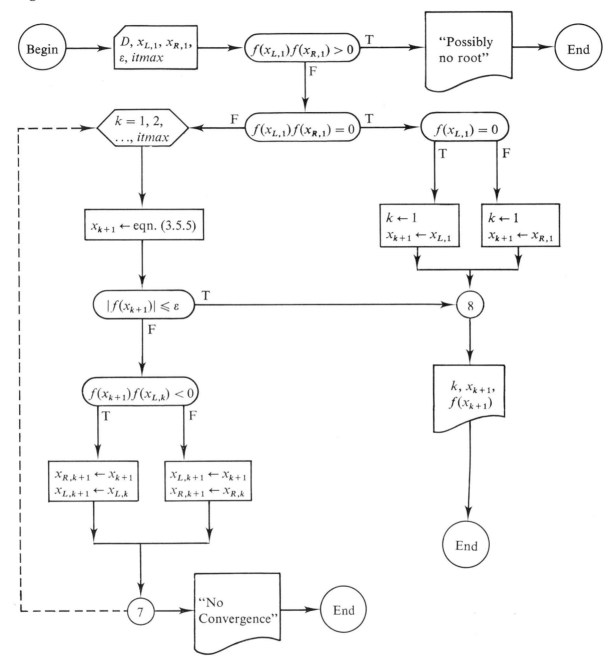

FORTRAN *Implementation*

List of Principal Variables

Program Symbol	Definition
CAMF	Function that computes the value of $f(x)$, in. (see equation 3.5.3).
D	Cam follower displacement, D, in.
EPS	Tolerance for convergence criterion, ε, in.
FX2, FXL, FXR	$f(x_{k+1})$, $f(x_{L,k})$, and $f(x_{R,k})$, in.
ITER	Iteration counter, k.
ITMAX	Maximum number of iterations permitted, *itmax*.
X2, XL, XR	x_{k+1}, $x_{L,k}$, and $x_{R,k}$, radians.

Program Listing

```
C           APPLIED NUMERICAL METHODS, EXAMPLE 3.5
C           DISPLACEMENT OF A CAM FOLLOWER USING A METHOD OF FALSE POSITION
C
C           THIS PROGRAM FINDS X2, THE ANGULAR DISPLACEMENT (IN RADIANS)
C           OF A CAM ON THE ANGULAR INTERVAL (XL,XR) WHICH CORRESPONDS
C           TO A GIVEN FOLLOWER DISPLACEMENT D, USING THE REGULA FALSI
C           ALGORITHM.  THE CAM DISPLACEMENT EQUATION IS DEFINED BY THE
C           STATEMENT FUNCTION CAMF.  FXL, FXR, AND FX2 ARE THE VALUES
C           OF CAMF AT XL, XR, AND X2 RESPECTIVELY.   ITERATION CONTINUES
C           UNTIL THE ITERATION COUNTER ITER EXCEEDS ITMAX OR UNTIL THE
C           MAGNITUDE OF FX2 IS LESS THAN OR EQUAL TO EPS.
C
C           ..... DEFINE CAM FUNCTION .....
            CAMF(X) = 0.5 + 0.5*(EXP(-X/6.283185)*SIN(X)) - D
C
C           ..... READ AND PRINT DATA .....
      1     READ (5,100)  D, XL, XR, EPS, ITMAX
            WRITE (6,200)  D, XL, XR, EPS, ITMAX
C
C           ..... EVALUATE FUNCTION AT ENDS OF INTERVAL .....
            FXL = CAMF(XL)
            FXR = CAMF(XR)
C
C           ..... CHECK FOR PRESENCE OF A ROOT .....
            IF ( FXL*FXR )   5, 3, 2
      2       WRITE (6,201)
              GO TO 1
      3     ITER = 1
            IF ( FXL.NE.0. )   GO TO 4
              X2 = XL
              FX2 = 0.
              GO TO 8
      4       X2 = XR
              FX2 = 0.
              GO TO 8
C
C           ..... BEGIN REGULA FALSI ITERATION .....
      5     DO 7   ITER=1,ITMAX
            X2 = (XL*FXR - XR*FXL)/(FXR - FXL)
            FX2 = CAMF(X2)
C
C           ..... CHECK FOR CONVERGENCE .....
            IF ( ABS(FX2).LE.EPS )   GO TO 8
C
C           ..... KEEP RIGHT OR LEFT SUBINTERVAL .....
            IF ( FX2*FXL.LT.0. )   GO TO 6
              XL = X2
              FXL = FX2
              GO TO 7
      6       XR = X2
              FXR = FX2
      7     CONTINUE
            WRITE (6,202)  ITMAX
C
      8     WRITE (6,203)  ITER, X2, FX2
            GO TO 1
C
C           ..... FORMATS FOR INPUT AND OUTPUT STATEMENTS .....
    100     FORMAT( 5X, F10.6, 2(10X,F10.6) / 5X, F10.6, 15X, I3 )
    200     FORMAT( 1H0/10H0D        = , F10.6/ 10H XL      = , F10.6/
          1    10H XR      = ,  F10.6/ 10H EPS      = , F10.6/ 10H ITMAX = , I3)
    201     FORMAT( 42H0POSSIBLY NO ROOT ON THE STARTING INTERVAL )
    202     FORMAT( 21H0NO CONVERGENCE AFTER, I3, 11H ITERATIONS )
    203     FORMAT( 10H0ITER      = , I3/ 10H X2       = , F10.6/ 10H FX2      = ,
          1    F10.6 )
C
            END
```

Program Listing (*Continued*)

Data

```
D   =      0.500000     XL =     0.700000     XR =     3.700000
EPS =      0.000010     ITMAX =       50
D   =      0.750000     XL =     0.250000     XR =     1.500000
EPS =      0.000050     ITMAX =       50
D   =      0.700000     XL =     3.140000     XR =     5.000000
EPS =      0.000001     ITMAX =      100
D   =      1.000000     XL =     0.000000     XR =     3.140000
EPS =      0.000100     ITMAX =      100
```

Computer Output

```
D      =     0.500000
XL     =     0.700000
XR     =     3.700000
EPS    =     0.000010
ITMAX  =     50

ITER   =     5
X2     =     3.141594
FX2    =    -0.000000



D      =     0.750000
XL     =     0.250000
XR     =     1.500000
EPS    =     0.000050
ITMAX  =     50

ITER   =     5
X2     =     0.580566
FX2    =     0.000043



D      =     0.700000
XL     =     3.139999
XR     =     5.000000
EPS    =     0.000001
ITMAX  =   100

POSSIBLY NO ROOT ON THE STARTING INTERVAL



D      =     1.000000
XL     =     0.0
XR     =     3.139999
EPS    =     0.000100
ITMAX  =   100

POSSIBLY NO ROOT ON THE STARTING INTERVAL
```

Discussion of Results

The computer output shows results for two data sets that yield solutions and two that do not. (The exact solution for the first data set is $x = \pi$.) The program can be used to find the angular displacement corresponding to a given follower displacement for *any* cam; only the function CAMF need be modified to include the appropriate radius function, $r(x)$.

3.9 Rutihauser's QD Algorithm

A modernization of the classical method of Bernoulli is afforded by the QD (quotient-difference) algorithm. The scheme starts in the manner described in Section 3.3. Thus let u_k, $0 \leqslant k \leqslant n-1$, be given numbers (in practice, chosen by techniques described later). For $k \geqslant n$, define

$$u_k = -\sum_{j=1}^{n} a_j u_{k-j}. \qquad (3.35)$$

The coefficients a_j are, of course, those of the polynomial

$$f(x) = \sum_{i=0}^{n} a_i x^{n-i},$$

whose zeros we again seek.

As in Bernoulli's method, we form the sequence $\{q_k^{(1)}\}$ where

$$q_k^{(1)} = \frac{u_{k+1}}{u_k}. \qquad (3.36)$$

Under suitable circumstances, if α_1 is a uniquely determined dominant zero, $\lim_{k \to \infty} q_k^{(1)} = \alpha_1$. Rutishauser's extension of Bernoulli's method builds additional sequences, $\{q_k^{(2)}\}$, $\{q_k^{(3)}\}$, ..., $\{q_k^{(n)}\}$, which can converge to $\alpha_2, \alpha_3, \ldots, \alpha_n$, respectively. As with Bernoulli's method, it is also possible to use subsidiary sequences when complex conjugate roots occur, and so on.

To define the new sequences $\{q_k^{(m)}\}$, $m = 2, 3, \ldots, n$, it is convenient to construct sequences $\{e_k^{(m)}\}$, $m = 0, 1, 2, \ldots, n-1$. We then have

$$e_k^{(m)} = [q_{k+1}^{(m)} - q_k^{(m)}] + e_{k+1}^{(m-1)}, \qquad (3.37a)$$

$$q_k^{(m+1)} = \frac{e_{k+1}^{(m)}}{e_k^{(m)}} q_{k+1}^{(m)}. \qquad (3.37b)$$

Clearly, nothing has been defined unless $e_k^{(0)}$ is known. We have, always,

$$e_k^{(0)} = 0.$$

For $n = 4$, the relations are shown schematically in Table 3.9. For obvious reasons, relations (3.37) are sometimes called *rhombus rules*. If a rhombus is centered on a q-column, pairs are added, as indicated; if a rhombus is centered on an e-column, pairs are multiplied.

As might be expected for a scheme involving division, it is difficult to guarantee feasibility for every starting procedure $u_0, u_1, \ldots, u_{n-1}$, and for every solution set $\alpha_1, \alpha_2, \ldots, \alpha_n$. Some results are known ([1], p. 166).

Consider first the condition

$$|\alpha_1| > |\alpha_2| > \cdots > |\alpha_n| > 0. \qquad (3.38)$$

It is then known that *if the QD sequences exist*, then $\lim_{k \to \infty} q_k^{(m)} = \alpha_m$ and $\lim_{k \to \infty} e_k^{(m)} = 0$.

Consider next the condition

$$|\alpha_1| \geqslant |\alpha_2| \geqslant \cdots \geqslant |\alpha_n| > 0, \qquad (3.39)$$

again requiring that the QD sequences exist. Then, for every m such that $|\alpha_{m-1}| > |\alpha_m| > |\alpha_{m+1}|$,

$$\lim_{k \to \infty} q_k^{(m)} = \alpha_m.$$

Also, for every m such that $|\alpha_m| > |\alpha_{m+1}|$,

$$\lim_{k \to \infty} e_k^{(m)} = 0.$$

Here, $|\alpha_0|$ is interpreted as ∞ and $|\alpha_{n+1}|$ as 0.

We thus see that the columns of a QD table can be divided into subtables by those $e^{(m)}$ columns that approach zero. Then all the $q^{(l)}$ columns contained in a subtable pertain to α_l values having the same modulus. Thus if a subtable has a single $q^{(l)}$ column, α_l is its limit.

One necessary and sufficient condition is known for the existence of the elements of the QD scheme. It is the non-vanishing of the determinants

$$H_k^{(m)} = \begin{vmatrix} u_k & u_{k+1} & \cdots & u_{k+m-1} \\ u_{k+1} & u_{k+2} & \cdots & u_{k+m} \\ \vdots & \vdots & & \vdots \\ u_{k+m-1} & u_{k+m} & \cdots & u_{k+2m-2} \end{vmatrix}, \qquad (3.40)$$

$k \geqslant 0$ and $1 \leqslant m \leqslant n$.

Table 3.9   Column Generation of the QD Algorithm

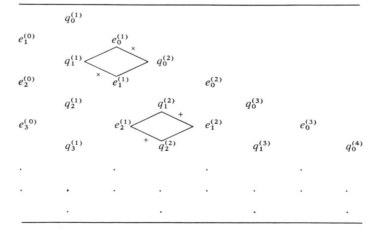

Sufficient conditions for the nonvanishing of the determinants of (3.40) are that

$$\alpha_i > 0, \qquad 1 \leqslant i \leqslant n, \qquad (3.41)$$

and, for $0 \leqslant k \leqslant n - 1$,

$$u_k = S_{k+1} = \sum_{i=1}^{n} \alpha_i^{k+1}. \qquad (3.42)$$

The S_j above are Newton's symmetric functions, and are given by Chrystal [5] in terms of the polynomial coefficients by the recursion relation

$$S_j + a_1 S_{j-1} + \cdots + a_{j-1}S_1 + ja_j = 0, \qquad 1 \leqslant j \leqslant n.$$

Thus if the zeros α_i are distinct, we have, by (3.12), for all values of k,

$$u_k = \sum_{i=1}^{n} \alpha_i^{k+1}. \qquad (3.43)$$

If the values of u_k are given as described in (3.42), it develops that the relation (3.43) is valid for all choices of α_i. Let the distinct zeros of $\sum_{i=0}^{n} a_i x^{n-i}$ be $\beta_1, \beta_2, \ldots, \beta_s$, and let their respective multiplicities be $t_1, t_2, \ldots, t_s$. This means that if

$$u_k = -[a_1 u_{k-1} + a_2 u_{k-2} + \cdots + (k+1)a_{k+1}], \qquad (3.44)$$

then, for all $k \geqslant 0$:

$$u_k = t_1 \beta_1^{k+1} + t_2 \beta_2^{k+1} + \cdots + t_s \beta_s^{k+1}. \qquad (3.45)$$

Another starting procedure is essentially that employed in Section 3.3 for Bernoulli's method. Let $u_0 = 1$ and, for $1 \leqslant k \leqslant n - 1$,

$$u_k = -\sum_{j=1}^{k} a_j u_{k-j}. \qquad (3.46)$$

While this does not guarantee the existence of all elements in the QD system, it does guarantee their existence for iterative indices sufficiently large ([1], p. 165).

The question of stability remains. The method described above is numerically unstable if the columns of numbers are generated in the order $e_k^{(1)}, q_k^{(2)}, e_k^{(2)}, q_k^{(3)} \ldots$. Fortunately, this can be avoided if the numbers generated are built row by row, rather than column by column. This has been implemented for the starting procedure of (3.46).

The relationships (3.37a) and (3.37b) are first rephrased as

$$q_{k+1}^{(m)} = e_k^{(m)} - e_{k+1}^{(m-1)} + q_k^{(m)}, \qquad (3.47a)$$

$$e_{k+1}^{(m)} = \frac{q_k^{(m+1)}}{q_{k+1}^{(m)}} e_k^{(m)}. \qquad (3.47b)$$

Thus, if a row of q's and the succeeding row of e's are known, we may build the next row of q's and then the next row of e's. To do this, we need proper starting values. For the case presented in (3.46), these are given by

$$q_0^{(1)} = -a_1, \qquad q_{1-m}^{(m)} = 0, \qquad m = 2, 3, \ldots, n, \qquad (3.48a)$$

$$e_{1-m}^{(m)} = \frac{a_{m+1}}{a_m}, \qquad m = 1, 2, \ldots, n - 1. \qquad (3.48b)$$

In addition, we require that

$$e_k^{(0)} = e_k^{(n)} = 0. \qquad (3.49)$$

It is known ([1], p. 171) that if the numbers generated by (3.47), (3.48), and (3.49) exist, then they are the same as those generated by (3.37) and (3.46), together with $e_k^{(0)} = 0$ for all k. Table 3.10 shows the beginning rows for $n = 4$ (compare with Table 3.9).

Table 3.10 Row Generation of the QD Algorithm

	$q_0^{(1)}$		$q_{-1}^{(2)}$		$q_{-2}^{(3)}$		$q_{-3}^{(4)}$	
$e_1^{(0)}$		$e_0^{(1)}$		$e_{-1}^{(2)}$		$e_{-2}^{(3)}$		$e_{-3}^{(4)}$
	$q_1^{(1)}$		$q_0^{(2)}$		$q_{-1}^{(3)}$		$q_{-2}^{(4)}$	
$e_2^{(0)}$		$e_1^{(1)}$		$e_0^{(2)}$		$e_{-1}^{(3)}$		$e_{-2}^{(4)}$
	$q_2^{(1)}$		$q_1^{(2)}$		$q_0^{(3)}$		$q_{-1}^{(4)}$	
$e_3^{(0)}$		$e_2^{(1)}$		$e_1^{(2)}$		$e_0^{(3)}$		$e_{-1}^{(4)}$

Problems

3.1 Modify the program of Example 3.1 so that Graeffe's root-squaring method is implemented as a subroutine, named GRAEFF, with argument list

(N, A, ITMAX, TOP, EPS, IPRINT,
ROOTR, ROOTI, PVAL, RTRUE)

where the first six arguments are defined in Example 3.1.

Develop a criterion for establishing that roots of equal magnitude (real or complex conjugate) may be present, so that equation (3.8) may be applied to find the real and imaginary parts of such roots. Upon return from the subroutine, ROOTR(I) and ROOTI(I) should contain the real and imaginary parts of the Ith root, PVAL(I) should contain the value of the polynomial at the Ith root, and RTRUE(I) should contain .TRUE. or .FALSE. according as the magnitude of PVAL(I) is smaller or not smaller than the value of EPS. There should be N entries in each of the four vectors.

Write a main program that reads values for N, ITMAX, TOP, EPS, IPRINT, and A(1), ..., A(N + 1), as in Example 3.1, calls upon GRAEFF to find estimates of the N roots of the polynomial whose coefficients are in A(1), ..., A(N + 1), prints the values returned by GRAEFF, and returns to read another data set. Test the program with the data used for Example 3.1.

3.2 Starting with a polynomial of degree n, $p_n(x) = \sum\limits_{i=0}^{n} a_i x^i$, it was shown in Section 1.4, that a factor $(x - x_k)$ can be removed from $p_n(x)$ by synthetic division, leading to

$$p_n(x) = (x - x_k)q_{n-1}(x) + R_0,$$

$$q_{n-1}(x) = \sum\limits_{i=1}^{n} b_i x^{i-1} = (x - x_k)q_{n-2}(x) + R_1,$$

$$q_{n-2}(x) = \sum\limits_{i=2}^{n} c_i x^{i-2},$$

where

$$b_n = a_n,$$
$$b_i = b_{i+1} x_k + a_i, \quad i = n-1, n-2, \ldots, 0,$$
$$c_n = b_n,$$
$$c_i = c_{i+1} x_k + b_i, \quad i = n-1, n-2, \ldots, 1.$$

Show that introduction of these relationships into Newton's algorithm of (3.29) leads to

$$x_{k+1} = x_k - \frac{b_0(x_k)}{c_1(x_k)},$$

an iterative method for finding a root, $\alpha = \lim\limits_{k \to \infty} x_k$, of $p_n(x)$. This root-finding procedure is known as *iterated synthetic division*.

If the polynomial $p_n(x)$ has a root near zero, what would be a good guess for x_1? Generalize the algorithm, so that up to n real roots of $p_n(x)$ may be extracted, one at a time.

3.3 Write a function, named PROOT, that implements the iterated synthetic division algorithm described in Problem 3.2. Let the argument list be

(N, A, X1, EPS, ITMAX, ITER),

where N is the degree of the polynomial $p_n(x)$, whose real coefficients $a_0, a_1, \ldots, a_n$ are available in A(1), ..., A(N + 1), X1 is the starting point, x_1, for Newton's algorithm, and EPS is a small positive number used in the tests for termination of the iteration:

$$\left| \frac{x_{k+1} - x_k}{x_{k+1}} \right| < \text{EPS, if } |x_{k+1}| > \text{EPS},$$

$$|b_0(x_{k+1})| < \text{EPS, if } |x_{k+1}| < \text{EPS}.$$

ITMAX is the maximum allowable number of iterations, and ITER should, on return, contain the number of iterations actually performed. If neither of the tests is satisfied after ITMAX iterations, computation should cease, and ITER should be assigned the value ITMAX + 1.

Write a main program that reads and prints values for N, A(1), ..., A(N + 1), X1, EPS, and ITMAX, calls upon PROOT to return an estimate of a root as its value, prints the value of PROOT(N, ..., ITER) and ITER, and returns to read another data set. Test the function with several of the polynomials used as test data for Example 3.1, and compare the roots with those found by Graeffe's method.

How would you modify PROOT to allow the extraction of up to n real roots of $p_n(x)$?

3.4 Show that a straightforward application of the method of successive substitutions (rather than Newton's method) to find a root of $p_n(x)$ by iterated synthetic division (see Problem 3.2) leads to an alternative algorithm (*Lin's iteration* [29])

$$x_{k+1} = -\frac{a_0(x_k)}{b_1(x_k)},$$

which is equivalent to

$$x_{k+1} = -\frac{a_0(x_k) x_k}{f(x_k) - a_0(x_k)}.$$

Find the asymptotic convergence factor for this iterative scheme, and determine a necessary condition for convergence to a root.

3.5 Since complex roots of a polynomial with real coefficients occur in conjugate pairs (if at all), isolation of quadratic factors from polynomials of degree greater than two is an important approach to the solution of polynomial equations. Once a quadratic factor has been found, then two real or complex roots may be found directly with the quadratic formula; no further iteration is required. One suitable approach is to use the method of iterative factorization of Section 3.4. A simpler, though less efficient, iterative procedure for finding quadratic factors can be developed, based on synthetic division by a quadratic factor.

Starting with the polynomial

$$p_n(x) = \sum\limits_{i=0}^{n} a_i x^i,$$

and an arbitrary quadratic factor $(x^2 + px + q)$, rewrite $p_n(x)$ as

$$p_n(x) = (x^2 + px + q)(b_n x^{n-2} + b_{n-1} x^{n-3} + \cdots + b_2) + b_1 x + b_0.$$

Show that $(x^2 + px + q)$ will be a perfect factor of $p_n(x)$ if and only if

$$a_1 - pb_2 - qb_3 = 0,$$
$$a_0 - qb_2 \quad\quad = 0,$$

and that application of the method of successive substitutions (see Section 5.8) to solution of these simultaneous equations leads to the "improved" estimates of p and q,

$$\bar{p} = \frac{a_1 - qb_3}{b_2},$$

$$\bar{q} = \frac{a_0}{b_2}.$$

This procedure is known as *Lin's method* (see also Problem 3.4).

Use Lin's method to find quadratic factors of

$$p_n(x) = x^4 - 2x^3 + 1.25x^2 - 0.25x - 0.75,$$

starting with $p = 0, q = 0$.

3.6 Show that application of the Newton-Raphson algorithm (see Section 5.9) to solution of the simultaneous equations of Problem 3.5 leads to

$$\frac{\partial b_1}{\partial p}\Delta p + \frac{\partial b_1}{\partial q}\Delta q = -b_1,$$

$$\left(\frac{\partial b_0}{\partial p} + b_1\right)\Delta p + \frac{\partial b_0}{\partial q}\Delta q = -b_0,$$

where $\Delta p = \bar{p} - p$ and $\Delta q = \bar{q} - q$. Introduce the recursion relations

$$c_n = b_n,$$
$$c_{n-1} = b_{n-1} - p,$$
$$c_j = b_j - pc_{j+1} - qc_{j+2}, \quad j = n-2, n-3, \ldots, 1,$$

where the b_j are those of Problem 3.5, and show that the equations developed above can be rewritten in the form

$$c_2\Delta p + c_3\Delta q = b_1,$$
$$-(pc_2 + qc_3)\Delta p + c_2\Delta q = b_0.$$

This iterative algorithm for finding ever-improving estimates of $\bar{p}$ and $\bar{q}$ is known as *Bairstow's method*.

Find quadratic factors for the polynomial given in Problem 3.5, starting with $p = 0, q = 0$, and compare the results with those found using Lin's method.

3.7 Write a program that implements Bernoulli's method of Section 3.3 for finding the dominant root or two roots of largest moduli, of the nth-degree polynomial

$$p_n(x) = \sum_{i=0}^{n} a_i x^{n-i},$$

where the a_i are real and $a_0 \neq 0$. The program should compute the sequences $\{u_k\}$, $\{v_k\}$, and $\{t_k\}$ of (3.9) and (3.10). Satisfactory values for the starting sequence are $u_k = 0$, for $0 \leq k < n - 1$, and $u_{n-1} = 1$. The elements u_n, u_{n+1}, and u_{n+2} should be computed first, followed by the computation of v_k, $k = 1, 2, \ldots, n+1$, and t_k, $k = 2, 3, \ldots, n+1$. The ratio tests of (3.11) and (3.13) should be applied to establish convergence to a root(s). Suggested versions of these tests are:

$$\left|\frac{u_{i+2}/u_{i+1}}{u_{i+1}/u_i} - 1\right| < \varepsilon,$$

$$\left|\frac{v_i/v_{i-1}}{v_{i-1}/v_{i-2}} - 1\right| < \varepsilon,$$

$$\left|\frac{t_{i+1}/v_i}{t_i/v_{i-1}} - 1\right| < \varepsilon.$$

Here, ε is a small positive number.

In each case, i assumes the values $n, n - 1, \ldots, n - m + 1$, where m is the number of such ratios which are to be tested in the sequence. If the first of these tests is passed, then the dominant root can be found from (3.11); if one of the latter two is passed, then two roots (possibly multiple, real or complex) can be found as discussed in Section 3.3.

Since convergence may be slow, storage for the sequences $\{u_k\}$, $\{v_k\}$, and $\{t_k\}$ should be limited to length $n + 3$. This can be accomplished if, after each iteration, the three most recently computed values of u_k (u_n, u_{n+1}, and u_{n+2} for the first iteration) are transferred to the locations originally occupied by u_0, u_1, and u_2. This overstoring procedure can be continued indefinitely until one of the ratio tests is passed or until the maximum allowable number of iterations has been exceeded. Also, since the numbers u_k may stray from the floating-point (real) number range, the n most recently computed elements of the sequence $\{u_k\}$ should be "normalized" after each iteration, by dividing each element by the average magnitude of the n most recently computed elements in the sequence $\{u_k\}$.

The program should read, as data, values for $n, a_0, a_1, \ldots, a_n, m, \varepsilon$, and the maximum number of iterations permitted. Test the program with a variety of polynomials, including some of those used to test the Graeffe's method program of Example 3.1.

3.8 It is stated on page 220 that the eigenvalues λ of an $n \times n$ matrix are the roots of its characteristic equation, $\sum_{i=0}^{n} a_i \lambda^i = 0$. Write a program that will read values for $n, a_0, a_1, \ldots, a_n$, and ε (a tolerance), and proceed to compute (possibly with the aid of one of the functions already developed) and print values for the eigenvalues $\lambda_1, \lambda_2, \ldots, \lambda_n$, known to be real, each within $\pm\varepsilon$. Test your program with the following characteristic equations, mentioned on pages 220, 224, and 225.

(a) $\lambda^4 + 20\lambda^3 - 700\lambda^2 - 8000\lambda + 120000 = 0,$

(b) $-\lambda^3 + 42\lambda^2 - 539\lambda + 2058 = 0,$

(c) $-\lambda^4 - 16\lambda^3 - 93\lambda^2 - 232\lambda - 209 = 0.$

3.9 As a continuation of Problem 3.8, write a program that will handle the possibility of complex eigenvalues. Test your program with the following characteristic equation,

$$\lambda^4 - 16\lambda^3 + 78\lambda^2 - 412\lambda + 624 = 0,$$

which corresponds to one of the matrices in Example 4.3, and has roots $\lambda = 12, 1 \pm 5i$, and 2.

3.10 When using the technique of Laplace transformation for solving problems, we are frequently confronted with the task of splitting the ratio of two polynomials,

$$F(s) = \frac{p_m(s)}{q_n(s)},$$

into partial fractions. The degree n of the polynomial in the denominator exceeds the degree m in the numerator. $F(s)$ is the Laplace transform of the function, $f(t)$ for example, that is being sought. A key step is to find the zeros $\alpha_1, \alpha_2, \ldots, \alpha_n$ (possibly complex) of $q_n(s)$. If there are no repeated zeros, let

$$\frac{p_m(s)}{q_n(s)} = \sum_{i=1}^{n} \frac{a_i}{s - \alpha_i}.$$

By multiplying through by $s - \alpha_i$, letting s approach α_i, and using Taylor's expansion, we obtain

$$a_i = \frac{p_m(\alpha_i)}{q_n'(\alpha_i)}.$$

If there is a repeated root, for example, $\alpha_1 = \alpha_2 = \cdots = \alpha_k = \beta$, let

$$\frac{p_m(s)}{q_n(s)} = \frac{r(s)}{(s - \beta)^k} = \sum_{i=1}^{k} \frac{b_i}{(s - \beta)^i} + \sum_{i=k+1}^{n} \frac{a_i}{s - \alpha_i}.$$

The reader should then be able to discover formulas giving the a_i and b_i for this case.

Once in partial fraction form, the transform $F(s)$ may be inverted by referring to tables (Spiegel [21], for example) to give the function $f(t)$ that is the required solution to the problem.

Discuss the possibility of automating the above procedure by computer—that is, of writing a program that will:

(a) accept coefficients for the polynomials $p_m(s)$ and $q_n(s)$,
(b) determine the zeros $\alpha_1, \alpha_2, \ldots, \alpha_n$ of $q_n(s)$,
(c) decompose $F(s)$ into partial fractions of appropriate form, and
(d) invert $F(s)$ to give $f(t)$, which is then suitably displayed (possibly being plotted against t).

If the scheme seems feasible, write a program to implement it, using polynomials generated in Problems 3.11 and 3.12 as test data.

3.11 At time $t = 0$, the switch is closed in the circuit of Fig. P3.11, which is intended to act as a band-pass filter for frequencies between roughly 3000 and 6000 cps.

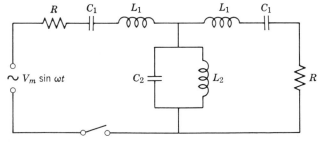

Figure P3.11

Following the method given in Skilling [20], the Laplace transform of the current leaving the generator is given by

$$I(s) = \frac{V_m \omega}{(s^2 + \omega^2)[R + \dfrac{1}{sC_1} + sL_1 + g(s)]},$$

where

$$\frac{1}{g(s)} = \frac{1}{sL_1 + \dfrac{1}{sC_1} + R} + sC_2 + \frac{1}{sL_2}.$$

Express $I(s)$ as the ratio of two polynomials, $p_m(s)/q_n(s)$ (see Problem 3.10). Write a program that will find the zeros of $q_n(s)$. Then invert $I(s)$ with the aid of tables ([21], for example) to give the actual current as a function of time.

Suggested Test Data

$V_m = 10$ volts, $R = 100$ ohms, $C_1 = 0.25 \times 10^{-6}$, $C_2 = 1 \times 10^{-6}$ farads, $L_1 = 0.005$, $L_2 = 0.001$ henrys, with $\omega = 10^4$, 3×10^4, and 10^5 sec^{-1}.

3.12 At time $t = 0$, the switch in the circuit of Fig. P3.12

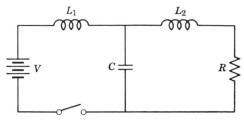

Figure P3.12

is closed. Following the method in Skilling [20], the Laplace transform of the current through the resistor is given by

$$I(s) = \frac{V}{s\{sL_1[1 + sC(sL_2 + R)] + sL_2 + R\}}.$$

If $V = 10$ volts, $L_1 = 0.02$, $L_2 = 0.1$ henrys, $C = 0.5 \times 10^{-6}$ farads, and $R = 50$ ohms, express $I(s)$ in terms of partial fractions (see Problem 3.10). With the aid of a table of Laplace transforms (Spiegel [21], for example), obtain the current through the resistor as a function of time.

3.13 Consider the algorithm of (3.22), $x_{j+1} = F(x_j)$. Let the discrepancy of the nth iterate, x_n, from the true solution, α, be ε_n, so that we may write $x_n = \alpha + \varepsilon_n$. Assuming that $F(x)$ is suitably differentiable, expand $F(x)$ in a Taylor's series about α and show that

$$\varepsilon_{n+1} = F'(\alpha)\varepsilon_n + \frac{F''(\alpha)\varepsilon_n^2}{2!} + \frac{F'''(\alpha)\varepsilon_n^3}{3!} + \cdots.$$

3.14 If the *order* of an iteration (3.22) is defined to be the order of the lowest-order nonzero derivative of $F(x)$ at the solution α, show that for simple roots, Newton's method is a second-order (quadratic) process, while for multiple roots, Newton's method is a first-order process.

3.15 (a) Show that an alternative formulation of Newton's method (see Section 3.7 and Fig. 3.3) can be developed by expansion of $f(z)$ in a Taylor's series about z_0, followed by truncation of the series after the first-derivative term.

(b) Show graphically that for $f(x)$ real, Newton's method exhibits *monotonic convergence* to α (that is, convergence from one side only) if $f(x_0)f''(x_0) > 0$ and $f(x)$ and $f''(x)$ do not change sign on (x_0, α).

(c) Show that Newton's method exhibits *oscillatory convergence* (that is, successive iterates alternate from one side of α to the other) if $f(x_0)f''(x_0) < 0$ and $f(x)$ and $f''(x)$ do not change sign on the interval (x_0, x_1) where $x_0 < \alpha < x_1$.

3.16 Based upon the notions of inverse interpolation (see Problems 1.14 and 1.15) and of iterated linear interpolation (see Problems 1.11, 1.12, and 1.13), develop a root-finding method for a function $f(x)$, single valued on an interval $[x_0, x_n]$ known to contain a zero. Use your method to find the root of the function

$$f(x) = x^3 - 3x + 1$$

with $x_0 = 0$, $x_1 = 0.1$, ..., $x_5 = 0.5$. Compare your results for interpolation of degrees 1 through 5 with the true solution 0.347296 (see Section 3.5).

Suppose that $f(x)$ can be calculated for any x. How would you modify the method just developed to achieve greater accuracy with improved computational efficiency? What conditions must be imposed on $f(x)$ in the interval of interest to insure convergence to a root?

3.17 This problem does not involve numerical methods directly; however, it establishes two functions that will be needed in Problems 3.18, 5.27, 5.30, and 6.34.

Consider two infinitely long surfaces, 1 and 2, that are generated by moving the curves AB and CD in Fig. P3.17a, normal to the plane of the paper. Suppose we wish to evaluate F_{12}, the fraction of thermal radiation emitted by surface 1 that is directly intercepted by surface 2. In the *string method* (see Hottel and Sarofim [23], for example), four threads are stretched tightly between AD, BC, AC, and BD. The geometric view factor F_{12} (see Problem 2.41) is then given in terms of the lengths of the threads by

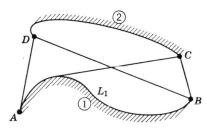

Figure P3.17a

$$F_{12} = \frac{BD + AC - AD - BC}{2L_1},$$

where L_1 is the distance between A and B along the surface AB.

Two infinitely long parallel cylinders of diameter d have their axes a distance w apart, as shown in Fig. P3.17b. Show by the string method that

$$F_{12} = \frac{1}{\pi d}\left(d \sin^{-1}\frac{d}{w} + \sqrt{w^2 - d^2} - w\right).$$

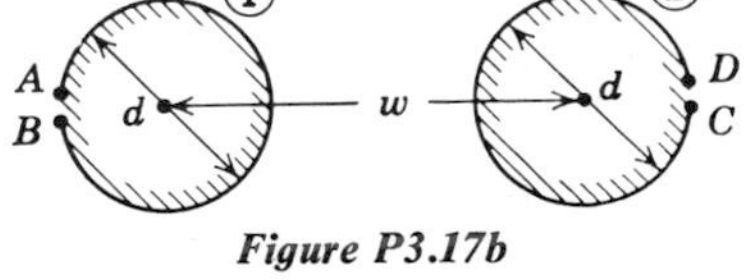

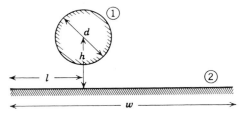

Figure P3.17b

(The points A, B, C, and D between which the threads may be stretched are shown in Fig. P3.17b.) Write a function named CYLCYL that will compute F_{12}. Anticipate that a typical reference will be

F12 = CYLCYL (D, W)

Also write a function named CYLPLN that will compute F_{12} for the infinitely long cylinder and plane shown in Fig. P3.17c. Anticipate that a typical reference will be

F12 = CYLPLN (D, H, L, W)

where the arguments have obvious counterparts in Fig. P3.17c.

Figure P3.17c

3.18 (a) An experiment is to be performed in which the two cylinders of Problem 3.17 are to be spaced so that F_{12} has a specified value θ. Write a program that will use the function CYLCYL to compute the appropriate value of w/d, if such exists, for $\theta = 0.5$, 0.2, 0.1, 0.05, 0.02, and 0.01.

(b) The cylinder and plane of Problem 3.17 are situated with $h = d$ and $l = w/2$. Write a program that will use the function CYLPLN to compute those values of w/d, if any, for which F_{12} equals 0.01, 0.02, 0.05, 0.1, 0.2, 0.49, and 0.5.

3.19 Consider the following approach to the problem of finding a solution to the equation $f(x) = 0$. Start with three points, $(x_0, f(x_0))$, $(x_1, f(x_1))$, and $(x_2, f(x_2))$. Find the second-degree interpolating polynomial (use Lagrange's form (1.43)) passing through the three points, so that

$$(x) \doteq p_2(x) = a_0 + a_1 x + a_2 x^2.$$

Now, solve for the two roots of $p_2(x)$ using the quadratic formula. Let the two roots be r_1 and r_2, and evaluate the corresponding functional values, $f(r_1)$ and $f(r_2)$. Let x_3 be r_1 or r_2, depending on which of $|f(r_1)|$ or $|f(r_2)|$ is smaller. Next, fit the points $(x_1, f(x_1))$, $(x_2, f(x_2))$, and $(x_3, f(x_3))$ with a second-degree interpolating polynomial, solve for the roots, choose x_4 to be that root which yields the smaller magnitude for the functional value, etc. Continue this process of fitting successive second-degree polynomials until, if convergence occurs, the functional value assumes some arbitrarily small value. Note that this procedure, known as *Muller's method* [26], allows the isolation of complex as well as real roots of $f(x)$.

Implement Muller's method as a function, named MULLER, with argument list

(X, F, EPS, ITMAX, ITER)

where X is a vector of length three containing x_1, x_2, and x_3 in X(1), X(2), and X(3), respectively, F is another function that computes $f(x)$ when required, EPS is a small positive number used in the convergence test for terminating the iteration, ITMAX is a maximum allowable number of iterations, should convergence not take place, and ITER is the number of iterations actually performed (set to ITMAX + 1 for failure to converge). The final estimate of the root should be returned as the value of MULLER. Assume that all the roots of $f(x)$ are real; if the algorithm yields complex roots at some stage, the function should set ITER to zero and return to the calling program. Test the program with some trial functions whose roots are known.

How would you modify the function so that it could isolate complex conjugate roots of a polynomial with real coefficients?

3.20   The 6J5 triode shown in Fig. P3.20 is used for amplifying an a-c input signal of small amplitude. The amplifier gain

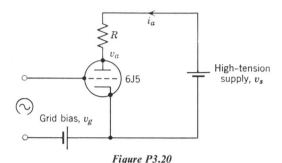

Figure P3.20

A (ratio of rms output a-c voltage developed across the load resistor R to the rms input voltage) is

$$A = -\frac{g_m r_p R}{r_p + R},$$

where r_p is the dynamic plate resistance and g_m is the transconductance (see Problem 2.48). If the high-tension supply voltage is constant at v_s, we have the following additional relation involving the anode voltage v_a and the anode current i_a as unknowns:

$$R i_a = v_s - v_a.$$

If v_g, v_s, and R are specified, devise a procedure for computing v_a and the amplifier gain A. Write a program to implement the method, making use of the functions already developed in Problems 1.42 and 2.48 for the 6J5 triode. Suggested test data (v_s and v_g in V, R in kΩ): $v_s = 300$, $v_g = -6.5$, $R = 10$; $v_s = 300$, $v_g = -16.2$, $R = 22$; $v_s = 300$, $v_g = -2.3$, $R = 22$.

3.21   The first-order irreversible chemical reaction $A \rightarrow B$ has a reaction rate constant k hr^{-1} at a temperature T. A stirred batch reactor is charged with V cu ft of reactant solution of initial concentration a_0 lb moles/cu ft and is operated isothermally at a temperature T for t_0 hours. The reaction products are then removed for product separation, and the reactor vessel is cleaned for subsequent reloading with fresh reactant.

The reactor is operated cyclicly; that is, the process of loading fresh reactant, allowing the reaction to proceed, dumping the product, and cleaning the reactor is repeated indefinitely. If the down time between reaction cycles is t_c hours, show that the reaction time t_0 required to maximize the overall yield of product B per hour is given by the solution of the equation

$$t_0 - \ln(t_0 k + t_c k + 1)/k = 0.$$

Solve this equation for the following test data:

V	(cu ft)	10	10	10	10
a_0	(lb moles/cu ft)	0.1	0.1	0.1	0.1
k	(hr^{-1})	2.5	2.5	1.0	1.0
t_c	(hr)	0.5	1.0	1.0	2.0

3.22   The isothermal irreversible second-order constant volume reaction $A + B \rightarrow C + D$ has a velocity constant k. A

volumetric flow rate v of a solution containing equal inlet concentrations a_0 each of A and B is fed to two CSTRs (continuous stirred tank reactors) in series, each of volume V. Denoting the exit concentrations of A from the first and second CSTRs by a_1 and a_2, respectively, rate balances give:

$$k a_1^2 = \frac{v(a_0 - a_1)}{V},$$

$$k a_2^2 = \frac{v(a_1 - a_2)}{V}.$$

If $k = 0.075$ liter/g mole min, $v = 30$ liter/min, $a_0 = 1.6$ g moles/liter, and the final conversion is 80% (that is, $a_2/a_0 = 0.2$), determine the necessary volume V (liter) of each reactor. For an extension to n CSTRs in series, see Problem 5.31.

3.23   Assume that three successive iterates, x_k, x_{k+1}, and x_{k+2}, have been obtained using (3.22), $x_{j+1} = F(x_j)$, and that α is the required solution of $f(x) = 0$. Using the mean-value theorem (see Section 1.6), show that

$$x_{k+1} - \alpha = (x_k - \alpha) F'(\xi_1),$$
$$x_{k+2} - \alpha = (x_{k+1} - \alpha) F'(\xi_2),$$

where ξ_1 is in (x_k, α) and ξ_2 is in (x_{k+1}, α).

If $\xi_1 = \xi_2$, show that the solution α is given by

$$\alpha = x_{k+2} - \frac{(\Delta x_{k+1})^2}{\Delta^2 x_k},$$

where $\Delta x_{k+1} = x_{k+2} - x_{k+1}$ and $\Delta^2 x_k = x_{k+2} - 2x_{k+1} + x_k$.

3.24   In general, ξ_1 and ξ_2 of Problem 3.23 will *not* be equal. However, if x_k, x_{k+1}, and x_{k+2} are near α, then $\xi_1 \doteq \xi_2$, so that the next iterate may be taken as

$$\bar{x}_{k+3} = x_{k+2} - \frac{(\Delta x_{k+1})^2}{\Delta^2 x_k}.$$

If $x_{j+1} = F(x_j)$ is a first-order process (see Problem 3.14), this extrapolation technique usually accelerates convergence to α, that is, $|\bar{x}_{k+3} - \alpha| < |x_{k+3} - \alpha|$, where $x_{k+3} = F(x_{k+2})$.

The iterative process that employs the sequence of calculations

$$x_2 = F(x_1),$$
$$x_3 = F(x_2),$$
$$\bar{x}_4 = x_3 - (\Delta x_2)^2/\Delta^2 x_1,$$
$$x_5 = F(\bar{x}_4),$$
$$x_6 = F(x_5),$$
$$\bar{x}_7 = x_6 - (\Delta x_5)^2/\Delta^2 \bar{x}_4,$$
$$x_8 = F(\bar{x}_7),$$
$$\text{etc.,}$$

is known as *Aitken's Δ^2 process.*

Use Aitken's Δ^2 process to find the three roots of $f(x) = x^3 - 3x + 1 = 0$ with

$$x_{j+1} = (x_j^3 + 1)/3, \qquad x_1 = 0.5;$$

$$x_{j+1} = \frac{3}{2} x_j - \frac{1}{6}(x_j^3 + 1), \quad x_1 = 1.5 \text{ and } x_1 = -1.5.$$

In each case, compare the sequence of iterates with the results of Table 3.5.

3.25 Devise a procedure, based on one of the standard equation-solving techniques, for evaluating $x^{1/n}$. Assume that x is a real positive number, that n is a positive integer, and that the real positive nth root is required.

3.26 Devise a procedure for evaluating the n complex roots, $x^{1/n}$, of a real positive number x. Assume that n is a positive integer.

3.27 Determine the first ten positive roots of the equation

$$\cosh \phi \cos \phi = -1,$$

which is important in the theory of vibrating reeds (see Wylie [18], for example). These roots may be compared with similar values found in Problem 4.32.

3.28 Compute to at least six significant figures the first 50 positive roots of the equation $\beta \tan \beta = h$, for $h = 0.1$, 1, and 10. These roots will be needed later in Problem 7.24.

3.29 Write a subroutine, named WARD, that implements Ward's method (see Section 3.6) for finding a root, $\alpha = \beta + i\gamma$, of a function $f(z)$ of the complex variable $z = x + iy$, where

$$f(z) = u(x,y) + iv(x,y).$$

Let a typical call on the subroutine be

CALL WARD (X, Y, FR, FI, HX, HY, EPSHX, EPSHY, ITMAX, W)

Here, FR and FI are functions of two variables, X and Y, that return the real part of $f(z)$, that is, $u(X,Y)$, and the imaginary part of $f(z)$, that is, $v(X,Y)$, respectively, when needed. Upon entering the routine, the first estimates of β and γ should be available in X and Y. The searching strategy should employ HX and HY as the initial step sizes in the x and y directions respectively. The searching step sizes should be halved when appropriate (without modifying the values of HX and HY in the calling program) until the step size in the x direction is smaller than EPSHX and the step size in the y direction is smaller than EPSHY, or until the total number of calls upon FR(X, Y) and FI(X, Y) exceeds ITMAX. In either event, upon return, X and Y should contain the final estimates of β and γ, respectively; W should be assigned the value of $w(x,y)$ for the final iteration, where $w(x,y) = |u(x,y)| + |v(x,y)|$.

Write a short calling program, and appropriate functions FR and FI, to find a root of

$$f(z) = z^4 - 2z^3 + 1.25z^2 - 0.25z - 0.75$$

with various starting points, including $z = 1 + i$. Compare your results with those of Tables 3.6 and 3.7.

3.30 Van der Waals's equation of state for an imperfect gas is

$$\left(P + \frac{a}{v^2}\right)(v - b) = RT,$$

where P is the pressure (atm), v is the molal volume (liters/mole), T is the absolute temperature ($°K$), R is the gas constant (0.082054 liter atm/mole $°K$), and a and b are constants that depend on the particular gas.

Write a program that will read values for P, T, a, and b as data, and that will compute the corresponding value(s) of v that satisfies the van der Waals equation. The test values in Table P3.30 for a (liter² atm/mole²) and b (liter/mole) are given by Keller [27].

Table P3.30

Gas	a	b
Carbon dioxide	3.592	0.04267
Dimethylaniline	37.49	0.1970
Helium	0.03412	0.02370
Nitric oxide	1.340	0.02789

Note: If $T \geqslant T_c$, where $T_c = 8a/27Rb$ is the critical temperature (above which a gas cannot be liquefied), there will be only one real root for v; otherwise, there will be either one or three real roots, depending on the particular values of P and T. If there are three roots, $v_1 < v_2 < v_3$, then v_1 and v_3 correspond to the liquid and vapor molal volumes, respectively, and v_2 has no physical significance. In any event, investigate the results for a wide range of values for P and T.

3.31 In a *hydraulic jump*, a liquid stream of depth D_1, flowing with velocity u_1, suddenly increases its depth to D_2, with a corresponding reduction in velocity. On the basis of mass and momentum balances, it can be shown that

$$D_2 = \frac{D_1}{2}\left[\sqrt{1 + \frac{8u_1^2}{gD_1}} - 1\right],$$

in which g is the gravitational acceleration. A hydraulic jump is possible only if $u_1 > \sqrt{gD_1}$.

If values of u_1 and D_2 are known, devise one or more schemes for determining: (a) if a hydraulic jump is possible, and (b), if so, the corresponding value of D_1. Write a program to implement the method; the input data will consist of pairs of values for u_1 and D_2.

3.32 Write a function, named CPOLY, with argument list (N, X), that evaluates the nth-degree polynomial $C_n(x)$ (see Problem 2.27) at argument $x = $ X, where $n = $ N may be any of 2, 3, 4, 5, 6, 7, 9. The coefficients of the polynomials should be preset in a suitable arrangement using a DATA (or equivalent) statement. The value of $C_n(x)$ should be returned as the value of CPOLY.

Next, write a main program that uses the half-interval method (see Fig. 3.5) to find the roots of each of the seven polynomials evaluated by CPOLY (see Problem 2.28 for a further use for the roots). The program should read a value for DELTA, an error tolerance for the roots, equivalent to Δ_n in (3.33), then calculate the n roots of $C_n(x)$, for $n = 2, 3, 4, 5, 6, 7, 9$, and print the results in tabular form.

Calculational effort can be reduced considerably by noting the following:

(a) All n roots of $C_n(x)$ lie on $(-1,1)$.

(b) For n even, $C_n(x)$ is an even function of x. Hence, the n roots occur in $n/2$ root-pairs, symmetrically arranged about the origin. Attention can be confined to $(-1,0)$ or $(0,1)$.

(c) For n odd, $C_n(x)$ is an odd function of x. Hence, there is a root at the origin, and the remaining $n - 1$ roots occur in $(n - 1)/2$ root-pairs, symmetrically arranged about the origin. Again, attention can be confined to $(-1,0)$ or $(0,1)$.

(d) No two roots for any of the polynomials are more closely spaced than 0.05.

A strategy similar to that used in Example 3.4 may be employed for solving the problem. Note that, because the above comments also hold for the Legendre polynomials, the program of Example 3.4 could be modified to halve approximately the number of calculations required to isolate the roots.

3.33 Devise two or more practical schemes for evaluating, within a prescribed tolerance ε, all the roots of the nth-degree Laguerre polynomial. Write a program that implements one of these methods. The input data should consist of values for n and ε. Your program should automatically generate the necessary coefficients of the appropriate Laguerre polynomial, according to equation (2.69). Check your computed values with those in Table 2.4.

The problem may be repeated for the Hermite polynomials, summarized in equation (2.75). The computed roots may be checked against those given in Table 2.6.

3.34 For the isentropic flow of a perfect gas from a reservoir through a converging-diverging nozzle, operating with sonic velocity at the throat, it may be shown that

$$\frac{A_t^2}{A^2} = \left(\frac{\gamma+1}{2}\right)^{(\gamma+1)/(\gamma-1)} \left(\frac{2}{\gamma-1}\right)\left[\left(\frac{P}{P_1}\right)^{2/\gamma} - \left(\frac{P}{P_1}\right)^{(\gamma+1)/\gamma}\right].$$

Here, P is the pressure at a point where the cross-sectional area of the nozzle is A, P_1 is the reservoir pressure, A_t is the throat area, and γ is the ratio of the specific heat at constant pressure to that at constant volume.

If A_t, γ, P_1, and $A\;(>A_t)$ are known, devise a scheme for computing the *two* possible pressures P that satisfy the above equation. Implement your method on the computer.

Suggested Test Data

$A_t = 0.1$ sq ft, $\gamma = 1.41$, $P_1 = 100$ psia, and $A = 0.12$ sq ft.

3.35 A spherical pocket of high-pressure gas, initially of radius r_0 and pressure p_0, expands radially outwards in an adiabatic submarine explosion. For the special case of a gas with $\gamma = 4/3$ (ratio of specific heat at constant pressure to that at constant volume) the radius r at any subsequent time t is given by [22]:

$$\frac{t}{r_0}\sqrt{\frac{p_0}{\rho}} = \left(1 + \frac{2}{3}\alpha + \frac{1}{5}\alpha^2\right)(2\alpha)^{1/2},$$

in which $\alpha = (r/r_0) - 1$, ρ is the density of water, and consistent units are assumed. During the adiabatic expansion, the gas pressure is given by $p/p_0 = (r_0/r)^{3\gamma}$.

Develop a procedure for computing the pressure and radius of the gas at any time.

Suggested Test Data (Not in Consistent Units)

$p_0 = 10^4$ lb$_f$/sq in, $\rho = 64$ lb$_m$/cu ft, $r_0 = 1$ ft, $t = 0.5, 1, 2, 3, 5,$ and 10 milliseconds.

3.36 F moles/hr of an n-component natural gas stream are introduced as feed to the flash vaporization tank shown in Fig. P3.36. The resulting vapor and liquid streams are withdrawn at the rates of V and L moles/hr, respectively. The mole fractions of the components in the feed, vapor, and liquid streams are designated by z_i, y_i, and x_i, respectively ($i = 1, 2, \ldots, n$).

Assuming vapor/liquid equilibrium and steady-state operation, we have

Overall balance $F = L + V$,

Individual balance $z_i F = x_i L + y_i V,$

Equilibrium relation $K_i = y_i/x_i.$ $\Big\}\; i = 1, 2, \ldots, n.$

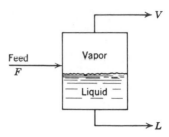

Figure P3.36

Here, K_i is the equilibrium constant for the ith component at the prevailing temperature and pressure in the tank. From these equations and the fact that $\sum_{i=1}^{n} x_i = \sum_{i=1}^{n} y_i = 1$, show that

$$\sum_{i=1}^{n} \frac{z_i(K_i - 1)}{V(K_i - 1) + F} = 0.$$

Write a program that reads values for F, the z_i, and the K_i as data, and then uses Newton's method to solve the last equation above for V. The program should also compute the values of L, the x_i, and the y_i by using the first three equations given above.

The test data [16], shown in Table P3.36, relate to the flashing of a natural gas stream at 1600 psia and 120°F.

Table P3.36

Component	i	z_i	K_i
Carbon dioxide	1	0.0046	1.65
Methane	2	0.8345	3.09
Ethane	3	0.0381	0.72
Propane	4	0.0163	0.39
Isobutane	5	0.0050	0.21
n-Butane	6	0.0074	0.175
Pentanes	7	0.0287	0.093
Hexanes	8	0.0220	0.065
Heptanes+	9	0.0434	0.036
		1.0000	

Assume that $F = 1000$ moles/hr. A small tolerance ε and an upper limit on the number of iterations should also be read as data. What would be a good value V_1 for starting the iteration?

3.37 For turbulent flow of a fluid in a smooth pipe, the following relation exists between the friction factor c_f and the Reynolds number Re (see, for example, Kay [17]):

$$\sqrt{\frac{1}{c_f}} = -0.4 + 1.74 \ln(Re\sqrt{c_f}).$$

Compute c_f for $Re = 10^4$, 10^5, and 10^6.

3.38 For steady flow of an incompressible fluid in a rough pipe of length L ft and inside diameter D in., the pressure drop ΔP lb$_f$/sq in. is given by

$$\Delta P = \frac{f_M \rho u_m^2 L}{24 g_c D},$$

where ρ is the fluid density (lb$_m$/cu ft), u_m is the mean fluid velocity (ft/sec), and f_M is the Moody friction factor (dimensionless). For the indicated units, the conversion factor g_c

equals 32.2 lb_m ft/lb_f sec². The friction factor f_M is a function of the pipe roughness ε (in.) and the Reynolds number,

$$Re = \frac{D\rho u_m}{12\mu},$$

where μ is the fluid viscosity in lb_m/ft sec. For $Re \leqslant 2000$,

$$f_M = 64/Re,$$

while for $Re > 2000$, f_M is given by the solution of the *Colebrook equation*,

$$\frac{1}{\sqrt{f_M}} = -2 \log_{10}\left(\frac{\varepsilon}{3.7D} + \frac{2.51}{Re\sqrt{f_M}}\right).$$

A good starting guess for the iterative solution of this equation may be found from the *Blasius equation*,

$$f_M = 0.316 Re^{-0.25},$$

appropriate for turbulent flow in smooth ($\varepsilon = 0$) pipes.

Write a function, named PDROP, that could be called with the statement

DELTAP = PDROP (Q, D, L, RHO, MU, E)

where the value of PDROP is the pressure drop in lb_f/sq in. for a flow rate of Q gal/min of a fluid with density RHO and viscosity MU through a pipe of length L, inside diameter D, and roughness E. Note that MU and L must be of type REAL

To test PDROP, write a program that reads values for Q, D, L, RHO, MU, and E, calls upon PDROP to compute the pressure drop, prints the data and result, and returns to read another data set.

Suggested Test Data

Q	(gal/min)	170	4
D	(in.)	3.068	0.622
L	(ft)	10000	100
RHO	(lb_m/cu ft)	62.4	80.2
MU	(lb_m/ft sec)	0.0007	0.05
E	(in.)	0.002	0.0005

3.39 As shown in Fig. P3.39, a centrifugal pump is used to transfer a liquid from one tank to another, with both tanks at the same level.

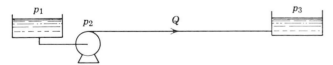

Figure P3.39

The pump raises the pressure of the liquid from p_1 (atmospheric pressure) to p_2, but this pressure is gradually lost because of friction inside the long pipe and, at the exit, p_3 is back down to atmospheric pressure.

The pressure rise in psig across the pump is given approximately by the empirical relation

$$p_2 - p_1 = a - bQ^{1.5},$$

where a and b are constants that depend on the particular pump being used, and Q is the flow rate in gpm. Also, from equations (5.4.2) and (5.4.3), the pressure drop in a horizontal pipe of length L feet and internal diameter D in. is given by

$$p_2 - p_3 = 2.16 \times 10^{-4}\frac{f_M \rho L Q^2}{D^5},$$

where ρ is the density (lb_m/cu ft) of the liquid being pumped. For the present purposes, the Moody friction factor f_M is treated as a constant although, as discussed in Problem 3.38, it really depends on the pipe roughness and on the Reynolds number in the pipe.

Write a program whose input will include values for a, b, ρ, L, D, f_M, ε (a tolerance used in convergence testing), and n (maximum number of iterations), and that will proceed to compute the flow rate Q. The program output should consist of printed values for the specified input data, the solution Q, the intermediate pressure p_2, and the actual number of iterations used. If the method fails to converge, a message should be printed to that effect. Use the two sets of test data shown in Table P3.39. Select values of ε and n that seem appropriate.

Table P3.39

	Set 1	Set 2
D, in.	1.049	2.469
L, ft	50.0	210.6
ρ, lb_m/cu ft (kerosene)	51.4	—
(water)	—	62.4
f_M, dimensionless	0.032	0.026
a, psi	16.7	38.5
b, psi/(gpm)$^{1.5}$	0.052	0.0296

3.40 Rework Problem 3.39, now allowing for a variation of the Moody friction factor f_M with pipe roughness and Reynolds number, as in Problem 3.38. Use the same two sets of test data, and assume in both cases that the pipe roughness is 0.0005 ft, corresponding to galvanized iron pipe. Appropriate viscosities (at 68°F, in centipoise) are $\mu = 2.46$ (kerosene) and 1.005 (water). For each data set, the program should print values for f_M and the Reynolds number.

3.41 A semi-infinite medium is at a uniform initial temperature T_0. For $t > 0$, a constant heat flux density q is maintained into the medium at the surface $x = 0$. If the thermal conductivity and thermal diffusivity of the medium are k and α, respectively, it can be shown that the resulting temperature $T = T(x,t)$ is given by

$$T = T_0 + \frac{q}{k}\left[2\sqrt{\frac{\alpha t}{\pi}}\, e^{-x^2/4\alpha t} - x \operatorname{erfc}\frac{x}{2\sqrt{\alpha t}}\right].$$

If all other values are given, devise a scheme for finding the time t taken for the temperature at a distance x to reach a preassigned value T^*. Implement your method on the computer.

Suggested Test Data

$T_0 = 70°F$, $q = 300$ BTU/hr sq ft, $k = 1.0$ BTU/hr ft °F, $\alpha = 0.04$ sq ft/hr, $x = 1.0$ ft, and $T^* = 120°F$.

3.42 A bare vertical wall of a combustion chamber containing hot gases is exposed to the surrounding air. Heat is lost at a rate q BTU/hr sq ft by conduction through the wall and by subsequent radiation and convection to the surroundings, assumed to behave as a black-body radiator. Let T_g, T_w, and T_a denote the temperatures of the gases, the exposed surface of the wall, and the air, respectively. If σ is the Stefan-Boltzmann constant, 0.171×10^{-8} BTU/hr sq ft °R⁴, and ε, t, and k denote the emissivity, thickness, and thermal conductivity, respectively, of the wall, we have

$$q = k(T_g - T_w)/t = \varepsilon\sigma(T_{wR}^4 - T_{aR}^4) + h(T_w - T_a).$$

The extra subscript R emphasizes that the absolute or Rankine temperature must be used in the radiation term ($°R = °F + 460$). The convection heat transfer coefficient h, BTU/hr sq ft °F, is given by the correlation $h = 0.21\,(T_w - T_a)^{1/3}$, suggested by Rohsenow and Choi [24].

Assuming that T_g, T_a, ε, k, and t are specified, rearrange the above relations to give a single equation in the outside wall temperature T_w. Compute T_w for the following test data: $T_a = 100°$F, $t = 0.0625$ ft, with (a) $T_g = 2100°$F, $k = 1.8$ (fused alumina) BTU/hr ft °F, $\varepsilon = 0.39$, (b) $T_g = 1100$, $k = 25.9$ (steel), $\varepsilon = 0.14$ (freshly polished) and $\varepsilon = 0.79$ (oxidized). In each case, also compute q and the relative importance of radiation and convection as mechanisms for transferring heat from the hot wall to the air.

3.43 The rate $qd\lambda$ at which radiant energy leaves unit area of the surface of a black body within the wavelength range λ to $\lambda + d\lambda$, is given by Planck's law:

$$qd\lambda = \frac{2\pi hc^2\,d\lambda}{\lambda^5(e^{hc/k\lambda T} - 1)}, \qquad \frac{\text{ergs}}{\text{cm}^2\text{sec}}$$

where c = speed of light, 2.997925×10^{10} cm/sec,

    h = Planck's constant, 6.6256×10^{-27} erg sec,

    k = Boltzmann's constant, 1.38054×10^{-16} erg/°K,

    T = absolute temperature, °K,

    λ = wavelength, cm.

For a given surface temperature T, devise a scheme for determining the wavelength λ_{max} for which the radiant energy is the most intense, that is, λ corresponding to $dq/d\lambda = 0$. Write a program that implements the scheme. The input data should consist of values for T, such as 1000, 2000, 3000, 4000°K; the output should consist of printed values for λ_{max} and the corresponding value of q. Verify that Wien's displacement law, $\lambda_{max}T$ = constant, is obeyed.

3.44 Write a function, named INVERF, that computes the *inverse error function*, x, where the error function is given by

$$\text{erf } x = \frac{2}{\sqrt{\pi}}\int_0^x e^{-t^2}\,dt.$$

The function should have arguments (ERFX,TOL) where ERFX is the specified value of the error function ($0 \leqslant$ ERFX < 1) for which the inverse error function, x, is desired, and TOL is the maximum error allowed in the calculated estimate of x. The final estimated value of the inverse error function should be returned as the value of INVERF (real).

The *regula falsi* method of (3.34) should be used to find the

x corresponding to ERFX, and a composite Gauss-Legendre quadrature (see Problem 2.21) should be used to evaluate the error function when needed. Since, to ten significant figures, erf $x = 1.000000000$ for $x > 10.$, $x_{L1} = 0$ and $x_{R1} = 10.$ are satisfactory starting values for (3.34).

Write a short main program to test INVERF. Suggested values for ERFX and the corresponding tabulated values for x are:

ERFX	x
0.0000000000	0.00
0.1124629161	0.10
0.7111556337	0.75
0.8427007929	1.00
0.9661051465	1.50
0.9953222650	2.00
1.0000000000	10.00

3.45 Repeat Problem 2.15, with the following variation. Assume that the exchanger length L is a known quantity, to be included in the data, and that the resulting exit temperature T_2 is to be computed by the program. The problem is now to find the root of

$$f(T_2) = \frac{m}{\pi D}\int_{T_1}^{T_2} \frac{c_p dT}{h(T_s - T)} - L = 0,$$

for which the *regula falsi*, half-interval, or false-position method could be used.

An alternative method for finding T_2 is discussed in Problem 6.19.

3.46 A vertical mast of length L has Young's modulus E and a weight w per unit length; its second moment of area is I. Timoshenko [25] shows that the mast will just begin to buckle under its own weight when $\beta = 4wL^3/9EI$ is the smallest root of

$$1 + \sum_{n=1}^{\infty} c_n\beta^n = 0.$$

The first coefficient is $c_1 = -3/8$, and the subsequent ones are given by the recursion relation

$$c_n = -\frac{3c_{n-1}}{4n(3n - 1)}.$$

Determine the appropriate value of β.

3.47 The stream function

$$\psi = Uy\left(1 - \frac{a^2}{r^2}\right) + \kappa \ln\frac{r}{a}$$

represents inviscid fluid flow past a circular cylinder of radius a with two effects superimposed [22]: (a) a stream whose velocity is uniformly U in the negative x direction far away from the cylinder, and (b) an anticlockwise circulation of strength κ round the cylinder. Here, $r = (x^2 + y^2)^{1/2}$ is the radial distance from the center of the cylinder, whose cross section is shown in Fig. P3.47. Note that the streamline $\psi = 0$ includes the surface of the cylinder.

Write a program that will produce graphical output (in the style of Examples 6.3, 6.5, 7.1 and 8.5) showing points lying on selected streamlines within the dimensionless interval

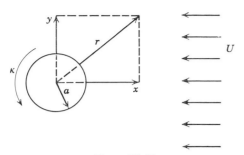

Figure P3.47

$x/a = \pm 5$. For a given ψ, increment x/a in steps of Δ between these limits, and use the above equation to compute the corresponding dimensionless ordinates y/a.

Suggested Test Data

$\Delta = 0.5$, with ψ/aU (dimensionless) varying from -2.5 to 2.5 in ten equal steps, for $\kappa/aU = 1, 2$, and 3 in turn.

This problem could be extended to compute the streamlines for flow past an aerofoil [22].

3.48 The analytical solution of Problem 7.31 is given on page 285 of Carslaw and Jaeger [28]. In slightly rearranged form, we have

$$\frac{T_A - T_s}{T_f - T_s} = \frac{\text{erf} \dfrac{x}{2\sqrt{\alpha_A t}}}{\text{erf } \eta},$$

$$\frac{T_0 - T_B}{T_0 - T_f} = \frac{\text{erfc} \dfrac{x}{2\sqrt{\alpha_B t}}}{\text{erfc}(\eta\sqrt{\alpha_A/\alpha_B})},$$

$$d = 2\eta\sqrt{\alpha_A t},$$

where η is the solution of

$$\frac{e^{-\eta^2}}{\text{erf } \eta} - \frac{k_B}{k_A}\frac{\alpha_A^{1/2}}{\alpha_B^{1/2}}\left(\frac{T_0 - T_f}{T_f - T_s}\right)\frac{e^{-\alpha_A\eta^2/\alpha_B}}{\text{erfc}(\eta\sqrt{\alpha_A/\alpha_B})} = \frac{\eta L\pi^{1/2}}{c_{pA}(T_f - T_s)}.$$

See Problem 7.31 for the definitions and units of all quantities.

In this connection, write a program that will read values for T_0 (suggested test value $= 37$), $T_s(20)$, $T_f(32)$, $k_A(1.30)$, $k_B(0.343)$, $\rho_A(57.3)$, $\rho_B(62.4)$, $c_{pA}(0.502)$, $c_{pB}(1.01)$, $L(144)$, and ε, and that will then proceed to solve the last equation above for η, within the specified tolerance ε. The value of η thus computed can then be used to evaluate the analytical solution for the purpose mentioned in Problem 7.31.

3.49 Methane and excess moist air are fed continuously to a torch. Write a program that will compute, within 5°F, the adiabatic flame temperature T^* for complete combustion according to the reaction

$$CH_4 + 2O_2 = CO_2 + 2H_2O.$$

The data for the program should include the table of thermal properties given below, together with values for T_m and T_a (the incoming methane and air temperatures, respectively, °F), p (the percentage of excess air over that theoretically required), and w (lb moles water vapor per lb mole incoming air on a dry basis). Assume that dry air contains 79 mole % nitrogen and 21 mole % oxygen.

The heat capacities for the five components present can be computed as a function of temperature from the general relation

$$c_{p_i} = a_i + b_i T_k + c_i T_k^2 + d_i/T_k^2 \text{ cal/g mole °K},$$

where $i = 1, 2, 3, 4$, and 5 for CH_4, O_2, N_2, H_2O (vapor), and CO_2, respectively, and T_k is in °K. Table P3.49 [19] also shows the standard heat of formation at 298°K, $\Delta H^f_{i,298}$ cal/g mole, for each component.

Table P3.49

i	a_i	b_i	c_i	d_i	$\Delta H^f_{i,298}$
1	5.34	0.0115	0.0	0.0	$-17889.$
2	8.27	0.000258	0.0	$-187700.$	0.0
3	6.50	0.00100	0.0	0.0	0.0
4	8.22	0.00015	1.34×10^{-6}	0.0	$-57798.$
5	10.34	0.00274	0.0	$-195500.$	$-94052.$

Suggested Test Data

$T_m = T_a = 60°\text{F}$, $p = 0$ to 100% in steps of 10%, $w = 0$ and 0.015.

3.50 Producer gas consisting of 35 mole % carbon monoxide and 65 mole % nitrogen is to be burned with an oxidant (either dry air or pure oxygen) in an adiabatic reactor; all gases enter at a temperature T_0 °F. The pressure is uniformly P atm throughout the system. For the reaction,

$$CO + \tfrac{1}{2}O_2 = CO_2,$$

which does not necessarily go to completion, the standard free energy and enthalpy changes at 298°K are [19] $\Delta G^0_{298} = -61,452$ and $\Delta H^0_{298} = -67,636$ cal/g mole, respectively. The standard states for all components are pure gases at one atmosphere, and ideal gas behavior may be assumed.

The constant-pressure heat capacities for the four components present can be computed as functions of temperature T_k °K from the general relation

$$c_{p_i} = a_i + b_i T_k + c_i T_k^2 \text{ cal/g mole °K}.$$

For the gases involved, the constants are shown in Table P3.50.

Table P3.50

Gas	i	a_i	$b_i \times 10^3$	$c_i \times 10^6$
CO	1	6.25	2.091	-0.459
O_2	2	6.13	2.990	-0.806
CO_2	3	6.85	8.533	-2.475
N_2	4	6.30	1.819	-0.345

Write a program that will compute, within 5°F, the adiabatic flame temperature T^* and the fractional conversion z of carbon monoxide, investigating both oxidants in turn. Assume that air is 79 mole % nitrogen and 21 mole % oxygen.

Suggested Test Data

$T_0 = 200°\text{F}$, $P = 1$ and 10 atm, f (oxidant supplied, as a fraction of the stoichiometric amount required) varying from 0.6 to 1.8 in steps of 0.1.

How much of each type of oxidant should be used to obtain the highest possible flame temperature?

3.51 Write a general-purpose subroutine, named QD, that implements the quotient-difference algorithm of Section 3.9, for estimating the roots of a polynomial function of a complex variable,

$$p_n(z) = a_0 z^n + a_1 z^{n-1} + \cdots + a_n,$$

where the coefficients may be complex. As an embellishment, consider the possibility of having QD improve each of the root estimates, using Newton's method.

Bibliography

1. P. Henrici, *Elements of Numerical Analysis*, Wiley, New York, 1964.
2. H. A. Luther, "A Class of Iterative Techniques for the Factorization of Polynomials," *Communications of the A.C.M.*, **7**, 177–179 (1964).
3. J. A. Ward, "The Down-Hill Method of Solving $f(z) = 0$," *Journal of the A.C.M.*, **4**, 148–150 (1957).
4. F. B. Hildebrand, *Introduction to Numerical Analysis*, McGraw-Hill, New York, 1956.
5. G. Chrystal, *Textbook of Algebra*, I, Chelsea, New York, 1952.
6. H. A. Luther, "An Iterative Factorization Technique for Polynomials," *Communications of the A.C.M.*, **6**, 108–110 (1963).
7. H. S. Wilf, *Mathematics for the Physical Sciences*, Wiley, New York, 1962.
8. A. M. Ostrowski, *Solution of Equations and Systems of Equations*, Academic Press, New York, 1966.
9. C. Fröberg, *Introduction to Numerical Analysis*, Addison-Wesley, Reading, Massachusetts, 1965.
10. *Modern Computing Methods*, Notes on Applied Science, No. 16, Her Majesty's Stationery Office, London, 1961.
11. A. S. Householder, *Principles of Numerical Analysis*, McGraw-Hill, New York, 1953.
12. D. R. Hartree, *Numerical Analysis*, Oxford University Press, London, 1958.
13. E. L. Stiefel, *An Introduction to Numerical Mathematics*, Academic Press, New York, 1963.
14. J. F. Traub, *Iterative Methods for the Solution of Equations*, Prentice-Hall, Englewood Cliffs, New Jersey, 1964.
15. C. F. Prutton and S. H. Maron, *Fundamental Principles of Physical Chemistry*, Macmillan, New York, 1953.
16. D. L. Katz *et al.*, *Handbook of Natural Gas Engineering*, McGraw-Hill, New York, 1959.
17. J. M. Kay, *An Introduction to Fluid Mechanics and Heat Transfer*, 2nd ed., Cambridge University Press, London, 1963.
18. C. R. Wylie, *Advanced Engineering Mathematics*, McGraw-Hill, New York, 1951.
19. J. H. Perry, ed., *Chemical Engineers' Handbook*, 3rd ed., McGraw-Hill, New York, 1950.
20. H. H. Skilling, *Electrical Engineering Circuits*, 2nd ed., Wiley, 1965.
21. M. R. Spiegel, *Theory and Problems of Laplace Transforms*, Schaum Publishing Co., New York, 1965.
22. L. M. Milne-Thomson, *Theoretical Hydrodynamics*, 4th ed., Macmillan, London, 1960.
23. H. C. Hottel and A. F. Sarofim, *Radiative Transfer*, McGraw-Hill, New York, 1967.
24. W. M. Rohsenow and H. Y. Choi, *Heat, Mass, and Momentum Transfer*, Prentice-Hall, Englewood Cliffs, New Jersey, 1961.
25. S. Timoshenko, *Theory of Elastic Stability*, McGraw-Hill, New York, 1936.
26. D. E. Muller, "A Method for Solving Algebraic Equations Using an Automatic Computer," *Math. Tables Aids Comput.*, **10**, 205–208 (1956).
27. R. Keller, *Basic Tables in Chemistry*, McGraw-Hill, New York, 1967.
28. H. S. Carslaw and J. C. Jaeger, *Conduction of Heat in Solids*, 2nd ed., Oxford University Press, London, 1959.
29. S. Lin, "A Method for Finding Roots of Algebraic Equations," *J. Math. and Phys.* **22**, 60–77 (1943).

CHAPTER 4

Matrices and Related Topics

4.1 Notation and Preliminary Concepts

This section serves to summarize the knowledge assumed concerning determinants, matrices, and simultaneous equations. The elements are real or complex numbers. At the same time, the notational pattern is established. Let

$$\mathbf{A} = (a_{ij}) = \begin{bmatrix} a_{11} & a_{12} & \cdots & a_{1n} \\ \vdots & & & \vdots \\ a_{m1} & a_{m2} & \cdots & a_{mn} \end{bmatrix},$$

$$\mathbf{B} = (b_{ij}) = \begin{bmatrix} b_{11} & b_{12} & \cdots & b_{1p} \\ \vdots & & & \vdots \\ b_{n1} & b_{n2} & \cdots & b_{np} \end{bmatrix},$$

$$\mathbf{C} = (c_{ij}) = \begin{bmatrix} c_{11} & c_{12} & \cdots & c_{1p} \\ \vdots & & & \vdots \\ c_{n1} & c_{n2} & \cdots & c_{np} \end{bmatrix},$$

$$\mathbf{D} = (d_{ij}) = \begin{bmatrix} d_{11} & d_{12} & \cdots & d_{1q} \\ \vdots & & & \vdots \\ d_{p1} & d_{p2} & \cdots & d_{pq} \end{bmatrix},$$

be $m \times n$, $n \times p$, $n \times p$, and $p \times q$ matrices respectively. By the *matrix sum* $\mathbf{E} = \mathbf{B} + \mathbf{C}$, we mean the $n \times p$ matrix $\mathbf{E} = (e_{ij})$ in which $e_{ij} = b_{ij} + c_{ij}$ for permissible values of the indices. Moreover, $\mathbf{B} + \mathbf{C} = \mathbf{C} + \mathbf{B}$. By the *matrix product* $\mathbf{F} = \mathbf{AB}$, we mean an $m \times p$ matrix $\mathbf{F} = (f_{ij})$ in which $f_{ij} = \sum_{k=1}^{n} a_{ik} b_{kj}$. It is always true that $\mathbf{A}(\mathbf{B} + \mathbf{C}) = \mathbf{AB} + \mathbf{AC}$ and $(\mathbf{B} + \mathbf{C})\mathbf{D} = \mathbf{BD} + \mathbf{CD}$, so long as the dimensions are compatible; it may not be true that $\mathbf{AB} = \mathbf{BA}$ even though $m = n = p$. Should $\mathbf{AB} = \mathbf{BA}$, $\mathbf{A}$ and $\mathbf{B}$ are said to *commute*. The $n \times p$ matrix, all of whose entries are zero, is called *the null matrix*; the context serves to specify the number of rows and columns. The null matrix is commonly denoted $\mathbf{0}$. Thus, if for all indices i and j, $b_{ij} = -c_{ij}$, $\mathbf{B} + \mathbf{C} = \mathbf{0}$.

Example. In particular, if

$$\mathbf{A} = \begin{bmatrix} 1 & 2 & -1 \\ 3 & 4 & 2 \end{bmatrix}, \quad \mathbf{B} = \begin{bmatrix} -1 & 3 \\ 2 & 1 \\ 0 & 3 \end{bmatrix}, \quad \mathbf{C} = \begin{bmatrix} 1 & 2 \\ -3 & 1 \\ 2 & 4 \end{bmatrix},$$

then

$$\mathbf{B} + \mathbf{C} = \begin{bmatrix} 0 & 5 \\ -1 & 2 \\ 2 & 7 \end{bmatrix}, \qquad \mathbf{A}(\mathbf{B} + \mathbf{C}) = \begin{bmatrix} -4 & 2 \\ 0 & 37 \end{bmatrix},$$

$$(\mathbf{B} + \mathbf{C})\mathbf{A} = \begin{bmatrix} 15 & 20 & 10 \\ 5 & 6 & 5 \\ 23 & 32 & 12 \end{bmatrix},$$

If

$$\mathbf{A} = \begin{bmatrix} 1 & 3 & 1 \\ 2 & 0 & -1 \\ 4 & 1 & 2 \end{bmatrix}, \qquad \mathbf{B} = \begin{bmatrix} 2 & 1 & 3 \\ -3 & 1 & 2 \\ 3 & 1 & 2 \end{bmatrix},$$

then

$$\mathbf{A}^2 = \begin{bmatrix} 11 & 4 & 0 \\ -2 & 5 & 0 \\ 14 & 14 & 7 \end{bmatrix}, \qquad \mathbf{AB} = \begin{bmatrix} -4 & 5 & 11 \\ 1 & 1 & 4 \\ 11 & 7 & 18 \end{bmatrix},$$

$$\mathbf{BA} = \begin{bmatrix} 16 & 9 & 7 \\ 7 & -7 & 0 \\ 13 & 11 & 6 \end{bmatrix}, \qquad \mathbf{B}^2 = \begin{bmatrix} 10 & 6 & 14 \\ -3 & 0 & -3 \\ 9 & 6 & 15 \end{bmatrix},$$

$$\mathbf{A} - \mathbf{B} = \begin{bmatrix} -1 & 2 & -2 \\ 5 & -1 & -3 \\ 1 & 0 & 0 \end{bmatrix}, \qquad \mathbf{A} + \mathbf{B} = \begin{bmatrix} 3 & 4 & 4 \\ -1 & 1 & 1 \\ 7 & 2 & 4 \end{bmatrix},$$

$$(\mathbf{A} - \mathbf{B})(\mathbf{A} + \mathbf{B}) = \begin{bmatrix} -19 & -6 & -10 \\ -5 & 13 & 7 \\ 3 & 4 & 4 \end{bmatrix},$$

$$\mathbf{A}^2 - \mathbf{B}^2 = \begin{bmatrix} 1 & -2 & -14 \\ 1 & 5 & 3 \\ 5 & 8 & -8 \end{bmatrix}.$$

Notice that $(\mathbf{A} - \mathbf{B})(\mathbf{A} + \mathbf{B}) \neq \mathbf{A}^2 - \mathbf{B}^2$. It will be found that $(\mathbf{A} - \mathbf{B})(\mathbf{A} + \mathbf{B}) = \mathbf{A}^2 - \mathbf{BA} + \mathbf{AB} - \mathbf{B}^2$.

Let $\bar{a}_{ij}$ denote the *complex conjugate* of the complex number a_{ij}, and let $\overline{\mathbf{A}}$ denote the matrix derived from $\mathbf{A}$ by replacing a_{ij} by $\bar{a}_{ij}$. Because the conjugate of the sum of two numbers is the sum of their conjugates, and the conjugate of the product is the product of the conjugates, it follows that $\overline{\mathbf{AB}} = \overline{\mathbf{A}}\ \overline{\mathbf{B}}$.

By the *transpose* $\mathbf{A}^t$ of the $m \times n$ matrix $\mathbf{A}$ we mean the matrix (g_{ij}) such that $g_{ij} = a_{ji}$. It is true that $(\mathbf{B} + \mathbf{C})^t = \mathbf{B}^t + \mathbf{C}^t$ and that $(\mathbf{AB})^t = \mathbf{B}^t \mathbf{A}^t$ (more generally that $(\mathbf{ABD})^t = \mathbf{D}^t \mathbf{B}^t \mathbf{A}^t$, etc.).

210

By the *conjugate transpose* $\mathbf{A}^*$ of matrix $\mathbf{A}$, we mean $(\overline{\mathbf{A}})^t$. Clearly, $(\overline{\mathbf{A}})^t = \overline{(\mathbf{A}^t)}$ and $(\mathbf{AB})^* = \mathbf{B}^*\mathbf{A}^*$. A matrix $\mathbf{A}$ is *Hermitian* if and only if $\mathbf{A}^* = \mathbf{A}$ (this requires of course that $m = n$). A matrix $\mathbf{A}$ is *symmetric* if and only if $\mathbf{A} = \mathbf{A}^t$. A *real matrix* is Hermitian if and only if it is symmetric.

Example. Choose

$$\mathbf{A} = \begin{bmatrix} 2+i & -2-i & -1+3i \\ i & -3+2i & 2 \\ 3-2i & 1+i & -1+i \end{bmatrix}.$$

Then

$$\overline{\mathbf{A}} = \begin{bmatrix} 2-i & -2+i & -1-3i \\ -i & -3-2i & 2 \\ 3+2i & 1-i & -1-i \end{bmatrix},$$

$$\overline{\mathbf{A}}^t = \begin{bmatrix} 2-i & -i & 3+2i \\ -2+i & -3-2i & 1-i \\ -1-3i & 2 & -1-i \end{bmatrix},$$

$$\mathbf{AA}^* = \begin{bmatrix} 20 & 3+11i & 5+6i \\ 3-11i & 18 & -5+6i \\ 5-6i & -5-6i & 17 \end{bmatrix}.$$

Note that $\mathbf{AA}^*$ is Hermitian.

$\mathbf{H}$ is a *diagonal matrix* if and only if $\mathbf{H}$ is a *square* ($n \times n$) *matrix* (h_{ij}) and $h_{ij} = 0$ if $i \neq j$. If we let $h_i = h_{ii}$, a diagonal matrix is often denoted $[h_1, h_2, \ldots, h_n]$ (with or without the commas). An alternate nomenclature is diag $(h_1 h_2 \ldots h_n)$. Observe that $\mathbf{AH}$ is the $m \times n$ matrix $(h_j a_{ij})$ and that $\mathbf{HB}$ is the $n \times p$ matrix $(h_i b_{ij})$. These features of multiplication by diagonal matrices are of special interest in the study of eigenvectors and eigenvalues described later.

$\mathbf{H}$ is a *scalar matrix* if and only if $\mathbf{H}$ is a diagonal matrix all of whose elements h_{ii} have the common value h. We write $h\mathbf{A} = \mathbf{A}h = \mathbf{AH}$ and $h\mathbf{B} = \mathbf{B}h = \mathbf{HB}$. The real or complex numbers used as the elements of the matrices are sometimes called *scalars*, and formations such as $h\mathbf{A}$ and $\mathbf{A}h$ are referred to as *scalar multiplications*. If the common value h is the number one, the resulting matrix is called the *identity matrix* and denoted $\mathbf{I}$ (the context serves to describe the *order*, namely the number of rows n in an $n \times n$ matrix). Thus $\mathbf{IA} = \mathbf{AI} = \mathbf{A}$.

If $m = n$, so that $\mathbf{A}$ is square, and if $\mathbf{K}$ is a matrix such that $\mathbf{AK} = \mathbf{I}$, then $\mathbf{K}$ is unique, is called the *inverse* of $\mathbf{A}$, and is denoted $\mathbf{A}^{-1}$. It is then true that $\mathbf{A}^{-1}\mathbf{A} = \mathbf{AA}^{-1} = \mathbf{I}$. The square matrix $\mathbf{A}$ is called *nonsingular* if and only if $\mathbf{A}^{-1}$ exists. If $m = n = p$ and both $\mathbf{A}^{-1}$ and $\mathbf{B}^{-1}$ exist, then $(\mathbf{AB})^{-1} = \mathbf{B}^{-1}\mathbf{A}^{-1}$. A square matrix $\mathbf{A}$ is *unitary* if and only if $\mathbf{A}^* = \mathbf{A}^{-1}$, and *orthogonal* if and only if $\mathbf{A}^* = \mathbf{A}^{-1} = \mathbf{A}^t$.

Example. If, for the matrix $\mathbf{A}$, we take

$$\mathbf{A} = \begin{bmatrix} \dfrac{2}{\sqrt{15}} & \dfrac{3-i}{\sqrt{15}} & \dfrac{i}{\sqrt{15}} \\[2mm] \dfrac{1-i}{\sqrt{5}} & \dfrac{i}{\sqrt{5}} & \dfrac{1-i}{\sqrt{5}} \\[2mm] \dfrac{5i}{5\sqrt{3}} & \dfrac{1-3i}{5\sqrt{3}} & \dfrac{2-6i}{5\sqrt{3}} \end{bmatrix},$$

it will be found that $\mathbf{A}^*\mathbf{A} = \mathbf{I}$, whence $\mathbf{A}$ is unitary.

The (main) *diagonal* of a square matrix $\mathbf{A}$ of order n consists of the elements, a_{ii}, $1 \leqslant i \leqslant n$. If all the elements below the diagonal are zero, $\mathbf{A}$ is called *upper triangular*. If, in addition, all elements on the diagonal are zero, $\mathbf{A}$ is called *strictly upper triangular*. *Lower triangular* and *strictly lower triangular* matrices are similarly defined.

It is often convenient to consider matrices whose elements are also matrices, in the sense of partitioning. Thus let

$$\mathbf{A} = \left[\begin{array}{ccc|cc} a_{11} & a_{12} & a_{13} & a_{14} & a_{15} \\ \hline a_{21} & a_{22} & a_{23} & a_{24} & a_{25} \\ a_{31} & a_{32} & a_{33} & a_{34} & a_{35} \end{array} \right],$$

$$\mathbf{B} = \left[\begin{array}{ccc|c} b_{11} & b_{12} & b_{13} & b_{14} \\ b_{21} & b_{22} & b_{23} & b_{24} \\ b_{31} & b_{32} & b_{33} & b_{34} \\ \hline b_{41} & b_{42} & b_{43} & b_{44} \\ b_{51} & b_{52} & b_{53} & b_{54} \end{array} \right],$$

where the broken lines indicate partitioning of $\mathbf{A}$ and $\mathbf{B}$ as indicated below:

$$\mathbf{A} = \begin{bmatrix} \mathbf{A}_{11} & \mathbf{A}_{12} \\ \mathbf{A}_{21} & \mathbf{A}_{22} \end{bmatrix}, \qquad \mathbf{B} = \begin{bmatrix} \mathbf{B}_{11} & \mathbf{B}_{12} \\ \mathbf{B}_{21} & \mathbf{B}_{22} \end{bmatrix},$$

Here

$$\mathbf{A}_{11} = [a_{11} \quad a_{12} \quad a_{13}], \qquad \mathbf{A}_{12} = [a_{14} \quad a_{15}],$$

$$\mathbf{A}_{21} = \begin{bmatrix} a_{21} & a_{22} & a_{23} \\ a_{31} & a_{32} & a_{33} \end{bmatrix}, \qquad \mathbf{A}_{22} = \begin{bmatrix} a_{24} & a_{25} \\ a_{34} & a_{35} \end{bmatrix},$$

$$\mathbf{B}_{11} = \begin{bmatrix} b_{11} & b_{12} & b_{13} \\ b_{21} & b_{22} & b_{23} \\ b_{31} & b_{32} & b_{33} \end{bmatrix}, \qquad \mathbf{B}_{12} = \begin{bmatrix} b_{14} \\ b_{24} \\ b_{34} \end{bmatrix},$$

$$\mathbf{B}_{21} = \begin{bmatrix} b_{41} & b_{42} & b_{43} \\ b_{51} & b_{52} & b_{53} \end{bmatrix}, \qquad \mathbf{B}_{22} = \begin{bmatrix} b_{44} \\ b_{54} \end{bmatrix}.$$

Note that

$$\mathbf{AB} = \begin{bmatrix} \mathbf{A}_{11}\mathbf{B}_{11} + \mathbf{A}_{12}\mathbf{B}_{21} & \mathbf{A}_{11}\mathbf{B}_{12} + \mathbf{A}_{12}\mathbf{B}_{22} \\ \mathbf{A}_{21}\mathbf{B}_{11} + \mathbf{A}_{22}\mathbf{B}_{21} & \mathbf{A}_{21}\mathbf{B}_{12} + \mathbf{A}_{22}\mathbf{B}_{22} \end{bmatrix}.$$

This effect (that is, analogy with ordinary matrix multiplication) is valid for any partitioning that gives meaning to the various constituents.

If $\mathbf{A}$ is an $n \times n$ square matrix, there is an associated number called the *determinant* of $\mathbf{A}$ and denoted $\det(\mathbf{A})$, dct $\mathbf{A}$, or $|\mathbf{A}|$. It is defined as

$$\det(\mathbf{A}) = |\mathbf{A}| = \Sigma \operatorname{sgn}(p_1 p_2 \ldots p_n) a_{1p_1} a_{2p_2} \ldots a_{np_n},$$

where each product $a_{1p_1} a_{2p_2} \ldots a_{np_n}$ consists of one and only one number from each row and column of $\mathbf{A}$, and where the sum extends over all possible permutations $p_1 p_2 \ldots p_n$ of the numbers 1 to n. Also, $\operatorname{sgn}(p_1 p_2 \ldots p_n)$ is one or minus one accordingly as the permutation is even or odd. The permutation $p_1 p_2 \ldots p_n$ is odd if an odd number of interchanges is required to return the numbers to natural order. Thus 1, 3, 2 is odd, while 1, 3, 4, 2 is even. It should be emphasized that this definition is not of immediate value in finding the number $\det(\mathbf{A})$. For example, if $n = 10$, the number of products required is $10! = 3,628,800$. The definition is, of course, requisite to an understanding of determinants and, on occasion, is needed for special purposes in automatic computation.

Useful properties are

$$\det(\mathbf{A}^t) = \det(\mathbf{A}), \qquad \det(\mathbf{A}\mathbf{B}) = \det(\mathbf{A}) \det(\mathbf{B}),$$

$$\det(\mathbf{A}^{-1}) = [\det(\mathbf{A})]^{-1}, \qquad \det(\overline{\mathbf{A}}) = \overline{\det(\mathbf{A})},$$

$$\det(\mathbf{A}^*) = \overline{\det(\mathbf{A})}.$$

If $\mathbf{A}$ is a *triangular matrix* then $\det(\mathbf{A})$ is the product of the diagonal entries. Diagonal matrices are an important special case.

A determinant, called the *minor* of a_{ij}, is associated with each element a_{ij} of a square matrix $\mathbf{A}$ of order n, and is defined as the determinant of the submatrix, formed by deleting from $\mathbf{A}$ the elements of the row and column in which a_{ij} lies. When this minor is multiplied by $(-1)^{i+j}$, the resulting number is called the *cofactor* of a_{ij}. Let this cofactor be denoted A_{ij}. Then, as special cases of Laplace's expansion, we have for each row r and each column s

$$\det(\mathbf{A}) = \sum_{j=1}^{n} a_{rj} A_{rj} = \sum_{i=1}^{n} a_{is} A_{is}.$$

Suppose a matrix has two identical rows. Interchanging these rows cannot alter the value of the determinant, yet by the definition the sign must change. Therefore, its determinantal value is zero. From this we see that if $r \neq t$

$$\sum_{j=1}^{n} a_{rj} A_{tj} = 0.$$

Because of the properties of transposes, if $s \neq t$,

$$\sum_{i=1}^{n} a_{is} A_{it} = 0.$$

With each square matrix $\mathbf{A} = (a_{ij})$ we associate a matrix $\mathbf{K} = (k_{ij})$ where $k_{ij} = A_{ji}$. This matrix is called the

adjoint of $\mathbf{A}$ and is denoted $\operatorname{adj}(\mathbf{A})$. Because of the properties described above, it is seen that

$$\mathbf{A} \operatorname{adj}(\mathbf{A}) = \det(\mathbf{A})\mathbf{I}.$$

If $\det(\mathbf{A}) \neq 0$ then $\mathbf{A}^{-1}$ may be written as (f_{ij}) where $f_{ij} = A_{ji}/\det(\mathbf{A})$. It is also seen, since $\det(\det(\mathbf{A})\mathbf{I}) = [\det(\mathbf{A})]^n$, that $\det(\operatorname{adj}(\mathbf{A})) = [\det(\mathbf{A})]^{n-1}$. If $\det(\mathbf{A}) = 0$, $\mathbf{A}^{-1}$ does not exist, for in that event, we would need $\det(\mathbf{A}^{-1}) \det(\mathbf{A}) = \det(\mathbf{I}) = 1$.

Example. Let the determinant for the unitary matrix $\mathbf{A}$ of page 211 be found by expanding in terms of the elements of the first column. The cofactor of $2/\sqrt{15}$ is $(8 + 6i)/(5\sqrt{15})$, that for $(1 - i)/\sqrt{5}$ is $(3 + 21i)/(5\sqrt{45})$, and that for $5i/(5\sqrt{3})$ is $(3 - 4i)/\sqrt{75}$. Thus

$$\det(\mathbf{A}) = \frac{2(8 + 6i)}{75} + \frac{(1 - i)(3 + 21i)}{75} + \frac{5i(3 - 4i)}{75} = \frac{4 + 3i}{5}.$$

Also,

$$\operatorname{adj}(\mathbf{A}) = \begin{bmatrix} \dfrac{8 + 6i}{5\sqrt{15}} & \dfrac{3 + 21i}{5\sqrt{45}} & \dfrac{3 - 4i}{\sqrt{75}} \\[2ex] \dfrac{9 + 13i}{5\sqrt{15}} & \dfrac{9 - 12i}{5\sqrt{45}} & \dfrac{-1 + 3i}{\sqrt{75}} \\[2ex] \dfrac{3 - 4i}{5\sqrt{15}} & \dfrac{3 + 21i}{5\sqrt{45}} & \dfrac{-2 + 6i}{\sqrt{75}} \end{bmatrix}.$$

Consider now all possible square submatrices formed from an $m \times n$ matrix $\mathbf{A}$ by deleting rows and columns. Consider in particular those whose determinants are not zero. Then by the *rank* of $\mathbf{A}$, we mean the order of such a nonsingular submatrix of highest possible order. By a previous paragraph, a square matrix $\mathbf{A}$ of order n is nonsingular if and only if its rank is n. Also, the adjoint of $\mathbf{A}$ is nonsingular if and only if $\mathbf{A}$ is nonsingular.

Concerning simultaneous linear equations, note that a solution exists if and only if the matrix of the coefficients has the same rank as the *augmented matrix* (that formed by placing the column of constants next to the matrix of coefficients). We also need to know that m *homogeneous* equations in n unknowns have a nontrivial solution (one not all zeros) if and only if the rank of the matrix of the coefficients is less than n.

Example. It will be found that the equations

$$5x_1 + 3x_2 - x_3 = 8$$
$$x_1 - x_2 + 2x_3 = 5$$
$$2x_1 - 3x_2 + 4x_3 = 8$$

have the unique solution $x_1 = 1, x_2 = 2, x_3 = 3$; also, it will be found that the determinant of the matrix of coefficients has the value

$$\begin{vmatrix} 5 & 3 & -1 \\ 1 & -1 & 2 \\ 2 & -3 & 4 \end{vmatrix} = 11.$$

Thus the rank of the matrix of the coefficients, namely,

$$\begin{bmatrix} 5 & 3 & -1 \\ 1 & -1 & 2 \\ 2 & -3 & 4 \end{bmatrix},$$

is three, as is that of the augmented matrix

$$\begin{bmatrix} 5 & 3 & -1 & 8 \\ 1 & -1 & 2 & 5 \\ 2 & -3 & 4 & 8 \end{bmatrix}.$$

In contrast, the equations

$$5x_1 + 3x_2 - x_3 = 8$$
$$x_1 - x_2 + 2x_3 = 5$$
$$6x_1 + 2x_2 + x_3 = 12$$

have no solution. This is allied to the fact that

$$\begin{vmatrix} 5 & 3 & -1 \\ 1 & -1 & 2 \\ 6 & 2 & 1 \end{vmatrix} = 0, \qquad \begin{vmatrix} 5 & 3 & 8 \\ 1 & -1 & 5 \\ 6 & 2 & 12 \end{vmatrix} = 8.$$

The same coefficient matrices provide examples of homogeneous equations. The equations

$$5x_1 + 3x_2 - x_3 = 0$$
$$x_1 - x_2 + 2x_3 = 0$$
$$2x_1 - 3x_2 + 4x_3 = 0$$

have only the solution $x_1 = x_2 = x_3 = 0$. However, the equations

$$5x_1 + 3x_2 - x_3 = 0$$
$$x_1 - x_2 + 2x_3 = 0$$
$$6x_1 + 2x_2 + x_3 = 0$$

have the nontrivial solution $x_1 = -5t$, $x_2 = 11t$, $x_3 = 8t$, where t is arbitrary.

4.2 Vectors

In the treatment of vectors, several approaches are possible; we choose to define a *vector* **v** as an $n \times 1$ (column) matrix whose elements are real or complex, as desired. Using the scalar multiplication for matrices previously described and the properties of matrices previously developed, it is a routine matter to show that the postulates for a *vector space* are satisfied by the set V_n of all such $n \times 1$ matrices. The verification should be made [2].

For this vector space V_n, an *inner product* (*dot product*) of two vectors **u** and **v** is defined as

$$(\mathbf{u}, \mathbf{v}) = \mathbf{u}^* \mathbf{v}, \qquad (4.1)$$

where, on the right, matrix multiplication is intended. Thus if $n = 3$, $\mathbf{u} = [2 + 3i, 3 - i, 4 + i]^t$ and $\mathbf{v} = [1 + i, 1 - i, 2]^t$, then $(\mathbf{u}, \mathbf{v})$ is $(2 - 3i)(1 + i) + (3 + i)(1 - i) + (4 - i)2$ or $17 - 5i$. Since the fundamental postulates satisfied (designed for a more general treatment) will be an expediting feature, they are listed and should be

verified. For a scalar c and vectors **u**, **v** and **w**, the inner product is a complex number such that

$$(\mathbf{u}, \mathbf{v}) = \overline{(\mathbf{v}, \mathbf{u})}$$
$$(\mathbf{u}, c\mathbf{v}) = c(\mathbf{u}, \mathbf{v})$$
$$(\mathbf{u} + \mathbf{v}, \mathbf{w}) = (\mathbf{u}, \mathbf{w}) + (\mathbf{v}, \mathbf{w}) \qquad (4.2)$$
$$(\mathbf{u}, \mathbf{v} + \mathbf{w}) = (\mathbf{u}, \mathbf{v}) + (\mathbf{u}, \mathbf{w})$$
$$(\mathbf{u}, \mathbf{u}) \geq 0, (\mathbf{u}, \mathbf{u}) = 0 \text{ if and only if } \mathbf{u} = \mathbf{0}.$$

It is possible to show [from (4.2) directly, if desired] that

$$(c\,\mathbf{u}, \mathbf{v}) = \bar{c}\,(\mathbf{u}, \mathbf{v}). \qquad (4.3)$$

The vectors **u** and **v** are *orthogonal* if and only if $(\mathbf{u}, \mathbf{v}) = 0$. The *length* of a vector **u**, denoted $\|\mathbf{u}\|$, is $\sqrt{(\mathbf{u}, \mathbf{u})}$. A *normalized* or *unit* vector is one whose length is unity. A (finite) set of vectors $\mathbf{u}_1, \mathbf{u}_2, \ldots, \mathbf{u}_n$ is an *orthogonal* set if and only if $(\mathbf{u}_i, \mathbf{u}_j) = 0$ for $i \neq j$, and is *orthonormal* if each vector is also of unit length. If $\mathbf{u}_1, \mathbf{u}_2, \ldots, \mathbf{u}_n$ form an orthonormal set of n vectors for V_n, it is seen by direct multiplication that $\overline{[\mathbf{u}_1 \, \mathbf{u}_2 \cdots \mathbf{u}_n]}^t [\mathbf{u}_1 \, \mathbf{u}_2 \cdots \mathbf{u}_n] = \mathbf{I}$. Thus such a matrix is unitary; from any such matrix, a set of n orthonormal vectors can be extracted.

The $p \times n$ matrices $\mathbf{A}_1, \mathbf{A}_2, \ldots, \mathbf{A}_m$ are *linearly dependent* if and only if there exist scalars $c_1, c_2, \ldots, c_m$, not all zero, such that

$$c_1 \mathbf{A}_1 + c_2 \mathbf{A}_2 + \cdots + c_m \mathbf{A}_m = \mathbf{0}. \qquad (4.4)$$

If such numbers cannot be found, the set is a *linearly independent* set. The definitions are applicable, in particular, to the $n \times 1$ matrices $\mathbf{u}_1, \mathbf{u}_2, \ldots, \mathbf{u}_m$.

Example. Let vectors be defined as follows:

$$\mathbf{u}_1 = \begin{bmatrix} 3 \\ 1 \\ 2 \\ -1 \\ 4 \end{bmatrix}, \quad \mathbf{u}_2 = \begin{bmatrix} 4 \\ 1 \\ 2 \\ -3 \\ 5 \end{bmatrix}, \quad \mathbf{u}_3 = \begin{bmatrix} 1 \\ 2 \\ 3 \\ 4 \\ 6 \end{bmatrix}, \quad \mathbf{u}_4 = \begin{bmatrix} -2 \\ 5 \\ 7 \\ 17 \\ 12 \end{bmatrix}.$$

It will be found that $\mathbf{u}_1 - 2\mathbf{u}_2 + 3\mathbf{u}_3 - \mathbf{u}_4$ is the zero vector; thus the vectors are linearly dependent.

The vectors,

$$\mathbf{v}_1 = \begin{bmatrix} \dfrac{1}{\sqrt{5}} \\ 0 \\ \dfrac{2}{\sqrt{5}} \end{bmatrix}, \quad \mathbf{v}_2 = \begin{bmatrix} \dfrac{2}{3} \\ \dfrac{2}{3} \\ -\dfrac{1}{3} \end{bmatrix}, \quad \mathbf{v}_3 = \begin{bmatrix} \dfrac{-4}{3\sqrt{5}} \\ \dfrac{5}{3\sqrt{5}} \\ \dfrac{2}{3\sqrt{5}} \end{bmatrix},$$

are orthonormal, hence also linearly independent.

A *vector space* is of *dimension* q if and only if q linearly independent vectors belong to the space and any set of $q + 1$ (or more) vectors from the space is linearly dependent. Should such a set of linearly independent vectors exist, every vector of the space can be expressed as a *linear combination* of these vectors. For this reason, such a set is called a *basis* for the space. In the case of the vector space V_n of all $n \times 1$ matrices, let $\boldsymbol{\varepsilon}_1 = [1, 0, 0, \ldots, 0]^t$, $\boldsymbol{\varepsilon}_2 = [0, 1, 0, \ldots, 0]^t$ and in general $\boldsymbol{\varepsilon}_i$ be the column matrix whose first $i - 1$ rows and whose last $n - i$ rows all are zero, while the element in the ith row is one. This set is clearly linearly independent. If $\mathbf{u} = [u_1, u_2, \ldots u_n]^t$ is any vector of V_n, then

$$\mathbf{u} = \sum_{i=1}^{n} u_i \boldsymbol{\varepsilon}_i. \qquad (4.5)$$

Now consider a set $\mathbf{u}_1, \mathbf{u}_2, \ldots, \mathbf{u}_{n+1}$, of vectors from V_n. Let $\mathbf{u}_j = \sum_{i=1}^{n} u_{ji} \boldsymbol{\varepsilon}_i$. Then constants $c_1, c_2, \ldots, c_{n+1}$, not all zero, exist such that

$$\sum_{j=1}^{n+1} c_j \mathbf{u}_j = \sum_{i=1}^{n} \boldsymbol{\varepsilon}_i \sum_{j=1}^{n+1} c_j u_{ji} = \mathbf{0},$$

for any n linear homogeneous equations (in this instance $\sum_{j=1}^{n+1} c_j u_{ji} = 0$, $i = 1, 2, \ldots, n$) in more than n unknowns (here $c_1, c_2, \ldots, c_{n+1}$) always have a nontrivial solution. Thus the dimension of V_n is n. The vectors $\boldsymbol{\varepsilon}_i$, $1 \leqslant i \leqslant n$, constitute a particular (orthogonal) basis, often called the *initial basis*.

Indeed, any n nonzero orthogonal vectors of V_n form a basis for V_n. Let $\mathbf{v}_1, \mathbf{v}_2, \ldots, \mathbf{v}_n$ be such a set. If we assume the existence of scalars $c_1, c_2, \ldots, c_n$, such that

$$c_1 \mathbf{v}_1 + c_2 \mathbf{v}_2 + \cdots + c_n \mathbf{v}_n = \mathbf{0},$$

it follows that

$$\sum_{i=1}^{n} (\mathbf{v}_j, c_i \mathbf{v}_i) = (\mathbf{v}_j, \mathbf{0})$$

or

$$c_j (\mathbf{v}_j, \mathbf{v}_j) = 0,$$

whence $c_j = 0$ and the set is linearly independent. In similar fashion, if $\mathbf{u}$ is any vector of V_n, then

$$\mathbf{u} = \sum_{j=1}^{n} \frac{(\mathbf{v}_j, \mathbf{u})}{(\mathbf{v}_j, \mathbf{v}_j)} \mathbf{v}_j.$$

Example. The orthogonal vectors

$$\mathbf{v}_1 = \begin{bmatrix} 1 \\ 0 \\ 2 \end{bmatrix}, \qquad \mathbf{v}_2 = \begin{bmatrix} 2 \\ 2 \\ -1 \end{bmatrix}, \qquad \mathbf{v}_3 = \begin{bmatrix} -4 \\ 5 \\ 2 \end{bmatrix},$$

are a basis for the set of all vectors $\mathbf{v}^t = [x \; y \; z]$. Indeed, following the technique described above, for arbitrary values of x, y, and z,

$$\mathbf{v} = \frac{x + 2z}{5} \mathbf{v}_1 + \frac{2x + 2y - z}{9} \mathbf{v}_2 + \frac{5y - 4x + 2z}{45} \mathbf{v}_3.$$

If m vectors $\mathbf{u}_1, \mathbf{u}_2, \ldots, \mathbf{u}_m$ are given, then the $n \times m$ matrix $\mathbf{U} = [\mathbf{u}_1 \, \mathbf{u}_2 \ldots \mathbf{u}_m]$ is defined in partitioned form. Conversely, any $n \times m$ matrix $\mathbf{U}$ determines uniquely m column matrices which may be construed as vectors. For any $n \times m$ matrix $\mathbf{U}$, the maximum number of linearly independent columns is called the *column rank*; the maximum number of linearly independent rows is called the *row rank*. It can be shown that these numbers are the same, and are the same number as the (determinant) rank of $\mathbf{U}$ previously defined. If we know that row rank is determinant rank, a knowledge of transposed matrices and determinants convinces us that column rank is the same number. No attempt is made here to show that row rank is determinant rank. It is worth observing that $\mathbf{U}$, $\mathbf{U}^*$, and $\mathbf{U}^t$ all have the same rank. If $\mathbf{U}^{-1}$ exists, it has the same rank as $\mathbf{U}$ and, in such event, the rank is the order.

A feature of value, concerning matrices of order n whose rank r is less than n, is that they can always be written as the product of an $n \times r$ matrix and an $r \times n$ matrix, each of rank r. Formal proof is not difficult; however, we merely indicate the proof for a matrix of order 4 and rank 2. Let the first two columns be linearly independent; then the matrix may be written (and rephrased) as

$$\begin{bmatrix} a_{11} & a_{12} & \alpha_1 a_{11} + \alpha_2 a_{12} & \beta_1 a_{11} + \beta_2 a_{12} \\ a_{21} & a_{22} & \alpha_1 a_{21} + \alpha_2 a_{22} & \beta_1 a_{21} + \beta_2 a_{22} \\ a_{31} & a_{32} & \alpha_1 a_{31} + \alpha_2 a_{32} & \beta_1 a_{31} + \beta_2 a_{32} \\ a_{41} & a_{42} & \alpha_1 a_{41} + \alpha_2 a_{42} & \beta_1 a_{41} + \beta_2 a_{42} \end{bmatrix}$$

$$= \begin{bmatrix} a_{11} & a_{12} \\ a_{21} & a_{22} \\ a_{31} & a_{32} \\ a_{41} & a_{42} \end{bmatrix} \begin{bmatrix} 1 & 0 & \alpha_1 & \beta_1 \\ 0 & 1 & \alpha_2 & \beta_2 \end{bmatrix}.$$

Conversely, if two such matrices, each of rank 2, are multiplied together, we can always find, in the product matrix, a minor that is the product of two nonvanishing determinants, one from each factor. This is readily seen by partitioning, so that the submatrices of rank two (one from each factor) can be seen to yield a submatrix in the product, also of rank two. Moreover, three or more columns must be linearly dependent.

Another factorization theorem applies to nonsingular matrices. The leading submatrices of a square matrix $\mathbf{A} = (a_{ij})$ are the matrices

$$[a_{11}], \quad \begin{bmatrix} a_{11} & a_{12} \\ a_{21} & a_{22} \end{bmatrix}, \quad \begin{bmatrix} a_{11} & a_{12} & a_{13} \\ a_{21} & a_{22} & a_{23} \\ a_{31} & a_{32} & a_{33} \end{bmatrix}, \quad \ldots, \quad \mathbf{A}.$$

The corresponding determinants are commonly denoted $\Delta_1, \Delta_2, \ldots, \Delta_n$. If all the leading submatrices of a square matrix are nonsingular, it may be written as the product (and indeed in more than one way) of a lower triangular matrix $\mathbf{L}$ and an upper triangular matrix $\mathbf{U}$. Proof is by induction and is sketched (for convenience), using always a one for the diagonal elements of $\mathbf{L}$. (Any nonzero element may be used.) Clearly, if the rank r is one, $[a_{11}] = [1][u_{11}]$ where $u_{11} = a_{11}$. Now assume that, for all matrices of order $r - 1$ (having the requisite properties), the proposition is true. Let $\mathbf{u}^t = [a_{r1} \, a_{r2} \ldots a_{r,r-1}]$

and $\mathbf{v}^t = [a_{1r}, a_{2r} \ldots a_{r-1,r}]$. Then, using partitioning, any suitable matrix $\mathbf{A} = (a_{ij})$ leads to

$$\mathbf{A}_r = \begin{bmatrix} \mathbf{A}_{r-1} & \mathbf{v} \\ \mathbf{u}^t & a_{rr} \end{bmatrix},$$

where $\mathbf{A}_{r-1}$ is the $(r-1)$th leading submatrix of $\mathbf{A}$. $\mathbf{A}_{r-1}$ has the form $\mathbf{L}_{r-1}\mathbf{U}_{r-1}$, where the diagonal elements of the lower triangular matrix $\mathbf{L}_{r-1}$ are all ones. Since the determinant of a triangular matrix is the product of its diagonal entries, and the determinant of the product is the product of the determinants, we are assured that $\mathbf{L}_{r-1}$ and $\mathbf{U}_{r-1}$ are nonsingular. Let $\mathbf{s}^t = \mathbf{u}^t \mathbf{U}_{r-1}^{-1}$ and let $\mathbf{w} = \mathbf{L}_{r-1}^{-1}\mathbf{v}$. Then

$$\mathbf{A}_r = \begin{bmatrix} \mathbf{L}_{r-1} & \mathbf{0} \\ \mathbf{s}^t & 1 \end{bmatrix} \begin{bmatrix} \mathbf{U}_{r-1} & \mathbf{w} \\ \mathbf{0} & b_{rr} \end{bmatrix},$$

where $b_{rr} = a_{rr} - \mathbf{s}^t\mathbf{w}$.

The requirement that $\Delta_i \neq 0$, $1 \leqslant i \leqslant n$, seems very restrictive. However, it will be seen in the section on symmetric and Hermitian matrices that an extremely important class, the definite matrices, do have this property.

In the section on the method of Rutishauser (see equations 4.46), an approach more suitable for automatic calculation will be found.

Example. An example is furnished by the following matrix:

$$\mathbf{A} = \begin{bmatrix} 3 & 1 & 2 \\ 9 & 7 & 12 \\ 6 & 4 & 10 \end{bmatrix}.$$

Here $\Delta_1 = 3$, $\Delta_2 = 12$, $\Delta_3 = 36$, and

$$\mathbf{A} = \begin{bmatrix} 1 & 0 & 0 \\ 3 & 2 & 0 \\ 2 & 1 & 3 \end{bmatrix} \begin{bmatrix} 3 & 1 & 2 \\ 0 & 2 & 3 \\ 0 & 0 & 1 \end{bmatrix}.$$

EXAMPLE 4.1

MATRIX OPERATIONS

Problem Statement

Write subroutines that will use double-precision arithmetic to perform the commonly used matrix and vector operations, such as addition, multiplication, etc.

Method of Solution

The operations are embodied in a single subroutine with multiple entries, and are listed in Table 4.1.1; this table also serves in place of a flow diagram. The following notation is used:

Matrices: $\mathbf{A}$, $\mathbf{B}$, $\mathbf{C}$ (all $m \times n$); $\mathbf{T}$ ($m \times p$); $\mathbf{U}$ ($n \times p$); $\mathbf{V}$ ($n \times m$).
Column Vectors: $\mathbf{x}$, $\mathbf{y}$ (both $n \times 1$); $\mathbf{z}$ ($m \times 1$).
Scalar: s.

Although the above subroutines are not used here, several of them will be employed extensively in Example 4.2.

Table 4.1.1   Subroutines for Manipulating Matrices and Vectors

Typical Call	Operation	Formula Used
CALL MATMLT (A, U, T, M, N, P)	$\mathbf{T} \leftarrow \mathbf{AU}$	$t_{ij} = \sum_{k=1}^{n} a_{ik} u_{kj}$
CALL MATADD (A, B, C, M, N)	$\mathbf{C} \leftarrow \mathbf{A} + \mathbf{B}$	$c_{ij} = a_{ij} + b_{ij}$
CALL MATSUB (A, B, C, M, N)	$\mathbf{C} \leftarrow \mathbf{A} - \mathbf{B}$	$c_{ij} = a_{ij} - b_{ij}$
CALL MATVEC (A, X, Z, M, N)	$\mathbf{z} \leftarrow \mathbf{Ax}$	$z_i = \sum_{j=1}^{n} a_{ij} x_j$
CALL SCAVEC (S, X, Y, N)	$\mathbf{y} \leftarrow s\mathbf{x}$	$y_i = s x_i$
CALL SCAMAT (S, A, B, M, N)	$\mathbf{B} \leftarrow s\mathbf{A}$	$b_{ij} = s a_{ij}$
CALL VECVEC (X, Y, S, N)	$s \leftarrow \mathbf{x}^t \mathbf{y}$	$s = \sum_{i=1}^{n} x_i y_i$
CALL VECMAT (Z, A, X, M, N)	$\mathbf{x}^t \leftarrow \mathbf{z}^t \mathbf{A}$	$x_j = \sum_{k=1}^{m} z_k a_{kj}$
CALL MATEQ (A, B, M, N)	$\mathbf{B} \leftarrow \mathbf{A}$	$b_{ij} = a_{ij}$
CALL VECLEN (X, S, N)	$s \leftarrow \|\mathbf{x}\|$	$s = \left(\sum_{i=1}^{n} x_i^2 \right)^{1/2}$
CALL VECEQ (X, Y, N)	$\mathbf{y} \leftarrow \mathbf{x}$	$y_i = x_i$
CALL TRNSPZ (A, V, M, N)	$\mathbf{V} \leftarrow \mathbf{A}^t$	$v_{ji} = a_{ij}$

FORTRAN *Implementation*

The subroutine calls are listed in Table 4.1.1; the argument names are self-explanatory.

Example 4.1   Matrix Operations   **217**

Program Listing

```
C           APPLIED NUMERICAL METHODS, EXAMPLE 4.1
C           SUBROUTINES FOR MANIPULATIONS OF MATRICES AND VECTORS.
C
C      ..... T(M,P) = A(M,N) * U(N,P) .....
       SUBROUTINE MATMLT (A, U, T, M, N, P)
       REAL*8 A, B, C, T, U, V, X, Y, Z, S, SUMSQX
       INTEGER P
       DIMENSION A(10,10), B(10,10), C(10,10), T(10,10), U(10,10),
      1 V(10,10), X(10), Y(10), Z(10)
       DO 1  I = 1, M
       DO 1  J = 1, P
     1 T(I,J) = 0.
       DO 2  I = 1, M
       DO 2  J = 1, P
       DO 2  K = 1, N
     2 T(I,J) = A(I,K)*U(K,J) + T(I,J)
       RETURN
C
C      ..... C(M,N) = A(M,N) + B(M,N) .....
       ENTRY MATADD (A, B, C, M, N)
       DO 3  I = 1, M
       DO 3  J = 1, N
     3 C(I,J) = A(I,J) + B(I,J)
       RETURN
C
C      ..... C(M,N) = A(M,N) - B(M,N) .....
       ENTRY MATSUB (A, B, C, M, N)
       DO 4  I = 1, M
       DO 4  J = 1, N
     4 C(I,J) = A(I,J) - B(I,J)
       RETURN
C
C      ..... Z(M) = A(M,N) * X(N) .....
       ENTRY MATVEC (A, X, Z, M, N)
       DO 5  I = 1, M
     5 Z(I) = 0.
       DO 6  I = 1, M
       DO 6  J = 1, N
     6 Z(I) = A(I,J)*X(J) + Z(I)
       RETURN
C
C      ..... Y(N) = S * X(N) .....
       ENTRY SCAVEC (S, X, Y, N)
       DO 7  I = 1, N
     7 Y(I) = S*X(I)
       RETURN
C
C      ..... B(M,N) = S*A(M,N) .....
       ENTRY SCAMAT (S, A, B, M, N)
       DO 8  I = 1, M
       DO 8  J = 1, N
     8 B(I,J) = S*A(I,J)
       RETURN
C
C      ..... S = X(N) * Y(N) .....
       ENTRY VECVEC (X, Y, S, N)
       S = 0.
       DO 9  I = 1, N
     9 S = S + X(I)*Y(I)
       RETURN
C
C      ..... X(N) = Z(M) * A(M,N) .....
       ENTRY VECMAT (Z, A, X, M, N)
       DO 10  J = 1, N
       X(J) = 0.
       DO 10  K = 1, M
    10 X(J) = X(J) + Z(K)*A(K,J)
       RETURN
```

Program Listing (*Continued*)

```
C
C        ..... B(M,N) = A(M,N) .....
         ENTRY MATEQ (A, B, M, N)
         DO 11  I = 1, M
         DO 11  J = 1, N
   11    B(I,J) = A(I,J)
         RETURN
C
C        ..... VECTOR LENGTH S, OF X(N) .....
         ENTRY VECLEN (X, S, N)
         SUMSQX = 0.
         DO 12  I = 1, N
   12    SUMSQX = SUMSQX + X(I)*X(I)
         S = DSQRT(SUMSQX)
         RETURN
C
C        ..... Y(N) = X(N) .....
         ENTRY VECEQ (X, Y, N)
         DO 13  I = 1, N
   13    Y(I) = X(I)
         RETURN
C
C        ..... V(N,M) = A(M,N) TRANSPOSED .....
         ENTRY TRNSPZ (A, V, M, N)
         DO 14  I = 1, M
         DO 14  J = 1, N
   14    V(J,I) = A(I,J)
         RETURN
         END
```

4.3 Linear Transformations and Subspaces

A set of vectors W from a vector space V may be said to form a (vector) *subspace* of V if and only if, for every scalar c and every pair of vectors $\mathbf{u}$ and $\mathbf{v}$ in W, it is true that both $\mathbf{u} + \mathbf{v}$ and $c\mathbf{u}$ are vectors of W. Let $\mathbf{A}$ be any (fixed) $n \times n$ matrix. Then the set of all vectors of the form $\mathbf{Au}$, where $\mathbf{u}$ is any (variable) vector of V_n, constitutes a subspace of V_n. For $\mathbf{Au}$ is an $n \times 1$ matrix; therefore, it is an element of V_n. Moreover, it is readily verified that

$$\mathbf{u} + \mathbf{v} = \mathbf{Au}_1 + \mathbf{Av}_1 = \mathbf{A}(\mathbf{u}_1 + \mathbf{v}_1),$$
$$c\mathbf{u} = c\mathbf{Au}_1 = \mathbf{A}c\mathbf{u}_1. \tag{4.6}$$

That the set of all vectors $\mathbf{Au}$ is a subspace of V_n means, in part, that a set of linearly independent vectors of the form $\mathbf{Au}$ will serve as a basis for the space of all vectors of that form. Note that $\mathbf{A\varepsilon}_1$ is the first column of $\mathbf{A}$, $\mathbf{A\varepsilon}_2$ is the second column of $\mathbf{A}$, and so on. Since $\mathbf{u} = \sum_{j=1}^{n} u_j \mathbf{\varepsilon}_j$, by an obvious extension of equation (4.6), it is seen that

$$\mathbf{Au} = \sum_{j=1}^{n} u_j \mathbf{A\varepsilon}_j.$$

Then for a basis of the space, we may choose any maximum number of linearly independent columns of $\mathbf{A}$. It is seen that the dimension of the subspace W of vectors $\mathbf{Au}$ is the rank of $\mathbf{A}$.

A *transformation* of a space V into a subspace W of V may be viewed as a device for associating with each element of V a uniquely defined image in W (more precisely, such a transformation is a many-one correspondence from V to a subset of V). Expressed in *operator* form, $\mathbf{Tu} = \mathbf{v}$, meaning that the *transform* or image of $\mathbf{u}$ is $\mathbf{v}$. The transformation is *linear* if and only if for all $\mathbf{u}$ and $\mathbf{v}$ in V and any scalar c,

$$\mathbf{T}(\mathbf{u} + \mathbf{v}) = \mathbf{Tu} + \mathbf{Tv};$$

and

$$\mathbf{T}(c\mathbf{u}) = c\mathbf{Tu}.$$

Observe immediately, reading equation (4.6) in reverse, that square matrices $\mathbf{A}$ of order n may be viewed as *linear operators* for V_n.

Let $\mathbf{A}$ be an $n \times n$ matrix and $\mathbf{u}$ a vector of V_n such that $\mathbf{Au} = \mathbf{0}$. If $\mathbf{A}$ is nonsingular, its determinant is not zero, and the set of simultaneous linear equations, represented by $\mathbf{Au} = \mathbf{0}$, has only the trivial solution $\mathbf{u} = \mathbf{0}$. If, however, $\mathbf{A}$ is singular [that is, $\det(\mathbf{A}) = 0$], then $\mathbf{u}$ exists such that $\mathbf{u} \neq \mathbf{0}$ and $\mathbf{Au} = \mathbf{0}$, for in such cases, the simultaneous equations involved have a nontrivial solution. The set of all vectors, whose image (using a fixed matrix $\mathbf{A}$) is the null-vector, is a subspace of V_n. This is readily verified in the manner by which equation (4.6) was established. This set is called the *null-space* of $\mathbf{A}$. Its rank is called the *nullity* of $\mathbf{A}$, and it will be shown that the

rank of $\mathbf{A}$ plus the nullity of $\mathbf{A}$ is the dimension of V_n. (The trivial space consisting of the null-vector only has rank zero.)

To demonstrate the proposition above, let $\mathbf{e}_1, \mathbf{e}_2, \ldots, \mathbf{e}_m$ be a basis for the null-space of $\mathbf{A}$. Let $\mathbf{e}_{m+1}, \ldots, \mathbf{e}_n$ be additional vectors such that $\mathbf{e}_1, \mathbf{e}_2, \ldots, \mathbf{e}_n$ *in toto* constitute a basis for V_n. Since every vector $\mathbf{u} = \sum_{i=1}^{n} u_i \mathbf{e}_i$ transforms as $\sum_{i=m+1}^{n} u_i \mathbf{Ae}_i$, it follows that every vector of the space W of all transforms is a linear combination of the vectors $\mathbf{Ae}_i$, $m + 1 \leqslant i \leqslant n$. But these are linearly independent, for if it were not so, some nontrivial linear combination $\sum_{i=m+1}^{n} b_i \mathbf{Ae}_i$ would be $\mathbf{0}$, whence $\mathbf{A} \sum_{i=m+1}^{n} b_i \mathbf{e}_i$ would be zero. In that event $\sum_{i=m+1}^{n} b_i \mathbf{e}_i = \mathbf{0}$, which contradicts the assumption that the vectors $\mathbf{e}_1, \mathbf{e}_2, \ldots, \mathbf{e}_n$ are a basis for V_n.

An important theorem involving nullity is Sylvester's law of nullity, which states that the nullity of the product of two matrices equals or exceeds the nullity of either factor, and that the nullity of the product cannot exceed the sum of the nullities of the factors.

It is intuitively obvious that the set of all vectors of V_n such that the nth row is zero constitutes a subspace of V_n. It can be phrased formally if for the matrix $\mathbf{A}$ the diagonal matrix $[1, 1, \ldots, 1, 0]$ is used, where every diagonal entry but the last is unity.

In future consideration of the transformation of vectors by square matrices $\mathbf{A}$, an extremely useful relation is the *transfer rule*:

$$(\mathbf{u}, \mathbf{Av}) = (\mathbf{A^*u}, \mathbf{v}). \tag{4.7}$$

Proof is straightforward: $\mathbf{u^*}(\mathbf{Av}) = (\mathbf{A^*u})^*\mathbf{v}$ since $(\mathbf{A^*u})^* = \mathbf{u^*A}$.

Example. As an example of a null-space, consider

$$\mathbf{A} = \begin{bmatrix} 2 & 1 & 3 & -1 & 1 \\ 1 & 4 & -2 & 1 & 3 \\ 3 & -1 & 2 & 1 & 4 \\ 0 & 6 & -1 & -1 & 0 \\ -2 & 5 & -4 & 0 & -1 \end{bmatrix},$$

and let $\mathbf{x}^t = [x_1\ x_2\ x_3\ x_4\ x_5]$. The simultaneous equations $\mathbf{Ax} = \mathbf{0}$ have the solution $\mathbf{x} = r\mathbf{v}_1 + s\mathbf{v}_2$, where r and s are arbitrary and $\mathbf{v}_1^t = [-5, 2, 5, 7, 0]$, $\mathbf{v}_2^t = [-13, 1, 6, 0, 7]$. Thus the nullity of $\mathbf{A}$ is at least two. Since the third-order determinant in the upper-left corner has the value -35, the rank of $\mathbf{A}$ is at least three. Hence the nullity is two and the rank is three.

Associated with every square matrix $\mathbf{A}$ is a special set of vectors, called *eigenvectors*, and a related set of scalars, called *eigenvalues*. Formally, the vector $\mathbf{u}$ is an eigenvector of $\mathbf{A}$ if and only if $\mathbf{u}$ is a nonzero vector and λ is a scalar (which may be zero), such that

$$\mathbf{Au} = \lambda \mathbf{u}. \tag{4.8}$$

The scalar λ is an eigenvalue of $\mathbf{A}$ if and only if there exists a nonzero vector $\mathbf{u}$ such that (4.8) holds. It is seen that the eigenvectors pertaining to $\mathbf{A}$ are those nonzero vectors whose images are scalar multiples of the original. It will shortly appear that the number of eigenvalues is finite; however, it is clear that any nonzero scalar multiple of an eigenvector is also an eigenvector.

From (4.8), observe for eigenvectors and eigenvalues that $(\mathbf{A} - \lambda \mathbf{I})\mathbf{u} = \mathbf{0}$ must be satisfied. Let

$$\phi(\lambda) = \det(\mathbf{A} - \lambda \mathbf{I}). \tag{4.9}$$

$\phi(\lambda)$ is the *characteristic function* of matrix $\mathbf{A}$. Since n homogeneous equations in n unknowns have a nontrivial solution if and only if the rank of the coefficient matrix is less than n, it follows that λ is an eigenvalue for $\mathbf{A}$ if and only if λ is any scalar such that

$$\phi(\lambda) = \det(\mathbf{A} - \lambda \mathbf{I}) = 0. \tag{4.10}$$

Equation (4.10) is the *characteristic equation* for matrix $\mathbf{A}$. If $\mathbf{A} = (a_{ij})$, then

$$\mathbf{A} - \lambda \mathbf{I} = \begin{bmatrix} a_{11} - \lambda & a_{12} & a_{13} & \dots & a_{1n} \\ a_{21} & a_{22} - \lambda & a_{23} & \dots & a_{2n} \\ a_{31} & a_{32} & a_{33} - \lambda & \dots & a_{3n} \\ \vdots & \vdots & \vdots & & \vdots \\ a_{n1} & a_{n2} & a_{n3} & \dots & a_{nn} - \lambda \end{bmatrix}.$$

Observe that the characteristic function of $\mathbf{A}^t$ is also the characteristic function for $\mathbf{A}$. This follows since $(\mathbf{A} - \lambda \mathbf{I})^t = \mathbf{A}^t - \lambda \mathbf{I}^t = \mathbf{A}^t - \lambda \mathbf{I}$. But $\det(\mathbf{B}^t) = \det(\mathbf{B})$; thus we see that $\det(\mathbf{A} - \lambda \mathbf{I}) = \det(\mathbf{A}^t - \lambda \mathbf{I})$. Moreover, if $\mathbf{A}$ is real and λ_1, λ_2 are two eigenvalues for $\mathbf{A}$ such that $\bar{\lambda}_2 \neq \lambda_1$, then an eigenvector $\mathbf{v}$, such that $\mathbf{A}^t \mathbf{v} = \lambda_2 \mathbf{v}$, is perpendicular to an eigenvector $\mathbf{u}$ such that $\mathbf{A}\mathbf{u} = \lambda_1 \mathbf{u}$. For by (4.7), $(\mathbf{v}, \mathbf{A}\mathbf{u}) = (\mathbf{v}, \lambda_1 \mathbf{u}) = \lambda_1(\mathbf{v}, \mathbf{u})$ and $(\mathbf{v}, \mathbf{A}\mathbf{u}) = (\mathbf{A}^t \mathbf{v}, \mathbf{u}) = (\lambda_2 \mathbf{v}, \mathbf{u}) = \bar{\lambda}_2 (\mathbf{v}, \mathbf{u})$. Thus $(\mathbf{v}, \mathbf{u}) = 0$.

Now let λ_i be an eigenvalue for $\mathbf{A}$ and let $\mathbf{A} - \lambda_i \mathbf{I}$ be of rank $n - 1$. Then $\text{adj}(\mathbf{A} - \lambda_i \mathbf{I})$ is not the null-matrix, although, since $\det(\mathbf{A} - \lambda_i \mathbf{I}) = 0, (\mathbf{A} - \lambda_i \mathbf{I}) \text{adj}(\mathbf{A} - \lambda_i \mathbf{I}) = 0$. If this adjoint be written in partitioned form as $[\mathbf{u}_1 \mathbf{u}_2 \dots \mathbf{u}_n]$, it is seen that $(\mathbf{A} - \lambda_i \mathbf{I})\mathbf{u}_k = \mathbf{0}$ or $\mathbf{A}\mathbf{u}_k = \lambda_i \mathbf{u}_k$. Thus any nonzero column may be used as an eigenvector corresponding to λ_i. Starting with $\text{adj}(\mathbf{A} - \lambda_i \mathbf{I}) \times (\mathbf{A} - \lambda_i \mathbf{I}) = \mathbf{0}$, it is found that the transpose of a nonzero row of the adjoint will serve as an eigenvector for $\mathbf{A}^t$. It is interesting to observe that, under these circumstances, $\text{adj}(\mathbf{A} - \lambda_i \mathbf{I}) = \mathbf{u}\mathbf{v}^t$ where $\mathbf{u}$ is an eigenvector for $\mathbf{A}$ corresponding to λ_i and $\mathbf{v}$ is an eigenvector for $\mathbf{A}^t$, also corresponding to λ_i. For by Sylvester's law of nullity, if r be the rank of the adjoint, $n - 0 \leqslant n - (n-1) + n - r$ or $r \leqslant 1$. Since $r \neq 0$, $r = 1$. Then $\text{adj}(\mathbf{A} - \lambda_i \mathbf{I}) = \mathbf{u}\mathbf{v}^t$, as explained on page 214.

Example. An example of some of the foregoing concepts can be found by using the matrix

$$\mathbf{A} = \begin{bmatrix} 17 & -1 & -27 & -6 \\ 6 & -14 & -54 & -24 \\ 1 & 1 & -29 & -4 \\ -9 & -19 & 51 & 6 \end{bmatrix}.$$

Direct expansion gives the characteristic function $\lambda^4 + 20\lambda^3 - 700\lambda^2 - 8000\lambda + 120000$, so that the eigenvalues are -30, -20, 10, and 20. The adjoint of $\mathbf{A} - 10\mathbf{I}$ is

$$\begin{bmatrix} 3600 & -1620 & 2340 & 1980 \\ -7200 & 3240 & -4680 & -3960 \\ -1200 & 540 & -780 & -660 \\ 10800 & -4860 & 7020 & 5940 \end{bmatrix},$$

thus an eigenvector for $\lambda = 10$ is $[3, -6, -1, 9]^t$. For eigenvectors corresponding to -30, -20, and 20, respectively, it is found that $[87, 546, 91, 181]^t$, $[-1, 2, -3, 7]^t$ and $[7, 6, 1, -9]^t$ may be used.

Reverting to consideration of the characteristic function of (4.10), after due reflection, we see that

$$\phi(\lambda) = (-1)^n(\lambda^n - \sigma_1 \lambda^{n-1} + \dots + (-1)^n \sigma_n), \tag{4.11}$$

where the σ_i (in addition to being the elementary symmetric functions of the roots $\lambda_1, \lambda_2, \dots, \lambda_n$) are certain combinations of the minors of $\mathbf{A}$. One can show that the sum of the diagonal entries of $\mathbf{A}$ is the sum of the eigenvalues of $\mathbf{A}$. This sum is called the *spur* or *trace* of $\mathbf{A}$. Thus,

$$Sp(\mathbf{A}) = \sum_{i=1}^{n} \lambda_i = \sum_{i=1}^{n} a_{ii}. \tag{4.12}$$

Also, the product of the eigenvalues is the determinant of $\mathbf{A}$. Thus,

$$\prod_{i=1}^{n} \lambda_i = \det(\mathbf{A}). \tag{4.13}$$

More generally, each σ_i is the sum of the ith order principal minors of $\mathbf{A}$, it being understood that the principal minors of a square matrix are those minors whose diagonal entries are diagonal entries of $\mathbf{A}$.

Consider next a theorem of interest involving square matrices of order n and to the effect that if

$$|a_{ii}| > \sum_{\substack{j=1 \\ j \neq i}}^{n} |a_{ij}|, \qquad 1 \leqslant i \leqslant n, \tag{4.14}$$

or if

$$|a_{ii}| > \sum_{\substack{j=1 \\ j \neq i}}^{n} |a_{ji}|, \qquad 1 \leqslant i \leqslant n, \tag{4.15}$$

then $\mathbf{A}$ is nonsingular. Proof is sketched for the second version. Suppose $\mathbf{A}$ is singular. Then so is $\mathbf{A}^t$, and there exists a nonzero vector $\mathbf{u}$ such that $\mathbf{A}^t \mathbf{u} = \mathbf{0}$. Let u_m be the component of $\mathbf{u}$ of maximum absolute value. Then $\sum_{j=1}^{n} a_{jm} u_j = 0$ and

$$|a_{mm}||u_m| = \left| \sum_{\substack{j=1 \\ j \neq m}}^{n} a_{jm} u_j \right| \leqslant \sum_{\substack{j=1 \\ j \neq m}}^{n} |a_{jm}||u_m|.$$

It follows that

$$|a_{mm}| \leqslant \sum_{\substack{j=1 \\ j \neq m}}^{n} |a_{jm}| < |a_{mm}|.$$

Since this cannot be, $\mathbf{A}$ is not singular.

When $\mathbf{A} - \lambda\mathbf{I}$ is used in the role of matrix $\mathbf{A}$ in the relations of (4.14) or (4.15), an immediate consequence is that every eigenvalue of a square matrix $\mathbf{A}$ lies (in the complex plane) in at least one of the circles

$$|\lambda - a_{ii}| \leqslant \sum_{\substack{j=1 \\ j \neq i}}^{n} |a_{ij}|, \qquad 1 \leqslant i \leqslant n, \qquad (4.16)$$

as well as in at least one of the circles

$$|\lambda - a_{ii}| \leqslant \sum_{\substack{j=1 \\ j \neq i}}^{n} |a_{ji}|, \qquad 1 \leqslant i \leqslant n. \qquad (4.17)$$

For by the paragraph above, if

$$|\lambda - a_{ii}| = \sum_{\substack{j=1 \\ j \neq i}}^{n} |a_{ij}|$$

for all permissible values of the indices, then $\mathbf{A} - \lambda\mathbf{I}$ is nonsingular. This establishes (4.16); (4.17) follows in like fashion.

Example. This section closes with an example of a use for eigenvalues, for finding a general solution for the system

$$\frac{dy_i}{dx} = a_{i1}y_1 + a_{i2}y_2 + \cdots + a_{in}y_n, \qquad 1 \leqslant i \leqslant n,$$

where the a_{ij} are constants. It is seen by substitution that $y_i = u_i e^{\lambda x}$ is a solution if and only if, for $\mathbf{A} = (a_{ij})$, $\det(\mathbf{A} - \lambda\mathbf{I}) = 0$ and $[u_1 \ u_2 \ldots u_n]^t$ is an eigenvector associated with λ. Should there be n distinct eigenvalues $\lambda_1, \lambda_2, \ldots, \lambda_n$ and corresponding eigenvectors $\mathbf{u}_1, \mathbf{u}_2, \ldots, \mathbf{u}_n$, then by superposition, the solution is

$$y_i = \sum_{j=1}^{n} c_j u_{ji} e^{\lambda_j x},$$

where $\mathbf{u}_j = [u_{j1}, u_{j2}, \ldots, u_{jn}]^t$, and $c_1, c_2, \ldots, c_n$ are arbitrary. If there are multiple roots for the characteristic equation, the solution is more elaborate.

4.4 Similar Matrices and Polynomials in a Matrix

Consider the matrices

$$\mathbf{A} = \begin{bmatrix} 1 & 0 \\ 0 & 1 \end{bmatrix}, \qquad \mathbf{B} = \begin{bmatrix} 1 & 0 \\ 1 & 1 \end{bmatrix}, \qquad \mathbf{C} = \begin{bmatrix} 1 & 0 \\ 2 & 1 \end{bmatrix}.$$

All have the characteristic function $(1 - \lambda)^2$, and $\mathbf{A}$ has two linearly independent eigenvectors, say $[1, 2]^t$ and $[2, 1]^t$. $\mathbf{B}$ and $\mathbf{C}$ have, except for a scalar multiplier, only one eigenvector, which may be taken as $[0, 1]^t$. Clearly, eigenvalues alone do not describe a matrix, nor do eigenvalues and eigenvectors completely determine it. Further insight can be gained by considering eigenvalues and eigenvectors for the matrix

$$\mathbf{A} = \begin{bmatrix} a & 0 & 0 & 0 \\ 0 & b & 0 & 0 \\ 0 & 0 & c & 0 \\ 0 & 0 & 1 & c \end{bmatrix},$$

under various assumptions such as $a = b = c$, $a = b$, or

$a \neq c$. There are certain unifying principles, and we proceed with a partial description.

If $\mathbf{P}$ is a nonsingular square matrix of order n, then for arbitrary vectors $\mathbf{u}$, the relation

$$\mathbf{u} = \mathbf{Pv} \qquad (4.18)$$

can be construed as a change in coordinates. Under these circumstances, given $\mathbf{v}$, we can find $\mathbf{u}$, or, given $\mathbf{u}$, we can find $\mathbf{v}$ as $\mathbf{P}^{-1}\mathbf{u}$. Consider now the eigenvector-eigenvalue relation $\mathbf{Au}_i = \lambda_i\mathbf{u}_i$ under such a change of variable. Letting $\mathbf{B} = \mathbf{P}^{-1}\mathbf{AP}$, from $\mathbf{Bv}_i = \mathbf{P}^{-1}\mathbf{APv}_i = \lambda_i\mathbf{v}_i$, and

$$\mathbf{v}_i = \mathbf{P}^{-1}\mathbf{u}_i, \qquad (4.19)$$

we see that the matrix $\mathbf{B}$ has the same eigenvalues as $\mathbf{A}$ and eigenvectors related by the matrix $\mathbf{P}$. The matrix $\mathbf{B}$ is said to be *similar* to the matrix $\mathbf{A}$ if and only if there exists a matrix $\mathbf{P}$ such that $\mathbf{B} = \mathbf{P}^{-1}\mathbf{AP}$.

Assume now that the eigenvalues of matrix $\mathbf{A}$ are all distinct, and denote them by $\lambda_1, \lambda_2, \ldots, \lambda_n$. Let the associated eigenvectors be $\mathbf{u}_1, \mathbf{u}_2, \ldots, \mathbf{u}_n$. It will soon appear that the eigenvectors are linearly independent. Hence if $\mathbf{U}$ is the matrix whose ith column is $\mathbf{u}_i$, it follows from $\mathbf{AU} = \mathbf{U} \operatorname{diag}(\lambda_1, \lambda_2, \ldots, \lambda_n)$ that

$$\mathbf{U}^{-1}\mathbf{AU} = \operatorname{diag}(\lambda_1, \lambda_2, \ldots, \lambda_n), \qquad (4.20)$$

and $\mathbf{A}$ is similar to a diagonal matrix whose diagonal elements are the eigenvalues of $\mathbf{A}$. To see that the eigenvectors are linearly independent, suppose that the first m are linearly independent, but that $\mathbf{u}_n = \sum_{i=1}^{m} c_i\mathbf{u}_i$. Then

$$\mathbf{Au}_n = \mathbf{A}\sum_{i=1}^{m} c_i\mathbf{u}_i = \sum_{i=1}^{m} c_i\mathbf{Au}_i = \sum_{i=1}^{m} c_i\lambda_i\mathbf{u}_i.$$

It would be also true that

$$\mathbf{Au}_n = \lambda_n\mathbf{u}_n = \lambda_n\sum_{i=1}^{m} c_i\mathbf{u}_i.$$

Thus $\sum_{i=1}^{m} c_i(\lambda_n - \lambda_i)\mathbf{u}_i = \mathbf{0}$. This contradicts the assumed independence of the first m eigenvectors.

Example. A numerical example is found in

$$\mathbf{A} = \begin{bmatrix} 17 & 17 & 27 & 12 \\ 6 & -14 & -54 & -24 \\ 1 & 1 & -29 & -4 \\ -9 & -19 & 51 & 6 \end{bmatrix},$$

$$\mathbf{U} = \begin{bmatrix} \dfrac{3}{10} & \dfrac{7}{20} & \dfrac{-3}{10} & \dfrac{-1}{20} \\[2mm] \dfrac{-6}{10} & \dfrac{6}{20} & \dfrac{6}{10} & \dfrac{2}{20} \\[2mm] \dfrac{-1}{10} & \dfrac{1}{20} & \dfrac{1}{10} & \dfrac{-3}{20} \\[2mm] \dfrac{9}{10} & \dfrac{-9}{20} & \dfrac{1}{10} & \dfrac{7}{20} \end{bmatrix},$$

together with $\lambda_1 = 10$, $\lambda_2 = 20$, $\lambda_3 = -30$, $\lambda_4 = -20$. It is readily verified that

$$\mathbf{U}^{-1} = \begin{bmatrix} 1 & 0 & 2 & 1 \\ 2 & 1 & 0 & 0 \\ 0 & 1 & 3 & 1 \\ 0 & 1 & -6 & 0 \end{bmatrix}.$$

and that $\mathbf{AU} = \mathbf{U}$ diag $(10, 20, -30, -20)$ and that each is, in fact,

$$\begin{bmatrix} 3 & 7 & 9 & 1 \\ -6 & 6 & -18 & -2 \\ -1 & 1 & -3 & 3 \\ 9 & -9 & -3 & -7 \end{bmatrix}.$$

It can be shown that every matrix is similar to a matrix of specifiable structure called the *Jordan canonical form*. Matrices of the type,

$$[\lambda], \quad \begin{bmatrix} \lambda & 0 \\ 1 & \lambda \end{bmatrix}, \quad \begin{bmatrix} \lambda & 0 & 0 \\ 1 & \lambda & 0 \\ 0 & 1 & \lambda \end{bmatrix}, \quad \begin{bmatrix} \lambda & 0 & 0 & 0 \\ 1 & \lambda & 0 & 0 \\ 0 & 1 & \lambda & 0 \\ 0 & 0 & 1 & \lambda \end{bmatrix}, \quad \dots,$$

are called *canonical boxes*. Every matrix is similar to a matrix based on the use of these canonical boxes to build a *quasidiagonal matrix*. An example is

$$\begin{bmatrix} \lambda_1 & 0 & 0 & 0 & 0 & 0 & 0 \\ 0 & \lambda_2 & 0 & 0 & 0 & 0 & 0 \\ 0 & 1 & \lambda_2 & 0 & 0 & 0 & 0 \\ 0 & 0 & 0 & \lambda_3 & 0 & 0 & 0 \\ 0 & 0 & 0 & 0 & \lambda_4 & 0 & 0 \\ 0 & 0 & 0 & 0 & 1 & \lambda_4 & 0 \\ 0 & 0 & 0 & 0 & 0 & 1 & \lambda_4 \end{bmatrix},$$

where the λ_i are any numbers, repeated or not. It is easy to show that one and only one eigenvector corresponds to each canonical box (except for a scalar multiplier).

Now let $a_0, a_1, \dots, a_m$ be any scalars and let $\mathbf{A}$ be a square matrix. Then by a polynomial in matrix $\mathbf{A}$, we mean an expression of the form

$$g(\mathbf{A}) = \sum_{i=0}^{m} a_i \mathbf{A}^{m-i},$$

where, by $\mathbf{A}^0$, we understand the identity matrix $\mathbf{I}$. Let $\mathbf{B}$ be any nonsingular matrix, and observe that $\mathbf{B}^{-1}\mathbf{A}^2\mathbf{B} = \mathbf{B}^{-1}\mathbf{A}\mathbf{B}\mathbf{B}^{-1}\mathbf{A}\mathbf{B}$. Proceeding by induction, it becomes clear that for nonsingular matrices $\mathbf{B}$,

$$g(\mathbf{B}^{-1}\mathbf{A}\mathbf{B}) = \mathbf{B}^{-1}g(\mathbf{A})\mathbf{B}. \quad (4.21)$$

There is a simple connection between the eigenvalues of the matrix $g(\mathbf{A})$ and those of the matrix $\mathbf{A}$. Indeed, if $\lambda_1, \lambda_2, \dots, \lambda_n$ be the eigenvalues of $\mathbf{A}$, then $g(\lambda_1)$, $g(\lambda_2)$, $\dots, g(\lambda_n)$ are the eigenvalues of $g(\mathbf{A})$. We give a demonstration only for the case where the eigenvectors of $\mathbf{A}$ are distinct. Let $\mathbf{P}$ be a matrix whose columns are eigenvectors for $\mathbf{A}$, so that $\mathbf{AP} = \mathbf{P}$ diag $(\lambda_1, \lambda_2, \dots, \lambda_n)$ and $\mathbf{P}^{-1}\mathbf{AP} = $ diag $(\lambda_1, \lambda_2, \dots, \lambda_n)$. It follows from (4.21) that

$$g(\mathbf{P}^{-1}\mathbf{AP}) = \mathbf{P}^{-1}g(\mathbf{A})\mathbf{P}.$$

It is not difficult to see that, if we denote diag $(\lambda_1, \lambda_2, \dots, \lambda_n)$ by Λ, then $\Lambda^2 = $ diag $(\lambda_1^2, \lambda_2^2, \dots, \lambda_n^2)$ and, in general, $\Lambda^k = $ diag $(\lambda_1^k, \lambda_2^k, \dots, \lambda_n^k)$. Also, for arbitrary scalars, c_1 and c_2, and diagonal matrices $\mathbf{D}_1 = $ diag $(e_1, e_2, \dots, e_n)$ and $\mathbf{D}_2 = $ diag $(f_1, f_2, \dots, f_n)$,

$$c_1\mathbf{D}_1 + c_2\mathbf{D}_2$$
$$= \text{diag}\,(c_1 e_1 + c_2 f_1, c_1 e_2 + c_2 f_2, \dots, c_1 e_n + c_2 f_n).$$

Applying these concepts to the above, the net result is that

$$\mathbf{P}^{-1}g(\mathbf{A})\mathbf{P} = \text{diag}\,[g(\lambda_1), g(\lambda_2), \dots, g(\lambda_n)],$$

or

$$g(\mathbf{A})\mathbf{P} = \mathbf{P}\,\text{diag}\,[g(\lambda_1), g(\lambda_2), \dots, g(\lambda_n)]. \quad (4.22)$$

For distinct eigenvectors, then, it is clear that the eigenvalues of $g(\mathbf{A})$ are $g(\lambda_i)$ and, in addition, that the eigenvectors of $g(\mathbf{A})$ are the same as those of $\mathbf{A}$.

Example. As a case in point, consider $g(x) = x^2 - 4$ and

$$\mathbf{A} = \begin{bmatrix} 11 & 6 & -2 \\ -2 & 18 & 1 \\ -12 & 24 & 13 \end{bmatrix}.$$

The eigenvalues of $\mathbf{A}$ are found to be 7, 14, and 21 with the eigenvectors $[1, 0, 2]^t$, $[2, 1, 0]^t$, and $[0, 1, 3]^t$, respectively. It develops that $g(\mathbf{A})$ is

$$\begin{bmatrix} 129 & 126 & -42 \\ -70 & 332 & 35 \\ -336 & 672 & 213 \end{bmatrix},$$

with eigenvectors as above and eigenvalues 45, 192, and 437, respectively.

The use of similar matrices, and certain analogies between polynomials $f(x)$, in an indeterminate x, and matrix polynomials $f(\mathbf{A})$, combine to produce powerful results. We proceed with an example.

First of all, it develops that a necessary and sufficient condition for $\lim_{k \to \infty} \mathbf{A}^k$ to be zero ($\mathbf{A}$ being a square matrix) is that all the eigenvalues of $\mathbf{A}$ shall be, in absolute value, less than one. If $\mathbf{A} = \mathbf{P}^{-1}\Lambda\mathbf{P}$, where $\Lambda = [\lambda_1, \lambda_2, \dots, \lambda_n]$, this is obvious, since $\mathbf{A}^k = \mathbf{P}^{-1}\Lambda^k\mathbf{P}$ and $\Lambda^k = [\lambda_1^k, \lambda_2^k, \dots, \lambda_n^k]$. Proof can also be accomplished if $\mathbf{A}$ is not similar to a diagonal matrix. On the strength of the above statement, we now show that a necessary and sufficient condition that the matric series

$$\mathbf{I} + \mathbf{A} + \mathbf{A}^2 + \cdots + \mathbf{A}^k + \cdots$$

converge is that all eigenvalues of $\mathbf{A}$ be less than unity in modulus. In such event,

$$(\mathbf{I} - \mathbf{A})^{-1} = \mathbf{I} + \mathbf{A} + \mathbf{A}^2 + \cdots + \mathbf{A}^k + \cdots. \quad (4.23)$$

Here, the meaning of the equal sign is that each element of the matrix on the left is the sum of an infinite series built from corresponding elements on the right. It is necessary that $\lim_{k \to \infty} \mathbf{A}^k$ be zero; therefore, by the above, each eigenvalue must be less than unity in modulus. Now let all eigenvalues have an absolute value less than unity, and consider sufficiency. Since $\det(\mathbf{I} - \mathbf{A}) = 0$ implies 1 is an eigenvalue, it follows that $\det(\mathbf{I} - \mathbf{A}) \neq 0$, and that $(\mathbf{I} - \mathbf{A})^{-1}$ exists. The identity

$$(\mathbf{I} + \mathbf{A} + \mathbf{A}^2 + \cdots + \mathbf{A}^k)(\mathbf{I} - \mathbf{A}) = \mathbf{I} - \mathbf{A}^{k+1}$$

is easy to establish. Then *postmultiplication* by $(\mathbf{I} - \mathbf{A})^{-1}$ gives

$$\mathbf{I} + \mathbf{A} + \mathbf{A}^2 + \cdots + \mathbf{A}^k = (\mathbf{I} - \mathbf{A})^{-1} - \mathbf{A}^{k+1}(\mathbf{I} - \mathbf{A})^{-1}.$$

Since $\lim_{k \to \infty} \mathbf{A}^{k+1} = \mathbf{0}$, (4.23) follows.

At this juncture, note that if, for a square matrix $\mathbf{B}$, an upper bound can be found for the moduli of the eigenvalues, then a closely related matrix $\mathbf{A}$ can be found whose eigenvalues are less than unity in absolute value and whose eigenvectors are those of $\mathbf{B}$. Let such an upper bound be p. Then let $\mathbf{A} = (1/p)\mathbf{B}$; it follows that if $\mathbf{B}\mathbf{u} = \lambda\mathbf{u}$ then

$$\frac{1}{p}\mathbf{B}\mathbf{u} = \mathbf{A}\mathbf{u} = \frac{\lambda}{p}\mathbf{u}. \tag{4.24}$$

It is not necessary to know the eigenvalues to find such a bound p. Two simple tests may be derived from (4.16) and (4.17). Let λ_k denote any eigenvalue of $\mathbf{A} = (a_{ij})$. The first of the relations mentioned above yields the inequality

$$|\lambda_k| \leqslant \max\left(\sum_{j=1}^{n} |a_{ij}|\right); \tag{4.25}$$

the second leads to

$$|\lambda_k| \leqslant \max\left(\sum_{i=1}^{n} |a_{ij}|\right). \tag{4.26}$$

Let the eigenvalue λ_k lie in the circle with center at a_{mm} and with radius equal to

$$\sum_{\substack{j=1 \\ j \neq m}}^{n} |a_{mj}|.$$

Then, since $|\lambda_k| - |a_{mm}| \leqslant |\lambda_k - a_{mm}|$, it is seen that $|\lambda_k| \leqslant \sum_{j=1}^{n} |a_{mj}|$. From this, (4.25) follows. Proof of (4.26) is similar.

The matrix $\mathbf{A}$ of page 222 will serve to illustrate the above. By (4.25), $|\lambda_k| \leqslant 49$. This is verified, since $\lambda_1 = 7$, $\lambda_2 = 14$, $\lambda_3 = 21$. By (4.26), $|\lambda_k| \leqslant 48$, a slightly sharper result.

The ideas of the paragraph above will find application, for example, in the following chapter in conjunction with the iterative solution of simultaneous linear equations. A related concept involves the inequality

$$Sp((\mathbf{AB})^*\mathbf{AB}) \leqslant Sp(\mathbf{A}^*\mathbf{A})Sp(\mathbf{B}^*\mathbf{B}). \tag{4.27}$$

This important inequality is an extension of the Cauchy-Schwarz inequality, which in vector form may be written [1]

$$(\mathbf{v}, \mathbf{w})(\mathbf{w}, \mathbf{v}) \leqslant (\mathbf{v}, \mathbf{v})(\mathbf{w}, \mathbf{w}). \tag{4.28}$$

In (4.28) let $\mathbf{v} = [a_{i1}\ a_{i2}\ \ldots\ a_{in}]^t$ and $\mathbf{w} = [\bar{b}_{1j}\ \bar{b}_{2j}\ \ldots\ \bar{b}_{nj}]^t$. Then (4.28) becomes

$$\sum_{m=1}^{n} \bar{a}_{im}\bar{b}_{mj} \sum_{m=1}^{n} b_{mj}a_{im} \leqslant \sum_{m=1}^{n} \bar{a}_{im}a_{im} \sum_{m=1}^{n} b_{mj}\bar{b}_{mj}.$$

Now sum both sides from $i = 1$ to $i = p$ and from $j = 1$ to $j = q$ (assuming $\mathbf{A}$ is $p \times n$ and $\mathbf{B}$ is $n \times q$). The result is (4.27). For a square matrix $\mathbf{A}$, since $Sp(\mathbf{A}^*\mathbf{A}) = \sum_{k=1}^{n} \sum_{i=1}^{n} a_{ik}\bar{a}_{ik}$, it follows that if $Sp(\mathbf{A}^*\mathbf{A}) \leqslant u < 1$, then $Sp(\mathbf{A}^m\mathbf{A}^{*m}) < u^m$; whence $\lim_{m \to \infty} \mathbf{A}^m = \mathbf{0}$ and (4.23) is true.

If we apply (4.27) to an eigenvalue-eigenvector relation $\mathbf{A}\mathbf{u} = \lambda\mathbf{u}$, we get

$$Sp(\mathbf{u}^*\mathbf{A}^*\mathbf{A}\mathbf{u}) \leqslant Sp(\mathbf{A}^*\mathbf{A})Sp(\mathbf{u}^*\mathbf{u}).$$

But $Sp(\mathbf{u}^*\mathbf{A}^*\mathbf{A}\mathbf{u}) = Sp(\bar{\lambda}\lambda\mathbf{u}^*\mathbf{u}) = |\lambda|^2 Sp(\mathbf{u}^*\mathbf{u})$. Thus, for any eigenvalue,

$$|\lambda|^2 \leqslant \sum_{i=1}^{n} \sum_{k=1}^{n} |a_{ik}|^2.$$

Still another relation, for real square matrices, is Schur's inequality, which states that $\lambda_1^2 + \lambda_2^2 + \cdots + \lambda_n^2 = Sp(\mathbf{A}^2) \leqslant Sp(\mathbf{A}^*\mathbf{A}) = \sum_{i=1}^{n} \sum_{k=1}^{n} a_{ik}^2$. Proof is accomplished directly. $Sp(\mathbf{A}^2)$ is $\sum_{i=1}^{n} a_{ii}^2 + \sum_{j,i=1, j \neq i}^{n} a_{ij}a_{ji}$. But for any two real numbers a and b, $2ab \leqslant a^2 + b^2$. Therefore, $a_{ij}a_{ji} \leqslant \frac{1}{2}(a_{ij}^2 + a_{ji}^2)$ and

$$Sp(\mathbf{A}^2) \leqslant \sum_{i=1}^{n} a_{ii}^2 + \sum_{\substack{j,i=1 \\ j \neq i}}^{n} \tfrac{1}{2}(a_{ij}^2 + a_{ji}^2) = Sp(\mathbf{A}^*\mathbf{A}).$$

We conclude this section with the famous Cayley-Hamilton theorem which states that if $\phi(\lambda)$ is the characteristic function for the matrix $\mathbf{A}$, then $\phi(\mathbf{A})$ is the null matrix. To understand this, note that for positive integral values of k, $\mathbf{A}^k - \lambda^k\mathbf{I} = (\mathbf{A} - \lambda\mathbf{I})(\mathbf{A}^{k-1} + \lambda\mathbf{A}^{k-2} + \cdots + \lambda^{k-1}\mathbf{I})$. This means that

$$\phi(\mathbf{A}) - \phi(\lambda)\mathbf{I} = (\mathbf{A} - \lambda\mathbf{I})\boldsymbol{\psi},$$

where $\boldsymbol{\psi}$ is a polynomial in λ and $\mathbf{A}$.

Since $\text{adj}(\mathbf{A} - \lambda\mathbf{I})$ is composed from the cofactors of $\mathbf{A} - \lambda\mathbf{I}$, it also is a polynomial in λ with matric coefficients. Moreover, $\phi(\lambda)\mathbf{I} = (\mathbf{A} - \lambda\mathbf{I})\,\text{adj}(\mathbf{A} - \lambda\mathbf{I})$. Adding this to the above, we obtain

$$\phi(\mathbf{A}) = (\mathbf{A} - \lambda\mathbf{I})\mathbf{C},$$

where $\mathbf{C}$ is a polynomial in λ with matric coefficients. Since the right side will involve λ nontrivially if $\mathbf{C}$ is not zero, and since $\phi(\mathbf{A})$ is independent of λ, it follows that $\phi(\mathbf{A})$ is zero.

Example. As an illustration, consider again the matrix $\mathbf{A}$ of page 222. $\mathbf{A}^2$ and $\mathbf{A}^3$ are found to be

$$\mathbf{A}^2 = \begin{bmatrix} 133 & 126 & -42 \\ -70 & 336 & 35 \\ -336 & 672 & 217 \end{bmatrix},$$

$$\mathbf{A}^3 = \begin{bmatrix} 1715 & 2058 & -686 \\ -1862 & 6468 & 931 \\ -7644 & 15288 & 4165 \end{bmatrix}.$$

The characteristic function is $-\lambda^3 + 42\lambda^2 - 539\lambda + 2058$, and it is found that $-\mathbf{A}^3 + 42\mathbf{A}^2 - 539\mathbf{A} + 2058\mathbf{I} = \mathbf{0}$.

4.5 Symmetric and Hermitian Matrices

Recall that a matrix $\mathbf{A}$ is Hermitian if and only if $\mathbf{A} = \mathbf{A}^* = \overline{\mathbf{A}}^t$. $\mathbf{A}$ is symmetric if and only if $\mathbf{A} = \mathbf{A}^t$. Thus $\mathbf{A}$ is symmetric and Hermitian if and only if $\mathbf{A}$ is real and self-transpose.

An *Hermitian form* is an expression of the type

$$\sum_{i,j=1}^{n} a_{ij}\bar{u}_i u_j, \qquad a_{ij} = \bar{a}_{ji},$$

where the u_i are construed as complex variables and the a_{ij} as constants. It is apparent that such a form may always be written

$$(\mathbf{u}, \mathbf{A}\mathbf{u}), \text{ where } \mathbf{A} = \mathbf{A}^*. \qquad (4.29)$$

A *quadratic form* is an expression of the type

$$\sum_{i,j=1}^{n} a_{ij}u_i u_j, \qquad a_{ij} = a_{ji},$$

where the a_{ij} are construed as constants and the u_i as variables. We are here concerned only with *real quadratic forms*. In that event the quadratic form may be written as

$$(\mathbf{u}, \mathbf{A}\mathbf{u}), \text{ where } \mathbf{A} = \overline{\mathbf{A}} = \mathbf{A}^t, \text{ and } \mathbf{u} \text{ is real.} \quad (4.30)$$

If $\mathbf{u}$ and $\mathbf{A}$ satisfy either (4.29) or (4.30), then:

(a) For all $\mathbf{u}$, $(\mathbf{u}, \mathbf{A}\mathbf{u})$ is real.

(b) Every eigenvalue of $\mathbf{A}$ is real.

(c) Eigenvectors corresponding to distinct eigenvalues are orthogonal.

To prove (a), note that $(\mathbf{u}, \mathbf{A}\mathbf{u}) = (\mathbf{A}^*\mathbf{u}, \mathbf{u}) = (\mathbf{A}\mathbf{u}, \mathbf{u}) = \overline{(\mathbf{u}, \mathbf{A}\mathbf{u})}$ (see equations (4.2) and (4.7)). To show (b), $(\mathbf{u}, \mathbf{A}\mathbf{u}) = (\mathbf{u}, \lambda\mathbf{u}) = \lambda(\mathbf{u}, \mathbf{u})$; since $(\mathbf{u}, \mathbf{A}\mathbf{u})$ and $(\mathbf{u}, \mathbf{u})$ are real, so is λ. In case (c), $(\mathbf{u}_1, \mathbf{A}\mathbf{u}_2) = \lambda_2(\mathbf{u}_1, \mathbf{u}_2)$ and $(\mathbf{u}_1, \mathbf{A}\mathbf{u}_2) = (\mathbf{A}\mathbf{u}_1, \mathbf{u}_2) = \bar{\lambda}_1(\mathbf{u}_1, \mathbf{u}_2) = \lambda_1(\mathbf{u}_1, \mathbf{u}_2)$. Then $\lambda_1 \neq \lambda_2$ and $\lambda_1(\mathbf{u}_1, \mathbf{u}_2) = \lambda_2(\mathbf{u}_1, \mathbf{u}_2)$ imply $(\mathbf{u}_1, \mathbf{u}_2) = 0$.

An example of a quadratic form is given by $4x_1^2 - 2x_1x_2 + 4x_2^2 - 2x_2x_3 + 4x_3^2 - 2x_3x_4 + 4x_4^2$. Since this may be written as $3x_1^2 + (x_1 - x_2)^2 + 2x_2^2 + (x_2 - x_3)^2 + 2x_3^2 + (x_3 - x_4)^2 + 3x_4^2$, it is clear that the form is also positive definite (see below).

A matrix $\mathbf{A}$ is unitary if and only if $\mathbf{A}^* = \mathbf{A}^{-1}$. A real matrix $\mathbf{A}$ is orthogonal if and only if $\mathbf{A}^t = \mathbf{A}^{-1}$. A matrix $\mathbf{A}$ is *isometric* if and only if, for all n-dimensional vectors $\mathbf{u}$, $\mathbf{v}$, it is true that $(\mathbf{u}, \mathbf{v}) = (\mathbf{A}\mathbf{u}, \mathbf{A}\mathbf{v})$. If $\mathbf{w} = \mathbf{A}\mathbf{u}$ be interpreted as a change of variable, it is seen that for an isometric transformation, $(\mathbf{u}, \mathbf{u}) = (\mathbf{A}\mathbf{u}, \mathbf{A}\mathbf{u}) = (\mathbf{w}, \mathbf{w})$; therefore, length is preserved. Clearly a real unitary matrix is an orthogonal matrix. It develops that a matrix $\mathbf{A}$ is isometric if and only if it is unitary. For suppose $\mathbf{A}$ is unitary; then $(\mathbf{A}\mathbf{u}, \mathbf{A}\mathbf{v}) = (\mathbf{A}^*\mathbf{A}\mathbf{u}, \mathbf{v}) = (\mathbf{u}, \mathbf{v})$. Next consider $(\mathbf{A}\mathbf{u}, \mathbf{A}\mathbf{v}) = (\mathbf{u}, \mathbf{v})$ for all $\mathbf{u}$ and $\mathbf{v}$. It is true, in particular, if $\mathbf{v} = (\mathbf{A}^*\mathbf{A} - \mathbf{I})\mathbf{u}$. Then $(\mathbf{A}\mathbf{u}, \mathbf{A}(\mathbf{A}^*\mathbf{A} - \mathbf{I})\mathbf{u}) = (\mathbf{u}, (\mathbf{A}^*\mathbf{A} - \mathbf{I})\mathbf{u})$ implies $(\mathbf{A}^*\mathbf{A}\mathbf{u}, (\mathbf{A}^*\mathbf{A} - \mathbf{I})\mathbf{u}) = (\mathbf{u}, (\mathbf{A}^*\mathbf{A} - \mathbf{I})\mathbf{u})$ or $((\mathbf{A}^*\mathbf{A} - \mathbf{I})\mathbf{u}, (\mathbf{A}^*\mathbf{A} - \mathbf{I})\mathbf{u}) = 0$ for all $\mathbf{u}$. This means $\mathbf{A}^*\mathbf{A} - \mathbf{I} = \mathbf{0}$ or $\mathbf{A}^* = \mathbf{A}^{-1}$.

It is next indicated that if $\mathbf{A}$ is any Hermitian matrix, then there exists a unitary matrix $\mathbf{P}$ such that

$$\mathbf{A} = \mathbf{P}\mathbf{\Lambda}\mathbf{P}^*, \qquad \mathbf{P}^* = \mathbf{P}^{-1}, \qquad (4.31)$$

where $\mathbf{\Lambda} = [\lambda_1\ \lambda_2\ \cdots\ \lambda_n]$ and $\lambda_1, \lambda_2, \ldots, \lambda_n$ are the (real) eigenvalues of $\mathbf{A}$. Should the eigenvalues be distinct, there are n orthogonal eigenvectors, thus n linearly independent eigenvectors. Then it follows, as in establishing (4.20), that (4.31) is true. To guarantee that $\mathbf{P}^* = \mathbf{P}^{-1}$, we need only require that each eigenvector be normalized in forming $\mathbf{P}$. We then see by direct multiplication that $\mathbf{P}^*\mathbf{P} = \mathbf{I}$, hence $\mathbf{P}^* = \mathbf{P}^{-1}$. No proof is attempted here for the case of multiple eigenvalues, though the theorem remains true (see Jacobi's method, page 250).

An Hermitian matrix $\mathbf{A}$ is *positive definite* if and only if, for all $\mathbf{u} \neq \mathbf{0}$, $(\mathbf{u}, \mathbf{A}\mathbf{u}) > 0$. Such a matrix is *positive semi-definite* if and only if, for $\mathbf{u} \neq \mathbf{0}$, $(\mathbf{u}, \mathbf{A}\mathbf{u}) \geqslant 0$. Corresponding statements define *negative definite* and *negative semidefinite Hermitian* matrices. Hermitian matrices thus far not characterized are called *indefinite*.

It is a simple matter to verify that for the real Hermitian matrix

$$\mathbf{A} = \begin{bmatrix} -4 & .. & 1 & 0 \\ 1 & -4 & 1 \\ 0 & 1 & -4 \end{bmatrix},$$

we may use $\mathbf{\Lambda} = [-4 - \sqrt{2}, -4, -4 + \sqrt{2}]$ and

$$\mathbf{P} = \begin{bmatrix} 1/2 & \sqrt{2}/2 & 1/2 \\ -\sqrt{2}/2 & 0 & \sqrt{2}/2 \\ 1/2 & -\sqrt{2}/2 & 1/2 \end{bmatrix}.$$

Recall that the leading submatrices of a square matrix $\mathbf{A}$ are those square matrices of order m, $1 \leqslant m \leqslant n$, formed from the first m rows and columns of $\mathbf{A}$, and that the corresponding determinants have been denoted $\Delta_1, \Delta_2, \ldots, \Delta_m, \ldots, \Delta_n$. Let the submatrices be denoted $\mathbf{A}^{(1)}, \mathbf{A}^{(2)}, \ldots, \mathbf{A}^{(m)}, \ldots, \mathbf{A}^{(n)}$. A theorem of consequence concerning Hermitian matrices states that between two distinct eigenvalues of $\mathbf{A}^{(k+1)}$ there lies at least one eigenvalue of $\mathbf{A}^{(k)}$ which may coincide with either of these two eigenvalues. Moreover, if λ is a multiple eigenvalue of order p for $\mathbf{A}^{(k+1)}$, then it is an eigenvalue of order at least $p - 1$ for $\mathbf{A}^{(k)}$. For brevity in presentation, let

$$\mathbf{B} = \mathbf{A}^{(k)}, \qquad \mathbf{C} = \mathbf{A}^{(k+1)} = \begin{bmatrix} \mathbf{B} & \mathbf{w} \\ \mathbf{w}^* & \beta \end{bmatrix}, \qquad \mathbf{B}\mathbf{U} = \mathbf{U}\mathbf{\Lambda},$$

where $\mathbf{U}$ is unitary and $\mathbf{\Lambda}$ is the matrix diag $(\lambda_1\ \lambda_2\ \cdots\ \lambda_k)$. Let λ be an eigenvalue of $\mathbf{C}$ and $[\mathbf{v}^t\alpha]^t$ the corresponding eigenvector, $\mathbf{v}$ being a $k \times 1$ matrix. Thus

$$\begin{bmatrix} \mathbf{B} & \mathbf{w} \\ \mathbf{w}^* & \beta \end{bmatrix}\begin{bmatrix} \mathbf{v} \\ \alpha \end{bmatrix} = \lambda\begin{bmatrix} \mathbf{v} \\ \alpha \end{bmatrix},$$

whence

$$\mathbf{B}\mathbf{v} + \alpha\mathbf{w} = \lambda\mathbf{v}, \qquad \mathbf{w}^*\mathbf{v} + \alpha\beta = \lambda\alpha. \qquad (4.32)$$

Let $\mathbf{v} = \mathbf{U}\mathbf{x}$. Then the first of these equations (4.32) yields $\mathbf{U}\boldsymbol{\Lambda}\mathbf{x} + \alpha\mathbf{w} = \lambda\mathbf{U}\mathbf{x}$; then $\boldsymbol{\Lambda}\mathbf{x} + \alpha\mathbf{U}^*\mathbf{w} = \lambda\mathbf{x}$ and $(\lambda\mathbf{I} - \boldsymbol{\Lambda})\mathbf{x} = \alpha\mathbf{U}^*\mathbf{w}$. When the latter is substituted in the second equation of (4.32), there results

$$\mathbf{w}^*\mathbf{U}(\lambda\mathbf{I} - \boldsymbol{\Lambda})^{-1}\alpha\mathbf{U}^*\mathbf{w} + \alpha\beta = \lambda\alpha.$$

This is, of course, valid only if λ is not an eigenvalue of $\mathbf{B}$.

The factor α may be removed, since we may view the components of the matrix $\mathbf{A}$ as variables. Since $\lambda\mathbf{I} - \boldsymbol{\Lambda}$ is diagonal, its inverse is $\text{diag}(\mu_1\,\mu_2\cdots\mu_k)$ where $\mu_i = 1/(\lambda - \lambda_i)$. Using this leads to the equation

$$\lambda - \beta = \sum_{j=1}^{k} \frac{|(\mathbf{w}, \mathbf{u}_j)|^2}{\lambda - \lambda_j}, \qquad (4.33)$$

where $\mathbf{U} = [\mathbf{u}_1, \mathbf{u}_2, \ldots, \mathbf{u}_k]$. Should $(\mathbf{w}, \mathbf{u}_j) = 0$, it is easy to verify that $\begin{bmatrix} \mathbf{v} \\ \alpha \end{bmatrix} = \begin{bmatrix} \mathbf{u}_j \\ 0 \end{bmatrix}$ is an eigenvector and λ_j an eigenvalue for $\mathbf{A}^{(k+1)}$. Should λ_j be a multiple root such that for l different indices $j_1, j_2, \ldots, j_l$, λ_j is the eigenvalue for $\mathbf{u}_{j_i}$ and $(\mathbf{w}, \mathbf{u}_{j_i}) \neq 0$, then λ_j is an eigenvalue of multiplicity at least $l - 1$ for $\mathbf{A}^{(k+1)}$. This is illustrated for $l = 2$, and for convenience we suppose $(\mathbf{w}, \mathbf{u}_1)$ and $(\mathbf{w}, \mathbf{u}_2)$ are not zero, while both $\mathbf{u}_1$ and $\mathbf{u}_2$ have the eigenvalue λ_1. Then investigation shows that the vector $\begin{bmatrix} \gamma\mathbf{u}_1 + \delta\mathbf{u}_2 \\ 0 \end{bmatrix}$, with proper choice of γ and δ, will serve as an eigenvector of $\mathbf{A}^{(k+1)}$ corresponding to the eigenvalue λ_1. We need only require that $\gamma\mathbf{w}^*\mathbf{u}_1 + \delta\mathbf{w}^*\mathbf{u}_2 = 0$, with γ and δ not both zero. Thus under all circumstances (4.33) leads to a polynomial equation of requisite degree for determining the eigenvalues of $\mathbf{C}$ distinct from those of $\mathbf{B}$. (If all the eigenvalues of $\mathbf{B}$ are eigenvalues of $\mathbf{C}$, and $(\mathbf{w}, \mathbf{u}_j) = 0$ for all values of j, then $\lambda = \beta$ is the new eigenvalue and may equal a previous eigenvalue.) The remaining details are omitted, with the remark that a sketch of a simple situation involving real values of λ_j is informative. This sketch may take the form of plotting $z = \lambda - \beta$ and

$$z = \sum_{j=1}^{k} \frac{|\mathbf{w}, \mathbf{u}_j|^2}{\lambda - \lambda_j}$$

on the same coordinate plane.

Example. An example is furnished by the matrix

$$\begin{bmatrix} -4 & 1 & 0 & 0 \\ 1 & -4 & 1 & 0 \\ 0 & 1 & -4 & 1 \\ 0 & 0 & 1 & -4 \end{bmatrix}$$

The leading submatrix $[-4]$ has the characteristic function $-4 - \lambda$ and the eigenvalue -4. The leading submatrix $\begin{bmatrix} -4 & 1 \\ 1 & -4 \end{bmatrix}$ has the characteristic function $15 + 8\lambda + \lambda^2$ and the eigenvalues -3 and -5. The leading submatrix of order three has the characteristic function $-56 - 46\lambda - 12\lambda^2 - \lambda^3$ and the eigenvalues $-4 - \sqrt{2}$, -4, and $-4 + \sqrt{2}$. The matrix itself has the characteristic function $209 + 232\lambda + 93\lambda^2 + 16\lambda^3 + \lambda^4$ and the eigenvalues $(-9 - \sqrt{5})/2$, $(-7 - \sqrt{5})/2$, $(-9 + \sqrt{5})/2$, and $(-7 + \sqrt{5})/2$.

If the matrix $\mathbf{A}$ is Hermitian, each of the following statements give a necessary and sufficient condition for $\mathbf{A}$ to be positive definite:

(*a*) All the eigenvalues of $\mathbf{A}$ are positive.

(*b*) The coefficients of the characteristic equation for $\mathbf{A}$ alternate in sign.

(*c*) Each leading submatrix of $\mathbf{A}$ is positive definite.

(*d*) $\Delta_m > 0$, $\quad 1 \leqslant m \leqslant n$.

First consider (*a*). If $\mathbf{A}$ is positive definite, then $(\mathbf{u}, \mathbf{A}\mathbf{u}) > 0$, $(\mathbf{u}, \mathbf{u}) > 0$ and $\mathbf{A}\mathbf{u} = \lambda\mathbf{u}$ imply $\lambda > 0$, because $(\mathbf{u}, \mathbf{A}\mathbf{u}) = \lambda(\mathbf{u}, \mathbf{u})$. Now suppose $\lambda_1, \lambda_2, \ldots, \lambda_n$ positive. Since $\mathbf{A}$ is Hermitian, it has n corresponding eigenvectors $\mathbf{x}_1, \mathbf{x}_2, \ldots, \mathbf{x}_n$ that are orthonormal. Then for any $\mathbf{u}$,

$$\mathbf{u} = c_1\mathbf{x}_1 + c_2\mathbf{x}_2 + \cdots + c_n\mathbf{x}_n,$$

whence

$$\mathbf{u} = (\mathbf{x}_1, \mathbf{u})\mathbf{x}_1 + (\mathbf{x}_2, \mathbf{u})\mathbf{x}_2 + \cdots + (\mathbf{x}_n, \mathbf{u})\mathbf{x}_n.$$

Moreover,

$$\mathbf{A}\mathbf{u} = \lambda_1(\mathbf{x}_1, \mathbf{u})\mathbf{x}_1 + \lambda_2(\mathbf{x}_2, \mathbf{u})\mathbf{x}_2 + \cdots + \lambda_n(\mathbf{x}_n, \mathbf{u})\mathbf{x}_n,$$

so that

$$(\mathbf{u}, \mathbf{A}\mathbf{u}) = \lambda_1|(\mathbf{x}_1, \mathbf{u})|^2 + \lambda_2|(\mathbf{x}_2, \mathbf{u})|^2 + \cdots + \lambda_n|(\mathbf{x}_n, \mathbf{u})|^2.$$

To establish (*b*), observe that if the coefficients of the characteristic equation alternate in sign, there can be no negative root. Since the matrix is Hermitian, all roots are real, hence all are positive. Then, by (*a*), $\mathbf{A}$ is positive definite. Conversely, if $\mathbf{A}$ is positive definite, then all eigenvalues are positive and the coefficients of the characteristic equation alternate in sign.

Consider next (*c*) and suppose $\mathbf{A}$ is positive definite. Let $\mathbf{u} = [u_1, u_2, \ldots, u_m, 0, \ldots, 0]^t$ be nonzero, yet such that the last $n - m$ entries are zeros. The inner product $(\mathbf{u}, \mathbf{A}\mathbf{u}) > 0$; it is also the inner product for an arbitrary vector in m-dimensional space, one which uses as its matrix the leading submatrix of order m. Hence this submatrix is positive definite. The condition of part (*c*) is obviously sufficient, since $\mathbf{A}$ itself is then positive definite.

Turning to part (*d*), suppose $\mathbf{A}$ is positive definite. Since the determinant of a matrix is the product of its eigenvalues, from part (*c*) it follows that each $\Delta_m > 0$. To see that the condition of (*d*) is sufficient, proceed by induction. The proposition is obviously true for $n = 1$. Now assume the proposition to be true for all Hermitian matrices of order k and consider one, say $\mathbf{A}^{(k+1)}$ of order $k + 1$. Let λ be (if possible) a negative eigenvalue for $\mathbf{A}^{(k+1)}$. Then since $\Delta_{k+1} > 0$, and Δ_{k+1} is the product of all eigenvalues for $\mathbf{A}^{(k+1)}$, $\mathbf{A}^{(k+1)}$ has a second negative eigenvalue. By the theorem just presented, $\mathbf{A}^{(k)}$ has an eigenvalue which is negative. This cannot be; thus the eigenvalues of $\mathbf{A}$ are positive and $\mathbf{A}$ is positive definite.

Example. An example of a positive definite quadratic form is $13y_1^2 + 9y_2^2 + 57y_3^2 + 8y_1y_2 + 8y_1y_3 - 6y_2y_3$. That this is positive definite may be seen by writing it as $5y_1^2 + (2y_1 + 2y_2)^2 + 4y_2^2 + (2y_1 + 2y_3)^2 + 44y_3^2 + (y_2 - 3y_3)^2$. When written in the form $(\mathbf{y}, \mathbf{Ay})$ where $\mathbf{y}^* = [y_1\ y_2\ y_3]$,

$$\mathbf{A} = \begin{bmatrix} 13 & 4 & 4 \\ 4 & 9 & -3 \\ 4 & -3 & 57 \end{bmatrix}.$$

The first two leading submatrices have the corresponding quadratic forms $13y_1^2$ and $13y_1^2 + 8y_1y_2 + 9y_2^2$. These are seen to be positive definite. The characteristic function is $5400 - 1330\lambda + 79\lambda^2 - \lambda^3$ and the eigenvalues are positive, since the functional values for $\lambda = 0, 10, 20$, and 60 are $5400, -1000, 2400$, and -6400, respectively.

For positive definite Hermitian matrices $\mathbf{A}$, it is true that

$$\lambda_n \leqslant \frac{(\mathbf{u}, \mathbf{Au})}{(\mathbf{u}, \mathbf{u})} \leqslant \frac{(\mathbf{Au}, \mathbf{Au})}{(\mathbf{u}, \mathbf{Au})} \leqslant \lambda_1, \qquad (4.34)$$

where λ_n is the least and λ_1 the greatest of the eigenvalues of $\mathbf{A}$, and $\mathbf{u}$ is any vector of proper dimension. That

$$\frac{(\mathbf{u}, \mathbf{Au})}{(\mathbf{u}, \mathbf{u})} \leqslant \frac{(\mathbf{Au}, \mathbf{Au})}{(\mathbf{u}, \mathbf{Au})}$$

follows quickly from (4.28) if for $\mathbf{v}$ we use $\mathbf{u}$ and for $\mathbf{w}$ we use $\mathbf{Au}$ [note too that $(\mathbf{u}, \mathbf{Au}) = (\mathbf{Au}, \mathbf{u})$]. Now let $\mathbf{\Lambda} = \mathrm{diag}(\lambda_1, \lambda_2, \ldots, \lambda_n)$, and $\mathbf{A} = \mathbf{P}^*\mathbf{\Lambda P}$. Then

$$\frac{(\mathbf{u}, \mathbf{Au})}{(\mathbf{u}, \mathbf{u})} = \frac{(\mathbf{Pu}, \mathbf{\Lambda Pu})}{(\mathbf{Pu}, \mathbf{Pu})} = (\mathbf{x}, \mathbf{\Lambda x}),$$

where $\mathbf{x} = \mathbf{Pu}/\|\mathbf{Pu}\|$; thus $(\mathbf{x}, \mathbf{x}) = 1$. But

$$(\mathbf{x}, \mathbf{\Lambda x}) = \sum_{i=1}^{n} \lambda_i x_i \bar{x}_i \geqslant \lambda_n \sum_{i=1}^{n} x_i \bar{x}_i = \lambda_n.$$

Now let $\mathbf{u} = \mathbf{A}^{-1}\mathbf{v}$. Then

$$\frac{(\mathbf{Au}, \mathbf{Au})}{(\mathbf{u}, \mathbf{Au})} = \frac{(\mathbf{Au}, \mathbf{Au})}{(\mathbf{Au}, \mathbf{u})} = \frac{(\mathbf{v}, \mathbf{v})}{(\mathbf{v}, \mathbf{A}^{-1}\mathbf{v})} = \frac{1}{\dfrac{(\mathbf{v}, \mathbf{A}^{-1}\mathbf{v})}{(\mathbf{v}, \mathbf{v})}} = \frac{1}{(\mathbf{y}, \mathbf{\Lambda}^{-1}\mathbf{y})},$$

where $(\mathbf{y}, \mathbf{y}) = 1$ and $\mathbf{y} = \mathbf{Pv}/\|\mathbf{Pv}\|$. Since

$$\mathbf{\Lambda}^{-1} = \mathrm{diag}(\lambda_1^{-1}, \lambda_2^{-1}, \ldots, \lambda_n^{-1}),$$

it follows that

$$\frac{1}{(\mathbf{y}, \mathbf{\Lambda}^{-1}\mathbf{y})} = \frac{1}{\displaystyle\sum_{i=1}^{n} \frac{1}{\lambda_i} y_i \bar{y}_i} \leqslant \frac{1}{\dfrac{1}{\lambda_1}} = \lambda_1.$$

Since the guarantee for convergence using the power method (Section 4.6) is based on the existence of n linearly independent eigenvectors, and since Hermitian matrices fulfill this requirement, the method is adapted to them. Moreover, once an eigenvalue and its corresponding eigenvector have been found, there is in this case a particularly simple theory for continuing. Let the eigenvalues

and corresponding eigenvectors be $\lambda_1, \lambda_2, \ldots, \lambda_n$ and $\mathbf{u}_1, \mathbf{u}_2, \ldots, \mathbf{u}_n$ (ordering by magnitude is not demanded). The eigenvectors must be orthogonal and we may, in addition, require that they be of unit length. Let $\mathbf{A}_1 = \mathbf{A}$, and define recursively

$$\mathbf{A}_{k+1} = \mathbf{A}_k - \lambda_k \mathbf{u}_k \mathbf{u}_k^*.$$

For $k = 1$, it is a simple matter to see that $\mathbf{A}_2 \mathbf{u}_1 = \mathbf{A}_1 \mathbf{u}_1 - \lambda_1 \mathbf{u}_1 = \mathbf{0}$, and that, for $i \neq 1$, $\mathbf{A}_2 \mathbf{u}_i = \mathbf{A}_1 \mathbf{u}_i - \lambda_1 \mathbf{u}_1 (\mathbf{u}_1, \mathbf{u}_i) = \mathbf{A}_1 \mathbf{u}_i = \lambda_i \mathbf{u}_i$. Thus $\mathbf{A}_2$ has the same eigenvalues and eigenvectors as $\mathbf{A}_1$, except for λ_1 which has been replaced by 0. It is seen that the process continues: the eigenvectors are retained, and the eigenvalues are successively replaced by zero.

If, in addition, the Hermitian matrix is positive definite, all eigenvalues are real and positive. It is still necessary to consider multiple roots for the characteristic equation.

4.6 The Power Method of Mises

In Sections 4.6–4.9, we consider various methods for determining eigenvalues and eigenvectors. For additional information concerning such methods, see Bodewig [1] and Faddeev and Faddeeva [5].

When the eigenvalues of a matrix $\mathbf{A}$ are so ordered that $|\lambda_1| \geqslant |\lambda_2| \geqslant \cdots \geqslant |\lambda_n|$, and when $|\lambda_1| > |\lambda_2|$ or $\lambda_1 = \lambda_2 = \cdots = \lambda_i$ and $|\lambda_1| > |\lambda_{i+1}|$, it is customary to call λ_1 the *dominant eigenvalue*. If the matrix is of order n, has n linearly independent eigenvectors $\mathbf{u}_1, \mathbf{u}_2, \ldots, \mathbf{u}_n$ and a dominant eigenvalue λ_1, then λ_1 and an associated eigenvector, $\mathbf{w}_1$, of unit length, can be approximated as follows. Suppose first that $|\lambda_1| > |\lambda_2|$. Let $\mathbf{v}_0$ be an (almost) arbitrary vector to be described more exactly later. Define the sequence $\mathbf{v}_m$ by

$$\mathbf{v}_m = \mathbf{Av}_{m-1}/\|\mathbf{Av}_{m-1}\|, \qquad m \geqslant 1. \qquad (4.35)$$

Then

$$\lim_{m \to \infty} \mathbf{v}_m = \mathbf{w}_1, \qquad \lim_{m \to \infty} \|\mathbf{Av}_{m-1}\| = |\lambda_1|. \qquad (4.36)$$

To see this, let $\mathbf{v}_0$ be any vector:

$$\mathbf{v}_0 = c_1 \mathbf{u}_1 + c_2 \mathbf{u}_2 + \cdots + c_n \mathbf{u}_n,$$

provided only that $c_1 \neq 0$. (Since $\mathbf{u}_1$ is not known, there is an element of hazard in choosing $\mathbf{v}_0$. However, even though the $\mathbf{v}_0$ chosen should have a zero component involving $\mathbf{u}_1$, a round-off error might eventually provide such a component.) Then

$$\mathbf{v}_1 = \beta_1 \mathbf{Av}_0 = \beta_1 [c_1 \lambda_1 \mathbf{u}_1 + c_2 \lambda_2 \mathbf{u}_2 + \cdots + c_n \lambda_n \mathbf{u}_n];$$

and, in general,

$$\mathbf{v}_m = \beta_m [c_1 \lambda_1^m \mathbf{u}_1 + \cdots + c_n \lambda_n^m \mathbf{u}_n], \qquad (4.37)$$

where β_m is merely a normalizing factor. For large values of m, this is substantially $\beta_m c_1 \lambda_1^m \mathbf{u}_1$, which in turn is $\mathbf{u}_1/\|\mathbf{u}_1\|$.

Should the dominant eigenvalue have multiplicity i, it is seen that $\mathbf{v}_m$ is substantially

$$\beta_m [c_1 \lambda_1^m \mathbf{u}_1 + c_2 \lambda_1^m \mathbf{u}_2 + \cdots + c_i \lambda_1^m \mathbf{u}_i]$$

and (4.36) is still valid if $\mathbf{w}_1$ be interpreted as one of a family of unit eigenvectors associated with λ_1. It is possible to find the remaining eigenvectors associated with λ_1 by repeating the process using a different vector $\mathbf{v}_0$, the procedure being most effective if the multiplicity is known. An alternate procedure is to solve the system of linear equations $\mathbf{A}\mathbf{u} = \lambda_1 \mathbf{u}$.

When an eigenvalue λ_1 (not necessarily dominant) and an associated eigenvector $\mathbf{w}_1$ have been found for matrix $\mathbf{A}$, it is often possible to proceed with the process. Suppose, for example, that a unit vector $\mathbf{h}_1$ can be found such that $\mathbf{A}^*\mathbf{h}_1 = \bar{\lambda}_1\mathbf{h}_1$. (Note that $\bar{\lambda}_1$ is an eigenvalue for $\mathbf{A}^*$.) Then let $\mathbf{B}$ be defined by

$$\mathbf{B} = \mathbf{A} - \lambda_1 \mathbf{h}_1 \mathbf{h}_1^*.$$

Observe that if $\mathbf{A}\mathbf{w} = \lambda\mathbf{w}$ and $\lambda \neq \lambda_1$, then $\mathbf{h}_1^*\mathbf{w} = 0$. For $\mathbf{h}_1^*\mathbf{A}\mathbf{w} = \lambda\mathbf{h}_1^*\mathbf{w}$ and also $\mathbf{h}_1^*\mathbf{A}\mathbf{w} = (\mathbf{A}^*\mathbf{h}_1)^*\mathbf{w} = (\bar{\lambda}_1\mathbf{h}_1)^*\mathbf{w} = \lambda_1\mathbf{h}_1^*\mathbf{w}$. Then from $\lambda\mathbf{h}_1^*\mathbf{w} = \lambda_1\mathbf{h}_1^*\mathbf{w}$, we find $\mathbf{h}_1^*\mathbf{w} = 0$. This means that $\mathbf{B}\mathbf{w} = \mathbf{A}\mathbf{w} - \lambda_1\mathbf{h}_1 \times 0$ or $\mathbf{B}\mathbf{w} = \mathbf{A}\mathbf{w} = \lambda\mathbf{w}$. Thus $\mathbf{B}$ has all the eigenvalues of $\mathbf{A}$ that are different from λ_1. Also the trace of $\mathbf{B}$ is λ_1 less than the trace of $\mathbf{A}$. For $Sp(\mathbf{h}_1\mathbf{h}_1^*) = (\mathbf{h}_1, \mathbf{h}_1) = 1$; hence $Sp(\lambda_1\mathbf{h}_1\mathbf{h}_1^*) = \lambda_1$ and $Sp(\mathbf{B}) = Sp(\mathbf{A}) - \lambda_1$. Therefore, if λ_1 is not a multiple root of the characteristic equation for $\mathbf{A}$, the matrix $\mathbf{B}$ will yield all the remaining eigenvalues and eigenvectors of $\mathbf{A}$. Compare this procedure, when $\mathbf{A} = \mathbf{A}^*$, with the method described at the end of Section 4.5.

In some physical problems, one is primarily concerned with the dominant eigenvalue. In others, the eigenvalue of concern is the one of least absolute value. It is now shown that the eigenvalues of $\mathbf{A}^{-1}$ are the reciprocals of those for $\mathbf{A}$. For $\mathbf{A}$ nonsingular and $\det(\mathbf{A} - (1/\mu)\mathbf{I}) = 0$

imply $\det((1/\mu)\mathbf{I}(\mathbf{A}\mu - \mathbf{I})) = 0$, hence $\det(\mathbf{A}\mu - \mathbf{I}) = 0$. Then since $\det(\mathbf{A}^{-1}(\mathbf{A}\mu - \mathbf{I})) = \det(\mathbf{A}^{-1})\det(\mathbf{A}\mu - \mathbf{I})$, it follows that $\det(\mu\mathbf{I} - \mathbf{A}^{-1}) = 0$. Procedures for finding $\mathbf{A}^{-1}$ are covered in Chapter 5.

At this point, it is worth noting that every polynomial of the form $\sum_{i=0}^{n} a_i x^{n-i}$, where $a_0 = 1$, determines a *companion* matrix

$$\mathbf{A} = \begin{bmatrix} -a_1 & -a_2 & -a_3 & \cdots & -a_{n-1} & -a_n \\ 1 & 0 & 0 & \cdots & 0 & 0 \\ 0 & 1 & 0 & \cdots & 0 & 0 \\ 0 & 0 & 1 & \cdots & 0 & 0 \\ \cdots & \cdots & \cdots & \cdots & \cdots & \cdots \\ 0 & 0 & 0 & \cdots & 1 & 0 \end{bmatrix}, \quad (4.38)$$

and that its characteristic function is precisely

$$(-1)^n \sum_{i=0}^{n} a_i x^{n-i}.$$

This can be verified by induction or by multiplying each column in $\mathbf{A} - x\mathbf{I}$ in succession by x (starting with the first) and adding to the next. When the resulting determinant is evaluated in terms of the last column, the statement becomes evident. Now use this companion matrix in connection with Mises' process, and for the initial vector $\mathbf{v}_0$ use

$$\mathbf{v}_0 = [u_{n-1}, u_{n-2}, \ldots, u_0]^t,$$

where the meaning of the components of $\mathbf{v}_0$ is that given in Bernoulli's method. For this particular matrix, the two methods are seen to coincide. Also, note that methods of finding eigenvalues, which do not depend on direct solution of the characteristic equation, might prove useful in finding the zeros of polynomial functions.

EXAMPLE 4.2

THE POWER METHOD

Problem Statement

Write a program, based on the method of Section 4.6, that determines the eigenvalues and eigenvectors of an $n \times n$ real matrix $\mathbf{A}$.

Method of Solution

The method for determining λ_1 and $\mathbf{u}_1$ is expressed in equations (4.35) and (4.36). Note that after the mth iteration, the old eigenvector estimate $\mathbf{v}_{m-1}$ is discarded in favor of the new $\mathbf{v}_m$. Hence, we need only use a single vector, $\mathbf{v}$, for containing successive such estimates, apart from the starting vector $\mathbf{v}_0$, which is reserved for an additional purpose indicated below.

An alternative procedure is used here for finding the remaining eigenvalues and eigenvectors, assuming that there are no repeated eigenvalues. To obtain λ_2, first observe that the vector

$$(\mathbf{A} - \lambda_1 \mathbf{I})\mathbf{v}_0 = (\lambda_1 - \lambda_1)c_1 \mathbf{u}_1 + (\lambda_2 - \lambda_1)c_2 \mathbf{u}_2$$
$$+ \cdots + (\lambda_n - \lambda_1)c_n \mathbf{u}_n$$

does not contain a component $\mathbf{u}_1$. Thus, a repetition of the procedure with a starting vector $\mathbf{Bv}_0$, where $\mathbf{B} = \mathbf{A} - \lambda_1 \mathbf{I}$, will yield λ_2 and $\mathbf{u}_2$. Similarly, once λ_1 and λ_2

are known, a starting vector $\mathbf{Bv}_0$, where $\mathbf{B} = (\mathbf{A} - \lambda_1 \mathbf{I}) \times (\mathbf{A} - \lambda_2 \mathbf{I})$, will generate λ_3 and $\mathbf{u}_3$, etc.

Because round-off error is likely to introduce unwanted components involving $\mathbf{u}_1$, $\mathbf{u}_2$, etc., we must periodically eliminate such quantities. This is achieved by replacing the current approximation $\mathbf{v}$ with $\mathbf{Bv}/\|\mathbf{Bv}\|$, after every m_{freq} iterations.

Computations for each eigenvalue are discontinued, when, from one iteration to the next, there is little further fractional change in the length of $\mathbf{v}$. Thus, if $l = \|\mathbf{Av}_m\|$ and $l_0 = \|\mathbf{Av}_{m-1}\|$, convergence is assumed if

$$\left| \frac{l - l_0}{l_0} \right| < \varepsilon,$$

where ε is a preassigned small quantity. If convergence does not occur within m_{max} iterations, the calculations are discontinued.

From equation (4.36), note that the power method yields only the *magnitude* of the eigenvalues. To append their correct signs, we must compare the first nonzero elements of $\mathbf{v}$ on two successive iterations. If these elements are of the same sign, then $\lambda_i = l$; otherwise, $\lambda_i = -l$.

Example 4.2   The Power Method   **229**

Flow Diagram

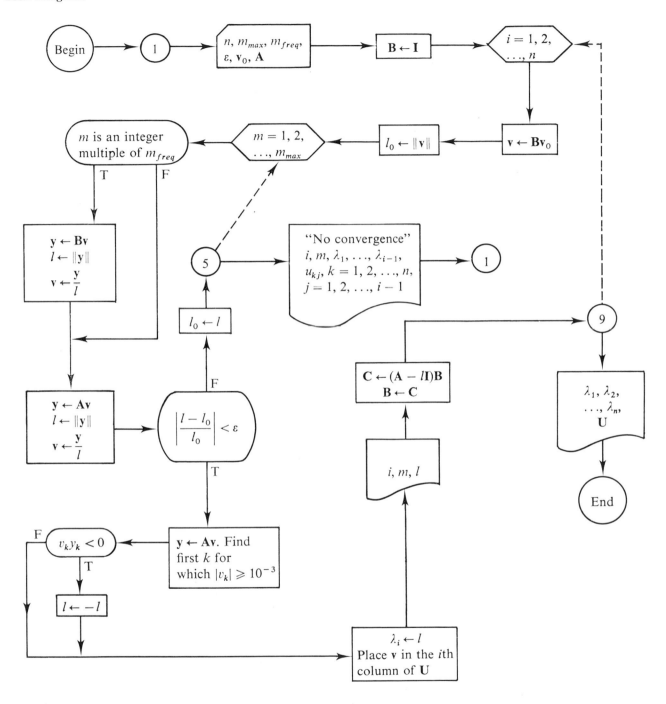

FORTRAN *Implementation*

List of Principal Variables

Program Symbol	Definition
A	Matrix $\mathbf{A}$, whose eigenvalues are required.
B	Repeated product matrix, $\mathbf{B} = (\mathbf{A} - \lambda_1 \mathbf{I})(\mathbf{A} - \lambda_2 \mathbf{I}) \ldots$
C, D	Matrices used for intermediate storage.
EPS	Tolerance, ε, used in convergence test.
IDENT	Identity matrix, $\mathbf{I}$.
L	Length, l, of $\mathbf{v}$.
LZERO	l_0, used for temporary storage of l.
LAMBDA	Vector containing eigenvalues, λ_i.
M	Iteration counter, m.
N	Number of rows, n, of matrix $\mathbf{A}$.
MFREQ	Number of iterations, m_{freq}, between periodic reorthogonalization of $\mathbf{v}$.
MMAX	Maximum number of iterations permitted, m_{max}.
U	Matrix $\mathbf{U}$ whose columns contain the eigenvectors of $\mathbf{A}$.
V	Current approximation, $\mathbf{v}$, to eigenvector.
VZERO	Starting guess, $\mathbf{v}_0$, for eigenvector.
Y	Vector for temporary storage, $\mathbf{y}$.

Example 4.2   The Power Method   **231**

Program Listing

```
C           APPLIED NUMERICAL METHODS, EXAMPLE 4.2
C           POWER METHOD FOR DETERMINING EIGENVALUES AND EIGENVECTORS.
C
C           THE FOLLOWING PROGRAM MAKES EXTENSIVE USE OF THE MATRIX
C           OPERATIONS DEFINED IN THE SUBROUTINES OF EXAMPLE 4.1
C
        IMPLICIT REAL*8(A-H, O-Z)
        REAL*8 L, LZERO, LAMBDA, IDENT
        DIMENSION A(10,10), B(10,10), C(10,10), D(10,10), IDENT(10,10),
       1 U(10,10), LAMBDA(10), V(10), VZERO(10), Y(10)
C
C           ..... READ AND CHECK INPUT DATA .....
    1   READ (5,100) N, MMAX, MFREQ, EPS, (VZERO(I), I = 1, N)
        WRITE (6,200) N, MMAX, MFREQ, EPS
        WRITE (6,207) (VZERO(I), I = 1, N)
        READ (5,101) ((A(I,J), J = 1, N), I = 1, N)
        WRITE (6,201)
        DO 15  I = 1, N
   15   WRITE (6,207) (A(I,J), J = 1, N)
C
C           ..... INITIALLY EQUATE B TO THE IDENTITY MATRIX .....
        DO 2  I = 1, N
        DO 2  J = 1, N
    2   IDENT(I,J) = 0.
        DO 3  I = 1, N
    3   IDENT(I,I) = 1.
        CALL MATEQ (IDENT, B, N, N)
C
C           ..... PERFORM POWER METHOD FOR ALL N EIGENVALUES .....
        DO 11  I = 1, N
C
C           ..... MODIFY STARTING VECTOR SO THAT IT IS ORTHO-
C                 GONAL TO ALL PREVIOUSLY COMPUTED EIGENVECTORS .....
        CALL MATVEC (B, VZERO, V, N, N)
        CALL VECLEN (V, LZERO, N)
C
C           ..... PERFORM SUCCESSIVE POWER METHOD ITERATIONS .....
        DO 5  M = 1, MMAX
C
C           ..... PERIODICALLY RE-ORTHOGONALIZE THE VECTOR V .....
        IF ((M/MFREQ)*MFREQ .NE. M) GO TO 4
            CALL MATVEC (B, V, Y, N, N)
            CALL VECLEN (Y, L, N)
            CALL SCAVEC (1.0/L, Y, V, N)
C
C           ..... COMPUTE NEW VECTOR V AND ITS LENGTH .....
    4   CALL MATVEC (A, V, Y, N, N)
        CALL VECLEN (Y, L, N)
        CALL SCAVEC (1.0/L, Y, V, N)
C
C           ..... CHECK FOR CONVERGENCE .....
        IF (DABS((L - LZERO)/LZERO) .LT. EPS) GO TO 7
    5   LZERO = L
C
C           ..... SALVAGE PARTIAL RESULTS IF METHOD DID NOT CONVERGE .....
        IM1 = I - 1
        WRITE (6,202) I, M, (LAMBDA(K), K = 1, IM1)
        WRITE (6,203)
        DO 6  K = 1, N
    6   WRITE (6,207) (U(K,J), J = 1, IM1)
        GO TO 1
C
C           ..... ESTABLISH THE SIGN OF THE EIGENVALUE .....
    7   CALL MATVEC (A, V, Y, N, N)
        DO 8  K = 1, N
        IF (DABS(V(K)) .LT. 1.0D-3) GO TO 8
            IF (V(K)*Y(K) .LT. 0.0) L = - L
            GO TO 9
    8   CONTINUE
```

Program Listing (*Continued*)

```
C
C         ..... STORE CURRENT EIGENVALUE AND EIGENVECTOR .....
    9   LAMBDA(I) = L
        DO 10  K = 1, N
   10   U(K,I) = V(K)
        WRITE (6,204) I, M, L
C
C         ..... MODIFY MATRIX B .....
        IF (I .GE. N) GO TO 11
            CALL SCAMAT (L, IDENT, C, N, N)
            CALL MATSUB (A, C, D, N, N)
            CALL MATMLT (D, B, C, N, N, N)
            CALL MATEQ (C, B, N, N)
   11   CONTINUE
C
C         ..... PRINT EIGENVALUES AND EIGENVECTORS .....
        WRITE (6,205) (LAMBDA(I), I = 1, N)
        WRITE (6,206)
        DO 12  I = 1, N
   12   WRITE (6,207) (U(I,J), J = 1, N)
        GO TO 1
C
C         ..... FORMATS FOR INPUT AND OUTPUT STATEMENTS .....
  100   FORMAT (3(12X, I3), 12X, E8.2/ (10X, 8F5.1))
  101   FORMAT (10X, 8F5.1)
  200   FORMAT (1H1, 4X, 47H POWER METHOD FOR DETERMINING EIGENVALUES, WIT
       1H/ 1H0, 6X, 10H N      = , I4/ 7X, 10H MMAX   = , I4/
       2   7X, 10H MFREQ  = , I4/ 7X, 10H EPS    = , E12.3/ 1H0,
       3 4X, 39H STARTING VECTOR VZERO(1)...VZERO(N) IS)
  201   FORMAT (1H0, 4X, 39H THE STARTING MATRIX A(1,1)...A(N,N) IS)
  202   FORMAT (1H0, 4X, 37H NO CONVERGENCE.  PARTIAL RESULTS ARE/ 1H0,
       1 6X, 6H I  = , I2, 10X, 9H M      = , I3/ 1H0,
       2 6X, 27H LAMBDA(1)...LAMBDA(I-1) = / (7X, 10F11.6))
  203   FORMAT (1H0, 4X, 27H FIRST I-1 EIGENVECTORS ARE)
  204   FORMAT (1H0, 6X, 6H I  = , I2, 5X, 9H M      = , I3,
       1 5X, 6H L  = , F11.6)
  205   FORMAT (1H0, 4X, 38H EIGENVALUES LAMBDA(1)...LAMBDA(N) ARE/
       1 (7X, 10F11.6))
  206   FORMAT (1H0, 4X, 39H EIGENVECTORS ARE SUCCESSIVE COLUMNS OF)
  207   FORMAT (7X, 10F11.6)
C
        END
```

Data

```
        N    =    3,   MMAX = 100,  MFREQ =   15,     EPS  =  1.0E-9
VZERO  = 1.   1.   1.
A      = 11.   6.  -2.  -2.  18.   1. -12.  24.
         13.
        N    =    4,   MMAX =  50,  MFREQ =    1,     EPS  =  1.0E-9
VZERO  = 1.   0.   0.   0.
A      = 10.   9.   7.   5.   9.  10.   8.   6.
          7.   8.  10.   7.   5.   6.   7.   5.
        N    =    8,   MMAX = 300,  MFREQ =   10,     EPS  =  1.0E-9
VZERO  = 1.   0.   0.   0.   0.   0.   0.   0.
A      = 2.  -1.   0.   0.   0.   0.   0.   0.
         -1.   2.  -1.   0.   0.   0.   0.   0.
          0.  -1.   2.  -1.   0.   0.   0.   0.
          0.   0.  -1.   2.  -1.   0.   0.   0.
          0.   0.   0.  -1.   2.  -1.   0.   0.
          0.   0.   0.   0.  -1.   2.  -1.   0.
          0.   0.   0.   0.   0.  -1.   2.  -1.
          0.   0.   0.   0.   0.   0.  -1.   2.
```

Example 4.2   The Power Method   **233**

Computer Output

Results for the 1st Data Set

```
POWER METHOD FOR DETERMINING EIGENVALUES, WITH

N      =     3
MMAX   =   100
MFREQ  =    15
EPS    =     0.100D-08

STARTING VECTOR VZERO(1)...VZERO(N) IS
     1.000000   1.000000   1.000000

THE STARTING MATRIX A(1,1)...A(N,N) IS
    11.000000    6.000000   -2.000000
    -2.000000   18.000000    1.000000
   -12.000000   24.000000   13.000000

    I  =  1      M    =   43      L  =    21.000000

    I  =  2      M    =   29      L  =    14.000000

    I  =  3      M    =   16      L  =     7.000000

EIGENVALUES LAMBDA(1)...LAMBDA(N) ARE
    21.000000  14.000000   7.000000

EIGENVECTORS ARE SUCCESSIVE COLUMNS OF
     0.000000   0.894427  -0.447214
     0.316228   0.447214   0.000000
     0.948683  -0.000000  -0.894427
```

Results for the 2nd Data Set

```
POWER METHOD FOR DETERMINING EIGENVALUES, WITH

N      =     4
MMAX   =    50
MFREQ  =     1
EPS    =     0.100D-08

STARTING VECTOR VZERO(1)...VZERO(N) IS
     1.000000   0.0        0.0        0.0

THE STARTING MATRIX A(1,1)...A(N,N) IS
    10.000000    9.000000    7.000000    5.000000
     9.000000   10.000000    8.000000    6.000000
     7.000000    8.000000   10.000000    7.000000
     5.000000    6.000000    7.000000    5.000000

    I  =  1      M    =    7      L  =    30.288685

    I  =  2      M    =   10      L  =     3.858057

    I  =  3      M    =    5      L  =     0.843107

    I  =  4      M    =    2      L  =     0.010150

EIGENVALUES LAMBDA(1)...LAMBDA(N) ARE
    30.288685   3.858057   0.843107   0.010150

EIGENVECTORS ARE SUCCESSIVE COLUMNS OF
     0.520925  -0.625397   0.567641  -0.123697
     0.551955  -0.271600  -0.760318   0.208554
     0.528567   0.614861   0.301652   0.501565
     0.380262   0.396306  -0.093305  -0.830444
```

Computer Output (*Continued*)

Results for the 3rd Data Set

```
POWER METHOD FOR DETERMINING EIGENVALUES, WITH

N     =    8
MMAX  =  300
MFREQ =   10
EPS   =    0.100D-08

STARTING VECTOR VZERO(1)...VZERO(N) IS
   1.000000   0.0        0.0        0.0        0.0        0.0        0.0        0.0

THE STARTING MATRIX A(1,1)...A(N,N) IS
   2.000000  -1.000000   0.0        0.0        0.0        0.0        0.0        0.0
  -1.000000   2.000000  -1.000000   0.0        0.0        0.0        0.0        0.0
   0.0       -1.000000   2.000000  -1.000000   0.0        0.0        0.0        0.0
   0.0        0.0       -1.000000   2.000000  -1.000000   0.0        0.0        0.0
   0.0        0.0        0.0       -1.000000   2.000000  -1.000000   0.0        0.0
   0.0        0.0        0.0        0.0       -1.000000   2.000000  -1.000000   0.0
   0.0        0.0        0.0        0.0        0.0       -1.000000   2.000000  -1.000000
   0.0        0.0        0.0        0.0        0.0        0.0       -1.000000   2.000000
```

```
I  =  1      M  =  97     L  =    3.879385

I  =  2      M  = 137     L  =    3.532089

I  =  3      M  =  95     L  =    3.000000

I  =  4      M  =  56     L  =    2.347296

I  =  5      M  =  34     L  =    1.652704

I  =  6      M  =  19     L  =    1.000000

I  =  7      M  =  11     L  =    0.467911

I  =  8      M  =  31     L  =    3.879385
```

```
EIGENVALUES LAMBDA(1)...LAMBDA(N) ARE
   3.879385   3.532089   3.000000   2.347296   1.652704   1.000000   0.467911   3.879385

EIGENVECTORS ARE SUCCESSIVE COLUMNS OF
   0.161294   0.303060   0.408279   0.464259   0.464251   0.408251   0.303013   0.161251
  -0.303111  -0.464290  -0.408259  -0.161224   0.161239   0.408252   0.464243  -0.303045
   0.408334   0.408248  -0.000027  -0.408262  -0.408248   0.000004   0.408249   0.408276
  -0.464277  -0.161183   0.408268   0.303003  -0.303022  -0.408247   0.161231  -0.464254
   0.464209  -0.161277  -0.408228   0.303023   0.303004  -0.408250  -0.161229   0.464232
  -0.408162   0.408248  -0.000027  -0.408234   0.408248  -0.000004  -0.408247  -0.408220
   0.302915  -0.464196   0.408238  -0.161235  -0.161221   0.408244  -0.464242   0.302981
  -0.161166   0.302966  -0.408218   0.464227  -0.464234   0.408246  -0.303013  -0.161209
```

Example 4.2 The Power Method **235**

Discussion of Results

The power method has been applied to three matrices. The results for the first matrix agree completely with the exact values given on page 222. The second matrix has extremely well-spaced eigenvalues, and convergence rapidly occurs to values that are virtually identical with those computed in Examples 4.3 and 4.4. The third matrix arises typically when treating unsteady-state heat conduction in a slab as a characteristic-value problem (see Section 7.26). Although the eigenvalues again agree, to six significant figures, with those computed in Examples 4.3 and 4.4, the eigenvectors are accurate only to about three or four significant figures. The eigenvectors could be obtained more accurately by increasing MMAX and reducing EPS. However, the total number of iterations is already fairly large, and we have chosen to leave the results as they are. Note that the eigenvectors of the third matrix are alternately symmetric and antisymmetric; a starting vector $v_0 = [1, 1, 1, 1, 1, 1, 1, 1]^t$ would have been a particularly unfortunate choice. Note that the method fails to generate the smallest eigenvalue; instead, the largest eigenvalue is duplicated. This difficulty could probably be overcome by searching for more suitable values of m_{max}, m_{freq}, and ε.

For complete success, the method demands double-precision arithmetic, as used here. Otherwise, the successive starting vectors are insufficiently orthogonal to the earlier eigenvectors; consequently, convergence may not occur to the smaller eigenvalues. The periodic reorthogonalization of the current vector v is particularly important for the second test matrix, because of its well-spaced eigenvalues.

4.7 Method of Rutishauser [4]

Throughout this section, for $i \geqslant 1$, $\mathbf{L}'$, $\mathbf{L}_i$, $\mathbf{L}_i'$ will be used to denote lower triangular matrices whose diagonal elements are all ones, while $\mathbf{R}$, $\mathbf{R}'$, $\mathbf{R}_i$, $\mathbf{R}_i'$ will be used to denote upper triangular matrices (here $\mathbf{R}'$, for instance, is not the transpose of $\mathbf{R}$—for this we consistently use the notation $\mathbf{R}^t$).

Let $\mathbf{A} = \mathbf{A}_1$ be a real square matrix such that $\mathbf{A}_1 = \mathbf{L}_1 \mathbf{R}_1$ (this can always be accomplished if, as previously shown, $\mathbf{A}$ is positive definite). Define $\mathbf{A}_2$ as $\mathbf{R}_1 \mathbf{L}_1$. It may be that $\mathbf{A}_2 = \mathbf{L}_2 \mathbf{R}_2$. If so, define $\mathbf{A}_3$ as $\mathbf{R}_2 \mathbf{L}_2$. In general, assume that

$$\mathbf{A}_k = \mathbf{L}_k \mathbf{R}_k, \quad \mathbf{A}_{k+1} = \mathbf{R}_k \mathbf{L}_k. \tag{4.39}$$

Note that in such event

$$\mathbf{A}_{k+1} = \mathbf{L}_k^{-1} \mathbf{A}_k \mathbf{L}_k = \mathbf{R}_k \mathbf{A}_k \mathbf{R}_k^{-1}. \tag{4.40}$$

Since the product of lower (upper) triangular matrices is also lower (upper) triangular, and since the inverse of a lower (upper) triangular matrix is also of the same kind, it is readily verified that if

$$\mathbf{L}_k' = \mathbf{L}_1 \mathbf{L}_2 \cdots \mathbf{L}_k; \quad \mathbf{R}_k' = \mathbf{R}_k \mathbf{R}_{k-1} \cdots \mathbf{R}_1; \tag{4.41}$$

then

$$\mathbf{A}_{k+1} = \mathbf{L}_k'^{-1} \mathbf{A} \mathbf{L}_k' = \mathbf{R}_k' \mathbf{A} \mathbf{R}_k'^{-1}. \tag{4.42}$$

This shows that $\mathbf{A}_k$ is similar to $\mathbf{A}$; therefore, as previously shown, it has the same eigenvalues and related eigenvectors. Suppose now that

$$\lim_{k \to \infty} \mathbf{L}_k' = \mathbf{L}'. \tag{4.43}$$

This means that

$$\lim_{k \to \infty} \mathbf{L}_k = \mathbf{I}, \ \lim_{k \to \infty} \mathbf{A}_k = \lim_{k \to \infty} \mathbf{R}_k = \mathbf{R}, \tag{4.44}$$

where $\mathbf{R}$ is upper triangular. There results from (4.42)

$$\mathbf{L}' \mathbf{R} \mathbf{L}'^{-1} = \mathbf{A}, \tag{4.45}$$

where $\mathbf{R}$ not only has the same eigenvalues as $\mathbf{A}$, but has them as its diagonal entries (if $\mathbf{A}$ is to be real, this means $\mathbf{A}$ must have only real eigenvalues). If $\mathbf{R}\mathbf{v} = \lambda\mathbf{v}$, then $\mathbf{A}\mathbf{L}'\mathbf{v} = \lambda\mathbf{L}'\mathbf{v}$. Thus we see that when convergence takes place, a knowledge of $\mathbf{L}'$ and $\mathbf{R}$ will yield all eigenvalues and eigenvectors for $\mathbf{A}$, provided that we can find the eigenvectors for $\mathbf{R}$. This is particularly straightforward if there are no multiple eigenvalues. Consider, for example,

$$\mathbf{R} = \begin{bmatrix} r_{11} & r_{12} & r_{13} & r_{14} \\ 0 & r_{22} & r_{23} & r_{24} \\ 0 & 0 & r_{33} & r_{34} \\ 0 & 0 & 0 & r_{44} \end{bmatrix}.$$

Solve the system $\mathbf{R}\mathbf{v} = r_{11}\mathbf{v}$, where $\mathbf{v}^t = [1, 0, 0, 0]$, to obtain the eigenvector for r_{11}. Solve the system $\mathbf{R}\mathbf{v} = r_{22}\mathbf{v}$, where $\mathbf{v}^t = [a, 1, 0, 0]$, to obtain the eigenvector

$$\left[\frac{r_{12}}{r_{22} - r_{11}}, 1, 0, 0 \right]^t$$

for r_{22}. Solve the system $\mathbf{R}\mathbf{v} = r_{33}\mathbf{v}$, where $\mathbf{v}^t = [a, b, 1, 0]$, to obtain the eigenvector for r_{33}, etc. The technique for individual eigenvectors is that of back substitution in Gaussian elimination (see page 270).

In application, we can adopt the philosophy of using the results if convergence occurs. We emphasize that convergence does take place for positive definite matrices. A technique is still needed for writing a suitable matrix $\mathbf{B}$ as $\mathbf{CD}$ where $\mathbf{C}$ is lower triangular (with ones on the diagonal) and $\mathbf{D}$ is upper triangular. Let $\mathbf{B} = (b_{ij})$, $\mathbf{C} = (c_{ij})$, $\mathbf{D} = (d_{ij})$, it being understood that

$$c_{ij} = 0 \quad \text{for} \quad i < j \leqslant n, \quad c_{ii} = 1;$$
$$d_{ij} = 0 \quad \text{for} \quad i > j.$$

Since $b_{ij} = \sum_{k=1}^{n} c_{ik} d_{kj}$, by the above,

$$b_{ij} = \sum_{k=1}^{i-1} c_{ik} d_{kj} + d_{ij}, \quad i \leqslant j,$$

$$b_{ij} = \sum_{k=1}^{j-1} c_{ik} d_{kj} + c_{ij} d_{jj}, \quad i > j.$$

Thus

$$d_{ij} = b_{ij} - \sum_{k=1}^{i-1} c_{ik} d_{kj}, \quad i \leqslant j;$$

$$c_{ij} = \frac{1}{d_{jj}} \left[b_{ij} - \sum_{k=1}^{j-1} c_{ik} d_{kj} \right], \quad i > j. \tag{4.46}$$

In connection with a possibility for convergence, it is assumed that $\mathbf{A}$ is real and that $|\lambda_1| > |\lambda_2| > \cdots > |\lambda_n|$, so that in addition, the eigenvalues are real. Note first that from (4.39), it is possible to see that

$$\mathbf{A}^k = \mathbf{L}_k' \mathbf{R}_k', \tag{4.47}$$

because

$$\mathbf{L}_k' \mathbf{R}_k' = (\mathbf{L}_1 \mathbf{L}_2 \cdots \mathbf{L}_{k-2}) \mathbf{L}_{k-1} \mathbf{L}_k \mathbf{R}_k \mathbf{R}_{k-1} (\mathbf{R}_{k-2} \cdots \mathbf{R}_2 \mathbf{R}_1)$$
$$= (\mathbf{L}_1 \mathbf{L}_2 \cdots \mathbf{L}_{k-2}) \mathbf{L}_{k-1} \mathbf{R}_{k-1} \mathbf{L}_{k-1} \mathbf{R}_{k-1} (\mathbf{R}_{k-2} \cdots \mathbf{R}_2 \mathbf{R}_1)$$
$$= (\mathbf{L}_1 \mathbf{L}_2 \cdots \mathbf{L}_{k-2}) \mathbf{R}_{k-2} \mathbf{L}_{k-2} \mathbf{R}_{k-2} \mathbf{L}_{k-2} (\mathbf{R}_{k-2} \cdots \mathbf{R}_2 \mathbf{R}_1)$$
$$= (\mathbf{L}_1 \mathbf{R}_1)^k$$
$$= \mathbf{A}^k.$$

It is possible to show [4] that instead of the formula listed in (4.46), we can write, for all indices i and j,

$$c_{ij} = \frac{\det(\mathbf{D}_{ji})}{\det(\mathbf{D}_{jj})}, \quad \mathbf{D}_{ji} = \begin{bmatrix} b_{11} & b_{12} & \cdots & b_{1j} \\ b_{21} & b_{22} & \cdots & b_{2j} \\ \vdots & \vdots & & \vdots \\ b_{j-1,1} & b_{j-1,2} & \cdots & b_{j-1,j} \\ b_{i1} & b_{i2} & \cdots & b_{ij} \end{bmatrix}.$$

Let $\mathbf{U} = (u_{ij})$ be a matrix such that $\mathbf{AU} = \mathbf{U} \operatorname{diag}(\lambda_1 \lambda_2 \ldots \lambda_n)$ and let $\mathbf{V} = (v_{ij}) = (\mathbf{U}^{-1})^t$. Thus

$$\mathbf{A}^k = \mathbf{U} \operatorname{diag}(\lambda_1^k \lambda_2^k \cdots \lambda_n^k) \mathbf{V}^t.$$

Then

$$
\mathbf{A}^k =
\begin{bmatrix}
u_{11} & u_{12} & \cdots & u_{1n} \\
u_{21} & u_{22} & \cdots & u_{2n} \\
\vdots & \vdots & & \vdots \\
u_{n1} & u_{n2} & \cdots & u_{nn}
\end{bmatrix}
\begin{bmatrix}
v_{11}\lambda_1^k & v_{21}\lambda_1^k & \cdots & v_{n1}\lambda_1^k \\
v_{12}\lambda_2^k & v_{22}\lambda_2^k & \cdots & v_{n2}\lambda_2^k \\
\vdots & \vdots & & \vdots \\
v_{1n}\lambda_n^k & v_{2n}\lambda_n^k & \cdots & v_{nn}\lambda_n^k
\end{bmatrix}.
$$

From this it follows for $\mathbf{B} = \mathbf{A}^k = \mathbf{CD}$, that $c_{ij} = \det(\mathbf{D}_{ji})/\det(\mathbf{D}_{jj})$, where

$$
\mathbf{D}_{ji} =
\begin{bmatrix}
u_{11} & u_{12} & \cdots & u_{1n} \\
u_{21} & u_{22} & \cdots & u_{2n} \\
\vdots & \vdots & & \vdots \\
u_{j-1,1} & u_{j-1,2} & \cdots & u_{j-1,n} \\
u_{i1} & u_{i2} & \cdots & u_{in}
\end{bmatrix}
\begin{bmatrix}
v_{11}\lambda_1^k & v_{21}\lambda_1^k & \cdots & v_{j1}\lambda_1^k \\
v_{12}\lambda_2^k & v_{22}\lambda_2^k & \cdots & v_{j2}\lambda_2^k \\
\vdots & \vdots & & \vdots \\
v_{1n}\lambda_n^k & v_{2n}\lambda_n^k & \cdots & v_{jn}\lambda_n^k
\end{bmatrix}.
$$

As k increases, because the λ_i are in order of decreasing magnitude, the value of $\det(\mathbf{D}_{ji})$ approaches that of $\det(\mathbf{D}'_{ji})$ where

$$
\mathbf{D}'_{ji} =
\begin{bmatrix}
u_{11} & u_{12} & \cdots & u_{1j} \\
u_{21} & u_{22} & \cdots & u_{2j} \\
\vdots & \vdots & & \vdots \\
u_{j-1,1} & u_{j-1,2} & \cdots & u_{j-1,j} \\
u_{i1} & u_{i2} & \cdots & u_{ij}
\end{bmatrix}
\begin{bmatrix}
v_{11}\lambda_1^k & v_{21}\lambda_1^k & \cdots & v_{j1}\lambda_1^k \\
v_{12}\lambda_2^k & v_{22}\lambda_2^k & \cdots & v_{j2}\lambda_2^k \\
\vdots & \vdots & & \vdots \\
v_{1j}\lambda_j^k & v_{2j}\lambda_j^k & \cdots & v_{jj}\lambda_j^k
\end{bmatrix}.
$$

That is,

$$
\mathbf{D}'_{ji} =
\begin{bmatrix}
u_{11} & u_{12} & \cdots & u_{1j} \\
u_{21} & u_{22} & \cdots & u_{2j} \\
\vdots & \vdots & & \vdots \\
u_{j-1,1} & u_{j-1,2} & \cdots & u_{j-1,j} \\
u_{i1} & u_{i2} & \cdots & u_{ij}
\end{bmatrix}
\operatorname{diag}(\lambda_1^k \lambda_2^k \cdots \lambda_j^k)
\begin{bmatrix}
v_{11} & v_{21} & \cdots & v_{j1} \\
v_{12} & v_{22} & \cdots & v_{j2} \\
\vdots & \vdots & & \vdots \\
v_{1j} & v_{2j} & \cdots & v_{jj}
\end{bmatrix}.
$$

To aid in seeing this, observe that $\mathbf{D}_{ji}$ is the sum of similar terms, all other terms having a middle factor, $\operatorname{diag}(\lambda_{l_1}^k \lambda_{l_2}^k \cdots \lambda_{l_j}^k)$, which for k large is small compared to the one shown. Use partitioning to see that $\mathbf{D}'_{ji}$ contains all terms of the type described. Thus for k large, c_{ij} is approximated by

$$
\frac{\det(\mathbf{D}'_{ji})}{\det(\mathbf{D}'_{jj})} = \frac{\det(\mathscr{D}_{ji})}{\det(\mathscr{D}_{jj})}
$$

where

$$
\mathscr{D}_{ji} =
\begin{bmatrix}
u_{11} & u_{12} & \cdots & u_{1j} \\
u_{21} & u_{22} & \cdots & u_{2j} \\
\vdots & \vdots & & \vdots \\
u_{j-1,1} & u_{j-1,2} & \cdots & u_{j-1,j} \\
u_{i1} & u_{i2} & \cdots & u_{ij}
\end{bmatrix}.
$$

This means that $\mathbf{L}' = \lim_{k \to \infty} \mathbf{L}'_k = \mathbf{L}_u$ if $\det(\mathbf{U}_j)\det(\mathbf{V}_j) \neq 0$, where

$$
\mathbf{U}_j =
\begin{bmatrix}
u_{11} & u_{12} & \cdots & u_{1j} \\
\vdots & \vdots & & \vdots \\
u_{j1} & u_{j2} & \cdots & u_{jj}
\end{bmatrix},
\qquad
\mathbf{V}_j =
\begin{bmatrix}
v_{11} & v_{21} & \cdots & v_{j1} \\
\vdots & \vdots & & \vdots \\
v_{1j} & v_{2j} & \cdots & v_{jj}
\end{bmatrix}.
$$

Here, $\mathbf{U} = \mathbf{L}_u\mathbf{R}_u$ expresses $\mathbf{U}$ as the product of a lower triangular matrix (with ones on the diagonal) by an upper triangular matrix. Therefore also, $\mathbf{R} = \mathbf{R}_u \operatorname{diag}(\lambda_1\lambda_2 \ldots \lambda_n)\mathbf{R}_u^{-1}$.

There is a modification which can be used in conjunction with real matrices $\mathbf{A}$ whose eigenvalues may be complex.

EXAMPLE 4.3

RUTISHAUSER'S METHOD

Problem Statement

Write a subroutine, called RUTIS, that will apply Rutishauser's LR transformation to a given matrix, and that will also find the eigenvectors as a byproduct. The subroutine should incorporate the following features: (a) economy of storage, (b) special handling of tridiagonal matrices, to take advantage of their high proportion of zeros, (c) acceleration of convergence, when appropriate, and (d) double-precision arithmetic. Check the subroutine for several test matrices by writing a main program that handles input and output and calls on RUTIS.

Method of Solution and FORTRAN Implementation

This example elaborates considerably on the basic LR method. The resulting program is long and involved, but because certain extra features are included, it is computationally quite efficient. The complete method is most easily discussed by referring partly to program symbols from the outset.

The calling statement for the subroutine will be

CALL RUTIS (N, A, ANEW, U, FREQ, ITMAX, EPS1, EPS2, EPS3,

EPS4, EIGVEC, STRIPD, SWEEP, TAG1, TAG2, ITER)

The various arguments are defined as follows:

subsequent transformed matrices $\mathbf{A}_2$, $\mathbf{A}_3$, ..., $\mathbf{A}_k$, and their lower and upper triangular decomposition matrices $\mathbf{L}$ and $\mathbf{R}$ (with the exception of the diagonal of $\mathbf{L}$, which consists of 1's, and need not be stored). This arrangement results in considerable economy of storage. The upper triangular portion of matrix $\mathbf{X}$ is reserved for the eigenvectors of $\mathbf{A}_k$; its lower triangular portion stores the accumulated product $\mathbf{L}_k' = \mathbf{L}_1 \mathbf{L}_2 \ldots \mathbf{L}_k$. The diagonal elements of $\mathbf{X}$ are all 1's and may be regarded as common to both the eigenvector and accumulated product portions. Matrix $\mathbf{U}$ is employed only for storing the normalized eigenvectors of $\mathbf{A}$.

The following algorithms are used in the subroutine:
(1) Decomposition of matrix $\mathbf{A}_k$ into the product of lower and upper triangular matrices $\mathbf{L}_k$ and $\mathbf{R}_k$ ($\mathbf{A}_k \to \mathbf{L}_k \mathbf{R}_k$):

$$
\left.
\begin{aligned}
r_{ij} &= a_{ij} - \sum_{k=1}^{i-1} l_{ik} r_{kj}, \qquad i = 1, 2, \ldots, j \\
_{ij} &= \frac{a_{ij} - \sum_{k=1}^{j-1} l_{ik} r_{kj}}{r_{jj}}, \qquad i = j+1, \ldots, n
\end{aligned}
\right\} j = 1, 2, \ldots, n.
$$

Note: (a) Also $l_{jj} = 1$, $j = 1, 2, \ldots, n$, but need not be stored.

Program Symbol	Definition
A	Array containing the $n \times n$ starting matrix, $\mathbf{A}$.
ANEW	Array that is to contain the final transformed matrix.
EIGVEC	Logical variable, having the value T/F (true/false) if the eigenvectors are/are not required.
EPS1	Tolerance used in convergence testing. If the sum, SUBSUM, of the absolute values of the subdiagonal elements of the transformed matrix falls below EPS1, the LR transformations will be discontinued.
EPS2, EPS3	Tolerances. The eigenvectors of $\mathbf{A}$ will be computed if and only if: (a) EIGVEC = T, (b) no two eigenvalues lie within a small amount EPS2 of each other (if they do, TAG2 will be returned as T), and (c) SUBSUM is not greater than EPS3 (if it is, TAG1 will be returned as T).
EPS4	Tolerance for the sweeping procedure (see below), which will occur only if: (a) SWEEP = T and (b) SUBSUM < EPS4.
FREQ	Number of LR steps elapsing between successive "sweeps," if any.
ITER	Returned as the number of LR steps actually performed by the subroutine.
ITMAX	Maximum number of LR steps to be performed.
N	Dimension of starting matrix, n.
STRIPD	Logical variable, having the value T/F if $\mathbf{A}$ is/is not tridiagonal. Used to avoid unnecessary multiplication of zeros.
SWEEP	Logical variable, having the value T/F if the sweeping procedure (see below) is/is not to be applied.
U	$n \times n$ matrix whose columns contain the eigenvectors of $\mathbf{A}$.

The subroutine employs two additional $n \times n$ working matrices, $\mathbf{B}$ and $\mathbf{X}$. As soon as RUTIS is entered, $\mathbf{B}$ is equated to the starting matrix $\mathbf{A}$, which is left untouched, should it be required further in the main program. Matrix $\mathbf{B}$ is then employed for storing, in turn, all

(b) Any element a_{ij} is used only once, namely, to compute the corresponding r_{ij} or l_{ij}. Hence the elements of $\mathbf{R}$ and $\mathbf{L}$ can replace those of $\mathbf{A}$ as soon as they are calculated.

Example 4.3   Rutishauser's Method   **239**

(c) In the program, **A**, **L**, and **R** occupy the same array (B) and are therefore referred to by the common symbol B.

(d) For the special case of a tridiagonal starting matrix, all subsequent LR transformations also yield tridiagonal matrices, and the above algorithm would result in an unnecessarily high proportion of multiplications involving zero. We therefore introduce two integer vectors, BEGIN and FINISH, such that for any column J, BEGIN(J) and FINISH(J) contain the row subscript of the first and last nonzero elements, respectively. For full matrices, BEGIN(J) and FINISH(J) are always 1 and N respectively, but they will be suitably modified for tridiagonal matrices. In the program, the lower and upper limits on I in the above algorithm will appear as BEGIN(J) and FINISH(J), respectively, and the lower limit on K will be BEGIN(J).

(2) Recombination of lower and upper triangular matrices, in reverse order, to give transformed matrix $\mathbf{A}_{k+1}$ ($\mathbf{A}_{k+1} \leftarrow \mathbf{R}_k\mathbf{L}_k$):

$$\left.\begin{aligned} a_{ij} &= \sum_{k=i}^{n} r_{ik}l_{kj} = r_{ii}l_{ij} + \sum_{k=i+1}^{n} r_{ik}l_{kj}, \\ &\qquad j = 1, 2, \ldots, i-1 \\ a_{ij} &= r_{ij} + \sum_{k=j+1}^{n} r_{ik}l_{kj}, \\ &\qquad j = i, i+1, \ldots, n \end{aligned}\right\} i = 1, 2, \ldots, n.$$

Note: (a) As soon as an element a_{ij} has been computed, the corresponding element r_{ij} or l_{ij} is no longer needed. Hence, the elements of **A** can replace those of **R** or **L** as soon as they are calculated.

(b) In the program, for reasons previously stated, the lower and upper limits on J are BEGIN(I) and FINISH(I), respectively. The upper limit on K is FINISH(I) for J < I and FINISH(J) for J ⩾ I.

(3) Determination of the accumulated lower triangular product matrix: $\mathbf{L}'_{k+1} \leftarrow \mathbf{L}'_k\mathbf{L}_{k+1}$, where the newest matrix $\mathbf{L}'_{k+1}$ has elements given by

$$\left.\begin{aligned} l'_{ij} \leftarrow l_{ij} + l'_{ij} + \sum_{k=j+1}^{i-1} l'_{ik}l_{kj}, \\ j = 1, 2, \ldots, i-1, \end{aligned}\right\} i = 1, 2, \ldots, n.$$

Note: (a) The substitution operator ← merely emphasizes that a newly computed element of $\mathbf{L}'_{k+1}$ occupies the same storage location as the corresponding element of $\mathbf{L}'_k$.

(b) In the program, **L′** is stored in the matrix **X**.

(4) Determination of the eigenvectors (to be placed in the upper triangular portion of matrix **X**) of the final transformed matrix (occupying the upper triangular portion of matrix **B**, since the strictly lower triangular portion should now consist of numbers very close to zero):

$$\left.\begin{aligned} x_{jj} &= 1, \\ x_{ij} &= \frac{a_{ij} + \sum_{k=i+1}^{j-1} a_{ik}x_{kj}}{a_{jj} - a_{ii}}, \\ &\qquad i = j-1, j-2, \ldots, 1, \end{aligned}\right\} j = 1, 2, \ldots, n.$$

Note that the eigenvectors can only be determined using this algorithm if no two eigenvalues are very close together.

(5) Determination of the starting matrix eigenvectors, as successive columns of matrix **U**:

$$\left.\begin{aligned} u_{ij} &= x_{ij} + \sum_{k=1}^{i-1} l'_{ik}x_{kj}, \quad j = i, i+1, \ldots, n, \\ u_{ij} &= l'_{ij} + \sum_{k=1}^{j-1} l'_{ik}x_{kj}, \quad j = 1, 2, \ldots, i-1, \end{aligned}\right\} i = 1, 2, \ldots, n.$$

(6) The algorithm given below relates to the acceleration of convergence by "sweeping." Note first that the subdiagonal elements of $\mathbf{A}_k$ tend to zero most quickly when **A** has eigenvalues whose moduli are well-spaced. For less favorable cases, convergence may not be especially rapid.

Since the LR algorithm is only a means to the ultimate end of producing an upper triangular matrix, an alternative transformation could be used at any stage should a better one be available. The convergence can indeed be accelerated by the following technique, once a matrix $\mathbf{A}_m$ has been obtained whose subdiagonal elements have been made moderately small by the conventional LR transformation.

Let

$$\mathbf{A}_{m+1} = \mathbf{L}_m^{-1}\mathbf{A}_m\mathbf{L}_m,$$

where

$$\mathbf{L}_m = \begin{bmatrix} 1 & & & & \\ v_2 & 1 & & \text{\Large 0} & \\ v_3 & & 1 & & \\ \vdots & & & \ddots & \\ v_m & & \text{\Large 0} & & 1 \end{bmatrix}, \quad \mathbf{L}_m^{-1} = \begin{bmatrix} 1 & & & & \\ -v_2 & 1 & & \text{\Large 0} & \\ -v_3 & & 1 & & \\ \vdots & & & \ddots & \\ -v_m & & \text{\Large 0} & & 1 \end{bmatrix}.$$

By multiplying out, the v's could be chosen so as to bring all the subdiagonal elements of the first column of $\mathbf{A}_{m+1}$ to zero; however, finding these values of v would require an excessive amount of computation. But, by neglecting quadratic terms in the v's and product terms of the v's with the subdiagonal elements of columns 2, 3, 4, ..., $n-1$ of $\mathbf{A}_m$, it can be shown readily that a choice of v's determined by the following equations will, in most cases, effect a substantial reduction in the magnitude of the subdiagonal elements of column 1:

$$\begin{bmatrix} a_{22} - a_{11} & a_{23} & a_{24} & \cdot & \cdot & \cdot & a_{2n} \\ & a_{33} - a_{11} & a_{34} & & & & a_{3n} \\ & & a_{44} - a_{11} & & & & a_{4n} \\ & & & \cdot & & & \vdots \\ & \text{\Large 0} & & & \cdot & & \\ & & & & & & a_{nn} - a_{11} \end{bmatrix} \begin{bmatrix} v_2 \\ v_3 \\ v_4 \\ \vdots \\ \\ v_n \end{bmatrix} = - \begin{bmatrix} a_{21} \\ a_{31} \\ a_{41} \\ \vdots \\ \\ a_{n1} \end{bmatrix}.$$

Further transformations

$$\mathbf{A}_{m+2} = \mathbf{L}_{m+1}^{-1} \mathbf{A}_{m+1} \mathbf{L}_{m+1},$$

$$\mathbf{A}_{m+3} = \mathbf{L}_{m+2}^{-1} \mathbf{A}_{m+2} \mathbf{L}_{m+2}, \text{ etc.},$$

where

$$\mathbf{L}_{m+1} = \begin{bmatrix} 1 & & & & & \\ & 1 & & & \text{\Large 0} & \\ v_3 & 1 & & & & \\ v_4 & & 1 & & & \\ \vdots & & & \cdot & & \\ \vdots & & & & \cdot & \\ v_n & & & & & 1 \end{bmatrix},$$

$$\mathbf{L}_{m+2} = \begin{bmatrix} 1 & & & & & \\ & 1 & & & \text{\Large 0} & \\ & & 1 & & & \\ & v_4 & 1 & & & \\ & \vdots & & \cdot & & \\ & \vdots & & & \cdot & \\ & v_n & & & & 1 \end{bmatrix}, \text{ etc.},$$

(and the v's are chosen properly, but will vary from one column to the next) will also reduce the subdiagonal elements of the remaining columns substantially.

In the subroutine, the elements v_i, which are stored in the vector $\mathbf{V}$, are determined for a particular column j from the relation

$$v_i = \frac{a_{ij} + \displaystyle\sum_{k=i+1}^{n} a_{ik} v_k}{a_{jj} - a_{ii}}, \left.\begin{array}{l} \\ \\ i = n, n-1, \ldots, j+1, \end{array}\right\} j = 1, 2, \ldots, n-1.$$

This process of "sweeping" through the columns may be repeated with ever-increasing effect. Finally, note that if the sweeping procedure is applied to a tridiagonal matrix, it will introduce small nonzero values into elements that were previously zero. The technique of (1d) above is then no longer advantageous, but this is of little consequence, since the very introduction of the sweeping procedure means that the required degree of convergence will soon occur.

We have not attempted to write a concise flow diagram for this example. Instead, the overall approach can be understood best by reading the program comment cards in conjunction with the above algorithms.

Example 4.3   Rutishauser's Method

241

Program Listing

Main Program

```
C          APPLIED NUMERICAL METHODS, EXAMPLE 4.3
C          EIGENVALUES BY RUTISHAUSER'S LEFT-RIGHT TRANSFORMATION.
C
C          THE FOLLOWING MAIN PROGRAM HANDLES INPUT AND OUTPUT ONLY, AND
C          CALLS ON THE SUBROUTINE RUTIS TO IMPLEMENT THE ALGORITHM.
C
           IMPLICIT REAL*8 (A-H, O-Z)
           INTEGER FREQ
           LOGICAL EIGVEC, STRIPD, SWEEP, TAG1, TAG2
           DIMENSION A(11,11), ANEW(11,11), U(11,11)
           ICOUNT = 1
           WRITE (6,200)
           READ (5,100) EPS1, EPS2, EPS3, EPS4, FREQ, SWEEP
           WRITE (6,201) EPS1, EPS2, EPS3, EPS4, FREQ, SWEEP
C
C          ..... READ STARTING MATRIX A AND OTHER PARAMETERS .....
     1     WRITE (6,202) ICOUNT
           ICOUNT = ICOUNT + 1
           READ (5,101) N, ITMAX, EIGVEC, STRIPD
           WRITE (6,203) N, ITMAX, EIGVEC, STRIPD
           DO 2 I = 1, N
     2     READ (5,102) (A(I,J), J = 1, N)
           WRITE (6,204)
           DO 3 I = 1, N
     3     WRITE (6,205) (A(I,J), J = 1, N)
C
C          ..... CALL ON RUTIS TO FIND EIGENVALUES AND EIGENVECTORS.....
           CALL RUTIS (N, A, ANEW, U, FREQ, ITMAX, EPS1, EPS2, EPS3,
          1 EPS4, EIGVEC, STRIPD, SWEEP, TAG1, TAG2, ITER)
C
C          .....PRINT VARIOUS RESULTS, AS APPROPRIATE .....
           WRITE (6,206) ITER, TAG1, TAG2
           WRITE (6,207)
           DO 4 I = 1, N
     4     WRITE (6,205) (ANEW(I,J), J = 1, N)
           IF (EIGVEC) GO TO 5
              WRITE (6,208)
              GO TO 1
     5     IF (.NOT. TAG1) GO TO 6
              WRITE (6,209)
              GO TO 1
     6     IF (.NOT. TAG2) GO TO 7
              WRITE (6,210)
              GO TO 1
     7     WRITE (6,211)
           DO 8 I = 1, N
     8     WRITE (6,205) (U(I,J), J = 1, N)
           GO TO 1
C
C          ..... FORMATS FOR INPUT AND OUTPUT STATEMENTS .....
   100     FORMAT (6X, E7.1, 10X, E7.1, 10X, E7.1, 10X, F4.1/
          1 6X, I3, 11X, L2)
   101     FORMAT (3X, I3, 11X, I4, 2(12X, L2))
   102     FORMAT (10X, 14F5.1)
   200     FORMAT (62H1     DETERMINATION OF EIGENVALUES OF A MATRIX BY RUTISH
          1AUSER'S/ 47H     LEFT-RIGHT TRANSFORMATION, WITH PARAMETERS/1H )
   201     FORMAT (7X, 10H EPS1   = , E12.3/ 7X, 10H EPS2   = , E12.3/
          1        7X, 10H EPS3   = , E12.3/ 7X, 10H EPS4   = , F6.1/
          2        7X, 10H FREQ   = , I4   / 7X, 10H SWEEP  = , L4   )
   202     FORMAT (1H1, 4X, 7HEXAMPLE, I3, 17H, WITH PARAMETERS/1H )
   203     FORMAT (7X, 10H N      = , I4   / 7X, 10H ITMAX  = , I4   /
          1        7X, 10H EIGVEC = , L4   / 7X, 10H STRIPD = , L4   )
   204     FORMAT (29H0     THE STARTING MATRIX A IS)
   205     FORMAT ( 7X, 10F10.6)
   206     FORMAT (1H0, 6X, 10H ITER   = , I4/ 7X, 10H TAG1   = , L4/
          1        7X, 10H TAG2   = , L4)
   207     FORMAT (35H0     THE TRANSFORMED MATRIX ANEW IS)
   208     FORMAT (30H0     EIGENVECTORS NOT REQUIRED)
   209     FORMAT (45H0     EIGENVECTORS NOT COMPUTED BECAUSE ONE OR/
          1 41H     MORE SUB-DIAGONAL ELEMENTS TOO LARGE)
```

Program Listing (*Continued*)

```
  210  FORMAT (46H0    EIGENVECTORS NOT COMPUTED BECAUSE PAIR OF/
     1 26H     EIGENVALUES TOO CLOSE)
  211  FORMAT (62H0    THE FOLLOWING MATRIX CONTAINS THE NORMALIZED EIGEN
     1VECTORS)
C
       END
```

Subroutine RUTIS

```
C          DETERMINATION OF THE EIGENVALUES OF AN NXN REAL MATRIX A,
C          BY RUTISHAUSER'S LEFT-RIGHT TRANSFORMATION.   NOTE
C          (1)    THE UPPER AND LOWER TRIANGULAR MATRICES (WITH THE
C                 EXCEPTION OF THE UNIT DIAGONAL OF THE LATTER) INTO WHICH A
C                 IS FACTORIZED, AND ALL SUCCESSIVE TRANSFORMATIONS OF A,
C                 OCCUPY ARRAY B.
C          (2)    THE ACCUMULATED PRODUCT OF THE LOWER TRIANGULAR
C                 DECOMPOSITION MATRICES IS STORED IN ARRAY X.
C          (3)    THE PROGRAM STOPS EITHER WHEN ITMAX SUCCESSIVE
C                 DECOMPOSITIONS AND MULTIPLICATIONS HAVE BEEN MADE, OR WHEN
C                 THE SUM (SUBSUM) OF THE ABSOLUTE VALUES OF THE SUB-
C                 DIAGONAL ELEMENTS OF THE TRANSFORMED MATRIX FALLS BELOW A
C                 SMALL VALUE EPS1.
C          (4)    FOR THE SPECIAL CASE OF AN INITIAL TRIDIAGONAL MATRIX,
C                 SETTING THE LOGICAL VARIABLE STRIPD = .TRUE. WILL
C                 REDUCE THE COMPUTATION TIME CONSIDERABLY.
C          (5)    IF THE LOGICAL VARIABLE SWEEP = .TRUE., A SPECIAL ROUTINE
C                 IS INTRODUCED TO ACCELERATE CONVERGENCE, PROVIDED THAT
C                 SUBSUM IS LESS THAN EPS4.
C          (6)    THE EIGENVECTORS OF A WILL BE COMPUTED AND STORED IN
C                 THE ARRAY U IF THE PARAMETER EIGVEC = .TRUE., PROVIDED
C                 THAT NO TWO EIGENVALUES LIE WITHIN A SMALL VALUE EPS2 OF
C                 EACH OTHER, AND THAT SUBSUM IS NOT GREATER THAN EPS3.
C
       SUBROUTINE RUTIS (N, A, B, U, FREQ, ITMAX, EPS1, EPS2,
     1 EPS3, EPS4, EIGVEC, STRIPD, SWEEP, TAG1, TAG2, ITER)
       IMPLICIT REAL*8 (A-H, O-Z)
       REAL*8 A, B, U, EPS1, EPS2, EPS3, EPS4, LENGTH
       DIMENSION A(11,11), B(11,11), U(11,11), V(11), X(11,11)
       INTEGER BEGIN(11), FINISH(11), FREQ
       LOGICAL EIGVEC, STRIPD, SWEEP, TAG1, TAG2
       NM1 = N - 1
       DO 1  I = 1, N
       DO 1  J = 1, N
       X(I,J) = 0.
    1  B(I,J) = 0.
       L = 0
       TAG1 = .FALSE.
       TAG2 = .FALSE.
C
C          ..... DETERMINE THE VECTORS BEGIN AND FINISH .....
       IF (.NOT. STRIPD) GO TO 3
          BEGIN(1) = 1
          BEGIN(N) = NM1
          FINISH(1) = 2
          FINISH(N) = N
          IF (N .LE. 2) GO TO 5
          DO 2  J = 2, NM1
          BEGIN(J) = J - 1
    2     FINISH(J) = J + 1
       GO TO 5
    3     DO 4  J = 1, N
          BEGIN(J) = 1
    4     FINISH(J) = N
    5  CONTINUE
       DO 6  I = 1, N
       JLOW = BEGIN(I)
       JHIGH = FINISH(I)
       DO 6  J = JLOW, JHIGH
    6  B(I,J) = A(I,J)
```

Example 4.3   Rutishauser's Method   **243**

Program Listing (*Continued*)

```
C
C         ..... START LEFT-RIGHT TRANSFORMATION, ITERATING UNTIL
C               CONVERGENCE SATISFACTORY OR ITERATIONS EXCEED ITMAX .....
          DO 51  ITER = 1, ITMAX
C
C         ..... THE MATRIX B IS DECOMPOSED INTO
C               UPPER AND LOWER TRIANGULAR FACTORS .....
          DO 10  J = 1, N
          ILOW = BEGIN(J)
          DO 8  I = ILOW, J
          SUM = 0.
          IM1 = I - 1
          KLOW = BEGIN(I)
          IF (KLOW .GT. IM1) GO TO 8
             DO 7  K = KLOW, IM1
   7         SUM = SUM + B(I,K)*B(K,J)
   8      B(I,J) = B(I,J) - SUM
          JP1 = J + 1
          IHIGH = FINISH(J)
          IF (JP1 .GT. IHIGH) GO TO 15
          DO 10  I = JP1, IHIGH
          SUM = 0.
          KLOW = BEGIN(I)
          JM1 = J - 1
          IF (KLOW .GT. JM1) GO TO 10
             DO 9  K = KLOW, JM1
   9         SUM = SUM + B(I,K)*B(K,J)
  10      B(I,J) = (B(I,J) - SUM)/B(J,J)
C
C         ..... THE ACCUMULATED PRODUCT OF THE SUCCESSIVE LOWER
C               TRIANGULAR DECOMPOSITION MATRICES IS COMPUTED .....
  15      IF (.NOT. EIGVEC) GO TO 18
             DO 17  I = 2, N
             IM1 = I - 1
             DO 17  J = 1, IM1
             X(I,J) = B(I,J) + X(I,J)
             KLOW = J + 1
             IF (KLOW .GT. IK1) GO TO 17
                DO 16  K = KLOW, IM1
  16            X(I,J) = X(I,J) + X(I,K)*B(K,J)
  17         CONTINUE
C
C         ..... AND THE FACTORS ARE COMBINED IN REVERSE ORDER .....
  18      DO 24  I = 1, N
          JLOW = BEGIN(I)
          IM1 = I - 1
          IF (JLOW .GT. IM1) GO TO 21
             DO 20  J = JLOW, IM1
             B(I,J) = B(I,I)*B(I,J)
             IP1 = I + 1
             KHIGH = FINISH(I)
             IF (IP1 .GT. KHIGH) GO TO 20
                DO 19  K = IP1, KHIGH
  19            B(I,J) = B(I,J) + B(I,K)*B(K,J)
  20         CONTINUE
  21      JHIGH = FINISH(I)
          DO 23  J = I, JHIGH
          JP1 = J + 1
          KHIGH = FINISH(J)
          IF (JP1 .GT. KHIGH) GO TO 23
             DO 22  K = JP1, KHIGH
  22         B(I,J) = B(I,J) + B(I,K)*B(K,J)
  23      CONTINUE
  24      CONTINUE
          DO 25  I = 1, N
          JLOW = BEGIN(I)
          JHIGH = FINISH(I)
          DO 25  J = JLOW, JHIGH
  25      IF (DABS(B(I,J)) .LT. 1.0D-10) B(I,J) = 0.
          L = L + 1
```

Program Listing (*Continued*)

```
C
C          ..... THE SUM OF THE ABSOLUTE VALUES OF THE
C                SUB-DIAGONAL ELEMENTS IS COMPUTED .....
           SUBSUM = 0.
           DO 26  I = 2, N
   26      SUBSUM = SUBSUM + DABS(B(I,I-1))
C
C          ..... DETERMINE COLUMN VECTORS FOR SWEEPING PROCEDURE .....
           IF (.NOT.(L.EQ.FREQ .AND. SUBSUM.LT.EPS4 .AND. SWEEP)) GO TO 42
               DO 37  J = 1, NM1
C
C              ..... REJECT CASES FOR WHICH DIAG. ELEMENTS TOO CLOSE .....
               DO 30  I = 1, N
   30          IF (DABS(B(J,J) - B(I,I)).LT.EPS2 .AND. J.NE.I) GO TO 37
               JP1 = J + 1
               DO 32  IT = JP1, N
               I = N + JP1 - IT
               V(I) = B(I,J)
               IP1 = I + 1
               IF (I .EQ. N) GO TO 32
                   DO 31  K = IP1, N
   31              V(I) = V(I) + B(I,K)*V(K)
   32          V(I) = V(I)/(B(J,J) - B(I,I))
C
C              ..... MODIFY LOWER TRIANGULAR PRODUCT MATRIX .....
               DO 34  IT = JP1, N
               I = N + JP1 - IT
               X(I,J) = X(I,J) + V(I)
               IM1 = I - 1
               IF (JP1 .GT. IM1) GO TO 34
                   DO 33  K = JP1, IM1
   33              X(I,J) = X(I,J) + X(I,K)*V(K)
   34          CONTINUE
C
C              ..... POSTMULTIPLY B WITH SWEEPING MATRIX .....
               DO 35  I = 1, N
               DO 35  K = JP1, N
   35          B(I,J) = B(I,J) + B(I,K)*V(K)
C
C              ..... PREMULTIPLY B WITH INVERSE OF SWEEPING MATRIX .....
               DO 36  I = JP1, N
               DO 36  K = 1, N
   36          B(I,K) = B(I,K) - V(I)*B(J,K)
   37          CONTINUE
               IF (.NOT. STRIPD) GO TO 41
                   DO 40  J = 1, N
                   BEGIN(J) = 1
   40              FINISH(J) = N
   41          CONTINUE
   42      CONTINUE
C
C          ..... CHECK FOR CONVERGENCE .....
           IF (.NOT.(L.EQ.FREQ .OR. ITER.EQ.ITMAX .OR. SUBSUM.LT.EPS1))
          1                                                    GO TO 50
               L = 0
   50      CONTINUE
   51      IF (SUBSUM .LT. EPS1) GO TO 52
   52      DO 53  I = 1, N
   53      X(I,I) = 0.
C
C          ..... CHECK TO SEE IF EIGENVECTORS ARE REQUIRED OR IF
C                ANY TWO EIGENVALUES ARE CLOSER TOGETHER THAN EPS2 .....
           IF (.NOT. EIGVEC) GO TO 72
           IF (SUBSUM .LE. EPS3) GO TO 54
               TAG1 = .TRUE.
               GO TO 72
   54      DO 55  I = 1, NM1
           IP1 = I + 1
           DO 55  J = IP1, N
           IF (DABS(B(I,I) - B(J,J)) .GE. EPS2) GO TO 55
               TAG2 = .TRUE.
               GO TO 72
   55      CONTINUE
```

Example 4.3   Rutishauser's Method   **245**

Program Listing (*Continued*)

```
C
C         ..... COMPUTE EIGENVECTORS OF TRANSFORMED MATRIX .....
          DO 62   J = 1, N
          X(J,J) = 1.
          IF (J .EQ. 1) GO TO 62
             JM1 = J - 1
             DO 61   IT = 1, JM1
             I = J - IT
             SUM = B(I,J)
             IP1 = I + 1
             IF (IP1 .GT. JM1) GO TO 61
                DO 60   K = IP1, JM1
   60           SUM = SUM + B(I,K)*X(K,J)
   61        X(I,J) = SUM/(B(J,J) - B(I,I))
   62     CONTINUE
C
C         ..... COMPUTE EIGENVECTORS OF ORIGINAL MATRIX .....
          DO 67   I = 1, N
          IM1 = I - 1
          IF (I .EQ. 1) GO TO 65
             DO 64   J = 1, IM1
             U(I,J) = X(I,J)
             JM1 = J - 1
             IF (J .EQ. 1) GO TO 64
                DO 63   K = 1, JM1
   63           U(I,J) = U(I,J) + X(I,K)*X(K,J)
   64        CONTINUE
   65     DO 67   J = I, N
          U(I,J) = X(I,J)
          IM1 = I - 1
          IF (I .EQ. 1) GO TO 67
             DO 66   K = 1, IM1
   66        U(I,J) = U(I,J) + X(I,K)*X(K,J)
   67     CONTINUE
C
C         ..... NORMALIZE THE EIGENVECTORS .....
          DO 71   J = 1, N
          SUMSQ = 0.
          DO 70   I = 1, N
   70     SUMSQ = SUMSQ + U(I,J)**2
          LENGTH = DSQRT (SUMSQ)
          DO 71   I = 1, N
   71     U(I,J) = U(I,J)/LENGTH
C
   72     CONTINUE
          RETURN
C
          END
```

Data

```
EPS1 = 1.0E-7    EPS2 = 1.0E-3    EPS3 = 1.0E-4    EPS4 = 0.1
FREQ =  5      SWEEP = T
N =  4    ITMAX =  25    EIGVEC = T    STRIPD = F
A(1,1)  =   10.    9.    7.    5.
             9.   10.    8.    6.
             7.    8.   10.    7.
             5.    6.    7.    5.
N =  4    ITMAX =  25    EIGVEC = T    STRIPD = F
A(1,1)  =    6.    4.    4.    1.
             4.    6.    1.    4.
             4.    1.    6.    4.
             1.    4.    4.    6.
N =  4    ITMAX =  25    EIGVEC = F    STRIPD = F
A(1,1)  =    4.   -5.    0.    3.
             0.    4.   -3.   -5.
             5.   -3.    4.    0.
             3.    0.    5.    4.
```

Program Listing (*Continued*)

Data (*Continued*)

```
N =  8     ITMAX = 100     EIGVEC = T     STRIPD = T
A(1,1)  =    2.  -1.   0.   0.   0.   0.   0.   0.
            -1.   2.  -1.   0.   0.   0.   0.   0.
             0.  -1.   2.  -1.   0.   0.   0.   0.
             0.   0.  -1.   2.  -1.   0.   0.   0.
             0.   0.   0.  -1.   2.  -1.   0.   0.
             0.   0.   0.   0.  -1.   2.  -1.   0.
             0.   0.   0.   0.   0.  -1.   2.  -1.
             0.   0.   0.   0.   0.   0.  -1.   2.
N =  9     ITMAX = 100     EIGVEC = T     STRIPD = T
A(1,1)  =   2.5 -2.   0.   0.   0.   0.   0.   0.   0.
            -1.   2.  -1.   0.   0.   0.   0.   0.   0.
             0.  -1.   2.  -1.   0.   0.   0.   0.   0.
             0.   0.  -1.   2.  -1.   0.   0.   0.   0.
             0.   0.   0.  -1.   2.  -1.   0.   0.   0.
             0.   0.   0.   0.  -1.   2.  -1.   0.   0.
             0.   0.   0.   0.   0.  -1.   2.  -1.   0.
             0.   0.   0.   0.   0.   0.  -1.   2.  -1.
             0.   0.   0.   0.   0.   0.   0.  -2.   2.5
```

Computer Output

```
DETERMINATION OF EIGENVALUES OF A MATRIX BY RUTISHAUSER'S
LEFT-RIGHT TRANSFORMATION, WITH PARAMETERS

    EPS1   =    0.100D-06
    EPS2   =    0.100D-02
    EPS3   =    0.100D-03
    EPS4   =    0.1
    FREQ   =    5
    SWEEP  =    T


  EXAMPLE   1, WITH PARAMETERS

    N      =    4
    ITMAX  =    25
    EIGVEC =    T
    STRIPD =    F

THE STARTING MATRIX A IS
    10.000000   9.000000   7.000000   5.000000
     9.000000  10.000000   8.000000   6.000000
     7.000000   8.000000  10.000000   7.000000
     5.000000   6.000000   7.000000   5.000000

    ITER   =    11
    TAG1   =    F
    TAG2   =    F

THE TRANSFORMED MATRIX ANEW IS
    30.288685  42.270007  10.019862   5.000000
     0.0        3.858057   1.007116   0.702164
     0.0        0.0        0.843107  -0.316835
     0.0        0.0        0.0        0.010150

THE FOLLOWING MATRIX CONTAINS THE NORMALIZED EIGENVECTORS
     0.520925  -0.625396   0.567641   0.123697
     0.551955  -0.271601  -0.760318  -0.208554
     0.528568   0.614861   0.301652  -0.501565
     0.380262   0.396306  -0.093305   0.830444
```

Example 4.3 Rutishauser's Method **247**

Computer Output (*Continued*)

EXAMPLE 2, WITH PARAMETERS

```
     N      =     4
     ITMAX  =    25
     EIGVEC =     T
     STRIPD =     F
```

THE STARTING MATRIX A IS
```
     6.000000   4.000000   4.000000   1.000000
     4.000000   6.000000   1.000000   4.000000
     4.000000   1.000000   6.000000   4.000000
     1.000000   4.000000   4.000000   6.000000
```

```
     ITER   =    12
     TAG1   =     F
     TAG2   =     T
```

THE TRANSFORMED MATRIX ANEW IS
```
    15.000000   4.999915   5.000000   1.000000
    -0.000000   5.000000  -0.000000   3.000000
    -0.000000  -0.000000   5.000000   3.000051
     0.0        0.000000   0.000000  -1.000000
```

EIGENVECTORS NOT COMPUTED BECAUSE PAIR OF
EIGENVALUES TOO CLOSE

EXAMPLE 3, WITH PARAMETERS

```
     N      =     4
     ITMAX  =    25
     EIGVEC =     F
     STRIPD =     F
```

THE STARTING MATRIX A IS
```
     4.000000  -5.000000   0.0        3.000000
     0.0        4.000000  -3.000000  -5.000000
     5.000000  -3.000000   4.000000   0.0
     3.000000   0.0        5.000000   4.000000
```

```
     ITER   =    25
     TAG1   =     F
     TAG2   =     F
```

THE TRANSFORMED MATRIX ANEW IS
```
    12.000000  -8.678738   3.000000   3.000000
     0.000000   2.131230  -5.000000  -2.000000
    -0.000000   5.255936  -0.131230  -3.452492
     0.0       -0.000000  -0.000000   2.000000
```

EIGENVECTORS NOT REQUIRED

EXAMPLE 4, WITH PARAMETERS

```
     N      =     8
     ITMAX  =   100
     EIGVEC =     T
     STRIPD =     T
```

THE STARTING MATRIX A IS
```
     2.000000  -1.000000   0.0        0.0        0.0        0.0        0.0        0.0
    -1.000000   2.000000  -1.000000   0.0        0.0        0.0        0.0        0.0
     0.0       -1.000000   2.000000  -1.000000   0.0        0.0        0.0        0.0
     0.0        0.0       -1.000000   2.000000  -1.000000   0.0        0.0        0.0
     0.0        0.0        0.0       -1.000000   2.000000  -1.000000   0.0        0.0
     0.0        0.0        0.0        0.0       -1.000000   2.000000  -1.000000   0.0
     0.0        0.0        0.0        0.0        0.0       -1.000000   2.000000  -1.000000
     0.0        0.0        0.0        0.0        0.0        0.0       -1.000000   2.000000
```

```
     ITER   =    41
     TAG1   =     F
     TAG2   =     F
```

THE TRANSFORMED MATRIX ANEW IS
```
     3.879385  -1.000000   0.0        0.0        0.0        0.0        0.0        0.0
     0.0        3.532089  -1.000000   0.0        0.0        0.0        0.0        0.0
     0.0        0.000000   3.000000  -1.000000   0.0        0.0        0.0        0.0
     0.0        0.0        0.0        2.347296  -1.000000   0.0        0.0        0.0
     0.0        0.0        0.0        0.0        1.652704  -1.000000   0.0        0.0
     0.0        0.0        0.0        0.0        0.0        1.000000  -1.000000   0.0
     0.0        0.0        0.0        0.0        0.0        0.0        0.467911  -1.000000
     0.0        0.0        0.0        0.0        0.0        0.0        0.0        0.120615
```

THE FOLLOWING MATRIX CONTAINS THE NORMALIZED EIGENVECTORS
```
     0.161230   0.303013   0.408248   0.464243   0.464243   0.408248   0.303013   0.161230
    -0.303013  -0.464243  -0.408248  -0.161230   0.161230   0.408248   0.464243   0.303013
     0.408248   0.408248  -0.000000  -0.408248  -0.408248   0.000000   0.408248   0.408248
    -0.464243  -0.161230   0.408248   0.303013  -0.303013  -0.408248   0.161230   0.464243
     0.464243  -0.161230  -0.408248   0.303013   0.303013  -0.408248  -0.161230   0.464243
    -0.408248   0.408248  -0.000000  -0.408248   0.408248  -0.000000  -0.408248   0.408248
     0.303013  -0.464243   0.408248  -0.161230  -0.161230   0.408248  -0.464243   0.303013
    -0.161230   0.303013  -0.408248   0.464243  -0.464243   0.408248  -0.303013   0.161230
```

Computer Output (*Continued*)

```
EXAMPLE  5,  WITH PARAMETERS

    N     =    9
  ITMAX   =  100
  EIGVEC  =    T
  STRIPD  =    T

THE STARTING MATRIX A IS
   2.500000 -2.000000  0.0        0.0        0.0        0.0        0.0        0.0        0.0
  -1.000000  2.000000 -1.000000   0.0        0.0        0.0        0.0        0.0        0.0
   0.0      -1.000000  2.000000  -1.000000   0.0        0.0        0.0        0.0        0.0
   0.0       0.0      -1.000000   2.000000  -1.000000   0.0        0.0        0.0        0.0
   0.0       0.0       0.0       -1.000000   2.000000  -1.000000   0.0        0.0        0.0
   0.0       0.0       0.0        0.0       -1.000000   2.000000  -1.000000   0.0        0.0
   0.0       0.0       0.0        0.0        0.0       -1.000000   2.000000  -1.000000   0.0
   0.0       0.0       0.0        0.0        0.0        0.0       -1.000000   2.000000  -1.000000
   0.0       0.0       0.0        0.0        0.0        0.0        0.0       -2.000000   2.500000

  ITER    =   61
  TAG1    =    F
  TAG2    =    F


THE TRANSFORMED MATRIX ANEW IS
   4.000000 -2.000000  0.0        0.0        0.0        0.0        0.0        0.0        0.0
   0.000000  4.088793 -1.000000   0.0        0.0        0.0        0.0        0.0        0.0
   0.0       0.0       3.539881  -1.000000   0.0        0.0        0.0        0.0        0.0
   0.0       0.0       0.0        2.889229  -1.000000   0.0        0.0        0.0        0.0
   0.0       0.0       0.0        0.0        2.122634  -1.000000   0.0        0.0        0.0
   0.0       0.0       0.0        0.0        0.0        1.355416  -1.000000   0.0        0.0
   0.0       0.0       0.0        0.0        0.0        0.0        0.702349  -1.000000   0.0
   0.0       0.0       0.0        0.0        0.0        0.0        0.0        0.255356  -1.000000
   0.0       0.0       0.0        0.0        0.0        0.0        0.0        0.0        0.046343

THE FOLLOWING MATRIX CONTAINS THE NORMALIZED EIGENVECTORS
   0.516398 -0.441843  0.441028   0.439670   0.437037   0.431576   0.418417   0.379102   0.251665
  -0.387298  0.350999 -0.229308  -0.085566   0.082461   0.246988   0.376084   0.425475   0.308750
   0.258199 -0.291320 -0.087920  -0.363582  -0.447150  -0.272372   0.069609   0.363200   0.351526
  -0.129099  0.257509  0.364695   0.408873  -0.027626  -0.422554  -0.285756   0.208180   0.378011
  -0.000000 -0.246562 -0.473667  -0.000000   0.450538  -0.000000  -0.440421  -0.000000   0.386978
   0.129099  0.257509  0.364695  -0.408873  -0.027626   0.422555  -0.285756  -0.208180   0.378011
  -0.258199 -0.291320 -0.087920   0.363582  -0.447150   0.272372   0.069609  -0.363200   0.351526
   0.387298  0.350999 -0.229308   0.085566   0.082462  -0.246988   0.376084  -0.425475   0.308750
  -0.516398 -0.441843  0.441028  -0.439670   0.437037  -0.431576   0.418417  -0.379102   0.251665
```

Example 4.3 Rutishauser's Method **249**

Discussion of Results (Examples 1–5)

(1) The eigenvalues are 30.288685, 3.858057, 0.843107, and 0.010150; they are remarkably well-spaced. The condition SUBSUM < EPS1 $(=10^{-7})$ stopped the iterations.

(2) The eigenvalues, 15.0, 5.0, 5.0, and −1.0, include a coincident pair. The eigenvectors were requested but were not computed because a pair of eigenvalues was found to be closer together than EPS2 = 0.001.

(3) The eigenvalues, 12.0, 1.0 ± 5.0i, and 2.0, include a complex conjugate pair. In such cases, it is typical that a two-row minor, in this example

$$\begin{vmatrix} a_{22} & a_{23} \\ a_{32} & a_{33} \end{vmatrix},$$

does not converge, but that the eigenvalues of its matrix do converge (to 1.0 + 5.0i and 1.0 − 5.0i).

(4) This tridiagonal matrix arises when treating unsteady-state heat conduction in a slab as a characteristic-value problem (see Section 7.26). Note that the eigenvectors are alternately antisymmetric and symmetric.

(5) This unsymmetrical tridiagonal matrix arises when treating flow of a reacting fluid between two parallel plates as a characteristic-value problem (see Problem 7.24).

4.8 Jacobi's Method for Symmetric Matrices

We consider here an iterative method, credited to Jacobi, for transforming a real symmetric matrix $\mathbf{A}$ into diagonal form. This method consists of applying to $\mathbf{A}$ a succession of plane rotations designed to reduce the off-diagonal elements to zero. Let $\mathbf{A}_0 = \mathbf{A}$ and let $\mathbf{U}_i$, $i \geq 1$, be orthogonal matrices. Define $\mathbf{A}_1 = \mathbf{U}_1^{-1}\mathbf{A}_0\mathbf{U}_1$, $\mathbf{A}_2 = \mathbf{U}_2^{-1}\mathbf{A}_1\mathbf{U}_2$, and, in general,

$$\mathbf{A}_{k+1} = \mathbf{U}_{k+1}^{-1}\mathbf{A}_k\mathbf{U}_{k+1}. \tag{4.48}$$

Then if $\mathbf{U}_k' = \mathbf{U}_1\mathbf{U}_2 \ldots \mathbf{U}_k$,

$$\mathbf{A}_{k+1} = \mathbf{U}_{k+1}'^{-1}\mathbf{A}\mathbf{U}_{k+1}', \tag{4.49}$$

and $\mathbf{A}_{k+1}$ has the same eigenvalues as $\mathbf{A}$. Moreover, for all indices k, $\mathbf{A}_k$ is real and symmetric.

Recall that $Sp(\mathbf{A}^*\mathbf{A}) = \sum_{i=1}^{n}\sum_{j=1}^{n} a_{ij}\bar{a}_{ij}$, or, for $\mathbf{A}$ real and symmetric, $Sp(\mathbf{A}^2) = \sum_{i=1}^{n}\sum_{j=1}^{n} a_{ij}^2$. If $\mathbf{T}$ is any nonsingular transformation, $\mathbf{T}^{-1}\mathbf{A}^2\mathbf{T}$ has the same eigenvalues as $\mathbf{A}^2$, and thus $Sp(\mathbf{T}^{-1}\mathbf{A}^2\mathbf{T}) = Sp(\mathbf{A}^2)$, since it is the sum of the eigenvalues. Thus, if $\mathbf{A}_k = (a_{ij}^{(k)})$, we have, for (4.48)

$$\sum_{i=1}^{n}\sum_{j=1}^{n}(a_{ij}^{(k)})^2 = \sum_{i=1}^{n}\sum_{j=1}^{n} a_{ij}^2.$$

If, now, the sequence $\{\mathbf{U}_k\}$ can be so chosen that

$$\sum_{i=1}^{n}(a_{ii}^{(k+1)})^2 > \sum_{i=1}^{n}(a_{ii}^{(k)})^2,$$

the sequence

$$\left\{\sum_{i=1}^{n}(a_{ii}^{(k)})^2\right\}$$

will be convergent, since it is monotonic and bounded above by $Sp(\mathbf{A}^2)$. If, in addition,

$$\sum_{i=1}^{n}\sum_{j=1}^{n}(a_{ij}^{(k)})^2 - \sum_{i=1}^{n}(a_{ii}^{(k)})^2$$

approaches zero, then

$$\lim_{k\to\infty}\mathbf{A}_k = \text{diag}(\lambda_1 \lambda_2 \ldots \lambda_n); \tag{4.50}$$

and, if $\lim_{k\to\infty}\mathbf{U}_k' = \mathbf{U}$,

$$\mathbf{A}\mathbf{U} = \mathbf{U}\,\text{diag}(\lambda_1 \lambda_2 \ldots \lambda_n). \tag{4.51}$$

The further character of $\mathbf{U}_{k+1}$ is now described. Let $a_{ij}^{(k)}(i \neq j)$ be a nonzero element of $\mathbf{A}_k$. Let the matrix $\mathbf{U}_{k+1}$ be the $n \times n$ identity matrix $\mathbf{I}$ except that the ith row has been replaced by a row of zeros, other than $\cos\alpha$ in column i and $\sin\alpha$ in column j, while the jth row has been replaced by a row of zeros, other than $\sin\alpha$ in column i and $-\cos\alpha$ in column j. The method of choosing α will be detailed shortly. Note that $\mathbf{U}_{k+1}$ is self-inverse. The result of both premultiplying and postmultiplying $\mathbf{A}_k$ by $\mathbf{U}_{k+1}$ is to leave the elements of $\mathbf{A}_k$ unaltered, except those in rows i and j and columns i and j. At the moment, we

concern ourselves only with $a_{ij}^{(k+1)}$, $a_{ii}^{(k+1)}$ and $a_{jj}^{(k+1)}$. When $\mathbf{A}_k$ is premultiplied by $\mathbf{U}_{k+1}$, the new entry in the ii position is $a_{ii}^{(k)}\cos\alpha + a_{ij}^{(k)}\sin\alpha$, that in the ij position is $a_{ij}^{(k)}\cos\alpha + a_{jj}^{(k)}\sin\alpha$, that in the jj position is $a_{ij}^{(k)}\sin\alpha - a_{jj}^{(k)}\cos\alpha$, and that in the ji position is $-a_{ij}^{(k)}\cos\alpha + a_{ii}\sin\alpha$. When the result this far is postmultiplied by $\mathbf{U}_{k+1}$, we have

$$a_{ii}^{(k+1)} = a_{ii}^{(k)}\cos^2\alpha + a_{jj}^{(k)}\sin^2\alpha + 2a_{ij}^{(k)}\sin\alpha\cos\alpha;$$

$$a_{jj}^{(k+1)} = a_{ii}^{(k)}\sin^2\alpha + a_{jj}^{(k)}\cos^2\alpha - 2a_{ij}^{(k)}\sin\alpha\cos\alpha;$$

$$a_{ij}^{(k+1)} = (a_{ii}^{(k)} - a_{jj}^{(k)})\sin\alpha\cos\alpha - a_{ij}^{(k)}(\cos^2\alpha - \sin^2\alpha).$$

Now choose α so that $a_{ij}^{(k+1)} = 0$. Then

$$a_{ii}^{(k+1)} = a_{ii}^{(k)}\frac{1+\cos 2\alpha}{2} + a_{jj}^{(k)}\frac{1-\cos 2\alpha}{2} + a_{ij}^{(k)}\sin 2\alpha;$$

$$a_{jj}^{(k+1)} = a_{ii}^{(k)}\frac{1-\cos 2\alpha}{2} + a_{jj}^{(k)}\frac{1+\cos 2\alpha}{2} - a_{ij}^{(k)}\sin 2\alpha;$$

and, unless $a_{ii}^{(k)} = a_{jj}^{(k)}$,

$$\tan 2\alpha = 2a_{ij}^{(k)}/(a_{ii}^{(k)} - a_{jj}^{(k)}), \tag{4.52}$$

where

$$-\frac{\pi}{4} < \alpha < \frac{\pi}{4}.$$

Direct verification shows that

$$(a_{ii}^{(k+1)})^2 + (a_{jj}^{(k+1)})^2 = (a_{ii}^{(k)})^2 + (a_{jj}^{(k)})^2 + 2(a_{ij}^{(k)})^2. \tag{4.53}$$

Thus, since the sum of the squares of all entries is constant, the diagonal terms have gained in dominance. It can also be verified that

$$a_{ii}^{(k+1)} + a_{jj}^{(k+1)} = a_{ii}^{(k)} + a_{jj}^{(k)};$$

$$a_{ii}^{(k+1)} = \tfrac{1}{2}(a_{ii}^{(k)} + a_{jj}^{(k)}) + \theta_{ij}^{(k)};$$

$$a_{jj}^{(k+1)} = \tfrac{1}{2}(a_{ii}^{(k)} + a_{jj}^{(k)}) - \theta_{ij}^{(k)};$$

$$(\theta_{ij}^{(k)})^2 = \left(\frac{a_{ii}^{(k)} - a_{jj}^{(k)}}{2}\right)^2 + (a_{ij}^{(k)})^2;$$

$$\theta_{ij}^{(k)} = a_{ij}^{(k)}/\sin 2\alpha;$$

$$\theta_{ij}^{(k)} = \left(\frac{a_{ii}^{(k)} - a_{jj}^{(k)}}{2}\right)/\cos 2\alpha. \tag{4.54}$$

Using (4.53), it is relatively easy to prove that the process actually does have the desired result if at each stage the off-diagonal element of largest value is used in the role of $a_{ij}^{(k)}$ above. Let

$$S_k = \sum_{i=1}^{n}\sum_{j=1}^{n}(a_{ij}^{(k)})^2 - \sum_{i=1}^{n}(a_{ii}^{(k)})^2.$$

The number of nonzero off-diagonal elements contributing to S_k does not exceed $r = n^2 - n - 2$ (since at least two elements are zeroed at each iteration). Hence, the largest of the quantities $(a_{ij}^{(k)})^2$ equals or exceeds S_k/r. When the next step is performed, we have

$$S_{k+1} \leqslant S_k - \frac{2}{r} S_k = \mu S_k,$$

where $0 < \mu < 1$. Thus $S_k \leqslant \mu^{k-1} S_1$, and it is clear that S_k has the limit zero.

If the program is carried out on a computer, the time taken to search for the largest current $|a_{ij}^{(k)}|$ may be considerable. It is therefore natural to inquire whether it suffices to choose the position (i, j) of the element to be zeroed at step $k + 1$ in some definite sequence, say in the order $(1,2), (1,3), \ldots, (1,n), (2,3), (2,4), \ldots, (2,n), \ldots, (n - 1,n)$, then return to $(1,2)$ and sweep through the same sequence again. That this leads to the desired result has been established by Forsythe and Henrici [3].

In the limit we have

$$\text{diag}\,(\lambda_1\, \lambda_2 \ldots \lambda_n) = \mathbf{U}^t \mathbf{A} \mathbf{U}, \qquad (4.55)$$

where $\mathbf{U} = \lim_{k \to \infty} \mathbf{U}_1 \mathbf{U}_2 \ldots \mathbf{U}_k$. Thus the columns of $\mathbf{U}$ are the eigenvectors of $\mathbf{A}$. Observe that we have proved, as a by-product, that a real Hermitian matrix of order n has n linearly independent eigenvectors, mutually orthogonal.

Since the matrices of the sequence $\mathbf{A}_k$ formed by the process described are symmetric, we can economize on storage by storing about half the original matrix, and overwriting all subsequent matrices in the same storage locations. Schematically, for $n = 5$, we have

$$
\begin{array}{ccccc}
a_{11} & a_{12} & a_{13} & a_{14} & a_{15} \\
 & a_{22} & a_{23} & a_{24} & a_{25} \\
 & & a_{33} & a_{34} & a_{35} \\
 & & & a_{44} & a_{45} \\
 & & & & a_{55}.
\end{array}
$$

If we need the column $[a_{12}\, a_{22}\, a_{32}\, a_{42}\, a_{52}]^t$ of the original matrix, we use the "bent" arrangement

$$
\begin{array}{l}
a_{12} \\
a_{22} \quad a_{23} \quad a_{24} \quad a_{25}.
\end{array}
$$

The number of storage locations for this arrangement is $(n^2 + n)/2$.

The program for determining the quantities $\sin \alpha$ and $\cos \alpha$ from $\tan 2\alpha$ needs care if accuracy is to be maintained. If we have $\tan 2\alpha = a/b$, we write this in the form $\tan 2\alpha = p/q$, where $q = |b|$ and $p = a$ (sign b). Then $\sec^2 2\alpha = 1 + p^2/q^2$ and $\cos^2 2\alpha = q^2/(p^2 + q^2)$, whence

$$\cos 2\alpha = q/\sqrt{p^2 + q^2},$$

and, as required, $-\pi/4 < \alpha < \pi/4$. (This assumes $a_{ii}^{(k)} \neq a_{jj}^{(k)}$, in which event $\alpha = \pi/4$.) Thus, since $\cos 2\alpha = 2 \cos^2 \alpha - 1$,

$$\cos \alpha = \sqrt{\tfrac{1}{2}(1 + q/\sqrt{p^2 + q^2})}. \qquad (4.56)$$

Since $q \geqslant 0$, there is no loss of accuracy. Note that (4.56) is valid for determining $\cos \alpha$, even though q should be zero. To obtain $\sin \alpha$ from $\tan 2\alpha = p/q$, $\sin 2\alpha = p/\sqrt{p^2 + q^2}$ (even if $q = 0$) and

$$\sin \alpha = \frac{p}{2 \cos \alpha \sqrt{p^2 + q^2}}. \qquad (4.57)$$

A refinement of the procedure is as follows. Suppose that at an early stage of the iteration $a_{ij}^{(k)}$ is already small. There will be little virtue in making this zero since it will not mean decreasing the sum of the squares of the off-diagonal elements appreciably. Therefore, during the kth sweep of the off-diagonal elements systematically, a rotation is omitted if $|a_{ij}^{(k-1)}| \leqslant \epsilon_k$. The set of values ϵ_k might be a decreasing set and ϵ_k should be zero after a small number of sweeps have been made.

If no eigenvectors are required, then the rotation matrices $\mathbf{U}_k$ can be discarded as used. If required, the product $\mathbf{I}\, \mathbf{U}_1\, \mathbf{U}_2 \ldots \mathbf{U}_k$ may be formed in n^2 additional locations, wherein the identity matrix $\mathbf{I}$ is stored initially.

EXAMPLE 4.4

JACOBI'S METHOD

Problem Statement

Write a program that implements Jacobi's method for finding the eigenvalues and eigenvectors of an $n \times n$ real symmetric matrix $\mathbf{A}$.

Method of Solution

The program given below follows in detail the procedure described in Section 4.8. However, we can dispense with the iteration index k, so that the starting matrix and all its subsequent transformations will be denoted by the common symbol $\mathbf{A}$. The product of the successive orthogonal annihilation matrices is the matrix $\mathbf{T} = \mathbf{IU}_1\mathbf{U}_2\mathbf{U}_3\ldots$

The program takes account of the symmetry of the starting matrix and its subsequent transformations, so that the calculations do not involve elements in the strictly lower triangular portion of $\mathbf{A}$. That is, the "bent" vector arrangement of Section 4.8 is used. Unfortunately, because of FORTRAN restrictions, we must also reserve storage for the lower triangular portion of $\mathbf{A}$, even though it is not used. In some other programming languages, such as MAD (Michigan Algorithm Decoder), that permit the definition of unique subscription functions, it would be simple to compact $\mathbf{A}$ into triangular rather than square shape.

For each Jacobi iteration, each element in the strictly upper triangular portion of $\mathbf{A}$ is annihilated row by row, in the order: $a_{12}, a_{13}, \ldots, a_{1n};\ a_{23}, a_{24}, \ldots, a_{2n};\ \ldots;$ $a_{n-1,n}$. If an element a_{ij} is already smaller in magnitude than some value ε_2, it is simply bypassed in the iterations.

Before the first iteration, the sum of squares S of all elements in the full matrix $\mathbf{A}$ is computed. The sum of the squares of the diagonal elements of $\mathbf{A}$ before and after each complete Jacobi iteration is computed and saved in σ_1 and σ_2, respectively. The criterion for ending the procedure is normally

$$1 - \frac{\sigma_1}{\sigma_2} < \varepsilon_3.$$

At this point, both σ_1 and σ_2 should almost equal S; in fact, this correspondence could alternatively be used as the criterion for termination. An upper limit, k_{max}, is also placed on the total number of iterations. The eigenvalues $\lambda_1, \lambda_2, \ldots, \lambda_n$ are the diagonal elements of the final transformed matrix $\mathbf{A}$. The elements of the corresponding eigenvectors are in successive columns of $\mathbf{T}$.

The following flow diagram is intended to give an overall picture of the method. However, because of the special nature of the rotation matrix, $\mathbf{U}^{-1}\mathbf{AU}$ does not have to be expanded fully in the program; in fact, only elements in the ith and jth row and in the ith and jth column of $\mathbf{A}$ will be modified at each step. It is also unnecessary for $\mathbf{U}$ to appear specifically, since it is simply $\mathbf{I}$ modified by $\sin \alpha$ and $\cos \alpha$ in a few (known) positions. The product matrix $\mathbf{T}$, however, is updated at each step.

Example 4.4   Jacobi's Method   **253**

Flow Diagram

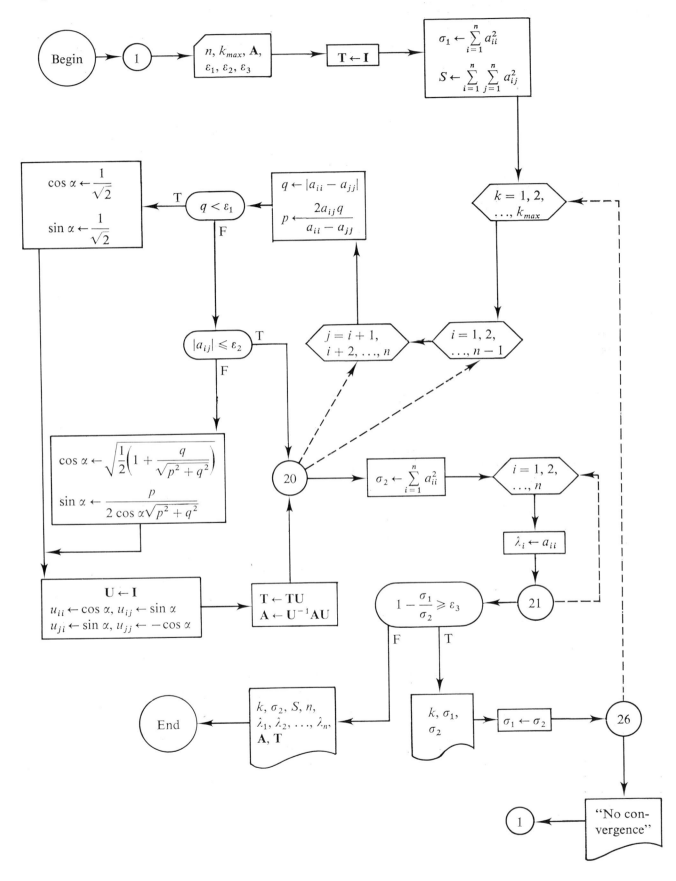

FORTRAN *Implementation*

List of Principal Variables

Program Symbol	Definition
A	Upper triangular matrix, **A**.
AIK	Vector used for temporary storage.
CSA, SNA	$\cos \alpha$ and $\sin \alpha$ (see equations (4.56) and (4.57)).
EIGEN	Vector of the eigenvalues $\lambda_1, \lambda_2, \ldots, \lambda_n$.
EPS1	Tolerance, ε_1; for $q < \varepsilon_1$, $\alpha = \pi/4$.
EPS2	Tolerance, ε_2; a_{ij} is bypassed if $|a_{ij}| < \varepsilon_2$.
EPS3	Tolerance, ε_3, used in termination criterion.
ITER	Counter, k, for the number of complete Jacobi iterations.
ITMAX	Maximum number of iterations permitted, k_{max}.
N	Dimension, n, of the matrix **A**.
OFFDSQ	Sum of squares of off-diagonal elements of **A**.
P, Q	p and q (see equation (4.56)).
S	Sum of squares of all elements in the full starting matrix.
SIGMA1, SIGMA2	Sums, σ_1 and σ_2, of the squares of the diagonal elements of **A** before and after an iteration, respectively.
SPQ	$(p^2 + q^2)^{1/2}$.
T	Product of rotation matrices; ultimately contains eigenvectors.

Example 4.4   Jacobi's Method   **255**

Program Listing

```
C              APPLIED NUMERICAL METHODS, EXAMPLE 4.4
C              EIGENVALUES AND EIGENVECTORS BY THE JACOBI METHOD.
C
C              ONLY THE UPPER TRIANGULAR PART OF THE REAL SYMMETRIC STARTING
C              MATRIX A IS READ.    T IS AN N BY N ORTHOGONAL MATRIX, BEING THE
C              PRODUCT OF THE SEQUENCE OF TRANSFORMATION MATRICES USED TO ANN-
C              IHILATE SUCCESSIVELY THE OFF-DIAGONAL ELEMENTS OF A, AND CON-
C              SEQUENTLY TO REDUCE A ITERATIVELY TO NEAR-DIAGONAL FORM.
C              SIGMA1 AND SIGMA2 ARE THE VALUES OF SIGMA A(I,I)**2 BEFORE AND
C              AFTER ONE COMPLETE ITERATION.  SINCE ANNIHILATION OF AN ELEMENT
C              MAY CAUSE ANOTHER ALREADY-ANNIHILATED ELEMENT TO ASSUME A
C              NON-ZERO VALUE, THE ITERATIVE PROCESS IS REPEATED UNTIL
C              THE CONVERGENCE TEST IS PASSED (1 - SIGMA1/SIGMA2 LESS THAN
C              EPS3) OR ITMAX COMPLETE ITERATIONS HAVE FAILED TO PRODUCE CON-
C              VERGENCE.   AN OFF-DIAGONAL ELEMENT SMALLER IN MAGNITUDE THAN
C              EPS2 IS IGNORED IN THE ANNIHILATION PROCESS.   EPS1 IS
C              COMPARED WITH (A(I,I) - A(J,J)) TO DETERMINE THE
C              METHOD OF COMPUTING CSA AND SNA, THE COSINE AND SINE OF
C              THE ROTATION ANGLE, RESPECTIVELY.   WHEN A HAS
C              BEEN REDUCED TO DIAGONAL FORM, THE EIGENVALUES WILL BE
C              FOUND IN THE DIAGONAL POSITIONS AND ARE SAVED IN EIGEN(1)...
C              EIGEN(N).   THE ASSOCIATED EIGENVECTORS ARE IN CORRESPONDING
C              COLUMNS OF THE FINAL TRANSFORMATION MATRIX T.   S IS THE SUM OF
C              SQUARES OF ALL ELEMENTS IN THE ORIGINAL MATRIX A, AND
C              SHOULD THEORETICALLY EQUAL THE FINAL VALUE OF SIGMA2.
C
       IMPLICIT REAL*8 (A-H, O-Z)
       DIMENSION A(20,20), T(20,20), AIK(20), EIGEN(20)
C
C      ..... READ PARAMETERS AND ESTABLISH STARTING MATRIX A .....
    1  DO 2  I = 1, 20
       DO 2  J = 1, 20
       T(I,J) = 0.0
    2  A(I,J) = 0.0
       READ (5,101) N, ITMAX, EPS1, EPS2, EPS3, ((A(I,J), J = I, N),
      1                                                     I = 1, N)
       NM1 = N - 1
       WRITE (6,200) N, ITMAX, EPS1, EPS2, EPS3
       DO 3  I = 1, N
    3  WRITE (6,201) (A(I,J), J = 1, N)
C
C      ..... SET UP INITIAL MATRIX T, COMPUTE SIGMA1 AND S .....
       SIGMA1 = 0.0
       OFFDSQ = 0.0
       DO 5  I = 1, N
       SIGMA1 = SIGMA1 + A(I,I)**2
       T(I,I) = 1.0
       IP1 = I + 1
       IF (I .GE. N) GO TO 6
       DO 5  J = IP1, N
    5  OFFDSQ = OFFDSQ + A(I,J)**2
    6  S = 2.0*OFFDSQ + SIGMA1
C
C      ..... BEGIN JACOBI ITERATION .....
       DO 26  ITER = 1, ITMAX
       DO 20  I = 1, NM1
       IP1 = I + 1
       DO 20  J = IP1, N
       Q = DABS(A(I,I) - A(J,J))
C
C      ..... COMPUTE SINE AND COSINE OF ROTATION ANGLE .....
       IF (Q .LE. EPS1) GO TO 9
          IF (DABS(A(I,J)) .LE. EPS2) GO TO 20
          P = 2.0*A(I,J)*Q/(A(I,I) - A(J,J))
          SPQ = DSQRT(P*P + Q*Q)
          CSA = DSQRT((1.0 + Q/SPQ)/2.0)
          SNA = P/(2.0*CSA*SPQ)
          GO TO 10
    9     CSA = 1.0/DSQRT(2.0D0)
          SNA = CSA
   10  CONTINUE
```

Program Listing (*Continued*)

```
C
C          ..... UPDATE COLUMNS I AND J OF T - EQUIVALENT TO
C                MULTIPLICATION BY THE ANNIHILATION MATRIX .....
           DO 11  K = 1, N
           HOLDKI = T(K,I)
           T(K,I) = HOLDKI*CSA + T(K,J)*SNA
     11    T(K,J) = HOLDKI*SNA - T(K,J)*CSA
C
C          ..... COMPUTE NEW ELEMENTS OF A IN ROWS I AND J .....
           DO 16  K = I, N
           IF (K .GT. J) GO TO 15
              AIK(K) = A(I,K)
              A(I,K) = CSA*AIK(K) + SNA*A(K,J)
              IF (K .NE. J) GO TO 14
                 A(J,K) = SNA*AIK(K) - CSA*A(J,K)
     14       GO TO 16
     15       HOLDIK = A(I,K)
              A(I,K) = CSA*HOLDIK + SNA*A(J,K)
              A(J,K) = SNA*HOLDIK - CSA*A(J,K)
     16    CONTINUE
C
C          ..... COMPUTE NEW ELEMENTS OF A IN COLUMNS I AND J .....
           AIK(J) = SNA*AIK(I) - CSA*AIK(J)
C
C          ..... WHEN K IS LARGER THAN I .....
           DO 19  K = 1, J
           IF (K .LE. I) GO TO 18
              A(K,J) = SNA*AIK(K) - CSA*A(K,J)
              GO TO 19
     18       HOLDKI = A(K,I)
              A(K,I) = CSA*HOLDKI + SNA*A(K,J)
              A(K,J) = SNA*HOLDKI - CSA*A(K,J)
     19    CONTINUE
     20    A(I,J) = 0.0
C
C          ..... FIND SIGMA2 FOR TRANSFORMED A AND TEST FOR CONVERGENCE .....
           SIGMA2 = 0.0
           DO 21  I = 1, N
           EIGEN(I) = A(I,I)
     21    SIGMA2 = SIGMA2 + EIGEN(I)**2
           IF (1.0 - SIGMA1/SIGMA2 .GE. EPS3) GO TO 25
              WRITE (6,204) ITER, SIGMA2, S, N
              WRITE (6,201) (EIGEN(I), I = 1, N)
              WRITE (6,205)
              DO 23  I = 1, N
     23       WRITE (6,201) (A(I,J), J = 1, N)
              WRITE (6,206)
              DO 24  I = 1, N
     24       WRITE (6,201) (T(I,J), J = 1, N)
              GO TO 1
     25    WRITE (6,202) ITER, SIGMA1, SIGMA2
     26    SIGMA1 = SIGMA2
C
C          ..... IF ITER EXCEEDS ITMAX, NO CONVERGENCE .....
           WRITE (6,203) ITER, S, SIGMA1, SIGMA2
           DO 27  I = 1, N
     27    WRITE (6,201) (A(I,J), J = 1, N)
           WRITE (6,207)
           DO 28  I = 1, N
     28    WRITE (6,201) (T(I,J), J = 1, N)
           GO TO 1
C
C          ..... FORMATS FOR INPUT AND OUTPUT STATEMENTS .....
    101    FORMAT (2(12X, I3)/ 3(11X, E9.2)/ (10X, 6F10.4))
    200    FORMAT (1H1, 4X, 54H DETERMINATION OF EIGENVALUES BY JACOBI'S METH
          1OD, WITH/1H0, 6X, 10H N      = , I4/
          2 7X, 10H ITMAX  = , I4/ 7X, 10H EPS1    = , E12.3/
          3 7X, 10H EPS2   = , E12.3/ 7X, 10H EPS3    = , E12.3/1H0,
          4 4X, 39H THE STARTING MATRIX A(1,1)...A(N,N) IS/1H )
    201    FORMAT (7X, 10F11.7)
```

Example 4.4   Jacobi's Method   **257**

Program Listing (*Continued*)

```
202   FORMAT (1H0, 6X, 10H ITER    = , I5, 10X, 10H SIGMA1 = , F10.5,
      1 10X, 10H SIGMA2 = , F10.5)
203   FORMAT (1H0, 4X, 21H NO CONVERGENCE, WITH// 7X, 10H ITER   = , I5,
      1 5X, 10H S       = , F10.5, 5X, 10H SIGMA1 = , F10.5,
      2 5X, 10H SIGMA2 = , F10.5// 5X, 24H THE CURRENT A MATRIX IS/1H )
204   FORMAT (1H0, 4X, 31H CONVERGENCE HAS OCCURRED, WITH/1H0,
      1 6X, 10H ITER    = , I5, 5X, 10H SIGMA2 = , F10.5,
      2 5X, 10H S       = , F10.5, 5X, 10H N       = , I5/1H0,
      3 4X, 36H EIGENVALUES EIGEN(1)...EIGEN(N) ARE/1H )
205   FORMAT (1H0, 4X, 34H THE FINAL TRANSFORMED MATRIX A IS/1H )
206   FORMAT (1H0, 4X, 68H EIGENVECTORS ARE IN CORRESPONDING COLUMNS OF
      1THE FOLLOWING T MATRIX/1H )
207   FORMAT (1H0, 4X, 24H THE CURRENT T MATRIX IS/1H )
C
      END
```

```
      N   =    4,  ITMAX  =   50,
      EPS1 = 1.00E-10,   EPS2 = 1.00E-10,   EPS3 =  1.00E-5,
A(1,1) =      10.0         9.0         7.0        5.0        10.0         8.0
              6.0        10.0         7.0        5.0
      N   =    4,  ITMAX  =   50,
      EPS1 = 1.00E-10,   EPS2 = 1.00E-10,   EPS3 =  1.00E-5,
A(1,1) =       6.0         4.0         4.0        1.0         6.0         1.0
              4.0         6.0         4.0        6.0
      N   =    8,  ITMAX  =   50,
      EPS1 = 1.00E-10,   EPS2 = 1.00E-10,   EPS3 =  1.00E-5,
A(1,1) =       2.0        -1.0         0.0        0.0         0.0         0.0
              0.0         0.0         2.0       -1.0         0.0         0.0
              0.0         0.0         0.0        2.0        -1.0         0.0
              0.0         0.0         0.0        2.0        -1.0         0.0
              0.0         0.0         2.0       -1.0         0.0         0.0
              2.0        -1.0         0.0        2.0        -1.0         2.0
```

Computer Output

Results for the 1st Data Set

```
DETERMINATION OF EIGENVALUES BY JACOBI'S METHOD, WITH

N      =     4
ITMAX  =    50
EPS1   =     0.100D-09
EPS2   =     0.100D-09
EPS3   =     0.100D-04

THE STARTING MATRIX A(1,1)...A(N,N) IS

10.0000000   9.0000000   7.0000000   5.0000000
 0.0        10.0000000   8.0000000   6.0000000
 0.0         0.0        10.0000000   7.0000000
 0.0         0.0         0.0         5.0000000

ITER   =     1           SIGMA1 = 325.00000        SIGMA2 = 930.00845

ITER   =     2           SIGMA1 = 930.00845        SIGMA2 = 932.99695

CONVERGENCE HAS OCCURRED, WITH

ITER   =     3      SIGMA2 = 933.00000      S     = 933.00000      N     =     4

EIGENVALUES EIGEN(1)...EIGEN(N) ARE

 30.2886853   0.8431071   3.8580575   0.0101500
```

Computer Output (*Continued*)

```
THE FINAL TRANSFORMED MATRIX A IS

 30.2886853 -0.0000070  0.0000001  0.0000000
  0.0         0.8431071 -0.0000000 -0.0000000
  0.0         0.0        3.8580575  0.0
  0.0         0.0        0.0        0.0101500

EIGENVECTORS ARE IN CORRESPONDING COLUMNS OF THE FOLLOWING T MATRIX

  0.5209249  0.5676405 -0.6253962 -0.1236975
  0.5519547 -0.7603186 -0.2716010  0.2085536
  0.5285679  0.3016522  0.6148613  0.5015651
  0.3802621 -0.0933051  0.3963056 -0.8304438
```

Results for the 2nd Data Set

```
DETERMINATION OF EIGENVALUES BY JACOBI'S METHOD, WITH

N     =    4
ITMAX =   50
EPS1  =    0.100D-09
EPS2  =    0.100D-09
EPS3  =    0.100D-04

THE STARTING MATRIX A(1,1)...A(N,N) IS

  6.0000000  4.0000000  4.0000000  1.0000000
  0.0        6.0000000  1.0000000  4.0000000
  0.0        0.0        6.0000000  4.0000000
  0.0        0.0        0.0        6.0000000

ITER  =    1          SIGMA1 =  144.00000        SIGMA2 =  274.60799

ITER  =    2          SIGMA1 =  274.60799        SIGMA2 =  275.99999

CONVERGENCE HAS OCCURRED, WITH

ITER  =    3     SIGMA2 =  276.00000     S    =  276.00000     N      =    4

EIGENVALUES EIGEN(1)...EIGEN(N) ARE

 15.0000000 -1.0000000  5.0000000  5.0000000

THE FINAL TRANSFORMED MATRIX A IS

 15.0000000 -0.0000000 -0.0000000 -0.0000000
  0.0        -1.0000000 -0.0000000 -0.0000000
  0.0         0.0        5.0000000  0.0
  0.0         0.0        0.0        5.0000000

EIGENVECTORS ARE IN CORRESPONDING COLUMNS OF THE FOLLOWING T MATRIX

  0.5000000  0.5000000 -0.2669908  0.6547640
  0.5000000 -0.5000000 -0.6547640 -0.2669908
  0.5000000 -0.5000000  0.6547640  0.2669908
  0.5000000  0.5000000  0.2669908 -0.6547640




DETERMINATION OF EIGENVALUES BY JACOBI'S METHOD, WITH

N     =    8
ITMAX =   50
EPS1  =    0.100D-09
EPS2  =    0.100D-09
EPS3  =    0.100D-04
```

Example 4.4   Jacobi's Method   **259**

Computer Output (*Continued*)

Results for the 3rd Data Set

THE STARTING MATRIX A(1,1)...A(N,N) IS

```
2.0000000 -1.0000000  0.0        0.0        0.0        0.0        0.0        0.0
0.0        2.0000000 -1.0000000  0.0        0.0        0.0        0.0        0.0
0.0        0.0        2.0000000 -1.0000000  0.0        0.0        0.0        0.0
0.0        0.0        0.0        2.0000000 -1.0000000  0.0        0.0        0.0
0.0        0.0        0.0        0.0        2.0000000 -1.0000000  0.0        0.0
0.0        0.0        0.0        0.0        0.0        2.0000000 -1.0000000  0.0
0.0        0.0        0.0        0.0        0.0        0.0        2.0000000 -1.0000000
0.0        0.0        0.0        0.0        0.0        0.0        0.0        2.0000000
```

```
ITER   =   1          SIGMA1 =   32.00000        SIGMA2 =   44.11429

ITER   =   2          SIGMA1 =   44.11429        SIGMA2 =   45.91432

ITER   =   3          SIGMA1 =   45.91432        SIGMA2 =   45.99973
```

CONVERGENCE HAS OCCURRED, WITH

```
ITER   =   4      SIGMA2 =   46.00000      S    =   46.00000       N    =   8
```

EIGENVALUES EIGEN(1)...EIGEN(N) ARE

```
0.1206148  3.8793852  3.5320889  0.4679111  1.0000000  3.0000000  2.3472964  1.6527036
```

THE FINAL TRANSFORMED MATRIX A IS

```
0.1206148  0.0000279  0.0000036 -0.0000060 -0.0000001  0.0000000  0.0000000  0.0000000
0.0        3.8793852  0.0000043 -0.0000064 -0.0000001  0.0000000 -0.0000000 -0.0000000
0.0        0.0        3.5320889 -0.0000014 -0.0000000 -0.0000000 -0.0000000 -0.0000000
0.0        0.0        0.0        0.4679111 -0.0000000 -0.0000000  0.0000000 -0.0000000
0.0        0.0        0.0        0.0        1.0000000 -0.0000000  0.0000000  0.0000000
0.0        0.0        0.0        0.0        0.0        3.0000000  0.0000000  0.0000000
0.0        0.0        0.0        0.0        0.0        0.0        2.3472964  0.0
0.0        0.0        0.0        0.0        0.0        0.0        0.0        1.6527036
```

EIGENVECTORS ARE IN CORRESPONDING COLUMNS OF THE FOLLOWING T MATRIX

```
0.1612335 -0.1612278 -0.3030153 -0.3030098  0.4082483 -0.4082483 -0.4642428 -0.4642428
0.3030237  0.3030041  0.4642461 -0.4642384  0.4082483  0.4082483  0.1612298 -0.1612298
0.4082519 -0.4082470 -0.4082540 -0.4082403  0.0000000 -0.0000000  0.4082483  0.4082483
0.4642493  0.4642371  0.1612351 -0.1612227 -0.4082483 -0.4082483 -0.3030130  0.3030130
0.4642368 -0.4642480  0.1612236  0.1612387 -0.4082482  0.4082483 -0.3030130 -0.3030130
0.4082438  0.4082511 -0.4082435  0.4082548  0.0000000 -0.0000000  0.4082483 -0.4082483
0.3030032 -0.3030201  0.4642389  0.4642484  0.4082483 -0.4082483  0.1612298  0.1612298
0.1612254  0.1612330 -0.3030110  0.3030156  0.4082483  0.4082483 -0.4642428  0.4642428
```

Discussion of Results

The eigenvalues and eigenvectors have been computed for three test matrices. The results are virtually identical with those produced by Rutishauser's method in Example 4.3. The sums of the squares of the diagonal elements of **A** after each iteration are as follows:

Iteration	Matrix 1	Matrix 2	Matrix 3
0 (start)	325.00000	144.00000	32.00000
1	930.00845	274.60799	44.11429
2	932.99695	275.99999	45.91432
3	933.00000	276.00000	45.99973
4	—	—	46.00000

Since the sums of the squares of all the elements in the starting matrices were 933, 276, and 46, respectively, all off-diagonal elements have been reduced to the vanishing point. Convergence is rapid in all cases; even the 8×8 matrix in the third data set requires only four Jacobi sweeps to meet the convergence criterion.

4.9 Method of Danilevski

Let $\mathbf{A} = (a_{ij})$ be a square matrix of order n and suppose that $a_{12} \neq 0$. Let $\mathbf{M}^{(1)} = (m_{ij}^{(1)})$ be a matrix such that $m_{ij}^{(1)} = \delta_{ij}$ (the Kronecker delta, that is, $\delta_{ij} = 0$ for

$$\mathbf{B}_{11} = \begin{bmatrix} 0 & 1 & 0 & 0 & \cdots & 0 & 0 & 0 \\ 0 & 0 & 1 & 0 & \cdots & 0 & 0 & 0 \\ \hdotsfor{8} \\ 0 & 0 & 0 & 0 & \cdots & 0 & 1 & 0 \\ 0 & 0 & 0 & 0 & \cdots & 0 & 0 & 1 \\ b_{m1} & b_{m2} & b_{m3} & b_{m4} & \cdots & b_{m,m-2} & b_{m,m-1} & b_{mm} \end{bmatrix},$$

$i \neq j$ and $\delta_{ij} = 1$ for $i = j$) unless $i = 2$. Let $m_{22}^{(1)} = 1/a_{12}$ and let $m_{2j}^{(1)} = -a_{1j}/a_{12}$ if $j \neq 2$. Let the inverse of $\mathbf{M}^{(1)}$ be $\mathbf{P}^{(1)}$. Then if $\mathbf{P}^{(1)} = (p_{ij}^{(1)})$, it is easy to verify that $p_{ij}^{(1)} = \delta_{ij}$ if $i \neq 2$, while $p_{2j}^{(1)} = a_{1j}$. It is also seen that if $\mathbf{M}^{(1)}$ is used as a postmultiplier for $\mathbf{A}$, and $\mathbf{P}^{(1)}$ as a premultiplier, the result is a matrix $\mathbf{A}^{(2)} = (a_{ij}^{(2)})$ such that $a_{12}^{(2)} = 1$ while $a_{1j}^{(2)} = 0$ if $j \neq 2$.

If a_{12} is zero, or if it be desired to base the effect on some other nonzero element of the first row, any element of that row, other than the first, can be brought to this location by an interchange of two columns. If this is followed by an interchange of the corresponding rows, the resulting matrix will always be similar to $\mathbf{A}$.

Now let $\mathbf{M}^{(2)} = (m_{ij}^{(2)})$ be a matrix such that $m_{ij}^{(2)} = \delta_{ij}$ unless $i = 3$. Assuming $a_{23}^{(2)} \neq 0$, let $m_{33}^{(2)} = 1/a_{23}^{(2)}$ and $m_{3j}^{(2)} = -a_{2j}^{(2)}/a_{23}^{(2)}$ if $j \neq 3$. Let the inverse of $\mathbf{M}^{(2)}$ be $\mathbf{P}^{(2)} = (p_{ij}^{(2)})$. Then $p_{ij}^{(2)} = \delta_{ij}$ if $i \neq 3$, while $p_{3j}^{(2)} = a_{2j}^{(2)}$. It is also seen that if $\mathbf{M}^{(2)}$ be used as a postmultiplier for $\mathbf{A}^{(2)}$ and $\mathbf{P}^{(2)}$ as a premultiplier, the result is a matrix $\mathbf{A}^{(3)} = (a_{ij}^{(3)})$ such that $a_{12}^{(3)} = 1$, $a_{1j}^{(3)} = 0$ if $j \neq 2$, $a_{23}^{(3)} = 1$, $a_{2j}^{(3)} = 0$ if $j \neq 3$.

If $a_{23}^{(2)}$ is zero, or if it be desired to base the effect on some other nonzero element of the second row, any element of this row, other than the first two, can be brought to the proper location by an interchange of two columns. If this is followed by an interchange of the corresponding rows, the resulting matrix is similar to $\mathbf{A}^{(2)}$ and the first row is unaltered.

Continuing in this manner we arrive at a matrix $\mathbf{B}$, similar to $\mathbf{A}$ and having one of three possible forms. If the process can continue unhindered, then we find

$$\mathbf{B} = \begin{bmatrix} 0 & 1 & 0 & 0 & \cdots & 0 & 0 & 0 \\ 0 & 0 & 1 & 0 & \cdots & 0 & 0 & 0 \\ \hdotsfor{8} \\ 0 & 0 & 0 & 0 & \cdots & 0 & 1 & 0 \\ 0 & 0 & 0 & 0 & \cdots & 0 & 0 & 1 \\ b_{n1} & b_{n2} & b_{n3} & b_{n4} & \cdots & b_{n,n-2} & b_{n,n-1} & b_{nn} \end{bmatrix}.$$

It may be that all elements of the first row, other than perhaps a_{11}, are zero. In such event $\mathbf{B}$ may be represented in partitioned form as

$$\mathbf{B} = \begin{bmatrix} \mathbf{B}_{11} & \mathbf{0} \\ \mathbf{B}_{21} & \mathbf{B}_{22} \end{bmatrix}, \qquad (4.58)$$

where $\mathbf{B}_{11} = b_{11} = a_{11}$ and $\mathbf{0}$ denotes the $1 \times (n-1)$ null matrix.

Finally, the process may be continued for a time, stopping when all choices for the pivot element lead to a zero. In such event $\mathbf{B}$ has the form of (4.58), where now

(4.59)

while $\mathbf{0}$ denotes the $m \times (n-m)$ null matrix, and $\mathbf{B}_{21}, \mathbf{B}_{22}$ have no special character.

The procedure is continued, treating $\mathbf{B}_{22}$ as $\mathbf{A}$ itself was treated (except that it is not considered as detached from $\mathbf{B}$). The final result may be written $\mathbf{C} = \mathbf{M}^{-1}\mathbf{A}\mathbf{M}$, where a typical form for $\mathbf{C}$ might be

$$\mathbf{C} = \begin{bmatrix} \mathbf{C}_{11} & \mathbf{0} & \mathbf{0} & \mathbf{0} \\ \mathbf{C}_{21} & \mathbf{C}_{22} & \mathbf{0} & \mathbf{0} \\ \mathbf{C}_{31} & \mathbf{C}_{32} & \mathbf{C}_{33} & \mathbf{0} \\ \mathbf{C}_{41} & \mathbf{C}_{42} & \mathbf{C}_{43} & \mathbf{C}_{44} \end{bmatrix}. \qquad (4.60)$$

Here the "diagonal" matrices $\mathbf{C}_{11}, \mathbf{C}_{22}, \mathbf{C}_{33}$, and $\mathbf{C}_{44}$ have the form (4.59), or are 1×1 matrices, zero or otherwise.

The result of first importance is that from the matrices $\mathbf{C}_{11}, \mathbf{C}_{22}, \mathbf{C}_{33}$, and $\mathbf{C}_{44}$ we may quickly find a factored form for the characteristic function of $\mathbf{A}$. This is because the characteristic function for $\mathbf{A}$ is that for $\mathbf{C}$, and the characteristic function for $\mathbf{C}$ is the product of those for $\mathbf{C}_{11}, \mathbf{C}_{22}, \mathbf{C}_{33}$, and $\mathbf{C}_{44}$.

When the characteristic function is known, it may be that its zeros can be found. With this information, the matrix $\mathbf{C}$ and the matrix $\mathbf{M}$ may be used to find the eigenvectors of $\mathbf{A}$, for the eigenvectors of $\mathbf{A}$ are $\mathbf{M}$ times the eigenvectors of $\mathbf{C}$.

The formation of the characteristic vectors of $\mathbf{C}$ will be illustrated only for the case where $\mathbf{C}$ has the form

$$\mathbf{C} = \begin{bmatrix} \mathbf{C}_{11} & \mathbf{0} & \mathbf{0} & \mathbf{0} \\ \mathbf{0} & \mathbf{C}_{22} & \mathbf{0} & \mathbf{0} \\ \mathbf{0} & \mathbf{0} & \mathbf{C}_{33} & \mathbf{0} \\ \mathbf{0} & \mathbf{0} & \mathbf{0} & \mathbf{C}_{44} \end{bmatrix},$$

and each $\mathbf{C}_{ii}$ has the form of (4.59). Suppose $\mathbf{C}_{11}$ is $p \times p$, $\mathbf{C}_{22}$ is $q \times q$, $\mathbf{C}_{33}$ is $r \times r$, and $\mathbf{C}_{44}$ is $s \times s$. Let the last row of $\mathbf{C}_{11}$ be $[e_1 \, e_2 \ldots e_p]$, those for $\mathbf{C}_{22}, \mathbf{C}_{33}$, and $\mathbf{C}_{44}$ being $[f_1 \, f_2 \ldots f_q]$, $[g_1 \, g_2 \ldots g_r]$, and $[h_1 \, h_2 \ldots h_s]$, respectively. Just as with the companion matrix (4.32), the characteristic function of $\mathbf{C}_{11}$ is

$$(-1)^{p-1}\left(-\lambda^p + \sum_{i=1}^{p} e_i \lambda^{i-1}\right),$$

and similarly for $\mathbf{C}_{22}, \mathbf{C}_{33}$, and $\mathbf{C}_{44}$.

Let α be an eigenvalue of $\mathbf{C}$ and let x, y, z, t be arbitrary for the moment. Then from the nature of C_{11}, etc., we see that an eigenvector u corresponding to α must be such that $u^t = [x, \alpha x, \ldots \alpha^{p-1}x, y, \alpha y, \ldots \alpha^{q-1}y, z, \alpha z, \ldots \alpha^{r-1}z, t, \alpha t, \ldots \alpha^{s-1}t]$. In addition, we must have

$$x \sum_{i=1}^{p} e_i \alpha^{i-1} = \alpha^p x, \quad y \sum_{i=1}^{q} f_i \alpha^{i-1} = \alpha^q y, \quad z \sum_{i=1}^{r} g_i \alpha^{i-1} = \alpha^r z,$$

and

$$t \sum_{i=1}^{s} h_i \alpha^{i-1} = \alpha^s t.$$

Thus we see that if α is a zero for the characteristic func-tion of C_{11} only, then x is arbitrary and $y = z = t = 0$. Moreover, even if α is a multiple eigenvalue, there is still only (essentially) one eigenvector. If, say, α is an eigenvalue for both C_{11} and C_{33} but not C_{22} and C_{44}, then x and z are arbitrary, while y and t are zero. In such event, there are two linearly independent eigenvectors for α. In general, all eigenvectors can be found from the eigenvectors for the component matrices by using zeros in the rows corresponding to other component matrices. For the case examined last, the eigenvectors would be $u_1^t = [1, \alpha, \ldots \alpha^{p-1}, 0, 0, \ldots 0, 0, 0, \ldots 0, 0, 0, \ldots 0]$ and $u_2^t = [0, 0, \ldots 0, 0, 0, \ldots 0, 1, \alpha, \ldots \alpha^{q-1}, 0, 0, \ldots 0]$.

Problems

4.1 Show that if $\mathbf{B}_1$ is a close approximation to $\mathbf{A}^{-1}$, then an even better approximation $\mathbf{B}_2$ is given by

$$\mathbf{B}_2 = \mathbf{B}_1(2\mathbf{I} - \mathbf{A}\mathbf{B}_1).$$

4.2 If $\mathbf{A}$, $\mathbf{B}$, and $\mathbf{C}$ are nonsingular square matrices, prove that $(\mathbf{ABC})^{-1} = \mathbf{C}^{-1}\mathbf{B}^{-1}\mathbf{A}^{-1}$.

4.3 Prove that $(\mathbf{AB})^t = \mathbf{B}^t\mathbf{A}^t$.

4.4 Show that the matrix

$$\mathbf{A} = \begin{bmatrix} \dfrac{2+6i}{5\sqrt{3}} & \dfrac{1+i}{\sqrt{5}} & \dfrac{-i}{\sqrt{15}} \\[2mm] \dfrac{1+3i}{5\sqrt{3}} & \dfrac{-i}{\sqrt{5}} & \dfrac{3+i}{\sqrt{15}} \\[2mm] \dfrac{-5i}{5\sqrt{3}} & \dfrac{1+i}{\sqrt{5}} & \dfrac{2}{\sqrt{15}} \end{bmatrix}$$

is unitary, and find its adjoint in two ways.

4.5 A point P has position vector $\mathbf{x}$ relative to an origin O in rectangular coordinates. If the axes are rotated, but still remain orthogonal, the new position vector of P may be expressed by the linear transformation $\mathbf{A}\mathbf{x}$. By noting that the distance OP is unchanged, show that $\mathbf{A}$ is an orthogonal matrix, that is, one for which $\mathbf{A}^t = \mathbf{A}^{-1}$.

4.6 Find all solutions of the simultaneous equations

$$\begin{aligned} 2x_1 - 3x_2 + 4x_3 + 5x_4 + 2x_5 &= 2, \\ 3x_1 + x_2 \quad - x_4 - 3x_5 &= -4, \\ -x_1 + 4x_2 - 2x_3 + 3x_4 + x_5 &= 1, \\ -9x_1 - 6x_2 + 6x_3 + 17x_4 + 17x_5 &= 21. \end{aligned}$$

4.7 It is shown (page 213) for orthonormal vectors $\mathbf{u}_1$, $\mathbf{u}_2, \ldots, \mathbf{u}_n$, that $[\mathbf{u}_1\,\mathbf{u}_2 \ldots \mathbf{u}_n]^*[\mathbf{u}_1\,\mathbf{u}_2 \ldots \mathbf{u}_n] = \mathbf{I}$. Prove that also $[\mathbf{u}_1\,\mathbf{u}_2 \ldots \mathbf{u}_n][\mathbf{u}_1\,\mathbf{u}_2 \ldots \mathbf{u}_n]^* = \mathbf{I}$.

4.8 Express the singular matrix

$$\begin{bmatrix} 1 & 5 & 2 & 3 \\ -2 & -4 & -1 & 0 \\ 3 & 5 & 4 & 2 \\ 4 & 2 & 0 & -5 \end{bmatrix}$$

as the product of two matrices.

4.9 Matrices such as

$$\mathbf{X}_3 = \begin{bmatrix} x_0 & x_1 & x_2 \\ x_2 & x_0 & x_1 \\ x_1 & x_2 & x_0 \end{bmatrix}$$

are called *circulants*. Find all eigenvalues and corresponding eigenvectors for $\mathbf{X}_3$. Use the results to build a matrix $\mathbf{U}$ such that $\mathbf{U}^{-1}\mathbf{X}_3\mathbf{U}$ is diagonal (see equation (4.20)).

4.10 Find one eigenvalue and a corresponding eigenvector for the general circulant

$$\begin{bmatrix} x_0 & x_1 \ldots x_n \\ x_n & x_0 \ldots x_{n-1} \\ \vdots & \vdots & \vdots \\ x_1 & x_2 \ldots x_0 \end{bmatrix}.$$

4.11 Show that if

$$\mathbf{A} = \begin{bmatrix} \cos\theta & \sin\theta \\ -\sin\theta & \cos\theta \end{bmatrix},$$

then, for $n = \pm 1, \pm 2, \ldots$

$$\mathbf{A}^n = \begin{bmatrix} \cos n\theta & \sin n\theta \\ -\sin n\theta & \cos n\theta \end{bmatrix}.$$

4.12 Devise a problem, similar to the previous problem, using $\cosh\theta$ and $\sinh\theta$.

4.13 Prove that the set of all nonsingular diagonal matrices of order n is a commutative group under matrix multiplication.

4.14 Verify Sylvester's law of nullity for the two matrices

$$\begin{bmatrix} 1 & 5 & 2 & 3 \\ -2 & -4 & -1 & 0 \\ 3 & 5 & 4 & 2 \\ 4 & 2 & 0 & -5 \end{bmatrix}, \quad \begin{bmatrix} 2 & 3 & 1 & 12 \\ -1 & 1 & -3 & -1 \\ 4 & -2 & 10 & 8 \\ 2 & 5 & -1 & 16 \end{bmatrix}.$$

4.15 Find the general solution of the simultaneous differential equations

$$\begin{aligned} \frac{dy_1}{dx} &= \alpha y_1 - \beta y_2 + \beta y_3, \\ \frac{dy_2}{dx} &= -\beta y_1 + \alpha y_2 - \beta y_3, \\ \frac{dy_3}{dx} &= \beta y_1 - \beta y_2 + \alpha y_3. \end{aligned}$$

Caution: the matrix of coefficients has a repeated eigenvalue.

4.16 Write a program for finding, by the method of Leverrier, the characteristic polynomial for a square matrix $\mathbf{A}$ of order n. (A related method due to Faddeev is to be preferred if the eigenvectors, or the inverse, or the adjoint is desired as well; see Problem 4.17.)

The method is described for the polynomial

$$\lambda^n - \sigma_1\lambda^{n-1} + \sigma_2\lambda^{n-2} + \cdots + (-1)^n\sigma_n,$$

as displayed in equation (4.11). Let $s_1 = \sum_{i=1}^n \lambda_i$ be the sum of the zeros of the above polynomial and, more generally, let $s_k = \sum_{i=1}^n \lambda_i^k$ be the sum of the kth powers of these zeros. Then, by Newton's formulas [13], for $k = 1, 2, \ldots, n$,

$$k\sigma_k = s_1\sigma_{k-1} - s_2\sigma_{k-2} + \cdots \pm s_{k-1}\sigma_1 \mp s_k,$$

so that $\sigma_1, \sigma_2, \ldots, \sigma_n$ can be calculated if $s_1, s_2, \ldots, s_n$ are known. But the spur of any matrix $\mathbf{M}$ is the sum of its eigenvalues, so that (see page 220) $s_1 = Sp(\mathbf{A})$ and, in general, $s_k = Sp(\mathbf{A}^k)$.

4.17 Write a program for finding, by the method of Faddeev, the characteristic polynomial $\phi(\lambda) = \det(\mathbf{A} - \lambda\mathbf{I}) = (-1)^n\Delta(\lambda)$ where, as in equation (4.11), we write

$$\Delta(\lambda) = \lambda^n - \sigma_1\lambda^{n-1} + \sigma_2\lambda^{n-2} + \cdots + (-1)^n\sigma_n.$$

Since this method involves also the computation of $\mathbf{B}_1, \mathbf{B}_2, \ldots, \mathbf{B}_{n-1}$, where

$$\mathbf{B}(\lambda) = \text{adj}(\lambda\mathbf{I} - \mathbf{A})$$
$$= \lambda^{n-1}\mathbf{I} - \mathbf{B}_1\lambda^{n-2} + \mathbf{B}_2\lambda^{n-3} + \cdots + (-1)^{n-1}\mathbf{B}_{n-1},$$

the program can be written so that we also find:

(a) adj $(\mathbf{A}) = (-1)^{n-1}$ adj $(-\mathbf{A}) = \mathbf{B}_{n-1}$,

(b) $\mathbf{A}^{-1} = \sigma_n^{-1}$ adj $\mathbf{A} = \sigma_n^{-1}\mathbf{B}_{n-1}$, provided that $\mathbf{A}$ is non-singular,

(c) for any known eigenvalue λ_i, a corresponding eigenvector, $\boldsymbol{\mu}_i$, by taking any nonzero column (see page 220) of $\mathbf{B}(\lambda_i)$.

The process, which follows, is established in Gantmacher [11]:

$$\mathbf{A}_1 = \mathbf{A}, \qquad \sigma_1 = Sp(\mathbf{A}_1), \qquad \mathbf{B}_1 = \sigma_1\mathbf{I} - \mathbf{A}_1,$$

$$\mathbf{A}_2 = \mathbf{A}\mathbf{B}_1, \qquad \sigma_2 = \frac{1}{2}Sp(\mathbf{A}_2), \qquad \mathbf{B}_2 = \sigma_2\mathbf{I} - \mathbf{A}_2,$$

$$\vdots \qquad\qquad \vdots \qquad\qquad \vdots$$

$$\mathbf{A}_j = \mathbf{A}\mathbf{B}_{j-1}, \qquad \sigma_j = \frac{1}{j}Sp(\mathbf{A}_j), \qquad \mathbf{B}_j = \sigma_j\mathbf{I} - \mathbf{A}_j,$$

$$\vdots \qquad\qquad \vdots \qquad\qquad \vdots$$

$$\mathbf{A}_n = \mathbf{A}\mathbf{B}_{n-1}, \qquad \sigma_n = \frac{1}{n}Sp(\mathbf{A}_n), \qquad \mathbf{B}_n = \sigma_n\mathbf{I} - \mathbf{A}_n = 0.$$

4.18 Read the first two paragraphs of Problem 5.13 and assume the following:

(a) The total strain energy of the frame is given by $U = \frac{1}{2}\mathbf{s}^t\mathbf{F}\mathbf{s}$.

(b) The elements of the vector $\mathbf{r} = [r_1 \, r_2 \ldots r_i \ldots r_n]^t$ of loads in the n selected redundant members adjust themselves so that the strain energy is minimized. That is, $\partial U/\partial r_i = 0$, $i = 1, 2, \ldots, n$.

(c) The m corresponding elements δ_j and p_j of the displacement and applied load vectors $\boldsymbol{\delta}$ and $\mathbf{p}$ are related by $\delta_j = \partial U/\partial p_j$, $j = 1, 2, \ldots, m$.

Prove the validity of the relations for $\boldsymbol{\Gamma}$ and $\mathbf{s}$ given in Problem 5.13.

4.19 A matrix occurring frequently in the numerical solution of partial differential equations is the $n \times n$ tridiagonal matrix [9]:

$$\mathbf{T}_n = \begin{bmatrix} -2 & 1 & 0 & 0 \ldots 0 & 0 \\ 1 & -2 & 1 & 0 \ldots 0 & 0 \\ 0 & 1 & -2 & 1 \ldots 0 & 0 \\ \vdots & & & & \vdots \\ 0 & 0 & 0 & 0 \ldots 1 & -2 \end{bmatrix},$$

wherein all entries are zero except the diagonal entries, always -2, and the infra- and super-diagonal entries, always 1. Show that the eigenvalues and corresponding eigenvectors are given by

$$\lambda_i = -4\sin^2\left(\frac{i\pi}{2n+2}\right),$$

$$\mathbf{u}_i = \left[\sin\frac{i\pi}{n+1} \quad \sin\frac{2i\pi}{n+1} \quad \cdots \quad \sin\frac{ni\pi}{n+1}\right]^t,$$

where $i = 1, 2, \ldots, n$.

4.20 The explicit method for the numerical solution of $u_t = u_{xx}$ is discussed in Section 7.5 (see also p. 61 of Smith [9]). If $\mathbf{v}_n = [v_{1,n}\, v_{2,n} \ldots v_{M-1,n}]^t$ is the vector of solutions at

time-level n, and the boundary values $g_0(t_n)$ and $g_1(t_n)$ are zero, show that

$$\mathbf{v}_{n+1} = \mathbf{A}\mathbf{v}_n,$$

in which $\mathbf{A} = \mathbf{I} + r\mathbf{T}_{M-1}$, where $r = \Delta t/(\Delta x)^2$ and $\mathbf{T}_{M-1}$ is the matrix of Problem 4.19 (now with $M - 1$ rows and columns).

The eigenvalue approach for discussing stability of the method involves proving whether the eigenvalues of $\mathbf{A}$ are less than one in magnitude (see page 222). Show that these eigenvalues are

$$1 - 4r\sin^2\frac{i\pi}{2M}, \qquad i = 1, 2, \ldots, M-1,$$

and that stability occurs if $r \leqslant \frac{1}{2}$.

4.21 In the Crank-Nicolson scheme for the numerical solution of $u_t = u_{xx}$ (page 451, also [9], p. 64), the eigenvalue approach for discussing stability involves proving that the eigenvalues of $\mathbf{A} = (2\mathbf{I} - r\mathbf{T}_{M-1})^{-1}(2\mathbf{I} + r\mathbf{T}_{M-1})$ are less than one in magnitude. Use Problem 4.19 to show that the eigenvalues are

$$\frac{2 - 4r\sin^2\dfrac{i\pi}{2M}}{2 + 4r\sin^2\dfrac{i\pi}{2M}}, \qquad i = 1, 2, \ldots, M-1,$$

and that the procedure is always stable.

4.22 In item (6) under "Method of Solution" in Example 4.3 (Rutishauser's method), verify:

(a) The matrix labeled $\mathbf{L}_m^{-1}$ as the inverse of that labeled $\mathbf{L}_m$,

(b) the simultaneous equations given for $v_2, v_3, \ldots v_n$,

(c) the general formula given for v_i.

4.23 Consider the horizontal motion of the mass-spring system shown in Fig. P4.23. The horizontal deflections x_1

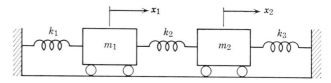

Figure P4.23

and x_2 are measured relative to the position of static equilibrium. The spring stiffnesses k_1, k_2, and k_3 are the forces required to extend or compress each spring by unit length.

(a) Show that the equations of motion are

$$m_1\ddot{x}_1 = -k_1x_1 + k_2(x_2 - x_1),$$
$$m_2\ddot{x}_2 = k_2(x_1 - x_2) - k_3x_2.$$

(b) If the deflection vector is $\mathbf{x} = [x_1 \, x_2]^t$, rewrite the equations of motion in the form $\ddot{\mathbf{x}} = \mathbf{A}\mathbf{x}$.

(c) Show that the substitution $\mathbf{x} = \mathbf{b}e^{j\omega t}$, where $j = \sqrt{-1}$, leads to the eigenvalue problem

$$\mathbf{A}\mathbf{b} = \lambda\mathbf{b},$$

where $\lambda = -\omega^2$. The possible values that ω may assume are the natural circular frequencies of vibration of the system.

(d) If $k_1 = k_2 = k_3 = 1$ $\mathrm{lb}_m/\mathrm{sec}^2$, and $m_1 = m_2 = 1$ lb_m, find the eigenvalues and eigenvectors of $\mathbf{A}$.

(e) If the initial conditions at $t = 0$ are $x_1 = 1$, $x_2 = \dot{x}_1 = \dot{x}_2 = 0$, show that

$$\mathbf{x} = \begin{bmatrix} \dfrac{1}{2} \\[2mm] \dfrac{1}{2} \end{bmatrix} \cos t + \begin{bmatrix} \dfrac{1}{2} \\[2mm] -\dfrac{1}{2} \end{bmatrix} \cos \sqrt{3}\, t.$$

4.24 Generalize Problem 4.23 to the situation involving n masses, $m_1, m_2, \ldots, m_n$, connected by $n + 1$ springs of stiffnesses $k_1, k_2, \ldots, k_{n+1}$.

Write a program that will read values for these masses and spring stiffnesses as data, and that will proceed to compute the resulting natural frequencies ω and the associated amplitude vectors **b**.

Test the program for a variety of mass-spring systems, and investigate, as special cases, the effect of making a particular mass or spring constant either very large or very small.

4.25 Figure P4.25 is a simplified representation of the main three rotating masses in a two-cylinder engine driving a flywheel on the same shaft.

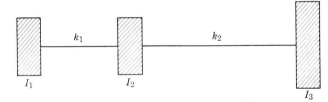

Figure P4.25

I_1, I_2, and I_3 are the moments of inertia (lb$_f$ in. sec^2) of the rotating masses. The shaft stiffnesses k_1 and k_2 are the torques (lb$_f$ in.) required to twist each section through unit angle. Let θ_1, θ_2, and θ_3 be the angular displacements of the rotating masses.

(a) By equating torque to the product of moment of inertia and angular acceleration, show that

$$I_1\ddot{\theta}_1 = k_1(\theta_2 - \theta_1),$$
$$I_2\ddot{\theta}_2 = k_1(\theta_1 - \theta_2) + k_2(\theta_3 - \theta_2),$$
$$I_3\ddot{\theta}_3 = k_2(\theta_2 - \theta_3).$$

(b) Following the general pattern of Problem 4.23, compute the natural frequencies and the associated vectors of relative displacements for each mode of torsional oscillations if $I_1 = I_2 = 4$, $I_3 = 20$ lb$_f$ in. sec^2, $k_1 = 8 \times 10^6$, and $k_2 = 10^7$ lb$_f$ in./radian.

4.26 Write a program that will generalize the situation in Problem 4.25 to that of n rotating masses on a shaft.

Test the program with the data of Problem 4.25, and also for the following four-cylinder engine and flywheel: $I_1 = I_2 = I_3 = I_4 = 4$, $I_5 = 20$ lb$_f$ in. sec^2, $k_1 = k_2 = k_3 = 8 \times 10^6$, $k_4 = 10^7$ lb$_f$ in./radian. Also investigate the effect of adding a generator ($I_6 = 8$) connected by a shaft ($k_5 = 2$), (a) next to the flywheel, and (b) next to the first cylinder.

4.27 The transverse deflection y of a beam obeys the differential equation

$$\frac{d^2y}{dx^2} = -\frac{M}{EI},$$

where x is the axial distance along the beam, M is the local bending moment (considered positive if it tends to make the beam convex in the direction y, as shown), E is Young's modulus, and I is the appropriate cross-sectional moment of inertia.

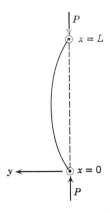

Figure P4.27

A column of length L, shown in Fig. P4.27, is subjected to an axial load P at its pin-jointed ends, which are free to move vertically. By taking moments, we find that $M = Py$, giving

$$\frac{d^2y}{dx^2} = -\frac{Py}{EI}.$$

Show that a nontrivial solution of this differential equation occurs only when P has one of the *characteristic values*

$$P = \frac{n^2\pi^2 EI}{L^2}, \qquad n = 1, 2, 3, \ldots,$$

and that the solution is then $y = A \sin(n\pi x/L)$, where A is an arbitrary constant. Note that for $n = 1$, we have $P = \pi^2 EI/L^2$ (known as the *Euler load*), under which the column will just begin to buckle.

What will happen if P does not equal one of these characteristic values?

4.28 Approximate the solution to Problem 4.27 by the following finite-difference method. Divide the beam into $n + 1$ segments, each of length $\Delta x = L/(n + 1)$, by introducing points labelled $0, 1, 2, \ldots, i, \ldots, n, n + 1$, as shown in Fig. P4.28.

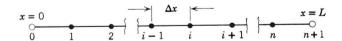

Figure P4.28

From equation (7.7), the approximation to the differential equation at the ith point is

$$\frac{y_{i-1} - 2y_i + y_{i+1}}{(\Delta x)^2} = -\frac{Py_i}{EI}.$$

(a) By considering points $i = 1, 2, \ldots, n$ in turn, show that the vector of deflections, $\mathbf{y} = [y_1 y_2 \ldots y_n]^t$, obeys

$$\mathbf{Ay} = \frac{P(\Delta x)^2}{EI}\mathbf{y},$$

where

$$A = \begin{bmatrix} 2 & -1 & & & & & 0 \\ -1 & 2 & -1 & & & & \\ & -1 & 2 & -1 & & & \\ & & \cdots\cdots\cdots & & & \\ & 0 & & -1 & 2 & -1 \\ & & & & -1 & 2 \end{bmatrix}.$$

(b) How are the characteristic loads P and the corresponding deflections $\mathbf{y}$ related to the eigenvalues and eigenvectors of $\mathbf{A}$?

(c) The eigenvalues of $\mathbf{A}$ are computed, for $n = 8$, in Example 4.3. Compare the resulting characteristic loads and relative deflections with the exact solution given in Problem 4.27.

4.29 A vertical column of length L, clamped at the bottom, is subjected to a vertically downward load P at its free end, as shown in Fig. P4.29. The column does not necessarily have a uniform cross-sectional moment of inertia I along its height.

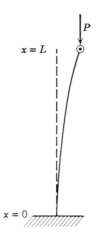

Figure P4.29

Show, by developing the situation into a matrix eigenvalue problem, how the axial buckling load could be estimated.

4.30 A vertical column, pin-jointed at both ends, is tapered so that its minimum cross-sectional moment of inertia varies linearly from I_0 at the bottom $(x = 0)$ to I_L at the top $(x = L)$.

By following a finite-difference procedure similar to that of Problem 4.28, determine the least axial load under which the column would start to buckle. At this point, what would be the axial shape of the column?

The following test data are suggested: $E = 30 \times 10^6$ lb$_f$/sq in., $L = 48$ in., $I_0 = 0.002$ in.^{4}, $I_L = 0.001$ in.^{4}, $n = 4$ and 9 (that is, investigate the results first using five, and then ten subdivisions).

4.31 A beam of length L is pin-jointed at both ends. Transverse deflections y of the beam vary with time t and distance x along the beam according to the partial differential equation

$$\frac{\partial^2}{\partial x^2}\left(EI\frac{\partial^2 y}{\partial x^2}\right) = -A\rho\frac{\partial^2 y}{\partial t^2},$$

where $E =$ Young's modulus, $I =$ second moment of area,

$A =$ cross-sectional area, and $\rho =$ density. Substitution of a solution of the form $y = X(x)e^{j\omega t}$ (where $j = \sqrt{-1}$ and ω is a circular frequency of natural vibrations) into the above equation leads to the following ordinary differential equation for the function X:

$$\frac{d^2}{dx^2}\left(EI\frac{d^2 X}{dx^2}\right) = A\rho\omega^2 X.$$

At both ends we have $X = 0$ and $d^2 X/dx^2 = 0$.

By subdividing the beam into $n + 1$ equal segments and following the general finite-difference approach of Problem 4.28, show that the determination of the frequency and relative displacements for each natural mode of vibration amounts to finding the eigenvalues and eigenvectors of a matrix. If required, additional information concerning finite-difference approximations and the representation of boundary conditions can be found in Sections 7.3 and 7.17, and in Example 7.9.

For a certain small light-alloy beam or reed, $E = 10^7$ lb$_f$/in.^{2}, $L = 10$ in., $\rho = 170$ lb$_m$/ft^3, and b (breadth) $= 0.5$ in. The thickness t varies linearly from one end to the other according to $t = t_0 + (t_L - t_0)(x/L)$. At any section, $A = bt$ and $I = bt^3/12$. Using $n = 5$ and $n = 10$ in turn, compute the various modes of vibration for (a) $t_0 = t_L = 0.02$ in. and (b) $t_0 = 0.02$ in., $t_L = 0.025$ in. The conversion 1 lb$_f$ ≡ 32.2 lb$_m$ ft/sec^2 will be needed. Also note that, analytically, for the case of constant thickness, $\omega = (EI/A\rho)^{1/2}p^2$, where p is a root of $\sin pL = 0$ [14].

4.32 Repeat Problem 4.31 for the case of a small cantilever that is clamped at $x = 0$ ($X = 0$, $dX/dx = 0$) and is completely free at $x = L$ ($d^2 X/dx^2 = 0$, $d^3 X/dx^3 = 0$). Investigate the cases of (a) $t_0 = t_L = 0.02$ in., (b) $t_0 = 0.02$ in., $t_L = 0.025$ in., and (c) $t_0 = 0.025$ in., $t_L = 0.02$ in. Analytically, for the case of constant thickness, $\omega = (EI/A\rho)^{1/2}p^2$, where p is a root of $\cosh pL \cos pL = -1$ (see Problem 3.27).

4.33 The transverse deflections w of a two-dimensional vibrating membrane with fixed perimeter are governed by

$$\frac{\partial^2 w}{\partial x^2} + \frac{\partial^2 w}{\partial y^2} = \frac{m}{T}\frac{\partial^2 w}{\partial t^2},$$

where T is the tension per unit length throughout the membrane and m is the mass per unit area; consistent units are assumed. Substitution of a solution of the form $w = U(x, y)e^{j\omega t}$ (where $j = \sqrt{-1}$ and ω is a circular frequency of natural vibrations) leads to the following equation for the function U:

$$\frac{\partial^2 U}{\partial x^2} + \frac{\partial^2 U}{\partial y^2} = -\frac{m\omega^2}{T}U.$$

By following a finite-difference approach similar to that in Problem 4.28, show that the determination of the frequency and relative displacements for each natural mode of vibration amounts to finding the eigenvalues and eigenvectors of a matrix.

Determine the natural frequencies and modes of vibration for the trapezoidal-shaped membrane of Fig. P4.33, with $\sqrt{T/m} = 2000$ in./sec. Suggested grid size: $\Delta x = 1$ in., $\Delta y = 2$ in., using symmetry to reduce the number of points to be considered.

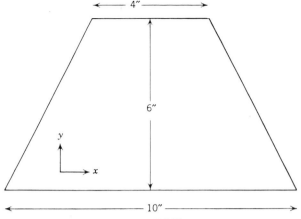

Figure P4.33

4.34 In many practical problems involving vibrations, one is often primarily concerned only with λ_{min} and λ_{max}, the eigenvalues of least and greatest magnitude.

In this connection, write a program that will use the power method to determine λ_{min} and λ_{max} and the associated eigenvectors for an $n \times n$ real matrix $\mathbf{A}$, which is read as data.

4.35 Write a general-purpose program that, given a real matrix $\mathbf{A}$ of order n, computes the coefficients of the characteristic equation (or factors of the characteristic equation) using the method of Danilevski, described in Section 4.9. The program should read the n^2 elements of $\mathbf{A} = (a_{ij})$ into the first n rows of the matrix $\mathbf{A}$, and read values for a small tolerance ε and any desired printing control variables. $\mathbf{A}$ should be transformed in place by the sequence of matrices $\mathbf{M}^{(1)}, \mathbf{M}^{(2)}, \ldots, \mathbf{M}^{(n)}$ described in the text. The matrices $\mathbf{M}^{(i)}$ need not appear explicitly, but the composite similarity matrix $\mathbf{M}$ should be constructed in the second n rows of $\mathbf{A}$ during the course of the iteration. The matrix $\mathbf{C}$ of (4.60) may be built up in the first n rows of $\mathbf{A}$ (the original matrix $\mathbf{A}$ will be destroyed in the process).

Before the Danilevski procedure is applied to the ith row of $\mathbf{A}$, all elements to the right of the diagonal should be examined to find the element of greatest magnitude, in column k for example. Exchange columns k and $i + 1$ and rows k and $i + 1$ to maintain the similarity of $\mathbf{A}$ as described in the text. If the largest element is smaller in magnitude than ε, simply clear the row to zero and proceed to the next row.

The coefficients of the characteristic equation (or coefficients of factors of the characteristic equation) should be stored in the vector $\mathbf{B}$ and printed when found.

As an indication of the errors resulting from the procedure, the starting matrix $\mathbf{A}$ can be regenerated as

$$\mathbf{A} = \mathbf{MCM}^{-1}.$$

After recovering all the coefficients of the characteristic equation:

(a) Evaluate $\mathbf{T} = \mathbf{MC}$, temporarily saving the results in a matrix T.

(b) Invert $\mathbf{M}$ in place in the second n rows of A, using the function SIMUL (see Example 5.2).

(c) Compute $\mathbf{A} = \mathbf{TM}^{-1}$, where the reconstructed elements of $\mathbf{A}$ are overstored in the first n rows of A.

(d) Print out the reconstructed matrix and compare it with the original matrix $\mathbf{A}$.

As test data for the program, use the first three matrices investigated in Example 4.3 and the matrix of (3.1.10) for Cases A and B of Example 3.1. The roots of the characteristic equations for these matrices (that is, the eigenvalues of the matrices) have been found in data sets 8, 11, 9, 14, and 15, respectively, of Example 3.1.

4.36 Consider the following transformation of a symmetrical $n \times n$ starting matrix $\mathbf{A}_1 = \mathbf{A} = (a_{ij})$, to give a second matrix $\mathbf{A}_2$:

$$\mathbf{A}_2 = \mathbf{P}_2 \mathbf{A}_1 \mathbf{P}_2^t,$$

where $\mathbf{P}_2 = \mathbf{I} - 2\mathbf{v}_2 \mathbf{v}_2^t$ and the column vector $\mathbf{v}_2$ is such that $\mathbf{v}_2^t \mathbf{v}_2 = 1$. Show that $\mathbf{P}_2$ is both orthogonal and symmetric and hence that the eigenvalues of $\mathbf{A}_2$ are the same as those of $\mathbf{A}_1$.

Now define

$$s^2 = \sum_{i=2}^{n} a_{i1}^2,$$

$$x_2^2 = \frac{1}{2}\left(1 \pm \frac{a_{21}}{s}\right),$$

$$x_i = \pm \frac{a_{i1}}{2x_2 s}, \qquad i = 3, 4, \ldots, n,$$

in which either both plus signs or both minus signs are taken. Prove that if $\mathbf{v}_2 = [0, x_2, x_3, \ldots, x_n]^t$, $\mathbf{A}_2$ will have zeros in the third through last elements of its first row and first column. Demonstrate that $n - 3$ analogous further transformations, $\mathbf{A}_3 = \mathbf{P}_3 \mathbf{A}_2 \mathbf{P}_3^t$, $\mathbf{A}_4 = \mathbf{P}_4 \mathbf{A}_3 \mathbf{P}_4^t$, etc., can be made that will ultimately yield a symmetric matrix $\mathbf{A}_{n-2}$ that is tridiagonal.

Let $a_1, a_2, \ldots, a_n$ be the diagonal elements of $\mathbf{A}_{n-2}$ and let its subdiagonal (and superdiagonal) elements be $b_1, b_2, \ldots, b_{n-1}$. Show that $p_n(\lambda)$, the characteristic polynomial of $\mathbf{A}_{n-2}$, is given by the following recursion relations:

$$p_0(\lambda) = 1,$$
$$p_1(\lambda) = a_1 - \lambda,$$
$$p_i(\lambda) = (a_i - \lambda)p_{i-1}(\lambda) - b_{i-1}^2 p_{i-2}(\lambda), \qquad i = 2, 3, \ldots, n.$$

The above forms the basis for the *Givens-Householder method* for determining the eigenvalues (and eigenvectors) of a symmetric matrix. For a comprehensive discussion, see Ralston and Wilf [15].

Bibliography

1. E. Bodewig, *Matrix Calculus*, North-Holland Publishing Co., Amsterdam, 1959.
2. N. H. McCoy, *Introduction to Modern Algebra*, Allyn and Bacon, New York, 1960.
3. G. E. Forsythe and P. Henrici, "The Cyclic Jacobi Method for Computing the Principal Values of a Complex Matrix," *Trans. Amer. Math. Soc.*, **94**, 1–23 (1960).
4. H. Rutishauser, "Solution of Eigenvalue Problems with the LR-Transformation," *Natl. Bureau of Standards Appl. Math. Series*, **49**, 47–81 (1958).
5. D. K. Faddeev and V. N. Faddeeva, *Computational Methods of Linear Algebra*, Freeman, San Francisco, 1963.
6. H. W. Turnbull and A. C. Aitken, *An Introduction to the Theory of Canonical Matrices*, Dover, New York, 1961.
7. L. A. Pipes, *Matrix Methods for Engineering*, Prentice-Hall, Englewood Cliffs, New Jersey, 1963.
8. F. B. Hildebrand, *Methods of Applied Mathematics*, Prentice-Hall, Englewood Cliffs, New Jersey, 1965.
9. G. D. Smith, *Numerical Solution of Partial Differential Equations*, Oxford University Press, London, 1965.
10. E. D. Nering, *Linear Algebra and Matrix Theory*, Wiley, New York, 1963.
11. F. R. Gantmacher, *The Theory of Matrices*, Chelsea, New York, 1960.
12. K. Hoffman and R. Kunze, *Linear Algebra*, Prentice-Hall, Englewood Cliffs, New Jersey, 1961.
13. G. Chrystal, *Textbook of Algebra*, Vol. 1, Chelsea, New York, 1952.
14. A. H. Church, *Mechanical Vibrations*, 2nd ed., Wiley, New York, 1963.
15. A. Ralston and H. S. Wilf, ed., *Mathematical Methods for Digital Computers*, Vol. 2, Wiley, New York, 1967.

CHAPTER 5

Systems of Equations

5.1 Introduction

This chapter is concerned with methods for solving the following system of n simultaneous equations in the n unknowns $x_1, x_2, \ldots, x_n$:

$$
\begin{aligned}
f_1(x_1,x_2,\ldots,x_n) &= 0, \\
f_2(x_1,x_2,\ldots,x_n) &= 0, \\
&\vdots \\
f_n(x_1,x_2,\ldots,x_n) &= 0.
\end{aligned}
\tag{5.1}
$$

The general case, in which the functions $f_1, f_2, \ldots, f_n$ do not admit of any particular simplification, is treated in Sections 5.8 and 5.9. However, if these functions are linear in the x's, (5.1) can be rewritten as:

$$
\begin{aligned}
b_{11}x_1 + b_{12}x_2 + \cdots + b_{1n}x_n &= u_1, \\
b_{21}x_1 + b_{22}x_2 + \cdots + b_{2n}x_n &= u_2, \\
&\vdots \\
b_{n1}x_1 + b_{n2}x_2 + \cdots + b_{nn}x_n &= u_n.
\end{aligned}
\tag{5.2}
$$

More concisely, we have

$$
\mathbf{Bx} = \mathbf{u},
\tag{5.3}
$$

in which $\mathbf{B}$ is the matrix of coefficients, $\mathbf{u} = [u_1, u_2, \ldots, u_n]^t$ is the right-hand side vector, and $\mathbf{x} = [x_1, x_2, \ldots, x_n]^t$ is the solution vector. Assuming negligible computational round-off error, *direct* methods for solving (5.2) exactly, in a finite number of operations, are discussed in Sections 5.3, 5.4, and 5.5. These direct techniques are useful when the number of equations involved is not too large (typically of the order of 40 or fewer equations). *Iterative* methods for solving (5.2) approximately are described in Sections 5.6 and 5.7. These iterative techniques are more appropriate when dealing with a large number of simultaneous equations (typically of the order of 100 equations or more), which will often possess certain other special characteristics.

5.2 Elementary Transformations of Matrices

Before studying systems of equations, it is useful to consider the three types of *elementary matrices*:

1. An elementary matrix of the *first kind* is an $n \times n$ diagonal matrix $\mathbf{Q}$, formed by taking the identity matrix $\mathbf{I}$ and replacing the ith diagonal element with a nonzero constant q. For example, with $n = 4$ and $i = 3$,

$$
\mathbf{Q} = \begin{bmatrix} 1 & 0 & 0 & 0 \\ 0 & 1 & 0 & 0 \\ 0 & 0 & q & 0 \\ 0 & 0 & 0 & 1 \end{bmatrix}.
$$

Note that $\det \mathbf{Q} = q$, and that the inverse matrix $\mathbf{Q}^{-1} = \operatorname{diag}(1, 1, 1/q, 1)$ is again like $\mathbf{I}$, this time with $1/q$ in the ith diagonal position.

2. An elementary matrix of the *second kind* is an $n \times n$ matrix $\mathbf{R}$, formed by interchanging any two rows i and j of $\mathbf{I}$. For example, with $n = 4$, $i = 1$, and $j = 3$,

$$
\mathbf{R} = \begin{bmatrix} 0 & 0 & 1 & 0 \\ 0 & 1 & 0 & 0 \\ 1 & 0 & 0 & 0 \\ 0 & 0 & 0 & 1 \end{bmatrix}.
$$

Note that $\det \mathbf{R} = -1$, and that $\mathbf{R}$ is self-inverse, that is, $\mathbf{RR}^{-1} = \mathbf{I}$.

3. An elementary matrix of the *third kind* is an $n \times n$ matrix $\mathbf{S}$, formed by inserting a nonzero constant s into the i, j $(i \neq j)$ element of $\mathbf{I}$. (This may also be construed as taking $\mathbf{I}$ and adding a multiple s of each element in row j to the corresponding element in row i.) For example, with $n = 4$, $i = 3$, and $j = 1$,

$$
\mathbf{S} = \begin{bmatrix} 1 & 0 & 0 & 0 \\ 0 & 1 & 0 & 0 \\ s & 0 & 1 & 0 \\ 0 & 0 & 0 & 1 \end{bmatrix}.
$$

Note that $\det \mathbf{S} = 1$.

Premultiplication of an arbitrary $n \times p$ matrix $\mathbf{A}$ by one of these elementary matrices produces an *elementary transformation* of $\mathbf{A}$, also termed an *elementary row operation*, on $\mathbf{A}$. As examples, we form the products $\mathbf{QA}$, $\mathbf{RA}$, and $\mathbf{SA}$, with $n = 3$, $i = 2$, $j = 3$, and $p = 4$.

1.
$$
\mathbf{QA} = \begin{bmatrix} 1 & 0 & 0 \\ 0 & q & 0 \\ 0 & 0 & 1 \end{bmatrix} \begin{bmatrix} a_{11} & a_{12} & a_{13} & a_{14} \\ a_{21} & a_{22} & a_{23} & a_{24} \\ a_{31} & a_{32} & a_{33} & a_{34} \end{bmatrix}
$$

$$
= \begin{bmatrix} a_{11} & a_{12} & a_{13} & a_{14} \\ qa_{21} & qa_{22} & qa_{23} & qa_{24} \\ a_{31} & a_{32} & a_{33} & a_{34} \end{bmatrix}.
$$

2.
$$\mathbf{RA} = \begin{bmatrix} 1 & 0 & 0 \\ 0 & 0 & 1 \\ 0 & 1 & 0 \end{bmatrix} \begin{bmatrix} a_{11} & a_{12} & a_{13} & a_{14} \\ a_{21} & a_{22} & a_{23} & a_{24} \\ a_{31} & a_{32} & a_{33} & a_{34} \end{bmatrix}$$

$$= \begin{bmatrix} a_{11} & a_{12} & a_{13} & a_{14} \\ a_{31} & a_{32} & a_{33} & a_{34} \\ a_{21} & a_{22} & a_{23} & a_{24} \end{bmatrix}.$$

3.
$$\mathbf{SA} = \begin{bmatrix} 1 & 0 & 0 \\ 0 & 1 & s \\ 0 & 0 & 1 \end{bmatrix} \begin{bmatrix} a_{11} & a_{12} & a_{13} & a_{14} \\ a_{21} & a_{22} & a_{23} & a_{24} \\ a_{31} & a_{32} & a_{33} & a_{34} \end{bmatrix}$$

$$= \begin{bmatrix} a_{11} & a_{12} & a_{13} & a_{14} \\ a_{21}+sa_{31} & a_{22}+sa_{32} & a_{23}+sa_{33} & a_{24}+sa_{34} \\ a_{31} & a_{32} & a_{33} & a_{34} \end{bmatrix}.$$

It is apparent that premultiplication by the elementary matrices produces the following transformations of $\mathbf{A}$:

1. $\mathbf{QA}$: Multiplication of all elements of one row by a scalar.
2. $\mathbf{RA}$: Interchange of two rows.
3. $\mathbf{SA}$: Addition of a scalar multiple of elements of one row to the corresponding elements of another row.

Observe that in each case the original elementary matrix can be formed from the identity matrix $\mathbf{I}$ by manipulating it exactly as we wish to have $\mathbf{A}$ manipulated.

Postmultiplication of an arbitrary $p \times n$ matrix $\mathbf{A}$ by one of the elementary matrices is called an *elementary column operation*. The three types of operations produce the following results:

1. $\mathbf{AQ}$: Multiplication of all elements of one column by a scalar.
2. $\mathbf{AR}$: Interchange of two columns.
3. $\mathbf{AS}$: Addition of a scalar multiple of elements of one column to the corresponding elements of another column.

If $\mathbf{A}$ is any matrix and $\mathbf{T}$ is the matrix resulting from elementary row or column operations on $\mathbf{A}$, $\mathbf{T}$ and $\mathbf{A}$ are termed *equivalent matrices*. For the examples given above, if $\mathbf{A}$ is a *square* matrix,

$$\det(\mathbf{QA}) = \det \mathbf{Q} \times \det \mathbf{A} = q \det \mathbf{A};$$
$$\det(\mathbf{RA}) = \det \mathbf{R} \times \det \mathbf{A} = -\det \mathbf{A};$$
$$\det(\mathbf{SA}) = \det \mathbf{S} \times \det \mathbf{A} = \det \mathbf{A}.$$

Thus, multiplication of all the elements of one row of a square matrix by a scalar also multiplies the determinant of the matrix by that scalar. Interchange of two rows changes the sign of the determinant (but not its magnitude), and addition of a scalar multiple of elements of one row to the corresponding elements of another row has no effect on the determinant.

Clearly, the product of elementary matrices is nonsingular, for each component has an inverse. It is also true that every nonsingular matrix can be written as a product of elementary matrices.

5.3 Gaussian Elimination

The *direct* methods of solving equations (5.2) are based on manipulations using the techniques expressed by the elementary matrices of Section 5.2. We now describe one such method, known as *Gaussian elimination*. Consider a general system of three linear equations:

$$b_{11}x_1 + b_{12}x_2 + b_{13}x_3 = u_1,$$
$$b_{21}x_1 + b_{22}x_2 + b_{23}x_3 = u_2, \qquad (5.4)$$
$$b_{31}x_1 + b_{32}x_2 + b_{33}x_3 = u_3.$$

As a first step, replace the second equation by the result of adding to it the first equation multiplied by $-b_{21}/b_{11}$. Similarly, replace the third equation by the result of adding to it the first equation multiplied by $-b_{31}/b_{11}$. The result is the system

$$b_{11}x_1 + b_{12}x_2 + b_{13}x_3 = u_1,$$
$$b'_{22}x_2 + b'_{23}x_3 = u'_2, \qquad (5.5)$$
$$b'_{32}x_2 + b'_{33}x_3 = u'_3.$$

in which the b' and u' are the new coefficients resulting from the above manipulations. Now multiply the second equation of (5.5) by $-b'_{32}/b'_{22}$, and add the result to the third equation of (5.5). The result is the triangular system

$$b_{11}x_1 + b_{12}x_2 + b_{13}x_3 = u_1,$$
$$b'_{22}x_2 + b'_{23}x_3 = u'_2, \qquad (5.6)$$
$$b''_{33}x_3 = u''_3,$$

in which b''_{33} and u''_3 result from the arithmetic operations. The system (5.6) is readily solved by the process of *back-substitution*, in which x_3 is obtained from the last equation; this allows x_2 to be obtained from the second equation, and then x_1 can be found from the first equation.

The above method seems primitive at a first glance, but by the time it has been made suitable for implementation by automatic machines, it furnishes a powerful tool not only for solving equations (5.2), but also for finding the inverse of the related matrix of coefficients $\mathbf{B}$, the determinant of $\mathbf{B}$, the adjoint of $\mathbf{B}$, etc.

Insofar as reaching (5.6) is concerned, all can be explained in terms of elementary matrices of the third kind. Note that matrices alone suffice, the presence of x_1, x_2, and x_3 being superfluous. Define an *augmented matrix* $\mathbf{C}$ consisting of the original coefficient matrix $\mathbf{B}$ with the right-hand side vector $\mathbf{u}$ appended to it. That is,

$$\mathbf{C} = [\mathbf{B}\,|\,\mathbf{u}] = \begin{bmatrix} b_{11} & b_{12} & b_{13} & u_1 \\ b_{21} & b_{22} & b_{23} & u_2 \\ b_{31} & b_{32} & b_{33} & u_3 \end{bmatrix},$$

in which the broken line denotes matrix partitioning.

Also define three elementary matrices of the third kind:

$$S_1 = \begin{bmatrix} 1 & 0 & 0 \\ -\dfrac{b_{21}}{b_{11}} & 1 & 0 \\ 0 & 0 & 1 \end{bmatrix}, \quad S_2 = \begin{bmatrix} 1 & 0 & 0 \\ 0 & 1 & 0 \\ -\dfrac{b_{31}}{b_{11}} & 0 & 1 \end{bmatrix},$$

$$S_3 = \begin{bmatrix} 1 & 0 & 0 \\ 0 & 1 & 0 \\ 0 & -\dfrac{b'_{32}}{b'_{22}} & 1 \end{bmatrix}.$$

The operations producing (5.6) from (5.4) can then be expressed as

$$S_3 S_2 S_1 C = \begin{bmatrix} b_{11} & b_{12} & b_{13} & u_1 \\ 0 & b'_{22} & b'_{23} & u'_2 \\ 0 & 0 & b''_{33} & u''_3 \end{bmatrix}.$$

The back-substitution is expressed in terms of premultiplication by elementary matrices of the first and third kinds. Let Q_1, Q_2, and Q_3 denote the three matrices of the first kind which are needed. For example,

$$Q_1 = \begin{bmatrix} 1 & 0 & 0 \\ 0 & 1 & 0 \\ 0 & 0 & \dfrac{1}{b''_{33}} \end{bmatrix}.$$

Then, with three more matrices of the third kind, which we call S_4, S_5, and S_6, the complete sequence of operations results in

$$Q_3 S_6 S_5 Q_2 S_4 Q_1 S_3 S_2 S_1 C = \begin{bmatrix} 1 & 0 & 0 & x_1 \\ 0 & 1 & 0 & x_2 \\ 0 & 0 & 1 & x_3 \end{bmatrix}.$$

Let E denote the product of these nine elementary matrices. Then $EC = E[B \vdots u] = [I \vdots x]$, whence $EB = I$ and $E = B^{-1}$. Hence, as a byproduct of solving equations such as (5.4) by elimination, we see that proper planning can produce B^{-1}. Clearly, we need not solve equations at all if only the inverse is needed, for in that event the column u is superfluous.

Since $EB = I$, $\det(E) \det(B) = \det(I) = 1$. From Section 5.2, the determinant of an S or third-kind elementary matrix is unity, whereas the determinant of a Q or first-kind matrix equals the value of that diagonal element which is usually not unity. Hence $\det(E) = \det(Q_3) \times \det(Q_2) \det(Q_1)$. That is, $\det(E)$ is the product of the diagonal elements (such as $1/b''_{33}$) of the matrices Q_1, Q_2, and Q_3 used in the elimination process. This means that $\det(B)$ is the product of their reciprocals.

The above arithmetic operations can be separated into two types: (*a*) *normalization* steps in which the diagonal elements are converted to unity, and (*b*) *reduction* steps in which the off-diagonal elements are converted to zero.

Note that by augmenting the coefficient matrix with several right-hand side vectors, we can solve several sets of simultaneous equations, each having the same coefficient matrix, at little extra computational cost.

Example. Consider the system of equations

$$2x_1 - 7x_2 + 4x_3 = 9,$$
$$x_1 + 9x_2 - 6x_3 = 1,$$
$$-3x_1 + 8x_2 + 5x_3 = 6,$$

for which the solution is $x_1 = 4$, $x_2 = 1$, and $x_3 = 2$. The augmented matrix $[B \vdots u \vdots I]$ will be formed, and the Gaussian elimination procedure just described will be carried out, except that the normalization steps will be introduced in a somewhat different order. Starting with the matrix,

$$\begin{bmatrix} 2 & -7 & 4 & 9 & 1 & 0 & 0 \\ 1 & 9 & -6 & 1 & 0 & 1 & 0 \\ -3 & 8 & 5 & 6 & 0 & 0 & 1 \end{bmatrix},$$

we multiply the top row by 1/2, add −1 times the new first row to the second row, and 3 times the new first row to the third row. The result is

$$\begin{bmatrix} 1 & -\dfrac{7}{2} & 2 & \dfrac{9}{2} & \dfrac{1}{2} & 0 & 0 \\ 0 & \dfrac{25}{2} & -8 & -\dfrac{7}{2} & -\dfrac{1}{2} & 1 & 0 \\ 0 & -\dfrac{5}{2} & 11 & \dfrac{39}{2} & \dfrac{3}{2} & 0 & 1 \end{bmatrix}. \quad (5.7)$$

This is equivalent to having formed the equations

$$x_1 - \frac{7}{2}x_2 + 2x_3 = \frac{9}{2},$$

$$\frac{25}{2}x_2 - 8x_3 = -\frac{7}{2},$$

$$-\frac{5}{2}x_2 + 11x_3 = \frac{39}{2}.$$

Note that the operations performed are equivalent to the matrix multiplication,

$$\begin{bmatrix} \dfrac{1}{2} & 0 & 0 \\ -\dfrac{1}{2} & 1 & 0 \\ \dfrac{3}{2} & 0 & 1 \end{bmatrix} \begin{bmatrix} 2 & -7 & 4 & 9 & 1 & 0 & 0 \\ 1 & 9 & -6 & 1 & 0 & 1 & 0 \\ -3 & 8 & 5 & 6 & 0 & 0 & 1 \end{bmatrix}$$

which yields as a result

$$\begin{bmatrix} 1 & -\dfrac{7}{2} & 2 & \dfrac{9}{2} & \dfrac{1}{2} & 0 & 0 \\ 0 & \dfrac{25}{2} & -8 & -\dfrac{7}{2} & -\dfrac{1}{2} & 1 & 0 \\ 0 & -\dfrac{5}{2} & 11 & \dfrac{39}{2} & \dfrac{3}{2} & 0 & 1 \end{bmatrix}.$$

Returning to (5.7), multiply the second row by 2/25, and then add 5/2 times the new second row to the third row. The result is:

$$\begin{bmatrix} 1 & -\dfrac{7}{2} & 2 & \dfrac{9}{2} & \dfrac{1}{2} & 0 & 0 \\[2ex] 0 & 1 & -\dfrac{16}{25} & -\dfrac{7}{25} & -\dfrac{1}{25} & \dfrac{2}{25} & 0 \\[2ex] 0 & 0 & \dfrac{47}{5} & \dfrac{94}{5} & \dfrac{7}{5} & \dfrac{1}{5} & 1 \end{bmatrix}.$$

The *forward course* has now been completed and, corresponding to (5.6), we may write

$$x_1 - \frac{7}{2} x_2 + 2x_3 = \frac{9}{2},$$

$$x_2 - \frac{16}{25} x_3 = -\frac{7}{25},$$

$$\frac{47}{5} x_3 = \frac{94}{5}.$$

To carry out the back-substitution, start by multiplying the last row by 5/47. Then multiply the new last row by 16/25 and add to the second row. Multiply this same last row by −2 and add to the first row. The result is

$$\begin{bmatrix} 1 & -\dfrac{7}{2} & 0 & \dfrac{1}{2} & \dfrac{19}{94} & -\dfrac{2}{47} & -\dfrac{10}{47} \\[2ex] 0 & 1 & 0 & 1 & \dfrac{13}{235} & \dfrac{22}{235} & \dfrac{16}{235} \\[2ex] 0 & 0 & 1 & 2 & \dfrac{7}{47} & \dfrac{1}{47} & \dfrac{5}{47} \end{bmatrix}.$$

Finally, multiply the second row by 7/2 and add to the first. The result is

$$\begin{bmatrix} 1 & 0 & 0 & 4 & \dfrac{93}{235} & \dfrac{67}{235} & \dfrac{6}{235} \\[2ex] 0 & 1 & 0 & 1 & \dfrac{13}{235} & \dfrac{22}{235} & \dfrac{16}{235} \\[2ex] 0 & 0 & 1 & 2 & \dfrac{7}{47} & \dfrac{1}{47} & \dfrac{5}{47} \end{bmatrix}.$$

This means, of course, that $x_1 = 4$, $x_2 = 1$, $x_3 = 2$ and the inverse of the matrix of coefficients is

$$\begin{bmatrix} \dfrac{93}{235} & \dfrac{67}{235} & \dfrac{6}{235} \\[2ex] \dfrac{13}{235} & \dfrac{22}{235} & \dfrac{16}{235} \\[2ex] \dfrac{7}{47} & \dfrac{1}{47} & \dfrac{5}{47} \end{bmatrix}.$$

The determinant of the coefficient matrix **B** equals the product of the reciprocals of the diagonal elements appearing in the **Q**-type matrices involved in the above transformation.

Inspection shows that the relevant diagonal elements are simply the multiplying factors used in the normalization steps, so that

$$\det \mathbf{B} = \left[\frac{1}{2} \times \frac{2}{25} \times \frac{5}{47} \right]^{-1} = 235.$$

5.4 Gauss–Jordan Elimination

A variation that accomplishes the effect of back-substitution simultaneously with the reduction of the subdiagonal elements will now be illustrated, again for the system,

$$2x_1 - 7x_2 + 4x_3 = 9,$$
$$x_1 + 9x_2 - 6x_3 = 1,$$
$$-3x_1 + 8x_2 + 5x_3 = 6.$$

Suppose that $\mathbf{B}^{-1}$ is required and form the augmented matrix $[\mathbf{B} \mid \mathbf{u} \mid \mathbf{I}]$:

$$\begin{bmatrix} 2 & -7 & 4 & 9 & 1 & 0 & 0 \\ 1 & 9 & -6 & 1 & 0 & 1 & 0 \\ -3 & 8 & 5 & 6 & 0 & 0 & 1 \end{bmatrix}.$$

As before, normalize the first row by dividing by the *pivot* element 2; then reduce the remaining elements of the first column to zero by subtracting the new first row from the second row, and also by subtracting −3 times the new first row from the third row. The result is

$$\begin{bmatrix} 1 & -\dfrac{7}{2} & 2 & \dfrac{9}{2} & \dfrac{1}{2} & 0 & 0 \\[2ex] 0 & \dfrac{25}{2} & -8 & -\dfrac{7}{2} & -\dfrac{1}{2} & 1 & 0 \\[2ex] 0 & -\dfrac{5}{2} & 11 & \dfrac{39}{2} & \dfrac{3}{2} & 0 & 1 \end{bmatrix}.$$

Next, normalize the second row by dividing by the pivot element 25/2; then reduce the remaining elements of the second column to zero by subtracting $-(7/2)$ times the new second row from the first row, and $-(5/2)$ times the new second row from the third row. Note that the reduction process now involves both the subdiagonal *and* superdiagonal elements. The result is

$$\begin{bmatrix} 1 & 0 & -\dfrac{6}{25} & \dfrac{88}{25} & \dfrac{9}{25} & \dfrac{7}{25} & 0 \\[2ex] 0 & 1 & -\dfrac{16}{25} & -\dfrac{7}{25} & -\dfrac{1}{25} & \dfrac{2}{25} & 0 \\[2ex] 0 & 0 & \dfrac{47}{5} & \dfrac{94}{5} & \dfrac{7}{5} & \dfrac{1}{5} & 1 \end{bmatrix}.$$

Finally, normalize the last row by dividing by the pivot element 47/5; then reduce the remaining elements of the third column to zero by subtracting $-(6/25)$ and $-(16/25)$

times the new third row from the first and second rows, respectively. The resulting matrix is $[\mathbf{I} \mid \mathbf{x} \mid \mathbf{B}^{-1}]$, where $\mathbf{x}$ is the solution vector, and $\mathbf{B}^{-1}$ is the inverse of the original matrix of coefficients:

$$\begin{bmatrix} 1 & 0 & 0 & 4 & \dfrac{93}{235} & \dfrac{67}{235} & \dfrac{6}{235} \\ 0 & 1 & 0 & 1 & \dfrac{13}{235} & \dfrac{22}{235} & \dfrac{16}{235} \\ 0 & 0 & 1 & 2 & \dfrac{7}{47} & \dfrac{1}{47} & \dfrac{5}{47} \end{bmatrix}.$$

The determinant of the original coefficient matrix is again the product of the pivot elements and thus equals $2 \times 25/2 \times 47/5$ or 235.

We conclude this section by developing an algorithm for the above procedure, which is called *Gauss-Jordan elimination*. Let the starting array be the $n \times (n + m)$ augmented matrix $\mathbf{A}$, consisting of an $n \times n$ coefficient matrix with m appended columns:

$$\begin{bmatrix} a_{11} & a_{12} & \cdots & a_{1n} & a_{1,n+1} & a_{1,n+2} & \cdots & a_{1,n+m} \\ a_{21} & a_{22} & \cdots & a_{2n} & a_{2,n+1} & a_{2,n+2} & \cdots & a_{2,n+m} \\ \vdots & \vdots & & \vdots & \vdots & \vdots & & \vdots \\ a_{n1} & a_{n2} & \cdots & a_{nn} & a_{n,n+1} & a_{n,n+2} & \cdots & a_{n,n+m} \end{bmatrix}.$$

Let $k = 1, 2, \ldots, n$ be the pivot counter, so that a_{kk} is the pivot element for the kth pass of the reduction. It is understood that the values of the elements of $\mathbf{A}$ will be modified during computation. The algorithm is

Normalization

$$a_{kj} \leftarrow \frac{a_{kj}}{a_{kk}}, \qquad j = n + m, n + m - 1, \ldots, k$$

Reduction

$$\left.\begin{array}{l} a_{ij} \leftarrow a_{ij} - a_{ik}a_{kj}, \\ j = n + m, n + m - 1, \ldots, k \end{array}\right\} \begin{array}{l} i = 1, 2, \ldots, n \\ (i \neq k) \end{array} \right\} k = 1, 2, \ldots, n. \qquad (5.8)$$

Note (*a*) Since no nonzero elements appear to the left of a_{kk} in the kth row at the beginning of the kth pass, it is unnecessary to normalize a_{kj} for $j < k$; (*b*) In order to avoid premature modification of elements in the pivot column, the column counter j is always decremented from its highest value $(n + m)$ until the pivot column is reached.

Thus far, elementary matrices of the second kind have not been used; neither has mention been made of the fact that at some stage, say the first, a potential divisor or pivot, such as b_{11}, may be zero. In this event, we can think of interchanging rows, which is expressible, of course, in terms of elementary row operations of the second kind. A related problem is that of maintaining sufficient accuracy during intermediate calculations in order to achieve specified accuracy in the final results. This might be expected for a nearly singular system; it can also happen when the magnitude of one of the pivot elements is relatively small. Consider, for instance, the system

$$0.0003\, x_1 + 3.0000\, x_2 = 2.0001,$$
$$1.0000\, x_1 + 1.0000\, x_2 = 1.0000,$$

which has the exact solution $x_1 = 1/3$, $x_2 = 2/3$. If the equations are solved using pivots on the matrix diagonal, as indicated in the previous examples, there results

$$1.0000\, x_1 + 10000\, x_2 = 6667,$$
$$x_2 = 6666/9999.$$

If x_2 from the second equation is taken to be 0.6667, then from the first equation $x_1 = 0.0000$; for $x_2 = 0.66667$, $x_1 = 0.30000$; for $x_2 = 0.666667$, $x_1 = 0.330000$, etc. The solution depends highly on the number of figures retained. If the equations are solved in reverse order, that is, by interchanging the two rows and proceeding as before, then x_2 is found to be $1.9998/2.9997 \doteq 0.66667$ while $x_1 = 0.33333$. This example indicates the advisa-

bility of choosing as the pivot the coefficient of largest absolute value in a column, rather than merely the first in line. The handling of the situation is developed in more detail in Example 5.2.

EXAMPLE 5.1

GAUSS-JORDAN REDUCTION
VOLTAGES AND CURRENTS IN AN ELECTRICAL NETWORK

Problem Statement

Write a program that implements the Gauss-Jordan elimination algorithm outlined in (5.8) to solve n simultaneous linear equations. The program should allow concurrent solution for m solution vectors.

As one of the data sets for the program, use the linear equations whose solutions are the potentials at nodes (junctions) 1 through 6 in the electrical network of Fig. 5.1.1. The values of the resistances are shown in ohms, and the potential applied between A and B is 100 volts.

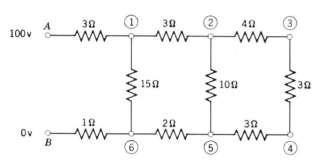

Figure 5.1.1 *Electrical network*

Method of Solution

The reduction algorithm: The starting matrix $\mathbf{A} = (a_{ij})$ is assumed to be the $n \times (n + m)$ augmented matrix of coefficients of page 273, where the column vectors $\mathbf{a}_j = [a_{1j}, a_{2j}, \ldots, a_{nj}]^t$, for $j = 1, 2, \ldots, n$, correspond to the matrix $\mathbf{B}$ of (5.3). The vectors $\mathbf{a}_j$, for $j = n + 1$, $n + 2, \ldots, n + m$, are m right-hand side vectors for which solutions are desired.

The *diagonal pivot strategy* of (5.8), that uses, as the n pivot elements, the elements along the main diagonal of the matrix of coefficients (the first n columns of $\mathbf{A}$) leads to the transformation

$$\mathbf{A} \leftarrow \mathbf{B}^{-1}\mathbf{A}. \qquad (5.1.1)$$

Here, as in (5.8), the left arrow is intended to mean *substitution in place*. The first n columns of $\mathbf{A}$ are transformed to the identity matrix $\mathbf{I}$ (the n unit vectors, in order), while the column vectors, $\mathbf{a}_j, j = n + 1, \ldots, n + m$, are transformed to the solution vectors $\mathbf{B}^{-1}\mathbf{a}_j$. Note that if any of the appended columns, $\mathbf{a}_j, j = n + 1, \ldots, n + m$, are unit vectors initially, then the transformation (5.1.1) leads to the corresponding columns of the inverse of the matrix of coefficients, $\mathbf{B}^{-1}$, as illustrated by the example of Section 5.4.

If a variable d is initialized with the value 1 before the elimination algorithm is begun, then it may be updated

with each cycle of the algorithm, to yield the determinant of $\mathbf{B}$ upon completion of the nth cycle. The complete algorithm is

Initialization

$$d \leftarrow 1$$

Updating the determinant

$$d \leftarrow d\, a_{kk}$$

Normalization

$$a_{kj} \leftarrow a_{kj}/a_{kk},$$
$$j = n + m, n + m - 1, \ldots, k$$

$\left.\rule{0pt}{8em}\right\} k = 1, 2, \ldots, n.$

Reduction

$$a_{ij} \leftarrow a_{ij} - a_{ik}a_{kj},$$
$$\begin{cases} j = n + m, n + m - 1, \ldots, k \\ i = 1, 2, \ldots, n \\ i \neq k \end{cases}$$

Should a_{ik} already be equal to zero, the reduction step for the ith row may be ignored.

A zero or very small pivot element may be encountered in the elimination process (this may or may not indicate that the coefficient matrix in the first n columns of $\mathbf{A}$ is singular or nearly singular). A test for pivot magnitude,

$$|a_{kk}| > \varepsilon, \qquad (5.1.2)$$

is made before the normalization step for the kth cycle, $k = 1, 2, \ldots, n$, to insure against extremely small divisors in normalization. If test (5.1.2) is failed, computation is stopped for the offending set of equations.

Electrical network equations: From *Ohm's Law*, I_{pq}, the current flowing from node p to node q in leg pq of the network, is given by

$$I_{pq} = \frac{v_p - v_q}{R_{pq}}, \qquad (5.1.3)$$

where v_p and v_q are the voltages at nodes p and q, respectively, and R_{pq} is the resistance of leg pq. For R_{pq} in units of ohms (Ω), the current is given in amperes. The equations relating the voltages at the nodes of the network may be found by applying *Kirchoff's Current Law*: the sum of the currents arriving at each node must be zero. This is simply a conservation law for charge, and indicates that current may not be accumulated or generated at any node of the network. Application of these two

Example 5.1   Gauss-Jordan Reduction   **275**

laws at node 1 leads to

$$I_{A1} + I_{21} + I_{61} = \frac{100 - v_1}{3} + \frac{v_2 - v_1}{3} + \frac{v_6 - v_1}{15} = 0$$

or

$$11v_1 - 5v_2 - v_6 = 500.$$

Similar equations may be written for each of the nodes in the network, leading to the system of six simultaneous linear equations:

Node	Equation					
1	$11v_1 -$	$5v_2$			$- v_6$	$= 500$
2	$-20v_1 +$	$41v_2 - 15v_3$		$- 6v_5$		$= 0$
3		$- 3v_2 +$	$7v_3 - 4v_4$			$= 0$
4			$- v_3 + 2v_4 -$	v_5		$= 0$
5		$- 3v_2$	$- 10v_4 +$	$28v_5 - 15v_6$		$= 0$
6	$- 2v_1$			$- 15v_5 + 47v_6$		$= 0$

(5.1.4)

Flow Diagram

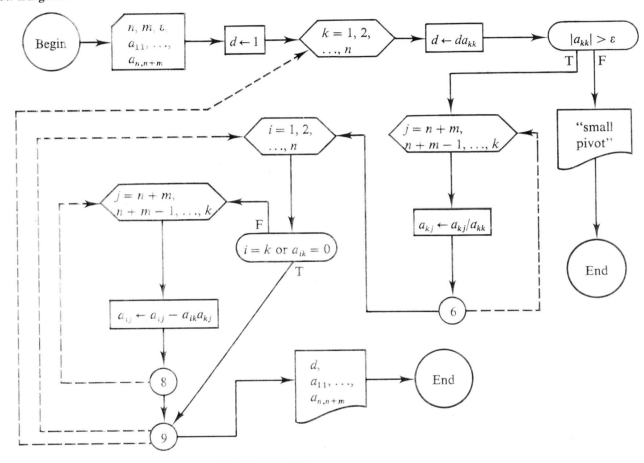

FORTRAN *Implementation*

List of Principal Variables

Program Symbol	Definition
A	Augmented matrix of coefficients, $\mathbf{A} = (a_{ij})$.
DETER	d, determinant of the original coefficient matrix (the first n columns of $\mathbf{A}$).
EPS	Minimum allowable magnitude, ε, for a pivot element.
I, J	Row and column subscripts, i and j.
K	Cycle counter and pivot element subscript, k.
KP1	$k + 1$.
M	Number of solution vectors, m.
N	Number of equations, n.
NPLUSM	$n + m$.

Program Listing

```
C              APPLIED NUMERICAL METHODS, EXAMPLE 5.1
C              GAUSS-JORDAN REDUCTION
C
C              THIS PROGRAM FINDS M SOLUTION VECTORS CORRESPONDING
C              TO A SET OF N SIMULTANEOUS LINEAR EQUATIONS USING THE GAUSS-
C              JORDAN REDUCTION ALGORITHM WITH THE DIAGONAL PIVOT STRATEGY.
C              THE N BY N MATRIX OF COEFFICIENTS APPEARS IN THE FIRST N
C              COLUMNS OF THE MATRIX A. M RIGHT-HAND SIDE VECTORS ARE
C              APPENDED AS THE (N+1)TH TO (N+M)TH COLUMNS OF A.  ON THE
C              K(TH) PASS OF THE ELIMINATION SCHEME, K(TH) ROW ELEMENTS ARE
C              NORMALIZED BY DIVIDING BY THE PIVOT ELEMENT A(K,K).  DETER,
C              THE DETERMINANT OF THE COEFFICIENT MATRIX, IS UPDATED PRIOR
C              TO ELIMINATION OF ALL NONZERO ELEMENTS (EXCEPT FOR THE PIVOT
C              ELEMENT) IN THE K(TH) COLUMN.  SHOULD A PIVOT ELEMENT BE
C              ENCOUNTERED WHICH IS SMALLER IN MAGNITUDE THAN EPS, COMPUTATION
C              IS DISCONTINUED AND AN APPROPRIATE COMMENT IS PRINTED.
C              THE SOLUTION VECTORS CORRESPONDING TO THE ORIGINAL RIGHT-
C              HAND SIDE VECTORS ARE STORED IN COLUMNS N+1 TO N+M OF A.
C
       IMPLICIT  REAL*8(A-H, O-Z)
       DIMENSION A(50,51)
C
    1  READ (5,100) N,M,EPS
       NPLUSM = N + M
       WRITE (6,200) N,M,EPS,N,NPLUSM
       DO 2   I = 1, N
       READ (5,101) (A(I,J),J=1,NPLUSM)
    2  WRITE (6,201) (A(I,J),J=1,NPLUSM)
C
C      ..... BEGIN ELIMINATION PROCEDURE .....
       DETER = 1.
       DO 9   K = 1, N
C
C      ..... UPDATE THE DETERMINANT VALUE .....
       DETER = DETER*A(K,K)
C
C      ..... CHECK FOR PIVOT ELEMENT TOO SMALL .....
       IF(DABS(A(K,K)).GT.EPS )    GO TO 5
          WRITE (6,202)
          GO TO 1
C
C      ..... NORMALIZE THE PIVOT ROW .....
    5  KP1 = K + 1
       DO 6   J = KP1, NPLUSM
    6  A(K,J) = A(K,J)/A(K,K)
       A(K,K) = 1.
C
C      ..... ELIMINATE K(TH) COLUMN ELEMENTS EXCEPT FOR PIVOT .....
       DO 9   I = 1, N
       IF ( I.EQ.K .OR. A(I,K).EQ.0. )    GO TO 9
          DO 8   J = KP1, NPLUSM
    8     A(I,J) = A(I,J) - A(I,K)*A(K,J)
          A(I,K) = 0.
    9  CONTINUE
C
       WRITE (6,203) DETER,N,NPLUSM
       DO 10 I = 1, N
   10  WRITE (6,201) (A(I,J),J=1,NPLUSM)
       GO TO 1
C
C      ..... FORMATS FOR INPUT AND OUTPUT STATEMENTS .....
  100  FORMAT ( 2(10X, I2, 8X), 10X, E7.1 )
  101  FORMAT ( 20X, 5F10.5 )
  200  FORMAT ( 10H1N      = , I8 / 10H M       = , I8 / 10H EPS     = ,
      1 1PE14.1/22H0             A(1,1)...A(, I2, 1H,, I2, 1H) / 1H  )
  201  FORMAT ( 1H , 7F13.7 )
  202  FORMAT ( 37H0SMALL PIVOT - MATRIX MAY BE SINGULAR )
  203  FORMAT ( 10H0DETER  = , E14.6/ 22H0              A(1,1)...A(, I2, 1H,,
      1  I2, 1H) / 1H  )
C
       END
```

Example 5.1   Gauss-Jordan Reduction   **277**

Program Listing (*Continued*)

Data

```
N     =    3          M     =    4          EPS   =   1.0E-10
A(1,1)...A(1,5) =      2.00000   -7.00000    4.00000   9.00000    1.00000
A(1,6)...A(1,7) =      0.00000    0.00000
A(2,1)...A(2,5) =      1.00000    9.00000   -6.00000   1.00000    0.00000
A(2,6)...A(2,7) =      1.00000    0.00000
A(3,1)...A(3,5) =     -3.00000    8.00000    5.00000   6.00000    0.00000
A(3,6)...A(3,7) =      0.00000    1.00000
N     =    3          M     =    4          EPS   =   1.0E-10
A(1,1)...A(1,5) =      2.00000   -7.00000    4.00000   9.00000    1.00000
A(1,6)...A(1,7) =      0.00000    0.00000
A(2,1)...A(2,5) =     -3.00000    8.00000    5.00000   6.00000    0.00000
A(2,6)...A(2,7) =      1.00000    0.00000
A(3,1)...A(3,5) =      1.00000    9.00000   -6.00000   1.00000    0.00000
A(3,6)...A(3,7) =      0.00000    1.00000
N     =    3          M     =    4          EPS   =   1.0E-10
A(1,1)...A(1,5) =      1.00000    9.00000   -6.00000   1.00000    1.00000
A(1,6)...A(1,7) =      0.00000    0.00000
A(2,1)...A(2,5) =      2.00000   -7.00000    4.00000   9.00000    0.00000
A(2,6)...A(2,7) =      1.00000    0.00000
A(3,1)...A(3,5) =      2.00000   -7.00000    4.00000   9.00000    0.00000
A(3,6)...A(3,7) =      0.00000    1.00000
N     =    3          M     =    4          EPS   =   1.0E-20
A(1,1)...A(1,5) =      0.00000   -7.00000    4.00000   1.00000    1.00000
A(1,6)...A(1,7) =      0.00000    0.00000
A(2,1)...A(2,5) =      1.00000    9.00000   -6.00000   1.00000    0.00000
A(2,6)...A(2,7) =      1.00000    0.00000
A(3,1)...A(3,5) =     -3.00000    8.00000    5.00000   6.00000    0.00000
A(3,6)...A(3,7) =      0.00000    1.00000
N     =    3          M     =    4          EPS   =   1.0E-20
A(1,1)...A(1,5) =      1.00000    9.00000   -6.00000   1.00000    1.00000
A(1,6)...A(1,7) =      0.00000    0.00000
A(2,1)...A(2,5) =      0.00000   -7.00000    4.00000   1.00000    0.00000
A(2,6)...A(2,7) =      1.00000    0.00000
A(3,1)...A(3,5) =     -3.00000    8.00000    5.00000   6.00000    0.00000
A(3,6)...A(3,7) =      0.00000    1.00000
N     =    6          M     =    1          EPS   =   1.0E-20
A(1,1)...A(1,5) =     11.00000   -5.00000    0.00000   0.00000    0.00000
A(1,6)...A(1,7) =     -1.00000  500.00000
A(2,1)...A(2,5) =    -20.00000   41.00000  -15.00000   0.00000   -6.00000
A(2,6)...A(2,7) =      0.00000    0.00000
A(3,1)...A(3,5) =      0.00000   -3.00000    7.00000  -4.00000    0.00000
A(3,6)...A(3,7) =      0.00000    0.00000
A(4,1)...A(4,5) =      0.00000    0.00000   -1.00000   2.00000   -1.00000
A(4,6)...A(4,7) =      0.00000    0.00000
A(5,1)...A(5,5) =      0.00000   -3.00000    0.00000 -10.00000   28.00000
A(5,6)...A(5,7) =    -15.00000    0.00000
A(6,1)...A(6,5) =     -2.00000    0.00000    0.00000   0.00000  -15.00000
A(6,6)...A(6,7) =     47.00000    0.00000
N     =    2          M     =    3          EPS   =   1.0E-20
A(1,1)...A(1,5) =      1.00000    1.00000    1.00000   1.00000    0.00000
A(2,1)...A(2,5) =      0.00003    3.00000    2.900001  0.00000    1.00000
N     =    2          M     =    3          EPS   =   1.0E-20
A(1,1)...A(1,5) =      0.00003    3.00000    2.900001  1.00000    0.00000
A(2,1)...A(2,5) =      1.00000    1.00000    1.00000   0.00000    1.00000
```

Computer Output

Results for the 1st Data Set

```
N     =        3
M     =        4
EPS   =        1.0D-10

          A(1,1)...A( 3, 7)
```

Computer Output (*Continued*)

```
      2.0000000     -7.0000000      4.0000000      9.0000000      1.0000000      0.0            0.0
      1.0000000      9.0000000     -6.0000000      1.0000000      0.0            1.0000000      0.0
     -3.0000000      8.0000000      5.0000000      6.0000000      0.0            0.0            1.0000000

   DETER  =    0.235000D 03

                 A(1,1)...A( 3,  7)

      1.0000000      0.0            0.0            4.0000000      0.3957447      0.2851064      0.0255319
      0.0            1.0000000      0.0            1.0000000      0.0553191      0.0936170      0.0680851
      0.0            0.0            1.0000000      2.0000000      0.1489362      0.0212766      0.1063830
```

Results for the 2nd Data Set

```
   N      =        3
   M      =        4
   EPS    =        1.0D-10

                 A(1,1)...A( 3,  7)

      2.0000000     -7.0000000      4.0000000      9.0000000      1.0000000      0.0            0.0
     -3.0000000      8.0000000      5.0000000      6.0000000      0.0            1.0000000      0.0
      1.0000000      9.0000000     -6.0000000      1.0000000      0.0            0.0            1.0000000

   DETER  =   -0.235000D 03

                 A(1,1)...A( 3,  7)

      1.0000000      0.0            0.0            4.0000000      0.3957447      0.0255319      0.2851064
      0.0            1.0000000      0.0            1.0000000      0.0553191      0.0680851      0.0936170
      0.0            0.0            1.0000000      2.0000000      0.1489362      0.1063830      0.0212766
```

Results for the 3rd Data Set

```
   N      =        3
   M      =        4
   EPS    =        1.0D-10

                 A(1,1)...A( 3,  7)

      1.0000000      9.0000000     -6.0000000      1.0000000      1.0000000      0.0            0.0
      2.0000000     -7.0000000      4.0000000      9.0000000      0.0            1.0000000      0.0
      2.0000000     -7.0000000      4.0000000      9.0000000      0.0            0.0            1.0000000

   SMALL PIVOT - MATRIX MAY BE SINGULAR
```

Results for the 4th Data Set

```
   N      =        3
   M      =        4
   EPS    =        1.0D-20

                 A(1,1)...A( 3,  7)

      0.0           -7.0000000      4.0000000      1.0000000      1.0000000      0.0            0.0
      1.0000000      9.0000000     -6.0000000      1.0000000      0.0            1.0000000      0.0
     -3.0000000      8.0000000      5.0000000      6.0000000      0.0            0.0            1.0000000

   SMALL PIVOT - MATRIX MAY BE SINGULAR
```

Example 5.1   Gauss-Jordan Reduction   **279**

Computer Output (*Continued*)

Results for the 5th Data Set

```
N      =        3
M      =        4
EPS    =        1.0D-20

           A(1,1)...A( 3,  7)

      1.0000000      9.0000000     -6.0000000      1.0000000      1.0000000      0.0            0.0
      0.0           -7.0000000      4.0000000      1.0000000      0.0            1.0000000      0.0
     -3.0000000      8.0000000      5.0000000      6.0000000      0.0            0.0            1.0000000

DETER  =   -0.490000D 02

           A(1,1)...A( 3,  7)

      1.0000000      0.0            0.0            4.0000000      1.3673469      1.8979592      0.1224490
      0.0            1.0000000      0.0            1.0000000      0.2448980      0.2653061      0.0816327
      0.0            0.0            1.0000000      2.0000000      0.4285714      0.7142857      0.1428571
```

Results for the 6th Data Set

```
N      =        6
M      =        1
EPS    =        1.0D-20

           A(1,1)...A( 6,  7)

     11.0000000     -5.0000000      0.0            0.0            0.0           -1.0000000    500.0000000
    -20.0000000     41.0000000    -15.0000000      0.0           -6.0000000      0.0            0.0
      0.0           -3.0000000      7.0000000     -4.0000000      0.0            0.0            0.0
      0.0            0.0           -1.0000000      2.0000000     -1.0000000      0.0            0.0
      0.0           -3.0000000      0.0          -10.0000000     28.0000000    -15.0000000      0.0
     -2.0000000      0.0            0.0            0.0          -15.0000000     47.0000000      0.0

DETER  =    0.150000D 07

           A(1,1)...A( 6,  7)

      1.0000000      0.0            0.0            0.0            0.0            0.0           70.0000000
      0.0            1.0000000      0.0            0.0            0.0            0.0           52.0000000
      0.0            0.0            1.0000000      0.0            0.0            0.0           40.0000000
      0.0            0.0            0.0            1.0000000      0.0            0.0           31.0000000
      0.0            0.0            0.0            0.0            1.0000000      0.0           22.0000000
      0.0            0.0            0.0            0.0            0.0            1.0000000      10.0000000
```

Results for the 7th Data Set (*double precision*)

```
N      =        2
M      =        3
EPS    =        1.0D-20

           A(1,1)...A( 2,  5)

      1.0000000      1.0000000      1.0000000      1.0000000      0.0
      0.0000300      3.0000000      2.9000010      0.0            1.0000000

DETER  =    0.299997D 01

           A(1,1)...A( 2,  5)

      1.0000000      0.0            0.0333333      1.0000100     -0.3333367
      0.0            1.0000000      0.9666667     -0.0000100      0.3333367
```

Computer Output (*Continued*)

Results for the 8th Data Set (*double precision*)

```
N       =           2
M       =           3
EPS     =           1.0D-20

            A(1,1)...A( 2, 5)

    0.0000300     3.0000000     2.9000010     1.0000000     0.0
    1.0000000     1.0000000     1.0000000     0.0           1.0000000

DETER  =  -0.299997D 01

            A(1,1)...A( 2, 5)

    1.0000000     0.0           0.0333333    -0.3333367     1.0000100
    0.0           1.0000000     0.9666667     0.3333367    -0.0000100
```

Results for the 7th Data Set (*single precision*)

```
N       =           2
M       =           3
EPS     =           1.0E-20

            A(1,1)...A( 2, 5)

    1.0000000     1.0000000     1.0000000     1.0000000     0.0
    0.0000300     3.0000000     2.9000006     0.0           1.0000000

DETER  =   0.299997E 01

            A(1,1)...A( 2, 5)

    1.0000000     0.0           0.0333335     1.0000095    -0.3333367
    0.0           1.0000000     0.9666665    -0.0000100     0.3333367
```

Results for the 8th Data Set (*single precision*)

```
N       =           2
M       =           3
EPS     =           1.0E-20

            A(1,1)...A( 2, 5)

    0.0000300     3.0000000     2.9000006     1.0000000     0.0
    1.0000000     1.0000000     1.0000000     0.0           1.0000000

DETER  =  -0.299997E 01

            A(1,1)...A( 2, 5)

    1.0000000     0.0           0.0625000    -0.3281250     1.0000095
    0.0           1.0000000     0.9666665     0.3333367    -0.0000100
```

Example 5.1 Gauss-Jordan Reduction **281**

Discussion of Results

Except for the last two sets of results shown in the computer output, all calculations were done using double-precision arithmetic. The first data set consists of the three equations used as the illustrative example in Section 5.4. The starting matrix **A** consists of the coefficient matrix **B** and four right-hand side vectors, including the three unit vectors in order, that is,

$$\mathbf{A} = [\mathbf{B} \mathop{|} \mathbf{u} \mathop{|} \mathbf{I}].$$

After the transformations resulting from the Gauss-Jordan algorithm using the diagonal pivot strategy, the final **A** matrix contains

$$\mathbf{A} = [\mathbf{I} \mathop{|} \mathbf{x} \mathop{|} \mathbf{B}^{-1}].$$

The second data set is for the same set of equations, except that the first two are interchanged. The solutions, **x**, are identical with those for the first data set, but, of course, the inverse matrix $\mathbf{B}^{-1}$ is different.

The third data set contains two identical equations, so that the coefficient matrix, **B**, is singular, and $\mathbf{B}^{-1}$ does not exist. This singularity will cause a zero pivot element (or, allowing for some round-off error, a pivot element of very small magnitude) to be encountered at some stage of the algorithm, in this case, during the third cycle.

The fourth data set consists of three equations; x_1 does not appear in the first equation. Since $a_{11} = 0$, the potential pivot for the first cycle fails the pivot magnitude test (5.1.2), and the comment regarding possible singularity of the coefficient matrix is printed. In fact, the coefficient matrix is not singular, as evidenced by the results for the fifth data set, in which the first two of the equations for the fourth data set have been interchanged. This illustrates one of the important weaknesses of the diagonal pivot strategy, that is, the appearance of a very small pivot element on the diagonal does not necessarily mean that the coefficient matrix is singular. By reordering the rows (equations) or columns (variables) of the matrix, it may be possible to find n pivot elements of significant magnitude; if this is possible the matrix is not singular and the equations have a unique solution, even though the right-hand side vector may be the null vector (the equations would be homogeneous in that case).

The sixth data set contains the equations of (5.1.4) describing the unknown potentials at the six nodes of the electrical network shown in Figure 5.1.1. The solutions in volts are

$$
\begin{aligned}
v_1 &= 70 \\
v_2 &= 52 \\
v_3 &= 40 \\
v_4 &= 31 \\
v_5 &= 22 \\
v_6 &= 10.
\end{aligned}
$$

Results for the seventh data set are shown for calculations done in both double- and single-precision arithmetic. For the IBM 360/67, single- and double-precision word sizes are the equivalent of 6-7 and 15-16 decimal digits, respectively. The equations are

$$
\begin{aligned}
x_1 + x_2 &= 1 \\
0.00003x_1 + 3x_2 &= 2.900001.
\end{aligned} \tag{5.1.5}
$$

The solutions are

$$
\begin{aligned}
x_1 &= 1/30 \\
x_2 &= 29/30.
\end{aligned} \tag{5.1.6}
$$

The results for the seventh data set using double-precision arithmetic are accurate to the seven decimal places shown in the computer output. Results for single-precision computations on the same data set are somewhat less accurate, with five or six figure agreement in most cases. Note that the number 2.900001 has been approximated as 2.9000006; the seventh decimal digit cannot be entered accurately because of the word-size limitation.

The eighth data set is identical with the seventh, except that the two equations are interchanged, leading to the system:

$$
\begin{aligned}
0.00003x_1 + 3x_2 &= 2.900001 \\
x_1 + x_2 &= 1.
\end{aligned} \tag{5.1.7}
$$

The solutions are again given by (5.1.6). Results for the double-precision calculations are again exact to the number of figures shown in the output, that is,

$$
\begin{aligned}
x_1 &= 0.0333333 \\
x_2 &= 0.9666667.
\end{aligned}
$$

For the single-precision calculations, however, the computed results are

$$
\begin{aligned}
x_1 &= 0.0625000 \\
x_2 &= 0.9666665.
\end{aligned}
$$

The almost meaningless value computed for x_1 results from the use of the very tiny (compared with other coefficients) pivot on the first cycle, $a_{11} = 0.00003$, as discussed in Section 5.4. This unfortunate proneness to error of the diagonal pivot strategy for some systems of equations can be overcome often, though not always, by arranging the equations to produce diagonal dominance in the coefficient matrix. This simply means that the magnitudes of the coefficients on the main diagonal of the coefficient matrix should be as large as possible, relative to the off-diagonal elements. An alternative (and preferred) strategy is to modify the Gauss-Jordan reduction scheme to allow in effect row and/or column interchanges to insure that selected pivots are those available elements of greatest magnitude. This approach, known as the *maximum pivot strategy*, will be developed in Example 5.2.

EXAMPLE 5.2

CALCULATION OF THE INVERSE MATRIX USING THE MAXIMUM PIVOT STRATEGY
MEMBER FORCES IN A PLANE TRUSS

Problem Statement

Write a function named SIMUL that solves a set of n simultaneous linear equations,

$$
\begin{aligned}
a_{11}x_1 + a_{12}x_2 + \cdots + a_{1n}x_n &= a_{1,n+1} \\
a_{21}x_1 + a_{22}x_2 + \cdots + a_{2n}x_n &= a_{2,n+1} \\
\vdots \qquad\qquad \vdots \qquad \vdots & \qquad\qquad (5.2.1) \\
a_{n1}x_1 + a_{n2}x_2 + \cdots + a_{nn}x_n &= a_{n,n+1}
\end{aligned}
$$

using Gauss-Jordan reduction with the maximum pivot strategy, described in the next section. The subroutine should have three alternative modes of operation, controlled by one of its arguments:

Mode 1. The equations of (5.2.1) should be solved and the solutions saved, in order, in a vector **x**.

Mode 2. The equations should be solved as in mode 1. In addition, the inverse of the matrix of coefficients should be calculated "in place," that is, the inverse should be overstored in the first n columns of the matrix **A**, without use of any auxiliary matrices (see next section).

Mode 3. In this case, the matrix **A** contains only n columns. The inverse should be computed "in place" as in mode 2.

In each case, the value of SIMUL should be the determinant of the matrix of coefficients.

Write a main program to test SIMUL. As one of the data sets for the program, use the linear equations whose solutions are the member forces in the statically determinate, simply supported, eleven-member plane truss shown in Fig. 5.2.1.

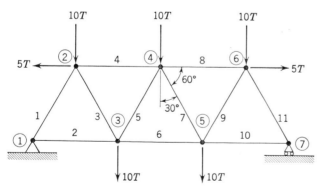

Figure 5.2.1 *Statically determinate, simply supported, eleven-member plane truss.*

The Maximum Pivot Strategy

In the Gauss-Jordan reduction with the diagonal pivot strategy, discussed in Section 5.4, and implemented in computer program form in Example 5.1, the pivot for the kth cycle is chosen to be the element in the a_{kk} position, that is, an element on the diagonal. As discussed in Example 5.1, this strategy can lead to computational difficulty for some systems of equations. Should a_{kk} be equal to zero, then the normalization steps of the algorithm must not be carried out. When a_{kk} is of relatively small magnitude when compared with other elements in the first n columns of **A**, the normalization and reduction operations can often be carried out; but computed results may be inaccurate because of round-off error (see results for the eighth data set in Example 5.1).

In such cases, provided that the matrix of coefficients is not near-singular, it is usually possible to overcome the problem by rearranging the rows or columns of the coefficient matrix; this is equivalent to reordering the equations or renumbering the variables, respectively. An alternative possibility is to choose *any* element of significant magnitude that is still available for pivoting (not in a row or column already containing a pivot) as the pivot for the kth pass. Usually the largest such element is preferred, as its use is likely to introduce the least round-off error in the reduction pass; the technique is termed the Gauss-Jordan reduction with the maximum pivot strategy. It is only necessary to keep lists of the row and column subscripts of successive pivot elements. Let r_k and c_k be, respectively, the row and column subscript of the kth pivot element, p_k.

The algorithm, closely related to that of Example 5.1, is

Initialization

$\quad d \leftarrow 1$

Choosing the pivot

$\quad p_k = a_{r_k c_k}, \ |a_{r_k c_k}| = \underset{i,j}{max} \ |a_{ij}|,$

$\qquad \begin{cases} i = 1, 2, \ldots, n, \\ i \neq r_1, r_2, \ldots, r_{k-1}, \\ j = 1, 2, \ldots, n, \\ j \neq c_1, c_2, \ldots, c_{k-1}, \end{cases}$

Updating the determinant

$\quad d \leftarrow d p_k$

Normalization

$\quad a_{r_k j} \leftarrow a_{r_k j}/p_k, \quad j = 1, 2, \ldots, n+1,$

Reduction

$\quad a_{ij} \leftarrow a_{ij} - a_{i c_k} a_{r_k j},$

$\qquad \begin{cases} j = 1, 2, \ldots, n+1, \\ i = 1, 2, \ldots, n, \\ i \neq r_k \end{cases}$

$\Bigg\} \ k = 1, 2, \ldots, n.$

The elements r_k and c_k must be assigned the appropriate values, once the kth pivot, p_k, has been selected. Here, as before, d is the determinant (possibly with incorrect sign) of the matrix of coefficients. After reduction is completed, the first n rows of $\mathbf{A}$ will contain a (possibly) permuted identity matrix. The $(n+1)$th column will contain the solution vector $\mathbf{x} = [x_1, x_2, \ldots, x_n]^t$, although the elements will usually be out of order. The solutions can be unscrambled by using the information saved in the vectors r and c, as follows:

$$x_{c_k} = a_{r_k, n+1}, \qquad k = 1, 2, \ldots, n. \qquad (5.2.2)$$

The resulting transformed coefficient matrix has a determinant equal to ± 1 (it is either an elementary matrix of the second kind or is the identity matrix itself). Therefore the value computed for the determinant, d, may be of incorrect sign. It is necessary to establish whether an even or odd number of row interchanges is required to reorder the final permuted matrix as the identity matrix. The problem can be solved by forming an auxiliary vector, j, such that

$$j_{r_k} = c_k, \qquad k = 1, 2, \ldots, n, \qquad (5.2.3)$$

and then counting the number of pairwise interchanges required to put the vector j into ascending sequence. If the number of interchanges is even, then the sign of d is correct; if not, the sign of d is incorrect.

The method is probably best illustrated with a numerical example. Consider the set of equations used in Section 5.4, but taken in a different order to illustrate the procedure better. The solutions, as before, are $\mathbf{x} = [4, 1, 2]^t$.

$$\begin{aligned} -3x_1 + 8x_2 + 5x_3 &= 6 \\ 2x_1 - 7x_2 + 4x_3 &= 9 \\ x_1 + 9x_2 - 6x_3 &= 1. \end{aligned}$$

The augmented coefficient matrix for this system is

$$\begin{bmatrix} -3 & 8 & 5 & 6 \\ 2 & -7 & 4 & 9 \\ 1 & \textcircled{9} & -6 & 1 \end{bmatrix}.$$

Then, for $k = 1$, that is for the first pass, element a_{32} has the greatest magnitude of the nine possible coefficients and $p_1 = 9$, $r_1 = 3$, $c_1 = 2$. The determinant value, d, is updated from its initial value of 1 to 9. After the normalization steps for the first cycle, the transformed matrix is

$$\begin{bmatrix} -3 & 8 & 5 & 6 \\ 2 & -7 & 4 & 9 \\ 1/9 & 1 & -2/3 & 1/9 \end{bmatrix}.$$

The reduction steps lead to

$$\begin{bmatrix} -35/9 & 0 & \textcircled{31/3} & 46/9 \\ 25/9 & 0 & -2/3 & 88/9 \\ 1/9 & 1 & -2/3 & 1/9 \end{bmatrix}.$$

For the second cycle, only a_{11}, a_{13}, a_{21}, and a_{23} are available as potential pivots. Since a_{13} has the greatest magnitude of the four candidates, $p_2 = 31/3$, $r_2 = 1$, $c_2 = 3$. The determinant value is updated to $9 \times 31/3 = 93$. After the normalization and reduction steps, the matrix becomes

$$\begin{bmatrix} -35/93 & 0 & 1 & 46/93 \\ \textcircled{235/93} & 0 & 0 & 940/93 \\ -13/93 & 1 & 0 & 41/93 \end{bmatrix}.$$

For the third and last cycle, only a_{21} is available for pivoting. Then $p_3 = 235/93$, $r_3 = 2$, $c_3 = 1$. The determinant value is updated to $93 \times 235/93 = 235$, and after normalization and reduction, the matrix is

$$\begin{bmatrix} 0 & 0 & 1 & 2 \\ 1 & 0 & 0 & 4 \\ 0 & 1 & 0 & 1 \end{bmatrix}.$$

Note that the first three columns contain a permuted identity matrix, and that the fourth contains the solutions, although not in the natural order. The r and c vectors contain the values:

k	r_k	c_k
1	3	2
2	1	3
3	2	1.

From (5.2.2), the solutions are

$$\begin{aligned} x_1 &= a_{2,4} = 4 \\ x_2 &= a_{3,4} = 1 \\ x_3 &= a_{1,4} = 2. \end{aligned}$$

The auxiliary vector j, formed according to (5.2.3), is

$$\begin{aligned} j_1 &= 3 \\ j_2 &= 1 \\ j_3 &= 2. \end{aligned}$$

Since two pairwise interchanges are required to put j into ascending sequence, the sign of d is correct, and the determinant of the original matrix of coefficients is 235.

The Inverse Matrix

The inverse matrix could be developed by appending an $n \times n$ identity matrix to the augmented matrix of coefficients, and carrying out the maximum pivot strategy as described in the preceding paragraphs. In that case, the normalization and reduction steps would be applied to all $2n + 1$ columns of the matrix, rather than just the first $n + 1$ columns. The initial matrix for the preceding numerical example would be

$$\begin{bmatrix} -3 & 8 & 5 & 6 & 1 & 0 & 0 \\ 2 & -7 & 4 & 9 & 0 & 1 & 0 \\ 1 & 9 & -6 & 1 & 0 & 0 & 1 \end{bmatrix}.$$

The transformed matrix resulting from the three cycles of the reduction algorithm would be

Cycle 1. $\begin{bmatrix} -35/9 & 0 & 31/3 & 46/9 & 1 & 0 & -8/9 \\ 25/9 & 0 & -2/3 & 88/9 & 0 & 1 & 7/9 \\ 1/9 & 1 & -2/3 & 1/9 & 0 & 0 & 1/9 \end{bmatrix}$

Cycle 2. $\begin{bmatrix} -35/93 & 0 & 1 & 46/93 & 3/31 & 0 & -8/93 \\ 235/93 & 0 & 0 & 940/93 & 2/31 & 1 & 67/93 \\ -13/93 & 1 & 0 & 41/93 & 2/31 & 0 & 5/93 \end{bmatrix}$

Cycle 3. $\begin{bmatrix} 0 & 0 & 1 & 2 & 5/47 & 7/47 & 1/47 \\ 1 & 0 & 0 & 4 & 6/235 & 93/235 & 67/235 \\ 0 & 1 & 0 & 1 & 16/235 & 13/235 & 22/235 \end{bmatrix}.$

Note that after the first cycle only the last column of the original identity matrix has been changed. Since the contents of the column containing the pivot element (column 2 in this case) are known to be a one in the pivot position and zeros elsewhere, there is no need to retain them. The elements of the developing inverse (in this case in column 7) can be overstored in place in the pivot column. Similar behavior can be observed for the results of the second and third cycle reduction calculations.

The maximum pivot strategy already developed may be modified slightly to implement the inverse calculation without the necessity of appending n additional columns to the coefficient matrix or of using other auxiliary matrices. The procedures for calculating the determinant and selecting the pivot element are unchanged. All elements of the row containing the pivot element, row r_k, are normalized as before, except the pivot element itself, which is replaced by its reciprocal. Thus the normalization step is given by

$$a_{r_k j} \leftarrow a_{r_k j}/p_k, \qquad j = 1, 2, \ldots, n + 1, \qquad j \neq c_k,$$
$$a_{r_k c_k} \leftarrow 1/p_k. \tag{5.2.4}$$

The reduction calculations are carried out as before, except for the elements in the column containing the pivot element. The reduction calculations are described by

For the numerical example, the introduction of (5.2.4) and (5.2.5) into the maximum pivot strategy leads to the following three matrices after the first, second, and third cycles of the algorithm, respectively.

$$\begin{bmatrix} -35/9 & -8/9 & 31/3 & 46/9 \\ 25/9 & 7/9 & -2/3 & 88/9 \\ 1/9 & 1/9 & -2/3 & 1/9 \end{bmatrix}$$

$$\begin{bmatrix} -35/93 & -8/93 & 3/31 & 46/93 \\ 235/93 & 67/93 & 2/31 & 940/93 \\ -13/93 & 5/93 & 2/31 & 41/93 \end{bmatrix}$$

$$\begin{bmatrix} 7/47 & 1/47 & 5/47 & 2 \\ 93/235 & 67/235 & 6/235 & 4 \\ 13/235 & 22/235 & 16/235 & 1 \end{bmatrix}.$$

The solution vector is unscrambled as before, and the determination of the appropriate sign for the determinant is unchanged. The elements of the inverse matrix are, of course, not in natural order unless all pivot elements are on the main diagonal of the coefficient matrix. The unscrambling process involves both row and column interchange. Let y be an n element vector. Then the inverse can be properly ordered using the following scheme in sequence:

$$\begin{aligned} y_{c_i} &\leftarrow a_{r_i j}, & i = 1, 2, \ldots, n, \\ a_{ij} &\leftarrow y_i, & i = 1, 2, \ldots, n, \end{aligned} \Big\} j = 1, 2, \ldots, n, \tag{5.2.6}$$

$$\begin{aligned} y_{r_j} &\leftarrow a_{i c_j}, & j = 1, 2, \ldots, n, \\ a_{ij} &\leftarrow y_j, & j = 1, 2, \ldots, n, \end{aligned} \Big\} i = 1, 2, \ldots, n.$$

For the numerical example, (5.2.6) leads to the unscrambled inverse:

$$\begin{bmatrix} 6/235 & 93/235 & 67/235 \\ 16/235 & 13/235 & 22/235 \\ 5/47 & 7/47 & 1/47 \end{bmatrix}.$$

$$a_{ij} \leftarrow a_{ij} - a_{i c_k} a_{r_k j}, \quad j = 1, 2, \ldots, n + 1, j \neq c_k, \Big| i = 1, 2, \ldots, n,$$
$$a_{i c_k} \leftarrow -a_{i c_k}/p_k, \qquad\qquad\qquad\qquad\qquad \Big| i \neq r_k. \tag{5.2.5}$$

Example 5.2   Inverse Matrix Using the Maximum Pivot Strategy   **285**

Method of Solution

The function SIMUL implements the algorithm described in the preceding sections. The alternative modes of operation are controlled by a computational switch s; modes 1, 2, and 3 (see Problem Statement) are activated for $s > 0$, $s = 0$, and $s < 0$, respectively. Before a potential pivot, $a_{r_k c_k}$, is used as p_k in the normalization steps, a test for pivot magnitude,

$$|a_{r_k c_k}| < \varepsilon, \qquad (5.2.7)$$

is made to insure against pivots of very small magnitude. If test (5.2.7) is passed, the matrix is singular or near-singular; computation is stopped, and SIMUL returns to the calling program with zero as the determinant value.

The main program reads values for n, s, ε and appropriate elements of the $n \times (n + 1)$ or $n \times n$ matrix A, calls on SIMUL to carry out the desired Gauss-Jordan calculations, and prints the results.

Next, consider the simply supported, eleven-member plane truss of Fig. 5.2.1. Since the number of joints, N_j, and the number of members, N_m, are related by $2N_j - 3 = N_m$, the truss is statically determinate, and the eleven member forces may be found by solving eleven force balances at appropriate joints in the structure. Let h_i be the applied force in the horizontal direction (positive if directed toward the right) at the ith joint, and

v_i be the applied force in the vertical direction (positive if directed downward) at the ith joint. Make two force balances (horizontal and vertical) at joints 2, 3, 4, 5, and 6, and one force balance (horizontal only) at the roller-supported joint 7. Let $\bar{c} = \cos 30°$ and $\bar{s} = \sin 30°$, and let f_i be the tensile force in member i (positive if in tension, negative if in compression). Then the eleven force balances are

$$\text{joint 2} \quad \begin{cases} h_2 + f_4 + \bar{s}f_3 - \bar{s}f_1 & = 0 \\ v_2 + \bar{c}f_1 + \bar{c}f_3 & = 0 \end{cases}$$

$$\text{joint 3} \quad \begin{cases} h_3 - f_2 - \bar{s}f_3 + \bar{s}f_5 + f_6 & = 0 \\ v_3 - \bar{c}f_3 - \bar{c}f_5 & = 0 \end{cases}$$

$$\text{joint 4} \quad \begin{cases} h_4 - f_4 - \bar{s}f_5 + \bar{s}f_7 + f_8 & = 0 \\ v_4 + \bar{c}f_5 + \bar{c}f_7 & = 0 \end{cases}$$

$$\text{joint 5} \quad \begin{cases} h_5 - f_6 - \bar{s}f_7 + \bar{s}f_9 + f_{10} & = 0 \\ v_5 - \bar{c}f_7 - \bar{c}f_9 & = 0 \end{cases}$$

$$\text{joint 6} \quad \begin{cases} h_6 - f_8 - \bar{s}f_9 + \bar{s}f_{11} & = 0 \\ v_6 + \bar{c}f_9 + \bar{c}f_{11} & = 0 \end{cases}$$

$$\text{joint 7} \quad h_7 - f_{10} - \bar{s}f_{11} \qquad = 0.$$

Rearranging these equations into the form of (5.2.1), the augmented matrix of coefficients is

$$\begin{bmatrix}
\bar{s} & 0 & -\bar{s} & -1 & 0 & 0 & 0 & 0 & 0 & 0 & 0 & h_2 \\
-\bar{c} & 0 & -\bar{c} & 0 & 0 & 0 & 0 & 0 & 0 & 0 & 0 & v_2 \\
0 & 1 & \bar{s} & 0 & -\bar{s} & -1 & 0 & 0 & 0 & 0 & 0 & h_3 \\
0 & 0 & \bar{c} & 0 & \bar{c} & 0 & 0 & 0 & 0 & 0 & 0 & v_3 \\
0 & 0 & 0 & 1 & \bar{s} & 0 & -\bar{s} & -1 & 0 & 0 & 0 & h_4 \\
0 & 0 & 0 & 0 & -\bar{c} & 0 & -\bar{c} & 0 & 0 & 0 & 0 & v_4 \\
0 & 0 & 0 & 0 & 0 & 1 & \bar{s} & 0 & -\bar{s} & -1 & 0 & h_5 \\
0 & 0 & 0 & 0 & 0 & 0 & \bar{c} & 0 & \bar{c} & 0 & 0 & v_5 \\
0 & 0 & 0 & 0 & 0 & 0 & 0 & 1 & \bar{s} & 0 & -\bar{s} & h_6 \\
0 & 0 & 0 & 0 & 0 & 0 & 0 & 0 & -\bar{c} & 0 & -\bar{c} & v_6 \\
0 & 0 & 0 & 0 & 0 & 0 & 0 & 0 & 0 & 1 & \bar{s} & h_7
\end{bmatrix}.$$

Here, $\bar{s} = 0.5$ and $\bar{c} \doteq 0.86603$. For the truss of Fig. 5.2.1, $h_2 = -5$, $v_2 = 10$, $h_3 = 0$, $v_3 = 10$, $h_4 = 0$, $v_4 = 10$, $h_5 = 0$, $v_5 = 10$, $h_6 = 5$, $v_6 = 10$, $h_7 = 0$.

Flow Diagram

Main Program

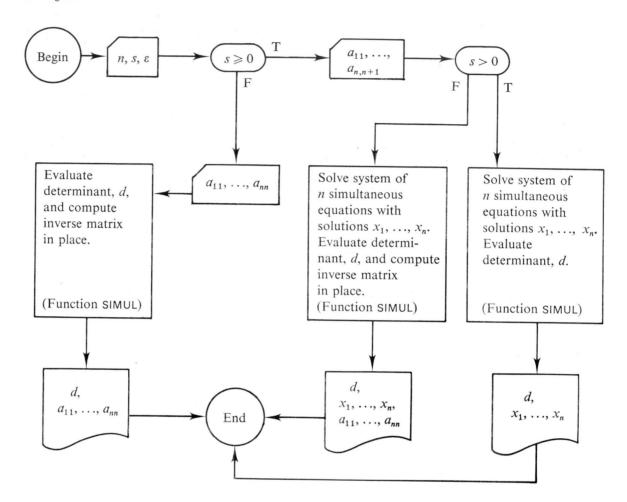

Example 5.2   Inverse Matrix Using the Maximum Pivot Strategy   **287**

Function SIMUL (Arguments: n, $\mathbf{A}$, $\mathbf{x}$, ε, s, N_d)

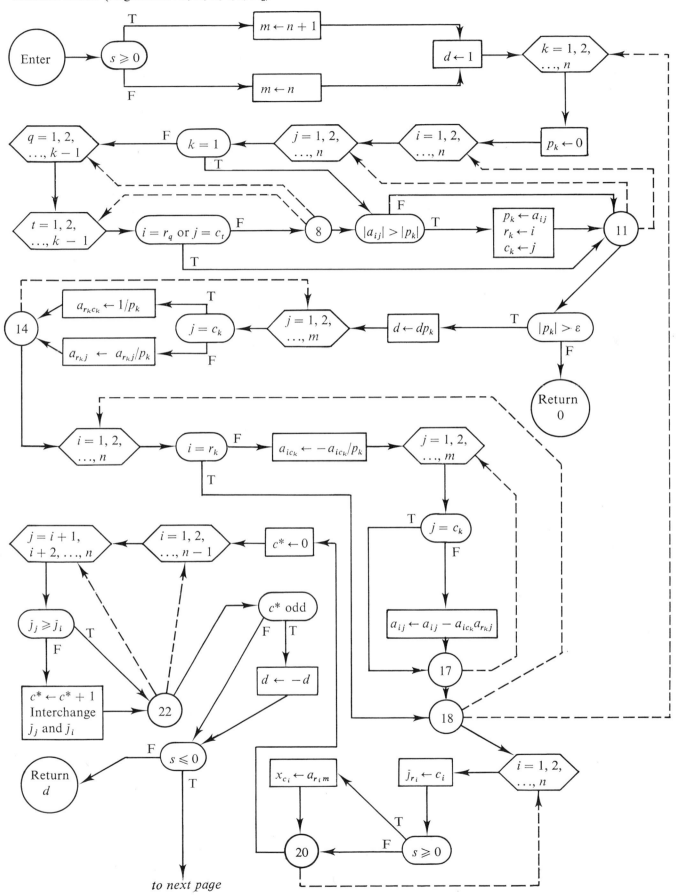

to next page

from previous page

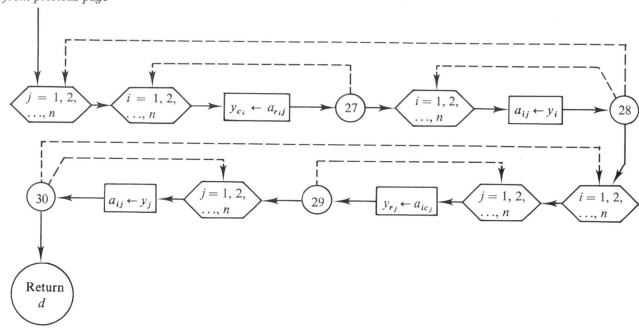

FORTRAN *Implementation*

List of Principal Variables

Program Symbol	Definition
(Main)	
A	Augmented matrix of coefficients, $\mathbf{A} = (a_{ij})$.
DETER	d, determinant of the original coefficient matrix (the first n columns of $\mathbf{A}$).
EPS	Minimum allowable magnitude, ε, for a pivot element.
I, J	Row and column subscripts, i and j.
INDIC	Computational switch, s.
MAX	Number of columns in $\mathbf{A}$, either n or $n + 1$.
N	Number of rows in $\mathbf{A}$, n.
X	Vector of solutions, x_i.
(Function SIMUL)	
AIJCK	a_{ic_k}.
INTCH	c^*, number of pairwise interchanges required to order elements of vector j.
IP1, KM1, NM1	$i + 1$, $k - 1$, and $n - 1$, respectively.
IROW	Vector of pivot element row subscripts, r_k.
JCOL	Vector of pivot element column subscripts, c_k.
IROWI, IROWJ, IROWK, JCOLI, JCOLJ, JCOLK	r_i, r_j, r_k, c_i, c_j, and c_k, respectively.
ISCAN, JSCAN	Indices q and t, used in scan of vectors c and r during pivot element search.
JORD	The vector j.
JTEMP	Temporary variable used in ordering the j vector.
K	Cycle counter and pivot element subscript, k.
NRC	N_d, row and column dimensions of storage for the matrix A (assumed to be square).
PIVOT	Pivot element, p_k.
Y	Vector y, used in unscrambling the inverse matrix.

Example 5.2   Inverse Matrix Using the Maximum Pivot Strategy   **289**

Program Listing

Main Program

```
C          APPLIED NUMERICAL METHODS, EXAMPLE 5.2
C          CALCULATION OF THE INVERSE MATRIX IN PLACE
C
C          THIS PROGRAM READS VALUES OF N, INDIC, AND EPS.  IF INDIC IS
C          NEGATIVE, ELEMENTS OF AN N BY N MATRIX A ARE READ, AND THEN THE
C          FUNCTION SIMUL IS CALLED TO COMPUTE THE INVERSE OF A IN PLACE.
C          IF INDIC IS ZERO, ELEMENTS OF AN N BY N+1 MATRIX A ARE READ,
C          AND THEN THE FUNCTION SIMUL IS CALLED TO SOLVE THE SYSTEM OF
C          LINEAR EQUATIONS WHOSE COEFFICIENT MATRIX IS IN THE FIRST N
C          COLUMNS OF A AND VECTOR OF RIGHT HAND SIDES IS APPENDED IN
C          COLUMN N+1.  THE N SOLUTIONS APPEAR IN X(1)...X(N) AND THE
C          INVERSE OF THE COEFFICIENT MATRIX APPEARS IN THE FIRST N
C          COLUMNS OF A.  IF INDIC IS POSITIVE, THE LATTER PROCEDURE IS
C          FOLLOWED, EXCEPT THAT THE INVERSE IS NOT COMPUTED IN PLACE.
C          SIMUL RETURNS AS ITS VALUE THE DETERMINANT OF THE FIRST N
C          COLUMNS OF A.  EPS IS THE MINIMUM PIVOT MAGNITUDE PERMITTED BY
C          SIMUL.  SHOULD NO ACCEPTABLE PIVOT BE FOUND, SIMUL RETURNS A
C          TRUE ZERO AS ITS VALUE.  DETER, THE DETERMINANT OF THE MATRIX
C          OF COEFFICIENTS IS RETURNED AS THE VALUE OF SIMUL.
C
       IMPLICIT  REAL*8(A-H, O-Z)
       DIMENSION X(50), A(51,51)
C
C      ..... READ AND PRINT MATRIX A .....
    1  READ (5,100) N,INDIC,EPS
       WRITE (6,200) N,INDIC,EPS
       MAX = N
       IF ( INDIC.GE.0 )    MAX = N + 1
       DO 4   I = 1, N
       READ (5,101) (A(I,J),J=1,MAX)
    4  WRITE (6,201) (A(I,J),J=1,MAX)
C
C      ..... CALL SIMUL .....
       DETER = SIMUL ( N, A, X, EPS, INDIC, 51 )
C
C      ..... PRINT SOLUTIONS .....
       IF ( INDIC.GE.0 )    GO TO 8
       WRITE (6,202) DETER
       DO 7   I = 1, N
    7  WRITE (6,201) (A(I,J),J=1,N)
       GO TO 1
    8  WRITE (6,203) DETER,N,(X(I),I=1,N)
       IF ( INDIC.NE.0 )    GO TO 1
    9  WRITE (6,204)
       DO 10   I = 1, N
   10  WRITE (6,201) (A(I,J),J=1,N)
       GO TO 1
C
C      ..... FORMATS FOR INPUT AND OUTPUT STATEMENTS .....
  100  FORMAT ( 10X, I2, 18X, I2, 18X, E7.1 )
  101  FORMAT ( 20X, 5F10.5 )
  200  FORMAT ( 10H1N     = , I4/ 10H INDIC  = , I4/ 10H EPS     = ,
      1    E10.1/ 23H0THE STARTING MATRIX IS /1H  )
  201  FORMAT ( 1H , 7F13.6 )
  202  FORMAT ( 10H0DETER  = , F12.6/ 22H0THE INVERSE MATRIX IS / 1H  )
  203  FORMAT ( 10H0DETER  = , F12.6/ 24H0THE SOLUTIONS X(1)...X(, I2,
      1    5H) ARE / 1H / (1H , 7F13.6) )
  204  FORMAT ( 22H0THE INVERSE MATRIX IS / 1H  )
C
       END
```

Program Listing (*Continued*)

Function SIMUL

```
          FUNCTION SIMUL( N, A, X, EPS, INDIC, NRC )
C
C          WHEN INDIC IS NEGATIVE, SIMUL COMPUTES THE INVERSE OF THE N BY
C          N MATRIX A IN PLACE.  WHEN INDIC IS ZERO, SIMUL COMPUTES THE
C          N SOLUTIONS X(1)...X(N) CORRESPONDING TO THE SET OF LINEAR
C          EQUATIONS WITH AUGMENTED MATRIX OF COEFFICIENTS IN THE N BY
C          N+1 ARRAY A AND IN ADDITION COMPUTES THE INVERSE OF THE
C          COEFFICIENT MATRIX IN PLACE AS ABOVE.  IF INDIC IS POSITIVE,
C          THE SET OF LINEAR EQUATIONS IS SOLVED BUT THE INVERSE IS NOT
C          COMPUTED IN PLACE. THE GAUSS-JORDAN COMPLETE ELIMINATION METHOD
C          IS EMPLOYED WITH THE MAXIMUM PIVOT STRATEGY.  ROW AND COLUMN
C          SUBSCRIPTS OF SUCCESSIVE PIVOT ELEMENTS ARE SAVED IN ORDER IN
C          THE IROW AND JCOL ARRAYS RESPECTIVELY.  K IS THE PIVOT COUNTER,
C          PIVOT THE ALGEBRAIC VALUE OF THE PIVOT ELEMENT, MAX
C          THE NUMBER OF COLUMNS IN A AND DETER THE DETERMINANT OF THE
C          COEFFICIENT MATRIX.  THE SOLUTIONS ARE COMPUTED IN THE (N+1)TH
C          COLUMN OF A AND THEN UNSCRAMBLED AND PUT IN PROPER ORDER IN
C          X(1)...X(N) USING THE PIVOT SUBSCRIPT INFORMATION AVAILABLE
C          IN THE IROW AND JCOL ARRAYS.  THE SIGN OF THE DETERMINANT IS
C          ADJUSTED, IF NECESSARY, BY DETERMINING IF AN ODD OR EVEN NUMBER
C          OF PAIRWISE INTERCHANGES IS REQUIRED TO PUT THE ELEMENTS OF THE
C          JORD ARRAY IN ASCENDING SEQUENCE WHERE JORD(IROW(I)) = JCOL(I).
C          IF THE INVERSE IS REQUIRED, IT IS UNSCRAMBLED IN PLACE USING
C          Y(1)...Y(N) AS TEMPORARY STORAGE.  THE VALUE OF THE DETERMINANT
C          IS RETURNED AS THE VALUE OF THE FUNCTION.  SHOULD THE POTENTIAL
C          PIVOT OF LARGEST MAGNITUDE BE SMALLER IN MAGNITUDE THAN EPS,
C          THE MATRIX IS CONSIDERED TO BE SINGULAR AND A TRUE ZERO IS
C          RETURNED AS THE VALUE OF THE FUNCTION.
C
          IMPLICIT  REAL*8(A-H, O-Z)
          REAL*8   A, X, EPS, SIMUL
          DIMENSION IROW(50), JCOL(50), JORD(50), Y(50), A(NRC,NRC), X(N)
C
          MAX = N
          IF ( INDIC.GE.0 )   MAX = N + 1
C
C         .....IS N LARGER THAN 50 .....
          IF ( N.LE.50 )   GO TO 5
          WRITE (6,200)
          SIMUL = 0.
          RETURN
C
C         ..... BEGIN ELIMINATION PROCEDURE .....
    5     DETER = 1.
          DO 18   K = 1, N
          KM1 = K - 1
C
C         ..... SEARCH FOR THE PIVOT ELEMENT .....
          PIVOT = 0.
          DO 11   I = 1, N
          DO 11   J = 1, N
C         ..... SCAN IROW AND JCOL ARRAYS FOR INVALID PIVOT SUBSCRIPTS .....
          IF ( K.EQ.1 )   GO TO 9
          DO 8    ISCAN = 1, KM1
          DO 8    JSCAN = 1, KM1
          IF ( I.EQ.IROW(ISCAN) )   GO TO 11
    8     IF ( J.EQ.JCOL(JSCAN) )   GO TO 11
    9     IF (DABS(A(I,J)).LE.DABS(PIVOT) )   GO TO 11
          PIVOT = A(I,J)
          IROW(K) = I
          JCOL(K) = J
   11     CONTINUE
C
C         ..... INSURE THAT SELECTED PIVOT IS LARGER THAN EPS .....
          IF ( DABS(PIVOT).GT.EPS )   GO TO 13
          SIMUL = 0.
          RETURN
C
C         ..... UPDATE THE DETERMINANT VALUE .....
   13     IROWK = IROW(K)
          JCOLK = JCOL(K)
          DETER = DETER*PIVOT
```

Example 5.2   Inverse Matrix Using the Maximum Pivot Strategy   **291**

Program Listing (*Continued*)

```
C
C        ..... NORMALIZE PIVOT ROW ELEMENTS .....
         DO 14    J = 1, MAX
   14    A(IROWK,J) = A(IROWK,J)/PIVOT
C
C        ..... CARRY OUT ELIMINATION AND DEVELOP INVERSE .....
         A(IROWK,JCOLK) = 1./PIVOT
         DO 18    I = 1, N
         AIJCK = A(I,JCOLK)
         IF ( I.EQ.IROWK )    GO TO 18
         A(I,JCOLK) = - AIJCK/PIVOT
         DO 17    J = 1, MAX
   17    IF ( J.NE.JCOLK )    A(I,J) = A(I,J) - AIJCK*A(IROWK,J)
   18    CONTINUE
C
C        ..... ORDER SOLUTION VALUES (IF ANY) AND CREATE JORD ARRAY .....
         DO 20    I = 1, N
         IROWI = IROW(I)
         JCOLI = JCOL(I)
         JORD(IROWI) = JCOLI
   20    IF ( INDIC.GE.0 )    X(JCOLI) = A(IROWI,MAX)
C
C        ..... ADJUST SIGN OF DETERMINANT .....
         INTCH = 0
         NM1 = N - 1
         DO 22    I = 1, NM1
         IP1 = I + 1
         DO 22    J = IP1, N
         IF ( JORD(J).GE.JORD(I))    GO TO 22
         JTEMP = JORD(J)
         JORD(J) = JORD(I)
         JORD(I) = JTEMP
         INTCH = INTCH + 1
   22    CONTINUE
         IF ( INTCH/2*2.NE.INTCH )    DETER = - DETER
C
C        ..... IF INDIC IS POSITIVE RETURN WITH RESULTS .....
   24    IF ( INDIC.LE.0 )    GO TO 26
         SIMUL = DETER
         RETURN
C
C        ..... IF INDIC IS NEGATIVE OR ZERO, UNSCRAMBLE THE INVERSE
C              FIRST BY ROWS .....
   26    DO 28    J = 1, N
         DO 27    I = 1, N
         IROWI = IROW(I)
         JCOLI = JCOL(I)
   27    Y(JCOLI) = A(IROWI,J)
         DO 28    I = 1, N
   28    A(I,J) = Y(I)
C        ..... THEN BY COLUMNS .....
         DO 30    I = 1, N
         DO 29    J = 1, N
         IROWJ = IROW(J)
         JCOLJ = JCOL(J)
   29    Y(IROWJ) = A(I,JCOLJ)
         DO 30    J = 1, N
   30    A(I,J) = Y(J)
C
C        ..... RETURN FOR INDIC NEGATIVE OR ZERO .....
         SIMUL = DETER
         RETURN
C
C        ..... FORMAT FOR OUTPUT STATEMENT .....
  200    FORMAT( 10H0N TOO BIG )
C
         END
```

Program Listing (*Continued*)

Data

```
N       =   3         INDIC  =  -1        EPS    =   1.0E-20
A(1,1)...A(1,3) =       -3.00000    8.00000    5.00000
A(2,1)...A(2,3) =        2.00000   -7.00000    4.00000
A(3,1)...A(3,3) =        1.00000    9.00000   -6.00000
N       =   3         INDIC  =   0        EPS    =   1.0E-20
A(1,1)...A(1,4) =       -3.00000    8.00000    5.00000    6.00000
A(2,1)...A(2,4) =        2.00000   -7.00000    4.00000    9.00000
A(3,1)...A(3,4) =        1.00000    9.00000   -6.00000    1.00000
N       =   3         INDIC  =   1        EPS    =   1.0E-20
A(1,1)...A(1,4) =       -3.00000    8.00000    5.00000    6.00000
A(2,1)...A(2,4) =        2.00000   -7.00000    4.00000    9.00000
A(3,1)...A(3,4) =        1.00000    9.00000   -6.00000    1.00000
N       =   3         INDIC  =   0        EPS    =   1.0E-10
A(1,1)...A(1,4) =        2.00000   -7.00000    4.00000    9.00000
A(2,1)...A(2,4) =        1.00000    9.00000   -6.00000    1.00000
A(3,1)...A(3,4) =       -3.00000    8.00000    5.00000    6.00000
N       =   3         INDIC  =   0        EPS    =   1.0E-10
A(1,1)...A(1,4) =        1.00000    9.00000   -6.00000    1.00000
A(2,1)...A(2,4) =        2.00000   -7.00000    4.00000    9.00000
A(3,1)...A(3,4) =        2.00000   -7.00000    4.00000    9.00000
N       =   3         INDIC  =   0        EPS    =   1.0E-10
A(1,1)...A(1,4) =        0.00000   -7.00000    4.00000    1.00000
A(2,1)...A(2,4) =        1.00000    9.00000   -6.00000    1.00000
A(3,1)...A(3,4) =       -3.00000    8.00000    5.00000    6.00000
N       =   2         INDIC  =   0        EPS    =   1.0E-20
A(1,1)...A(1,3) =        1.00000    1.00000    1.00000
A(2,1)...A(2,3) =        0.00003    3.00000    2.900001
N       =   2         INDIC  =   0        EPS    =   1.0E-20
A(1,1)...A(1,3) =        0.00003    3.00000    2.900001
A(2,1)...A(2,3) =        1.00000    1.00000    1.00000
N       =  11         INDIC  =   0        EPS    =   1.0E-10
A(1,1)...A(1,5) =        0.50000    0.00000   -0.50000   -1.00000    0.00000
A(1,6)...A(1,10) =       0.00000    0.00000    0.00000    0.00000    0.00000
A(1,11)...A(1,12) =      0.00000   -5.00000
A(2,1)...A(2,5) =       -0.86603    0.00000   -0.86603    0.00000    0.00000
A(2,6)...A(2,10) =       0.00000    0.00000    0.00000    0.00000    0.00000
A(2,11)...A(2,12) =      0.00000   10.00000
A(3,1)...A(3,5) =        0.00000    1.00000    0.50000    0.00000   -0.50000
A(3,6)...A(3,10) =      -1.00000    0.00000    0.00000    0.00000    0.00000
A(3,11)...A(3,12) =      0.00000    0.00000
A(4,1)...A(4,5) =        0.00000    0.00000    0.86603    0.00000    0.86603
A(4,6)...A(4,10) =       0.00000    0.00000    0.00000    0.00000    0.00000
A(4,11)...A(4,12) =      0.00000   10.00000
A(5,1)...A(5,5) =        0.00000    0.00000    0.00000    1.00000    0.50000
A(5,6)...A(5,10) =       0.00000   -0.50000   -1.00000    0.00000    0.00000
A(5,11)...A(5,12) =      0.00000    0.00000
A(6,1)...A(6,5) =        0.00000    0.00000    0.00000    0.00000   -0.86603
A(6,6)...A(6,10) =       0.00000   -0.86603    0.00000    0.00000    0.00000
A(6,11)...A(6,12) =      0.00000   10.00000
A(7,1)...A(7,5) =        0.00000    0.00000    0.00000    0.00000    0.00000
A(7,6)...A(7,10) =       1.00000    0.50000    0.00000   -0.50000   -1.00000
A(7,11)...A(7,12) =      0.00000    0.00000
A(8,1)...A(8,5) =        0.00000    0.00000    0.00000    0.00000    0.00000
A(8,6)...A(8,10) =       0.00000    0.86603    0.00000    0.86603    0.00000
A(8,11)...A(8,12) =      0.00000   10.00000
A(9,1)...A(9,5) =        0.00000    0.00000    0.00000    0.00000    0.00000
A(9,6)...A(9,10) =       0.00000    0.00000    1.00000    0.50000    0.00000
A(9,11)...A(9,12) =     -0.50000    5.00000
A(10,1)...A(10,5) =      0.00000    0.00000    0.00000    0.00000    0.00000
A(10,6)...A(10,10) =     0.00000    0.00000    0.00000   -0.86603    0.00000
A(10,11)...A(10,12)=    -0.86603   10.00000
A(11,1)...A(11,5) =      0.00000    0.00000    0.00000    0.00000    0.00000
A(11,6)...A(11,10) =     0.00000    0.00000    0.00000    0.00000    1.00000
A(11,11)...A(11,12)=     0.50000    0.00000
```

Computer Output

Results for the 1st Data Set

```
  N    =   3
  INDIC =  -1
  EPS  =   0.1D-19

THE STARTING MATRIX IS

   -3.000000    8.000000    5.000000    6.000000
    2.000000   -7.000000    4.000000    9.000000
    1.000000    9.000000   -6.000000    1.000000

DETER =   235.000000

THE SOLUTIONS X(1)...X( 3) ARE

    4.000000    1.000000    2.000000

THE INVERSE MATRIX IS

    0.025532    0.395745    0.285106
    0.068085    0.055319    0.093617
    0.106383    0.148936    0.021277
```

Results for the 2nd Data Set

```
  N    =   3
  INDIC =   0
  EPS  =   0.1D-19

THE STARTING MATRIX IS

   -3.000000    8.000000    5.000000    6.000000
    2.000000   -7.000000    4.000000    9.000000
    1.000000    9.000000   -6.000000    1.000000

DETER =   235.000000

THE SOLUTIONS X(1)...X( 3) ARE

    4.000000    1.000000    2.000000

THE INVERSE MATRIX IS

    0.025532    0.395745    0.285106
    0.068085    0.055319    0.093617
    0.106383    0.148936    0.021277
```

Results for the 3rd Data Set

```
  N    =   3
  INDIC =   1
  EPS  =   0.1D-19

THE STARTING MATRIX IS

   -3.000000    8.000000    5.000000    6.000000
    2.000000   -7.000000    4.000000    9.000000
    1.000000    9.000000   -6.000000    1.000000

DETER =   235.000000

THE SOLUTIONS X(1)...X( 3) ARE

    4.000000    1.000000    2.000000
```

Results for the 4th Data Set

```
  N    =   3
  INDIC =   0
  EPS  =   0.1D-09

THE STARTING MATRIX IS

    2.000000   -7.000000    4.000000    9.000000
    1.000000    9.000000   -6.000000    1.000000
   -3.000000    8.000000    5.000000    6.000000

DETER =   235.000000

THE SOLUTIONS X(1)...X( 3) ARE

    4.000000    1.000000    2.000000

THE INVERSE MATRIX IS

    0.395745    0.285106    0.025532
    0.055319    0.093617    0.068085
    0.148936    0.021277    0.106383
```

Computer Output (Continued)

Results for the 5th Data Set

```
N     =    3
INDIC =    0
EPS   =    0.1D-09

THE STARTING MATRIX IS

   1.000000       9.000000      -6.000000       1.000000
   2.000000      -7.000000       4.000000       9.000000
   2.000000      -7.000000       4.000000       9.000000

DETER  =    0.0

THE SOLUTIONS X(1)...X( 3) ARE

   4.000000       1.000000       2.000000

THE INVERSE MATRIX IS

  -0.040000       0.080000      -0.640000
   0.360000       0.280000      -0.240000
  -1.000000       0.000000      -0.000000
```

Results for the 6th Data Set

```
N     =    3
INDIC =    0
EPS   =    0.1D-09

THE STARTING MATRIX IS

   0.0           -7.000000       4.000000       1.000000
   1.000000       9.000000      -6.000000       1.000000
  -3.000000       8.000000       5.000000       6.000000

DETER  =   49.000000

THE SOLUTIONS X(1)...X( 3) ARE

   4.000000       1.000000       2.000000

THE INVERSE MATRIX IS

   1.897959       1.367347       0.122449
   0.265306       0.244898       0.081633
   0.714286       0.428571       0.142857
```

Results for the 7th Data Set

```
N     =    2
INDIC =    0
EPS   =    0.1D-19

THE STARTING MATRIX IS

   1.000000       1.000000       1.000000
   0.000030       3.000000       2.900001

DETER  =    2.999970

THE SOLUTIONS X(1)...X( 2) ARE

   0.033333       0.966667

THE INVERSE MATRIX IS

   1.000010      -0.333337
  -0.000010       0.333337
```

Results for the 8th Data Set

```
N     =    2
INDIC =    0
EPS   =    0.1D-19

THE STARTING MATRIX IS

   0.000030       3.000000       2.900001
   1.000000       1.000000       1.000000

DETER  =   -2.999970

THE SOLUTIONS X(1)...X( 2) ARE

   0.033333       0.966667

THE INVERSE MATRIX IS

  -0.333337       1.000010
   0.333337      -0.000010
```

Example 5.2   Inverse Matrix Using the Maximum Pivot Strategy   **295**

Computer Output (*Continued*)

Results for the 9th Data Set

```
N      =     11
INDIC  =      0
EPS    =      0.1D-09
```

THE STARTING MATRIX IS

```
    0.500000      0.0         -0.500000    -1.000000     0.0          0.0          0.0
    0.0           0.0          0.0          0.0         -5.000000
   -0.866030      0.0         -0.866030     0.0          0.0          0.0          0.0
    0.0           0.0          0.0          0.0         10.000000
    0.0           1.000000     0.500000     0.0         -0.500000    -1.000000     0.0
    0.0           0.0          0.0          0.0          0.0
    0.0           0.0          0.866030     0.0          0.866030     0.0          0.0
    0.0           0.0          0.0          0.0         10.000000
    0.0           0.0          0.0          1.000000     0.500000     0.0         -0.500000
   -1.000000      0.0          0.0          0.0          0.0
    0.0           0.0          0.0          0.0         -0.866030     0.0         -0.866030
    0.0           0.0          0.0          0.0         10.000000
    0.0           0.0          0.0          0.0          0.0          1.000000     0.500000
    0.0          -0.500000    -1.000000     0.0          0.0
    0.0           0.0          0.0          0.0          0.0          0.0          0.866030
    0.0           0.866030     0.0          0.0         10.000000
    0.0           0.0          0.0          0.0          0.0          0.0          0.0
    1.000000      0.500000     0.0         -0.500000     5.000000
    0.0           0.0          0.0          0.0          0.0          0.0          0.0
    0.0          -0.866030     0.0         -0.866030    10.000000
    0.0           0.0          1.000000     0.500000     0.0
```

DETER =   1.461457

THE SOLUTIONS X(1)...X(11) ARE

```
  -28.867360     14.433680     17.320416    -18.093888    -5.773472     25.980624    -5.773472
  -18.093888     17.320416     14.433680    -28.867360
```

THE INVERSE MATRIX IS

```
    0.333333     -0.962245    -0.0         -0.769796     0.333333    -0.577347    -0.0
   -0.384898      0.333333    -0.192449    -0.0
    0.833333      0.481123     1.000000     0.384898     0.833333     0.288674     1.000000
    0.192449      0.833333     0.096225     1.000000
   -0.333333     -0.192449    -0.0          0.769796    -0.333333     0.577347    -0.0
    0.384898     -0.333333     0.192449    -0.0
   -0.666667     -0.384898    -0.0         -0.769796     0.333333    -0.577347    -0.0
   -0.384898      0.333333    -0.192449    -0.0
    0.333333      0.192449    -0.0          0.384898     0.333333    -0.577347    -0.0
   -0.384898      0.333333    -0.192449    -0.0
    0.500000      0.288674    -0.0          0.577347     0.500000     0.866021     1.000000
    0.577347      0.500000     0.288674     1.000000
   -0.333333     -0.192449    -0.0         -0.384898    -0.333333    -0.577347    -0.0
    0.384898     -0.333333     0.192449    -0.0
   -0.333333     -0.192449    -0.0         -0.384898    -0.333333    -0.577347    -0.0
   -0.769796      0.666667    -0.384898    -0.0
    0.333333      0.192449    -0.0          0.384898     0.333333     0.577347    -0.0
    0.769796      0.333333    -0.192449    -0.0
    0.166667      0.096225    -0.0          0.192449     0.166667     0.288674    -0.0
    0.384898      0.166667     0.481123     1.000000
   -0.333333     -0.192449     0.0         -0.384898    -0.333333    -0.577347     0.0
   -0.769796     -0.333333    -0.962245     0.0
```

Discussion of Results

All calculations were carried out using double-precision arithmetic. Results for the first three data sets show the output for the three modes of operation of SIMUL. The equations are those used as a numerical example in the discussion of the maximum pivot strategy. Equations for the fourth data set are those used as an illustrative example in Section 5.4.

The coefficient matrix for the fifth data set is singular (two of the equations are identical); this is indicated by the zero determinant value. In this case, the entries in the **x** vector are meaningless (left over from the previous problem), and the numbers printed under the inverse matrix label are the contents of **A** when the singularity was discovered.

The equations of the sixth data set are the same as those for the fourth data set in Example 5.1. Note that the appearance of a zero on the diagonal in the a_{11} position causes no difficulty when the maximum pivot strategy is employed (compare with the results in Example 5.1).

Results for the seventh and eighth data sets show that the order of equations is immaterial when the maximum pivot strategy is employed.

Results for the ninth data set include the member forces in the plane frame of Fig. 5.2.1. The forces are listed in Table 5.2.1.

Table 5.2.1 Member Forces in the Plane Frame

Member	Force (Tons)	Tension or Compression
1	28.867	Compression
2	14.434	Tension
3	17.320	Tension
4	18.094	Compression
5	5.773	Compression
6	25.981	Tension
7	5.773	Compression
8	18.094	Compression
9	17.320	Tension
10	14.434	Tension
11	28.867	Compression

Note that for the symmetrically distributed load, member forces are also symmetric. Once the inverse matrix has been computed, the member forces for the given structure may be calculated for *any* combination of vertical and horizontal forces applied at the joints (any other applied forces can be decomposed into their horizontal and vertical components) by evaluating the matrix product of the inverse matrix and the new right-hand side vector.

5.5 A Finite Form of the Method of Kaczmarz

We consider the solution of (5.2) under the assumption that **B** is nonsingular. The procedure consists in first converting the system of (5.2) into an equivalent system,

$$\mathbf{Ax} = \mathbf{v}, \qquad \mathbf{A}^* = \mathbf{A}^{-1}, \tag{5.9}$$

such that (5.9) and (5.2) have the same solution vector **x**. Then, using an arbitrary initial vector, $\mathbf{r}_0$, we define

$$\mathbf{r}_j = \mathbf{r}_{j-1} - [(\boldsymbol{\alpha}_j, \mathbf{r}_{j-1}) - v_j]\boldsymbol{\alpha}_j, \qquad 1 \leqslant j \leqslant n, \tag{5.10}$$

where $\mathbf{A} = (a_{ij})$ and $\boldsymbol{\alpha}_j = [\bar{a}_{j1}, \bar{a}_{j2}, \ldots, \bar{a}_{jn}]^t$. Then $\mathbf{Ar}_n = \mathbf{v}$ and

$$\mathbf{Br}_n = \mathbf{u}. \tag{5.11}$$

We show that (5.10) defines a vector $\mathbf{r}_n$ such that $\mathbf{Ar}_n = \mathbf{v}$. Notice first that the equations of (5.9) may be written

$$(\boldsymbol{\alpha}_i, \mathbf{x}) = v_i, \qquad 1 \leqslant i \leqslant n.$$

Notice next that, multiplying (5.10) on the left by $\boldsymbol{\alpha}_j$,

$$(\boldsymbol{\alpha}_j, \mathbf{r}_j) = v_j,$$

so that the jth equation of (5.9) is satisfied by $\mathbf{r}_j$. However,

$$(\boldsymbol{\alpha}_i, \mathbf{r}_j) = (\boldsymbol{\alpha}_i, \mathbf{r}_{j-1}), \qquad i \neq j,$$

since $(\boldsymbol{\alpha}_i, \boldsymbol{\alpha}_j) = 0$ for $i \neq j$. Thus, if $i < j$, $(\boldsymbol{\alpha}_i, \mathbf{r}_j) = (\boldsymbol{\alpha}_i, \mathbf{r}_{j-1}) = \cdots = (\boldsymbol{\alpha}_i, \boldsymbol{\alpha}_i) = v_i$. We see inductively that $\mathbf{Ar}_n = \mathbf{v}$, and the unique solution of (5.9) has been found.

Turn now to the solution of (5.2). Let $\mathbf{B}^* = [\boldsymbol{\beta}_1, \boldsymbol{\beta}_2, \ldots, \boldsymbol{\beta}_n]$ where $\boldsymbol{\beta}_i = [\bar{b}_{i1}, \bar{b}_{i2}, \ldots, \bar{b}_{in}]^t$. A system equivalent to (5.2) and having the properties of (5.9) is built in orthodox manner from the linearly independent vectors $\boldsymbol{\beta}_i$ by using the *Gram-Schmidt* orthogonalization procedure, as follows. Let

$$\boldsymbol{\gamma}_1 = \boldsymbol{\beta}_1;$$

$$\boldsymbol{\alpha}_i = \frac{\boldsymbol{\gamma}_i}{\sqrt{(\boldsymbol{\gamma}_i, \boldsymbol{\gamma}_i)}}, \qquad 1 \leqslant i \leqslant n; \tag{5.12}$$

$$\boldsymbol{\gamma}_j = \boldsymbol{\beta}_j - \sum_{i=1}^{j-1} (\boldsymbol{\alpha}_i, \boldsymbol{\beta}_j)\boldsymbol{\alpha}_i, \qquad 2 \leqslant j \leqslant n.$$

Then it is readily found that $(\boldsymbol{\alpha}_i, \boldsymbol{\alpha}_i) = 1$, while $(\boldsymbol{\alpha}_i, \boldsymbol{\alpha}_j) = 0$ if $i \neq j$ is shown to be true inductively. Thus, if $\mathbf{A}^* = [\boldsymbol{\alpha}_1, \boldsymbol{\alpha}_2, \ldots, \boldsymbol{\alpha}_n]^t$, then $\mathbf{A}^* = \mathbf{A}^{-1}$. This is verified by direct multiplication. Finally, let

$$v_1 = \frac{u_1}{\sqrt{(\boldsymbol{\gamma}_1, \boldsymbol{\gamma}_1)}},$$

$$v_j = \frac{1}{\sqrt{(\boldsymbol{\gamma}_j, \boldsymbol{\gamma}_j)}} \left\{ u_j - \sum_{i=1}^{j-1} (\boldsymbol{\beta}_j, \boldsymbol{\alpha}_i) v_i \right\}. \tag{5.13}$$

With these definitions, a solution of (5.9) is a solution of (5.2). For, if $(\boldsymbol{\alpha}_j, \mathbf{x}) - v_j = 0$, $1 \leqslant j \leqslant n$, then by (5.12),

$$(\boldsymbol{\beta}_j, \mathbf{x}) - \sum_{i=1}^{j-1} (\boldsymbol{\beta}_j, \boldsymbol{\alpha}_i)(\boldsymbol{\alpha}_i, \mathbf{x}) - (\boldsymbol{\gamma}_j, \mathbf{x}) = 0$$

or

$$(\boldsymbol{\beta}_j, \mathbf{x}) - \sum_{i=1}^{j-1} (\boldsymbol{\beta}_j, \boldsymbol{\alpha}_i)v_i - \sqrt{(\boldsymbol{\gamma}_j, \boldsymbol{\gamma}_j)}\,v_j = 0.$$

Then, by (5.13),

$$(\boldsymbol{\beta}_j, \mathbf{x}) = u_j.$$

In application, all can be accomplished by using the array $[\mathbf{B} \vdots \mathbf{u}]$ and forming in the same locations the array $[\mathbf{A} \vdots \mathbf{v}]$. If it is desired to vary the vector **u** after **A** has been built, it will be necessary to record the n numbers $\sqrt{(\boldsymbol{\gamma}_i, \boldsymbol{\gamma}_i)}$ and the $(n^2 - n)/2$ numbers $(\boldsymbol{\beta}_j, \boldsymbol{\alpha}_i)$, $1 \leqslant i < j$, $2 \leqslant j \leqslant n$. The building of the matrix $[\mathbf{A} \vdots \mathbf{v}]$ from $[\mathbf{B} \vdots \mathbf{u}]$ can be visualized best by writing the conjugates of relations (5.12) [but not of (5.13)]. Then observe that the first row of $[\mathbf{A} \vdots \mathbf{v}]$ is formed from the first row of $[\mathbf{B} \vdots \mathbf{u}]$, the second row of $[\mathbf{A} \vdots \mathbf{v}]$ from the second row of $[\mathbf{B} \vdots \mathbf{u}]$ and the just established row of $[\mathbf{A} \vdots \mathbf{v}]$, etc. Each operation involved can be viewed as tantamount to premultiplication by an elementary matrix of the first or third kind. Thus there exists a nonsingular matrix $\boldsymbol{\phi}$ such that

$$\boldsymbol{\phi}[\mathbf{B} \vdots \mathbf{u}] = [\mathbf{A} \vdots \mathbf{v}].$$

It will be seen that

$$\det(\boldsymbol{\phi}) = \prod_{i=1}^{n} \frac{1}{\sqrt{(\boldsymbol{\gamma}_i, \boldsymbol{\gamma}_i)}}. \tag{5.14}$$

This knowledge can be useful in case the matrix **B** is *ill-conditioned*, that is, has rows or columns so nearly dependent on each other that rounding or truncation errors can cause the calculated determinantal value to deviate markedly from its true value. Now recall that $|\det(\mathbf{A})| = 1$ to realize that (5.14) can accomplish the purpose cited. Note also that the sequences $\{\boldsymbol{\alpha}_j\}$, $\{v_j\}$, and $\{\mathbf{r}_j\}$ can progress together, so that the method can properly be called an n-step method.

After orthogonalization, it is also possible to find the solution vector **x** as $\mathbf{A}^*\mathbf{v}$.

Example. As a simple illustration of the Kaczmarz method, we consider the following problem, also discussed in Sections 5.6 and 5.7:

$$\begin{aligned} 4x_1 + 2x_2 + x_3 &= 11, \\ -x_1 + 2x_2 &= 3, \\ 2x_1 + x_2 + 4x_3 &= 16. \end{aligned}$$

The matrix $[\mathbf{B} \vdots \mathbf{u}]$ is

$$\begin{bmatrix} 4 & 2 & 1 & 11 \\ -1 & 2 & 0 & 3 \\ 2 & 1 & 4 & 16 \end{bmatrix}.$$

The first row of $[\mathbf{A} \vdots \mathbf{v}]$ is that of $[\mathbf{B} \vdots \mathbf{u}]$ divided by $\sqrt{4^2 + 2^2 + 1^2}$ or $\left[\dfrac{4}{\sqrt{21}}, \dfrac{2}{\sqrt{21}}, \dfrac{1}{\sqrt{21}}, \dfrac{11}{\sqrt{21}}\right]$. Prior to normalizing, the second row is

$$[-1, 2, 0, 3] - 0\left[\frac{4}{\sqrt{21}}, \frac{2}{\sqrt{21}}, \frac{1}{\sqrt{21}}, \frac{11}{\sqrt{21}}\right] = [-1, 2, 0, 3].$$

The normalizing factor is $\sqrt{1^2 + 2^2}$, so that the second row of $[\mathbf{A} \vdots \mathbf{v}]$ is $\left[\dfrac{-1}{\sqrt{5}}, \dfrac{2}{\sqrt{5}}, 0, \dfrac{3}{\sqrt{5}}\right]$. Prior to normalizing, the third row is

$$[2, 1, 4, 16] - \left(\frac{14}{\sqrt{21}}\right)\left[\frac{4}{\sqrt{21}}, \frac{2}{\sqrt{21}}, \frac{1}{\sqrt{21}}, \frac{11}{\sqrt{21}}\right]$$

$$+ 0\left[\frac{-1}{\sqrt{5}}, \frac{2}{\sqrt{5}}, 0, \frac{3}{\sqrt{5}}\right] \quad \text{or} \quad \left[-\frac{2}{3}, -\frac{1}{3}, \frac{10}{3}, \frac{26}{3}\right].$$

Thus for $[\mathbf{A} \vdots \mathbf{v}]$, we have

$$\begin{bmatrix} \dfrac{4}{\sqrt{21}} & \dfrac{2}{\sqrt{21}} & \dfrac{1}{\sqrt{21}} & \dfrac{11}{\sqrt{21}} \\[2ex] -\dfrac{1}{\sqrt{5}} & \dfrac{2}{\sqrt{5}} & 0 & \dfrac{3}{\sqrt{5}} \\[2ex] -\dfrac{2}{\sqrt{105}} & -\dfrac{1}{\sqrt{105}} & \dfrac{10}{\sqrt{105}} & \dfrac{26}{\sqrt{105}} \end{bmatrix}.$$

Using $\mathbf{r}_0 = [1, 1, 1]^t$, we find

$$\mathbf{r}_1 = [1, 1, 1]^t - \left(-\frac{4}{\sqrt{21}}\right)\left[\frac{4}{\sqrt{21}}, \frac{2}{\sqrt{21}}, \frac{1}{\sqrt{21}}\right]^t$$

$$= \left[\frac{37}{21}, \frac{29}{21}, \frac{25}{21}\right]^t.$$

Then

$$\mathbf{r}_2 = \left[\frac{37}{21}, \frac{29}{21}, \frac{25}{21}\right]^t - \left(\frac{-2}{\sqrt{5}}\right)\left[\frac{-1}{\sqrt{5}}, \frac{2}{\sqrt{5}}, 0\right]^t$$

$$= \left[\frac{143}{105}, \frac{229}{105}, \frac{25}{21}\right]^t.$$

There results

$$\mathbf{r}_3 = \left[\frac{143}{105}, \frac{229}{105}, \frac{25}{21}\right]^t - \left(-\frac{19}{\sqrt{105}}\right)\left[\frac{-2}{\sqrt{105}}, \frac{-1}{\sqrt{105}}, \frac{10}{\sqrt{105}}\right]^t$$

$$= [1, 2, 3]^t.$$

5.6   Jacobi Iterative Method

Consider again the solution of the linear system $\mathbf{Bx} = \mathbf{u}$:

$$\begin{aligned} b_{11}x_1 + b_{12}x_2 + \cdots + b_{1n}x_n &= u_1, \\ b_{21}x_1 + b_{22}x_2 + \cdots + b_{2n}x_n &= u_2, \\ \vdots \qquad\qquad\qquad &\quad \vdots \\ b_{n1}x_1 + b_{n2}x_2 + \cdots + b_{nn}x_n &= u_n. \end{aligned} \qquad (5.2)$$

We now formulate the *Jacobi iterative method* for *approximating* the solution of (5.2). The degree of

approximation, however, can normally be improved by expending more computational effort, that is, by performing an increased number of iterations.

First, solve for the x_i, giving:

$$\begin{aligned} x_1 &= (u_1 - b_{12}x_2 - b_{13}x_3 - \cdots - b_{1n}x_n)/b_{11}, \\ x_2 &= (u_2 - b_{21}x_1 - b_{23}x_3 - \cdots - b_{2n}x_n)/b_{22}, \\ \vdots &\qquad\qquad\qquad\qquad\qquad\qquad \vdots \\ x_n &= (u_n - b_{n1}x_1 - b_{n2}x_2 - \cdots - b_{n,n-1}x_{n-1})/b_{nn}. \end{aligned} \qquad (5.15)$$

The system (5.15) can be written more concisely as

$$x_i = \frac{\left(u_i - \displaystyle\sum_{\substack{j=1 \\ j \neq i}}^{n} b_{ij}x_j\right)}{b_{ii}}, \quad i = 1, 2, \ldots, n. \qquad (5.16)$$

Note that the above rearrangement is predicated on $b_{ii} \neq 0$. Usually, we try to reorder the equations and the unknowns so that *diagonal dominance* is obtained, that is, so that each diagonal element b_{ii} is larger, in absolute value, than the magnitudes of other entries in row i and column i. In this connection, also see equations (5.21).

Next, make starting guesses for the x's and insert these values into the right-hand sides of (5.15). The resulting new approximations for the x's are resubstituted into the right-hand sides of (5.15), and the process is repeated. Hopefully, the x's thus computed will show little further change after several such iterations have been made.

Example. Consider the equations

$$\begin{aligned} 4x_1 + 2x_2 + x_3 &= 11, \\ -x_1 + 2x_2 \qquad &= 3, \\ 2x_1 + x_2 + 4x_3 &= 16, \end{aligned}$$

which have the solution vector $\mathbf{x} = [1, 2, 3]^t$, that is, $x_1 = 1$, $x_2 = 2$, and $x_3 = 3$. Rewrite the equations as

$$x_1 = \frac{11}{4} - \frac{1}{2}x_2 - \frac{1}{4}x_3,$$

$$x_2 = \frac{3}{2} + \frac{1}{2}x_1,$$

$$x_3 = 4 - \frac{1}{2}x_1 - \frac{1}{4}x_2,$$

and arbitrarily choose a starting vector $\mathbf{x}_0 = [1, 1, 1]^t$ in which the subscript denotes the *zero*th stage of iteration. Using a second subscript to denote the iteration number, the first iteration gives

$$x_{11} = \frac{11}{4} - \frac{1}{2} \times 1 - \frac{1}{4} \times 1 = 2,$$

$$x_{21} = \frac{3}{2} + \frac{1}{2} \times 1 = 2,$$

$$x_{31} = 4 - \frac{1}{2} \times 1 - \frac{1}{4} \times 1 = \frac{13}{4}.$$

That is, $\mathbf{x}_1 = [2, 2, 13/4]^t$. Similarly, the next four iterations yield

$$\mathbf{x}_2 = \left[\frac{15}{16}, \frac{5}{2}, \frac{5}{2}\right]^t,$$

$$\mathbf{x}_3 = \left[\frac{7}{8}, \frac{63}{32}, \frac{93}{32}\right]^t,$$

$$\mathbf{x}_4 = \left[\frac{133}{128}, \frac{31}{16}, \frac{393}{128}\right]^t,$$

$$\mathbf{x}_5 = \left[\frac{519}{512}, \frac{517}{256}, \frac{767}{256}\right]^t.$$

The approximation computed at the fifth iteration is roughly within 1% of the exact solution. The accuracy could be improved by performing more iterations. Observe that a whole new solution vector is computed before it is used in the next iteration.

In order to establish a criterion for the convergence of the Jacobi method, regard the rearranged equations (5.15) as the system

$$\mathbf{x} = \mathbf{A}\mathbf{x} + \mathbf{v}, \tag{5.17}$$

in which

$$\mathbf{A} = -\begin{bmatrix} 0 & \dfrac{b_{12}}{b_{11}} & \dfrac{b_{13}}{b_{11}} & \cdots & \dfrac{b_{1n}}{b_{11}} \\ \dfrac{b_{21}}{b_{22}} & 0 & \dfrac{b_{23}}{b_{22}} & \cdots & \dfrac{b_{2n}}{b_{22}} \\ \vdots & & & & \vdots \\ \dfrac{b_{n1}}{b_{nn}} & \dfrac{b_{n2}}{b_{nn}} & \cdots & \dfrac{b_{n,n-1}}{b_{nn}} & 0 \end{bmatrix}, \quad \mathbf{v} = \begin{bmatrix} \dfrac{u_1}{b_{11}} \\ \dfrac{u_2}{b_{22}} \\ \vdots \\ \dfrac{u_n}{b_{nn}} \end{bmatrix}. \tag{5.18}$$

If the starting vector $\mathbf{x}_0$ is near the solution vector $\mathbf{x}$, convergence will be faster. In any event, define

$$\mathbf{x}_{k+1} = \mathbf{A}\mathbf{x}_k + \mathbf{v}, \tag{5.19}$$

in which the subscript k is the iteration number. This means that

$$\mathbf{x}_k = \mathbf{A}^k \mathbf{x}_0 + [\mathbf{I} + \mathbf{A} + \mathbf{A}^2 + \cdots + \mathbf{A}^{k-1}]\mathbf{v}.$$

From this, we see that convergence normally requires that

$$\lim_{k \to \infty} \mathbf{A}^k = \mathbf{0}. \tag{5.20}$$

From (4.23), it is also a necessary and sufficient condition that

$$\lim_{k \to \infty} [\mathbf{I} + \mathbf{A} + \mathbf{A}^2 + \cdots + \mathbf{A}^k] = (\mathbf{I} - \mathbf{A})^{-1}.$$

Thus, when (5.20) is satisfied, $\mathbf{x} = \lim_{k \to \infty} \mathbf{x}_k$ exists and $\mathbf{x} = \mathbf{0} + (\mathbf{I} - \mathbf{A})^{-1}\mathbf{v}$; that is $(\mathbf{I} - \mathbf{A})\mathbf{x} = \mathbf{v}$ or $\mathbf{x} = \mathbf{A}\mathbf{x} + \mathbf{v}$.

Thus, convergence hinges on the truth of (5.20). From page 222, (5.20) is true if and only if all eigenvalues of $\mathbf{A}$ are in modulus less than unity. For this to be so, from (4.25), (4.26), and the subsequent development, we have the sufficient conditions

$$\left. \begin{aligned} \sum_{i=1}^{n} |a_{ij}| &\leqslant \mu < 1, & 1 \leqslant j \leqslant n, \\[1em] \sum_{j=1}^{n} |a_{ij}| &\leqslant \mu < 1, & 1 \leqslant i \leqslant n, \\[1em] \sum_{i=1}^{n} \sum_{j=1}^{n} |a_{ij}|^2 &\leqslant \mu < 1. & \end{aligned} \right\} \tag{5.21}$$

or

or

By using (5.18), these sufficiency conditions can also be translated into an equivalent set of conditions on the elements of the original coefficient matrix $\mathbf{B}$. For example, the second condition of (5.21) becomes

$$\sum_{\substack{j=1 \\ j \neq i}}^{n} |b_{ij}| < |b_{ii}|, \quad 1 \leqslant i \leqslant n. \tag{5.22}$$

If, as frequently occurs, matrix $\mathbf{B}$ is *irreducible* (that is, the solution of the original system of equations cannot be reduced to the solution of two or more systems of lower order), the sufficiency condition can be relaxed (for example, see Ralston and Wilf [1]) to

$$\sum_{\substack{j=1 \\ j \neq i}}^{n} |b_{ij}| \leqslant |b_{ii}|, \quad 1 \leqslant i \leqslant n, \tag{5.23}$$

with strict inequality holding for at least one value of i.

5.7 Gauss-Seidel Iterative Method

The linear system considered is again that of (5.2) rephrased in the form (5.15) or (5.17). In the iterations, however, the newly-computed components of the $\mathbf{x}$ vector are always used in the right-hand sides as soon as they are obtained. This contrasts with the Jacobi method, in which the new components are not used until all n components have been found.

Example. The Gauss-Seidel method is applied to the short example considered under the Jacobi method. The form used is

$$x_1 = \frac{11}{4} - \frac{1}{2}x_2 - \frac{1}{4}x_3,$$

$$x_2 = \frac{3}{2} + \frac{1}{2}x_1,$$

$$x_3 = 4 - \frac{1}{2}x_1 - \frac{1}{4}x_2,$$

with the understanding that the most recently available x's are always used in the right-hand sides. Again $\mathbf{x}_0$ is chosen as $[1, 1, 1]^t$. The first iteration gives

$$x_{11} = \frac{11}{4} - \frac{1}{2} \times 1 - \frac{1}{4} \times 1 = 2,$$

$$x_{21} = \frac{3}{2} + \frac{1}{2} \times 2 = \frac{5}{2},$$

$$x_{31} = 4 - \frac{1}{2} \times 2 - \frac{1}{4} \times \frac{5}{2} = \frac{19}{8}.$$

That is,

$$\mathbf{x}_1 = \left[2, \frac{5}{2}, \frac{19}{8}\right]^t.$$

Similarly, the next two iterations yield

$$\mathbf{x}_2 = \left[\frac{29}{32}, \frac{125}{64}, \frac{783}{256}\right]^t,$$

$$\mathbf{x}_3 = \left[\frac{1033}{1024}, \frac{4095}{2048}, \frac{24541}{8192}\right]^t.$$

Observe that in this example the rate of convergence is much faster than that in the Jacobi method.

In order to investigate the conditions for the convergence of the Gauss-Seidel method, we first phrase the iteration in terms of the individual components. Let x_{ik} denote the kth approximation to the ith component of the solution vector $\mathbf{x} = [x_1, x_2, \ldots, x_n]^t$. Let $[x_{10}, x_{20}, \ldots, x_{n0}]^t$ be an arbitrary initial approximation (though, as with the Jacobi method, if a good estimate is known, it should be used for efficiency). Let $\mathbf{A}$ and $\mathbf{v}$ be the same as given in (5.18), and define

$$x_{ik} = \sum_{j=1}^{i-1} a_{ij} x_{jk} + \sum_{j=i+1}^{n} a_{ij} x_{j,k-1} + v_i, \quad (5.24)$$

for $1 \leqslant i \leqslant n$ and $1 \leqslant k$. When $i = 1$, $\sum_{j=1}^{i-1} a_{ij} x_{jk}$ is interpreted as zero, and when $i = n$, $\sum_{j=i+1}^{n} a_{ij} x_{j,k-1}$ is likewise interpreted as zero.

Write $\mathbf{A} = \mathbf{A_L} + \mathbf{A_R}$ where

$$\mathbf{A_L} = \begin{bmatrix} 0 & 0 & \cdots & 0 & 0 \\ a_{21} & 0 & \cdots & 0 & 0 \\ \vdots & & & & \vdots \\ a_{n1} & a_{n2} & \cdots & a_{n,n-1} & 0 \end{bmatrix},$$

$$\mathbf{A_R} = \begin{bmatrix} 0 & a_{12} & \cdots & a_{1n} \\ 0 & 0 & \cdots & a_{2n} \\ \vdots & & & \vdots \\ 0 & 0 & \cdots & 0 \end{bmatrix}.$$

Thus $\mathbf{A_L}$ is a strictly lower-triangular matrix whose subdiagonal entries are the elements of $\mathbf{A}$ in their natural positions. A similar description applies to $\mathbf{A_R}$. It is seen that, if $\mathbf{x}_k = [x_{1k}, x_{2k}, \ldots, x_{nk}]^t$,

$$\mathbf{x}_k = \mathbf{A_L} \mathbf{x}_k + \mathbf{A_R} \mathbf{x}_{k-1} + \mathbf{v}.$$

This can be paraphrased as

$$\mathbf{x}_k = (\mathbf{I} - \mathbf{A_L})^{-1} \mathbf{A_R} \mathbf{x}_{k-1} + (\mathbf{I} - \mathbf{A_L})^{-1} \mathbf{v}, \quad (5.25)$$

which is then of the Jacobi form. This means that a necessary and sufficient condition for the convergence of (5.24) is that the eigenvalues of $(\mathbf{I} - \mathbf{A_L})^{-1} \mathbf{A_R}$ be less than unity in modulus. The eigenvalues of $(\mathbf{I} - \mathbf{A_L})^{-1} \mathbf{A_R}$ are found by solving $\det((\mathbf{I} - \mathbf{A_L})^{-1} \mathbf{A_R} - \lambda \mathbf{I}) = 0$, or $\det([\mathbf{I} - \mathbf{A_L}]^{-1} \times [\mathbf{A_R} - \lambda(\mathbf{I} - \mathbf{A_L})]) = 0$, or $\det(\mathbf{A_R} - \lambda \mathbf{I} + \lambda \mathbf{A_L}) = 0$. Thus the Gauss-Seidel process converges if and only if the zeros of the determinant of

$$\begin{bmatrix} -\lambda & a_{12} & a_{13} & \cdots & a_{1n} \\ a_{21}\lambda & -\lambda & a_{23} & \cdots & a_{2n} \\ a_{31}\lambda & a_{32}\lambda & -\lambda & \cdots & a_{3n} \\ \vdots & & & & \vdots \\ a_{n1}\lambda & a_{n2}\lambda & a_{n3}\lambda & \cdots & -\lambda \end{bmatrix} \quad (5.26)$$

are less than one in absolute value.

Since $a_{ii} = 0$, $1 \leqslant i \leqslant n$, while $a_{ij} = -b_{ij}/b_{ii}$ for $i \neq j$, the determinant of (5.26) has the same zeros as the determinant of

$$\begin{bmatrix} b_{11}\lambda & b_{12} & b_{13} & \cdots & b_{1n} \\ b_{21}\lambda & b_{22}\lambda & b_{23} & \cdots & b_{2n} \\ b_{31}\lambda & b_{32}\lambda & b_{33}\lambda & \cdots & b_{3n} \\ \vdots & & & & \vdots \\ b_{n1}\lambda & b_{n2}\lambda & b_{n3}\lambda & \cdots & b_{nn}\lambda \end{bmatrix}. \quad (5.27)$$

It develops that conditions analogous to the first two of (5.21) prove sufficient to guarantee convergence, namely,

$$\sum_{\substack{j=1 \\ j \neq i}}^{n} \left| \frac{b_{ij}}{b_{ii}} \right| \leqslant \mu < 1 \quad \text{or} \quad \sum_{\substack{j=1 \\ j \neq i}}^{n} \left| \frac{b_{ji}}{b_{jj}} \right| \leqslant \mu < 1, \quad 1 \leqslant i \leqslant n. \quad (5.28)$$

The first of these may be demonstrated as follows. We have already seen in (4.14) that since

$$|b_{ii}| > \sum_{\substack{j=1 \\ j \neq i}}^{n} |b_{ij}|,$$

$\mathbf{B}$ is nonsingular. Thus a solution vector $\mathbf{x}$ exists such that $\mathbf{x} = \mathbf{A}\mathbf{x} + \mathbf{v}$, whence

$$x_i = \sum_{\substack{j=1 \\ j \neq i}}^{n} a_{ij} x_j + v_i,$$

in which $a_{ij} = -b_{ij}/b_{ii}$. Subtracting this from (5.24) yields

$$|x_{ik} - x_i| \leqslant \sum_{j=1}^{i-1} |a_{ij}| |x_{jk} - x_j| + \sum_{j=i+1}^{n} |a_{ij}| |x_{j,k-1} - x_j|. \quad (5.29)$$

Let e_k denote the maximum of the numbers $|x_{ik} - x_i|$ as i varies. Then

$$|x_{1k} - x_1| \leqslant \sum_{j=2}^{n} |a_{1j}| e_{k-1} \leqslant \mu e_{k-1} < e_{k-1}.$$

Substituting this in (5.29) yields

$$|x_{2k} - x_2| \leqslant |a_{21}| e_{k-1} + \sum_{j=3}^{n} |a_{2j}| e_{k-1} \leqslant \mu e_{k-1}.$$

Continuing as indicated gives $|x_{ik} - x_i| \leqslant \mu e_{k-1}, 1 \leqslant i \leqslant n$. This means, of course, that $|x_{ik} - x_i| \leqslant \mu^k e_0$, whence, since $0 < \mu < 1$, $\lim_{k \to \infty} x_{ik} = x_i$.

More interesting still than the sufficiency conditions of (5.28) is the fact that convergence always takes place if the matrix **B** of (5.3) is positive definite. To demonstrate this, let $\mathbf{B} = \mathbf{D} + \mathbf{L} + \bar{\mathbf{L}}^t$ where $\mathbf{D} = \bar{\mathbf{D}}$ is the matrix $\text{diag}(b_{11}, b_{22}, \ldots, b_{nn})$, and **L** is the strictly lower-triangular matrix formed from the elements of **B** below the diagonal. Starting from (5.25), it is seen that a necessary and sufficient condition for convergence is that all eigenvalues of $(\mathbf{I} - \mathbf{A_L})^{-1}\mathbf{A_R}$ be of modulus less than unity. But $\mathbf{A_L} = -\mathbf{D}^{-1}\mathbf{L}$ and $\mathbf{A_R} = -\mathbf{D}^{-1}\mathbf{L}^*$. Thus $(\mathbf{I} - \mathbf{A_L})^{-1}\mathbf{A_R} = -(\mathbf{D} + \mathbf{L})^{-1}\mathbf{L}^*$. The eigenvalues of this matrix, except for sign, are those of $(\mathbf{D} + \mathbf{L})^{-1}\mathbf{L}^*$, which we consider instead. Let λ_i be an eigenvalue of this matrix, and let $\mathbf{w}_i$ be the corresponding eigenvector. Since **B** is positive definite,

$$(\mathbf{w}_i, \mathbf{Bw}_i) = (\mathbf{w}_i, \mathbf{Dw}_i) + (\mathbf{w}_i, \mathbf{Lw}_i) + (\mathbf{w}_i, \mathbf{L}^*\mathbf{w}_i) > 0. \quad (5.30)$$

But $(\mathbf{D} + \mathbf{L})^{-1}\mathbf{L}^*\mathbf{w}_i = \lambda_i \mathbf{w}_i$, so that $\mathbf{L}^*\mathbf{w}_i = \lambda_i \mathbf{Dw}_i + \lambda_i \mathbf{Lw}_i$; then

$$(\mathbf{w}_i, \mathbf{L}^*\mathbf{w}_i) = \lambda_i [(\mathbf{w}_i, \mathbf{Dw}_i) + (\mathbf{w}_i, \mathbf{Lw}_i)]. \quad (5.31)$$

Taking the conjugate of both sides, $(\mathbf{L}^*\mathbf{w}_i, \mathbf{w}_i) = (\mathbf{w}_i, \mathbf{Lw}_i)$ $= \bar{\lambda}_i [(\mathbf{Dw}_i, \mathbf{w}_i) + (\mathbf{Lw}_i, \mathbf{w}_i)]$, or

$$(\mathbf{w}_i, \mathbf{Lw}_i) = \bar{\lambda}_i [(\mathbf{w}_i, \mathbf{Dw}_i) + (\mathbf{w}_i, \mathbf{L}^*\mathbf{w}_i)]. \quad (5.32)$$

Combining (5.31) and (5.32) gives

$$(\mathbf{w}_i, \mathbf{L}^*\mathbf{w}_i) = \frac{\lambda_i + \lambda_i \bar{\lambda}_i}{1 - \lambda_i \bar{\lambda}_i}(\mathbf{w}_i, \mathbf{Dw}_i),$$

$$(\mathbf{w}_i, \mathbf{Lw}_i) = \frac{\bar{\lambda}_i + \bar{\lambda}_i \lambda_i}{1 - \bar{\lambda}_i \lambda_i}(\mathbf{w}_i, \mathbf{Dw}_i).$$

Substituting directly in (5.30) yields

$$\frac{(1 + \lambda_i)(1 + \bar{\lambda}_i)}{1 - \bar{\lambda}_i \lambda_i}(\mathbf{w}_i, \mathbf{Dw}_i) > 0.$$

Since **D** is itself positive definite, $(\mathbf{w}_i, \mathbf{Dw}_i) > 0$; hence $1 - \bar{\lambda}_i \lambda_i > 0$, or $|\lambda_i| < 1$.

Thus, sufficiency has been shown. It is also possible to prove that if the matrix **B** is Hermitian and all diagonal elements are positive, then convergence requires that **B** be positive definite.

The solution of systems of equations by iterative procedures such as the Jacobi and Gauss-Seidel methods is sometimes termed *relaxation* (the errors in the initial estimate of the solution vector are decreased or relaxed as calculation continues). The Gauss-Seidel and related methods are used extensively in the solution of large systems of linear equations, generated as the result of the finite-difference approximation of partial differential equations (see Chapter 7).

EXAMPLE 5.3

GAUSS-SEIDEL METHOD

Problem Statement

Write a program that implements the Gauss-Seidel method, described in Section 5.7, for solving the following system of n simultaneous linear equations:

$$
\begin{aligned}
a_{11}x_1 + a_{12}x_2 + \cdots + a_{1n}x_n &= a_{1,n+1} \\
a_{21}x_1 + a_{22}x_2 + \cdots + a_{2n}x_n &= a_{2,n+1} \\
&\ \ \vdots \\
a_{n1}x_1 + a_{n2}x_2 + \cdots + a_{nn}x_n &= a_{n,n+1},
\end{aligned}
\tag{5.3.1}
$$

in which the a_{ij} are constants.

Method of Solution

In order to reduce the number of divisions required in the calculations, the coefficients of (5.3.1) are first normalized by dividing all elements in row i by a_{ii}, $i = 1, 2, \ldots, n$, to produce an augmented coefficient matrix of the form

$$
\begin{bmatrix}
1 & a'_{12} & a'_{13} & \cdots & a'_{1n} & a'_{1,n+1} \\
a'_{21} & 1 & a'_{23} & \cdots & a'_{2n} & a'_{2,n+1} \\
\vdots & & & & \vdots & \vdots \\
a'_{n1} & a'_{n2} & a'_{n3} & \cdots & 1 & a'_{n,n+1}
\end{bmatrix},
\tag{5.3.2}
$$

where $a'_{ij} = a_{ij}/a_{ii}$.

In terms of this notation, the approximation to the solution vector after the kth iteration,

$$
\mathbf{x}_k = [x_{1k}, x_{2k}, \ldots, x_{nk}]^t,
$$

is modified by the algorithm

$$
x_{i,k+1} = a'_{i,n+1} - \sum_{j=1}^{i-1} a'_{ij}x_{j,k+1} - \sum_{j=i+1}^{n} a'_{ij}x_{jk},
\tag{5.3.3}
$$
$$
i = 1, 2, \ldots, n,
$$

to produce the next approximation

$$
\mathbf{x}_{k+1} = [x_{1,k+1}, x_{2,k+1}, \ldots, x_{n,k+1}]^t.
$$

Since, in the Gauss-Seidel method, the new values $x_{i,k+1}$ replace the old values x_{ik} as soon as computed, the iteration subscript k can be omitted, and (5.3.3) becomes

$$
x_i = a'_{i,n+1} - \sum_{\substack{j=1 \\ j \neq i}}^{n} a'_{ij}x_j, \qquad i = 1, 2, \ldots, n,
\tag{5.3.4}
$$

in which the most recently available x_j values are always used on the right-hand side. Hopefully, the x_i values computed by iterating with (5.3.4) will converge to the solution of (5.3.1).

The convergence criterion is

$$
|x_{i,k+1} - x_{ik}| < \varepsilon, \qquad i = 1, 2, \ldots, n,
\tag{5.3.5}
$$

that is, no element of the solution vector may have its magnitude changed by an amount greater than ε as a result of one Gauss-Seidel iteration. Since convergence may not occur, an upper limit on the number of iterations, k_{max}, is also specified.

Example 5.3   Gauss-Seidel Method   **303**

Flow Diagram

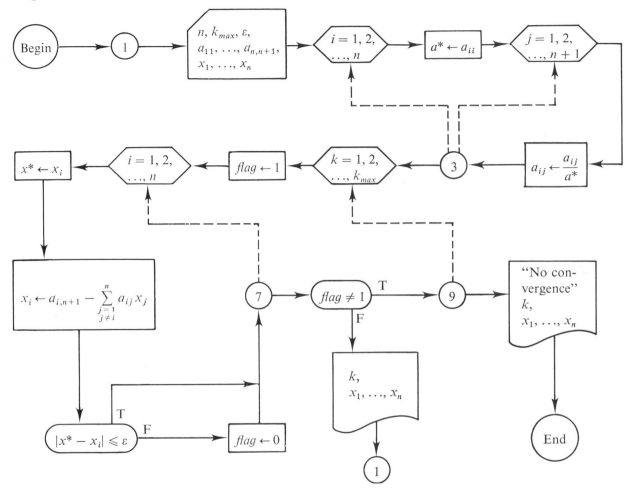

FORTRAN *Implementation*

        List of Principal Variables

Program Symbol	*Definition*
A	$n \times (n + 1)$ augmented coefficient matrix, containing elements a_{ij}.
ASTAR, XSTAR	Temporary storage locations for elements of A and X, respectively.
EPS	Tolerance used in convergence test, ε.
FLAG	A flag used in convergence testing; it has the value 1 for successful convergence, and the value 0 otherwise.
ITER	Iteration counter, k.
ITMAX	The maximum number of iterations allowed, k_{max}.
N	Number of simultaneous equations, n.
X	Vector containing the elements of the current approximation to the solution vector, $\mathbf{x}_k$.

Program Listing

```
C             APPLIED NUMERICAL METHODS, EXAMPLE 5.3
C             GAUSS-SEIDEL ITERATION FOR N SIMULTANEOUS LINEAR EQUATIONS.
C
C             THE ARRAY A CONTAINS THE N X N+1 AUGMENTED COEFFICIENT MATRIX.
C             THE VECTOR X CONTAINS THE LATEST APPROXIMATION TO THE SOLUTION.
C             THE COEFFICIENT MATRIX SHOULD BE DIAGONALLY DOMINANT AND
C             PREFERABLY POSITIVE DEFINITE.   ITMAX IS THE MAXIMUM NUMBER OF
C             ITERATIONS ALLOWED.   EPS IS USED IN CONVERGENCE TESTING.  IN
C             TERMINATING THE ITERATIONS, NO ELEMENT OF X MAY UNDERGO A MAG-
C             NITUDE CHANGE GREATER THAN EPS FROM ONE ITERATION TO THE NEXT.
C
      INTEGER FLAG
      DIMENSION A(20,20), X(20)
C
C      ..... READ AND CHECK INPUT PARAMETERS,
C             COEFFICIENT MATRIX, AND STARTING VECTOR .....
    1 READ (5,100) N, ITMAX, EPS
      WRITE (6,200) N, ITMAX, EPS
      NP1 = N + 1
      READ (5,101) ((A(I,J), J = 1, NP1), I = 1, N)
      READ (5,101) (X(I), I = 1, N)
      DO 2  I = 1, N
    2 WRITE (6,201) (A(I,J), J = 1, NP1)
      WRITE (6,202) (X(I), I = 1, N)
C
C      ..... NORMALIZE DIAGONAL ELEMENTS IN EACH ROW .....
      DO 3  I = 1, N
      ASTAR = A(I,I)
      DO 3  J = 1, NP1
    3 A(I,J) = A(I,J)/ASTAR
C
C      ..... BEGIN GAUSS-SEIDEL ITERATIONS .....
      DO 9  ITER = 1, ITMAX
      FLAG = 1
      DO 7  I = 1, N
      XSTAR = X(I)
      X(I) = A(I,NP1)
C
C      ..... FIND NEW SOLUTION VALUE, X(I) .....
      DO 5  J = 1, N
      IF (I .EQ. J) GO TO 5
        X(I) = X(I) - A(I,J)*X(J)
    5 CONTINUE
C
C      ..... TEST X(I) FOR CONVERGENCE .....
      IF (ABS(XSTAR - X(I)) .LE. EPS) GO TO 7
        FLAG = 0
    7 CONTINUE
      IF (FLAG .NE. 1) GO TO 9
        WRITE (6,203) ITER, (X(I), I = 1, N)
        GO TO 1
    9 CONTINUE
C
C      ..... REMARK IF METHOD DID NOT CONVERGE .....
      WRITE (6,204) ITER, (X(I), I = 1, N)
      GO TO 1
C
C      ..... FORMATS FOR INPUT AND OUTPUT STATEMENTS .....
  100 FORMAT (6X, I4, 16X, I4, 14X, F10.6)
  101 FORMAT (10X, 6F10.5)
  200 FORMAT (72H1 SOLUTION OF SIMULTANEOUS LINEAR EQUATIONS BY GAUSS-SE
     1IDEL METHOD, WITH           /1H0, 5X, 9HN        = , I4/
     2 6X, 9HITMAX   = , I4/ 6X, 9HEPS       = , F10.5/ 47H0 THE COEFFICIENT
     3 MATRIX A(1,1)...A(N+1,N+1) IS)
  201 FORMAT (1H0, 11F10.5)
  202 FORMAT (36H0 THE STARTING VECTOR X(1)...X(N) IS/ (1H0, 10F10.5))
  203 FORMAT (35H0 PROCEDURE CONVERGED, WITH ITER = , I4/
     1 32H0 SOLUTION VECTOR X(1)...X(N) IS/ (1H0, 10F10.5))
  204 FORMAT (16H0 NO CONVERGENCE/ 10H0 ITER  = , I4/
     1 31H0 CURRENT VECTOR X(1)...X(N) IS/ (1H0, 10F10.5))
C
      END
```

Example 5.3   Gauss-Seidel Method   **305**

Program Listing (*Continued*)

Data

```
N  =   4         ITMAX  =   15     EPS     =  0.0001
A(1,1) =    5.0          1.0          3.0          0.0         16.0          1.0
                        4.0          1.0          1.0         11.0         -1.0          2.0
                        6.0         -2.0         23.0          1.0         -1.0          1.0
                        4.0         -2.0
X(1)   =    1.0          2.0          3.0          4.0
N  =   4         ITMAX  =   15     EPS     =  0.0001
A(1,1) =    5.0          1.0          3.0          0.0         16.0          1.0
                        4.0          1.0          1.0         11.0         -1.0          2.0
                        6.0         -2.0         23.0          1.0         -1.0          1.0
                        4.0         -2.0
X(1)   =   50.0         50.0         50.0         50.0
N  =   6         ITMAX  =   50     EPS     =  0.0001
A(1,1) =    4.0         -1.0          0.0         -1.0          0.0          0.0
                      100.0         -1.0          4.0         -1.0          0.0         -1.0
                        0.0          0.0          0.0         -1.0          4.0          0.0
                        0.0         -1.0          0.0         -1.0          0.0          0.0
                        4.0         -1.0          0.0        100.0          0.0         -1.0
                        0.0         -1.0          4.0         -1.0          0.0          0.0
                        0.0         -1.0          0.0         -1.0          4.0          0.0
X(1)   =    0.0          0.0          0.0          0.0          0.0          0.0
```

Computer Output

Results for the 1st Data Set

```
SOLUTION OF SIMULTANEOUS LINEAR EQUATIONS BY GAUSS-SEIDEL METHOD, WITH

    N      =     4
    ITMAX  =    15
    EPS    =     0.00010

THE COEFFICIENT MATRIX A(1,1)...A(N+1,N+1) IS

   5.00000    1.00000    3.00000    0.0       16.00000

   1.00000    4.00000    1.00000    1.00000   11.00000

  -1.00000    2.00000    6.00000   -2.00000   23.00000

   1.00000   -1.00000    1.00000    4.00000   -2.00000

THE STARTING VECTOR X(1)...X(N) IS

   1.00000    2.00000    3.00000    4.00000

PROCEDURE CONVERGED, WITH ITER =    12

SOLUTION VECTOR X(1)...X(N) IS

   0.99998    2.00000    2.99999   -0.99999
```

Partial Results for the 2nd Data Set (*Same Equations as 1st Set*)

```
THE STARTING VECTOR X(1)...X(N) IS

  50.00000   50.00000   50.00000   50.00000

PROCEDURE CONVERGED, WITH ITER =    13

SOLUTION VECTOR X(1)...X(N) IS

   1.00002    2.00000    3.00001   -1.00001
```

Computer Output (*Continued*)

Results for the 3rd Data Set

```
SOLUTION OF SIMULTANEOUS LINEAR EQUATIONS BY GAUSS-SEIDEL METHOD, WITH

     N     =     6
     ITMAX =    50
     EPS   =     0.00010

THE COEFFICIENT MATRIX A(1,1)...A(N+1,N+1) IS

   4.00000   -1.00000    0.0      -1.00000    0.0       0.0     100.00000

  -1.00000    4.00000   -1.00000   0.0       -1.00000   0.0       0.0

   0.0       -1.00000    4.00000   0.0        0.0      -1.00000    0.0

  -1.00000    0.0        0.0       4.00000   -1.00000   0.0     100.00000

   0.0       -1.00000    0.0      -1.00000    4.00000  -1.00000    0.0

   0.0        0.0       -1.00000   0.0       -1.00000   4.00000    0.0

THE STARTING VECTOR X(1)...X(N) IS

   0.0        0.0        0.0       0.0        0.0       0.0

PROCEDURE CONVERGED, WITH ITER =    13

SOLUTION VECTOR X(1)...X(N) IS

  38.09517   14.28566    4.76188  38.09518   14.28568   4.76189
```

Example 5.3 Gauss-Seidel Method **307**

Discussion of Results

The first two data sets relate to the simultaneous equations

$$5x_1 + x_2 + 3x_3 \qquad = 16$$
$$x_1 + 4x_2 + x_3 + x_4 = 11$$
$$-x_1 + 2x_2 + 6x_3 - 2x_4 = 23$$
$$x_1 - x_2 + x_3 + 4x_4 = -2,$$

which have the solution $\mathbf{x} = [1, 2, 3, -1]^t$. Even though the second choice of starting vector is much poorer than the first, there is only a marginal difference in the number of iterations required for the specified convergence. The third data set arises from the finite-difference solution of an elliptic partial differential equation; it is, in fact, the system (7.82) with $g_{15} = g_{16} = 100$ and g_7 through $g_{14} = 0$.

Finally, note that convergence is guaranteed in all three cases, since each coefficient matrix satisfies conditions (5.28).

5.8 Iterative Methods for Nonlinear Equations

Sections 5.8 and 5.9 are concerned with finding the solution, or solutions, of the system

$$
\begin{aligned}
f_1(x_1, x_2, \cdots, x_n) &= 0, \\
f_2(x_1, x_2, \cdots, x_n) &= 0, \\
&\vdots \qquad\qquad \vdots \\
f_n(x_1, x_2, \cdots, x_n) &= 0,
\end{aligned}
\tag{5.33}
$$

involving n real functions of the n real variables $x_1, x_2, \ldots, x_n$. Following the previous notation, $\mathbf{x} = [x_1, x_2, \ldots, x_n]^t$, we shall write $f_i(\mathbf{x}) = f_i(x_1, x_2, \ldots, x_n)$. Here, and in the subsequent development, $1 \leqslant i \leqslant n$. Then let $\boldsymbol{\alpha} = [\alpha_1, \alpha_2, \ldots, \alpha_n]^t$ be a solution of (5.33), that is, let $f_i(\boldsymbol{\alpha}) = 0$.

Let the n functions $F_i(\mathbf{x})$ be such that

$$
x_i = F_i(\mathbf{x})
\tag{5.34}
$$

implies $f_j(\mathbf{x}) = 0$, $1 \leqslant j \leqslant n$. Basically, the n equations (5.34) will constitute a suitable rearrangement of the original system (5.33). In particular, let

$$
\alpha_i = F_i(\boldsymbol{\alpha}).
\tag{5.35}
$$

Let the starting vector $\mathbf{x}_0 = [x_{10}, x_{20}, \ldots, x_{n0}]^t$ be an approximation to $\boldsymbol{\alpha}$. Define successive new estimates of the solution vector, $\mathbf{x}_k = [x_{1k}, x_{2k} \ldots, x_{nk}]^t$, $k = 1, 2, \ldots$, by computing the individual elements from the recursion relations

$$
x_{ik} = F_i(x_{1,k-1}, x_{2,k-1}, \ldots, x_{n,k-1}) = F_i(\mathbf{x}_{k-1}).
\tag{5.36}
$$

Suppose there is a region R describable as $|x_j - \alpha_j| \leqslant h$, $1 \leqslant j \leqslant n$, and for $\mathbf{x}$ in R there is a positive number μ, less than one, such that

$$
\sum_{j=1}^{n} \left| \frac{\partial F_i(\mathbf{x})}{\partial x_j} \right| \leq \mu.
\tag{5.37}
$$

Then, if the starting vector $\mathbf{x}_0$ lies in R, we show that the iterative method expressed by (5.36) converges to a solution of the system (5.33), that is,

$$
\lim_{k \to \infty} \mathbf{x}_k = \boldsymbol{\alpha}.
\tag{5.38}
$$

Using the mean-value theorem, the truth of (5.38) is established by first noting from (5.35) and (5.36), that

$$
x_{ik} - \alpha_i = F_i(\mathbf{x}_{k-1}) - F_i(\boldsymbol{\alpha})
$$

$$
= \sum_{j=1}^{n} (x_{j,k-1} - \alpha_j) \frac{\partial F_i[\boldsymbol{\alpha} + \xi_{i,k-1}(\mathbf{x}_{k-1} - \boldsymbol{\alpha})]}{\partial x_j},
\tag{5.39}
$$

in which $0 < \xi_{i,k-1} < 1$. That is,

$$
|x_{ik} - \alpha_i| \leqslant h \sum_{j=1}^{n} \left| \frac{\partial F_i}{\partial x_j} \right| \leqslant \mu h < h,
$$

showing that the points $\mathbf{x}_k$ lie in R. Also, by induction, from (5.38) and (5.39),

$$
|x_{ik} - \alpha_i| \leqslant \mu \max_j (|x_{j,k-1} - \alpha_j|) \leqslant \mu^k h.
$$

Therefore, (5.38) is true, and the procedure converges to a solution of (5.33). Note that if the $F_i(\mathbf{x})$ are linear, we have the Jacobi method, and the sufficient conditions of (5.37) are the same as the second set of sufficient conditions in (5.21).

For the nonlinear equations, there is also a counterpart to the Gauss-Seidel method, previously used in Sec. 5.7 for the linear case. We proceed as before, except that (5.36) is replaced by

$$
x_{ik} = F_i(x_{1k}, x_{2k}, \ldots, x_{i-1,k}, x_{i,k-1}, \ldots, x_{n,k-1}).
$$

That is, the most recently computed elements of the solution vector are always used in evaluating the F_i. The proof of convergence according to (5.38) is much the same as for the Jacobi-type iteration. We have

$$
x_{1k} - \alpha_1 = \sum_{j=1}^{n} (x_{j,k-1} - \alpha_j) \cdot \frac{\partial F_1(\boldsymbol{\varepsilon}_{1k})}{\partial x_j},
$$

where

$$
\boldsymbol{\varepsilon}_{1k} = [\alpha_1 + \xi_{ik}(x_{1,k-1} - \alpha_1), \ldots, \alpha_n + \xi_{ik}(x_{n,k-1} - \alpha_n)]^t.
$$

It will appear inductively that the above is true, because the various points concerned remain in R. If e_{k-1} is the largest of the numbers $|x_{j,k-1} - \alpha_j|$, then $|x_{1k} - \alpha_1| \leqslant \mu e_{k-1} < e_{k-1} < h$. It follows that

$$
x_{2k} - \alpha_2 = (x_{1k} - \alpha_1) \frac{\partial F_2(\boldsymbol{\varepsilon}_{2k})}{\partial x_1}
$$

$$
+ \sum_{j=2}^{n} (x_{j,k-1} - \alpha_j) \frac{\partial F_2(\boldsymbol{\varepsilon}_{2k})}{\partial x_j},
$$

where $\boldsymbol{\varepsilon}_{2k} = [\alpha_1 + \xi_{2k}(x_{1k} - \alpha_1), \alpha_2 + \xi_{2k}(x_{2,k-1} - \alpha_2), \ldots, \alpha_n + \xi_{2k}(x_{n,k-1} - \alpha_n)]^t$. That is, $|x_{2k} - \alpha_2| \leqslant \mu e_{k-1} < e_{k-1} < h$, and, in general, $|x_{ik} - \alpha_i| \leqslant \mu e_{k-1} < e_{k-1} < h$. Therefore, $|x_{ik} - \alpha_i| \leqslant \mu^k h$, and convergence according to (5.38) is again established. Observe that the first of the sufficiency conditions of (5.28) has been reaffirmed under slightly more general circumstances.

Example. To illustrate the above techniques, choose the equations

$$
f_1(x_1, x_2) = \frac{1}{2} \sin(x_1 x_2) - \frac{x_2}{4\pi} - \frac{x_1}{2} = 0,
$$

$$
f_2(x_1, x_2) = \left(1 - \frac{1}{4\pi}\right)(e^{2x_1} - e) + \frac{e x_2}{\pi} - 2 e x_1 = 0.
$$

Rewrite these equations in a form which is consistent with (5.34),

$$x_1 = F_1(x_1, x_2) = \sin(x_1 x_2) - \frac{x_2}{2\pi},$$

$$x_2 = F_2(x_1, x_2) = 2\pi x_1 - \left(\pi - \frac{1}{4}\right)(e^{2x_1 - 1} - 1),$$

and choose the starting values $x_{10} = 0.4$, $x_{20} = 3.0$. Within slide-rule accuracy, the Jacobi-type iteration gives

$$x_{11} = \sin(1.2) - \frac{3}{2\pi} = 0.455,$$

$$x_{21} = 2\pi \times 0.4 - 2.89(e^{-0.2} - 1) = 3.03;$$

$$x_{12} = \sin(1.379) - \frac{3.03}{2\pi} = 0.499,$$

$$x_{22} = 2\pi \times 0.455 - 2.89(e^{-0.09} - 1) = 3.11;$$

similarly, $x_{13} = 0.505$, $x_{23} = 3.14$; $x_{14} = 0.500$, $x_{24} = 3.14$; $x_{15} = 0.500$, $x_{25} = \pi$.

Using the same arrangement of the equations in conjunction with the same starting values, iteration of the Gauss-Seidel type gives

$$x_{11} = \sin(1.2) - \frac{3}{2\pi} = 0.455,$$

$$x_{21} = 2\pi \times 0.455 - 2.89(e^{-0.2} - 1) = 3.11;$$

$$x_{12} = \sin(1.415) - \frac{3.11}{2\pi} = 0.493,$$

$$x_{22} = 2\pi \times 0.493 - 2.89(e^{-0.014} - 1) = 3.14;$$

similarly, $x_{13} = 0.500$, $x_{23} = \pi$; $x_{14} = 0.500$, $x_{24} = \pi$, etc.

There is less risk involved in using an approximate slide-rule approach in these iterative calculations than might be supposed. Unlike the exact methods, such as Gaussian elimination for linear equations, there is no inherited round-off error from one step to the next. This follows, since the results at each stage of the iteration can be viewed as a new guess or initial approximation to the solution vector. Substantial error can be tolerated, provided that there is no gross error in the final stages of calculation. These remarks apply to the iterative solution of linear equations as well.

EXAMPLE 5.4

FLOW IN A PIPE NETWORK
SUCCESSIVE-SUBSTITUTION METHOD

Problem Statement

A network consists of a number of horizontal pipes, of specified diameters and lengths, that are joined at n nodes, numbered $i = 1, 2, \ldots, n$. The pressure is specified at some of these nodes. There is at most a single pipe connected directly between any two nodes.

Write a program that will accept information concerning the above, and that will proceed to compute: (a) the pressures at all remaining nodes, and (b) the flow rate (and direction of flow) in each pipe.

Method of Solution

For flow of a liquid from point i to point j in a horizontal pipe, the pressure drop is given by the *Fanning* equation:

$$p_i - p_j = \frac{1}{2} f_M \rho u_m^2 \frac{L}{D}. \qquad (5.4.1)$$

Here, f_M is the dimensionless *Moody* friction factor, ρ is the liquid density, u_m is the mean velocity, and L and D are the length and diameter of the pipe, respectively. Since the volumetric flow rate is $Q = (\pi D^2/4) u_m$, equation (5.4.1) becomes

$$p_i - p_j = \frac{8 f_M \rho Q^2 L}{\pi^2 D^5}.$$

Here, all quantities are in consistent units. However, if p_i and p_j are expressed in psi (lb_f/sq in.), ρ in lb_m/cu ft, Q in gpm (gallons/min), L in ft, and D in inches, we obtain

$$p_i - p_j = C \frac{LQ^2}{D^5}, \qquad (5.4.2)$$

where

$$C = \frac{8 \times 12^5}{\pi^2 \times 144 \times 32.2 \times (7.48 \times 60)^2} f_M \rho. \qquad (5.4.3)$$

Let $c_{ij} = CL_{ij}/D_{ij}^5$, where the subscripts ij now emphasize that we are concerned with the pipe joining nodes i and j. The flow rate Q_{ij} between nodes i and j is then given by

$$|p_i - p_j| = c_{ij} Q_{ij}^2, \qquad (5.4.4)$$

in which Q_{ij} is plus or minus for flow from i to j or *vice versa*, respectively. In the following version, Q_{ij} will

automatically have the correct sign:

$$Q_{ij} = (p_i - p_j) \sqrt{\frac{1}{c_{ij} |p_i - p_j|}}.$$

At any *free* node j, where the pressure is not specified, the sum of the flows from neighboring nodes i must be zero:

$$\sum_i Q_{ij} = \sum_i (p_i - p_j) \sqrt{\frac{1}{c_{ij} |p_i - p_j|}} = 0. \qquad (5.4.5)$$

When applied at all the free nodes, equation (5.4.5) yields a system of nonlinear simultaneous equations in the unknown pressures. We shall solve this system by the successive-substitution type of method described in Section 5.8. First, note that $(p_i - p_j)$ is more sensitive than $(|p_i - p_j|)^{1/2}$ to variations in p_j. Thus an appropriate version, analogous to equation (5.34), is

$$p_j = \frac{\sum_i a_{ij} p_i}{\sum_i a_{ij}}, \qquad (5.4.6)$$

in which

$$a_{ij} = (c_{ij} |p_i - p_j|)^{-1/2}. \qquad (5.4.7)$$

Equation (5.4.6) is applied repeatedly at all free nodes until either each computed pressure p_j does not change by more than a small amount ε from one iteration to the next, or a preassigned number of iterations, *itmax*, has been exceeded. The most recently estimated values of p_i will always be used in the right-hand side of equation (5.4.6).

In order to implement the above, we also introduce the following:

(a) A vector of logical values, $\bar{p}_1, \bar{p}_2, \ldots, \bar{p}_n$ (PGIVEN in the program), such that $\bar{p}_j$ is true (T) if the pressure is specified at node j, and false (F) if it is not.

(b) A matrix of logical values, $I_{11} \ldots I_{nn}$ (the *incidence* matrix INCID in the program), such that I_{ij} is true if there is a pipe directly joining nodes i and j, and false if not.

Since the incidence, diameter, and length matrices are symmetric (for example, $D_{ji} = D_{ij}$), we need supply only the lower triangular portions of such matrices as data. The input data will also include a complete set of pressures, $p_1, p_2, \ldots, p_n$; some of these will be the known pressures, and the remainder will be the starting guesses at the free nodes.

Example 5.4   Flow in a Pipe Network (Successive-Substitution Method)   311

Flow Diagram

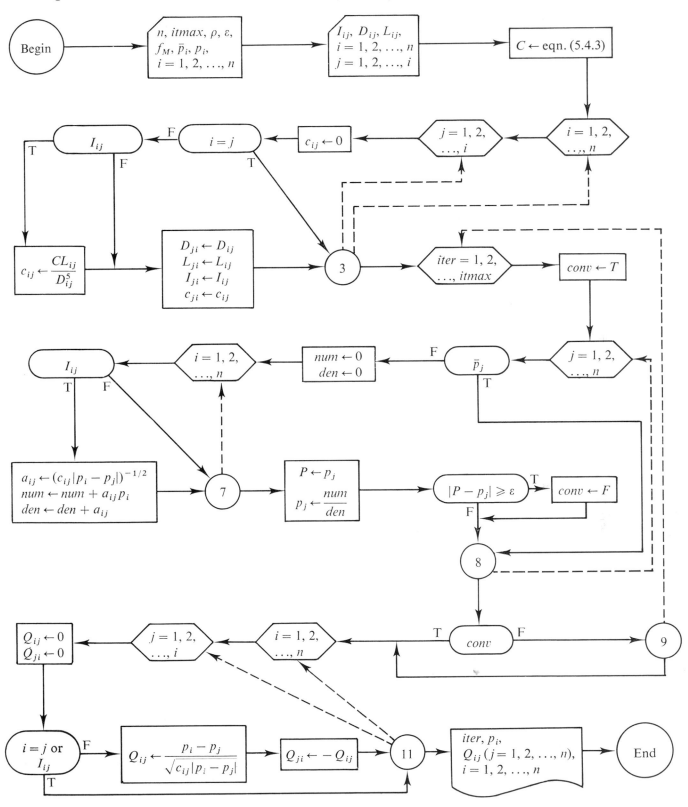

FORTRAN *Implementation*

List of Principal Variables

Program Symbol	Definition
A	Matrix, whose elements a_{ij} are defined by (5.4.7).
C	Matrix, whose elements c_{ij} relate the flow rate to the pressure drop in the pipe joining nodes i and j.
CONV	Logical variable used in testing for convergence, *conv*.
D, L	Matrices, whose elements D_{ij} and L_{ij} give the diameter (in.) and length (ft) of the pipe joining nodes i and j.
DENOM, NUMER	Storage for the denominator and numerator of (5.4.6), *den* and *num*, respectively.
EPS	Tolerance, ε, used in testing for convergence.
F	Moody friction factor, f_M (assumed constant).
FACTOR	The constant, C, in equation (5.4.3).
I, J	Indices for representing the nodes i and j.
INCID	Matrix of logical values, $\mathbf{I}$; if I_{ij} is T, there is a pipe joining nodes i and j; if F, there is not.
ITER	Counter on the number of iterations, *iter*.
IPRINT	Logical variable, which must have the value T if intermediate approximations to the pressures are to be printed.
ITMAX	Upper limit on the number of iterations, *itmax*.
N	Total number of nodes, n.
P	Vector of pressures, p_i (psi), at each node.
PGIVEN	Vector of logical values, $\bar{p}_i$, at each node. If $\bar{p}_i$ is T, the pressure is specified at node i; if F, it is not.
Q	Matrix, whose elements Q_{ij} give the flow rate (gpm) from node i to node j.
RHO	Density of the liquid in the pipes, ρ (lb_m/cu ft).
SAVEP	Temporary storage for old pressure p_j during convergence testing, P.

Example 5.4   Flow in a Pipe Network (Successive-Substitution Method)   **313**

Program Listing

```
C           APPLIED NUMERICAL METHODS, EXAMPLE 5.4
C           FLOW IN A PIPE NETWORK - SUCCESSIVE SUBSTITUTION METHOD
C
C           THIS PROGRAM READS A DESCRIPTION OF THE TOPOLOGY OF AN
C           ARBITRARY N NODE PIPE NETWORK WITH PRESSURES SPECIFIED AT
C           PARTICULAR NODES, AND THEN COMPUTES THE PRESSURES AT THE
C           REMAINING NODES AND THE INTER-NODAL FLOW RATES USING A METHOD
C           OF SUCCESSIVE SUBSTITUTIONS.  IF INCID(I,J) IS TRUE, THEN NODES
C           I AND J ARE CONNECTED BY A PIPE SEGMENT OF DIAMETER D(I,J)
C           INCHES AND LENGTH L(I,J) FEET.  IF PGIVEN(I) IS TRUE, THE
C           PRESSURE AT NODE I, P(I) PSI, IS FIXED. OTHERWISE, P(I) ASSUMES
C           SUCCESSIVE ESTIMATES OF THE PRESSURE AT NODE I.  RHO IS THE
C           FLUID DENSITY IN LB/CU FT AND F THE PIPE FRICTION FACTOR,
C           ASSUMED IDENTICAL FOR ALL PIPE SEGMENTS.  ITER IS THE ITERATION
C           COUNTER.  ITERATION IS STOPPED WHEN ITER EXCEEDS ITMAX OR WHEN
C           NO NODAL PRESSURE CHANGES BY AN AMOUNT GREATER THAN EPS PSI
C           BETWEEN TWO SUCCESSIVE ITERATIONS.   Q(I,J) IS THE FLOW RATE IN
C           GAL/MIN BETWEEN NODES I AND J.  WHEN Q(I,J) IS POSITIVE, FLUID
C           FLOWS FROM NODE I TO NODE J.   THE MATRICES A AND C ARE
C           DESCRIBED IN THE TEXT.  WHEN IPRINT IS TRUE, INTERMEDIATE
C           APPROXIMATIONS OF THE NODAL PRESSURES ARE PRINTED.
C
      LOGICAL IPRINT, PGIVEN, INCID, CONV
      REAL   L, NUMER
      DIMENSION P(10), PGIVEN(10), A(10,10), C(10,10), D(10,10),
     1   L(10,10), INCID(10,10), Q(10,10)
C
C           ..... READ DATA .....
    1 READ (5,100)  N, ITMAX, RHO, EPS, F, IPRINT, (PGIVEN(I), I=1,N)
      READ (5,101)  (P(I), I=1,N)
      DO 2   I=1,N
      READ (5,102)  (INCID(I,J), J=1,I)
      READ (5,101)  (D(I,J), J=1,I)
    2 READ (5,101)  (L(I,J), J=1,I)
C
C           ..... SET UP UPPER TRIANGULAR PARTS OF SYMMETRIC MATRICES D, L,
C                 AND INCID AND COMPUTE ELEMENTS OF C MATRIX .....
      FACTOR = 8.*12.**5*RHO*F/(3.1415926**2*32.2*(60.*7.48)**2*144.)
      DO 3   I=1,N
      DO 3   J=1,I
      C(I,J) = 0.
      IF ( I.EQ.J )   GO TO 3
      IF ( INCID(I,J) )   C(I,J) = FACTOR*L(I,J)/D(I,J)**5
      D(J,I) = D(I,J)
      L(J,I) = L(I,J)
      INCID(J,I) = INCID(I,J)
      C(J,I) = C(I,J)
    3 CONTINUE
C
C           ..... PRINT OUT INITIAL INFORMATION ABOUT NETWORK .....
      WRITE (6,200)  N,ITMAX,RHO,EPS,F,IPRINT,(I,P(I),PGIVEN(I),I=1,N)
      WRITE (6,201)
      DO 4   I=1,N
    4 WRITE (6,202)  I, I, N, (INCID(I,J), J=1,N)
      WRITE (6,201)
      DO 5   I=1,N
    5 WRITE (6,203)  I, I, N, (D(I,J), J=1,N)
      WRITE (6,201)
      DO 6   I=1,N
    6 WRITE (6,204)  I, I, N, (L(I,J), J=1,N)
```

Systems of Equations

Program Listing (*Continued*)

```
C
C     ..... COMPUTE SUCCESSIVE ESTIMATES OF PRESSURES AT NODES .....
      IF ( IPRINT )   WRITE (6,205) (I, I=1,N)
      DO 9   ITER=1,ITMAX
      CONV = .TRUE.
      DO 8   J=1,N
      IF ( PGIVEN(J) )   GO TO 8
      NUMER = 0.
      DENOM = 0.
      DO 7   I=1,N
      IF ( .NOT.INCID(I,J) )   GO TO 7
        A(I,J) = 1.0/SQRT(C(I,J)*ABS(P(I)-P(J)))
        NUMER = NUMER + A(I,J)*P(I)
        DENOM = DENOM + A(I,J)
    7 CONTINUE
      SAVEP = P(J)
      P(J) = NUMER/DENOM
      IF ( ABS(SAVEP-P(J)).GE.EPS )   CONV = .FALSE.
    8 CONTINUE
      IF ( IPRINT )   WRITE (6,206)  ITER, (P(I), I=1,N)
    9 IF ( CONV )   GO TO 10
      WRITE (6,207)  ITMAX
C
C     ..... COMPUTE FLOWS IN INDIVIDUAL NETWORK BRANCHES .....
   10 DO 11   I=1,N
      DO 11   J=1,I
      Q(I,J) = 0.
      Q(J,I) = 0.
      IF ( I.EQ.J .OR. .NOT.INCID(I,J) )   GO TO 11
      Q(I,J) = (P(I)-P(J))/SQRT(C(I,J)*ABS(P(I)-P(J)))
      Q(J,I) = - Q(I,J)
   11 CONTINUE
C
C     ..... PRINT FINAL PRESSURES AND FLOWS .....
      WRITE (6,208)  ITER, N
      DO 12   I=1,N
   12 WRITE (6,209)  I, P(I), (Q(I,J), J=1,N)
      GO TO 1
C
C     ..... FORMATS FOR INPUT AND OUTPUT STATEMENTS .....
  100 FORMAT( 3X,I2,17X,I3,15X,F5.1,15X,E5.0/ 4X,F6.3,14X,L1 /
     1    (30X, 20(L1,1X)) )
  101 FORMAT( 30X, 5F8.3 )
  102 FORMAT( 30X,20(L1,1X) )
  200 FORMAT( 23H1FLOW IN A PIPE NETWORK/ 10H0N        = , I3/ 10H ITMAX
     1= , I3/ 10H RHO      = , F7.3/ 10H EPS     = , E10.2/ 10H F       = ,
     2  F7.3/ 10H IPRINT = , 2X, L1/ 3H0 I, 6X, 4HP(I), 4X,9HPGIVEN(I)/
     3  (1H , I2, F10.3, 6X, L1) )
  201 FORMAT( 1H0/1H0 )
  202 FORMAT( 7H0INCID(, I2, 13H, 1)...INCID(, I2,1H,,I2, 3H) = ,
     1  40(L1,1X)/ (1H , 29X, 40(L1,1X)) )
  203 FORMAT( 3H0D(, I2, 9H, 1)...D(, I2,1H,,I2, 1H), 9X, 1H= , 8F10.3 /
     1    (1H , 29X, 8F10.3) )
  204 FORMAT( 3H0L(, I2, 9H, 1)...L(, I2,1H,,I2, 1H), 9X, 1H= , 8F10.3 /
     1    (1H , 29X, 8F10.3) )
  205 FORMAT( 1H0/ 5H0ITER, 7X, 16HPRESSURE AT NODE/ (1H ,11X,8(I1,9X)))
  206 FORMAT( 1H , I3, 3X, 8F10.4/ (1H , 6X, 8F10.4) )
  207 FORMAT( 35H0SOLUTIONS FAILED TO CONVERGE AFTER, I3,11H ITERATIONS)
  208 FORMAT( 1H0/26H0PRESSURES AND FLOWS AFTER, I3, 15H ITERATIONS ARE/
     1    3H0 I,5X,4HP(I),7X,16HQ( I, 1)...Q( I,,I2,1H) / 1H , 7X, 3HPSI,
     2  14X, 7HGAL/MIN// )
  209 FORMAT( 1H , I2, F10.4, 5X, 8F10.3/ (1H , 17X, 8F10.3) )
C
      END
```

Example 5.4 Flow in a Pipe Network (Successive-Substitution Method)   **315**

Program Listing (*Continued*)

Data

```
N = 5              ITMAX =100          RHO = 50.0          EPS = 1.E-4
F =  0.056          IPRINT = T
PGIVEN(1)...PGIVEN(5)      =   T F T F F
P(1)...P(5)                =      50.000   20.000    0.000   40.000   30.000
INCID(1,1)                 =   F
D(1,1)                     =       0.000
L(1,1)                     =       0.000
INCID(2,1)...INCID(2,2)    =   T F
D(2,1)...D(2,2)            =       3.000    0.000
L(2,1)...L(2,2)            =     150.000    0.000
INCID(3,1)...INCID(3,3)    =   F T F
D(3,1)...D(3,3)            =       0.000    3.000    0.000
L(3,1)...L(3,3)            =       0.000  150.000    0.000
INCID(4,1)...INCID(4,4)    =   T F F F
D(4,1)...D(4,4)            =       4.000    0.000    0.000    0.000
L(4,1)...L(4,4)            =     100.000    0.000    0.000    0.000
INCID(5,1)...INCID(5,5)    =   F T F T F
D(5,1)...D(5,5)            =       0.000    4.000    0.000    4.000    0.000
L(5,1)...L(5,5)            =       0.000  100.000    0.000  100.000    0.000
```

Computer Output

```
FLOW IN A PIPE NETWORK

N      =    5
ITMAX  = 100
RHO    =   50.000
EPS    =    0.10E-03
F      =    0.056
IPRINT =    T

I       P(I)      PGIVEN(I)
1     50.000          T
2     20.000          F
3      0.0            T
4     40.000          F
5     30.000          F
```

```
INCID( 1, 1)...INCID( 1, 5) =F T F T F

INCID( 2, 1)...INCID( 2, 5) =T F T F T

INCID( 3, 1)...INCID( 3, 5) =F T F F F

INCID( 4, 1)...INCID( 4, 5) =T F F F T

INCID( 5, 1)...INCID( 5, 5) =F T F T F
```

```
D( 1, 1)...D( 1, 5)    =      0.0       3.000     0.0       4.000     0.0

D( 2, 1)...D( 2, 5)    =      3.000     0.0       3.000     0.0       4.000

D( 3, 1)...D( 3, 5)    =      0.0       3.000     0.0       0.0       0.0

D( 4, 1)...D( 4, 5)    =      4.000     0.0       0.0       0.0       4.000

D( 5, 1)...D( 5, 5)    =      0.0       4.000     0.0       4.000     0.0
```

Computer Output (*Continued*)

L(1, 1)...L(1, 5)	=	0.0	150.000	0.0	100.000	0.0
L(2, 1)...L(2, 5)	=	150.000	0.0	150.000	0.0	100.000
L(3, 1)...L(3, 5)	=	0.0	150.000	0.0	0.0	0.0
L(4, 1)...L(4, 5)	=	100.000	0.0	0.0	0.0	100.000
L(5, 1)...L(5, 5)	=	0.0	100.000	0.0	100.000	0.0

ITER	PRESSURE AT NODE				
	1	2	3	4	5
1	50.0000	27.4553	0.0	40.0000	31.6616
2	50.0000	30.3218	0.0	40.4145	33.1600
3	50.0000	31.9882	0.0	40.9944	34.4999
4	50.0000	33.2753	0.0	41.6180	35.7211
5	50.0000	34.3876	0.0	42.2345	36.8321
6	50.0000	35.3809	0.0	42.8204	37.8350
7	50.0000	36.2724	0.0	43.3644	38.7339
8	50.0000	37.0706	0.0	43.8616	39.5349
9	50.0000	37.7819	0.0	44.3111	40.2451
10	50.0000	38.4132	0.0	44.7139	40.8726
11	50.0000	38.9714	0.0	45.0728	41.4253
12	50.0000	39.4634	0.0	45.3909	41.9110
13	50.0000	39.8960	0.0	45.6718	42.3370
14	50.0000	40.2756	0.0	45.9191	42.7100
15	50.0000	40.6081	0.0	46.1362	43.0361
16	50.0000	40.8989	0.0	46.3266	43.3211
17	50.0000	41.1530	0.0	46.4931	43.5698
18	50.0000	41.3748	0.0	46.6387	43.7867
19	50.0000	41.5682	0.0	46.7658	43.9758
20	50.0000	41.7368	0.0	46.8767	44.1406
21	50.0000	41.8837	0.0	46.9734	44.2841
22	50.0000	42.0117	0.0	47.0576	44.4090
23	50.0000	42.1230	0.0	47.1310	44.5178
24	50.0000	42.2200	0.0	47.1949	44.6125
25	50.0000	42.3043	0.0	47.2505	44.6948
26	50.0000	42.3777	0.0	47.2989	44.7665
27	50.0000	42.4416	0.0	47.3411	44.8288
28	50.0000	42.4971	0.0	47.3777	44.8831
29	50.0000	42.5454	0.0	47.4096	44.9302
30	50.0000	42.5874	0.0	47.4373	44.9713
31	50.0000	42.6239	0.0	47.4615	45.0070
32	50.0000	42.6557	0.0	47.4825	45.0380
33	50.0000	42.6833	0.0	47.5007	45.0650
34	50.0000	42.7073	0.0	47.5166	45.0884
35	50.0000	42.7281	0.0	47.5303	45.1088
36	50.0000	42.7463	0.0	47.5424	45.1265
37	50.0000	42.7621	0.0	47.5528	45.1420
38	50.0000	42.7758	0.0	47.5619	45.1554
39	50.0000	42.7878	0.0	47.5697	45.1670
40	50.0000	42.7981	0.0	47.5766	45.1772
41	50.0000	42.8071	0.0	47.5826	45.1860
42	50.0000	42.8150	0.0	47.5878	45.1937
43	50.0000	42.8218	0.0	47.5923	45.2003
44	50.0000	42.8277	0.0	47.5962	45.2061
45	50.0000	42.8329	0.0	47.5996	45.2112
46	50.0000	42.8374	0.0	47.6026	45.2155
47	50.0000	42.8413	0.0	47.6051	45.2193
48	50.0000	42.8447	0.0	47.6074	45.2227
49	50.0000	42.8476	0.0	47.6093	45.2255
50	50.0000	42.8502	0.0	47.6110	45.2280
51	50.0000	42.8524	0.0	47.6125	45.2302
52	50.0000	42.8543	0.0	47.6138	45.2321
53	50.0000	42.8560	0.0	47.6149	45.2337
54	50.0000	42.8574	0.0	47.6158	45.2352
55	50.0000	42.8587	0.0	47.6167	45.2364

Example 5.4   Flow in a Pipe Network (Successive-Substitution Method)   **317**

Computer Output (*Continued*)

56	50.0000	42.8598	0.0	47.6174	45.2375
57	50.0000	42.8608	0.0	47.6181	45.2385
58	50.0000	42.8616	0.0	47.6186	45.2393
59	50.0000	42.8624	0.0	47.6191	45.2400
60	50.0000	42.8630	0.0	47.6195	45.2406
61	50.0000	42.8636	0.0	47.6199	45.2411
62	50.0000	42.8640	0.0	47.6202	45.2416
63	50.0000	42.8644	0.0	47.6205	45.2420
64	50.0000	42.8648	0.0	47.6207	45.2424
65	50.0000	42.8651	0.0	47.6209	45.2427
66	50.0000	42.8654	0.0	47.6211	45.2429
67	50.0000	42.8656	0.0	47.6212	45.2432
68	50.0000	42.8658	0.0	47.6214	45.2434
69	50.0000	42.8660	0.0	47.6215	45.2435
70	50.0000	42.8662	0.0	47.6216	45.2437
71	50.0000	42.8663	0.0	47.6217	45.2438
72	50.0000	42.8664	0.0	47.6218	45.2439
73	50.0000	42.8665	0.0	47.6218	45.2440
74	50.0000	42.8666	0.0	47.6219	45.2441

```
PRESSURES AND FLOWS AFTER 74 ITERATIONS ARE
```

I	P(I)	Q(I, 1)...Q(I, 5)				
	PSI	GAL/MIN				
1	50.0000	0.0	138.242	0.0	200.677	0.0
2	42.8666	-138.242	0.0	338.885	0.0	-200.654
3	0.0	0.0	-338.885	0.0	0.0	0.0
4	47.6219	-200.677	0.0	0.0	0.0	200.664
5	45.2441	0.0	200.654	0.0	-200.664	0.0

Discussion of Results

The data used above relate to the network shown in Fig. 5.4.1, with $f_M = 0.056$, $\rho = 50$ lb$_m$/cu ft, and two pressures fixed: $p_1 = 50$, $p_3 = 0$ psi.

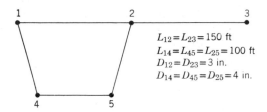

$L_{12} = L_{23} = 150$ ft
$L_{14} = L_{45} = L_{25} = 100$ ft
$D_{12} = D_{23} = 3$ in.
$D_{14} = D_{45} = D_{25} = 4$ in.

Figure 5.4.1 Pipe network for example calculation.

Although the method is computationally straightforward, it needs many iterations to give a reasonable degree of convergence. Also, referring to equation (5.4.7), we can see that a starting guess of $p_i = p_j$ for any two nodes that are directly connected would be unfortunate.

Note that the bulk of the pressure drop occurs in the pipe 2-3, and that the flow in the branch 1-4-5-2 is appreciably greater than that in the pipe 1-2, even though the latter is much shorter. Both these observations can be reconciled by noting that pressure drop is proportional to Q^2/D^5, and that pipe 2-3 must take the combined flows along 1-4-5-2 and 1-2.

The method can be extended to more complex situations, in which we could allow for (a) f_M being a function of Reynolds number and pipe roughness, instead of being treated as a constant, and (b) pumps and valves in some of the branches, etc. Also, the logical arrays used above could find a similar application in solving for the currents in a network of resistors, with known voltages applied at some of the nodes (although this would lead to a set of simultaneous *linear* equations).

5.9 Newton-Raphson Iteration for Nonlinear Equations

The equations to be solved are again those of (5.33), and we retain the nomenclature of the previous section. The Newton-Raphson process, to be described, is once more iterative in character. We first define

$$f_{ij}(\mathbf{x}) = \frac{\partial f_i(\mathbf{x})}{\partial x_j}. \qquad (5.40)$$

Next define the matrix $\boldsymbol{\phi}(\mathbf{x})$ as

$$\boldsymbol{\phi}(\mathbf{x}) = (f_{ij}(\mathbf{x})), \qquad 1 \leqslant i \leqslant n, 1 \leqslant j \leqslant n. \quad (5.41)$$

Thus $\det(\boldsymbol{\phi}(\mathbf{x}))$ is the *Jacobian* of the system (5.33) evaluated for the vector $\mathbf{x} = [x_1, x_2, \ldots, x_n]^t$. Now define the vector $\mathbf{f}(\mathbf{x})$ as

$$\mathbf{f}(\mathbf{x}) = [f_1(\mathbf{x}), f_2(\mathbf{x}), \ldots, f_n(\mathbf{x})]^t. \qquad (5.42)$$

With these definitions in mind, and with the starting vector $\mathbf{x}_0 = [x_{10}, x_{20}, \ldots, x_{n0}]^t$, let

$$\mathbf{x}_{k+1} = \mathbf{x}_k + \boldsymbol{\delta}_k, \qquad (5.43)$$

where $\boldsymbol{\delta}_k$ is the solution vector for the set of simultaneous linear equations

$$\boldsymbol{\phi}(\mathbf{x}_k)\,\boldsymbol{\delta}_k = -\mathbf{f}(\mathbf{x}_k). \qquad (5.44)$$

The fundamental theorem concerning convergence is much less restrictive than those of the previous sections. We have the result that if the components of $\boldsymbol{\phi}(\mathbf{x})$ are continuous in a neighborhood of a point $\boldsymbol{\alpha}$ such that $\mathbf{f}(\boldsymbol{\alpha}) = \mathbf{0}$, if $\det(\boldsymbol{\phi}(\boldsymbol{\alpha})) \neq 0$, and if $\mathbf{x}_0$ is "near" $\boldsymbol{\alpha}$, then $\lim_{k \to \infty} \mathbf{x}_k = \boldsymbol{\alpha}$.

An outline for a method of proof follows. By (5.42) and (5.44), since $f_i(\boldsymbol{\alpha}) = 0$,

$$\boldsymbol{\delta}_k = \boldsymbol{\phi}^{-1}(\mathbf{x}_k)[\mathbf{f}(\boldsymbol{\alpha}) - \mathbf{f}(\mathbf{x}_k)]. \qquad (5.45)$$

By the mean-value theorem,

$$f_i(\mathbf{x}_k) - f_i(\boldsymbol{\alpha}) = \sum_{j=1}^{n} f_{ij}(\boldsymbol{\alpha} + \xi_{ik}(\mathbf{x}_k - \boldsymbol{\alpha}))(x_{jk} - \alpha_j),$$

where $0 < \xi_{ik} < 1$. For the ith row of a matrix $\boldsymbol{\psi}$ use

$$[f_{i1}(\boldsymbol{\alpha} + \xi_{ik}(\mathbf{x}_k - \boldsymbol{\alpha})), \ldots, f_{in}(\boldsymbol{\alpha} + \xi_{ik}(\mathbf{x}_k - \boldsymbol{\alpha}))].$$

Then

$$\mathbf{x}_{k+1} - \boldsymbol{\alpha} = \mathbf{x}_k - \boldsymbol{\alpha} + \boldsymbol{\delta}_k = \boldsymbol{\phi}^{-1}(\mathbf{x}_k)[\boldsymbol{\phi}(\mathbf{x}_k) - \boldsymbol{\psi}](\mathbf{x}_k - \boldsymbol{\alpha}).$$

Since the entries in the matrix $\boldsymbol{\phi}(\mathbf{x}_k) - \boldsymbol{\psi}$ are differences of the type $f_{ij}(\mathbf{x}_k) - f_{ij}(\boldsymbol{\alpha} + \xi_{ik}(\mathbf{x}_k - \boldsymbol{\alpha}))$, they can be kept uniformly small if the starting vector $\mathbf{x}_0$ lies in an initially chosen region R describable as $|x_i - \alpha_i| \leqslant h$, $1 \leqslant i \leqslant n$. Concurrent with this is the fact that since $\det(\boldsymbol{\phi}(\mathbf{x})) \neq 0$, $\det(\boldsymbol{\phi}(\mathbf{x}_k))$ can be bounded from zero. The net result is that, for $0 < \mu < 1$, $|x_{ik} - \alpha_i| \leqslant h\mu^k$, $1 \leqslant i \leqslant n$. Thus the sequence $\{\mathbf{x}_k\}$ converges to $\boldsymbol{\alpha}$.

Example. To illustrate the procedure, the equations of the previous section are used, namely

$$f_1(x_1, x_2) = \frac{1}{2}\sin(x_1 x_2) - \frac{x_2}{4\pi} - \frac{x_1}{2} = 0$$

$$f_2(x_1, x_2) = \left(1 - \frac{1}{4\pi}\right)(e^{2x_1} - e) + \frac{ex_2}{\pi} - 2ex_1 = 0.$$

It is readily seen that

$$\frac{\partial f_1}{\partial x_1} = -\frac{1}{2} + \frac{x_2 \cos(x_1 x_2)}{2}, \qquad \frac{\partial f_1}{\partial x_2} = -\frac{1}{4\pi} + \frac{x_1 \cos(x_1 x_2)}{2},$$

$$\frac{\partial f_2}{\partial x_1} = -2e + \left(2 - \frac{1}{2\pi}\right)e^{2x_1}, \qquad \frac{\partial f_2}{\partial x_2} = \frac{e}{\pi}.$$

The increments Δx_1 and Δx_2 in x_1 and x_2 are determined by

$$\frac{\partial f_1}{\partial x_1}\Delta x_1 + \frac{\partial f_1}{\partial x_2}\Delta x_2 = -f_1,$$

$$\frac{\partial f_2}{\partial x_1}\Delta x_1 + \frac{\partial f_2}{\partial x_2}\Delta x_2 = -f_2.$$

Or, writing the determinant D of the coefficient matrix (the Jacobian),

$$D = \frac{\partial f_1}{\partial x_1}\frac{\partial f_2}{\partial x_2} - \frac{\partial f_1}{\partial x_2}\frac{\partial f_2}{\partial x_1},$$

then

$$\Delta x_1 = \left(\frac{f_2 \dfrac{\partial f_1}{\partial x_2} - f_1 \dfrac{\partial f_2}{\partial x_2}}{D}\right), \Delta x_2 = \left(\frac{f_1 \dfrac{\partial f_2}{\partial x_1} - f_2 \dfrac{\partial f_1}{\partial x_1}}{D}\right).$$

For ease in verification, detailed results are tabulated in Table 5.1. Once again, calculations have been carried out by slide rule. The entries -0.0000 designate tiny negative values.

Table 5.1 Newton-Raphson Solution for $\mathbf{x}_0 = \begin{bmatrix} 0.4 \\ 3.0 \end{bmatrix}$

k	x_1	x_2	f_1	f_2	$\dfrac{\partial f_1}{\partial x_1}$	$\dfrac{\partial f_1}{\partial x_2}$	$\dfrac{\partial f_2}{\partial x_1}$	$\dfrac{\partial f_2}{\partial x_2}$	D	Δx_1	Δx_2
0	0.400	3.000	0.0272	−0.0324	0.0435	−0.0071	−1.34	0.865	0.0281	−0.831	−1.249
1	−0.431	1.751	−0.266	1.74	0.138	−0.236	−4.66	0.865	−0.982	0.186	−1.018
2	−0.245	0.733	−0.0251	0.0303	−0.139	−0.200	−4.31	0.865	−0.984	−0.016	−0.114
3	−0.261	0.619	0.0009	0.0003	−0.195	−0.208	−4.35	0.865	−1.07	0.0007	0.003
4	−0.260	0.622	0.0000	0.0000	−0.193	−0.208	−4.34	0.865	−1.07	0.0000	0.0000
5	−0.260	0.622	0.0000	0.0000							

Note that despite using the same initial value, this solution differs from that obtained in Section 5.8. However, the starting values $x_{10} = 0.6$, $x_{20} = 3.0$ do lead to the alternative solution $x_1 = 0.5$, $x_2 = \pi$. Values are given in Table 5.2.

k	x_1	x_2	f_1	f_2	$\dfrac{\partial f_1}{\partial x_1}$	$\dfrac{\partial f_1}{\partial x_2}$	$\dfrac{\partial f_2}{\partial x_1}$	$\dfrac{\partial f_2}{\partial x_2}$	$\mathbf{D}$	Δx_1	Δx_2
1	0.600	3.000	−0.0518	−0.112	−0.841	−0.148	0.675	0.865	−0.627	−0.098	0.206
2	0.502	3.206	−0.0066	0.0549	−0.563	−0.0894	−0.411	0.865	−0.524	−0.001	−0.064
3	0.501	3.142	−0.0003	0.0000	−0.503	−0.0801	−0.426	0.865	−0.470	−0.0006	−0.0004
4	0.500	3.142	−0.0000	−0.0000	−0.500	−0.0796	−0.433	0.865	−0.467	−0.0000	−0.0000
5	0.500	3.142	−0.0000	0.0000							

EXAMPLE 5.5

CHEMICAL EQUILIBRIUM
NEWTON-RAPHSON METHOD

Problem Statement

The principal reactions in the production of synthesis gas by partial oxidation of methane with oxygen are:

$$CH_4 + \tfrac{1}{2}O_2 \rightleftharpoons CO + 2H_2 \qquad (5.5.1)$$

$$CH_4 + H_2O \rightleftharpoons CO + 3H_2 \qquad (5.5.2)$$

$$H_2 + CO_2 \rightleftharpoons CO + H_2O \qquad (5.5.3)$$

Write a program that finds the O_2/CH_4 reactant ratio that will produce an adiabatic equilibrium temperature of $2200°F$ at an operating pressure of 20 atmospheres, when the reactant gases are preheated to an entering temperature of $1000°F$.

Assuming that the gases behave ideally, so that the component activities are identical with component partial pressures, the equilibrium constants at $2200°F$ for the three equations are respectively:

$$K_1 = \frac{p_{CO}p_{H_2}^2}{p_{CH_4}p_{O_2}^{1/2}} = 1.3 \times 10^{11}, \qquad (5.5.4)$$

$$K_2 = \frac{p_{CO}p_{H_2}^3}{p_{CH_4}p_{H_2O}} = 1.7837 \times 10^5, \qquad (5.5.5)$$

$$K_3 = \frac{p_{CO}p_{H_2O}}{p_{CO_2}p_{H_2}} = 2.6058. \qquad (5.5.6)$$

Here p_{CO}, p_{CO_2}, p_{H_2O}, p_{H_2}, p_{CH_4} and p_{O_2} are the partial pressures of CO (carbon monoxide), CO_2 (carbon dioxide), H_2O (water vapor), H_2 (hydrogen), CH_4 (methane), and O_2 (oxygen), respectively.

Enthalpies of the various components at $1000°F$ and $2200°F$ are listed in Table 5.5.1.

Table 5.5.1 Component Enthalpies in BTU/lb mole

Component	1000°F	2200°F
CH_4	−13492	8427
H_2O	−90546	−78213
CO_2	−154958	−139009
CO	−38528	−28837
H_2	10100	18927
O_2	10690	20831

A fourth reaction may also occur at high temperatures:

$$C + CO_2 \rightleftharpoons 2CO \qquad (5.5.7)$$

At $2200°F$, any carbon formed would be deposited as a solid; the equilibrium constant is given by

$$K_4 = \frac{p_{CO}^2}{a_C p_{CO_2}} = 1329.5, \qquad (5.5.8)$$

where a_C is the activity of carbon in the solid state. Do not include reaction (5.5.7) in the equilibrium analysis. After establishing the equilibrium composition, considering only the homogeneous gaseous reactions given by (5.5.1), (5.5.2), and (5.5.3), determine the thermodynamic likelihood that solid carbon would appear as a result of reaction (5.5.7). Assume that the activity of solid carbon is unaffected by pressure and equals unity.

Use the Newton-Raphson method to solve the system of simultaneous nonlinear equations developed as the result of the equilibrium analysis.

Method of Solution

Because of the magnitude of K_1, the equilibrium constant for reaction (5.1.1), the first reaction can be assumed to go to completion at $2200°F$, that is, virtually no unreacted oxygen will remain in the product gases at equilibrium.

Let the following nomenclature be used:

x_1 mole fraction of CO in the equilibrium mixture

x_2 mole fraction of CO_2 in the equilibrium mixture

x_3 mole fraction of H_2O in the equilibrium mixture

x_4 mole fraction of H_2 in the equilibrium mixture

x_5 mole fraction of CH_4 in the equilibrium mixture

x_6 number of moles of O_2 per mole of CH_4 in the feed gases

x_7 number of moles of product gases in the equilibrium mixture per mole of CH_4 in the feed gases.

Then a system of seven simultaneous equations may be generated from three atom balances, an energy balance, a mole fraction constraint, and two equilibrium relations.

Atom conservation balances. The number of atoms of each element entering equals the number of atoms of each element in the equilibrium mixture.

$$\text{Oxygen: } x_6 = (\tfrac{1}{2}x_1 + x_2 + \tfrac{1}{2}x_3)x_7. \qquad (5.5.9)$$

$$\text{Hydrogen: } 4 = (2x_3 + 2x_4 + 4x_5)x_7. \qquad (5.5.10)$$

$$\text{Carbon: } 1 = (x_1 + x_2 + x_5)x_7. \qquad (5.5.11)$$

Energy (enthalpy) balance. Since the reaction is to be conducted adiabatically, that is, no energy is added to

321

or removed from the reacting gases, the enthalpy (H) of the reactants must equal the enthalpy of the products.

$$[H_{CH_4} + x_6 H_{O_2}]_{1000°F} = x_7[x_1 H_{CO} + x_2 H_{CO_2} + x_3 H_{H_2O}$$

$$+ x_4 H_{H_2} + x_5 H_{CH_4}]_{2200°F}.$$
$$(5.5.12)$$

Mole fraction constraint.

$$x_1 + x_2 + x_3 + x_4 + x_5 = 1. \qquad (5.5.13)$$

Equilibrium relations.

$$K_2 = \frac{P^2 x_1 x_4^3}{x_3 x_5} = 1.7837 \times 10^5, \qquad (5.5.14)$$

$$K_3 = \frac{x_1 x_3}{x_2 x_4} = 2.6058. \qquad (5.5.15)$$

The relationships (5.5.14) and (5.5.15) follow directly from (5.5.5) and (5.5.6), respectively, where P is the total pressure and $p_{CO} = P x_1$, etc. In addition, there are five side conditions,

$$x_i \geqslant 0, \qquad i = 1, 2, \ldots, 5. \qquad (5.5.16)$$

These conditions insure that all mole fractions in the equilibrium mixture are nonnegative, that is, any solution of equations (5.5.9) to (5.5.15) that contains negative mole fractions is physically meaningless. From physical-chemical principles, there is one and only one solution of the equations that satisfies conditions (5.5.16). Any irrelevant solutions may be detected easily.

The seven equations may be rewritten in the form

$$f_i(\mathbf{x}) = 0, \qquad i = 1, 2, \ldots, 7, \qquad (5.5.17)$$

where $\mathbf{x} = [x_1 \ x_2 \ x_3 \ x_4 \ x_5 \ x_6 \ x_7]^t$, as follows:

$$f_1(\mathbf{x}) = \frac{1}{2} x_1 + x_2 + \frac{1}{2} x_3 - \frac{x_6}{x_7} = 0 \qquad (5.5.18a)$$

$$f_2(\mathbf{x}) = x_3 + x_4 + 2x_5 - \frac{2}{x_7} = 0 \qquad (5.5.18b)$$

$$f_3(\mathbf{x}) = x_1 + x_2 + x_5 - \frac{1}{x_7} = 0 \qquad (5.5.18c)$$

$$f_4(\mathbf{x}) = -28837 x_1 - 139009 x_2 - 78213 x_3 + 18927 x_4$$

$$+ 8427 x_5 + \frac{13492}{x_7} - 10690 \frac{x_6}{x_7} = 0 \qquad (5.5.18d)$$

$$f_5(\mathbf{x}) = x_1 + x_2 + x_3 + x_4 + x_5 - 1 = 0 \qquad (5.5.18e)$$

$$f_6(\mathbf{x}) = P^2 x_1 x_4^3 - 1.7837 \times 10^5 x_3 x_5 = 0 \qquad (5.5.18f)$$

$$f_7(\mathbf{x}) = x_1 x_3 - 2.6058 x_2 x_4 = 0. \qquad (5.5.18g)$$

The system of simultaneous nonlinear equations has the form of (5.33), and will be solved using the Newton-Raphson method, described in Section 5.9. The partial

derivatives of (5.40) may be found by partial differentiation of the seven functions, $f_i(\mathbf{x})$, with respect to each of the seven variables. For example,

$$\frac{\partial f_1}{\partial x_1} = \frac{1}{2}, \qquad \frac{\partial f_1}{\partial x_4} = 0, \qquad \frac{\partial f_1}{\partial x_7} = \frac{x_6}{x_7^2}.$$

$$\frac{\partial f_1}{\partial x_2} = 1, \qquad \frac{\partial f_1}{\partial x_5} = 0, \qquad (5.5.19)$$

$$\frac{\partial f_1}{\partial x_3} = \frac{1}{2}, \qquad \frac{\partial f_1}{\partial x_6} = -\frac{1}{x_7},$$

The Newton-Raphson method may be summarized as follows:

1. Choose a starting vector $\mathbf{x}_k = \mathbf{x}_0 = [x_{10}, x_{20}, \ldots, x_{70}]$, where $\mathbf{x}_0$ is hopefully near a solution $\boldsymbol{\alpha}$.

2. Solve the system of linear equations (5.44),

$$\boldsymbol{\phi}(\mathbf{x}_k)\boldsymbol{\delta}_k = -\mathbf{f}(\mathbf{x}_k),$$

where

$$\phi_{ij}(\mathbf{x}_k) = \frac{\partial f_i}{\partial x_j}(\mathbf{x}_k), \qquad \begin{matrix} i = 1, 2, \ldots, 7, \\ j = 1, 2, \ldots, 7, \end{matrix} \qquad (5.5.20)$$

and

$$\mathbf{f}(\mathbf{x}_k) = [f_1(\mathbf{x}_k), f_2(\mathbf{x}_k), \ldots, f_7(\mathbf{x}_k)]^t, \qquad (5.5.21)$$

for the increment vector

$$\boldsymbol{\delta}_k = [\delta_{1k}, \delta_{2k}, \ldots, \delta_{7k}]^t. \qquad (5.5.22)$$

3. Update the approximation to the root for the next iteration.

$$\mathbf{x}_{k+1} = \mathbf{x}_k + \boldsymbol{\delta}_k.$$

4. Check for possible convergence to a root $\boldsymbol{\alpha}$. One such test might be

$$|\delta_{ik}| < \varepsilon_2, \qquad i = 1, 2, \ldots, 7. \qquad (5.5.23)$$

If (5.5.23) is true for all i, then $\mathbf{x}_{k+1}$ is taken to be the root. If test (5.5.23) is failed for any i, then the process is repeated starting with step 2. The iterative process is continued until test (5.5.23) is passed for some k, or when k exceeds some specified upper limit.

In the programs that follow, the elements of the augmented matrix

$$\mathbf{A} = [\boldsymbol{\phi}(\mathbf{x}_k) \ \vdots \ -\mathbf{f}(\mathbf{x}_k)] \qquad (5.5.24)$$

are evaluated by a subroutine named CALCN. The system of linear equations (5.44) is solved by calling on the function SIMUL, described in detail in Example 5.2.

The main program is a general one, in that it is not specifically written to solve only the seven equations of interest. By properly defining the subroutine CALCN, the main program could be used to solve any system of n

Example 5.5   Chemical Equilibrium (Newton-Raphson Method)   **323**

simultaneous nonlinear equations. The main program reads data values for *itmax*, *iprint*, *n*, ε_1, ε_2, and x_1, x_2, ..., x_n. Here, *itmax* is the maximum number of Newton-Raphson iterations, *iprint* is a variable that controls printing of intermediate output, *n* is the number of

nonlinear equations, ε_1 is the minimum pivot magnitude allowed in the Gauss-Jordan reduction algorithm, ε_2 is a small positive number used in test (5.5.23), and x_1, x_2, ..., x_n are the initial estimates x_{10}, x_{20}, ..., x_{n0}, that is, the elements of $\mathbf{x}_0$.

Flow Diagram

Main Program

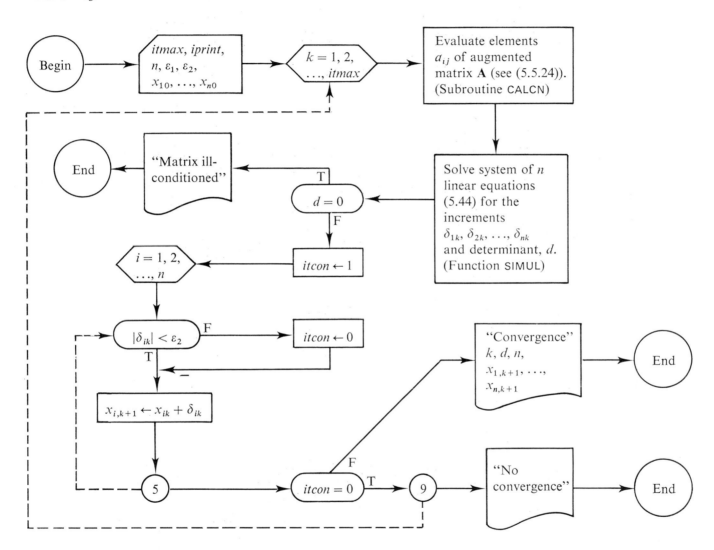

Subroutine CALCN (Arguments: $\mathbf{x}_k$, $\mathbf{A}$, N)

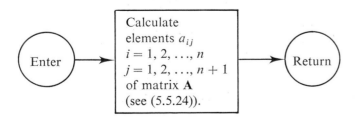

FORTRAN *Implementation*

List of Principal Variables

Program Symbol	Definition

(Main)

A	Augmented matrix of coefficients, **A** (see (5.5.24)).
DETER	d, determinant of the matrix ϕ (the Jacobian).
EPS1	ε_1, minimum pivot magnitude permitted in subroutine SIMUL.
EPS2	ε_2, small positive number, used in convergence test (5.5.23).
I	Subscript, i.
IPRINT	Print control variable, *iprint*. If *iprint* = 1, intermediate solutions are printed after each iteration.
ITCON	Used in convergence test (5.5.23). ITCON = 1 if (5.5.23) is passed for all i, $i = 1, 2, \ldots, n$; otherwise ITCON = 0.
ITER	Iteration counter, k.
ITMAX	Maximum number of iterations permitted, *itmax*.
N	Number of nonlinear equations, n.
XINC	Vector of increments, δ_{ik}.
XOLD	Vector of approximations to the solution, x_{ik}.
SIMUL	Function developed in Example 5.2. Solves the system of n linear equations (5.44) for the increments, δ_{ik}, $i = 1, 2, \ldots, n$.

(Subroutine CALCN)

DXOLD	Same as XOLD. Used to avoid an excessive number of references to subroutine arguments in CALCN.
I, J	i and j, row and column subscripts, respectively.
NRC	N, dimension of the matrix A in the calling program. A is assumed to have the same number of rows and columns.
P	Pressure, P, atm.

Example 5.5   Chemical Equilibrium (Newton-Raphson Method)   **325**

Program Listing

Main Program

```
C           APPLIED NUMERICAL METHODS, EXAMPLE 5.5
C           CHEMICAL EQUILIBRIUM - NEWTON-RAPHSON METHOD
C
C           THIS PROGRAM SOLVES N SIMULTANEOUS NON-LINEAR EQUATIONS
C           IN N UNKNOWNS BY THE NEWTON-RAPHSON ITERATIVE PROCEDURE.
C           INITIAL GUESSES FOR VALUES OF THE UNKNOWNS ARE READ INTO
C           XOLD(1)...XOLD(N).  THE PROGRAM FIRST CALLS ON THE SUBROUTINE
C           CALCN TO COMPUTE THE ELEMENTS OF A, THE AUGMENTED MATRIX OF
C           PARTIAL DERIVATIVES, THEN ON FUNCTION SIMUL (SEE PROBLEM 5.2)
C           TO SOLVE THE GENERATED SET OF LINEAR EQUATIONS FOR THE CHANGES
C           IN THE SOLUTION VALUES XINC(1)...XINC(N).  DETER IS THE
C           JACOBIAN COMPUTED BY SIMUL.  THE SOLUTIONS ARE UPDATED AND THE
C           PROCESS CONTINUED UNTIL ITER, THE NUMBER OF ITERATIONS,
C           EXCEEDS ITMAX OR UNTIL THE CHANGE IN EACH OF THE N VARIABLES
C           IS SMALLER IN MAGNITUDE THAN EPS2 (ITCON = 1 UNDER THESE
C           CONDITIONS).  EPS1 IS THE MINIMUM PIVOT MAGNITUDE PERMITTED
C           IN SIMUL.  WHEN IPRINT = 1, INTERMEDIATE SOLUTION VALUES ARE
C           PRINTED AFTER EACH ITERATION.
C
      DIMENSION XOLD(21), XINC(21), A(21,21)
C
C     ..... READ AND PRINT DATA .....
    1 READ (5,100) ITMAX,IPRINT,N,EPS1,EPS2,(XOLD(I),I=1,N)
      WRITE (6,200) ITMAX,IPRINT,N,EPS1,EPS2,N,(XOLD(I),I=1,N)
C
C     ..... NEWTON-RAPHSON ITERATION .....
      DO 9   ITER = 1, ITMAX
C
C     ..... CALL ON CALCN TO SET UP THE A MATRIX .....
      CALL CALCN( XOLD, A, 21 )
C
C     ..... CALL SIMUL TO COMPUTE JACOBIAN AND CORRECTIONS IN XINC .....
      DETER = SIMUL( N, A, XINC, EPS1, 1, 21 )
      IF ( DETER.NE.0. )   GO TO 3
         WRITE (6,201)
         GO TO 1
C
C     ..... CHECK FOR CONVERGENCE AND UPDATE XOLD VALUES .....
    3 ITCON = 1
      DO 5   I = 1, N
      IF ( ABS(XINC(I)).GT.EPS2 )   ITCON = 0
    5 XOLD(I) = XOLD(I) + XINC(I)
      IF ( IPRINT.EQ.1 )   WRITE (6,202) ITER,DETER,N,(XOLD(I),I=1,N)
      IF ( ITCON.EQ.0 )   GO TO 9
         WRITE (6,203) ITER,N,(XOLD(I),I=1,N)
         GO TO 1
    9 CONTINUE
C
      WRITE (6,204)
      GO TO 1
C
C     ..... FORMATS FOR INPUT AND OUTPUT STATEMENTS .....
  100 FORMAT ( 10X,I3,17X,I1,19X,I3/ 10X,E7.1,13X,E7.1/ (20X, 5F10.3) )
  200 FORMAT ( 10H1ITMAX = , I8/ 10H IPRINT = , I8/  10H N     = ,
     1   I8/  10H EPS1   = , 1PE14.1/ 10H EPS2   = , 1PE14.1/
     2   26H0            XOLD(1)...XOLD(, I2, 1H)/ 1H / (1H ,1P4E16.6) )
  201 FORMAT ( 38H0MATRIX IS ILL-CONDITIONED OR SINGULAR )
  202 FORMAT ( 10H0ITER   = ,I8/  10H DETER  = , E18.5/
     2   26H             XOLD(1)...XOLD(, I2, 1H) / (1H ,1P4E16.6) )
  203 FORMAT ( 24H0SUCCESSFUL CONVERGENCE / 10H0ITER   = , I3/
     2   26H0            XOLD(1)...XOLD(, I2, 1H) / 1H / (1H ,1P4E16.6) )
  204 FORMAT ( 15H NO CONVERGENCE )
C
      END
```

Program Listing (*Continued*)

Subroutine CALCN

```
          SUBROUTINE CALCN( DXOLD, A, NRC )
C
C             THIS SUBROUTINE SETS UP THE AUGMENTED MATRIX OF PARTIAL
C             DERIVATIVES REQUIRED FOR THE SOLUTION OF THE NON-LINEAR
C             EQUATIONS WHICH DESCRIBE THE EQUILIBRIUM CONCENTRATIONS
C             OF CHEMICAL CONSTITUENTS RESULTING FROM PARTIAL OXIDATION
C             OF METHANE WITH OXYGEN TO PRODUCE SYNTHESIS GAS.  THE PRESSURE
C             IS 20 ATMOSPHERES.  SEE TEXT FOR MEANINGS OF XOLD(1)...XOLD(N)
C             AND A LISTING OF THE EQUATIONS.  DXOLD HAS BEEN USED AS THE
C             DUMMY ARGUMENT FOR XOLD TO AVOID AN EXCESSIVE NUMBER OF
C             REFERENCES TO ELEMENTS IN THE ARGUMENT LIST.
C
          DIMENSION XOLD(20), DXOLD(NRC), A(NRC,NRC)
C
          DATA  P / 20. /
C
C         ..... SHIFT ELEMENTS OF DXOLD TO XOLD AND CLEAR A ARRAY .....
          DO 1   I = 1, 7
          XOLD(I) = DXOLD(I)
          DO 1   J = 1, 8
        1 A(I,J) = 0.
C
C         ..... COMPUTE NON-ZERO ELEMENTS OF A .....
          A(1,1) = 0.5
          A(1,2) = 1.0
          A(1,3) = 0.5
          A(1,6) = -1.0/XOLD(7)
          A(1,7) = XOLD(6)/XOLD(7)**2
          A(1,8) = -XOLD(1)/2. - XOLD(2) - XOLD(3)/2. + XOLD(6)/XOLD(7)
          A(2,3) = 1.0
          A(2,4) = 1.0
          A(2,5) = 2.0
          A(2,7) = 2.0/XOLD(7)**2
          A(2,8) = -XOLD(3) - XOLD(4) - 2.0*XOLD(5) + 2.0/XOLD(7)
          A(3,1) = 1.0
          A(3,2) = 1.0
          A(3,5) = 1.0
          A(3,7) = 1.0/XOLD(7)**2
          A(3,8) = -XOLD(1) - XOLD(2) - XOLD(5) + 1.0/XOLD(7)
          A(4,1) = -28837.
          A(4,2) = -139009.
          A(4,3) = -78213.
          A(4,4) = 18927.
          A(4,5) = 8427.
          A(4,6) = -10690./XOLD(7)
          A(4,7) = (-13492. + 10690.*XOLD(6))/XOLD(7)**2
          A(4,8) = 28837.*XOLD(1) + 139009.*XOLD(2) + 78213.*XOLD(3)
        1         -18927.*XOLD(4) - 8427.*XOLD(5) - 13492./XOLD(7) + 10690.
        2         *XOLD(6)/XOLD(7)
          A(5,1) = 1.0
          A(5,2) = 1.0
          A(5,3) = 1.0
          A(5,4) = 1.0
          A(5,5) = 1.0
          A(5,8) = 1.0 - XOLD(1) - XOLD(2) - XOLD(3) - XOLD(4) - XOLD(5)
          A(6,1) = P*P*XOLD(4)**3
          A(6,3) = -1.7837E5*XOLD(5)
          A(6,4) = 3.0*P*P*XOLD(1)*XOLD(4)**2
          A(6,5) = -1.7837E5*XOLD(3)
          A(6,8) = 1.7837E5*XOLD(5)*XOLD(3) - P*P*XOLD(1)*XOLD(4)**3
          A(7,1) = XOLD(3)
          A(7,2) = -2.6058*XOLD(4)
          A(7,3) = XOLD(1)
          A(7,4) = -2.6058*XOLD(2)
          A(7,8) = 2.6058*XOLD(4)*XOLD(2) - XOLD(1)*XOLD(3)
          RETURN
C
          END
```

Example 5.5 Chemical Equilibrium (Newton-Raphson Method) **327**

Program Listing (*Continued*)

Data

```
ITMAX   =    50        IPRINT =   1           N      =   7
EPS1    =  1.0E-10     EPS2   =  1.0E-05
XOLD(1)...XOLD(5) =        0.500     0.000     0.000     0.500     0.000
XOLD(6)...XOLD(7) =        0.500     2.000
ITMAX   =    50        IPRINT =   0           N      =   7
EPS1    =  1.0E-10     EPS2   =  1.0E-05
XOLD(1)...XOLD(5) =        0.200     0.200     0.200     0.200     0.200
XOLD(6)...XOLD(7) =        0.500     2.000
ITMAX   =    50        IPRINT =   1           N      =   7
EPS1    =  1.0E-10     EPS2   =  1.0E-05
XOLD(1)...XOLD(5) =        0.220     0.075     0.001     0.580     0.125
XOLD(6)...XOLD(7) =        0.436     2.350
```

Computer Output

Results for the 1st Data Set

```
ITMAX   =         50
IPRINT  =          1
N       =          7
EPS1    =      1.0E-10
EPS2    =      1.0E-05

            XOLD(1)...XOLD( 7)

    5.000000E-01     0.0           0.0           5.000000E-01
    0.0             5.000000E-01   2.000000E 00

ITER    =          1
DETER   =      -0.97077E 07
            XOLD(1)...XOLD( 7)
    2.210175E-01     2.592762E-02   6.756210E-02   4.263276E-01
    2.591652E-01     3.343250E-01   1.975559E 00

ITER    =          2
DETER   =      -0.10221E 10
            XOLD(1)...XOLD( 7)
    3.101482E-01     7.142063E-03   5.538273E-02   5.791981E-01
    4.812878E-02     4.681466E-01   2.524948E 00

ITER    =          3
DETER   =      -0.41151E 09
            XOLD(1)...XOLD( 7)
    3.202849E-01     9.554777E-03   4.671279E-02   6.129664E-01
    1.048106E-02     5.533223E-01   2.880228E 00

ITER    =          4
DETER   =      -0.22807E 09
            XOLD(1)...XOLD( 7)
    3.228380E-01     9.224802E-03   4.603060E-02   6.180951E-01
    3.811378E-03     5.758237E-01   2.974139E 00

ITER    =          5
DETER   =      -0.20218E 09
            XOLD(1)...XOLD( 7)
    3.228708E-01     9.223551E-03   4.601713E-02   6.181716E-01
    3.716873E-03     5.767141E-01   2.977859E 00

ITER    =          6
DETER   =      -0.20134E 09
            XOLD(1)...XOLD( 7)
    3.228708E-01     9.223547E-03   4.601710E-02   6.181716E-01
    3.716847E-03     5.767153E-01   2.977863E 00
```

Computer Output (*Continued*)

```
SUCCESSFUL CONVERGENCE

ITER   =   6

          XOLD(1)...XOLD( 7)

   3.228708E-01     9.223547E-03     4.601710E-02     6.181716E-01
   3.716847E-03     5.767153E-01     2.977863E 00
```

Results for the 3rd Data Set

```
ITMAX  =        50
IPRINT =         1
N      =         7
EPS1   =       1.0E-10
EPS2   =       1.0E-05

          XOLD(1)...XOLD( 7)

   2.200000E-01     7.499999E-02     9.999999E-04     5.800000E-01
   1.250000E-01     4.360000E-01     2.349999E 00

ITER   =         1
DETER  =      -0.61808E 08
          XOLD(1)...XOLD( 7)
   6.951495E-01    -8.022028E-02     1.272939E-02     1.217132E 00
  -8.447912E-01     1.314754E 00     5.969404E 00

ITER   =         2
DETER  =       0.12576E 09
          XOLD(1)...XOLD( 7)
   4.958702E-01    -1.698154E-02     5.952045E-03     9.518250E-01
  -4.366657E-01     2.379797E 00     1.043425E 01

ITER   =         3
DETER  =       0.77199E 07
          XOLD(1)...XOLD( 7)
   4.559822E-01    -9.799302E-04    -7.583648E-04     9.107630E-01
  -3.650070E-01     2.509821E 00     1.107038E 01

ITER   =         4
DETER  =       0.53378E 07
          XOLD(1)...XOLD( 7)
   4.569673E-01    -4.071472E-04    -2.142648E-03     9.152630E-01
  -3.696806E-01     2.608933E 00     1.149338E 01

ITER   =         5
DETER  =       0.49739E 07
          XOLD(1)...XOLD( 7)
   4.569306E-01    -4.071994E-04    -2.125205E-03     9.151721E-01
  -3.695704E-01     2.610552E 00     1.150046E 01

ITER   =         6
DETER  =       0.49611E 07
          XOLD(1)...XOLD( 7)
   4.569306E-01    -4.071984E-04    -2.125199E-03     9.151720E-01
  -3.695703E-01     2.610549E 00     1.150045E 01

SUCCESSFUL CONVERGENCE

ITER   =   6

          XOLD(1)...XOLD( 7)

   4.569306E-01    -4.071984E-04    -2.125199E-03     9.151720E-01
  -3.695703E-01     2.610549E 00     1.150045E 01
```

Example 5.5 Chemical Equilibrium (Newton-Raphson Method)   **329**

Discussion of Results

Results are shown for the first and third data sets only. For the first two data sets, the Newton-Raphson iteration converged to the same solution, one that satisfies the side conditions (5.5.16). Results for the third data set cannot be physically meaningful, because the solution has negative mole fractions for CO_2, H_2O, and CH_4. The equilibrium compositions, reactant ratio O_2/CH_4

Table 5.5.2 Equilibrium Gas Mixture

x_1, mole fraction CO	0.322871
x_2, mole fraction CO_2	0.009224
x_3, mole fraction H_2O	0.046017
x_4, mole fraction H_2	0.618172
x_5, mole fraction CH_4	0.003717
x_6, feed ratio O_2/CH_4	0.576715
x_7, total moles of product	2.977863

in the feed gases, and the total number of moles of product per mole of CH_4 in the feed are tabulated in Table 5.5.2. Thus the required feed ratio is 0.5767 moles of oxygen per mole of methane in the feed gases.

To establish if carbon is likely to be formed according to reaction (5.5.7) at 2200°F for a gas of the computed composition, it is necessary to calculate the magnitude of

$$\overline{K} = \frac{p_{CO}^2}{a_C p_{CO_2}} = \frac{P x_1^2}{a_C x_2}. \qquad (5.5.25)$$

If $\overline{K}$ is larger than K_4 from (5.5.8), then there will be a tendency for reaction (5.5.7) to shift toward the left; carbon will be formed. Assuming that $a_C = 1$,

$$\overline{K} = \frac{20 \times (0.322871)^2}{1 \times 0.009224} \doteq 226.03 < K_4 = 1329.5. \quad (5.5.26)$$

Therefore there will be no tendency for carbon to form.

Problems

5.1   Write the following simultaneous equations in matrix form:

$$x_1 + 3x_2 = 5,$$
$$4x_1 - x_2 = 12.$$

By means of a hand calculation, implement the Gauss-Jordan reduction scheme with the diagonal pivot criterion to compute:

(a) x_1 and x_2.
(b) The inverse of the coefficient matrix.
(c) The determinant of the coefficient matrix.

5.2   Solve the following three equations using the Gauss-Jordan reduction scheme with the maximum pivot criterion:

$$x_1 + 2x_2 + 8x_3 = -3,$$
$$2x_1 - 4x_2 - 6x_3 = 0,$$
$$-2x_1 + 4x_2 + 2x_3 = 4.$$

Do not interchange rows or columns. Show the status of the augmented matrix after each complete pass of the elimination procedure.

5.3   Define the *norm* of an $n \times n$ real matrix $\mathbf{A}$ by

$$\|\mathbf{A}\| = \max_{\|\mathbf{x}\| \neq 0} \frac{\|\mathbf{Ax}\|}{\|\mathbf{x}\|}.$$

Alternatively, this may be written as

$$\|\mathbf{A}\| = \max_{\|\mathbf{x}\| = 1} \|\mathbf{Ax}\|.$$

Thus geometrically, $\|\mathbf{A}\|$ may be viewed as the length of the longest vector in the image set $\{\mathbf{Ax}\}$ of all possible unit vectors $\{\mathbf{x}\}$ (the unit sphere) under the transformation $\mathbf{x} \rightarrow \mathbf{Ax}$. As a consequence of the definition,

$$\|c\mathbf{A}\| = |c| \|\mathbf{A}\|,$$
$$\|\mathbf{Ax}\| \leq \|\mathbf{A}\| \|\mathbf{x}\|.$$

Now consider the problem of solving the equations (5.2),

$$\mathbf{Bx} = \mathbf{u},$$

when the elements of $\mathbf{B}$ are known exactly, but the elements of $\mathbf{u}$ are not known with certainty. In particular, suppose that a vector $\mathbf{u} + \delta\mathbf{u}$ is used as the right-hand side vector (presumably the elements of $\delta\mathbf{u}$ would be small, so that $\mathbf{u} + \delta\mathbf{u}$ is fairly close to $\mathbf{u}$ itself). If $\mathbf{x} + \delta\mathbf{x}$ is the solution of the system

$$\mathbf{B}(\mathbf{x} + \delta\mathbf{x}) = \mathbf{u} + \delta\mathbf{u},$$

show that the relative uncertainty in $\mathbf{x}$ introduced by the uncertainty in $\mathbf{u}$ is given by

$$\frac{\|\delta\mathbf{x}\|}{\|\mathbf{x}\|} \leq \text{cond}(\mathbf{B}) \frac{\|\delta\mathbf{u}\|}{\|\mathbf{u}\|}.$$

Here, cond($\mathbf{B}$), the *condition number* [14], is given by

$$\text{cond}(\mathbf{B}) = \|\mathbf{B}\| \|\mathbf{B}^{-1}\| \geq 1.$$

If cond($\mathbf{B}$) is small (of order unity), then $\mathbf{B}$ is said to be *well conditioned*, while if cond($\mathbf{B}$) is large, then $\mathbf{B}$ is said to be poorly conditioned or *ill conditioned*.

5.4   As a continuation of Problem 5.3, assume that the elements of the right-hand side vector $\mathbf{u}$ are known exactly, but that the elements of $\mathbf{B}$ are not known with certainty. Let the approximation of $\mathbf{B}$ be denoted as $\mathbf{B} + \delta\mathbf{B}$ with the remaining notation the same as before. Show that

$$\frac{\|\delta\mathbf{x}\|}{\|\mathbf{x} + \delta\mathbf{x}\|} \leq \text{cond}(\mathbf{B}) \frac{\|\delta\mathbf{B}\|}{\|\mathbf{B}\|}.$$

5.5   Let $\mathbf{x}_1$ be the solution to the system of linear equations

$$\mathbf{Bx} = \mathbf{u}$$

found by one of the elimination algorithms. Assuming that some round-off errors are present in $\mathbf{x}_1$, let the error vector $\boldsymbol{\varepsilon}_1$ be defined by

$$\boldsymbol{\varepsilon}_1 = \mathbf{x} - \mathbf{x}_1,$$

and the residual vector $\mathbf{r}_1$ be defined by

$$\mathbf{r}_1 = \mathbf{u} - \mathbf{Bx}_1.$$

Show that if the system of equations

$$\mathbf{B}\boldsymbol{\delta}_1 = \mathbf{r}_1$$

could be solved *exactly*, then the solution

$$\mathbf{x}_2 = \mathbf{x}_1 + \boldsymbol{\delta}_1$$

would solve the original system $\mathbf{Bx} = \mathbf{u}$, *exactly*.

5.6   In practice, the solution vector $\boldsymbol{\delta}_1$ of Problem 5.5 will *not* be computed exactly, and x_2 will be taken as the next iterate in the solution scheme

$$\boldsymbol{\varepsilon}_k = \mathbf{x} - \mathbf{x}_k,$$
$$\mathbf{r}_k = \mathbf{u} - \mathbf{Bx}_k,$$
$$\mathbf{B}\boldsymbol{\delta}_k = \mathbf{r}_k,$$
$$\mathbf{x}_{k+1} = \mathbf{x}_k + \boldsymbol{\delta}_k.$$

Forsythe and Moler [14] point out that the residuals $\mathbf{r}_k$ must generally be computed with a higher precision than that used for the rest of the calculations. The iterative improvement algorithm may be terminated when $\|\boldsymbol{\delta}_k\|$ is sufficiently small (typically when the single-precision results for $\mathbf{x}_k$ stabilize).

Consider the equations

$$2x_1 - 7x_2 + 4x_3 = 9,$$
$$x_1 + 9x_2 - 6x_3 = 1,$$
$$-3x_1 + 8x_2 + 5x_3 = 6.$$

Assuming that at some stage in the calculations

$$\mathbf{x}_k = [3.97, 1.10, 1.90]^t,$$

carry out one iteration of the correction scheme to find $\mathbf{x}_{k+1}$, retaining six significant digits in the computation of $\mathbf{r}_k$, and three significant digits elsewhere.

5.7   How would you modify the programs of Examples 5.1 and 5.2 to accommodate the iterative improvement of the solution vector outlined in Problems 5.5 and 5.6?

5.8 Assume that an approximate inverse, Q_k, of matrix **B** is available. Using techniques analogous to those outlined in Problems 5.5 and 5.6, show that if a residual matrix R_k is defined to be

$$R_k = I - BQ_k,$$

then the next iterate should be

$$Q_{k+1} = Q_k + Q_k R_k,$$

and a general recursion formula,

$$Q_{k+1} = Q_k(2I - BQ_k),$$

can be used to calculate it.

How would the function SIMUL of Example 5.2 have to be modified to employ this iterative improvement algorithm for evaluation of B^{-1}? Make the changes, and test the program thoroughly. Among the test matrices, include the *Hilbert matrix*.

$$H_n = 1/(i+j-1), \qquad i, j = 1, 2, \ldots, n,$$

for $n = 4$, 5, and 6. The Hilbert matrix is very ill conditioned, even for small n [15], and is often used as a test matrix for demonstrating effectiveness of inversion routines.

5.9 Write a function, named DPOLY, that returns, as its value (see Problem 2.51),

$$\left. \frac{d^m p_n(x)}{dx^m} \right|_{x_i} = \sum_{j=0}^{n} a_j f(x_j).$$

The routine should have the argument list

(N, X, Y, M, I, A, Q, NQROW, NQCOL, TRUBL),

where N and M are equivalent to n and m, respectively, X is an array containing $x_0, \ldots, x_n$ in X(1), ..., X(N + 1), Y is an array containing the functional values $f(x_0), \ldots, f(x_n)$ in Y(1), ..., Y(N + 1,) and I is the subscript of the desired argument, X(I) (note that $I = i + 1$). Q is a matrix dimensioned to have NQROW rows and NQCOL columns in the calling program (to insure a compatible storage arrangement). DPOLY should set up the augmented matrix of coefficients of the simultaneous linear equations whose solutions are the a_j, $j = 0, \ldots, n$, in the first N + 1 rows and N + 2 columns of the matrix Q (see Problem 2.51) and call on an appropriate linear equation solver (such as the function SIMUL of Example 5.2) to evaluate the a_j. DPOLY should store $a_0, \ldots, a_n$ in A(1), ..., A(N + 1), evaluate the appropriate derivative at the specified argument, and return to the calling program. TRUBL (logical) should be set to .FALSE. if no computational problems are encountered and to .TRUE. otherwise.

Write a short main program that reads and prints essential data, calls upon DPOLY to evaluate the required derivative and coefficients A(1), ..., A(N + 1), prints the results, and returns to read more data. As trial problems, generate the formulas developed in Problems 2.49 and 2.50.

5.10 Jenkins and White [8] give precisely determined values, shown in Table P5.10, for the refractive index, n, at various wavelengths, λ (angstrom units), for borosilicate crown glass.

Table P5.10

λ	n
6563	1.50883
6439	1.50917
5890	1.51124
5338	1.51386
5086	1.51534
4861	1.51690
4340	1.52136
3988	1.52546

Use the 2nd, 4th, and 7th entries in Table P5.10 to determine the constants A, B, and C in Cauchy's equation for refractive index:

$$n = A + \frac{B}{\lambda^2} + \frac{C}{\lambda^4}.$$

Investigate the merits of Cauchy's equation for predicting the remaining entries in the table.

5.11 When a pure sample gas is bombarded by low energy electrons in a mass spectrometer, the galvanometer shows peak heights that correspond to individual m/e (mass-to-charge) ratios for the resulting mixture of ions. For the ith peak produced by a pure sample j, one can then assign a sensitivity s_{ij} (peak height per micron of Hg sample pressure). These coefficients are unique for each type of gas.

A distribution of peak heights may also be obtained for an n-component gas *mixture* that is to be analyzed for the partial pressures $p_1, p_2, \ldots, p_n$ of each of its constituents. The height h_i of a certain peak is a linear combination of the products of the individual sensitivities and partial pressures:

$$\sum_{j=1}^{n} s_{ij} p_j = h_i.$$

In general, more than n peaks may be available. However, if the n most distinct ones are chosen, we have $i = 1, 2, \ldots, n$, so that the individual partial pressures are given by the solution of n simultaneous linear equations.

Write a program that will accept values for the number of components N, the sensitivities S(1,1) ... S(N,N), and the peak heights H(1) ... H(N). The program should then compute and print values for the individual partial pressures P(1) ... P(N). An elimination procedure should be used in the computations.

Suggested Test Data

The sensitivities given in Table P5.11 were reported by Carnahan [9], in connection with the analysis of a hydrocarbon gas mixture.

A particular gas mixture (sample #39G) produced the following peak heights: $h_1 = 17.1$, $h_2 = 65.1$, $h_3 = 186.0$, $h_4 = 82.7$, $h_5 = 84.2$, $h_6 = 63.7$, and $h_7 = 119.7$. The measured total pressure of the mixture was 39.9 microns of Hg, which can be compared with the sum of the computed partial pressures.

Table P5.11

Peak Index i	m/e	Component Index, j						
		1	2	3	4	5	6	7
		Hydrogen	Methane	Ethylene	Ethane	Propylene	Propane	n-Pentane
1	2	16.87	0.1650	0.2019	0.3170	0.2340	0.1820	0.1100
2	16	0.0	27.70	0.8620	0.0620	0.0730	0.1310	0.1200
3	26	0.0	0.0	22.35	13.05	4.420	6.001	3.043
4	30	0.0	0.0	0.0	11.28	0.0	1.110	0.3710
5	40	0.0	0.0	0.0	0.0	9.850	1.684	2.108
6	44	0.0	0.0	0.0	0.0	0.2990	15.98	2.107
7	72	0.0	0.0	0.0	0.0	0.0	0.0	4.670

5.12 Could Problem 5.11 be solved by the Gauss-Seidel method?

5.13 Here and in Problems 5.14 and 5.15 we consider the loading of statically *indeterminate* pin-jointed frames. All supports are rigid, and the frames fit perfectly when unloaded. The following notation is used consistently for members: E = Young's modulus, L = length, A = cross-sectional area, and I = second moment of area about the neutral axis.

Let $\mathbf{p}$ = vector (column) of applied loads, $\boldsymbol{\delta}$ = corresponding displacement vector of deflections (one for each applied load), $\mathbf{s}$ = vector of resulting internal loads in members (including redundants—see below). Tensions and extensions are considered positive; compressions and contractions negative. Let $\mathbf{F}$ be a diagonal matrix with entries L/AE for individual members ($\mathbf{F}$ is the unassembled flexibility matrix), and let $\boldsymbol{\Gamma}$ be the flexibility matrix for the assembled structure, such that $\boldsymbol{\delta} = \boldsymbol{\Gamma}\mathbf{p}$. For the frame, choose arbitrarily a sufficient number of redundant members (whose internal loads are given by the vector $\mathbf{r}$, which will also be contained as part of $\mathbf{s}$), such that without them the structure would be statically *determinate*. Let $\mathbf{B}_0$ be a matrix such that $\mathbf{s} = \mathbf{B}_0\mathbf{p}$ would give the internal loads in the absence of the redundant members, and let $\mathbf{B}_1$ be a matrix such that $\mathbf{s} = \mathbf{B}_1\mathbf{r}$ would give the internal loads in the absence of any applied loads; combined, the effect is $\mathbf{s} = \mathbf{B}_0\mathbf{p} + \mathbf{B}_1\mathbf{r}$. It may then be shown (see McMinn [10], Robinson [11], or Problem 4.18, for example) that

$$\boldsymbol{\Gamma} = \mathbf{B}_0^t \mathbf{F} \mathbf{B},$$

$$\mathbf{s} = \mathbf{B}\mathbf{p},$$

where

$$\mathbf{B} = \mathbf{B}_0 - \mathbf{B}_1(\mathbf{B}_1^t \mathbf{F} \mathbf{B}_1)^{-1}\mathbf{B}_1^t \mathbf{F} \mathbf{B}_0.$$

Consider the frame shown in Fig. P5.13, with $AE = 50 \times 10^6$ lb$_f$ for all members. Number the members 1 through 5; these numbers will then identify the rows of the $\mathbf{F}$, $\mathbf{B}_0$, and $\mathbf{B}_1$ matrices as corresponding to the individual members.

Choosing AC as the redundant member, we have

$$\mathbf{p} = \begin{bmatrix} 500 \\ 1000 \end{bmatrix}, \quad \mathbf{F} = \frac{1}{50 \times 10^6} \begin{bmatrix} 30 & 0 & 0 & 0 & 0 \\ 0 & 40 & 0 & 0 & 0 \\ 0 & 0 & 30 & 0 & 0 \\ 0 & 0 & 0 & 50 & 0 \\ 0 & 0 & 0 & 0 & 50 \end{bmatrix},$$

$$\mathbf{B}_0 = \begin{bmatrix} 1 & \frac{3}{4} \\ 0 & 1 \\ 0 & 0 \\ 0 & -\frac{5}{4} \\ 0 & 0 \end{bmatrix}, \quad \text{and} \quad \mathbf{B}_1 = \begin{bmatrix} -\frac{3}{5} \\ -\frac{4}{5} \\ -\frac{3}{5} \\ 1 \\ 1 \end{bmatrix}.$$

Note that the successive columns of $\mathbf{B}_0$ and $\mathbf{B}_1$ can be found easily by considering from statics alone the internal forces that result from unit loads applied in turn (a) horizontally at B,

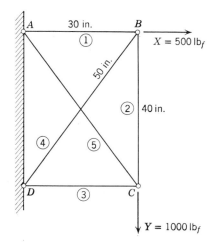

Figure P5.13

(b) vertically at C, and (c) along the redundant member. The number of columns in $\mathbf{B}_0$ equals the number of applied loads; the number in $\mathbf{B}_1$ equals the number of redundant members (here, just one). The ordering of rows and columns in the above matrices is arbitrary but must be self-consistent. For example, if the applied load vector were taken as $\mathbf{v} = [1000, 500]^t$ instead of $[500, 1000]^t$, the columns of $\mathbf{B}_0$ would have to be interchanged.

Determine the displacement and internal load vectors $\boldsymbol{\delta}$ and $\mathbf{s}$ for the frame.

5.14 Following in the style of Problem 5.13, choose an appropriate set of redundant members and evaluate $\mathbf{p}$, $\mathbf{F}$, $\mathbf{B}_0$, and $\mathbf{B}_1$ for the pin-jointed frame shown in Fig. P5.14. Assume $AE = 50 \times 10^6$ lb$_f$ throughout.

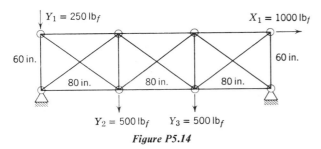

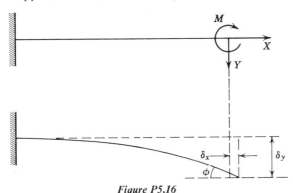

Figure P5.14

5.15 Write a computer program that will simulate the loading of a statically indeterminate pin-jointed frame, as discussed in Problem 5.13. The input should include **p**, **F**, $\mathbf{B}_0$, and $\mathbf{B}_1$. The output should include **B**, **Γ**, **s**, and **δ**. Test the program with the data of Problems 5.13 and 5.14.

5.16 Horizontal and vertical loads X and Y, and a moment M are applied to the cantilever of length L shown in Fig. P5.16.

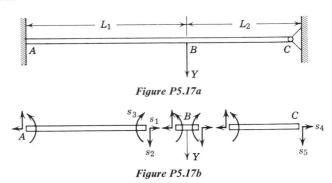

Figure P5.17a

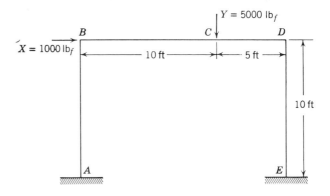

Figure P5.17b

where the internal loads (one, s_3, is a moment) are indicated in Fig. P5.17b. The unassembled flexibility matrix is

$$
\mathbf{F} =
\begin{bmatrix}
\dfrac{L_1}{EA} & 0 & 0 & 0 & 0 \\[2mm]
0 & \dfrac{L_1^3}{3EI} & \dfrac{L_1^2}{2EI} & 0 & 0 \\[2mm]
0 & \dfrac{L_1^2}{2EI} & \dfrac{L_1}{EI} & 0 & 0 \\[2mm]
0 & 0 & 0 & \dfrac{L_2}{EA} & 0 \\[2mm]
0 & 0 & 0 & 0 & \dfrac{L_2^3}{3EI}
\end{bmatrix}.
$$

Choosing s_4 and s_5 as the redundant loads, write down **p**, $\mathbf{B}_0$, and $\mathbf{B}_1$, and use the computer program developed in Problem 5.15 to solve for the resulting internal loads and the deflection at B. Assume $E = 30 \times 10^6$ lb$_f$/in.^{2}, $A = 3.53$ in.^{2} and $I - 20.99$ in.^{4} throughout (appropriate for a 6×3 steel I beam), with $L_1 = 10$ ft, $L_2 = 5$ ft, and $Y = 1000$ lb$_f$. Comment on the computed values of s_1 and s_4.

5.18 The portal frame shown in Fig. P5.18 is clamped rigidly at A and E, and B and D are rigid corners. $E = 30 \times 10^6$

At the free end, the horizontal extension δ_x, the downward deflection δ_y, and the slope ϕ (approximately equal to the angle with the horizontal for small ϕ) are related to the loads as follows:

$$
\begin{bmatrix} \delta_x \\[2mm] \delta_y \\[2mm] \phi \end{bmatrix}
=
\begin{bmatrix}
\dfrac{L}{EA} & 0 & 0 \\[2mm]
0 & \dfrac{L^3}{3EI} & \dfrac{L^2}{2EI} \\[2mm]
0 & \dfrac{L^2}{2EI} & \dfrac{L}{EI}
\end{bmatrix}
\begin{bmatrix} X \\[2mm] Y \\[2mm] M \end{bmatrix}
$$

Here, $E = $ Young's modulus, $A = $ cross-sectional area, and $I = $ second moment of area for the cantilever. The above 3×3 matrix is the *flexibility* matrix **Γ** for the cantilever.

Evaluate $\mathbf{K} = \mathbf{\Gamma}^{-1}$, the *stiffness* matrix for the cantilever.

5.17 In the pin-jointed frames of Problems 5.13 and 5.14 the members were subjected to axial loads only. However, the method outlined in Problem 5.13 may be applied to more general structures, in which shears and bending moments also exist. The following modifications are necessary: (a) the applied and internal load vectors must now include shears and bending moments in addition to axial loads, and (b) the individual diagonal elements of the F matrix (previously L/AE for each member) must be replaced by the appropriate flexibility matrix for each member (such as the 3×3 matrix of Problem 5.16).

As a simple example, consider the beam of Fig. P5.17a, clamped at A and pin-jointed at C. Let $\mathbf{s} = [s_1 s_2 s_3 s_4 s_5]^t$,

Figure P5.18

lb$_f$/in.^{2} throughout, $A = 5.3$ in.^{2} and $I = 55.63$ in.^{4} for AB and DE, and $A = 11.77$ in.^{2} and $I = 204.8$ in.^{4} for BCD. Compute all the internal loads and the displacements of B and C.

5.19 Consider the frame of Problem 5.14. By removing the diagonal members that slant up to the right, and by substituting a horizontal roller joint for the right-hand pin-jointed support, the problem becomes statically determinate.

In this event (with the same loads) compute the new internal loads in the members and the reactions at the two supports.

5.20 This problem is "open-ended," in that the degree of complexity possible depends on the skill and imagination of the programmer, and his familiarity with structural problems.

The ultimate goal is to have the computer design a structure so that no member is oversized. Ideally, input to the program would consist of basic information concerning the configuration of the structure and the loads to be imposed on it, together with an inventory of the available members and the various working stresses for the materials involved. The output would consist of specifications for all members together with the corresponding internal loads and deflections. Economic factors might also be considered.

Establish a feasible scheme for accomplishing all or part of the above goal, and write and test a computer program that will implement the scheme.

5.21 Let **A** be an n by n square matrix whose leading submatrices have nonzero determinants, so that **A** may be factored (in more than one way) as

$$\mathbf{A} = \mathbf{L}_1 \mathbf{U}_1$$

where (see Section 4.2) **L** and **U** are lower and upper triangular matrices, respectively. Show that:

(a) Under the same hypotheses, **A** may be factored *uniquely* as

$$\mathbf{A} = \mathbf{L} \mathbf{U}_2$$

where $\mathbf{U}_2$ is an upper triangular matrix and **L** is a lower triangular matrix whose diagonal elements are all unity.

(b) The matrix $\mathbf{U}_2$ of part (a) may be factored uniquely as

$$\mathbf{U}_2 = \mathbf{D}\mathbf{U}$$

where **U** is an upper triangular matrix whose diagonal elements are all unity, and **D** is a diagonal matrix whose elements are the corresponding elements of $\mathbf{U}_2$.

5.22 Since the leading submatrices of a symmetric, positive definite matrix **A** have nonzero determinants (see Section 4.5), **A** satisfies the hypotheses of Problem 5.21. Show that:

(a) **A** can be written in the form

$$\mathbf{A} = \mathbf{L}\mathbf{D}\mathbf{U} = (\mathbf{L}\mathbf{D}^{1/2})(\mathbf{D}^{1/2}\mathbf{U}) = \mathbf{S}^t\mathbf{S}$$

where $\mathbf{D} = \text{diag}(d_1, d_2, \ldots, d_n)$, $\mathbf{D}^{1/2} = \text{diag}(d_1^{1/2}, d_2^{1/2}, \ldots, d_n^{1/2})$, and $\mathbf{S} = \mathbf{D}^{1/2}\mathbf{U}$.

(b) The matrix $\mathbf{S} = (s_{ij})$ has the following elements:

$$s_{11} = \sqrt{a_{11}},$$

$$s_{1j} = a_{1j}/s_{11}, \qquad j = 2, 3, \ldots, n,$$

$$s_{ii} = \sqrt{a_{ii} - \sum_{k=1}^{i-1} s_{ki}^2}, \qquad i = 2, 3, \ldots, n,$$

$$s_{ij} = \frac{1}{s_{ii}}\left(a_{ij} - \sum_{k=1}^{i-1} s_{ki}s_{kj}\right), \qquad i = 2, 3, \ldots, n,$$
$$\qquad\qquad j = i+1, i+2, \ldots, n,$$

$$s_{ij} = 0, \qquad\qquad i > j.$$

This algorithm is known as *Cholesky's method* or the *square-root method* for factoring a positive definite matrix [14].

5.23 Show that the inverse of an $n \times n$ symmetric, positive definite matrix **A** is given by

$$\mathbf{A}^{-1} = \mathbf{S}^{-1}(\mathbf{S}^{-1})^t,$$

where **S** is the matrix factor found by Cholesky's method (see Problem 5.21b.)

Write a subroutine, named CHOLSK, with argument list (N,A) that inverts, in place, an N by N symmetric, positive definite matrix with elements A(1,1), ..., A(N,N). Organize computations so that the elements of **S** are overstored in the appropriate elements of A. Then the inverse of the *triangular* matrix **S** should be developed in A using the diagonal-pivot strategy (why not the maximum-pivot strategy?). Finally $\mathbf{A}^{-1}$ should be computed, in place, in A. No auxiliary matrices should be used in the subroutine.

5.24 A particular type of electrical network consists of several known resistors that are joined at n nodes, numbered $i = 1, 2, \ldots, n$. The voltage V is specified at two or more of these nodes. There is at most a single resistor, R_{pq}, connected between any two nodes p and q.

Write a program that will accept information concerning the above (in the manner of Example 5.4) and that will proceed to compute: (a) the voltages at all remaining nodes, and (b) the current I_{pq} (and direction of flow) in each resistor.

Suggested Test Data

Use the network of Example 5.1 and also that shown in Fig. P5.24, in which the resistances are in ohms.

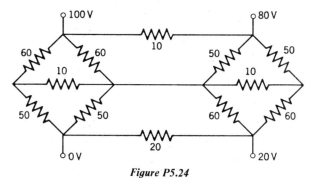

Figure P5.24

5.25 Consider the radiant heat transfer to and from the two surfaces i and j shown in Fig. P5.25. Define $T = $ absolute

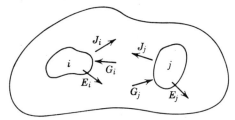

Figure P5.25

temperature, $\varepsilon = $ emissivity, $\alpha = $ absorptivity, $\rho = 1 - \alpha = $ reflectance, $\sigma = $ Stefan-Boltzmann constant, $A = $ area, $E = \varepsilon A \sigma T^4$, $G = $ total rate of radiation arriving at a surface (BTU/hr, for example), and $J = $ total rate of radiation leaving a surface (emitted plus reflected), with subscripts indicating the appropriate surface. Also let the geometric view factor F_{ij} be the fraction of the radiation leaving surface i that is directly intercepted by surface j.

Now consider an enclosure consisting of n surfaces (one or more of which will comprise the enclosing surface). At steady state, show that

$$\left.\begin{array}{l} J_i = E_i + (1 - \alpha_i)G_i, \\ G_i = \sum_{j=1}^{n} F_{ji}J_j, \end{array}\right\} \quad i = 1, 2, \ldots, n.$$

If ε, α, T, and hence E are known for every surface, show that the J_i are given by the solution of the n simultaneous linear equations:

where

$$\left.\begin{array}{l} \sum_{j=1}^{n} a_{ij}J_j = b_i, \\[4pt] a_{ij} = F_{ji} \text{ for } i \neq j, \\ a_{ii} = F_{ii} - 1/\rho_i, \\ b_i = -E_i/\rho_i, \end{array}\right\} \quad i = 1, 2, \ldots, n.$$

Give an expression for Q_i, the rate at which heat must be supplied (or removed, if negative) internally to each surface in order to maintain its temperature constant.

5.26 Extend Problem 5.25 to the case in which m of the n surfaces are *refractory* or insulating. A refractory surface i radiates and reflects at the same rate that energy falls on it; that is, $J_i = G_i$.

If the surfaces i are numbered so that the m refractories are $i = n - m + 1, n - m + 2, \ldots, n$, show that the J_i are again the solution of the simultaneous equations given in Problem 5.25, except that the coefficients of the last m equations are now

$$\left.\begin{array}{l} a_{ij} = F_{ji} \text{ for } i \neq j, \\ a_{ii} = F_{ii} - 1, \\ b_i = 0, \end{array}\right\} \quad i = n - m + 1, n - m + 2, \ldots, n.$$

How can the individual refractory temperatures be determined?

5.27 Figure P5.27 shows the cross section of a long experimental hydrocarbon-cracking furnace; heat is radiated steadily from the cylindrical electrical heating elements 1 and 2 to the

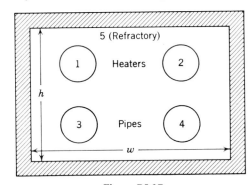

Figure P5.27

pipes 3 and 4, through which a fluid is circulating. The elements and pipes have a common diameter d, and are located centrally in their respective quadrants. Assume that T_1, T_2, T_3, T_4, h, w, and d have been specified, and that ε and α are known for all surfaces. All view factors can be obtained by using (a) the string method (see Problem 3.17), (b) the reciprocity relation $A_iF_{ij} = A_jF_{ji}$, and (c) the fact that $\sum_{j=1}^{n}F_{ij} = 1$ for all surfaces i.

Based on the discussion in Problems 5.25 and 5.26, write a program that will compute (a) all the view factors needed (the functions developed in Problem 3.17 should help), (b) E_i, G_i, and J_i for each surface, (c) Q_i, the rate of heat supply or removal for each heating element and pipe, and (d) T_5, the refractory temperature (assumed uniform over all four walls). Assume that the problem is essentially two-dimensional; that is, neglect longitudinal temperature variations along the furnace. Base all calculations for areas and heat fluxes on unit length of the furnace. Investigate both the arrangement shown in Fig. P5.27 and also that in which heater 2 and pipe 4 are interchanged.

Suggested Test Data

$d = 1$ in., $T_3 = T_4 = 950°F$, $\varepsilon_1 = \varepsilon_2 = 0.75$, $\varepsilon_3 = \varepsilon_4 = 0.79$, $\varepsilon_5 = 0.63$, with gray surfaces ($\alpha = \varepsilon$) throughout; investigate (a) $T_1 = T_2 = 1600°F$, $h = 4$, $w = 6$ in., (b) $T_1 = T_2 = 1600°F$, $h = 6$, $w = 9$ in., and (c) $T_1 = 1700$, $T_2 = 1500°F$, $h = 6$, $w = 9$ in. Note that in all radiation calculations, the temperature must be converted to $°R(=°F + 460)$. The Stefan-Boltzmann constant is $\sigma = 0.171 \times 10^{-8}$ BTU/hr sq ft $°R^4$.

5.28 In Problem 5.27, the entire refractory wall was assumed to be at a uniform temperature. Check the validity of this assumption by subdividing the refractory into four *separate* refractory surfaces, each with its own individual temperature, T_5 through T_8, for example. (The subdivisions need not coincide with the four individual walls.) Repeat the calculations with the previous test data.

Investigate the possibility of writing a general program that will handle n subdivisions of the refractory, where n can be read as data. If this appears feasible, implement it on the computer in preference to writing a program that can only handle exactly four subdivisions.

5.29 Solve Problem 5.27 (or 5.28) with either of the following modifications:

(a) A third pipe (also at 950°F, for example), running along the middle of the furnace.

(b) With both T_3 and T_4 fixed (at 950°F, for example), determine the necessary heater temperature that would deliver a specified heat flux (1000 BTU/hr per foot length, for example) to each of the pipes.

5.30 Figure P5.30 shows two parallel horizontal pipes, each of outside diameter d, and separated by a distance d, that are located centrally in a horizontal thin metal shield whose cross section is a rectangle of height H and width w. The pipes carry a hot fluid, and their surfaces are maintained at temperatures T_1 and T_2. The pipes lose heat by radiation to the metal shield, with subsequent radiation *and* convection to the

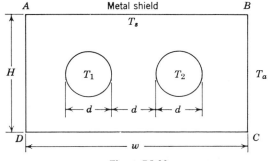

Figure P5.30

atmosphere outside, which behaves as a black-body enclosure at a temperature T_a. There is negligible temperature drop across each wall of the shield, but the shield temperature is not necessarily uniform all the way round. The local rate of heat loss q from unit area of the outside of the shield to the atmosphere is given by

$$q = \varepsilon \sigma (T_s^4 - T_a^4) + h(T_s - T_a),$$

where ε_s is the emissivity of the shield and σ is the Stefan-Boltzmann constant. The convective heat transfer coefficient h, BTU/hr sq ft °F, depends on the particular surface, the temperature difference $\Delta T = T_s - T_a$, °F, and the height H, feet, according to the following dimensional correlations (Perry [13]):

$$AB: h = 0.38(\Delta T)^{0.25},$$
$$CD: h = 0.20(\Delta T)^{0.25},$$
$$AD \text{ and } BC: h = 0.28(\Delta T/H)^{0.25}.$$

Assume that T_1, T_2, T_a, H, w, and d have been specified, and that ε and α are known for all surfaces. View factors inside the shield can be obtained by using (a) the string method (see Problem 3.17), (b) the reciprocity relation $A_i F_{ij} = A_j F_{ji}$, and (c) the fact that $\sum_{j=1}^{n} F_{ij} = 1$ for all surfaces i. Assume that the problem is essentially two-dimensional; that is, neglect longitudinal temperature variations. Base all calculations for areas and heat fluxes on unit length of the pipes.

Write a program that will extend the method discussed in Problems 5.25 and 5.26 to compute (a) all the relevant view factors (the functions developed in Problem 3.17 should help), (b) E_i, G_i, and J_i for each surface, (c) the net rate of heat loss for each pipe, and (d) the temperature or temperatures of the shield. Subdivide the shield surface into as many individual sections as seem desirable, and neglect conduction between such sections.

Suggested Test Data

$T_a = 60$°F, $d = 3$ in., $\varepsilon_1 = \varepsilon_2 = 0.79$, $\varepsilon_s = 0.66$ (both sides), with gray surfaces ($\alpha = \varepsilon$) throughout; investigate the four possible combinations of (a) $T_1 = T_2 = 900$°F, and (b) $T_1 = 900$, $T_2 = 600$°F, in conjunction with (a) $H = 6$, $w = 12$ in., and (b) $H = 10$, $w = 20$ in. Note that in all radiation calculations, the temperature must be converted to °R($=$°F $+ 460$°). The Stefan-Boltzmann constant is $\sigma = 0.171 \times 10^{-8}$ BTU/hr sq ft °R^4.

For a modification that allows for conduction around the perimeter of the shield, see Problem 6.34.

5.31 Extend the situation of Problem 3.22 to n similar CSTRs in series. The relevant equations will now be

$$ka_i^2 = \frac{v(a_{i-1} - a_i)}{V}, \qquad i = 1, 2, \ldots, n.$$

Using the same parameters as in Problem 3.22, find V when $n = 2, 3, 4, 5$, and 10.

5.32 Referring to Problem 3.20, we can dispense with the grid-bias battery by replacing it with a short circuit and inserting instead a resistor R_c between the cathode and ground. The grid voltage then becomes

$$v_g = -i_a R_c,$$

where i_a is the anode current (unknown as yet).

If v_s, R, and R_c are specified, devise a numerical procedure for computing v_a, i_a, v_g, and A (defined in Problem 3.20). Write a program that implements the method, making use of the functions already developed in Problems 1.42 and 2.48 for the 6J5 triode.

Suggested Test Data (v_s in V, R and R_c in kΩ)

$v_s = 300$, $R = 10$, $R_c = 0.47$; $v_s = 300$, $R = 22$, $R_c = 0.47$; $v_s = 300$, $R = 22$, $R_c = 1.5$.

5.33 A horizontal pipe of internal and external diameters d_1 and d_2, respectively, is covered with a uniform thickness t of insulating material, which has an external diameter d_3. The thermal conductivities of the pipe wall and insulation are k_w and k_i, respectively. The inside surface of the pipe is maintained at a high temperature T_1 by a rapid stream of hot gases. Heat is lost at a rate Q BTU/hr per foot length of pipe by conduction through the pipe wall and insulation, and by subsequent convection and radiation to the surrounding air.

If $\varepsilon = $ emissivity of the outer surface of the insulation, T_2 and $T_3 = $ temperatures of the outer surfaces of the pipe and insulation, respectively, $\sigma = $ the Stefan-Boltzmann constant, 0.171×10^{-8} BTU/hr sq ft °R^4, and $T_a = $ temperature of the surroundings, assumed to behave as a black-body radiator, we have:

$$Q = \frac{2\pi k_w (T_1 - T_2)}{\ln(d_2/d_1)} = \frac{2\pi k_i (T_2 - T_3)}{\ln(d_3/d_2)}$$
$$= \pi d_3 [\varepsilon \sigma (T_{3R}^4 - T_{aR}^4) + h(T_3 - T_a)].$$

The extra subscript R emphasizes that in the radiation term, the absolute or Rankine temperature must be used (°R $=$ °F $+ 460$°).

The heat transfer coefficient h, BTU/hr sq ft °F, for convection between the insulation and air is given by the dimensional correlation (Rohsenow and Choi [12]):

$$d_3^3 \Delta T < 1000: \quad h = 0.25(\Delta T/d_3)^{1/4},$$
$$d_3^3 \Delta T \geqslant 1000: \quad h = 0.18(\Delta T)^{1/3},$$

in which $\Delta T = T_3 - T_a$ °F, and d_3 is in feet.

If T_1, T_a, d_1, d_2, d_3 or t, k_w, k_i, and ε are specified, devise a scheme for solving the above equations for the unknowns ΔT, T_2, T_3, h, and Q. Test the method for $T_1 = 1000$, $T_a = 60$°F, $k_w = 25.9$ (steel), $k_i = 0.120$ (asbestos) BTU/hr ft °F, with (a) $d_1 = 1.049$, $d_2 = 1.315$ in. (convert to feet for consistency) and (b) $d_1 = 6.065$, $d_2 = 6.625$ in. For both pipes, consider all combinations of $t = 0$ (no insulation), 0.1, 0.5, 1, 2, and 6 in. (again convert to feet), with $\varepsilon = 0.93$ (untreated surface) and $\varepsilon = 0.52$ (coat of aluminum paint). Plot the rate of heat loss and the outer temperature of the insulation against the insulation thickness for the four combinations of pipe and emissivity.

5.34 The following equations can be shown to relate the temperatures and pressures on either side of a detonation wave that is moving into a zone of unburned gas:

$$\frac{\gamma_2 m_2 T_1}{m_1 T_2} \left(\frac{P_2}{P_1}\right)^2 - (\gamma_2 + 1)\frac{P_2}{P_1} + 1 = 0,$$

$$\frac{\Delta H_{R1}}{c_{p2} T_1} + \frac{T_2}{T_1} - 1 = \frac{(\gamma_2 - 1)m_2}{2\gamma_2 m_1}\left(\frac{P_2}{P_1} - 1\right)\left(1 + \frac{m_1 T_2 P_1}{m_2 T_1 P_2}\right).$$

Here, T = absolute temperature, P = absolute pressure, γ = ratio of specific heat at constant pressure to that at constant volume, m = mean molecular weight, ΔH_R = heat of reaction, c_p = specific heat, and the subscripts 1 and 2 refer to the unburned and burned gas, respectively.

Write a program that will accept values for m_1, m_2, γ_2, ΔH_{R1}, c_{p2}, T_1, and P_1 as data, and that will proceed to compute and print values for T_2 and P_2. Run the program with the following data, which apply to the detonation of a mixture of hydrogen and oxygen: $m_1 = 12$ g/g mole, $m_2 = 18$ g/g mole, $\gamma_2 = 1.31$, $\Delta H_{R1} = -58,300$ cal/g mole, $c_{p2} = 9.86$ cal/g mole °K, $T_1 = 300$°K, and $P_1 = 1$ atm.

5.35 Read Sections 8.19 and 8.20 as an introduction to this problem. Then consider a regression plane whose equation is

$$z = \alpha + \beta x + \gamma y,$$

but now suppose that the m observed points (x_i, y_i, z_i), $i = 1, 2, \ldots, m$, contain random errors in *all* the variables. As an alternative to the usual least-squares procedure, it is plausible to choose α, β, and γ so as to minimize the sum of the squares of the *normal distances* of each point from the regression plane.

Let P be the point in the plane that is closest to the origin O, and denote the spherical coordinates of P as (r, θ, ϕ). The equation of the regression plane can then be rewritten as

$$x \sin\theta \cos\phi + y \sin\theta \sin\phi + z \cos\theta - r = 0.$$

Show that the problem now amounts to minimizing

$$S = \sum_{i=1}^{m} (x_i \sin\theta \cos\phi + y_i \sin\theta \sin\phi + z_i \cos\theta - r)^2,$$

and that setting $\partial S/\partial\theta = \partial S/\partial\phi = \partial S/\partial r = 0$ yields three simultaneous nonlinear equations in θ, ϕ, and r.

Write a program that will accept the coordinates of the m data points and that will proceed to determine α, β, and γ according to the above criterion. For a sample set of data, compare these regression coefficients with those determined by the usual method of least squares, using $z = \alpha + \beta x + \gamma y$, $x = \alpha_1 + \beta_1 y + \gamma_1 z$, and $y = \alpha_2 + \beta_2 x + \gamma_2 z$ in turn.

5.36 Write a program that solves a system of n simultaneous linear equations,

$$a_{11}x_1 + a_{12}x_2 + \cdots + a_{1n}x_n = a_{1,n+1},$$
$$a_{21}x_1 + a_{22}x_2 + \cdots + a_{2n}x_n = a_{2,n+1},$$
$$\vdots \qquad\qquad \vdots \qquad\qquad \vdots$$
$$a_{n1}x_1 + a_{n2}x_2 + \cdots + a_{nn}x_n = a_{n,n+1},$$

using the method of Kaczmarz, described in Section 5.5. The program should read and print values for n, a_{11}, ..., $a_{n,n+1}$, initial values for x_1, ..., x_n (the starting trial vector), and a small positive number, ε, to be used in testing for singularity or near singularity. Next, the solution should be generated using the method of Kaczmarz. Should

$$\|\gamma_j\| < \varepsilon, \qquad j = 1, 2, \ldots, n,$$

print a comment to the effect that the coefficient matrix is singular or ill-conditioned, and stop computation for that data set. If a solution can be found, print it. In any event, return to read another data set. As test data, select some of the equations from the data for programs in Examples 5.1 and 5.2.

5.37 Write the system of equations (5.2) in matrix form as

$$\mathbf{Bx} = \mathbf{u}.$$

(a) Show that the Jacobi iteration of (5.15) may be written in the form

$$\mathbf{x}_{k+1} = \mathbf{D}^{-1}\mathbf{u} - \mathbf{D}^{-1}(\mathbf{L} + \mathbf{U})\mathbf{x}_k,$$

where $\mathbf{x}_k$ and $\mathbf{x}_{k+1}$ are the estimated solution vectors before and after the kth iteration, respectively, $\mathbf{U}$ is a strictly upper-triangular matrix containing the superdiagonal elements of $\mathbf{B}$, $\mathbf{L}$ is a strictly lower-triangular matrix containing the subdiagonal elements of $\mathbf{B}$, and $\mathbf{D}$ is a diagonal matrix containing the elements on the principal diagonal of $\mathbf{B}$.

(b) Let

$$\mathbf{C} = -\mathbf{D}^{-1}(\mathbf{L} + \mathbf{U}),$$

so that the iteration may be rewritten as

$$\mathbf{x}_{k+1} = \mathbf{D}^{-1}\mathbf{u} + \mathbf{Cx}_k.$$

Let $\boldsymbol{\alpha}$ be the solution of (5.2) and $\boldsymbol{\varepsilon}_k$ be a vector of displacements

$$\boldsymbol{\varepsilon}_k = \boldsymbol{\alpha} - \mathbf{x}_k.$$

Show that if $\mathbf{x}_0$ is the starting vector, then the error vector for $\mathbf{x}_{k+1}$ is given by

$$\boldsymbol{\varepsilon}_{k+1} = \mathbf{C}^{k+1}\boldsymbol{\varepsilon}_0,$$

so that convergence normally requires that $\lim_{k \to \infty} \mathbf{C}^k = \mathbf{0}$, and that the argument is equivalent to that of (5.17) through (5.20).

5.38 Using the nomenclature of Problem 5.37, show that the Gauss-Seidel iteration of Section 5.7 may be written as

$$\mathbf{x}_{k+1} = (\mathbf{L} + \mathbf{D})^{-1}\mathbf{u} - (\mathbf{L} + \mathbf{D})^{-1}\mathbf{Ux}_k,$$

and that the error vector for $\mathbf{x}_{k+1}$ is given by

$$\boldsymbol{\varepsilon}_{k+1} = \mathbf{G}^{k+1}\boldsymbol{\varepsilon}_0,$$

where $\mathbf{G} = -(\mathbf{L} + \mathbf{D})^{-1}\mathbf{U}$.

5.39 Consider the system of three simultaneous linear equations:

$$3x_1 - 2x_2 + 7x_3 = 20,$$
$$x_1 + 6x_2 - x_3 = 10,$$
$$10x_1 - 2x_2 + 7x_3 = 29.$$

(a) Without rearranging the equations, try to find the solutions iteratively using either the Jacobi or Gauss-Seidel methods with starting values (0,0,0) and (1.01,2.01,2.99) for (x_1, x_2, x_3).

(b) Rearrange the equations to conform to criteria (5.21) and repeat part (a).

5.40 Consider Q gpm of water flowing from point 1 to point 2 in an inclined pipe of length L ft and diameter D in. Starting from the equation in part (a) of Problem 5.46 and assuming a constant value of the Moody friction factor f_M, the following equation can be shown to hold approximately for turbulent flow in pipes of average roughness:

$$(z_2 - z_1) + 2.31(p_2 - p_1) + 8.69 \times 10^{-4}Q^2 L/D^5 = 0.$$

Here, p is the pressure in psig and z is the elevation in feet.

Also, a typical head-discharge curve for a centrifugal pump can be represented by

$$\Delta p = \alpha - \beta Q^2,$$

in which Δp is the pressure increase in psig across the pump, Q is the flow rate in gpm, and α and β are constants depending on the particular pump.

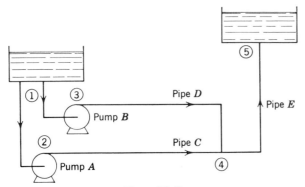

Figure P5.40

Consider the piping system shown in Fig. P5.40. The pressures p_1 and p_5 are both essentially atmospheric (0 psig); there is an increase in elevation between points 4 and 5, but pipes C and D are horizontal. Based on the above, the governing equations are:

$$Q_E = Q_C + Q_D,$$
$$p_2 = \alpha_A - \beta_A Q_C^2,$$
$$p_3 = \alpha_B - \beta_B Q_D^2,$$
$$2.31(p_4 - p_2) + 8.69 \times 10^{-4} Q_C^2 L_C / D_C^5 = 0,$$
$$2.31(p_4 - p_3) + 8.69 \times 10^{-4} Q_D^2 L_D / D_D^5 = 0,$$
$$z_5 - z_4 + 2.31(0 - p_4) + 8.69 \times 10^{-4} Q_E^2 L_E / D_E^5 = 0.$$

Write a program that will accept values for α_A, β_A, α_B, β_B, $z_5 - z_4$, D_C, L_C, D_D, L_D, D_E, and L_E, and that will solve the above equations for the unknowns Q_C, Q_D, Q_E, p_2, p_3, and p_4. One suggested set of test data is $z_5 - z_4 = 70$ ft, with:

Pump	α, psi	β, psi/(gpm)^2
A	156.6	0.00752
B	117.1	0.00427

Pipe	D, in.	L, ft
C	1.278	125
D	2.067	125
E	2.469	145

Assume that the above pipe lengths have already included the equivalent lengths of all fittings and valves.

5.41 Rework Example 5.4 (flow in a pipe network, solved by the successive-substitution method) using the Newton-Raphson technique instead. Is one method decidedly better than the other in this case from the viewpoints of (a) simplicity, and (b) computational efficiency?

5.42 Expand each of the f_i, $i = 1, 2, \ldots, n$, of (5.33) in a Taylor's series in n variables, $x_1, x_2, \ldots, x_n$, about the kth iterate, $\mathbf{x}_k = [x_{k,1}, x_{k,2}, \ldots, x_{k,n}]^t$, of the Newton-Raphson iteration to yield

$$f_i(\boldsymbol{\alpha}) = f_i(\mathbf{x}_k) + \sum_{j=1}^{n} (\alpha_j - x_{k,j}) \frac{\partial f_i(\mathbf{x}_k)}{\partial x_j}$$
$$+ O[(\alpha_i - x_{k,i})^2], \qquad i = 1, 2, \ldots, n,$$

where $\boldsymbol{\alpha} = [\alpha_1, \alpha_2, \ldots, \alpha_n]^t$. Let $\boldsymbol{\alpha}$ be a solution of (5.33), so that $f_i(\boldsymbol{\alpha}) = 0$, $i = 1, 2, \ldots, n$. Drop the second-order terms in the Taylor's series, and replace α_j by the jth element of the $(k+1)$th iterate, $x_{k+1,j}$ (hopefully a good approximation of α_j), to yield

$$\sum_{j=1}^{n} (x_{k+1,j} - x_{k,j}) \frac{\partial f_i(\mathbf{x}_k)}{\partial x_j} = -f(\mathbf{x}_{k+1}), \qquad i = 1, 2, \ldots, n.$$

Show that this system of equations is equivalent to (5.44) for the Newton-Raphson iteration. Note that this is the n-dimensional equivalent of the development of Newton's method for a function of one variable suggested in Problem 3.15.

5.43 In the Newton-Raphson method of Section 5.9 (see also Example 5.5), the matrix $\boldsymbol{\phi}(\mathbf{x}_k)$ of equations (5.44) is evaluated and inverted once for each pass of the iterative algorithm. Since nearly all the computing time required for solution to the system of nonlinear equations by this technique is consumed in the evaluation and inversion of the successive $\boldsymbol{\phi}_k$, investigate the possibility of using a calculated $\boldsymbol{\phi}^{-1}(\mathbf{x}_k)$ for more than one iteration. For example, consider the sequence

$$\boldsymbol{\delta}_k = -\boldsymbol{\phi}^{-1}(\mathbf{x}_k)\mathbf{f}(\mathbf{x}_k),$$
$$\mathbf{x}_{k+1} = \mathbf{x}_k + \boldsymbol{\delta}_k,$$
$$\boldsymbol{\delta}_{k+1} = -\boldsymbol{\phi}^{-1}(\mathbf{x}_k)\mathbf{f}(\mathbf{x}_{k+1}),$$
$$\mathbf{x}_{k+2} = \mathbf{x}_{k+1} + \boldsymbol{\delta}_{k+1},$$
$$\boldsymbol{\delta}_{k+2} = -\boldsymbol{\phi}^{-1}(\mathbf{x}_k)\mathbf{f}(\mathbf{x}_{k+2}),$$
$$\mathbf{x}_{k+3} = \mathbf{x}_{k+2} + \boldsymbol{\delta}_{k+2},$$
etc.

Develop criteria for deciding when to recompute the elements of $\boldsymbol{\phi}(\mathbf{x})$ and its inverse.

5.44 The calling program in Example 5.5 is well suited for the general problem of solving n simultaneous nonlinear equations by the Newton-Raphson method, since all information about the specific equation set (except for the initial guess for the solution vector) is contained in the subroutine CALCN. In most practical problems, however, the equations contain parameters (such as the pressure P in CALCN) which the user would also like to read in as data. How would you modify the calling program and the essential structure of CALCN to allow this, so that further modifications of the calling program would be unnecessary for other systems of equations with different parameters?

5.45 The principal chemical reactions occurring in the production of synthesis gas are listed in Example 5.5 (see (5.5.1), (5.5.2), and (5.5.3)). Write a program (modelled closely on the programs of Example 5.5) to find the O_2/CH_4 ratio that will produce an adiabatic equilibrium temperature of $T_e \, ^\circ F$ at an operating pressure of P atm if the inlet CH_4 gas is preheated to a temperature of $T_m \, ^\circ F$ and the oxygen, introduced in the form of an oxygen-nitrogen mixture (possibly air) containing x_0 mole percent oxygen, is preheated to $T_a \, ^\circ F$.

The heat capacities for the seven possible gaseous components can be computed as a function of temperature from the general relation

$$c_{p_i}(T_k) = a_i + b_i T_k + c_i T_k^2 + d_i / T_k^2 \text{ cal/g mole } ^\circ K,$$

where $i = 1, 2, 3, 4, 5, 6$, and 7 for CO, CO_2, H_2O, H_2, CH_4, O_2, and N_2, respectively, and T_k is in °K (°K = °C + 273.15). Table P5.45a [13] also shows the standard heat of formation at 298°K, $\Delta H^f_{i,298}$ cal/g mole, for each component.

Table P5.45a

i	a_i	b_i	c_i	d_i	$\Delta H^f_{i,298}$
1	6.60	0.00120	0.0	0.0	$-26416.$
2	10.34	0.00274	0.0	$-195500.$	$-94052.$
3	8.22	0.00015	1.34×10^{-6}	0.0	$-57798.$
4	6.62	0.00081	0.0	0.0	0.0
5	5.34	0.0115	0.0	0.0	$-17889.$
6	8.27	0.000258	0.0	$-187700.$	0.0
7	6.50	0.00100	0.0	0.0	0.0

The program should read in and print out the essential data, solve the nonlinear equations using the Newton-Raphson method, print the computed results, and return to read another data set. If the composition of the incoming oxygen/nitrogen stream makes it impossible to achieve the specified temperature T_e, the program should write an appropriate comment and continue to the next data set (Table P5.45b).

Suggested Test Data

Table P5.45b

T_e (°F)	T_m (°F)	T_a (°F)	P (atm)	x_0 (%)
1500	500	500	1	21
1500	100	100	1	100
1500	500	100	20	100
1500	100	500	20	21
2200	1000	1000	20	100
2200	1000	500	1	21
2200	500	1000	1	21
2200	100	100	1	100

5.46 Extend Example 5.4 (flow in a pipe network) so that the program can handle one or more of the following additional features:

(a) Elevation change between nodes. If z_i and z_j denote the elevations in feet of nodes i and j, the Fanning equation, (5.4.1), will become

$$p_i - p_j = \frac{1}{2}f_M \rho u_m^2 \frac{L}{D} + \rho g(z_j - z_i).$$

(b) Moody friction factor f_M now considered a function of Reynolds number and pipe roughness (see Problem 3.38).

(c) Specified steady flow rate Q_i gpm injected into node i from outside the network. This would be an alternative to specifying the pressure at certain nodes. For a specified withdrawal, Q_i would be negative.

(d) Centrifugal pump connected between nodes i and j (the possibility of a direct connection pipe between these nodes is then ignored). Assume for simplicity that the head-discharge curve for such a pump can be expressed using two constants, α_{ij} and β_{ij}, in the form

$$p_j - p_i = \alpha_{ij} - \beta_{ij}Q_{ij}^2.$$

The pump is assumed to operate only for flow in the direction *i to j*; however, the possibility that Q_{ij} might be forced to be negative because of other factors should not be neglected.

(e) Fittings and valves located in certain pipes. This is not an essential feature since the pressure drop across a valve or fitting is normally reckoned as being that across an equivalent length of pipe, which can then be lumped in with the actual length.

Consider using the Newton-Raphson procedure for solving the resulting simultaneous nonlinear equations, especially if Problem 5.41 has already been attempted. Depending on which of the above features have been accounted for, devise a few appropriate piping networks for testing your program (a simple case could be based on Fig. P5.40).

Bibliography

1. A. Ralston and H. S. Wilf, *Mathematical Methods for Digital Computers*, Wiley, New York, 1960.
2. J. F. Traub, *Iterative Methods for the Solution of Equations*, Prentice-Hall, Englewood Cliffs, New Jersey, 1964.
3. L. Fox, *An Introduction to Numerical Linear Algebra*, Oxford University Press, New York, 1965.
4. K. S. Kunz, *Numerical Analysis*, McGraw-Hill, New York, 1957.
5. A. M. Ostrowski, *Solution of Equations and Systems of Equations*, Academic Press, New York, 1966.
6. D. K. Faddeev and V. N. Faddeeva, *Computational Methods of Linear Algebra*, Freeman, San Francisco, 1963.
7. B. Wendroff, *Theoretical Numerical Analysis*, Academic Press, New York, 1966.
8. F. A. Jenkins and H. E. White, *Fundamentals of Optics*, 2nd ed., McGraw-Hill, New York, 1951.
9. B. Carnahan, *Radiation Induced Cracking of Pentanes and Dimethylbutanes*, Ph.D. Thesis, University of Michigan, 1964.
10. S. J. McMinn, *Matrices for Structural Analysis*, E. & F. N. Spon Ltd., London, 1962.
11. J. Robinson, *Structural Matrix Analysis for the Engineer*, Wiley, New York, 1966.
12. W. M. Rohsenow and H. Y. Choi, *Heat, Mass, and Momentum Transfer*, Prentice-Hall, Englewood Cliffs, New Jersey, 1961.
13. J. H. Perry, ed., *Chemical Engineers' Handbook*, 3rd ed., McGraw-Hill, New York, 1950.
14. G. Forsythe and C. B. Moler, *Computer Solution of Linear Algebraic Systems*, Prentice-Hall, Englewood Cliffs, New Jersey, 1967.
15. J. Todd, "Computational Problems Concerning the Hilbert Matrix," *J. Research Natl. Bur. Standards, Series B.*, **65**, 19–22 (1961).

CHAPTER 6

The Approximation of the Solution of Ordinary Differential Equations

6.1 Introduction

The behavior of many physical processes, particularly those in systems undergoing time-dependent changes (transients), can be described by ordinary differential equations. Thus, methods of solution for these equations are of great importance to engineers and scientists. Although many important differential equations can be solved by well-known analytical techniques, a greater number of physically significant differential equations cannot be so solved. Fortunately, the solutions of these equations can usually be generated numerically. This chapter will describe the more important of these numerical procedures.

Nth Order Ordinary Differential Equations. Consider the solution of nth-order ordinary differential equations of the form

$$F\left(x, y, \frac{dy}{dx}, \frac{d^2y}{dx^2}, \frac{d^3y}{dx^3}, \ldots, \frac{d^ny}{dx^n}\right) = 0. \qquad (6.1)$$

An equation of type (6.1) is termed *nth-order* because the highest derivative is of order n, and *ordinary* because only total derivatives appear (no partial derivatives are present, or alternatively, there is only one independent variable, x). A function $y(x)$ that satisfies this equation, implying that it is at least n times differentiable, is said to be a *solution* of the equation. To obtain a *unique solution* [in general, there are many functions $y(x)$ that satisfy (6.1)], it is necessary to supply some additional information, namely, values of $y(x)$ and/or of its derivatives at some specific values of x. For an nth-order equation, n such conditions are normally sufficient to determine a unique solution $y(x)$. If all n conditions are specified at the same value of x (x_0, for example), then the problem is termed an *initial-value problem*. When more than one value of x is involved, the problem is termed a *boundary-value problem*.

Any nth-order ordinary differential equation may be written as a system of n first-order equations by defining $n - 1$ new variables. For example, consider the second-order equation (Bessel's equation),

$$x^2 \frac{d^2y}{dx^2} + x \frac{dy}{dx} + (x^2 - p^2)y = 0, \qquad (6.2)$$

where p is a constant. By defining one new variable, $z = dy/dx$, the second-order equation can be rewritten as a pair of first-order equations:

$$\frac{dy}{dx} - z = 0$$
$$x^2 \frac{dz}{dx} + xz + (x^2 - p^2)y = 0. \qquad (6.3)$$

Since any higher-order equation (or a system of such equations) can be rewritten in similar fashion, the numerical solution of first-order equations only will be described.

6.2 Solution of First-Order Ordinary Differential Equations

A first-order equation is, by definition, of the form

$$F\left(x, y, \frac{dy}{dx}\right) = 0,$$

or, alternatively,

$$\frac{dy}{dx} = f(x, y). \qquad (6.4)$$

We desire a solution $y(x)$ which satisfies both (6.4) and one specified initial condition. In general, it is impossible to determine $y(x)$ in functional (analytical) form. Instead, the interval in the independent variable x over which a solution is desired, $[a,b]$, is divided into subintervals or *steps*. The value of the true solution $y(x)$ is approximated at $n + 1$ evenly spaced values of x, $(x_0, x_1, \ldots, x_n)$, so that h, the *step size*, is given by

$$h = \frac{b - a}{n},$$

and

$$x_i = x_0 + ih, \qquad i = 0, 1, \ldots, n. \qquad (6.5)$$

Thus the solution is given in *tabular* form for $n + 1$ *discrete* values of x only (see Fig. 6.1). This table of values contains sampled values of one particular approximation of the solution of the equation.

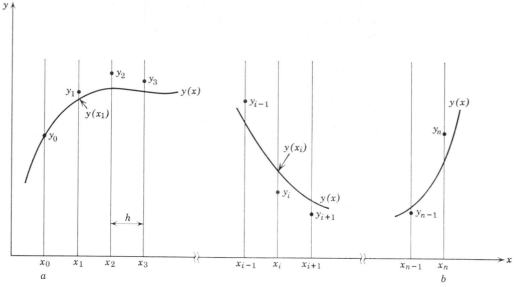

Figure 6.1   Numerical solution of a first-order differential equation.

Let the true solution $y(x)$ at the indicated base points be denoted by $y(x_i)$, and the computed approximation of $y(x)$ at these same points be denoted by y_i, so that

$$y_i \doteq y(x_i). \tag{6.6}$$

The true derivative dy/dx at the base points will be approximated by $f(x_i, y_i)$, abbreviated as f_i, so that

$$f_i = f(x_i, y_i) \doteq f(x_i, y(x_i)). \tag{6.7}$$

When the requisite numerical calculations are done exactly, that is, without round-off error (see below), the difference between the computed value y_i and the true value $y(x_i)$ is termed the *discretization* or *truncation error*, ε_i:

$$\varepsilon_i = y_i - y(x_i). \tag{6.8}$$

The discretization error encountered in integrating a differential equation across one step is sometimes called the *local truncation error*. The discretization error is determined solely by the particular numerical solution procedure selected, that is, by the nature of the approximations present in the method; this type of error is independent of computing equipment characteristics.

An inherently different kind of error results from computing-machine design. In practice, computers have only a finite memory and therefore a finite number size (scientific computers usually have a *fixed word-length*, that is, the number of digits retained for any computed result is fixed, usually 7–12 significant digits). Thus any irrational number, or indeed any number with more significant digits than can be retained, that occurs in a sequence of calculations must be approximated by "rounded" values. The error involved is termed *round-off error*, and for any particular numerical method is determined by the computing characteristics of the machine

which does the calculations, the order of the machine operations used to implement the algorithm, etc. Some upper bound can usually be found for the discretization error for a particular method; on the other hand, round-off error-generation is extremely complex and unpredictable. However, because of this very unpredictability, numerical analysts have been fairly successful in developing a probabilistic theory of round-off error, on the assumption that local round-off error, that is, the error caused by round-off in integrating a differential equation across one step, is a random variable (see [2] for an excellent description of this work). The only errors which will be examined in any detail here are those related to discretization, that is, those inherent in the numerical procedures.

The common numerical algorithms for solving a first-order ordinary differential equation with initial condition $y(x_0)$ are based on one of two approaches:

1. Direct or indirect use of Taylor's expansion of the *object* or *solution function* $y(x)$.
2. Use of open or closed integration formulas similar to those already developed in Chapter 2.

The various procedures can be classified roughly into two groups, the so-called one-step and multistep methods. *One-step methods* permit calculation of y_{i+1} given the differential equation and information at x_i only, that is, a value y_i. *Multistep methods* require, in addition, values of y_j and/or f_j at other (usually several) values x_j outside the integration interval under consideration, $[x_i, x_{i+1}]$.

One disadvantage of the multistep methods is that more information is required to start the procedure than is normally directly available. Usually an initial condition, say $y(x_0)$, is given; subsequent values, $y(x_1)$, $y(x_2)$, etc., are not known. Some other method (usually a one-step method) must be used to get started. Another difficulty encountered in the multistep methods is that it is rather difficult to change the step-size h once the calculation is under way. On the other hand, since each new application of a one-step method is equivalent to restarting the procedure, such a change of step-size causes no trouble. The multistep methods require considerably less computation, compared with the one-step methods, to produce results of comparable accuracy. The advantages and disadvantages of each group of methods will become more apparent with the development of the numerical procedures.

Taylor's Expansion Approach. One method of approximating the solution of (6.4) numerically is to express the solution $y(x)$ about some starting point x_0 by using a Taylor's expansion:

$$y(x_0 + h) = y(x_0) + hf(x_0, y(x_0))$$

$$+ \frac{h^2}{2!} f'(x_0, y(x_0))$$

$$+ \frac{h^3}{3!} f''(x_0, y(x_0)) + \cdots. \qquad (6.9)$$

Here, $f'(x, y(x))$ denotes $(d/dx)f(x, y(x))$, $f''(x, y(x))$ denotes $(d^2/dx^2)f(x, y(x))$, etc. If $y(x_0)$ is specified as the initial condition, $f(x_0, y(x_0))$ can be computed directly from the differential equation (6.4)

$$\frac{dy}{dx} = f(x, y).$$

To evaluate the higher-order derivatives of (6.9), we must differentiate $f(x, y)$ by using the chain rule, since f is a function of both x and y:

$$\frac{df}{dx} = \frac{\partial f}{\partial x} + \frac{\partial f}{\partial y} \frac{dy}{dx}. \qquad (6.10)$$

Example. Consider a case for which $f(x, y)$ is a function of x alone:

$$\frac{dy}{dx} = f(x, y) = x^2, \qquad (6.11)$$

subject to the initial condition $y(x_0) = y_0$. From (6.10),

$$\begin{aligned}
f'(x, y) &= 2x, & f'(x_0, y_0) &= 2x_0; \\
f''(x, y) &= 2, & f''(x_0, y_0) &= 2; \\
f'''(x, y) &= 0, & f'''(x_0, y_0) &= 0; \qquad (6.12) \\
&\vdots & &\vdots \\
f^{(n)}(x, y) &= 0, & f^{(n)}(x_0, y_0) &= 0, \; n > 3.
\end{aligned}$$

Expansion of $y(x)$ about x_0 by substitution of (6.12) into the Taylor's series of (6.9) yields

$$y(x_0 + h) = y(x_0) + hx_0^2 + h^2 x_0 + \frac{h^3}{3}. \qquad (6.13)$$

Analytic integration of (6.11) after separation of variables gives

$$\int_{y(x_0)}^{y(x_0 + h)} dy = \int_{x_0}^{x_0 + h} x^2 dx = \frac{x^3}{3} \Big]_{x_0}^{x_0 + h},$$

$$y(x_0 + h) = y(x_0) + hx_0^2 + h^2 x_0 + \frac{h^3}{3}, \qquad (6.14)$$

which is identical to (6.13). There is no truncation error for the algorithm of (6.13) because all high-order derivatives $f^{(n)}(x, y)$, $n > 3$, vanish.

Example. Consider a case for which $f(x, y)$ is a function of y alone:

$$\frac{dy}{dx} = f(x, y) = 2y, \qquad (6.15)$$

subject to the initial condition $y(x_0) = y_0$. Differentiating (6.15) by using the chain rule (6.10) yields:

$$\begin{aligned}
f'(x, y) &= 4y, & f'(x_0, y_0) &= 4y_0; \\
f''(x, y) &= 8y, & f''(x_0, y_0) &= 8y_0; \\
f'''(x, y) &= 16y, & f'''(x_0, y_0) &= 16y_0; \qquad (6.16) \\
&\vdots & &\vdots \\
f^{(n)}(x, y) &= 2^{n+1}y, & f^{(n)}(x_0, y_0) &= 2^{n+1}y_0.
\end{aligned}$$

The expansion of $y(x)$ about x_0, using (6.16) in the Taylor's series of (6.9), gives

$$y(x_0 + h) = y(x_0) + 2hy(x_0) + \frac{4h^2 y(x_0)}{2!} + \frac{8h^3 y(x_0)}{3!} + \cdots$$

$$= y(x_0) \left[1 + 2h + \frac{(2h)^2}{2!} + \frac{(2h)^3}{3!} + \frac{(2h)^4}{4!} + \cdots \right]. \qquad (6.17)$$

After separation of variables, direct integration of (6.15) gives

$$\int_{y(x_0)}^{y(x_0 + h)} \frac{dy}{y} = 2 \int_{x_0}^{x_0 + h} dx,$$

and produces the solution

$$y(x_0 + h) = y(x_0) e^{2h}. \qquad (6.18)$$

Since $\{1 + 2h + [(2h)^2/2!] + \cdots\}$ is the Taylor's expansion of e^{2h} about $h = 0$, the two solutions (6.17) and (6.18) agree with an accuracy determined by the number of terms retained in the series. If terms up to that including $f^{(n-1)}$ are retained, then the error is given by

$$\epsilon = y(\xi) \frac{(2h)^{n+1}}{(n+1)!}, \qquad \xi \text{ in } (x_0, x_0 + h).$$

Example. Consider a more general, but still simple, example for which $f(x, y)$ is a function of both variables,

$$\frac{dy}{dx} = f(x, y) = x + y, \qquad (6.19)$$

subject to the initial condition $y(x_0) = y_0$. Differentiation of (6.19) yields:

$$f'(x,y) = 1 + x + y, \qquad f'(x_0,y_0) = x_0 + y_0 + 1;$$
$$f''(x,y) = 1 + x + y, \qquad f''(x_0,y_0) = x_0 + y_0 + 1; \qquad (6.20)$$
$$\vdots \qquad\qquad \vdots$$
$$f^{(n)}(x,y) = 1 + x + y, \qquad f^{(n)}(x_0,y_0) = x_0 + y_0 + 1.$$

Expansion of $y(x)$ in a Taylor's series about $x = x_0$ yields

$$y(x_0 + h) = y(x_0) + \frac{h(x_0 + y(x_0))}{1!} + \frac{h^2(1 + x_0 + y(x_0))}{2!}$$
$$+ \frac{h^3(1 + x_0 + y(x_0))}{3!} + \frac{h^4(1 + x_0 + y(x_0))}{4!} + \cdots.$$

By adding and subtracting $(x_0 + h + 1)$ on the right-hand side,

$$y(x_0 + h) = -x_0 - h - 1 + (1 + x_0 + y(x_0))$$
$$+ h(1 + x_0 + y(x_0))$$
$$+ \frac{h^2(1 + x_0 + y(x_0))}{2!} + \cdots$$
$$= -x_0 - h - 1 + (1 + x_0 + y(x_0))$$
$$\times \left[1 + h + \frac{h^2}{2!} + \frac{h^3}{3!} + \frac{h^4}{4!} + \cdots \right]. \qquad (6.21)$$

The differential equation is linear and can be solved analytically by using the integrating factor e^{-x}. Multiplying (6.19) by e^{-x}, integrating both sides, and solving for y yields

$$y = -(x + 1) + Ce^x, \qquad (6.22)$$

where C is the integration constant. Evaluation of the integration constant at $(x_0, y(x_0))$ gives

$$C = e^{-x_0}(1 + x_0 + y(x_0)),$$

so that the solution of the initial-value problem is given by

$$y = -x - 1 + (1 + x_0 + y(x_0))e^{-x_0} e^x. \qquad (6.23)$$

For $y = y(x_0 + h)$, (6.23) becomes

$$y(x_0 + h) = -x_0 - h - 1 + (1 + x_0 + y(x_0))e^h. \qquad (6.24)$$

Since $[1 + h + (h^2/2!) + \cdots]$ of (6.21) is Taylor's expansion of e^h, the analytical solution again agrees with that found by the Taylor's expansion approach. The error caused by truncation after the term containing $f^{(n-1)}$ is given by

$$\frac{(1 + \xi + y(\xi))}{(n + 1)!} h^{n+1}, \qquad \xi \text{ in } (x_0, x_0 + h).$$

A procedure for stepping from one value of x to another, that is, from x_0 to $x_0 + h$, follows from expansion of $y(x)$ about x_0. Similarly, algorithms for stepping* from x_i to

* Throughout the remainder of this chapter, we shall consider the step-size h to be a positive number, that is, integration will be carried out for increasing values of the independent variable x. Most of the algorithms to be developed, however, apply for negative h as well.

$x_{i+1} = x_i + h$ can be based upon the Taylor's expansion of $y(x)$ about x_i:

$$y(x_{i+1}) = y(x_i + h) = y(x_i) + hf(x_i, y(x_i)) + \frac{h^2 f'(x_i, y(x_i))}{2!}$$
$$+ \frac{h^3 f''(x_i, y(x_i))}{3!} + \frac{h^4 f'''(x_i, y(x_i))}{4!} + \cdots$$
$$+ \frac{h^n f^{(n-1)}(x_i, y(x_i))}{n!} + \frac{h^{n+1} f^{(n)}(\xi, y(\xi))}{(n + 1)!},$$
$$x_i < \xi < x_{i+1}. \qquad (6.25)$$

The algorithms, formed by dropping the last term on the right-hand side of (6.25) and replacing $y(x_{i+1})$ on the left-hand side by y_{i+1}, are said to be of *order* h^n. The error is of order h^{n+1}. The local truncation error $\varepsilon_{i+1} - \varepsilon_i$, introduced by one application is therefore bounded as follows:

$$|\varepsilon_{i+1} - \varepsilon_i| \leqslant \frac{h^{n+1}}{(n + 1)!} M, \qquad (6.26)$$

where

$$M \geqslant |f^{(n)}(\eta, y(\eta))|_{\max}, \qquad x_i \leqslant \eta \leqslant x_{i+1}.$$

Unfortunately, in the general case, the differentiation of $f(x,y)$ becomes enormously complicated. Except for the simplest case,

$$y(x_{i+1}) = y(x_i) + hf(x_i, y(x_i)) + O(h^2), \qquad (6.27)$$

the direct Taylor's expansion of (6.25) is not often used to solve first-order differential equations. Here "$O(\ )$" means "terms of order $(\ )$." (In view of the recent development of computer programs which formally differentiate arbitrary symbolic expressions [1], this argument against the direct Taylor's expansion, with high-order terms included, may well vanish at some future time.)

Since $y(x_0)$ is usually the only value of $y(x_i)$ that is known exactly (assuming that the initial condition is free of error), $y(x_i)$ in (6.27) must in general be replaced by y_i. The algorithm then assumes the form

$$y_1 = y(x_0) + hf(x_0, y(x_0)) \qquad (6.28a)$$
$$y_{i+1} = y_i + hf(x_i, y_i) = y_i + hf_i, \qquad i \geqslant 1, \quad (6.28b)$$

which is called *Euler's method*.

6.3 Euler's Method

Because it is the simplest method and the most amenable to an analysis of error propagation, Euler's one-step method of (6.28) will be discussed in some detail, even though accuracy limitations preclude its use for most practical problems. There is a simple geometric interpretation for (6.28a). The solution across the interval $x_0 \leqslant x \leqslant x_1$ is assumed to follow the line tangent to $y(x)$ at x_0 (see

Fig. 6.2). When Euler's method is applied repeatedly across several intervals in sequence, the numerical solution traces out a polygon segment with sides of slopes f_i, $i = 0, 1, 2, \ldots, n - 1$.

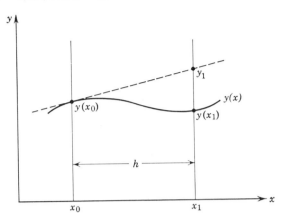

Figure 6.2 Euler's method.

As an example, consider the differential equation of (6.19),

$$\frac{dy}{dx} = x + y,$$

subject to the initial condition $x_0 = 0$, $y(x_0) = y_0 = 0$ (see Example 6.1). The solution already developed in (6.23) for this initial condition is

$$y = e^x - x - 1.$$

The Euler solution is shown in Table 6.1, using a step-size $h = 0.1$ and an upper limit of integration $x_{10} = 1.0$. Column 3 contains the values of y_i computed from (6.28) with all figures retained in the calculation (no round-off error). Column 4 contains the computed

derivatives, again with all figures retained. Column 5 shows the true solutions rounded to four figures. Column 6 contains the overall truncation error (rounded to four figures) at each value of x_i. Columns 7 and 8 contain the results which are computed when only four figures are retained at each stage of the calculations. In column 7, the four figures retained are truncated, that is, less significant figures are simply dropped. In column 8, the four figures retained are rounded values. Column 9 shows the values which would be computed by using true y values, that is, $y(x_i)$ rather than y_i, at the beginning of each new step [see (6.27)]. Column 10 shows the local truncation error for each interval when $y(x_i)$ is used to begin each step. Column 11 shows the value of the maximum local truncation error computed from the Taylor's expansion error term with $n = 1$ (see (6.25)),

$$|\varepsilon_{i+1} - \varepsilon_i| = \frac{h^2}{2!} |f'(\xi, y(\xi))|, \qquad x_i < \xi < x_{i+1}.$$

(6.29)

For the given equation, $f(x, y) = x + y$, the derivative in (6.29) is given by

$$f'(x, y) = \frac{d^2 y}{dx^2} = e^x.$$

Since the maximum value of e^x, $x_i \leqslant x \leqslant x_{i+1}$ occurs at $x = x_{i+1}$, the maximum value of the local truncation error (6.29) is given by

$$|\varepsilon_{i+1} - \varepsilon_i|_{max} = \frac{h^2}{2!} e^{x_{i+1}}.$$

(6.30)

Unfortunately, this error bound is valid only for the algorithm of (6.28a) and that obtained from (6.27),

$$y_{i+1} = y(x_i) + h f(x_i, y(x_i)).$$

(6.31)

Table 6.1   Solution of Equation (6.19) by Euler's Method

		$y(0) = 0$					$h = 0.1$			
				True y Rounded $y(x_i)$	Overall Truncation Error Rounded $\varepsilon_i = y_i - y(x_i)$	Truncated at Four Figures y_i	Rounded to Four Figures y_i	y_i Value Computed Using $y(x_{i-1})$	Local Truncation Error Using $y(x_{i-1})$	$e_{max}^x \dfrac{h^2}{2!}$
i	x_i	y_i	$f(x_i, y_i)$							
(1)	(2)	(3)	(4)	(5)	(6)	(7)	(8)	(9)	(10)	(11)
0	0.0	0.0000	0.0000	0.0000	0.0000	0.0000	0.0000	0.0000	—	—
1	0.1	0.0000	0.1000	0.0052	−0.0052	0.0000	0.0000	0.0000	−0.0052	0.0055
2	0.2	0.0100	0.2100	0.0214	−0.0114	0.0100	0.0100	0.0157	−0.0057	0.0061
3	0.3	0.0310	0.3310	0.0499	−0.0189	0.0310	0.0310	0.0435	−0.0064	0.0067
4	0.4	0.0641	0.4641	0.0918	−0.0277	0.0641	0.0641	0.0849	−0.0069	0.0075
5	0.5	0.11051	0.61051	0.1487	−0.0382	0.1105	0.1105	0.1410	−0.0077	0.0082
6	0.6	0.171561	0.771561	0.2221	−0.0505	0.1715	0.1716	0.2136	−0.0085	0.0091
7	0.7	0.2487171	0.9487171	0.3138	−0.0651	0.2486	0.2488	0.3043	−0.0095	0.0101
8	0.8	0.34358881	1.14358881	0.4255	−0.0819	0.3434	0.3437	0.4152	−0.0103	0.0111
9	0.9	0.457947691	1.357947691	0.5596	−0.1017	0.4577	0.4581	0.5480	−0.0116	0.0123
10	1.0	0.5937424601	1.5937424601	0.7183	−0.1246	0.5934	0.5939	0.7056	−0.0127	0.0136

For the general integration between x_i and x_{i+1}, that is, the results of column 3, the actual algorithm is given by (6.28b) as

$$y_{i+1} = y_i + hf(x_i, y_i).$$

The value of y_i used for every interval except the first, where $y_0 = y(x_0)$, is inexact, being the result of previous calculations which involved earlier truncation errors.

6.4   Error Propagation in Euler's Method

Let us examine the *propagation* of local discretization errors in Euler's method of (6.28) applied to the integration of the initial-value problem

$$\frac{dy}{dx} = f(x, y), \qquad y(x_0) = y_0. \qquad (6.32)$$

Assume that $f(x, y)$ and its first-order partial derivatives are continuous and bounded in the region $a \leqslant x \leqslant b$, $-\infty < y < \infty$, and that $a < x_0 < x_n < b$. Assume also that a solution $y(x)$ exists. Then there must exist constants M and K such that

$$|y''(x)| = \left| \frac{\partial f(x, y)}{\partial x} + f(x, y) \frac{\partial f(x, y)}{\partial y} \right| \leqslant M \quad (6.33)$$

and

$$|f(x, y^*) - f(x, y)| = \left| \frac{\partial f(x, \alpha)}{\partial y} \right| |y^* - y| \leqslant K |y^* - y|, \qquad (6.34)$$

where $y^* < \alpha < y$ for (x, y) and (x, y^*) in the region. Relationship (6.34) follows directly from the differential mean-value theorem of page 9.

As in (6.8), denote the error between the approximate and exact solutions by ε_i, that is, let

$$\varepsilon_i = y_i - y(x_i).$$

Then the additional error, $\Delta \varepsilon_i$, generated in traversing the ith step, is

$$\Delta \varepsilon_i = \Delta y_i - \Delta y(x_i), \qquad (6.35)$$

or

$$\varepsilon_{i+1} - \varepsilon_i = y_{i+1} - y_i - [y(x_{i+1}) - y(x_i)], \quad (6.36)$$

subject to the condition $\varepsilon_0 = 0$. From Euler's algorithm of (6.28b),

$$y_{i+1} - y_i = hf(x_i, y_i),$$

whereas, from Taylor's expansion (6.25),

$$y(x_{i+1}) - y(x_i) = hf(x_i, y(x_i)) + \frac{h^2}{2!} f'(\xi, y(\xi)),$$

$$x_i < \xi < x_{i+1}. \quad (6.37)$$

Thus (6.35) is equivalent to

$$\Delta \varepsilon_i = h[f(x_i, y_i) - f(x_i, y(x_i))] - \frac{h^2}{2} f'(\xi, y(\xi)). \qquad (6.38)$$

Then, from (6.33) and (6.34),

$$|\Delta \varepsilon_i| = |\varepsilon_{i+1} - \varepsilon_i| \leqslant hK|y_i - y(x_i)| + \frac{M}{2!} h^2,$$

or

$$|\varepsilon_{i+1} - \varepsilon_i| \leqslant hK|\varepsilon_i| + \frac{M}{2!} h^2. \qquad (6.39)$$

Since $|\varepsilon_{i+1}| \leqslant |\varepsilon_{i+1} - \varepsilon_i| + |\varepsilon_i|$, (6.39) can be rewritten as

$$|\varepsilon_{i+1}| \leqslant (1 + hK)|\varepsilon_i| + \frac{M}{2} h^2, \qquad i \geqslant 0. \quad (6.40)$$

To determine $|\varepsilon_i|$, (6.40) can be applied i times with the starting value $\varepsilon_0 = 0$. However, (6.40) has a general solution of the form

$$|\varepsilon_i| \leqslant \frac{Mh}{2K} [(1 + hK)^i - 1]. \qquad (6.41)$$

That (6.41) is a solution of (6.40) is not immediately apparent, but this can be proved by induction as follows. Consider a general inequality of the form

$$|\varepsilon_{i+1}| \leqslant A|\varepsilon_i| + B, \qquad i \geqslant 0, \qquad (6.42)$$

where A and B are independent of i. The proposed solution of (6.42), for $A > 0$, $B \geqslant 0$, $A \neq 1$, is

$$|\varepsilon_i| \leqslant A^i |\varepsilon_0| + \left(\frac{A^i - 1}{A - 1} \right) B, \qquad i > 0. \quad (6.43)$$

For $i = 1$, (6.43) is identical with (6.42). For a general value of i, substitution of (6.43) into (6.42) yields

$$|\varepsilon_{i+1}| \leqslant A \left\{ A^i |\varepsilon_0| + \left(\frac{A^i - 1}{A - 1} \right) B \right\} + B$$

$$= A^{i+1} |\varepsilon_0| + \left\{ A \left(\frac{A^i - 1}{A - 1} \right) + 1 \right\} B$$

$$= A^{i+1} |\varepsilon_0| + \left(\frac{A^{i+1} - 1}{A - 1} \right) B,$$

which is just (6.43) with i incremented by unity. Thus, by induction, (6.43) is a solution of (6.42). The error for Euler's method (6.40) is a special form of (6.43), since $\varepsilon_0 = 0$. In this case, $A = (1 + hK)$, $B = Mh^2/2$, so that the solution is

$$|\varepsilon_i| \leqslant A^i |\varepsilon_0| + \left(\frac{A^i - 1}{A - 1} \right) B = \left(\frac{A^i - 1}{A - 1} \right) B$$

$$= \left[\frac{(1 + hK)^i - 1}{1 + hK - 1} \right] \frac{M}{2} h^2$$

$$= \frac{Mh}{2K} [(1 + hK)^i - 1],$$

which is the given solution (6.41).

The solution of (6.41) can be simplified further, since

$$(1 + hK) < e^{hK}, \tag{6.44}$$

which follows from Taylor's expansion of e^{hK}. Substitution of (6.44) into (6.41) gives

$$|\varepsilon_i| \leqslant \frac{Mh}{2K}(e^{ihK} - 1) \leqslant \frac{Mh}{2K}e^{ihK}. \tag{6.45}$$

For $nh = x_n - x_0 = L$, the constant total interval of integration, (6.45) can be written as

$$|\varepsilon_n| \leqslant \frac{Mh}{2K}e^{LK}.$$

Then, as h approaches zero, the error approaches zero, because

$$\lim_{h \to 0} |\varepsilon_n| \leqslant \lim_{h \to 0} \frac{Mh}{2K}e^{LK} = 0.$$

Notice that this is true despite the fact that $n \to \infty$ as $h \to 0$. A numerical procedure for which, when $0 \leqslant i \leqslant n$,

$$\lim_{h \to 0} |\varepsilon_i| = 0,$$

is said to be *convergent*. Thus, Euler's method converges with an overall truncation error for which

$$|\varepsilon_i| = |y_i - y(x_i)| = O(h). \tag{6.46}$$

Note that although the *local* truncation error (6.29) for Euler's method is of order h^2, (6.46) shows that the *total* truncation error is of order h.

For the equation of (6.19)

$$f(x,y) = x + y,$$

subject to the initial condition $y(x_0) = y(0) = 0$, the analytical solution is

$$y = e^x - x - 1.$$

Since M can be taken as an upper bound of the magnitude of $f'(x,y)$ on the interval $[x_0, x_i]$, let

$$M = |f'(x,y)|_{max} = |e^x|_{max}. \tag{6.47}$$

Also, K can be taken as an upper bound on the partial derivative of $f(x,y)$ with respect to y, that is,

$$K = |f_y(x,y)|_{max} = 1. \tag{6.48}$$

Using these values for M and K, and with $h = 0.1$ as before, an upper bound on the truncation error $|\varepsilon_i|$ is, from (6.41),

$$|\varepsilon_i| \leqslant \frac{0.1e^{x_i}}{2}[(1 + 0.1)^i - 1]. \tag{6.49}$$

Values of $|\varepsilon_i|_{max}$ computed from the right-hand side of (6.49) are listed below. As expected, all these error bounds (Table 6.2) are greater than the true truncation error (from Table 6.1, column 6).

Table 6.2 *Total Truncation Error for Euler's Method Solution of Equation (6.19)*

i	x_i	$|\varepsilon_i|_{max}$	$\varepsilon_i = y_i - y(x_i)$
0	0.0	—	0.0000
1	0.1	0.0055	−0.0052
2	0.2	0.0128	−0.0114
3	0.3	0.0222	−0.0189
4	0.4	0.0349	−0.0277
5	0.5	0.0502	−0.0382
6	0.6	0.0704	−0.0505
7	0.7	0.0960	−0.0651
8	0.8	0.1226	−0.0819
9	0.9	0.1678	−0.1017
10	1.0	0.2175	−0.1246

EXAMPLE 6.1

EULER'S METHOD

Problem Statement

Write a program that uses Euler's method to solve the first-order equation (6.19),

$$f(x, y) = x + y,$$

with the initial condition $y(x_0) = y(0) = 0$. Integrate the equation on the interval $0 \leqslant x \leqslant x_{max}$ using several different step sizes, h. Print the results after every k steps (i.e., for $x = x_0, x_k, x_{2k}, \ldots$) and compare the results with the true solution (6.23):

$$y(x_i) = e^{x_i} - x_i - 1, \qquad i = 0, k, 2k, 3k, \ldots.$$

Method of Solution

Euler's algorithm (6.28),

$$y_i = y_{i-1} + hf(x_{i-1}, y_{i-1})$$
$$= y_{i-1} + h(x_{i-1} + y_{i-1}),$$

is used to implement the solution of (6.19).

Flow Diagram

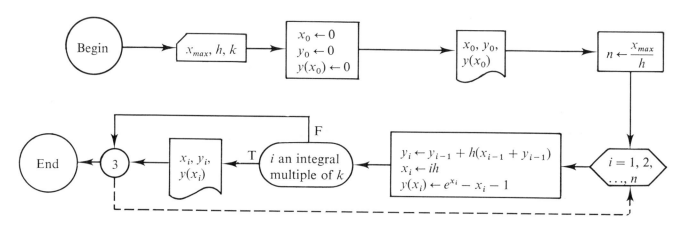

FORTRAN *Implementation*

List of Principal Variables

Program Symbol	Definition
H	Step size, h.
I	Step counter, i.
IPRINT	Number of steps between printout, k.
NSTEPS	Total number of steps, x_{max}/h.
TRUEY	True solution, $y(x_i)$.
X	Independent variable, x_i.
XMAX	Maximum value of the independent variable, x_{max}.
Y	Computed solution, y_i.

Example 6.1 Euler's Method **349**

Program Listing

```
C           APPLIED NUMERICAL METHODS, EXAMPLE 6.1
C           EULER'S METHOD
C
C           THIS PROGRAM USES EULERS METHOD TO COMPUTE THE SOLUTION OF THE
C           ORDINARY DIFFERENTIAL EQUATION  DY/DX = X+Y  ON THE INTERVAL
C           (0,XMAX) WITH STEPSIZE H AND INITIAL CONDITION Y(0) = 0.
C           I IS THE COUNTER FOR THE NUMBER OF APPLICATIONS OF THE METHOD.
C           NSTEPS IS THE TOTAL NUMBER OF STEPS FOR EULER'S METHOD.
C           TRUEY IS THE ANALYTICAL SOLUTION  Y(X) = EXP(X) - X - 1.
C           SOLUTIONS ARE PRINTED AFTER EVERY IPRINT STEPS.
C
            IMPLICIT  REAL*8(A-H, O-Z)
C
C           ..... READ DATA AND SET INITIAL CONDITIONS .....
      1     READ (5,100)  XMAX, H, IPRINT
            WRITE (6,200)  XMAX, H, IPRINT
            X = 0.
            Y = 0.
            TRUEY = 0.
            WRITE (6,201)  X, Y, TRUEY
C
C           ..... EULERS METHOD INTEGRATION .....
            NSTEPS = (XMAX + H/2.)/H
            DO 3  I = 1, NSTEPS
            Y = Y + H*(X + Y)
            X = FLOAT(I)*H
            TRUEY = DEXP(X) - X - 1.
      3     IF (I/IPRINT*IPRINT.EQ.I)  WRITE (6,201)  X, Y, TRUEY
            GO TO 1
C
C           ..... FORMATS FOR INPUT AND OUTPUT STATEMENTS .....
    100     FORMAT ( 10X,F10.6,17X,F10.6,20X,I5 )
    200     FORMAT ( 10H1XMAX   = , F12.6/ 10H H       = , F12.6/ 10H IPRINT =
          1 I5/ 1H0, 6X, 1HX, 15X, 1HY, 13X, 5HTRUEY/ 1H )
    201     FORMAT ( 1H , F10.6, 2F16.6 )
C
            END
```

Data

XMAX	=	1.000000	H	=	1.000000	IPRINT	=	1
XMAX	=	1.000000	H	=	0.500000	IPRINT	=	1
XMAX	=	1.000000	H	=	0.250000	IPRINT	=	1
XMAX	=	1.000000	H	=	0.100000	IPRINT	=	1
XMAX	=	1.000000	H	=	0.010000	IPRINT	=	10
XMAX	=	1.000000	H	=	0.001000	IPRINT	=	100
XMAX	=	1.000000	H	=	0.000100	IPRINT	=	1000
XMAX	=	1.000000	H	=	0.000010	IPRINT	=	10000

Computer Output

Results for the 1st Data Set

```
XMAX   =    1.000000
H      =    1.000000
IPRINT =    1

        X                 Y              TRUEY

   0.0               0.0            0.0
   1.000000          0.0            0.718282
```

Computer Output (*Continued*)

Results for the 2nd Data Set

```
XMAX    =      1.000000
H       =      0.500000
IPRINT  =      1
```

X	Y	TRUEY
0.0	0.0	0.0
0.500000	0.0	0.148721
1.000000	0.250000	0.718282

Results for the 3rd Data Set

```
XMAX    =      1.000000
H       =      0.250000
IPRINT  =      1
```

X	Y	TRUEY
0.0	0.0	0.0
0.250000	0.0	0.034025
0.500000	0.062500	0.148721
0.750000	0.203125	0.367000
1.000000	0.441406	0.718282

Results for the 4th Data Set

```
XMAX    =      1.000000
H       =      0.100000
IPRINT  =      1
```

X	Y	TRUEY
0.0	0.0	0.0
0.100000	0.0	0.005171
0.200000	0.010000	0.021403
0.300000	0.031000	0.049859
0.400000	0.064100	0.091825
0.500000	0.110510	0.148721
0.600000	0.171561	0.222119
0.700000	0.248717	0.313753
0.800000	0.343589	0.425541
0.900000	0.457948	0.559603
1.000000	0.593742	0.718282

Results for the 5th Data Set

```
XMAX    =      1.000000
H       =      0.010000
IPRINT  =      10
```

X	Y	TRUEY
0.0	0.0	0.0
0.100000	0.004622	0.005171
0.200000	0.020190	0.021403
0.300000	0.047849	0.049859
0.400000	0.088864	0.091825
0.500000	0.144632	0.148721
0.600000	0.216697	0.222119
0.700000	0.306763	0.313753
0.800000	0.416715	0.425541
0.900000	0.548633	0.559603
1.000000	0.704814	0.718282

Example 6.1   Euler's Method   **351**

Computer Output (*Continued*)

Results for the 6th Data Set

```
XMAX    =       1.000000
H       =       0.001000
IPRINT  =   100
```

X	Y	TRUEY
0.0	0.0	0.0
0.100000	0.005116	0.005171
0.200000	0.021281	0.021403
0.300000	0.049656	0.049859
0.400000	0.091527	0.091825
0.500000	0.148309	0.148721
0.600000	0.221573	0.222119
0.700000	0.313048	0.313753
0.800000	0.424651	0.425541
0.900000	0.558497	0.559603
1.000000	0.716924	0.718282

Results for the 7th Data Set

```
XMAX    =       1.000000
H       =       0.000100
IPRINT  =   1000
```

X	Y	TRUEY
0.0	0.0	0.0
0.100000	0.005165	0.005171
0.200000	0.021391	0.021403
0.300000	0.049839	0.049859
0.400000	0.091795	0.091825
0.500000	0.148680	0.148721
0.600000	0.222064	0.222119
0.700000	0.313682	0.313753
0.800000	0.425452	0.425541
0.900000	0.559492	0.559603
1.000000	0.718146	0.718282

Results for the 8th Data Set

```
XMAX    =       1.000000
H       =       0.000010
IPRINT  =  10000
```

X	Y	TRUEY
0.0	0.0	0.0
0.100000	0.005170	0.005171
0.200000	0.021402	0.021403
0.300000	0.049857	0.049859
0.400000	0.091822	0.091825
0.500000	0.148717	0.148721
0.600000	0.222113	0.222119
0.700000	0.313746	0.313753
0.800000	0.425532	0.425541
0.900000	0.559592	0.559603
1.000000	0.718268	0.718282

Discussion of Results

Equation (6.19) has been solved on the interval [0,1] using Euler's method with several different step sizes, $h = 1.0, 0.5, 0.25, 0.1, 0.01, 0.001, 0.0001,$ and 0.00001. The errors in the computed solution at $x = 1$ as a function of the step size are shown in Table 6.1.1 and Fig. 6.1.1. As expected from the error analysis of Section 6.4, the error decreases linearly with h for small h (see (6.46)).

Table 6.1.1 Error in Euler's Method Solution at $x = 1$

Step size, h	Error at $x = 1$
1.0	0.718282
0.5	0.468282
0.25	0.276876
0.1	0.124540
0.01	0.013468
0.001	0.001358
0.0001	0.000136
0.00001	0.000014

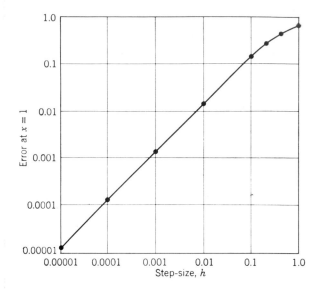

Figure 6.1.1   Error in Euler's method solution at $x = 1$.

EXAMPLE 6.2

ETHANE PYROLYSIS IN A TUBULAR REACTOR

Problem Statement

The pyrolysis of ethane in the temperature range 1200 to 1700°F is represented essentially by the irreversible first-order chemical reaction

$$C_2H_6 \rightarrow C_2H_4 + H_2, \qquad (6.2.1)$$

ethane → ethylene + hydrogen.

Pure ethane is fed at a rate of 1800 lb/hr at 1200°F to a 4.026 in. I.D. steel tube contained in an ethane pyrolysis furnace. Heat is supplied by the furnace to the tube at a rate of 5000 BTU/hr sq ft (of inside tube area). The tube contains no internal obstructions (e.g., catalyst) and any pressure drop along the length of the tube can be ignored; the mean pressure for the gases in the tube may be assumed equal to 30 psia. Assuming plug flow in the tube, write a program that will calculate the length of tube required to produce 75 percent decomposition of the ethane to ethylene and hydrogen. The program should include provision for reading important parameters (ethane feed rate, inlet temperature, tube diameter, mean pressure, etc.) and printing temperature (°F) and conversion profiles along the length of the tube (ft) at desired intervals.

Required thermodynamic properties (standard heats of formation, ΔH_f, temperature-dependent specific heat capacities, c_p), kinetic information (the temperature-dependent rate constant for reaction (6.2.1)), and physical constants are shown in Table 6.2.1.

Table 6.2.1 *Data for Ethane Pyrolysis Reaction**

	ΔH_f at 298°K (cal/g mole)	c_p (cal/g mole °K)
C_2H_6(gas)	−20236	$3.75 + 35.7 \times 10^{-3}\bar{T} - 10.12 \times 10^{-6}\bar{T}^2$
C_2H_4(gas)	12496	$5.25 + 24.2 \times 10^{-3}\bar{T} - 6.88 \times 10^{-6}\bar{T}^2$
H_2(gas)	0	$7.00 - 0.385 \times 10^{-3}\bar{T} + 0.6 \times 10^{-6}\bar{T}^2$

Reaction rate constant: $k = 5.764 \times 10^{16}e^{-41,310/T}$ (sec)$^{-1}$.
Atomic Weights: $C = 12, H = 1$.
Gas Constant: $R = 10.73$ psia cu ft/lb mole °R.

* $\bar{T}$ is temperature in °K (Kelvin).

Method of Solution

The problem is stated in mixed units, but will be solved using the BTU, lb mole, °R (Rankine), ft, and hr system. Adopt the following notation:

A = Cross-sectional area of tube, sq ft.
c = Concentration of ethane, lb moles/cu ft.
c_p = Specific heat capacity, BTU/lb mole°R.
k = Reaction rate constant, sec^{-1}.
L = Length measured from reactor inlet, ft.
n_0 = Inlet molal feed rate of ethane, lb moles/hr.

$n_{C_2H_4}$ = Molal flow rate of ethylene at any point, lb moles/hr.
$n_{C_2H_6}$ = Molal flow rate of ethane at any point, lb moles/hr.
n_{H_2} = Molal flow rate of hydrogen at any point, lb moles/hr.
P = Total pressure, psia.
q = Heat input from furnace, BTU/hr ft (of tube length).
r = Specific reaction rate, lb moles ethane/cu ft hr.
T = Absolute temperature, °R.
$\bar{T}$ = Absolute temperature, °K.
V = Reactor volume, cu ft.
x = Mole fraction of ethane.
z = Fraction of ethane converted to ethylene and hydrogen.
ΔH_f = Heat of formation, cal/g mole.
ΔH_R = Heat of reaction, BTU/lb mole.

The following conversion constants will be useful in generating a consistent set of units for the solution of the problem:

The Kelvin, Rankine, and Fahrenheit temperature scales are related by:

$$°R = °F + 460,$$

$$°K = °R/1.8.$$

The value of the specific heat capacity in cal/g mole °K is numerically equal to the specific heat capacity in BTU/lb mole °R.

The heat of reaction ΔH_R in BTU/lb mole is equal to 1.8 times its numerical value in cal/g mole.

The molal flow rates of the three constituents are:

	C_2H_6	=	C_2H_4	+	H_2
Inlet molal flow rate:	n_0		0		0
Molal flow rate when the conversion is z:	$n_0(1 - z)$		$n_0 z$		$n_0 z$

Thus the total number of moles flowing at any point in the tubular reactor is $n_0(1 + z)$ and the corresponding mole fraction of ethane is $x = (1 - z)/(1 + z)$.

We now establish steady-state material and energy balances over a differential element dL of reactor length, shown in Fig. 6.2.1.

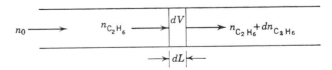

Figure 6.2.1 Differential element of tubular reactor.

353

Material balance. The material balance for ethane over the differential volume element $dV = A\,dL$ is:

Flowing In + From Reaction = Flowing Out

$$n_{C_2H_6} + r\,dV = n_{C_2H_6} + dn_{C_2H_6}. \tag{6.2.2}$$

Rearranging (6.2.2),

$$r = \frac{dn_{C_2H_6}}{dV} = \frac{d[n_0(1-z)]}{A\,dL} = -\frac{n_0}{A}\frac{dz}{dL}. \tag{6.2.3}$$

But for the given first-order irreversible reaction, the rate, r, is

$$r = -3600kc, \tag{6.2.4}$$

where the conversion constant 3600 sec/hr is introduced for dimensional consistency. At the low pressure of the reacting gas mixture, the ideal gas law holds, so that (6.2.4) becomes

$$r = -3600k\frac{xP}{RT} = -3600k\frac{1-z}{1+z}\frac{P}{RT}. \tag{6.2.5}$$

From (6.2.3), (6.2.5), and Table 6.2.1, the conversion z as a function of reactor length, L, is described by the solution of the first-order ordinary differential equation

$$\frac{dz}{dL} = \frac{3600AP}{n_0R}\frac{k}{T}\frac{1-z}{1+z}$$

$$= \left(\frac{2.075 \times 10^{20}AP}{n_0R}\right)\left(\frac{e^{-41310/T}}{T}\right)\left(\frac{1-z}{1+z}\right). \tag{6.2.6}$$

For a given tube I.D., reactor pressure, and inlet ethane flow rate, the first factor on the right-hand side of (6.2.6) is constant; the second factor is a function of temperature only.

Energy balance. The energy balance over the differential volume element dV must account for heat liberated due to reaction, heat introduced from the furnace through the tube wall, and sensible heat effects (because of temperature change) in the flowing gas stream. For a change dz in conversion in the differential element, the heat liberated by the reaction is $n_0\,dz(-\Delta H_R)$. The energy introduced into the differential element through the tube wall is $q\,dL$. The corresponding gain in enthalpy of the flowing gases is given by

$$\Delta H_s = [n_{C_2H_6}c_{pC_2H_6} + n_{C_2H_4}c_{pC_2H_4} + n_{H_2}c_{pH_2}]\,dT$$

$$= [n_0(1-z)c_{pC_2H_6} + n_0z(c_{pC_2H_4} + c_{pH_2})]\,dT, \tag{6.2.7}$$

where dT is the temperature change across the differential element. The energy balance is

$$n_0\,dz(-\Delta H_R) + q\,dL = n_0[(1-z)c_{pC_2H_6}$$

$$+ z(c_{pC_2H_4} + c_{pH_2})]\,dT. \tag{6.2.8}$$

Then the change in temperature as a function of length is described by the first-order ordinary differential equation

$$\frac{dT}{dL} = \frac{\dfrac{q}{n_0} + (-\Delta H_R)\dfrac{dz}{dL}}{(1-z)c_{pC_2H_6} + z(c_{pC_2H_4} + c_{pH_2})}. \tag{6.2.9}$$

Provided that the temperature $\overline{T}$ is computed from temperature T, the heat capacity relationships from Table 6.2.1 can be introduced directly into the denominator of (6.2.9).

The heat of reaction, ΔH_R, varies with temperature according to

$$\frac{d(\Delta H_R)}{dT} = c_{pC_2H_4} + c_{pH_2} - c_{pC_2H_6}. \tag{6.2.10}$$

The heat of reaction at 298°K can be calculated from the heats of formation of Table 6.2.1 as $12496 + 20236 = 32732$ cal/g mole °K. Introducing the heat capacity relationships of Table 6.2.1 into (6.2.10), and integrating, yields the heat of reaction at any temperature T (°R),

$$\Delta H_R = 1.8[32732 + 8.50(\overline{T} - 298)$$

$$- 0.005942(\overline{T}^2 - 298^2)$$

$$+ 1.28 \times 10^{-6}(\overline{T}^3 - 298^3)] \text{ BTU/lb mole.} \tag{6.2.11}$$

Algorithm. Equations (6.2.6) and (6.2.9) are two coupled nonlinear first-order ordinary differential equations which must be solved simultaneously. The length L is the independent variable, and z and T are the dependent (solution) variables. The initial conditions are

$$z(L_0) = z_0 = z(0) = 0 \text{ (no conversion at inlet)},$$

$$T(L_0) = T_0 = T(0) = T_f \text{ (inlet feed temperature)}.$$

The two differential equations can be solved in parallel using Euler's method of (6.28). Let the step size be denoted by ΔL. Then (6.28) becomes

$$z_i = z_{i-1} + \Delta L\left(\frac{dz}{dL}\right)_{i-1}, \tag{6.2.12}$$

$$T_i = T_{i-1} + \Delta L\left(\frac{dT}{dL}\right)_{i-1}. \tag{6.2.13}$$

Here, z_i and T_i are, respectively, the conversion and temperature at $L_i = i\Delta L$. At the beginning of the ith step the values of z_{i-1} and T_{i-1} have already been calculated. The values of dz/dL and dT/dL for equations (6.2.12) and (6.2.13) can be computed from (6.2.6) and (6.2.9). Then z_i and T_i can be computed from (6.2.12) and (6.2.13). The process is repeated for subsequent steps until z_i exceeds some desired upper limit z_{max}, $0 < z_{max} \leqslant 1$. The program contains provision for printing values for L_i, z_i, and T_i (converted to °F) at specified intervals in i.

Example 6.2   Ethane Pyrolysis in a Tubular Reactor   **355**

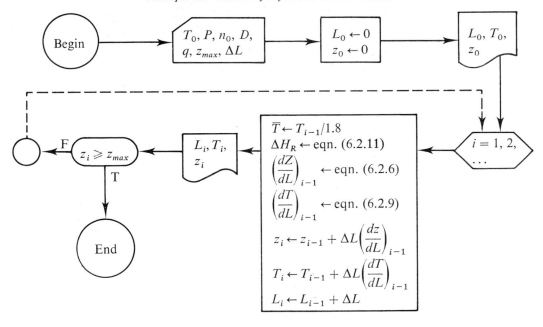

FORTRAN *Implementation*

List of Principal Variables

Program Symbol	Definition
AL	Length, L_i, ft.
CONV	Desired conversion fraction for ethane, z_{max}.
CP	Denominator of equation (6.2.9), BTU/lb mole °R.
DH	ΔH_R, BTU/lb mole (see equation (6.2.11)).
DI	Internal diameter of reactor tube, D, in.
DL	Length increment, ΔL, ft.
DTDL	$(dT/dL)_{i-1}$, °R/ft.
DZDL	$(dz/dL)_{i-1}$, ft^{-1}.
FACTOR	$2.075 \times 10^{20} AP/n_0 R$ (see equation (6.2.6)).
I	Step counter, i.
IPRINT	Intermediate print control. Results are printed after every IPRINT steps.
P	Pressure in the reactor, P, psia.
Q	q/n_0, BTU/lb mole ft.
QPERSF	Heat input from furnace, BTU/hr sq ft (of inside tube surface area).
RATEMS	Inlet mass feed rate of ethane, lb/hr.
T, TF, TK	Temperature, °R, °F, and °K, respectively.
Z	Fraction of ethylene converted, z_i.

Program Listing

```
C              APPLIED NUMERICAL METHODS, EXAMPLE 6.2
C              PYROLYSIS OF ETHANE IN A TUBULAR REACTOR
C
C              THIS PROGRAM USES EULER'S METHOD TO SOLVE A SYSTEM OF TWO
C              FIRST ORDER ORDINARY DIFFERENTIAL EQUATIONS DESCRIBING THE
C              AXIAL TEMPERATURE (T) AND CONVERSION (Z) PROFILES FOR
C              PYROLYSIS OF ETHANE IN A TUBULAR REACTOR.  THE DISTANCE FROM
C              THE TUBE ENTRANCE, AL, IS THE INDEPENDENT VARIABLE AND DL IS
C              THE STEP-SIZE USED IN THE INTEGRATION PROCEDURE.  DTDL AND
C              DZDL ARE THE DERIVATIVES OF TEMPERATURE AND CONVERSION WITH
C              RESPECT TO LENGTH AT THE BEGINNING OF EACH STEP.  TF IS THE
C              FAHRENHEIT AND TK THE KELVIN EQUIVALENT OF THE TEMPERATURE
C              T WHICH HAS UNITS OF DEGREES RANKINE.  INPUT DATA INCLUDE
C              THE INLET TEMPERATURE TF, INLET PRESSURE P, MASS RATE OF
C              ETHYLENE FEED RATEMS, INTERNAL DIAMETER OF THE TUBE DI,
C              HEAT INPUT RATE FROM THE FURNACE QPERSF, THE STEP-SIZE DL,
C              THE MAXIMUM CONVERSION DESIRED CONV, AND THE FREQUENCY OF
C              PRINTOUT IPRINT.  DH IS THE HEAT OF REACTION AND CP A HEAT
C              CAPACITY TERM.  Q, FACTOR AND CP ARE DESCRIBED IN THE TEXT.
C              INTEGRATION PROCEEDS DOWN THE TUBE UNTIL THE INDICATED
C              CONVERSION FRACTION CONV IS REACHED.  I IS THE STEP COUNTER.
C
C         ..... READ AND PRINT DATA - COMPUTE CONSTANT PARAMETERS .....
    1    READ (5,100)  TF, P, RATEMS, DI, QPERSF, CONV, DL, IPRINT
         WRITE (6,200) TF, P, RATEMS, DI, QPERSF, CONV, DL, IPRINT
         Q = QPERSF*30./RATEMS*3.14159*DI/12.
         FACTOR = 2.07504E20*3.14159*DI*DI*P*30./(144.*4.*10.73*RATEMS)
C
C         ..... SET INITIAL CONDITIONS .....
         AL = 0.
         Z = 0.
         T = TF + 460.
         WRITE (6,201)  AL, TF, Z
C
C         ..... INTEGRATE EQUATIONS ACROSS IPRINT STEPS .....
    2    DO 3  I = 1, IPRINT
C
C         ..... DERIVATIVES FROM MATERIAL AND ENERGY BALANCES .....
         TK = T/1.8
         DH = 1.8*(32732. + 8.50*(TK-298.) - 5.942E-3*(TK*TK - 298.*298.)
    1       + 1.28E-6*(TK*TK*TK - 298.*298.*298.))
         CP = (1.0-Z)*(3.75+35.7E-3*TK-10.12E-6*TK*TK)+Z*(12.25+23.815E-3
    1       *TK-6.28E-6*TK*TK)
         DZDL = FACTOR*EXP(-41310./TK)*(1.-Z)/(T*(1.+Z))
         DTDL = (Q-DH*DZDL)/CP
C
C         ..... APPLY EULER'S ALGORITHM .....
         T = T + DTDL*DL
         Z = Z + DZDL*DL
         AL = AL + DL
    3    IF (Z.GE.CONV)  GO TO 4
C
C         ..... PRINT SOLUTIONS, CONTINUE INTEGRATION IF NOT DONE .....
    4    TF = T - 460.
         WRITE (6,201)  AL, TF, Z
         IF (Z.LT.CONV)  GO TO 2
         GO TO 1
C
C         ..... FORMATS FOR INPUT AND OUTPUT STATEMENTS .....
  100    FORMAT ( 9X,F8.3,19X,F8.3,19X,F8.3/ 9X,F8.3,19X,F8.3,19X,F8.3/
    1    9X,F8.3,19X,I4 )
  200    FORMAT ( 10H1TF      = , F10.4/ 10H P       = , F10.4/10H RATEMS = ,
    1    F10.4/ 10H DI      = , F10.4/ 10H QPERSF = , F10.4/ 10H CONV    =
    2     , F10.4/ 10H DL     = , F10.4/ 10H IPRINT = , I5/ 1H0, 3X,
    3    1HL,    12X, 2HTF, 13X, 1HZ / 1H  )
  201    FORMAT ( 1H ,F7.2,F14.2,F14.6 )
C
         END
```

Example 6.2   Ethane Pyrolysis in a Tubular Reactor   357

Program Listing (*Continued*)

Data

TF	= 1200.000	P	= 30.000	RATEMS	= 1800.000	
DI	= 4.026	QPERSF	= 5000.000	CONV	= 0.750	
DL	= 0.100	IPRINT	= 500			
TF	= 1200.000	P	= 30.000	RATEMS	= 1800.000	
DI	= 4.026	QPERSF	= 5000.000	CONV	= 0.750	
DL	= 0.500	IPRINT	= 100			
TF	= 1200.000	P	= 30.000	RATEMS	= 1800.000	
DI	= 4.026	QPERSF	= 5000.000	CONV	= 0.750	
DL	= 1.000	IPRINT	= 50			
TF	= 1200.000	P	= 30.000	RATEMS	= 1800.000	
DI	= 4.026	QPERSF	= 5000.000	CONV	= 0.750	
DL	= 5.000	IPRINT	= 10			
TF	= 1200.000	P	= 30.000	RATEMS	= 1800.000	
DI	= 4.026	QPERSF	= 5000.000	CONV	= 0.750	
DL	= 10.000	IPRINT	= 5			
TF	= 1200.000	P	= 30.000	RATEMS	= 1800.000	
DI	= 4.026	QPERSF	= 5000.000	CONV	= 0.750	
DL	= 25.000	IPRINT	= 2			
TF	= 1200.000	P	= 30.000	RATEMS	= 1800.000	
DI	= 4.026	QPERSF	= 5000.000	CONV	= 0.750	
DL	= 50.000	IPRINT	= 1			
TF	= 1200.000	P	= 30.000	RATEMS	= 1800.000	
DI	= 4.026	QPERSF	= 5000.000	CONV	= 0.750	
DL	= 100.000	IPRINT	= 1			
TF	= 1200.000	P	= 30.000	RATEMS	= 1800.000	
DI	= 4.026	QPERSF	= 5000.000	CONV	= 0.750	
DL	= 200.000	IPRINT	= 1			

Computer Output

Results for the 1st Data Set

```
TF     = 1200.0000
P      =   30.0000
RATEMS = 1800.0000
DI     =    4.0260
QPERSF = 5000.0000
CONV   =    0.7500
DL     =    0.1000
IPRINT =  500
```

L	TF	Z
0.0	1200.00	0.0
50.00	1335.39	0.008140
99.99	1383.61	0.055868
149.99	1392.91	0.122008
199.98	1399.55	0.189402
249.98	1406.27	0.256761
299.91	1413.24	0.323986
349.84	1420.57	0.391026
399.77	1428.36	0.457829
449.69	1436.77	0.524321
499.62	1445.99	0.590402
549.55	1456.32	0.655929
599.47	1468.19	0.720684
622.44	1474.34	0.750122

Results for the 2nd Data Set

```
TF     = 1200.0000
P      =   30.0000
RATEMS = 1800.0000
DI     =    4.0260
QPERSF = 5000.0000
CONV   =    0.7500
DL     =    0.5000
IPRINT =  100
```

L	TF	Z
0.0	1200.00	0.0
50.00	1335.60	0.008074
100.00	1383.74	0.055868
150.00	1392.94	0.122087
200.00	1399.58	0.189522
250.00	1406.30	0.256910
300.00	1413.27	0.324163
350.00	1420.60	0.391233
400.00	1428.40	0.458066
450.00	1436.82	0.524587
500.00	1446.05	0.590699
550.00	1456.39	0.656254
600.00	1468.27	0.721037
623.00	1474.43	0.750487

Computer Output (*Continued*)

Results for the 3rd Data Set

```
TF      =   1200.0000
P       =     30.0000
RATEMS  =   1800.0000
DI      =      4.0260
QPERSF  =   5000.0000
CONV    =      0.7500
DL      =      1.0000
IPRINT  =     50
```

L	TF	Z
0.0	1200.00	0.0
50.00	1335.83	0.007985
100.00	1383.87	0.055825
150.00	1392.96	0.122105
200.00	1399.59	0.189550
250.00	1406.30	0.256943
300.00	1413.28	0.324200
350.00	1420.61	0.391274
400.00	1428.41	0.458111
450.00	1436.82	0.524637
500.00	1446.06	0.590752
550.00	1456.39	0.656312
600.00	1468.28	0.721099
623.00	1474.45	0.750550

Results for the 4th Data Set

```
TF      =   1200.0000
P       =     30.0000
RATEMS  =   1800.0000
DI      =      4.0260
QPERSF  =   5000.0000
CONV    =      0.7500
DL      =      5.0000
IPRINT  =     10
```

L	TF	Z
0.0	1200.00	0.0
50.00	1337.62	0.007255
100.00	1384.86	0.055487
150.00	1393.04	0.122204
200.00	1399.60	0.189685
250.00	1406.31	0.257083
300.00	1413.29	0.324344
350.00	1420.62	0.391422
400.00	1428.42	0.458263
450.00	1436.83	0.524793
500.00	1446.07	0.590912
550.00	1456.40	0.656478
600.00	1468.28	0.721270
625.00	1475.01	0.753274

Results for the 5th Data Set

```
TF      =   1200.0000
P       =     30.0000
RATEMS  =   1800.0000
DI      =      4.0260
QPERSF  =   5000.0000
CONV    =      0.7500
DL      =     10.0000
IPRINT  =      5
```

L	TF	Z
0.0	1200.00	0.0
50.00	1339.92	0.006322
100.00	1385.94	0.055145
150.00	1393.09	0.122351
200.00	1399.62	0.189851
250.00	1406.33	0.257251
300.00	1413.30	0.324513
350.00	1420.63	0.391593
400.00	1428.43	0.458435
450.00	1436.84	0.524966
500.00	1446.07	0.591088
550.00	1456.41	0.656656
600.00	1468.28	0.721453
630.00	1476.42	0.759823

Results for the 6th Data Set

```
TF      =   1200.0000
P       =     30.0000
RATEMS  =   1800.0000
DI      =      4.0260
QPERSF  =   5000.0000
CONV    =      0.7500
DL      =     25.0000
IPRINT  =      2
```

L	TF	Z
0.0	1200.00	0.0
50.00	1346.70	0.003620
100.00	1383.72	0.056787
150.00	1392.21	0.123360
200.00	1399.38	0.190552
250.00	1406.29	0.257858
300.00	1413.32	0.325095
350.00	1420.67	0.392169
400.00	1428.47	0.459012
450.00	1436.88	0.525547
500.00	1446.10	0.591674
550.00	1456.43	0.657250
600.00	1468.28	0.722059
625.00	1474.99	0.754075

Example 6.2   Ethane Pyrolysis in a Tubular Reactor   **359**

Computer Output (*Continued*)

Results for the 7th Data Set

```
TF      =  1200.0000
P       =    30.0000
RATEMS  =  1800.0000
DI      =     4.0260
QPERSF  =  5000.0000
CONV    =     0.7500
DL      =    50.0000
IPRINT  =     1
```

L	TF	Z
0.0	1200.00	0.0
50.00	1354.47	0.000906
100.00	1424.49	0.038377
150.00	1253.04	0.191834
200.00	1400.97	0.194216
250.00	1404.87	0.262969
300.00	1417.56	0.327482
350.00	1412.98	0.400319
400.00	1443.19	0.456346
450.00	1402.88	0.546592
500.00	1484.75	0.577684
550.00	1331.53	0.723643
600.00	1472.32	0.727250
650.00	1478.11	0.795021

Results for the 8th Data Set

```
TF      =  1200.0000
P       =    30.0000
RATEMS  =  1800.0000
DI      =     4.0260
QPERSF  =  5000.0000
CONV    =     0.7500
DL      =   100.0000
IPRINT  =     1
```

L	TF	Z
0.0	1200.00	0.0
100.00	1508.94	0.001811
200.00	-1684.50	1.718774

Results for the 9th Data Set

```
TF      =  1200.0000
P       =    30.0000
RATEMS  =  1800.0000
DI      =     4.0260
QPERSF  =  5000.0000
CONV    =     0.7500
DL      =   200.0000
IPRINT  =     1
```

L	TF	Z
0.0	1200.00	0.0
200.00	1817.89	0.003623
400.00	-939566.44	495.893799

Discussion of Results

The program has been run using the parameters given in the problem statement with several different values for the length increment, ΔL. All calculations have been made using single-precision arithmetic (note the influence of round-off error in the tabulated values for L in the results for the first data set). The total reactor length and the temperature at the reactor outlet corresponding to 75 percent conversion of ethane, determined by linear interpolation on the computed results, are shown in Table 6.2.2.

Table 6.2.2   Reactor Length and Outlet Temperature for 75 Percent Conversion of Ethane

Length Increment (ft)	Reactor Length (ft)	Outlet Temperature (°F)
0.1	622.4	1474.3
0.5	622.6	1474.3
1.0	622.6	1474.3
5.0	622.4	1474.3
10.0	622.3	1474.3
25.0	621.8	1474.1
50.0	616.8	1474.3
100.0	—	—
200.0	—	—

The results are almost identical for length increments of 0.1 ft to 25 ft, suggesting that the truncation errors are small and the results accurate. There is very little conversion of ethane in the first 50 ft of tube length; the gas temperature is rising (because of heat input from the furnace through the tube wall) but the reaction velocity constant is quite small, and only a small amount of decomposition takes place. Once the temperature is high enough, the rate of reaction becomes significant. The temperature rises only very slowly thereafter; the heat introduced from the furnace is roughly balanced by the heat of reaction for the endothermic (energy-consuming) pyrolysis reaction. Euler's method produces rather accurate results (not generally the case) for substantial length increments, because the derivatives of (6.2.6) and (6.2.9) are small and virtually constant over a substantial portion of the reactor length.

Significant errors begin to show up in the results for a length increment of 50 ft. Notice the curious oscillation of temperature down the length of the reactor; this behavior would be quite unreasonable from physical and chemical considerations. Euler's method produces these oscillations because the temperature at the beginning of a length increment is assumed to hold throughout the entire increment. When the temperature is rather low, the rate of reaction will be low, and heat from the furnace will be absorbed primarily as sensible heat, raising the temperature at the beginning of the next segment. This higher temperature will lead to a high reaction rate and to the consumption of all of the heat from the furnace (and some of the sensible heat of the reacting gases) by the decomposition reaction, leading to a lower gas temperature at the beginning of the next increment. As the length increment is made larger, these oscillations become more serious. For length increments of 100 and 200 ft, the results become completely meaningless. This problem has also been solved by using the integration function of Example 6.3 named RUNGE, which employs the fourth-order Runge-Kutta method described in the next section (results not shown). Results were virtually identical with those for the Euler method solution for the smaller step sizes; the Runge-Kutta solutions were unstable for $\Delta L > 25$ ft.

It should be mentioned that the method of solution outlined earlier assumes that the pressure is constant throughout the length of the reactor. This assumption would be unwarranted for certain combinations of feed rate and tube diameter (see Problem 6.20 at the end of the chapter).

6.5 Runge-Kutta Methods

The solution of a differential equation by direct Taylor's expansion of the object function is generally not practical if derivatives of higher order than the first are retained. For all but the simplest equations, the necessary higher-order derivatives tend to become quite complicated. In addition, as shown by the preceding examples, each problem results in a specific series for its solution. Thus, when higher-order error terms are desired, no simple algorithm analogous to Euler's method can be developed directly from the Taylor's expansion.

Fortunately, it is possible to develop one-step procedures which involve only first-order derivative evaluations, but which also produce results equivalent in accuracy to the higher-order Taylor formulas. These algorithms are called the *Runge-Kutta* methods. Approximations of the second, third, and fourth orders (that is, approximations with accuracies equivalent to Taylor's expansions of $y(x)$ retaining terms in h^2, h^3, and h^4, respectively) require the estimation of $f(x, y)$ at two, three, and four values, respectively, of x on the interval $x_i \leqslant x \leqslant x_{i+1}$. Methods of order m, where m is greater than four, require derivative evaluations at more than m nearby points [14].

All the Runge-Kutta methods have algorithms of the form

$$y_{i+1} = y_i + h\phi(x_i, y_i, h). \qquad (6.50)$$

Here, ϕ, termed the *increment* function by Henrici [2], is simply a suitably chosen approximation to $f(x, y)$ on the interval $x_i \leqslant x \leqslant x_{i+1}$. Because there is a considerable amount of algebra involved in the development of

where p and q are constants to be established later. The quantities hk_1 and hk_2 have a simple geometric interpretation, which will become apparent once p and q are determined.

First, expand k_2 in a Taylor's series for a function of two variables*, and drop all terms in which the exponent of h is greater than one:

$$
\begin{aligned}
k_2 &= f(x_i + ph, y_i + qhf(x_i, y_i)) \\
&= f(x_i, y_i) + phf_x(x_i, y_i) \\
&\quad + qhf(x_i, y_i)f_y(x_i, y_i) + O(h^2). \qquad (6.54)
\end{aligned}
$$

From (6.53) and (6.54), (6.52) becomes

$$
\begin{aligned}
y_{i+1} &= y_i + h[af(x_i, y_i) + bf(x_i, y_i)] \\
&\quad + h^2[bpf_x(x_i, y_i) + bqf(x_i, y_i)f_y(x_i, y_i)] + O(h^3). \\
&\qquad\qquad\qquad\qquad\qquad\qquad\qquad\qquad (6.55)
\end{aligned}
$$

Next, expand the object function $y(x)$ about x_i by using Taylor's series (6.25), as before:

$$
\begin{aligned}
y(x_i + h) = y(x_{i+1}) &= y(x_i) + hf(x_i, y(x_i)) \\
&+ \frac{h^2}{2}f'(x_i, y(x_i)) + \frac{h^3}{3!}f''(\xi, y(\xi)),
\end{aligned}
$$
$$
x_i < \xi < x_{i+1}. \quad (6.56)
$$

By chain-rule differentiation (6.10), $f'(x_i, y(x_i))$ is given by

$$f'(x_i, y(x_i)) = f_x(x_i, y(x_i)) + f_y(x_i, y(x_i))f(x_i, y(x_i)).$$

Finally, equate terms in like powers of h in (6.55) and (6.56):

Power of h	Expansion of $y(x)$	Runge-Kutta Algorithm
0	$y(x_i)$	y_i
1	$f(x_i, y(x_i))$	$(a + b)f(x_i, y_i)$
2	$\frac{1}{2}[f_x(x_i, y(x_i)) + f_y(x_i, y(x_i))f(x_i, y(x_i))]$	$[bpf_x(x_i, y_i) + bqf_y(x_i, y_i)f(x_i, y_i)]$

the higher-order Runge-Kutta formulas, only the simplest of these procedures (the second-order algorithm) will be developed in detail. The derivation of other Runge-Kutta formulas is analogous to the one which follows.

Let ϕ be a weighted average of two derivative evaluations k_1 and k_2 on the interval $x_i \leqslant x \leqslant x_{i+1}$, that is,

$$\phi = ak_1 + bk_2, \qquad (6.51)$$

which leads to the Runge-Kutta algorithm

$$y_{i+1} = y_i + h(ak_1 + bk_2). \qquad (6.52)$$

Let

$$
\begin{aligned}
k_1 &= f(x_i, y_i), \\
k_2 &= f(x_i + ph, y_i + qhf(x_i, y_i)) \\
&= f(x_i + ph, y_i + qhk_1),
\end{aligned} \qquad (6.53)
$$

Assuming that $y_i = y(x_i)$ and that we want equality of the coefficients of h^2 for all suitably differentiable functions $f(x, y)$, we find that $a + b = 1$, $bp = 1/2$, and $bq = 1/2$. Thus

$$
\begin{aligned}
a &= 1 - b, \\
p = q &= \frac{1}{2b}.
\end{aligned} \qquad (6.57)
$$

Since the three equations of (6.57) contain four unknowns, the system is underdetermined, that is, there is one variable, say b, which may be chosen arbitrarily. The two common choices are $b = \frac{1}{2}$ and $b = 1$.

---

* The first few terms of the two-variable Taylor's series are:

$$
\begin{aligned}
f(x + r, y + s) = f(x, y) &+ rf_x(x, y) + sf_y(x, y) + r^2f_{xx}(x, y)/2 \\
&+ rsf_{xy}(x, y) + s^2f_{yy}(x, y)/2 + O[(|r| + |s|)^3].
\end{aligned}
$$

For b = $\frac{1}{2}$. $a = \frac{1}{2}$, $p = 1$, $q = 1$. Then (6.52) becomes

$$y_{i+1} = y_i + \frac{h}{2}[f(x_i,y_i) + f(x_i + h,y_i + hf(x_i,y_i))],$$

(6.58)

which can also be written

$$y_{i+1} = y_i + \frac{h}{2}[f(x_i,y_i) + f(x_{i+1},\bar{y}_{i+1})],$$ (6.59)

where

$$\bar{y}_{i+1} = y_i + hf(x_i,y_i).$$ (6.60)

The one-step algorithm of (6.59) and (6.60) is known as the *improved Euler's method* or *Heun's method*, and has the geometric interpretation shown in Fig. 6.3a.

equations, (6.60) and (6.59), leads to the simplest of the so-called *predictor-corrector* methods which are described in more detail in Section 6.11.

For b = 1. $a = 0$, $p = 1/2$, $q = 1/2$. Then (6.55) becomes

$$y_{i+1} = y_i + hf\left(x_i + \frac{h}{2}, \bar{y}_{i+1/2}\right),$$ (6.61)

where

$$\bar{y}_{i+1/2} = y_i + \frac{h}{2}f(x_i,y_i).$$ (6.62)

The one-step algorithm of (6.61) and (6.62) is called the *improved polygon method* or the *modified Euler's method*, illustrated in Fig. 6.3b. Again, Euler's method is employed twice in sequence. First, from (6.62), an approximation

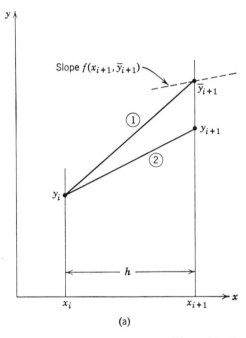

(a)

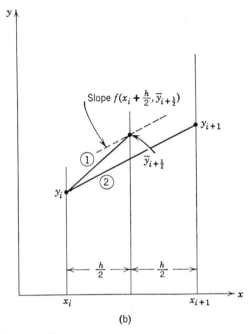

(b)

Figure 6.3   Second-order Runge-Kutta procedures.

Essentially, Euler's method is employed twice in sequence. First, equation (6.60) is used to predict $\bar{y}_{i+1}$, a preliminary estimate of y_{i+1}. That is, $\bar{y}_{i+1}$ is the ordinate, at $x = x_{i+1}$, of the straight line ①, passing through (x_i,y_i) with slope $f(x_i,y_i) = k_1$. Second, an improved estimate y_{i+1} is obtained from equation (6.59); the slope of line ②, used for this purpose, is the weighted average of approximations to f at the two ends of the interval. Note that although the true derivative at x_{i+1} is $f(x_{i+1}, y(x_{i+1}))$, it is approximated by $f(x_{i+1},\bar{y}_{i+1})$, since $y(x_{i+1})$ is unknown.

Euler's algorithm of (6.60) may be viewed as a *predicting* equation for $\bar{y}_{i+1}^{(1)}$ (the first approximation to y_{i+1}), whereas (6.59) may be considered a *correcting* equation to produce an improved estimate of y_{i+1}. Equation (6.59) may be used iteratively to produce a sequence of corrected y_{i+1} values, $\bar{y}_{i+1}^{(2)}, \bar{y}_{i+1}^{(3)}, \ldots, \bar{y}_{i+1}^{(m)}$. In this case, the pair of

$\bar{y}_{i+1/2}$ is obtained at the halfway point $x_i + h/2$. Second, (6.61) evaluates $f(x,y)$ for $x = x_i + h/2$, $y = \bar{y}_{i+1/2}$, and uses this as the average derivative for proceeding over the whole interval.

The higher-order Runge-Kutta methods are developed analogously. For example, the increment function for the third-order method is

$$\phi = ak_1 + bk_2 + ck_3,$$

where k_1, k_2, and k_3 approximate the derivative at various points on the integration interval $x_i \leqslant x \leqslant x_{i+1}$. In this case,

$$k_1 = f(x_i,y_i),$$

$$k_2 = f(x_i + ph, y_i + phk_1),$$

$$k_3 = f(x_i + rh, y_i + shk_1 + (r - s)hk_2).$$

The *third-order* Runge-Kutta algorithms are given by

$$y_{i+1} = y_i + h(ak_1 + bk_2 + ck_3). \qquad (6.63)$$

To determine the constants a, b, c, p, r, and s, we first expand k_2 and k_3 about (x_i, y_i) in Taylor's series as functions of two variables. The object function $y(x)$ is expanded in a Taylor's series as before, (6.25). Coefficients of like powers of h through the h^3 terms in (6.63) and (6.25) are equated to produce a formula with a local truncation error of order h^4. Details of the argument are essentially the same as in the development of the second-order methods.

Again, there are fewer equations than unknowns:

$$a + b + c = 1,$$
$$bp + cr = \tfrac{1}{2},$$
$$bp^2 + cr^2 = \tfrac{1}{3},$$
$$cps = \tfrac{1}{6}.$$

Two of the constants a, b, c, p, r, and s are arbitrary. For one set of constants, selected by Kutta, the third-order method is:

$$y_{i+1} = y_i + \frac{h}{6}(k_1 + 4k_2 + k_3),$$

$$k_1 = f(x_i, y_i),$$
$$k_2 = f(x_i + \tfrac{1}{2}h, y_i + \tfrac{1}{2}h, k_1), \qquad (6.64)$$
$$k_3 = f(x_i + h, y_i + 2hk_2 - hk_1).$$

Note that if $f(x,y)$ is a function of x only, then (6.64) reduces to Simpson's rule (2.21b).

All the *fourth-order* formulas are of the form

$$y_{i+1} = y_i + h(ak_1 + bk_2 + ck_3 + dk_4), \qquad (6.65)$$

where k_1, k_2, k_3, and k_4 are approximate derivative values computed on the interval $x_i \leqslant x \leqslant x_{i+1}$. Several fourth-order algorithms are used. The following is attributed to Runge:

$$y_{i+1} = y_i + \frac{h}{6}(k_1 + 2k_2 + 2k_3 + k_4),$$

$$k_1 = f(x_i, y_i),$$
$$k_2 = f(x_i + \tfrac{1}{2}h, y_i + \tfrac{1}{2}hk_1), \qquad (6.66)$$
$$k_3 = f(x_i + \tfrac{1}{2}h, y_i + \tfrac{1}{2}hk_2),$$
$$k_4 = f(x_i + h, y_i + hk_3).$$

Again, note that (6.66) reduces to Simpson's rule if $f(x,y)$ is a function of x only. Another fourth-order method, ascribed to Kutta, is:

$$y_{i+1} = y_i + \frac{h}{8}(k_1 + 3k_2 + 3k_3 + k_4),$$

$$k_1 = f(x_i, y_i),$$
$$k_2 = f(x_i + \tfrac{1}{3}h, y_i + \tfrac{1}{3}hk_1), \qquad (6.67)$$
$$k_3 = f(x_i + \tfrac{2}{3}h, y_i - \tfrac{1}{3}hk_1 + hk_2),$$
$$k_4 = f(x_i + h, y_i + hk_1 - hk_2 + hk_3).$$

This reduces to Simpson's second rule (2.21c) if $f(x,y)$ is a function of x only.

The most widely used fourth-order method (and very likely the most widely used single-step method for solving ordinary differential equations as well) is the one credited to Gill [6]:

$$y_{i+1} = y_i + \frac{h}{6}\left[k_1 + 2\left(1 - \frac{1}{\sqrt{2}}\right)k_2 \right.$$
$$\left. + 2\left(1 + \frac{1}{\sqrt{2}}\right)k_3 + k_4 \right],$$

$$k_1 = f(x_i, y_i),$$
$$k_2 = f(x_i + \tfrac{1}{2}h, y_i + \tfrac{1}{2}hk_1), \qquad (6.68)$$
$$k_3 = f\left(x_i + \frac{1}{2}h, y_i + \left(-\frac{1}{2} + \frac{1}{\sqrt{2}}\right)hk_1 \right.$$
$$\left. + \left(1 - \frac{1}{\sqrt{2}}\right)hk_2 \right),$$
$$k_4 = f\left(x_i + h, y_i - \frac{1}{\sqrt{2}}hk_2 + \left(1 + \frac{1}{\sqrt{2}}\right)hk_3 \right).$$

Originally, the constants were chosen to reduce the amount of temporary storage required in the solution of sizable systems of first-order equations. With the advent of machines having large memories, the necessity for saving a few memory locations has largely disappeared, but the Runge-Kutta subroutines in most computer-program libraries still employ the Gill constants.

Runge-Kutta formulas of higher order can be developed by extending the procedures outlined in this section (families of fifth-order formulas can be found in [25, 40, 41].)

6.6   Truncation Error, Stability, and Step-Size Control in the Runge-Kutta Algorithms

Since the mth-order Runge-Kutta algorithms of Section 6.5 were generated by requiring that (6.50) agree with the Taylor's expansion of the solution function $y(x)$ through terms of order h^m, the local truncation error e_t is of the form

$$e_t = Kh^{m+1} + O(h^{m+2}), \qquad (6.69)$$

where K depends (in a complicated way usually) upon $f(x,y)$ and its higher-order partial derivatives. If one assumes that h is sufficiently small, so that the error is dominated by the first term in (6.69), it is possible, though not at all simple, to find bounds for K [7, 8]. In general, such bounds depend upon bounds for $f(x, y)$ and its various partial derivatives, and upon the particular Runge-Kutta method used. Ralston [8] shows that particular choices of the free parameters in the underdetermined equations for the constants in the algorithm [for example, (6.57)] will minimize the upper bound on K.

In order to choose a reasonable step size, one needs some estimate of the error being committed in integrating across one step. On the one hand, the step size should be small enough to achieve required accuracy (if possible); on the other, it should be as large as possible in order to keep rounding errors (a function of the number of arithmetic operations performed) under control and to avoid an excessive number of derivative evaluations. This latter consideration is very important, particularly when the differential equation is complicated and each derivative evaluation requires substantial computing time. For the *m*th-order methods of the previous section, the derivative must be evaluated *m* times for *each* integration step.

One approach to this problem is to assume that the local truncation errors have the form Kh^{m+1} with K constant, and that the local truncation error, committed in traversing one step, dominates the change in total error for the step. Then an estimate of the local truncation error can be found by integrating between two points, say x_n and x_{n+1}, using two different step sizes h_1 and h_2 to evaluate y_{n+1}; let the corresponding solutions be $y_{n+1,1}$ and $y_{n+1,2}$. Then if y_{n+1}^* is the "true" solution, we can employ Richardson's extrapolation technique described on page 78 as follows*:

$$y_{n+1}^* - y_{n+1,1} = Kh_1^{m+1}\frac{(x_{n+1} - x_n)}{h_1},$$

$$y_{n+1}^* - y_{n+1,2} = Kh_2^{m+1}\frac{(x_{n+1} - x_n)}{h_2}. \tag{6.70}$$

Dividing the first of these equations by the second, and solving for y_{n+1}^* yields

$$y_{n+1}^* = \frac{y_{n+1,1} - y_{n+1,2}(h_1/h_2)^m}{1 - (h_1/h_2)^m}. \tag{6.71}$$

If we choose $h_2 = h_1/2$, (6.71) becomes

$$y_{n+1}^* = \frac{y_{n+1,1} - 2^m y_{n+1,2}}{1 - 2^m}, \tag{6.72}$$

and an estimate of the local truncation error for the solution $y_{n+1,1}$, assuming that $(x_{n+1} - x_n) = h_1$, is given by (6.70) and (6.72) as

$$e_t = Kh_1^{m+1} = \frac{2^m(y_{n+1,2} - y_{n+1,1})}{2^m - 1}. \tag{6.73}$$

For the fourth-order Runge-Kutta method, $m = 4$ and (6.73) becomes

$$e_t = Kh_1^5 = \frac{16}{15}(y_{n+1,2} - y_{n+1,1}). \tag{6.74}$$

Unfortunately, if we use (6.73) as a monitoring procedure for the integration step size on every integration interval, the total number of calculations is approximately trebled over the number required for integration using just one step size, h_1. As a compromise, we could use the monitoring procedure less frequently, for instance, for every kth step.

Another criterion, suggested by Collatz [9] for the Runge-Kutta method of (6.66), is to calculate $|(k_3 - k_2)/(k_2 - k_1)|$ after each integration step. If the ratio becomes large (more than a few hundredths [10]), then the step size should be decreased. This is only a very qualitative guideline, but has the virtue that the added computation is negligible.

If m is odd, Call and Reeves [11] suggest integrating in the reverse direction, from x_{n+1} to x_n with h replaced by $-h$, after having integrated across the step in the forward direction. The truncation error is estimated as half the difference between y_n and y_n^*, where y_n^* is the solution found as a result of the reverse integration. Unfortunately, when m is even, the method fails, since the truncation errors in one direction exactly cancel those in the other and, aside from rounding errors, $y_n = y_n^*$.

Determining a bound for the accumulated or propagated error for the Runge-Kutta algorithms is difficult [12,13]. Reported bounds are usually very conservative [7]; in addition, the parameters essential for their computation are only rarely available. In general, if the local truncation error for a one-step method is of $O(h^{m+1})$, then the accumulated error will be of $O(h^m)$, [3,4], that is, the reduction in the order of the error is similar to that observed for Euler's method.

All the Runge-Kutta methods can be shown [2] to be convergent, that is, $\lim_{h\to 0}(y_i - y(x_i)) = 0$ (see page 347). Another criterion for selecting an algorithm for the solution of a differential equation with given initial conditions is *stability*. Stability is a somewhat ambiguous term and appears in the literature with a variety of qualifying adjectives (inherent, partial, relative, weak, strong, absolute, etc.). In general, a solution is said to be *unstable* if errors introduced at some stage in the calculations (for example, from erroneous initial conditions or local truncation or round-off errors) are propagated without bound throughout subsequent calculations.

Certain equations with specified initial conditions cannot be solved by any step-by-step integration procedure without exhibiting instability, and are said to be *inherently* unstable. For example, consider the equation of (6.19),

$$\frac{dy}{dx} = f(x,y) = x + y,$$

for which the analytical solution is given by (6.23) as

$$y(x) = -x - 1 + [1 + x_0 + y(x_0)]e^{-x_0}e^x.$$

With the initial condition $y(0) = -1$, the analytical solution is

$$y(x) = -x - 1.$$

---

* Throughout this section, n should be considered as a general subscript, and not the subscript of the final base point as in (6.5).

Thus the exponential term in the general solution vanishes because of the particular choice of the initial condition. Even a very tiny change in the initial condition (for example, $y(0) = -0.99999$) will eventually cause a drastic change in the magnitude (even the sign in this case) of the solution for large values of x. Therefore, even though the multiple of the exponential term is quite small, the contribution of the exponential term will eventually swamp the contribution of the linear terms in the solution. When such an equation is solved by using one of the one-step methods, each new step may be viewed as the solution of a new initial-value problem. Even if the initial condition is error-free for the first step, the initial conditions for subsequent steps will inevitably contain errors introduced by truncation and round-off in preceding steps; the calculated solution for large x will bear no resemblance to the true solution.

Inherent instability is associated with the equation being solved and the initial conditions specified, but does not depend on the particular algorithm being used. Depending on the equation being solved, its initial conditions, *and* the particular one-step method being used, another form of instability, *partial instability* [15], may be observed, even when the equation is not inherently unstable. This phenomenon is related to the step size chosen, and is perhaps seen most easily by examining the Euler's method of algorithm of (6.28b). From (6.38), the total error at x_{i+1} is related to the total error at x_i by

$$\varepsilon_{i+1} = \varepsilon_i + h[f(x_i, y_i) - f(x_i, y(x_i))] - \frac{h^2}{2} f'(\xi, y(\xi)),$$
$$(6.75)$$

where $x_i < \xi < x_{i+1}$. From the differential mean-value theorem of page 9, we may write

$$f(x_i, y_i) - f(x_i, y(x_i)) = (y_i - y(x_i)) \frac{\partial f}{\partial y}\Big|_{x_i, \alpha}$$

with α in $(y_i, y(x_i))$. Since $[y_i - y(x_i)]$ is just ε_i, (6.75) may be written

$$\varepsilon_{i+1} = \varepsilon_i \left(1 + h \frac{\partial f}{\partial y}\Big|_{x_i, \alpha}\right) - \frac{h^2}{2} f'(\xi, y(\xi)),$$

$$\xi \text{ in } (x_i, x_{i+1}), \quad \alpha \text{ in } (y_i, y(x_i)). \quad (6.76)$$

The first term on the right-hand side of (6.76) is the contribution of the propagated error to the error at x_{i+1} while the second term is the local truncation error. Clearly, if $\partial f/\partial y$ is negative, then a value of h can be found which will make $[1 + h(\partial f/\partial y)] < 1$, and the error will tend to diminish or die out: the solution will be stable. If $[1 + h(\partial f/\partial y)] > 1$, that is, for $\partial f/\partial y$ positive, the error at x_i will be amplified in traversing the ith step, and the solution will tend toward instability. Even in these cases, however, it may be possible to keep the propagation

error under control, especially during the early course of the integration, by choosing a sufficiently small h, that is, by keeping the *propagation factor* $[1 + h(\partial f/\partial y)]$ close to 1.

Suppose that $\partial f/\partial y$ is positive and constant, so that the propagation factor is greater than one for all h and the error does increase without bound for increasing x as shown by (6.76). For example, consider equation (6.15),

$$\frac{dy}{dx} = 2y,$$

for which the solution (6.18) is

$$y(x) = y(x_0)e^{2(x - x_0)}.$$

Will the unbounded growth of the error invalidate the computed solution? Not necessarily, since the solution itself is unbounded for increasing x. The most important criterion is not that the *absolute* error ε_i be bounded, but that the *relative* error ε_i/y_i not grow appreciably.

Similar, though more complicated, propagation factors can be developed for higher-order one-step methods [3]. The quantity $h(\partial f/\partial y)$, sometimes called the *step factor*, contributes to these propagation factors in a manner comparable to that for Euler's method. Collatz [9] suggests that the step factor be kept essentially constant during the course of the integration, leading to another method of controlling the step size.

6.7 Simultaneous Ordinary Differential Equations

Consider the solution of the following system of n simultaneous first-order ordinary differential equations in the dependent variables $y_1, y_2, \ldots, y_n$:

$$\frac{dy_1}{dx} = f_1(x, y_1, y_2, \ldots, y_n),$$

$$\frac{dy_2}{dx} = f_2(x, y_1, y_2, \ldots, y_n),$$

$$\vdots \qquad\qquad (6.77)$$

$$\frac{dy_n}{dx} = f_n(x, y_1, y_2, \ldots, y_n),$$

with initial conditions given at a common point (x_0), that is,

$$y_1(x_0) = y_{1,0},$$
$$y_2(x_0) = y_{2,0},$$
$$\vdots \qquad\qquad (6.78)$$
$$y_n(x_0) = y_{n,0}.$$

The solution of such a system is, at least in principle, no more difficult than the solution of a single first-order equation. The algorithm selected is applied to each of the n equations in parallel at each step.

Since a single high-order equation

$$\frac{d^m y}{dx^m} = F\left(x, y, \frac{dy}{dx}, \frac{d^2 y}{dx^2}, \ldots, \frac{d^{m-1} y}{dx^{m-1}}\right), \qquad (6.79)$$

with appropriate initial conditions

$$y(x_0), \frac{dy(x_0)}{dx}, \ldots, \frac{d^{m-1} y(x_0)}{dx^{m-1}},$$

can always be rewritten as a system of first-order equations of the form of (6.77) [see, for example, (6.2), (6.3)], the numerical methods developed in this chapter may be applied indirectly to solve higher-order initial-value problems as well. Initial-value problems involving systems of equations of mixed order may also be reduced to the form of (6.77) in most cases. Depending on how the differential equations are coupled, some of the derivatives in (6.77) may be functions of other derivatives, that is,

$$\frac{dy_j}{dx} = f_j(x, y_1, y_2, \ldots, y_n, f_1, f_2 \ldots, f_{j-1}, f_{j+1}, \ldots f_n).$$

If the equations can be ordered so that, for all j, $dy_j/dx = f_j(x, y_1, y_2, \ldots, y_n, f_1, f_2, \ldots, f_{j-1})$, then the integration schemes of the preceding sections can always be applied. If such an ordering is impossible, then one may compute the particular (dy_j/dx) which cannot be so ordered from

$$\frac{dy_j}{dx} = f_j(x, y_1, y_2, \ldots, y_n, f_1, f_2, \ldots, f_{j-1}, f_{j+1}^*, \ldots, f_n^*)$$

where the starred derivatives must be known or assumed at x_0. Thereafter, one can usually use the most recently computed values for them.

Error analyses comparable to those of Section 6.4 are virtually impossible to implement for the higher-order Runge-Kutta schemes for systems of differential equations. The step-size control mechanisms and stability considerations outlined in the preceding section carry over to the multiple-equation case without appreciable change. In practice, we often solve the equations using different step sizes and observe the behavior of the solutions with regard to apparent convergence and stability.

EXAMPLE 6.3

FOURTH-ORDER RUNGE-KUTTA METHOD
TRANSIENT BEHAVIOR OF A RESONANT CIRCUIT

Problem Statement

Write a general-purpose function named RUNGE that solves a system of n first-order ordinary differential equations

$$\frac{dy_1}{dx} = f_1(x, y_1, y_2, \ldots, y_n)$$

$$\frac{dy_2}{dx} = f_2(x, y_1, y_2, \ldots, y_n) \qquad (6.3.1)$$

$$\vdots$$

$$\frac{dy_n}{dx} = f_n(x, y_1, y_2, \ldots, y_n),$$

using the fourth-order Runge-Kutta method with Runge's constants (6.66).

Consider the circuit of Fig. 6.3.1 containing a capacitor of C farads, a resistor of R ohms, and an inductance of L henries. Assume that the capacitor is initially charged

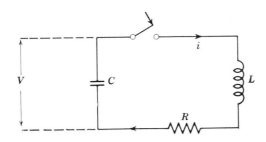

Figure 6.3.1   Electrical circuit.

to a voltage V_0, and that suddenly the switch is closed at time $t = 0$. Show that the ordinary differential equation describing V, the damped oscillation of voltage across the capacitor is given as a function of time by

$$LC \frac{d^2 V}{dt^2} + RC \frac{dV}{dt} + V = 0, \qquad (6.3.2)$$

subject to the initial conditions

$$V(0) = V_0,$$
$$\frac{dV}{dt}(0) = 0. \qquad (6.3.3)$$

Let

$$\bar{\alpha}^2 = \frac{1}{LC} - \frac{R^2}{4L^2}, \qquad (6.3.4)$$
$$\alpha = \sqrt{|\bar{\alpha}^2|},$$

and show that the following analytical solutions satisfy (6.3.2) with conditions (6.3.3):

For $\bar{\alpha}^2 > 0$ (the under-damped or oscillatory case):

$$V = \frac{V_0 \exp\left(-\frac{Rt}{2L}\right) \cos\left(\alpha t - \tan^{-1}\left(\frac{R}{2L\alpha}\right)\right)}{\alpha \sqrt{CL}}. \qquad (6.3.5)$$

For $\bar{\alpha}^2 = 0$ (the critically-damped case):

$$V = V_0 \exp\left(-\frac{Rt}{2L}\right)\left(1 + \frac{Rt}{2L}\right). \qquad (6.3.6)$$

For $\bar{\alpha}^2 < 0$ (the over-damped case):

$$V = V_0 \exp\left(-\frac{Rt}{2L}\right)\left[\left(\frac{1}{2} + \frac{R}{4L\alpha}\right) \exp(\alpha t)\right.$$
$$\left. + \left(\frac{1}{2} - \frac{R}{4L\alpha}\right) \exp(-\alpha t)\right]. \qquad (6.3.7)$$

Write a test program that calls on RUNGE to solve the differential equation (6.3.2) with initial conditions (6.3.3), and then compares the numerical solution with the value of the appropriate analytical solution. For test purposes, consider the following cases:

$$V_0 = 100 \text{ volts}$$
$$C = 2 \times 10^{-6} \text{ farads}$$
$$L = 0.5 \text{ henries}$$
$$R = 0, 100, 1000, \text{ and } 1500 \text{ ohms}.$$

Use step-size $h = 0.0001$ sec and tabulate the solutions at reasonable intervals in time during the first $t_{max} = 0.2$ sec. Observe the effects of step-size variation by finding numerical solutions for the cases:

$$V_0 = 100 \text{ volts}$$
$$C = 2 \times 10^{-6} \text{ farads}$$
$$L = 0.5 \text{ henries}$$
$$R = 100 \text{ ohms}$$
$$h = 0.00001, 0.0001, 0.001, 0.002, 0.005, 0.01.$$

Method of Solution

The fourth-order Runge-Kutta algorithm of (6.66) for the one-step integration of a single first-order equation (6.4) with one appropriate initial condition, $y_i \doteq y(x_i)$, may be written for a system of n first-order equations (6.3.1) with n initial conditions,

$$y_{ji} \doteq y_j(x_i), \qquad j = 1, 2, \ldots, n.$$

Here, y_{ji} is the solution of the jth equation in (6.3.1) at x_i. The initial conditions for the zeroth step, $y_{j0}, j = 1, 2, \ldots, n$, will usually be known exactly. Thereafter, the initial conditions for the ith step will be approximations to the true initial conditions, $y_j(x_i), j = 1, 2, \ldots, n$, since

367

they will result from applications of the Runge-Kutta method on the $(i-1)$th interval. For a system of n equations, the one-step integration across the ith interval may be described by:

$$y_{j,i+1} = y_{ji} + h\phi_j = y_{ji} + h(\tfrac{1}{6}k_{j1} + \tfrac{1}{3}k_{j2} + \tfrac{1}{3}k_{j3} + \tfrac{1}{6}k_{j4})$$
$$(6.3.8a)$$

$$k_{j1} = f_j(x_i, y_{1i}, y_{2i}, \ldots, y_{ni}), \qquad (6.3.8b)$$

$$y_{ji}^* = y_{ji} + \tfrac{1}{2}hk_{j1}, \qquad (6.3.8c)$$

$$k_{j2} = f_j(x_i + \tfrac{1}{2}h, y_{1i}^*, y_{2i}^*, \ldots, y_{ni}^*), \qquad (6.3.8d)$$

$$\bar{y}_{ji} = y_{ji} + \tfrac{1}{2}hk_{j2}, \qquad (6.3.8e)$$

$$k_{j3} = f_j(x_i + \tfrac{1}{2}h, \bar{y}_{1i}, \bar{y}_{2i}, \ldots, \bar{y}_{ni}), \qquad (6.3.8f)$$

$$\bar{y}_{ji}^* = y_{ji} + hk_{j3}, \qquad (6.3.8g)$$

$$k_{j4} = f_j(x_i + h, \bar{y}_{1i}^*, \bar{y}_{2i}^*, \ldots, \bar{y}_{ni}^*). \qquad (6.3.8h)$$

The relationships in (6.3.8) are applied in parallel at each point in the algorithm for all n equations, that is, for $j = 1, 2, \ldots, n$.

Because the Runge-Kutta method is a one-step method, the subscript i throughout (6.3.8) is, in a sense, superfluous. In addition, because the k_{j1} are not needed after the y_{ji}^* are computed, and the y_{ji}^* in turn are not needed after the k_{j2} are computed, etc., it is possible to write a general-purpose Runge-Kutta function and calling program which require relatively few memory locations for retention of the many variables appearing in (6.3.8). The entire algorithm of (6.3.8) will be implemented in program form as outlined below.

Let four vectors of length at least n be denoted by the names Y, $\bar{Y}$, F, and ϕ. Before carrying out the Runge-Kutta integration for the ith step, the following variables must be initialized:

$x \leftarrow x_i$, value of the independent variable.

$h \leftarrow h$, step size for integration across the ith step, $x_{i+1} - x_i$.

$n \leftarrow n$, number of first-order differential equations.

$Y_j \leftarrow y_{ji}, j = 1, 2, \ldots, n$, solution values for the n equations at x_i.

Then (6.3.8) may be described by a five-pass procedure.

Pass 1

1. Calculate the values $f_j, j = 1, 2, \ldots, n$, using the current x and Y_j values. These are equivalent to the values $k_{j1}, j = 1, 2, \ldots, n$, of (6.3.8b).

$$F_j \leftarrow f_j(x, Y_1, Y_2, \ldots, Y_n) = k_{j1}$$
$$= f_j(x_i, y_{1i}, y_{2i}, \ldots, y_{ni}), \quad j = 1, 2, \ldots, n.$$
$$(6.3.9)$$

Pass 2

2. Save the current values $Y_j, j = 1, 2, \ldots, n$, in another vector of equal length, $\bar{Y}$. This assigns the solution values at the beginning of the ith step to the vector $\bar{Y}$.

$$\bar{Y}_j \leftarrow Y_j = y_{ji}, \qquad j = 1, 2, \ldots, n. \quad (6.3.10)$$

3. Begin accumulation of the values $\phi_j, j = 1, 2, \ldots, n$, in (6.3.8a).

$$\phi_j \leftarrow F_j = k_{j1}, \qquad j = 1, 2, \ldots, n. \quad (6.3.11)$$

4. Compute the values $y_{ji}^*, j = 1, 2, \ldots, n$, in (6.3.8c) and assign them to elements of the vector Y.

$$Y_j \leftarrow \bar{Y}_j + \frac{h}{2} F_j = y_{ji}^* = y_{ji} + \frac{h}{2} k_{j1}, \quad j = 1, 2, \ldots, n.$$
$$(6.3.12)$$

5. Increment x to the value needed in (6.3.8d).

$$x \leftarrow x + \frac{h}{2} = x_i + \frac{h}{2}. \quad (6.3.13)$$

6. Calculate the values $f_j, j = 1, 2, \ldots, n$, using the current x and Y_j values. These are equivalent to the values $k_{j2}, j = 1, 2, \ldots, n$, of (6.3.8d).

$$F_j \leftarrow f_j(x, Y_1, Y_2, \ldots, Y_n) = k_{j2}$$
$$= f_j\left(x_i + \frac{h}{2}, y_{1i}^*, y_{2i}^*, \ldots, y_{ni}^*\right), \quad j = 1, 2, \ldots, n.$$
$$(6.3.14)$$

Pass 3

7. Add the contribution of k_{j2} to $\phi_j, j = 1, 2, \ldots, n$, in (6.3.8a).

$$\phi_j \leftarrow \phi_j + 2F_j = k_{j1} + 2k_{j2}. \quad (6.3.15)$$

8. Compute the values $\bar{y}_{ji}, j = 1, 2, \ldots, n$, in (6.3.8e) and assign them to elements of the vector Y.

$$Y_j \leftarrow \bar{Y}_j + \frac{h}{2} F_j = \bar{y}_{ji} = y_{ji} + \frac{h}{2} k_{j2}, \quad j = 1, 2, \ldots, n.$$
$$(6.3.16)$$

9. Calculate the values $f_j, j = 1, 2, \ldots, n$, using the current x and Y_j values. These are equivalent to the values $k_{j3}, j = 1, 2, \ldots, n$, of (6.3.8f).

$$F_j \leftarrow f_j(x, Y_1, Y_2, \ldots, Y_n) = k_{j3}$$
$$= f_j\left(x_i + \frac{h}{2}, \bar{y}_{1i}, \bar{y}_{2i}, \ldots, \bar{y}_{ni}\right), \quad j = 1, 2, \ldots, n.$$
$$(6.3.17)$$

Pass 4

10. Add the contribution of k_{j3} to $\phi_j, j = 1, 2, \ldots, n$, in (6.3.8a).

$$\phi_j \leftarrow \phi_j + 2F_j = k_{j1} + 2k_{j2} + 2k_{j3}, \quad j = 1, 2, \ldots, n.$$
$$(6.3.18)$$

11. Compute the values $\bar{y}_{ji}^*, j = 1, 2, \ldots, n$, in (6.3.8g) and assign them to elements of the vector Y.

$$Y_j \leftarrow \bar{Y}_j + hF_j = \bar{y}_{ji}^* = y_{ji} + hk_{j3}, \quad j = 1, 2, \ldots, n.$$
$$(6.3.19)$$

12. Increment x to the value needed in (6.3.8h).

$$x \leftarrow x + \frac{h}{2} = x_i + h = x_{i+1}. \qquad (6.3.20)$$

13. Calculate the values $f_j, j = 1, 2, \ldots, n$, using the current x and Y_j values. These are equivalent to the values $k_{j4}, j = 1, 2, \ldots, n$, of (6.3.8h).

$$F_j \leftarrow f_j(x, Y_1, Y_2, \ldots, Y_n) = k_{j4}$$
$$= f_j(x_i + h, \bar{y}_{1i}^*, \bar{y}_{2i}^*, \ldots, \bar{y}_{ni}^*), \qquad j = 1, 2, \ldots, n. \qquad (6.3.21)$$

Pass 5

14. Complete the evaluation of $\phi_j, j = 1, 2, \ldots, n$, in (6.3.8a).

$$\phi_j \leftarrow (\phi_j + F_j)/6 = (k_{j1} + 2k_{j2} + 2k_{j3} + k_{j4})/6. \qquad (6.3.22)$$

15. Compute the values $y_{j,i+1}, j = 1, 2, \ldots, n$, in (6.3.8a) and assign them to elements of the Y vector.

$$Y_j \leftarrow \bar{Y}_j + h\phi_j = y_{ji} + h\phi_j, \qquad j = 1, 2, \ldots, n. \qquad (6.3.23)$$

As a consequence of the procedure described by (6.3.9) to (6.3.23), h and n remain unchanged, and x and the vector Y contain:

$x = x_{i+1}$, value of the independent variable.

$Y_j = y_{j,i+1}, \qquad j = 1, 2, \ldots, n$, solution values for the n equations at x_{i+1}.

All initial values have been assigned for the next integration step, from x_{i+1} to x_{i+2}. The step size, h, may be changed if desired (see Section 6.6). The five-pass procedure of (6.3.9) to (6.3.23) may be repeated for the next step.

Note that the parts of the procedure given by (6.3.9), (6.3.14), (6.3.17), and (6.3.21) are identical,

$$F_j \leftarrow f_j(x, Y_1, Y_2, \ldots, Y_n), \qquad j = 1, 2, \ldots, n, \qquad (6.3.24)$$

and are the only ones that refer directly to the n differential equations, $f_j, j = 1, 2, \ldots, n$, of (6.3.1). Therefore, it is possible to write a general-purpose function called RUNGE that implements all parts of the procedure outlined, *except* for initialization of n, x, h, and $Y_j, j = 1, 2, \ldots, n$, and steps (6.3.9), (6.3.14), (6.3.17), and (6.3.21). The calling program will then contain all information about the specific system of differential equations, and be responsible for printing results, changing the step size, terminating the integration process, and evaluating the F_j when needed.

The five passes of the algorithm can be handled by five different calls upon RUNGE, as shown schematically in Fig. 6.3.2. Let a step counter, m, preset to 0, be maintained by the function RUNGE, and let the value returned by RUNGE signal the calling program to indicate whether the $F_j, j = 1, 2, \ldots, n$, of (6.3.24) are to be computed (following the first four passes) or not (when integration across one step is completed following the fifth pass). Let the value returned be 1 when the F_j are to be evaluated and 0 when one complete integration step is completed.

The main program used to test the function RUNGE solves the second-order ordinary differential equation (6.3.2) subject to initial conditions (6.3.3). Since the charge, q, on a capacitor is related to the capacitance, C, and voltage, V, by

$$q = CV, \qquad (6.3.25)$$

the current, i, into the capacitor is given by

$$i = -\frac{dq}{dt} = -C\frac{dV}{dt}. \qquad (6.3.26)$$

The voltage, V, across a resistor and inductance in series is given by

$$V = L\frac{di}{dt} + Ri. \qquad (6.3.27)$$

Then, from (6.3.26) and (6.3.27), the voltage across the capacitor as a function of time is given by (6.3.2),

$$\frac{d^2V}{dt^2} = -\frac{R}{L}\frac{dV}{dt} - \frac{1}{LC}V. \qquad (6.3.28)$$

The initial conditions are

$$V(0) = V_0,$$
$$\frac{dV}{dt}(0) = 0. \qquad (6.3.29)$$

Differentiation of the three proposed solutions, (6.3.5), (6.3.6), and (6.3.7), and substitution into (6.3.28), shows that, for the given value of $\bar{\alpha}^2$, each satisfies (6.3.28) and initial conditions (6.3.29).

The second-order equation (6.3.28) must be rewritten as a system of two first-order equations. Let

$$Y_1 = V,$$
$$Y_2 = \frac{dV}{dt}, \qquad (6.3.30)$$
$$x = t.$$

Then

$$F_1 = \frac{dY_1}{dx} = \frac{dV}{dt} = Y_2,$$

$$F_2 = \frac{dY_2}{dx^2} = \frac{d^2V}{dt^2} = -\frac{R}{L}\frac{dV}{dt} - \frac{1}{LC}V = -\frac{R}{L}Y_2 - \frac{1}{LC}Y_1. \qquad (6.3.31)$$

The initial conditions of (6.3.29) are

$$Y_{1,0} = V_0,$$
$$Y_{2,0} = 0. \qquad (6.3.32)$$

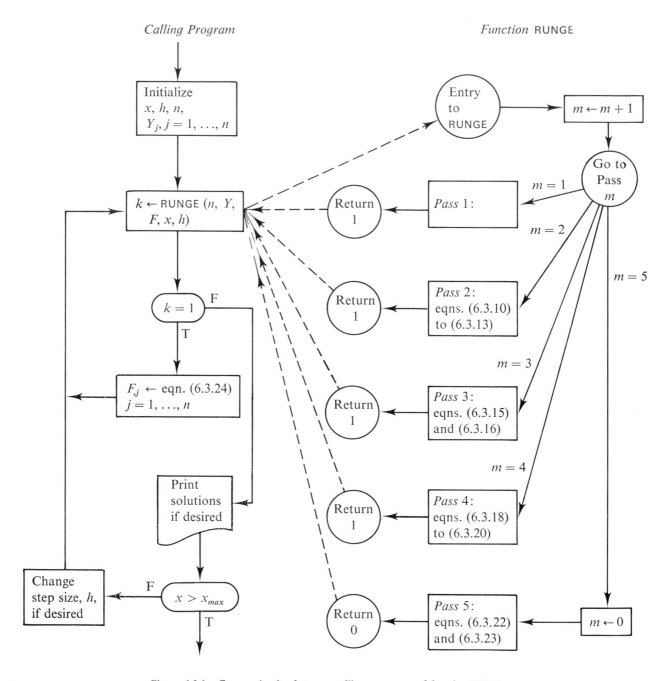

Figure 6.3.2   Communication between calling program and function RUNGE.

Flow Diagram

Main Program

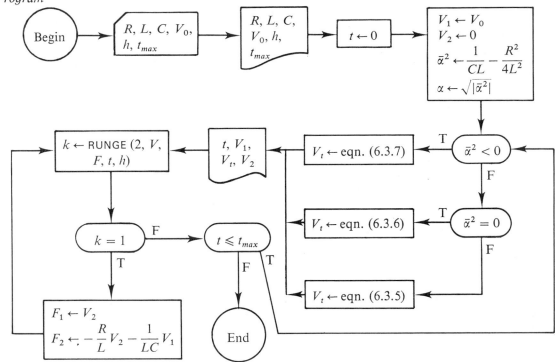

Function RUNGE   (Dummy arguments: n, Y, F, x, h; calling arguments: 2, V, F, t, h)

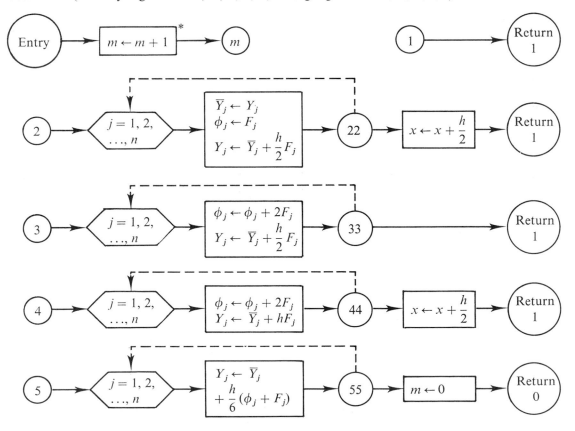

* m is assumed to be preset to zero, before RUNGE is called for the first time.

FORTRAN *Implementation*

List of Principal Variables

Program Symbol	Definition
(Main)	
ALPHA, ALPHSQ	α and $\bar{\alpha}^2$, respectively.
C	Capacitance, C, farads.
F	Vector of derivative approximations, F_j (see (6.3.24)).
H	Step size, h.
HL	Inductance, L, henries.
ICOUNT	Step counter.
IFREQ	Frequency of intermediate printout. Solutions are printed at $t = 0$ and after every IFREQ steps thereafter.
IFPLOT	Variable to control plotting of solutions on printer. If IFPLOT = 1, a plot is prepared by calling on PLOT1, PLOT2, etc.; if IFPLOT $\neq$ 1, no plot is prepared.
IMAGE	Large vector used to store image of plot before printing.
K	Value returned by RUNGE. If K = 1, the elements of F are to be calculated, if K $\neq$ 1, one step of the integration is completed.
PLOT1, PLOT2, PLOT3, PLOT4	Subroutines used for preparing on-line graph of V against t. See Examples 7.1 and 8.5 for further details.
R	Resistance, R, ohms.
RO2L	$R/(2L)$.
T	Time, t, sec.
TMAX	Upper limit of integration, t_{max}, sec.
TRUV	True voltage at time t, V_t, calculated from analytical solutions of (6.3.2) subject to initial conditions (6.3.3).
V	Vector of solutions of (6.3.2) computed by the function RUNGE. V(1) = V, volts. V(2) = dV/dt, volts/sec.
VZERO	Initial voltage across capacitor, V_0, volts.
(Function RUNGE)	
J	Subscript, j
M	Pass counter for the Runge-Kutta algorithm, m. Must be preset to 0 before first call upon RUNGE.
N	Number of equations, n.
PHI	Vector of values, ϕ_j.
SAVEY	Vector of initial conditions, $\bar{Y}_j$ (see (6.3.10)).
X	Independent variable, x.
Y	Vector of dependent variable (solution) values, Y_j.

Program Listing

Main Program

```
C        APPLIED NUMERICAL METHODS, EXAMPLE 6.3
C        ELECTRICAL TRANSIENTS USING THE RUNGE-KUTTA METHOD
C
C        THIS TEST PROGRAM CALLS ON THE FUNCTION RUNGE TO SOLVE
C        THE DIFFERENTIAL EQUATION V'' = -R*V'/HL - V/(HL*C) SUBJECT
C        TO THE INITIAL CONDITIONS V(0.0) = VZERO AND V'(0.0) = 0.0.
C        V(1) AND V(2) ARE THE VALUES OF V AND V' RESPECTIVELY.  F(1)
C        AND F(2) ARE THE DERIVATIVES OF V(1) AND V(2) RESPECTIVELY.
C        R, HL, AND C ARE THE RESISTANCE, INDUCTANCE, AND CAPACITANCE
C        (IN OHMS, HENRIES, AND FARADS) OF A CIRCUIT (SEE FIGURE)
C        IN WHICH THE CAPACITOR IS CHARGED TO A VOLTAGE VZERO AT TIME
C        ZERO.  T (TIME IN SECONDS) IS THE INDEPENDENT VARIABLE, H IS
C        THE STEPSIZE, AND TMAX THE UPPER INTEGRATION LIMIT USED IN
C        THE RUNGE-KUTTA INTEGRATION.  THE EQUATION WITH THE GIVEN
C        INITIAL CONDITIONS DESCRIBES THE DAMPED OSCILLATION OF VOLTAGE
C        ACROSS THE CAPACITOR UPON CLOSURE OF THE CIRCUIT.  TRUV IS
C        THE ANALYTICAL SOLUTION WHICH APPLIES FOR THE UNDER-DAMPED,
C        CRITICALLY DAMPED OR OVER-DAMPED CASE DEPENDING ON THE VALUE
C        OF ALPHSQ=1/(C*HL)-R*R/(4*HL*HL) (POSITIVE, ZERO, AND NEGATIVE
C        VALUE RESPECTIVELY).  K IS THE VALUE RETURNED BY THE FUNCTION
C        RUNGE.  IT EQUALS  1  WHEN THE DERIVATIVES ARE TO BE
C        CALCULATED AND  0  WHEN INTEGRATION ACROSS ONE STEP IS
C        COMPLETE.  ICOUNT IS A STEP COUNTER.  RESULTS ARE PRINTED
C        AFTER EVERY IFREQ INTEGRATION STEPS.  IF IFPLOT = 1, THE
C        RESULTS ARE ALSO PLOTTED USING THE LIBRARY SUBROUTINES
C        PLOT1, PLOT2, PLOT3, AND PLOT4.
C
      IMPLICIT  REAL*8(A-H, O-Z)
      INTEGER  RUNGE
      DIMENSION F(2), V(2), IMAGE(1500)
C
C     ..... READ AND PRINT DATA .....
    1 READ (5,100) R,HL,C,VZERO,H,TMAX,IFREQ,IFPLOT
      WRITE (6,200) R,HL,C,VZERO,H,TMAX,IFREQ,IFPLOT
C
C     ..... INITIALIZE T, V(1), V(2), AND ICOUNT .....
      T = 0.0
      V(1) = VZERO
      V(2) = 0.0
      ICOUNT = 0
C
C     ..... COMPUTE ALPHSQ AND ALPHA, PRINT HEADINGS ....,
      ALPHSQ = 1./(C*HL) - R*R/(4.0*HL*HL)
      ALPHA = DSQRT(DABS(ALPHSQ))
      RO2L = R/(2.*HL)
      IF ( IFPLOT.NE.1 )   GO TO 3
         CALL PLOT1( 0, 5, 11, 6, 19 )
         CALL PLOT2( IMAGE,TMAX,0.,DABS(VZERO),-DABS(VZERO) )
    3 WRITE (6,201)
C
C     ..... IS CIRCUIT OVER-, CRITICALLY-, OR UNDER-DAMPED .....
C     ..... COMPUTE ANALYTICAL SOLUTION, PRINT AND PLOT .....
    4 IF (ALPHSQ)   5, 6, 7
    5    TRUV = VZERO*DEXP(-RO2L*T)*((1.+RO2L/ALPHA)*DEXP(ALPHA*T)
     1          +(1.-RO2L/ALPHA)*DEXP(-ALPHA*T))/2.0
         GO TO 8
    6    TRUV = VZERO*DEXP(-RO2L*T)*(1. + RO2L*T)
         GO TO 8
    7    TRUV = VZERO*DEXP(-RO2L*T)*DCOS(ALPHA*T-DATAN(RO2L/ALPHA))
     1          /(ALPHA*DSQRT(C*HL))
    8 IF ( IFPLOT.NE.1 )   GO TO 10
         CALL PLOT3( 1H*,  T,  V(1), 1, 8 )
   10 WRITE (6,202) T,V(1),TRUV,V(2)
C
C     ..... CALL ON THE FOURTH-ORDER RUNGE-KUTTA FUNCTION .....
   11 K = RUNGE( 2, V, F, T, H )
```

Program Listing (*Continued*)

```
C
C          ..... WHENEVER K=1, COMPUTE DERIVATIVE VALUES .....
           IF ( K.NE.1 )    GO TO 13
              F(1) = V(2)
              F(2) = -R*V(2)/HL -V(1)/(HL*C)
              GO TO 11
C
C          ..... IF T EXCEEDS TMAX, TERMINATE INTEGRATION .....
   13      IF ( T.LE.TMAX )    GO TO 16
              IF ( IFPLOT.NE.1 )    GO TO 1
                 WRITE (6,203)
                 CALL PLOT4( 7, 7HVOLTAGE )
                 WRITE (6,204)
                 GO TO 1
   16      ICOUNT = ICOUNT + 1
C
C          ..... PRINT RESULTS OR CALL DIRECTLY ON RUNGE .....
           IF ( ICOUNT.NE.IFREQ )    GO TO 11
           ICOUNT = 0
           GO TO 4
C
C          ..... FORMATS FOR INPUT AND OUTPUT STATEMENTS .....
  100      FORMAT ( 9X, F7.2,14X,F6.2,14X,E6.1/ 10X,F6.2,14X,F7.5,13X,F6.3/
     1       10X,I4,16X,I1 )
  200      FORMAT ( 10H1R      = ,F14.5/ 10H HL      = ,F14.5/10H C      = ,
     1       E14.1   /10H VZERO  = ,F14.5/ 10H H       = ,F14.5/10H TMAX   = ,
     2       F14.5/ 10H IFREQ  = ,I8  / 10H IFPLOT = , I8 )
  201      FORMAT ( 64H0        T             CALC. V           TRUE   V
     1       CALC. V' / 1H )
  202      FORMAT ( 1H , F10.5, 2F18.8, F18.5 )
  203      FORMAT ( 1H1 )
  204      FORMAT ( 1H0, 54X, 16HTIME - (SECONDS) )
C
           END
```

Function RUNGE

```
           FUNCTION RUNGE( N, Y, F, X, H )
C
C          THE FUNCTION RUNGE EMPLOYS THE FOURTH-ORDER RUNGE-KUTTA METHOD
C          WITH RUNGE'S COEFFICIENTS TO INTEGRATE A SYSTEM OF N SIMULTAN-
C          EOUS FIRST ORDER ORDINARY DIFFERENTIAL EQUATIONS F(J)=DY(J)/DX,
C          (J=1,2,...,N), ACROSS ONE STEP OF LENGTH H IN THE INDEPENDENT
C          VARIABLE X, SUBJECT TO INITIAL CONDITIONS Y(J), (J=1,2,...,N).
C          EACH F(J), THE DERIVATIVE OF Y(J), MUST BE COMPUTED FOUR TIMES
C          PER INTEGRATION STEP BY THE CALLING PROGRAM.  THE FUNCTION MUST
C          BE CALLED FIVE TIMES PER STEP (PASS(1)...PASS(5)) SO THAT THE
C          INDEPENDENT VARIABLE VALUE (X) AND THE SOLUTION VALUES
C          (Y(1)...Y(N)) CAN BE UPDATED USING THE RUNGE-KUTTA ALGORITHM.
C          M IS THE PASS COUNTER.  RUNGE RETURNS AS ITS VALUE 1.0 TO
C          SIGNAL THAT ALL DERIVATIVES (THE F(J)) BE EVALUATED OR 0.0 TO
C          SIGNAL THAT THE INTEGRATION PROCESS FOR THE CURRENT STEP IS
C          FINISHED.  SAVEY(J) IS USED TO SAVE THE INITIAL VALUE OF Y(J)
C          AND PHI(J) IS THE INCREMENT FUNCTION FOR THE J(TH) EQUATION.
C          AS WRITTEN, N MAY BE NO LARGER THAN 50.
C
           IMPLICIT  REAL*8(A-H, O-Z)
           REAL*8  Y, F, X, H
           INTEGER  RUNGE
           DIMENSION PHI(50), SAVEY(50), Y(N), F(N)
           DATA M/0/
C
           M = M + 1
           GO TO (1,2,3,4,5), M
C
C          ..... PASS 1 .....
    1      RUNGE = 1
           RETURN
```

Program Listing (*Continued*)

```
C
C       ..... PASS 2 .....
    2   DO 22   J = 1, N
        SAVEY(J) = Y(J)
        PHI(J) = F(J)
   22   Y(J) = SAVEY(J) + 0.5*H*F(J)
        X = X + 0.5*H
        RUNGE = 1
        RETURN
C
C       ..... PASS 3 .....
    3   DO 33   J = 1, N
        PHI(J) = PHI(J) + 2.0*F(J)
   33   Y(J) = SAVEY(J) + 0.5*H*F(J)
        RUNGE = 1
        RETURN
C
C       ..... PASS 4 .....
    4   DO 44   J = 1, N
        PHI(J) = PHI(J) + 2.0*F(J)
   44   Y(J) = SAVEY(J) + H*F(J)
        X = X + 0.5*H
        RUNGE = 1
        RETURN
C
C       ..... PASS 5 .....
    5   DO 55   J = 1, N
   55   Y(J) = SAVEY(J) + (PHI(J) + F(J))*H/6.0
        M = 0
        RUNGE = 0
        RETURN
C
        END
```

Data

R	= 100.00	HL	= 0.50	C	= 2.0E-6
VZERO	= 10.00	H	= 0.00001	TMAX	= 0.025
IFREQ	= 25	IFPLOT	= 1		
R	= 0.00	HL	= 0.50	C	= 2.0E-6
VZERO	= 10.00	H	= 0.00010	TMAX	= 0.020
IFREQ	= 10	IFPLOT	= 0		
R	= 1000.00	HL	= 0.50	C	= 2.0E-6
VZERO	= 10.00	H	= 0.00010	TMAX	= 0.020
IFREQ	= 10	IFPLOT	= 0		
R	= 1500.00	HL	= 0.50	C	= 2.0E-6
VZERO	= 10.00	H	= 0.00010	TMAX	= 0.020
IFREQ	= 10	IFPLOT	= 0		
R	= 100.00	HL	= 0.50	C	= 2.0E-6
VZERO	= 10.00	H	= 0.00001	TMAX	= 0.020
IFREQ	= 100	IFPLOT	= 0		
R	= 100.00	HL	= 0.50	C	= 2.0E-6
VZERO	= 10.00	H	= 0.00010	TMAX	= 0.020
IFREQ	= 10	IFPLOT	= 0		
R	= 100.00	HL	= 0.50	C	= 2.0E-6
VZERO	= 10.00	H	= 0.00100	TMAX	= 0.020
IFREQ	= 1	IFPLOT	= 0		
R	= 100.00	HL	= 0.50	C	= 2.0E-6
VZERO	= 10.00	H	= 0.00200	TMAX	= 0.020
IFREQ	= 1	IFPLOT	= 0		
R	= 100.00	HL	= 0.50	C	= 2.0E-6
VZERO	= 10.00	H	= 0.00500	TMAX	= 0.020
IFREQ	= 1	IFPLOT	= 0		
R	= 100.00	HL	= 0.50	C	= 2.0E-6
VZERO	= 10.00	H	= 0.01000	TMAX	= 0.020
IFREQ	= 1	IFPLOT	= 0		

Computer Output

Plotted Results for 1st Data Set

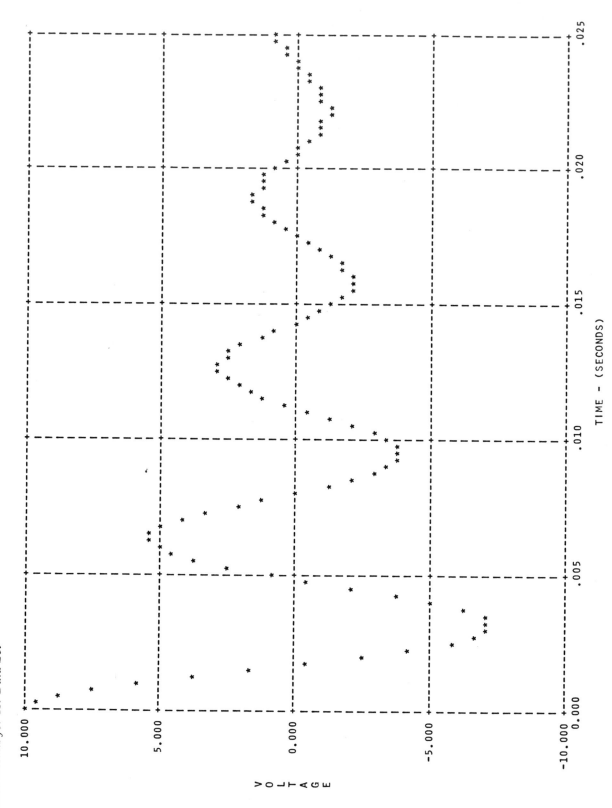

Computer Output (*Continued*)

Results for the 2nd Data Set

R	=	1500.00000
HL	=	0.50000
C	=	0.2D-05
VZERO	=	10.00000
H	=	0.00010
TMAX	=	0.02000
IFREQ	=	10
IFPLOT	=	0

T	CALC. V	TRUE V	CALC. V'
0.0	10.00000000	10.00000000	0.0
0.00100	5.40302967	5.40302306	-8414.70478
0.00200	-4.16145269	-4.16146837	-9092.97992
0.00300	-9.89991939	-9.89992497	-1441.22445
0.00400	-6.53645953	-6.53643621	7568.00114
0.00500	2.83658106	2.83662185	9589.20120
0.00600	9.60168495	9.60170287	2794.20166
0.00700	7.53905707	7.53905707	-6569.81898
0.00800	-1.45493381	-1.45500034	-9893.58664
0.00900	-9.11126613	-9.11130262	-4121.25037
0.01000	-8.39075464	-8.39071529	5440.17766
0.01100	0.44165561	0.44253698	9999.89484
0.01200	8.43847910	8.43853959	5365.80880
0.01300	9.07450499	9.07446781	-4201.56862
0.01400	1.36748601	1.36737218	-9906.04804
0.01500	-7.59679023	-7.59687913	-6502.96626
0.01600	-9.57662243	-9.57659480	2878.90274
0.01700	-2.75176585	-2.75163338	9613.92474
0.01800	6.60306659	6.60316708	7509.96179
0.01900	9.88705680	9.88704618	-1498.61414
0.02000	4.08096657	4.08082062	-9129.37207

Results for the 3rd Data Set

R	=	1000.00000
HL	=	0.50000
C	=	0.2D-05
VZERO	=	10.00000
H	=	0.00010
TMAX	=	0.02000
IFREQ	=	10
IFPLOT	=	0

T	CALC. V	TRUE V	CALC. V'
0.0	10.00000000	10.00000021	0.0
0.00100	7.35757855	7.35758878	-3678.78080
0.00200	4.06005539	4.06005848	-2706.69810
0.00300	1.99148127	1.99148272	-1493.60923
0.00400	0.91578189	0.91578194	-732.62484
0.00500	0.40427710	0.40427682	-336.89732
0.00600	0.17351291	0.17351265	-148.72525
0.00700	0.07295073	0.07295056	-63.83185
0.00800	0.03019173	0.03019164	-26.83708
0.00900	0.01234103	0.01234098	-11.10692
0.01000	0.00499402	0.00499399	-4.54001
0.01100	0.00200422	0.00200420	-1.83720
0.01200	0.00079875	0.00079875	-0.73731
0.01300	0.00031645	0.00031645	-0.29384
0.01400	0.00012473	0.00012473	-0.11641
0.01500	0.00004894	0.00004894	-0.04589
0.01600	0.00001913	0.00001913	-0.01801
0.01700	0.00000745	0.00000745	-0.00704
0.01800	0.00000289	0.00000289	-0.00274
0.01900	0.00000112	0.00000112	-0.00106
0.02000	0.00000043	0.00000043	-0.00041

Results for the 4th Data Set

R	=	500.00000
HL	=	0.50000
C	=	0.2D-05
VZERO	=	10.00000
H	=	0.00010
TMAX	=	0.02000
IFREQ	=	10
IFPLOT	=	0

T	CALC. V	TRUE V	CALC. V'
0.0	10.00000000	10.00000000	0.0
0.00100	7.86644015	7.86645599	-2726.04778
0.00200	5.44495442	5.44495666	-2059.45739
0.00300	3.72182288	3.72182306	-1420.22445
0.00400	2.54061638	2.54061634	-970.32090
0.00500	1.73404656	1.73404650	-662.33895
0.00600	1.18352059	1.18352054	-452.06406
0.00700	0.80777456	0.80777452	-308.54239
0.00800	0.55132090	0.55132087	-210.58584
0.00900	0.37628658	0.37628655	-143.72868
0.01000	0.25682246	0.25682244	-98.09745
0.01100	0.17528602	0.17528600	-66.95330
0.01200	0.11963591	0.11963590	-45.69685
0.01300	0.08165369	0.08165368	-31.18893
0.01400	0.05573013	0.05573013	-21.28702
0.01500	0.03803683	0.03803683	-14.52878
0.01600	0.02596083	0.02596083	-9.91616
0.01700	0.01771874	0.01771874	-6.76796
0.01800	0.01209337	0.01209336	-4.61925
0.01900	0.00825394	0.00825394	-3.15273
0.02000	0.00563347	0.00563347	-2.15179

Results for the 5th Data Set

R	=	100.00000
HL	=	0.50000
C	=	0.2D-05
VZERO	=	10.00000
H	=	0.00001
TMAX	=	0.02000
IFREQ	=	100
IFPLOT	=	0

T	CALC. V	TRUE V	CALC. V'
0.0	10.00000000	10.00000000	0.0
0.00100	5.68971891	5.68971891	-7627.57679
0.00200	-2.58070263	-2.58070263	-7516.15502
0.00300	-7.20135221	-7.20135221	-1161.42920
0.00400	-4.98325602	-4.98325602	5009.24394
0.00500	0.98550667	0.98550668	5886.96794
0.00600	5.05105559	5.05105559	1699.75050
0.00700	4.17040640	4.17040639	-3144.92073
0.00800	-0.25968420	-0.25968843	-4490.61851
0.00900	-3.44002905	-3.44002905	-1850.17734
0.01000	-3.56851681	-3.56851681	1853.45707
0.01100	-0.50285277	-0.50285276	3341.17931
0.01200	2.26240109	2.26240109	1774.88989
0.01300	2.64105351	2.64105351	-986.56352
0.01400	0.75017631	0.75017631	-2425.30898
0.01500	-1.42309381	-1.42309381	-1582.15077
0.01600	-2.01649802	-2.01649802	426.63595
0.01700	-0.82191085	-0.82191085	1715.75924
0.01800	0.84106437	0.84106437	1341.39588
0.01900	1.50170200	1.50170199	-82.94375
0.02000	0.79116024	0.79116024	-1179.97420

Computer Output (Continued)

Results for the 6th Data Set

```
R      =   100.00000
HL     =     0.50000
C      =     0.2D-05
VZERO  =    10.00000
H      =     0.00010
TMAX   =     0.02000
IFREQ  =    10
IFPLOT =     0
```

T	CALC. V	TRUE V	CALC. V'
0.0	10.00000000	10.00000000	0.0
0.00100	5.68972630	5.68971891	-7627.57558
0.00200	-2.58069239	-2.58070263	-7516.16529
0.00300	-7.20135522	-7.20135221	-1161.44732
0.00400	-4.98327674	-4.98325602	5009.23693
0.00500	0.98548526	0.98550668	5886.98405
0.00600	5.05105572	5.05105559	1699.77815
0.00700	4.17043109	4.17040639	-3144.90741
0.00800	-0.02594075	-0.02596843	-4490.63369
0.00900	-3.44002437	-3.44002905	-1850.20820
0.01000	-3.36854000	-3.36851681	1853.43882
0.01100	-0.50288259	-0.50285276	3341.19041
0.01200	2.26237181	2.26240109	1774.91974
0.01300	2.64107247	2.64105351	-986.54239
0.01400	0.75020528	0.75017631	-2425.31507
0.01500	-1.42308113	-1.42309381	-1582.17716
0.01600	-2.01651180	-2.01649802	426.61590
0.01700	-0.82193704	-0.82191085	1715.76066
0.01800	0.84104973	0.84106437	1341.41766
0.01900	1.50171074	1.50170199	-82.92239
0.02000	0.79118262	0.79116024	-1179.97185

Results for the 7th Data Set

```
R      =   100.00000
HL     =     0.50000
C      =     0.2D-05
VZERO  =    10.00000
H      =     0.00100
TMAX   =     0.02000
IFREQ  =     1
IFPLOT =     0
```

T	CALC. V	TRUE V	CALC. V'
0.0	10.00000000	10.00000000	0.0
0.00100	5.73333333	5.68971891	-7563.33333
0.00200	-2.43329000	-2.58070263	-7528.54200
0.00300	-7.08917553	-7.20135221	-1357.16829
0.00400	-5.07580444	-4.98325602	4797.40409
0.00500	0.71830874	0.98550668	5863.82444
0.00600	4.84683623	5.05105559	1931.64399
0.00700	4.23981951	4.17040639	-2850.54126
0.00800	0.27487048	-0.02596843	-4409.83527
0.00900	-3.17771301	-3.44002905	-2069.13818
0.01000	-3.38684697	-3.36851681	1530.09602
0.01100	-0.78452964	-0.50285276	3207.38778
0.01200	1.97605730	2.26240109	1947.09739
0.01300	2.60599417	2.64105351	-672.75310
0.01400	0.98504840	0.75017631	-2254.64438
0.01500	-1.14050162	-1.42309381	-1596.63518
0.01600	-1.93710934	-2.01649802	146.50624
0.01700	-0.99980180	-0.82191085	1526.93576
0.01800	0.58165271	0.84106437	1400.65212
0.01900	1.39284077	1.50170199	-151.24523
0.02000	0.91295386	0.79116024	-989.61633

Results for the 8th Data Set

```
R      =   100.00000
HL     =     0.50000
C      =     0.2D-05
VZERO  =    10.00000
H      =     0.00200
TMAX   =     0.02000
IFREQ  =     1
IFPLOT =     0
```

T	CALC. V	TRUE V	CALC. V'
0.0	10.00000000	10.00000000	0.0
0.00200	-0.93333333	-2.58070263	-5813.33333
0.00400	-3.29237333	-4.98325602	1761.05244
0.00600	1.33104667	5.05105559	1544.84977
0.00800	0.77384165	-0.02596843	-1097.58231
0.01000	-0.71028640	-3.36851681	-219.80669
0.01200	-0.27256191	2.26240109	458.98464
0.01400	-0.06058560	0.75017631	-60.45841
0.01600	-0.07909051	-2.01649802	-145.77724
0.01800	0.04561918	0.84106437	65.77534
0.02000		0.79116024	32.19144

Results for the 9th Data Set

```
R      =   100.00000
HL     =     0.50000
C      =     0.2D-05
VZERO  =    10.00000
H      =     0.00500
TMAX   =     0.02000
IFREQ  =     1
IFPLOT =     0
```

T	CALC. V	TRUE V	CALC. V'
0.0	10.00000000	10.00000000	0.0
0.00500	176.66666667	0.98550668	72916.66667
0.01000	2589.42708333	-3.36851681	268725.69444
0.01500	26185.00361690	-1.42309381	70188368.05556
0.02000	-49188.45317322	0.79116024	1533284857.10237

Computer Output (*Continued*)

Results for the 10th Data Set

```
R      =       100.00000
HL     =         0.50000
C      =         0.2D-05
VZERO  =        10.00000
H      =         0.01000
TMAX   =         0.02000
IFREQ  =       1
IFPLOT =       0
```

T	CALC. V	TRUE V	CALC. V'
0.0	10.00000000	10.00000000	0.0
0.01000	3843.33333333	-3.36851681	-33333.33333
0.02000	1477009.99999999	0.79116024	-25600000.00000

Discussion of Results

All calculations have been made using double-precision arithmetic. Only the plotted output is shown for the under-damped solution resulting from the input parameters of the 1st data set. Results for the 2nd, 3rd, and 4th data sets correspond to an undamped ($R = 0$), critically-damped ($R = 1000$), and over-damped solution, respectively. For the step size used, $h = 0.0001$, the numerical solutions agree with the appropriate analytical solution of (6.3.5), (6.3.6), and (6.3.7) to five or six significant figures.

Results for data sets 5 through 10 show the influence of the step-size h, on the numerical solution for an under-damped case (see plotted output for data set 1). Table 6.3.1 shows the calculated solution, V, the true solution, V_t, and the error, $V - V_t$, at time $t = 2$ sec. Because double-precision arithmetic has been used throughout, and the total number of integration steps is no larger than 2000 for any case, the error may be attributed solely to truncation effects; any round-off error is negligible in comparison.

Table 6.3.1 *Comparison of Numerical and Analytical Solutions at Time $t = 2$ sec.*

Step size, h (Sec)	Numerical Solution, V (Volts)	Analytical Solution, V_t (Volts)	Error $V - V_t$ (Volts)
0.00001	0.79116024	0.79116024	0.00000000
0.0001	0.79118262	0.79116024	0.00002238
0.001	0.91295386	0.79116024	0.12179362
0.002	0.04561918	0.79116024	−0.74554106
0.005	−49188.45317322	0.79116024	−49189.24433346
0.01	1477009.99999999	0.79116024	1477009.20883975

For small step sizes, the solutions computed by the Runge-Kutta fourth-order method are extremely accurate. The truncation error increases with increasing step size, until the solution eventually "blows up" and bears no resemblance to the true solution. This is not surprising, in view of the fact that the period of oscillation for the solution is $2\pi/\alpha \doteq 0.00628$ sec. As the step length approaches the period of oscillation, virtually all local information about the curvature of the solution function, V_t, is lost.

6.8   Multistep Methods

The one-step methods of previous sections have approximated the solution of the first-order equation

$$\frac{dy}{dx} = f(x,y)$$

with initial condition $y_0 = y(x_0)$. This has been accomplished for Euler's method (6.28) by integration across a series of single intervals to yield successively,

$$y_1 = y_0 + \int_{x_0}^{x_1} f_0 \, dx,$$

$$y_2 = y_1 + \int_{x_1}^{x_2} f_1 \, dx, \qquad (6.80)$$

$$\vdots$$

$$y_{i+1} = y_i + \int_{x_i}^{x_{i+1}} f_i \, dx.$$

For an integration involving $k+1$ intervals terminating at x_{i+1}, this can be written as

$$y_{i+1} = y_{i-k} + \int_{x_{i-k}}^{x_{i+1}} \psi_i(x) \, dx, \qquad (6.81)$$

where $\psi_i(x)$ is a step-function with ordinates $f_j - f(x_j, y_j)$ on the half-open intervals $[x_j, x_{j+1})$, $j = i - k, \ldots, i$. The integral in (6.81) can be viewed as the area between the limits x_{i-k} and x_{i+1} shown in Fig. 6.4.

It seems clear that replacement of the function $\psi_i(x)$ in (6.81) by an interpolating polynominal $\phi(x)$ that passes through the points (x_j, f_j) for j near i might well lead to more accurate algorithms.

The derivations are similar to those used in generating the open and closed integration formulas of Chapter 2, except that the interpolating polynomial is determined by derivative values $f(x_j, y_j)$ instead of functional values y_j. The number of values of f_j required depends on: (a) the desired degree of the interpolating polynomial, and (b) the availability of the values f_j. Assuming that the integration has already proceeded to the base point x_i, the values of all the f_j, $0 \leqslant j \leqslant i$, are known. In general, f_{i+1} will be unknown, since f is a function of both x and y,

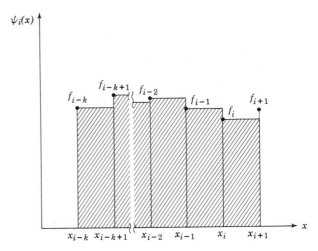

Figure 6.4   Multistep integration.

and y_{i+1} has not yet been computed. All the common multistep methods are described by

$$y_{i+1} = y_{i-k} + \int_{x_{i-k}}^{x_{i+1}} \phi(x) \, dx, \qquad (6.82)$$

where $\phi(x) = \sum_{j=0}^{r} a_j x^j$. Here, r is the degree of the interpolating polynomial.

6.9   Open Integration Formulas

Since the x_j are evenly spaced, and the values $f_i, f_{i-1}, f_{i-2}, \ldots, f_{i-r}$, are known, $\phi(x)$ is given in simplest form by Newton's interpolation formula based on the backward finite differences of x_i, already developed in (1.61):

$$\phi(x_i + \alpha h) = f_i + \alpha \nabla f_i + \alpha(\alpha + 1) \frac{\nabla^2 f_i}{2!}$$

$$+ \alpha(\alpha + 1)(\alpha + 2) \frac{\nabla^3 f_i}{3!}$$

$$+ \cdots + \alpha(\alpha + 1)(\alpha + 2) \cdots (\alpha + r - 1) \frac{\nabla^r f_i}{r!},$$

where $f_i = f(x_i, y_i)$, and $x = x_i + \alpha h$, that is, $\alpha = (x - x_i)/h$. For the base-point values x_{i-p}, α assumes integral values $-p$. Since $dx = h \, d\alpha$, the integral of (6.82) is, in terms of the variable α,

$$\int_{x_{i-k}}^{x_{i+1}} \phi(x) \, dx = h \int_{-k}^{1} \phi(x_i + \alpha h) \, d\alpha = h \int_{-k}^{1} \left[f_i + \alpha \nabla f_i + \alpha(\alpha + 1) \frac{\nabla^2 f_i}{2!} + \alpha(\alpha + 1)(\alpha + 2) \frac{\nabla^3 f_i}{3!} + \cdots \right.$$

$$\left. + \alpha(\alpha + 1)(\alpha + 2) \cdots (\alpha + r - 1) \frac{\nabla^r f_i}{r!} \right] d\alpha. \qquad (6.83)$$

That is,

$$\int_{x_{i-k}}^{x_{i+1}} \phi(x) \, dx = h \left[\alpha f_i + \frac{\alpha^2}{2} \nabla f_i + \alpha^2 \left(\frac{\alpha}{3} + \frac{1}{2} \right) \frac{\nabla^2 f_i}{2!} \right.$$

$$\left. + \alpha^2 \left(\frac{\alpha^2}{4} + \alpha + 1 \right) \frac{\nabla^3 f_i}{3!} + \alpha^2 \left(\frac{\alpha^3}{5} + \frac{3\alpha^2}{2} + \frac{11\alpha}{3} + 3 \right) \frac{\nabla^4 f_i}{4!} + \cdots \right]_{-k}^{1}. \qquad (6.84)$$

With a suitable renumbering of subscripts, (6.84) can be shown to be equivalent to the open Newton-Cotes integration formulas of (2.30).

For $k = 0,1,2,$ and 3, equation (6.84) leads to the following algorithms:

$k = 0$:

$$y_{i+1} = y_i + h\left(f_i + \frac{1}{2}\nabla f_i + \frac{5}{12}\nabla^2 f_i\right.$$

$$\left. + \frac{3}{8}\nabla^3 f_i + \frac{251}{720}\nabla^4 f_i + \cdots\right). \quad (6.85a)$$

$k = 1$:

$$y_{i+1} = y_{i-1} + h\left(2f_i + 0\nabla f_i + \frac{1}{3}\nabla^2 f_i\right.$$

$$\left. + \frac{1}{3}\nabla^3 f_i + \frac{29}{90}\nabla^4 f_i + \cdots\right). \quad (6.85b)$$

$k = 2$:

$$y_{i+1} = y_{i-2} + h\left(3f_i - \frac{3}{2}\nabla f_i + \frac{3}{4}\nabla^2 f_i\right.$$

$$\left. + \frac{3}{8}\nabla^3 f_i + \frac{27}{80}\nabla^4 f_i + \cdots\right). \quad (6.85c)$$

$k = 3$:

$$y_{i+1} = y_{i-3} + h\left(4f_i - 4\nabla f_i + \frac{8}{3}\nabla^2 f_i\right.$$

$$\left. + 0\nabla^3 f_i + \frac{14}{45}\nabla^4 f_i + \cdots\right). \quad (6.85d)$$

As illustrated by the shaded area of Fig. 6.5, equation (6.85a) involves approximate integration for any suitably differentiable function, $\psi(x)$, that passes through the points $(x_{i-r}, f_{i-r}), (x_{i-r+1}, f_{i-r+1}), \ldots, (x_{i-1}, f_{i-1}), (x_i, f_i)$. The interval of integration is, of course, $[x_i, x_{i+1}]$. Equation (6.85b) uses the same points, but the interval of

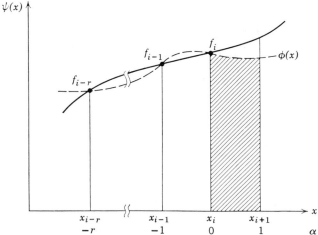

Figure 6.5 Open multistep integration.

integration is $[x_{i-1}, x_{i+1}]$. Similar statements hold for the other members of (6.85). All the information required, that is, $y_i, f(x_i, y_i), y_{i-1}, f(x_{i-1}, y_{i-1}) \ldots$ etc., is known, since the integration is presumed to have proceeded to x_i already.

Note that for the *odd* values of k, the coefficient of the kth backward difference is zero. For this reason, the most commonly used formulas of this type are for k odd with just $k + 1$ terms retained (that is, $r = k$). The $(k + 1)$th term is zero in these cases, so that the interpolating polynomial is actually of degree $r - 1$ rather than of degree r as would be expected. Of course, any number of terms could be retained. When the formula is terminated with the $(r + 1)$th term, that is, when the last included term involves $\nabla^r f_i / r!$, the error term is

$$h^{r+2} \int_{-k}^1 \frac{\alpha(\alpha + 1)(\alpha + 2)\cdots(\alpha + r)}{(r + 1)!}\psi^{(r+1)}(\xi)\, d\alpha,$$

$$x_{i-k} < \xi < x_{i+1}. \quad (6.86)$$

From (6.85), the most important *open* formulas are:

$k = 0, r = 3$:

$$y_{i+1} = y_i + h\left(f_i + \frac{1}{2}\nabla f_i + \frac{5}{12}\nabla^2 f_i + \frac{3}{8}\nabla^3 f_i\right),$$

$$R = \frac{251}{720}h^5 f^{(4)}(\xi). \quad (6.87a)$$

$k = 1, r = 1$:

$$y_{i+1} = y_{i-1} + h(2f_i + 0\nabla f_i), \qquad R = \frac{1}{3}h^3 f^{(2)}(\xi).$$

$$(6.87b)$$

$k = 3, r = 3$:

$$y_{i+1} = y_{i-3} + h\left(4f_i - 4\nabla f_i + \frac{8}{3}\nabla^2 f_i + 0\nabla^3 f_i\right),$$

$$R = \frac{14}{45}h^5 f^{(4)}(\xi). \quad (6.87c)$$

$k = 5, r = 5$:

$$y_{i+1} = y_{i-5} + h\left(6f_i - 12\nabla f_i + 15\nabla^2 f_i - 9\nabla^3 f_i\right.$$

$$\left. + \frac{33}{10}\nabla^4 f_i + 0\nabla^5 f_i\right), \qquad R = \frac{41}{140}h^7 f^{(6)}(\xi). \quad (6.87d)$$

In each case, ξ lies somewhere between the smallest and largest of the x_j involved in the formula. The error terms R of equations (6.87), computed from (6.86), are the local truncation errors for one application of the formulas, assuming that $\psi(x) = f(x, y)$, and that $y_j = y(x_j)$ and $f_j = f(x_j, y(x_j))$ for those j involved in the formulas. However, since the y_j and f_j, except for y_0 and f_0, are computed numerically and thus are usually inexact, the error terms are approximations only.

In terms of the derivative estimates f_j, instead of their backward differences, these open formulas become:

$k = 0, r = 3$:

$$y_{i+1} = y_i + \frac{h}{24}(55f_i - 59f_{i-1} + 37f_{i-2} - 9f_{i-3}),$$
$$R = O(h^5). \quad (6.88a)$$

$k = 1, r = 1$:

$$y_{i+1} = y_{i-1} + 2hf_i, \qquad R = O(h^3). \quad (6.88b)$$

$k = 3, r = 3$:

$$y_{i+1} = y_{i-3} + \frac{4h}{3}(2f_i - f_{i-1} + 2f_{i-2}), \qquad R = O(h^5). \quad (6.88c)$$

$k = 5, r = 5$:

$$y_{i+1} = y_{i-5} + \frac{3h}{10}(11f_i - 14f_{i-1} + 26f_{i-2}$$
$$- 14f_{i-3} + 11f_{i-4}), \qquad R = O(h^7). \quad (6.88d)$$

All of these formulas involve use of the interpolating polynomial passing through known points (x_j, f_j),

$(j = i, i-1, i-2, \ldots, i-r)$. Thus, since the integration covers the whole interval $[x_{i-k}, x_{i+1}]$, the polynomial effectively extrapolates over the interval $[x_i, x_{i+1}]$. The situation for the case $k = 3$, $r = 3$ is shown in Fig. 6.6.

6.10 Closed Integration Formulas

A set of *closed* integration formulas of the multistep form (6.82),

$$y_{i+1} = y_{i-k} + \int_{x_{i-k}}^{x_{i+1}} \phi(x)\,dx,$$

can be generated in analogous fashion, where $\phi(x)$ is the interpolating polynomial which fits not only the previously calculated values f_i, f_{i-1}, f_{i-2}, but the unknown f_{i+1} as well. As before, the transformation of variable $x = x_i + \alpha h$ yields

$$y_{i+1} = y_{i-k} + h \int_{-k}^{1} \phi(x_i + \alpha h)\,d\alpha. \quad (6.89)$$

However, $\phi(x_i + \alpha h)$ is now expressed in terms of the backward-difference formula based at x_{i+1} instead of x_i [see (6.83) for comparison]:

$$y_{i+1} = y_{i-k} + h \int_{-k}^{1} \left[f_{i+1} + (\alpha - 1)\nabla f_{i+1} + \frac{(\alpha - 1)\alpha}{2!}\nabla^2 f_{i+1} \right.$$
$$\left. + \frac{(\alpha - 1)(\alpha)(\alpha + 1)}{3!}\nabla^3 f_{i+1} + \cdots \frac{(\alpha - 1)(\alpha)(\alpha + 1)\cdots(\alpha + r - 2)}{r!}\nabla^r f_{i+1} \right] d\alpha, \quad (6.90)$$

or

$$y_{i+1} = y_{i-k} + h \left[\alpha f_{i+1} + \alpha\left(\frac{\alpha}{2} - 1\right)\nabla f_{i+1} + \frac{\alpha^2\left(\frac{\alpha}{3} - \frac{1}{2}\right)}{2!}\nabla^2 f_{i+1} \right.$$
$$\left. + \frac{\alpha^2\left(\frac{\alpha^2}{4} - \frac{1}{2}\right)}{3!}\nabla^3 f_{i+1} + \frac{\left(\frac{\alpha^5}{5} + \frac{\alpha^4}{2} - \frac{\alpha^3}{3} - \alpha^2\right)}{4!}\nabla^4 f_{i+1} + \cdots \right]_{-k}^{1}. \quad (6.91)$$

Equation (6.91) is simply the analogue of the general Newton-Cotes closed integration formula (2.14), with the interpolating polynomial written in terms of the backward differences of $f(x_{i+1}, y_{i+1})$. For $k = 0, 1, 3$, and 5, equation (6.91) leads to the following:

$k = 0$:

$$y_{i+1} = y_i + h\left(f_{i+1} - \frac{1}{2}\nabla f_{i+1} - \frac{1}{12}\nabla^2 f_{i+1} \right.$$
$$\left. - \frac{1}{24}\nabla^3 f_{i+1} - \frac{19}{720}\nabla^4 f_{i+1} + \cdots \right). \quad (6.92a)$$

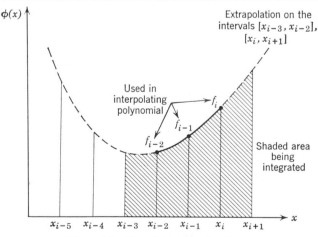

Figure 6.6 *Open integration for the case $k = 3$, $r = 3$ (eqn. 6.88c).*

$k = 1$:

$$y_{i+1} = y_{i-1} + h\left(2f_{i+1} - 2\nabla f_{i+1} + \frac{1}{3}\nabla^2 f_{i+1}\right.$$

$$\left. + 0\nabla^3 f_{i+1} - \frac{1}{90}\nabla^4 f_{i+1} + \cdots\right). \quad (6.92b)$$

$k = 3$:

$$y_{i+1} = y_{i-3} + h\left(4f_{i+1} - 8\nabla f_{i+1} + \frac{20}{3}\nabla^2 f_{i+1}\right.$$

$$\left. - \frac{8}{3}\nabla^3 f_{i+1} + \frac{14}{45}\nabla^4 f_{i+1} + 0\nabla^5 f_{i+1} + \cdots\right). \quad (6.92c)$$

$k = 5$:

$$y_{i+1} = y_{i-5} + h\left(6f_{i+1} - 18\nabla f_{i+1} + 27\nabla^2 f_{i+1}\right.$$

$$\left. - 24\nabla^3 f_{i+1} + \frac{123}{10}\nabla^4 f_{i+1} - \frac{33}{10}\nabla^5 f_{i+1} + \cdots\right). \quad (6.92d)$$

For these formulas, the error term for truncation after the term involving the rth difference is

$$h^{r+2}\int_{-k}^{1}\frac{(\alpha-1)(\alpha)(\alpha+1)(\alpha+2)\cdots(\alpha+r-1)}{(r+1)!}$$

$$\times \psi^{(r+1)}(\xi)\,d\alpha, \qquad x_{i-k} < \xi < x_{i+1}. \quad (6.93)$$

For k odd, the coefficient of $\nabla^{k+2}f_{i+1}$ vanishes. Therefore, the most frequently used formulas of this type are for k odd, with $r = k + 2$. Three of the more important *closed* formulas are:

$k = 0, r = 3$;

$$y_{i+1} = y_i + h\left(f_{i+1} - \frac{1}{2}\nabla f_{i+1} - \frac{1}{12}\nabla^2 f_{i+1} - \frac{1}{24}\nabla^3 f_{i+1}\right),$$

$$R = -\frac{19}{720}h^5 f^{(4)}(\xi). \quad (6.94a)$$

$k = 1, r = 3$:

$$y_{i+1} = y_{i-1} + h\left(2f_{i+1} - 2\nabla f_{i+1} + \frac{1}{3}\nabla^2 f_{i+1} + 0\nabla^3 f_{i+1}\right),$$

$$R = -\frac{1}{90}h^5 f^{(4)}(\xi). \quad (6.94b)$$

$k = 3, r = 5$:

$$y_{i+1} = y_{i-3} + h\left(4f_{i+1} - 8\nabla f_{i+1} + \frac{20}{3}\nabla^2 f_{i+1}\right.$$

$$\left. - \frac{8}{3}\nabla^3 f_{i+1} + \frac{14}{45}\nabla^4 f_{i+1}\right), \qquad R = -\frac{8}{945}h^7 f^{(6)}(\xi). \quad (6.94c)$$

The error terms R computed by (6.93) are the local truncation errors for one application of the integration formulas, provided that $\psi(x) = f(x,y)$ and that $y_j = y(x_j)$ and $f_j = f(x_j, y(x_j))$ for those j involved in the formulas. In each case, ξ lies somewhere between the smallest and largest of the x_j involved in the formula.

In terms of the derivatives f_j instead of the backward differences, these formulas become:

$k = 0, r = 3$:

$$y_{i+1} = y_i + \frac{h}{24}(9f_{i+1} + 19f_i - 5f_{i-1} + f_{i-2}),$$

$$R = O(h^5). \quad (6.95a)$$

$k = 1, r = 3$:

$$y_{i+1} = y_{i-1} + \frac{h}{3}(f_{i+1} + 4f_i + f_{i-1}), \qquad R = O(h^5). \quad (6.95b)$$

$k = 3, r = 5$:

$$y_{i+1} = y_{i-3} + \frac{2h}{45}(7f_{i+1} + 32f_i + 12f_{i-1}$$

$$+ 32f_{i-2} + 7f_{i-3}), \qquad R = O(h^7). \quad (6.95c)$$

The situation for the case $k = 1, r = 3$ is shown in Fig. 6.7.

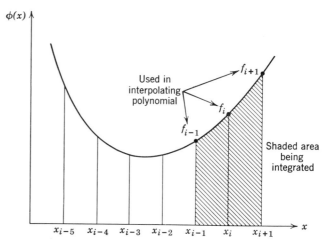

Figure 6.7 *Closed integration for the case $k = 1, r = 3$ (eqn. 6.95b).*

6.11 Predictor-Corrector Methods

Assuming that we have available the necessary starting values (usually a one-step Runge-Kutta method is used to generate the approximate solutions y_1, y_2, etc., near the starting point), the open integration formulas of (6.88) are very straightforward algorithms for step-by-step solution of first-order ordinary differential equations. For example, to solve the equation

$$\frac{dy}{dx} = f(x,y)$$

with initial condition $y(x_0)$ given, one of the fourth-order Runge-Kutta methods of Section 6.5 could be used to compute y_1, y_2, y_3 (and f_1, f_2, f_3). Starting with $i = 3$, equation (6.88c) could be used to generate *explicitly* the successive values $y_4, y_5, \ldots, y_n$. A fourth-order Runge-Kutta method would be preferred for producing starting values for (6.88c), since the local truncation error is of order h^5 as it is for (6.88c).

A closed integration formula with accuracy of order h^5 is given by (6.95b). In this case, a fourth-order Runge-Kutta method could be used to compute y_1 (and f_1). Thereafter, starting with $i = 1$, equation (6.95b) could be used to produce successively $y_2, y_3, \ldots, y_n$. Unfortunately, (6.95b) cannot be used to solve for y_{i+1} directly, since $f_{i+1} = f(x_{i+1}, y_{i+1})$ is generally unknown. Except for the rather special case for which $f(x,y)$ is a function of x only, (6.95b) is an *implicit* equation in y_{i+1} which must be solved iteratively by one of the methods of Chapter 3.

One approach is to solve (6.95b) by the method of successive substitutions described in Section 3.5. If $y_{i+1,j}$ is the jth successive approximation to the solution of (6.95b), then the recursion relation comparable to (3.22) is given by

$$y_{i+1,j+1} = y_{i-1} + \frac{h}{3}[f(x_{i+1}, y_{i+1,j}) + 4f_i + f_{i-1}],$$

$$j = 0, 1, \ldots. \quad (6.96)$$

Thus the procedure for solving (6.95b) is to assume a value for $y_{i+1,0}$, compute $f(x_{i+1}, y_{i+1,0})$, find $y_{1+1,1}$ from (6.96), then calculate $f(x_{i+1}, y_{i+1,1})$, find $y_{i+1,2}$ from (6.96), etc. The process continues until the sequence $y_{i+1,0}, y_{i+1,1}, y_{i+1,2}$ converges, that is, until $y_{i+1,j+1}$ differs from $y_{i+1,j}$ by some acceptably small amount.

Under what conditions will this iterative procedure converge? Since y_{i-1}, f_i, f_{i-1}, h, and x_{i+1} are constant for a given i, (6.96) may be written

$$y_{i+1,j+1} = \frac{h}{3}f(x_{i+1}, y_{i+1,j}) + C \quad (6.97)$$

$$= F(y_{i+1,j})$$

where C is a constant. From the discussion on page 168, convergence will take place if $|F'(y_{i+1})|$ is less than one. Thus (6.96) converges, provided that the asymptotic convergence factor

$$|F'(y_{i+1})| = \frac{h}{3}\left|\frac{\partial f}{\partial y_{i+1}}\right| < 1. \quad (6.98)$$

Then the step-size h must satisfy the condition

$$h < \frac{3}{\left|\dfrac{\partial f}{\partial y_{i+1}}\right|}. \quad (6.99)$$

The closed multistep method of (6.95b) is more complicated than the open multistep method of (6.88c) because of the iterative calculation (6.96) required for each step of the algorithm. Nevertheless, the open formula is not often used by itself to generate a sequence of solution values $y_4, y_5, \ldots, y_n$. The closed method is preferred because its local truncation error is considerably smaller than that for the open method, even though the two formulas are of the same order. This can be seen by comparing the error terms of (6.87c) and (6.94b):

Open formula (6.88c) error: $\quad \dfrac{14}{45}h^5 f^{(4)}(\xi)$,

$$\xi \text{ in } (x_{i-3}, x_{i+1}). \quad (6.100)$$

Closed formula (6.95b) error: $\quad -\dfrac{1}{90}h^5 f^{(4)}(\bar{\xi})$,

$$\bar{\xi} \text{ in } (x_{i-1}, x_{i+1}). \quad (6.101)$$

These truncation error terms apply strictly only when $y_i = y(x_i), y_{i-1} = y(x_{i-1}), \ldots$, and $f_i = f(x_i, y(x_i)), f_{i-1} = f(x_{i-1}, y(x_{i-1})), \ldots$; in most real situations these quantities will have been computed numerically. Therefore, (6.100) and (6.101) should be viewed as approximations only. Assuming that $f^{(4)}(\xi)$ is effectively equal to $f^{(4)}(\bar{\xi})$, a reasonable assumption for sufficiently small h, (6.95b) is significantly more accurate than (6.88c).

Comparison of other open and closed multistep methods of comparable order, for example, (6.88a) and (6.95a), or (6.88d) and (6.95c), indicates that the closed formulas are, in general, considerably more accurate than the open ones. This is not surprising, since the open formulas involve *extrapolation* of the polynomial $\phi(x)$ of equation (6.82) on the interval $[x_i, x_{i+1}]$, while the closed formulas involve *interpolation*.

The closed methods can be used alone to generate approximations to the solution of differential equations, provided that the necessary starting values are available (or can be found by using a self-starting one-step method) and that the step size chosen satisfies the appropriate convergence criterion [for example, (6.99)]. Since each iteration of a closed formula [for example, (6.96)] requires one evaluation of the derivative $f(x_{i+1}, y_{i+1,j})$, it is important that convergence be *very* rapid. The number of iterations required for convergence depends on many factors; the two factors over which the programmer has most control are the initial guess, $y_{i+1,0}$, and the step size h.

In practice it has been found that if more than one or two iterations are required for convergence, the multistep methods cannot compete effectively with the one-step methods of preceding sections. For example, the fourth-order Runge-Kutta methods require four derivative evaluations for each step with the advantages that starting values are needed at just one point, and that the step size can be adjusted from step to step with little difficulty. On the other hand, the fourth order method of (6.96) has the disadvantage that it is not self-starting, since values of the solution are needed at both x_0 and x_1 before the method can be applied for the first time; in addition, as described in the next section, a change in the step size, while possible, is rather cumbersome. The principal advantage of (6.96) is that it can be used to produce solutions to differential equations (with accuracy comparable to that for a fourth-order Runge-Kutta method) with as few as *two* derivative evaluations per step, $f(x_{i+1}, y_{i+1,0})$, and $f(x_{i+1}, y_{i+1,1})$.

Fortunately, we already have very good algorithms for estimating $y_{i+1,0}$, namely, the open formulas of Sections 6.9. The usual practice is to select an open and closed formula with comparable order for the local truncation error. The open formula is used to *predict* the value $y_{i+1,0}$, and the closed formula is then used to *correct* the estimate by an iterative computation similar to (6.96). The open formula is usually called the *predictor* and the closed formula is called the *corrector*; algorithms which use the predictor and corrector as outlined above are called *predictor-corrector methods* (see also page 362). Three of the commonly used predictor-corrector methods are the fourth-order and sixth-order *Milne methods* [5] and the fourth-order *modified Adams* or *Adams-Moulton method* which use predictors and correctors already developed in Sections 6.9 and 6.10.

Fourth-order Milne method:
Predictor:

$$y_{i+1} = y_{i-3} + \frac{4h}{3}(2f_i - f_{i-1} + 2f_{i-2}), \qquad R = O(h^5).$$
$$(6.88c)$$

Corrector:

$$y_{i+1} = y_{i-1} + \frac{h}{3}(f_{i+1} + 4f_i + f_{i-1}), \qquad R = O(h^5).$$
$$(6.95b)$$

Sixth-order Milne method:
Predictor:

$$y_{i+1} = y_{i-5} + \frac{3h}{10}(11f_i - 14f_{i-1} + 26f_{i-2}$$
$$- 14f_{i-3} + 11f_{i-4}), \qquad R = O(h^7). \quad (6.88d)$$

Corrector:

$$y_{i+1} = y_{i-3} + \frac{2h}{45}(7f_{i+1} + 32f_i + 12f_{i-1}$$
$$+ 32f_{i-2} + 7f_{i-3}), \qquad R = O(h^7). \quad (6.95c)$$

Modified Adams or Adams-Moulton method:
Predictor:

$$y_{i+1} = y_i + \frac{h}{24}(55f_i - 59f_{i-1} + 37f_{i-2} - 9f_{i-3}),$$
$$R = O(h^5). \quad (6.88a)$$

Corrector:

$$y_{i+1} = y_i + \frac{h}{24}(9f_{i+1} + 19f_i - 5f_{i-1} + f_{i-2}),$$
$$R = O(h^5). \quad (6.95a)$$

Many other predictor-corrector methods are also used (see Section 6.13 for another important method). The general naming conventions for the integration methods that employ the open and closed integration formulas are as follows:

Name of Method	Mode of Operation
Adams or Adams-Bashforth	Use of predictor equations only.
Moulton	Iterative use of corrector equations only.
Modified Adams	Use of predictor followed by iterative use of corrector, $k = 0$ for both equations.
Milne	Use of predictor followed by iterative use of corrector, $k \neq 0$ for either equation.

6.12 Truncation Error, Stability, and Step-Size Control in the Multistep Algorithms

One of the virtues of the predictor-corrector methods of the preceding section is that we can estimate and then correct for local truncation errors, by assuming that the error terms [for example, (6.100) and (6.101)] apply. The approach is probably best illustrated by an example. Consider the fourth-order Milne method of (6.88c) and (6.95b). Given the differential equation $dy/dx = f(x,y)$, a specified step-size h, and starting values for y_0, y_1, y_2, y_3, f_0, f_1, f_2, and f_3 (usually y_0 is given, and y_1, y_2, and y_3 are computed by using a fourth-order Runge-Kutta method), the algorithm proceeds step-by-step for $i = 3, 4, 5, \ldots$ (here $x_i = x_0 + ih$) as follows:

1. Calculate $y_{i+1,0}$ using the predictor (6.88c),

$$y_{i+1,0} = y_{i-3} + \tfrac{4}{3}h(2f_i - f_{i-1} + 2f_{i-2}). \quad (6.102)$$

2. Compute $f(x_{i+1}, y_{i+1,0})$, and then solve the corrector (6.95b) iteratively using (6.96),

$$y_{i+1,j+1} = y_{i-1} + \frac{h}{3}[f(x_{i+1}, y_{i+1,j}) + 4f_i + f_{i-1}],$$
$$j = 0, 1, \ldots.$$

The iteration on j is continued until a specified convergence criterion is met, for example,

$$\left| \frac{y_{i+1,j+1} - y_{i+1,j}}{y_{i+1,j+1}} \right| < \varepsilon, \qquad (6.103)$$

where ε is some small positive number. If (6.103) fails to converge, then criterion (6.98) is being violated, and computation must be stopped; action must be taken to decrease the step size and try again as described below. Since computational efficiency requires that (6.96) converge very rapidly, h should be such that the asymptotic convergence factor $|F'(y_{i+1})| \ll 1$ in (6.98). In fact, h should be small enough so that the convergence test (6.103) is passed after just *one* or at most *two* iterations. Note that the derivative $f(x_{i+1}, y_{i+1,j})$ must be evaluated once for each value of j.

3. Let k be the number of iterations required to solve (6.96). Then, for the standard predictor-corrector algorithm, y_{i+1} is equated to $y_{i+1,k}$, and f_{i+1} is computed by using the new y_{i+1}. In general, $k + 1$ evaluations of $f(x_{i+1}, y_{i+1})$ are required for each step, k to satisfy the convergence criterion (6.103), and one to compute $f_{i+1} = f(x_{i+1}, y_{i+1,k})$ for use in subsequent calculations. Next, i is incremented by one, and steps 1, 2, and 3 are repeated for the next integration step.

4. The local truncation error in using the Milne method to integrate across the interval $[x_i, x_{i+1}]$ can be estimated by assuming that the error terms of (6.100) and (6.101) apply. In fact, they apply strictly only when $y_{i-3}, y_{i-1}, f_{i-2}, f_{i-1}$, and f_i in (6.102) and (6.96) are exact, which they will not be in most cases. Nevertheless, if these quantities were known exactly and no round-off errors were introduced, we could then write

$$y(x_{i+1}) - y_{i+1,0} = \frac{14}{45} h^5 f^{(4)}(\xi), \qquad \xi \text{ in } (x_{i-3}, x_{i+1}), \qquad (6.104)$$

$$y(x_{i+1}) - y_{i+1,k} = -\frac{1}{90} h^5 f^{(4)}(\bar{\xi}), \qquad \bar{\xi} \text{ in } (x_{i-1}, x_{i+1}). \qquad (6.105)$$

If we assume that $f^{(4)}(\xi)$ is approximately equal to $f^{(4)}(\bar{\xi})$, a reasonable assumption since h is presumed to be small, then division of (6.104) by (6.105) leads to

$$y(x_{i+1}) \doteq \frac{1}{29} (28 y_{i+1,k} + y_{i+1,0}). \qquad (6.106)$$

The estimate of the local truncation error e_t for the corrector equation then follows as

$$e_t = \frac{1}{90} h^5 f^{(4)}(\bar{\xi}) \doteq \frac{1}{29} (y_{i+1,k} - y_{i+1,0}). \qquad (6.107)$$

5. In a modification of the standard fourth-order Milne method, (6.106) is used to modify the solution $y_{i+1,k}$ of the corrector equation; the approximate solution at x_{i+1} is computed as

$$y_{i+1} = \frac{1}{29} (28 y_{i+1,k} + y_{i+1,0}). \qquad (6.108)$$

Equation (6.108) may be rewritten as

$$y_{i+1} = y_{i+1,0} + \frac{28}{29} (y_{i+1,k} - y_{i+1,0})$$

$$\doteq y_{i+1,0} + 28 e_t. \qquad (6.109)$$

If we assume that the local truncation error varies only slowly from step to step so that e_t for the interval $[x_i, x_{i+1}]$ is approximately equal to that for the interval $[x_{i-1}, x_i]$, then we can modify $y_{i+1,0}$ as calculated from the predictor equation (6.102) to find an improved starting value for the iterative solution of (6.96). Let the improved $y_{i+1,0}$ be denoted $y^*_{i+1,0}$. Since e_t for the interval $[x_{i-1}, x_i]$ is, from (6.107), approximately $(y_{i,k} - y_{i,0})/29$, we can estimate $y^*_{i+1,0}$ from (1.109) as

$$y^*_{i+1,0} = y_{i+1,0} + \frac{28}{29} (y_{i,k} - y_{i,0}). \qquad (6.110)$$

Using $y^*_{i+1,0}$ rather than $y_{i+1,0}$ as the starting value for the solution of (6.96) in no way changes the value of $y_{i+1,k}$, and hence the preceding analysis remains unchanged. Because $y^*_{i+1,0}$ is, for most cases, a better value than $y_{i+1,0}$ computed from (6.102), the only effect of (6.110) is to speed convergence of the iterative solution of (6.96) and possibly to reduce the number of derivative evaluations required.

A similar approach may be used for the other predictor-corrector algorithms of Section 6.11. Clearly, it is much simpler to compute an estimate of the local truncation error for the multistep methods than for the Runge-Kutta methods (see page 364).

Step-size control is another matter entirely. The step size must be small enough to satisfy the convergence criterion for the corrector equation [for example, (6.99)], preferably small enough to insure convergence in just one or two iterations, and it must be small enough to satisfy any restrictions on the magnitude of the local truncation error [for example, (6.107)]. On the other hand, the step size should preferably be large enough so that round-off errors and the number of derivative evaluations will be minimized. The latter consideration is especially important when the derivative function is complicated, and each evaluation requires substantial computing time. The principal advantage of the multistep methods, namely that they require fewer derivative evaluations per step than do the one-step methods of comparable accuracy, will be lost if the step size is chosen to be smaller than necessary.

Fortunately, relationships such as (6.103) and (6.107) provide sufficient information to determine when the step size should be increased or decreased. Unfortunately, the mechanism for implementing such changes is not very straightforward. The difficulty is that when the step size is changed, the necessary starting values for the predictor and corrector will not usually be available. Assume that integration has proceeded without difficulty to base point x_i using step-size h_1, and that integration across the interval $[x_i, x_{i+1}]$ leads to convergence problems for the corrector (for example, if more than one or two iterations are required) or to a truncation error larger than desirable. Then one approach would be to decrease the step size by some amount and restart the integration procedure at x_i using the new step-size h_2. For an arbitrary h_2, about the only choice available is to use a one-step method to generate the necessary starting values $y_{i+1}, y_{i+2}, \ldots$, etc., required to reintroduce the multistep method for subsequent integration. A similar procedure can be followed if the estimated truncation error is much smaller than actually required and the corrector equation requires only one or two iterations for convergence, except that the new step-size h_2 is now larger than h_1.

If the new step-size h_2 is chosen to be $2h_1$ and a sufficient number of "old" values, $y_{i-1}, y_{i-2}, \ldots$, and $f_{i-1}, f_{i-2}, \ldots$, have been retained, then the change is relatively simple. One need only reassign subscripts so that the "old" y_{i-3} becomes the "new" y_{i-2}, the "old" y_{i-5} becomes the "new" y_{i-3}, etc.

If the new step-size h_2 is chosen to be $h_1/2$, then *some* but not all of the solution and derivative values for the predictor and corrector will be available. The old y_{i-1} becomes the new y_{i-2}, the old y_{i-2} becomes the new y_{i-4}, etc.; certain values, y_{i-1}, y_{i-3}, etc., will be missing. One approach is to use a one-step method to compute y_{i-1} starting with the new y_{i-2}, and to compute y_{i-3} starting with the new y_{i-4}; another approach is to interpolate on the available new values $y_i, y_{i-2}, y_{i-4}, \ldots$, to estimate the missing new values $y_{i-1}, y_{i-3}, \ldots$.

In practice, the step-size h is usually changed by doubling or halving it as described above. Clearly, too-frequent changes in the step size will vitiate the principal advantage of the multistep methods—their computational speed.

In the early 1950's, when computers were first widely used for solving ordinary differential equations, investigators discovered that for some equations certain of the multistep methods led to computational errors far larger than expected from local truncation errors (equations with known analytical solutions were used in these studies). It was also discovered that a decrease in step size often resulted in an *increase* in the observed error, even when round-off errors were known to be insignificant. In some cases, the numerical solution showed little, if any, relationship to the true solution of the equation being solved.

Subsequent analysis has shown that, under certain conditions, some of the multistep methods exhibit catastrophic instabilities which render the numerical solution meaningless. Such instabilities develop even though the equations are inherently stable (see page 364), and cannot in general be removed by step size adjustment (hence the instability cannot be a partial instability as described on page 365).

Virtually all stability analyses reported in the literature have been performed for the simple linear ordinary differential equation

$$\frac{dy}{dx} = f(x,y) = \alpha y, \tag{6.111}$$

where α is a constant. Often the analyses begin with an arbitrary equation, but assumptions to retain only linear terms and to require that $\partial f / \partial y$ be constant soon follow and the equation actually being studied is (6.111).

If the corrector equation in a predictor-corrector method is iterated to convergence for each integration step, then any error in the observed solution can be attributed solely to the corrector. Hence, it is sufficient to study the propagation of error by the corrector equation alone. When the corrector is not iterated to convergence, but is employed just once (often the case in practice), then the stability analysis must include errors generated by both the predictor and corrector equations [7]. To illustrate, we shall assume that the corrector is iterated to convergence.

Since the corrector equation (6.95b) for the fourth-order Milne method is observed to produce catastrophic instabilities for solution of some differential equations (but excellent results for others), a stability analysis will illustrate the general approach. Other multistep methods can be analyzed similarly.

The Milne corrector is

$$y_{i+1} = y_{i-1} + \frac{h}{3}(f_{i+1} + 4f_i + f_{i-1}).$$

Substitution of (6.111) leads to

$$\left(1 - \frac{\alpha h}{3}\right)y_{i+1} - 4\left(\frac{\alpha h}{3}\right)y_i - \left(1 + \frac{\alpha h}{3}\right)y_{i-1} = 0, \tag{6.112}$$

which is a *linear homogeneous difference equation* of order two. Note that for a fixed h, the coefficients are constants, and that the convergence criterion of (6.98) requires that

$$\frac{h}{3}|\alpha| < 1. \tag{6.113}$$

The theory of the solution of linear difference equations such as (6.112) is closely related to the theory for the solution of linear ordinary differential equations. We shall give only a brief outline of the theory here; those unfamiliar with it are referred to the excellent introduction to difference equations by Conte [30].

If we let y_k be a function defined for a set of integers k, then a *linear difference equation of order n* is a linear relation involving $y_k, y_{k+1}, \ldots, y_{k+n}$, that is, it is of the form

$$a_0 y_k + a_1 y_{k+1} + a_2 y_{k+2} + \cdots + a_n y_{k+n} = b, \quad (6.114)$$

where the coefficients $a_0, \ldots, a_n$ and b may be functions of k but not of y. If b is zero, the equation is considered to be *homogeneous*; otherwise it is called *nonhomogeneous*.

The theory for solution of homogeneous linear difference equations with *constant* coefficients is similar to that for homogeneous linear differential equations with constant coefficients. In this case, we look for a solution of the form $y_k = \gamma^k$. Substitution of this solution into (6.114), with $b = 0$ and $a_0, \ldots, a_n$ constant, yields

$$a_0 \gamma^k + a_1 \gamma^{k+1} + \cdots + a_n \gamma^{k+n} = 0,$$

which, upon division by γ^k, becomes

$$a_0 + a_1 \gamma + a_2 \gamma^2 + \cdots + a_n \gamma^n = 0. \quad (6.115)$$

Equation (6.115) is called the *characteristic equation* and is a polynomial of degree n in the variable γ. If the n roots, $\gamma_1, \ldots, \gamma_n$ of (6.115) are distinct, then $\gamma_1^k, \gamma_2^k, \ldots, \gamma_n^k$ are all solutions of (6.114).

The complete solution of the homogeneous form of (6.114) is then given by the linear combination

$$y_k = c_1 \gamma_1^k + c_2 \gamma_2^k + \cdots + c_n \gamma_n^k, \quad (6.116)$$

where $c_1, \ldots, c_n$ are constants. Each term γ_j^k is a *particular* solution of the homogeneous equation. Complex and multiple roots of (6.115) may be handled in a fashion similar to that used for linear ordinary differential equations.

For the homogeneous linear difference equation of (6.112), the characteristic equation is

$$\left(1 - \frac{\alpha h}{3}\right)\gamma^2 - 4\left(\frac{\alpha h}{3}\right)\gamma - \left(1 + \frac{\alpha h}{3}\right) = 0. \quad (6.117)$$

This is a quadratic equation in γ which, from the quadratic formula, has the two roots

$$\gamma_1 = \frac{\dfrac{2\alpha h}{3} + \sqrt{1 + \dfrac{\alpha^2 h^2}{3}}}{1 - \dfrac{\alpha h}{3}}, \quad (6.118)$$

$$\gamma_2 = \frac{\dfrac{2\alpha h}{3} - \sqrt{1 + \dfrac{\alpha^2 h^2}{3}}}{1 - \dfrac{\alpha h}{3}}. \quad (6.119)$$

Milne and Reynolds [31] have tabulated the values of these two roots for values of αh between -1 and 1. Root γ_1 is positive for all αh in this range and is monotone increasing from 0.366 at $\alpha h = -1$ to 2.732 at $\alpha h = 1$. Root γ_2 is negative for all αh in this range and is monotone increasing from -1.366 at $\alpha h = -1$ to -0.732 at $\alpha h = 1$. A critical feature of γ_2 is that for negative αh, it is smaller than -1 and for positive αh, it is larger than -1. If we set h equal to zero, the roots are $\gamma_1 = 1$ and $\gamma_2 = -1$. Since the convergence criterion (6.113) requires that $|\alpha h|$ be smaller than 3, and for rapid convergence preferably much less than 3, values of αh between -1 and 1 are those which would be encountered in practice.

Now, if γ_1 and γ_2 are expanded in a power series [31], they are, respectively,

$$\gamma_1 = 1 + \alpha h + \frac{(\alpha h)^2}{2!} + \frac{(\alpha h)^3}{3!} + \frac{(\alpha h)^4}{4!} + \frac{(\alpha h)^5}{72} + \cdots$$

$$= e^{\alpha h} + \frac{(\alpha h)^5}{180} + \cdots, \quad (6.120)$$

$$\gamma_2 = -1 + \frac{(\alpha h)}{3} - \frac{(\alpha h)^2}{18} - \frac{(\alpha h)^3}{54} + \frac{5(\alpha h)^4}{648} + \frac{5(\alpha h)^5}{1944} + \cdots \quad (6.121)$$

The solution of the original difference equation (6.112) assumes the form (6.116)

$$y_i = c_1 \gamma_1^i + c_2 \gamma_2^i \quad (6.122)$$

or, from (6.120),

$$y_i \doteq c_1 e^{i\alpha h} + c_2 \gamma_2^i. \quad (6.123)$$

Since $x_i = x_0 + ih$, we may write (6.123) as

$$y_i = c_1 e^{\alpha(x_i - x_0)} + c_2 \gamma_2^i. \quad (6.124)$$

The analytical solution of the original differential equation (6.111) is given by

$$\left. \begin{array}{l} y(x) = y(x_0)e^{\alpha(x - x_0)} \\ y(x_i) = c e^{\alpha x_i} \end{array} \right\} \quad (6.125)$$

or

where c is a constant determined by the initial conditions. Clearly, the particular solution of the homogeneous difference equation (6.112) which corresponds to the root γ_1 is the desired solution of the differential equation (6.125). Note that the *difference* equation has a *second* particular solution $c_2 \gamma_2^i$ which has no relationship whatsoever to the exact solution of the differential equation. Such solutions are called *parasitic* or *extraneous* solutions, and will always be present when a difference equation of order greater than one is used to generate the solution of a first-order ordinary differential equation. We must investigate the nature of the parasitic solution to see if it will in fact be of no significance, or might possibly overwhelm the true solution and render the numerical solution meaningless.

First consider the case $\alpha > 0$. Since h is positive, αh will be positive, and the solution of the difference equation associated with γ_1 will *grow* exponentially as $ce^{\alpha x_i}$, approximating a true solution to the differential equation. For positive αh, the root γ_2 is a negative fraction greater than -1. Therefore, the particular solution γ_2^i will *decay* with increasing i, and will have only minor influence on the complete solution. Thus errors introduced at various stages during computation (by local truncation errors or round-off errors) will not be amplified in succeeding steps because of the presence of the parasitic solution.

Next, consider the case $\alpha < 0$. Since h is positive, αh will be negative, and the solution of the difference equation associated with γ_1 will *decay* exponentially as $ce^{\alpha x_i}$, approximating a true solution to the differential equation. For negative αh, the root γ_2 is a negative number less than -1. Hence the particular solution γ_2^i will *grow* in magnitude with increasing i. In fact, because γ_2 is negative, the solution will *oscillate* in sign from step to step. In this case any errors introduced during the computation will be amplified during succeeding steps with alternating signs. Eventually, this parasitic solution will swamp the true solution and the numerical results will be meaningless.

Methods which exhibit stable behavior for the solution of equation (6.111) for some values of αh and unstable behavior for other values of αh are said to be *weakly stable*, *weakly unstable*, or *marginally stable*. Hence the fourth-order Milne corrector is a marginally stable method. This does not mean that the method should not be used, but only that it should not be used when the true solution of the equation is a nonincreasing (decaying) function. Under other circumstances, the Milne corrector is perfectly suitable and, because of its small truncation error, even desirable.

Similar analyses can be carried out for any of the multistep algorithms. In each case, the appropriate homogeneous linear difference equation with constant coefficients is found for equation (6.111). The characteristic equation is then solved for the roots $\gamma_1, \gamma_2, \ldots, \gamma_n$, where n, the order of the equation, is equal to the difference of the largest and smallest subscript which appears in the multistep equation. For example, for the Milne corrector, the largest subscript is $i + 1$ and the smallest is $i - 1$; the order of the difference equation and thus the number of solutions is $(i + 1) - (i - 1)$ or 2.

Let γ_1 be the root of the characteristic equation which is associated with the true solution of (6.111); then γ_1 is called the *principal zero* or *root*. If

$$|\gamma_j| < |\gamma_1|, \qquad j = 2, 3, \ldots, n, \qquad (6.126)$$

the method is called *relatively stable*. In this case, the approximation to the true solution will dominate the parasitic solutions associated with the roots γ_j, $j = 2, 3, \ldots, n$. If the true solution of (6.111) decays with increasing i, then the parasitic solutions must decay even

more rapidly. If the true solution of (6.111) grows with increasing i, then the parasitic solutions must either decay or grow less rapidly than the true solution.

A method is called *strongly stable* if

$$|\gamma_j| < 1, \qquad j = 2, 3, \ldots, n. \qquad (6.127)$$

Thus, for a method to be strongly stable, all parasitic solutions must decay with increasing i.

Dahlquist [32] has shown that if the truncation error for a multistep method is of $O(h^{p+1})$, and n is the order of the difference equation, then to achieve either strong or marginal stability, p must satisfy the relationship

$$p \leqslant n + 2. \qquad (6.128)$$

Moreover, $p = n + 2$ is possible only when n is even and the method is marginally stable (for example, Milne's fourth-order corrector for which $n = 2$ and $p = 4$). Thus one can increase the accuracy of a method (increase the order of the truncation error) only by increasing the value of n, and consequently, the number of parasitic solutions associated with the difference equation. Thus, diminished stability is the price one must pay for increased accuracy in a multistep method. Stability analyses for several new predictor-corrector algorithms have been published in recent years [33, 34, 35, 36, 37, 39].

All the preceding stability analyses have dealt with the solution of the very simple linear equation of (6.111). The question of applicability of the conclusions of the simple stability analyses to more general nonlinear equations remains unanswered. Henrici [2] believes that the variability of $\partial f/\partial x$ may make a significant difference in the stability of a method, for example, changing a strongly stable method into a marginally stable one for certain equations. Computational experiments have shown, however, that conclusions about stability, following from a stability analysis for equation (6.111), correlate rather well with observed behavior of the multistep methods when used for other equations as well.

Simultaneous ordinary differential equations (see Section 6.7) may be solved by multistep methods as well as by one-step methods. The appropriate algorithm is implemented for each equation in parallel at each step. The criteria for solution of simultaneous corrector equations by the usual method of successive substitutions are those outlined in Section 5.8. Henrici has devoted an entire book [28] to a study of the solution of systems of equations by multistep methods.

6.13   Other Integration Formulas

Hamming [21, 22] has investigated a general class of corrector formulas of the form

$$y_{i+1} = a_0 y_i + a_1 y_{i-1} + a_2 y_{i-2}$$
$$+ h(b_{-1} f_{i+1} + b_0 f_i + b_1 f_{i-1} + b_2 f_{i-2}) + O(h^5),$$
$$(6.129)$$

which includes the correctors for the fourth-order Milne and Adams-Moulton predictor-corrector methods. Five of the seven constants in (6.129) can be eliminated by requiring that the formula be exact for polynomials of degree four or less, that is, exact for the functions $y(x) = 1, x, x^2, x^3, x^4$. This process is called the method of undetermined coefficients, and leads to the following relationships among the constants, taking a_1 and a_2 as the parameters:

$$a_0 = 1 - a_1 - a_2 \qquad b_0 = \frac{1}{24}(19 + 13a_1 + 8a_2)$$

$$a_1 = a_1 \qquad b_1 = \frac{1}{24}(-5 + 13a_1 + 32a_2)$$

$$a_2 = a_2 \qquad b_2 = \frac{1}{24}(1 - a_1 + 8a_2)$$

$$b_{-1} = \frac{1}{24}(9 - a_1).$$

$$(6.130)$$

The derivation of the error term for (6.129) for $y(x)$ not a polynomial of degree 4 or less is rather complicated [7, 22] and will not be discussed here.

Hamming [22] has studied the stability characteristics of (6.129) and selected the remaining parameters a_1 and a_2 to achieve much stronger stability than is exhibited by the Milne method corrector; the price paid is some increase in the magnitude of the truncation error. The form of (6.129), selected by Hamming, as representing the best compromise between stability and accuracy, is

$$y_{i+1} = \frac{9}{8}y_i - \frac{1}{8}y_{i-2} + \frac{3}{8}h(f_{i+1} + 2f_i - f_{i-1}). \quad (6.131)$$

Assuming that y_i, y_{i-2}, f_i, and f_{i-1} are known exactly, the local truncation error for (6.131) is

$$e_t = \frac{1}{40}h^5 f^{(4)}(\xi), \qquad \xi \text{ in } (x_{i-2}, x_{i+1}). \quad (6.132)$$

For practical step sizes, (6.131) is stable in the sense of (6.127).

The Hamming corrector can be used with any suitable predictor. *Hamming's predictor-corrector method* employs the fourth-order Milne method predictor; the technique of modifying both the predicted and corrected value of the solution already outlined for the fourth-order Milne method on pages 386 and 387 is usually followed. The complete algorithm is:

1. Starting values for $y_0, y_1, y_2, y_3, f_0, f_1, f_2$, and f_3 must be available. Usually y_0 will be the only known condition, and a fourth-order Runge-Kutta method will be used to compute y_1, y_2, and y_3. The derivatives f_0, f_1, f_2, and f_3 can be computed from the differential equation $dy/dx = f(x, y)$. Steps 2 through 6 are then repeated for $i = 3, 4, \ldots$.

2. The predicted solution $y_{i+1,0}$ is computed using the fourth-order Milne predictor as in (6.102),

$$y_{i+1,0} = y_{i-3} + \frac{4}{3}h(2f_i - f_{i-1} + 2f_{i-2}).$$

3. The predicted value is modified, by assuming that the local truncation error on successive intervals does not change appreciably, to yield

$$y^*_{i+1,0} = y_{i+1,0} + \frac{112}{121}(y_{i,k} - y_{i,0}). \quad (6.133)$$

This modification is analogous to that of (6.110) for Milne's method. For the case $i = 3$, this step is bypassed, since there will be no values for the elements on the right-hand side of (6.133). Here, $y_{i,k}$ is the solution of the corrector equation (6.134) from the preceding step.

4. Hamming's corrector equation of (6.131) is solved iteratively using the successive substitution algorithm

$$y_{i+1,j+1} = \frac{1}{8}\{9y_i - y_{i-2} + 3h[f(x_{i+1}, y_{i+1,j})$$
$$+ 2f_i - f_{i-1}]\}, \qquad j = 0, 1, \ldots, k. \quad (6.134)$$

The initial value for $y_{i+1,j}$ on the right-hand side is $y^*_{i+1,0}$ from step 3. In theory, iteration is continued until some convergence test has been satisfied [for example, see (6.103)]. In practice, the corrector is usually applied just once; the step size is chosen to insure that convergence effectively takes place in just one iteration.

5. The values $y_{i+1,k}$ from step 4 and $y_{i+1,0}$ from step 2 are next used to estimate the truncation error e_t for the corrector equation from

$$e_t \doteq \frac{9}{121}(y_{i+1,k} - y_{i+1,0}), \quad (6.135)$$

which follows directly from the error terms for the predictor (6.104) and corrector (6.132), respectively, using an analysis identical with that outlined on page 387 for Milne's method [see (6.107)].

6. The final value for the solution y_{i+1} is then computed from

$$y_{i+1} = y_{i+1,k} - \frac{9}{121}(y_{i+1,k} - y_{i+1,0}), \quad (6.136)$$

which is analogous to (6.108) for Milne's method. The derivative is computed at this final value and called f_{i+1}. If the local truncation error estimate is within allowable limits, the counter i is advanced by one and steps 2 through 6 are repeated for the next integration interval. If the local truncation error estimate from (6.135) is outside allowable limits, the step size is adjusted in some fashion (see page 388), and then the integration process is continued.

This fourth-order Hamming's method is now among the most popular of the multi-step methods.

Many other one-step and multistep algorithms are available for solution of first-order ordinary differential equations. Milne [5] and Henrici [2] give particularly complete coverage of the multistep methods.

Recently, Butcher [23, 24, 25] has developed several one-step methods of orders five to seven. Gear [26] and Butcher [27, 38] have developed some modified multi-step methods of orders four to seven, that have some of the characteristics of both one-step methods (derivative evaluations are made in the interior of the integration step) and multistep methods (information from previous steps is used). Waters [29] has compared the performance of several of these methods with the commonly used algorithms (fourth-order Runge-Kutta method, etc.) from the standpoint of accuracy and computation time. He solves a system of ordinary differential equations for which the evaluation of derivatives requires relatively little computing time.

There is also a variety of one-step and multistep methods suitable for direct integration of equations of order two or more; the higher-order equation need not be reduced to a system of first-order equations before carrying out the numerical solution. Henrici [2] has pointed out that solutions generated by these direct methods are no more accurate than those found by reducing the equation to a system of first order equations and then solving the system using methods for first-order equations. However, for equations of special form (for example, second-order differential equations that do not contain a term in the first derivative), the direct methods may save some computation.

EXAMPLE 6.4

HAMMING'S METHOD

Problem Statement

Write a general-purpose function named HAMING that solves a system of n first-order ordinary differential equations

$$\frac{dy_1}{dx} = f_1(x, y_1, y_2, \ldots, y_n)$$

$$\frac{dy_2}{dx} = f_2(x, y_1, y_2, \ldots, y_n) \qquad (6.4.1)$$

$$\vdots$$

$$\frac{dy_n}{dx} = f_n(x, y_1, y_2, \ldots, y_n),$$

using Hamming's predictor-corrector method outlined in Section 6.13.

Write a main program that solves the second-order ordinary differential equation

$$\frac{d^2y}{dx^2} = -y, \qquad (6.4.2)$$

subject to the initial conditions

$$y(0) = 0, \qquad \frac{dy}{dx}(0) = 1. \qquad (6.4.3)$$

The program should call on the fourth-order Runge-Kutta function RUNGE, developed in Example 6.3, to find the essential starting values for Hamming's algorithm and, thereafter, should call on HAMING to calculate estimates of y and dy/dx on the interval $[0, x_{max}]$. Evaluate the numerical solutions for several different step sizes, h, and compare the numerical results with the true solutions

$$y(x) = \sin x$$
$$\frac{dy}{dx} = \cos x. \qquad (6.4.4)$$

Method of Solution

Let $y_{j,i}$ be the final modification of the estimated solution for the jth dependent variable, y_j, at x_i, resulting from Hamming's method (see (6.136)), and let $f_{j,i}$ be the calculated estimate of f_j at x_i, that is,

$$y_{j,i} \doteq y_j(x_i),$$
$$f_{j,i} = f_j(x_i, y_{1,i}, y_{2,i}, \ldots, y_{n,i}). \qquad (6.4.5)$$

Assume that $y_{j,i}, y_{j,i-1}, y_{j,i-2}, y_{j,i-3}, f_{j,i}, f_{j,i-1}, f_{j,i-2}$ have already been found and are available for $j = 1, 2, \ldots, n$. Let an estimate of the local truncation error (6.135) for the corrector equation (6.131) for the jth dependent variable be denoted $e_{j,i}$. Then, assuming that the $e_{j,i}, j = 1, 2, \ldots, n$, are available, the procedure outlined

for Hamming's method in Section 6.13 may be modified to handle a system of n simultaneous first-order ordinary differential equations by simply appending a leading subscript, j, to all y and f terms in (6.131) to (6.136).

In terms of the new nomenclature, steps 2 through 6 of the outline in Section 6.13 are:

2. The predicted solutions $y_{j,i+1,0}$ are computed using the Milne predictor (6.102):

$$y_{j,i+1,0} = y_{j,i-3} + \tfrac{4}{3}h(2f_{j,i} - f_{j,i-1} + 2f_{j,i-2}),$$
$$j = 1, 2, \ldots, n. \quad (6.4.6)$$

3. The predicted solutions, $y_{j,i+1,0}$, are modified (assuming that the local truncation error estimates, $e_{j,i+1}, j = 1, 2, \ldots, n$, will not be significantly different from the estimates $e_{j,i}, j = 1, 2, \ldots, n$) as in (6.133):

$$y^*_{j,i+1,0} = y_{j,i+1,0} + \tfrac{112}{9}e_{j,i}, \qquad j = 1, 2, \ldots, n. \quad (6.4.7)$$

4. The jth corrector equation corresponding to (6.134) is applied for each dependent variable:

$$y_{j,i+1,1} = \tfrac{1}{8}[9y_{j,i} - y_{j,i-2} + 3h(f^*_{j,i+1,0} + 2f_{j,i} - f_{j,i-1})],$$
$$j = 1, 2, \ldots, n, \quad (6.4.8)$$

where

$$f^*_{j,i+1,0} = f(x_{i+1}, y^*_{1,i+1,0}, y^*_{2,i+1,0}, \ldots, y^*_{n,i+1,0}). \quad (6.4.9)$$

The corrector equations in (6.4.8) are being applied just once for each variable, the customary practice. The corrector equations could, however, be applied more than once, as in (6.134). Note that the subscript j in (6.134) is an iteration counter, and is not the index, j, on the dependent variables used throughout this example.

5. Estimate the local truncation error for each of the corrector equations on the current interval as in (6.135):

$$e_{j,i+1} = \tfrac{9}{121}(y_{j,i+1,1} - y_{j,i+1,0}), \qquad j = 1, 2, \ldots, n. \quad (6.4.10)$$

6. Make the final modifications of the solutions of the corrector equations as in (6.136):

$$y_{j,i+1} = y_{j,i+1,1} - e_{j,i+1}, \qquad j = 1, 2, \ldots, n. \quad (6.4.11)$$

After evaluating the $y_{j,i+1}$, the n values $f_{j,i+1}$ may be computed from (6.4.5) as

$$f_{j,i+1} = f_j(x_{i+1}, y_{1,i+1}, y_{2,i+1}, \ldots, y_{n,i+1}), \quad j = 1, 2, \ldots, n. \quad (6.4.12)$$

If desired, the entire process may be repeated for the next interval by starting again at step 2.

If HAMING is to be a general-purpose function, suitable for integrating *any* set of n first-order equations, then the evaluation of the derivative estimates in (6.4.9) and (6.4.12) must be done outside the function HAMING.

One way to implement the sequence (6.4.6) to (6.4.12) is to separate HAMING into two parts, one to handle the prediction portion of the algorithm (equations (6.4.6) and (6.4.7)), and the other to handle the correction portion of the algorithm (equations (6.4.8), (6.4.10), and (6.4.11)). The function can then return to the calling program after each portion, requesting that the derivative estimates of (6.4.9) and (6.4.12) be calculated in the main program or elsewhere, when needed.

A simplified diagram of the calling procedure for HAMING is shown in Fig. 6.4.1. Note that all direct references to the first-order equations are confined to the calling program. Therefore, the function HAMING can be written to solve an arbitrary system of n first-order equations, provided that the $5n + 2$ essential numbers, x_i, h, and

$$\left. \begin{array}{lll} y_{j,i-3}, & f_{j,i}, & e_{j,i}, \\ & f_{j,i-1}, & \\ & f_{j,i-2}, & \end{array} \right\} j = 1, 2, \ldots, n, \quad (6.4.13)$$

are available for the function to use upon entry to the predictor section, and the $6n + 1$ essential numbers, h, and

$$\left. \begin{array}{ll} y_{j,i}, & f^*_{j,i+1,0}, \\ y_{j,i-2}, & f_{j,i}, \\ y_{j,i+1,0}, & f_{j,i-1}, \end{array} \right\} j = 1, 2, \ldots, n, \quad (6.4.14)$$

are available for the function to use upon entry to the corrector section.

The simplest way to communicate the necessary numbers in (6.4.13) and (6.4.14) is to maintain tables available to both the calling program and the function HAMING. Most of the bookkeeping tasks of updating the tables, etc., can be assigned to the function, so that the calling program has little to do except to set up the necessary tables prior to the first call upon HAMING, and to evaluate the derivative estimates of (6.4.9) and (6.4.12). Let a 4 by n matrix Y, a 3 by n matrix F, and an n-element vector $\bar{e}$

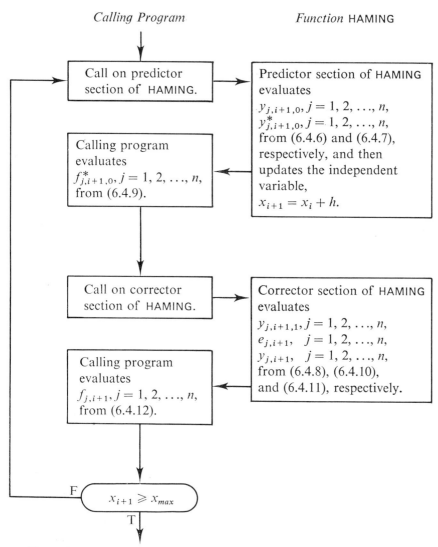

Figure 6.4.1 *Communication between a calling program and the function* HAMING.

Example 6.4 Hamming's Method   **395**

be assigned to the calling program, and available to the function HAMING through the argument list. Then write the calling program and function HAMING, so that the matrices Y and F, and the vector $\bar{e}$, have the following contents at the indicated points in the algorithm.

Before entry into the predictor section of HAMING:

$$Y = \begin{bmatrix} y_{1,i} & y_{2,i} & \cdots & y_{j,i} & \cdots & y_{n,i} \\ y_{1,i-1} & y_{2,i-1} & \cdots & y_{j,i-1} & \cdots & y_{n,i-1} \\ y_{1,i-2} & y_{2,i-2} & \cdots & y_{j,i-2} & \cdots & y_{n,i-2} \\ y_{1,i-3} & y_{2,i-3} & \cdots & y_{j,i-3} & \cdots & y_{n,i-3} \end{bmatrix},$$

(6.4.15)

$$F = \begin{bmatrix} f_{1,i} & f_{2,i} & \cdots & f_{j,i} & \cdots & f_{n,i} \\ f_{1,i-1} & f_{2,i-1} & \cdots & f_{j,i-1} & \cdots & f_{n,i-1} \\ f_{1,i-2} & f_{2,i-2} & \cdots & f_{j,i-2} & \cdots & f_{n,i-2} \end{bmatrix},$$

(6.4.16)

$$\bar{e} = \begin{bmatrix} e_{1,i} & e_{2,i} & \cdots & e_{j,i} & \cdots & e_{n,i} \end{bmatrix}^t.$$

(6.4.17)

After return from the predictor section of HAMING:

$$Y = \begin{bmatrix} y_{1,i+1,0}^{*} & y_{2,i+1,0}^{*} & \cdots & y_{j,i+1,0}^{*} & \cdots & y_{n,i+1,0}^{*} \\ y_{1,i} & y_{2,i} & \cdots & y_{j,i} & \cdots & y_{n,i} \\ y_{1,i-1} & y_{2,i-1} & \cdots & y_{j,i-1} & \cdots & y_{n,i-1} \\ y_{1,i-2} & y_{2,i-2} & \cdots & y_{j,i-2} & \cdots & y_{n,i-2} \end{bmatrix},$$

(6.4.18)

$$F = \begin{bmatrix} f_{1,i} & f_{2,i} & \cdots & f_{j,i} & \cdots & f_{n,i} \\ f_{1,i} & f_{2,i} & \cdots & f_{j,i} & \cdots & f_{n,i} \\ f_{1,i-1} & f_{2,i-1} & \cdots & f_{j,i-1} & \cdots & f_{n,i-1} \end{bmatrix},$$

(6.4.19)

$\bar{e}$ is unchanged from (6.4.17).

Before entry into the corrector section of HAMING:

Y is unchanged from (6.4.18),

$$F = \begin{bmatrix} f_{1,i+1,0}^{*} & f_{2,i+1,0}^{*} & \cdots & f_{j,i+1,0}^{*} & \cdots & f_{n,i+1,0}^{*} \\ f_{1,i} & f_{2,i} & \cdots & f_{j,i} & \cdots & f_{n,i} \\ f_{1,i-1} & f_{2,i-1} & \cdots & f_{j,i-1} & \cdots & f_{n,i-1} \end{bmatrix},$$

(6.4.20)

$\bar{e}$ is unchanged from (6.4.17).

After return from the corrector section of HAMING:

$$Y = \begin{bmatrix} y_{1,i+1} & y_{2,i+1} & \cdots & y_{j,i+1} & \cdots & y_{n,i+1} \\ y_{1,i} & y_{2,i} & \cdots & y_{j,i} & \cdots & y_{n,i} \\ y_{1,i-1} & y_{2,i-1} & \cdots & y_{j,i-1} & \cdots & y_{n,i-1} \\ y_{1,i-2} & y_{2,i-2} & \cdots & y_{j,i-2} & \cdots & y_{n,i-2} \end{bmatrix},$$

(6.4.21)

F is unchanged from (6.4.20),

$$\bar{e} = \begin{bmatrix} e_{1,i+1} & e_{2,i+1} & \cdots & e_{j,i+1} & \cdots & e_{n,i+1} \end{bmatrix}^t.$$

(6.4.22)

If the calling program uses (6.4.12) to replace the elements in the first row of F after the return from the corrector section of HAMING, so that

$$F = \begin{bmatrix} f_{1,i+1} & f_{2,i+1} & \cdots & f_{j,i+1} & \cdots & f_{n,i+1} \\ f_{1,i} & f_{2,i} & \cdots & f_{j,i} & \cdots & f_{n,i} \\ f_{1,i-1} & f_{2,i-1} & \cdots & f_{j,i-1} & \cdots & f_{n,i-1} \end{bmatrix},$$

(6.4.23)

then the matrices Y and F and vector $\bar{e}$ are ready for a call on the predictor section of HAMING for the next integration step. The independent variable is incremented in the predictor section, that is,

$$x_{i+1} = x_i + h,$$

(6.4.24)

so that the calling program will automatically have the proper value to calculate the $f_{j,i+1,0}^{*}$ and $f_{j,i+1}$ from (6.4.9) and (6.4.12), respectively.

Assuming that the integration process begins at $x = x_0$ and that the only known conditions on (6.4.1) are

$$y_{1,0} = c_1$$
$$y_{2,0} = c_2$$
$$\vdots$$
$$y_{n,0} = c_n,$$

(6.4.25)

there is not enough information available to calculate the elements of (6.4.15), (6.4.16), and (6.4.17). Therefore, HAMING cannot be called directly when $x_i = x_0$. The usual procedure is to use a one-step method to integrate across the first three steps to evaluate

$$\left.\begin{matrix} y_{j,1} \\ y_{j,2} \\ y_{j,3} \end{matrix}\right\} \quad j = 1, 2, \ldots, n.$$

(6.4.26)

With (6.4.25) and (6.4.26), the matrix Y of (6.4.15) is known for $i = 3$. The matrix F of (6.4.16) may be evaluated from (6.4.26) and (6.4.1) for $i = 3$. The vector of local truncation error estimates (6.4.17) for $i = 3$ is normally unknown, and should be set to zero unless better values are available from other sources. HAMING may then be called for the first time.

In the calling program that follows, the function RUNGE, already developed in Example 6.3, is used to generate the solutions of (6.4.26). Since RUNGE implements the fourth-order Runge-Kutta method, the solutions of (6.4.26) should be comparable in accuracy with the solutions generated by the Hamming's predictor-corrector algorithm, also a fourth-order method.

The main program reads data values for n, x_0, h, x_{max}, int, $y_{1,0}$, $y_{2,0}$, ..., $y_{n,0}$. Here, int is the number of integration steps between the printing of solution values. This program is a reasonably general one. However, the defining statements for computation of the derivative estimates (6.4.9) and (6.4.12) would be different for each system of differential equations.

For test purposes, the differential equation solved is (6.4.2), subject to the initial conditions of (6.4.3). First, the second-order equation must be rewritten as a system of two first-order equations. Let

$$y_1 = y$$

$$y_2 = \frac{dy}{dx}. \tag{6.4.27}$$

Then

$$\frac{dy_1}{dx} = f_1(x, y_1, y_2) = \frac{dy}{dx} = y_2$$

$$\frac{dy_2}{dx} = f_2(x, y_1, y_2) = \frac{d^2 y}{dx^2} = -y = -y_1, \tag{6.4.28}$$

so that

$$f_{1,i} = y_{2,i}$$

$$f_{2,i} = -y_{1,i}. \tag{6.4.29}$$

The initial conditions of (6.4.3) are

$$y_{1,0} = 0$$

$$y_{2,0} = 1. \tag{6.4.30}$$

Example 6.4   Hamming's Method   **397**

Flow Diagram

Main Program

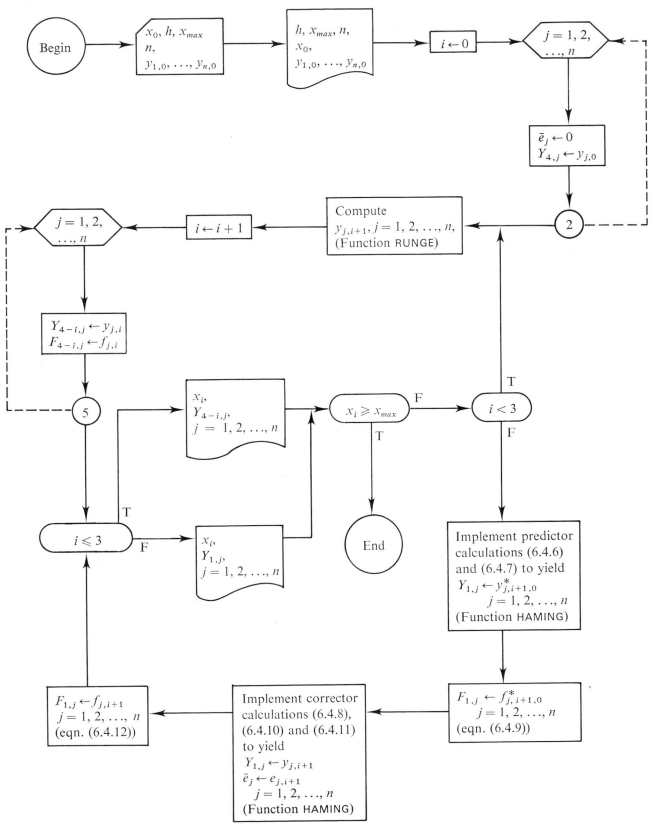

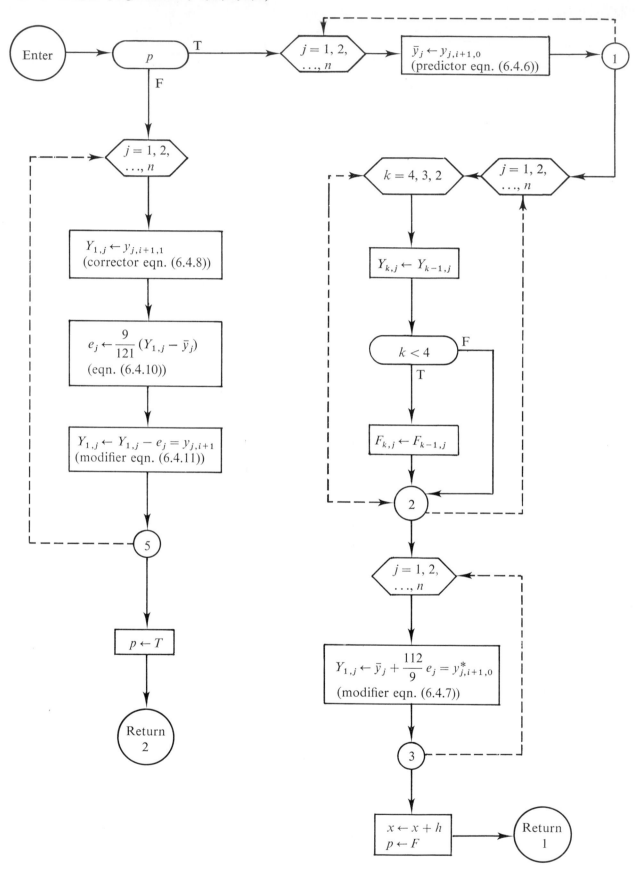

Function HAMING (Arguments: n, Y, F, x, h, $\bar{e}$)

Example 6.4   Hamming's Method   399

FORTRAN *Implementation*

List of Principal Variables

Program Symbol	Definition

(Main)

COUNT — Step counter, i

F — F, a 3 by n matrix of derivative estimates (see (6.4.16), (6.4.19), (6.4.20), and (6.4.23)).

FR — Vector of values, $f_{j,i}$, $j = 1, 2, \ldots, n$. Used by RUNGE.

H — h, step size.

ISUB — $4 - i$, a subscript.

INT — Print control parameter, *int*. Solutions are printed at x_0 and every *int* steps thereafter.

J — j, index on the dependent variables.

M — Value returned by the function HAMING.

N — n, number of first-order ordinary differential equations.

RUNGE — Function that implements the fourth-order Runge-Kutta method to solve a system of n first-order ordinary differential equations. See Example 6.3 for details.

TE — Vector of local truncation error estimates, $e_{j,i}$, $j = 1, 2, \ldots, n$.

X — Independent variable, x_i.

XMAX — Upper integration limit, x_{max}.

Y — Y, a 4 by n matrix of solution values (see (6.4.15), (6.4.18), and (6.4.21)).

YR — Vector of values $y_{j,i}$, $j = 1, 2, \ldots, n$. Used by RUNGE.

(Function HAMING)

K — k, a subscript.

K5 — $5 - k$.

PRED — Logical variable, p. If true, the predictor section of HAMING is executed; if false, the corrector section of HAMING is executed.

YPRED — Vector of predicted solutions, $\bar{y}_j = y_{j,i+1,0}$, $j = 1, 2, \ldots, n$, (see (6.4.6)).

Program Listing

Main Program

```
C              APPLIED NUMERICAL METHODS, EXAMPLE 6.4
C              HAMMING'S PREDICTOR-CORRECTOR METHOD
C
C              THIS TEST PROGRAM SOLVES A SYSTEM OF N FIRST-ORDER ORDINARY
C              DIFFERENTIAL EQUATIONS USING THE HAMMING PREDICTOR-CORRECTOR
C              METHOD.  THE PROGRAM READS A STARTING VALUE FOR THE INDEPENDENT
C              VARIABLE, X, THE INTEGRATION STEPSIZE, H, THE UPPER LIMIT OF
C              INTEGRATION, XMAX, AND N INITIAL CONDITIONS YR(1)...YR(N).   Y
C              AND F ARE MATRICES CONTAINING SOLUTION AND DERIVATIVE VALUES
C              AND ARE DESCRIBED IN THE TEXT. TE(J) IS THE TRUNCATION ERROR
C              ESTIMATE FOR THE JTH CORRECTOR EQUATION.  COUNT IS THE STEP
C              COUNTER.  THE FUNCTION RUNGE (SEE EXAMPLE 6.3) IS CALLED TO
C              INTEGRATE ACROSS THE FIRST THREE STEPS AND YIELDS THE STARTING
C              VALUES NEEDED FOR HAMMING'S METHOD.  THEREAFTER, THE EQUATIONS
C              ARE INTEGRATED USING ALTERNATELY THE PREDICTOR AND CORRECTOR
C              PORTIONS OF THE FUNCTION HAMING.  THE EQUATIONS BEING SOLVED
C              AS AN EXAMPLE ARE THOSE OF (6.4.2).  TO SOLVE ANOTHER SYSTEM OF
C              EQUATIONS, ALL STATEMENTS REFERENCING THE SYMBOLS F AND FR
C              (DERIVATIVES FOR USE BY HAMING AND RUNGE, RESPECTIVELY) MUST BE
C              REPLACED BY STATEMENTS DEFINING THE DERIVATIVES FOR THE NEW
C              SYSTEM.  THE SOLUTIONS ARE PRINTED AT THE INITIAL X AND AFTER
C              EVERY INT INTEGRATION STEPS THEREAFTER.
C
               IMPLICIT  REAL*8(A-H, O-Z)
               INTEGER   COUNT, RUNGE, HAMING
               DIMENSION TE(20), YR(20), FR(20), Y(4,20), F(3,20)
C
C              ..... READ IN PARAMETERS AND INITIAL CONDITIONS .....
      1  READ (5,100)   X, H, XMAX, INT, N, (YR(J), J=1,N)
C
C              ..... PRINT PARAMETERS, HEADING AND INITIAL CONDITIONS .....
         WRITE (6,200)   H, XMAX, INT, N, (J, J=1,N)
         WRITE (6,201)   X, (YR(J), J=1,N)
C
C              ..... INITIALIZE STEP COUNTER AND FIRST ROW OF Y MATRIX.
C                    SET INITIAL TRUNCATION ERRORS TO ZERO .....
         COUNT = 0
         DO 2  J=1,N
         TE(J) = 0.
      2  Y(4,J) = YR(J)
C
C              ..... CALL RUNGE TO INTEGRATE ACROSS FIRST THREE STEPS .....
      3  IF (RUNGE(N,YR,FR,X,H) .NE. 1)   GO TO 4
            FR(1) = YR(2)
            FR(2) = -YR(1)
            GO TO 3
C
C              ..... PUT APPROPRIATE INITIAL VALUES IN THE Y AND F MATRICES .....
      4  COUNT = COUNT + 1
         ISUB = 4 - COUNT
         DO 5  J=1,N
      5  Y(ISUB,J) = YR(J)
         F(ISUB,1) = YR(2)
         F(ISUB,2) = - YR(1)
C
C              ..... PRINT SOLUTIONS AFTER EVERY INT STEPS .....
      6  IF ( COUNT/INT*INT .NE. COUNT )   GO TO 7
         IF ( COUNT.LE.3 )   WRITE (6,202)   X, (Y(ISUB,J), J=1,N)
         IF ( COUNT.GT.3 )   WRITE (6,202)   X, (Y(1,J), J=1,N)
C
C              ..... IF X EXCEEDS XMAX, TERMINATE INTEGRATION .....
      7  IF ( X.GT.XMAX-H/2. )   GO TO 1
C
C              ..... CALL RUNGE OR HAMING TO INTEGRATE ACROSS NEXT STEP .....
         IF ( COUNT.LT.3 )   GO TO 3
C
C              ..... CALL HAMING (PREDICTION OR CORRECTION) .....
      8  M = HAMING( N,Y,F,X,H,TE )
            F(1,1) = Y(1,2)
            F(1,2) = - Y(1,1)
            IF ( M.EQ.1 )   GO TO 8
```

Example 6.4 Hamming's Method **401**

Program Listing (*Continued*)

```
C
C     ..... INCREMENT STEP COUNTER AND CONTINUE INTEGRATION .....
      COUNT = COUNT + 1
      GO TO 6
C
C     ..... FORMATS FOR INPUT AND OUTPUT STATEMENTS .....
  100 FORMAT( 5X, F10.4, 10X, F10.6, 12X, F10.4/ 5X, I5, 15X, I2/
     1   (20X, 4F12.5) )
  200 FORMAT( 10H1H       = , E15.3/ 10H XMAX  = , F12.4/ 10H INT    = ,
     1   I7/ 10H N      = ,I7/1H0/ 1H0, 5X,1HX,10X, 4(2HY(,I2,1H),10X)/
     2   (1H ,16X, 4(2HY(,I2,1H),10X)) )
  201 FORMAT( 1H0, F10.4, 4E15.7/ (1H , 10X, 4E15.7) )
  202 FORMAT( 1H , F10.4, 4E15.7/ (1H , 10X, 4E15.7) )
C
      END
```

Function HAMING

```
      FUNCTION HAMING( N, Y, F, X, H, TE )
C
C        HAMING IMPLEMENTS HAMMING'S PREDICTOR-CORRECTOR ALGORITHM TO
C        SOLVE N SIMULTANEOUS FIRST-ORDER ORDINARY DIFFERENTIAL
C        EQUATIONS.   X IS THE INDEPENDENT VARIABLE AND H IS THE
C        INTEGRATION STEPSIZE.   THE ROUTINE MUST BE CALLED TWICE FOR
C        INTEGRATION ACROSS EACH STEP.  ON THE FIRST CALL, IT IS ASSUMED
C        THAT THE SOLUTION VALUES AND DERIVATIVE VALUES FOR THE N
C        EQUATIONS ARE STORED IN THE FIRST N COLUMNS OF THE FIRST
C        FOUR ROWS OF THE Y MATRIX AND THE FIRST THREE ROWS OF THE F
C        MATRIX RESPECTIVELY.   THE ROUTINE COMPUTES THE N PREDICTED
C        SOLUTIONS YPRED(J), INCREMENTS X BY H AND PUSHES ALL
C        VALUES IN THE Y AND F MATRICES DOWN ONE ROW.   THE PREDICTED
C        SOLUTIONS YPRED(J) ARE MODIFIED, USING THE TRUNCATION ERROR
C        ESTIMATES TE(J) FROM THE PREVIOUS STEP, AND SAVED IN THE FIRST
C        ROW OF THE Y MATRIX. HAMING RETURNS TO THE CALLING PROGRAM WITH
C        THE VALUE 1 TO INDICATE THAT ALL DERIVATIVES SHOULD BE COMPUTED
C        AND STORED IN THE FIRST ROW OF THE F ARRAY BEFORE THE SECOND
C        CALL IS MADE ON HAMING.  ON THE SECOND ENTRY TO THE FUNCTION
C        (DETERMINED BY THE LOGICAL VARIABLE PRED), HAMING USES THE
C        HAMMING CORRECTOR TO COMPUTE NEW SOLUTION ESTIMATES, ESTIMATES
C        THE TRUNCATION ERRORS TE(J) FOR THE CURRENT STEP, IMPROVES
C        THE CORRECTED SOLUTIONS USING THE NEW TRUNCATION ERROR
C        ESTIMATES, SAVES THE IMPROVED SOLUTIONS IN THE FIRST ROW OF THE
C        Y MATRIX, AND RETURNS TO THE CALLING PROGRAM WITH A VALUE 2 TO
C        INDICATE COMPLETION OF ONE FULL INTEGRATION STEP.
C
      IMPLICIT  REAL*8(A-H, O-Z)
      REAL*8  Y, F, X, H, TE
      INTEGER HAMING
      LOGICAL  PRED
      DIMENSION YPRED(20), TE(N), Y(4,N), F(3,N)
      DATA  PRED / .TRUE. /
C
C     ..... IS CALL FOR PREDICTOR OR CORRECTOR SECTION .....
      IF (.NOT.PRED)   GO TO 4
C
C     ..... PREDICTOR SECTION OF HAMING .....
C     ..... COMPUTE PREDICTED Y(J) VALUES AT NEXT POINT .....
      DO 1   J=1,N
    1 YPRED(J) = Y(4,J) + 4.*H*(2.*F(1,J) - F(2,J) + 2.*F(3,J))/3.
C
C     ..... UPDATE THE Y AND F TABLES .....
      DO 2    J=1,N
      DO 2    K5=1,3
      K = 5 - K5
      Y(K,J) = Y(K-1,J)
    2 IF (K.LT.4)  F(K,J) = F(K-1,J)
```

Program Listing (*Continued*)

```
C
C       ..... MODIFY PREDICTED Y(J) VALUES USING THE TRUNCATION ERROR
C             ESTIMATES FROM THE PREVIOUS STEP, INCREMENT X VALUE .....
        DO 3  J=1,N
     3  Y(1,J) = YPRED(J) + 112.*TE(J)/9.
        X = X + H
C
C       ..... SET PRED AND REQUEST UPDATED DERIVATIVE VALUES .....
        PRED = .FALSE.
        HAMING = 1
        RETURN
C
C       ..... CORRECTOR SECTION OF HAMING .....
C       ..... COMPUTE CORRECTED AND IMPROVED VALUES OF THE Y(J) AND SAVE
C             TRUNCATION ERROR ESTIMATES FOR THE CURRENT STEP .....
     4  DO 5  J=1,N
        Y(1,J) = (9.*Y(2,J)-Y(4,J) + 3.*H*(F(1,J)+2.*F(2,J)-F(3,J)))/8.
        TE(J) = 9.*(Y(1,J) - YPRED(J))/121.
     5  Y(1,J) = Y(1,J) - TE(J)
C
C       ..... SET PRED AND RETURN WITH SOLUTIONS FOR CURRENT STEP .....
        PRED = .TRUE.
        HAMING = 2
        RETURN
C
        END
```

Data

```
X =        0.0000      H =     1.000000    XMAX =       5.0000
INT =    1              N =    2
YR(1)...YR(2)=                 0.00000     1.00000
X =        0.0000      H =     0.500000    XMAX =       5.0000
INT =    1              N =    2
YR(1)...YR(2)=                 0.00000     1.00000
X =        0.0000      H =     0.250000    XMAX =       5.0000
INT =    2              N =    2
YR(1)...YR(2)=                 0.00000     1.00000
X =        0.0000      H =     0.125000    XMAX =       5.0000
INT =    4              N =    2
YR(1)...YR(2)=                 0.00000     1.00000
X =        0.0000      H =     0.062500    XMAX =       5.0000
INT =    8              N =    2
YR(1)...YR(2)=                 0.00000     1.00000
X =        0.0000      H =     0.031250    XMAX =       5.0000
INT =   16              N =    2
YR(1)...YR(2)=                 0.00000     1.00000
X =        0.0000      H =     0.015625    XMAX =       5.0000
INT =   32              N =    2
YR(1)...YR(2)=                 0.00000     1.00000
```

Computer Output

Results for the 1st Data Set

```
H       =       0.100D 01
XMAX    =       5.0000
INT     =       1
N       =       2


     X           Y( 1)            Y( 2)

   0.0        0.0              0.1000000D 01
   1.0000     0.8333333D 00    0.5416667D 00
   2.0000     0.9027778D 00   -0.4010417D 00
   3.0000     0.1548032D 00   -0.9695457D 00
   4.0000    -0.6638999D 00   -0.6880225D 00
   5.0000    -0.1045312D 01    0.1429169D 00
```

Example 6.4   Hamming's Method   **403**

Computer Output (*Continued*)

Results for the 2nd Data Set

```
H       =       0.500D 00
XMAX    =       5.0000
INT     =       1
N       =       2
```

X	Y(1)	Y(2)
0.0	0.0	0.1000000D 01
0.5000	0.4791667D 00	0.8776042D 00
1.0000	0.8410373D 00	0.5405884D 00
1.5000	0.9971298D 00	0.7142556D-01
2.0000	0.9104181D 00	-0.4146978D 00
2.5000	0.6001440D 00	-0.8012885D 00
3.0000	0.1423377D 00	-0.9912065D 00
3.5000	-0.3510641D 00	-0.9387887D 00
4.0000	-0.7588721D 00	-0.6554891D 00
4.5000	-0.9810034D 00	-0.2112528D 00
5.0000	-0.9627114D 00	0.2857746D 00

Results for the 3rd Data Set

```
H       =       0.250D 00
XMAX    =       5.0000
INT     =       2
N       =       2
```

X	Y(1)	Y(2)
0.0	0.0	0.1000000D 01
0.5000	0.4794100D 00	0.8775872D 00
1.0000	0.8414639D 00	0.5403375D 00
1.5000	0.9975084D 00	0.7075958D-01
2.0000	0.9093144D 00	-0.4161486D 00
2.5000	0.5984732D 00	-0.8011617D 00
3.0000	0.1410964D 00	-0.9900096D 00
3.5000	-0.3508261D 00	-0.9364535D 00
4.0000	-0.7568475D 00	-0.6536075D 00
4.5000	-0.9775539D 00	-0.2107270D 00
5.0000	-0.9589062D 00	0.2837483D 00

Results for the 4th Data Set

```
H       =       0.125D 00
XMAX    =       5.0000
INT     =       4
N       =       2
```

X	Y(1)	Y(2)
0.0	0.0	0.1000000D 01
0.5000	0.4794249D 00	0.8775832D 00
1.0000	0.8414708D 00	0.5403028D 00
1.5000	0.9974948D 00	0.7073750D-01
2.0000	0.9092971D 00	-0.4161466D 00
2.5000	0.5984717D 00	-0.8011433D 00
3.0000	0.1411195D 00	-0.9899918D 00
3.5000	-0.3507835D 00	-0.9364555D 00
4.0000	-0.7568022D 00	-0.6536421D 00
4.5000	-0.9775289D 00	-0.2107944D 00
5.0000	-0.9589223D 00	0.2836631D 00

Results for the 5th Data Set

```
H       =       0.625D-01
XMAX    =       5.0000
INT     =       8
N       =       2
```

X	Y(1)	Y(2)
0.0	0.0	0.1000000D 01
0.5000	0.4794255D 00	0.8775826D 00
1.0000	0.8414710D 00	0.5403023D 00
1.5000	0.9974950D 00	0.7073721D-01
2.0000	0.9092974D 00	-0.4161468D 00
2.5000	0.5984721D 00	-0.8011436D 00
3.0000	0.1411200D 00	-0.9899925D 00
3.5000	-0.3507832D 00	-0.9364566D 00
4.0000	-0.7568025D 00	-0.6536436D 00
4.5000	-0.9775301D 00	-0.2107958D 00
5.0000	-0.9589242D 00	0.2836622D 00

Results for the 6th Data Set

```
H       =       0.312D-01
XMAX    =       5.0000
INT     =       16
N       =       2
```

X	Y(1)	Y(2)
0.0	0.0	0.1000000D 01
0.5000	0.4794255D 00	0.8775826D 00
1.0000	0.8414710D 00	0.5403023D 00
1.5000	0.9974950D 00	0.7073720D-01
2.0000	0.9092974D 00	-0.4161468D 00
2.5000	0.5984721D 00	-0.8011436D 00
3.0000	0.1411200D 00	-0.9899925D 00
3.5000	-0.3507832D 00	-0.9364567D 00
4.0000	-0.7568025D 00	-0.6536436D 00
4.5000	-0.9775301D 00	-0.2107958D 00
5.0000	-0.9589243D 00	0.2836622D 00

Results for the 7th Data Set

```
H       =       0.156D-01
XMAX    =       5.0000
INT     =       32
N       =       2
```

X	Y(1)	Y(2)
0.0	0.0	0.1000000D 01
0.5000	0.4794255D 00	0.8775826D 00
1.0000	0.8414710D 00	0.5403023D 00
1.5000	0.9974950D 00	0.7073720D-01
2.0000	0.9092974D 00	-0.4161468D 00
2.5000	0.5984721D 00	-0.8011436D 00
3.0000	0.1411200D 00	-0.9899925D 00
3.5000	-0.3507832D 00	-0.9364567D 00
4.0000	-0.7568025D 00	-0.6536436D 00
4.5000	-0.9775301D 00	-0.2107958D 00
5.0000	-0.9589243D 00	0.2836622D 00

Discussion of Results

Double-precision arithmetic has been used for all calculations. Differential equation (6.4.2) with initial conditions given by (6.4.3) has been solved on the interval [0,5] with step-size $h = 1.0, 0.5, 0.25, 0.125, 0.0625, 0.03125,$ and 0.015625. To seven-place accuracy, the true solutions

$$y_1 = y = \sin x,$$

$$y_2 = \frac{dy}{dx} = \cos x, \qquad (6.4.31)$$

are listed in Table 6.4.1.

Table 6.4.1   True Solutions, $y(x)$ and dy/dx

x	$y(x) = \sin x$	$dy/dx = \cos x$
0.0	0.0000000	1.0000000
1.0	0.8414710	0.5403023
2.0	0.9092974	−0.4161468
3.0	0.1411200	−0.9899925
4.0	−0.7568025	−0.6536436
5.0	−0.9589243	0.2836622

Table 6.4.2. shows the computed results at $x = 5$ for the various step sizes used.

Table 6.4.2   Calculated Solutions at $x = 5$

Step size, h	y_1	y_2
1.0	−1.045312	0.1429169
0.5	−0.9627114	0.2857746
0.25	−0.9589062	0.2837483
0.125	−0.9589223	0.2836631
0.0625	−0.9589242	0.2836622
0.03125	−0.9589243	0.2836622
0.015625	−0.9589243	0.2836622
True Values	−0.9589243	0.2836622

Results for step-sizes 0.03125 and 0.015625 (data sets 6 and 7) agree with the true values to seven figures. Results for the larger step sizes are not of acceptable accuracy. The program has been run with even larger values of h (results not shown) as well. For h large enough, the solutions "blow up" in a fashion similar to that already observed for the Runge-Kutta method in Example 6.3.

In view of the periodic nature of the solution functions, it is not surprising that as the step size approaches the length of the functional period, the solutions become meaningless. Clearly, for step sizes larger than the period, virtually all local information about the curvature of the function is lost; it would be unreasonable to expect accurate solutions in such cases.

6.14 Boundary-Value Problems

The numerical methods described so far have assumed the availability of initial conditions to start the solution procedure. In many problems, conditions on the equation are given as boundary rather than initial values. Consider, for example, a second-order equation of the form

$$F\left(x, y, \frac{dy}{dx}, \frac{d^2y}{dx^2}\right) = 0 \qquad (6.137)$$

subject to the boundary conditions $y(a) = \alpha$, $y(b) = \beta$. The numerical solution of this problem is generally much more complicated than the solution for the corresponding initial-value problem.

The usual algorithms for the solution of boundary-value problems fall into two general classes: the finite-difference methods and the shooting methods.

The *finite-difference methods* involve approximation of the differential equation at the $n + 2$ base points $x_0, x_1, \ldots, x_{n+1}$; each derivative is replaced by a finite-difference representation as described in detail in Chapter 7 (see, in particular, Section 7.3). For the two-point boundary value problem of (6.137), the initial condition at $x_0 = a$, that is, $y_0 = \alpha$, and the boundary condition at $x_{n+1} = b$, that is, $y_{n+1} = \beta$, can be introduced directly into the first and the nth finite-difference equation respectively. If y_0 and y_{n+1} are specified, then the finite-difference procedure leads to a system of n simultaneous equations in the n unknowns $y_1, y_2, \ldots, y_n$, the approximate solutions at the interior base points $x_1, x_2, \ldots, x_n$. Usually, though not necessarily, the base points are equally spaced on the interval $[x_0, x_{n+1}]$. For more complicated initial or boundary conditions, the methods of Section 7.17 may be used.

If the original differential equation is *linear* (that is, if the differential equation is linear in the dependent variable y and all its derivatives), then the set of equations generated is also linear. The system of simultaneous equations can be solved with the iterative methods of Chapter 5 (for example, the Gauss-Seidel method) if n is large or by the elimination methods of Chapter 5 if n is small (say $n < 40$). If, as usually happens for equations of order 2, the system of linear equations has a tridiagonal coefficient matrix, the special form of the Gaussian elimination method described in Section 7.9 may be used, even for n rather large (say n up to 500).

Since the finite-difference methods for solution of linear ordinary differential equations are identical with those described in detail in Chapter 7 for solution of linear partial differential equations (but simpler, since the ordinary differential equation has only one independent variable), they will not be pursued further here. The reader is referred to [16] for detailed numerical solutions of several simple linear boundary-value problems by finite-difference methods.

Unfortunately, when the differential equation is *nonlinear*, the system of finite-difference equations is also nonlinear. In addition to the problems of uniqueness associated with the solution of nonlinear equations, the generation of *any* solution may be very difficult, especially when many base points are used. In some cases [17], one can linearize the equations, solve the equations iteratively, then relinearize about the new solution, find a new solution iteratively, etc. In effect, a complex problem has been replaced by another problem which is somewhat less complex.

The *shooting methods* reduce the solution of a boundary-value problem to the iterative solution of an initial-value problem [18]. The usual approaches involve a trial-and-error procedure. That boundary point having the most known conditions is selected as the initial point. Any other missing initial conditions are *assumed*, and the initial-value problem is solved using one of the step-by-step procedures from the previous sections. Unless the computed solution agrees with the known boundary conditions (unlikely on the first try), the initial conditions are adjusted and the problem is solved again. The process is repeated until the assumed initial conditions yield, within specified tolerances, a solution that agrees with the known boundary conditions.

In (6.137), for example, the missing initial value $dy(a)/dx$ is assumed to be c_1, for instance, and the integration from a to b is carried out by using one of the standard procedures for initial-value problems. Equation (6.137) would normally be rewritten as a system of two first-order equations. Let γ_1 be the computed solution at $x = b$ (see Fig. 6.8). The procedure is repeated by using

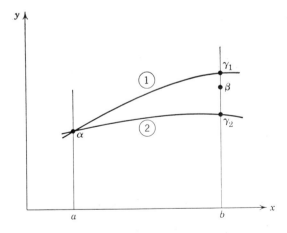

Figure 6.8 A trial-and-error solution of a boundary-value problem.

another assumed value for the missing initial condition, for instance, $dy(a)/dx = c_2$. For this case, let γ_2 be the computed solution at $x = b$. If γ_1 and γ_2 encompass the desired $y(b) = \beta$ as shown in Fig. 6.8, and if (6.137) is well behaved, then an estimate of a new trial value, c_3, for the initial condition can be found by the linear interpolation

$$c_3 = c_1 + \frac{(c_2 - c_1)(\gamma_1 - \beta)}{(\gamma_1 - \gamma_2)}. \qquad (6.138)$$

This procedure can be repeated by using another linear or perhaps a quadratic or higher-order interpolation to produce a sequence of new values $c_4, c_5, c_6, \ldots$, until a selected assumed value of the initial condition produces the boundary-value solution as accurately as desired. This interpolation procedure will be most successful when applied to linear or nearly linear equations; for highly nonlinear equations the approach may be completely unsatisfactory.

Obviously, any other trial-and-error procedure which results in a sequence of ever-improving initial condition estimates is also acceptable. For example, one could use a root-finding procedure, such as the half-interval method, on the function

$$g(c) = y(b,c) - \beta, \qquad (6.139)$$

where $y(b,c)$ is the computed value of $y(b)$ with initial condition c. This technique is used in the solution of the boundary-value problem of Example 6.5. Yet another approach is to define a nonnegative objective function

$$g(c) = |y(b,c) - \beta| \qquad (6.140)$$

and to use one of the standard one-dimensional minimization strategies, such as the "golden-section" or Fibonacci search [19]. When several initial conditions must be assumed, one can frequently define a multidimensional objective function similar to (6.140) and then use one of the multidimensional optimization algorithms, such as the direct search of Hooke and Jeeves [20], to find the missing conditions.

When the boundary-value problem involves a system of many differential equations, or when the specified conditions apply to several different values of the independent variable (the so-called multiple-point boundary-value problem), the solution procedure increases greatly in complexity. In some cases, it may be possible to restate the problem in simpler form by a suitable transformation of variables; in others, a rather drastic change in form, for example, rewriting the problem in terms of integral rather than differential equations, may prove fruitful. In any event, as should be apparent from the preceding paragraphs, there are no known algorithms which *a priori* guarantee successful solution of a given boundary-value problem.

EXAMPLE 6.5

A BOUNDARY-VALUE PROBLEM IN FLUID MECHANICS

Introduction

Consider the *Blasius* problem [42], in which a thin plate is placed in, and parallel to, a fluid stream of velocity u_∞ and kinematic viscosity v, as shown in Fig. 6.5.1. We wish to find how u and v, the velocity components in the x and y directions, vary in the region close to the plate, known as the *boundary layer*.

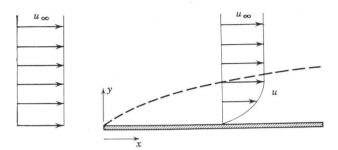

Figure 6.5.1   The boundary layer on a flat plate.

The governing equations of motion and continuity are

$$u \frac{\partial u}{\partial x} + v \frac{\partial u}{\partial y} = v \frac{\partial^2 u}{\partial y^2}, \qquad (6.5.1)$$

$$\frac{\partial u}{\partial x} + \frac{\partial v}{\partial y} = 0, \qquad (6.5.2)$$

subject to the boundary conditions

$$y = 0: \quad u = v = 0, \qquad (6.5.3)$$

$$y = \infty: u = u_\infty. \qquad (6.5.4)$$

By introducing the dimensionless coordinate

$$\eta = y \sqrt{\frac{u_\infty}{vx}},$$

and a stream function

$$\psi = \sqrt{vxu_\infty} f(\eta)$$

such that

$$u = \frac{\partial \psi}{\partial y}, \qquad v = -\frac{\partial \psi}{\partial x},$$

equations (6.5.1) and (6.5.2) reduce to a single ordinary differential equation in the dimensionless stream function $f(\eta)$:

$$f f'' + 2f''' = 0. \qquad (6.5.5)$$

The boundary conditions now become

$$\eta = 0: \quad f = 0, \; f' = 0, \qquad (6.5.6)$$

$$\eta = \infty: \quad f' = 1. \qquad (6.5.7)$$

From the above equations involving stream function,

we can derive the following relations for dimensionless velocities U and V:

$$U = \frac{u}{u_\infty} = f', \qquad (6.5.8)$$

$$V = \frac{v}{\frac{1}{2}\sqrt{\frac{vu_\infty}{x}}} = \eta f' - f. \qquad (6.5.9)$$

Thus, once (6.5.5) has been solved for f, we can predict the velocity field from (6.5.8) and (6.5.9).

Problem Statement

Perform a fourth-order Runge-Kutta solution of (6.5.5) and its associated boundary conditions. The program should print tabulated values of η, f, f' ($= U$), f'', and V ($= \eta f' - f$), and should produce a graph of U and V versus η on the on-line printer.

Method of Solution

By defining $g_1 = f$, $g_2 = f'$, and $g_3 = f''$, we can replace equation (6.5.5) by an equivalent set of three first-order equations:

$$\frac{dg_1}{d\eta} = g_2,$$

$$\frac{dg_2}{d\eta} = g_3, \qquad (6.5.10)$$

$$\frac{dg_3}{d\eta} = -\frac{1}{2}g_1 g_3,$$

subject to

$$\eta = 0: \quad g_1 = g_2 = 0, \qquad (6.5.11)$$

$$\eta = \infty: \quad g_2 = 1. \qquad (6.5.12)$$

Starting at $\eta = 0$, the integration of (6.5.10) over successive steps $\Delta\eta$ is achieved by the fourth-order Runge-Kutta function RUNGE; this is described fully in Example 6.3, and the details will not be repeated here.

Since we have initial conditions (at $\eta = 0$) for g_1 and g_2 only, we search for a value of g_3 at $\eta = 0$ that will generate a solution that yields $g_2 = 1$ at $\eta = \infty$. This is accomplished by the half-interval method, discussed previously in Section 3.8 and Example 3.4.

In practice, condition (6.5.12) must be replaced by the approximate condition

$$\eta = \eta_{max}: \quad g_2 = 1, \qquad (6.5.13)$$

where η_{max} is arbitrary, as long as it is chosen large enough so that the solution shows little further change for η larger than η_{max}. This corresponds to the physical fact that the mainstream velocity is effectively equal to u_∞ far from the plate.

We start with two limits, g_{3L} and g_{3R}, between which the missing initial condition, g_{30}, is thought to lie. The solution of (6.5.10) is performed iteratively n times, improving at each iteration the value chosen for g_{30}. At each iteration, we set $g_{30} = (g_{3L} + g_{3R})/2$, in which one of the limits g_{3L} or g_{3R} of the current interval has been adjusted according to the half-interval method. The criterion for the adjustment is whether or not the computed $g_2(\eta_{max})$ exceeds 1. If it does, g_{3R} at the next iteration is equated to the current midpoint g_{30}, and g_{3L} is not changed. However, if $g_2(\eta_{max}) \leqslant 1$, we equate the next g_{3L} to the current g_{30} and leave g_{3R} unchanged.

The following flow diagram illustrates the essential basic steps. In the actual program, however, there are further elaborations involving arrangements for periodic printing and plotting of graphs.

Flow Diagram

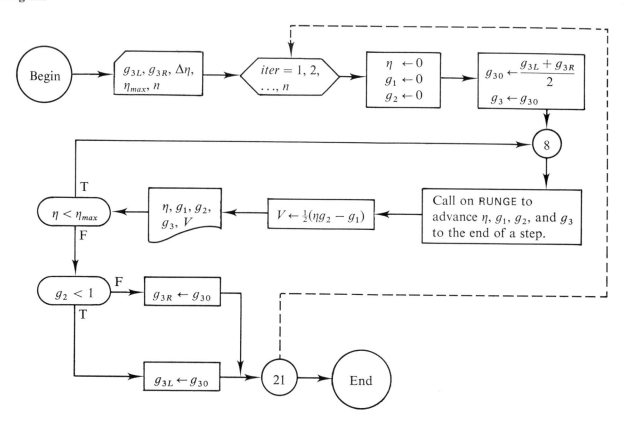

Example 6.5   A Boundary-Value Problem in Fluid Mechanics   **409**

FORTRAN *Implementation*

List of Principal Variables

Program Symbol	Definition
DETA	Step size, $\Delta\eta$.
DG	Vector containing values of the three derivatives, $dg_1/d\eta$, $dg_2/d\eta$, and $dg_3/d\eta$.
ETA	Dimensionless distance, η.
ETAMAX	Maximum value of η, η_{max}, for which solutions are required.
G	Vector containing values of g_1, g_2, and g_3.
G3LEFT G3RITE	Lower and upper limits, g_{3L} and g_{3R}, for the current interval containing the initial value of g_3.
G3ZERO	Initial value of g_3, g_{30}.
IFPLOT	Integer, having the value 1 if a graph is required.
IMAGE	Storage vector used by the plotting subroutines.
ITER	Iteration counter.
N	Upper limit on the number of half-interval iterations, n.
NCOPY	Number of copies of the graph that are required.
NIBETP	Number of half-interval iterations between printouts.
NSBETP	Number of Runge-Kutta steps, within any one half-interval iteration, between printouts.
NSTEPS	Counter on the number of steps $\Delta\eta$.
ORD	Value of dimensionless velocity, V, to be plotted as the ordinate of the graph.
PLOT1, PLOT2, PLOT3, PLOT4	Subroutines used for preparing on-line graph of U and V against η. See Examples 7.1 and 8.5 for further details.
RUNGE	Function for implementing the fourth-order Runge-Kutta procedure (see Example 6.3).
SIGNL	Has the value -1, if $g_2(\eta_{max}) < 1$ when $g_3(0) = g_{3L}$; otherwise, the value is $+1$.

Program Listing

Main Program

```
C              APPLIED NUMERICAL METHODS, EXAMPLE 6.5
C              A BOUNDARY VALUE PROBLEM IN FLUID MECHANICS
C
C              THIS PROGRAM CALLS ON THE FOURTH ORDER RUNGE KUTTA METHOD SUB-
C              ROUTINE RUNGE TO SOLVE THE 'BLASIUS' PROBLEM WHICH DESCRIBES
C              BOUNDARY LAYER FLOW ALONG A THIN FLAT PLATE IMMERSED IN A FLUID
C              OF UNIFORM VELOCITY AT ZERO INCIDENCE ANGLE.  G(1), G(2) AND
C              G(3) ARE THE DEPENDENT VARIABLES, ETA THE INDEPENDENT VARIABLE,
C              DETA THE STEPSIZE, AND DG(1), DG(2) AND DG(3) THE DERIVATIVES.
C              THE BOUNDARY CONDITIONS ARE G(1)=0., G(2)=0. AT ETA=0. AND
C              G(2)=1. AT ETA=INFINITY (ETAMAX).  THE MISSING INITIAL
C              CONDITION, G(3) AT ETA=0., IS FOUND BY A HALF INTERVAL
C              ITERATIVE PROCEDURE.  ITER IS THE ITERATION COUNTER AND THE
C              INTERVAL OF UNCERTAINTY AFTER ITER PASSES IS (G3LEFT,G3RITE).
C              G3ZERO IS THE MID-INTERVAL VALUE USED FOR THE INITIAL VALUE OF
C              G(3).  SIGNL = -1 IF G(2) AT ETAMAX IS SMALLER THAN 1.0
C              WHEN G(3) AT ETA = 0 IS EQUAL TO G3LEFT.  OTHERWISE, SIGNL = 1.
C              N IS THE TOTAL NUMBER OF INTERVAL HALVING OPERATIONS, SO THAT
C              THE INITIAL INTERVAL OF UNCERTAINTY IN G(3) AT ETA=0. IS
C              REDUCED BY A FACTOR OF 2.**(-N).  SOLUTION VALUES ARE PRINTED
C              ON THE FIRST, NTH AND INTEGRAL MULTIPLES OF NIBETP ITERATIONS.
C              SOLUTIONS ARE PRINTED AFTER EVERY NSBETP STEPS (NSTEPS IS THE
C              STEP COUNTER).  WHEN IFPLOT = 1, VALUES OF G(2) AND
C              ORD=0.5*(ETA*G(2)-G(1)) VERSUS ETA ARE PLOTTED ON THE LAST
C              ITERATION.  NCOPY COPIES OF THE GRAPH ARE PRINTED.
C
       IMPLICIT  REAL*8(A-H, O-Z)
       INTEGER  RUNGE
       DIMENSION  G(3), DG(3), IMAGE(1500)
C
     1 READ (5,100)  G3LEFT, G3RITE, SIGNL, DETA, ETAMAX, NIBETP, NSBETP,
      1  N, IFPLOT, NCOPY
       WRITE (6,200)  G3LEFT, G3RITE, SIGNL, DETA, ETAMAX, NIBETP, NSBETP,
      1  N, IFPLOT, NCOPY
C
C      ..... HALF INTERVAL ITERATION FOR INITIAL G(3) VALUE ...
       DO 21  ITER = 1, N
C
C      ..... SET, PRINT AND PLOT INITIAL CONDITIONS .....
       NSTEPS = 0
       ETA = 0.
       G(1) = 0.
       G(2) = 0.
       G3ZERO = (G3LEFT + G3RITE)/2.
       G(3) = G3ZERO
       IF (.NOT.(ITER/NIBETP*NIBETP.EQ.ITER.OR.ITER.EQ.1.OR.ITER.EQ.N))
      1  GO TO 8
       ORD = 0.
       WRITE (6,201)  ITER,G3LEFT,G3ZERO,G3RITE,ETA,G(1),G(2),G(3),ORD
       IF (ITER.NE.N .OR. IFPLOT.NE.1)  GO TO 8
          CALL PLOT1( 0, 6, 9, 6, 19 )
          CALL PLOT2( IMAGE, ETAMAX, 0., 1.25, 0. )
          CALL PLOT3( 1H*, ETA, G(2), 1, 8 )
C
C      ..... CALL ON RUNGE-KUTTA SUBROUTINE .....
     8 IF (RUNGE( 3, G, DG, ETA, DETA ) .NE. 1 )  GO TO 10
       DG(1) = G(2)
       DG(2) = G(3)
       DG(3) = -G(1)*G(3)/2.
       GO TO 8
C
C      ..... PRINT SOLUTIONS, PLOT G(2) AND ORD VALUES .....
    10 IF (.NOT.(ITER/NIBETP*NIBETP.EQ.ITER.OR.ITER.EQ.1.OR.ITER.EQ.N))
      1  GO TO 17
       NSTEPS = NSTEPS + 1
       IF (NSTEPS.NE.NSBETP)  GO TO 17
          NSTEPS = 0
          ORD = 0.5*(ETA*G(2) - G(1))
          WRITE (6,202)  ETA, G(1), G(2), G(3), ORD
          IF (ITER.NE.N .OR. IFPLOT.NE.1)  GO TO 17
             CALL PLOT3( 1H*, ETA, G(2), 1, 8 )
             CALL PLOT3( 1HX, ETA, ORD, 1, 8 )
```

Example 6.5 A Boundary-Value Problem in Fluid Mechanics **411**

Program Listing (*Continued*)

```
C
C      ..... INTEGRATE ACROSS ANOTHER STEP IF REQUIRED .....
   17  IF (ETA .LT. ETAMAX-DETA/2.)  GO TO 8
C
C      ..... FIND INTERVAL HALF WITH THE SIGN CHANGE .....
   18  IF ((G(2)-1.)*SIGNL .GT. 0.)  GO TO 20
          G3RITE = G3ZERO
          GO TO 21
   20     G3LEFT = G3ZERO
   21  CONTINUE
C
C      ..... WRITE NCOPY COPIES OF THE GRAPH IF REQUESTED .....
       IF (IFPLOT.NE.1)  GO TO 1
          DO 23  I = 1, NCOPY
             WRITE (6,203)
             CALL PLOT4( 22, 22HG2          AND          ORD )
   23        WRITE (6,204)
          GO TO 1
C
C      ..... FORMATS FOR INPUT AND OUTPUT STATEMENTS .....
  100  FORMAT ( 10X,F10.7,20X,F10.7,19X,F3.0/10X,F10.7,20X,F10.7,19X,I3/
      1    10X,I2,28X,I2,28X,I2/ 10X,I2 )
  200  FORMAT ( 10H1G3LEFT = , F10.6/ 10H G3RITE = , F10.6/10H SIGNL   = ,
      1    F3.0/ 10H DETA   = , F10.6/ 10H ETAMAX = , F10.6/10H NIBETP = ,
      2    I3/ 10H NSBETP = , I3/ 10H N      = , I3/ 10H IFPLOT = , I3/
      3    10H NCOPY  = , I3 )
  201  FORMAT ( 10H1ITER    = , I3/ 10H G3LEFT = , F10.6/ 10H G3ZERO = ,
      1    F10.6/ 10H G3RITE = , F10.6/ 7H0   ETA, 11X, 4HG(1), 12X,
      2    4HG(2), 12X, 4HG(3), 12X, 3HORD/  1H0, F7.4, 2F16.7, 2F16.8 )
  202  FORMAT ( 1H , F7.4, 2F16.7, 2F16.8 )
  203  FORMAT ( 1H1, 52X, 19HTHE BLASIUS PROBLEM/ 1H0 )
  204  FORMAT ( 1H0, 60X, 3HETA/ 1H ,11X,29HPLOTTING CHARACTER (*) = G(2)
      1    / 1H ,11X,28HPLOTTING CHARACTER (X) = ORD )
C
       END
```

Data

G3LEFT = 0.1000000	G3RITE = 0.5000000	SIGNL = -1
DETA = 0.1000000	ETAMAX = 10.0000000	NIBETP = 10
NSBETP = 2	N = 20	IFPLOT = 1
NCOPY = 1		

Computer Output

```
G3LEFT =   0.100000
G3RITE =   0.500000
SIGNL  = -1.
DETA   =   0.100000
ETAMAX =  10.000000
NIBETP =  10
NSBETP =   2
N      =  20
IFPLOT =   1
NCOPY  =   1
```

Computer Output (*Continued*)

Results for the 1st Half-Interval Iteration

```
ITER    =    1
G3LEFT  =    0.100000
G3ZERO  =    0.300000
G3RITE  =    0.500000
```

ETA	G(1)	G(2)	G(3)	ORD
0.0	0.0	0.0	0.30000000	0.0
0.2000	0.0059999	0.0599970	0.29994001	0.00299976
0.4000	0.0239962	0.1199520	0.29952042	0.01199232
0.6000	0.0539709	0.1797574	0.29838480	0.02694178
0.8000	0.0958775	0.2392351	0.29618689	0.04775530
1.0000	0.1496269	0.2981396	0.29260209	0.07425638
1.2000	0.2150748	0.3561641	0.28734261	0.10616110
1.4000	0.2920100	0.4129493	0.28017536	0.14305952
1.6000	0.3801453	0.4680962	0.27094067	0.18440433
1.8000	0.4791112	0.5211829	0.25956977	0.22950905
2.0000	0.5884528	0.5717839	0.24609846	0.27755748
2.2000	0.7076318	0.6194919	0.23067436	0.32762517
2.4000	0.8360321	0.6639404	0.21355575	0.37871245
2.6000	0.9729702	0.7048249	0.19510072	0.42978727
2.8000	1.1177093	0.7419206	0.17574671	0.47983427
3.0000	1.2694769	0.7750961	0.15598188	0.52790577
3.2000	1.4274840	0.8043197	0.13631121	0.57316950
3.4000	1.5909456	0.8296594	0.11722104	0.61494820
3.6000	1.7590994	0.8512760	0.09914617	0.65274702
3.8000	1.9312237	0.8694095	0.08244318	0.68626629
4.0000	2.1066511	0.8843623	0.06737276	0.71539902
4.2000	2.2847795	0.8964782	0.05409218	0.74021444
4.4000	2.4650776	0.9061224	0.04265794	0.76093052
4.6000	2.6470882	0.9136624	0.03303667	0.77787931
4.8000	2.8304259	0.9194510	0.02512223	0.79146938
5.0000	3.0147737	0.9238145	0.01875577	0.80214937
5.2000	3.1998762	0.9270438	0.01374639	0.81037566
5.4000	3.3855324	0.9293899	0.00988988	0.81658642
5.6000	3.5715874	0.9310630	0.00698428	0.82118282
5.8000	3.7579243	0.9322343	0.00484134	0.82451747
6.0000	3.9444568	0.9330392	0.00329392	0.82688922
6.2000	4.1311225	0.9335821	0.00219967	0.82854309
6.4000	4.3178774	0.9339414	0.00144176	0.82967386
6.6000	4.5046908	0.9341749	0.00092751	0.83043193
6.8000	4.6915418	0.9343239	0.00058564	0.83093028
7.0000	4.8784166	0.9344171	0.00036294	0.83125155
7.2000	5.0653063	0.9344744	0.00022076	0.83145467
7.4000	5.2522049	0.9345089	0.00013179	0.83158061
7.6000	5.4391089	0.9345294	0.00007722	0.83165720
7.8000	5.6260161	0.9345413	0.00004441	0.83170288
8.0000	5.8129251	0.9345480	0.00002507	0.83172961
8.2000	5.9998351	0.9345518	0.00001389	0.83174494
8.4000	6.1867457	0.9345539	0.00000755	0.83175358
8.6000	6.3736566	0.9345550	0.00000403	0.83175834
8.8000	6.5605677	0.9345556	0.00000211	0.83176093
9.0000	6.7474788	0.9345559	0.00000109	0.83176230
9.2000	6.9343900	0.9345561	0.00000055	0.83176301
9.4000	7.1213012	0.9345562	0.00000027	0.83176338
9.6000	7.3082125	0.9345562	0.00000013	0.83176356
9.8000	7.4951237	0.9345562	0.00000006	0.83176365
10.0000	7.6820350	0.9345562	0.00000003	0.83176370

Example 6.5   A Boundary-Value Problem in Fluid Mechanics   **413**

Computer Output (*Continued*)

Results for the 20th (final) Half-Interval Iteration

```
ITER    =   20
G3LEFT  =    0.332057
G3ZERO  =    0.332058
G3RITE  =    0.332058
```

ETA	G(1)	G(2)	G(3)	ORD
0.0	0.0	0.0	0.33205757	0.0
0.2000	0.0066410	0.0664078	0.33198407	0.00332028
0.4000	0.0265599	0.1327643	0.33147008	0.01327289
0.6000	0.0597347	0.1989374	0.33007936	0.02981386
0.8000	0.1061083	0.2647093	0.32738950	0.05282956
1.0000	0.1655719	0.3297803	0.32300734	0.08210419
1.2000	0.2379489	0.3937764	0.31658941	0.11729136
1.4000	0.3229819	0.4562621	0.30786560	0.15789252
1.6000	0.4203211	0.5167571	0.29666365	0.20324514
1.8000	0.5295185	0.5747585	0.28293119	0.25252343
2.0000	0.6500249	0.6297661	0.26675170	0.30475369
2.2000	0.7811939	0.6813108	0.24835105	0.35884491
2.4000	0.9222908	0.7289824	0.22809187	0.41363344
2.6000	1.0725068	0.7724555	0.20645472	0.46793874
2.8000	1.2309782	0.8115101	0.18400666	0.52062503
3.0000	1.3968092	0.8460449	0.16136037	0.57066276
3.2000	1.5690961	0.8760819	0.13912809	0.61718306
3.4000	1.7469513	0.9017617	0.11787627	0.65951923
3.6000	1.9295265	0.9233301	0.09808630	0.69723100
3.8000	2.1160312	0.9411185	0.08012594	0.73010945
4.0000	2.3057479	0.9555187	0.06423415	0.75816339
4.2000	2.4980413	0.9669575	0.05051979	0.78159014
4.4000	2.6923627	0.9758713	0.03897266	0.80073545
4.6000	2.8882498	0.9826839	0.02948383	0.81604812
4.8000	3.0853226	0.9877899	0.02187126	0.82803458
5.0000	3.2832757	0.9915423	0.01590688	0.83721795
5.2000	3.4818697	0.9942459	0.01134187	0.84410461
5.4000	3.6809213	0.9961557	0.00792775	0.84915981
5.6000	3.8802930	0.9974782	0.00543204	0.85279243
5.8000	4.0798843	0.9983759	0.00364849	0.85534799
6.0000	4.2796234	0.9989733	0.00240211	0.85710820
6.2000	4.4794599	0.9993630	0.00155023	0.85829528
6.4000	4.6793593	0.9996121	0.00098067	0.85907921
6.6000	4.8792986	0.9997683	0.00060808	0.85958615
6.8000	5.0792626	0.9998643	0.00036959	0.85990719
7.0000	5.2792417	0.9999221	0.00022019	0.86010631
7.2000	5.4792299	0.9999562	0.00012859	0.86022727
7.4000	5.6792232	0.9999759	0.00007361	0.86029924
7.6000	5.8792197	0.9999871	0.00004130	0.86034118
7.8000	6.0792178	0.9999933	0.00002271	0.86036512
8.0000	6.2792168	0.9999967	0.00001224	0.86037851
8.2000	6.4792164	0.9999985	0.00000647	0.86038585
8.4000	6.6792162	0.9999995	0.00000335	0.86038978
8.6000	6.8792161	1.0000000	0.00000170	0.86039185
8.8000	7.0792161	1.0000002	0.00000085	0.86039292
9.0000	7.2792162	1.0000003	0.00000041	0.86039346
9.2000	7.4792163	1.0000004	0.00000020	0.86039372
9.4000	7.6792164	1.0000004	0.00000009	0.86039385
9.6000	7.8792164	1.0000004	0.00000004	0.86039391
9.8000	8.0792165	1.0000005	0.00000002	0.86039394
10.0000	8.2792166	1.0000005	0.00000001	0.86039395

Computer Output (*Continued*)

Plotted Results for the Final Iteration

THE BLASIUS PROBLEM

PLOTTING CHARACTER (*) = G(2)
PLOTTING CHARACTER (X) = ORD

Example 6.5   A Boundary-Value Problem in Fluid Mechanics   **415**

Discussion of Results

The results of the computations, performed in double-precision arithmetic, are displayed above only for the first and 20th (final) half-interval iteration. The success of the method can be seen by examining $g_2(\eta_{max})$, which differs only marginally from the required value of 1. The corresponding values for $g_2(\eta_{max})$ at the end of the 1st and 10th iterations were 0.9345562 and 1.0007317, respectively. The results for the final iteration agree to at least six significant digits with those reported in Reference 42. Observe that U essentially attains its mainstream value for $\eta = 6$ or greater. Since $\partial u/\partial x$ is everywhere negative (at a given distance from the plate, the u velocity is retarded in the direction of flow), a positive V velocity occurs in order to satisfy the continuity equation (6.5.2).

Problems

6.1 Rewrite the following system of ordinary differential equations as a system of first-order ordinary differential equations:

$$\frac{d^3y}{dx^3} = x^2 y \frac{d^2y}{dx^2} - y \frac{dz}{dx},$$

$$\frac{d^2z}{dx^2} = zx \frac{dz}{dx} + 4 \frac{dy}{dx}.$$

6.2 Solve the ordinary differential equation

$$\frac{d^2y}{dx^2} = -4y$$

with initial conditions

$$y(0) = 1,$$

$$\left.\frac{dy}{dx}\right|_{x=0} = 0,$$

using the Taylor's expansion approach described in Section 6.2, and compare with the analytical solution.

6.3 Write a program, similar to that of Example 6.1, that employs either the improved Euler method of (6.59) and (6.60) or the modified Euler method of (6.61) and (6.62) to solve the first-order equation (6.19)

$$f(x,y) = x + y,$$

with initial condition $y(x_0) = y(0) = 0$. Integrate the equation on the interval $0 \leqslant x \leqslant 2$ using several different step sizes, $h = 1., 0.5, 0.25, 0.1, 0.05, 0.025, 0.01, 0.005, 0.0025, 0.001,$ $0.0005, 0.00025, 0.0001$. Initially, and after every k steps of the procedure, print the current results $(x_i, y_i, f(x_i, y_i)$ the true solution, $y(x_i)$, and the discretization error, ε_i).

Plot the discretization error, ε_i, at $x = 2$ against h, h^2, and h^3, and determine the apparent order of the error for small step sizes.

6.4 Consider the first-order equation,

$$\frac{dy}{dx} = 100y - 101e^{-x} - 100,$$

with the initial condition,

$$y(0) = 2.$$

Ignoring round-off error, show that the discretization error for the solution of this equation with the given condition by Euler's method is

$$\varepsilon_{i+1} = \varepsilon_i(1 + 100h) - \frac{h^2}{2} e^{-\xi_{i+1}}, \quad x_i < \xi_{i+1} < x_{i+1},$$

or

$$\varepsilon_i = \varepsilon_0(1 + 100h)^i - \frac{h^2}{2} [e^{-\xi_i} + (1 + 100h)e^{-\xi_{i-1}}$$
$$+ \cdots + (1 + 100h)^{i-1}e^{-\xi_1}].$$

Consider the solution of the equation on the interval $0 \leqslant x \leqslant 1$. Investigate the stability of Euler's method in the solution of the given equation for an initial error $\varepsilon_0 = 0.0001$, and various step-sizes $h = 0.01, 0.001, \ldots,$ etc.

6.5 Show that the algorithm

$$y_{i+1} = y_i + \frac{h}{4}(k_1 + 3k_3),$$

$$k_1 = f(x_i, y_i),$$

$$k_2 = f(x_i + h/3, y_i + hk_1/3),$$

$$k_3 = f(x_i + 2h/3, y_i + 2hk_2/3),$$

is a third-order Runge-Kutta method with accuracy comparable to that of (6.64).

6.6 Develop a general formulation of the fourth-order Runge-Kutta methods, comparable to that described in detail for the second-order methods, and outlined for the third-order methods, in Section 6.5. Starting with (6.65), expand each of the k_i, $i = 2, 3, 4$, in a Taylor's series as a function of two variables, and equate the coefficient of each power of $h \leqslant 4$ in (6.65) to that of the same power of h in (6.25). What is the system of equations describing the fourth-order parameters, comparable to (6.57) for the second-order methods? How many parameters must be specified to determine a particular fourth-order method? Show that (6.66), (6.67), and (6.68) satisfy the system of equations developed above.

6.7 Choose, arbitrarily, a sufficient number of parameters to specify a particular fourth-order Runge-Kutta method (see Problem 6.6), and develop a new Runge-Kutta formula of your own. Write a function, named MYRK and modelled after the function RUNGE of Example 6.3, that could be used in place of RUNGE to solve systems of first-order ordinary differential equations. Write a main program that calls on MYRK to solve equation (6.4.2) with initial conditions (6.4.3), for a variety of step sizes. Compare the results with those of Example 6.4, for comparable step sizes.

6.8 The differential equation

$$\frac{dy}{dx} - 3x^4 - x + 2 = 0,$$

with

$$x_0 = 0, \ y(x_0) = 0,$$

is to be integrated from $x_0 = 0$ to $x_{10} = 5$, using the third-order Runge-Kutta algorithm of (6.64), with a step-size $h = 1/2$.

Without performing the actual integration, compute an *upper bound* for the total error in the computed value of y at x_{10}. Assume negligible round-off error; that is, the total error is given by the total truncation error,

$$\varepsilon_{10} = y_{10} - y(x_{10}).$$

6.9 Consider the second-order ordinary differential equation

$$\frac{d^2y}{dx^2} = y''(x) = g(x,y),$$

in which the first derivative, $y'(x)$, does not appear explicitly. The following Runge-Kutta method has been developed for integrating equations of this type without requiring the second-order equation to be rewritten as a system of two first-order equations:

$$y_{i+1} = y_i + \frac{h}{6}(k_1 + 4k_2 + k_3),$$

$$y'_{i+1} = h\left[y_i' + \frac{h}{6}(k_1 + 2k_2)\right],$$

$$k_1 = g(x_i, y_i),$$

$$k_2 = g(x_i + h/2, y_i + hy_i'/2 + h^2 k_1/8),$$

$$k_3 = g(x_i + h, y_i + hy_i' + h^2 k_2/2).$$

The initial conditions $y(x_0)$ and $y'(x_0)$ must be specified. Derive this algorithm, and show that it is a third-order method.

6.10 Write a general-purpose function, named RKGILL, that solves a system of n simultaneous first-order ordinary differential equations (6.77)

$$\frac{dy_j}{dx} = f_j(x, y_1, y_2, \ldots, y_n), \qquad j = 1, 2, \ldots, n,$$

using the fourth-order Runge-Kutta method with Gill's coefficients (6.68). The function should be more general than the function RUNGE of Example 6.3, in that RKGILL should automatically adjust the step-size h, based on upper "bounds" for the local truncation errors to be supplied by the user in a vector argument. Use the Richardson extrapolation technique outlined in (6.70) to (6.74) to estimate the truncation errors. Develop appropriate criteria for determining when to change the step-size h. Halving or doubling the step size should be acceptable in most cases. Keep in mind that unnecessary halving of h or delayed doubling of h will greatly increase the number of calculations required for a given problem solution, as will too frequent estimation of the truncation errors.

RKGILL should keep "historical" information to relieve the user of unnecessary bookkeeping. Arguments for the routine should include both the lower and upper integration limits. In addition, it will be convenient to have all derivative evaluations (equivalent to computing the F_j of (6.3.9), (6.3.14), etc.) handled by a separate subroutine with argument list (X, Y, F), where X, Y, and F have the meanings of like symbols in Example 6.3. The name of this subroutine should, itself, be an argument of RKGILL, so that RKGILL can call directly for calculation of derivatives without returning to the calling program.

The user will normally want to print results in tabular form, for independent variable values that are integral multiples of the *original* step size. Therefore, the routine RKGILL should have as one of its arguments, an integer frequency for printing control purposes. This means that all independent variable values associated with the user-specified printout of solutions must occur as the right-hand side (for positive step sizes) of some integration step. It may be necessary to reduce drastically the step size (always by some factor of two) *temporarily* to accommodate proper printing. Note that if the printing frequency is one, then RKGILL should *never* increase the step size beyond its original value, even when the error criteria would indicate that this should be done.

To avoid the necessity of storing tabular information, or of having RKGILL implement the printing of solutions, the function should return to the calling program whenever solutions are to be printed. The calling program should then print any results desired according to any appropriate format. The function RKGILL should return a logical value, .FALSE., to signal that integration is not yet complete, or .TRUE., to indicate that the upper integration limit has been reached. If RKGILL returns the value .FALSE., then the calling program should return to RKGILL immediately after printing.

Test the program thoroughly with a variety of functions, to insure that the step-size adjustment and printing control features are functioning properly. Once checked out, RKGILL can be used to solve many of the equations in the problems that follow.

6.11 The corrector equation, (6.95c), for Milne's sixth-order method, can be used iteratively to produce a sequence of corrected values,

$$y_{i+1,j} = y_{i-3} + \frac{2h}{45}(7f_{i+1,j} + 32f_i + 12f_{i-1} + 32f_{i-2} + 7f_{i-3}),$$

where

$$f_{i+1,j} = f(x_{i+1}, y_{i+1,j}).$$

If the differential equation being solved is $dy/dx = f(x,y)$, under what conditions will this iterative procedure converge to a limiting value $y_{i+1,\infty}$?

6.12 Conduct a stability analysis of the sixth-order Milne corrector (6.95c) for the solution of (6.111).

(a) Find the linear homogeneous difference equation corresponding to the corrector.

(b) Find the characteristic equation of the difference equation of part (a).

(c) How many roots are there for (b)?

(d) For what range of αh should the behavior of (c) be examined?

(e) Investigate the behavior of the roots on the interval selected in part (d), using one of the root-finding techniques discussed in Chapter 3.

(f) If possible, expand the roots of (b) as power series in the parameter αh, as in (6.120) and (6.121).

(g) What is the complete solution to the difference equation?

(h) Identify the solution associated with the principal root and the parasitic solutions (from part (g)).

(i) Show that the sixth-order Milne corrector is marginally stable.

6.13 Conduct a stability analysis, similar to that of Problem 6.12, for the corrector (6.95a) of the fourth-order modified Adams method. Does this corrector give rise to parasitic solutions? Compare the stability of (6.95a) with the stability of (6.95c).

6.14 Develop an algorithm, based on the modified Adams predictor-corrector method ((6.88a) and (6.95a)) that will allow the solution of a single nth-order ordinary differential equation,

$$\frac{d^n y}{dx^n} = f\left(x, \frac{d^{n-1}y}{dx^{n-1}}, \frac{d^{n-2}y}{dx^{n-2}}, \ldots, \frac{dy}{dx}, y\right),$$

with n initial conditions, y, dy/dx, ..., $d^{n-1}y/dx^{n-1}$, all specified at $x = x_0$, without requiring the decomposition of the nth-order equation into a system of n first-order equations.

How would you implement your algorithm as a general-purpose subroutine?

6.15 Write a general-purpose function, named AUTOHM that solves a system of n simultaneous first-order ordinary differential equations (6.77),

$$\frac{dy_j}{dx} = f_j(x, y_1, y_2, \ldots, y_n), \qquad j = 1, 2, \ldots, n,$$

using the fourth-order Hamming corrector (6.131) with the fourth-order Milne predictor (6.102). The function should be more general than the function HAMING of Example 6.4, in that AUTOHM should automatically adjust the step-size h, based on upper "bounds" for the local truncation errors to be supplied by the user in a vector argument. Develop appropriate criteria for determining when to change the step size by either halving it or doubling it. Keep in mind that too frequent modification of the step size may cause an excessive number of calculations to be done.

In the manner of the function RKGILL described in Problem 6.10, evaluations of derivatives should be performed by a separate subroutine. Arguments for AUTOHM should include the upper and lower integration limits, the name of the function that evaluates the derivatives, a starting step size, an integer frequency for printing control (see Problem 6.10), a vector of error bounds, all tables necessary for communication of information, etc. AUTOHM should return the value .FALSE. when the calling program is to print results and then call immediately upon AUTOHM to continue the integration, or .TRUE. when integration to the upper limit is complete.

Starting values for the solution should be generated internally by AUTOHM using a fourth-order Runge-Kutta method. The user should be required to supply the n solution values *only* at x_0, and call upon AUTOHM directly. The function RKGILL of Problem 6.10 could be called to do this; however, a preferred way of starting would be to use the following Runge-Kutta method (here written for a single equation):

$$y_{i+1} = y_i + 0.17476028226269037 \, hk_1$$
$$- 0.55148066287873294 \, hk_2$$
$$+ 1.2055355993965235 \, hk_3$$
$$+ 0.17118478121951903 \, hk_4,$$

$$k_1 = f(x_i, y_i),$$

$$k_2 = f(x_i + 0.4h, y_i + 0.4 \, hk_1),$$

$$k_3 = f(x_i + 0.45573725421878943 \, h, \, y_i$$
$$+ 0.29697760924775360 \, hk_1$$
$$+ 0.15875964497103583 \, hk_2),$$

$$k_4 = f(x_i + h, y_i + 0.21810038822592047 \, hk_1$$
$$- 3.0509651486929308 \, hk_2$$
$$+ 3.8328647604670103 \, hk_3).$$

Ralston [8] shows that of all fourth-order Runge-Kutta methods, this one has the smallest bound for the local truncation error. It has rather poor stability to rounding errors, but this is not important, since only three steps of the

algorithm are required to get the starting values for Hamming's method.

Adequate "old" information regarding the y_j and f_j, $j = 1$, 2, ..., n, should be retained at all times to allow doubling of the step size, without recomputing any functional values before continuing the integration with the new step size. When the step size is halved, functional information at two new base points will be required. Use the Runge-Kutta method outlined above to find the missing values.

Test the program thoroughly with the equations used to test RKGILL of Problem 6.10. Once checked out, AUTOHM can be used to solve many of the equations in the problems that follow.

6.16 Investigate the following procedure, related to the principle of spline function approximation (see Problem 1.24), for approximating the solution of

$$\frac{dy}{dx} = f(x), \qquad a = x_0 \leqslant x \leqslant x_n = b$$

subject to the initial condition $y(x_0) = y_0$.

Introduce a series of equally spaced base points, $x_i = ih$, $i = 0, 1, \ldots, n$, where the spacing is $h = (b - a)/n$. Assume that over each interval $[x_i, x_{i+1}]$, $i = 0, 1, \ldots, n - 1$, the solution is approximated by the second-degree polynomial,

$$p_{2,i}(x) = a_i + b_i x + c_i x^2, \qquad i = 0, 1, \ldots, n - 1.$$

Also, assume that successive such polynomials and their first derivatives match each other in value at intermediate base points, so that

$$a_i + b_i x_i + c_i x_i^2 = a_{i-1} + b_{i-1} x_i + c_{i-1} x_i^2$$
$$b_i + 2c_i x_i = b_{i-1} + 2c_{i-1} x_i = f(x_i), i = 1, 2, \ldots, n - 1.$$

In addition, to insure that the initial condition is obeyed, and that the differential equation is satisfied at the end points, let

$$a_0 + b_0 x_0 + c_0 x_0^2 = y_0,$$
$$b_0 + 2c_0 x_0 = f(x_0),$$
$$b_{n-1} + 2c_{n-1} x_n = f(x_n).$$

(a) Show that the complete solution to the problem amounts to solving $3n$ simultaneous equations in the coefficients a_i, b_i, c_i, $i = 0, 1, \ldots, n - 1$.

(b) What is the most efficient way of solving these simultaneous equations?

(c) Apply the method to the solution of

$$\frac{dy}{dx} = \frac{\cos x}{(1 + 4 \sin^2 x)^{1/2}}$$

on the interval [1,2] with $y_0 = 2$. Use several different step sizes such as 0.5, 0.25, 0.1, 0.05, 0.025, 0.01, 0.005, 0.001. If possible, compare the computational work performed and the accuracy obtained with those for solution by the Euler and Runge-Kutta methods for the same problem. In any event, compare the results with the analytical solution.

6.17 Extend the method of Problem 6.16 to the solution of equations of the form

$$\frac{dy}{dx} = f(x, y).$$

Note that relations such as

$$b_i + 2c_i x_i = b_{i-1} + 2c_{i-1} x_i = f(x_i, y_i)$$

will now be involved, so that initial guesses must be made for the unknown y_i, $i = 1, 2, \ldots, n$, in order to solve the system of equations for the $a_i, b_i, c_i, i = 0, 1, \ldots, n-1$. Devise an iterative scheme and convergence criteria for the iterative improvement of the solutions y_i, $i = 1, 2, \ldots, n$.

Apply the method you develop to the solution of

$$\frac{dy}{dx} = x + y,$$

with initial condition $y(0) = y_0 = 0$. Try the approach with various step sizes and compare the solutions with the analytical solution and solutions found by other integration procedures.

6.18 Extend the methods of Problems 6.16 and 6.17 by approximating the solution $y(x)$ on each interval $[x_i, x_{i+1}]$, $i = 0, 1, \ldots, n-1$, with the third-degree polynomial

$$p_{3,i}(x) = a_i + b_i x + c_i x^2 + d_i x^3.$$

6.19 Repeat Problem 2.15, with the following variation. Assume that the exchanger length L is a known quantity, to be included in the data, and that the resulting exit temperature T_2 is to be computed by the program. First note that the differential form of the heat balance given in Problem 2.15 is

$$\frac{dT}{dx} = \frac{\pi D h(T_s - T)}{m c_p},$$

where x is the distance from the heat-exchanger inlet. The problem then amounts to a step-by-step solution of a first-order differential equation, with the initial condition that $T = T_1$ at $x = 0$; the solution is terminated when the specified length L is reached, at which stage T is the required temperature T_2.

6.20 Modify Example 6.2, concerning the pyrolysis of ethane in a tubular reactor, now removing the earlier simplifying assumption of constant pressure throughout the reactor. Assume that the pressure drop along the reactor is almost entirely due to wall friction (and not to the acceleration of the gases), so that a momentum balance yields

$$\frac{dP}{dL} = -\frac{f_M \rho u^2}{2D}.$$

Here, D is the internal diameter of the tube, u is the mean velocity, ρ is the density, and f_M is the dimensionless Moody friction factor (see Example 5.4 and Problem 3.38).

The above differential equation will now augment those involving dz/dL and dT/dL. Note that u and ρ may be expressed in terms of known quantities by making the substitutions $m = \rho u A$ and $\rho = MP/RT$, where m is the total mass flow rate and $M = 30/(1 + z)$ is the mean molecular weight at any point. Other symbols and suggested test data are basically the same as given in Example 6.2. However, include a value for f_M (such as 0.022) in the data; also investigate the consequences of specifying different pipe diameters (such as $D = 5.047, 4.026, 3.548,$ and 3.068 in.). As usual, use consistent units when substituting actual values into the above differential equation for dP/dL.

6.21 Example 6.2 assumed for simplicity that the thermal cracking of ethane yields two products only—ethylene and hydrogen. The situation is really more complicated, as evidenced by Shah [50], who discusses several additional reactions that may occur during the thermal decomposition of ethane (and also of propane).

Shah's paper includes all of the relevant reaction rates, specific heats, and heats of reaction. Armed with this information, which is too lengthy to be summarized here, the reader may wish to devise and solve further problems in the area of thermal cracking.

6.22 A periodic voltage $V = V_m \sin \omega t$ is applied to terminal A of the rectifying and ripple-filter circuit shown in Fig. P6.22. The particular diode rectifier used has essentially

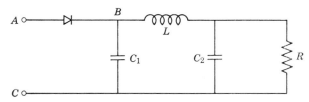

Figure P6.22

negligible resistance for current flowing from A to B, but has infinite resistance in the reverse direction. Terminal C is grounded.

After many cycles of continuous operation, determine the variation with time of: (a) the voltage across capacitor C_1, (b) the voltage across the load resistor R, and (c) the current through the inductance. For the load, also determine the ripple factor (root mean square deviation of voltage from its mean value, divided by that mean value).

Suggested Test Data

$V_m = 160$ volts, $\omega = 120\pi$ sec^{-1}, $C_1 = 4$, $C_2 = 8$, then $C_1 = 8$, $C_2 = 4$ microfarads, $L = 5$ henries, with $R = 220$ and 2200 ohms for each combination of capacitances.

6.23 A periodic square-wave voltage of amplitude V_m and period T is applied to terminal A in Fig. P6.23; terminal C is

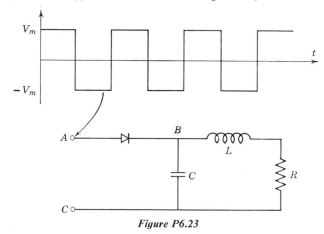

Figure P6.23

grounded. The rectifier is such that for $v_a \geqslant v_b$, the current i_{ab} flowing from A to B obeys the relation

$$i_{ab} = k(v_a - v_b)^{3/2},$$

in which k is a constant; however, when $v_a < v_b$, no current flows between A and B in either direction.

Write a program that will compute the variation with time t of the voltages across (a) the capacitor and (b) the resistor. Discontinue the calculations when either t exceeds an upper limit t_{max} or the fractional voltage change from one cycle to the next (compared at corresponding times) falls below a small value ε.

Suggested Test Data

$V_m = 100$ V, $T = 0.1$, 0.01, and 0.001 sec, $C = 10$ μF, $L = 2.5$ H, $R = 500$ Ω, with $k = 0.003$ and 0.0003 A/V$^{3/2}$ for each value of T; $\varepsilon = 0.001$ and $t_{max} = 100T$.

6.24 Problem 5.24 was concerned with writing a general program that could simulate any electrical network consisting entirely of resistors, with known voltages applied at certain points.

Discuss the possibility of extending this idea to the digital simulation of a completely general network, in which not only resistors, but capacitors, inductances, switches, electronic vacuum tubes, a-c sources, etc., may be present.

6.25 Figure P6.25 shows the cross section of an electron lens that is discussed in Problem 7.26 (q.v.).

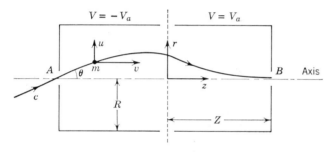

Figure P6.25

An electron of charge $-e$ and mass m enters the small hole at A with velocity c at an angle θ to the axis of the lens. Inside the hollow cylinders, the electric field is $\mathbf{E} = -\nabla V$, and the force on the electron is $\mathbf{F} = -e\mathbf{E}$. Hence the subsequent radial and axial velocity components u and v are modified according to:

$$m\frac{du}{dt} = e\frac{\partial V}{\partial r},$$

$$m\frac{dv}{dt} = e\frac{\partial V}{\partial z}.$$

Hopefully, the anode voltage V_a and the distances R and Z will be arranged so that the electron will be travelling along the z axis by the time it escapes through the small hole at B.

Making use of the potential distributions computed in Problem 7.26, write another program that will investigate the effectiveness of the lens for several different values of the parameters c, θ, V_a, R, and Z. Note that $e = 1.602 \times 10^{-19}$ coulombs and $m = 9.108 \times 10^{-31}$ kg.

6.26 The pin-ended strut shown in Fig. P6.26 is subjected to an axial load P. The lateral deflection y is governed by [43]:

$$\frac{d^2y}{dx^2} + \frac{P}{EI}\left[1 + \left(\frac{dy}{dx}\right)^2\right]^{3/2} y = 0,$$

where $E =$ Young's modulus, and I is the appropriate cross-sectional moment of inertia of the strut. (For small deflec-

tions—not the situation here—the slope dy/dx is frequently neglected).

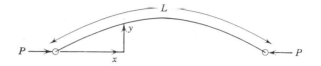

Figure P6.26

If the length of the strut is L, assumed constant, at what value of PL^2/EI will the central deflection y_c be such that $y_c/L = 0.3$?

6.27 A mast of length L, clamped vertically at its base B, has Young's modulus E and second cross-sectional moment of area I. If the mast is long enough, it will bend over due to its self-weight, w per unit length. As shown in Fig. P6.27, let s

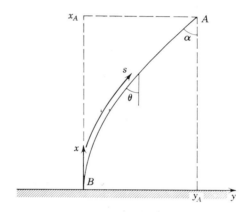

Figure P6.27

denote distance measured along the mast from B, $y = y(s)$ the horizontal deflection at any point, $x = x(s)$ the vertical height at any point, and $\theta = \theta(s)$ the angle between the mast and the vertical. Note that $dy/ds = \sin\theta$. The governing equation is

$$EI\frac{d\theta}{ds} = \int_s^L w[y(\zeta) - y(s)]d\zeta,$$

which may be differentiated with respect to s to yield a second-order ordinary differential equation. The boundary conditions are $\theta = 0$ at $s = 0$, and $d\theta/ds = 0$ at $s = L$.

Compute those values of the dimensionless group $\gamma = wL^3/EI$ for which x_A/L equals 0.99, 0.95, 0.9, 0.5, and 0. What will be the corresponding values of y_A/L and α (the value of θ at the free end A)? Determine the value of γ for which the mast just begins to lean over. What does this mean in practical terms for a light-alloy pole of O.D. 2 in. and wall thickness 0.1 in., for which $w = 0.705$ lb$_f$/ft, $E = 10^7$ lb$_f$/sq in., and $I = 0.270$ in.^{4}?

Timoshenko [44] gives a simplified treatment of this problem, in which the curvature $d\theta/ds$ is approximated by d^2y/dx^2 (see Problem 3.46).

6.28 The installation shown in Fig. P6.28 delivers water from a reservoir of constant elevation H to a turbine. The surge tank of diameter D is intended to prevent excessive pressure rises in the pipe whenever the valve is closed quickly during an emergency.

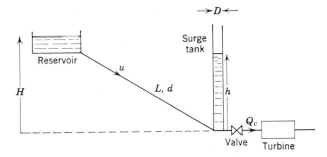

Figure P6.28

Assuming constant density, and neglecting the effect of acceleration of water in the surge tank, a momentum balance on the water in the pipe leads to

$$g(H - h) - \frac{1}{2} f_M \frac{L}{d} u^2 = L \frac{du}{dt}.$$

Here, h = height of water in the surge tank (h_0 under steady conditions), f_M = Moody friction factor, u = mean velocity in the pipe, g = gravitational acceleration, and t = time. Also, continuity requires that

$$\frac{\pi d^2}{4} u = \frac{\pi D^2}{4} \frac{dh}{dt} + Q_v.$$

The flow rate Q_v through the valve in the period $0 \leqslant t \leqslant t_c$ during which it is being closed is approximated by

$$Q_v = k\left(1 - \frac{t}{t_c}\right)(h - h^*)^{1/2},$$

where the constant k depends on the particular valve and the downstream head h^* depends on the particular emergency at the turbine.

During and after an emergency shutdown of the valve, compute the variation with time of the level in the surge tank.

Suggested Test Data

$g = 32.2$ ft/sec², $H = 100$ ft, $h_0 = 88$ ft, $f_M = 0.024$, $L = 2000$ ft, $d = 2$ ft, $t_c = 6$ sec, $k = 21.4$ ft²·⁵/sec, and $D = 4$, 6, 10, and 15 ft. Take two extreme values for h^*: (a) its original steady value, $h_0 - Q_{v0}^2/k^2$, where Q_{v0} is the original steady flow rate, and (b) zero.

6.29 A projectile of mass m and maximum diameter d is fired with muzzle velocity V_0 at an angle of fire θ_0 above the horizontal. The subsequent velocity components u and v in the horizontal and vertical directions x and y, respectively, obey the ordinary differential equations

$$m \frac{du}{dt} = -F_D \cos \theta,$$

$$m \frac{dv}{dt} = -mg - F_D \sin \theta.$$

Here, θ = angle of projectile path above the horizontal, and g = gravitational acceleration. The drag force F_D is given by $F_D = C_D A \rho V^2/2$, where V = speed of projectile, $A = \pi d^2/4$ = projected area, and ρ = density of air. Consistent units are assumed in the above equations.

The drag coefficient C_D varies with the Mach number $M = V/c$, where c = velocity of sound in air. Representative values (see Streeter [45], for example) are:

M:	0	0.5	0.75	1	1.25	1.5	2	2.5	3
C_D:	1.6	1.8	2.1	4.8	5.8	5.4	4.8	4.2	3.9

The range on horizontal terrain is to be R. Write a program that will determine if this range can be achieved and, if so, the two possible angles of fire, the total times of flight, and the velocities on impact. In each case, also determine the error in the range that would result from a ± 10 minute of arc error in the firing angle.

Suggested Test Data

$m = 100$ lb$_m$, $g = 32.2$ ft/sec², $d = 6$ in., $V_0 = 2154$ ft/sec, $\rho = 0.0742$ lb$_m$/cu ft, $c = 1137$ ft/sec, with $R = 0.5, 1, 2, 4, 6, 8$, and 10 thousand yards.

6.30 Let the suspension of a vehicle of mass M be represented by the lumped spring-dashpot system shown in Fig. P6.30. At time $t = 0$ the vehicle is travelling steadily with its

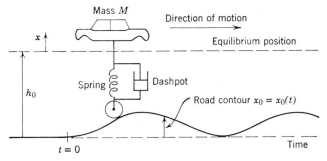

Figure P6.30

center of gravity at an equilibrium distance h_0 above the ground, and it has no vertical velocity. For subsequent times $(t > 0)$ the contour of the road (the displacement of the road surface from the reference level at time zero) is given by an arbitrary function $x_0 = x_0(t)$.

If the *stiffness* (restoring force/extension) of the spring is k, and the damping coefficient of the dashpot is r, then show that $x(t)$, the displacement of the center of gravity of the vehicle as a function of time, is the solution of the second-order ordinary differential equation

$$M \frac{d^2x}{dt^2} = -k(x - x_0) - r\left(\frac{dx}{dt} - \frac{dx_0}{dt}\right),$$

with the initial conditions

$$x(0) = 0,$$

$$\left.\frac{dx}{dt}\right|_{t=0} = 0.$$

Let the road contour function be given by

$$x_0(t) = A(1 - \cos \omega t),$$

where $2A$ is the full displacement of the road surface from the reference level.

Note that the under-, critically-, and over-damped cases correspond to $r/2\sqrt{kM}$ being less than, equal to, and greater than unity, respectively.

Write a program that uses the model outlined above to simulate the behavior of a specified suspension system, over the time period $0 \leqslant t \leqslant t_{max}$. The program should read values for M, R, K, A, W, TMAX, DT, and FREQ, where W corresponds to ω, DT is the step size to be used in integrating the differential equation, and FREQ is an integer used to control printing frequency, such that the values of t, x, dx/dt, d^2x/dt^2, and $x_0(t)$ are printed initially and every FREQ time steps thereafter. The remaining program symbols have obvious interpretations. The equation should be solved using a one-step method, and the program should allow for the processing of several sets of data.

Suggested Test Data

M = 3680 lb_m, K = 640 lb_f/in., A = 2 in., W = 7 rad/sec, and TMAX = 10 sec. Investigate R = 80, 160, and 240 lb_f sec/in. in turn. The values of DT and FREQ will depend on the integration method chosen. In any event, each of the data sets listed above should be processed with more than one step size. For each situation, plot x, x_0, dx/dt, and d^2x/dt^2 as functions of time.

6.31 Let the damping coefficient, r, of Problem 6.30 be a nonlinear function of the relative velocities of the two parts of the dashpot:

$$r = r_0 \left(1 + c \left| \frac{dx}{dt} - \frac{dx_0}{dt} \right|^{1/2} \right).$$

Rerun the simulation of Problem 6.30 with this definition of the damping coefficient. Investigate all nine combinations of $r_0 = 80$, 160, and 240 lb_f sec/in., with $c = 0.1$, 1, and 10 $(sec/in.)^{1/2}$.

6.32 Extend Example 6.5 to include heat transfer for a plate at a temperature θ_w and a fluid whose temperature is θ_∞ far away from the plate. Neglecting viscous dissipation and conduction in the x direction, the partial differential equation governing the variation of temperature θ is

$$u \frac{\partial \theta}{\partial x} + v \frac{\partial \theta}{\partial y} = \frac{k}{\rho c_p} \frac{\partial^2 \theta}{\partial y^2},$$

subject to the boundary conditions

$$y = 0: \quad \theta = \theta_w,$$
$$y = \infty: \quad \theta = \theta_\infty.$$

Here, k, ρ, and c_p are the thermal conductivity, density, and specific heat of the fluid.

Show that the above relations can be reexpressed as

$$\frac{d^2T}{d\eta^2} + \frac{fPr}{2} \frac{dT}{d\eta} = 0,$$

subject to

$$\eta = 0: \quad T = 1,$$
$$\eta = \infty: \quad T = 0,$$

where f and η are defined in Example 6.5, $Pr = \nu \rho c_p / k$ is the Prandtl number of the fluid, and $T = (\theta - \theta_\infty)/(\theta_w - \theta_\infty)$ is a dimensionless temperature.

Obtain solutions that will enable T to be plotted against η for $Pr = 0.1$, 1, 10, 100, and 1000.

6.33 A hot vertical wall, maintained at a temperature θ_w, is situated in a fluid of infinite extent. Far away from the wall, the fluid has temperature θ_0 and zero velocity. Because of the buoyant effect on heating, natural convection occurs in the fluid. Let $u = u(x,y)$ and $v = v(x,y)$ denote the resulting fluid velocities in the x and y directions (horizontal and vertical distances from the bottom of the wall, respectively). Also use $\theta = \theta(x,y)$ to denote the fluid temperature, and let Pr, β, and ν be its Prandtl number, volume coefficient of expansion, and kinematic viscosity, respectively.

The steady motion is governed by the suitably simplified equations of continuity, momentum, and energy (see Schlichting [42], for example). By using the similarity transformation

$$\eta = \left[\frac{\beta g (\theta_w - \theta_0) y^4}{4 \nu^2 x} \right]^{1/4},$$

it may be shown that dimensionless velocities and temperature are given by

$$U = \frac{u}{2\sqrt{\beta g x (\theta_w - \theta_0)}} = \frac{d\zeta}{d\eta},$$

$$V = v \left[\frac{4x}{\beta g (\theta_w - \theta_0) \nu^2} \right]^{1/4} = \eta \frac{d\zeta}{d\eta} - 3\zeta,$$

$$T = \frac{\theta - \theta_0}{\theta_w - \theta_0},$$

where the functions $\zeta = \zeta(\eta)$ and $T = T(\eta)$ are solutions of the simultaneous ordinary differential equations

$$\frac{d^3\zeta}{d\eta^3} + 3\zeta \frac{d^2\zeta}{d\eta^2} - 2\left(\frac{d\zeta}{d\eta}\right)^2 + T = 0,$$

$$\frac{d^2T}{d\eta^2} + 3Pr\zeta \frac{dT}{d\eta} = 0.$$

Show that the boundary conditions on ζ and T are:

$$\eta = 0: \quad \zeta = \frac{d\zeta}{d\eta} = 0, \qquad T = 1,$$

$$\eta = \infty: \quad \frac{d\zeta}{d\eta} = 0, \qquad T = 0.$$

Note that in a finite-difference procedure, $\eta = \infty$ would be approximated by $\eta = \eta_{max}$, where η_{max} is large enough so that its exact value has negligible influence on the solution.

Solve the above differential equations, and construct plots of U, V, and T against η. What is the value of the dimensionless temperature gradient at the wall, $(dT/d\eta)_{\eta=0}$?

6.34 Extend Problem 5.30 by allowing for heat conduction around the perimeter of the shield. Let t and k be the thickness and thermal conductivity of the shield, x be distance measured around the perimeter, and $T_s = T_s(x)$ be the shield temperature at any point. If q_r denotes the local rate of radiant heat absorption by unit area of the inside of the shield, show that T_s obeys the differential equation

$$kt \frac{d^2T_s}{dx^2} + q_r - q = 0,$$

where q is defined in Problem 5.30.

Attempt to devise a method for computing T_s as a function of position; if the scheme appears feasible, implement it on the computer. Use the data of Problem 5.30, with $k = 25.9$ BTU/hr ft °F and $t = 0.1$ in.

6.35 Ethylene oxide is to be produced by passing a mixture of ethylene and oxygen through a reactor consisting of a bundle of parallel vertical tubes that are packed with catalyst particles consisting of silver on an alumina base, as described by Wan [46]. The reaction is

$$8C_2H_4 + 9O_2 = 6C_2H_4O + 4CO_2 + 4H_2O.$$

The large heat of reaction serves to generate steam from boiling water surrounding the tubes. Nitrogen may also be added to the feed gases as an inert diluent in order to moderate the rate of reaction.

By making certain simplifying assumptions and using standard design correlations (see Perry [47] and Rohsenow and Choi [48]), the following equations can be shown to govern the variations of pressure, conversion, and gas and catalyst temperatures along the tubes (mass transfer is not a limiting factor):

Pressure Along Tubes

$$\frac{dp}{dL} = -\frac{G^2(1-\varepsilon)}{\rho_g d_p \varepsilon^3}\left[\frac{150(1-\varepsilon)}{Re} + 1.75\right].$$

Conversion Along Tubes

$$\frac{dz}{dL} = \frac{r\rho_c}{N_0}.$$

Gas Temperature Along Tubes

$$\frac{dT_g}{dL} = \frac{r\rho_c(-\Delta H_R)}{Gc_p} - \frac{4H}{Gc_p D}(T_g - T_w),$$

where H follows the dimensional correlation

$$H = 0.0750\, c_p G^{0.8} D^{-0.2}.$$

Reaction Rate

$$r = 1.17 \times 10^6 (e^{-17,490/T_c}) P x_1^{0.328} x_2^{0.672}.$$

Catalyst/Gas Temperature Difference

$$a_v(T_c - T_g)h = r(-\Delta H_R)\rho_c,$$

with

$$\frac{hd_p}{k} = 0.80\, Re^{0.7}\, Pr^{1/3}.$$

Equation of State

$$\rho_g = \frac{MP}{RT_g}.$$

The following notation is used here:

a_v — Surface area of catalyst per unit packed volume, ft^{-1}.

c_p — Mean specific heat of gas, BTU/lb$_m$ °F. Assume that $c_p = (0.585 + 0.260n + 0.269g)/(1 + u + 1.143g)$, an average value for the feed gas over the temperature range of most interest, holds throughout the reactor.

D — Tube internal diameter, ft.

d_p — Catalyst particle diameter, ft.

G — Gas superficial mass flow rate, lb$_m$/sq ft hr.

g — Moles oxygen per mole ethylene in feed.

h, H — Heat transfer coefficients between catalyst and gas, and between gas and cooling water, BTU/hr sq ft °F.

k — Mean gas thermal conductivity, BTU/hr ft °F.

L — Length along tube, ft; L_{max} = value at exit.

M — Mean molecular weight of gas at any point, lb$_m$/lb mole.

n — Moles nitrogen per mole ethylene in feed.

N_0 — Lb moles ethylene/hr sq ft entering the reactor.

P — Absolute pressure, atm. P_0 = inlet value.

p — Absolute pressure, lb$_m$/ft hr^2. Conversion factors 32.2 lb$_m$ ft/lb$_f$ sec^2, 144 sq in./sq ft, and 14.7 psia/atm will be needed to convert to practical units.

Pr — Prandtl number of the gas, $\mu c_p/k$.

r — Specific reaction rate, lb mole ethylene oxide formed per lb$_m$ catalyst per hour.

R — Gas constant, 0.7302 atm cu ft/lb mole °R.

Re — Particle Reynolds number, $d_p G/\mu$.

T_g, T_c, T_w — Gas, catalyst, and water temperatures, °R. Extra subscript Γ denotes °F, and 0 denotes inlet value.

T_{max} — Temperature above which there is a danger of explosion, °R.

x_1, x_2 — Mole fractions of ethylene and oxygen, respectively.

Y — Total yield of ethylene oxide, lb moles/hr sq ft.

z — Conversion, moles ethylene oxide formed per mole of ethylene in the feed.

ΔH_R — Mean heat of reaction, BTU/lb mole of ethylene oxide formed.

ε — Void fraction in packed tube.

ρ_c — Bulk catalyst density, lb$_m$/cu ft.

ρ_g — Gas density, lb$_m$/cu ft.

μ — Mean gas viscosity, lb$_m$/ft hr.

On the basis of material balances, first establish the relations:

$$x_1 = \frac{1 - \frac{4}{3}z}{1 + g + n - \frac{z}{2}},$$

$$x_2 = \frac{g - \frac{3}{2}z}{1 + g + n - \frac{z}{2}},$$

$$N_0 = \frac{G}{28 + 32g + 28n}.$$

A preliminary design has suggested the following values (units as above): $\rho_c = 83.5$, $T_{wF} = 300$, $D = 1/12$, $d_p = 0.0033$, $T_{max} = 1010$, $\varepsilon = 0.57$, $\mu = 0.0595$, $k = 0.028$, $a_v = 782$, $P_0 = 15$, but these may need modification.

Suitable values for G, g, n, T_{gF0}, and L_{max} are still to be chosen. Investigate the performance of the reactor for several different combinations of these variables, bearing in mind the following desirable features: (a) high overall yield Y, (b) T_g must never exceed T_{max}, (c) dT_g/dL must not be negative at the inlet (reaction self-extinguishing), (d) P must always be positive, and (e) for control purposes, a change of $1°F$ in the gas temperature at inlet should not produce too large a change in its value at the exit (no more than $10°F$, for example).

Tentative ranges for investigation are: $G = 5,000$ to $40,000$; $g = 0.2$ to 0.6; $n = 0$ to 4; $T_{gF0} = 350$ to 500; $L_{max} = 2$ to 6.

6.36 Figure P6.36 shows a cross section of a long cooling fin of width W, thickness t, and thermal conductivity k, that is

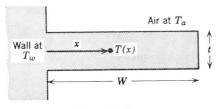

Figure P6.36

bonded to a hot wall, maintaining its base (at $x = 0$) at a temperature T_w. Heat is conducted steadily through the fin and is lost from the sides of the fin by convection to the surrounding air with a heat transfer coefficient h. (Radiation is neglected at sufficiently low temperatures.)

Show that the fin temperature T, assumed here to depend only on the distance x along the fin, obeys the differential equation

$$kt \frac{d^2T}{dx^2} = 2h(T - T_a),$$

where T_a is the mean temperature of the surrounding air. (Fourier's law gives the heat flux density as $q = -k\,dT/dx$ for steady conduction in one dimension.) If the surface of the fin is vertical, h obeys the dimensional correlation $h = 0.21(T - T_a)^{1/3}$ BTU/hr sq ft °F, with both temperatures in °F (Rohsenow and Choi [48]).

What are the boundary conditions on T? Write a program that will compute: (a) the temperature distribution along the fin, and (b) the total rate of heat loss from the fin to the air per foot length of fin.

Suggested Test Data

$T_w = 200°F$, $T_a = 70°F$, $t = 0.25$ in; investigate all eight combinations of $k = 25.9$ (steel) and 220 (copper) BTU/hr ft °F, $W = 0.5$, 1, 2, and 5 in.

If available, compare the results with those obtained from Problem 7.42, in which temperature variations across the fin are taken into account.

6.37 *Note.* Before attempting this problem, the reader should become familiar with Example 2.1 and the discussion in Problems 3.17 and 5.25.

Figure P6.37 shows a horizontal cross section of a very tall vertical wall that is maintained at a uniformly high temperature T_w and whose surface has an emissivity ε_w. A large number of vertical metallic cooling fins, spaced on a pitch d, are bonded

to the wall for its entire height. Each fin has width W, thickness t, thermal conductivity k, and surface emissivity ε_f. The wall and fins transfer heat by combined convection *and* radiation to the surrounding air, which has a mean temperature T_a and also behaves as a black-body enclosure at that temperature.

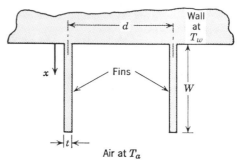

Figure P6.37

Assume that (a) both wall and fins have gray surfaces, and (b) the heat transfer coefficient for *convection* between the wall and fins to the surrounding air approximately obeys the correlation $h = 0.21(\Delta T)^{1/3}$ BTU/hr sq ft °F, in which the temperature difference ΔT between the hot surface and air is in °F (see Rohsenow and Choi [48]). Also, neglect temperature variations across the thickness of the fins; the local fin temperature T_f then obeys the differential equation

$$kt \frac{d^2T_f}{dx^2} = 2q_f,$$

where q_f is the local rate of heat loss per unit area from one side of a fin and x is distance along a fin.

Write a program that will accept values for the parameters T_w, T_a, ε_w, ε_f, W, t, d, and k, and then compute the average net rate of heat loss $\bar{q}$ from the wall and fins, based on unit area of the wall surface. Find $\bar{q}$ for several different representative values of the parameters. Discuss the possibility of designing fins that would maximize $\bar{q}$ for a specified weight of metal in the fins.

6.38 Consider two wildlife animal species: A, which has an abundant supply of natural food, and B, which depends entirely for its food supply by preying on A. At a given time t, let N_A and N_B be the populations of A and B, respectively, in a given natural area.

By making certain simple assumptions, show that the following differential equations could describe the growth or decay of the two polulations:

$$\frac{dN_A}{dt} = \alpha N_A - \beta N_A N_B,$$

$$\frac{dN_B}{dt} = -\gamma N_B + \delta N_A N_B.$$

What significance do you attach to the positive constants α, β, γ, and δ?

Write a program that will solve the above equations for a wide variety of initial conditions and values for α, β, γ, and δ. If possible, arrange for the program to plot N_A and N_B against t.

6.39 Before attempting this problem, the reader should have solved Problem 7.27, in the suggested dimensionless form, for several dimensionless velocity ratios $u_B/u_A = 0.5, 1.0, 2.0, 3.0$. The dimensionless stream function Ψ should be available in tabular form for all the grid points of the finite-difference solution for each of these dimensionless velocity ratios.

Vitols [49] has studied the motion of particles in flow regimes described by the solutions of Problem 7.27, where the inner cylinder represents an aspirated particle-sampling probe immersed in a flowing fluid containing solid particles (for example, sampling for fly ash in an industrial stack). The outer cylinder in Fig. P7.27 need not be taken as the radius of an outer container (stack, for example), but simply as an imaginary stream tube, far enough away from the probe so that there is no radial velocity component of any significance.

Because of inertial and drag forces, a particle flowing at free-stream velocity far upstream of the probe will not necessarily follow a streamline in the vicinity of the probe, where radial and axial velocity components of the fluid may be changing markedly. This effect is illustrated in Fig. 6.39a and 6.39b for u_B/u_A less than one and greater than one, respectively.

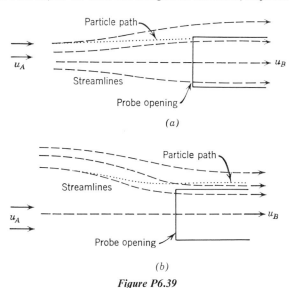

(a)

(b)

Figure P6.39

Thus if the estimated density of particles in the free stream is taken as the number of particles collected by the sampler divided by the volume of gas passing through the probe, the calculated values may differ markedly from the true situation. The total volume of gas passing through the probe will be that enclosed by the stream tube that impinges on the outer circumference of the probe opening. For $u_B/u_A < 1$, particles from outside the limiting stream tube will enter the sampler while, for $u_B/u_A > 1$, particles originally inside the limiting stream tube will pass outside the probe.

Now, consider a particle that just impinges on the outer circumference of the probe. All particles of the same diameter within a cylindrical envelope generated by this limiting particle trajectory will be collected by the probe. Thus the actual density or number of particles per unit volume in the sampled gas is given by

$$\frac{N_p}{\pi r_B^2 u_B}\left[\frac{r_{s,\infty}}{r_{p,\infty}}\right]^2,$$

where N_p is the number of particles collected per unit time, $r_{s,\infty}$ is the upstream radius of the stream tube that impinges on the probe circumference and $r_{p,\infty}$ is the upstream radius of the limiting particle-trajectory envelope. In both cases, "upstream" means far enough removed from the probe to ignore radial velocity effects.

Thus, to calculate the true particle density for spherical particles of a given diameter, we must know $r_{s,\infty}$ and $r_{p,\infty}$ for each dimensionless velocity ratio u_B/u_A. The quantity $r_{s,\infty}$ will be known once the dimensionless stream function has been determined, as in Problem 7.27. It remains to determine $r_{p,\infty}$.

Vitols [49] has shown that the motion of an individual spherical particle can be described by the following ordinary differential equations:

$$\frac{d\bar{v}_{\bar{r}}}{d\tau} = \frac{C_D Re}{24}\frac{(\bar{u}_{\bar{r}} - \bar{v}_{\bar{r}})}{K},$$

$$\frac{d\bar{v}_{\bar{z}}}{d\tau} = \frac{C_D Re}{24}\frac{(\bar{u}_{\bar{z}} - \bar{v}_{\bar{z}})}{K},$$

where

$$Re = Re_0[(\bar{u}_{\bar{r}} - \bar{v}_{\bar{r}})^2 + (\bar{u}_{\bar{z}} - \bar{v}_{\bar{z}})^2]^{1/2},$$

$$K = \frac{\sigma d^2 u_A}{18\mu r_B} = \text{particle inertia parameter,}$$

$$Re_0 = \frac{\rho d u_A}{\mu} = \text{free-stream Reynolds number.}$$

Here,

$C_D = $ dimensionless drag coefficient for spheres
$d = $ particle diameter, cm
$u_A = $ free-stream velocity, cm/sec
$\sigma = $ particle density, gm/cm³
$\mu = $ absolute viscosity of fluid, poise
$r_B = $ probe radius, cm
$\rho = $ fluid density, gm/cm³
$u = $ local fluid velocity, cm/sec
$v = $ local particle velocity, cm/sec
$t = $ time, seconds
$r = $ radial coordinate of particle position, cm
$z = $ axial coordinate (origin at probe) of particle position, cm.

The following are dimensionless:

$\bar{u} = $ local fluid velocity, u/u_A
$\bar{v} = $ local particle velocity, v/u_A
$\tau = $ time, tu_A/r_B
$\bar{r} = $ radial coordinate, r/r_B
$\bar{z} = $ axial coordinate, z/r_B
$\bar{v}_{\bar{r}} = d\bar{r}/d\tau$, radial component of particle velocity
$\bar{v}_{\bar{z}} = d\bar{r}/d\tau$, axial component of particle velocity
$\bar{u}_{\bar{r}} = d\bar{u}/d\bar{r}$, radial component of fluid velocity
$\bar{u}_{\bar{z}} = d\bar{u}/d\bar{z}$, axial component of fluid velocity.

Several assumptions are inherent in the development of this equation, including (a) uniform particle distribution, (b) no gravitational or electrostatic forces of consequence, (c) monodisperse spherical particles with diameter very small in relation to diameter of probe opening, and (d) free-stream flow that is steady, incompressible, and irrotational.

The drag coefficient C_D is a function of Reynold's number and is available in tabular form. For industrial sampling applications, the Reynolds number is normally in the range 1.0 to 100. Some values for spherical particles are shown in the Table P6.39 [47]:

Table P6.39

Re	C_D
0.1	240
0.5	49.5
1.0	26.5
5.0	6.9
10.0	4.1
20.0	2.55
50.0	1.50
100.0	1.07

Write a program that accepts, as data, values for the dimensionless velocity ratio u_B/u_A (possible values correspond to those for which the stream functions are available), K (industrial cases encountered usually have values of K from 1 to 100), and Re_0 (normally between 1 and 100 for practical applications). The program should then integrate the two second-order nonlinear ordinary differential equations to establish the position $(\bar{r}, \bar{z})$ of a given particle in the flow field at any time τ, given an initial position $(\bar{r}_0, \bar{z}_0)$ at time $\tau = 0$. The initial position should be situated far enough upstream (several dimensionless probe radii) so that the initial particle velocity in the radial direction is zero and in the axial direction is the free stream velocity.

Note that as the particle moves in time, the velocity components for the fluid, $\bar{u}_{\bar{r}}$ and $\bar{u}_{\bar{z}}$, must be computed as functions of location by numerical differentiation of the dimensionless stream function (available in tabular form from Problem 7.27). In addition, the Reynolds number and the corresponding drag coefficient C_D must be evaluated for local conditions.

The program should automatically adjust the initial location of the particle $(\bar{r}_0, \bar{z}_0)$ until it finds the radius $\bar{r}_{p,\infty} = r_{p,\infty}/r_B = \bar{r}_0$. Thus the problem may be viewed as a boundary value problem for which three conditions are initial conditions $(\bar{z}_0, \bar{v}_{\bar{r}}, \bar{v}_{\bar{z}})$ and one is a boundary condition, namely that at some time $\tau > 0$, the particle will hit the "target" (the lip of the probe) at location $\bar{r} = 1$, $\bar{z} = 0$. The desired solution of the problem is $\bar{r}_{p,\infty}$.

As trial values, solve the problem for the following [49]:

u_B/u_A	0.5	1.5	2.0	3.0
Re_0	12.0	15.0	16.6	23.2
K	13.9	17.4	19.3	35.5

6.40 Discuss the possibility of extending Problem 6.39 to account for spherical particles whose diameters conform to a specified statistical distribution.

6.41 A jet of fluid of constant density ρ originates from a point source in a fluid that is otherwise stagnant, as shown in Fig. P6.41. Let u and v be the fluid velocities in the r (radial) and z (axial) directions, respectively. Assuming a uniform pres-

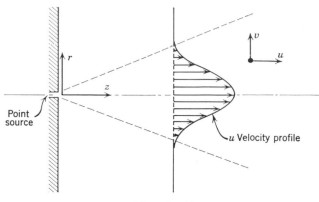

Figure P6.41

sure throughout, momentum in the z direction is conserved, so that

$$2\pi\rho \int_0^\infty u^2 r \, dr$$

is constant. Also assume a solution of the form $u(r,z) = \phi(z)f(\eta)$, where $\eta = r/z$, and let

$$F(\eta) = \int_0^\eta f(\eta) \, \eta \, d\eta.$$

Using the continuity equation,

$$\frac{\partial u}{\partial z} + \frac{1}{r} \frac{\partial (vr)}{\partial r} = 0,$$

show that

$$u = \frac{A}{\eta z} \frac{dF}{d\eta},$$

$$v = \frac{A}{z} \left(\frac{dF}{d\eta} - \frac{F}{\eta} \right),$$

where A is a constant.

If momentum is transported only by turbulent shear, and turbulent normal stresses are ignored, a simplified Reynold's equation results. Tollmien [51] has studied this problem; assuming a Prandtl mixing length l of the form $l = cz$, it can be shown that

$$u \frac{du}{\partial z} + v \frac{\partial u}{\partial r} = -\frac{1}{r} \frac{\partial}{\partial r} \left[rc^2 z^2 \left(\frac{\partial u}{\partial r} \right)^2 \right].$$

By substituting the above relationships into this equation and integrating once, show that F obeys the ordinary differential equation

$$F \frac{dF}{d\eta} = c^2 \left[\frac{d^2 F}{d\eta^2} - \frac{1}{\eta} \frac{dF}{d\eta} \right]^2.$$

Eliminate c by introducing a new independent variable $\zeta = c^{-2/3}\eta$. Arbitrarily assuming that $uz/A = 1$ on the centerline, what are the boundary conditions on F? Solve the final equation with the selected boundary conditions and construct a graph showing how uz/A and vz/A vary with ζ.

6.42 A pile AB of total length L has Young's modulus E and cross-sectional moment of inertia I. It is driven vertically down for a depth D into the ground. A horizontal force P is applied to the pile through a pin joint at its exposed end A.

The following differential equation [52] governs y, the horizontal deflection of the pile from its undisturbed position, as a function of x, the vertical distance measured down from A:

$$EI \frac{d^4 y}{dx^4} = w.$$

Here, w is the load in the y direction on unit length of the pile which, due to the ground resistance, is given by a known function, $w = f(x,y)$.

What are the boundary conditions on y? Discuss methods for computing $y = y(x)$ in the following three cases:

(a) $f(x,y) = -ky$, where k is a constant that is independent of depth.

(b) $f(x,y) = -k(x)y$, where k is a known function of depth.

(c) $f(x,y) = -k(x)g(y)$, where both k and g are known functions.

Would an algorithm for solving a *pentadiagonal system* of linear equations be applicable to any of the above cases? Can such an algorithm be developed? (See Section 7.9 for the solution of a tridiagonal system of equations.)

6.43 Sulfuryl chloride vapor decomposes according to the irreversible first-order endothermic reaction

$$SO_2Cl_2 \rightarrow SO_2 + Cl_2.$$

Thermodynamic and kinetic information is available (Table P6.43) with temperature T_k in degrees Kelvin.

Table P6.43

	ΔH_f at 298°K (cal/g mole)	c_p (cal/g mole °K)
SO_2Cl_2 (gas)	−82,040	$13.00 + 24.0 \times 10^{-3}T_k - 14.4 \times 10^{-6}T_k^2$
SO_2 (gas)	−70,940	$8.12 + 6.825 \times 10^{-3}T_k - 2.103 \times 10^{-6}T_k^2$
Cl_2 (gas)	0	$7.575 + 2.424 \times 10^{-3}T_k - 0.965 \times 10^{-6}T_k^2$

Reaction rate constant: $k = 6.427 \times 10^{15}\, e^{-50,610/RT_k}\ sec^{-1}$

Atomic weights: S = 32.07, O = 16.0, Cl = 35.46

Gas constant: $R = 1.987$ cal/g mole °K

In a proposed experiment, m pounds per hour of sulfuryl chloride vapor are to be fed at an inlet pressure p_0 and an inlet temperature T_0 to a long coiled tube of internal and external diameters d_1 and d_2, respectively. The tube, which has a thermal conductivity k_t and whose surface is gray with emissivity ε, is situated inside a furnace that acts, to a first

approximation, as a black-body radiator at a temperature T_f. Considering radiation from the furnace to the tube, conduction through the tube wall, and heat transfer by convection from the inside tube wall to the reacting gases, we have:

$$q = \pi d_2 \varepsilon \sigma (T_f^4 - T_2^4) = \frac{2\pi k_t(T_2 - T_1)}{\ln \dfrac{d_2}{d_1}} = \pi d_1 h(T_1 - T_g).$$

Here, q is the rate of heat transfer to the gas per unit length of tube, T_g, T_1, and T_2 are the temperatures of the gas, inside tube wall, and outside tube wall, respectively, and σ is the Stefan-Boltzmann constant: consistent units are assumed and absolute temperatures must be used in the radiant-transfer term.

The following *dimensional* correlation is available [47] for the heat transfer coefficient h (BTU/hr sq ft °F) between the inside tube wall and gas:

$$h = 16.6\bar{c}_p G^{0.8} d_1^{-0.2},$$

where $\bar{c}_p$ is the local mean specific heat of the gas (BTU/lb °F), G is the gas mass velocity (lb/sec sq ft), and d_1 the inside tube diameter (in.).

Pressure p varies with length L along the tube according to the differential equation given in Problem 6.20. Differential equations describing dT_g/dL and dz/dL, where z is the fractional conversion, may be obtained by methods similar to those presented in Example 6.2.

Write a program that computes and prints values for T_g, T_1, and T_2 (all in °F), p (psia), and z at convenient intervals along the reactor tube until either z exceeds a value z_{max}, L exceeds a value L_{max}, or p falls below a value p_{min}.

Suggested Test Data (*Not in Consistent Units*)

$d_1 = 0.5$ in.
$d_2 = 0.625$ in.
$T_0 = 250°F$
f_M (Moody friction factor) $= 0.026$
$z_{max} = 0.90$
$\varepsilon = 0.92$
$\sigma = 1.355 \times 10^{-12}$ cal/sec sq cm °K⁴
$k_t = 12.8$ BTU/hr ft °F
$p_{min} = 5$ psia
$L_{max} = 200$ ft.

Investigate the behavior of the reactor for all combinations of:

$m = 10, 30, 100$ lb/hr
$p_0 = 14.7, 50$ psia
$T_f = 600, 900, 1200°K.$

Bibliography

1. B. W. Arden, *An Introduction to Digital Computing*, Addison-Wesley, Reading, Massachusetts, 1963.
2. P. Henrici, *Discrete Variable Methods in Ordinary Differential Equations*, Wiley, New York, 1962.
3. F. B. Hildebrand, *Introduction to Numerical Analysis*, McGraw-Hill, New York, 1956.
4. L. Lapidus, *Digital Computation for Chemical Engineers*, McGraw-Hill, New York, 1962.
5. W. E. Milne, *Numerical Solution of Differential Equations*, Wiley, New York, 1953.
6. S. Gill, "A Process for the Step-by-Step Integration of Differential Equations in an Automatic Computing Machine," *Proc. Cambridge Phil. Soc.*, **47**, 96–108 (1951).
7. A. Ralston, *A First Course in Numerical Analysis*, McGraw-Hill, New York, 1965.
8. A. Ralston, "Runge-Kutta Methods with Minimum Error Bounds," *Math. Comp.*, **16**, 431–437 (1962).
9. L. Collatz, *The Numerical Treatment of Differential Equations*, Third Ed., Springer-Verlag, Berlin, 1960.
10. D. D. McCracken and W. S. Dorn, *Numerical Methods and FORTRAN Programming*, Wiley, New York, 1964.
11. D. H. Call and R. F. Reeves, "Error Estimation in Runge-Kutta Procedures," *Communications of the A.C.M.*, **1**, 7–8 (1958).
12. J. W. Carr, III, "Error Bounds for the Runge-Kutta Single-Step Integration Process," *Journal of the A.C.M.*, **5**, 39–44 (1958).
13. B. A. Galler and D. P. Rosenberg, "A Generalization of a Theorem of Carr on Error Bounds for Runge-Kutta Procedures," *Journal of the A.C.M.*, **7**, 57–60 (1960).
14. P. Henrici, "The Propagation of Error in the Digital Integration of Ordinary Differential Equations," *Error in Digital Computation—I*, (L. B. Rall, editor), 185–205, Wiley, New York, 1965.
15. L. Fox (ed.), *Numerical Solution of Ordinary and Partial Differential Equations*, Addison-Wesley, Reading, Massachusetts, 1962.
16. R. Beckett and J. Hurt, *Numerical Calculations and Algorithms*, McGraw-Hill, New York, 1967.
17. J. F. Holt, "Numerical Solution of Nonlinear Two-Point Boundary Problems by Finite Difference Methods," *Communications of the A.C.M.*, **7**, 366–373 (1964).
18. D. D. Morrison, J. D. Riley, and J. F. Zancanaro, "Multiple Shooting Method for Two-Point Boundary Value Problems," *Communications of the A.C.M.*, **5**, 613–614 (1962).
19. D. Wilde, *Optimum Seeking Methods*, Prentice-Hall, Englewood Cliffs, New Jersey, 1964.
20. R. Hooke and T. A. Jeeves, "Direct Search Solution of Numerical and Statistical Problems," *Journal of the A.C.M.*, **8**, 212–229 (1961).
21. R. W. Hamming, "Stable Predictor-Corrector Methods for Ordinary Differential Equations," *Journal of the A.C.M.*, **6**, 37–47 (1959).
22. R. W. Hamming, *Numerical Methods for Scientists and Engineers*, McGraw-Hill, New York, 1962.
23. J. C. Butcher, "Integration of Processes based on Radau Quadrature Formulas," *Math. Comp.*, **18**, 233–244 (1964).
24. J. C. Butcher, "Implicit Runge-Kutta Processes," *Math. Comp.*, **18**, 50–64 (1964).
25. J. C. Butcher, "On Runge-Kutta Processes of Higher Order," *J. Austral. Math. Soc.*, **4**, 179–194 (1964).
26. C. W. Gear, "Hybrid Methods for Initial Value Problems in Ordinary Differential Equations," *Journal of the S.I.A.M.*, **2**, 69–86 (1965).
27. J. C. Butcher, "A Modified Multi-Step Method for the Numerical Integration of Ordinary Differential Equations," *Journal of the A.C.M.*, **12**, 124–135 (1965).
28. P. Henrici, *Error Propagation for Difference Methods*, Wiley, New York, 1963.
29. J. Waters, "Methods of Numerical Integration Applied to a System Having Trivial Function Evaluations," *Communications of the A.C.M.*, **9**, 293–296 (1966).
30. S. D. Conte, *Elementary Numerical Analysis*, McGraw-Hill, New York, 1965.
31. W. E. Milne and R. R. Reynolds, "Stability of a Numerical Solution of Differential Equations," *Journal of the A.C.M.*, **6**, 196–203 (1959).
32. G. Dahlquist, "Convergence and Stability in the Numerical Integration of Ordinary Differential Equations," *Math. Scand.*, **4**, 33–53 (1956).
33. W. E. Milne and R. R. Reynolds, "Fifth-Order Methods for the Numerical Solution of Ordinary Differential Equations," *Journal of the A.C.M.*, **9**, 64–70 (1962).
34. P. E. Chase, "Stability Properties of Predictor-Corrector Methods for Ordinary Differential Equations," *Journal of the A.C.M.*, **9**, 457–468 (1962).
35. W. B. Gragg and H. J. Stetter, "Generalized Multistep Predictor-Corrector Methods," *Journal of the A.C.M.*, **11**, 188–209 (1964).
36. R. L. Crane and R. W. Klopfenstein, "A Predictor-Corrector Algorithm with an Increased Range of Absolute Stability," *Journal of the A.C.M.*, **12**, 227–241 (1965).
37. F. T. Krogh, "Predictor-Corrector Methods of High Order with Improved Stability", *Journal of the A.C.M.*, **13**, 374–385 (1966).
38. J. C. Butcher, "A Multistep Generalization of Runge-Kutta Methods with Four or Five Stages," *Journal of the A.C.M.*, **14**, 84–99 (1967).
39. J. J. Kohfeld and G. T. Thompson, "Multistep Methods with Modified Predictors and Correctors," *Journal of the A.C.M.*, **14**, 155–166 (1967).
40. H. A. Luther and H. P. Konen, "Some Fifth-Order Classical Runge-Kutta Formulas," *S.I.A.M. Review*, **7**, 551–558 (1965).
41. H. A. Luther, "Further Explicit Fifth-Order Runge-Kutta Formulas," *S.I.A.M. Review*, **8**, 374–380 (1966).
42. H. Schlichting, *Boundary Layer Theory*, 4th ed., McGraw-Hill, New York, 1960.
43. M. R. Horne and W. Merchant, *The Stability of Frames*, Pergamon Press, New York, 1965.
44. S. Timoshenko, *Theory of Elastic Stability*, McGraw-Hill, New York, 1936.
45. V. L. Streeter, *Fluid Mechanics*, 4th ed., McGraw-Hill, New York, 1966.
46. Shen-Wu Wan, "Oxidation of Ethylene to Ethylene Oxide," *Ind. Eng. Chem.*, **45**, 234–238 (1953).
47. J. H. Perry, ed., *Chemical Engineers' Handbook*, 3rd ed., McGraw-Hill, New York, 1950.
48. W. M. Rohsenow and H. Y. Choi, *Heat, Mass, and Momentum Transfer*, Prentice-Hall, Englewood Cliffs, New Jersey, 1961.
49. V. Vitols, *Determination of Theoretical Collection Efficiencies of Aspirated Particulate Matter Sampling Probes Under Anisokinetic Flow*, Ph.D. Thesis, The University of Michigan, 1964.
50. M. J. Shah, "Computer Control of Ethylene Production," *Ind. Eng. Chem.*, **59**, 70–85 (1967).
51. W. Tollmien, "*Calculation of Turbulent Expansion Processes*," NACA TM 1085 (translation) (1945).
52. W. F. Hughes and E. W. Gaylord, *Basic Equations of Engineering Science*, Schaum Publishing Company, New York, 1964.

CHAPTER 7

Approximation of the Solution of Partial Differential Equations

7.1 Introduction

Linear partial differential equations (PDEs) of the second order are frequently referred to as being of the elliptic, hyperbolic, or parabolic type. Such a classification is possible if the equation has been reduced, by a suitable transformation of the independent variables, to the form

$$\sum_{i=1}^{n} A_i \frac{\partial^2 u}{\partial x_i^2} + \sum_{i=1}^{n} B_i \frac{\partial u}{\partial x_i} + Cu + D = 0,$$

in which the coefficients A_i, evaluated at the point $(x_1, x_2, \ldots, x_n)$, may be 1, -1, or zero. Here, u is the dependent variable, and the x_i are the independent variables. Note the absence of mixed derivatives $\partial^2 u / \partial x_i \, \partial x_j \, (i \neq j)$ in this form. The following are the main possibilities of interest:

1. If all the A_i are nonzero and have the same sign, the PDE is of *elliptic* type.
2. If all the A_i are nonzero and have, with one exception, the same sign, the PDE is of *hyperbolic* type.
3. If one A_i is zero (A_k, for instance) and the remaining A_i are nonzero and of the same sign, and if the coefficient B_k of $\partial u / \partial x_k$ is nonzero, the PDE is of *parabolic* type.

Since the coefficients A_i, B_i, C, and D are functions of the independent variables $x_1, x_2, \ldots, x_n$, the classification of a PDE may vary according to the particular point being considered in the $(x_1, x_2, \ldots, x_n)$ space. Very frequently, one of the independent variables will be time t and the remainder (for our purposes up to three in number) will be distance coordinates x, y, and z. The reader should verify that the PDEs

$$\frac{\partial^2 u}{\partial x^2} + \frac{\partial^2 u}{\partial y^2} = 0, \qquad \frac{\partial^2 u}{\partial x^2} + \frac{\partial^2 u}{\partial y^2} = \frac{\partial^2 u}{\partial t^2},$$

$$\frac{\partial^2 u}{\partial x^2} + \frac{\partial^2 u}{\partial y^2} = \frac{\partial u}{\partial t}.$$

are of elliptic, hyperbolic, and parabolic type, respectively. Further details of the classification of PDEs are given by Petrovsky [20].

This chapter is devoted largely to parabolic and elliptic PDEs. The former are frequently regarded here as equations of a time-dependent nature, requiring both an initial condition and subsequent time-dependent boundary conditions for their solutions, whereas the latter are boundary-value problems having time-independent solutions. The various computer examples deal with fairly simple problems, often concerning heat conduction. However, the same basic principles can be extended to a wide variety of more complex situations, several of which are outlined in Section 7.2.

When using a finite-difference technique to solve a PDE (plus associated boundary and initial conditions), a network of *grid points* is first established throughout the region of interest occupied by the independent variables. Suppose, for example, we have two distance coordinates x and y, and time t as independent variables, and that the respective grid spacings are Δx, Δy, and Δt. Subscripts, i, j, and n may then be used to denote that space point having coordinates $i\Delta x$, $j\Delta y$, $n\Delta t$, also called the grid-point (i, j, n). Let the exact solution to the PDE be $u = u(x, y, t)$, and let its approximation, to be determined at each grid point by the method of finite differences, be $v_{i,j,n}$. We also use $u_{i,j,n}$ to denote the exact solution $u(i\Delta x, j\Delta y, n\Delta t)$ at a particular grid-point (i, j, n).

The partial derivatives of the original PDE are then approximated by suitable finite-difference expressions involving Δx, Δy, Δt, and the $v_{i,j,n}$. This procedure leads to a set of algebraic equations in the $v_{i,j,n}$, whose values may then be determined. By making the grid spacings sufficiently small, it is hoped that $v_{i,j,n}$ will become a sufficiently close approximation to $u_{i,j,n}$ at any grid-point (i, j, n).

7.2 Examples of Partial Differential Equations

The following PDEs, several of which bear obvious similarities to the types mentioned in Section 7.1, are typical of those of practical importance to the engineer. The symbol ∇^2 denotes the Laplacian operator.

Unsteady Heat-Conduction Equation. One-dimensional unsteady heat conduction in a rod is governed by

$$\frac{\partial}{\partial x}\left(k \frac{\partial T}{\partial x}\right) = \rho c_p \frac{\partial T}{\partial t},$$

where T denotes temperature, and k, ρ, and c_p are the thermal conductivity, density, and specific heat of the rod. If k is constant, this equation may be rewritten as

$\alpha \partial^2 T/\partial x^2 = \partial T/\partial t$, in which $\alpha = k/\rho c_p$ is the thermal diffusivity. The introduction of new variables $X = x/L$ and $\tau = \alpha t/L^2$, where L is a characteristic dimension, leads to $\partial^2 T/\partial X^2 = \partial T/\partial \tau$. A similar equation governs the interdiffusion of two substances.

Vorticity Transport Equation. The vorticity ζ of an incompressible fluid in two-dimensional motion varies according to

$$\frac{\partial \zeta}{\partial t} + u \frac{\partial \zeta}{\partial x} + v \frac{\partial \zeta}{\partial y} = v\nabla^2 \zeta,$$

where u and v are the x and y velocity components, and v is the kinematic viscosity.

Poisson's Equation. Poisson's equation is $\nabla^2 \psi = -\sigma$. Three important applications occur: (*a*) in *fluid dynamics*, with $\psi = $ stream function and $\sigma = $ vorticity, (*b*) in *electrostatics*, with $\psi = $ electric potential and $\sigma = $ ratio of charge density to dielectric constant, and (*c*) in *elasticity*, with $\sigma = 2$, ψ is a function from which the angle of twist of a cylinder under torsion can be calculated.

Laminar Flow Heat-Exchanger Equation. The following equation governs variations of temperature T with radial and axial distances r and z for steady, laminar flow in a cylindrical heat exchanger:

$$\frac{\partial^2 T}{\partial r^2} + \frac{1}{r}\frac{\partial T}{\partial r} + \frac{\partial^2 T}{\partial z^2} = \frac{\rho u c_p}{k}\frac{\partial T}{\partial z}.$$

Here, ρ, c_p, and k are the density, specific heat, and thermal conductivity of the fluid, and the axial velocity u is a known function of r. Note how the character of the equation changes if the term $\partial^2 T/\partial z^2$, corresponding to axial conduction, can be neglected.

Telephone Equation. The following equation can be used to predict variations of voltage V along a transmission cable:

$$\frac{\partial^2 V}{\partial x^2} = LC\frac{\partial^2 V}{\partial t^2} + (RC + GL)\frac{\partial V}{\partial t} + RGV.$$

Here, R and L denote the resistance and inductance per unit length of the cable, and C and G denote the capacitance and conductance to ground per unit length of the cable.

Wave Equation. The angle of twist ϕ at any section of a circular shaft undergoing torsional vibrations is governed by

$$\frac{\partial^2 \phi}{\partial t^2} = \frac{G}{\rho}\frac{\partial^2 \phi}{\partial x^2},$$

where G is the rigidity modulus of the shaft and ρ is its density.

Biharmonic Equation. The transverse deflection w of a thin plate of flexural rigidity D subject to a normal load q per unit area is governed by $\nabla^4 w = q/D$.

Vibrating Beam Equation. The transverse deflection y of a vibrating beam obeys

$$\frac{\partial^2 y}{\partial t^2} + \frac{EI}{A\rho}\frac{\partial^4 y}{\partial x^4} = 0,$$

in which $E = $ modulus of elasticity, $I = $ cross-sectional moment of inertia, $A = $ cross-sectional area, and $\rho = $ density.

Ion-Exchange Equation. For flow of a solution through a packed column containing an ion-exchange resin,

$$v\frac{\partial c}{\partial x} + \varepsilon\frac{\partial c}{\partial t} + r = 0.$$

Here, $c = $ concentration of a particular ion in solution, $r = $ rate at which that ion is adsorbed per unit volume of column, $\varepsilon = $ bed void fraction, and $v = $ superficial liquid velocity. A similar type of equation governs regenerative heat transfer.

7.3 The Approximation of Derivatives by Finite Differences

Here, suppose for simplicity that $u = u(x,y)$. Assuming that u possesses a sufficient number of partial derivatives, the values of u at the two points (x,y) and $(x + h, y + k)$ are related by the Taylor's expansion:

$$u(x + h, y + k)$$

$$= u(x,y) + \left(h\frac{\partial}{\partial x} + k\frac{\partial}{\partial y}\right)u(x,y)$$

$$+ \frac{1}{2!}\left(h\frac{\partial}{\partial x} + k\frac{\partial}{\partial y}\right)^2 u(x,y) + \cdots$$

$$+ \frac{1}{(n-1)!}\left(h\frac{\partial}{\partial x} + k\frac{\partial}{\partial y}\right)^{n-1} u(x,y) + R_n, \quad (7.1)$$

where the remainder term is given by

$$R_n = \frac{1}{n!}\left(h\frac{\partial}{\partial x} + k\frac{\partial}{\partial y}\right)^n u(x + \xi h, y + \xi k),$$

$$0 < \xi < 1. \quad (7.2)$$

That is,

$$R_n = O[(|h| + |k|)^n]. \quad (7.3)$$

By (7.3), we mean there exists a positive constant M such that $|R_n| \leqslant M(|h| + |k|)^n$ as both h and k tend to zero.

The space point $(i\,\Delta x, j\,\Delta y)$, also called the grid-point (i,j), is surrounded by the neighboring grid points shown in Fig. 7.1. Expanding in Taylor's series for $u_{i-1,j}$ and $u_{i+1,j}$ about the central value $u_{i,j}$, we obtain

$$u_{i-1,j} \doteq u_{i,j} - \Delta x u_x + \frac{(\Delta x)^2}{2!} u_{xx}$$

$$- \frac{(\Delta x)^3}{3!} u_{xxx} + \frac{(\Delta x)^4}{4!} u_{xxxx},$$

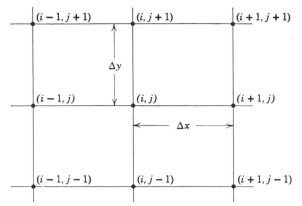

Figure 7.1   Arrangement of grid points.

$$u_{i+1,j} \doteq u_{i,j} + \Delta x u_x + \frac{(\Delta x)^2}{2!} u_{xx}$$

$$+ \frac{(\Delta x)^3}{3!} u_{xxx} + \frac{(\Delta x)^4}{4!} u_{xxxx}.$$

Here, $u_x \equiv \partial u / \partial x$, $u_{xx} \equiv \partial^2 u / \partial x^2$, etc., and all derivatives are evaluated at the grid-point (i,j). By taking these equations singly, and by adding or subtracting one from the other, we obtain the following finite-difference formulas for the first- and second-order derivatives at (i,j):

$$\frac{\partial u}{\partial x} = \frac{u_{i+1,j} - u_{i,j}}{\Delta x} + O(\Delta x), \tag{7.4}$$

$$\frac{\partial u}{\partial x} = \frac{u_{i,j} - u_{i-1,j}}{\Delta x} + O(\Delta x), \tag{7.5}$$

$$\frac{\partial u}{\partial x} = \frac{u_{i+1,j} - u_{i-1,j}}{2 \Delta x} + O[(\Delta x)^2], \tag{7.6}$$

$$\frac{\partial^2 u}{\partial x^2} = \frac{u_{i-1,j} - 2u_{i,j} + u_{i+1,j}}{(\Delta x)^2} + O[(\Delta x)^2]. \tag{7.7}$$

Formulas (7.4), (7.5), and (7.6) are known as the forward, backward, and central difference forms respectively. Similar forms exist for $\partial u / \partial y$ and $\partial^2 u / \partial y^2$. It may also be shown that

$$\frac{\partial^2 u}{\partial x \, \partial y} = \frac{u_{i+1,j+1} - u_{i-1,j+1} - u_{i+1,j-1} + u_{i-1,j-1}}{4 \Delta x \, \Delta y}$$

$$+ O[(\Delta x + \Delta y)^2]. \tag{7.8}$$

For a square grid ($\Delta x = \Delta y$), the following *nine-point* approximation is available for the Laplacian in two dimensions and will have the specified truncation error, provided that $u_{xx} + u_{yy} = 0$ is being solved:

$$\frac{\partial^2 u}{\partial x^2} + \frac{\partial^2 u}{\partial y^2} = \frac{\begin{bmatrix} u_{i-1,j+1} + 4u_{i,j+1} + u_{i+1,j+1} \\ + 4u_{i-1,j} - 20u_{i,j} + 4u_{i+1,j} \\ + u_{i-1,j-1} + 4u_{i,j-1} + u_{i+1,j-1} \end{bmatrix}}{6(\Delta x)^2}$$

$$+ O[(\Delta x)^4]. \tag{7.9}$$

By taking more and more neighboring points, an unlimited number of other approximations can be obtained, but the above forms are the most compact.

For convenience, the central-difference operator δ_x will be used occasionally. It is defined by

$$\delta_x u_{i,j} = \frac{u_{i+\frac{1}{2},j} - u_{i-\frac{1}{2},j}}{\Delta x}, \tag{7.10}$$

whence

$$\delta_x^2 u_{i,j} = \frac{u_{i-1,j} - 2u_{i,j} + u_{i+1,j}}{(\Delta x)^2}. \tag{7.11}$$

7.4   A Simple Parabolic Differential Equation

Consider an insulated bar with an initial temperature distribution at $t = 0$, having ends that are subsequently maintained at temperatures which may be functions of time. The temperature distribution $u(x,t)$ in the bar at any $t > 0$ may be found by defining suitable dimensionless variables and by assuming that the physical properties of the bar are constant. The problem can then

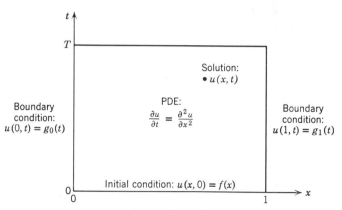

Figure 7.2   The differential problem.

be described by the following differential equation and initial and boundary conditions, also illustrated in Fig. 7.2.

$$\frac{\partial u}{\partial t} = \frac{\partial^2 u}{\partial x^2}, \quad \text{for } 0 < x < 1, \quad 0 < t < T, \tag{7.12}$$

$$u(x,0) = f(x), \qquad 0 \leqslant x \leqslant 1,$$

$$u(0,t) = g_0(t), \qquad 0 < t \leqslant T, \tag{7.13}$$

$$u(1,t) = g_1(t), \qquad 0 < t \leqslant T.$$

Here, $f(x)$ is the *initial* condition, and $g_0(t)$ and $g_1(t)$ are the *boundary* conditions. The latter are of a particularly simple type, since they specify the temperature itself at the ends of the bar. On page 462, we consider boundary conditions of a more general nature which involve also the derivatives of the dependent variable.

7.5   The Explicit Form of the Difference Equation

In order to approximate the solution of (7.12) and (7.13), a network of grid points is first established throughout the region $0 \leqslant x \leqslant 1$, $0 \leqslant t \leqslant T$, as shown in Fig. 7.3,

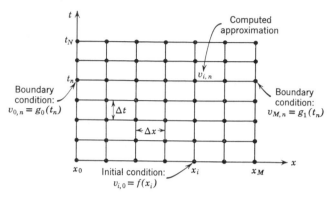

Figure 7.3   The difference problem.

with grid spacings $\Delta x = 1/M$, $\Delta t = T/N$, where M and N are arbitrary integers. In this problem, it is easy to ensure that grid points lie on the boundaries of x and t, although, as we shall see later, this correspondence is seldom possible in two-dimensional problems when the boundaries are irregularly shaped. For any grid-point (i,n) that does not have $i = 0$, $i = M$, or $n = 0$, the derivatives of (7.12) are now replaced by the finite-difference forms suggested by (7.4) and (7.7):

$$\frac{v_{i,n+1} - v_{i,n}}{\Delta t} = \frac{v_{i-1,n} - 2v_{i,n} + v_{i+1,n}}{(\Delta x)^2},$$

or, defining

$$\lambda = \frac{\Delta t}{(\Delta x)^2}, \tag{7.14}$$

then

$$v_{i,n+1} = \lambda v_{i-1,n} + (1 - 2\lambda)v_{i,n} + \lambda v_{i+1,n}. \tag{7.15}$$

In Fig. 7.4, the crosses and circles indicate those grid points involved in the time and space differences respectively.

If all the $v_{i,n}$ are known at any time level t_n, equation (7.15) enables $v_{i,n+1}$ to be calculated directly (that is, *explicitly*) at the time level t_{n+1} for $1 \leqslant i \leqslant M - 1$. For the boundary points $i = 0$, $i = M$, we also have

$$\begin{aligned} v_{0,n+1} &= g_0(t_{n+1}), \\ v_{M,n+1} &= g_1(t_{n+1}). \end{aligned} \tag{7.16}$$

Since the initial values of v are prescribed at $t = 0$ by

$$v_{i,0} = f(x_i), \tag{7.17}$$

the values of v can evidently be obtained at all the grid points by repeated application of (7.15) and (7.16); we must calculate all values of v at any one time level before advancing to the next time-step.

If the initial and boundary conditions do not match at $(0,0)$ and $(1,0)$, $u(x,t)$ will be discontinuous at these corners, and the question arises as to what values should be assigned to, for example, $v_{0,0}$. It appears reasonable in

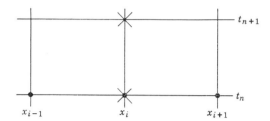

Figure 7.4   The explicit form.

such a case to use the arithmetic average of the values given by $f(x)$ as $x \to 0$ and $g_0(t)$ as $t \to 0$; in programming, it is often simpler to use either one value or the other and to recognize that a small error is thereby introduced.

Example. Consider the heat-conduction problem of (7.12) and (7.13), with the simple conditions $f(x) = 0$ and $g_0(t) = g_1(t) = 100$. Arbitrarily choose $\Delta x = 0.2$ and $\Delta t = 0.01$, corresponding to $\lambda = 1/4$, so that (7.15) becomes

$$v_{i,n+1} = \frac{v_{i-1,n} + 2v_{i,n} + v_{i+1,n}}{4}.$$

We may then verify the tabulated values of $v_{i,n}$ in Table 7.1, computed to two decimal places.

Table 7.1   Illustration of the Explicit Method

Time Sub-script, n	Space Subscript, i					
	0	1	2	3	4	5
0	0	0	0	0	0	0
1	100	0	0	0	0	100
2	100	25	0	0	25	100
3	100	37.5	6.25	6.25	37.5	100
4	100	45.31	14.06	14.06	45.31	100
5	100	51.17	21.87	21.87	51.17	100
6	100	56.05	29.19	29.19	56.05	100

etc.

A gradual diffusion of heat into the bar is evidenced by the general rise in temperature. Clearly, other values of Δx and Δt could be chosen (subject to a restriction mentioned below), each producing slightly different approximations to the true solution $u(x,t)$.

7.6   Convergence of the Explicit Form

Having constructed a plausible procedure for obtaining the values of v, we must now consider the important question of whether these values actually represent a good approximation to the solution of the original PDE (7.12) at the grid points.

The departure of the finite-difference approximation from the solution of the PDE at any grid point is known as the local *discretization error* w. That is,

$$w = u - v. \tag{7.18}$$

The finite-difference method is said to converge if $w \to 0$ as the grid spacings Δx and Δt tend to zero. We now show that a sufficient condition for convergence of the explicit method is that $0 < \lambda \leq \frac{1}{2}$. The computational procedure is assumed to be capable of an exact representation of the solution of the finite-difference equation. This is not quite true in practice, since only a finite number of digits can be retained by the computer and the phenomenon of *round-off error* is introduced.

From Taylor's expansion, supposing as usual that u possesses a sufficient number of partial derivatives,

$$u_{i,n+1} = u_{i,n} + \Delta t u_t + \frac{(\Delta t)^2}{2!} u_{tt} + O[(\Delta t)^3], \tag{7.19}$$

$$u_{i\pm 1,n} = u_{i,n} \pm \Delta x u_x + \frac{(\Delta x)^2}{2!} u_{xx} \pm \frac{(\Delta x)^3}{3!} u_{xxx}$$
$$+ \frac{(\Delta x)^4}{4!} u_{xxxx} \pm \frac{(\Delta x)^5}{5!} u_{xxxxx} + O[(\Delta x)^6]. \tag{7.20}$$

In (7.19) and (7.20), the derivatives are evaluated at $(i\Delta x, n\Delta t)$. Employing equations (7.12), $u_t = u_{xx}$, and (7.14), $\lambda = \Delta t/(\Delta x)^2$, in conjunction with (7.19) and (7.20), it is readily seen that

$$u_{i,n+1} = \lambda u_{i-1,n} + (1 - 2\lambda)u_{i,n} + \lambda u_{i+1,n} + z_{i,n}, \tag{7.21}$$

where

$$\frac{z_{i,n}}{\Delta t} = \frac{\Delta t}{2} u_{tt} - \frac{(\Delta x)^2}{12} u_{xxxx} + O[(\Delta t)^2]$$
$$+ O[(\Delta x)^4]. \tag{7.22}$$

Subtracting (7.15) from (7.21) and applying (7.18),

$$w_{i,n+1} = \lambda w_{i-1,n} + (1 - 2\lambda)w_{i,n} + \lambda w_{i+1,n} + z_{i,n}. \tag{7.23}$$

Now suppose that $0 < \lambda \leq \frac{1}{2}$. The coefficients λ and $(1 - 2\lambda)$ are nonnegative and we therefore have the inequality

$$|w_{i,n+1}| \leq \lambda|w_{i-1,n}| + (1 - 2\lambda)|w_{i,n}| + \lambda|w_{i+1,n}| + |z_{i,n}|.$$

Let $w_{max}(n)$ be the upper bound of $|w_{i,j}|$, $0 \leq j \leq n$, $1 \leq i \leq M - 1$, and let $z_{max}(n)$ be the upper bound of $|z_{i,j}|$, $0 \leq j \leq n$, $1 \leq i \leq M - 1$. Then

$$w_{max}(n + 1) \leq w_{max}(n) + z_{max}(n).$$

Therefore, over the whole region $0 \leq t \leq T$, since $w_{max}(0) = 0$ and since $z_{max}(n)$ does not decrease with time,

$$w_{max}(N) \leq N z_{max}(N - 1),$$

that is,

$$w_{max}(N) \leq T \left| \frac{\Delta t}{2} u_{tt} - \frac{(\Delta x)^2}{12} u_{xxxx} \right.$$
$$\left. + O[(\Delta t)^2] + O[(\Delta x)^4] \right|_{max}. \tag{7.24}$$

From (7.24), we conclude that, provided $0 < \lambda \leq \frac{1}{2}$, the discretization error is $O[(\Delta x)^2]$ and thus the explicit finite-difference representation converges as $\Delta x \to 0$. Finally, since $u_t = u_{xx}$, it follows that $u_{tt} = u_{txx} = u_{xxt} = u_{xxxx}$; therefore, for the special choice of $\lambda = \frac{1}{6}$, the discretization error is actually $O[(\Delta x)^4]$.

EXAMPLE 7.1

UNSTEADY-STATE HEAT CONDUCTION IN AN INFINITE, PARALLEL-SIDED SLAB (EXPLICIT METHOD)

Problem Statement

An infinite parallel-sided slab ($0 \leqslant x \leqslant L$) of thermal diffusivity α is initially (at time $t = 0$) at a uniform temperature θ_0. Its two faces are subsequently maintained at a constant temperature θ_1. Find how the temperature θ inside the slab varies with time and position.

Method of Solution

The heat conduction equation is $\alpha \, \partial^2\theta/\partial x^2 = \partial\theta/\partial t$. By defining the dimensionless variables

$$T = \frac{\theta - \theta_0}{\theta_1 - \theta_0}, \qquad \tau = \frac{\alpha t}{L^2}, \qquad X = \frac{x}{L},$$

the problem can be rewritten as that of solving

$$\frac{\partial T}{\partial \tau} = \frac{\partial^2 T}{\partial X^2},$$

subject to the associated conditions

$$\tau = 0: \quad T = 0 \text{ for } 0 \leqslant X \leqslant 1,$$

$$\tau > 0: \quad T = 1 \text{ at } X = 0 \text{ and } X = 1.$$

The problem is thus a special case of that stated in equations (7.12) and (7.13); the initial and boundary conditions now have the simple forms $f(X) = 0$, $g_0(\tau) = g_1(\tau) = 1$. The following program, however, obtains its initial and boundary conditions by calling on appropriate predefined functions (F, G0, G1). Thus, by modifying these

functions, the problem could be solved for arbitrary initial and boundary conditions.

The computations follow the explicit procedure summarized by equations (7.14) through (7.17). Note that the subscripts denoting time (n and $n + 1$ in equation (7.15)) can be discarded by using T_i (TOLD(I)) in the program) to denote the known temperature at point i, and T_i' (TNEW(I)) to denote the temperature about to be computed at the end of the time-step. After all the T_i' have been computed, they are referred to as T_i, and the process is repeated over subsequent time-steps; since we thereby avoid the storage of temperatures that are no longer wanted, the memory requirements are considerably reduced.

The input data to the program include $\Delta\tau$ (the time-step), M (the number of increments ΔX), and T_{max} (the maximum temperature of interest at the center of the slab). We avoid excessive output by printing the results only periodically, after a certain number of time-steps have elapsed. This periodic printing is achieved by incrementing a counter once every time-step, and testing to see if it is an integer multiple of the specified number of steps. If so, the temperatures computed for that time are printed. A similar procedure is also incorporated into several of the subsequent examples in this chapter.

We also use certain plotting subroutines, available at the University of Michigan computing center, for displaying graphically the computed temperatures on the printout.

Flow Diagram (excluding details of plotting points)

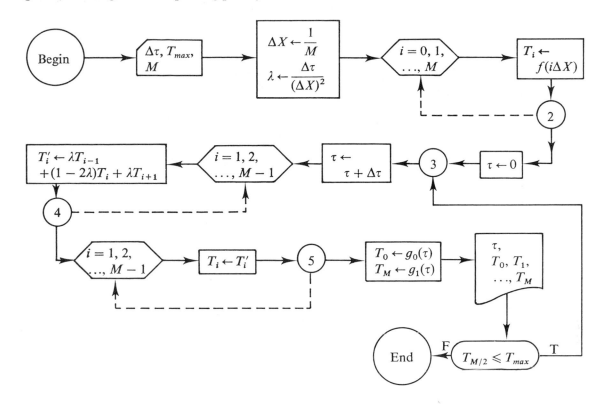

FORTRAN *Implementation*

List of Principal Variables

Program Symbol	Definition
CONST	$1 - 2\lambda$.
DX	Space increment, ΔX.
DTAU	Time-step, $\Delta\tau$.
F	Function giving the initial condition, $f(X)$.
G0, G1	Functions giving the boundary conditions, $g_0(\tau)$ and $g_1(\tau)$.
I	Subscript denoting the ith grid point. Due to FORTRAN limitations, we have $1 \leqslant I \leqslant M + 1$, corresponding to $0 \leqslant i \leqslant M$ in the text.
ICOUNT	Counter on the number of time-steps.
IFREQ, IFRPLT	Number of time-steps elapsing between successive printings and plots of temperatures, respectively.
M	Number of intervals ΔX into which the slab is divided by the grid points.
PLOT1, PLOT2, PLOT3, PLOT4	Subroutines used for preparing on-line graph of computed temperatures (see below).
RATIO	$\lambda = \Delta\tau/(\Delta X)^2$.
TAU	Time, τ.
TMAX	Maximum center temperature to be computed.
TOLD, TNEW	Vectors containing temperatures at the beginning and end of a time-step, respectively.
X	Vector containing the X-coordinate of each grid point.

PLOT1 and PLOT2 reserve a region of storage, known as the graph *image*, which will eventually contain all characters, blanks, etc., constituting the final graph; these subroutines also place symbols appropriate to the horizontal and vertical grid lines, and to the numbers along the axes, into the image. PLOT3 places the plotting character (*) for the series of points (X(I), T(I)), I = 1, 2, ..., M + 1, into locations in the image governed by the coordinates of these points. PLOT4 controls the printing of the graph image and inserts an appropriate label for the ordinate.

Program Listing

```
C              APPLIED NUMERICAL METHODS, EXAMPLE 7.1
C              UNSTEADY-STATE HEAT CONDUCTION IN A PARALLEL-SIDED SLAB,
C              SOLVED BY THE EXPLICIT METHOD.
C
C              THE INITIAL TEMPERATURE DISTRIBUTION IS GIVEN BY THE FUNCTION
C              F(X).   THE BOUNDARY TEMPERATURES AT X = 0 AND X = 1 ARE
C              GIVEN BY THE FUNCTIONS G0(TAU) AND G1(TAU), RESPECTIVELY.
C              THE TEMPERATURES ARE PRINTED EVERY IFREQ TIME-STEPS, UNTIL THE
C              CENTER TEMPERATURE EXCEEDS TMAX.
C
C              ..... DEFINITIONS OF FUNCTIONS FOR COMPUTING
C                    INITIAL AND BOUNDARY CONDITIONS .....
               F(DIST) = 0.0
               G0(TIME) = 1.0
               G1(TIME) = 1.0
C
               DIMENSION TOLD(21), TNEW(21), X(21), ARRAY(2500)
C
C              ..... READ AND CHECK DATA, AND COMPUTE CONSTANTS .....
     1         READ (5,100) DTAU, TMAX, M, IFREQ, IFRPLT
               INT = M/10
               FLOATM = M
               DX = 1.0/FLOATM
               RATIO = DTAU/(DX*DX)
               WRITE (6,200) DX, DTAU, TMAX, M, IFREQ, RATIO, IFRPLT
               CONST = 1.0 - 2.0*RATIO
C
C              ..... ESTABLISH GRAPH SIZE FOR PLOTTING ROUTINE .....
               CALL PLOT1 (0, 6, 9, 5, 19)
               CALL PLOT2 (ARRAY(1), 1.0, 0.0, 1.0, 0.0)
C
C              ..... SET AND PRINT INITIAL TEMPERATURES .....
               MP1 = M + 1
               DO 2  I = 1, MP1
               FLOATI = I
               X(I) = (FLOATI - 1.0)/FLOATM
     2         TOLD(I) = F(FLOATI*DX)
               TAU = 0.0
               WRITE (6,201)
               WRITE (6,202) TAU, (TOLD(I), I = 1, MP1, INT)
               ICOUNT = 0
C
C              ..... COMPUTE TEMPERATURES FOR SUCCESSIVE TIME-STEPS .....
     3         TAU = TAU + DTAU
               ICOUNT = ICOUNT + 1
               DO 4  I = 2, M
     4         TNEW(I) = RATIO*(TOLD(I-1) + TOLD(I+1)) + CONST*TOLD(I)
C
C              ..... SUBSTITUTE NEW TEMPERATURES IN TOLD .....
               DO 5  I = 2, M
     5         TOLD(I) = TNEW(I)
C
C              ..... SET BOUNDARY CONDITIONS .....
               TOLD(1) = G0(TAU)
               TOLD(MP1) = G1(TAU)
C
C              ..... PRINT T'S AND STORE PLOTTING POINTS WHEN APPROPRIATE .....
               IF ((ICOUNT/IFREQ)*IFREQ .NE. ICOUNT) GO TO 3
                  MOVER2 = M/2
                  WRITE (6,202) TAU, (TOLD(I), I = 1, MP1, INT)
                  IF ((ICOUNT/IFRPLT)*IFRPLT .NE. ICOUNT) GO TO 8
                     CALL PLOT3 (1H*, X(1), TOLD(1), MP1, 4)
     8            IF (TNEW(MOVER2) .LE. TMAX) GO TO 3
C
C              ..... PRINT GRAPH OF TEMPERATURE T VS. DISTANCE X .....
     9         WRITE (6,203)
               CALL PLOT4 (27, 27HDIMENSIONLESS TEMPERATURE T)
               WRITE (6,204)
               GO TO 1
```

Program Listing (*Continued*)

```
C
C       ..... FORMATS FOR INPUT AND OUTPUT STATEMENTS .....
  100   FORMAT (6X, F7.4, 10X, F5.2, 6X, I3, 10X, I3, 11X, I3)
  200   FORMAT (82H1    UNSTEADY-STATE HEAT CONDUCTION IN A SLAB, EXPLICIT
       1METHOD, WITH THE PARAMETERS/ 12H0    DX   = , F10.5/
       212H    DTAU = , F10.5/ 12H    TMAX = , F10.5/ 12H    M     = ,
       3I4/ 12H    IFREQ = , I4/ 12H    RATIO = , F10.5/
       4 12H    IFRPLT = , I4)
  201   FORMAT (8H0    TIME, 18X, 39HVALUES OF TEMPERATURE AT ALL GRIDPOINT
       1S)
  202   FORMAT (1H , F7.3/(1H , 7X, 11F8.5))
  203   FORMAT (1H1)
  204   FORMAT (1H0, 38X, 25H DIMENSIONLESS DISTANCE X)
C
        END
```

Data

```
DTAU = 0.005 ,   TMAX = 0.95,   M = 10,   IFREQ = 5,    IFRPLT = 10
DTAU = 0.0025,   TMAX = 0.95,   M = 10,   IFREQ = 10,   IFRPLT = 20
DTAU = 0.001 ,   TMAX = 0.95,   M = 10,   IFREQ = 25,   IFRPLT = 50
DTAU = 0.001 ,   TMAX = 0.95,   M = 20,   IFREQ = 25,   IFRPLT = 50
```

Computer Output (*for 4th Data Set*)

```
UNSTEADY-STATE HEAT CONDUCTION IN A SLAB, EXPLICIT METHOD, WITH THE PARAMETERS

DX    =    0.05000
DTAU  =    0.00100
TMAX  =    0.95000
M     =   20
IFREQ =   25
RATIO =    0.40000
IFRPLT =  50

TIME            VALUES OF TEMPERATURE AT ALL GRIDPOINTS
0.0
        0.0     0.0     0.0     0.0     0.0     0.0     0.0     0.0     0.0     0.0     0.0
0.025
        1.00000 0.65225 0.36671 0.17539 0.07450 0.04429 0.07450 0.17539 0.36671 0.65225 1.00000
0.050
        1.00000 0.75439 0.53563 0.36562 0.25878 0.22245 0.25878 0.36562 0.53563 0.75439 1.00000
0.075
        1.00000 0.81085 0.64050 0.50568 0.41936 0.38967 0.41936 0.50568 0.64050 0.81085 1.00000
0.100
        1.00000 0.85258 0.71962 0.61414 0.54645 0.52312 0.54645 0.61414 0.71962 0.85258 1.00000
0.125
        1.00000 0.88492 0.78111 0.69873 0.64584 0.62762 0.64584 0.69873 0.78111 0.88492 1.00000
0.150
        1.00000 0.91015 0.82909 0.76477 0.72347 0.70924 0.72347 0.76477 0.82909 0.91015 1.00000
0.175
        1.00000 0.92984 0.86656 0.81633 0.78408 0.77297 0.78408 0.81633 0.86656 0.92984 1.00000
0.200
        1.00000 0.94522 0.89580 0.85659 0.83141 0.82273 0.83141 0.85659 0.89580 0.94522 1.00000
0.225
        1.00000 0.95723 0.91864 0.88802 0.86836 0.86159 0.86836 0.88802 0.91864 0.95723 1.00000
0.250
        1.00000 0.96660 0.93647 0.91256 0.89721 0.89192 0.89721 0.91256 0.93647 0.96660 1.00000
0.275
        1.00000 0.97392 0.95039 0.93172 0.91974 0.91561 0.91974 0.93172 0.95039 0.97392 1.00000
0.300
        1.00000 0.97963 0.96126 0.94669 0.93733 0.93410 0.93733 0.94669 0.96126 0.97963 1.00000
0.325
        1.00000 0.98410 0.96975 0.95837 0.95106 0.94854 0.95106 0.95837 0.96975 0.98410 1.00000
0.350
        1.00000 0.98758 0.97638 0.96749 0.96178 0.95982 0.96178 0.96749 0.97638 0.98758 1.00000
```

Computer Output (*Continued*)

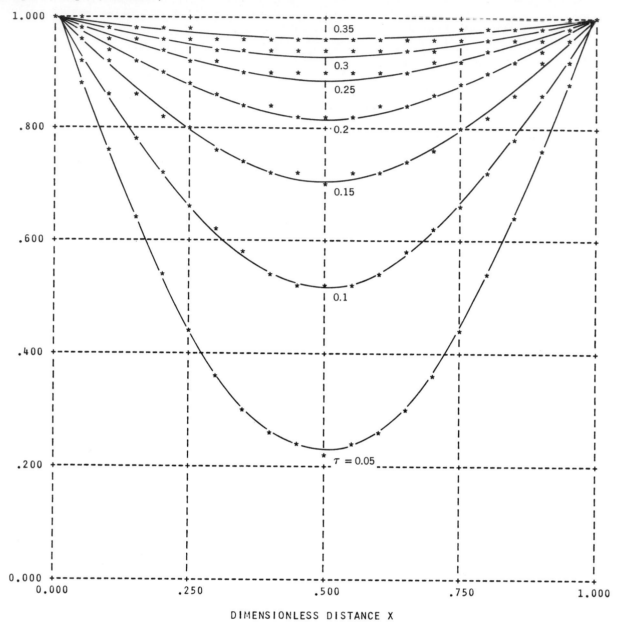

DIMENSIONLESS DISTANCE X

Discussion of Results

The computer output is reproduced above for the 4th data set only. Each row of numbers represents the temperatures computed for the indicated value of time, as in Table 7.1. The lines joining the points on the graph have been added by hand. The accuracy of the computations for all data sets may be checked from Table 7.1.1, which compares values of the dimensionless center temperature T_c with those given by Olson and Schultz [17] corresponding to the known analytical solution:

Table 7.1.1   Values of Center Temperature, T_c

Time, τ	0.05	0.1	0.15	0.2	0.25
T_c (exact)	0.228	0.526	0.710	0.823	0.892
T_c (Set 1, $M = 10$, $\lambda = 0.5$)	0.219	0.526	0.713	0.826	0.895
T_c (Set 2, $M = 10$, $\lambda = 0.25$)	0.216	0.520	0.707	0.822	0.891
T_c (Set 3, $M = 10$, $\lambda = 0.1$)	0.226	0.523	0.708	0.822	0.891
T_c (Set 4, $M = 20$, $\lambda = 0.4$)	0.222	0.523	0.709	0.823	0.892

Considering the relatively small number of grid points used, the agreement is satisfactory. Better accuracy could be achieved by taking more grid points.

7.7   The Implicit Form of the Difference Equation

In the explicit method previously described, $v_{i,n}$ depends only on $v_{i-1,n-1}$, $v_{i,n-1}$, and $v_{i+1,n-1}$. Referring to Fig. 7.5, only those values of v within the pyramid-shaped area A can have any influence on the value of $v_{i,n}$, whereas it is known that the solution $u(x,y)$ of the PDE depends also on the values of u both in A and in B for times earlier than t_n.

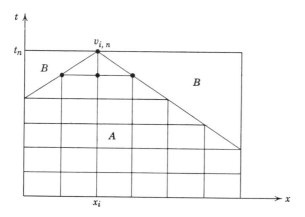

Figure 7.5   Limitation of the explicit method.

Furthermore, the requirement $0 < \Delta t/(\Delta x)^2 \leqslant \frac{1}{2}$ places an undesirable restriction on the time increment which can be used. For problems extending over large values of time, this could result in excessive amounts of computation.

The *implicit* method, now to be described, overcomes both these difficulties at the expense of a somewhat more complicated calculational procedure. It consists of representing u_{xx} by a finite-difference form evaluated at the advanced point of time t_{n+1}, instead of at t_n as in the explicit method. Referring again to the problem of equations (7.12) and (7.13), the difference equation becomes

$$\frac{v_{i,n+1} - v_{i,n}}{\Delta t} = \frac{v_{i-1,n+1} - 2v_{i,n+1} + v_{i+1,n+1}}{(\Delta x)^2}. \quad (7.25)$$

That is, the following relation exists between the values of v at the four points shown in the space-time grid of Fig. 7.6:

$$-\lambda v_{i-1,n+1} + (1 + 2\lambda)v_{i,n+1} - \lambda v_{i+1,n+1} = v_{i,n}. \quad (7.26)$$

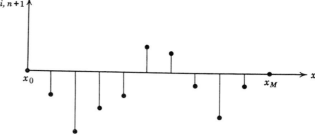

Figure 7.6   The implicit form.

The boundary and initial conditions of the explicit method still hold:

$$v_{0,n+1} = g_0(t_{n+1}),$$
$$v_{M,n+1} = g_1(t_{n+1}), \quad (7.27)$$
$$v_{i,0} = f(x_i).$$

At any one time level, equation (7.26) will be written once for each point $1 \leqslant i \leqslant M - 1$, resulting in a system of $M - 1$ simultaneous equations in the $M - 1$ unknowns $v_{i,n+1}$. The methods of solution for such a system will be discussed after we consider the convergence of the implicit method.

7.8   Convergence of the Implicit Form

Following a procedure similar to that for the explicit case, it is easily shown with the aid of Taylor's expansion that

$$u_{i,n+1} - u_{i,n} = \lambda u_{i-1,n+1} - 2\lambda u_{i,n+1}$$
$$+ \lambda u_{i+1,n+1} + z_{i,n}, \quad (7.28)$$

where

$$\frac{z_{i,n}}{\Delta t} = -\left[\frac{\Delta t}{2} u_{tt} + \frac{(\Delta x)^2}{12} u_{xxxx}\right] + O[(\Delta t)^2] + O[(\Delta x)^4].$$

In this equation, u_{tt} and u_{xxxx} are evaluated at the gridpoint $(i, n + 1)$. More simply,

$$\frac{z_{i,n}}{\Delta t} = O[\Delta t + (\Delta x)^2]. \quad (7.29)$$

Thus, from (7.18), (7.26), and (7.28), the discretization error satisfies the equation

$$w_{i,n+1} - w_{i,n} = \lambda w_{i-1,n+1} - 2\lambda w_{i,n+1}$$
$$+ \lambda w_{i+1,n+1} + z_{i,n}. \quad (7.30)$$

Now, at any time level t_{n+1}, w is zero at the boundary points $(0, n + 1)$ and $(M, n + 1)$. In between, it will have a maximum and/or a minimum (if it is not zero everywhere), as shown in Fig. 7.7.

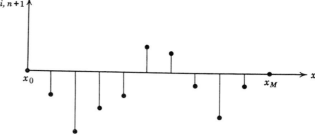

Figure 7.7   The discretization error.

From Fig. 7.7, it can be seen that the expression $(\lambda w_{i-1,n+1} - 2\lambda w_{i,n+1} + \lambda w_{i+1,n+1})$ of (7.30) will be nonpositive where $w_{i,n+1}$ has a maximum and nonnegative where $w_{i,n+1}$ has a minimum. (We are concerned here with absolute and not local or relative maxima and minima.)

Let w_{n+1}^+ and w_{n+1}^- be the respective maximum and minimum values of $w_{i,n+1}$ for $1 \leq i \leq M - 1$. Let z_n^+ and z_n^- be the values of $z_{i,n}$ at those points that have the respective maximum and minimum values of $w_{i,n+1}$. Then, from (7.30),

$$w_{n+1}^+ \leq w_n^+ + z_n^+,$$
$$w_{n+1}^- \geq w_n^- + z_n^-.$$

Let $w_{max}(n)$ be the upper bound of $|w_{i,j}|$ for $0 \leq j \leq n$, $1 \leq i \leq M - 1$, and let $z_{max}(n)$ be the upper bound of $|z_{i,j}|$ for $0 \leq j \leq n$, $1 \leq i \leq M - 1$. Then $w_{max}(n + 1) \leq w_{max}(n) + z_{max}(n)$. Thus, over the whole region of $0 \leq t \leq T$, since $w_{max}(0) = 0$ and since $z_{max}(n)$ does not decrease with time,

$$w_{max}(N) \leq N z_{max}(N - 1);$$

that is, from (7.29),

$$w_{max}(N) \leq T[O(\Delta t + (\Delta x)^2)]. \tag{7.31}$$

Therefore, we conclude that the implicit method converges to the solution of the PDE as $\Delta t \to 0$ and $\Delta x \to 0$, regardless of the value of the ratio $\Delta t/(\Delta x)^2$.

7.9 Solution of Equations Resulting from the Implicit Method

Having established the convergence of the implicit scheme, we now return to study the solution of the $M - 1$ linear equations which result at each time step, namely,

of three variables per equation, the solution can be expressed very concisely.

We first demonstrate the validity of a *recursion solution* of the form

$$v_i = \gamma_i - \frac{c_i}{\beta_i} v_{i+1},$$

in which the constants β_i and γ_i are to be determined. Substitution into the ith equation of (7.33) gives

$$a_i \left(\gamma_{i-1} - \frac{c_{i-1}}{\beta_{i-1}} v_i \right) + b_i v_i + c_i v_{i+1} = d_i.$$

That is,

$$v_i = \frac{d_i - a_i \gamma_{i-1}}{b_i - \frac{a_i c_{i-1}}{\beta_{i-1}}} - \frac{c_i v_{i+1}}{b_i - \frac{a_i c_{i-1}}{\beta_{i-1}}},$$

which verifies the above form, subject to the following recursion relations:

$$\beta_i = b_i - \frac{a_i c_{i-1}}{\beta_{i-1}}, \qquad \gamma_i = \frac{d_i - a_i \gamma_{i-1}}{\beta_i}.$$

Also, from the first equation of (7.33),

$$v_1 = \frac{d_1}{b_1} - \frac{c_1}{b_1} v_2,$$

whence $\beta_1 = b_1$ and $\gamma_1 = d_1/\beta_1$. Finally, substitution of

$$(1 + 2\lambda)v_{1,n+1} - \lambda v_{2,n+1} = v_{1,n} + \lambda g_0(t_{n+1}),$$

$$-\lambda v_{i-1,n+1} + (1 + 2\lambda)v_{i,n+1} - \lambda v_{i+1,n+1} = v_{i,n}, \qquad \text{for } 2 \leq i \leq M - 2, \tag{7.32}$$

$$-\lambda v_{M-2,n+1} + (1 + 2\lambda)v_{M-1,n+1} = v_{M-1,n} + \lambda g_1(t_{n+1}).$$

Expressed more clearly, equations (7.32) are a special form of the system

$$
\begin{aligned}
b_1 v_1 + c_1 v_2 &= d_1 \\
a_2 v_1 + b_2 v_2 + c_2 v_3 &= d_2 \\
a_3 v_2 + b_3 v_3 + c_3 v_4 &= d_3 \\
\cdots\cdots\cdots\cdots\cdots\cdots \\
a_i v_{i-1} + b_i v_i + c_i v_{i+1} &= d_i \\
\cdots\cdots\cdots\cdots\cdots\cdots \\
a_{N-1} v_{N-2} + b_{N-1} v_{N-1} + c_{N-1} v_N &= d_{N-1} \\
a_N v_{N-1} + b_N v_N &= d_N.
\end{aligned}
\tag{7.33}
$$

In going from (7.32) to (7.33), the subscripts $(n + 1)$ on the v's have been dropped, and the right-hand sides of (7.32), each of which is a known quantity, are called $d_1, d_2, \ldots, d_N$ for simplicity, with $N = M - 1$. The matrix of coefficients a, b, and c alone is called a *tridiagonal matrix*. The system (7.33) is readily solved by a Gaussian elimination method (pp. 270 and 272); with a maximum

the recursion solution into the last equation of (7.33) yields

$$v_N = \frac{d_N - a_N v_{N-1}}{b_N} = \frac{d_N - a_N \left(\gamma_{N-1} - \frac{c_{N-1}}{\beta_{N-1}} v_N \right)}{b_N},$$

whence

$$v_N = \frac{d_N - a_N \gamma_{N-1}}{b_N - \dfrac{a_N c_{N-1}}{\beta_{N-1}}} = \gamma_N.$$

To summarize, the complete algorithm for the solution of the tridiagonal system is

$$v_N = \gamma_N,$$

$$v_i = \gamma_i - \frac{c_i v_{i+1}}{\beta_i}, \qquad i = N-1, N-2, \ldots, 1,$$

$$(7.34)$$

where the β's and γ's are determined from the recursion formulas

$$\beta_1 = b_1, \qquad \gamma_1 = d_1/\beta_1,$$

$$\beta_i = b_i - \frac{a_i c_{i-1}}{\beta_{i-1}}, \qquad i = 2, 3, \ldots, N, \qquad (7.35)$$

$$\gamma_i = \frac{d_i - a_i \gamma_{i-1}}{\beta_i}, \qquad i = 2, 3, \ldots, N.$$

One of the disadvantages of a Gaussian elimination method is that round-off error may accumulate seriously. However, Douglas [7] has conducted an analysis of the scheme of (7.34) and (7.35) and expects the round-off error to be small in comparison with the discretization error for usual choices of Δx and Δt.

We can now compare the amounts of computation required by the explicit and implicit methods. In making a rough estimate, we consider here only the number of multiplication and division steps. For $M - 1$ points at each time level, the explicit scheme of (7.15) requires $2M - 2$ multiplication steps. Now if, as is the case with (7.32), the coefficients a, b, and c of (7.33) remain constant, the β_i of (7.35) can be predetermined. In this case, the implicit scheme referred to requires some $3M - 3$ steps. The absence of a restriction on the size of $\Delta t/(\Delta x)^2$ in the implicit method generally outweighs this moderate increase in computational effort.

Finally, note that (7.33) might also be solved by the Gauss-Seidel iteration scheme, discussed in Section 7.24. However, *each* iteration consumes $2M - 2$ steps, and since several iterations will generally be required for satisfactory convergence, such a procedure is not recommended.

EXAMPLE 7.2

UNSTEADY-STATE HEAT CONDUCTION IN AN INFINITE PARALLEL-SIDED SLAB (IMPLICIT METHOD)

Problem Statement

Use the implicit method to solve the same problem that has already been stated in Example 7.1.

Method of Solution

The implicit technique employs the algorithm expressed in equations (7.34) and (7.35) for the solution of the $M-1$ algebraic equations (7.32) in temperature that result at each time-step. For convenience in later examples, this algorithm is written as a subroutine named TRIDAG, for which a typical call might be

$$\text{CALL TRIDAG (IF, L, A, B, C, D, V)}$$

Here, the last five argument names are vectors that are used to store the corresponding elements appearing in equation (7.33). In order to make the subroutine more general, two additional integers, IF and L, have been introduced into the argument list. These correspond to the first and last subscripts, f and l, of the unknowns; that is, the unknowns are assumed to be v_f, v_{f+1}, ..., v_{l-1}, v_l. In the present application of solving equation (7.32), $f = 1$ and $l = M - 1$.

Flow Diagram

Main Program

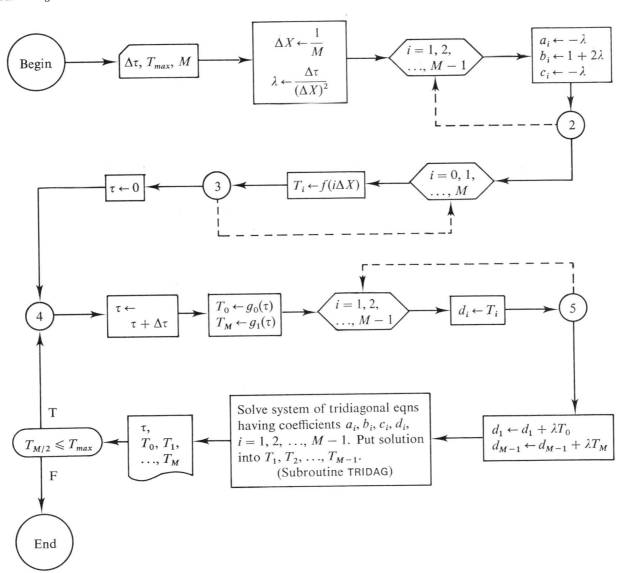

Subroutine TRIDAG (Dummy arguments: f, l, a, b, c, d, v;

calling arguments: $1, M - 1, a, b, c, d, T$)

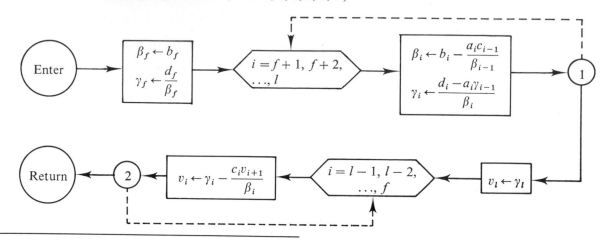

FORTRAN *Implementation*

List of Principal Variables

Program Symbol   *Definition*

The variable names are the same as those listed in Example 7.1, except that TOLD, TNEW, IFRPLT, and the plotting routines have been deleted, and the following have been added:

(Main)

A, B, C, D	Coefficient vectors defined in equations (7.33).
T	Vector of temperatures at each grid point.
TRIDAG	Subroutine for solving system of simultaneous equations having a tridiagonal coefficient matrix.

(Subroutine
  TRIDAG)

BETA, GAMMA	Vectors of intermediate coefficients β_i and γ_i, defined in equations (7.35).
IF, L	Subscripts f and l, corresponding to the first and last equations to be solved.
V	Vector containing the computed solution.

Because of FORTRAN limitations, the subscripts in the text $(i = 0, 1, ..., M)$ are advanced by one when they appear in the program $(I = 1, 2, ..., M + 1)$.

Program Listing

Main Program

```
C               APPLIED NUMERICAL METHODS, EXAMPLE 7.2
C               UNSTEADY-STATE HEAT CONDUCTION IN A PARALLEL-SIDED SLAB,
C               SOLVED BY THE IMPLICIT METHOD.
C
C               THE INITIAL TEMPERATURE DISTRIBUTION IS GIVEN BY THE FUNCTION
C               F(X).   THE BOUNDARY TEMPERATURES AT X = 0 AND X = 1 ARE
C               GIVEN BY THE FUNCTIONS G0(TAU) AND G1(TAU), RESPECTIVELY.
C               THE TEMPERATURES ARE PRINTED EVERY IFREQ TIME-STEPS, UNTIL THE
C               CENTER TEMPERATURE EXCEEDS TMAX.   THE TRIDIAGONAL SYSTEM OF
C               EQUATIONS RESULTING AT EACH TIME-STEP IS SOLVED BY THE
C               SUBROUTINE TRIDAG.
C
C       ..... DEFINITIONS OF FUNCTIONS FOR COMPUTING
C               INITIAL AND BOUNDARY CONDITIONS .....
        F(DIST) = 0.0
        G0(TIME) = 1.0
        G1(TIME) = 1.0
C
        DIMENSION A(21), B(21), C(21), D(21), T(21)
C
C       ..... CHECK INPUT PARAMETERS AND SET ARRAYS A, B, AND C .....
      1 READ (5,100) DTAU, TMAX, M, IFREQ
        FLOATM = M
        DX = 1.0/FLOATM
        RATIO = DTAU/(DX*DX)
        WRITE (6,200) DX, DTAU, TMAX, M, IFREQ, RATIO
        DO 2  I = 2, M
        A(I) = - RATIO
        B(I) = 1.0 + 2.0*RATIO
      2 C(I) = - RATIO
C
C       ..... SET AND PRINT INITIAL TEMPERATURES .....
        MP1 = M + 1
        DO 3  I = 1, MP1
        FLOATI = I
      3 T(I) = F(FLOATI*DX)
        TAU = 0.0
        WRITE (6,201)
        WRITE (6,202) TAU, (T(I), I = 1, MP1)
        ICOUNT = 0
C
C       ..... PERFORM CALCULATIONS OVER SUCCESSIVE TIME-STEPS .....
      4 TAU = TAU + DTAU
        ICOUNT = ICOUNT + 1
C
C       ..... SET BOUNDARY VALUES .....
        T(1) = G0(TAU)
        T(MP1) = G1(TAU)
C
C       ..... COMPUTE RIGHT-HAND SIDE VECTOR D .....
        DO 5  I = 2, M
      5 D(I) = T(I)
        D(2) = D(2) + RATIO*T(1)
        D(M) = D(M) + RATIO*T(MP1)
C
C       ..... COMPUTE NEW TEMPERATURES .....
        CALL TRIDAG (2, M, A, B, C, D, T)
C
C       ..... PRINT TEMPERATURES WHEN APPROPRIATE .....
        IF ((ICOUNT/IFREQ)*IFREQ .NE. ICOUNT) GO TO 4
        MOVER2 = M/2
        WRITE (6,202) TAU, (T(I), I = 1, MP1)
        IF (T(MOVER2) .LE. TMAX) GO TO 4
        GO TO 1
```

Program Listing (*Continued*)

```
C
C        ..... FORMATS FOR INPUT AND OUTPUT STATEMENTS .....
 100    FORMAT (6X, F7.4, 10X, F5.2, 6X, I3, 10X, I3)
 200    FORMAT (82H1   UNSTEADY-STATE HEAT CONDUCTION IN A SLAB, IMPLICIT
        1METHOD, WITH THE PARAMETERS/ 12H0    DX    =  , F10.5/
        212H    DTAU  = , F10.5/ 12H    TMAX = , F10.5/ 12H    M     = ,
        3I4/ 12H    IFREQ = , I4/ 12H    RATIO = , F10.5)
 201    FORMAT (8H0   TIME, 18X, 39HVALUES OF TEMPERATURE AT ALL GRIDPOINT
        1S)
 202    FORMAT (1H , F7.3/(1H , 7X, 11F8.5))
C
        END
```

Subroutine TRIDAG

```
C          SUBROUTINE FOR SOLVING A SYSTEM OF LINEAR SIMULTANEOUS
C          EQUATIONS HAVING A TRIDIAGONAL COEFFICIENT MATRIX.
C          THE EQUATIONS ARE NUMBERED FROM IF THROUGH L, AND THEIR
C          SUB-DIAGONAL, DIAGONAL, AND SUPER-DIAGONAL COEFFICIENTS
C          ARE STORED IN THE ARRAYS A, B, AND C.   THE COMPUTED
C          SOLUTION VECTOR V(IF)...V(L) IS STORED IN THE ARRAY V.
C
        SUBROUTINE TRIDAG (IF, L, A, B, C, D, V)
        DIMENSION A(1), B(1), C(1), D(1), V(1), BETA(101), GAMMA(101)
C
C        ..... COMPUTE INTERMEDIATE ARRAYS BETA AND GAMMA .....
        BETA(IF) = B(IF)
        GAMMA(IF) = D(IF)/BETA(IF)
        IFP1 = IF + 1
        DO 1 I = IFP1, L
        BETA(I) = B(I) - A(I)*C(I-1)/BETA(I-1)
   1    GAMMA(I) = (D(I) - A(I)*GAMMA(I-1))/BETA(I)
C
C        ..... COMPUTE FINAL SOLUTION VECTOR V .....
        V(L) = GAMMA(L)
        LAST = L - IF
        DO 2 K = 1, LAST
        I = L - K
   2    V(I) = GAMMA(I) - C(I)*V(I+1)/BETA(I)
        RETURN
C
        END
```

Data

```
DTAU = 0.0025,   TMAX = 0.95,  M = 10,  IFREQ = 10
DTAU = 0.0125,   TMAX = 0.95,  M = 10,  IFREQ =  2
```

Computer Output (*for 2nd Data Set*)

```
UNSTEADY-STATE HEAT CONDUCTION IN A SLAB, IMPLICIT METHOD, WITH THE PARAMETERS

DX    =     0.10000
DTAU  =     0.01250
TMAX  =     0.95000
M     =    10
IFREQ =     2
RATIO =     1.25000

TIME                    VALUES OF TEMPERATURE AT ALL GRIDPOINTS
0.0
       0.0     0.0     0.0     0.0     0.0     0.0     0.0     0.0     0.0     0.0     0.0
0.025
       1.00000 0.59326 0.32471 0.17391 0.10104 0.07965 0.10104 0.17391 0.32471 0.59326 1.00000
```

Computer Output (*Continued*)

```
0.050
      1.00000 0.73394 0.51047 0.35033 0.25667 0.22612 0.25667 0.35033 0.51047 0.73394 1.00000
0.075
      1.00000 0.80014 0.62336 0.48730 0.40248 0.37377 0.40248 0.48730 0.62336 0.80014 1.00000
0.100
      1.00000 0.84392 0.70394 0.59387 0.52385 0.49986 0.52385 0.59387 0.70394 0.84392 1.00000
0.125
      1.00000 0.87671 0.76568 0.67782 0.62157 0.60222 0.62157 0.67782 0.76568 0.87671 1.00000
0.150
      1.00000 0.90227 0.81416 0.74429 0.69948 0.68404 0.69948 0.74429 0.81416 0.90227 1.00000
0.175
      1.00000 0.92246 0.85251 0.79702 0.76140 0.74913 0.76140 0.79702 0.85251 0.92246 1.00000
0.200
      1.00000 0.93845 0.88293 0.83887 0.81058 0.80084 0.81058 0.83887 0.88293 0.93845 1.00000
0.225
      1.00000 0.95114 0.90706 0.87209 0.84963 0.84189 0.84963 0.87209 0.90706 0.95114 1.00000
0.250
      1.00000 0.96121 0.92622 0.89846 0.88063 0.87448 0.88063 0.89845 0.92622 0.96121 1.00000
0.275
      1.00000 0.96921 0.94143 0.91939 0.90524 0.90036 0.90523 0.91939 0.94143 0.96921 1.00000
0.300
      1.00000 0.97556 0.95350 0.93600 0.92477 0.92090 0.92477 0.93600 0.95350 0.97556 1.00000
0.325
      1.00000 0.98059 0.96309 0.94920 0.94028 0.93720 0.94028 0.94920 0.96309 0.98059 1.00000
0.350
      1.00000 0.98459 0.97070 0.95967 0.95259 0.95015 0.95259 0.95967 0.97070 0.98459 1.00000
```

Discussion of Results

The printed output, which is given here only for the second data set, shows values of dimensionless temperature T for all grid points at every second time-step, i.e., for values of τ spaced by 0.025. Table 7.2.1 lists representative values of the dimensionless center temperature, T_c, for both data sets, in comparison with the known exact solution of Olson and Schultz [17].

Considering the fairly small number of grid points used, $\Delta\tau = 0.0025$ gives reasonably accurate results. Even $\Delta\tau = 0.0125$ would be adequate for rough engineering calculations, particularly if machine time were at a pre-mium; note that the corresponding value of λ is 1.25, appreciably above the upper limit of $\lambda = 0.5$ in an explicit procedure.

Table 7.2.1   Values of Center Temperature, T_c

Time, τ	0.05	0.10	0.15	0.20	0.25
Computed T_c ($\Delta\tau = 0.0025$)	0.231	0.520	0.704	0.817	0.887
Computed T_c ($\Delta\tau = 0.0125$)	0.226	0.500	0.684	0.801	0.874
Exact T_c	0.228	0.526	0.710	0.823	0.892

7.10 Stability

It has been shown in previous sections that, under certain conditions, the explicit and implicit finite-difference forms are convergent. The term *convergent* is understood to mean that the exact solution of the finite-difference problem (in the absence of round-off error) tends to the solution of the PDE as the grid spacings in time and distance tend to zero. There are two important concepts closely associated with the convergence of a particular finite-difference procedure, namely, those of *consistency* and *stability*. Indeed, Richtmyer [23] presents a theorem attributed to Lax [13] which demonstrates for linear PDE that, provided that a consistency criterion (to be discussed in the next section) is satisfied, stability is both a necessary and sufficient condition for convergence. A similar conclusion is also reached by Douglas [5].

Referring to a certain computational procedure, the term *stability* denotes a property of the particular finite-difference equation(s) used as the time increment is made vanishingly small. It means that there is an upper limit (as $\Delta t \to 0$) to the extent to which any piece of information, whether present in the initial conditions, or brought in via the boundary conditions, or arising from any sort of error in the calculations, can be amplified in the computations. The following is a brief outline of the treatment for determining the stability of finite-difference procedures, from von Neumann, first given by O'Brien, Hyman, and Kaplan [16] and also discussed in References 4, 5, 9, 12, 19, and 23. Stability alone does not necessarily mean that the deviation between the true solution to a certain PDE and its finite-difference approximation will be in any sense small. Rather, it implies the boundedness of the finite-difference solution, at a given time t, as Δt tends to zero.

Assume that at any stage, referred to here as $t = 0$, a Fourier expansion (either as an integral or as a finite series) can be made of some initial function $f(x)$, and that a typical term in the expansion, neglecting a constant coefficient, is $e^{j\beta x}$, where β is a positive constant, and j here denotes $\sqrt{-1}$. Assume further that a separation of time and space variables can be made, and that at a time t, this term has become $\psi(t)e^{j\beta x}$. By substituting in the original difference equation, the form of ψ can be found, and a criterion thereby established as to whether or not it remains bounded as t becomes large. To illustrate the method, three examples are now considered.

Example. The *explicit* finite-difference form of the PDE $u_t = u_{xx}$ is

$$\frac{v_{i,n+1} - v_{i,n}}{\Delta t} = \frac{v_{i-1,n} - 2v_{i,n} + v_{i+1,n}}{(\Delta x)^2}.$$

Substituting $v_{i,n} = \psi(t)e^{j\beta x}$, we have

$$\frac{\psi(t + \Delta t)e^{j\beta x} - \psi(t)e^{j\beta x}}{\Delta t}$$

$$= \frac{\psi(t)}{(\Delta x)^2}[e^{j\beta(x - \Delta x)} - 2e^{j\beta x} + e^{j\beta(x + \Delta x)}],$$

whence

$$\psi(t + \Delta t) = \psi(t)\left(1 - 4\lambda \sin^2 \frac{\beta \Delta x}{2}\right).$$

Since $\psi(0) = 1$, this has the solution

$$\psi(t) = \left(1 - 4\lambda \sin^2 \frac{\beta \Delta x}{2}\right)^{t/\Delta t}.$$

For stability, $\psi(t)$ must remain bounded as Δt, and thus Δx, approaches zero. Clearly, this requires

$$\left|1 - 4\lambda \sin^2 \frac{\beta \Delta x}{2}\right| \leqslant 1. \qquad (7.36)$$

An equivalent viewpoint is to define an *amplification factor* ξ as

$$\xi = \frac{\psi(t + \Delta t)}{\psi(t)} = 1 - 4\lambda \sin^2 \frac{\beta \Delta x}{2},$$

and to require that $|\xi| \leqslant 1$, which again leads to condition (7.36).

In general, components of all frequencies β may be present; if they are not present in the initial conditions, or not brought in by the boundary conditions, then they are likely to be introduced by round-off error. That is, we must guard against unbounded amplification of $\psi(t)$ for all β. Since $\sin^2(\beta \Delta x/2)$ is unity for some β, inspection shows that λ must be at most $\frac{1}{2}$ if condition (7.36) is to be satisfied. That is, for the explicit representation of $u_t = u_{xx}$, $\lambda = \Delta t/(\Delta x)^2 \leqslant \frac{1}{2}$ is a necessary (and sufficient) condition for stability. This is not, perhaps, a surprising result, since equation (7.15) is

$$v_{i,n+1} = \lambda v_{i-1,n} + (1 - 2\lambda)v_{i,n} + \lambda v_{i+1,n}.$$

Intuitively, we might expect $v_{i,n}$ to contribute towards $v_{i,n+1}$ in a "nonnegative" manner; this can occur only for $\lambda \leqslant \frac{1}{2}$.

The phenomenon of instability is easily demonstrated by reworking the example of page 432, with $\Delta x = 0.2$ and $\Delta t = 0.04$, so that $\lambda = 1$. In this case, (7.15) gives

$$v_{i,n+1} = v_{i-1,n} - v_{i,n} + v_{i+1,n}.$$

Table 7.2 shows the resulting computed values, which exhibit an obvious instability, even in the absence of round-off error.

Table 7.2 Instability of Explicit Method for $\lambda = 1$

Time Subscript, n	Space Subscript, i					
	0	1	2	3	4	5
0	0	0	0	0	0	0
1	100	0	0	0	0	100
2	100	100	0	0	100	100
3	100	0	100	100	0	100
4	100	200	0	0	200	100
5	100	−100	200	200	−100	100
6	100	400	−100	−100	400	100

etc.

Example. The *implicit* finite-difference form of the PDE $u_t = u_{xx}$ is

$$\frac{v_{i,n+1} - v_{i,n}}{\Delta t} = \frac{v_{i-1,n+1} - 2v_{i,n+1} + v_{i+1,n+1}}{(\Delta x)^2}.$$

The substitution $v_{i,n} = \psi(t)e^{J\beta x}$ results in an amplification factor

$$\xi = \frac{1}{1 + 4\lambda \sin^2 \dfrac{\beta \Delta x}{2}}.$$

Since $|\xi| \leqslant 1$ for all λ, the implicit procedure is unconditionally stable.

Example. The finite-difference equation proposed by Richardson [22] for the PDE $u_t = u_{xx}$ represents the time derivative by the formula (7.6), in which the truncation error is $O[(\Delta t)^2]$:

$$\frac{v_{i,n+1} - v_{i,n-1}}{2 \Delta t} = \frac{v_{i-1,n} - 2v_{i,n} + v_{i+1,n}}{(\Delta x)^2}. \tag{7.37}$$

Following the usual procedure, we arrive at a quadratic equation in the amplification factor:

$$\xi - \frac{1}{\xi} = -8\lambda \sin^2 \frac{\beta \Delta x}{2}. \tag{7.38}$$

By inspection, if the roots are ξ_1 and ξ_2, then $\xi_1 = -1/\xi_2$. The only possible solution satisfying $|\xi| \leqslant 1$ is $\xi_1 = 1, \xi_2 = -1$; but this solution contradicts the fact that, for a general β, the right-hand side of (7.38) is negative, irrespective of the value of λ. Therefore, we conclude that Richardson's method is unconditionally *unstable*. Leutert [14], however, has shown that if the initial conditions for the finite-difference solution are properly chosen (by a method in which they are closely related to, but not necessarily identical with, those in the differential problem), then Richardson's method converges for all λ. Unfortunately, considerations of round-off error would probably prevent this fact from being fully exploited in practice.

The corresponding method for investigating the stability of the finite-difference representation of a system of *simultaneous* partial differential equations is discussed under Example 7.5.

Richtmyer [23] indicates that, for stability, the amplification factor ξ should really obey the condition

$$|\xi| \leqslant 1 + O(\Delta t), \tag{7.39}$$

rather than the stricter condition $|\xi| \leqslant 1$ used here. Inequality (7.39) allows for the possibility that the true solution might have the form e^{At}, which is incompatible with the restriction $|\xi| \leqslant 1$. However, for problems in which it is thought that an increasing exponential solution is unlikely or even impossible, there seems to be a reasonable case in practice for ensuring that the difference procedure has an amplification factor $|\xi| \leqslant 1$, in order to prevent the amplification of any round-off error. Certainly, in the three examples considered, the condition of

either $|\xi| \leqslant 1$ or $|\xi| \leqslant 1 + O(\Delta t)$ leads to the same conclusion.

7.11 Consistency

The term *consistency*, applied to a certain finite-difference procedure, means that the procedure may in fact approximate the solution of the PDE under study, and not the solution of some other PDE. For example, consider the explicit approximation,

$$\frac{v_{i-1,n} - 2v_{i,n} + v_{i+1,n}}{(\Delta x)^2} = \frac{v_{i,n+1} - v_{i,n}}{\Delta t}, \tag{7.40}$$

of the one-dimensional heat-conduction equation

$$\frac{\partial^2 u}{\partial x^2} = \frac{\partial u}{\partial t}. \tag{7.12}$$

The *truncation error* of the approximation is defined as the difference between the finite differences and the derivatives they are intended to represent. With the aid of Taylor's expansion, it is readily shown that the truncation error corresponding to (7.40) and (7.12) is

$$\frac{u_{i-1,n} - 2u_{i,n} + u_{i+1,n}}{(\Delta x)^2} - \frac{u_{i,n+1} - u_{i,n}}{\Delta t} - \left[\frac{\partial^2 u}{\partial x^2} - \frac{\partial u}{\partial t}\right]_{i,n}$$
$$= O(\Delta t) + O[(\Delta x)^2].$$

Since the truncation error tends to zero as $\Delta t, \Delta x \to 0$, the explicit representation is consistent with the original PDE.

Consistency is often taken for granted. However, the following example shows that a certain amount of caution must be observed. Consider the explicit approximation to equation (7.12) proposed by DuFort and Frankel [8], namely,

$$\frac{v_{i-1,n} - v_{i,n-1} - v_{i,n+1} + v_{i+1,n}}{(\Delta x)^2} = \frac{v_{i,n+1} - v_{i,n-1}}{2\Delta t}.$$

It may be shown that this scheme is unconditionally stable. From Taylor's expansion the truncation error is

$$\frac{u_{i-1,n} - u_{i,n-1} - u_{i,n+1} + u_{i+1,n}}{(\Delta x)^2}$$

$$- \frac{u_{i,n+1} - u_{i,n-1}}{2\Delta t} - \left[\frac{\partial^2 u}{\partial x^2} - \frac{\partial u}{\partial t}\right]_{i,n}$$

$$= O[(\Delta x)^2] + O[(\Delta t)^2] + O\left(\frac{(\Delta t)^4}{(\Delta x)^2}\right) - \left(\frac{\Delta t}{\Delta x}\right)^2 \left(\frac{\partial^2 u}{\partial t^2}\right)_{i,n}.$$

The consistency of the DuFort-Frankel method depends on the way in which $\Delta t, \Delta x$ tend to zero. If $\Delta t/(\Delta x)^2$ is held constant as Δt and $\Delta x \to 0$, then the scheme is consistent with equation (7.12). On the other hand, if $\Delta t/\Delta x = c$, a constant, as Δt and $\Delta x \to 0$, then the term $c^2(\partial^2 u/\partial t^2)$ remains, and the difference procedure is consistent instead with an entirely different PDE, namely,

$$\frac{\partial^2 u}{\partial x^2} = \frac{\partial u}{\partial t} + c^2 \frac{\partial^2 u}{\partial t^2}.$$

7.12 The Crank-Nicolson Method

Both the explicit and implicit methods just described lead to discretization errors of $O[\Delta t + (\Delta x)^2]$. We will now develop a finite-difference method which reduces the dependency on the time increment from $O(\Delta t)$ to $O[(\Delta t)^2]$.

Recall that (7.6) gives an approximation to $\partial u/\partial t$ within $O[(\Delta t)^2]$. We can, therefore, write the following equation for the derivative $\partial u/\partial t$ at the half-way point $(i, n + \frac{1}{2})$ of Fig. 7.8a:

$$\frac{\partial u}{\partial t} = \frac{u_{i,n+1} - u_{i,n}}{\Delta t} + O[(\Delta t)^2]. \qquad (7.41)$$

(Notice that this is true even if $u_{xx} \neq u_t$.)

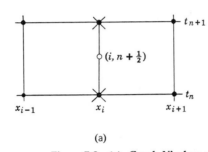

(a)

Also, by performing a Taylor's expansion, the following approximation can be derived for $\partial^2 u/\partial x^2$, again at the half-way point $(i, n + \frac{1}{2})$:

$$\frac{\partial^2 u}{\partial x^2} \doteq \theta \delta_x^2 u_{i,n+1} + (1 - \theta) \delta_x^2 u_{i,n}, \qquad (7.42)$$

where the value of θ is anywhere in the range $0 \leq \theta \leq 1$. The central-difference operator δ_x is used for conciseness; it is defined by (7.10).

In the Crank-Nicolson method [3], θ is chosen to be $1/2$ and the finite-difference equation, corresponding to (7.41) and (7.42) for the PDE $u_t = u_{xx}$, is

$$\frac{v_{i,n+1} - v_{i,n}}{\Delta t} = \frac{1}{2} \delta_x^2 v_{i,n+1} + \frac{1}{2} \delta_x^2 v_{i,n}. \qquad (7.43)$$

It may be shown that the Crank-Nicolson method is stable for all values of the ratio $\lambda = \Delta t/(\Delta x)^2$, and that it converges with discretization error $O[(\Delta t)^2 + (\Delta x)^2]$. Although this is a distinct improvement over the previous methods, the computation is only slightly more complicated than for the implicit method. Indeed, equation

(7.43), written out in full, becomes

$$-\lambda v_{i-1,n+1} + 2(1 + \lambda) v_{i,n+1} - \lambda v_{i+1,n+1}$$
$$= \lambda v_{i-1,n} + 2(1 - \lambda) v_{i,n} + \lambda v_{i+1,n}, \quad (7.44)$$

which is very similar to (7.26) for the implicit procedure.

Forsythe and Wasow [9] mention that if, instead of using the Crank-Nicolson value of $\theta = \frac{1}{2}$ in (7.42), the choice $\theta = (6\lambda - 1)/12\lambda$ is made, then the discretization error becomes $O[(\Delta x)^4]$, and that if λ is also chosen to be $1/\sqrt{20}$, the error is further reduced to $O[(\Delta x)^6]$. However, these authors also caution against expecting such improvements for an equation not of the simple form $u_t = u_{xx}$.

7.13 Unconditionally Stable Explicit Procedures

Although the familiar explicit method of Section 7.5 is stable only for $\lambda \leq \frac{1}{2}$, there are several other simple explicit procedures which are free from this restriction. Examples of such methods are illustrated below for the

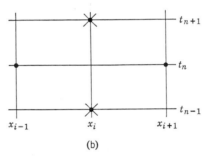

(b)

Figure 7.8 (a) Crank-Nicolson method. (b) DuFort-Frankel method.

solution of $u_t = u_{xx}$, but all can be extended to more than one space dimension.

DuFort-Frankel Method [8]

$$\frac{v_{i,n+1} - v_{i,n-1}}{2\Delta t} = \frac{v_{i-1,n} - v_{i,n-1} - v_{i,n+1} + v_{i+1,n}}{(\Delta x)^2}. \qquad (7.45)$$

Note that three time levels are involved, as shown in Fig. 7.8b.

Saul'yev Method. The following is a special case of the method given on page 29 et seq. of [31]. Advance to time level $n + 1$ by proceeding in the positive x-direction with

$$\frac{v_{i,n+1} - v_{i,n}}{\Delta t} = \frac{v_{i-1,n+1} - v_{i,n+1} - v_{i,n} + v_{i+1,n}}{(\Delta x)^2}, \qquad (7.46a)$$

and then advance to time level $n + 2$ by proceeding in the negative x-direction (over the same region) with

$$\frac{v_{i,n+2} - v_{i,n+1}}{\Delta t} = \frac{v_{i-1,n+1} - v_{i,n+1} - v_{i,n+2} + v_{i+1,n+2}}{(\Delta x)^2}. \qquad (7.46b)$$

Note that $v_{i-1,n+1}$ and $v_{i+1,n+2}$ in the first and second of these formulas will be known either from computations at the preceding grid point or from a boundary condition. This explicit *alternating-direction* procedure is then repeated for successive pairs of time-steps.

Larkin [30] also presents a modification of the Saul'yev method, in which the following two formulas are first used to compute two intermediate values p and q, both at time level $n + 1$:

$$\frac{p_{i,n+1} - v_{i,n}}{\Delta t} = \frac{p_{i-1,n+1} - p_{i,n+1} - v_{i,n} + v_{i+1,n}}{(\Delta x)^2}, \quad (7.47\text{a})$$

$$\frac{q_{i,n+1} - v_{i,n}}{\Delta t} = \frac{v_{i-1,n} - v_{i,n} - q_{i,n+1} + q_{i+1,n+1}}{(\Delta x)^2}. \quad (7.47\text{b})$$

The final approximation is then

$$v_{i,n+1} = \tfrac{1}{2}(p_{i,n+1} + q_{i,n+1}). \quad (7.47\text{c})$$

Barakat and Clark Method [26]. Both $p_{i,n}$ and $q_{i,n}$ are retained from the computations of the previous time-step. The formulas, for use in the forward ($+x$) and backward ($-x$) directions respectively, are

$$\frac{p_{i,n+1} - p_{i,n}}{\Delta t} = \frac{p_{i-1,n+1} - p_{i,n+1} - p_{i,n} + p_{i+1,n}}{(\Delta x)^2},$$
$$(7.48\text{a})$$

$$\frac{q_{i,n+1} - q_{i,n}}{\Delta t} = \frac{q_{i-1,n} - q_{i,n} - q_{i,n+1} + q_{i+1,n+1}}{(\Delta x)^2},$$
$$(7.48\text{b})$$

followed by

$$v_{i,n+1} = \tfrac{1}{2}(p_{i,n+1} + q_{i,n+1}). \quad (7.48\text{c})$$

7.14   The Implicit Alternating-Direction Method

It is now logical to progress to a parabolic PDE having two space coordinates. That is, let $u = u(x,y,t)$ and $v = v(i,j,n)$, where $y = j\Delta y$. A simple example arising from, say, unsteady-state heat conduction in a flat plate is:

$$\frac{\partial u}{\partial t} = \frac{\partial^2 u}{\partial x^2} + \frac{\partial^2 u}{\partial y^2}. \quad (7.49)$$

The explicit method of solution, in which the space derivatives are approximated at the time level t_n, leads to the difference equation

$$\frac{v_{i,j,n+1} - v_{i,j,n}}{\Delta t} = \delta_x^2 v_{i,j,n} + \delta_y^2 v_{i,j,n}. \quad (7.50)$$

The solution of (7.50) presents no difficulties and will not be discussed further, except to say that the following restriction between the time and space increments must be observed to ensure stability:

$$\Delta t \leqslant \frac{1}{2[(\Delta x)^{-2} + (\Delta y)^{-2}]}.$$

On the other hand, the *implicit* method leads to the difference equation

$$\frac{v_{i,j,n+1} - v_{i,j,n}}{\Delta t} = \delta_x^2 v_{i,j,n+1} + \delta_y^2 v_{i,j,n+1}, \quad (7.51)$$

which, when written out in full for the simple case of a square grid with $\Delta x = \Delta y$, has the form

$$-\lambda v_{i-1,j,n+1} - \lambda v_{i,j-1,n+1} + (1 + 4\lambda)v_{i,j,n+1}$$
$$- \lambda v_{i,j+1,n+1} - \lambda v_{i+1,j,n+1} = v_{i,j,n}.$$

Just as for the one-dimensional case, it may be shown that this scheme is stable, independent of λ. There are now five unknowns per equation, and the simple version of the Gaussian elimination method given by the algorithm (7.34) for the special tridiagonal system of (7.33) is no longer applicable. Gaussian elimination may still be used, however, but only at the expense of a considerable amount of computation. An alternative is to use the Gauss-Seidel iterative method discussed in Section 7.24, although this method may need a fair number of iterations for adequate convergence.

The *implicit alternating-direction method*, discussed by Peaceman and Rachford [19] and Douglas [4,6], avoids these disadvantages and yet still manages to use a system of equations with a tridiagonal coefficient matrix for which the algorithm of (7.34) affords a straightforward solution. Essentially, the principle is to employ *two* difference equations which are used in turn over successive time-steps each of duration $\Delta t/2$. The first equation is implicit only in the x-direction and the second is implicit only in the y-direction. Thus, if $v_{i,j}^*$ is an intermediate value at the end of the first time-step, we have

$$\frac{v_{i,j}^* - v_{i,j,n}}{\Delta t/2} = \delta_x^2 v_{i,j}^* + \delta_y^2 v_{i,j,n}, \quad (7.52\text{a})$$

followed by

$$\frac{v_{i,j,n+1} - v_{i,j}^*}{\Delta t/2} = \delta_x^2 v_{i,j}^* + \delta_y^2 v_{i,j,n+1}. \quad (7.52\text{b})$$

Written out in full and rearranged, with $\Delta x = \Delta y$ for simplicity, these equations become

$$-v_{i-1,j}^* + 2\left(\frac{1}{\lambda} + 1\right)v_{i,j}^* - v_{i+1,j}^*$$
$$= v_{i,j-1,n} + 2\left(\frac{1}{\lambda} - 1\right)v_{i,j,n} + v_{i,j+1,n}, \quad (7.53\text{a})$$

$$-v_{i,j-1,n+1} + 2\left(\frac{1}{\lambda} + 1\right)v_{i,j,n+1} - v_{i,j+1,n+1}$$
$$= v_{i-1,j}^* + 2\left(\frac{1}{\lambda} - 1\right)v_{i,j}^* + v_{i+1,j}^*. \quad (7.53\text{b})$$

The first equation is solved for the intermediate values v^*, which are then used in the second equation, thus leading to the solution $v_{i,j,n+1}$ at the end of the whole time interval Δt.

The stability of this procedure is investigated by the von Neumann method, previously outlined in Section 7.10 for one space variable. Substitution of the term $\psi(t)e^{j\alpha x}e^{j\beta y}$ (j here denotes $\sqrt{-1}$) into the difference equations (7.52a) and (7.52b), and elimination of the intermediate function $\psi(t + \Delta t/2)$, yields the following expression for the amplification factor across a whole time-step:

$$\xi = \frac{\psi(t + \Delta t)}{\psi(t)} = \left[\frac{1 - \dfrac{2\Delta t}{(\Delta x)^2}\sin^2\dfrac{\alpha\Delta x}{2}}{1 + \dfrac{2\Delta t}{(\Delta x)^2}\sin^2\dfrac{\alpha\Delta x}{2}}\right]$$

$$\times \left[\frac{1 - \dfrac{2\Delta t}{(\Delta y)^2}\sin^2\dfrac{\beta\Delta y}{2}}{1 + \dfrac{2\Delta t}{(\Delta y)^2}\sin^2\dfrac{\beta\Delta y}{2}}\right].$$

Clearly, $|\xi| \leqslant 1$ for any value of Δt, and the procedure is unconditionally stable. Convergence occurs with a discretization error $O[(\Delta t)^2 + (\Delta x)^2]$. We assume here, and in Section 7.15, that ratios such as $\Delta x/\Delta y$ are held constant.

The implicit alternating-direction procedure also finds an important application in the solution of elliptic PDEs (p. 508).

7.15 Additional Methods for Two and Three Space Dimensions

The implicit alternating-direction method can be extended to three space dimensions by using two intermediate values, but an examination of the corresponding amplification factor shows that it is unstable for $\lambda > 3/2$. Instead, the following alternating-direction modification of the Crank-Nicolson method is suggested by Douglas [24]:

$$\frac{v^* - v_n}{\Delta t} = \tfrac{1}{2}\delta_x^2(v^* + v_n) + \delta_y^2 v_n + \delta_z^2 v_n,$$

$$\frac{v^{**} - v_n}{\Delta t} = \tfrac{1}{2}\delta_x^2(v^* + v_n) + \tfrac{1}{2}\delta_y^2(v^{**} + v_n) + \delta_z^2 v_n, \quad (7.54)$$

$$\frac{v_{n+1} - v_n}{\Delta t} = \tfrac{1}{2}\delta_x^2(v^* + v_n) + \tfrac{1}{2}\delta_y^2(v^{**} + v_n) + \tfrac{1}{2}\delta_z^2(v_{n+1} + v_n).$$

Here, v^* and v^{**} denote the two intermediate values; the space subscripts are omitted for clarity. A general discussion of alternating-direction methods is also given by Douglas and Gunn [32].

Another procedure, given by Brian [27], is also available:

$$\frac{v^* - v_n}{\Delta t/2} = \delta_x^2 v^* + \delta_y^2 v_n + \delta_z^2 v_n,$$

$$\frac{v^{**} - v_n}{\Delta t/2} = \delta_x^2 v^* + \delta_y^2 v^{**} + \delta_z^2 v_n,$$

$$\frac{v^{***} - v_n}{\Delta t/2} = \delta_x^2 v^* + \delta_y^2 v^{**} + \delta_z^2 v^{***}, \quad (7.55)$$

$$\frac{v_{n+1} - v_n}{\Delta t} = \delta_x^2 v^* + \delta_y^2 v^{**} + \delta_z^2 v^{***}.$$

The third intermediate value v^{***} can actually be eliminated between the three equations to produce an equivalent system in which v^* and v^{**} can be regarded as successive approximations to v at the half time-step:

$$\frac{v^* - v_n}{\Delta t/2} = \delta_x^2 v^* + \delta_y^2 v_n + \delta_z^2 v_n,$$

$$\frac{v^{**} - v_n}{\Delta t/2} = \delta_x^2 v^* + \delta_y^2 v^{**} + \delta_z^2 v_n, \quad (7.56)$$

$$\frac{v_{n+1} - v^{**}}{\Delta t/2} = \delta_x^2 v^* + \delta_y^2 v^{**} + \delta_z^2 v_{n+1}.$$

Both of the above three-dimensional procedures are unconditionally stable and converge with discretization error $O[(\Delta t)^2 + (\Delta x)^2]$. Also, both procedures have obvious two-dimensional counterparts, although Brian's method then becomes identical with the implicit alternating-direction form.

EXAMPLE 7.3

UNSTEADY-STATE HEAT CONDUCTION IN A LONG BAR OF SQUARE CROSS SECTION
(IMPLICIT ALTERNATING-DIRECTION METHOD)

Problem Statement

An infinitely long bar of thermal diffusivity α has a square cross section of side $2a$. It is initially at a uniform temperature θ_0 and then suddenly has its surface maintained at a temperature θ_1. Compute the subsequent temperatures $\theta(x,y,t)$ inside the bar.

Method of Solution

If dimensionless distances, time, and temperature are defined by

$$X = \frac{x}{a}, \quad Y = \frac{y}{a}, \quad \tau = \frac{\alpha t}{a^2}, \quad \text{and} \quad T = \frac{\theta - \theta_0}{\theta_1 - \theta_0},$$

it may be shown that the unsteady-state conduction is governed by

$$\frac{\partial^2 T}{\partial X^2} + \frac{\partial^2 T}{\partial Y^2} = \frac{\partial T}{\partial \tau}. \quad (7.3.1)$$

Because of symmetry, it suffices to solve the problem in one quadrant only, such as that shown in Fig. 7.3.1. The center of the bar ($X = 0$, $Y = 0$) and one of its corners ($X = 1$, $Y = 1$) are regarded as the grid points $(0,0)$ and (n,n), respectively. From symmetry, there is no heat flux across the X and Y axes, which behave, in effect, as perfectly insulating boundaries across which the normal temperature gradient is zero. The initial and boundary conditions are:

$\tau = 0$: $\quad T = 0$ throughout the region,

$\tau > 0$: $\quad T = 1$ along the sides $X = 1$ and $Y = 1$,
$\quad \partial T/\partial X = 0$ and $\partial T/\partial Y = 0$ along the sides
$\quad X = 0$ and $Y = 0$, respectively.

The solution to the problem is by the implicit alternating-direction method described in the text and summarized by equations (7.53a) and (7.53b), with the first half time-step implicit in the X direction. Let T and T^* refer to temperatures at the beginning and end of a half

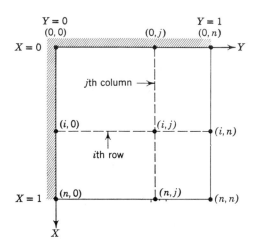

Figure 7.3.1 *Lower right-hand quadrant of cross section of bar.*

time-step $\Delta\tau/2$. Equation (7.53a) is applied to each point $i = 1, 2, \ldots, n - 1$ in the jth column; also, the method of Section 7.17 is used in conjunction with the effective boundary condition $\partial T/\partial X = 0$ at $X = 0$ to yield a finite-difference approximation of equation (7.3.1) at the boundary point $(0, j)$. We then have the following tridiagonal system for the jth column:

$$\left. \begin{array}{l} bT^*_{0,j} - 2T^*_{1,j} \qquad\qquad\qquad\qquad = d_0 \\ -T^*_{0,j} + bT^*_{1,j} - T^*_{2,j} \qquad\qquad\quad = d_1 \\ \cdots\cdots\cdots\cdots\cdots\cdots\cdots\cdots\cdots\cdots\cdots \\ \quad - T^*_{i-1,j} + bT^*_{i,j} - T^*_{i+1,j} \qquad = d_i \\ \cdots\cdots\cdots\cdots\cdots\cdots\cdots\cdots\cdots\cdots\cdots \\ \quad - T^*_{n-3,j} + bT^*_{n-2,j} - T^*_{n-1,j} = d_{n-2} \\ \qquad\qquad - T^*_{n-2,j} + bT^*_{n-1,j} = d_{n-1} \end{array} \right\} \quad (7.3.2)$$

with

$$\left. \begin{array}{l} d_i = T_{i,j-1} + fT_{i,j} + T_{i,j+1}, \quad \text{for} \quad i = 0, 1, \ldots, n - 2 \\ d_{n-1} = T_{n-1,j-1} + fT_{n-1,j} + T_{n-1,j+1} + T_{n,j} \end{array} \right\} \text{for } j \neq 0,$$

$$\left. \begin{array}{l} d_i = 2T_{i,1} + fT_{i,0}, \quad \text{for} \quad i = 0, 1, \ldots, n - 2 \\ d_{n-1} = 2T_{n-1,1} + fT_{n-1,0} + T_{n,0} \end{array} \right\} \text{for } j = 0,$$

where

$$b = 2(1/\lambda + 1),$$
$$f = 2(1/\lambda - 1),$$
$$\lambda = \Delta\tau/(\Delta x)^2.$$

Example 7.3   Implicit Alternating-Direction Method   **455**

Note: (a) the second form for the d_i, when $j = 0$, arises from consideration of the boundary condition $\partial T/\partial Y = 0$ at $Y = 0$, and (b) in the present problem, the boundary values $T_{n,j}$ and $T_{n,j}^*$ are synonymous (both equal 1).

Equation (7.3.2) is the same as (7.33) in form, and may be solved for the $T_{i,j}^*$ ($i = 0,1, \ldots, n-1$) by the algorithm of (7.34) and (7.35). The procedure is repeated for suc-cessive columns, $j = 0, 1, \ldots, n-1$ until all the $T_{i,j}^*$ are found at the end of the first half time-step.

The temperatures at the end of the second half time-step are found similarly, by applying equation (7.53b), or its equivalent at the boundary $Y = 0$, to each point in a row ($j = 0,1, \ldots, n-1$), for successive rows ($i = 0,1, \ldots, n-1$).

Flow Diagram

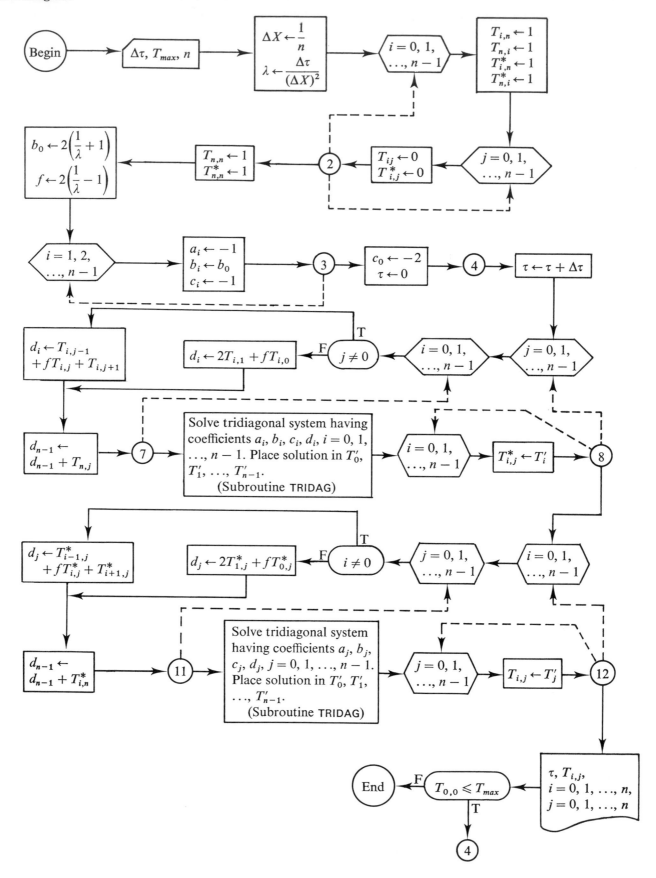

Example 7.3   Implicit Alternating-Direction Method   **457**

FORTRAN *Implementation*

List of Principal Variables

Program Symbol	*Definition*
A, B, C, D	Coefficient vectors defined in equations (7.33).
DTAU	Time-step, $\Delta\tau$.
DX	Space increment, ΔX.
F	$f = 2(1/\lambda - 1)$.
I, J	Row and column subscripts, i, j.
ICOUNT	Counter on the number of time-steps.
IFREQ	Number of time-steps between successive printings of temperatures.
N	Number of space increments between $X = 0$ and $X = 1$.
RATIO	$\lambda = \Delta\tau/(\Delta X)^2$.
T	Matrix of temperatures T at each grid point.
TAU	Time, τ.
TMAX	Maximum center temperature to be computed, T_{max}.
TPRIME	Vector for temporary storage of temperatures computed by TRIDAG. These values T' are then placed in the appropriate row of T or column of T^*.
TRIDAG	Subroutine for solving a tridiagonal system of simultaneous equations (see Example 7.2).
TSTAR	Matrix of temperatures T^* at the end of the first half time-step.

Because of FORTRAN limitations, all subscripts in the text are advanced by one when they appear in the program; e.g., $T_{0,0}$ and $T_{n,n}$ become T(1,1) and T(N+1, N+1), respectively.

Program Listing

```
C           APPLIED NUMERICAL METHODS, EXAMPLE 7.3
C           TWO-DIMENSIONAL UNSTEADY STATE HEAT CONDUCTION IN AN INFINITE
C           BAR OF SQUARE CROSS-SECTION, SOLVED BY THE I.A.D. METHOD.
C
C           AT TIME TAU = 0, THE TEMPERATURE IS ZERO EVERYWHERE, AND THE
C           FACES OF THE BAR ARE SUBSEQUENTLY MAINTAINED AT T = 1.
C           THE TEMPERATURES IN THE LOWER RIGHT-HAND QUADRANT ARE PRINTED
C           EVERY IFREQ TIME-STEPS, UNTIL THE CENTER TEMPERATURE EXCEEDS
C           TMAX.
C
      DIMENSION A(11), B(11), C(11), D(11), T(11, 11), TSTAR(11, 11),
     1 TPRIME(11)
C
C         ..... READ AND CHECK INPUT PARAMETERS .....
    1 READ (5,100) DTAU, TMAX, N, IFREQ
      NP1 = N + 1
      FLOATN = N
      DX = 1.0/FLOATN
      RATIO = DTAU/(DX*DX)
      WRITE (6,200) DTAU, DX, RATIO, TMAX, N, IFREQ
C
C         ..... SET INITIAL AND BOUNDARY VALUES .....
      DO 2  I = 1, N
      T(I,NP1) = 1.0
      T(NP1,I) = 1.0
      TSTAR(I,NP1) = 1.0
      TSTAR(NP1,I) = 1.0
      DO 2  J = 1, N
      T(I,J) = 0.0
    2 TSTAR(I,J) = 0.0
      T(NP1,NP1) = 1.0
      TSTAR(NP1,NP1) = 1.0
C
C         ..... SET COEFFICIENT ARRAYS A, B AND C .....
      B(1) = 2.0*(1.0/RATIO + 1.0)
      F = 2.0*(1.0/RATIO - 1.0)
      DO 3  I = 2, N
      A(I) = - 1.0
      B(I) = B(1)
    3 C(I) = - 1.0
      C(1) = - 2.0
      ICOUNT = 0
      TAU = 0.0
C
C         ..... PERFORM CALCULATIONS OVER SUCCESSIVE TIME-STEPS .....
    4 TAU = TAU + DTAU
      ICOUNT = ICOUNT + 1
C
C         ..... COMPUTE TEMPERATURES AT END OF HALF
C               TIME INCREMENT (IMPLICIT BY COLUMNS) .....
      DO 8  J = 1, N
      DO 7  I = 1, N
      IF (J .NE. 1) GO TO 6
          D(I) = 2.0*T(I,2) + F*T(I,1)
      GO TO 7
    6     D(I) = T(I,J-1) + F*T(I,J) + T(I,J+1)
    7 D(N) = D(N) + T(NP1,J)
      CALL TRIDAG (1, N, A, B, C, D, TPRIME)
      DO 8  I = 1, N
    8 TSTAR(I,J) = TPRIME(I)
C
C         ..... COMPUTE TEMPERATURES AT END OF WHOLE
C               TIME INCREMENT (IMPLICIT BY ROWS) .....
      DO 12  I = 1, N
      DO 11  J = 1, N
      IF (I .NE. 1) GO TO 10
          D(J) = 2.0*TSTAR(2,J) + F*TSTAR(1,J)
      GO TO 11
   10     D(J) = TSTAR(I-1,J) + F*TSTAR(I,J) + TSTAR(I+1,J)
   11 D(N) = D(N) + TSTAR(I,NP1)
      CALL TRIDAG (1, N, A, B, C, D, TPRIME)
      DO 12  J = 1, N
   12 T(I,J) = TPRIME(J)
```

Example 7.3   Implicit Alternating-Direction Method   **459**

Program Listing (*Continued*)

```
C
C       ..... PRINT TEMPERATURES THROUGHOUT THE QUADRANT .....
        IF (ICOUNT .NE. IFREQ) GO TO 15
           ICOUNT = 0
           WRITE (6,201) TAU
           DO 14   I = 1, NP1
   14      WRITE (6,202) (T(I,J), J = 1, NP1)
   15   IF (T(1,1) - TMAX) 4, 4, 1
C
C       ..... FORMATS FOR INPUT AND OUTPUT STATEMENTS .....
  100   FORMAT (6X, F6.3, 10X, F5.2, 7X, I3, 11X, I2)
  200   FORMAT (82H1   UNSTEADY STATE HEAT CONDUCTION IN A SQUARE BAR, I.A
       1.D. METHOD, WITH PARAMETERS/
       212H0   DTAU  = , F10.5/ 12H      DX    = , F10.5/
       312H    RATIO = , F10.5/ 12H      TMAX  = , F10.5/
       412H    N     = , I4/ 12H      IFREQ = , I4)
  201   FORMAT (20H0    AT A TIME TAU = , F8.5/ 32H0    TEMPERATURES IN QUAD
       1RANT ARE/1H /)
  202   FORMAT (4H    , 11F8.5)
C
        END
```

Data

```
DTAU = 0.05 ,   TMAX = 0.95,   N = 10,   IFREQ = 1
```

Computer Output

```
UNSTEADY STATE HEAT CONDUCTION IN A SQUARE BAR, I.A.D. METHOD, WITH PARAMETERS

DTAU  =    0.05000
DX    =    0.10000
RATIO =    5.00000
TMAX  =    0.95000
N     =   10
IFREQ =    1

AT A TIME TAU =   0.05000

TEMPERATURES IN QUADRANT ARE

  0.01579 0.01737 0.02272 0.03398 0.05566 0.09644 0.17262 0.31467 0.57943 1.07278 1.00000
  0.01737 0.01894 0.02428 0.03552 0.05717 0.09788 0.17394 0.31577 0.58010 1.07266 1.00000
  0.02272 0.02428 0.02959 0.04077 0.06230 0.10279 0.17844 0.31949 0.58238 1.07227 1.00000
  0.03398 0.03552 0.04077 0.05183 0.07311 0.11313 0.18790 0.32734 0.58720 1.07143 1.00000
  0.05566 0.05717 0.06230 0.07311 0.09391 0.13304 0.20613 0.34243 0.59646 1.06983 1.00000
  0.09644 0.09788 0.10279 0.11313 0.13304 0.17047 0.24041 0.37083 0.61389 1.06681 1.00000
  0.17262 0.17394 0.17844 0.18790 0.20613 0.24041 0.30445 0.42387 0.64644 1.06118 1.00000
  0.31467 0.31577 0.31949 0.32734 0.34243 0.37083 0.42387 0.52279 0.70714 1.05068 1.00000
  0.57943 0.58010 0.58238 0.58720 0.59646 0.61389 0.64644 0.70714 0.82028 1.03110 1.00000
  1.07278 1.07266 1.07227 1.07143 1.06983 1.06682 1.06118 1.05068 1.03110 0.99462 1.00000
  1.00000 1.00000 1.00000 1.00000 1.00000 1.00000 1.00000 1.00000 1.00000 1.00000 1.00000

AT A TIME TAU =   0.10000

TEMPERATURES IN QUADRANT ARE

  0.09333 0.09942 0.11890 0.15546 0.21508 0.30496 0.42973 0.58082 0.70958 0.66423 1.00000
  0.09942 0.10546 0.12481 0.16113 0.22035 0.30962 0.43356 0.58363 0.71153 0.66648 1.00000
  0.11890 0.12481 0.14374 0.17927 0.23721 0.32455 0.44581 0.59264 0.71777 0.67370 1.00000
  0.15546 0.16113 0.17927 0.21333 0.26886 0.35258 0.46881 0.60954 0.72948 0.68724 1.00000
  0.21508 0.22035 0.23721 0.26886 0.32048 0.39829 0.50631 0.63711 0.74858 0.70932 1.00000
  0.30496 0.30962 0.32455 0.35258 0.39829 0.46719 0.56284 0.67866 0.77737 0.74260 1.00000
  0.42973 0.43356 0.44581 0.46881 0.50631 0.56284 0.64132 0.73635 0.81733 0.78881 1.00000
  0.58082 0.58363 0.59264 0.60954 0.63711 0.67866 0.73635 0.80620 0.86573 0.84476 1.00000
  0.70958 0.71153 0.71777 0.72948 0.74858 0.77737 0.81733 0.86573 0.90697 0.89245 1.00000
  0.66423 0.66648 0.67370 0.68724 0.70932 0.74260 0.78881 0.84476 0.89245 0.87565 1.00000
  1.00000 1.00000 1.00000 1.00000 1.00000 1.00000 1.00000 1.00000 1.00000 1.00000 1.00000
```

Computer Output (*Continued*)

AT A TIME TAU = 0.20000

TEMPERATURES IN QUADRANT ARE

```
0.40354 0.41077 0.43205 0.46633 0.51243 0.57037 0.64334 0.73701 0.84127 0.84398 1.00000
0.41077 0.41790 0.43893 0.47279 0.51834 0.57558 0.64766 0.74020 0.84319 0.84587 1.00000
0.43205 0.43893 0.45919 0.49183 0.53574 0.59091 0.66039 0.74958 0.84885 0.85144 1.00000
0.46633 0.47279 0.49184 0.52251 0.56376 0.61560 0.68089 0.76470 0.85798 0.86041 1.00000
0.51243 0.51834 0.53574 0.56376 0.60145 0.64881 0.70846 0.78503 0.87025 0.87247 1.00000
0.57037 0.57558 0.59091 0.61560 0.64881 0.69054 0.74310 0.81057 0.88566 0.88762 1.00000
0.64334 0.64766 0.66039 0.68089 0.70846 0.74310 0.78673 0.84275 0.90508 0.90671 1.00000
0.73701 0.74020 0.74958 0.76470 0.78503 0.81057 0.84275 0.88405 0.93001 0.93121 1.00000
0.84127 0.84319 0.84885 0.85798 0.87025 0.88567 0.90508 0.93001 0.95776 0.95848 1.00000
0.84398 0.84587 0.85144 0.86041 0.87247 0.88762 0.90671 0.93121 0.95848 0.95919 1.00000
1.00000 1.00000 1.00000 1.00000 1.00000 1.00000 1.00000 1.00000 1.00000 1.00000 1.00000
```

AT A TIME TAU = 0.40000

TEMPERATURES IN QUADRANT ARE

```
0.77532 0.77809 0.78636 0.79998 0.81851 0.84105 0.86674 0.89726 0.93831 0.95512 1.00000
0.77809 0.78082 0.78899 0.80244 0.82074 0.84301 0.86838 0.89853 0.93907 0.95567 1.00000
0.78636 0.78899 0.79685 0.80980 0.82742 0.84886 0.87328 0.90231 0.94134 0.95732 1.00000
0.79997 0.80244 0.80980 0.82192 0.83842 0.85849 0.88136 0.90854 0.94508 0.96004 1.00000
0.81851 0.82074 0.82742 0.83842 0.85339 0.87160 0.89235 0.91701 0.95017 0.96374 1.00000
0.84105 0.84301 0.84886 0.85849 0.87160 0.88755 0.90572 0.92732 0.95636 0.96825 1.00000
0.86674 0.86838 0.87328 0.88136 0.89235 0.90572 0.92096 0.93906 0.96341 0.97338 1.00000
0.89726 0.89853 0.90231 0.90853 0.91701 0.92732 0.93906 0.95302 0.97179 0.97948 1.00000
0.93831 0.93907 0.94134 0.94508 0.95017 0.95636 0.96341 0.97179 0.98306 0.98768 1.00000
0.95512 0.95567 0.95732 0.96004 0.96375 0.96825 0.97338 0.97948 0.98768 0.99103 1.00000
1.00000 1.00000 1.00000 1.00000 1.00000 1.00000 1.00000 1.00000 1.00000 1.00000 1.00000
```

AT A TIME TAU = 0.75000

TEMPERATURES IN QUADRANT ARE

```
0.96003 0.96052 0.96199 0.96439 0.96767 0.97170 0.97650 0.98213 0.98705 0.99430 1.00000
0.96052 0.96101 0.96246 0.96483 0.96806 0.97205 0.97679 0.98235 0.98720 0.99437 1.00000
0.96199 0.96246 0.96385 0.96614 0.96925 0.97309 0.97765 0.98301 0.98768 0.99458 1.00000
0.96439 0.96483 0.96614 0.96828 0.97120 0.97479 0.97907 0.98408 0.98846 0.99492 1.00000
0.96766 0.96806 0.96925 0.97120 0.97384 0.97711 0.98099 0.98555 0.98952 0.99539 1.00000
0.97170 0.97205 0.97309 0.97479 0.97711 0.97997 0.98336 0.98735 0.99083 0.99596 1.00000
0.97650 0.97679 0.97765 0.97907 0.98099 0.98336 0.98618 0.98950 0.99238 0.99665 1.00000
0.98213 0.98235 0.98301 0.98408 0.98555 0.98735 0.98950 0.99201 0.99421 0.99745 1.00000
0.98704 0.98720 0.98768 0.98846 0.98952 0.99083 0.99238 0.99421 0.99580 0.99815 1.00000
0.99430 0.99437 0.99458 0.99492 0.99539 0.99597 0.99665 0.99745 0.99815 0.99919 1.00000
1.00000 1.00000 1.00000 1.00000 1.00000 1.00000 1.00000 1.00000 1.00000 1.00000 1.00000
```

Example 7.3   Implicit Alternating-Direction Method   **461**

Discussion of Results

The printed output gives values of the dimensionless temperature T_{ij} at every grid point in the quadrant $(i = 0, 1, \ldots, 10; \ j = 0, 1, \ldots, 10)$, for selected values of the dimensionless time τ. The time-step was chosen to be 0.05, twenty times as large as the maximum permissible if the problem had been solved by an explicit procedure. This large value for $\Delta\tau$ is responsible for the "impossible" temperatures, greater than 1, appearing at the end of the first time-step. Indeed, an oscillation of decreasing amplitude in the temperatures can be detected throughout the computations for those points just inside the surface of the bar. This phenomenon is characteristic of stable methods when rather large time-steps are employed.

The computed center temperatures, T_c, agree well with those published by Olson and Schultz [17], corresponding to the known analytical solution, as shown in Table 7.3.1.

Table 7.3.1
Comparison of Center Temperatures

Time, τ	T_c (computed)	T_c (exact)
0.1	0.09333	0.09883
0.2	0.40354	0.40354
0.3	0.63224	0.63179
0.4	0.77532	0.77486
0.5	0.86283	0.86252
0.6	0.91624	0.91607
0.7	0.94886	0.94877

7.16 Simultaneous First- and Second-Order Space Derivatives

This chapter is largely devoted to the treatment of simple unsteady-state and steady-state heat-conduction or diffusion equations. Although this approach is mainly for clarity, similar finite-difference methods can be extended to more involved situations. For example, the following approximation would be appropriate for a combination of first- and second-order space derivatives which occurs frequently in cylindrical coordinates:

$$\frac{\partial^2 u}{\partial r^2} + \frac{1}{r}\frac{\partial u}{\partial r} \doteq \frac{u_{i-1} - 2u_i + u_{i+1}}{(\Delta r)^2} + \frac{1}{i\Delta r}\frac{u_{i+1} - u_{i-1}}{2\Delta r}.$$

The representation of $\partial u/\partial r$ by the central difference does not add to the list of unknowns, namely, u_{i-1}, u_i, and u_{i+1}, already involved in the approximation of $\partial^2 u/\partial r^2$. Hence, the presence of a first-order space derivative often adds little to the complexity of the solution.

7.17 Types of Boundary Condition

For the sake of argument, assume we are dealing with a problem in which $u = u(x,y,t)$ satisfies the parabolic PDE, $u_{xx} + u_{yy} = u_t$, in a region R which has a boundary C, where R and C lie in the xy−plane. Until now, it has been assumed that u is specified as a function g of time and position on C. This, however, is not the only type of boundary condition; the derivatives u_n or u_s (n = normal, s = tangential) might be specified instead, or perhaps the boundary condition might involve the values u_n, u_s, and u. The three possibilities are termed the Dirichlet, Neumann, and third boundary conditions respectively [9]. To summarize, we have, on C

Dirichlet condition	$u = g$
Neumann condition	$\alpha u_n + \beta u_s = g$ (7.57)
Third condition	$\alpha u_n + \beta u_s + \gamma u = g$.

The translation into finite differences depends on the particular boundary condition. As an example, we deal here with a condition frequently encountered in problems of heat transfer, on, for instance, the straight boundary $x = 0$, namely,

$$-u_n + au = g. \tag{7.58}$$

The purpose of the finite-difference approach is to seek an approximation to the PDE, $u_t = u_{xx} + u_{yy}$, at every point where u is not already known. For a typical boundary point such as $(0,j)$ in Fig. 7.9, u_t and u_{yy} present no difficulty; u_{xx} is obtained from Taylor's expansion:

$$u_{1,j} = u_{0,j} + u_n\Delta x + \frac{(\Delta x)^2}{2!}u_{xx} + O[(\Delta x)^3],$$

that is

$$u_{xx} = \frac{2}{(\Delta x)^2}[u_{1,j} - u_{0,j} - u_n\Delta x] + O(\Delta x).$$

Using the boundary condition, $u_n = au - g$, we obtain

$$u_{xx} = \frac{2}{(\Delta x)^2}[u_{1,j} - (a\Delta x + 1)u_{0,j} + g\Delta x] + O(\Delta x). \tag{7.59}$$

The final finite-difference approximation at the point $(0,j)$ is then, in implicit form,

$$\frac{2}{(\Delta x)^2}[v_{1,j,n+1} - (a\Delta x + 1)v_{0,j,n+1} + g\Delta x]$$

$$+ \delta_y^2 v_{0,j,n+1} = \frac{v_{0,j,n+1} - v_{0,j,n}}{\Delta t}. \tag{7.60}$$

Formula (7.59) is not completely satisfactory, since, with its use, the approximations for u_{xx} and u_{yy} do not match, being $O(\Delta x)$ and $O[(\Delta y)^2]$, respectively. However, with the inclusion of the point $(2,j)$, a formula of $O[(\Delta x)^2]$ can be derived fairly easily for u_{xx}.

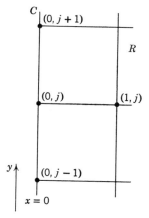

Figure 7.9   Boundary points.

For a heat-conduction problem in which $x = 0$ is an insulated boundary, the condition is $u_n = 0$. We then have $a = g = 0$, so that

$$u_{xx} = \frac{2}{(\Delta x)^2}[u_{1,j} - u_{0,j}] + O(\Delta x). \tag{7.61}$$

7.18 Finite-Difference Approximations at the Interface between Two Different Media

Consider, for simplicity, a one-dimensional unsteady-state heat-conduction problem involving two different substances A and B in contact, as shown in Fig. 7.10.

We wish to derive the relevant finite-difference approximation for the temperature θ_i at point i on the interface between A and B. The following procedure is based on the continuity of heat flux at the interface. Let A and B

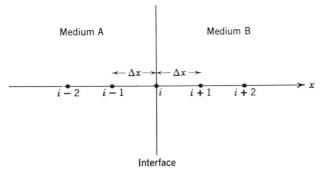

Figure 7.10 *Interface between different media.*

have thermal diffusivities α_A and α_B, and thermal conductivities k_A and k_B, and let the grid spacing be Δx in both media. Suppose that the new temperature θ'_i, after a time increment Δt, is to be calculated using an explicit representation.

Medium A. From Taylor's expansion, we have, approximately,

$$\theta_{i-1} \doteq \theta_i - \Delta x \left(\frac{\partial \theta}{\partial x} \right)_{iA} + \frac{(\Delta x)^2}{2} \left(\frac{\partial^2 \theta}{\partial x^2} \right)_{iA},$$

where the subscript iA denotes the derivative in medium A at the interface.
that is,

$$\left(\frac{\partial^2 \theta}{\partial x^2} \right)_{iA} \doteq \frac{2}{(\Delta x)^2} \left[\theta_{i-1} - \theta_i + \Delta x \left(\frac{\partial \theta}{\partial x} \right)_{iA} \right]. \quad (7.62)$$

Also, the time derivative is approximated by

$$\left(\frac{\partial \theta}{\partial t} \right)_{iA} \doteq \frac{\theta'_i - \theta_i}{\Delta t}. \quad (7.63)$$

The substitution of (7.62) and (7.63) into the unsteady-state heat-conduction equation $\alpha \, \partial^2 \theta / \partial x^2 = \partial \theta / \partial t$ gives

$$\frac{2\alpha_A}{(\Delta x)^2} \left[\theta_{i-1} - \theta_i + \Delta x \left(\frac{\partial \theta}{\partial x} \right)_{iA} \right] = \frac{\theta'_i - \theta_i}{\Delta t},$$

or

$$\Delta x \left(\frac{\partial \theta}{\partial x} \right)_{iA} = \frac{(\theta'_i - \theta_i)}{2\lambda \alpha_A} + (\theta_i - \theta_{i-1}), \quad (7.64)$$

where $\lambda = \Delta t / (\Delta x)^2$.

Medium B. It may similarly be shown that

$$-\Delta x \left(\frac{\partial \theta}{\partial x} \right)_{iB} = \frac{(\theta'_i - \theta_i)}{2\lambda \alpha_B} + (\theta_i - \theta_{i+1}). \quad (7.65)$$

The unwanted derivatives $(\partial \theta / \partial x)_{iA}$ and $(\partial \theta / \partial x)_{iB}$ may now be eliminated by observing that the heat flux must be continuous at the interface, so that

$$k_A \left(\frac{\partial \theta}{\partial x} \right)_{iA} = k_B \left(\frac{\partial \theta}{\partial x} \right)_{iB}. \quad (7.66)$$

Then, from (7.64), (7.65), and (7.66), it follows after a certain amount of simplification that

$$\theta'_i = \theta_i + \left[\frac{2\lambda \alpha_A}{\dfrac{\alpha_A}{\alpha_B} + \dfrac{k_A}{k_B}} \right] \left[\theta_{i+1} - \left(1 + \frac{k_A}{k_B} \right) \theta_i + \frac{k_A}{k_B} \theta_{i-1} \right],$$

$$(7.67)$$

which is the required explicit finite-difference representation. Note that for $\alpha_A = \alpha_B$ and $k_A = k_B$, equation (7.67) reduces to the familiar form

$$\theta'_i = \lambda' \theta_{i+1} + (1 - 2\lambda') \theta_i + \lambda' \theta_{i-1},$$

where $\lambda' = \lambda \alpha_A$.

7.19 Irregular Boundaries

In problems having simple geometry, we can usually arrange for certain grid points to lie on the boundaries. However, in cases in which the boundary does not fall on regular grid points (shown in Fig. 7.11) the boundary is considered to be *irregular*.

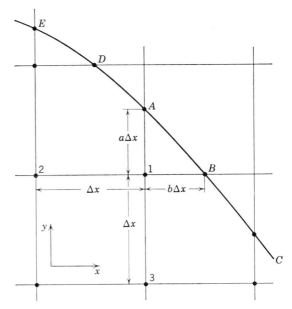

Figure 7.11 *Irregular boundary.*

Consider a square grid, and let the boundary conditions be of the *Dirichlet* type. That is, u is known along the curved boundary C, of which we shall use points A and B. For simplicity, we will abandon the subscript notation temporarily, and label the relevant interior grid points 1, 2, and 3, as indicated.

A typical problem might require the finite-difference approximation for $u_{xx} + u_{yy}$ at interior grid-point 1. The procedure is to write down the appropriate Taylor's expansions and to eliminate unwanted derivatives. Thus we have:

$$u_A = u_1 + a\,\Delta x u_y + \frac{(a\,\Delta x)^2}{2!}\,u_{yy} + O[(\Delta x)^3],$$

$$u_3 = u_1 - \Delta x u_y + \frac{(\Delta x)^2}{2!}\,u_{yy} + O[(\Delta x)^3],$$

$$u_B = u_1 + b\,\Delta x u_x + \frac{(b\,\Delta x)^2}{2!}\,u_{xx} + O[(\Delta x)^3],$$

$$u_2 = u_1 - \Delta x u_x + \frac{(\Delta x)^2}{2!}\,u_{xx} + O[(\Delta x)^3].$$

(7.68)

The elimination of u_x and u_y eventually leads to the result

$$u_{xx} + u_{yy} = \frac{2}{(\Delta x)^2}\left[\frac{u_2}{b+1} + \frac{u_3}{a+1} + \frac{u_A}{a(a+1)}\right.$$

$$\left. + \frac{u_B}{b(b+1)} - \frac{(a+b)u_1}{ab}\right] + O(\Delta x), \quad (7.69)$$

which is the required finite-difference approximation. The procedure is then repeated for other pairs of points, such as D and E in Fig. 7.11.

An easier, but less accurate, alternative is to approximate the curved boundary by a jagged series of steps constructed from the square grid.

The treatment of the *Neumann* type of boundary condition on an irregular boundary is more involved, and the reader is referred to Forsythe and Wasow [9].

7.20 The Solution of Nonlinear Partial Differential Equations

The fact that a given PDE may be nonlinear does not preclude its solution by one of the basic methods pre-sented in this chapter. One must bear in mind, however, that the object of any simple finite-difference representation is always to approximate the nonlinear PDE by an algebraic equation which is *linear* in its unknowns. This observation is illustrated by the following two examples:

1. The nonlinear term $u\,\partial u/\partial x$, where u is a varying fluid velocity, occurs in the Navier-Stokes equations describing unsteady fluid motion. Such a term is conveniently represented by regarding the coefficient u as constant over a single time-step and by approximating $\partial u/\partial x$ in the usual way, either explicitly or implicitly. Normally, u would be assigned its value at the beginning of the time-step; the computations might be repeated, however, using a mean value, once an estimate had been obtained for u at the end of the time-step. This procedure of reevaluating coefficients is called *iteration* across a time-step.

2. The term $\partial[D(\partial c/\partial x)]/\partial x$ arises typically in diffusion problems in which the diffusion coefficient D is a function of concentration c. For simplicity, if D is a linear function of c, with $D = \alpha c + \beta$, the term expands to

$$\frac{\partial}{\partial x}\left(D\,\frac{\partial c}{\partial x}\right) = D\,\frac{\partial^2 c}{\partial x^2} + \alpha\left(\frac{\partial c}{\partial x}\right)^2.$$

The first term, $D(\partial^2 c/\partial x^2)$, is treated by following the observations in (1) above. The term $(\partial c/\partial x)^2$ presents no problem in an explicit procedure. Implicitly, however, we would split it into the product $(\partial c/\partial x) \times (\partial c/\partial x)$ and treat the first factor $\partial c/\partial x$ as a "constant" coefficient. This representation might be particularly appropriate in a Crank-Nicolson procedure.

Examples 7.4 and 7.5 illustrate the solution of nonlinear PDE's.

EXAMPLE 7.4

UNSTEADY-STATE HEAT CONDUCTION IN A SOLIDIFYING ALLOY

Problem Statement

A cylindrical mold, shown in Fig. 7.4.1, is charged with a molten alloy of metals A and B at an initial temperature of $T_{liq} = 400°F$, the liquidus temperature of the alloy. The mold is well insulated, except at one end, which is maintained at the solidus temperature of the alloy, $T_{sol} = 150°F$, by a stream of oil.

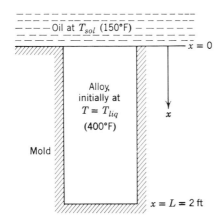

Figure 7.4.1 Solidification of alloy in mold.

Find the temperature profiles in the ingot as a function of time, up to the point when the face, $x = L = 2$ ft, has cooled to $T_{low} = 200°F$.

The following data are available for the alloy:

$\left. \begin{array}{l} \rho = 540 \text{ lb/cu ft,} \\ k = 10.1 \text{ BTU/hr ft °F,} \\ c_p = 0.038 \text{ BTU/lb °F,} \end{array} \right\}$ for both solid and liquid,

$\Delta H = $ latent heat of fusion $= 120.0$ BTU/lb.

The quantity α, given in Table 7.4.1 as a function of temperature T, has been determined from the phase equilibrium diagram sketched in Fig. 7.4.2. It gives the amount of solid formed corresponding to a small drop in temperature of the liquid/solid mixture.

Table 7.4.1 Values of α, lb Solid Formed per °F Fall per lb Mixture of Solid and Liquid

T (°F)	α (°F^{-1})	T (°F)	α (°F^{-1})	T (°F)	α (°F^{-1})
150	0.0119	240	0.00375	330	0.00200
160	0.0102	250	0.00341	340	0.00190
170	0.00874	260	0.00315	350	0.00181
180	0.00756	270	0.00291	360	0.00173
190	0.00657	280	0.00270	370	0.00167
200	0.00575	290	0.00252	380	0.00160
210	0.00509	300	0.00238	390	0.00153
220	0.00454	310	0.00223	400	0.00147
230	0.00412	320	0.00211		

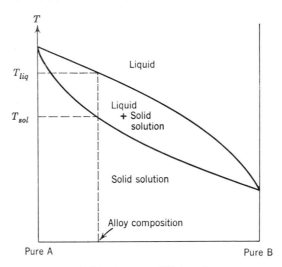

Figure 7.4.2 Phase equilibrium diagram.

Method of Solution

Performing a heat balance on a differential element, and considering a generation term arising from latent heat effects gives the differential equation governing the alloy temperature T as a function of distance x and time τ:

$$\frac{\partial^2 T}{\partial x^2} = \frac{\rho}{k}(c_p + \alpha \Delta H) \frac{\partial T}{\partial \tau}, \qquad (7.4.1)$$

where $\alpha = \alpha(T)$ is a known function of temperature. The boundary and initial conditions are

$$\tau = 0: \quad T = T_{liq} \quad \text{for} \quad 0 \leqslant x \leqslant L, \qquad (7.4.1a)$$

$$\tau > 0: \quad T = T_{sol} \quad \text{at} \quad x = 0, \qquad (7.4.1b)$$

$$\partial T / \partial x = 0 \quad \text{at} \quad x = L. \qquad (7.4.1c)$$

For the finite-difference solution, the interval $0 \leqslant x \leqslant L$ is subdivided by a grid whose points are spaced Δx apart, and temperatures at all grid points are computed at time intervals of $\Delta \tau$. The implicit finite-difference approximation of the PDE (7.4.1) is

$$T'_{i-1} - 2T'_i + T'_{i+1} = \gamma_i(T'_i - T_i), \qquad (7.4.2)$$

where

$$\gamma_i = \frac{\rho}{k}(c_p + \alpha \Delta H) \frac{(\Delta x)^2}{\Delta \tau}. \qquad (7.4.3)$$

The superscript prime here denotes a value at the end of a time-step and the subscript i designates the grid point with x coordinate $i \Delta x$. By applying equation (7.4.2) to the grid points $i = 1, 2, \ldots, n - 1$ in turn, and by employing a Taylor's expansion to obtain the approximation for use at the point on the insulated boundary, $i = n$, we have the tridiagonal system

$$(2 + \gamma_1)T_1' - T_2' \qquad\qquad\qquad = T_0' + \gamma_1 T_1$$
$$\cdots\cdots\cdots\cdots\cdots\cdots\cdots\cdots\cdots\cdots\cdots\cdots\cdots\cdots$$
$$-T_{i-1}' + (2 + \gamma_i)T_i' - T_{i+1}' \qquad\qquad = \gamma_i T_i \qquad\qquad (7.4.4)$$
$$\cdots\cdots\cdots\cdots\cdots\cdots\cdots\cdots\cdots\cdots\cdots\cdots\cdots$$
$$-2T_{n-1}' + (2 + \gamma_n)T_n' = \gamma_n T_n$$

Again, the subroutine TRIDAG (see Example 7.2) is used to solve the system (7.4.4). The coefficients $(2 + \gamma_i)$ appearing on the main diagonal are now functions of temperature and must be evaluated at each time-step. For this purpose, a table look-up function, named TLU, is employed to find the value of α (and hence of γ_i) corresponding to the particular temperature at each grid point. In the present example, computation is stopped when T_n has fallen to $T_{low} = 200°F$.

Note that equation (7.4.2) is the linearized finite-difference approximation of the nonlinear PDE (7.4.1). This simplification has been achieved by treating the coefficient γ_i as a constant at a point over any one time-step. The value of γ_i at each point is taken as that corresponding to α, and hence to the known T_i, at the beginning of the time-step.

Table Look-up Function

Suppose we have *ntab* tabulated pairs of values of x and z: $x_1, x_2, \ldots, x_{ntab}$, and $z_1, z_2, \ldots, z_{ntab}$. Then, given a value x^*, which need not coincide with one of the tabulated values of x, what is the corresponding value z^* of z? This simple problem is solved below by the function named TLU. A check is first made to see if x^* is within the range of the tabulated values x_i, which are assumed to be monotonically increasing. If x^* is outside this range, a warning "flag" is transmitted to the calling program. Otherwise, the function then locates the two tabulated values, such as x_{i-1} and x_i, between which x^* lies. Finally, linear interpolation gives the required value of z:

$$z^* = z_{i-1} + \frac{(x^* - x_{i-1})(z_i - z_{i-1})}{x_i - x_{i-1}}.$$

In the present application, the vector names x and z are replaced by T_{tab} and α_{tab}, which contain the tabulated values of T and α, respectively.

Example 7.4   Unsteady-State Heat Conduction in a Solidifying Alloy   **467**

Flow Diagram
Main Program

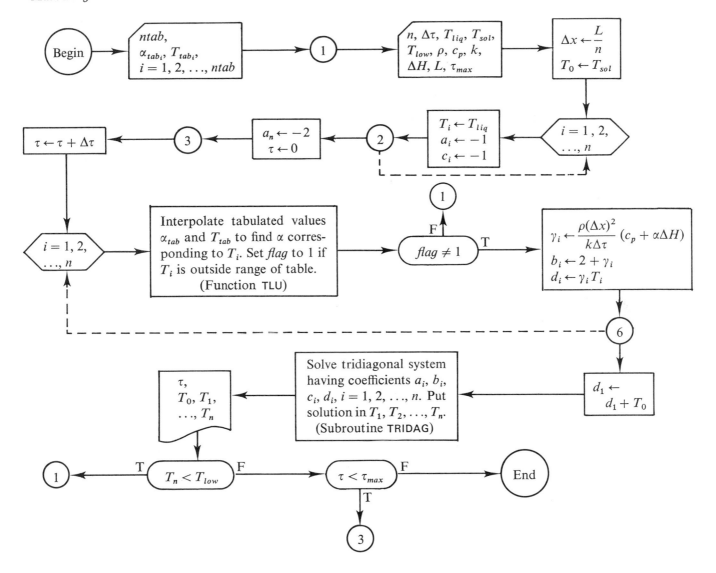

Function TLU (Dummy arguments: *ntab*, *z*, *x*, x^*, *flag*;
calling arguments: *ntab*, α_{tab}, T_{tab}, T_i, *flag*)

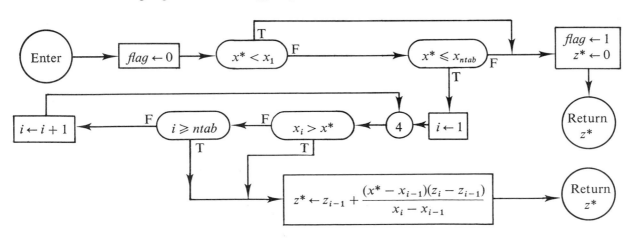

FORTRAN *Implementation*

Program Symbol (Main)	List of Principal Variables Definition
A, B, C, D	Coefficient vectors defined in equations (7.33).
ALFTAB	Vector of tabulated values, α_{tab}.
ALPHA	α, lb solid formed per °F fall in temperature per lb mixture of solid and liquid.
CP	Specific heat, c_p, BTU/lb °F.
DELTAH	Latent heat of fusion, ΔH, BTU/lb.
DTAU	Time-step, $\Delta\tau$, hrs.
DX	Space increment, Δx, ft.
FACTOR	$\dfrac{\rho(\Delta x)^2}{k\,\Delta\tau}$.
GAMMA†	Vector containing values of γ_i at each grid point.
I	Grid-point subscript, i.
ICOUNT	Counter on the number of time-steps.
IFREQ	Number of time-steps between successive printings of temperatures.
K	Thermal conductivity, k, BTU/hr ft °F.
L	Length of ingot, L, ft.
N	Number of intervals, n, into which the ingot is divided by the grid points.
NTABLE	Number of tabulated values of α and T, *ntab*.
RHO	Density, ρ, lb/cu ft.
T†	Vector of temperatures, T, °F.
TAU	Time, τ, hrs.
TAUMAX	Maximum value of time, τ_{max}, for which temperatures are to be computed.
TLIQ	Initial temperature, T_{liq}, °F.
TLOW	Lowest temperature at $x = L$ that is of interest, T_{low}, °F.
TLU	Table look-up function.
TRIDAG	Subroutine for solving tridiagonal system of equations (see Example 7.2).
TSOL	Applied surface temperature, T_{sol}, °F.
TTAB	Vector of tabulated values of temperature, T_{tab}.
(Function TLU)	
FLAG	A flag that is set to 1 if x^* is outside the range of tabulated values; otherwise, it is set to 0.
X, Z	Vectors of tabulated values of x and z.
XSTAR	Specified value, x^*. The corresponding value z^* is required.

† Because of FORTRAN limitations, subscripts on γ and T in the text are advanced by one when they appear in the program; e.g., T_0 through T_n become T(1) through T(N+1).

Example 7.4   Unsteady-State Heat Conduction in a Solidifying Alloy   **469**

Program Listing

Main Program

```
C           APPLIED NUMERICAL METHODS, EXAMPLE 7.4
C           SOLIDIFICATION OF AN ALLOY INGOT.
C
C           PROBLEM IN UNSTEADY-STATE HEAT CONDUCTION, WITH A LATENT
C           HEAT EFFECT, LEADING TO A NON-LINEAR PARTIAL DIFFERENTIAL
C           EQUATION.   A ONE-DIMENSIONAL MOLD, EXTENDING FROM X = 0
C           TO X = L FT., IS INITIALLY FILLED WITH A MOLTEN ALLOY AT
C           TLIQ DEGREES.   THE FACE X = L FT. IS INSULATED AND
C           THE FACE X = 0 FT. IS MAINTAINED AT TSOL DEGREES.    THE
C           FOLLOWING PROGRAM USES AN IMPLICIT FINITE-DIFFERENCE
C           SCHEME TO DETERMINE TEMPERATURES (T) IN THE COOLING INGOT
C           AS A FUNCTION OF DISTANCE (X) AND TIME (TAU).    THE SUB-
C           ROUTINE TRIDAG IS EMPLOYED TO SOLVE THE TRIDIAGONAL
C           SYSTEM OF EQUATIONS RESULTING AT EACH TIME-STEP.
C
      INTEGER FLAG
      REAL K, L
      DIMENSION A(20), B(20), C(20), D(20), GAMMA(20), T(20),
     1 ALFTAB(50), TTAB(50)
C
C     ..... READ AND CHECK TABLE LOOK-UP INFORMATION .....
      READ (5,100) NTABLE, (ALFTAB(I), I = 1, NTABLE)
      READ (5,101) (TTAB(I), I = 1, NTABLE)
      WRITE (6,200) NTABLE, (ALFTAB(I), I = 1, NTABLE)
      WRITE (6,201) (TTAB(I), I = 1, NTABLE)
C
C     ..... READ AND CHECK VALUES FOR EACH PARTICULAR RUN .....
    1 READ (5,102) N, IFREQ, DTAU, TLIQ, TSOL, TLOW, RHO, CP, K,
     1 DELTAH, L, TAUMAX
      WRITE (6,202) N, IFREQ, DTAU, TLIQ, TSOL, TLOW, RHO, CP, K,
     1 DELTAH, L, TAUMAX
C
C     ..... COMPUTE CONSTANTS AND SET INITIAL TEMPERATURES .....
      NP1 = N + 1
      FN = N
      DX = L/FN
      FACTOR = (RHO/K)*DX*DX/DTAU
      T(1) = TSOL
      DO 2  I = 2, NP1
      T(I) = TLIQ
      A(I) = - 1.0
    2 C(I) = - 1.0
      A(NP1) = - 2.0
      WRITE (6,203)
      ICOUNT = 0
      TAU = 0.0
      WRITE (6,204) TAU, (T(I), I = 1, NP1)
C
C     ..... COMPUTE NEW TEMPERATURES BY IMPLICIT METHOD .....
    3 TAU = TAU + DTAU
      ICOUNT = ICOUNT + 1
C
C     ..... TABLE LOOK-UP FOR ALPHA AND HENCE GAMMA(I) .....
      DO 6  I = 2, NP1
      ALPHA = TLU (NTABLE, ALFTAB, TTAB, T(I), FLAG)
      IF (FLAG .NE. 1) GO TO 5
         WRITE (6,205)
         GO TO 1
    5 GAMMA(I) = FACTOR*(CP + ALPHA*DELTAH)
C
C     ..... UPDATE TRIDIAGONAL COEFFICIENTS
C           AND COMPUTE NEW TEMPERATURES .....
      B(I) = 2.0 + GAMMA(I)
    6 D(I) = GAMMA(I)*T(I)
      D(2) = D(2) + T(1)
      CALL TRIDAG (2, NP1, A, B, C, D, T)
```

Program Listing (*Continued*)

```
C
C         ..... PRINT TEMPERATURES WHEN APPROPRIATE .....
          IF ((ICOUNT/IFREQ)*IFREQ .NE. ICOUNT) GO TO 8
          WRITE (6,204) TAU, (T(I), I = 1, NP1)
      8   CONTINUE
C
C         ..... HAS END TEMPERATURE FALLEN BELOW LOWER LIMIT .....
          IF (T(NP1) .LT. TLOW) GO TO 1
C
C         ..... CHECK TO SEE IF TIME HAS EXCEEDED ITS UPPER LIMIT .....
          IF (TAU - TAUMAX) 3, 1, 1
C
C         ..... FORMATS FOR INPUT AND OUTPUT STATEMENTS .....
  100   FORMAT (/ I10/ (7F10.8))
  101   FORMAT (7F10.6)
  102   FORMAT (7X, I4, 12X, I3/ 4(11X, F9.4))
  200   FORMAT (1H1, 4X, 48H UNSTEADY HEAT CONDUCTION IN A SOLIDIFYING ING
         1OT/1H0, 6X, 10H NTABLE = , I5/1H0,
         2 4X, 58H TABULATED VALUES OF ALPHA, ALFTAB(1)...ALFTAB(NTABLE) ARE
         3/1H0/(8X, 7F10.5))
  201   FORMAT (1H0, 4X, 61H TABULATED VALUES OF TEMPERATURE, TTAB(1)...TT
         1AB(NTABLE), ARE// (8X, 7F10.3))
  202   FORMAT (1H1, 4X, 31H THE PROBLEM WILL BE SOLVED FOR/1H0,
         1 6X, 10H N     = , I5/ 7X, 10H IFREQ  = , I5/
         2 7X, 10H DTAU  = , F10.4/ 7X, 10H TLIQ   = , F10.4/
         3 7X, 10H TSOL  = , F10.4/ 7X, 10H TLOW   = , F10.4/
         4 7X, 10H RHO   = , F10.4/ 7X, 10H CP     = , F10.4/
         5 7X, 10H K     = , F10.4/ 7X, 10H DELTAH = , F10.4/
         6 7X, 10H L     = , F10.4/ 7X, 10H TAUMAX = , F10.4)
  203   FORMAT (1H1, 4X, 53H FOLLOWING TABLE GIVES TEMPERATURES AT ALL GRI
         1DPOINTS /1H0, 4X, 5H TIME, 22X, 45H TEMPERATURES (X = 0 TO INSULAT
         2ED FACE X = L))
  204   FORMAT (5X, F5.2/ (10X, 11F8.2))
  205   FORMAT (1H0, 4X, 26H SCOPE OF TABLE INADEQUATE)
C
          END
```

Function TLU

```
C         ONE-DIMENSIONAL TABLE LOOK-UP PROGRAM.   CORRESPONDING VALUES
C         OF X (ALWAYS INCREASING) AND Z ARE STORED IN THE ARRAYS
C         X(1)...X(NTABLE) AND Z(1)...Z(NTABLE).   USING LINEAR INTER-
C         POLATION, THIS FUNCTION WILL GENERATE A VALUE OF Z CORRESPON-
C         DING TO A SPECIFIED VALUE OF X = XSTAR.
C
          FUNCTION TLU (NTABLE, Z, X, XSTAR, FLAG)
          INTEGER FLAG
          DIMENSION X(1), Z(1)
C
C         ..... CHECK TO SEE IF XSTAR LIES WITHIN THE SCOPE
C               OF THE TABULATED VALUES X(1)...X(NTABLE) .....
          FLAG = 0
          IF (XSTAR .LT. X(1)) GO TO 2
          IF (XSTAR .LE. X(NTABLE)) GO TO 3
      2   FLAG = 1
          TLU = 0.0
          RETURN
C
C         ..... SEARCH TO FIND TWO SUCCESSIVE ENTRIES,
C               X(I-1) AND X(I), BETWEEN WHICH XSTAR LIES .....
      3   I = 1
      4   IF (X(I) .GT. XSTAR) GO TO 7
          IF (I .GE. NTABLE) GO TO 7
          I = I + 1
          GO TO 4
C
C         ..... LINEARLY INTERPOLATE TO FIND CORRESPONDING VALUE OF Z .....
      7   TLU = Z(I-1) + (XSTAR - X(I-1))*(Z(I) - Z(I-1))/(X(I) - X(I-1))
          RETURN
C
          END
```

Example 7.4   Unsteady-State Heat Conduction in a Solidifying Alloy   **471**

Program Listing (*Continued*)

Data

```
VALUES OF NTABLE, AND ALFTAB AND TTAB VECTORS ARE
      26
0.0119     0.0102     0.00874    0.00756    0.00657    0.00575    0.00509
0.00454    0.00412    0.00375    0.00341    0.00315    0.00291    0.00270
0.00252    0.00238    0.00223    0.00211    0.00200    0.00190    0.00181
0.00173    0.00167    0.00160    0.00153    0.00147
150.0      160.0      170.0      180.0      190.0      200.0      210.0
220.0      230.0      240.0      250.0      260.0      270.0      280.0
290.0      300.0      310.0      320.0      330.0      340.0      350.0
360.0      370.0      380.0      390.0      400.0
      N  =  10     IFREQ  =  1
      DTAU    =     5.0       TLIQ   =   400.0     TSOL  =   150.0     TLOW  =   200.0
      RHO     =   540.0       CP     =   0.038     K     =    10.1     DELTAH =  120.0
      L       =     2.0       TAUMAX =   100.0
```

Computer Output

```
UNSTEADY HEAT CONDUCTION IN A SOLIDIFYING INGOT

   NTABLE =    26

TABULATED VALUES OF ALPHA, ALFTAB(1)...ALFTAB(NTABLE) ARE

      0.01190    0.01020    0.00874    0.00756    0.00657    0.00575    0.00509
      0.00454    0.00412    0.00375    0.00341    0.00315    0.00291    0.00270
      0.00252    0.00238    0.00223    0.00211    0.00200    0.00190    0.00181
      0.00173    0.00167    0.00160    0.00153    0.00147

TABULATED VALUES OF TEMPERATURE, TTAB(1)...TTAB(NTABLE), ARE

      150.000    160.000    170.000    180.000    190.000    200.000    210.000
      220.000    230.000    240.000    250.000    260.000    270.000    280.000
      290.000    300.000    310.000    320.000    330.000    340.000    350.000
      360.000    370.000    380.000    390.000    400.000


THE PROBLEM WILL BE SOLVED FOR

   N       =       10
   IFREQ   =        1
   DTAU    =        5.0000
   TLIQ    =      400.0000
   TSOL    =      150.0000
   TLOW    =      200.0000
   RHO     =      540.0000
   CP      =        0.0380
   K       =       10.1000
   DELTAH  =      120.0000
   L       =        2.0000
   TAUMAX  =      100.0000



FOLLOWING TABLE GIVES TEMPERATURES AT ALL GRIDPOINTS

   TIME                  TEMPERATURES (X = 0 TO INSULATED FACE X = L)
   0.0
        150.00  400.00  400.00  400.00  400.00  400.00  400.00  400.00  400.00  400.00  400.00
   5.00
        150.00  214.74  262.49  297.63  323.39  342.12  355.54  364.88  371.00  374.46  375.58
  10.00
        150.00  192.17  228.39  258.64  283.42  303.30  318.81  330.39  338.40  343.09  344.64
  15.00
        150.00  182.62  211.94  237.47  259.19  277.23  291.74  302.85  310.69  315.35  316.90
  20.00
        150.00  176.93  201.65  223.56  242.50  258.45  271.44  281.50  288.65  292.94  294.36
  25.00
        150.00  173.00  194.34  213.44  230.09  244.22  255.77  264.76  271.18  275.04  276.32
```

Computer Output (*Continued*)

```
30.00
        150.00  170.05  188.78  205.65  220.44  233.03  243.36  251.42  257.18  260.64  261.79
35.00
        150.00  167.73  184.37  199.43  212.67  223.99  233.29  240.55  245.75  248.88  249.92
40.00
        150.00  165.84  180.77  194.33  206.29  216.52  224.96  231.55  236.27  239.10  240.05
45.00
        150.00  164.28  177.77  190.07  200.94  210.26  217.95  223.97  228.29  230.88  231.75
50.00
        150.00  162.95  175.23  186.45  196.38  204.91  211.97  217.49  221.46  223.85  224.64
55.00
        150.00  161.82  173.05  183.33  192.46  200.31  206.81  211.90  215.56  217.76  218.49
60.00
        150.00  160.84  171.15  180.63  189.05  196.30  202.31  207.02  210.41  212.45  213.13
65.00
        150.00  159.98  169.49  178.25  186.05  192.78  198.36  202.74  205.89  207.78  208.42
70.00
        150.00  159.22  168.03  176.15  183.40  189.67  194.86  198.94  201.88  203.65  204.24
75.00
        150.00  158.55  166.73  174.28  181.04  186.89  191.74  195.56  198.31  199.96  200.51
80.00
        150.00  157.95  165.56  172.61  178.92  184.39  188.94  192.52  195.09  196.65  197.16
```

Example 7.4 Unsteady-State Heat Conduction in a Solidifying Alloy   **473**

Discussion of Results

This example has illustrated a finite-difference technique for solving a nonlinear PDE. In the present case, the nonlinearity has presented little complication.

The printout is for $n = 10$ and $\Delta\tau = 5$ hr; the resulting temperature profiles at $\tau = 0$, 5, 20 and 80 hr are plotted in Fig. 7.4.3. In order to investigate the effect of grid-spacing and time-step on the results, runs have also been made for values of n ranging from 5 to 30 and for values of $\Delta\tau$ ranging from 0.1 to 5 hr. The times taken for the end temperature to fall to 200°F have always agreed with one another to within 2%.

The above situation has obviously been idealised; more realistically, in alloy-casting practice, it is likely that heat conduction into the mold will be important and that appreciably higher temperatures will be involved.

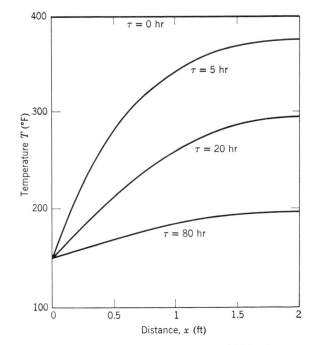

Figure 7.4.3   Temperature profiles in solidifying ingot.

EXAMPLE 7.5

NATURAL CONVECTION AT A HEATED VERTICAL PLATE

Introduction

The following is an example involving the solution of a set of three, simultaneous, nonlinear partial differential equations, employing an explicit technique.

Consider the problem, shown in Fig. 7.5.1, involving a semiinfinite heated vertical plate situated in an infinite

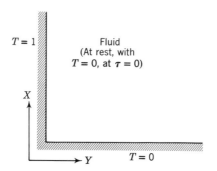

Figure 7.5.1 Heated vertical plate.

fluid that is initially cold and at rest. By taking the equations of momentum, energy, and continuity of a simplified boundary-layer type, by assuming the fluid to be incompressible except for a temperature-dependent buoyant effect, and by defining an appropriate dimensionless temperature T and dimensionless X and Y velocities U and V, Hellums [11] has shown that the governing equations are:

$$Momentum: \quad \frac{\partial U}{\partial \tau} + U\frac{\partial U}{\partial X} + V\frac{\partial U}{\partial Y} = T + \frac{\partial^2 U}{\partial Y^2}, \quad (7.5.1)$$

$$Energy: \quad \frac{\partial T}{\partial \tau} + U\frac{\partial T}{\partial X} + V\frac{\partial T}{\partial Y} = \frac{1}{Pr}\frac{\partial^2 T}{\partial Y^2}, \quad (7.5.2)$$

$$Continuity: \quad \frac{\partial U}{\partial X} + \frac{\partial V}{\partial Y} = 0, \quad (7.5.3)$$

where τ, X, and Y are dimensionless time and distance coordinates, respectively, and Pr is the Prandtl number of the fluid. Equations (7.5.1), (7.5.2), and (7.5.3) are subject to the initial and boundary conditions:

$$\left.\begin{array}{llll} X = 0: & U = V = T = 0, \\ Y = 0: & U = V = 0, T = 1, \\ Y = \infty: & U = V = T = 0, \\ \tau = 0: & U = V = T = 0. \end{array}\right\} \quad (7.5.4)$$

The first of these conditions corresponds to an unheated horizontal plate at $X = 0$.

Problem Statement

Solve the three simultaneous nonlinear PDEs (7.5.1), (7.5.2), and (7.5.3) for the dependent variables U, V, and T as functions of X, Y, and τ. In particular, obtain the final steady-state solution, if such exists.

Method of Solution

Although the primary goal is to obtain the steady-state solution, for which both $\partial U/\partial \tau$ and $\partial T/\partial \tau$ are zero, one way such a solution may be achieved is by considering the corresponding unsteady-state problem, already formulated above. Successive steps in time may then be regarded as successive approximations towards the final steady-state solution.

The space under investigation must be restricted to finite dimensions. Here, we consider a plate of height X_{max} ($=100$), and regard $Y = Y_{max}$ ($=25$) as corresponding to $Y = \infty$. As shown in Fig. 7.5.2, there are m and n grid spacings in the X and Y directions, respectively.

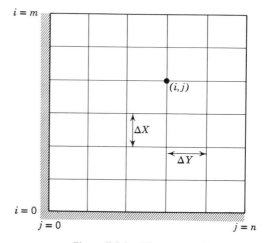

Figure 7.5.2 The space grid.

For simplicity, an explicit method will be used. Let U', V', and T' denote the values of U, V, and T at the end of a time-step. Then an appropriate set of finite-difference equations corresponding to equations (7.5.1), (7.5.2), and (7.5.3) is

$$\frac{U'_{i,j} - U_{i,j}}{\Delta \tau} + U_{i,j}\frac{U_{i,j} - U_{i-1,j}}{\Delta X} + V_{i,j}\frac{U_{i,j+1} - U_{i,j}}{\Delta Y}$$
$$= T'_{i,j} + \frac{U_{i,j+1} - 2U_{i,j} + U_{i,j-1}}{(\Delta Y)^2}, \quad (7.5.1a)$$

$$\frac{T'_{i,j} - T_{i,j}}{\Delta \tau} + U_{i,j}\frac{T_{i,j} - T_{i-1,j}}{\Delta X} + V_{i,j}\frac{T_{i,j+1} - T_{i,j}}{\Delta Y}$$
$$= \frac{1}{Pr}\frac{T_{i,j+1} - 2T_{i,j} + T_{i,j-1}}{(\Delta Y)^2}, \quad (7.5.2a)$$

$$\frac{U'_{i,j} - U'_{i-1,j}}{\Delta X} + \frac{V'_{i,j} - V'_{i,j-1}}{\Delta Y} = 0. \quad (7.5.3a)$$

During any one time-step, the coefficients $U_{i,j}$ and $V_{i,j}$ appearing in (7.5.1a) and (7.5.2a) are treated as constants. Then, at the end of any time-step $\Delta \tau$, the new

Example 7.5   Natural Convection at a Heated Vertical Plate   **475**

temperatures T' and the new velocity components U' and V' at all interior grid points may be obtained by successive applications of (7.5.2a), (7.5.1a), and (7.5.3a), respectively. This process is repeated in time and, provided the time-step is sufficiently small, U, V, and T should eventually converge to values which approximate the steady-state solution of equations (7.5.1), (7.5.2), and (7.5.3).

Stability of the Finite-Difference Equations

Since an explicit procedure is being used, we wish to know the largest time-step consistent with stability. The stability analysis for simultaneous PDEs in an extension of that employed earlier for a single PDE and is outlined here.

Equation (7.5.3a) will be ignored since $\Delta \tau$ does not appear in it. The general terms of the Fourier expansion for U and T at a time arbitrarily called $t = 0$ are both $e^{i\alpha X} e^{i\beta Y}$, apart from a constant. (Here, $i = \sqrt{-1}$). At a time τ later, these terms will become:

$$U: \quad \psi(\tau) e^{i\alpha X} e^{i\beta Y}, \qquad T: \quad \zeta(\tau) e^{i\alpha X} e^{i\beta Y}.$$

Substituting in (7.5.1a) and (7.5.2a), regarding the co-efficients U and V as constants over any one time-step, and denoting values after the time-step by ψ' and ζ' gives, upon simplification,

$$\frac{\psi' - \psi}{\Delta \tau} + U \frac{\psi(1 - e^{-i\alpha \Delta X})}{\Delta X} + V \frac{\psi(e^{i\beta \Delta Y} - 1)}{\Delta Y}$$
$$= \zeta' + \frac{2\psi(\cos \beta \, \Delta Y - 1)}{(\Delta Y)^2} \quad (7.5.1b)$$

$$\frac{\zeta' - \zeta}{\Delta \tau} + U \frac{\zeta(1 - e^{i\alpha \Delta X})}{\Delta X} + V \frac{\zeta(e^{i\beta \Delta Y} - 1)}{\Delta Y}$$
$$= \frac{2\zeta}{Pr} \frac{(\cos \beta \, \Delta Y - 1)}{(\Delta Y)^2}. \quad (7.5.2b)$$

Now define the following:

$$A = 1 - \frac{U \Delta \tau}{\Delta X}(1 - e^{i\alpha \Delta X})$$
$$- \frac{V \Delta \tau}{\Delta Y}(e^{i\beta \Delta Y} - 1) + \frac{2 \Delta \tau}{(\Delta Y)^2}(\cos \beta \, \Delta Y - 1)$$

$$B = 1 - \frac{U \Delta \tau}{\Delta X}(1 - e^{i\alpha \Delta X})$$
$$- \frac{V \Delta \tau}{\Delta Y}(e^{i\beta \Delta Y} - 1) + \frac{1}{Pr} \frac{2 \Delta \tau}{(\Delta Y)^2}(\cos \beta \, \Delta Y - 1).$$

Equations (7.5.1b) and (7.5.2b) are then

$$\psi' = A\psi + \Delta \tau \zeta' = A\psi + B\Delta \tau \zeta$$
$$\zeta' = B\zeta.$$

Expressed in matrix notation,

$$\begin{bmatrix} \psi' \\ \zeta' \end{bmatrix} = \begin{bmatrix} A & B \Delta \tau \\ 0 & B \end{bmatrix} \begin{bmatrix} \psi \\ \zeta \end{bmatrix},$$

that is,

$$\boldsymbol{\eta}' = \mathbf{C}\boldsymbol{\eta},$$

where $\boldsymbol{\eta}$ is the column vector whose elements are ψ and ζ. For stability, each eigenvalue λ_1, λ_2 of the amplification matrix $\mathbf{C}$ must not exceed unity in modulus. But $\lambda_1 = A$ and $\lambda_2 = B$. Hence the stability condition is

$$|A| \leqslant 1 \quad \text{and} \quad |B| \leqslant 1, \quad \text{for all } \alpha, \beta.$$

Assume that U is everywhere nonnegative and that V is everywhere nonpositive. This is to be expected, since the heated fluid rises in the positive X direction and fluid is drawn in from the positive Y direction to take its place. In any case, the final results confirm this assumption. Define

$$a = \frac{U \Delta \tau}{\Delta X}, \qquad b = \frac{|V| \Delta \tau}{\Delta Y}, \qquad \text{and} \qquad c = \frac{\Delta \tau}{(\Delta Y)^2}.$$

Hence

$$A = (1 - a - b - 2c) + ae^{-i\alpha \Delta X} + be^{i\beta \Delta Y} + 2c \cos \beta \Delta Y.$$

The coefficients a, b, and c are all real and nonnegative. By representing A on an Argand diagram, we can demonstrate that the maximum modulus of A occurs when $\alpha \Delta x = m\pi$ and $\beta \Delta Y = n\pi$, where m and n are integers, and hence occurs when A is real. For $\Delta \tau$ sufficiently large, the value of $|A|$ is greatest when both m and n are odd integers, in which case

$$A = (1 - a - b - 2c) - a - b - 2c = 1 - 2(a + b + 2c),$$

which becomes increasingly more negative as $\Delta \tau$ increases. To satisfy $|A| \leqslant 1$, the most negative allowable value is $A = -1$. Hence the stability condition is that

$$2(a + b + 2c) \leqslant 2,$$

that is,

$$\frac{U \Delta \tau}{\Delta X} + \frac{|V| \Delta \tau}{\Delta Y} + \frac{2 \Delta \tau}{(\Delta Y)^2} \leqslant 1. \quad (7.5.5)$$

Likewise, the second condition $|B| \leqslant 1$ requires that

$$\frac{U \Delta \tau}{\Delta X} + \frac{|V| \Delta \tau}{\Delta Y} + \frac{1}{Pr} \frac{2 \Delta \tau}{(\Delta Y)^2} \leqslant 1. \quad (7.5.6)$$

In the present problem, with $Pr = 0.733$, we need only be concerned with satisfying (7.5.6), since (7.5.5) follows automatically. The coefficients U and $|V|$, although treated as constants over any one time-step, will vary from one time-step to the next in a manner which cannot be predicted *a priori*. That is, the maximum permissible time-step consistent with stability is itself variable, but its value can always be checked, during computation if necessary.

Flow Diagram

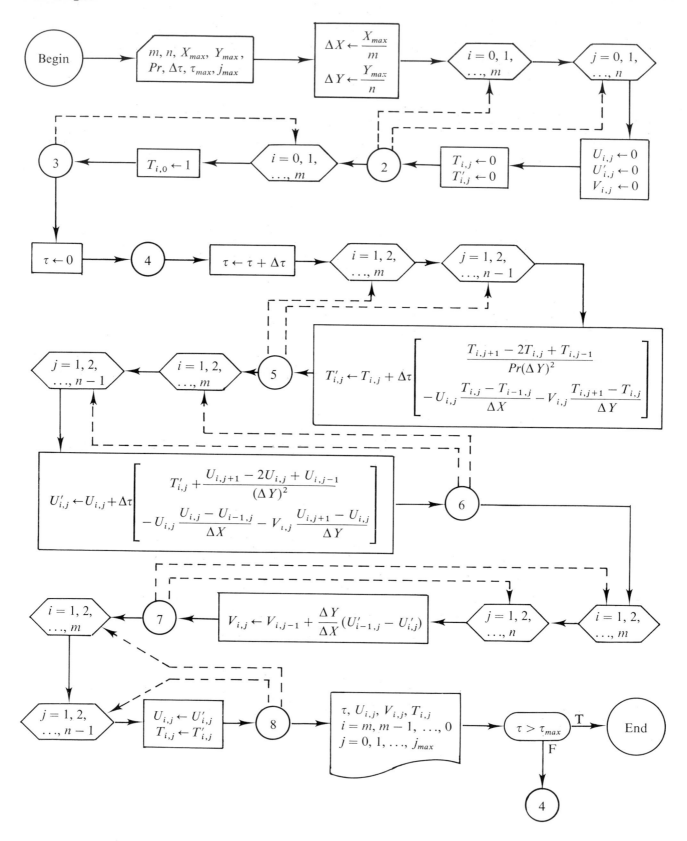

Example 7.5   Natural Convection at a Heated Vertical Plate   **477**

FORTRAN *Implementation*

List of Principal Variables

Program Symbol	Definition
DTAU	Time-step, $\Delta\tau$.
DX, DY	Space increments, ΔX and ΔY, respectively.
I, J	Grid-point subscripts, i, j.
ICOUNT	Counter on the number of time-steps.
IFREQ	Number of time-steps between successive printings of temperatures.
JMAX	Largest column subscript, j_{max}, for which printout is requested, in case n is too large for the width of the page.
M, N	Number of grid spacings m, n, in the X and Y directions, respectively.
PR	Prandtl number, Pr.
T, TNEW	Matrices of temperatures, T, T', at the beginning and end of a time-step, respectively.
TAU	Time, τ.
TAUMAX	Largest value of τ to be considered.
U, V	Matrices of velocities U and V in the X and Y directions, respectively.
UNEW	Matrix of velocities U' at the end of a time-step.
XMAX	Height of the plate, X_{max}.
YMAX	Maximum distance from the plate, Y_{max}.

Because of FORTRAN limitations, all subscripts in the text have been advanced by one in the program; e.g., $T_{m,n}$ becomes T(M + 1, N + 1).

Program Listing

```
C              APPLIED NUMERICAL METHODS, EXAMPLE 7.5
C              FREE CONVECTION AT A HEATED VERTICAL PLATE.
C
C              THE EQUATIONS OF MOTION (SIMPLIFIED BOUNDARY LAYER TYPE),
C              ENERGY AND CONTINUITY ARE SOLVED USING AN EXPLICIT PROCEDURE.
C
       DIMENSION U(41,41), UNEW(41,41), V(41,41), T(41,41), TNEW(41,41)
C
C      ..... READ AND CHECK INPUT PARAMETERS, AND COMPUTE CONSTANTS .....
     1 READ (5,100) M, N, IFREQ, JMAX, XMAX, YMAX, PR, DTAU, TAUMAX
       JMAXP1 = JMAX + 1
       MP1 = M + 1
       NP1 = N + 1
       FLOATM = M
       FLOATN = N
       DX = XMAX/FLOATM
       DY = YMAX/FLOATN
       DYSQ = DY*DY
       DYSQPR = DYSQ*PR
       YOVERX = DY/DX
       WRITE (6,200) M, N, IFREQ, JMAX, XMAX, YMAX, PR, DTAU, TAUMAX
C
C      ..... INITIALIZE VELOCITIES AND TEMPERATURES .....
       ICOUNT = 0
       DO 2  I = 1, MP1
       DO 2  J = 1, NP1
       U(I,J) = 0.0
       UNEW(I,J) = 0.0
       V(I,J) = 0.0
       T(I,J) = 0.0
     2 TNEW(I,J) = 0.0
       DO 3  I = 1, MP1
     3 T(I,1) = 1.0
C
C      ..... PERFORM CALCULATIONS OVER SUCCESSIVE TIME-STEPS .....
       TAU = 0.0
     4 TAU = TAU + DTAU
       ICOUNT = ICOUNT + 1
C
C      ..... CALCULATE NEW TEMPERATURES .....
       DO 5  I = 2, MP1
       DO 5  J = 2, N
     5 TNEW(I,J) = T(I,J) + DTAU*
     1             (((T(I,J+1) - 2.0*T(I,J) + T(I,J-1))/DYSQPR)
     2             - (U(I,J)*(T(I,J) - T(I-1,J))/DX)
     3             - (V(I,J)*(T(I,J+1) - T(I,J))/DY))
C
C      ..... CALCULATE NEW U VELOCITIES .....
       DO 6  I = 2, MP1
       DO 6  J = 2, N
     6 UNEW(I,J) = U(I,J) + DTAU*
     1             (((U(I,J+1) - 2.0*U(I,J) + U(I,J-1))/DYSQ)
     2             - (U(I,J)*(U(I,J) - U(I-1,J))/DX)
     3             - (V(I,J)*(U(I,J+1) - U(I,J))/DY) + TNEW(I,J))
C
C      ..... CALCULATE NEW V VELOCITIES .....
       DO 7  I = 2, MP1
       DO 7  J = 2, NP1
     7 V(I,J) = V(I,J-1) + YOVERX*(UNEW(I-1,J) - UNEW(I,J))
C
C      ..... SUBSTITUTE UNEW INTO U, AND TNEW INTO T .....
       DO 8  I = 2, MP1
       DO 8  J = 2, N
       U(I,J) = UNEW(I,J)
     8 T(I,J) = TNEW(I,J)
```

Example 7.5   Natural Convection at a Heated Vertical Plate   **479**

Program Listing (*Continued*)

```
C
C      ..... PRINT U, V AND T FIELDS WHEN APPROPRIATE .....
       IF (ICOUNT .NE. IFREQ) GO TO 13
          ICOUNT = 0
          WRITE (6,201) TAU
          WRITE (6,202)
          DO 10  K = 1, MP1
          I = MP1 - K + 1
   10     WRITE (6,205) (U(I,J), J = 1, JMAXP1)
          WRITE (6,203)
          DO 11  K = 1, MP1
          I = MP1 - K + 1
   11     WRITE (6,205) (V(I,J), J = 1, JMAXP1)
          WRITE (6,204)
          DO 12  K = 1, MP1
          I = MP1 - K + 1
   12     WRITE (6,205) (T(I,J), J = 1, JMAXP1)
   13  IF (TAU - TAUMAX) 4, 4, 1
C
C      ..... FORMATS FOR INPUT AND OUTPUT STATEMENTS .....
  100  FORMAT (3(10X, I3), 13X, I5, 15X, F8.2/ 4(12X, F8.3))
  200  FORMAT (56H1     FREE CONVECTION AT A VERTICAL PLATE, WITH PARAMETER
      1S/ 12H0     M     = , I4/ 12H      N     = , I4/
      2 12H      IFREQ = , I4/ 12H      JMAX  = , I4/
      3 12H      XMAX  = , F10.5/ 12H      YMAX  = , F10.5/
      4 12H      PR    = , F10.5/ 12H      DTAU  = , F10.5/
      5 13H      TAUMAX = , F9.5)
  201  FORMAT (25H1            AT A TIME TAU = , F8.3)
  202  FORMAT (45H0          THE FIELD OF VELOCITY COMPONENT U IS/1H /)
  203  FORMAT (45H0          THE FIELD OF VELOCITY COMPONENT V IS/1H /)
  204  FORMAT (33H0          THE TEMPERATURE FIELD IS/1H /)
  205  FORMAT (4H    , 11F8.3)
C
       END
```

Data

```
M   = 10    N  =  10   IFREQ = 20    JMAX   =   10     XMAX  =  100.0
YMAX = 25.0          PR  =  0.733   DTAU   =   0.5     TAUMAX =  80.05
```

Computer Output

```
FREE CONVECTION AT A VERTICAL PLATE, WITH PARAMETERS

M      =     10
N      =     10
IFREQ  =     20
JMAX   =     10
XMAX   =    100.00000
YMAX   =     25.00000
PR     =      0.73300
DTAU   =      0.50000
TAUMAX =     80.04999

   AT A TIME TAU =    80.000

   THE FIELD OF VELOCITY COMPONENT U IS

0.0    4.470   5.027   4.067   2.862   1.855   1.123   0.628   0.308   0.112   0.0
0.0    4.269   4.713   3.748   2.598   1.661   0.992   0.548   0.266   0.096   0.0
0.0    4.050   4.377   3.415   2.327   1.464   0.862   0.470   0.225   0.080   0.0
0.0    3.808   4.015   3.064   2.048   1.266   0.734   0.393   0.186   0.065   0.0
0.0    3.539   3.623   2.696   1.761   1.067   0.606   0.319   0.148   0.051   0.0
0.0    3.232   3.195   2.306   1.468   0.867   0.482   0.248   0.113   0.038   0.0
0.0    2.875   2.720   1.893   1.167   0.669   0.362   0.181   0.081   0.027   0.0
0.0    2.446   2.187   1.454   0.860   0.475   0.248   0.120   0.052   0.017   0.0
0.0    1.904   1.577   0.986   0.553   0.290   0.144   0.067   0.027   0.009   0.0
0.0    1.164   0.861   0.493   0.255   0.124   0.057   0.024   0.009   0.003   0.0
0.0    0.0     0.0     0.0     0.0     0.0     0.0     0.0     0.0     0.0     0.0

   THE FIELD OF VELOCITY COMPONENT V IS

0.0   -0.050  -0.129  -0.209  -0.275  -0.323  -0.356  -0.376  -0.386  -0.390  -0.390
0.0   -0.055  -0.139  -0.222  -0.290  -0.339  -0.372  -0.391  -0.401  -0.405  -0.405
0.0   -0.060  -0.151  -0.238  -0.308  -0.357  -0.390  -0.409  -0.419  -0.422  -0.422
0.0   -0.067  -0.165  -0.258  -0.329  -0.379  -0.411  -0.429  -0.439  -0.442  -0.442
0.0   -0.077  -0.184  -0.281  -0.355  -0.405  -0.436  -0.453  -0.462  -0.465  -0.465
0.0   -0.089  -0.208  -0.311  -0.386  -0.436  -0.466  -0.483  -0.491  -0.494  -0.494
0.0   -0.107  -0.241  -0.350  -0.427  -0.475  -0.504  -0.519  -0.526  -0.529  -0.529
0.0   -0.135  -0.288  -0.405  -0.482  -0.528  -0.554  -0.567  -0.573  -0.576  -0.576
0.0   -0.185  -0.364  -0.487  -0.562  -0.603  -0.625  -0.635  -0.640  -0.641  -0.641
0.0   -0.291  -0.506  -0.630  -0.693  -0.724  -0.739  -0.745  -0.747  -0.748  -0.748
0.0    0.0     0.0     0.0     0.0     0.0     0.0     0.0     0.0     0.0     0.0

   THE TEMPERATURE FIELD IS

1.000  0.704   0.450   0.269   0.155   0.087   0.047   0.025   0.012   0.004   0.0
1.000  0.696   0.437   0.257   0.145   0.080   0.043   0.022   0.011   0.004   0.0
1.000  0.685   0.423   0.243   0.135   0.073   0.039   0.020   0.009   0.003   0.0
1.000  0.673   0.406   0.228   0.124   0.066   0.034   0.017   0.008   0.003   0.0
1.000  0.658   0.386   0.211   0.112   0.058   0.030   0.015   0.007   0.002   0.0
1.000  0.640   0.362   0.192   0.099   0.050   0.025   0.012   0.005   0.002   0.0
1.000  0.615   0.332   0.169   0.084   0.041   0.020   0.009   0.004   0.001   0.0
1.000  0.579   0.294   0.142   0.067   0.032   0.015   0.007   0.003   0.001   0.0
1.000  0.522   0.241   0.108   0.048   0.022   0.010   0.004   0.002   0.001   0.0
1.000  0.406   0.159   0.064   0.026   0.011   0.004   0.002   0.001   0.000   0.0
1.000  0.0     0.0     0.0     0.0     0.0     0.0     0.0     0.0     0.0     0.0
```

Example 7.5   Natural Convection at a Heated Vertical Plate   **481**

Discussion of Results

The velocity and temperature fields are reproduced above only for $\tau = 80$. An examination of the complete printout, for $\tau = 10, 20, \ldots, 80$, shows little change in U, V, and T after $\tau = 40$ has been reached. Thus the results for $\tau = 80$ are essentially steady-state values. The computations are for a 10×10 grid; the value $Pr = 0.733$ is that for air chosen by several previous investigators. In each case, the first column of figures corresponds to the vertical plate, and the extreme right-hand column corresponds to $Y = 25$. All the values of V are negative, indicating that the horizontal velocity component is always directed towards the plate. The vertical velocity component U reaches a maximum a little way out from the plate, except near the bottom of the plate, and then decreases. The temperature T decreases monotonically away from the plate.

We can compare these results with those computed by Hellums [11] on a 39×39 grid with $\Delta\tau = 0.1$; his values agree almost perfectly with the analytical solution to the problem given by Ostrach [18]. For $X = 100$, representative steady-state values are given in Table 7.5.1; Hellums' results have been interpolated to correspond to the present grid.

The accuracy of the present results may be described as good, fair, or poor, depending on whether one is interested in the values of T, U, or V. However, note that the number of computations involved here (10×10 grid, $\Delta\tau = 0.5$) is roughly only one seventieth of the number required for a 39×39 grid with $\Delta\tau = 0.1$.

Note: It may easily be verified by subsitution that the new dependent variables $U/X^{1/2}$ and $VX^{1/4}$, together with T, are functions of just *two* new independent variables, namely, $Y/X^{1/4}$ and $\tau/X^{1/2}$. Thus the above results may be condensed very considerably, if required.

Table 7.5.1   Comparison of Steady-State Results for 10×10 Grid with Analytical Solution

Y		0	2.5	5.0	7.5	10.0	12.5	15.0
Analytical	U	0	4.65	5.29	4.15	2.78	1.65	0.92
solution (same	V	0	−0.030	−0.097	−0.177	−0.251	−0.305	−0.342
as 39×39 grid)	T	1	0.713	0.461	0.270	0.149	0.077	0.040
Results computed	U	0	4.47	5.03	4.08	2.87	1.86	1.13
for	V	0	−0.051	−0.130	−0.210	−0.276	−0.325	−0.358
10×10 grid	T	1	0.705	0.451	0.270	0.156	0.088	0.049

7.21 Derivation of the Elliptic Difference Equation

Let R be a finite connected region in the xy − plane, and let S denote the boundary of R (see Fig. 7.12).

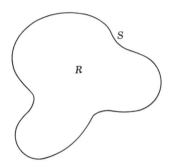

Figure 7.12   Region and boundary.

We seek to determine a numerical approximation v of the solution $u(x,y)$ of the boundary-value problem

$$\text{div}[k(x,y) \text{ grad } u] - C(x,y)u = f(x,y),$$

$$(x,y) \text{ in } R, \qquad (7.70)$$

$$u(x,y) = g(x,y), \qquad (x,y) \text{ on } S, \qquad (7.71)$$

where $k(x,y) > 0$ and $C(x,y) \geqslant 0$ in R.

An equation such as (7.70) would arise for steady-state heat conduction in a flat plate, whose thermal conductivity k depends on position, with an internal heat source (represented by f) and a heat-transfer effect at the surface of the plate (represented by C). Observe that the elliptic problem is time-independent.

We introduce a rectangular grid on the region R, so that every point (i,j) has four neighbors, as shown in Fig. 7.13.

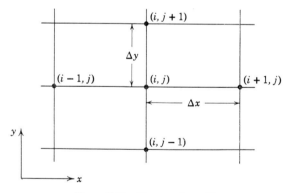

Figure 7.13   Rectangular grid.

It is a matter of convenience, but not of necessity, to make the grid spacings equal in the x and y directions. In the development that follows, we will assume that $\Delta x = \Delta y$, unless it is stated otherwise. A point (i,j) of the grid is said to be an *interior* point if its four neighbours lie within R, or on S, but not outside S. Other points

lying within R or on S, but which are not interior points, are called *boundary* points (see Fig. 7.14).

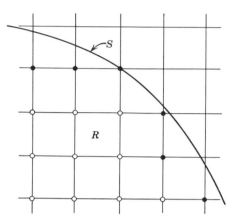

Figure 7.14   Interior ($\bigcirc$) and boundary ($\bullet$) points.

We then approximate the PDE of (7.70) at each interior point of the grid by the difference equation

$$\delta_x(k_{i,j}\delta_x v_{i,j}) + \delta_y(k_{i,j}\delta_y v_{i,j}) - C_{i,j}v_{i,j} = f_{i,j}, \quad (7.72)$$

where $k_{i,j} = k(i \Delta x, j \Delta y)$ and $C_{i,j} = C(i \Delta x, j \Delta y)$. At each boundary point of the grid, we set

$$v_{i,j} = g(\bar{i},\bar{j}), \qquad (7.73)$$

where $(\bar{i},\bar{j})$ is any point on S within a distance Δx of the boundary point (i, j).

In the general case, we order the points on the grid by assigning to each in succession an ordinal number k, and indicating it by P_k; we redesignate the value of v at this point by v_k. If the total number of interior points of the grid in R is n, it is convenient to number the points so that P_k is an interior point if and only if $1 \leqslant k \leqslant n$.

We then eliminate from the finite-difference equations the values of v at the boundary points by using the values prescribed in (7.73). We are then left with a system of n linear equations in the n values v_k, $k = 1,2, \ldots, n$ for the approximate function at the interior points. By defining the vector

$$\mathbf{v} = \begin{bmatrix} v_1 \\ v_2 \\ \vdots \\ v_n \end{bmatrix}, \qquad (7.74)$$

we can write this system of equations in the form

$$\mathbf{Av} = \mathbf{b}, \qquad (7.75)$$

where $\mathbf{A}$ is an $n \times n$ matrix whose entries are determined by the coefficients of the difference equation, and where the vector $\mathbf{b}$ is determined by the prescribed boundary values and the known terms in the differential equation. We are then left with the problem of solving (7.75) for $\mathbf{v}$.

7.22 Laplace's Equation in a Rectangle

As a special case, consider the problem of (7.70) and (7.71) in the rectangular region $R: 0 \leqslant x \leqslant \alpha, 0 \leqslant y \leqslant \beta$ (for simplicity, α and β are assumed to be in the ratio of two moderately small integers). We have:

$$\frac{\partial^2 u}{\partial x^2} + \frac{\partial^2 u}{\partial y^2} = 0 \text{ in } R, \qquad (7.76)$$

$$u(x,y) = g(x,y) \text{ on } S. \qquad (7.77)$$

Then, with integers M_x and M_y chosen so that

$$\Delta x = \frac{\alpha}{M_x} = \Delta y = \frac{\beta}{M_y}, \qquad (7.78)$$

we have the finite-difference problem

$$\frac{v_{i-1,j} - 2v_{i,j} + v_{i+1,j}}{(\Delta x)^2} + \frac{v_{i,j-1} - 2v_{i,j} + v_{i,j+1}}{(\Delta x)^2} = 0,$$

or

$$v_{i,j} - \tfrac{1}{4}(v_{i-1,j} + v_{i+1,j} + v_{i,j-1} + v_{i,j+1}) = 0,$$

$$(7.79)$$

$$i = 1, 2, \ldots, M_x - 1, \qquad j = 1, 2, \ldots, M_y - 1,$$

with

$$v_{0,j} = g_{0,j}, \qquad v_{M_x,j} = g_{M_x,j},$$
$$v_{i,0} = g_{i,0}, \qquad v_{i,M_y} = g_{i,M_y}. \qquad (7.80)$$

Suppose that $M_x = 4$ and $M_y = 3$, corresponding to the grid of Fig. 7.15. The points numbered 1 through 6 are

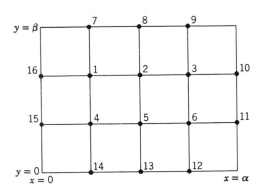

Figure 7.15 Grid points for a rectangle.

interior points; those numbered 7 through 16 are boundary points, at which the values of v are already known from equation (7.80). The corresponding system of equations, multiplied by a factor of four to remove fractions, is

$$\begin{array}{rcl}
4v_1 - v_2 \quad - v_4 & = g_7 + g_{16} \\
-v_1 + 4v_2 - v_3 \quad - v_5 & = g_8 \\
-v_2 + 4v_3 \quad - v_6 & = g_9 + g_{10} \\
-v_1 \quad + 4v_4 - v_5 & = g_{14} + g_{15} \\
-v_2 \quad - v_4 + 4v_5 - v_6 & = g_{13} \\
-v_3 \quad - v_5 + 4v_6 & = g_{11} + g_{12}.
\end{array} \qquad (7.81)$$

Or, written in the form $\mathbf{Av} = \mathbf{b}$,

$$\begin{bmatrix}
4 & -1 & 0 & -1 & 0 & 0 \\
-1 & 4 & -1 & 0 & -1 & 0 \\
0 & -1 & 4 & 0 & 0 & -1 \\
-1 & 0 & 0 & 4 & -1 & 0 \\
0 & -1 & 0 & -1 & 4 & -1 \\
0 & 0 & -1 & 0 & -1 & 4
\end{bmatrix}
\begin{bmatrix}
v_1 \\ v_2 \\ v_3 \\ v_4 \\ v_5 \\ v_6
\end{bmatrix}
=
\begin{bmatrix}
g_7 + g_{16} \\ g_8 \\ g_9 + g_{10} \\ g_{14} + g_{15} \\ g_{13} \\ g_{11} + g_{12}
\end{bmatrix}.$$

$$(7.82)$$

Observe that the coefficient matrix $\mathbf{A}$ is symmetric; note also that in any row of $\mathbf{A}$, the sum of the absolute values of the nondiagonal elements is less than the absolute value of the diagonal element. With larger choices of M_x and M_y, we would have certain interior points (in the rectangle of Fig. 7.15) none of whose neighbors were boundary points. In such cases, certain rows of the matrix $\mathbf{A}$ would have the sum of the absolute values of the non-diagonal elements *equal* to the absolute value of the diagonal element; however, the former inequality would still be preserved for certain other rows. The latter is an important property which, as we shall see shortly, helps to ensure the convergence of various iterative methods of solution.

The preceding discussion dealt with the theory of the method. In actual computation, to facilitate programming, it is probable that both subscripts (i,j) would be retained on v. Also, the complete matrix $\mathbf{A}$, consisting as it does of n^2 elements, is most unlikely to be stored in its entirety in the computer. We shall soon see why this is so. Finally, note that a matrix, formed as $\mathbf{A}$ is formed, is always positive definite.

7.23 Alternative Treatment of the Boundary Points

Let us now look more closely at the boundary condition (7.73). It presents no complications for the simple case shown in Fig. 7.15, in which certain grid points are arranged to lie on the boundary. Fig. 7.16, however, shows a typical situation involving a curved boundary S, on which u is assumed already specified. Point 1 is a boundary point, and condition (7.73) states that the value of v_1 shall be equated to some value of g *anywhere* on S between C and D (that is, within a distance Δx of point 1). Although simple, this is clearly not the most satisfactory of arrangements, and it is termed *interpolation of degree zero*.

If better accuracy is required, the procedure recommended is that of *interpolation of degree two*, considered earlier for parabolic equations on page 463. The Laplacian at point 1 is approximated by

$$\frac{\partial^2 u}{\partial x^2} + \frac{\partial^2 u}{\partial y^2} \doteq \frac{2}{(\Delta x)^2} \left[\frac{u_2}{b+1} + \frac{u_3}{a+1} + \frac{u_A}{a(a+1)} \right.$$
$$\left. + \frac{u_B}{b(b+1)} - \frac{(a+b)u_1}{ab} \right]. \qquad (7.69)$$

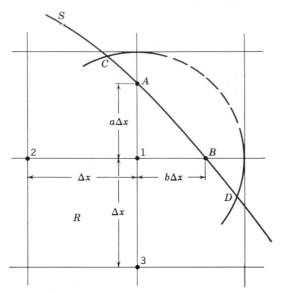

Figure 7.16   Curved boundary.

Thus, for the problem of solving Laplace's equation in a region with an irregular boundary, the following finite-difference equation holds at point 1 (which may be regarded as a typical boundary point):

$$ab(a + 1)v_2 + ab(b + 1)v_3 + b(b + 1)g_A$$
$$+ a(a + 1)g_B - (a + b)(a + 1)(b + 1)v_1 = 0. \quad (7.83)$$

The values of v (such as v_1) at the boundary points are unknown; therefore, they must be incorporated into the matrix equation $Av = b$ as if they were values of v at the interior points. In this case, the symmetry of the coefficient matrix will almost certainly be destroyed, but the methods of solution will, in general, not be invalidated.

Example. As a very simple illustration, it can be shown that the following equation gives the finite-difference approximation of $u_{xx} + u_{yy} = 0$ in the region of Fig. 7.17.

$$\begin{bmatrix} 4 & -1 & -1 & 0 \\ -3 & 18 & 0 & -4 \\ -1 & 0 & 4 & -1 \\ 0 & -1 & -1 & 4 \end{bmatrix} \begin{bmatrix} v_1 \\ v_2 \\ v_3 \\ v_4 \end{bmatrix} = \begin{bmatrix} g_5 + g_{12} \\ 8g_6 + 3g_7 \\ g_{10} + g_{11} \\ g_8 + g_9 \end{bmatrix}. \quad (7.84)$$

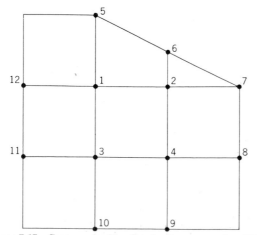

Figure 7.17   System of grid points leading to equation (7.84).

7.24   Iterative Methods of Solution

So far, we have formulated the numerical approximation of the boundary-value problem with the elliptic differential equation as the solution v of the linear algebraic system (7.75),

$$Av = b.$$

The solution of this system exists and is unique if and only if A is nonsingular, in which case

$$v = A^{-1}b. \quad (7.85)$$

Unfortunately, even though we may know that the matrix is nonsingular, the size of the system is usually so large that the derivation of the inverse by any direct method requires an excessive amount of calculation, quite apart from considerations of round-off error. It is, therefore, more convenient, in this case, to employ a method of *iteration* or *relaxation*. Two such methods were discussed in Chapter 5: the *Jacobi* (total-step or simultaneous displacement) and *Gauss-Seidel* (single-step or successive displacement) iteration procedures. In the solution of elliptic difference equations, the Jacobi method is a special case of the *Richardson* method [9], and the Gauss-Seidel method is also known as the *Liebmann* method.

Basically, each method involves transferring all the off-diagonal terms to the right-hand side, so that the *i*th equation reads

$$a_{ii}v_i = b_i - \sum_{\substack{j=1 \\ j \neq i}}^{n} a_{ij}v_j.$$

If approximations v to the exact solution of (7.75) are known, then new approximations v' can be computed from

$$v_i' = \frac{\left(b_i - \sum_{\substack{j=1 \\ j \neq i}}^{n} a_{ij}v_j\right)}{a_{ii}}, \qquad i = 1, 2, \ldots, n. \quad (7.86)$$

This procedure is repeated until the computed values show little further change. In the Jacobi method, the old values v are always used in the right-hand side of (7.86) until a complete set of new values v' has been computed. In the Gauss-Seidel method, however, the most recently available values of v are always used in the right-hand side of (7.86).

Sufficient conditions for the convergence of both methods are given in Sections 5.6 and 5.7; see also Ralston and Wilf [21]. Convergence is guaranteed if the coefficient matrix A of (7.75) satisfies:

1. A is an irreducible matrix; that is, the solution of the system (7.75) cannot be reduced to the solution of two or more systems of lower order.

2.

$$\sum_{\substack{j=1 \\ j \neq i}}^{n} |a_{ij}| \leqslant |a_{ii}|,$$

with strict inequality holding for at least one value of i.

It can be shown that the coefficient matrices that arise in the finite-difference approximations (7.72), (7.73) and (7.79), (7.80) for the boundary-value problem with the elliptic PDE always satisfy these conditions. The final solution is independent of the choice of starting values, although a poor initial estimate will require more iterations for convergence. In the solution of Laplace's equation, the Gauss-Seidel method converges more rapidly than the Jacobi method and will be preferred. In Section 7.25, we also consider other methods for accelerating the rate of convergence to the solution of (7.75).

In practice, we shall probably be solving upwards of one hundred simultaneous equations, but since five terms are the most that will appear on the left-hand side of each equation, the coefficient matrix **A** will contain a very high proportion of zero elements. Consequently, attempts to work entirely in terms of matrices and, in particular, to store all their elements are extremely wasteful of computer storage. Rather, the Jacobi and Gauss-Seidel iterative methods are effected in practice by the repeated application of a single algebraic equation throughout the whole system of grid points. Reverting to double space-subscripts, this amounts to computing a new approximation $v'_{i,j}$ at every interior grid point from the simple formula

$$v'_{i,j} = \frac{(v_{i-1,j} + v_{i+1,j} + v_{i,j-1} + v_{i,j+1})}{4}. \qquad (7.87)$$

EXAMPLE 7.6

STEADY-STATE HEAT CONDUCTION IN A SQUARE PLATE

Problem Statement

Find the steady-state temperature distribution in a square plate, one side of which is maintained at 100°, with the other three sides maintained at 0°, as shown in Fig. 7.6.1.

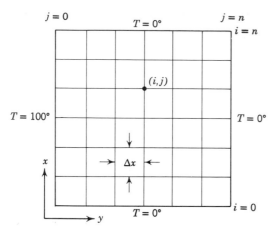

Figure 7.6.1 Heat conduction in a square plate.

Method of Solution

The problem is that of solving Laplace's equation in a rectangle (see Section 7.22). If each side of the square is divided into n increments Δx ($=\Delta y$), the problem involves the solution of a system of $(n-1)^2$ simultaneous equations (similar to (7.82)), with the temperatures at the interior grid points as the unknowns. The method of solution is to iterate through all the grid points, calculating a better approximation to the temperature at each point (i, j) in turn from equation (7.87):

$$T_{i,j} \leftarrow \frac{T_{i-1,j} + T_{i+1,j} + T_{i,j-1} + T_{i,j+1}}{4},$$

$$i = 1, 2, \ldots, n-1,$$

$$j = 1, 2, \ldots, n-1.$$

As soon as a new value of T is calculated at a point, its previous value is discarded. This is the Gauss-Seidel method of iteration (see Section 7.24). To start, a temperature of 0° is assumed everywhere within the plate. The process of iteration through all grid points is repeated until further iterations would produce, it is hoped, very little change in the computed temperatures. The following program stops if the sum ε, over all grid points, of the absolute values of the deviations of the temperatures from their previously computed values, falls below a small quantity ε_{max}. Computations will also be discontinued if the number of complete iterations, k, exceeds an upper limit, k_{max}.

Example 7.6   Steady-State Heat Conduction in a Square Plate   **487**

Flow Diagram

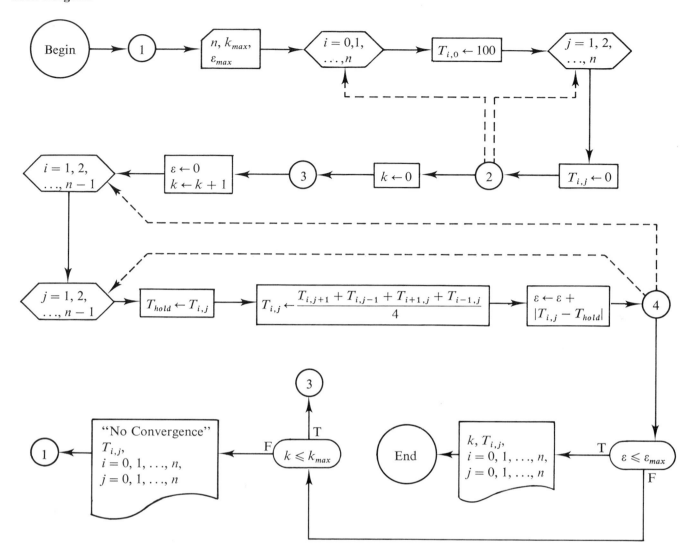

FORTRAN *Implementation*

List of Principal Variables

Program Symbol	Definition
EPS	Sum, ε, of absolute values of deviations of temperatures from their previously computed values.
EPSMAX	The largest tolerable value, ε_{max}, of ε.
HOLDT	Temporary storage, T_{hold}, for temperature while new value is being computed.
I, J	Grid-point subscripts, i, j.
ITER	Iteration counter, k.
ITMAX	Upper limit, k_{max}, on number of iterations.
N	Number of increments, n, into which the side of the square is divided.
T	Matrix of temperatures, T.

Because of FORTRAN limitations, the subscripts in the text are advanced by one in the program; e.g., $T_{0,0}$ through $T_{n,n}$ become (T1,1) through T(N+1,N+1).

Program Listing

```
C              APPLIED NUMERICAL METHODS, EXAMPLE 7.6
C              STEADY STATE HEAT CONDUCTION IN A SQUARE PLATE.
C
C              LEFT-HAND SIDE IS AT 100 DEGREES AND THE OTHER THREE SIDES ARE
C              AT 0 DEGREES.   THE PLATE HAS N GRID SPACINGS ALONG EACH SIDE.
C              A GAUSS-SEIDEL ITERATION IS EMPLOYED UNTIL EITHER THE SUM OF
C              THE ABSOLUTE VALUES OF THE DEVIATIONS OF THE TEMPERATURES FROM
C              THEIR LAST COMPUTED VALUES FALLS BELOW A SMALL QUANTITY EPSMAX,
C              OR, THE NUMBER OF ITERATIONS EXCEEDS ITMAX.
C
C              ..... READ AND CHECK INPUT PARAMETERS .....
        DIMENSION T(11,11)
      1 READ (5,100) N, ITMAX, EPSMAX
        WRITE (6,200) N, ITMAX, EPSMAX
C
C              ..... ESTABLISH INITIAL GUESSES FOR TEMPERATURE .....
        NP1 = N + 1
        DO 2  I = 1, NP1
        T(I,1) = 100.0
        DO 2  J = 2, NP1
      2 T(I,J) = 0.0
C
C              ..... CALCULATE SUCCESSIVELY BETTER APPROXIMATIONS FOR
C                    TEMPERATURES AT ALL GRID POINTS, ITERATING UNTIL
C                    SATISFACTORY CONVERGENCE IS ACHIEVED .....
        ITER = 0
      3 EPS = 0.0
        ITER = ITER + 1
        DO 4  I = 2, N
        DO 4  J = 2, N
        HOLDT = T(I,J)
        T(I,J) = (T(I,J+1) + T(I,J-1) + T(I+1,J) + T(I-1,J))/4.0
      4 EPS = EPS + ABS(T(I,J) - HOLDT)
C
C              ..... STOP ITERATIONS IF COMPUTED VALUES SHOW LITTLE FURTHER
C                    CHANGE, OR IF NUMBER OF ITERATIONS IS TOO LARGE .....
        IF (EPS .LE. EPSMAX) GO TO 6
        IF (ITER - ITMAX) 3, 3, 8
C
C              ..... PRINT VALUES OF THE ITERATION COUNTER
C                    ITER AND THE FINAL TEMPERATURE FIELD .....
      6 WRITE (6,201) ITER
        DO 7  I = 1, NP1
      7 WRITE (6,202) (T(I,J), J = 1, NP1)
        GO TO 1
C
C              ..... COMMENT IN CASE ITER EXCEEDS ITMAX .....
      8 WRITE (6,203)
        DO 9  I = 1, NP1
      9 WRITE (6,202) (T(I,J), J = 1, NP1)
        GO TO 1
C
C              ..... FORMATS FOR INPUT AND OUTPUT STATEMENTS .....
    100 FORMAT (11X, I4, 11X, I4, 12X, E8.1)
    200 FORMAT (62H1STEADY-STATE HEAT CONDUCTION IN A FLAT PLATE, WITH PAR
       1AMETERS/ 10H0N      = , I5/ 10H ITMAX  = , I5/
       210H EPSMAX = , E12.2)
    201 FORMAT (46H0CONVERGENCE CONDITION HAS BEEN REACHED AFTER ,
       1 I3, 11H ITERATIONS/ 34H0THE TEMPERATURE FIELD IS GIVEN BY)
    202 FORMAT (1H0, 11F9.4)
    203 FORMAT (42H0NO CONVERGENCE.   CURRENT VALUES OF T ARE)
C
        END
```

Data

```
        N    =   8,   ITMAX = 100,   EPSMAX =   1.0E-4
        N    =   4,   ITMAX =  50,   EPSMAX =   1.0E-5
```

Example 7.6   Steady-State Heat Conduction in a Square Plate   **489**

Computer Output

Results for the 1st Data Set

```
STEADY-STATE HEAT CONDUCTION IN A FLAT PLATE, WITH PARAMETERS

N     =     8
ITMAX =   100
EPSMAX =    0.10E-03

CONVERGENCE CONDITION HAS BEEN REACHED AFTER  88 ITERATIONS

THE TEMPERATURE FIELD IS GIVEN BY

100.0000    0.0       0.0       0.0       0.0       0.0       0.0       0.0       0.0

100.0000   48.2587   26.9301   16.3567   10.2941    6.4373    3.7683    1.7413    0.0

100.0000   66.1045   43.1052   28.2027   18.3822   11.6868    6.8946    3.1969    0.0

100.0000   73.0542   51.1835   34.9667   23.3455   15.0330    8.9266    4.1515    0.0

100.0000   74.9290   53.6078   37.1353   24.9999   16.1733    9.6273    4.4826    0.0

100.0000   73.0542   51.1835   34.9667   23.3455   15.0330    8.9266    4.1515    0.0

100.0000   66.1045   43.1052   28.2027   18.3822   11.6868    6.8946    3.1969    0.0

100.0000   48.2587   26.9301   16.3567   10.2941    6.4373    3.7683    1.7413    0.0

100.0000    0.0       0.0       0.0       0.0       0.0       0.0       0.0       0.0
```

Results for the 2nd Data Set

```
STEADY-STATE HEAT CONDUCTION IN A FLAT PLATE, WITH PARAMETERS

N     =     4
ITMAX =    50
EPSMAX =    0.10E-04

CONVERGENCE CONDITION HAS BEEN REACHED AFTER  22 ITERATIONS

THE TEMPERATURE FIELD IS GIVEN BY

100.0000    0.0       0.0       0.0       0.0

100.0000   42.8571   18.7500    7.1428    0.0

100.0000   52.6785   25.0000    9.8214    0.0

100.0000   42.8571   18.7500    7.1428    0.0

100.0000    0.0       0.0       0.0       0.0
```

Discussion of Results

The printout shows the distribution of temperature in the plate for both 8×8 and 4×4 grids. Even with such coarse grids, there is fairly good agreement between the two cases.

The computed temperatures may be compared with the analytical solution given by Carslaw and Jaeger [2]:

$$T(x, y) = \frac{4T_0}{\pi} \sum_{n=0}^{\infty} \frac{1}{(2n + 1)} \sin \frac{(2n + 1)\pi x}{a}$$

$$\times \sinh \frac{(a - y)(2n + 1)\pi}{a} \operatorname{cosech}(2n + 1)\pi,$$

where a is the side of the square, $T_0 \, (=100)$ is the temperature of the side $y = 0$, and the coordinate system is shown in Fig. 7.6.1.

EXAMPLE 7.7

DEFLECTION OF A LOADED PLATE

Problem Statement

Consider a simply supported square plate of side L that is subjected to a load q per unit area, as shown in Fig. 7.7.1. The deflection w in the z-direction is the solution of the *biharmonic* equation:

$$\nabla^4 w = \frac{\partial^4 w}{\partial x^4} + 2\frac{\partial^4 w}{\partial x^2 \partial y^2} + \frac{\partial^4 w}{\partial y^4} = \frac{q}{D}, \quad (7.7.1)$$

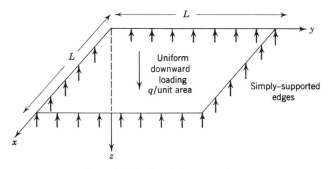

Figure 7.7.1   Loaded square plate.

subject to the boundary conditions $w = 0$ and $\partial^2 w/\partial \eta^2 = 0$ along its four edges, where η denotes the normal to the boundary. D is the flexural rigidity of the plate, given by

$$D = \frac{Et^3}{12(1-\sigma^2)}, \quad (7.7.2)$$

where E = Young's modulus, t = plate thickness, and σ = Poisson's ratio. For simplicity, suppose the loading is uniform so that q is constant.

Write a program for computing the deflections w at a grid of points with n intervals along each side of the square.

Method of Solution

By introducing the variable $u = \nabla^2 w$, the problem amounts to solving Poisson's equation twice in succession:

$$\nabla^2 u = q/D, \quad \text{with } u = 0 \text{ along the four edges}, \quad (7.7.3)$$

$$\nabla^2 w = u, \quad \text{with } w = 0 \text{ along the four edges}. \quad (7.7.4)$$

For this purpose, we employ a subroutine, named POISON, that uses the Gauss-Seidel method to approximate the solution of Poisson's equation:

$$\frac{\partial^2 \phi}{\partial x^2} + \frac{\partial^2 \phi}{\partial y^2} = \psi(x, y). \quad (7.7.5)$$

The finite-difference approximation of equation (7.7.5) is

$$\frac{\phi_{i-1,j} - 2\phi_{i,j} + \phi_{i+1,j}}{(\Delta x)^2} + \frac{\phi_{i,j-1} - 2\phi_{i,j} + \phi_{i,j+1}}{(\Delta y)^2} = \psi_{i,j}.$$

Thus, for $\Delta x = \Delta y$, the Gauss-Seidel method amounts to repeated application of

$$\phi_{i,j} \leftarrow \tfrac{1}{4}[\phi_{i-1,j} + \phi_{i+1,j} + \phi_{i,j-1} + \phi_{i,j+1} - (\Delta x)^2 \psi_{i,j}] \quad (7.7.6)$$

at every interior grid point. The subroutine is written for k_{max} applications of (7.7.6) through all interior grid points. Applied to equation (7.7.5), the call would be of the form

CALL POISON (N, L, PHI, PSI, KMAX)

Here, the matrix PSI would contain the known right-hand side values ψ and the subroutine would compute and store the values of ϕ in the matrix PHI. By using appropriate arguments, the subroutine will solve equations (7.7.3) and (7.7.4) in two successive calls.

Flow Diagram

Main Program

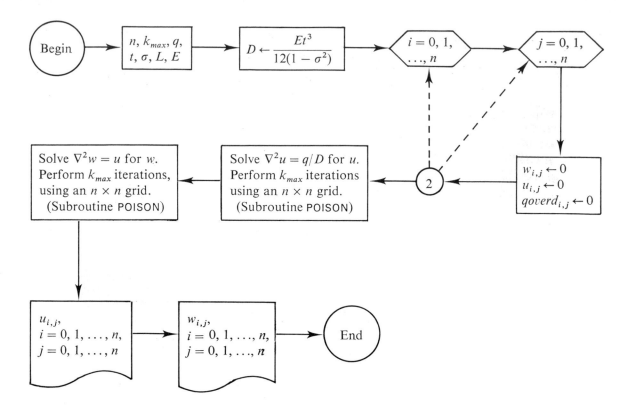

Subroutine POISON (Dummy arguments: $n, L, \phi, \psi, k_{max}$;
                        1st calling arguments, $n, L, u, qoverd, k_{max}$;
                        2nd calling arguments: n, L, w, u, k_{max})

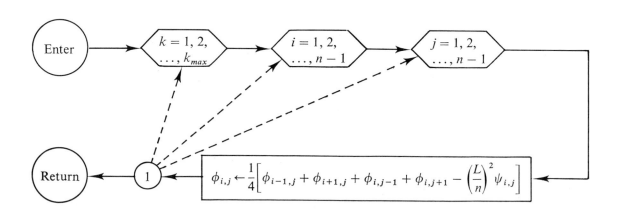

Example 7.7 Deflection of a Loaded Plate   **493**

FORTRAN *Implementation*

List of Principal Variables

Program Symbol   *Definition*

(Main)

D	Flexural rigidity, D, lb_f in.
E	Young's modulus, E, lb_f/sq in.
I, J	Grid-point subscripts, i, j. Because of FORTRAN limitations, we have $1 \leqslant I \leqslant N + 1$. corresponding to $0 \leqslant i \leqslant n$, and similarly for J.
ITMAX	Number of Gauss-Seidel iterations, k_{max}.
L	Length of side of square, L, in.
N	Number, n, of grid spacings along a side of the square.
POISON	Subroutine for solving Poisson's equation by the Gauss-Seidel method.
Q	Load per unit area of the plate, q, lb_f/sq in.
QOVERD	Matrix, with values of $qoverd = q/D$ at each grid point.
SIGMA	Poisson's ratio, σ.
T	Plate thickness, t, in.
U	Matrix of intermediate variable, $u = \nabla^2 w$, at each grid point.
W	Matrix of downwards deflection, w, in., at each grid point.

(Subroutine
 POISON)

ITER	Iteration counter, k.
PHI, PSI	Matrices of functions ϕ and ψ, occurring in Poisson's equation, $\nabla^2 \phi = \psi$.

Program Listing

Main Program

```
C           APPLIED NUMERICAL METHODS, EXAMPLE 7.7
C           DEFLECTION OF A UNIFORMLY-LOADED SQUARE PLATE.
C
C           THE BIHARMONIC EQUATION,  DELSQ(DELSQ(W)) = Q/D,
C           IS SOLVED IN ORDER TO FIND THE DOWNWARDS DEFLECTION W
C           THROUGHOUT A SIMPLY-SUPPORTED SQUARE PLATE OF SIDE L
C           AND FLEXURAL RIGIDITY D SUBJECTED TO A UNIFORM LOADING Q
C           PER UNIT AREA.
C
        REAL L
        DIMENSION U(11,11), W(11,11), QOVERD(11,11)
C
C       ..... READ AND PRINT DATA AND SET INITIAL ESTIMATES .....
      1 WRITE (6,200)
        READ (5,100) N, ITMAX, Q, T, SIGMA, L, E
        WRITE (6,201) N, ITMAX, Q, T, SIGMA, L, E
        NP1 = N + 1
        D = E*T**3/(12.0*(1.0 - SIGMA**2))
        RHS = Q/D
        DO 2  I = 1, NP1
        DO 2  J = 1, NP1
        W(I,J) = 0.0
        U(I,J) = 0.0
      2 QOVERD(I,J) = RHS
C
C       ..... SOLVE DELSQ(U) = Q/D .....
        CALL POISON (N, L, U, QOVERD, ITMAX)
C
C       ..... SOLVE DELSQ(W) = U .....
        CALL POISON (N, L, W, U, ITMAX)
C
C       ..... PRINT INTERMEDIATE U'S AND THE DEFLECTIONS W .....
        WRITE (6,202)
        DO 3  I = 1, NP1
      3 WRITE (6,203) (U(I,J), J = 1, NP1)
        WRITE (6,204)
        DO 4  I = 1, NP1
      4 WRITE (6,203) (W(I,J), J = 1, NP1)
        GO TO 1
C
C       ..... FORMATS FOR INPUT AND OUTPUT STATEMENTS .....
    100 FORMAT (3X, I2, 9X, I4, 2(6X, F4.1), 10X, F4.1, 6X, F5.1, 6X,
       1 E7.1)
    200 FORMAT ( 87H1      SOLUTION OF BIHARMONIC EQUATION FOR DEFLECTION O
       1F A UNIFORMLY-LOADED SQUARE PLATE)
    201 FORMAT (1H0, 10X, 8HN      = , I4/ 11X, 8HITMAX = , I4/
       1 11X, 8HQ      = , F10.5/ 11X, 8HT      = , F10.5/
       2 11X, 8HSIGMA = , F10.5/ 11X, 8HL      = , F10.5/
       3 11X, 8HE      = , E11.2)
    202 FORMAT (35H0      THE INTERMEDIATE VALUES U ARE)
    203 FORMAT (1H0, 4X, 9F10.6)
    204 FORMAT (33H0      THE FINAL DEFLECTIONS W ARE)
C
        END
```

Subroutine POISON

```
C           SUBROUTINE FOR SOLVING POISSON'S EQUATION,
C                   DELSQ(PHI) = PSI(X,Y),
C           IN A SQUARE OF SIDE L, ALONG WHICH THERE ARE N INCREMENTS.
C           ITMAX GAUSS-SEIDEL ITERATIONS ARE PERFORMED AT ALL GRID POINTS.
```

Example 7.7   Deflection of a Loaded Plate   **495**

Program Listing (*Continued*)

```
C
      SUBROUTINE POISON (N, L, PHI, PSI, ITMAX)
      REAL L
      DIMENSION PHI(11,11), PSI(11,11)
      FN = N
      DXSQ = (L/FN)**2
      DO 1  ITER = 1, ITMAX
      DO 1  I = 2, N
      DO 1  J = 2, N
    1 PHI(I,J) = 0.25*(PHI(I-1,J) + PHI(I+1,J) + PHI(I,J-1)
     1                          + PHI(I,J+1) - DXSQ*PSI(I,J))
      RETURN
C
      END
```

Data

```
N = 4, ITMAX =   5, Q = 1.0, T = 0.2, SIGMA = 0.3, L = 40.0, E = 30.0E6
N = 4, ITMAX =  25, Q = 1.0, T = 0.2, SIGMA = 0.3, L = 40.0, E = 30.0E6
N = 8, ITMAX =  25, Q = 1.0, T = 0.2, SIGMA = 0.3, L = 40.0, E = 30.0E6
N = 8, ITMAX = 100, Q = 1.0, T = 0.2, SIGMA = 0.3, L = 40.0, E = 30.0E6
```

Computer Output

Results for the 2nd Data Set

```
SOLUTION OF BIHARMONIC EQUATION FOR DEFLECTION OF A UNIFORMLY-LOADED SQUARE PLATE

      N     =    4
      ITMAX =   25
      Q     =    1.00000
      T     =    0.20000
      SIGMA =    0.30000
      L     =   40.00000
      E     =    0.30E 08

THE INTERMEDIATE VALUES U ARE

   0.0       0.0       0.0       0.0       0.0

   0.0      -0.003128 -0.003981 -0.003128  0.0

   0.0      -0.003981 -0.005119 -0.003981  0.0

   0.0      -0.003128 -0.003981 -0.003128  0.0

   0.0       0.0       0.0       0.0       0.0

THE FINAL DEFLECTIONS W ARE

   0.0       0.0       0.0       0.0       0.0

   0.0       0.248828  0.341249  0.248828  0.0

   0.0       0.341249  0.469218  0.341249  0.0

   0.0       0.248828  0.341249  0.248828  0.0

   0.0       0.0       0.0       0.0       0.0
```

Computer Output (*Continued*)

Results for the 4th Data Set

```
       SOLUTION OF BIHARMONIC EQUATION FOR DEFLECTION OF A UNIFORMLY-LOADED SQUARE PLATE

           N     =      8
           ITMAX =    100
           Q     =      1.00000
           T     =      0.20000
           SIGMA =      0.30000
           L     =     40.00000
           E     =      0.30E 08
```

THE INTERMEDIATE VALUES U ARE

0.0	0.0	0.0	0.0	0.0	0.0	0.0	0.0	0.0
0.0	-0.001294	-0.002020	-0.002396	-0.002513	-0.002396	-0.002020	-0.001294	0.0
0.0	-0.002020	-0.003251	-0.003914	-0.004123	-0.003914	-0.003251	-0.002020	0.0
0.0	-0.002396	-0.003914	-0.004749	-0.005014	-0.004749	-0.003914	-0.002396	0.0
0.0	-0.002513	-0.004123	-0.005014	-0.005299	-0.005014	-0.004123	-0.002513	0.0
0.0	-0.002396	-0.003914	-0.004749	-0.005014	-0.004749	-0.003914	-0.002396	0.0
0.0	-0.002020	-0.003251	-0.003914	-0.004123	-0.003914	-0.003251	-0.002020	0.0
0.0	-0.001294	-0.002020	-0.002396	-0.002513	-0.002396	-0.002020	-0.001294	0.0
0.0	0.0	0.0	0.0	0.0	0.0	0.0	0.0	0.0

THE FINAL DEFLECTIONS W ARE

0.0	0.0	0.0	0.0	0.0	0.0	0.0	0.0	0.0
0.0	0.077190	0.138200	0.176497	0.189490	0.176497	0.138200	0.077190	0.0
0.0	0.138200	0.248618	0.318392	0.342133	0.318392	0.248618	0.138200	0.0
0.0	0.176497	0.318392	0.408462	0.439175	0.408461	0.318391	0.176497	0.0
0.0	0.189490	0.342133	0.439175	0.472290	0.439175	0.342133	0.189490	0.0
0.0	0.176497	0.318392	0.408462	0.439175	0.408461	0.318391	0.176497	0.0
0.0	0.138200	0.248618	0.318392	0.342133	0.318392	0.248618	0.138200	0.0
0.0	0.077190	0.138200	0.176497	0.189490	0.176497	0.138200	0.077190	0.0
0.0	0.0	0.0	0.0	0.0	0.0	0.0	0.0	0.0

Example 7.7   Deflection of a Loaded Plate   **497**

Discussion of Results

The printout is shown only for the 2nd and 4th data sets, with $n = 4$ and $n = 8$. Judging by the symmetry of the computed values, convergence is probably complete to the number of significant figures printed (after 25 and 100 iterations, respectively). There is also little change in passing from $n = 4$ to $n = 8$, which suggests that the computed values are good approximations to the exact solution. The 1st and 3rd data sets, again for $n = 4$ and $n = 8$, but with only 5 and 25 iterations, respectively, did not give symmetrical values, indicating only partial convergence.

The above method could easily be extended to the case of an unevenly loaded plate, simply by inserting the appropriate local values in the matrix *qoverd*.

EXAMPLE 7.8

TORSION WITH CURVED BOUNDARY

Introduction

A steady torque T is applied to a cylindrical shaft that is clamped at one end. The cross section of the shaft is an ellipse with major and minor semiaxes α and β, shown in Fig. 7.8.1. If the modulus of rigidity of the shaft is G,

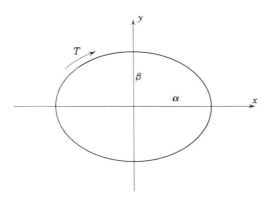

Figure 7.8.1   Torsion of an elliptical cylinder.

then the angle of twist θ, per unit length, is given by Hughes and Gaylord [33] as

$$\theta = \frac{T}{2G\int\psi\,dA},\qquad (7.8.1)$$

where the integral is over the whole cross-sectional area, and ψ is the solution of

$$\nabla^2\psi = -2,\qquad (7.8.2)$$

with

$$\psi = 0 \text{ on the surface of the ellipse.}$$

Since the analytical solution of (7.8.2) is

$$\psi = -\left(\frac{x^2}{\alpha^2} + \frac{y^2}{\beta^2} - 1\right)\left(\frac{\alpha^2\beta^2}{\alpha^2 + \beta^2}\right),\qquad (7.8.3)$$

it can be shown from (7.8.1) that the angle of twist per unit length is

$$\theta = \frac{T(\alpha^2 + \beta^2)}{\pi G\alpha^3\beta^3}.\qquad (7.8.4)$$

Problem Statement

Write a program that will perform a finite-difference solution of (7.8.2) and compare the computed results with the analytical solution given by (7.8.3). The purpose of this problem is primarily to illustrate the technique of *interpolation of degree two* at a curved boundary (see Section 7.23). Use a square grid, and assume that

$$\Delta x = \Delta y = \frac{\alpha}{n} = \frac{\beta}{m},$$

where m and n are integers.

Method of Solution

The general approach is to perform successive Gauss-Seidel iterations over all grid points. Because of symmetry, we shall consider only one quadrant of the ellipse, shown in Fig. 7.8.2.

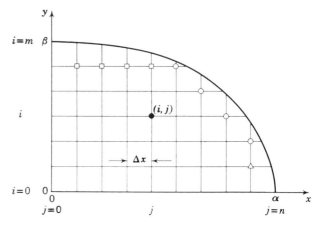

Figure 7.8.2   Quadrant of ellipse.

The grid points within the ellipse are subdivided into five main categories:

1. *Interior points.* The appropriate finite-difference approximation of (7.8.2) at the interior points is

$$\psi_{ij} = \tfrac{1}{4}[\psi_{i-1,j} + \psi_{i+1,j} + \psi_{i,j-1} + \psi_{i,j+1} + 2(\Delta x)^2].$$

2. *Lower Boundary Points* $(y = 0)$. Because of symmetry about the x axis,

$$\psi_{0,j} = \tfrac{1}{4}[2\psi_{1,j} + \psi_{0,j-1} + \psi_{0,j+1} + 2(\Delta x)^2],$$

$$j = 1, 2, \ldots, n - 1.$$

3. *Left-hand Boundary Points* $(x = 0)$. Because of symmetry about the y axis,

$$\psi_{i,0} = \tfrac{1}{4}[\psi_{i-1,0} + \psi_{i+1,0} + 2\psi_{i,1} + 2(\Delta x)^2],$$

$$i = 1, 2, \ldots, m - 1.$$

4. *Corner Point.* At the center of the ellipse,

$$\psi_{0,0} = \tfrac{1}{4}[2\psi_{1,0} + 2\psi_{0,1} + 2(\Delta x)^2].$$

5. *Points Near Curved Boundary.* These boundary points, indicated in Fig. 7.8.2 by the symbols $\bigcirc$, $\square$, and $\triangle$, require individual treatment, as described below.

The key to a detailed examination of the boundary points mentioned in (5) above is to find $jmax_i$, the column subscript of the rightmost grid point in each row $i (= 0, 1, \ldots, m)$. Since the equation of the ellipse is

$$\frac{x^2}{\alpha^2} + \frac{y^2}{\beta^2} = 1,$$

Example 7.8 Torsion with Curved Boundary   **499**

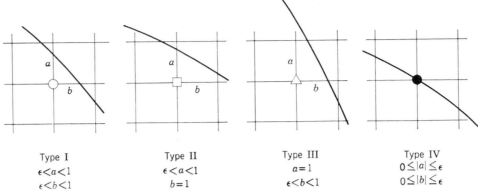

Figure 7.8.3 Types of boundary point.

it follows that

$$jmax_i = n\sqrt{1 - \frac{i^2}{m^2}},$$

truncated to the next lower integer.

As illustrated in Fig. 7.8.3, each boundary point in row i can now be placed into one of the following four categories:

Type I: Point $(i, jmax_i)$, if this is not of type III or IV.
Type II: Points (i, j), if any, for which $jmax_{i+1} < j < jmax_i$.
Type III: Point $(i, jmax_i)$, only if it is not of type IV and if $jmax_{i+1} = jmax_i$.
Type IV: Occurs if the curved boundary produces an intercept within $\pm\epsilon$ of a grid point, where $\epsilon \ll 1$.

The symbols $\bigcirc$, $\square$, and $\triangle$, in Figs. 7.8.2 and 7.8.3, indicate points of types I, II, and III, respectively. Note that for any row i, points of types I, III, and IV are mutually exclusive.

Consider a point (i, j), possibly having unequal "arms" to the right and above, as shown in Fig. 7.8.4. From

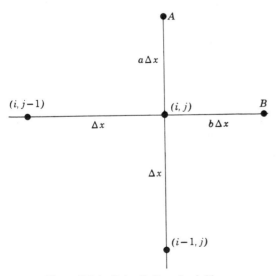

Figure 7.8.4 Point (i, j) and neighbors.

(7.69), the finite-difference approximation of (7.8.2) at such a point is

$$\nabla^2\psi \doteq \frac{2}{(\Delta x)^2}\left[\frac{\psi_{i,j-1}}{b+1} + \frac{\psi_{i-1,j}}{a+1} + \frac{\psi_A}{a(a+1)}\right.$$
$$\left. + \frac{\psi_B}{b(b+1)} - \frac{(a+b)\psi_{ij}}{ab}\right] = -2.$$

That is,

$$\psi_{ij} = c[d\psi_{i,j-1} + e\psi_{i-1,j} + f\psi_A + g\psi_B + (\Delta x)^2], \quad (7.8.5)$$

where

$$c = \frac{ab}{a+b}, \quad d = \frac{1}{b+1}, \quad e = \frac{1}{a+1}, \quad f = \frac{1}{a(a+1)},$$

$$g = \frac{1}{b(b+1)}. \quad (7.8.6)$$

Since $\psi = 0$ on the surface, we have the following special cases of (7.8.5) at the various types of point:

Type of Point (i,j)	ψ_A	ψ_B	a	b
I	0	0	a	b
II	0	$\psi_{i,j+1}$	a	1
III	$\psi_{i+1,j}$	0	1	b

For a point (i,j) of type IV, $\psi_{ij} = 0$. In particular, $\psi_{m,0} = \psi_{0,n} = 0$.

For computing purposes, we must also note that the horizontal and vertical arms extending from any point (i,j) to the curved boundary are such that

$$a = m\sqrt{1 - \frac{j^2}{n^2}} - i, \quad b = n\sqrt{1 - \frac{i^2}{m^2}} - j.$$

Once the boundary points have been classified (in the program, this is achieved by the subroutine BNDPTS) the Gauss-Seidel iteration technique is employed over all grid points, using the particular formula appropriate to each point. The iterations are discontinued when the sum ε over all grid points of the absolute values of the deviations of ψ from its previous value falls below some small quantity ε_{max}. An upper limit is also placed on the number of iterations.

Finally, the function COMPAR is called to determine the RMS (root mean square) deviation of ψ from its known analytical solution, (7.8.3).

We have not attempted to write a concise flow diagram for this example. Instead, the overall approach can be understood best by reading the above description in conjunction with the program comment cards.

FORTRAN *Implementation*

List of Principal Variables

Program Symbol	Definition
(Main)	
ALPHA, BETA	Semiaxes of the ellipse, α and β.
BNDPTS	Subroutine for locating the boundary points and their associated intercepts.
C, D, E, F, G,	Expressions defined in equation (7.8.6).
COMPAR	Function for determining the RMS deviation, RMSDEV, of the computed values ψ_{ij} from their known exact values.
DX	Space increment, $\Delta x = \Delta y$.
EPS	Sum ε of the absolute values of the deviations of the ψ_{ij} from their previously computed values.
I, J	Grid-point subscripts, i, j. Because of FORTRAN limitations, we have $1 \leq I \leq M + 1$ and $1 \leq J \leq N + 1$ in the program, corresponding to $0 \leq i \leq m$ and $0 \leq j \leq n$ in the text.
ITER	Counter on the number of Gauss-Seidel iterations.
ITMAX	Maximum allowable value of ITER.
ITYPE	Matrix giving the type of each boundary point (see Figs. 7.8.2 and 7.8.3).
JLOW, JHIGH	Vectors such that JLOW(I) and JHIGH(I) contain the column subscripts J of the first and last boundary points (of types I–IV) in row I.
JMAX	Vector such that JMAX(I) contains the column subscript J of the rightmost grid point in row I.
JR	Vector such that JR(I) contains the highest column subscript of a completely interior point in row I.
M, N	Number of intervals, m and n, into which the minor and major semiaxes of the ellipse are divided.
PSI	Matrix containing the values of ψ at each grid point.
SAVPSI	Temporary storage for the current value of ψ_{ij}.
(Subroutine BNDPTS)	
EPS	Small distance ϵ (see Fig. 7.8.3).
(Function COMPAR)	
C	$\alpha^2 \beta^2 / (\alpha^2 + \beta^2)$.
DEVSQ	The sum of the squares of the deviations.
IPTS	The total number of grid points.
TRUPSI	The true value of ψ at each grid point.

Example 7.8   Torsion with Curved Boundary   **501**

Program Listing

Main Program

```
C           APPLIED NUMERICAL METHODS, EXAMPLE 7.8
C           TORSION OF A CYLINDER OF ELLIPTICAL CROSS-SECTION.
C
C           INVOLVES GAUSS-SEIDEL TYPE SOLUTION OF POISSON'S EQUATION,
C                    DELSQ(PSI)  =  - 2,
C           THROUGHOUT THE UPPER RIGHT-HAND QUADRANT OF AN ELLIPSE.
C           THERE ARE N AND M GRID SPACINGS RESPECTIVELY ALONG THE
C           MAJOR AND MINOR AXES OF LENGTHS ALPHA AND BETA.    PSI IS
C           ZERO ALONG THE CURVED PORTION OF THE BOUNDARY.    INTER-
C           POLATION OF DEGREE TWO IS EMPLOYED AT THE BOUNDARY POINTS.
C
        DIMENSION JR(21), JMAX(21), PSI(21,21), C(21,21), D(21,21),
       1E(21,21), F(21,21), G(21,21), ITYPE(21,21)
C
C           ..... READ AND CHECK DATA, AND SET CONSTANTS .....
      1 READ (5,100) M, N, ITMAX, ALPHA, BETA, EPSMAX
        WRITE (6,200) M, N, ITMAX, ALPHA, BETA, EPSMAX
        MP1 = M + 1
        NP1 = N + 1
        FN = N
        DX = ALPHA/FN
        DXSQ = DX*DX
        TUDXSQ = 2.0*DX*DX
        DO 2  I = 1, MP1
        DO 2   J = 1, NP1
      2 PSI(I,J) = 0.0
        WRITE (6,201)
C
C           ..... CALL ON SUBROUTINE BNDPTS TO DETERMINE THE
C                 BOUNDARY POINTS AND THEIR ASSOCIATED INTERCEPTS .....
        CALL BNDPTS (M, N, JR, JMAX, ITYPE, C, D, E, F, G)
        WRITE (6,202) (JR(I), I = 2, M)
        WRITE (6,203) (JMAX(I), I = 1, MP1)
C
C           ..... COMPUTE SUCCESSIVELY BETTER APPROXIMATIONS FOR
C                 PSI AT ALL GRID POINTS, ITERATING BY GAUSS-SEIDEL
C                 METHOD UNTIL CONVERGENCE CRITERION IS SATISFIED .....
        ITER = 0
      3 ITER = ITER + 1
        EPS = 0.0
C
C           ..... POINTS ON STRAIGHT PORTIONS OF
C                 BOUNDARY, FIRST ALONG THE Y-AXIS .....
        DO 4  I = 2, M
        SAVPSI = PSI(I,1)
        PSI(I,1) = (PSI(I+1,1) + PSI(I-1,1) + 2.0*PSI(I,2) + TUDXSQ)/4.0
      4 EPS = EPS + ABS(PSI(I,1) - SAVPSI)
C
C           ..... AND THEN ALONG THE X-AXIS .....
        DO 5  J = 2, N
        SAVPSI = PSI(1,J)
        PSI(1,J) = (PSI(1,J-1) + PSI(1,J+1) + 2.0*PSI(2,J) + TUDXSQ)/4.0
      5 EPS = EPS + ABS(PSI(1,J) - SAVPSI)
C
C           ..... CENTER POINT .....
        SAVPSI = PSI(1,1)
        PSI(1,1) = (2.0*PSI(2,1) + 2.0*PSI(1,2) + TUDXSQ)/4.0
        EPS = EPS + ABS(PSI(1,1) - SAVPSI)
C
C           ..... INTERIOR POINTS .....
        DO 21  I = 2, M
        JHIGH = JR(I)
        IF (JHIGH .LT. 2) GO TO 21
          DO 6   J = 2, JHIGH
          SAVPSI = PSI(I,J)
          PSI(I,J) = (PSI(I-1,J) + PSI(I+1,J) + PSI(I,J-1)
       1                            + PSI(I,J+1) + TUDXSQ)/4.0
      6   EPS = EPS + ABS(PSI(I,J) - SAVPSI)
     21 CONTINUE
```

Program Listing (*Continued*)

```
C
C        ..... BOUNDARY POINTS (INTERPOLATION REQUIRED) .....
         DO 12  I = 2, M
         JLOW = JR(I) + 1
         JHIGH = JMAX(I)
         DO 12   J = JLOW, JHIGH
         IF (ITYPE(I,J) .EQ. 4) GO TO 12
            SUM = D(I,J)*PSI(I,J-1) + E(I,J)*PSI(I-1,J) + DXSQ
            IF (ITYPE(I,J) .NE. 2) GO TO 9
               SUM = SUM + G(I,J)*PSI(I,J+1)
               GO TO 11
    9       IF (ITYPE(I,J) .NE. 3) GO TO 11
               SUM = SUM + F(I,J)*PSI(I+1,J)
   11       SAVPSI = PSI(I,J)
            PSI(I,J) = C(I,J)*SUM
            EPS = EPS + ABS(PSI(I,J) - SAVPSI)
   12    CONTINUE
C
C        ..... CHECK TO SEE IF CONVERGENCE CRITERION IS SATIS-
C              FIED AND, IF SO, PRINT FINAL FIELD OF PSI VALUES .....
         IF (ITER .GE. ITMAX) GO TO 14
         IF (EPS - EPSMAX) 14, 3, 3
   14       WRITE (6,204) ITER, EPS
            DO 15  I = 1, MP1
            ISUB = M + 2 - I
            JHIGH = JMAX(ISUB)
   15       WRITE (6,205) (PSI(ISUB,J), J = 1, JHIGH)
C
C        ..... COMPUTE THE ROOT MEAN SQUARE DEVIATION
C              OF PSI FROM ITS KNOWN ANALYTICAL SOLUTION .....
         RMSDEV = COMPAR (M, N, JMAX, PSI, ALPHA, BETA)
         WRITE (6,206) RMSDEV
         GO TO 1
C
C        ..... FORMATS FOR INPUT AND OUTPUT STATEMENTS .....
  100    FORMAT (3(11X, I4)/ 2(12X, F8.1), 12X, F8.3)
  200    FORMAT (70H1      TORSION OF CYLINDER OF ELLIPTICAL CROSS-SECTION,
        1WITH PARAMETERS/ 12H0    M      = , I4/ 12H     N      = , I4/
        2 12H     ITMAX  = , I4/ 12H     ALPHA  = , F8.3/
        3 12H     BETA   = , F8.3 / 12H     EPSMAX = , F8.3)
  201    FORMAT (78H0      RESULTS ARE FOR INTERPOLATION OF DEGREE TWO, WITH
        1 GAUSS-SEIDEL ITERATION/ 80H0      THE FOLLOWING VALUES ENABLE THE
        2BOUNDARY AND INTERIOR POINTS TO BE LOCATED)
  202    FORMAT (33H0      VALUES OF JR(2)...JR(M) ARE/ (1H0, 5X, 11I5))
  203    FORMAT (39H0      VALUES OF JMAX(1)...JMAX(M+1) ARE/ (1H0, 5X,
        1 11I5))
  204    FORMAT (29H1      ITERATIONS STOPPED WITH/ 12H0    ITER   = , I4/
        1 12H0    EPS    = , E12.4/ 32H0      THE FIELD OF PSI VALUES IS)
  205    FORMAT (1H0, 11F9.4)
  206    FORMAT (60H0      RMS DEVIATION BETWEEN COMPUTED AND EXACT PSI VALU
        1ES IS/ 15H0      RMSDEV = , F10.5)
C
         END
```

Subroutine BNDPTS

```
C        SUBROUTINE FOR DETERMINING BOUNDARY POINTS AND INTERCEPTS.
C        FOR A GIVEN ROW I, (I,JR(I)) IS THE RIGHTMOST INTERIOR
C        POINT AND (I,JMAX(I)) IS THE RIGHTMOST BOUNDARY POINT.
C        A AND B ARE THE FRACTIONAL INTERCEPTS IN THE VERTICAL (Y)
C        AND HORIZONTAL (X) DIRECTIONS, RESPECTIVELY.
C
         SUBROUTINE BNDPTS (M, N, JR, JMAX, ITYPE, C, D, E, F, G)
         DIMENSION JR(21), JMAX(21), ITYPE(21,21), C(21,21), D(21,21),
        1E(21,1), F(21,21), G(21,21)
         EPS = 1.0E-6
         FM = M
         FN = N
         FMSQ = M*M
         FNSQ = N*N
         MP1 = M + 1
```

Example 7.8   Torsion with Curved Boundary   503

Program Listing (*Continued*)

```
C
C        ..... LOCATE EXTREME RIGHT-HAND POINT
C              (I,JMAX(I)) AND DETERMINE ITS TYPE .....
         JMAX(1) = N + 1
         DO 7  I = 2, MP1
         FIM1 = I - 1
         XOVRDX = FN*SQRT(1.0 - FIM1*FIM1/FMSQ)
         JM1 = XOVRDX + EPS
         FJM1 = JM1
         J = JM1 + 1
         JMAX(I) = J
         YOVRDX = FM*SQRT(1.0 - FJM1*FJM1/FNSQ)
         A = YOVRDX - FIM1
         B = XOVRDX - FJM1
         IF (ABS(A) .LT. EPS) GO TO 2
         IF (ABS(B) .GE. EPS) GO TO 3
    2       ITYPE(I,J) = 4
         GO TO 7
    3       IF (A .LE. 1.0) GO TO 5
            ITYPE(I,J) = 3
            A = 1.0
            F(I,J) = 0.5
         GO TO 6
    5       ITYPE(I,J) = 1
    6    CONTINUE
         C(I,J) = A*B/(A + B)
         D(I,J) = 1.0/(B + 1.0)
         E(I,J) = 1.0/(A + 1.0)
    7 CONTINUE
C
C        ..... LOCATE BOUNDARY POINTS OF TYPE 2 .....
         DO 11  I = 2, M
         FIM1 = I - 1
         J = JMAX(I) - 1
    8 IF (JMAX(I+1) .GE. J) GO TO 10
         FJM1 = J - 1
         A = FM*SQRT(1.0 - FJM1*FJM1/FNSQ) - FIM1
         ITYPE(I,J) = 2
         C(I,J) = A/(A + 1.0)
         D(I,J) = 0.5
         E(I,J) = 1.0/(A + 1.0)
         G(I,J) = 0.5
         J = J - 1
         GO TO 8
   10    CONTINUE
   11    JR(I) = J
         RETURN
C
         END




C        FUNCTION FOR COMPARING THE COMPUTED SOLUTION WITH ITS
C        KNOWN ANALYTICAL VALUE.
C
C
         FUNCTION COMPAR (M, N, JMAX, PSI, ALPHA, BETA)
         DIMENSION JMAX(21), PSI(21,21)
```

Program Listing (*Continued*)

Function **COMPAR**

```
C
C        ..... COMPUTE THE SUMS OF THE DEVIATIONS SQUARED .....
         IPTS = 0
         DEVSQ = 0.0
         FMSQ = M*M
         FNSQ = N*N
         C = (ALPHA*BETA)**2/(ALPHA**2 + BETA**2)
         MP1 = M + 1
         DO 1  I = 1, MP1
         FIM1 = I - 1
         JHIGH = JMAX(I)
         DO 1  J = 1, JHIGH
         FJM1 = J - 1
         IPTS = IPTS + 1
         TRUPSI = (1.0 - FIM1*FIM1/FMSQ - FJM1*FJM1/FNSQ)*C
       1 DEVSQ = DEVSQ + (PSI(I,J) - TRUPSI)**2
C
C        ..... COMPUTE THE ROOT MEAN SQUARE DEVIATION .....
         PTS = IPTS
         COMPAR = SQRT(DEVSQ/PTS)
         RETURN
C
         END
```

Data

```
M      =     4,   N      =    5,   ITMAX = 100,
ALPHA  =      10.0,   BETA   =      8.0,   EPSMAX =    10.0
M      =     4,   N      =    5,   ITMAX = 100,
ALPHA  =      10.0,   BETA   =      8.0,   EPSMAX =     1.0
M      =     4,   N      =    5,   ITMAX = 100,
ALPHA  =      10.0,   BETA   =      8.0,   EPSMAX =     0.1
M      =     4,   N      =    5,   ITMAX = 200,
ALPHA  =      10.0,   BETA   =      8.0,   EPSMAX =     0.01
M      =     4,   N      =    5,   ITMAX = 200,
ALPHA  =      10.0,   BETA   =      8.0,   EPSMAX =     0.001
M      =     8,   N      =   10,   ITMAX = 300,
ALPHA  =      10.0,   BETA   =      8.0,   EPSMAX =     1.0
M      =     8,   N      =   10,   ITMAX = 300,
ALPHA  =      10.0,   BETA   ,=      8.0,   EPSMAX =     0.1
M      =     8,   N      =   10,   ITMAX = 500,
ALPHA  =      10.0,   BETA   =      8.0,   EPSMAX =     0.01
```

```
    TORSION OF CYLINDER OF ELLIPTICAL CROSS-SECTION, WITH PARAMETERS

M      =    4
N      =    5
ITMAX  = 200
ALPHA  =   10.000
BETA   =    8.000
EPSMAX =    0.001

  RESULTS ARE FOR INTERPOLATION OF DEGREE TWO, WITH GAUSS-SEIDEL ITERATION

  THE FOLLOWING VALUES ENABLE THE BOUNDARY AND INTERIOR POINTS TO BE LOCATED

  VALUES OF JR(2)...JR(M) ARE

      4    4    1

  VALUES OF JMAX(1)...JMAX(M+1) ARE

      6    5    5    4    1
```

Example 7.8   Torsion with Curved Boundary

505

Computer Output

Results for the 5th Data Set

```
    ITERATIONS STOPPED WITH

ITER   =   75

EPS    =   0.9260E-03

   THE FIELD OF PSI VALUES IS

0.0

17.0729   15.5120   10.8291    3.0244

29.2678   27.7069   23.0240   15.2193    4.2926

36.5846   35.0237   30.3410   22.5363   11.6096

39.0236   37.4627   32.7799   24.9752   14.0486    0.0

   RMS DEVIATION BETWEEN COMPUTED AND EXACT PSI VALUES IS

   RMSDEV  =    0.00042




    TORSION OF CYLINDER OF ELLIPTICAL CROSS-SECTION, WITH PARAMETERS

M       =    8
N       =   10
ITMAX   =  500
ALPHA   =   10.000
BETA    =    8.000
EPSMAX  =    0.010

   RESULTS ARE FOR INTERPOLATION OF DEGREE TWO, WITH GAUSS-SEIDEL ITERATION

   THE FOLLOWING VALUES ENABLE THE BOUNDARY AND INTERIOR POINTS TO BE LOCATED

   VALUES OF JR(2)...JR(M) ARE

       9     9     9     8     7     5     1

   VALUES OF JMAX(1)...JMAX(M+1) ARE

      11    10    10    10     9     8     7     5     1


    ITERATIONS STOPPED WITH

ITER   =  232

EPS    =   0.9897E-02
```

Computer Output (*Continued*)
Results for the 8th Data Set

```
THE FIELD OF PSI VALUES IS

0.0

 9.1449    8.7547    7.5842    5.6333    2.9020

17.0702   16.6801   15.5096   13.5588   10.8277    7.3161    3.0240

23.7760   23.3859   22.2155   20.2648   17.5338   14.0223    9.7303    4.6579

29.2624   28.8723   27.7020   25.7514   23.0204   19.5090   15.2172   10.1450    4.2922

33.5294   33.1394   31.9691   30.0186   27.2877   23.7764   19.4847   14.4125    8.5599    1.9266

36.5772   36.1872   35.0170   33.0665   30.3356   26.8244   22.5328   17.4608   11.6082    4.9750

38.4057   38.0158   36.8456   34.8951   32.1644   28.6532   24.3617   19.2896   13.4371    6.8040

39.0155   38.6252   37.4550   35.5046   32.7738   29.2627   24.9712   19.8992   14.0467    7.4137    0.0

RMS DEVIATION BETWEEN COMPUTED AND EXACT PSI VALUES IS

RMSDEV  =    0.00471
```

Example 7.8   Torsion with Curved Boundary   **507**

Discussion of Results

Two sets of computed results are displayed above; in both cases, the value of RMSDEV is very low, indicating excellent accuracy in the computations. This is not altogether surprising because the analytical solution for ψ, given by (7.8.3), has a special form; in particular, it is such that ψ_{xxx}, ψ_{yyy}, and higher-order derivatives are zero. This means that the finite-difference approximation to $\nabla^2\psi$ at any grid point is *exact*, even for a very coarse grid spacing. The values of RMSDEV for all runs are given in Table 7.8.1.

For the reason stated above, observe that in this particular example there is essentially no improvement in accuracy when employing the finer grid. Note also from

Table 7.8.1   Summary of Results

	$(m=4, n=5)$			$(m=8, n=10)$	
ε_{max}	ITER	RMSDEV	ε_{max}	ITER	RMSDEV
10	14	3.26690			
1	29	0.34275	1	108	0.44685
0.1	44	0.03601	0.1	170	0.04488
0.01	60	0.00332	0.01	232	0.00471
0.001	75	0.00042			

Table 7.8.1 that the number of iterations for a given degree of convergence (indicated by the value of RMSDEV) is roughly proportional to the total number of grid points involved.

7.25   Successive Overrelaxation and Alternating-Direction Methods

We now consider two additional methods which accelerate convergence to the solution of the finite-difference equations arising from the elliptic problem $u_{xx} + u_{yy} = 0$. The first, known as the method of successive overrelaxation (S.O.R.), is again an iterative technique in which an improved estimate $v'_{i,j}$ is computed by applying the following formula at every grid point:

$$v'_{i,j} = v_{i,j} + \frac{\omega}{4}(v_{i-1,j} + v_{i+1,j} + v_{i,j-1} + v_{i,j+1} - 4v_{i,j}),$$

$$(7.88)$$

where ω is an arbitrary parameter. For $\omega = 1$, the procedure is identical to the Gauss-Seidel method. However, for a choice of ω in the range $1 < \omega < 2$, the convergence is more rapid. The location of the optimum value of the parameter, ω_{opt}, presents some difficulty and is discussed in detail by Forsythe and Wasow [9]. For the simple case of Laplace's equation in a square with Dirichlet boundary conditions, Young [25] and Frankel [10] show that ω_{opt} equals the smaller root of

$$t^2\omega^2 - 16\omega + 16 = 0,   (7.89)$$

with $t = 2\cos(\pi/n)$, where n is the total number of increments into which the side of the square is divided. The number of iterations required for a given degree of convergence falls very rapidly when the parameter is in the immediate vicinity of ω_{opt}, and it is generally better to overestimate ω_{opt} than to underestimate it.

The second method is introduced by noting that the solution of the elliptic problem may be regarded as the limiting solution (for large values of time) of the corresponding time-dependent initial-value problem. Thus to solve $u_{xx} + u_{yy} = 0$ in a region R, some initial condition is first assigned throughout R, and the problem $u_{xx} + u_{yy} = u_t$ is solved instead. Successive time-steps of the solution of this parabolic problem may be viewed as successive steps of iteration in the elliptic problem. The boundary conditions will, of course, be identical for both cases. In fact, it can readily be shown that the Jacobi scheme for $u_{xx} + u_{yy} = 0$ is equivalent to the ordinary explicit method for $u_{xx} + u_{yy} = u_t$ with $\lambda = \Delta t/(\Delta x)^2 = 1/4$.

With these observations in mind, the *implicit alternating-direction method* (I.A.D.), discussed by Peaceman and Rachford [19], now finds an obvious application to the solution of elliptic PDEs. Indeed, for a rectangular region, it is superior even to the method of successive overrelaxation. A single stage of iteration, in which new estimates $v'_{i,j}$ are obtained from previous approximations $v_{i,j}$ via intermediate values $v^*_{i,j}$, is achieved by applying the following two difference equations in the manner discussed in Section 7.14.

$$-v^*_{i-1,j} + (2 + \rho)v^*_{i,j} - v^*_{i+1,j}$$
$$= v_{i,j-1} + (\rho - 2)v_{i,j} + v_{i,j+1},   (7.90a)$$

$$-v'_{i,j-1} + (2 + \rho)v'_{i,j} - v'_{i,j+1}$$
$$= v^*_{i-1,j} + (\rho - 2)v^*_{i,j} + v^*_{i+1,j}.   (7.90b)$$

Equations (7.90a) and (7.90b) are implicit in the x and y directions, respectively. When applied to successive rows or columns of points, each involves the solution of a system of equations having a tridiagonal coefficient matrix. The iteration parameter ρ is analogous to $2/\lambda$ for the parabolic case, and may be varied from one application of (7.90a) and (7.90b) to the next. For Laplace's equation in a square, the optimum convergence occurs when ρ is given the *sequence* of values

$$\rho_k = 4\sin^2\frac{k\pi}{2n},   k = 1, 2, \ldots, n - 1,   (7.91)$$

where n is the number of increments into which the side of the square is divided. Birkhoff and Varga [1] show that the alternating-direction method is most advantageous for rectangular regions.

Certain problems in unsteady two-dimensional fluid flow (for example, see [15], [28], and [29]) involve the solution of an elliptic PDE at *each* time-step. In such cases, there is a strong motivation for finding the optimum values of either ω or ρ for use in the S.O.R. and I.A.D. methods, respectively. Frequently, this investigation has to be performed on a semiempirical basis.

7.26   Characteristic-Value Problems

Boundary-value problems require the solution of a differential equation of order two or greater to satisfy specified conditions at both ends of an interval. A very important class is that in which both the differential equation and the boundary conditions are homogeneous. The term *homogeneous* means that if a differential equation and/or the boundary conditions are satisfied by a function $y(x)$, for instance, then they are also satisfied by $Ay(x)$, where A is an arbitrary constant. Thus the following boundary condition is homogeneous:

$$y + c\frac{dy}{dx} = 0   (\text{at}   x = a, \text{for instance}).   (7.92)$$

The subsequent discussion applies only to cases in which both the differential equation and the associated boundary conditions are homogeneous. In the general problem of this type, an arbitrary parameter λ is involved, and we must determine those values of λ for which the problem admits of nontrivial solutions.

It is convenient to mention such problems here because PDEs are frequently solved by the technique of separation of variables, which decomposes the original PDE into two or more ordinary differential equations, each of which involves an arbitrary parameter λ. Consideration of the boundary values then determines those possible values of λ that lead to a meaningful solution. A class of problems of this type is of the Sturm-Liouville form:

$$\frac{d}{dx}\left[p(x)\frac{dy}{dx}\right] + [q(x) + \lambda r(x)]y = 0, \qquad a < x < b,$$

$$y + c_1\frac{dy}{dx} = 0 \qquad \text{at} \quad x = a, \tag{7.93}$$

$$y + c_2\frac{dy}{dx} = 0 \qquad \text{at} \quad x = b,$$

where $p(x)$, $q(x)$, and $r(x)$ are known functions that are continuous in the interval (a,b), and in general, $r(x) > 0$ within the interval. These problems do not in general admit of nontrivial solutions for any λ. Nontrivial solutions exist only for discrete values of λ that are known as the *characteristic values* of the problem; the corresponding solutions are called the *characteristic functions*. We study here a method for the approximate treatment of such problems.

Consider the following slightly simplified version of the general Sturm-Liouville problem:

$$\frac{d^2y}{dx^2} + [q(x) + \lambda r(x)]y = 0, \qquad a < x < b, \tag{7.94}$$

$$y(a) = y(b) = 0.$$

Subdivide the interval (a,b) into equal parts by inserting the points

$$a = x_0; \quad x_1, x_2, \ldots, x_n; \quad x_{n+1} = b,$$

where $$\tag{7.95}$$

$$x_k = x_0 + hk, \qquad h = (b - a)/(n + 1).$$

We then make the following substitutions in the boundary-value problem:

$$y(x_k) \doteq v_k; \qquad \frac{d^2y(x_k)}{dx^2} \doteq \frac{v_{k-1} - 2v_k + v_{k+1}}{h^2};$$

$$\tag{7.96}$$

$$q(x_k) = q_k; \qquad r(x_k) = r_k.$$

Thus the differential equation and boundary conditions (7.94) are replaced by the following system of difference equations involving the values of the approximate solution v_k at the points x_k, $k = 0, 1, \ldots, n+1$:

$$v_0 = v_{n+1} = 0,$$

$$-v_{k-1} + [(2 - q_kh^2) - \lambda h^2 r_k]v_k - v_{k+1} = 0,$$

$$k = 1, 2, \ldots, n. \tag{7.97}$$

This set of homogeneous linear equations will admit of a nontrivial solution $v_1, v_2, \ldots, v_n$ if and only if the determinant of the array of coefficients of these quantities vanishes.

Let the vector $\mathbf{v}$ be defined by

$$\mathbf{v} = \begin{bmatrix} v_1 \\ v_2 \\ \vdots \\ v_n \end{bmatrix}. \tag{7.98}$$

Then the system of equations (7.97) can be written in the form

$$\mathbf{Q}\mathbf{v} = \lambda h^2 \mathbf{R}\mathbf{v}, \tag{7.99}$$

where $\mathbf{Q}$ is the matrix

$$\mathbf{Q} = \begin{bmatrix} (2 - q_1h^2) & -1 & 0 & 0 & \cdots & 0 & 0 \\ -1 & (2 - q_2h^2) & -1 & 0 & \cdots & 0 & 0 \\ 0 & -1 & (2 - q_3h^2) & -1 & \cdots & 0 & 0 \\ \cdot & \cdot & \cdot & \cdot & \cdots & \cdot & \cdot \\ 0 & 0 & 0 & 0 & \cdots & -1 & (2 - q_nh^2) \end{bmatrix} \tag{7.100}$$

and $\mathbf{R}$ is the diagonal matrix with elements $r_1, r_2, \ldots, r_n$ along the main diagonal. For convenience, since $r(x) > 0$, we can set

$$\mathbf{v} = \mathbf{R}^{-1/2}\mathbf{x}, \tag{7.101}$$

$$\mathbf{A} = h^{-2}\mathbf{R}^{-1/2}\mathbf{Q}\mathbf{R}^{-1/2},$$

and replace (7.99) by the equivalent system

$$\mathbf{A}\mathbf{x} = \lambda \mathbf{x}. \tag{7.102}$$

Here, $\mathbf{A}$ is the symmetric matrix

$$\mathbf{A} = \begin{bmatrix} a_{11} & -a_{12} & 0 & \cdots & 0 & 0 \\ -a_{21} & a_{22} & -a_{23} & \cdots & 0 & 0 \\ 0 & -a_{32} & a_{33} & \cdots & 0 & 0 \\ \cdot & \cdot & \cdot & \cdots & \cdot & \cdot \\ 0 & 0 & 0 & \cdots & -a_{n,n-1} & a_{nn} \end{bmatrix},$$

$$\tag{7.103}$$

in which

$$a_{kk} = \frac{2 - h^2q_k}{h^2r_k},$$

$$a_{ij} = a_{ji} = \frac{1}{(r_ir_j)^{1/2}}, \qquad \text{where } |i - j| = 1.$$

The problem of finding the characteristic values of (7.94) is, therefore, very similar to that of finding the eigenvalues and eigenvectors of a square matrix. This problem is discussed more fully in Chapter 4.

EXAMPLE 7.9

UNSTEADY CONDUCTION BETWEEN CYLINDERS
(CHARACTERISTIC-VALUE PROBLEM)

Problem Statement

Find the temperature history $\theta(r,t)$ in the solid bounded by two infinite cylindrical surfaces of radii r_1 and r_2, as shown in Fig. 7.9.1. Initially (at $t = 0$), $\theta = 0$ everywhere,

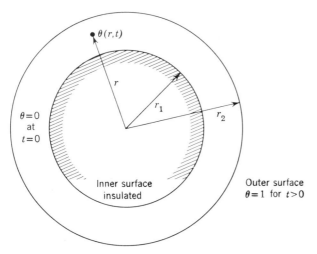

Figure 7.9.1 *Initial and boundary conditions for the hollow cylinder*

and for $t > 0$ the outer surface $r = r_2$ is maintained at $\theta = 1$. The inner surface $r = r_1$ behaves as a perfect insulator.

Method of Solution

The dimensionless heat conduction equation in radial coordinates is

$$\frac{\partial^2 \theta}{\partial r^2} + \frac{1}{r}\frac{\partial \theta}{\partial r} = \frac{\partial \theta}{\partial t}.$$

To reduce the situation to a characteristic-value problem, we must render the boundary conditions homogeneous, that is, of the form $\partial\theta/\partial r + a\theta = 0$.

By changing the variable to $\phi = 1 - \theta$, the governing differential equation becomes

$$\frac{\partial^2 \phi}{\partial r^2} + \frac{1}{r}\frac{\partial \phi}{\partial r} = \frac{\partial \phi}{\partial t}, \qquad (7.9.1)$$

subject to

(a) the initial condition: $\phi = 1$ at $t = 0$,
(b) the boundary conditions:
$$\left.\begin{array}{l} \partial\phi/\partial r = 0 \text{ at } r = r_1, \\ \phi = 0 \text{ at } r = r_2. \end{array}\right\} \quad (7.9.2)$$

Assuming that a separation of variables can be made,

$$\phi(r, t) = R(r)T(t), \qquad (7.9.3)$$

where R and T are functions of r and t only, respectively. Substituting in (7.9.1), we obtain

$$\frac{R''}{R} + \frac{1}{r}\frac{R'}{R} = \frac{T'}{T} = -\lambda. \qquad (7.9.4)$$

Since the parameter λ may assume a variety of values, the solution to the problem is written as

$$\phi(r,t) = \sum_j c_j R_j(r)e^{-\lambda_j t}, \qquad (7.9.5)$$

where the λ_j, c_j, and R_j are yet to be determined.

Consider that part of equation (7.9.4) involving R:

$$R'' + \frac{1}{r}R' + \lambda R = 0. \qquad (7.9.6)$$

We wish to determine those values that λ may assume, and the corresponding values of the function R. Divide the region between the cylindrical surfaces into n equal increments Δr, with grid points allocated as follows:

$$
\begin{array}{ccccccccc}
1 & 2 & 3 & i-1 & i & i+1 & n & n+1 \\
\cdot & \cdot & \cdot & \cdot & \cdot & \cdot & \cdot & \cdot \\
\uparrow & & & & & & & \uparrow
\end{array}
$$

Inner boundary $\qquad\qquad$ Outer boundary
$r = r_1$ (insulated) $\qquad$ $r = r_2$ ($\phi = 0$)

The finite-difference approximation to equation (7.9.6) is now considered at the various points.

(a) *General point* $(i = 2, 3, \ldots, n)$:

$$\frac{R_{i-1} - 2R_i + R_{i+1}}{(\Delta r)^2} + \frac{1}{r_i}\frac{R_{i+1} - R_{i-1}}{2\Delta r} + \lambda R_i = 0,$$

or, defining

$$D = \frac{2}{(\Delta r)^2}, \qquad E_i = \frac{1}{(\Delta r)^2}\left(1 - \frac{\Delta r}{2r_i}\right),$$

and

$$F_i = \frac{1}{(\Delta r)^2}\left(1 + \frac{\Delta r}{2r_i}\right),$$

we have

$$-E_i R_{i-1} + (D - \lambda)R_i - F_i R_{i+1} = 0.$$

(b) *Inner boundary point* $(i = 1)$:

$$R'/r = 0 \qquad \text{and} \qquad R'' = \frac{2}{(\Delta r)^2}(R_2 - R_1).$$

Hence,

$$(D - \lambda)R_1 - DR_2 = 0.$$

(c) *Outer boundary point* $(i = n + 1)$:
Since ϕ is always zero at $r = r_2$, we set $R_{n+1} = 0$.

We then have the following system of equations in the unknown R_i, $i = 1, 2, \ldots, n$:

$$DR_1 \quad - DR_2 \qquad\qquad\qquad\qquad = \lambda R_1$$
$$-E_2 R_1 + DR_2 \quad - F_2 R_3 \qquad\qquad\quad = \lambda R_2$$
$$-E_3 R_2 + DR_3 \quad - F_3 R_4 \qquad\quad = \lambda R_3$$
$$\cdots \quad \cdots \quad \cdots \quad \cdots \quad \cdots$$
$$-E_i R_{i-1} + DR_i \quad - F_i R_{i+1} \qquad = \lambda R_i$$
$$\cdots \quad \cdots \quad \cdots \quad \cdots \quad \cdots$$
$$-E_n R_{n-1} + DR_n = \lambda R_n.$$

Or, denoting the coefficient matrix by $\mathbf{A}$, and the column vector whose elements are $R_1, R_2, \ldots, R_n$ by $\mathbf{r}$,

$$\mathbf{A}\mathbf{r} = \lambda \mathbf{r}. \qquad (7.9.7)$$

In general, there will be n eigenvalues λ and n associated eigenvectors $\mathbf{r}$; let the jth such quantities be λ_j and $\mathbf{r}_j$.

Recognizing by subscript i that ϕ is required at some particular grid point and that there are n eigenvectors, equation (7.9.5) is

$$\phi_i(t) = \sum_{j=1}^{n} c_j r_{ij} e^{-\lambda_j t}, \qquad (7.9.8)$$

where r_{ij} is the ith element of the jth eigenvector. Again, the c_j will be determined by applying a property of orthogonality. Since $\mathbf{A}$ is unsymmetric, its eigenvectors are not orthogonal. This difficulty, however, may be overcome by denoting the transpose of $\mathbf{A}$ as $\mathbf{B} = \mathbf{A}^t$, and by denoting the eigenvectors of $\mathbf{B}$ by $\mathbf{s}$; the eigenvalues of matrix $\mathbf{B}$ are actually the same as those of matrix $\mathbf{A}$. Then, by a principle stated on page 220, if λ_1 and λ_2 are two eigenvalues of $\mathbf{A}$ (or $\mathbf{B}$) such that $\lambda_1 \neq \lambda_2$, then an eigenvector $\mathbf{s}$ such that $\mathbf{B}\mathbf{s} = \lambda_2 \mathbf{s}$ is orthogonal to an eigenvector $\mathbf{r}$ such that $\mathbf{A}\mathbf{r} = \lambda_1 \mathbf{r}$. In this event, $\mathbf{r}^t \mathbf{s} = 0$.

At time $t = 0$, by multiplying equation (7.9.8) through by s_{ip} (the ith element of the pth eigenvector of $\mathbf{B}$) and summing over all grid points i, we have

$$\sum_{i=1}^{n} s_{ip} \phi_i(0) = \sum_{i=1}^{n} \sum_{j=1}^{n} c_j s_{ip} r_{ij}.$$

But $\phi_i(0) = 1$ everywhere, from the initial condition (7.9.2). Also, by the orthogonality property of the eigenvectors, as long as there are no repeated eigenvalues,

$$\sum_{i=1}^{n} s_{ip} r_{ij} = 0, \qquad\qquad \text{if } p \neq j,$$
$$= \sum_{i=1}^{n} s_{ij} r_{ij}, \qquad \text{if } p = j. \qquad (7.9.9)$$

Hence,

$$c_j = \left(\sum_{i=1}^{n} s_{ij} \right) \Big/ \left(\sum_{i=1}^{n} s_{ij} r_{ij} \right). \qquad (7.9.10)$$

In the following program, the matrices $\mathbf{A}$ and $\mathbf{B}$ are first established and their eigenvalues and eigenvectors are then found by calling on the subroutine RUTIS. The eigenvectors of $\mathbf{A}$ and $\mathbf{B}$ are stored column by column in the matrices $\mathbf{R}$ and $\mathbf{S}$, respectively. The program checks to determine if the eigenvectors of $\mathbf{A}$ and $\mathbf{B}$ are indeed orthogonal by constructing a new matrix $\mathbf{P} = \mathbf{R}^t \mathbf{S}$ whose elements are such that

$$p_{ij} = \mathbf{r}_i^t \mathbf{s}_j^t = \sum_{k=1}^{n} r_{ki} s_{kj}. \qquad (7.9.11)$$

The off-diagonal elements ($i \neq j$) of $\mathbf{P}$ should be close to zero. Next, the coefficients c_j are evaluated from (7.9.10). This allows $\phi_i(t)$ to be computed from (7.9.8) for any time and grid point; hence the corresponding temperatures $\theta_i(t) = 1 - \phi_i(t)$ can be computed and tabulated. When evaluating (7.9.8), terms are ignored if the exponent $\lambda_j t$ is greater than 40.

Flow Diagram

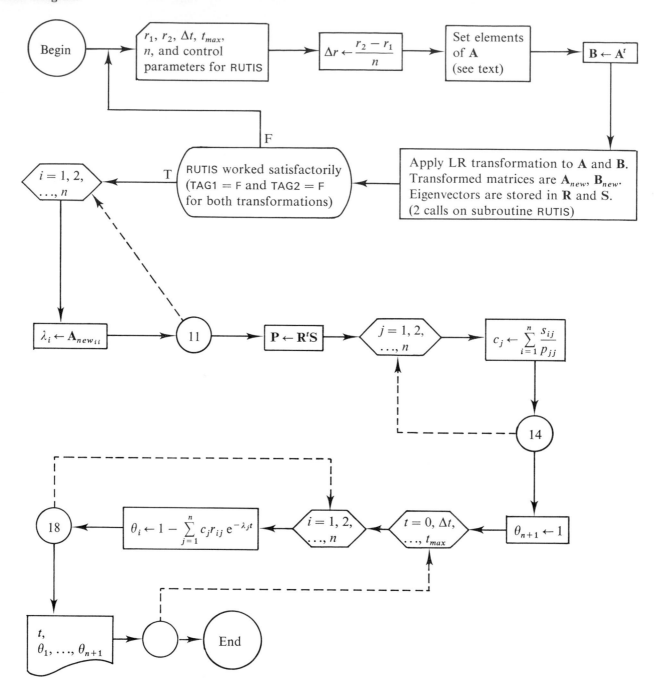

FORTRAN *Implementation*

List of Principal Variables

Program Symbol	*Definition*
A, B	Matrix **A** appearing in equation (7.9.7), and its transpose **B**.
ANEW, BNEW	Transformed matrices returned by RUTIS.
C	Vector of coefficients c_j, defined in (7.9.10).
DR	Radial grid spacing, Δr.
DT	Time interval between successive printings of temperatures.
FREQ, ITMAX, EPS1, EPS2, EPS3, EPS4, EIGVEC, STRIPD, SWEEP, TAG1, TAG2, ITER	Parameters for use in subroutine RUTIS (see Example 4.3).
LAMBDA	Vector of eigenvalues λ_i.
N	Number of grid points, n, at which temperatures are to be computed.
P	Matrix $\mathbf{P} = \mathbf{R}^t \mathbf{S}$, with elements given by (7.9.11).
R, S	Matrices whose columns contain eigenvectors **r** and **s** of **A** and **B**, respectively.
R1, R2	Radii of inner and outer cylinders, r_1 and r_2, respectively.
RUTIS	Subroutine for finding the eigenvalues and eigenvectors of a matrix (see Example 4.3).
T	Time, t.
THETA	Vector of temperatures, θ_i.
TMAX	Maximum value of time to be considered, t_{max}.

Program Listing

```
C           APPLIED NUMERICAL METHODS, EXAMPLE 7.9
C           UNSTEADY CONDUCTION BETWEEN CYLINDERS (EIGENVALUE PROBLEM).
C
      IMPLICIT REAL*8 (A-H, O-Z)
      REAL*8 LAMBDA
      INTEGER FREQ
      LOGICAL EIGVEC, STRIPD, SWEEP, TAG1, TAG2
      DIMENSION A(11,11), ANEW(11,11), R(11,11), P(11,11), C(11),
     1 THETA(11), LAMBDA(11), B(11,11), BNEW(11,11), S(11,11)
C
C     ..... CHECK PARAMETERS, ESTABLISH MATRIX A AND TRANSPOSE .....
    1 WRITE (6,200)
      READ (5,100) R1, R2, DT, TMAX, N, FREQ, ITMAX, EPS1, EPS2, EPS3,
     1 EPS4, EIGVEC, STRIPD, SWEEP
      WRITE (6,201) R1, R2, DT, TMAX, N, FREQ, ITMAX, EPS1, EPS2, EPS3,
     1 EPS4, EIGVEC, STRIPD, SWEEP
      FN = N
      DR = (R2 - R1)/FN
      DUM = 1./(DR*DR)
      D = 2.*DUM
      DO 2  I = 1, N
      THETA(I) = 0.0
      DO 2  J = 1, N
    2 A(I,J) = 0.0
      NM1 = N - 1
      NP1 = N + 1
      DO 3  I = 1, NM1
      A(I,I) = D
      FI = I
      A(I,I+1) = - DUM*(1. + 0.5/(R1/DR + FI - 1))
    3 A(I+1,I) = - DUM*(1. - 0.5/(R1/DR + FI))
      A(N,N) = D
      A(1,2) = - D
      DO 4  I = 1, N
      DO 4  J = 1, N
    4 B(I,J) = A(J,I)
      WRITE (6,203)
      DO 5  I = 1, N
    5 WRITE (6,204) (A(I,J), J = 1, N)
C
C
C     ..... CALL ON SUBROUTINE RUTIS, TO FIND THE
C           EIGENVALUES AND EIGENVECTORS OF A AND B .....
      WRITE (6,207)
      DO 8  I = 1, N
    8 WRITE (6,204) (B(I,J), J = 1, N)
      CALL RUTIS (N, A, ANEW, R, FREQ, ITMAX, EPS1, EPS2,
     1 EPS3, EPS4, EIGVEC, STRIPD, SWEEP, TAG1, TAG2, ITER)
      WRITE (6,202) TAG1, TAG2, ITER
      IF (TAG1 .OR. TAG2) GO TO 1
      WRITE (6,205)
      DO 6  I = 1, N
    6 WRITE (6,204) (ANEW(I,J), J = 1, N)
      WRITE (6,206)
      DO 7  I = 1, N
    7 WRITE (6,204) (R(I,J), J = 1, N)
      CALL RUTIS (N, B, BNEW, S, FREQ, ITMAX, EPS1, EPS2,
     1 EPS3, EPS4, EIGVEC, STRIPD, SWEEP, TAG1, TAG2, ITER)
      WRITE (6,202) TAG1, TAG2, ITER
      IF (TAG1 .OR. TAG2) GO TO 1
      WRITE (6,208)
      DO 9  I = 1, N
    9 WRITE (6,204) (BNEW(I,J), J = 1, N)
      WRITE (6,209)
      DO 10  I = 1, N
   10 WRITE (6,204) (S(I,J), J = 1, N)
      DO 11  I = 1, N
   11 LAMBDA(I) = ANEW(I,I)
```

Program Listing (*Continued*)

```
C
C       ..... CHECK ON ORTHOGONALITY OF EIGENVECTORS .....
        DO 12  I = 1, N
        DO 12  J = 1, N
        P(I,J) = 0.
        DO 12  K = 1, N
   12   P(I,J) = P(I,J) + R(K,I)*S(K,J)
        WRITE (6,210)
        DO 13  I = 1, N
   13   WRITE (6,204) (P(I,J), J = 1, N)
C
C       ..... DETERMINE COEFFICIENTS C(J) FROM INITIAL CONDITION .....
        DO 14  J = 1, N
        C(J) = 0.
        DO 14  I = 1, N
   14   C(J) = C(J) + S(I,J)/P(J,J)
        WRITE (6,211)
        WRITE (6,204) (C(J), J = 1, N)
C
C       ..... COMPUTE VALUES OF TEMPERATURE .....
        WRITE (6,212)
        THETA(NP1) = 1.
        MIN = 1
        T = 0.
   15   IF (T.GT.TMAX .OR. THETA(1).GT.0.95) GO TO 1
   16   IF (DABS(LAMBDA(MIN)*T) .LE. 40.) GO TO 17
            MIN = MIN + 1
            GO TO 16
   17   DO 18  I = 1, N
        THETA (I) = 1.
        DO 18  J = MIN, N
   18   THETA(I) = THETA(I) - C(J)*R(I,J)*DEXP(-LAMBDA(J)*T)
        WRITE (6,213) T, (THETA(J), J = 1, NP1)
        T = T + DT
        GO TO 15
C
C       ..... FORMATS FOR INPUT AND OUTPUT STATEMENTS .....
  100   FORMAT (4(12X, F6.1)/ 3(12X, I6)/ 4(12X, E6.0)/ 3(12X, L6))
  200   FORMAT (69H1     UNSTEADY STATE HEAT CONDUCTION BETWEEN CONCENTRIC C
       1YLINDERS, WITH/ 1H0)
  201   FORMAT (8X, 10H R1        = , F10.4/ 8X, 10H R2        = , F10.4/
       1 8X, 10H DT        = , F10.4/ 8X, 10H TMAX      = , F10.4/
       2 8X, 10H N         = , I5   / 8X, 10H FREQ      = , I5   /
       3 8X, 10H ITMAX     = , I5   / 8X, 10H EPS1      = , E10.1/
       4 8X, 10H EPS2      = , E10.1/ 8X, 10H EPS3      = , E10.1/
       5 8X, 10H EPS4      = , E10.1/ 8X, 10H EIGVEC    = , L5   /
       6 8X, 10H STRIPD    = , L5   / 8X, 10H SWEEP     = , L5)
  202   FORMAT (1H0, 7X, 10H TAG1      = , L5/ 8X, 10H TAG2      = , L5/
       1 8X, 10H ITER      = , I5)
  203   FORMAT (24H0     STARTING MATRIX A IS/1H )
  204   FORMAT (5X, 10F10.6)
  205   FORMAT (30H0     TRANSFORMED MATRIX ANEW IS/1H )
  206   FORMAT (46H0     MATRIX R, CONTAINING EIGENVECTORS OF A, IS/1H )
  207   FORMAT (26H0     TRANSPOSED MATRIX B IS/1H )
  208   FORMAT (30H0     TRANSFORMED MATRIX BNEW IS/1H )
  209   FORMAT (46H0     MATRIX S, CONTAINING EIGENVECTORS OF B, IS/1H )
  210   FORMAT (79H0     ORTHOGONALITY REQUIRES OFF-DIAGONAL ELEMENTS OF FOL
       1LOWING MATRIX TO BE ZERO/1H )
  211   FORMAT (36H0     THE COEFFICIENTS C(1)...C(N) ARE/1H )
  212   FORMAT (83H1     TIME            TEMPERATURES AT GRID POINTS (INN
       1ER SURFACE TO OUTER SURFACE)/1H )
  213   FORMAT (1H , F7.3/(8X, 11F8.5))
C
        END
```

Program Listing (*Continued*)

Data

```
R1      =    10.0,    R2      =   19.0,    DT      =    5.0,    TMAX    = 100.0,
N       =     9,      FREQ    =    5,      ITMAX   =   75,
EPS1    = 1.E-7,      EPS2    = 1.E-3,     EPS3    = 1.E-4,     EPS4    = 1.E-1,
EIGVEC  =     T,      STRIPD  =    T,      SWEEP   =    T.
```

Computer Output

```
UNSTEADY STATE HEAT CONDUCTION BETWEEN CONCENTRIC CYLINDERS, WITH

        R1      =     10.0000
        R2      =     19.0000
        DT      =      5.0000
        TMAX    =    100.0000
        N       =      9
        FREQ    =      5
        ITMAX   =     75
        EPS1    =      0.1D-06
        EPS2    =      0.1D-02
        EPS3    =      0.1D-03
        EPS4    =      0.1D 00
        EIGVEC  =      T
        STRIPD  =      T
        SWEEP   =      T

STARTING MATRIX A IS

   2.000000 -2.000000  0.0        0.0        0.0        0.0        0.0        0.0        0.0
  -0.954545  2.000000 -1.045455   0.0        0.0        0.0        0.0        0.0        0.0
   0.0      -0.958333  2.000000  -1.041667   0.0        0.0        0.0        0.0        0.0
   0.0       0.0      -0.961538   2.000000  -1.038462   0.0        0.0        0.0        0.0
   0.0       0.0       0.0       -0.964286   2.000000  -1.035714   0.0        0.0        0.0
   0.0       0.0       0.0        0.0       -0.966667   2.000000  -1.033333   0.0        0.0
   0.0       0.0       0.0        0.0        0.0       -0.968750   2.000000  -1.031250   0.0
   0.0       0.0       0.0        0.0        0.0        0.0       -0.970588   2.000000  -1.029412
   0.0       0.0       0.0        0.0        0.0        0.0        0.0       -0.972222   2.000000

TRANSPOSED MATRIX B IS

   2.000000 -0.954545  0.0        0.0        0.0        0.0        0.0        0.0        0.0
  -2.000000  2.000000 -0.958333   0.0        0.0        0.0        0.0        0.0        0.0
   0.0      -1.045455  2.000000  -0.961538   0.0        0.0        0.0        0.0        0.0
   0.0       0.0      -1.041667   2.000000  -0.964286   0.0        0.0        0.0        0.0
   0.0       0.0       0.0       -1.038462   2.000000  -0.966667   0.0        0.0        0.0
   0.0       0.0       0.0        0.0       -1.035714   2.000000  -0.968750   0.0        0.0
   0.0       0.0       0.0        0.0        0.0       -1.033333   2.000000  -0.970588   0.0
   0.0       0.0       0.0        0.0        0.0        0.0       -1.031250   2.000000  -0.972222
   0.0       0.0       0.0        0.0        0.0        0.0        0.0       -1.029412   2.000000

        TAG1    =       F
        TAG2    =       F
        ITER    =      41

TRANSFORMED MATRIX ANEW IS

   3.961222 -2.000000  0.0        0.0        0.0        0.0        0.0        0.0        0.0
   0.000000  3.723779 -1.045455   0.0        0.0        0.0        0.0        0.0        0.0
   0.000000  0.000000  3.279354  -1.041667   0.0        0.0        0.0        0.0        0.0
   0.0       0.000000  0.000000   2.680719  -1.038462   0.0        0.0        0.0        0.0
   0.0       0.0       0.0        0.0        2.000000  -1.035714   0.0        0.0        0.0
   0.0       0.0       0.0        0.0        0.0        1.319281  -1.033333   0.0        0.0
   0.0       0.0       0.0        0.0        0.0        0.0        0.720646  -1.031250   0.0
   0.0       0.0       0.0        0.0        0.0        0.0        0.0        0.276221  -1.029412
   0.0       0.0       0.0        0.0        0.0        0.0        0.0        0.0        0.038778
```

Computer Output (*Continued*)

MATRIX R, CONTAINING EIGENVECTORS OF A, IS

```
 0.458344  0.508351  0.515423  0.517336  0.517789  0.517336  0.515423  0.508351  0.458344
-0.449457 -0.438143 -0.329704 -0.176080 -0.000000  0.176080  0.329704  0.438143  0.449457
 0.424672  0.258277 -0.067135 -0.357701 -0.472764 -0.357701 -0.067135  0.258277  0.424672
-0.386060 -0.024312  0.385781  0.395747  0.000000 -0.395747 -0.385781  0.024312  0.386060
 0.335892 -0.198788 -0.413109  0.071789  0.437745  0.071789 -0.413109 -0.198788  0.335892
-0.276607  0.353487  0.151113 -0.415638 -0.000000  0.415638 -0.151113 -0.353486  0.276607
 0.210767 -0.403714  0.199366  0.206648 -0.409503  0.206648  0.199366 -0.403714  0.210767
-0.140992  0.342762 -0.389286  0.254041 -0.000000 -0.254041  0.389286 -0.342762  0.140992
 0.069893 -0.193320  0.295831 -0.362829  0.386103 -0.362829  0.295831 -0.193320  0.069893
```

```
       TAG1  =    F
       TAG2  =    F
       ITER  =    41
```

TRANSFORMED MATRIX BNEW IS

```
 3.961222 -0.954545  0.0       0.0       0.0       0.0       0.0       0.0       0.0
 0.000000  3.723779 -0.958333  0.0       0.0       0.0       0.0       0.0       0.0
 0.000000  0.000000  3.279354 -0.961538  0.0       0.0       0.0       0.0       0.0
 0.000000  0.000000  0.000000  2.680719 -0.964286  0.0       0.0       0.0       0.0
 0.0       0.0       0.0       0.0       2.000000 -0.966667  0.0       0.0       0.0
 0.0       0.0       0.0       0.0       0.0       1.319281 -0.968750  0.0       0.0
 0.0       0.0       0.0       0.0       0.0       0.0       0.720646 -0.970588  0.0
 0.0       0.0       0.0       0.0       0.0       0.0       0.0       0.276221 -0.972222
 0.0       0.0       0.0       0.0       0.0       0.0       0.0       0.0       0.038778
```

MATRIX S, CONTAINING EIGENVECTORS OF B, IS

```
 0.203792  0.208591  0.209275  0.209460  0.209503  0.209460  0.209275  0.208591  0.203792
-0.418715 -0.376687 -0.280487 -0.149373 -0.000000  0.149373  0.280487  0.376687  0.418715
 0.431590  0.242236 -0.062305 -0.331031 -0.437224 -0.331031 -0.062305  0.242236  0.431590
-0.425045 -0.024703  0.387864  0.396762  0.000000 -0.396762 -0.387864  0.024703  0.425045
 0.398258 -0.217516 -0.447289  0.077509  0.472310  0.077510 -0.447289 -0.217516  0.398258
-0.351392  0.414416  0.175303 -0.480811 -0.000000  0.480811 -0.175303 -0.414416  0.351392
 0.285602 -0.504854  0.246699  0.254988 -0.504958  0.254988  0.246699 -0.504854  0.285602
-0.202993  0.455422 -0.511814  0.333059 -0.000000 -0.333059  0.511814 -0.455422  0.202993
 0.106548 -0.271970  0.411823 -0.503666  0.535616 -0.503666  0.411823 -0.271970  0.106548
```

ORTHOGONALITY REQUIRES OFF-DIAGONAL ELEMENTS OF FOLLOWING MATRIX TO BE ZERO

```
 0.956210 -0.000000 -0.000000 -0.000000  0.000000  0.000000  0.000000  0.000000  0.000000
-0.000000  0.936469 -0.000000 -0.000000 -0.000000 -0.000000 -0.000000 -0.000000 -0.000000
-0.000000 -0.000000  0.935681 -0.000000  0.000000  0.000000  0.000000  0.000000  0.000000
-0.000000 -0.000000 -0.000000  0.935545  0.000000  0.000000  0.000000  0.000000  0.000000
 0.000000 -0.000000  0.000000  0.000000  0.935518 -0.000000  0.000000  0.000000  0.000000
 0.000000 -0.000000  0.000000  0.000000 -0.000000  0.935545 -0.000000 -0.000000 -0.000000
 0.000000 -0.000000  0.000000  0.000000  0.000000 -0.000000  0.935681  0.000000  0.000000
 0.000000 -0.000000  0.000000  0.000000  0.000000 -0.000000  0.000000  0.936469  0.000000
 0.000000 -0.000000  0.000000  0.000000  0.000000 -0.000000  0.000000  0.000000  0.956210
```

THE COEFFICIENTS C(1)...C(N) ARE

```
 0.028911 -0.080157  0.137941 -0.206408  0.294219 -0.419411  0.627712 -1.080612  2.953258
```

```
   TIME              TEMPERATURES AT GRID POINTS (INNER SURFACE TO OUTER SURFACE)

  0.0
        -0.00000-0.00000 0.00000 0.00000-0.00000 0.00000-0.00000 0.00000-0.00000 1.00000
  5.000
         0.01449 0.02003 0.03797 0.07379 0.13598 0.23392 0.37434 0.55712 0.77220 1.00000
 10.000
         0.11595 0.12905 0.16663 0.22819 0.31351 0.42164 0.54999 0.69388 0.84661 1.00000
 15.000
         0.25210 0.26556 0.30340 0.36313 0.44212 0.53733 0.64515 0.76137 0.88130 1.00000
 20.000
         0.37893 0.39071 0.42364 0.47514 0.54240 0.62234 0.71166 0.80680 0.90413 1.00000
```

Computer Output (*Continued*)

```
25.000
         0.48714 0.49702 0.52459 0.56759 0.62354 0.68978 0.76347 0.84170 0.92150 1.00000
30.000
         0.57722 0.58540 0.60822 0.64379 0.69002 0.74468 0.80541 0.86981 0.93546 1.00000
35.000
         0.65166 0.65841 0.67723 0.70657 0.74468 0.78973 0.83977 0.89281 0.94686 1.00000
40.000
         0.71303 0.71860 0.73411 0.75828 0.78969 0.82681 0.86803 0.91172 0.95624 1.00000
45.000
         0.76361 0.76819 0.78097 0.80089 0.82676 0.85734 0.89129 0.92728 0.96395 1.00000
50.000
         0.80527 0.80905 0.81958 0.83598 0.85729 0.88248 0.91045 0.94010 0.97031 1.00000
55.000
         0.83959 0.84270 0.85138 0.86489 0.88245 0.90319 0.92624 0.95066 0.97554 1.00000
60.000
         0.86786 0.87043 0.87757 0.88870 0.90317 0.92026 0.93924 0.95935 0.97985 1.00000
65.000
         0.89115 0.89326 0.89915 0.90832 0.92023 0.93431 0.94995 0.96652 0.98340 1.00000
70.000
         0.91034 0.91208 0.91692 0.92448 0.93429 0.94589 0.95877 0.97242 0.98633 1.00000
75.000
         0.92614 0.92757 0.93157 0.93779 0.94587 0.95543 0.96604 0.97728 0.98874 1.00000
80.000
         0.93916 0.94034 0.94363 0.94875 0.95541 0.96328 0.97202 0.98128 0.99072 1.00000
85.000
         0.94988 0.95085 0.95356 0.95779 0.96327 0.96975 0.97695 0.98458 0.99236 1.00000
90.000
         0.95872 0.95952 0.96175 0.96523 0.96975 0.97509 0.98102 0.98730 0.99370 1.00000
```

Discussion of Results

By examining the diagonal elements of the transformed matrices ANEW and BNEW, observe that matrices **A** and **B** have identical eigenvalues. The subdiagonal elements of ANEW and BNEW are zero, to six decimal places, indicating that RUTIS has performed a sufficient number of iterations (actually ITER = 41 in both cases). Note also that the off-diagonal elements of **P** (the last matrix printed) are virtually zero, which checks the orthogonality of the eigenvectors as expressed in equation (7.9.9).

Judging from the values of the coefficients c_j, the eigenvectors that are weighted the most heavily are those corresponding to the smallest eigenvalues, i.e., to the values of $e^{-\lambda_j t}$ that decay least rapidly with time. An additional check on the accuracy of the calculations is afforded by the values of temperature at $t = 0$; the first of these should be zero, in the absence of round-off error.

Finally, we mention that, once the eigenvalues and eigenvectors have been found, the effect of any other initial condition can be examined merely by recomputing the coefficients c_j. Also, the computed values of temperature do not depend on values of temperature at any previous time. These are two advantages which are not afforded by the conventional finite-difference solution of the parabolic equation (7.9.1).

Problems

7.1 Verify the following finite-difference approximations for use in two dimensions at the point (i,j):

(a) $\dfrac{\partial^4 u}{\partial x^4} = \dfrac{u_{i-2,j} - 4u_{i-1,j} + 6u_{i,j} - 4u_{i+1,j} + u_{i+2,j}}{(\Delta x)^4}$
$$+ O[(\Delta x)^2].$$

(b) $\dfrac{\partial u}{\partial x} = \dfrac{-3u_{i,j} + 4u_{i+1,j} - u_{i+2,j}}{2\Delta x} + O[(\Delta x)^2].$

(c) $\dfrac{\partial^2 u}{\partial x^2} = \dfrac{2u_{i,j} - 5u_{i+1,j} + 4u_{i+2,j} - u_{i+3,j}}{(\Delta x)^2} + O[(\Delta x)^2].$

Suggest possible uses of formulas (b) and (c).

7.2 Verify equation (7.8) for the finite-difference approximation of $\partial^2 u/\partial x \partial y$.

7.3 Verify equation (7.9) for the finite-difference approximation of the Laplacian during the solution of $u_{xx} + u_{yy} = 0$.

7.4 Rework the numerical example in Section 7.5, using the explicit method with $\Delta x = 0.2$ and $\Delta t = 0.02$, that is, $\lambda = 1/2$.

7.5 Rework the numerical example in Section 7.5, performing four time steps, using the implicit method with $\Delta x = 0.2$ and $\Delta t = 0.04$, that is, $\lambda = 1$.

7.6 The following finite-difference approximation has been suggested for the PDE $u_t = u_{xx} + u_{yy}$:

$$\frac{v_{i,j,n+1} - v_{i,j,n}}{\Delta t} = \delta_x^2 v_{i,j,n+1} + \delta_y^2 v_{i,j,n}.$$

Investigate the stability of this procedure.

7.7 Verify the formula given on page 453 for the amplification factor during the solution of $u_{xx} + u_{yy} = u_t$ by the implicit alternating-direction method.

7.8 Set up the analog of (7.52) for solving $u_{xx} + u_{yy} + u_{zz} = u_t$ by a simple extension of the implicit alternating-direction method. If $\Delta x = \Delta y = \Delta z$, show that the method will be unstable at least for $\lambda > 3/2$.

7.9 Investigate the stability of the following two procedures for solving $u_{xx} + u_{yy} + u_{zz} = u_t$: (a) the alternating-direction modification of the Crank-Nicolson method, (7.54), and (b) Brian's method, (7.55).

7.10 Show that Brian's method, (7.55), for solving $u_{xx} + u_{yy} + u_{zz} = u_t$, can be reexpressed in the form of (7.56).

7.11 The following nonlinear PDE governs unsteady heat conduction in a bar:

$$\frac{\partial}{\partial x}\left(k\frac{\partial T}{\partial x}\right) = \rho c_p \frac{\partial T}{\partial t}.$$

Here, the thermal conductivity k, density ρ, and specific heat c_p are known functions of temperature T.

What finite-difference approximation would you recommend for a Crank-Nicolson type solution?

7.12 In Section 7.17, the boundary condition $-u_n + au = g$ was coupled with the PDE $u_t = u_{xx} + u_{yy}$ to give equation (7.60).

As an alternative approach, the finite-difference approximation of the boundary condition *alone* could be employed at the boundary, giving, for example,

(a) $-\dfrac{-3v_{0,j,n+1} + 4v_{1,j,n+1} - v_{2,j,n+1}}{2\Delta x} + av_{0,j,n+1} = g,$

(b) $-\dfrac{v_{1,j,n+1} - v_{0,j,n+1}}{\Delta x} + av_{0,j,n+1} = g,$

depending on which approximation is used for u_n ($= \partial u/\partial x$). Although these formulas are implicit and relate to a two-dimensional problem, counterparts could easily be derived for explicit and/or one-dimensional problems. Also, the value of a and/or g might be zero in certain applications.

From the points of view of accuracy and computational convenience, investigate the desirability of this alternative way of accounting for boundary conditions.

7.13 One-dimensional unsteady heat conduction in a medium is governed by the equation $\alpha(\partial^2 T/\partial x^2) = \partial T/\partial t$, in which T is temperature (°F), x is distance (ft), t is time (hr), and α is the thermal diffusivity (sq ft/hr) of the medium.

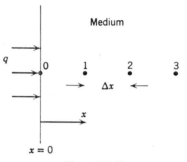

Figure P7.13

A heat flux density q (BTU/hr sq ft) is imposed on the boundary $x = 0$ of the medium shown in Fig. P7.13. If the thermal conductivity of the medium is k (BTU/hr sq ft °F), what is the explicit finite-difference approximation of the heat conduction equation at grid-point 1?

Note. Fourier's law of heat conduction is: $q = -k\,\partial T/\partial x$.

7.14 The equation $u_{xx} + u_{yy} = u_t$ is being solved explicitly for the region shown in Fig. P7.14. The boundary conditions are of the Dirichlet type. What formula should be used to compute $v_{A,n+1}$? Assume that $\Delta x = \Delta y$.

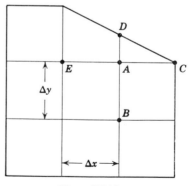

Figure P7.14

7.15 Compare the relative merits of (a) the Jacobi, (b) the Gauss-Seidel, and (c) the successive overrelaxation methods for solving the problem stated in Example 7.6 (solution of Laplace's equation in a square). To do this, perform a few hand calculations with four grid spacings along each side of the square, and see how quickly each method converges to the corresponding values computed in Example 7.6.

7.16 The cross section of a hollow square duct is shown in Fig. P7.16. The sides of the two squares are in the ratio 2:1. The interior and exterior surfaces of the duct are maintained at temperatures of 1000°F and 100°F, respectively.

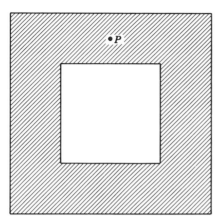

Figure P7.16

Assuming steady-state heat conduction, estimate the temperature at point P, located halfway between the midpoints of adjacent sides of the two squares.

7.17 Figure P7.17 shows a cross section of one quadrant of a circular duct that passes through a square block of refractory material of thermal conductivity $k = 0.26$ BTU/hr ft °F. The inner curved surface is maintained steadily at 1400°F by a hot gas, and the outer surface is constant at 100°F. If $r = 6$ in., estimate (a) the steady temperatures at the indicated grid points ($\Delta x = \Delta y = 3$ in.) and (b) the heat leakage per foot length of the duct. In this connection, what is the finite-difference approximation of $\nabla^2 T = 0$ at point P?

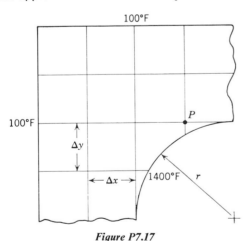

Figure P7.17

What would the corresponding answers be for $r = 12$ in., and $\Delta x = \Delta y = 6$ in.?

7.18 Show that the Jacobi iteration scheme for solving $u_{xx} + u_{yy} = 0$ is equivalent to the ordinary explicit method for solving $u_{xx} + u_{yy} = u_t$, with $\lambda = \Delta t/(\Delta x)^2 = 1/4$.

7.19 Set up a successive overrelaxation scheme for solving $\nabla^2 \psi = -\sigma$ in two space dimensions, with $\Delta x \neq \Delta y$. Assume that $\sigma = \sigma(x,y)$ is a known function of position (see Section 7.2(c)).

7.20 Consider the implicit alternating-direction solution of Laplace's equation in a square, for which the optimum sequence of iteration parameters ρ is given by equation (7.91). Investigate a possible connection between this sequence and the expression for the amplification factor given in Section 7.14 for the implicit alternating-direction solution of the corresponding parabolic problem.

7.21 Write a computer program to find the temperature history $\theta(r,t)$ inside an infinitely long cylinder of radius a that is initially at a uniform temperature θ_0 and is suddenly immersed in a bath of hot fluid maintained at a temperature θ_1. The heat-transfer coefficient between the bath and the cylindrical surface is h, and the thermal diffusivity and conductivity of the material of the cylinder are α and k, respectively.

To facilitate the solution, first define a dimensionless time, radius, and temperature by

$$\tau = \frac{\alpha t}{a^2}, \qquad R = \frac{r}{a}, \qquad \text{and} \qquad T = \frac{\theta - \theta_0}{\theta_1 - \theta_0}.$$

Noting that there is axial symmetry, the governing equations can be shown to be

Conduction equation

$$\frac{\partial T}{\partial \tau} = \frac{\partial^2 T}{\partial R^2} + \frac{1}{R}\frac{\partial T}{\partial R}.$$

Initial condition

$$\tau = 0, \, 0 \leqslant R \leqslant 1 : T = 0.$$

Boundary conditions

$$\tau > 0, \, R = 1 : \phi \frac{\partial T}{\partial R} = 1 - T, \quad \text{where} \quad \phi = \frac{k}{ha},$$

$$\tau > 0, \, R = 0 : \quad \frac{\partial T}{\partial R} = 0.$$

Then solve the problem by an implicit finite-difference technique, in which the radius from $R = 0$ to $R = 1$ is divided into n equal increments, giving $n + 1$ unknown temperatures at each time step. The grid points at $R = 0$ and $R = 1$ will need special approximations. A necessary first step at the center is to note, from L'Hospital's rule, that since $\partial T/\partial R \to 0$ as $R \to 0$, the conduction equation becomes $\partial T/\partial \tau = 2(\partial^2 T/\partial R^2)$ at $R = 0$.

The input data for the computer program should include values for n, $\Delta \tau$ (the time step), ϕ, and τ_{max} (the maximum value of τ for which the solution is of interest). Some control will also be needed for printing the computed temperatures at definite time intervals. Suggested values are: $n = 10$ and 20, $\Delta \tau = 0.005, 0.01, 0.02, 0.05,$ and $0.1, \phi = 0, 0.5,$ and $2, \tau_{max} = 1.5$.

Comment briefly on how the computed results depend on the particular choice of grid size and time increment.

7.22 Consider the problem illustrated in Fig. P7.22, of heat transfer to a viscous fluid of thermal diffusivity α flowing with mean velocity u_m through a heated tube of radius a. The temperature θ of the inlet fluid is θ_0, and the tube wall is at a constant temperature θ_1.

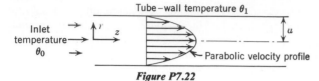

Figure P7.22

Let r and z be radial and axial coordinates. Define corresponding dimensionless coordinates by $R = r/a$ and $Z = \alpha z/(2u_m a^2)$. Assuming steady laminar flow with constant viscosity and negligible axial conduction (see, for example, page 616 of Goldstein [35]), the following PDE governs the dimensionless temperature $T = (\theta - \theta_0)/(\theta_1 - \theta_0)$:

$$\frac{\partial^2 T}{\partial R^2} + \frac{1}{R}\frac{\partial T}{\partial R} = (1 - R^2)\frac{\partial T}{\partial Z},$$

subject to the inlet condition $T = 0$ at $Z = 0$, $0 \leq R \leq 1$, and the boundary conditions $T = 1$ at $R = 1$, $Z > 0$, and $\partial T/\partial R = 0$ at $R = 0$, $Z > 0$.

Write a program that uses a finite-difference procedure for computing T as a function of R and Z. The input data should include values for: m (number of radial increments ΔR), ΔZ (axial step), and Z_{max} (maximum value of Z for which T is to be computed).

7.23 A problem closely related to (7.22) is that in which the tube wall is electrically heated at a known rate q (energy per unit area per unit time). See, for example, page 293 of Bird, Stewart, and Lightfoot [34]. In this case, if a new dimensionless temperature is defined by $T = (\theta - \theta_0)/(aq/k)$, where k is the thermal conductivity of the fluid, the PDE and inlet condition remain unchanged, but the boundary conditions become $\partial T/\partial R = 1$ at $R = 1$, $Z > 0$, still with $\partial T/\partial R = 0$ at $R = 0$, $Z > 0$.

Write a program that solves this new problem.

7.24 A liquid containing an inlet concentration c_0 of a dissolved reactant enters the region between two wide parallel plates, separated by a distance $2a$, as shown in Fig. P7.24.

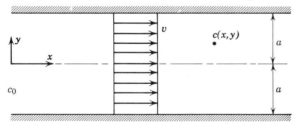

Figure P7.24

The liquid velocity is assumed to have the uniform value v. A first-order reaction occurs with velocity constant k at the plates, which are coated with a catalyst. Transport in the y direction, normal to the plates, is assumed to be by diffusion only, with diffusion coefficient D; in the x or axial direction, convection is assumed to predominate over diffusion. The problem is to find how the reactant concentration c varies with x and y.

By defining a dimensionless concentration $C = c/c_0$ and dimensionless distances $X = xD/a^2 v$ and $Y = y/a$, the governing equations can be expressed as shown below.

Transport Equation

For $X > 0$, $-1 < Y < 1$: $\dfrac{\partial^2 C}{\partial Y^2} = \dfrac{\partial C}{\partial X}.$

Inlet Condition

For $X = 0$, $-1 \leq Y \leq 1$: $C = 1.$

Boundary Conditions

At $Y = 1$, $X > 0$: $hC + \partial C/\partial Y = 0$,

$Y = -1$, $X > 0$: $hC - \partial C/\partial Y = 0$,

in which $h = ka/D$.

For values of $h = 0.1$, 1, and 10, obtain numerical values for C as a function of X and Y, until the centerline concentration falls to 5% of the inlet value, by each of the following methods. Take advantage of symmetry and solve the problem in the region for which $0 \leq Y \leq 1$ only.

Method I

Following an argument similar to that used by Carslaw and Jaeger (pages 114-120 of [2]), it may be shown that

$$C = 2 \sum_{n=1}^{\infty} \frac{(h^2 + \beta_n^2)\sin\beta_n}{\beta_n[(\beta_n^2 + h^2) + h]}\cos\beta_n Y\, e^{-\beta_n^2 X},$$

in which the β_n are the positive roots of $\beta\tan\beta = h$, with $\beta_1 < \beta_2 < \beta_3 \ldots$ (see Problem 3.28). Adequate convergence should be ensured by taking enough terms of the series into the summation.

Method II

Use a finite-difference procedure, such as the Crank-Nicolson, DuFort-Frankel, or Saul'yev method. The solution should be performed for several different values of ΔX and ΔY, in order to investigate the effect of grid spacing on convergence.

Method III

Treat the problem as a characteristic-value problem, in the manner of Example 7.9. A procedure, such as that given in Example 4.2 or 4.3, will be needed for finding the eigenvalues and eigenvectors of a matrix.

Comment as to which of the above methods, if any, would lend itself to the solution of a similar problem in which D and/or v were known functions of y.

7.25 A cylindrical cavity, 10 ft in diameter and 10 ft high, is situated deep in ground that is initially at a uniform temperature of 60°F. At a time $t = 0$, the cavity is filled with liquefied natural gas, maintaining its walls at -260°F. The liquefied gas that evaporates is recondensed and returned to the cavity. The temperature T in the surrounding ground obeys the equation

$$k\left(\frac{\partial^2 T}{\partial r^2} + \frac{1}{r}\frac{\partial T}{\partial r} + \frac{\partial^2 T}{\partial z^2}\right) = \rho c_p \frac{\partial T}{\partial t},$$

in which r and z are radial and vertical coordinates. The ground is dry and has the following properties: thermal conductivity $k = 2.2$ BTU/hr ft °F, density $\rho = 125$ lb/cu ft, and specific heat $c_p = 0.19$ BTU/lb °F.

Use a finite-difference method to solve for the transient temperatures in the ground. Hence, plot against time the total rate Q of heat conduction into the cylinder from the ground, in BTU/hr, for t up to 5 years. What method of solution would you use if the ground did contain an appreciable moisture content?

A more detailed discussion of this problem is given, for example, by Duffy et al. [37].

7.26 Figure P7.26 shows the cross section of two hollow cylindrical anodes that are used for focusing an electron beam passing along their axis. The anodes are separated by a small distance and are maintained at potentials $-V_a$ and $+V_a$.

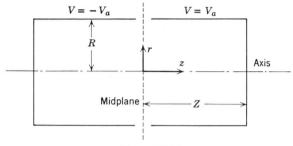

Figure P7.26

Assume here that the anodes are closed at their ends, although in practice threre would be a circular opening in each to allow passage of the electron beam. The distribution of potential is governed by Laplace's equation in cylindrical coordinates:

$$\frac{\partial^2 V}{\partial r^2} + \frac{1}{r}\frac{\partial V}{\partial r} + \frac{\partial^2 V}{\partial z^2} = 0.$$

Write a program that will use a finite-difference method to approximate the distribution of potential in the electron "lens" inside the anodes. Use symmetry to simplify the problem as much as possible. The input data should include values for: V_a, R, Z, m (number of axial grid spacings between $z = 0$ and $z = Z$), n (number of radial grid spacings between $r = 0$ and $r = R$), N (upper limit on the number of iterations to be performed), and ε (a tolerance used in testing for convergence, as in Example 7.6).

For a further description of this problem, see page 332 of Ramey [36]. Also, the motion of an electron inside the lens is discussed in Problem 6.25.

7.27 Figure P7.27 shows a diametral plane section of a pipe

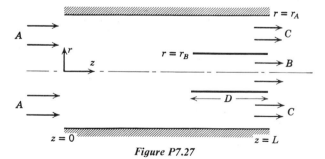

Figure P7.27

of radius r_A and length L with a coaxial tube of radius r_B inserted a distance D into the downstream end. An inviscid fluid enters steadily at A and separates into a central stream B and an annular stream C. At A, B, and C, the axial velocities u have the uniform values u_A, u_B, and u_C, and there is no radial flow at these sections ($v = 0$).

Write a program that accepts values for r_A, r_B, L, D, u_A, and

u_B, and that uses a finite-difference procedure to estimate values of the stream function ψ at a network of grid points inside the pipe. Arrange, if possible, for the computer printout to display points on several streamlines (lines of constant ψ) so that the flow pattern is represented directly.

Suggested Test Values

$r_A = 10$, $r_B = 4$, $L = 20$, $D = 8$ cm, $u_A = 20$, $u_B = 60$ cm/sec.

To achieve the above, first note that continuity gives u_C:

$$u_A r_A^2 = u_B r_B^2 + u_C(r_A^2 - r_B^2).$$

Also, the axially-symmetric stream function $\psi(r,z)$ is such that $u = (\partial\psi/\partial r)/r$, $v = -(\partial\psi/\partial z)/r$, and for irrotational flow (assumed here) it satisfies

$$\frac{\partial^2 \psi}{\partial r^2} - \frac{1}{r}\frac{\partial\psi}{\partial r} + \frac{\partial^2 \psi}{\partial z^2} = 0.$$

For the uniform velocity profiles, the stream function is of the form $\psi = \frac{1}{2}ur^2$, so by using u_A, u_B, and u_C in turn, the boundary conditions are specified at A, B, and C. Also, ψ has the values 0 on the center line, $\frac{1}{2}u_A r_A^2$ on the outer wall, and $\frac{1}{2}u_B r_B^2$ on the wall of the inner tube.

To allow greater generality, we suggest that the reader rephrase the problem in terms of the dimensionless variables $R = r/r_A$, $Z = z/r_A$, $\Psi = \psi/(\frac{1}{2}u_A r_A^2)$, with $\alpha = r_B/r_A$, $\beta = L/r_A$, and $\gamma = D/r_A$ as parameters.

For a particular application of the results computed here, see Problem 6.39.

7.28 A horizontal rectangular plate of uniform thickness t has length l and breadth b. The flexural rigidity of the plate is given by $D = Et^3/12(1 - \sigma^2)$, where $E =$ Young's modulus and $\sigma =$ Poisson's ratio. The edges of the plate are clamped rigidly, and the entire plate is subject to a uniform load q per unit area. Write a program that will determine the downwards deflection w as a function of position.

This problem parallels that of Example 7.7 and involves the solution of the biharmonic equation $\nabla^4 w = q/D$. However, the finite-difference scheme should be set up without anticipating that the grid spacings Δx and Δy are necessarily equal. Also, the boundary conditions along the edges will now be (a) $w = 0$, and (b) $\partial w/\partial\eta = 0$, where η is the direction normal to an edge.

The input data for the program should include values for t, l, b, E, σ, q, m, and n (number of grid spacings along the length and breadth, respectively), N (upper limit on the number of iterations), and ε (tolerance used in testing for convergence, as in Example 7.6). Actual values can be patterned after those used in Example 7.7.

The above problem may be modified to include (a) effect of arbitrary loading over the surface, (b) effect of one or more free edges, without support, and (c) deflection of a circular plate. The relevant equations for the latter two cases are given by Hughes and Gaylord on pages 83 and 149 of [33].

7.29 A steel shaft of a hexagonal cross section has a maximum diameter of 2 inches. If the modulus of rigidity of steel is $G = 11.5 \times 10^6$ lb$_f$/sq in., compute the torque needed to twist the shaft through an angle of $\theta = 0.002$ radians per foot.

Following Hughes and Gaylord [33], the required torque M is given by

$$M = 2G\theta \int \psi \, dA,$$

where the integral is over the cross section, and ψ is the solution of

$$\nabla^2 \psi = -2$$

throughout the cross section, subject to $\psi = 0$ on the surface.

7.30 (a) Figure P7.30 shows the cross section of an oil pipe-line that is half buried in relatively cool ground. The top half of the pipe is exposed to the sun, and the surface temperature of the pipe may be approximated by $T_s = A + B \sin\theta$, where A and B are constants.

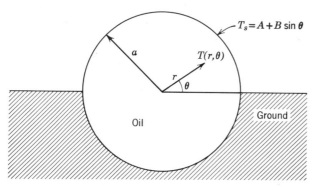

Figure P7.30

Assuming that the thermal conductivity of the oil is constant and that heat transfer across the section is by conduction only, the local oil temperature $T = T(r, \theta)$ is the solution of the simplified heat-conduction equation in cylindrical coordinates:

$$\frac{\partial^2 T}{\partial r^2} + \frac{1}{r} \frac{\partial T}{\partial r} + \frac{1}{r^2} \frac{\partial^2 T}{\partial \theta^2} = 0.$$

Write a program that will perform a finite-difference solution to find T as a function of r and θ. An iterative technique, such as the Gauss-Seidel method, or successive overrelaxation, is suggested. Observe that symmetry makes it necessary to consider only the region $-\pi/2 \leqslant \theta \leqslant \pi/2$, at most. The input data should include values for A, B, k (the number of radial spacings Δr), l (the number of angular increments $\Delta \theta$ between $\theta = -\pi/2$ and $\theta = \pi/2$), n (the upper limit on the number of iterations to be performed), and ε (a tolerance used in testing for convergence, as in Example 7.6). Suggested values are $A = 125°F$, $B = 50°F$, $k = l = 8$, $n = 150$, and $\varepsilon = 10^{-4}$.

(b) Assuming steady flow along the pipe, the axial velocity $v = v(r, \theta)$ of the oil obeys the following PDE (see, for example, page 22 of Hughes and Gaylord [33]):

$$\frac{dp}{dz} = \frac{1}{r} \frac{\partial}{\partial r} \left(\mu r \frac{\partial v}{\partial r} \right) + \frac{1}{r} \frac{\partial}{\partial \theta} \left(\frac{\mu}{r} \frac{\partial v}{\partial \theta} \right),$$

where dp/dz is the pressure gradient along the pipe, and μ is the viscosity of the oil, which varies with temperature according to the empirical law $\mu = \mu_0 e^{c/(T+d)}$, where μ_0, c, and d are constants.

Write an extension to the program in part (a) that will read values for dp/dz, μ_0, c, d, and a (the pipe radius), and proceed to compute the distribution of velocity v over the cross

section, based on the temperatures already computed in part (a). The following values are suggested: $dp/dz = -0.05$ lb$_f$/cu ft, $\mu_0 = 5 \times 10^{-9}$ lb$_f$ sec/sq ft, $c = 8000°$, $d = 460°$, and $a = 2/3$ ft.

(c) Finally, write an additional extension to the program that will estimate the total flow rate of oil, Q cu ft/sec, by evaluating numerically the integral

$$Q = \int_{r=0}^{a} \int_{\theta=0}^{2\pi} rv \, dr \, d\theta.$$

Compare this value of Q with that predicted by assuming a constant viscosity evaluated at the mean temperature $A°F$:

$$Q = \frac{\pi a^4}{8 \mu_0 e^{c/(A+d)}} \left(-\frac{dp}{dz} \right).$$

Note. the elliptic equations in parts (a) and (b) may also be solved by the implicit alternating-direction method (page 452).

7.31 A deep region of liquid is at a uniform initial temperature T_0. At a time $t = 0$, the temperature at the surface is lowered to T_s, at which value it is held constant. The liquid freezes at a temperature T_f, where $T_s < T_f \leqslant T_0$, so that a frozen region grows into the liquid, as shown in Fig. P7.31.

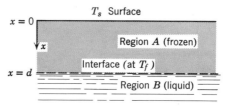

Figure P7.31

Neglecting possible convection currents and the small upwards motion due to contraction upon freezing, heat transfer is by conduction, and we have to solve

$$\alpha_A \frac{\partial^2 T_A}{\partial x^2} = \frac{\partial T_A}{\partial t} \quad \text{(Region } A),$$

$$\alpha_B \frac{\partial^2 T_B}{\partial x^2} = \frac{\partial T_B}{\partial t} \quad \text{(Region } B),$$

in which $\alpha = k/\rho c_p$ is the thermal diffusivity, with $k =$ thermal conductivity, $\rho =$ density, and $c_p =$ specific heat.

A heat balance at the interface results in the equation

$$v \rho L = k_A \left(\frac{\partial T_A}{\partial x} \right)_{x=d^-} - k_B \left(\frac{\partial T_B}{\partial x} \right)_{x=d^+},$$

which governs the velocity v of movement of the interface. Here, L is the latent heat of fusion, and d is the instantaneous x coordinate of the interface.

Write a program that uses an unconditionally stable finite-difference method to compute the location of the interface and the temperatures in regions A and B as functions of time. Pay particular attention to the problem of locating the interface which, in general, will lie *between* two consecutive grid points. The input data should consist of values for T_0, T_s, T_f, k_A, ρ_A, c_{pA}, k_B, ρ_B, c_{pB}, L, Δx, Δt, and t_{max} (the maximum time for which solutions are required). Suggested test data, which are relevant to the freezing of water, are: $T_0 = 37°F$, $T_s = 20°F$,

$T_f = 32°F$, $L = 144$ BTU/lb, $t_{max} = 20$ days, with other physical properties given in Table P7.31.

Table P7.31

	Region A (Ice)	Region B (Water)	Units
k	1.30	0.343	BTU/hr ft °F
ρ	57.3	62.4	lb/cu ft
c_p	0.502	1.01	BTU/lb °F

Note that since the density of water falls with decreasing temperature in the range under study, convection currents are likely to be absent. As usual, investigate the dependency of the computed results on particular choices of Δx and Δt. Check your results against those predicted by the analytical solution, given by Carslaw and Jaeger [2] and also discussed in Problem 3.48.

The above problem can be extended to a variety of more complicated situations, such as the freezing of the earth around: (a) an underground cavity containing liquefied natural gas at a very low temperature, (b) a row of buried pipes through which a cold refrigerant is circulating. Also, the contraction effect on freezing could be taken into consideration.

7.32 This problem considers an easier, but less rigorous, method for solving Problem 7.31. Basically, the technique is to treat the frozen and liquid regions as a single continuous phase, in which the physical properties depend on the local temperature.

As shown in Fig. P7.32, which is not to scale, the physical properties are assumed to change linearly in the region $T_f \pm \delta$. The peak in c_p now represents the latent-heat effect, and should be adjusted so that $\int_{T_f - \delta}^{T_f + \delta} c_p dT = L$.

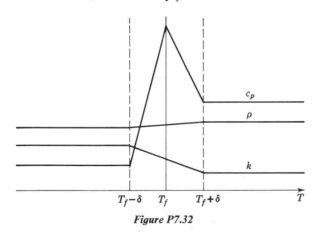

Figure P7.32

The problem is now to solve the single equation, $\alpha \partial^2 T / \partial x^2 = \partial T / \partial t$, which will be nonlinear, because α depends on the particular temperature at each point. The situation is somewhat similar to that in Example 7.4.

Write a program that implements the above method. The input data will be similar to those in Problem 7.31, with the addition of a value for δ. Different values for δ should be tried. If δ is too large, the results may be rather inaccurate; if too small, the resulting equations may be so highly nonlinear as to cause instabilities.

7.33 An ion-exchange column consists of a cylindrical tube of length L that is packed with beads of ion-exchange resin. A solution containing sodium ions (Na^+) flows through the column with a superficial velocity v. The resin adsorbs Na^+ from the solution and returns hydrogen ions (H^+) in exchange.

If the concentrations of Na^+ are c in the solution and q (based on the total packed volume) in the resin, material balances give the following equations:

$$v \frac{\partial c}{\partial x} + \varepsilon \frac{\partial c}{\partial t} + r = 0,$$

$$r = \frac{\partial q}{\partial t}.$$

Here, ε is the void fraction and r is the rate of adsorption, which varies with the particular conditions. For the Na^+/H^+ exchange process on Dowex-50 resin, the following expression is given by Gilliland and Baddour [38]:

$$r = k[c(q_0 - q) - \frac{q}{K}(c_0 - c)].$$

Here, c_0 is the concentration of Na^+ in the feed to the column ($x = 0$), q_0 is the total exchange capacity of the resin, and k and K are experimentally determined constants.

Devise a finite-difference scheme for predicting the variation of c and q with time t and distance x in the column. Write a computer program that implements the method.

Suggested Test Data

$\varepsilon = 0.45$, $c_0 = 0.1$ meq/cc, $q_0 = 0.86$ meq/cc, $k = 0.433$ cc/meq sec, $K = 1.50$, $L = 50$ cm, and $v = 0.50$ cm/sec. Stop the calculations when c at the column exit ($x = L$) reaches 95% of its inlet value.

7.34 This problem simulates the performance of a horizontal underground stratum of porous rock that is to be used seasonally for the storage and withdrawal of dry natural gas. Figure P7.34a shows a square grid ($\Delta x = \Delta y$) that approxima-

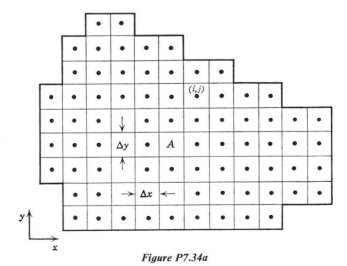

Figure P7.34a

tes a plan of the formation, which has a uniform vertical thickness h, and which is surrounded on all sides by impermeable rock. A cylindrical well for gas injection and withdrawal is located in block A.

At the end of the summer, when injection is complete, the reservoir pressure is uniformly at a high value p_0. Gas is then to be withdrawn from A at a well pressure p_{wA} that must at least equal a specified delivery pressure p_d. Over the subsequent period $0 \leqslant t \leqslant t_{max}$, the gas is scheduled to be withdrawn at a volumetric flow rate Q (referred to standard pressure and temperature p_s and T_s) that conforms to the pattern of anticipated demand shown in Fig. P7.34b. Following the guide-

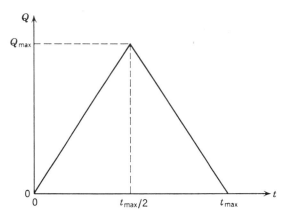

Figure P7.34b

lines below, write a program that will estimate the maximum feasible peak supply rate Q_{max}; the output from the program should also include the corresponding well pressure as a function of time.

The equations governing the variation of pressure throughout the reservoir are:

Continuity:
$$\frac{\partial}{\partial x}(\rho u) + \frac{\partial}{\partial y}(\rho v) + m = -\varepsilon \frac{\partial \rho}{\partial t}. \tag{1}$$

Darcy's law:
$$u = -\frac{k}{\mu}\frac{\partial p}{\partial x}, \quad v = -\frac{k}{\mu}\frac{\partial p}{\partial y}. \tag{2}$$

Ideal gas law:
$$\rho = \frac{Mp}{RT}. \tag{3}$$

Here, t = time, ε = rock porosity, k = rock permeability, ρ = gas density, μ = gas viscosity, p = pressure, u and v = superficial velocities in the x and y directions, m = mass rate of withdrawal of gas per unit volume of rock, M = molecular weight, R = gas constant, T = absolute temperature, and consistent units are assumed; ε, k, μ, M, and T are assumed constant.

The general practice for solving such problems is to introduce grid points, such as (i,j), at the *center* of each block; p_{ij} is then viewed as the *average* pressure for the block. Although the well is located in block A, the well pressure p_{wA} will be different from the average block pressure p_A. According to a simplified treatment (see Henderson, Dempsey, and Tyler [39], for example), in which the exact location of the well within the block is immaterial, the two pressures are related by

$$p_A^2 - p_{wA}^2 = \frac{m_A \mu RT}{\pi k h M}\left(\ln \frac{r_e}{r_w} - \frac{1}{2}\right), \tag{4}$$

in which $m_A = QMp_s/RT_s$ is the total mass rate of gas withdrawal from the well, r_w = radius of the well bore, and $\pi r_e^2 = \Delta x \Delta y$. For a given p_A and m_A, the corresponding p_{wA}

can be found from equation (4). If $p_{wA} \leqslant p_d$, then of course the scheme becomes unworkable within the framework of minimum delivery pressure as specified above.

Note that when developing a finite-difference formulation of equation (1), m will be zero for all blocks except A, in which we then have the relation $m(\Delta x)^2 h = m_A$.

Suggested Test Data (Not in Consistent Units)

$\Delta x = \Delta y = 400$ ft, $h = 27$ ft, $\varepsilon = 0.148$, $k = 168$ md (millidarcies; 1000 md $= 1$ darcy $\equiv 1$ centipoise sq cm/sec atm), $\mu = 0.0128$ centipoise, $M = 16$ lb$_m$/lb mole (that for methane), $R = 10.73$ psia cu ft/lb mole °R, $T = 545$°R, $r_w = 4$ in., $p_0 = 1185$ psia, $p_d = 520$ psia, $t_{max} = 100$ days, $T_s = 520$°R, and $p_s = 14.65$ psia.

7.35 Perform more elaborate calculations on the lines of Problem 7.34, but now allowing for one or more of the following modifications:

(a) Permeability and porosity no longer uniform, but varying from block to block.

(b) Multiple wells, all coming on stream simultaneously, with identical well pressures.

(c) Multiple wells, scheduled to come on stream in succession, so that the peak withdrawal rate is maximized.

(d) Nonideal gas behavior.

(e) Operation over several yearly cycles, with the reservoir pressure not necessarily uniform at the end of the injection period.

(f) Rectangular grid ($\Delta x \neq \Delta y$), often useful if the rock formation extends appreciably further in one horizontal direction than in the other.

7.36 An underground rock formation of porosity ε and permeability k is initially saturated with water of viscosity μ_0 and density ρ_0 at a pressure p_0. Part of the formation is to be sealed by injecting into it a grout solution at a constant pressure p_w from a vertical well. The well is fairly deep so that the flow is predominantly radially outward from the well bore, whose radius is r_w. The grout solution is made up in one batch, and its viscosity μ_1 increases everywhere with time t according to the relation

$$\mu_1(t) = a + \frac{b}{c - t},$$

where a, b, and c are experimentally determined constants.

Assuming that both the grout solution and the water are slightly compressible and obey the same equation of state, Saville [40] presents the following governing equations:

Continuity:
$$\frac{1}{r}\frac{\partial}{\partial r}(r\rho u) = -\varepsilon \frac{\partial \rho}{\partial t}.$$

Darcy's law:
$$u = -\frac{k}{\mu}\frac{\partial p}{\partial r}.$$

Equation of state:
$$\ln \frac{\rho}{\rho_0} = C(p - p_0).$$

Here, r = radial distance, p = pressure, ρ = density, C = composite compressibility of liquid and rock, u = superficial velocity, and μ = local viscosity (of grout solution or water, as appropriate).

The radius R of the grout/water interface progresses according to

$$\frac{dR}{dt} = -\frac{k}{\mu_0 \varepsilon} \left(\frac{\partial p}{\partial r}\right)_{R+},$$

where R^+ emphasizes that the pressure gradient is evaluated on the water side of the interface. Pressure and velocity are continuous across the interface.

Write a program that uses a finite-difference scheme for predicting the location of the interface as a function of time until it virtually ceases to advance.

Suggested Test Data (*Not in Consistent Units*)

$r_w = 3$ in., $\varepsilon = 0.15$, $\mu_0 = 1$ cp, $\rho_0 = 62.4$ lb/cu ft, $C = 7.2 \times 10^{-6}$ psia^{-1}, $k = 235$ md (millidarcies; 1000 md = 1 darcy $\equiv$ 1 cp sq cm/sec atm), $p_0 = 480$ psia, and $p_w = 850$ psia. Investigate two different grout solutions reported in [40]: *AM-9*, with $a = 1.0$ cp, $b = 3.5$ cp/min, $c = 74$ min; and *Siroc*, with $a = 5.3$ cp, $b = 4.9$ cp/hr, and $c = 6.7$ hr.

7.37 A circular hole of radius a is drilled through the center of a rectangular plate of length L and width w. A uniform tensile stress T is exerted at both ends of the plate, as shown in Fig. P7.37a.

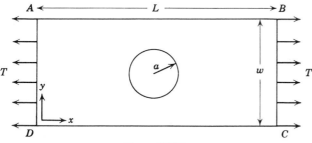

Figure P7.37a

The internal stresses σ_x, σ_y, and τ_{xy} (considered positive as shown in Fig. P7.37b) are given [33] by

$$\sigma_x = \Omega + \frac{\partial^2 \phi}{\partial y^2},$$

$$\sigma_y = \Omega + \frac{\partial^2 \phi}{\partial x^2},$$

$$\tau_{xy} = -\frac{\partial^2 \phi}{\partial x \partial y},$$

where the potential function Ω may be treated as zero in the present problem. The Airy stress function ϕ is the solution of the biharmonic equation

$$\nabla^4 \phi = \frac{\partial^4 \phi}{\partial x^4} + 2 \frac{\partial^4 \phi}{\partial x^2 \partial y^2} + \frac{\partial^4 \phi}{\partial y^4} = 0.$$

The boundary conditions are: $\sigma_x = T$ and $\tau_{xy} = 0$ along the ends AD and BC; $\sigma_y = \tau_{xy} = 0$ along the sides AB and CD; on the surface of the hole, both the normal and shear stresses are zero.

Write a computer program that will use a finite-difference method to approximate the distribution of stresses inside the plate.

Suggested Input Data

$w = 5$ in., $L = 5$ and 10 in., $a = 0.5$, 1, and 1.5 in., $T = 1000$ lb$_f$/sq in., together with appropriate values for m and n (the number of grid spacings Δx and Δy to be used along AB and DA, respectively), N (upper limit on number of iterations to be performed), and ε (a tolerance used in testing for convergence, as in Example 7.6).

For comparison, an approximate solution to the problem is given on page 80 of Timoshenko and Goodier [41].

7.38 Investigate the possibility of extending Problem 7.37 to the cases of elliptical holes with major axes oriented (a) along the plate, and (b) across the plate. (For large eccentricities, the solution is of particular interest because it approximates the effect of a crack in the plate.)

7.39 Figure P7.39 is a simplified view of the cross section of a wide concrete dam. The internal stresses σ_x, σ_y, and τ_{xy} obey the PDE given in Problem 7.37, except that the potential function is now $\Omega = -\rho_c g x$, where ρ_c is the density of concrete. The boundary conditions are zero normal and tangential stresses along $ABCD$, with $\tau_{xy} = 0$ and $\sigma_y = -\rho_w g x$ along AE, where ρ_w is the density of the water behind the dam. Along DE, assume as an approximation that τ_{xy} is constant and that σ_x at any point is proportional to the height of concrete above that point.

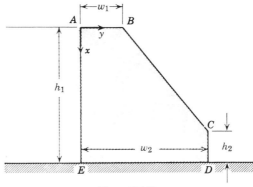

Figure P7.39

Write a program that employs a finite-difference method to approximate the distribution of stresses inside the dam.

Suggested Input Data

$w_1 = 50$, $w_2 = 200$, $h_1 = 250$, $h_2 = 50$ ft, $\rho_w = 62.4$, $\rho_c = 144$ lb$_m$/cu ft, $g = 32.2$ ft/sec^2, together with suitable values for m and n (the number of grid spacings Δx and Δy to be used along AE and ED, respectively), N and ε (defined in Problem 7.37).

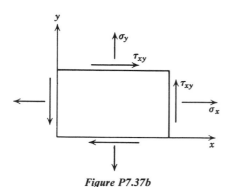

Figure P7.37b

The conversion factor 32.2 lb_m ft/lb_f sec^2 will also be needed in order to express the stresses in lb_f/sq in.

7.40 Write a computer program that uses either the Crank-Nicolson method or one of the unconditionally stable explicit methods of Section 7.13 to solve the problem of unsteady heat conduction across a slab, stated in Problem 7.1. Compare your results with those of Examples 7.1 and 7.2.

7.41 Solve Problem 7.22, concerning a laminar-flow heat exchanger, by treating it as a characteristic-value problem. A procedure, such as that given in Example 4.2 or 4.3, will be needed for finding the eigenvalues and eigenvectors of a matrix.

7.42 Figure P7.42 shows a cross section of a long cooling fin of width W, thickness t, and thermal conductivity k, that is bonded to a hot wall, maintaining its base (at $x = 0$) at a temperature T_w. Heat is conducted steadily through the fin in the plane of Fig. P7.42, so that the fin temperature T obeys Laplace's equation, $\partial^2 T/\partial x^2 + \partial^2 T/\partial y^2 = 0$. (Temperature variations along the length of the fin, in the z direction, are ignored.)

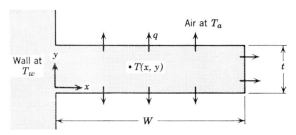

Figure P7.42

Heat is lost from the sides and tip of the fin by convection to the surrounding air (radiation is neglected at sufficiently low temperatures) at a local rate $q = h(T_s - T_a)$ BTU/hr sq ft. Here, T_s and T_a, °F are the temperatures at a point on the fin surface and of the air, respectively. If the surface of the fin is vertical, the heat transfer coefficient h obeys the dimensional correlation $h = 0.21(T_s - T_a)^{1/3}$, given by Rohsenow and Choi [42].

Write a program that will compute: (a) the temperature distribution inside the fin, and (b) the total rate of heat loss from the fin to the air per foot length of fin.

Suggested Test Data

$T_w = 200$°F, $T_a = 70$°F, $t = 0.25$ in.; investigate all eight combinations of $k = 25.9$ (steel) and 220 (copper) BTU/hr ft °F, $W = 0.5, 1, 2,$ and 5 in.

If available, comare the results with those obtained from Problem 6.36, in which temperature variations across the fin are ignored.

7.43 An infinitely long bar of thermal diffusivity α has a square cross section of side $2a$. It is initially at a uniform temperature θ_0 when it is placed quickly inside a furnace that behaves as a black-body enclosure at a temperature θ_b. If σ is the Stefan-Boltzmann constant and ε is the emissivity of the surface of the bar, the heat flux density (BTU/hr sq ft, for example) into the surface of the bar at any point is given by

$$q = \varepsilon\sigma(\theta_b^4 - \theta_s^4) = -k\left(\frac{\partial\theta}{\partial n}\right)_{n=0}.$$

Here, k is the thermal conductivity of the bar, n is distance measured normally inwards to the bar from the surface, θ_s is the current local surface temperature, and all temperatures are absolute.

Write down in detail the PDE, initial and boundary conditions that govern $\theta = \theta(x,y,t)$, the temperature inside the bar as a function of position coordinates x and y, and time t. Rewrite these governing equations in terms of the dimensionless variables

$$X = \frac{x}{a}, \qquad Y = \frac{y}{a}, \qquad \tau = \frac{\alpha t}{a^2}, \qquad \text{and} \qquad T = \frac{\theta - \theta_0}{\theta_b - \theta_0}.$$

Hence show that the general solution is of the form $T = T(X, Y, \tau, \beta, \gamma)$, where the dimensionless parameters β and γ are given by

$$\beta = \frac{k}{\varepsilon\sigma a\theta_b^3}, \qquad \gamma = \frac{\theta_0}{\theta_b}.$$

Let τ_{cf} be the dimensionless time taken for the dimensionless center temperature T_c to rise to a specified fractional value f. Write a computer program that will enable plots to be made of τ_{cf} against β, with γ as a parameter.

A steel bar has $a = 0.1$ ft, $\alpha = 0.322$ sq ft/hr, $\theta_0 = 520$°R, $k = 25.9$ BTU/hr ft °F, and $\varepsilon = 0.79$. It is placed inside a black-body enclosure with $\theta_b = 2520$°R; σ equals 0.171×10^{-8} BTU/hr sq ft °R^4. How long will it take for the center temperature to rise to 1520°R ($T_c = 0.5$)? How long, if $a = 0.2$ ft, with all other quantities unchanged?

7.44 In an experiment for simulating the effect of a hot refractory wall close to a tube in a pipestill, a long metal pipe is placed parallel to a very large wall that behaves as a black-body radiator at an absolute temperature T_w. The pipe, which has inside and outside radii r_1 and r_2, is separated by a distance D from the wall. The pipe wall has a thermal conductivity k and the outer surface has an emissivity ε. A well-mixed fluid at a temperature T_f flows rapidly through the pipe; the local heat flux density (BTU/hr sq ft, for example) from the inner pipe wall to the fluid is

$$q_1 = q_1(\phi) = h(T_1 - T_f),$$

where h is the relevant heat transfer coefficient and $T_1 = T_1(\phi)$ is the local inner-wall temperature. The polar coordinates (r, ϕ) are shown in Fig. P7.44.

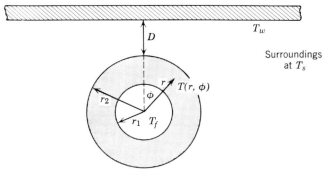

Figure P7.44

The corresponding radiant flux density to a point on the outer surface where the temperature is $T_2 = T_2(\phi)$ is

$$q_2 = q_2(\phi) = \varepsilon\sigma[F_{2w}(T_w^4 - T_2^4) + (1 - F_{2w})(T_s^4 - T_2^4)].$$

The geometric view factor $F_{2w} = F_{2w}(\phi)$ is the fraction of radiation leaving a small area on the outer pipe surface that is directly intercepted by the wall; the remaining fraction, $1 - F_{2w}$, is absorbed by the remainder of the surroundings. F_{2w} can be evaluated by the method discussed in Problem 3.17, modified so that one surface is a differential element of area. Ignore heat transfer by convection outside the tube.

Write a program that will compute the steady temperature distribution $T = T(r, \phi)$ throughout the pipe wall and the net rate of heat transfer to the fluid, per unit length of pipe.

Assume that the problem is essentially two-dimensional, in the plane of Fig. P7.44.

Suggested Test Data

$T_w = 1500°R$, $T_f = 760°R$, $T_s = 540°R$, $\varepsilon = 0.79$, $k = 12.8$ BTU/hr ft °R, $r_2 = 1$ in. Investigate all eight combinations of $r_1 = 0.5$ and 0.9 in., $D = 0.5$ and 2.5 in., $h = 20$ and 200 BTU/hr sq ft °R. The Stefan-Boltzmann constant is $\sigma = 0.171 \times 10^{-8}$ BTU/hr sq ft °R⁴.

Bibliography

1. G. Birkhoff and R. S. Varga, "Implicit Alternating Direction Methods," *Trans. Amer. Math. Soc.*, **92**, 13–24 (1959).

2. H. S. Carslaw and J. C. Jaeger, *Conduction of Heat in Solids*, 2nd ed., Oxford University Press, New York, 1959.

3. J. Crank and P. Nicolson, "A Practical Method for Numerical Evaluation of Solutions of Partial Differential Equations of the Heat Conduction Type," *Proc. Camb. Phil. Soc.*, **43**, 50–67 (1947).

4. J. Douglas, Jr., "On the Numerical Integration of $\partial^2 u/\partial x^2 + \partial^2 u/\partial y^2 = \partial u/\partial t$ by Implicit Methods," *J. Soc. Indust. Appl. Math.*, **3**, 42–65 (1955).

5. J. Douglas, Jr., "On the Relation between Stability and Convergence in the Numerical Solution of Linear Parabolic and Hyperbolic Differential Equations," *J. Soc. Indust. Appl. Math.*, **41**, 20–37 (1956).

6. J. Douglas, Jr. and H. H. Rachford, Jr., "On the Numerical Solution of Heat Conduction Problems in Two and Three Space Variables," *Trans. Amer. Math. Soc.*, **82**, 421–439 (1956).

7. J. Douglas, Jr., "The Effect of Round-off Error in the Numerical Solution of the Heat Equation," *Journal of the A.C.M.*, **6**, 48–58 (1959).

8. E. C. DuFort and S. P. Frankel, "Stability Conditions in the Numerical Treatment of Parabolic Differential Equations," *Math. Tables Aids Comput.*, **7**, 135–152 (1953).

9. G. E. Forsythe and W. R. Wasow, *Finite-Difference Methods for Partial Differential Equations*, Wiley, New York, 1960.

10. S. P. Frankel, "Convergence Rates of Iterative Treatments of Partial Differential Equations," *Math. Tables Aids Comput.*, **4**, 65–75 (1950).

11. J. D. Hellums and S. W. Churchill, "Transient and Steady State, Free and Natural Convection, Numerical Solutions: Part 1, The Isothermal, Vertical Plate," *A.I.Ch.E. Journal*, **8**, 690–692 (1962).

12. L. Lapidus, *Digital Computation for Chemical Engineers*, McGraw-Hill, New York, 1962.

13. P. D. Lax and R. D. Richtmyer, "Survey of the Stability of Linear Finite Difference Equations," *Comm. Pure Appl. Math.*, **9**, 267–293 (1956).

14. W. Leutert, "On the Convergence of Approximate Solutions of the Heat Equation to the Exact Solution," *Proc. Amer. Math. Soc.*, **2**, 433–439 (1951).

15. J. O. Wilkes and S. W. Churchill, "The Finite-Difference Computation of Natural Convection in a Rectangular Enclosure," *A.I.Ch.E. Journal*, **12**, 161–166 (1966).

16. G. O'Brien, M. Hyman, and S. Kaplan, "A Study of the Numerical Solution of Partial Differential Equations," *J. Math. Phys.*, **29**, 233–251 (1951).

17. F. C. W. Olson and O. T. Schultz, "Temperatures in Solids during Heating or Cooling," *Ind. Eng. Chem.*, **34**, 874–877 (1942).

18. S. Ostrach, *An Analysis of Laminar Free-Convection Flow and Heat Transfer about a Flat Plate Parallel to the Direction of the Generation Body Force*, Natl. Advisory Comm. Aeronaut. Tech. Report 1111, 1953.

19. D. W. Peaceman and H. H. Rachford, Jr., "The Numerical Solution of Parabolic and Elliptic Differential Equations," *J. Soc. Indust. Appl. Math.*, **3**, 28–41 (1955).

20. I. G. Petrovsky, *Lectures on Partial Differential Equations*, Interscience, New York, 1954.

21. A. Ralston and H. S. Wilf., *Mathematical Methods for Digital Computers*, Wiley, New York, 1960.

22. L. F. Richardson, "The Approximate Arithmetical Solution by Finite Differences of Physical Problems Involving Differential Equations with an Application to the Stresses in a Masonry Dam," *Philos. Trans. Roy. Soc. London, Series A*, **210**, 307–357 (1911).

23. R. D. Richtmyer, *Difference Methods for Initial Value Problems*, Interscience, New York, 1957.

24. J. Douglas, "Alternating Direction Methods for Three Space Variables," *Numerische Mathematik*, **4**, 41–63 (1962).

25. D. Young, "Iterative Methods for Solving Partial Difference Equations of Elliptic Type," *Trans. Amer. Math. Soc.*, **76**, 92–111 (1954).

26. H. Z. Barakat and J. A. Clark, "On the Solution of the Diffusion Equation by Numerical Methods," *Journal of Heat Transfer, Trans. A.S.M.E., Series C*, **88**, 421–427 (1966).

27. P. L. T. Brian, "A Finite-Difference Method of High-Order Accuracy for the Solution of Three-Dimensional Transient Heat Conduction Problems," *A.I.Ch.E. Journal*, **7**, 367–370 (1961).

28. J. Fromm, "The Time Dependent Flow of an Incompressible Viscous Fluid," *Methods in Computational Physics*, Vol. 3, pp. 345–382, Academic Press, New York, 1964.

29. J. E. Welch, F. H. Harlow, J. P. Shannon, and B. J. Daly, *The MAC Method; A Computing Technique for Solving Viscous, Incompressible, Transient Fluid-Flow Problems Involving Free Surfaces*, Los Alamos Scientific Laboratory of the Univ. of California, Los Alamos, 1966.

30. B. K. Larkin, "Some Stable Explicit Difference Approximations to the Diffusion Equation," *Math. of Comp.*, **18**, 196–202 (1964).

31. V. K. Saul'yev, *Integration of Equations of Parabolic Type by the Method of Nets*, Macmillan, New York, 1964.

32. J. Douglas and J. E. Gunn, "A General Formulation of Alternating Direction Methods, Part I, Parabolic and Hyperbolic Problems," *Numerische Mathematik*, **6**, 428–453 (1964).

33. W. F. Hughes and E. W. Gaylord, *Basic Equations of Engineering Science*, Schaum Publishing Company, New York, 1964.

34. R. B. Bird, W. E. Stewart, and E. N. Lightfoot, *Transport Phenomena*, Wiley, New York, 1960.

35. S. Goldstein, ed., *Modern Developments in Fluid Dynamics*, Oxford University Press, London, 1938.

36. R. L. Ramey, *Physical Electronics*, Wadsworth Publishing Company, 1961.

37. A. R. Duffy, J. E. Sorenson, R. E. Mesloh, and E. L. Smith, "Heat Transfer Characteristics of Belowground LNG Storage," *Chem. Eng. Progr.*, **63**, 55–61 (1967).

38. E. R. Gilliland and R. F. Baddour, "The Rate of Ion Exchange," *Ind. Eng. Chem.*, **45**, 330–337 (1953).

39. J. H. Henderson, J. R. Dempsey, and J. C. Tyler, "Use of Numerical Reservoir Models in the Development and Operation of Gas Storage Reservoirs," Paper No. SPE 2009, *Symposium on Numerical Simulation of Reservoir Performance*, Society of Petroleum Engineers, Dallas, 1968.

40. M. R. Tek, J. O. Wilkes, D. A. Saville, et al., *New Concepts in Underground Storage of Natural Gas*, The American Gas Association, New York, 1966.

41. S. Timoshenko and J. N. Goodier, *Theory of Elasticity*, 2nd ed., McGraw-Hill, New York, 1951.

42. W. M. Rohsenow and H. Y. Choi, *Heat, Mass, and Momentum Transfer*, Prentice-Hall, Englewood Cliffs, New Jersey, 1961.

CHAPTER 8

Statistical Methods

8.1   Introduction: The Use of Statistical Methods

In most branches of science and industry, methods of experimental measurement may be inexact, and measurements themselves may be restricted in quantity. For example, even simple linear measurement is subject to inaccuracies, and the results of a complicated experimental procedure may be influenced by many disturbing factors; also, the testing of mechanical failure of working parts is necessarily destructive, so usually only a small fraction is tested. In such cases, statistical methods may be used to advantage to obtain the best interpretation of the data. A statistical approach to a particular problem may enable the experimenter to design a method of solution that minimizes the effect of experimental error; it will also enable him to estimate the reliability of the results.

Frequently, in statistical problems, the technique is to examine relatively small amounts of experimental data and thus to generalize about larger amounts of data. In a typical statistical investigation which permits certain inferences to be drawn, we are usually confronted with the following sequence of steps:

1.   Specifying a mathematical model which represents the situation. This involves:

   (a) Assuming a distribution function for the data, based either on experience or on a distribution which might reasonably be expected to fit the data.
   (b) Identifying certain parameters of this distribution with what we wish to know about the actual situation.

Note here, especially, the danger of the misapplication of statistical methods. For example, the most elegant statistical analysis of a series of measurements made with a foot rule will be hopelessly inadequate if the rule is only $11\frac{3}{4}$ inches long. Or, the deduction that effect A is due to a cause B may be incorrect if in fact both A and B depend on some common cause C.

2.   Deciding on the procedure for taking experimental data or samples, if they are not already available in suitable form.

3.   Deciding on which statistics, computed from the data or samples, will be used for making the required inferences. After we have chosen the statistics, we shall probably have to consider their distribution in small samples, as opposed to the statistics in a much larger population.

4.   Finally, making the required inferences. For example:

   (a) An estimate of the unknown parameters of the assumed population distribution, together with confidence limits for these parameters.
   (b) A statement as to our confidence that the original mathematical model was a reasonable one.

The most frequently encountered statistical problems are those which involve one or more of the following features:

1.   *Reduction of data.* Much numerical information may often be condensed into a simple relationship, together with a statement as to the confidence we may place in the relationship.

2.   *Estimates and tests of significance.* From experimental data, certain population parameters can be estimated. It is usually possible to determine whether these estimates differ significantly from preconceived values.

3.   *Reliability of inferences depending on one or more variables.* For example, the total sulfur content in a bulk shipment is predicted from samples taken throughout the shipment, each of which is analyzed for sulfur, possibly by different methods and by different analysts. We then ask, what reliability may be attached to the prediction of total sulfur content in the shipment?

4.   *Relationships between two or more variables.* Suppose that some measurable quantity depends on one or more separate factors. Then, if it is possible by experimental design to control the separate factors at a series of fixed levels and to observe the measurable quantity at each level, the technique known as the *analysis of variance* is used to evaluate the dependency.

A less preferable method statistically, but often more practicable, is to observe the fluctuations in the measurable quantity and the separate factors, which arise naturally during the course of a particular operation, without attempting to control the separate factors at predetermined levels. In this case, methods of *regression analysis* are employed to evaluate the dependency.

531

8.2 Definitions and Notation

Statistics is the branch of scientific method of collecting, arranging, and using numerical facts or data arising from natural phenomena or experiment. A *statistic* is an item of information deduced from the application of statistical methods. A *population* is a collection of objects having in common some observable or measurable characteristic known as a *variate*. An *individual* is a single member of a population. A *sample* is a group of individuals drawn from a population, usually at random, so that each individual is equally likely to be selected. A *random variable* is a numerical quantity associated with the variate; its value for a given individual being determined by the value or nature of the variate for that particular individual. A *continuous variable* is one which can assume any value within some continuous range. A *discontinuous* or *discrete variable* is one which can assume only certain discrete values.

The *probability*, denoted by *Pr*, that a random variable *x*, belonging to an individual drawn from a population, shall have some particular value *A* equals the fraction of individuals in the population having that value *A* associated with them. The *frequency function*, $f(x)$, also known as the *probability density function*, of the random variable *x* is defined by

1. $f(x_0)dx$ = probability that the continuous random variable *x* shall have any value between x_0 and $x_0 + dx$.
2. $f(x_0)$ = probability that a discontinuous random variable *x* shall have the value x_0.

For a continuous distribution, a typical dependency of $f(x)$ on *x*, known as the *frequency distribution*, is shown in Fig. 8.1. Although special cases usually have some restriction on the range of *x* (for example, $x \geqslant 0$), we consider here the general case of $-\infty < x < +\infty$. Note, $Pr(x_1 \leqslant x \leqslant x_2) = \int_{x_1}^{x_2} f(x)\,dx$ = shaded area of Fig. 8.1, and $\int_{-\infty}^{\infty} f(x)\,dx = 1$, since all values of *x* must lie somewhere between the extreme limits.

The *cumulative frequency function*, $F(x_0)$, shown in Fig. 8.2, and also known as the *distribution function*, is defined as the probability that *x* shall not exceed a certain value x_0. Note that $F(x_0) = Pr(x \leqslant x_0) = \int_{-\infty}^{x_0} f(x)\,dx$, $F(-\infty) = 0$, and $F(\infty) = 1$. A discontinuous frequency distribution is shown in Fig. 8.3. Note that

$$Pr(x_1 \leqslant x \leqslant x_2) = \sum_{x_1}^{x_2} f(x),$$

and that $\sum_{-\infty}^{\infty} f(x) = 1$. The corresponding cumulative frequency function is given by $F(x_0) = \sum_{-\infty}^{x_0} f(x)$.

The term ave(y), where $y = y(x)$, means the arithmetic *average* of *y*, weighted according to the frequency distribution, so that

$$\text{ave}(y) = \int_{-\infty}^{\infty} y f(x)\,dx. \tag{8.1}$$

The integral sign would be replaced by a summation sign for a discontinuous distribution. The notation $E(y)$, indicating the *expected* value, is also used for ave(y).

Referring to a particular frequency distribution: (a) the *mode* is the most frequently occurring value of *x*, (b) the *mean* μ is the arithmetic average of *x* defined by

$$\mu = \text{ave}(x) = \int_{-\infty}^{\infty} x f(x)\,dx,$$

and (c) the *median* μ_e is that value of *x* such that half the population lies below it and half above it [that is, $F(\mu_e) = 1/2$].

These three statistics coincide for symmetrical distributions. For discontinuous distributions, the mean and median may lie between two possible values of *x*.

For a population, it is also convenient to define the *r*th *moment coefficients*, μ_r' and μ_r, about the origin and mean respectively. They are: (a) about the origin, $\mu_r' = \text{ave}(x^r)$, and (b) about the mean, $\mu_r = \text{ave}[(x - \mu)^r]$. Note that the mean $\mu = \mu_1'$. The moment μ_2 is an important statistic known as the *variance* of *x*; its square root is called the *standard deviation* σ. We have

$$\mu_2 = \text{ave}[(x - \mu)^2] = \text{var}(x) = \sigma^2. \tag{8.2}$$

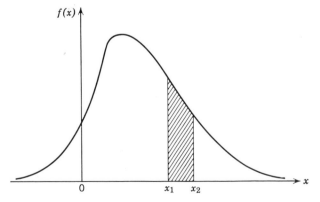

Figure 8.1 *Continuous frequency distribution.*

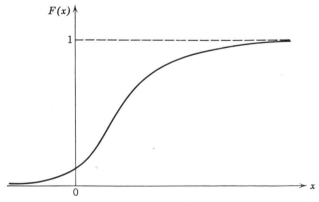

Figure 8.2 *Cumulative continuous frequency distribution.*

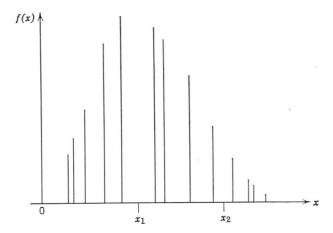

Figure 8.3 *Discontinuous frequency distribution.*

The mean of a particular distribution serves to locate it as a whole, whereas its variance indicates the magnitude of its spread about the mean.

8.3 Laws of Probability

Let A_1, A_2, A_3 represent either single numerical values or sets of numerical values; if the latter, let $x = A_1$ mean that x has some value within the set A_1. Then,

1. If A_1, A_2, and A_3 are mutually exclusive,

$$Pr(x = A_1 \text{ or } A_2 \text{ or } A_3) = Pr(x = A_1) + Pr(x = A_2)$$
$$+ Pr(x = A_3). \quad (8.3)$$

2. If x and y are two independent random variables that can have values $A_1^x, A_2^x, A_3^x \ldots$, and $A_1^y, A_2^y, A_3^y \ldots$, respectively, then

$$Pr(x = A_i^x \text{ and } y = A_j^y) = Pr(x = A_i^x) \times Pr(y = A_j^y). \quad (8.4)$$

8.4 Permutations and Combinations

1. The number of different arrangements, or *permutations*, of x items chosen from n distinct items is

$$P(n,x) = \frac{n!}{(n-x)!} \quad \text{(also written} \quad {}^nP_x). \quad (8.5)$$

Note that $0! = 1$.

2. The number of ways, or *combinations*, in which x items may be chosen from n distinct items, regardless of their order of arrangement, is

$$C(n,x) = \frac{n!}{(n-x)!\,x!} \quad \left(\text{also written} \quad \binom{n}{x} \text{ or } {}^nC_x\right). \quad (8.6)$$

3. If n items are made up of $x_1, x_2, x_3, \ldots$ items of types 1, 2, 3, $\ldots$ respectively, then the number of different arrangements of all the n items is

$$\frac{n!}{x_1!\,x_2!\,x_3!\cdots}.$$

8.5 Population Statistics

A few important relations concerning means and variances of populations will now be developed. These relations do not depend on any particular frequency distribution.

1. For *one random variable x*, by definition,

$$\text{ave}(x) = \mu,$$
$$\text{var}(x) = \sigma^2 = \text{ave}[(x - \mu)^2] = \text{ave}(x^2 - 2x\mu + \mu^2)$$
$$= \text{ave}(x^2) - 2\mu\,\text{ave}(x) + \mu^2,$$

that is,

$$\text{var}(x) = \text{ave}(x^2) - \mu^2. \quad (8.7)$$

2. For *two random variables x* and *y*, consider for the sake of argument a *discontinuous* distribution, and let

$f(x_i,y_j) = $ frequency function for the pair of values x_i, y_j,

$f(x_i) = $ frequency function for the value x_i, regardless of the value of y,

$f(y_j) = $ frequency function for the value y_j, regardless of the value of x.

Note that:

(a) $\sum\limits_{ij} f(x_i,y_j) = 1$,

(b) $f(x_i) = \sum\limits_{j} f(x_i,y_j)$ and $f(y_j) = \sum\limits_{i} f(x_i,y_j)$,

(c) $\text{ave}(x) = \sum\limits_{ij} x_i f(x_i,y_j) = \sum\limits_{i} x_i \sum\limits_{j} f(x_i,y_j)$
$$= \sum\limits_{i} x_i f(x_i),$$
$$\text{ave}(y) = \sum\limits_{j} y_j f(y_j).$$

Therefore,

$$\text{ave}(x + y) = \sum\limits_{ij} (x_i + y_j) f(x_i,y_j)$$
$$= \sum\limits_{ij} x_i f(x_i,y_j) + \sum\limits_{ij} y_j f(x_i,y_j)$$
$$= \text{ave}(x) + \text{ave}(y). \quad (8.8)$$

The *covariance*, σ_{xy}, of x and y is defined by

$$\text{cov}(x,y) = \sigma_{xy} = \text{ave}[(x - \mu_x)(y - \mu_y)]$$
$$= \text{ave}(xy - \mu_x y - \mu_y x + \mu_x \mu_y),$$

that is,

$$\sigma_{xy} = \text{ave}(xy) - \mu_x \mu_y. \quad (8.9)$$

The covariance is a measure of the dependency of x and y on each other. In particular, if x and y are *independent*,

$$f(x_i,y_j) = f(x_i)f(y_j),$$

that is,

$$\text{ave}(xy) = \sum\limits_{ij} x_i y_j f(x_i,y_j) = \sum\limits_{i} x_i f(x_i) \sum\limits_{j} y_j f(y_j) = \mu_x \mu_y.$$

Thus from (8.9), $\sigma_{xy} = 0$.

The above results can be reproduced for a continuous distribution by replacing summations with integrals.

3. A *linear combination* z of random variables $x_1, x_2, \ldots, x_n$ is defined by

$$z = a_1 x_1 + a_2 x_2 + \cdots + a_n x_n = \sum a_i x_i, \quad (8.10)$$

where the a's are constants, and the summation is understood to be over $i = 1, 2, \ldots, n$ unless otherwise stated.* Let $\mu_i = \text{ave}(x_i)$, $\sigma_i^2 = \text{var}(x_i)$, $\sigma_{ij} = \text{cov}(x_i, x_j)$. Then, by an extension of (8.8),

$$\mu = \text{ave}(z) = \text{ave}\left(\sum a_i x_i\right) = \sum a_i \,\text{ave}(x_i) = \sum a_i \mu_i, \quad (8.11)$$

$$\sigma^2 = \text{var}(z) = \text{ave}[(z - \mu)^2] = \text{ave}(z^2) - \mu^2.$$

By using (8.7) and (8.9), the reader can verify that this leads to

$$\sigma^2 = \sum a_i^2 \sigma_i^2 + 2 \sum_{i < j} a_i a_j \sigma_{ij}. \quad (8.12)$$

In particular, if all the x_i are mutually independent, $\sigma_{ij} = 0$ and $\sigma^2 = \Sigma a_i^2 \sigma_i^2$.

4. The mean and variance of an *arbitrary function* $z(x,y)$ of the two random variables x and y may be obtained *approximately* as follows. Taylor's expansion about $z(\mu_x, \mu_y)$, neglecting second-order terms, gives

$$z(x,y) \doteq z(\mu_x, \mu_y) + (x - \mu_x) z_x + (y - \mu_y) z_y,$$

where the partial derivatives z_x, z_y are evaluated at μ_x, μ_y.

---

* *Note.* Throughout this chapter, the summation parameter and its range will often be omitted for brevity, if the intended meaning is unambiguous. For example, the right-hand side of equation (8.12) is, more fully,

$$\sum_{i=1}^{n} a_i^2 \sigma_i^2 + 2 \sum_{i=1}^{j-1} \sum_{j=2}^{n} a_i a_j \sigma_{ij}.$$

Also, a summation such as $\Sigma_{i=1}^n x_i$ may be written as Σx_i or Σx.

Then, since $\text{ave}(x - \mu_x) = \text{ave}(y - \mu_y) = 0$:

$$\text{ave}(z) \doteq z(\mu_x, \mu_y),$$

$$\text{var}(z) \doteq z_x^2 \sigma_x^2 + z_y^2 \sigma_y^2 + 2 z_x z_y \sigma_{xy}.$$

Example. As an illustration of (1), (2), and (3) listed under Section 8.5, consider a population consisting of five cards numbered 0, 1, 2, 3, and 4 placed in a hat. We have

1. *One random variable x.* Let x = number on a card which is drawn at random from the hat and then replaced. Clearly,

$$\mu = \frac{0 + 1 + 2 + 3 + 4}{5} = 2,$$

$$\sigma^2 = \text{ave}(x^2) - \mu^2 = \frac{0 + 1 + 4 + 9 + 16}{5} - 2^2 = 2.$$

2. *Two random variables.* Let x and y be the numbers from the first and second draws. As for (1), $\mu_x = \mu_y = 2$, $\sigma_x^2 = \sigma_y^2 = 2$. Also, $\text{cov}(x,y) = \sigma_{xy} = \text{ave}(xy) - \mu_x \mu_y$. Suppose the second draw is made before the first card is replaced,

$$\sigma_{xy} = \frac{0(1 + 2 + 3 + 4) + 1(0 + 2 + 3 + 4) + \cdots}{20} - 2^2 = -0.5$$

However, if the first card is replaced before the second card is drawn,

$$\sigma_{xy} = \frac{0(0 + 1 + 2 + 3 + 4) + 1(0 + 1 + 2 + 3 + 4) + \cdots}{25} - 2^2 = 0,$$

confirming that for this case x and y are independent of each other.

3. *Linear combination.* Suppose $z = (x + y)$, without replacement. Then

$$\text{ave}(z) = 2 + 2 = 4,$$

$$\text{var}(z) = 2 + 2 + 2(-0.5) = 3.$$

EXAMPLE 8.1

DISTRIBUTION OF POINTS IN A BRIDGE HAND

Problem Statement

A bridge *deck* consists of 52 cards divided into four suits (spades, hearts, diamonds, and clubs), each of which contains four honor cards (one ace, one king, one queen, and one jack) and nine other cards. A bridge *hand* contains 13 cards which are assumed to be drawn at random from the deck. The honor point count of a hand is reckoned by assigning 4 points to each ace it contains, 3 to each king, 2 to each queen, 1 to each jack, and zero to the other cards (zero also for any other properties of the hand), and computing the total number of points thus assigned. The problem is to find the probability of obtaining any given point count from 0 (the minimum) through 37 (the maximum). These probabilities will then constitute the frequency function $f(p)$ for the distribution of a random variable p which equals the point count of a bridge hand.

Method of Solution

We first note that the total number of different possible hands is large, being $C(52,13) = 635,013,559,600$, and it is out of the question to generate and examine each hand for its point count. However, by focusing attention on the honor cards (the only cards that contribute to the point count), the problem can be simplified considerably.

The first step is to establish all the possible honor combinations that could occur in a hand. Let the number of jacks, queens, kings, and aces in any hand be j, q, k, and a, respectively. Now j, q, k, and a may independently assume any of the values 0, 1, 2, 3, or 4. Thus there are $5^4 = 625$ possible combinations, of which a few will eventually be rejected as containing more than 13 honors. The whole pattern can be generated by cyclically varying j, q, k, and a every 125th, 25th, 5th, and each hand, respectively, as shown in Table 8.1.1.

Second, the probability of obtaining a hand having N honor cards comprising j jacks, q queens, k kings, and a aces is found as follows. The probability of one particular sequence of N particular honor cards and any $13 - N$ nonhonor cards is

$$\frac{1}{52} \times \frac{1}{51} \times \cdots \times \frac{1}{53 - N} \times \frac{36}{52 - N} \times \cdots \times \frac{24 + N}{40}$$

$$= \frac{36!}{(23 + N)!} \times \frac{39!}{52!}.$$

But the number of different possible sequences involving the N particular honor cards is

$$P(13, j) \times P(13 - j, q) \times P(13 - j - q, k)$$

$$\times P(13 - j - q - k, a) = \frac{13!}{(13 - N)!}.$$

Hence, the probability r_N of being dealt N particular honor cards in any sequence within one hand is

$$r_N = \frac{13!}{(13 - N)!} \times \frac{36!}{(23 + N)!} \times \frac{39!}{52!}. \qquad (8.1.1)$$

Table 8.1.1

Hand Number (i)	Number of:				Point Count p $(j + 2q + 3k + 4a)$	Number of Honors, N $(j + q + k + a)$
	Jacks (j)	Queens (q)	Kings (k)	Aces (a)		
0	0	0	0	0	0	0
1	0	0	0	1	4	1
2	0	0	0	2	8	2
3	0	0	0	3	12	3
4	0	0	0	4	16	4
5	0	0	1	0	3	1
6	0	0	1	1	7	2
7	0	0	1	2	11	3
.	.	.	.	.	.	.
.	.	.	.	.	.	.
.	.	.	.	.	.	.
623	4	4	4	3	36	15
624	4	4	4	4	40	16

The cyclical pattern is easily generated by using integer division, in which the quotient is rounded down to the next lowest integer. For example, we use the formula $q \leftarrow i/25 - 5((i/25)/5)$ for the number of queens in hand i; this gives the pattern $q = 0, 1, 2, 3, 4, 0, 1, 2$, etc., in which the changes occur every 25th hand.

Note that the r_N may be generated from the recursion relation

$$r_{N+1} = r_N \times \frac{13 - N}{24 + N},$$

with

$$r_0 = \frac{36!}{23!} \times \frac{39!}{52!} = \frac{24 \times \cdots \times 36}{40 \times \cdots \times 52}.$$

But the N honor cards may be any j jacks, any q queens, any k kings, and any a aces, and hence may be selected in any of $C(4, j) \times C(4, q) \times C(4, k) \times C(4, a)$ ways. Note that since $C(n, x) = n!/x!(n - x)!$, we have $C(4, 0) = C(4, 4) = 1$, $C(4, 1) = C(4, 3) = 4$, and $C(4, 2) = 6$. Hence

the probability of obtaining N honor cards composed of any j jacks, q queens, k kings, and a aces is

$$C(4, j) \times C(4, q) \times C(4, k) \times C(4, a) \times r_N,$$

which can be computed fairly easily.

Finally, it is simple for the computer to work through the 625 possible combinations described above, summing the probabilities of all possibilities leading to a given point-count p, and hence to obtain the frequency function $f(p)$ for the distribution of point counts. The program given below also produces the cumulative frequency function $F(p)$, the mean μ, and variance σ^2 of the point-count distribution.

Flow Diagram

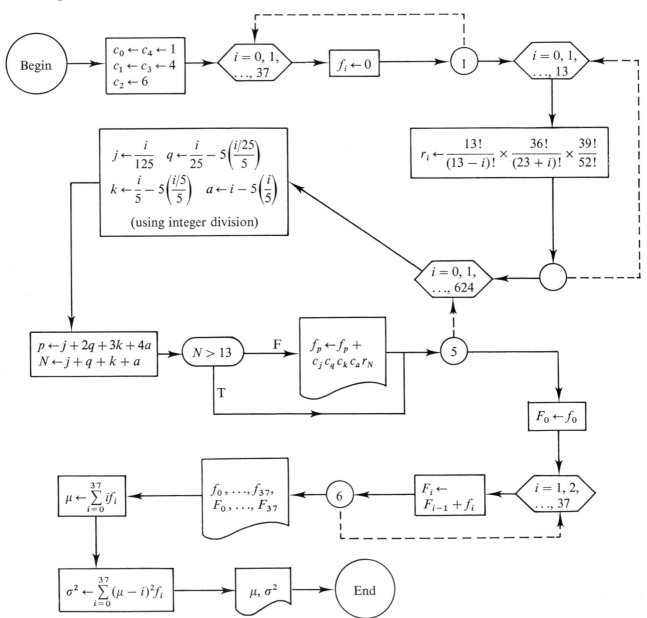

Example 8.1   Distribution of Points in a Bridge Hand   **537**

FORTRAN *Implementation*

List of Principal Variables

Program Symbol	Definition
AVG, VAR	Mean μ, and variance σ^2, of the point-count distribution.
C†	Vector containing the values $c_i = C(4,i)$, $i = 0, 1, 2, 3$, and 4.
CUMPRB†	Vector containing the probabilities F_p of obtaining any point count from 0 to p in any one hand.
NJ, NQ, NK, and NA	Number of jacks, queens, kings, and aces (j, q, k, and a), respectively.
NPTS	Point count, p.
NHONS	Number of honor cards, N.
PROB†	Vector containing the probabilities f_p of obtaining exactly p points in any one hand.
R†	Vector containing values r_N given by equation (8.1.1).

† Due to FORTRAN limitations, all subscripts in the program are advanced by one; e.g., r_0 through r_{13} in the text become R(1) through R(14) in the program.

Program Listing

```
C              APPLIED NUMERICAL METHODS, EXAMPLE 8.1
C              DISTRIBUTION OF POINTS IN A BRIDGE HAND.
C
C              THE TOTAL POINT COUNT OF A HAND IS COMPUTED WITH ACE = 4,
C              KING = 3, QUEEN = 2, AND JACK = 1 (POINTS ARE NOT COUNTED
C              HERE FOR DISTRIBUTIONAL OR OTHER FEATURES).   THE PROB-
C              ABILITY OF EACH POINT COUNT FROM 0 THROUGH 37 IS COMPUTED,
C              TAKING INTO ACCOUNT ALL THE POSSIBLE HONOR DISTRIBUTIONS
C              LEADING TO EACH PARTICULAR POINT COUNT.   THE PROBABILI-
C              TIES THEN REPRESENT THE FREQUENCY FUNCTION, FROM WHICH THE
C              CUMULATIVE FREQUENCY FUNCTION AND THE MEAN AND VARIANCE OF
C              THE POINT-COUNT DISTRIBUTION ARE ALSO OBTAINED.
C
       IMPLICIT REAL*8 (A-H, O-Z)
       DIMENSION C(5), R(14), PROB(38), CUMPRB(38)
C
C        ..... SET THE C ARRAY AND INITIALIZE PROB ARRAY .....
       DATA C/ 1.0, 4.0, 6.0, 4.0, 1.0/
       DO 1  I = 1, 38
     1 PROB(I) = 0.0
C
C        ..... COMPUTE COEFFICIENTS R(1) THROUGH R(14) .....
       R(1) = 24.0/40.0
       DO 2  I = 1, 12
       FI = I
     2 R(1) = R(1)*(24.0 + FI)/(40.0 + FI)
       DO 3 IP1 = 1, 13
       FIP1 = IP1
     3 R(IP1 + 1) = R(IP1)*(13.0 - FIP1 + 1.0)/(24.0 + FIP1 - 1.0)
C
C        ..... ESTABLISH HANDS CONTAINING ALL POSSIBLE HONOR
C              CARD DISTRIBUTIONS, AND COMPUTE THE CORRESPOND-
C              ING TOTAL POINTS AND HONOR CARDS FOR EACH CASE .....
       DO 5  IP1 = 1, 625
       I = IP1 - 1
       NJ = I/125
       NQ = I/25 - ((I/25)/5)*5
       NK = I/5 - ((I/5)/5)*5
       NA = I - (I/5)*5
       NPTS = NJ + 2*NQ + 3*NK + 4*NA
       NHONS = NJ + NQ + NK + NA
C
C        ..... COMPUTE PROBABILITIES OF ALL POINT COUNTS .....
       IF (NHONS .GT. 13) GO TO 5
       PROB(NPTS + 1) = PROB(NPTS + 1) + C(NJ + 1)*C(NQ + 1)*C(NK + 1)
     1                                        *C(NA + 1)*R(NHONS + 1)
     5 CONTINUE
C
C        ..... COMPUTE CUMULATIVE PROBABILITIES .....
       CUMPRB(1) = PROB(1)
       DO 6  I = 2, 38
     6 CUMPRB(I) = CUMPRB(I-1) + PROB(I)
C
C        ..... PRINT RESULTS IN TABULATED FORM .....
       WRITE (6,200)
       I = 0
       WRITE (6,201) I, PROB(1), CUMPRB(1)
       DO 7  I = 1, 26
     7 WRITE (6,201) I, PROB(I+1), CUMPRB(I+1)
       DO 8  I = 27, 37
     8 WRITE (6,202) I, PROB(I+1), CUMPRB(I+1)
C
C        ..... COMPUTE MEAN AND VARIANCE .....
       AVG = 0.0
       DO 9  I = 1, 37
       FI = I
     9 AVG = AVG + FI*PROB(I + 1)
       VAR = AVG*AVG*PROB(1)
       DO 10  I = 1, 37
       FI = I
    10 VAR = VAR + (FI - AVG)**2*PROB(I + 1)
       WRITE (6,203) AVG, VAR
       CALL EXIT
```

Example 8.1   Distribution of Points in a Bridge Hand   **539**

Program Listing (*Continued*)

```
C
C     ..... FORMATS FOR INPUT AND OUTPUT STATEMENTS .....
  200 FORMAT (1H1, 9X, 39HDISTRIBUTION OF POINTS IN A BRIDGE HAND/1H0,
     1 9X, 11HPOINT COUNT, 3X, 11HPROBABILITY, 3X, 12HCUMUL. PROB./1H )
  201 FORMAT (10X, I6, 9X, F10.8, 4X, F10.8)
  202 FORMAT (10X, I6, 8X, E11.4, 4X, F10.8)
  203 FORMAT (1H0, 9X, 7HMEAN = , F10.7/1H0, 9X, 11HVARIANCE = ,
     1 F10.7)
C
      END
```

Computer Output

```
DISTRIBUTION OF POINTS IN A BRIDGE HAND

POINT COUNT    PROBABILITY    CUMUL. PROB.

      0        0.00363896      0.00363896
      1        0.00788442      0.01152338
      2        0.01356119      0.02508457
      3        0.02462363      0.04970820
      4        0.03845438      0.08816259
      5        0.05186193      0.14002452
      6        0.06554096      0.20556547
      7        0.08028087      0.28584634
      8        0.08892189      0.37476823
      9        0.09356227      0.46833050
     10        0.09405114      0.56238164
     11        0.08944680      0.65182844
     12        0.08026865      0.73209709
     13        0.06914331      0.80124040
     14        0.05693323      0.85817363
     15        0.04423679      0.90241042
     16        0.03310918      0.93551960
     17        0.02361695      0.95913655
     18        0.01605084      0.97518740
     19        0.01036173      0.98554912
     20        0.00643536      0.99198448
     21        0.00377867      0.99576315
     22        0.00210043      0.99786358
     23        0.00111904      0.99898262
     24        0.00055903      0.99954165
     25        0.00026428      0.99980593
     26        0.00011668      0.99992261
     27        0.4907D-04      0.99997168
     28        0.1857D-04      0.99999024
     29        0.6672D-05      0.99999692
     30        0.2198D-05      0.99999911
     31        0.6113D-06      0.99999973
     32        0.1719D-06      0.99999990
     33        0.3521D-07      0.99999993
     34        0.7061D-08      0.99999994
     35        0.9827D-09      0.99999994
     36        0.9449D-10      0.99999994
     37        0.6299D-11      0.99999994

MEAN =   9.9999994

VARIANCE = 17.0588225
```

Discussion of Results

The computed probabilities, of obtaining any specified number of points in a bridge hand, are shown as the vertical lines of Fig. 8.1.1. Together, they constitute the frequency function $f(p)$ for the random variable p, the point count. The computed values for the mean (10.000) and variance (17.059) can actually be deduced theoretically as follows, without having to consider the exact form of the frequency function.

Regard the point-count p as the linear combination

$$p = y_1 + y_2 + \cdots + y_{13},$$

where $y_1, y_2, \ldots, y_{13}$ are the points associated with each card in the hand. Then, if E denotes expected or average value,

$$E(y_1) = E(y_2) = \cdots = E(y_{13})$$

$$= \frac{4 \times (4 + 3 + 2 + 1)}{52} = \frac{40}{52}.$$

Hence, $\mu = E(p) = 13 \times 40/52 = 10$. Also, $\text{var}(p) = E(p^2) - E^2(p)$. Now,

$$E(p^2) = E(y_1 + y_2 + \cdots + y_{13})^2$$

$$= E(y_1^2 + y_2^2 + \cdots + y_{13}^2 + \sum_{i \neq j} y_i y_j)$$

$$= 13 E(y_1^2) + 13 \times 12 \times E(y_1 y_2).$$

But $E(y_1 y_2)$ may be obtained by considering all the possible combinations of two honor cards in positions 1 and 2, such as: (a) two queens, giving $y_1 y_2 = 4$, which may occur in $C(4,2) = 6$ ways, or (b) one ace, one king, giving $y_1 y_2 = 12$, in $4 \times 4 = 16$ ways, etc. The total contribution to $y_1 y_2$ is $8 \times (4 + 3 + 2 + 1)^2 - 2 \times (4^2 + 3^2 + 2^2 + 1^2) = 740$, and there are $C(52,2) = 52 \times 51/2$ possible pairs of cards occupying places 1 and 2. Hence,

$$E(y_1 y_2) = \frac{2 \times 740}{52 \times 51}.$$

The variance of p is finally obtained by noting that

$$E(p^2) = 13 \times \frac{4 \times (4^2 + 3^2 + 2^2 + 1^2)}{52}$$

$$+ 13 \times 12 \times \frac{2 \times 740}{52 \times 51}$$

$$= 30 + (1480/17) = 117.059,$$

i.e., $\sigma^2 = \text{var}(p) = 117.059 - 10^2 = 17.059$.   Q.E.D.

The frequency function $f(p)$ is almost symmetrical about the mean $\mu = 10$; the symmetry is not perfect,

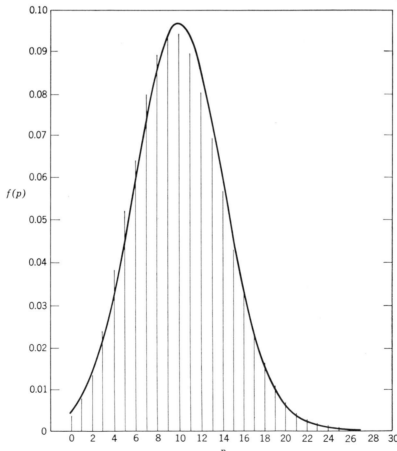

Figure 8.1.1 *Distribution of points in a bridge hand. The curve shows the frequency function for the normal distribution with mean* $= 100$ *and variance* $= 17.059$ *(standard deviation* $= 4.130$*).*

Example 8.1   Distribution of Points in a Bridge Hand   **541**

since negative point counts are impossible, whereas on the high side they may run up to 37, although with very small probability.

The smooth curve drawn on Fig. 8.1.1 represents the frequency function, (8.26), for the normal distribution with mean $\mu = 10$ and variance $\sigma^2 = 17.059$. The normal distribution will be discussed in more detail later; note here, however, that even though its frequency function is *continuous*, it does give a fairly good approximation to $f(p)$ for the *discontinuous* point-count distribution.

8.6   Sample Statistics

Consider a sample which comprises n independent observations on the random variable x.

1.   The *sample mean* $\bar{x}$ is defined by

$$\bar{x} = \frac{1}{n} \Sigma x_i, \tag{8.13}$$

that is,

$$\mu_{\bar{x}} = \text{ave}(\bar{x}) = \text{ave}\left[\frac{1}{n} \Sigma x_i\right] = \frac{1}{n} \Sigma \, \text{ave}(x_i) = \frac{1}{n} \Sigma \mu.$$

Thus, $\text{ave}(\bar{x}) = \mu$, so that the sample mean is an unbiased estimate of the population mean. The variance of the sample mean is

$$\sigma_{\bar{x}}^2 = \text{ave}[(\bar{x} - \mu_{\bar{x}})^2] = \text{ave}[(\bar{x})^2] - \mu_{\bar{x}}^2$$

$$= \text{ave}\left[\left(\frac{x_1 + x_2 + \cdots + x_n}{n}\right)^2\right] - \mu^2$$

$$= \frac{1}{n^2} \text{ave}\left[\Sigma x_i^2 + \sum_{i \neq j} x_i x_j\right] - \mu^2.$$

But $\text{ave}(x^2) = \sigma^2 + \mu^2$ and, if the x's are independent,

$$\text{ave}(x_i x_j) = \text{ave}(x_i) \, \text{ave}(x_j) = \mu^2,$$

that is,

$$\sigma_{\bar{x}}^2 = \frac{1}{n^2} \left[n(\sigma^2 + \mu^2) + n(n-1)\mu^2\right] - \mu^2 = \frac{\sigma^2}{n}. \tag{8.14}$$

2.   The *sample variance* s^2 is defined by

$$s^2 = \frac{\Sigma(x_i - \bar{x})^2}{n - 1}, \tag{8.15}$$

that is,

$$\text{ave}(s^2) = \text{ave}\left[\frac{\Sigma(x_i - \bar{x})^2}{n-1}\right] = \frac{1}{n-1} \text{ave}(\Sigma x_i^2 - n\bar{x}^2)$$

$$= \frac{1}{n-1}[\Sigma \, \text{ave}(x^2) - n \, \text{ave}(\bar{x}^2)].$$

But

$$\text{ave}(x^2) = \sigma^2 + \mu^2 \quad \text{and} \quad \text{ave}(\bar{x}^2) = \frac{\sigma^2}{n} + \mu^2,$$

that is,

$$\text{ave}(s^2) = \frac{1}{n-1}\left[n(\sigma^2 + \mu^2) - n\left(\frac{\sigma^2}{n} + \mu^2\right)\right] = \sigma^2.$$

Therefore, the sample variance is an unbiased estimate of the population variance, so that $(n - 1)$ and not n should be used in defining s^2. This allows for the fact that $\Sigma(x_i - m)^2$ is a minimum when m is the sample mean, whereas, if it were available, m should preferably be taken as the population mean, μ, in which case n and not $(n - 1)$ would be placed in the denominator of (8.15).

8.7   Moment-Generating Functions

The following population moments have already been defined:

about the origin

$$\mu_r' = \text{ave}(x^r) = \int_{-\infty}^{\infty} x^r f(x) \, dx; \tag{8.16}$$

about the mean

$$\mu_r = \text{ave}[(x - \mu_1')^r] = \int_{-\infty}^{\infty} (x - \mu_1')^r f(x) \, dx. \tag{8.17}$$

By expanding the last integrand, the μ_r may be obtained in terms of the μ_r'. In particular,

$$\mu_2(=\sigma^2) = \mu_2' - (\mu_1')^2 = \mu_2' - \mu^2 = \text{ave}[(x)^2] - \mu^2.$$

If several moments are required, it is sometimes a little tedious to perform several integrations of the type (8.16). For these cases, it is often more convenient to work not with the original frequency function $f(x)$ but with a derived function called the *moment generating function* (MGF). The MGF about the origin is defined, for an arbitrary parameter θ, by

$$M_x(\theta) = \text{ave}(e^{\theta x}) = \int_{-\infty}^{\infty} e^{\theta x} f(x) \, dx. \tag{8.18}$$

Since

$$e^{\theta x} = 1 + \theta x + \frac{\theta^2 x^2}{2!} + \cdots,$$

we have

$$M_x(\theta) = \int_{-\infty}^{\infty} f(x) \, dx + \theta \int_{-\infty}^{\infty} x f(x) \, dx$$

$$+ \frac{\theta^2}{2} \int_{-\infty}^{\infty} x^2 f(x) \, dx + \cdots$$

Thus,

$$\mu_r' = \left[\frac{d^r M_x(\theta)}{d\theta^r}\right]_{\theta = 0}. \tag{8.19}$$

In certain situations, the integral of (8.18) may not exist. In this case, it is convenient to define instead the *characteristic function*

$$\phi_x(\theta) = \text{ave}(e^{ix\theta}) \tag{8.20}$$

(where $i = \sqrt{-1}$) which will converge, and for which very similar results follow. For the present purposes, however, we assume that $M_x(\theta)$ does exist. The MGF has the following properties:

1.   There is a unique relation between $M_x(\theta)$ and $f(x)$; that is, each is defined by the other.

2.   Let x and y be two independent random variables whose frequency distributions are known. Then the MGF of the random variable $(x + y)$ is given by

$$M_{x+y}(\theta) = M_x(\theta) M_y(\theta). \tag{8.21}$$

Thus the statistics of the $(x + y)$ distribution are known immediately.

3. It yields the moment coefficients from equation (8.19).

4. There also exists an MGF about the mean,

$$M_{x-\mu}(\theta) = \text{ave}[e^{\theta(x-\mu)}] = e^{-\mu\theta} M_x(\theta),$$

for which similar results follow.

8.8 The Binomial Distribution

Consider a series of n independent observations on a random variable which can have only two values (for example, success or failure) with respective probabilities p and $q = 1 - p$. The probability of any one particular sequence of x successes and $n - x$ failures is $p^x q^{n-x}$. Also, the number of different such sequences, each containing x successes and $n - x$ failures, equals the number of ways x objects can be chosen from a total of n objects, that is, $\binom{n}{x}$.

Hence, the number of successes x is a random variable whose frequency distribution is

$$f(x) = \binom{n}{x} p^x q^{n-x}, \qquad (8.22)$$

where x may have the values $0, 1, 2, \ldots, n$. Since (8.22) represents the general term of the expansion $(p + q)^n$, such a distribution is called the *binomial* distribution. Note that Stirling's formula,

$$N! \doteq \sqrt{2\pi}\, N^{N+\frac{1}{2}} e^{-N},$$

may be of assistance in evaluating the various terms of (8.22) for cases of large n, if factorial tables are not available.

Example. Based on previous experience, a certain line of manufactured items is thought to contain 5% defectives. What is the probability that a sample of 5 items will not contain more than one defective item?

$$\text{Probability} = f(0) + f(1) = \binom{5}{0}(0.95)^5 + \binom{5}{1}(0.95)^4(0.05)$$

$$= 0.7738 + 0.2036 = 0.9774.$$

Thus there is a 97.7% chance of not more than one defective.

The *mean and variance* of the binomial distribution are easily obtained from the MGF, which is given by

$$M_x(\theta) = \text{ave}(e^{x\theta}) = \sum_{x=0}^{n} e^{x\theta} \binom{n}{x} p^x q^{n-x}$$

$$= \sum_{x=0}^{n} \binom{n}{x}(pe^\theta)^x q^{n-x} = (pe^\theta + q)^n. \qquad (8.23)$$

That is, $\mu_1' = (dM/d\theta)_{\theta=0} = np$, and $\mu_2' = (d^2M/d\theta^2)_{\theta=0} = n(n-1)p^2 + np$. Thus,

$$\mu = \text{ave}(x) = \mu_1' = np,$$

and

$$\sigma^2 = \text{var}(x) = \mu_2' - \mu^2 = np(1 - p) = npq.$$

8.9 The Multinomial Distribution

Suppose we have a random variable which can assume not only two values (as in the binomial distribution) but can fall into any one of k different classes with respective probabilities $f_1, f_2, \ldots, f_k$. Then for a total of n observations, the probability that $x_1, x_2, \ldots, x_k$ observations will fall into classes $1, 2, \ldots, k$, respectively, is given by the frequency function of the *multinomial distribution*:

$$f(x_1, x_2, \ldots, x_k) = \frac{n!}{x_1! x_2! \cdots x_k!} (f_1)^{x_1}(f_2)^{x_2} \cdots (f_k)^{x_k}. \qquad (8.24)$$

With respect to the variable x_i, the multinomial distribution has mean $= nf_i$ and variance $= nf_i(1 - f_i)$.

Example. A bag contains a large number of balls of which 50% are red, 30% black, and 20% white. A sample of 5 balls is drawn. What is the probability that 3 will be red, none black, and 2 white? We have $f_1 = 0.5, f_2 = 0.3, f_3 = 0.2$; whence

$$f(3,0,2) = \frac{5!}{3!\, 0!\, 2!}(0.5)^3(0.3)^0(0.2)^2 = 0.05.$$

That is, there is a 1 in 20 probability of the specified drawing occurring. Note that the requirement of a "a large number of balls" can be omitted if the balls are drawn one at a time and then replaced.

8.10 The Poisson Distribution

It may be shown fairly easily that as $n \to \infty$ while np remains finite (and equal to λ, for instance), the binomial distribution tends to the limit

$$f(x) = \frac{e^{-\lambda}\lambda^x}{x!}, \qquad x = 0, 1, 2, \ldots. \qquad (8.25)$$

The frequency function of (8.25) is that of the *Poisson* distribution, and is applicable to discrete events occurring at random in a continuum of time or space, when we regard as a random variable x the frequency or number of events occurring in a relatively small interval of that time or space.

For example, incidents of radioactive decay may occur from second to second in a Geiger counter; over a minute, we could say that they occurred at an *average* rate of λ incidents per second. Then the probabilities of $0, 1, 2, \ldots$ incidents occurring in any one second would be expected to equal the successive terms of the Poisson distribution, namely,

$$e^{-\lambda}\left[1 + \lambda + \frac{\lambda^2}{2!} + \frac{\lambda^3}{3!} + \cdots\right].$$

Note that in contrast to the binomial distribution, there is no upper limit to the number of incidents that might occur in a second, even though the chances of a large number would be very small. In other words, we cannot say how many incidents did *not* occur in a given second.

The MGF of the Poisson distribution is

$$M_x(\theta) = \text{ave}(e^{x\theta}) = \sum_{x=0}^{\infty} e^{x\theta} \frac{e^{-\lambda}\lambda^x}{x!}$$

$$= e^{-\lambda} \sum_{x=0}^{\infty} \frac{(\lambda e^{\theta})^x}{x!} = e^{-\lambda} e^{\lambda e^{\theta}}$$

$$= e^{\lambda(e^{\theta}-1)}.$$

Alternatively, if we take the MGF for the binomial distribution, equation (8.23), and let $n \to \infty$, $np \to \lambda$, we obtain

$$M_x(\theta) = [1 + p(e^{\theta} - 1)]^n$$

$$\doteq \left[1 + \frac{\lambda}{n}(e^{\theta} - 1)\right]^n \to e^{\lambda(e^{\theta}-1)}$$

that is,

$$\mu_1' = (dM/d\theta)_{\theta=0} = \lambda, \text{ and } \mu_2' = (d^2M/d\theta^2)_{\theta=0} = \lambda^2 + \lambda.$$

Thus

$$\mu = \text{ave}(x) = \mu_1' = \lambda, \quad \text{and} \quad \sigma^2 = \text{var}(x) = \mu_2' - \mu^2 = \lambda.$$

EXAMPLE 8.2

POISSON DISTRIBUTION RANDOM NUMBER GENERATOR

Problem Statement

Write a program that will generate a sequence of n random numbers coming from a population conforming to the Poisson distribution with mean λ. Compare the observed frequency of appearance of each particular number with its theoretical frequency.

Method of Solution

We shall make use of a "flat" random number generator, described below, which returns a random variable z as a decimal fraction having the uniform frequency function $h(z) = 1$ for $0 \leqslant z < 1$, and $h(z) = 0$ for all other values of z. Let $x_k = z_0 z_1 z_2 \ldots z_k$ be the product of a sequence of $k + 1$ such random variables. Then the lowest value of k, which first causes x_k to be less than or equal to $e^{-\lambda}$, will be a random variable having the Poisson distribution with mean λ. A sketch of the proof follows.

First note that if y and z are independent random variables, with frequency functions $g(y)$ and $h(z)$, respectively, it can be shown that $x = yz$ has the frequency function

$$f(x) = \int g(y) h(x/y) \frac{dy}{y}.$$

In general, the integration limits will be $y = -\infty$ and $y = +\infty$, but in the present case the particular forms of g and h will lead to much more restricted limits.

Let $f_k(x_k)$ be the frequency function for x_k. Since $f_0(x_0) = h(z_0) = 1$, we have, for $x_1 = x_0 z_1$,

$$f_1(x_1) = \int_{x_1}^{1} g(x_0) h(x_1/x_0) \frac{dx_0}{x_0}$$

$$= \int_{x_1}^{1} 1 \times 1 \times \frac{dx_0}{x_0} = -\ln x_1.$$

By induction, we can show that $x_k = x_{k-1} z_k$ has the frequency function

$$f_k(x_k) = \frac{(-1)^k}{k!} \ln^k x_k.$$

We also note the existence of the recursion relation $I_k = x \ln^k x - k I_{k-1}$ for evaluating integrals of the form $I_k = \int \ln^k x \, dx$. Hence, the probability that x_k not be greater than $e^{-\lambda}$ is

$$Pr(x_k \leqslant e^{-\lambda}) = \int_0^{e^{-\lambda}} f_k(x_k) \, dx_k$$

$$= \frac{(-1)^k}{k!} [x \ln^k x - k I_{k-1}]_0^{e^{-\lambda}},$$

that is,

$$Pr(x_k \leqslant e^{-\lambda}) = \frac{e^{-\lambda} \lambda}{k!} + Pr(x_{k-1} \leqslant e^{-\lambda}).$$

By induction, this means that

$$Pr(x_k \leqslant e^{-\lambda}) = e^{-\lambda} \left[\frac{\lambda^k}{k!} + \frac{\lambda^{k-1}}{(k-1)!} + \cdots + \frac{\lambda^2}{2!} + \lambda + 1 \right].$$

Thus, the probability that x_k does not fall above $e^{-\lambda}$ corresponds to the cumulative frequency function for the first $k + 1$ members of the Poisson distribution. Hence, we conclude that if $x_k \leqslant e^{-\lambda}$, but $x_{k-1} > e^{-\lambda}$, then k obeys the Poisson distribution with mean λ.

Generator for Uniformly Distributed Random Numbers

The multiplicative congruential method for generating a sequence of uniformly distributed pseudorandom integers x_i, $i = 2, 3, \ldots, n$, uses the recursion relation

$$x_i = a x_{i-1} (\text{mod } m),$$

in which a and m are integer constants. A random floating-point number z_i, uniformly distributed between 0 and 1, is then given by $z_i = x_i/m$. The modulus m is a large integer, usually of the form 2^α or 10^α (for binary and decimal machines, respectively), its magnitude being restricted by the available word length. The exact choice for m (and a) is usually only critical if we are trying to write a very efficient program in basic machine instructions; for example, on a binary machine, multiplication by an integeral power of two can be achieved by simply shifting digits the appropriate number of places, etc.

The method is discussed more fully in [7], [8], and [9]. To summarize, we can say the following:

(a) For $m = 2^\alpha$, appropriate for efficient machine-language programs with binary computers, the maximum period before the numbers start repeating is $m/4$. Assuming $\alpha > 2$, this maximum period will be achieved, provided that the starting value x_1 is odd, and that a differs by 3 from the nearest multiple of 8. A good choice for a is close to $2^{\alpha/2}$.

(b) For $m = 10^\alpha$ (decimal machines), the maximum period is $m/20$, which will be achieved, for $\alpha > 2$, provided that x_1 is odd and not a multiple of 5, and that a differs from the nearest multiple of 200 by one of the following numbers: 3, 11, 13, 19, 21, 27, 29, 37, 53, 59, 61, 67, 69, 77, 83, or 91. A good choice for a is close to $2^{\alpha/2}$.

The term *pseudorandom* is used to describe the successive values x_i; although they may have satisfactory randomness, a predetermined algebraic formula has been used for their generation. The fact that the period may be large does *not* guarantee that the particular sequence will necessarily possess acceptable random properties.

In the present example, we choose the values: $m = 2^{20}$, $a = 2^{10} + 3$, and $x_1 = 566{,}387$. Thus, the conditions mentioned in (a) above are satisfied, and we are also sure that the product ax_{i-1} will not exceed $2^{31} - 1$, which is the maximum allowable integer on the machine being used. For convenience, the above method is written as a subroutine named RANDOM. Note finally, that once x_i has been computed, x_{i-1} is no longer needed. Thus, all the x_i can be stored successively in the same memory location.

Flow Diagram

Main Program (Excluding details of sorting and comparing numbers that are generated)

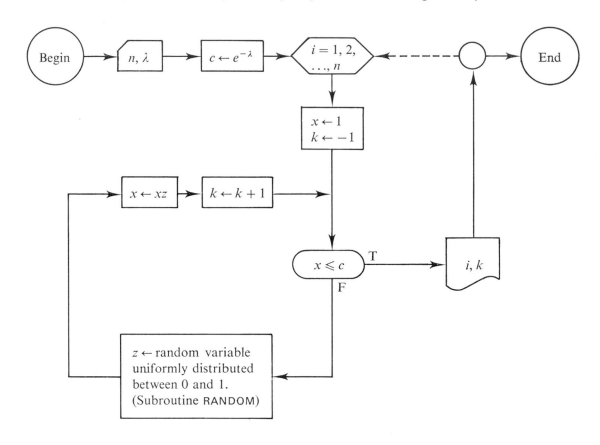

Subroutine RANDOM (Argument: z)

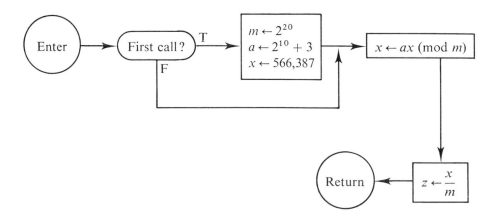

Example 8.2   Poisson Distribution Random Number Generator   **547**

FORTRAN *Implementation*

List of Principal Variables

Program Symbol	Definition
(Main)	
C	The constant $c = e^{-\lambda}$.
FACT	Vector whose kth element FACT(K) contains $k!$
IPRINT	Number of individual random numbers to be printed.
K	Random variable k obeying the Poisson distribution.
LAMBDA	Mean value, λ.
N	Total number, n, of random numbers to be generated.
NOBS	Vector containing observed frequencies of particular random numbers. NOBSZ is the observed frequency of zeros.
RANDOM	Subroutine that gives a random number z between 0 and 1 with uniform probability.
THEORN	Vector containing the theoretical frequencies of particular random numbers. THEORZ is the theoretical frequency of zeros.
X	Repeated product, $x_k = z_0 z_1 \ldots z_k$.
Z	Random number z, uniformly distributed between 0 and 1.
(Subroutine RANDOM)	
A	Multiplier, a.
I	An integer switch that is preset to 1 by using the DATA statement. It identifies the first entry; thereafter, it has the value 0.
M	Modulus, m.
X	Current random integer, x_i.

Program Listing

Main Program

```
C              APPLIED NUMERICAL METHODS, EXAMPLE 8.2
C              POISSON DISTRIBUTION RANDOM NUMBER GENERATOR.
C
C              THE SUBROUTINE RANDOM PRODUCES A RANDOM NUMBER UNIFORMLY
C              DISTRIBUTED BETWEEN 0 AND 1.    THIS IS THEN TRANSLATED INTO
C              A RANDOM VARIABLE K FOLLOWING THE POISSON DISTRIBUTION WITH
C              MEAN LAMBDA.    N SUCH NUMBERS ARE GENERATED.    NOBS(K) AND
C              THEORN(K) ARE THE OBSERVED AND THEORETICAL COUNTS FOR A
C              PARTICULAR VALUE OF K.
C
        DIMENSION NOBS(50), THEORN(50), FACT(50)
C
C        ..... READ AND CHECK DATA .....
        REAL LAMBDA
    1   READ (5,100) N, IPRINT, LAMBDA
        WRITE (6,200) N, IPRINT, LAMBDA
        FN = N
        NOBSZ = 0
        KMAX = 0
        DO 2   I = 1, 50
    2   NOBS(I) = 0
        C = EXP(- LAMBDA)
C
C        ..... GENERATE N POISSON DISTRIBUTION RANDOM NUMBERS .....
        WRITE (6,204)
        DO 11   I = 1, N
        X = 1.0
        K = - 1
    3   IF (X .LE. C) GO TO 5
C
C        ..... CALL ON FLAT R.N.G. FUNCTION RANDOM .....
        CALL RANDOM (Z)
        X = X*Z
        K = K + 1
        GO TO 3
C
C        ..... INCREASE KMAX TO LARGEST NUMBER YET GENERATED .....
    5   IF (K .LE. KMAX) GO TO 7
        KMAX = K
C
C        ..... PRINT THE FIRST IPRINT NUMBERS .....
    7   IF (I .GT. IPRINT) GO TO 9
        WRITE (6,201) I, K
C
C        ..... AUGMENT TOTAL COUNT OF NUMBER JUST GENERATED .....
    9   IF (K .NE. 0) GO TO 10
            NOBSZ = NOBSZ + 1
            GO TO 11
   10   NOBS(K) = NOBS(K) + 1
   11   CONTINUE
C
C        ..... COMPUTE THEORETICAL FREQUENCIES, PRINT NOBS AND THEORN .....
        WRITE (6,202)
        K = 0
        THEORZ = C*FN
        WRITE (6,203) K, NOBSZ, THEORZ
        K = 1
        FACT(1) = 1.0
        THEORN(1) = C*LAMBDA*FN
        WRITE (6,203) K, NOBS(1), THEORN(1)
        IF (KMAX .LT. 2) GO TO 1
        DO 12   K = 2, KMAX
        FK = K
        FACT(K) = FACT(K-1)*FK
        THEORN(K) = C*LAMBDA**K*FN/FACT(K)
   12   WRITE (6,203) K, NOBS(K), THEORN(K)
        GO TO 1
```

Example 8.2 Poisson Distribution Random Number Generator **549**

Program Listing (*Continued*)

```
C
C       ..... FORMATS FOR INPUT AND OUTPUT STATEMENTS .....
  100   FORMAT (10X, I5, 11X, I4, 13X, F7.3)
  200   FORMAT (1H1, 10X, 44HPOISSON DISTRIBUTION RANDOM NUMBER GENERATOR
     1 /1H0, 15X, 9HN      = , I4/ 16X, 9HIPRINT = , I4/
     2 16X, 9HLAMBDA = , F10.5)
  201   FORMAT (1H , 15X, 5HI   = , I5, 5X, 5HK   = , I5)
  202   FORMAT (1H0, 10X, 44HTHE OBSERVED AND THEORETICAL FREQUENCIES ARE
     1 /1H0, 15X, 25HK       NOBS       NTHEOR/1H )
  203   FORMAT (I17, I11, F13.4)
  204   FORMAT (1H0, 10X, 32HTHE FIRST FEW RANDOM NUMBERS ARE/1H )
C
        END
```

Subroutine **RANDOM**

```
C       SUBROUTINE FOR GENERATING RANDOM NUMBERS HAVING A UNIFORM
C       DISTRIBUTION, BY THE MIXED MULTIPLICATIVE CONGRUENTIAL METHOD.
C
        SUBROUTINE RANDOM (Z)
        DATA I/1/
        INTEGER A, X
        IF (I .EQ. 0) GO TO 1
        I = 0
        M = 2**20
        FM = M
        X = 566387
        A = 2**10 + 3
C
   1    X = MOD(A*X, M)
        FX = X
        Z = FX/FM
        RETURN
        END
```

Data

```
N   =  1000,  IPRINT =  20,   LAMBDA  =   2.0
N   =  1000,  IPRINT =  20,   LAMBDA  =   5.0
```

Computer Output

```
POISSON DISTRIBUTION RANDOM NUMBER GENERATOR          POISSON DISTRIBUTION RANDOM NUMBER GENERATOR

     N     = 1000                                          N     = 1000
     IPRINT =   20                                         IPRINT =   20
     LAMBDA =    2.00000                                   LAMBDA =    5.00000

THE FIRST FEW RANDOM NUMBERS ARE                      THE FIRST FEW RANDOM NUMBERS ARE

     I  =      1    K  =      5                            I  =      1    K  =      6
     I  =      2    K  =      2                            I  =      2    K  =      8
     I  =      3    K  =      1                            I  =      3    K  =      6
     I  =      4    K  =      4                            I  =      4    K  =      6
     I  =      5    K  =      0                            I  =      5    K  =      6
     I  =      6    K  =      2                            I  =      6    K  =      3
     I  =      7    K  =      2                            I  =      7    K  =      6
     I  =      8    K  =      0                            I  =      8    K  =      3
     I  =      9    K  =      4                            I  =      9    K  =      4
     I  =     10    K  =      2                            I  =     10    K  =      4
     I  =     11    K  =      1                            I  =     11    K  =      5
     I  =     12    K  =      3                            I  =     12    K  =      8
     I  =     13    K  =      3                            I  =     13    K  =      5
     I  =     14    K  =      1                            I  =     14    K  =      5
     I  =     15    K  =      1                            I  =     15    K  =      5
     I  =     16    K  =      1                            I  =     16    K  =      1
     I  =     17    K  =      3                            I  =     17    K  =      6
     I  =     18    K  =      2                            I  =     18    K  =      2
     I  =     19    K  =      4                            I  =     19    K  =      3
     I  =     20    K  =      0                            I  =     20    K  =      3

THE OBSERVED AND THEORETICAL FREQUENCIES ARE         THE OBSERVED AND THEORETICAL FREQUENCIES ARE

     K      NOBS       NTHEOR                              K      NOBS       NTHEOR

     0       142      135.3353                             0         5        6.7379
     1       267      270.6704                             1        54       33.6897
     2       274      270.6704                             2        88       84.2243
     3       179      180.4469                             3       159      140.3739
     4        87       90.2235                             4       179      175.4673
     5        42       36.0894                             5       161      175.4673
     6         7       12.0298                             6       135      146.2227
     7         2        3.4371                             7       100      104.4448
                                                           8        54       65.2780
                                                           9        38       36.2656
                                                          10        14       18.1328
                                                          11         8        8.2422
                                                          12         5        3.4342
```

Example 8.2   Poisson Distribution Random Number Generator **551**

Discussion of Results

One thousand random numbers have been generated for each of the cases $\lambda = 2$ and $\lambda = 5$. The observed distributions seem to conform reasonably to those predicted theoretically; this conclusion is further substantiated by using a χ^2 test in Example 8.4.

8.11 The Normal Distribution

Many random variables are distributed approximately according to the normal, or Gaussian, law. Such variables are characterized by random deviations on either side of a fairly well-defined central value or mean. For example, successive observations on (a) the heights of different men belonging to a certain race, (b) a particular experimental measurement subject to several random errors, or (c) the time taken to travel to work along a given route, would be expected to conform to the normal distribution law. Other variables might be transformed to give an approximately normal distribution, for example, the logarithm of the diameter of particles in a powder.

The frequency function of the normal distribution is

$$f(x) = \frac{1}{\sigma\sqrt{2\pi}} e^{-(x-\mu)^2/2\sigma^2}, \qquad (8.26)$$

which is shown in Fig. 8.4. The area under the curve is, of course, unity. It is shown below that μ and σ^2 are, in

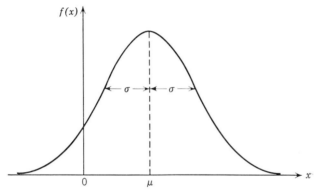

Figure 8.4   The normal distribution.

fact, the mean and variance of this distribution. It is shown in the next section that the frequency function (8.26) is in complete agreement with the concept of a large number of small random fluctuations, characterized by the parameter σ, about a central value, μ. The normal distribution can be used to represent a random variable, such as the height of men, not having negative values, provided that $f(x)$ has already fallen to a negligibly small value for small positive values of x.

The statistics of the distribution are obtained from the MGF. Noting that

$$\int_0^\infty e^{-ax^2}\, dx = \frac{1}{2}\sqrt{\frac{\pi}{a}},$$

then

$$M_x(\theta) = \frac{1}{\sigma\sqrt{2\pi}} \int_{-\infty}^\infty e^{x\theta} \exp\left[\frac{-(x-\mu)^2}{2\sigma^2}\right] dx$$

$$= \exp\left[\mu\theta + \frac{\sigma^2\theta^2}{2}\right]. \qquad (8.27)$$

Thus

$$\mu_1' = (dM/d\theta)_{\theta=0} = \mu, \quad \text{or} \quad \text{ave}(x) = \mu_1' = \mu,$$

and

$$\mu_2' = (d^2M/d\theta^2)_{\theta=0} = \mu^2 + \sigma^2,$$

$$\text{or} \quad \text{var}(x) = \mu_2' - \mu^2 = \sigma^2.$$

The standardized form is obtained by changing the variable to $\xi = (x-\mu)/\sigma$, which is termed an $N(0,1)$ variable because its distribution is normal with zero mean and unit variance. In fact, the corresponding frequency function $\phi(\xi)$ is given by

$$\phi(\xi) = \frac{1}{\sqrt{2\pi}} e^{-\xi^2/2}. \qquad (8.28)$$

Representative values of the frequency function $\phi(\xi)$ and the corresponding cumulative distribution function $\Phi(\xi)$, both correct to four decimal places, are given in Table 8.1, together with values of ξ_P (correct to about ± 0.002) which have a probability P of being exceeded. Table 8.1 is derived in Example 8.3. The levels $P = 0.2, 0.1$, etc., are frequently termed the 20%, 10% levels, etc.

Table 8.1   Values of the Standardized Normal Distribution

ξ	ϕ	Φ	ξ	ϕ	Φ
0.0	0.3989	0.5000	2.0	0.0540	0.9772
0.1	0.3970	0.5398	2.1	0.0440	0.9821
0.2	0.3910	0.5793	2.2	0.0355	0.9861
0.3	0.3814	0.6179	2.3	0.0283	0.9893
0.4	0.3683	0.6554	2.4	0.0224	0.9918
0.5	0.3521	0.6915	2.5	0.0175	0.9938
0.6	0.3332	0.7258	2.6	0.0136	0.9953
0.7	0.3122	0.7580	2.7	0.0104	0.9965
0.8	0.2897	0.7881	2.8	0.0079	0.9974
0.9	0.2661	0.8159	2.9	0.0060	0.9981
1.0	0.2420	0.8413	3.0	0.0044	0.9986
1.1	0.2178	0.8643	3.1	0.0033	0.9990
1.2	0.1942	0.8849	3.2	0.0024	0.9993
1.3	0.1714	0.9032	3.3	0.0017	0.9995
1.4	0.1497	0.9192	3.4	0.0012	0.9997
1.5	0.1295	0.9332	3.5	0.0009	0.9998
1.6	0.1109	0.9452	3.6	0.0006	0.9998
1.7	0.0940	0.9554	3.7	0.0004	0.9999
1.8	0.0790	0.9641	3.8	0.0003	0.9999
1.9	0.0656	0.9713	3.9	0.0002	1.0000
2.0	0.0540	0.9772	4.0	0.0001	1.0000

P	0.20	0.10	0.05	0.02	0.01
ξ_P	0.843	1.282	1.647	2.056	2.329

P	0.005	0.002	0.001
ξ_P	2.578	2.880	3.092

The normal distribution is probably the most important distribution in the whole of statistical theory. It is easily shown via the MGF that the linear combination $z = \sum a_i x_i$ of normally distributed variables x_i is itself normally

Example 8.2 Poisson Distribution Random Number Generator **553**

distributed (with mean $\sum a_i\mu_i$ and variance $\sum a_i^2\sigma_i^2$). In particular, for an $N(\mu,\sigma)$ population, the sample mean $\bar{x}$ is an $N(\mu,\sigma^2/n)$ variable.

Example. A population is known to be distributed as $N(40,9)$. What value would the mean of four items drawn at random from the population have a 1% probability of exceeding?

Assuming that the population is sufficiently large so that the items are independent of one another, then the mean of the four items is $\bar{x} = (x_1 + x_2 + x_3 + x_4)/4$, which is a linear combination of normally distributed variables and is itself normally distributed.

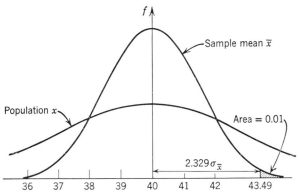

Figure 8.5 *Population and sample ($n = 4$) distributions.*

Then, $\sigma_{\bar{x}}^2 = \sigma^2/n = 9/4$, or $\sigma_{\bar{x}} = 1.5$. From Table 8.1, the value of ξ which has a $P = 0.01$ probability of being exceeded is $\xi_P = 2.329 = (\bar{x} - \mu)/\sigma_{\bar{x}}$. Thus the required value is $\bar{x} = 40 + 2.329 \times 1.5 = 43.49$ (see Fig. 8.5). That is, in the long run, the sample mean will exceed 43.49 once in every 100 samples.

8.12 Derivation of the Normal Distribution Frequency Function

Assume that superimposed on the "true" value m for any measurement x, there is a large number n of very small errors δ, of which X are in the positive direction; that is, $x = m + (2X - n)\delta$. Let the probability of any one error being in the positive direction be p. From the binomial distribution (8.22),

$$f(X) = \binom{n}{X} p^X (1 - p)^{n - X},$$

so the MGF for the distribution of x is

$$M_x(\theta) = \sum_{X=0}^{n} e^{[m + (2X - n)\delta]\theta} p^X (1 - p)^{n - X} \binom{n}{X}$$

$$= e^{m\theta} e^{-n\delta\theta} (pe^{2\delta\theta} + 1 - p)^n.$$

Now, if positive and negative errors are equally likely, $p = 1/2$, so that

$$M_x(\theta) = e^{m\theta} e^{-n\delta\theta} \left(\frac{1 + e^{2\delta\theta}}{2}\right)^n$$

$$= e^{m\theta} e^{-n\delta\theta} \left[\frac{1 + 1 + 2\delta\theta + 2\delta^2\theta^2 + (4/3)\delta^3\theta^3 + \cdots}{2}\right]^n$$

$$= e^{m\theta} e^{-n\delta\theta} \left[1 + \frac{n\delta\theta + n\delta^2\theta^2 + (2/3)n\delta^3\theta^3 + \cdots}{n}\right]^n.$$

Now let $n \to \infty$ and $\delta \to 0$, while $2n\delta^2 (= c^2$, for instance) remains finite, so that terms of $O(n\delta^3)$ tend to zero. The MGF then becomes

$$M_x(\theta) = \exp\left[m\theta + \frac{c^2\theta^2}{2}\right]. \tag{8.29}$$

But for $m = \mu$ and $c^2 = \sigma^2$ this is identical with the form obtained by the integration of

$$\int_{-\infty}^{\infty} e^{\theta x} \frac{1}{\sigma\sqrt{2\pi}} \exp\left[-\frac{(x - \mu)^2}{2\sigma^2}\right] dx.$$

EXAMPLE 8.3

TABULATION OF THE STANDARDIZED NORMAL DISTRIBUTION

Problem Statement

For a standardized normal variable ξ, the frequency function ϕ, the cumulative frequency function Φ, and the probability P that a certain value ξ_P will not be exceeded are illustrated in Fig. 8.3.1 and are defined by

$$\phi(\xi) = \frac{1}{\sqrt{2\pi}} e^{-\xi^2/2},$$

$$\Phi(\xi) = \int_{-\infty}^{\xi} \phi(\xi)\, d\xi = 0.5 + \int_{0}^{\xi} \phi(\xi)\, d\xi,$$

$$P = 1 - \Phi(\xi_P).$$

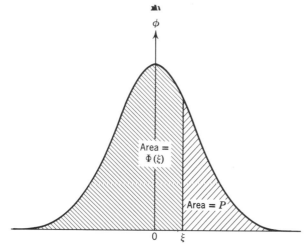

Figure 8.3.1   The standardized normal distribution.

The problem is to construct tables of: (a) ϕ and Φ versus ξ, for $0 \leqslant \xi \leqslant nh$, with increments in ξ of $2h$, and (b) ξ_P versus P, for certain values $P_1, P_2, \ldots, P_q$, with the knowledge that no value of ξ higher than nh will be involved.

Method of Solution

Note that owing to symmetry about the origin, only one-half of the distribution is considered. The computation is performed in three main steps. First, values of ϕ_j are calculated corresponding to $\xi_j = jh$, for $j = 0, 1, 2, \ldots, n$. Second, values of Φ_j are obtained at the alternate points $j = 0, 2, 4, \ldots, n$, where n is even, by repeated applications of Simpson's rule:

$$\Phi_j - \Phi_{j-2} = \int_{j-2}^{j} \phi(\xi)\, d\xi \doteq \frac{h}{3}(\phi_{j-2} + 4\phi_{j-1} + \phi_j),$$

with $\Phi_0 = 0.5$. Simpson's rule overestimates the integral by an amount $(h^5/90)d^4\phi(\eta)/d\xi^4$, where $\xi_{j-2} \leqslant \eta \leqslant \xi_j$. Now $d^4\phi/d\xi^4 = e^{-\zeta^2/2}(\xi^4 - 6\xi^2 + 3)/\sqrt{2\pi}$, which has a maximum value of 3, at $\xi = 0$. In the following program, $h = 0.05$ and $n = 80$, so a conservative estimate of the maximum error in Φ, occurring at $\xi = 4.0$, is $(0.05)^5 \times 3 \times 40/(90\sqrt{2\pi})$, which is less than 10^{-6}, an inconsequential amount. Third, the value of ξ_P corresponding to P, i.e., to $\Phi = 1 - P$, is found by a table look-up procedure followed by linear interpolation for ξ between two consecutive entries of Φ.

Example 8.3   Tabulation of the Standardized Normal Distribution   **555**

Flow Diagram

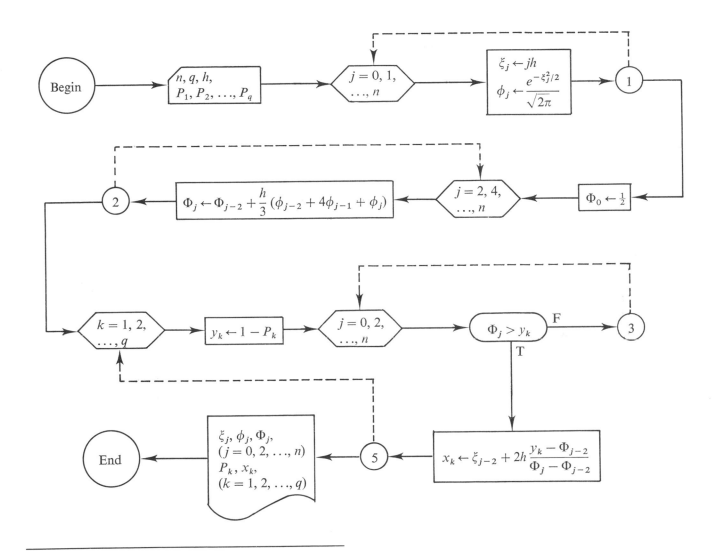

FORTRAN *Implementation*

List of Principal Variables

Program Symbol	Definition
CAPPHI	Vector containing values of the cumulative frequency function, Φ_j.
DXI	Increment, $\Delta\xi = h$.
JP1	Subscript equivalent to j. Due to FORTRAN limitations, we have $1 \leqslant$ JP1 $\leqslant$ N $+$ 1 in the program, corresponding to $0 \leqslant j \leqslant n$ in the text.
N	Total number n of increments $\Delta\xi$; n must be even.
NPROBS	Total number q of probabilities P to be tabulated. Only values from $P = 0$ to $P = 0.5$ are to occur.
PHI	Vector containing values of the frequency function, ϕ_j.
PROB	Vector containing specified values of P.
R	$1/\sqrt{2\pi}$.
X	Vector containing values of ξ_P.
XI	Vector containing values of the standardized normal variable, ξ_j.
Y	Vector containing values of $1 - P$.

Program Listing

```
C               APPLIED NUMERICAL METHODS, EXAMPLE 8.3
C               TABULATION OF VALUES OF THE STANDARDIZED NORMAL DISTRIBUTION.
C
C               THE FREQUENCY FUNCTION (F.F.) AND THE CUMULATIVE DISTRIBUTION
C               FUNCTION (C.D.F.) ARE TABULATED AGAINST THE STANDARDIZED NORMAL
C               VARIABLE (S.N.V.).   THE NUMBER OF ENTRIES AND THEIR SPACING
C               ARE CONTROLLED BY THE INPUT DATA.   THE INTEGRATION FOR THE
C               C.D.F. IS ACHIEVED USING SIMPSON'S RULE.   THOSE VALUES OF THE
C               S.N.V. WHICH HAVE SPECIFIED PROBABILITIES OF BEING EXCEEDED ARE
C               ALSO TABULATED.
C
        DIMENSION XI(100), PHI(100), CAPPHI(100), PROB(20), X(20), Y(20)
        R = 1.0/SQRT(2.0*3.14159)
        READ (5,100) N, NPROBS, DXI, (PROB(I), I = 1, NPROBS)
C
C               ..... COMPUTE FREQUENCY FUNCTION .....
        NP1 = N + 1
        DO 1  JP1 = 1, NP1
        FJ = JP1 - 1
        XI(JP1) = FJ*DXI
    1   PHI(JP1) = R*EXP(-XI(JP1)*XI(JP1)/2.0)
C
C               ..... COMPUTE CUMULATIVE DISTRIBUTION FUNCTION .....
        CAPPHI(1) = 0.5
        DO 2  JP1 = 3, NP1, 2
    2   CAPPHI(JP1) = CAPPHI(JP1-2) +
       1             (PHI(JP1-2) + 4.0*PHI(JP1-1) + PHI(JP1))*DXI/3.0
C
C               ..... COMPUTE VALUES OF S.N.V. WHICH HAVE
C                     SPECIFIED PROBABILITIES OF BEING EXCEEDED .....
        DO 5  K = 1, NPROBS
        Y(K) = 1.0 - PROB(K)
        DO 3  JP1 = 1, NP1, 2
        IF (CAPPHI(JP1) .GT. Y(K)) GO TO 4
    3   CONTINUE
    4   X(K) = XI(JP1-2) + (2.0*DXI)*
       1          (Y(K) - CAPPHI(JP1-2))/(CAPPHI(JP1) - CAPPHI(JP1-2))
    5   CONTINUE
C
C               ..... ARRANGE THE HEADINGS PROPERLY .....
        WRITE (6,200)
C
C               ..... AND PRINT THE RESULTS .....
        NOVER2 = N/2
        NOV2P1 = N/2 + 1
        DO 6  JP1 = 1, NOV2P1, 2
        ISUB = JP1 + NOVER2
    6   WRITE (6,201) XI(JP1), PHI(JP1), CAPPHI(JP1), XI(ISUB), PHI(ISUB),
       1 CAPPHI(ISUB)
C
C               ..... NOT FORGETTING THE PROBABILITIES .....
        WRITE (6,202)
        DO 7  J = 1, NPROBS
    7   WRITE (6,203) PROB(J), X(J)
        CALL EXIT
C
C               ..... FORMATS FOR INPUT AND OUTPUT STATEMENTS .....
  100   FORMAT (4X, I4, 13X, I3, 10X, F6.2/ /(5F10.5))
  200   FORMAT (1H1/  7X, 60HTABULATION OF VALUES OF THE STANDARDIZED NORM
       1AL DISTRIBUTION/1H0, 6X, 6HS.N.V., 2X, 9HFREQUENCY, 2X, 10HCUM.DIS
       2TR., 7X, 6HS.N.V., 2X, 9HFREQUENCY, 2X, 11HCUM. DISTR./8X, 4H(XI),
       33X, 8HFUNCTION, 4X, 8HFUNCTION, 10X, 4H(XI), 3X, 8HFUNCTION, 4X,
       48HFUNCTION/1H /)
  201   FORMAT (7X, F5.3, 4X, F7.5, 4X, F7.5, 10X, F5.3, 4X, F7.5,
       14X, F7.5)
  202   FORMAT (1H0,   10X, 4HPROB, 8X, 2HXI/1H /)
  203   FORMAT (7X, F8.4, 6X, F6.4)
C
        END
```

Example 8.3   Tabulation of the Standardized Normal Distribution   557

Program Listing (*Continued*)

Data

```
N  =  80,    NPROBS  =  8,    DXI  =  0.05
VALUES OF PROB(1)...PROB(NPROBS) ARE
   0.2        0.1        0.05      0.02       0.01
   0.005      0.002      0.001
```

Computer Output

TABULATION OF VALUES OF THE STANDARDIZED NORMAL DISTRIBUTION

S.N.V. (XI)	FREQUENCY FUNCTION	CUM.DISTR. FUNCTION	S.N.V. (XI)	FREQUENCY FUNCTION	CUM. DISTR. FUNCTION
0.0	0.39894	0.50000	2.000	0.05399	0.97725
0.100	0.39695	0.53983	2.100	0.04398	0.98214
0.200	0.39104	0.57926	2.200	0.03547	0.98610
0.300	0.38139	0.61791	2.300	0.02833	0.98928
0.400	0.36827	0.65542	2.400	0.02239	0.99180
0.500	0.35207	0.69146	2.500	0.01753	0.99379
0.600	0.33322	0.72575	2.600	0.01358	0.99534
0.700	0.31225	0.75804	2.700	0.01042	0.99653
0.800	0.28969	0.78814	2.800	0.00792	0.99744
0.900	0.26609	0.81594	2.900	0.00595	0.99813
1.000	0.24197	0.84134	3.000	0.00443	0.99865
1.100	0.21785	0.86433	3.100	0.00327	0.99903
1.200	0.19419	0.88493	3.200	0.00238	0.99931
1.300	0.17137	0.90320	3.300	0.00172	0.99952
1.400	0.14973	0.91924	3.400	0.00123	0.99966
1.500	0.12952	0.93319	3.500	0.00087	0.99977
1.600	0.11092	0.94520	3.600	0.00061	0.99984
1.700	0.09405	0.95543	3.700	0.00042	0.99989
1.800	0.07895	0.96407	3.800	0.00029	0.99993
1.900	0.06562	0.97128	3.900	0.00020	0.99995
2.000	0.05399	0.97725	4.000	0.00013	0.99997

PROB	XI
0.2000	0.8427
0.1000	1.2825
0.0500	1.6469
0.0200	2.0563
0.0100	2.3287
0.0050	2.5782
0.0020	2.8806
0.0010	3.0917

Discussion of Results

This example has illustrated the use of the computer in compiling tables of statistical functions. The values for the frequency function are correct to the fifth decimal place; those for the cumulative distribution function may be taken as correct within ± 0.00001. The values ξ_P, however, being obtained from a linear interpolation procedure, will be more seriously in error. Comparison with other tables [1] shows that the ξ_P computed here are too high by an amount not exceeding 0.002; for most work this error is acceptable.

8.13   The χ^2 Distribution

Let $\xi_1, \xi_2, \ldots, \xi_\nu$ be $N(0,1)$ variables, that is, ν variables drawn from a normally distributed population having zero mean and unit variance. The variable χ^2 is defined for a given value of ν by

$$\chi^2 = \xi_1^2 + \xi_2^2 + \cdots + \xi_\nu^2 = \sum_{i=1}^{\nu} \xi_i^2. \qquad (8.30)$$

The variable χ could have been defined as the square root of (8.30), but χ^2 is of greater practical utility. The frequency function for the distribution, which may be verified by showing that it has the same MGF as that of the sum of the squares of ν $N(0,1)$ variables, is

$$f(\chi^2) = \frac{1}{2^{\nu/2}\Gamma(\nu/2)}\, e^{-\chi^2/2}(\chi^2)^{\nu/2-1}. \qquad (8.31)$$

The gamma function is, by definition,

$$\Gamma(\alpha) = \int_0^\infty e^{-x} x^{\alpha-1}\, dx, \qquad \text{for} \quad \alpha > 0. \qquad (8.32)$$

For α an integer, it has the property that $\Gamma(\alpha+1) = \alpha!$.

The frequency function is shown in Fig. 8.6 for various values of the parameter ν, known as the number of *degrees of freedom*. From the viewpoint of tests of significance, which we shall be considering shortly, the information presented in Fig. 8.7 is more helpful. For any ν, Fig. 8.7 gives that value χ_P^2 which has a probability P of being exceeded. The MGF of the χ^2 distribution is

$$M_{\chi^2}(\theta) = \frac{1}{2^{\nu/2}\Gamma(\nu/2)} \int_0^\infty e^{\chi^2\theta} e^{-\chi^2/2}(\chi^2)^{(\nu/2)-1}\, d\chi^2$$

$$= \frac{1}{\Gamma(\nu/2)} \int_0^\infty e^{-(\chi^2/2)(1-2\theta)}(\chi^2/2)^{(\nu/2)-1}\, d(\chi^2/2).$$

Substituting

$$x = \frac{\chi^2}{2}(1 - 2\theta),$$

that is,

$$\frac{\chi^2}{2} = \frac{x}{1-2\theta} \qquad \text{and} \qquad d\left(\frac{\chi^2}{2}\right) = \frac{dx}{1-2\theta},$$

gives

$$M_{\chi^2}(\theta) = \frac{1}{\Gamma(\nu/2)}(1-2\theta)^{-\nu/2} \int_0^\infty e^{-x} x^{(\nu/2)-1}\, dx$$

$$= (1-2\theta)^{-\nu/2}.$$

We then conclude

1. $$\mu_1' = (dM/d\theta)_{\theta=0} = \nu,$$

and

$$\mu_2' = (d^2M/d\theta^2)_{\theta=0} = \nu(\nu + 2).$$

Thus

$$\mu = \text{ave}(\chi^2) = \nu,$$
$$\sigma^2 = \text{var}(\chi^2) = 2\nu.$$

2.   The MGF for the variable $x = \chi_1^2 + \chi_2^2$ is the product of the MGFs of χ_1^2 and χ_2^2, each of which is based on ν_1 and ν_2 degrees of freedom respectively, so that

$$M_x(\theta) = (1-2\theta)^{-\nu_1/2}(1-2\theta)^{-\nu_2/2} = (1-2\theta)^{-(\nu_1+\nu_2)/2}.$$

That is, x has the χ^2 distribution with $(\nu_1 + \nu_2)$ degrees of freedom.

Finally, note that χ^2 also has the properties:

1. χ^2 tends toward the normal distribution $N(\nu,2\nu)$ as ν becomes large. This tendency may be seen in Fig. 8.6.

2. $\sqrt{2\chi^2}$ tends toward $N(\sqrt{2\nu-1},\ 1)$ even more quickly than does (1) for large ν.

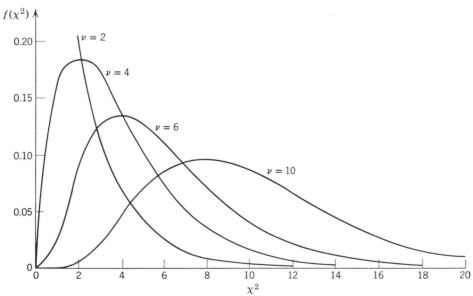

Figure 8.6 χ^2 *distribution frequency function.*

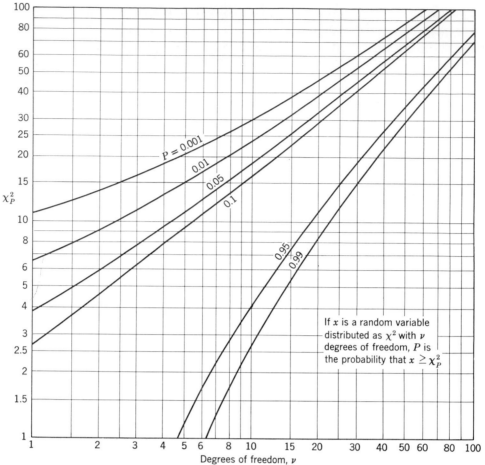

Figure 8.7 Probability points of the χ^2 distribution.

8.14 χ^2 as a Measure of Goodness-of-Fit

Consider a random variable which can fall into any one of k different classes with respective probabilities $f_1, f_2, \ldots, f_k$. For a total of n observations, the *expected* number falling in the ith class is nf_i. Let the actual *observed* number in the ith class be x_i. The x_i would obey the multinomial distribution (8.24), and on this basis it can be shown [3] that the variable

$$\chi^2 = \sum_i \frac{(\text{Observed} - \text{Expected})^2}{\text{Expected}} = \sum_{i=1}^{k} \frac{(x_i - nf_i)^2}{nf_i} \quad (8.33)$$

obeys the χ^2 distribution *approximately*. The approximation improves as the expected frequency nf_i in each class becomes greater. For every $nf_i > 20$, there is hardly any loss of accuracy. The relevant number of degrees of freedom is $k - r$, where r is the number of restrictions imposed on the f_i (see examples which follow).

The expected frequencies are usually based on the hypothesis of a particular distribution. Therefore, this hypothesis can be tested by evaluating χ^2 and checking to see if its value is reasonable in view of: (a) the number of degrees of freedom involved, and (b) the confidence level required, that is, how "sure" we wish to be.

Example. Suppose that 100 tosses of a coin produce 40 heads and 60 tails, and that we wish to know if the coin is biased in some way. On the assumption or *null hypothesis* that the coin is not biased, we should have expected 50 heads and 50 tails. The number of restrictions imposed on the f_i in this case is $r = 1$, since if the expected probability of obtaining a "head" $(= f_1$, for instance) is stated to be 1/2, then f_2 is automatically $1 - 1/2 = 1/2$ since there are no other alternatives. Hence there is just $\nu = k - r = 2 - 1 = 1$ degree of freedom. We have,

$$\chi^2 = \frac{(40.5 - 50)^2}{50} + \frac{(59.5 - 50)^2}{50} = 3.61.$$

Notice that 1/2 has been added to the 40 and subtracted from the 60. This procedure, known as *Yates's correction*, generally adds 1/2 to those frequencies falling below expectation, and subtracts 1/2 from those falling above it. Yates's correction compensates for the fact that a discontinuous distribution (binomial in this case) is being represented by the continuous χ^2 distribution. Figure 8.7 or statistical tables give the following values:

$\nu = 1$	1	1	1
$P = 0.1$	0.05	0.01	0.001
$\chi_P^2 = 2.71$	3.84	6.63	10.83

That is, the observed value of $\chi^2 = 3.61$ (or greater) can be expected to occur, on the average, about 6% of the time. This is as far as statistics goes; it leaves the interpretation to us. Although we personally may believe that the coin is biased, we would want stronger evidence before making such a statement public. The levels $P = 5\%$, 1%, and 0.1% are sometimes described as "probably significant," "significant," and "highly significant."

However, if 1000 tosses produced 400 heads and 600 tails, then

$$\chi^2 = \frac{(400.5 - 500)^2}{500} + \frac{(599.5 - 500)^2}{500} = 39.6,$$

a figure which so far exceeds even the "highly significant" level that we should have little hesitation in stating that the coin was biased in favor of tails. Even so, it should be recognized that there is a possibility, although an exceedingly remote one, of our being wrong.

It so happens that in the above example we could have predicted, directly from the binomial distribution, the probability of obtaining, for instance, 40 or fewer heads in 100 tosses. However, this would involve a fair amount of work in evaluating factorials and the χ^2 approach is preferred.

8.15 Contingency Tables

Suppose the success or failure of some experiment is classified as to whether treatment A or treatment B was used in the experiment. Table 8.2 shows such a cross classification, known as a *contingency table*.

Table 8.2   Contingency Table:
Observed Results

	Success	Failure	Totals
Treatment A	88	7	95
Treatment B	47	15	62
Totals	135	22	157

Can treatment B be correlated with a significantly higher failure rate than treatment A?

We shall use the χ^2 test for goodness-of-fit. As a null hypothesis we assume A and B have equal effects and pool the results to give the chance of a failure as $22/157 = 0.140$, whence the expected numbers of successes and failures for A and B can be calculated. These are shown in Table 8.3.

Table 8.3   Expected Frequencies on Basis of
Null Hypothesis

	Success	Failure	Totals
Treatment A	81.7	13.3	95
Treatment B	53.3	8.7	62
Totals	135	22	157

There is only one degree of freedom, since, for example, having specified that we expect treatment A to yield 13.3 failures, all the remaining entries can be obtained by difference from the subtotals. Taking into account Yates's correction, we have

$$\chi^2 = \frac{(87.5 - 81.7)^2}{81.7} + \frac{(47.5 - 53.3)^2}{53.3}$$

$$+ \frac{(7.5 - 13.3)^2}{13.3} + \frac{(14.5 - 8.7)^2}{8.7}$$

$$= 5.8^2 \left(\frac{1}{81.7} + \frac{1}{53.3} + \frac{1}{13.3} + \frac{1}{8.7} \right) = 7.43.$$

For $v = 1$ d.f., $\chi^2 = 6.63$ at the 1% level and 7.88 at the 0.5% level. That is, on the basis of our null hypothesis, there is a probability of about 1 in 150 of the observed χ^2 or higher occurring. Hence, we conclude that the null hypothesis is incorrect and that treatment B has a significantly higher failure rate than treatment A.

The above is the simplest possible example of a contingency table. For an $m \times n$ table in which m treatments are classified according to n results, the appropriate number of degrees of freedom is $v = (m - 1)(n - 1)$.

EXAMPLE 8.4

χ^2 TEST FOR GOODNESS-OF-FIT

Problem Statement

Write a program to compute χ^2 from equation (8.33):

$$\chi^2 = \sum_{i=1}^{k} \frac{(x_i - nf_i)^2}{nf_i}, \tag{8.33}$$

in which the following are read as data: x_i = number of observations falling into each class i, n = total number of observations, f_i = frequency function for each class i, and k = total number of classes. The program should incorporate the following features: (a) automatic regrouping of data to ensure that each class has at least l expected observations (recall that the χ^2 distribution is obeyed more exactly as l increases), (b) Yates's correction, and (c) optional input of the theoretically expected frequencies $x_i^e \,(=nf_i)$ for each class, instead of n and the f_i individually.

Method of Solution

The regrouping of data is achieved by examining each $x_i^e = nf_i$ in turn; if x_i^e is found to be less than the prescribed lower limit l, the observations for class i and one or more subsequent classes $(i + 1,\ i + 2,$ etc.) will be pooled in order to raise the combined expectation to at least l. The number of degrees of freedom v will be $(k_{new} - 1)$, where k_{new} is the number of regrouped classes. Let the regrouped observed and expected frequencies be denoted by y_i and y_i^e, respectively. Allowing for Yates's correction, χ^2 becomes

$$\chi^2 = \sum_{i=1}^{k_{new}} \frac{(|y_i - y_i^e| - \frac{1}{2})^2}{y_i^e}. \tag{8.4.1}$$

Example 8.4 χ² *Test for Goodness-of-Fit* **563**

Flow Diagram

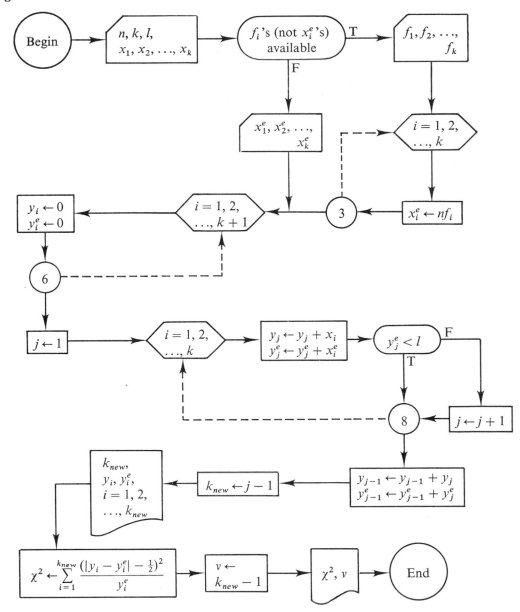

FORTRAN *Implementation*

List of Principal Variables

Program Symbol	Definition
CHISQ	χ^2, defined by equation (8.4.1).
F	Vector containing values of f_i.
JUSTF	Switch, with value 0 (the x_i^e to be read) or 1 (the f_i to be read).
K	Number of classes k; becomes KNEW after a possible regrouping of data.
L	Least number l expected to fall into a class.
N	Number of observations, n.
NU	Degrees of freedom, v.
XEXP	Vector containing theoretical frequencies x_i^e; becomes YEXP (with the y_i^e) after a possible regrouping.
XOBS	Vector containing observed frequencies x_i; becomes YOBS (with the y_i) after a possible regrouping.

Program Listing

```
C           APPLIED NUMERICAL METHODS, EXAMPLE 8.4
C           CHI-SQUARE FOR GOODNESS-OF-FIT.
C
C           THE DATA CONSIST OF THE NUMBER  OF OBSERVATIONS XOBS(I) FALLING
C           INTO EACH CLASS I OUT OF A TOTAL OF K CLASSES, AND EITHER THE
C           THEORETICALLY EXPECTED NUMBER XEXP(I) OR THE FREQUENCY
C           FUNCTION F(I) FOR EACH CLASS.    THERE ARE N TOTAL OBSERVATIONS.
C           THE VALUES OF XOBS ARE GROUPED BY THE PROGRAM SO THAT AT LEAST
C           A NUMBER L ARE EXPECTED IN EACH CLASS.   CHI-SQUARE IS THEN
C           COMPUTED OVER ALL THE CLASSES, USING YATES'S CORRECTION TO
C           ACCOUNT FOR THE FACT THAT CHI-SQUARE IS CONTINUOUS AND THAT THE
C           OBSERVATIONS ARE DISCRETE.
C
      DIMENSION XOBS(50), YOBS(50), YEXP(50), XEXP(50), F(50)
      INTEGER XOBS, YOBS
C
C     ..... READ AND CHECK DATA, COMPUTE XTHEOR IF NOT SUPPLIED .....
    1 READ (5,100) N, K, L, JUSTF, (XOBS(I), I = 1, K)
      WRITE (6,200) N, K, L, JUSTF
      FN = N
      IF (JUSTF .NE. 1) GO TO 4
         READ (5,102) (F(I), I = 1, K)
         DO 3  I = 1, K
    3       XEXP(I) = FN*F(I)
      GO TO 5
    4    READ (5,101) (XEXP(I), I = 1, K)
C
C     ..... GROUP THE OBSERVATIONS INTO CLASSES, WITH AT
C           LEAST L OBSERVATIONS EXPECTED IN EACH CLASS .....
    5 KP1 = K + 1
      DO 6  I = 1, KP1
      YOBS(I) = 0.0
    6 YEXP(I) = 0.0
      J = 1
      DO 8  I = 1, K
      YOBS(J) = YOBS(J) + XOBS(I)
      YEXP(J) = YEXP(J) + XEXP(I)
      FL = L
      IF (YEXP(J) .LT. L) GO TO 8
         J = J + 1
    8 CONTINUE
      YOBS(J-1) = YOBS(J-1) + YOBS(J)
      YEXP(J-1) = YEXP(J-1) + YEXP(J)
      KNEW = J - 1
C
C     ..... PRINT VALUES OF YOBS AND YEXP .....
      WRITE (6,201) KNEW, (YOBS(I), I = 1, KNEW)
      WRITE (6,202) KNEW, (YEXP(I), I = 1, KNEW)
C
C     ..... COMPUTE CHI-SQUARE AND NUMBER OF DEGREES OF FREEDOM .....
      CHISQ = 0.0
      DO 9  I = 1, KNEW
      FYOBS = YOBS(I)
    9 CHISQ = CHISQ + ((ABS(FYOBS - YEXP(I))) - 0.5)**2/YEXP(I)
      NU = KNEW - 1
      WRITE (6,203) CHISQ, NU
      GO TO 1
C
C     ..... FORMATS FOR INPUT AND OUTPUT STATEMENTS .....
  100 FORMAT (4(11X, I4)/ / (14I5))
  101 FORMAT (/ (7F10.5))
  102 FORMAT (/ (5E16.6))
  200 FORMAT (35H1 DETERMINATION OF CHI-SQUARE, WITH/1H0,
     1          5X, 8HN      = , I4/ 6X, 8HK      = , I4/
     2          6X, 8HL      = , I4/ 6X, 8HJUSTF = , I4)
  201 FORMAT (49H0 THE INPUT DATA (POSSIBLY REARRANGED) NOW FOLLOW/1H0,
     1          30H THE VALUES OF YOBS(1)...YOBS(, I2, 5H) ARE// (12I5))
  202 FORMAT (31H0 THE VALUES OF YEXP(1)...YEXP(, I2, 5H) ARE//( 7F9.3))
  203 FORMAT (33H0 THE RESULTS ARE        CHISQ = , F8.3, 5X, 6HNU = ,
     1 I4)
C
      END
```

Example 8.4   χ² Test for Goodness-of-Fit   565

Program Listing (*Continued*)

Data

```
        N  =  1000,      K  =    8,     L  =  20,    JUSTF =    0
NUMBER OF OBSERVATIONS XOBS(I) IN SUCCESSIVE CLASSES ARE
   142   267   274   179    87    42     7     2
THEORETICALLY EXPECTED NUMBERS XEXP(I) FOR SUCCESSIVE CLASSES ARE
 135.3353  270.6704  270.6704  180.4469   90.2235   36.0894   12.0298
    3.4371
        N  =  1000,      K  =   13,     L  =  20,    JUSTF =    0
NUMBER OF OBSERVATIONS XOBS(I) IN SUCCESSIVE CLASSES ARE
     5    54    88   159   179   161   135   100    54    38    14     8     5
THEORETICALLY EXPECTED NUMBERS XEXP(I) FOR SUCCESSIVE CLASSES ARE
    6.7379   33.6897   84.2243  140.3739  175.4673  175.4673  146.2227
  104.4448   65.2780   36.2656   18.1328    8.2422    3.4342
        N  =  5000,      K  =   38,     L  =  20,    JUSTF =    1
NUMBER OF OBSERVATIONS XOBS(I) IN SUCCESSIVE CLASSES ARE
    22    34    72   125   189   282   337   423   433   457   425   423   414   354
   314   213   171   123    65    47    36    21    14     3     1     0     2     0
     0     0     0     0     0     0     0     0     0     0
FREQUENCY FUNCTION F(I) FOR SUCCESSIVE CLASSES IS
    3.638960E-03    7.884410E-03    1.356119E-02    2.462363E-02    3.845438E-02
    5.186192E-02    6.554095E-02    8.028086E-02    8.892187E-02    9.356225E-02
    9.405112E-02    8.944678E-02    8.026863E-02    6.914330E-02    5.693321E-02
    4.423677E-02    3.310917E-02    2.361694E-02    1.605084E-02    1.036172E-02
    6.435350E-03    3.77867 E-03    2.10042 E-03    1.11903 E-03    5.5903  E-04
    2.6427  E-04    1.1668  E-04    4.907   E-05    1.857   E-05    6.672   E-06
    2.198   E-06    6.113   E-07    1.719   E-07    3.521   E-08    7.061   E-09
    9.827   E-10    9.449   E-11    6.299   E-12
```

Computer Output

Results for the 1st Data Set

```
DETERMINATION OF CHI-SQUARE, WITH

    N     = 1000
    K     =    8
    L     =   20
    JUSTF =    0

THE INPUT DATA (POSSIBLY REARRANGED) NOW FOLLOW

THE VALUES OF YOBS(1)...YOBS( 6) ARE
 142   267   274   179    87    51

THE VALUES OF YEXP(1)...YEXP( 6) ARE
 135.335  270.670  270.670  180.447    90.223    51.556

THE RESULTS ARE        CHISQ =    0.435    NU =    5
```

Results for the 2nd Data Set

```
DETERMINATION OF CHI-SQUARE, WITH

    N     = 1000
    K     =   13
    L     =   20
    JUSTF =    0

THE INPUT DATA (POSSIBLY REARRANGED) NOW FOLLOW

THE VALUES OF YOBS(1)...YOBS(10) ARE
  59    88   159   179   161   135   100    54    38    27
```

Computer Output (*Continued*)

```
THE VALUES OF YEXP(1)...YEXP(10) ARE
  40.428    84.224   140.374   175.467   175.467   146.223   104.445
  65.278    36.266    29.809

THE RESULTS ARE          CHISQ  =     14.647      NU  =      9
```

Results for the 3rd Data Set

```
DETERMINATION OF CHI-SQUARE, WITH

    N    = 5000
    K    =   38
    L    =   20
    JUSTF =   1

THE INPUT DATA (POSSIBLY REARRANGED) NOW FOLLOW

THE VALUES OF YOBS(1)...YOBS(21) ARE
  56     72    125    189    282    337    423    433    457    425    423    414
 354    314    213    171    123     65     47     36     41

THE VALUES OF YEXP(1)...YEXP(21) ARE
  57.617    67.806   123.118   192.272   259.310   327.704   401.404
 444.609   467.811   470.255   447.233   401.343   345.716   284.666
 221.184   165.546   118.085    80.254    51.809    32.177    40.077

THE RESULTS ARE          CHISQ  =     17.009      NU  =     20
```

Example 8.4 χ^2 Test for Goodness-of-Fit   **567**

Discussion of Results

The first two data sets are taken from Example 8.2, where we generated two sequences of 1000 numbers thought to obey the Poisson distribution; the frequency of appearance of each number was observed, together with its expected frequency. We are now computing χ^2 to test one against the other. From Fig. 8.7 or tables, the probabilities P, that the actual χ^2 or higher would occur by chance, are $P \doteq 0.97$ (Set 1) and $P \doteq 0.10$ (Set 2). Since neither P is abnormally low, we conclude that the random number generator satisfactorily conforms to the Poisson distribution. The first P is actually somewhat high, indicating an unusually good fit.

The authors have written a procedure, not reproduced here (but see Problem 8.22), that uses a random number generator to simulate the dealing of bridge hands and then tabulates their point counts. As a result, "experimental" point-count distributions can be produced for any number of hands. In the third data set above, we test one of these experimental distributions, based on 5000 hands, against the theoretical frequency function predicted in Example 8.1. For $\chi^2 = 17.009$ and $v = 20$, we find $P \doteq 0.65$, indicating an acceptable fit of the data by theory. When tested against the normal distribution curve of Fig. 8.1.1, in a calculation not given here, the same data give $\chi^2 = 54.406$ with $v = 20$, corresponding to the unacceptably low value of $P \doteq 0.00005$.

8.16   The Sample Variance

The sample variance has been defined by (8.15) as

$$s^2 = \frac{1}{n-1} \sum_{i=1}^{n} (x_i - \bar{x})^2.$$

It has been shown that $\text{ave}(s^2) = \sigma^2$, so that the sample variance is an unbiased estimate of the population variance.

It may be shown further [1] that for a population of normally distributed variables whose variance is σ^2, the variable

$$\chi^2 = (n-1)s^2/\sigma^2 \tag{8.34}$$

obeys the χ^2 distribution with $v = (n-1)$ d.f.

Suppose we have k samples obtained from populations having a common variance σ^2 (but possibly having different means). Let sample i contain n_i items and have variance s_i^2. Then, if $N = \sum_{i=1}^{k} n_i$, an unbiased *joint estimate* of σ^2 is given by

$$s^2 = \frac{(n_1 - 1)s_1^2 + (n_2 - 1)s_2^2 + \cdots + (n_k - 1)s_k^2}{n_1 + n_2 + \cdots + n_k - k}$$

$$= \frac{\sum_{i=1}^{k} (n_i - 1)s_i^2}{N - k}, \tag{8.35}$$

because

$$\text{ave}(s^2) = \frac{1}{N-k} \text{ave} \sum_{i=1}^{k} (n_i - 1)s_i^2$$

$$= \frac{1}{N-k} \sum_{i=1}^{k} (n_i - 1) \, \text{ave}(s_i^2)$$

$$= \frac{1}{N-k} \sum_{i=1}^{k} (n_i - 1)\sigma^2 = \sigma^2.$$

Also, from (8.35),

$$(N-k)\frac{s^2}{\sigma^2} = \sum_{i=1}^{k} (n_i - 1)\frac{s_i^2}{\sigma^2}. \tag{8.36}$$

If the populations are normally distributed, each term on the right-hand side of (8.36) behaves as χ^2, with $(n_i - 1)$ d.f. Hence the whole of the right-hand side behaves as χ^2, with $\sum_{i=1}^{k} (n_i - 1) = (N - k)$ d.f. That is, the variable

$$\chi^2 = (N-k)\frac{s^2}{\sigma^2} \tag{8.37}$$

also behaves as χ^2 with $(N - k)$ degrees of freedom.

Example. In a certain experiment, $s^2 = 100$ with $v = 10$ d.f. Establish an interval in which we can be 90% certain that the population variance σ^2 lies.

Since $vs^2/\sigma^2 = \chi^2$, then $\sigma^2 = vs^2/\chi^2$. From Fig. 8.7 or tables [4], for $v = 10$ d.f., χ^2 has a 5% chance of exceeding 18.31 and a 95% chance of exceeding 3.94. Thus, the lower limit of σ^2 is $10 \times 100/18.31 = 54.6$, and its upper limit is $10 \times 100/3.94 = 254$. (This is not the only 90% confidence interval; it is the one which is symmetrical with respect to the probabilities on χ^2.)

8.17   Student's *t* Distribution

If we wish to test the hypothesis that a sample whose mean is $\bar{x}$ could come from a normal distribution of mean μ and *known* variance σ^2, the procedure is easy, for the variable $(\bar{x} - \mu)\sqrt{n}/\sigma$ is $N(0,1)$, and can readily be compared with tabulated values. When σ^2 is unknown and has to be estimated from the sample variance s^2, the situation is somewhat different, and the following distribution is of assistance.

Assume two random variables: ξ, distributed as $N(0,1)$, and χ^2, distributed as chi-square with v d.f. Then, if ξ and χ^2 are independent, the random variable

$$t = \xi/\sqrt{\chi^2/v} \tag{8.38}$$

is called *Student's t* with v d.f. It has the frequency function

$$f(t) = \frac{1}{\sqrt{v\pi}} \frac{\Gamma\left(\dfrac{v+1}{2}\right)}{\Gamma\left(\dfrac{v}{2}\right)} \left(1 + \frac{t^2}{v}\right)^{-(v+1)/2}. \tag{8.39}$$

The distribution is very similar to $N(0,1)$, which it approximates closely for all but small values of v. Figure 8.8 shows values of t_P plotted against v, with P as a parameter such that P is the probability that $|t| \geqslant t_P$.

To illustrate the case in which σ^2 is unknown, consider a population $N(\mu,\sigma^2)$. The sample mean $\bar{x}$ is $N(\mu,\sigma^2/n)$. Hence, $\phi = (\bar{x} - \mu)\sqrt{n}/\sigma$ is $N(0,1)$; also, $\chi^2 = (n-1)s^2/\sigma^2$ is a chi-square variable with $(n-1)$ d.f. That is,

$$t = \frac{(\bar{x} - \mu)\sqrt{n}/\sigma}{\sqrt{\dfrac{(n-1)}{(n-1)}\dfrac{s^2}{\sigma^2}}} = \frac{(\bar{x} - \mu)\sqrt{n}}{s} \tag{8.40}$$

has the t distribution with $(n-1)$ d.f., which provides a test of significance for the deviation of a sample mean from its expected value when the population variance is unknown and must be estimated from the sample variance.

A simple extension provides a test of significance between *two sample means* $\bar{x}_1$ and $\bar{x}_2$, which will determine whether $\bar{x}_1$ and $\bar{x}_2$ could have come from the same population.

Assume first that the samples come from populations having a common variance σ^2; the validity of this assumption can be checked by the F test in Section 8.18. Then the linear combination $(\bar{x}_1 - \bar{x}_2)$ has the normal distribution with mean $(\mu_1 - \mu_2)$ and variance $\sigma^2(1/n_1 + 1/n_2)$. Thus

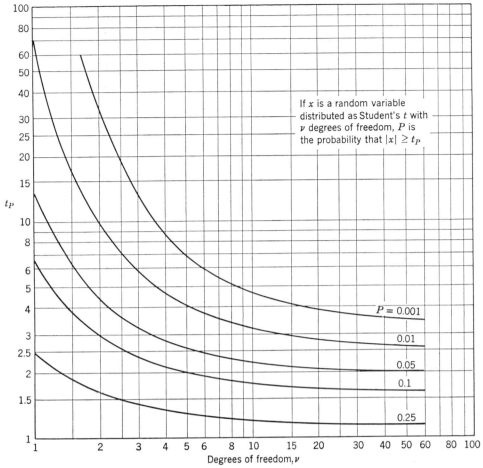

Figure 8.8 Probability points of Student's t distribution.

$$\frac{(\bar{x}_1 - \bar{x}_2) - (\mu_1 - \mu_2)}{\sigma \sqrt{\dfrac{1}{n_1} + \dfrac{1}{n_2}}}$$

is $N(0,1)$. Further, if the joint estimate of σ^2 from the samples is

$$s^2 = \frac{(n_1 - 1)s_1^2 + (n_2 - 1)s_2^2}{n_1 + n_2 - 2},$$

as indicated by (8.35), then $(n_1 + n_2 - 2)s^2/\sigma^2$ has the chi-square distribution with $(n_1 + n_2 - 2)$ d.f. Thus

$$t = \frac{(\bar{x}_1 - \bar{x}_2) - (\mu_1 - \mu_2)}{\sigma \sqrt{\dfrac{1}{n_1} + \dfrac{1}{n_2}} \sqrt{\dfrac{(n_1 + n_2 - 2)\, s^2}{(n_1 + n_2 - 2)\, \sigma^2}}} \qquad (8.41)$$

has the t distribution with $v = (n_1 + n_2 - 2)$ d.f.

Finally, as a null hypothesis, assume that the samples *do* come from the same population and hence that μ_1 and μ_2 are equal. That is,

$$t = \frac{\bar{x}_1 - \bar{x}_2}{s \sqrt{\dfrac{1}{n_1} + \dfrac{1}{n_2}}}, \qquad (8.42)$$

and will, with specified probability, be expected to fall within the appropriate tabulated values, unless the null hypothesis is incorrect and $\mu_1 \neq \mu_2$.

Example. Repeated analyses show that two batches of a manufactured chemical contain the following percentages of an impurity X. Is there a significant difference between the X-content of the two batches?

Table 8.4   Analyses for Percent X in Two
Batches of Chemical

| | Percent X | | | |
Analysis	Batch 1	Batch 2	x_1	x_2
1	3.36	3.79	3.6	7.9
2	3.57	3.57	5.7	5.7
3	3.24	3.72	2.4	7.2
4	3.34	3.68	3.4	6.8
5	3.46	3.75	4.6	7.5

In Table 8.4 the new variables x_1 and x_2 are given by $x = 10 \times (\%X - 3.00)$. This makes the arithmetic a little easier, especially if the calculation is being done by hand, but does not alter the final conclusions. Various sums are next calculated as shown in Table 8.5.

Table 8.5   *Calculation of Batch Means and Variances*

	Batch 1	Batch 2
Σx	19.7	35.1
Σx^2	83.93	249.23
$\bar{x} = \Sigma x / n$	3.94	7.02
$\bar{x}^2$	15.5236	49.2804
$\Sigma(x - \bar{x})^2 = (\Sigma x^2) - n\bar{x}^2$	6.312	2.828
$s^2 = \Sigma(x - \bar{x})^2/(n - 1)$	1.578	0.707

The joint estimate of σ^2 is $s^2 = (4 \times 1.578 + 4 \times 0.707)/8 = 1.1425$; that is, $s = 1.069$. On the basis of the null hypothesis that there is no difference between the X-content of the two batches, $\mu_1 = \mu_2$ and

$$t = \frac{\bar{x}_1 - \bar{x}_2}{s\sqrt{\dfrac{1}{n_1} + \dfrac{1}{n_2}}} = \frac{3.94 - 7.02}{1.069\sqrt{\dfrac{1}{5} + \dfrac{1}{5}}} = -4.555, \text{ with 8 d.f.}$$

But, from tables of the t distribution [4], $|t|$ based on 8 d.f. has a 0.2% probability of being greater than 4.50. Thus we conclude, with very little doubt, that the null hypothesis is incorrect and that there is a definite difference between the X-content of the two batches. In fact, taking into account the

method of deriving x_1 and x_2 from the percent X in the two batches, the best estimate we have is that the percent X is $(0.702 - 0.394) = 0.308$ higher in Batch 2 than in Batch 1.

Finally, we can qualify this statement by giving a *confidence interval* within which, with 95% probability, for instance, the difference lies. Now $t = 2.31$ with 8 d.f. at the $P = 5\%$ level. Thus the percent X in Batch 2 exceeds that in Batch 1 by an amount that has a 95% probability of lying within

$$0.308 \pm 2.31 \left(\frac{1.069}{10}\right)\sqrt{\frac{2}{5}} = 0.308 \pm 0.156.$$

8.18   The *F* Distribution

The ratio $F = s_1^2/s_2^2$ of two estimates of the variance of a normal population based on v_1 and v_2 d.f., respectively, has the frequency function

$$f(F) = \frac{(v_1/v_2)^{v_1/2}}{B(v_1/2, v_2/2)} F^{(v_1/2)-1}\left(1 + \frac{v_1}{v_2}F\right)^{-(v_1+v_2)/2}, \quad (8.43)$$

where

$$B(m,n) = \Gamma(m)\Gamma(n)/\Gamma(m + n) = \int_0^1 x^{m-1}(1 - x)^{n-1}\, dx$$

is the *beta function*.

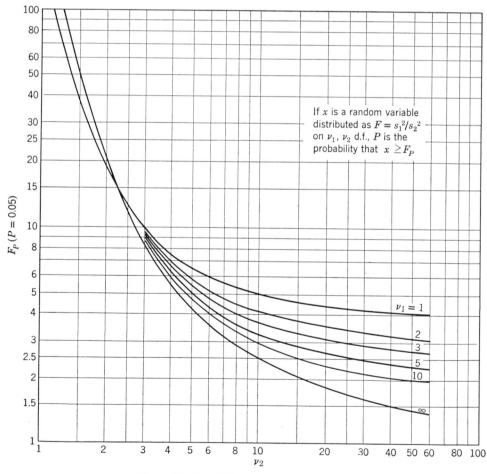

Figure 8.9 $P = 0.05$ *points of the F distribution.*

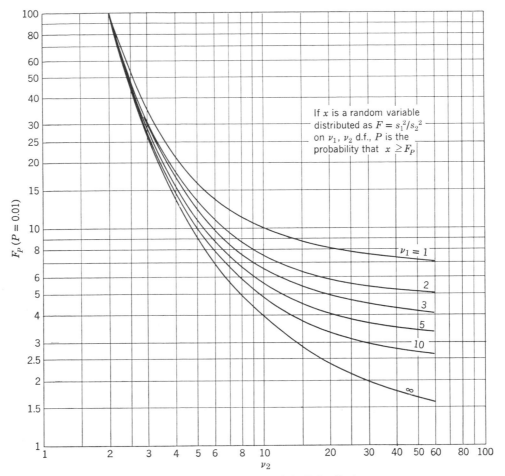

Figure 8.10 $P = 0.01$ *points of the F distribution.*

Figures 8.9 and 8.10 show F_P as a function of v_1 and v_2, such that F_P has a probability P of being exceeded. Evaluating F provides a test of significance between two estimates of a population variance. Note that a value F_{1-P,v_1,v_2} (such that there is a probability P of F falling below it) is given by $F_{1-P,v_1,v_2} = 1/F_{P,v_2,v_1}$.

Example. In our example of the t distribution, the two sample variances $s_1^2 = 1.578$ and $s_2^2 = 0.707$, each having 4 d.f., were pooled to give a joint estimate s^2 of a population variance. Was this pooling justified?

$F = s_1^2/s_2^2 = 1.578/0.707 = 2.23$. From Fig. 8.9 or tables [4], for $v_1 = 4$, $v_2 = 4$, there is a 5% probability that F will exceed 6.39, and a 5% probability that F will fall below $1/6.39 = 0.1565$. Our results are well within these limits and there is, therefore, no reason why the sample variances should not be pooled.

8.19 Linear Regression and Method of Least Squares

Suppose that, in an experiment, certain values of a variable y have been observed, each corresponding to a particular value of x, as shown in Fig. 8.11. If we wish to draw a straight line on the graph to represent the data as well as possible, considering experimental scatter, we must first postulate a model representing the situation.

Assume that each y_i is an observation from a normal population with mean $\alpha + \beta x_i$ and constant variance σ^2, and that the corresponding values x_i are known precisely. For example, y might be the result of a chemical analysis or the estimate of a product yield, whereas x might be an accurately known time, an accurately weighed amount of catalyst, or a carefully controlled temperature. The situation is indicated in Fig. 8.12, in which $y = \alpha + \beta x$ is the equation of the *regression line*. Using the experimental data, we wish to obtain estimates a, b, and s^2 of the model parameters α, β, and σ^2. Assuming that the measurement of y locates it within a small interval of extent Δy, the probability of observing the value y_1, is, for instance, from the normal distribution,

$$Pr(y_1) \doteq \frac{1}{\sigma\sqrt{2\pi}} e^{-(y_1-\alpha-\beta x_1)^2/2\sigma^2} \Delta y \doteq k e^{-(y_1-\alpha-\beta x_1)^2/2\sigma^2},$$

where k is a constant. Similar expressions hold for $Pr(y_2), \ldots, Pr(y_m)$, where m is the number of data points or observations. The probability P of all these values of y occurring simultaneously is

$$P = Pr(y_1)Pr(y_2)\cdots Pr(y_m) \doteq k^m e^{-\sum_{i=1}^{m}(y_i-\alpha-\beta x_i)^2/2\sigma^2}.$$

8.21 Alternative Formulation of Regression Equations

With a slight change in notation, let the multiple regression of (8.54) be rephrased as

$$y = \beta_1 x_1 + \beta_2 x_2 + \cdots + \beta_n x_n = \sum_{j=1}^{n} \beta_j x_j, \quad (8.62)$$

where $x_1, x_2, \ldots, x_n$ are again n different variables. The special case in which x_1, for instance, were constant would mean that β_1 had now assumed the role of the previous α. Suppose that m experimental observations have been made, and that x_{ij} is the value of the variable x_j at the ith observation. If y_i is the ith observed value of y, our task is now to minimize the sum of squares

$$S = \sum_{i=1}^{m} \left(y_i - \sum_{j=1}^{n} \beta_j x_{ij} \right)^2.$$

Setting $\partial S/\partial \beta_k = 0$ for $k = 1, 2, \ldots, n$, and replacing the β_j with their least-squares estimates b_j, we have

$$\sum_{i=1}^{m} x_{ik} \left(y_i - \sum_{j=1}^{n} b_j x_{ij} \right) = 0,$$

that is,

$$\sum_{j=1}^{n} b_j \sum_{i=1}^{m} x_{ik} x_{ij} = \sum_{i=1}^{m} x_{ik} y_i, \quad (8.63)$$
$$k = 1, 2, \ldots, n.$$

Now define $\mathbf{X}$ as the $m \times n$ matrix containing x_{ij} in its ith row and jth column:

$$\mathbf{X} = (x_{ij}) = \begin{bmatrix} x_{11} \cdots x_{1n} \\ \vdots \quad \vdots \\ x_{m1} \cdots x_{mn} \end{bmatrix}. \quad (8.64)$$

Also define the following column vectors:

$$\mathbf{y} = [y_1 \ y_2 \ldots y_m]^t, \quad (8.65)$$
$$\mathbf{b} = [b_1 \ b_2 \ldots b_n]^t. \quad (8.66)$$

The system of normal equations (8.63) can then be re-written in the equivalent form

$$\mathbf{X}^t \mathbf{X} \mathbf{b} = \mathbf{X}^t \mathbf{y}, \quad (8.67)$$

which has the solution

$$\mathbf{b} = (\mathbf{X}^t \mathbf{X})^{-1} \mathbf{X}^t \mathbf{y}. \quad (8.68)$$

We can also define an $n \times n$ symmetrical *variance-covariance* matrix $\mathbf{V}$ by

$$\mathbf{V} = (v_{ij}) = (\mathbf{X}^t \mathbf{X})^{-1} \sigma^2, \quad (8.69)$$

where, as usual, σ^2 is estimated from

$$s^2 = \frac{\mathbf{y}^t \mathbf{y} - \mathbf{b}^t \mathbf{X}^t \mathbf{y}}{m - n}. \quad (8.70)$$

It can be shown (see, for example, Draper and Smith [10]) that the diagonal and off-diagonal elements of $\mathbf{V}$ give, respectively, the variances and covariances of the b_j; that is, $\mathrm{var}(b_j) = v_{jj}$, and $\mathrm{cov}(b_i, b_j) = v_{ij}$.

8.22 Regression in Terms of Orthogonal Polynomials

Suppose that we are attempting the nth-order polynomial regression of y against x, and express the model in the form

$$y = \beta_0 P_0 + \beta_1 P_1 + \cdots + \beta_n P_n = \sum_{j=0}^{n} \beta_j P_j, \quad (8.71)$$

where P_j is a jth-order polynomial in x, and whose form is to be specified later. The problem is still to choose the β_j in order to minimize the sum of squares

$$S = \sum_{i=1}^{m} \left(y_i - \sum_{j=0}^{n} \beta_j P_{ij} \right)^2,$$

where P_{ij} is the value of the polynomial P_j, evaluated at the ith data value x_i, and m is the total number of data points. Proceeding as in Section 8.21, we obtain

$$\mathbf{P}^t \mathbf{P} \mathbf{b} = \mathbf{P}^t \mathbf{y}, \quad (8.72)$$

that is,

$$\mathbf{b} = (\mathbf{P}^t \mathbf{P})^{-1} \mathbf{P}^t \mathbf{y}, \quad (8.73)$$

in which $\mathbf{b} = [b_0 \ b_1 \ldots b_n]^t$, $\mathbf{y} = [y_1 \ y_2 \ldots y_m]^t$, and

$$\mathbf{P} = \begin{bmatrix} P_{10} & P_{11} & \cdots & P_{1n} \\ \vdots & & & \vdots \\ P_{m0} & P_{m1} & \cdots & P_{mn} \end{bmatrix}.$$

The matrix product $\mathbf{Q} = \mathbf{P}^t \mathbf{P}$ is an $(n+1) \times (n+1)$ matrix whose general element is

$$q_{kl} = \sum_{i=1}^{m} P_{ik} P_{il}. \quad (8.74)$$

If we could arrange for all the off-diagonal elements of Q to be zero, that is, for

$$q_{kl} = \sum_{i=1}^{m} P_{ik} P_{il} = 0, \quad k \neq l, \quad (8.75)$$

then the regression coefficients would be estimated simply by

$$b_j = \frac{\sum_{i=1}^{m} P_{ij} y_i}{\sum_{i=1}^{m} P_{ij}^2}, \quad j = 0, 1, \ldots, n. \quad (8.76)$$

Forsythe [11] has shown that a suitable set of polynomials, obeying the orthogonality property (8.75), is given by the recursion relations

$$P_k(x) = (x - \gamma_k)P_{k-1}(x) - \delta_k P_{k-2}(x),$$

$$k = 1, 2, \ldots, n$$

subject to

$$P_{-1}(x) = 0,$$

$$P_0(x) = 1,$$

where the γ_k and δ_k are determined from

$$\gamma_k = \frac{\sum\limits_{i=1}^{m} x_i P_{i,k-1}^2}{\sum\limits_{i=1}^{m} P_{i,k-1}^2},$$

$$\delta_k = \frac{\sum\limits_{i=1}^{m} x_i P_{i,k-1} P_{i,k-2}}{\sum\limits_{i=1}^{m} P_{i,k-2}^2}.$$

$$(8.77)$$

The advantage of the above technique is that the regression coefficients b_j are obtained without solving a system of simultaneous equations. Thus, any problems associated with the inversion of a near-singular matrix, occurring with n moderately large as explained in Example 8.5, are avoided. Also, if we wish to increase the order of the regression by one or more, the additional terms such as $\beta_{n+1}P_{n+1}$ can be calculated simply from (8.76) and (8.77) without having to recompute all the previous polynomials and their associated regression coefficients.

Finally, note that the variances of the b_j are again the diagonal elements of $(\mathbf{P}^t\mathbf{P})^{-1}\sigma^2$; their covariances are given by the off-diagonal elements, which are now all zero, since the b_j are mutually independent.

EXAMPLE 8.5

POLYNOMIAL REGRESSION WITH PLOTTING

Introduction

This example considers the problem of finding how high an order of polynomial must be used to give a reasonably good representation, as defined below, of a series of m data points (x,y). We also wish to estimate the corresponding regression coefficients.

The technique employs a least-squares fit of the data by successive polynomials of order $n = 1, 2$, etc., and examines the standard deviation s about the regression line in each case. We would expect s to decrease fairly rapidly with increasing n until a good fit were obtained, and that further increases in n might actually increase s again, due to the reduction of degrees of freedom in the denominator of (8.59). The following are possible arbitrary criteria for an optimum value of n: (a) that value which minimizes s, or (b) that value for which the next higher-order polynomial causes a 10% reduction in s.

Problem Statement

Write a subroutine, named REGR, that follows the method of Section 8.20 and performs an nth-order polynomial regression on a series of m data points (x,y). For simplicity, assume that estimates of the variances and covariances of the regression coefficients are not required. The calling statement should be

$$S = REGR \ (M, X, Y, N, A, B)$$

Flow Diagram

Main Program (Excluding details of plotting points)

in which the variables have obvious meanings. Test the subroutine by calling it from a main program that reads as data the values of m and the set of x and y coordinates. A succession of polynomial regressions, with orders between specified lower and upper limits n_{min} and n_{max}, should then be performed on this one set of data. The main program should also print, for comparison, a plot of the original data points together with a series of points lying on the regression curve.

Method of Solution

In the subroutine REGR, the sums $\sum y$, $\sum y^2$, $\sum x^i y$ $(i = 1, 2, \ldots, n)$ and $\sum x^i$ $(i = 1, 2, \ldots, 2n)$ are first computed. Note that for polynomial regression the variable x_i appearing in equation (8.54) becomes x^i. Hence a sum such as the $\sum x_i x_j$ of equation (8.55) becomes $\sum x^{i+j}$. The remainder of the subroutine is concerned with the solution of the system of equations (8.56) for the regression coefficients $b_1, b_2, \ldots, b_n$, and the subsequent calculation of a and s from equations (8.57) and (8.59), respectively.

In the main program, the coordinates of the m data points are stored as $x_1, x_2, \ldots, x_m$, and $y_1, y_2, \ldots, y_m$ by reading from cards. Once the regression coefficients have been found by calling on REGR, the coordinates of 26 points lying on the regression curve are computed and conveniently stored in $x_{m+1}, \ldots, x_{m+26}$, and $y_{m+1}, \ldots, y_{m+26}$. We then use certain plotting subroutines for displaying all these points (x_i, y_i), $i = 1, 2, \ldots, m + 26$, on the printout.

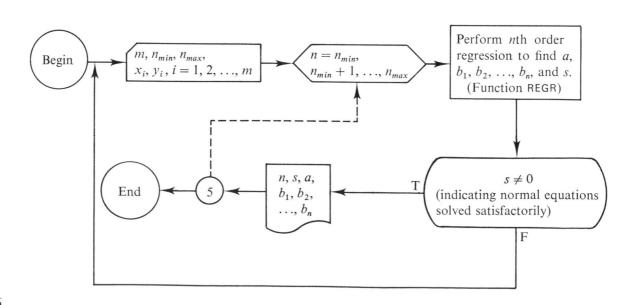

Example 8.5 Polynomial Regression with Plotting   **577**

Function REGR (Arguments: m, x, y, n, a, b)

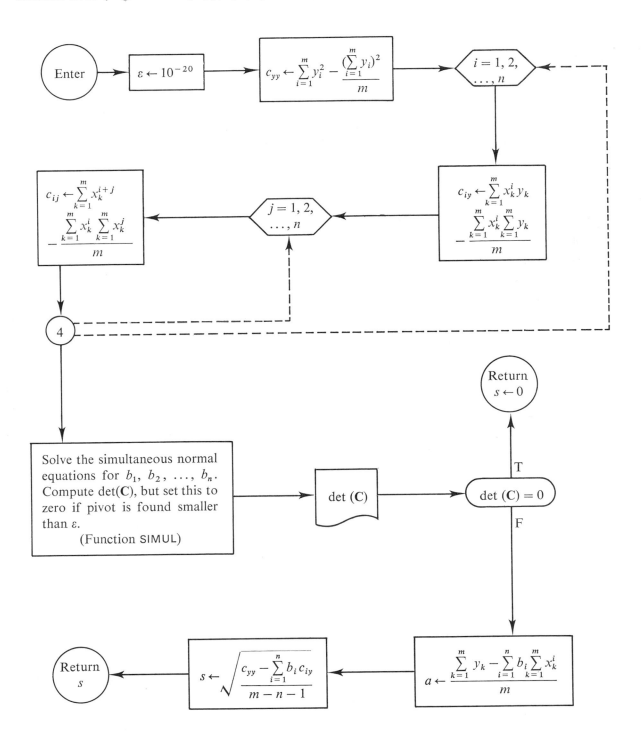

FORTRAN *Implementation*

List of Principal Variables

Program Symbol	Definition
(Main)	
A	Regression coefficient, a.
B	Vector containing regression coefficients b_i.
DELTAX	x-spacing for the 26 points on the regression curve.
M	Number of data points, m.
MAX, MIN	Upper and lower limits on order of regression, n_{max} and n_{min}.
N	Order, n, of polynomial regression.
POINT	Vector containing the plotting characters.
REGR	Function for performing nth-order regression.
S	Standard deviation, s, of the points about the regression line. However, as a warning signal, if SIMUL encounters a near-singular matrix, S is returned as zero.
PLOT1, PLOT2, PLOT3, PLOT4	Subroutines for plotting points on the printout (see Example 7.1). The plotting character for the points lying on the regression curve ($i = m + 1, \ldots, m + 26$) is chosen as the digit equal to n. An asterisk denotes the original data points ($i = 1, 2, \ldots, m$).
X, Y	Vectors containing the x and y coordinates of the data points.
(Function REGR)	
C	Matrix containing the coefficients c_{ij} of equations (8.56); the augmented part, the $(n + 1)$th column, contains the c_{iy}.
CYX	Vector containing the c_{iy}.
CYY	c_{yy}.
DET	Determinant of the coefficient matrix **C**.
EPS	Tolerance used by the function SIMUL.
SIMUL	Function for solving simultaneous equations (see Example 5.2).
SX, SYX	Vectors containing $\sum x^i$ and $\sum x^i y$.
SY, SYY	$\sum y$, $\sum y^2$.

Example 8.5   Polynomial Regression with Plotting

579

Program Listing

Main Program

```
C           APPLIED NUMERICAL METHODS, EXAMPLE 8.5
C           POLYNOMIAL REGRESSION WITH PLOTTING.
C
C           THIS MAIN PROGRAM READS THE HORIZONTAL AND VERTICAL COORDINATES
C           OF M DATA POINTS INTO THE X AND Y ARRAYS.   THE LEAST AND
C           GREATEST VALUES OF X SHOULD BE STORED IN X(1) AND X(M) RESPEC-
C           TIVELY.   THE FUNCTION REGR IS USED TO PERFORM SUCCESSIVE NTH-
C           ORDER REGRESSIONS, FROM N = MIN THROUGH N = MAX.   IN EACH
C           CASE, THE REGRESSION CURVE IS PLOTTED AGAINST THE ORIGINAL
C           DATA POINTS.
C
      IMPLICIT REAL*8(A-H, O-Z)
      DIMENSION X(100), Y(100), B(10), POINT(10), IMAGE(2500)
C
C     ..... SET PLOTTING CHARACTERS IN THE POINT ARRAY .....
      DATA POINT/ 1H1, 1H2, 1H3, 1H4, 1H5, 1H6, 1H7, 1H8, 1H9, 1H0/
C
C     ..... READ AND CHECK COORDINATES X(1)...X(M), Y(1)...Y(M),
C           AND LOWEST AND HIGHEST REGRESSION ORDERS MIN AND MAX .....
    1 READ (5,100) M, MIN, MAX, (X(I), I = 1, M)
      READ (5,101) (Y(I), I = 1, M)
      WRITE (6,200) M, (X(I), Y(I), I = 1, M)
      WRITE (6,201) MIN, MAX
      DO 5  N = MIN, MAX
      WRITE (6,202) N
C
C     ..... USE FUNCTION REGR TO PERFORM NTH-ORDER REGRESSION .....
      S = REGR (M, X, Y, N, A, B)
      IF (S .NE. 0.0) GO TO 3
         WRITE (6,203)
         GO TO 1
    3 WRITE (6,204) S, A, (I, B(I), I = 1, N)
C
C     ..... COMPUTE 26 POINTS LYING ON REGRESSION CURVE .....
      DELTAX = (X(M) - X(1))/25.0
      MP1 = M + 1
      MP26 = M + 26
      DO 4  I = MP1, MP26
      STEPS = I - M - 1
      X(I) = X(1) + STEPS*DELTAX
      Y(I) = A
      DO 4  J = 1, N
    4 Y(I) = Y(I) + B(J)*X(I)**J
C
C     ..... PLOT REGRESSION CURVE AGAINST ORIGINAL POINTS .....
      WRITE (6,205)
      CALL PLOT1 (0, 6, 8, 8, 14)
      CALL PLOT2 (IMAGE(1), 7.0, 0.0, 30.0, -20.0)
      CALL PLOT3 (POINT(N), X(MP1), Y(MP1), 26, 8)
      CALL PLOT3 (1H*, X(1), Y(1), M, 8)
      CALL PLOT4 (10, 10HORDINATE Y)
    5 WRITE (6,206)
      GO TO 1
C
C     ..... FORMATS FOR INPUT AND OUTPUT STATEMENTS .....
  100 FORMAT (3(7X, I3)/ (10X, 6F10.5))
  101 FORMAT (10X, 6F10.5)
  200 FORMAT (34H1 POLYNOMIAL REGRESSION, WITH M = , I2, 12H DATA POINTS
     1 // 8X, 5H X(I), 8X, 5H Y(I)// (2F13.2))
  201 FORMAT (58H0 THE LOWEST AND HIGHEST ORDER POLYNOMIALS TO BE TRIED
     1ARE// 6X, 7H MIN = , I3, 5X, 7H MAX = , I3)
  202 FORMAT (32H1 POLYNOMIAL REGRESSION OF ORDER/1H0, 5X, 7H N   = ,I3)
  203 FORMAT (69H0 MATRIX C IS NEAR-SINGULAR.   REGRESSION COEFFICIENTS
     1NOT DETERMINED)
  204 FORMAT (1H0, 5X, 5H S = , F10.6/ 6X, 5H A = , F10.6//
     1 (6X, 3H B(, I2, 4H) = , F11.6))
  205 FORMAT (1H1)
  206 FORMAT (1H0, 56X, 13H ABSCISSA (X))
C
      END
```

Program Listing (*Continued*)

Function REGR

```
C              FUNCTION REGR, WHICH CARRIES OUT AN NTH-ORDER POLYNOMIAL
C              REGRESSION ON M DATA POINTS CONTAINED IN THE X AND Y ARRAYS.
C              THE FUNCTION NORMALLY RETURNS THE STANDARD DEVIATION S OF THE
C              POINTS ABOUT THE REGRESSION CURVE.  THE REGRESSION COEFFICIENTS
C              ARE PLACED IN A AND B(1)...B(N).   HOWEVER, IF THE SIMULTANEOUS
C              EQUATION SOLVING ROUTINE SIMUL ENCOUNTERS A NEAR-SINGULAR
C              MATRIX, THE FUNCTION RETURNS THE VALUE 0.0
C
       FUNCTION REGR (M, X, Y, N, A, B)
       IMPLICIT REAL*8(A-H, O-Z)
       REAL*8 A, B, REGR, X, Y
       DATA EPS/ 1.0E-20/
       DIMENSION C(11,11), SX(20), SYX(10), CYX(10), X(100), Y(100),
      1B(10)
C
C      ..... COMPUTE SUMS OF POWERS AND PRODUCTS .....
       NTWO = 2*N
       NP1 = N + 1
       SY = 0.0
       SYY = 0.0
       DO 1  I = 1, N
       NPI = N + I
       SX(I) = 0.0
       SX(NPI) = 0.0
    1  SYX(I) = 0.0
       DO 3  I = 1, M
       SY = SY + Y(I)
       SYY = SYY + Y(I)**2
       DUM = 1.0
       DO 2  J = 1, N
       DUM = DUM*X(I)
       SX(J) = SX(J) + DUM
    2  SYX(J) = SYX(J) + Y(I)*DUM
       DO 3  J = NP1, NTWO
       DUM = DUM*X(I)
    3  SX(J) = SX(J) + DUM
C
C      ..... COMPUTE COEFFICIENTS C(I,J) .....
       FM = M
       CYY = SYY - SY*SY/FM
       DO 4  I = 1, N
       CYX(I) = SYX(I) - SY*SX(I)/FM
       C(I,NP1) = CYX(I)
       DO 4  J = 1, N
       IPJ = I + J
    4  C(I,J) = SX(IPJ) - SX(I)*SX(J)/FM
C
C      ..... CALL ON SIMUL TO SOLVE SIMULTANEOUS EQUATIONS .....
       DET = SIMUL (N, C, B, EPS, 1, 11)
       WRITE (6,200) DET
  200  FORMAT (13H0      DET = , E14.8)
       IF (DET .NE. 0.0) GO TO 6
       REGR = 0.0
       RETURN
C
C      ..... COMPUTE INTERCEPT A AND STANDARD DEVIATION S .....
    6  DUM = SY
       TEMP = CYY
       DO 7  I = 1, N
       DUM = DUM - B(I)*SX(I)
    7  TEMP = TEMP - B(I)*CYX(I)
       A = DUM/FM
       DENOM = M - N - 1
       S = DSQRT(TEMP/DENOM)
       REGR = S
       RETURN
C
       END
```

Example 8.5   Polynomial Regression with Plotting   **581**

Program Listing (*Continued*)

Data

```
M =    10   MIN =  1  MAX =   8
X(1) =     0.23      1.01      2.29      2.87      4.15      5.36
           5.51      6.36      6.84      7.00
Y(1) =     5.64      7.83     17.04     21.38     24.56     16.21
          14.57      0.78     -7.64    -12.52
```

Computer Output

```
POLYNOMIAL REGRESSION, WITH M = 10 DATA POINTS
         X(I)         Y(I)
         0.23         5.64
         1.01         7.83
         2.29        17.04
         2.87        21.38
         4.15        24.56
         5.36        16.21
         5.51        14.57
         6.36         0.78
         6.84        -7.64
         7.00       -12.52

THE LOWEST AND HIGHEST ORDER POLYNOMIALS TO BE TRIED ARE
     MIN =   1     MAX =   8
```

Computer Output (*Continued*)

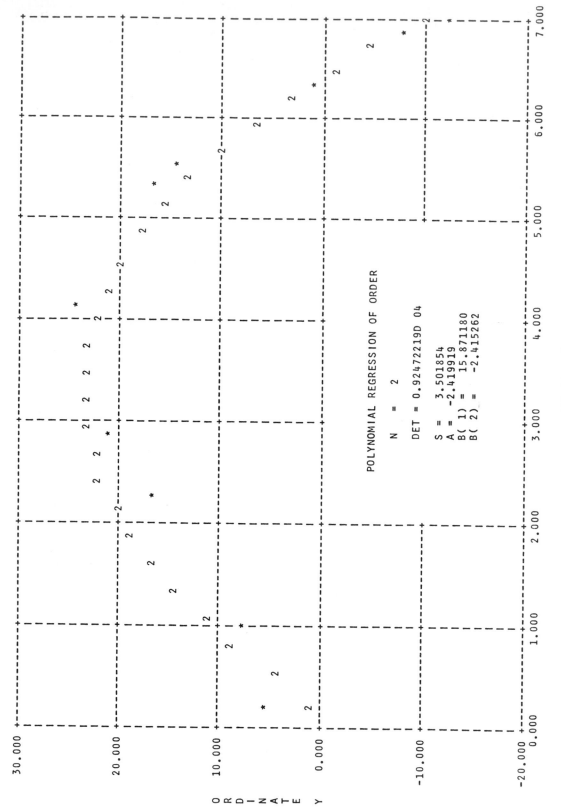

Example 8.5 Polynomial Regression with Plotting 583

Computer Output (*Continued*)

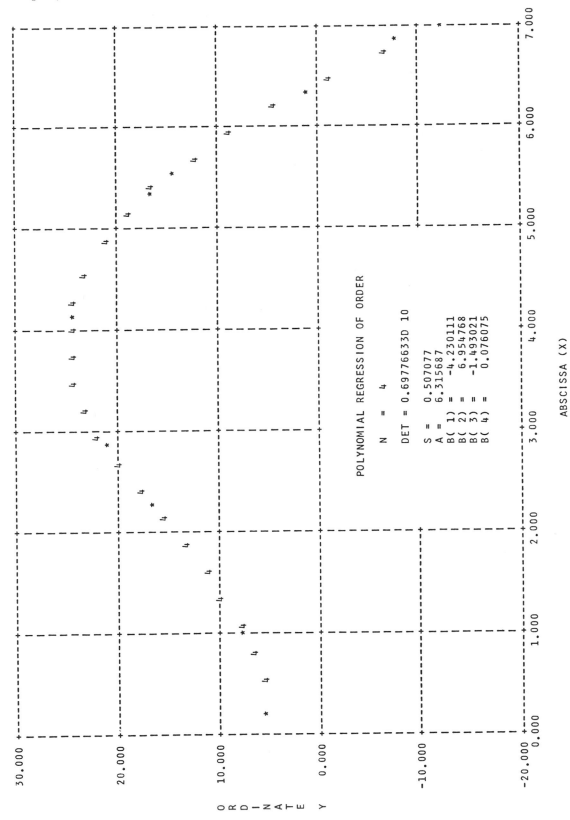

POLYNOMIAL REGRESSION OF ORDER

N = 4

DET = 0.69776633D 10

S = 0.507077
A = 6.315687
B(1) = -4.230111
B(2) = 6.954768
B(3) = -1.493021
B(4) = 0.076075

ABSCISSA (X)

Discussion of Results

For brevity, we have reproduced above only two of the eight printed graphs, namely, those for quadratic and quartic regression polynomials. Also, those parts of the output giving values of N, DET, S, A, and the B(I) have been superimposd on the graphs. The asterisks denote the original data points; the lines of repeated digits represent the regression curves and their orders.

An examination of the complete output shows the following standard deviations s for various orders of regression n:

The standard deviation falls rapidly with n increasing, but becomes less sensitive to change of n after the quartic is reached. A minimum in s is actually observed at $n = 4$, corresponding to the second graph. Thus, on the basis of either criterion stated in the introduction, we can say that the data are represented best by a quartic polynomial.

It is well known (e.g., see Hamming [5]) that the system of simultaneous normal equations resulting from polynomial regression is difficult to solve accurately if n is not fairly small. Even though double-precision arithmetic has been used in the program, this fact probably accounts for the reduction in s in going from $n = 7$ to $n = 8$.

n:	1	2	3	4	5	6	7	8
s:	11.657	3.502	1.224	0.507	0.565	0.592	0.688	0.376

8.23   Introduction to the Analysis of Variance

Table 8.6 presents the percentages of component X in five shipments of a certain chemical, as determined by four repeated analyses on each shipment.

Table 8.6   *Percentage of X in Chemical*

	Shipment				
Analysis	A	B	C	D	E
1	17.4	18.5	17.5	17.2	17.8
2	17.9	18.4	17.6	17.0	18.0
3	18.1	17.9	17.5	17.4	18.3
4	17.7	18.2	17.1	17.7	17.7

Can we say whether or not the shipments differ significantly in their percentage content of X, bearing in mind the errors introduced in the analyses?

This is a simple example of a problem in *analysis of variance*. Generally, such problems are characterized by a set of observations cross-classified according to various factors, each of which might occur at several different levels. We then ask which of the factors is significantly associated with variations in the observations. The field known as *design of experiments* deals with problems of assigning the most suitable combinations of factors under which observations should be made, particularly if the number of observations must be kept to a minimum.

Our simple example is referred to as having one *classification* (shipment number) with *replication* (successive analyses), represented algebraically by Table 8.7. The

Table 8.7   *Model for Analysis of Variance*

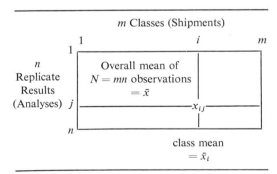

following model is now postulated. Assume that the replicate results in each class represent a sample of size n from a normally distributed population having mean $\mu + \delta_i$ and variance σ^2. Here μ is the overall mean of the population from which the shipments are drawn, and δ_i is a factor that allows for variation between shipments and comes from a population having variance σ_δ^2. The purpose of making repeated analyses is to obtain an

estimate of the analytical error represented by σ^2. Then any one observation is given by

$$x_{ij} = \mu + \delta_i + \varepsilon_{ij}, \qquad (8.78)$$

where ε_{ij} is a random variable, incurred by analytical error, being normally distributed with mean zero and variance σ^2.

Consider the deviation of any observation from the mean of the observations:

$$x_{ij} - \bar{x} = (x_{ij} - \bar{x}_i) + (\bar{x}_i - \bar{x}).$$

Squaring both sides and summing over i and j,

$$\sum_{ij} (x_{ij} - \bar{x})^2 = \sum_{ij} (x_{ij} - \bar{x}_i)^2 + 2 \sum_{ij} (x_{ij} - \bar{x}_i)(\bar{x}_i - \bar{x})$$
$$+ \sum_{ij} (\bar{x}_i - \bar{x})^2$$
$$= \sum_{ij} (x_{ij} - \bar{x}_i)^2 + 2 \sum_{i} (\bar{x}_i - \bar{x}) \underbrace{\sum_{j} (x_{ij} - \bar{x}_i)}_{\substack{\text{zero for all}\\ \text{classes}}}$$
$$+ n \sum_{i} (\bar{x}_i - \bar{x})^2.$$

Thus we have the result

$$\sum_{ij} (x_{ij} - \bar{x})^2 = \sum_{ij} (x_{ij} - \bar{x}_i)^2 + n \sum_{i} (\bar{x}_i - \bar{x})^2.$$

Total sum of squares of deviations from overall mean, S	$=$	Sum of squares of deviations from respective class means, $S_{j(i)}$	$+$	$n \times$ sum of squares of deviations of class means from overall mean, S_i

$$(8.79)$$

Now

$$\frac{\sum_{ij} (x_{ij} - \bar{x}_i)^2}{N - m} = \text{joint estimate of } \sigma^2,$$

on $N - m$ degrees of freedom, and

$$\frac{n \sum_{i} (\bar{x}_i - \bar{x})^2}{m - 1} = n \operatorname{var} \bar{x}_i$$

$$= \text{estimate of } n \operatorname{var}\left(\mu + \delta_i\right.$$
$$\left. + \frac{\varepsilon_{i1} + \varepsilon_{i2} + \cdots + \varepsilon_{in}}{n}\right)$$

$$= \text{estimate of } n\left(\sigma_\delta^2 + n \frac{\sigma^2}{n^2}\right)$$

$$= \text{estimate of } (n\sigma_\delta^2 + \sigma^2), \qquad \text{on } m - 1 \text{ d.f.}$$

We may now draw up an analysis of variance table (Table 8.8); the figures refer to computed values for the original numerical example of Table 8.6.

As a null hypothesis, assume that there is no variation in the percentage of X between shipments, and put $\sigma_\delta^2 = 0$.

Table 8.8   Analysis of Variance for One Classification with Replication

Source of Estimate	Sum of Squares	Degrees of Freedom	Mean Square	Quantity Which the Mean Square Estimates
Between Classes	$S_i = n \sum_i (\bar{x}_i - \bar{x})^2$ 2.307	$m - 1$ 4	$\dfrac{S_i}{m-1}$ 0.5767	$\sigma^2 + n\sigma_\delta^2$
Within Classes	$S_{j(i)} = \sum_{ij}(x_{ij} - \bar{x}_i)^2$ 1.105	$N - m$ 15	$\dfrac{S_{j(i)}}{N-m}$ 0.0737	σ^2
Total	$S = \sum_{ij}(x_{ij} - \bar{x})^2$ 3.412	$N - 1$ 19		

Then 0.5767 and 0.0737 are two estimates of σ^2 and may be checked using the F test. In fact, $F = 0.5767/0.0737 = 7.82$ based on $v_1 = 4$, $v_2 = 15$ d.f. But, from Fig. 8.10, $F = 4.89$ at the 1% level; also, from tables, a value of $F = 5.8029$ has only a 0.5% probability of being exceeded. Thus, we conclude that the null hypothesis is extremely likely to be an incorrect assumption and that there is a definite variation in the percentage of X between shipments. That is, the shipments are not of a uniform quality. Indeed, an estimate may now be made of σ_δ^2, should it be required.

Problems

8.1 The independent random variables y and z have frequency functions $g(y)$ and $h(z)$, respectively. Show that the random variable $x = yz$ has the frequency function

$$f(x) = \int_{-\infty}^{\infty} g(y)h(x/y)\frac{dy}{y}.$$

8.2 In a single bridge deal, what is the probability that the North and South hands will contain the entire club suit between them?

8.3 Write a program to compute the probability P that, from a group of n people, at least two will have the same birthday. The program should print values of n and P for $n = 2, 3, \ldots, n_{max}$, where the value of n_{max} is read as data.

8.4 Independent events are occurring randomly over a long period of time. The number of events per unit time, which obeys the Poisson distribution, is expected to be η. Show that the time-interval t, elapsing between successive events, has the frequency function $f(t) = \eta e^{-\eta t}$. Show also by integration that the mean value of t is $1/\eta$.

8.5 A liquid-phase chemical reaction occurs continuously in a tank of constant volume V cu.ft. The flow rates of reactant and product streams to and from the reactor are both v cu.ft/min (see Fig. P8.5).

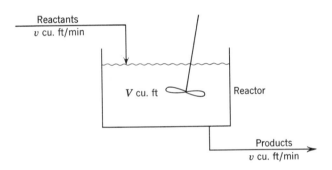

Figure P8.5

In analyzing the performance of the reactor, we may need to investigate the residence time t spent inside the reactor by a small particle of entering liquid before it escapes in the outlet stream. If the tank is well-stirred, we can suppose that the contents of the reactor consist of a large number of liquid particles, each of which has the same chance of escaping in the outlet stream during a small time interval. On the basis of this hypothesis, show that there is a distribution of residence times, with mean value V/v and variance $(V/v)^2$.

8.6 The Maxwell-Boltzmann distribution of molecular velocities v_i in a gas at an absolute temperature T has the frequency function

$$f(v_i) = \alpha e^{-\beta v_i^2}, \qquad i = 1, 2, 3,$$

where i refers to each of the x, y, and z directions, $\beta = m/2kT$, $m = $ mass of a molecule, $k = $ Boltzmann's constant, and $\alpha = (m/2\pi kT)^{1/2}$ is a constant such that

$$\int_{-\infty}^{\infty} f(v_i)\,dv_i = 1.$$

Show that the variable $t_i = v_i(2\beta)^{1/2}$ has the standardized normal distribution $N(0,1)$. Thus, if c is the molecular speed (that is, the RMS velocity), show that $E/(kT/2)$, where $E = mc^2/2$ is the kinetic energy, has the χ^2 distribution based on three degrees of freedom. Finally, prove that c has the frequency function

$$f(c) = 4\pi\alpha^3 c^2 e^{-\beta c^2}.$$

8.7 Theoretically investigate the basis for supposing that the variable of equation (8.33) approaches χ^2 as the expected frequency in each class becomes large.

8.8 $\chi^2_{P,\nu}$ is defined as that value which has a probability P of being exceeded by a χ^2 variable based on ν degrees of freedom. Write a program that will compute and tabulate $\chi^2_{P,\nu}$ for the following values of ν and P:

$$\nu: 1, 2, \ldots, 10, 12, 15, 20, 30, \ldots, 100$$
$$P: 0.01, 0.05, 0.1, 0.5$$

Note. The largest tabulated value will be $\chi^2_{0.01,100} \doteq 135.8$.

8.9 Table P8.9, for 1960–62 [17], shows the distribution of weights for a large number of U.S. males in specified age groups.

Table P8.9

Weight (Pounds)	18–24 years	35–44 years	55–64 years
	Number of Persons		
Below 100	—	—	22
100 – 109	—	46	19
110 – 119	145	42	174
120 – 129	524	210	492
130 – 139	798	737	566
140 – 149	1,305	1,017	921
150 – 159	1,122	1,820	1,049
160 – 169	1,052	1,672	1,100
170 – 179	766	1,799	922
180 – 189	656	1,458	769
190 – 199	208	964	586
200 – 209	154	692	455
210 – 219	137	403	245
220 – 229	198	234	114
230 – 239	21	129	9
240 – 249	38	82	9
Above 249	15	68	65
Total:	7,139	11,373	7,517

(a) Attempt to fit each set of data by a reasonably simple frequency function.

(b) Is there a significant difference between the mean weights for each possible pair of groups?

8.10 For a Student's t variable based on ν degrees of freedom, a value $t_{P,\nu}$ is defined such that P is the probability that $|t| \geqslant t_{P,\nu}$. Write a program that will compute and tabulate $t_{P,\nu}$ for the following values of ν and P:

$$\nu: 1, 2, \ldots, 10, 12, 15, 20, 30, 40, 50$$
$$P: 0.01, 0.05, 0.1, 0.25$$

Note. The largest tabulated value will be $t_{0.01,1} \doteq 63.7$.

8.11 F_{P,ν_1,ν_2} is defined as that value which has a probability P of being exceeded by an F variable based on ν_1 and ν_2

degrees of freedom. Write a program that will compute and tabulate F_{P,v_1,v_2} for the following values of P, v_1, and v_2:

$$P: 0.01, 0.05, 0.1$$

$$v_1: 1, 2, \ldots, 10, 12, 15, 20, 30, 40, 50$$

$$v_2: 1, 2, \ldots, 10, 12, 15, 20, 30, 40, 50$$

Note. The largest tabulated value will be $F_{0.01,50,1} \doteq 6300$. Values of F for the same v_1, but with v_2 or P larger, are considerably smaller. For example, $F_{0.01,50,2} \doteq 99.5$, $F_{0.1,50,1} \doteq 62.7$.

8.12 The *additive method* for generating random numbers, uniformly distributed between 0 and 1, uses the algorithm

$$x_i = x_{i-1} + x_{i-n} \pmod{m}, \qquad i = n+1, n+2, \ldots$$

in which all quantities are integers, and the magnitude of m is restricted by the available word length of the machine being used. The required random number between 0 and 1 is then $z_i = x_i/m$. The method requires that $x_1, x_2, \ldots, x_n$ be preset with uniformly distributed random numbers, whose values lie between 0 and 1. Green, Smith, and Klem [12] indicate that n should be at least 16 to ensure completely satisfactory random properties of the sequence, although a value as low as $n = 6$ can suffice for most purposes. Note that as soon as x_i has been computed, x_{i-n} is no longer needed. Thus, by suitable ordering and replacement, it is unnecessary to extend the x vector beyond its original n storage locations.

Write a subroutine named RANADD that will implement the above procedure. If possible, the call should be of the form

CALL RANADD (Z)

where Z is returned as the random number. However, if a statement, such as the DATA statement in FORTRAN IV, is not available for presetting vectors with numerical constants, alternative calls may have to be considered.

If $n = 16$ and $m = 10^9$, Table P8.12, taken from a table of random digits [13], might give suitable starting values for $x_1, x_2, \ldots, x_{16}$:

Table P8.12

356,120,997	988,919,262	437,131,844	459,225,517
739,989,737	666,850,663	149,716,880	491,221,612
789,764,838	252,429,765	378,688,294	737,326,323
016,664,811	951,830,262	566,387,005	194,272,481

These values can be truncated for use with machines whose word length does not permit integers as high as 10^9.

What are the main advantages and disadvantages of the additive method, particularly as compared to the multiplicative congruential method used in Example 8.2?

8.13 The mixed multiplicative congruential method for generating a sequence of uniformly distributed random integers x_i, $i = 2, 3, \ldots, n$, uses the recursion relation

$$x_i = ax_{i-1} + c \pmod{m},$$

in which a, c, and m are integer constants. A random floating-point number z_i, uniformly distributed between 0 and 1, is then given by $z_i = x_i/m$. The modulus m is a large integer, usually the form 2^z or 10^z (for binary and decimal machines,

respectively), its magnitude being restricted by the available word length.

It can be shown (see, for example, Refs. 7, 8, and 9) that the maximum period, before the sequence starts repeating, is m numbers, and that this period will be achieved provided that:

(i) c and m do not have a common divisor.
(ii) $a \pmod{p} = 1$, where p is any prime factor of m.
(iii) $a \pmod{4} = 1$, if m is a multiple of 4.

Note that if efficiency is very important, the choice of values for a, c, and m will also be influenced by the need to perform the computations in a small number of basic machine operations (for example, shifting and truncating).

(a) If $m = 2^z$, where α is a positive integer, show that conditions (i), (ii), and (iii) are satisfied if c is odd, and $a = 4i + 1$, where i is a positive integer.

(b) If $m = 10^z$, show that these conditions are satisfied if c is odd and not divisible by 5, and $a = 20i + 1$.

(c) Write a program that will implement the above method. The program should read values for x_1, a, c, m, and n (the total number of values z_i to be generated and printed), so that the merits of different choices can be compared.

(d) The authors have investigated the sequence using: $a = 2^{10} + 1$, $c = 1$, and $m = 2^{20}$. For two arbitrary starting values, $x_1 = 899,462$ and then $76,701$, they found that the resulting z_i were unsatisfactory. Let the program generate the first 200 numbers of these particular sequences, and comment on the ways in which the series of numbers is apparently not truly random.

(e) Discuss the feasibility of machine tests for evaluating the randomness of a series of supposedly random numbers.

(f) Attempt to find satisfactory values for a, c, and m. Then, rewrite the program as a subroutine named RANMMC, similar to that in Example 8.2. The call, with Z the number to be returned, will be

CALL RANMMC (Z)

8.14 The *run test*, used in checking for possible *serial association* in a supposedly random series of digits, examines the frequency of occurrence of repeated digits. A χ^2 test can then be used to compare the observed and expected frequencies. Here, we define a *run* of length r as occurring when any digit is not preceded by the same digit, but is followed by a sequence of $(r - 1)$, and no more, identical digits.

In a sequence of 100,000 random digits, each of which may be 0, 1, $\ldots$, 9, what is the expected frequency of occurrence of runs of length r, for $r = 1$ (digit not repeated), 2, 3, 4, 5, and 6?

8.15 Let x be a random number that is uniformly distributed between 0 and 1, and suppose that we wish to transform x into a random variable y that comes from a continuous distribution with arbitrary frequency function $f(y)$ and cumulative distribution function $F(y)$. Show graphically, or otherwise, that y given by

$$x = \int_{-\infty}^{y} dF$$

will be the required random variable.

8.16 Based on Problem 8.15, write a function named REXPON that accepts a value for x, and transforms it into a random variable y that obeys the exponential distribution $f(y) = \eta e^{-\eta y}$, with mean $1/\eta$. Anticipate that the call for the function will be

$$Y = \text{REXPON } (X, \text{ETA})$$

in which X, ETA, and Y have obvious interpretations.

8.17 Discuss the possibility of generating an $N(\mu, \sigma)$ random variable based on the method given in Problem 8.15.

8.18 If x_1 and x_2 are a pair of independent random variables uniformly distributed between 0 and 1, Box and Muller [14] indicate that the pair of values

$$y_1 = \sigma(-2 \ln x_1)^{1/2} \cos 2\pi x_2 + \mu,$$
$$y_2 = \sigma(-2 \ln x_1)^{1/2} \sin 2\pi x_2 + \mu,$$

will be normally distributed according to $N(\mu, \sigma)$.

(a) Write a subroutine named RNORML that implements Box and Muller's procedure. The call will be of the form

$$\text{CALL RNORML } (X1, X2, MU, SIGMA, Y1, Y2)$$

in which the arguments have obvious interpretations.

(b) Investigate the theoretical justification for the procedure.

8.19 Here, we investigate a statistical method for approximating the solution of Laplace's equation $\nabla^2 u = 0$ in a rectangular region with Dirichlet boundary conditions.

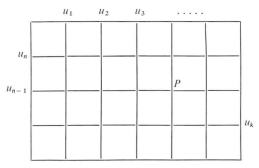

Figure P8.19

Introduce a square grid as shown in Fig. P8.19, and let u_k be the known value of u at the boundary point k ($k = 1, 2, \ldots, n$). Consider a *random walk*, in which we start from any point P and proceed, at random, along a series of grid lines until a point on the boundary is eventually reached. The steps of the walk are such that at any point there is an equal probability of proceeding to each of the four neighboring points. Starting from P, let f_{Pk} be the probability of reaching point k at the end of the walk. Then

$$v_P = \sum_{k=1}^{n} f_{Pk} u_k$$

is an approximation to u_P, the solution of $\nabla^2 u = 0$ at P.

(a) Verify the approximation v_P by showing that it satisfies: (i) the boundary condition u_k for P coincident with k, and (ii) equation (7.79), the finite-difference approximation of $\nabla^2 u = 0$.

(b) Write a program that implements the above procedure. The values f_{Pk} should be estimated by making a reasonably large number N of random walks from each point P, keeping track of how many times the walk terminates at each point k. A random number generator with a flat distribution should be used to decide which direction to take at each step of the walk.

(c) What are the advantages and disadvantages of this method for solving Laplace's equation, compared with conventional relaxation methods?

(d) Could the method be extended to obtain solutions for: (i) Poisson's equation, or (ii) a region with a curved boundary?

8.20 A chemical company is faced with the problem of disposing of a potential waste product. One possibility is to convert it into x tons per annum of a saleable product. The cost of the operation would be y \$/ton of product, all of which could then be sold at z \$/ton. The annual profit would be $P = x(z - y)$ dollars. Bearing in mind the uncertainties of production and marketing, the actual value of x is thought to be uniformly distributed between lower and upper limits x_1 and x_2, y is $N(a + b/x, \sigma_y^2)$, and z is $N(c - xd, \sigma_z^2)$, where estimated values are available for x_1, x_2, a, b, c, d, σ_y^2, and σ_z^2.

Before proceeding with the project, the company wishes to estimate the frequency function $f(P)$ for the annual profit. Since an analytical approach may be difficult, an alternative is to use a random number generator (see Example 8.2 and Problems 8.12, 8.13, and 8.18) to simulate the distributions of x, y, and z. An approximation to $f(P)$ may then be constructed from the results of a large number of trials.

Write a program that will implement the above technique, also known as *risk analysis*. Investigate the effect on $f(P)$ of different values for the various parameters. Also investigate the possibility of estimating the mean and variance of P by using a method similar to that in Section 8.5(4).

8.21 Write a program to simulate the formation of queues at the check-out stands of a supermarket, based on the following model.

The time-interval t, elapsing between the arrival of successive customers at the check-out stands, has the exponential distribution (see Prob. 8.4) $f(t) = \eta e^{-\eta t}$, in which η is the average number of customers arriving per unit time. There are n stands open, and each customer chooses the stand that has the least number of people waiting to be served. The time τ taken to pass through the stand, after waiting to be served, is normally distributed with mean μ and variance σ^2.

The program should simulate the passage of N customers through the stands. Exponential and normal distribution random number generators, such as those developed in Problems 8.16 and 8.18, should be used to generate successive values for t and τ. The program should read values for n, η, μ, σ^2 and N as data. The printed output should consist of (a) the observed frequency function for the number of customers waiting at a stand at any time, and (b) the observed frequency function for the total time taken to wait and be served.

Note. Many variations of this problem are obviously possible, and might include: (a) customer chooses the queue that he estimates has the least total number of *purchases* to be processed, (b) periodic closing down or addition of stands, (c) τ uniformly distributed between $\tau_{\min}$ and $\tau_{\max}$, etc.

8.22 Write a program that simulates the random dealing of n successive bridge hands, based on the following method.

First establish a code whereby the integers 1 through 52 represent the 52 cards in the deck, for example, let $1 \equiv 2$ of clubs, $2 \equiv 3$ of clubs, ..., $13 \equiv$ ace of clubs, $14 \equiv 2$ of diamonds, etc. Let these integers occupy, in any order, the 52 elements of the integer vector DECK(1) ... DECK(52). Also, obtain a random number generator that gives a sequence of values $x_1, x_2, \ldots$, uniformly distributed between 0 and 1. The first card is "dealt" by computing $i_1 = 1 + 52x_1$, rounding down to the next lower integer, and observing the card that is in DECK(i_1). The card so dealt is then effectively removed from the deck by interchanging DECK(i_1) and DECK(52). To deal the second card, compute $i_2 = 1 + 51x_2$, again rounded down, and examine DECK(i_2); then interchange DECK(i_2) and DECK(51). The process is repeated, and eventually the coded form of the first hand will be in DECK(40) ... DECK(52).

In addition, at least, the program should keep track of the distribution of point counts in the successive hands. These point counts can then be compared with those predicted in Example 8.1. Also, depending on the imagination and ability of the programmer, successive hands may be printed in a format similar to those found in bridge articles, that is, a listing of the hands sorted by suit and value.

8.23 During the batch saponification reaction between equimolar amounts of sodium hydroxide and ethyl acetate, the concentration c (gm.moles/liter) varies with time t (min) according to the equation

$$\frac{1}{c} = \frac{1}{c_0} + kt,$$

where c_0 is the initial concentration, and k (liter/gm.mole.min) is the reaction rate constant. The following results were obtained in the laboratory, at a temperature of 77°F:

$$1/c: 24.7 \quad 32.4 \quad 38.4 \quad 45.0 \quad 52.3 \quad 65.6$$
$$t: \quad 1 \qquad 2 \qquad 3 \qquad 4 \qquad 5 \qquad 7$$
$$1/c: 87.6 \quad 102 \quad 135 \quad 154 \quad 192$$
$$t: \quad 10 \qquad 12 \qquad 15 \qquad 20 \qquad 25$$

Obtain a least-squares estimate of (a) the reaction rate constant, and (b) the initial concentration.

8.24 The data in Table P8.24 have been published in *Time* [18] for the tar and nicotine content (in milligrams) of several brands of king-size filter and regular cigarettes.

Table P8.24

Filter		Regular	
Tar	Nicotine	Tar	Nicotine
8.3	0.32	32.4	1.69
12.3	0.46	33.0	1.75
18.8	1.10	34.1	1.48
22.9	1.32	34.8	1.89
23.1	1.26	36.7	1.73
24.0	1.44	37.2	2.11
27.3	1.42	38.5	2.35
30.0	1.96	41.1	2.45
35.9	2.23	41.5	1.97
41.6	2.20	43.4	2.64

(a) Perform the linear regression $y = \alpha + \beta x$ on each of these two sets of data, with $y =$ nicotine content and $x =$ tar content.

(b) Test the hypothesis that β is the same for both cases.

(c) For a given tar content, do the regular cigarettes contain significantly less nicotine than the filter variety?

8.25 In the linear regression $y = \alpha + \beta x$, the method of least squares assumes that the values x_i, $i = 1, 2, \ldots, m$ are known exactly, whereas the y_i are subject to random error.

Using the computer, perform experiments to see what happens if the x_i are *also* subject to random error. To achieve this, assume a model with known α and β. Then use a random number generator (see Example 8.2, and Problems 8.12, 8.13, and 8.18) to provide m "exact" values x_i over some interval, together with corresponding values y_i, distributed with constant variance about a mean $\alpha + \beta x_i$. Next, superimpose random errors on the x_i, and use these "inexact" values when computing the estimates a and b. Repeat the process many times, and finally compare the mean of the several values of a and b thus computed with the known parameters α and β.

8.26 Nedderman [6] used stereoscopic photography of tiny air bubbles to determine the velocity profile close to the wall for flow of water in a 1 in. I.D. tube. At a Reynolds number of 1200, he obtained the values given in Table P8.26.

Table P8.26

y, Distance from Wall (cm)	u, Velocity (cm/sec)	y	u
0.003	0.03	0.056	0.85
0.021	0.32	0.061	0.92
0.025	0.30	0.070	1.05
0.025	0.33	0.078	1.17
0.037	0.57	0.085	1.32
0.043	0.66	0.092	1.38
0.049	0.74	0.106	1.57
0.053	0.80	0.113	1.65
0.055	0.84		

Theoretically, the data should follow the law: $u = py + qy^2$, where p and q are constants.

(a) Use the method of least squares to estimate p and q, and find the corresponding standard deviation of the data about the regression line.

(b) Suppose that we are interested in predicting the value of the shear stress at the pipe wall, which is given by $\tau_w = \mu(du/dy)_{y=0} = \mu p$, where μ is the viscosity of water. Estimate the variance of p, so that we could then attempt to place confidence limits on the predicted value of τ_w.

(c) Would the data be fitted substantially better by the cubic formula: $u = py + qy^2 + ry^3$?

8.27 Consider the family of p straight lines

$$y = \alpha_k + \beta x, \qquad k = 1, 2, \ldots, p,$$

which have a common slope β but different intercepts α_k. Suppose that n_k pairs of experimental values are available for each line:

$$(x_{ik}, y_{ik}), \qquad i = 1, 2, \ldots, n_k; \qquad k = 1, 2, \ldots, p.$$

Devise a method for obtaining least-squares estimates of the parameters $\alpha_1, \alpha_2, \ldots, \alpha_k,$ and β, and write a program to implement the method. Note that this type of problem is also discussed by Ergun [15].

Test the program with the data (shown in Table P8.27), reported by Williams and Katz [16] in connection with a Wilson plot for evaluating the shell-side heat transfer coefficient in a heat exchanger.

(e) The values predicted for y by the regression equation at successive points $x_1, x_2, \ldots, x_m$.

8.31 The experimental data for heat transfer between viscous fluids and the shell side of a heat exchanger can be correlated fairly successfully by the equation

$$Nu = \alpha \, Re^\beta \, Pr^\gamma \, r^\delta,$$

where Nu, Re, and Pr are the Nusselt, Reynolds, and Prandtl

Table P8.27

k:	1		2		3		4		5	
n_k:	4		4		4		4		4	
	x	y	x	y	x	y	x	y	x	y
	166	2.58	168	2.44	167	2.22	163	2.02	163	1.87
	124	2.32	124	2.10	125	1.91	122	1.75	123	1.59
	102	2.11	102	1.93	101	1.71	101	1.56	99.8	1.42
	85.8	1.97	85.6	1.77	85.5	1.57	84.1	1.42	84.5	1.26

8.28 For the matrix formulation of multiple regression in Section 8.21, verify that equations (8.63) can be rewritten as (8.67).

8.29 In Section 8.22, multiple regression was discussed in terms of orthogonal polynomials. In this connection, verify the following:

(a) That the polynomials of (8.77) satisfy the orthogonality condition (8.75). (*Hint.* Suppose that P_k is about to be computed, and that all lower-order polynomials have already been proved to be mutually orthogonal. Multiply the first of equations (8.77) through by P_j, and sum over all the data points x_i, $i = 1, 2, \ldots, m$. Then consider the individual terms of the resulting equation for $j \le k - 3$, $j = k - 2$, and $j = k - 1$, in turn.)

(b) That equation (8.73) giving the regression coefficients, can be rewritten as (8.76).

8.30 Write a program that will perform the orthogonal polynomial regression discussed in Section 8.22. The program should accept the following input values: m (total number of data points), $x_1, x_2, \ldots, x_m, y_1, y_2, \ldots, y_m$, and n (order of regression).

The printed output should consist of values for:

(a) The estimated regression coefficients, $b_0, b_1, \ldots, b_n$.
(b) The variance-covariance matrix $\mathbf{V}$.
(c) The variance s^2 of the data about the regression line.
(d) The coefficients of the various powers of x appearing in all the orthogonal polynomials so that they can be reconstructed, if necessary.

numbers, r is the ratio of the viscosity at the mean fluid temperature to that at the wall temperature, and α, β, γ, and δ are constants.

Table P8.31 represents part of the data reported by Katz and Williams [16], and reexamined by Briggs, Katz, and Young [19], for heat transfer outside 3/4 in. O.D. plain tubes:

Table P8.31

Nu	Re	Pr	r
277	49,000	2.30	0.947
348	68,600	2.28	0.954
421	84,800	2.27	0.959
223	34,200	2.32	0.943
177	22,900	2.36	0.936
114.8	1,321	246	0.592
95.9	931	247	0.583
68.3	518	251	0.579
49.1	346	273	0.290
56.0	122.9	1,518	0.294
39.9	54.0	1,590	0.279
47.0	84.6	1,521	0.267
94.2	1,249	107.4	0.724
99.9	1,021	186	0.612
83.1	465	414	0.512
35.9	54.8	1,302	0.273

Obtain least-squares estimates of α, β, γ, and δ, and indicate how one might determine the confidence that could be placed in each such estimate.

Bibliography

1. C. A. Bennett and N. L. Franklin, *Statistical Analysis in Chemistry and the Chemical Industry*, Wiley, New York, 1954.

2. O. L. Davies, ed., *Statistical Methods in Research and Production*, 3rd ed., Oliver and Boyd, London, 1957.

3. M. G. Kendall, *The Advanced Theory of Statistics*, Vol. I, Griffin, London, 1948.

4. D. V. Lindley and J. C. P. Miller, *Cambridge Elementary Statistical Tables*, Cambridge University Press, 1953.

5. R. W. Hamming, *Numerical Methods for Scientists and Engineers*, McGraw-Hill, New York, 1962.

6. R. M. Nedderman, *Velocity Profiles in Thin Liquid Layers*, Ph.D. Thesis, Dept. of Chemical Engineering, University of Cambridge, 1960.

7. A. Ralston and H. S. Wilf, editors, *Mathematical Methods for Digital Computers*, Vol. 2, Wiley, New York, 1966.

8. J. M. Hammersley and D. C. Handscomb, *Monte Carlo Methods*, Methuen, London, 1964.

9. T. H. Naylor, J. L. Balintfy, D. S. Burdick, and K. Chu, *Computer Simulation Techniques*, Wiley, New York, 1966.

10. N. R. Draper and H. Smith, *Applied Regression Analysis*, Wiley, New York, 1966.

11. G. E. Forsythe, "Generation and Use of Orthogonal Polynomials for Data Fitting with a Digital Computer," *J. Soc. Indust. Appl. Math.*, **5**, 74–88 (1957).

12. B. F. Green, J. E. K. Smith, and L. Klem, "Empirical Tests of an Additive Random Number Generator," *Journal of the A.C.M.*, **6**, 527–537 (1959).

13. The Rand Corporation, *A Million Random Digits with 100,000 Normal Deviates*, The Free Press, Glencoe, Illinois, 1955.

14. G. E. P. Box and M. E. Muller, "A Note on the Generation of Random Normal Deviates," *Ann. Math. Stat.*, **29**, 610–611, 1958.

15. S. Ergun, "Application of the Principle of Least Squares to Families of Straight Lines," *Ind. Eng. Chem.*, **48**, 2063–2068 (1956).

16. R. B. Williams and D. L. Katz, *Performance of Finned Tubes in Shell-and-Tube Heat Exchangers*, University of Michigan Engineering Research Institute, Ann Arbor, 1951. See also: *Trans. ASME*, **74**, 1307–1320 (1952).

17. *Weight, Height, and Selected Body Dimensions of Adults: United States, 1960–1962*, National Center for Health Statistics, Series 11, No. 8, U.S. Dept. of Health, Education, and Welfare, Washington, D.C., 1965.

18. *Time* **89** (12), 51 (1967).

19. D. E. Briggs, D. L. Katz, and E. H. Young, "How to Design Finned-Tube Heat Exchangers," *Chem. Eng. Progr.*, **59**, 49–59 (1963).

APPENDIX

Presentation of Computer Examples

The following is an explanation of the various subdivisions appearing in the documentation of each computer example:

1. Problem Statement. Contains a statement of the problem to be solved, and may refer to the main text if appropriate. Occasionally preceded by an introductory section.

2. Method of Solution. Refers to algorithms already developed in the text whenever possible. Also gives notes on any special problems which may occur, and how they will be overcome.

3. Flow Diagram. The authors have avoided a flow diagram that merely repeats the program, step by step. Rather, the flow diagram is intended to clarify the computational procedure by reproducing only those steps that are essential to the algorithm. Thus, in the final program, there may be several additional steps that are *not* given in the flow diagram. Such steps frequently include: (a) printout of data that have just been read, often for checking purposes, (b) manipulations, such as the floating of an integer when it is to be added to a floating-point number, that are caused by limitations of FORTRAN, (c) calculation of intermediate constants used only as a computational convenience, (d) return to the beginning of the program to process another set of data, (e) printing headings and comments, (f) arranging for printout at definite intervals, during an iterative type of calculation, by setting up a counter and checking to see if it is an integral multiple of the specified frequency of printout, etc. The flow diagram convention is explained at the end of this appendix.

4. FORTRAN Implementation. This section serves as the main bridge between the algorithm of the text or flow diagram and the final FORTRAN program. It contains a list of the main variables used in the program, together with their definitions and, where applicable, their algebraic equivalents. These variable names, etc., are listed alphabetically under a heading describing the program in which they first appear, typically in the order: main program, first subroutine or function, second subroutine or function, etc. Variables in a subroutine or function whose meanings are identical with those already listed for an earlier program (for example, the main program or another subroutine or function) are not repeated.

In addition, we include here any particular programming points such as (a) descriptions of special subroutines, (b) shifting of subscripts by one in order to accommodate, for example, a_0 in the algebra as A(1) [and not as the illegal A(0)] in the program, etc.

All programs have been run on an IBM 360/67 computer using the IBM G or H level compilers. We have endeavored to write programs that follow the language rules for FORTRAN IV as outlined by the American Standards Association (ASA-FORTRAN),* and have not attempted to take advantage of special nonstandard features, such as mixed-mode expressions, of the G or H level FORTRAN IV languages.

5. Program Listing. Contains a printed list of the original FORTRAN IV program.

6. Data. Contains a printed list of the data cards, if any.

7. Computer Output. In this section, the printed computer output is reproduced. However, if the complete output is rather lengthy, only certain selected portions may be given. In this case, the remaining output is usually summarized somehow. Sometimes, clarifying notes, lines, etc., are added by hand to the printout. Occasionally, the printed output may be cut and reassembled if its clarity is thereby enhanced.

8. Discussion of Results. Contains a short critical discussion of the computed results, including comments on any particular programming difficulties and how they might be overcome.

* Subcommittee X3 of the American Standards Association. "FORTRAN vs. Basic FORTRAN," *Communications of the ACM*, Vol. 7, No. 10, 590–625, 1964.

Flow-Diagram Convention

The following boxes, each of characteristic shape, are used for constructing the flow diagrams in this text.

Substitution

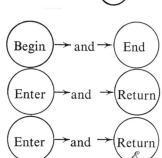

The value of the variable $\mathcal{V}$ is replaced by the value of the expression $\mathcal{E}$.

Label

1. When a path leaves from it, the label serves merely as an identification point in the flow diagram; $\mathcal{S}$ is usually the same as the statement number in the corresponding program.

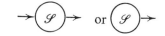

2. When a particular branch *terminates* in a label, control is transferred to the one (and only one) other point in the flow diagram where $\mathcal{S}$ occurs as in (1).

3. These special cases encompass the computations in a main program.

4. Indicate the start and finish of computations in a subrotuine.

5. Indicate the start and finish of computations in a function. The value of the expression $\mathcal{E}$ is returned by the function.

Conditional Branching

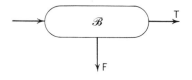

If the Boolean expression $\mathcal{B}$ is true, the branch marked T is followed; otherwise, the branch marked F (false) is followed.

Iteration

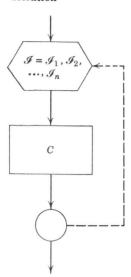

The counter $\mathscr{I}$ is incremented uniformly (in steps of $\mathscr{I}_2 - \mathscr{I}_1$) between its initial and final limits $\mathscr{I}_1$ and $\mathscr{I}_n$, respectively. For each such value of $\mathscr{I}$, the sequence of computations C is performed. The dotted line emphasizes the return for the next value of $\mathscr{I}$, and the small circle, which is usually inscribed with the corresponding statement number in the program, serves as a junction box.

Input and Output

The values for the variables comprising the list $\mathscr{L}$ are read as input data.

The values for the variables or expressions comprising the list $\mathscr{L}$ are printed. A message to be printed is enclosed in quotation marks.

Occasionally, there are special cases (particularly, calls on subroutines and functions) which do not fit conveniently into the above arrangement. However, the intended meaning is conveyed readily by suitable modification of the flow diagram. The flow diagram for a subroutine or function is separate from that for the calling program, and is started and concluded with the words "Enter" and "Return," as explained above. The arguments for subroutines and functions are also indicated.

Index

Numbers prefixed by E refer to Computer Examples; numbers prefixed by P refer to end-of-chapter Problems.